ACCOUNTING TRENDS & TECHNIQUES

IFRS Financial Statements

Best Practices in Presentation and Disclosure

12656-359

FOURTH EDITION

1 2 3 4 5 6 7 8 9 0 AAP 1 9 8 7 6 5 4 3 2

ISSN 1531-4340

ISBN 978-1-93735-142-7

Notice to readers: This book does not represent an official position of the American Institute of Certified Public Accountants,
and it is distributed with the understanding that the authors and publisher are not rendering legal, accounting,
or other professional services via this publication.

Director, Accounting & Auditing Publications: Amy Eubanks
Senior Technical Manager: Doug Bowman
Technical Manager: Anjali Patel
Developmental Editor: David Cohen
Project Manager: Charlotte Ingles

RECOGNITION

Author

Patricia Doran Walters, PhD, CFA

Director, Professional Program in Accounting
Associate Professor of Professional Practice
Neeley School of Business at Texas Christian University
President, Disclosure Analytics, Inc.

AICPA Staff

Anjali Patel, CPA

Technical Manager
Accounting and Auditing Publications

David Cohen

Developmental Editor
Professional Product Development

Special acknowledgment and sincere thanks are due to DisclosureNet™ Inc. and the following individuals for providing access to DisclosureNet™, a cloud-based public disclosure research tool offering global corporate filings, without which this book would not be possible:

Stephane Jasmin, President and Chief Executive Officer
Todd Peterson, Vice President, Client Service
Peter Kaju, Chief Financial Officer

ABOUT THIS EDITION OF *IFRS FINANCIAL STATEMENTS—BEST PRACTICES IN PRESENTATION AND DISCLOSURE*

Along with the other publications in AICPA's *Accounting Trends & Techniques* series, the former *IFRS Accounting Trends & Techniques* has a new name: *IFRS Financial Statements—Best Practices in Presentation and Disclosure (IFRS BPPD)*. The name has changed simply to provide users with a clearer sense of what this product delivers: IFRS presentation and disclosure examples carefully selected by AICPA experts accompanied by just the right amount of reporting guidance and relevant financial statement trends. *IFRS BPPD* remains the best source for reporting and disclosure examples from IFRS financial statements, just as the *Accounting Trends & Techniques* series remains the premier source for financial reporting information, with an unmatched legacy of innovation and practical application.

This 2012 edition features a number of significant enhancements over previous editions: The survey sample now includes 175 companies, 75% of which are new to this edition; the number of survey companies from Latin America (Argentina, Brazil, Chile) increased over 100% to 28; because both Canada and Korea adopted IFRSs in 2011 the survey sample now includes 18 companies from Canada and 8 from Korea; and for the first time the survey sample includes a Japanese company (a financial institution listed on the New York Stock Exchange).

Similar to the other titles in the *Accounting Trends & Techniques* series, IFRS BPPD includes helpful reporting guidance, compiles annual reporting and disclosure data, and presents illustrative reporting examples from an extensive analysis of the annual reports of entities across the globe and across numerous industries. The financial statements of those entities selected for this edition include a required statement of compliance confirming that the financial statements were prepared in conformity with International Financial Reporting Standards (IFRSs) as issued by the International Accounting Standards Board (IASB); this edition also includes survey entities for which the national standards applicable to their jurisdiction are essentially equivalent to IFRSs as issued by the IASB (for example, Australia). All but one entity, which is a farm-owned cooperative, are publicly traded.

To be included in the survey sample, entities domiciled in jurisdictions in which the required accounting standards may not be in full conformity with IFRSs, such as the European Union, were required to include either the phrase "as issued by the IASB" in the statement of compliance or a separate sentence that confirms the standards applied in the financial statements are not different from those issued by the IASB. Entities domiciled in jurisdictions where the national standards are essentially equivalent to IFRSs as issued by the IASB were not required to include this additional confirmation of compliance with IFRS as issued by the IASB. Survey entities that are also SEC registrants are required by the SEC to add the phrase "as issued by the IASB" to their statement of compliance.

IFRS BPPD provides preparers and auditors and other financial professionals with an invaluable resource for incorporating new and existing accounting and reporting guidance into financial statements using presentation techniques adopted by some of the most recognized entities in the world. *IFRS BPPD* can also be used internally by an entity's management and externally by investors, analysts, and academics to build their base of understanding and awareness of financial statement presentation and disclosure under IFRSs and the IFRS accounting policies prevalent in different industries around the world.

ORGANIZATION AND CONTENT

This 2012 edition of *IFRS BPPD* incorporates information from the annual reports of 175 carefully selected entities generally having annual fiscal periods ending between January and December 2011.

The content of *IFRS BPPD* addresses many of the common requirements most likely to be encountered when preparing or reviewing general purpose financial statements, including consolidated financial statements of commercial, industrial, and business reporting entities, as defined in *The Conceptual Framework for Financial Reporting* (IFRS *Conceptual Framework*) within the IASB's *IFRS 2012* bound volume. The IFRS *Conceptual Framework* sets forth the concepts that underlie the preparation and presentation of financial statements for external users and contains definitions of the elements of financial statements (that is, assets, liabilities, equity, income, and expenses).

Among other purposes, the IFRS *Conceptual Framework* assists preparers of financial statements in applying IFRSs and in dealing with topics that have yet to form the subject of a specific standard or interpretation. Although the framework is not a standard, the requirements of IAS 8, *Accounting Policies, Changes in Accounting Estimates and Errors*, essentially establish the IFRS *Conceptual Framework* as part of the IFRS hierarchy of accounting and reporting requirements.

To provide you with the most useful and comprehensive look at current financial reporting presentation and disclosure, *IFRS BPPD* is topically organized using familiar financial statement terminology and offers the following:

- Illustrative examples from the surveyed annual reports showing reporting policies, presentation, and disclosures
- Descriptive guidance that includes comparisons of the current reporting requirements under IFRSs and U.S. generally accepted accounting principles (U.S. GAAP). U.S. GAAP is generally considered to be the requirements of the Financial Accounting Standards Board (FASB) *Accounting Standards Codification*™ (ASC) and regulations of the U.S. Securities and Exchange Commission (SEC) for those foreign private issuers that are SEC registrants.
- Statistical tables that track reporting trends
- Detailed indexes

Different terms for the same underlying concepts within IFRSs and U.S. GAAP are identified to enhance relevance and understanding.

Illustrative Reporting Examples

IFRS BPPD presents carefully selected reporting examples excerpted from the audited annual reports of the survey entities to illustrate current reporting techniques and various presentation practices. Each edition of *IFRS BPPD* includes completely new reporting examples found to be particularly relevant and useful to financial statement preparers and other users in illustrating current reporting practices.

Reporting Guidance

IFRS BPPD offers discerning, plain English guidance covering the significant IFRSs and U.S. GAAP accounting and financial statement reporting requirements presented in narratives with a consistent format throughout the book. You'll find a strategic use of common headings (overview, recognition and measurement, presentation, and disclosure) in all sections; under those common headings are subheadings for IFRSs and U.S. GAAP. Although not a substitute for the authoritative accounting and reporting standards, the reporting guidance boils down the complex requirements with a focus on the reader's clear understanding of the content. The related authoritative sources for each requirement are cited within the narratives (for example, IFRS 3, *Business Combinations*, FASB ASC 310, *Receivables*, or Regulation S-K).

In 2012, the IASB issued two editions of the 2012 bound volume of IFRSs. One edition, *IFRS— Consolidated without early application* (referred to as the "blue book"), includes the latest consolidated version of the entire authoritative body of IFRSs as at December 31, 2011 that are required for annual reporting periods beginning on January 1, 2012. The other edition, *IFRS* (referred to as the "red book") includes all newly issued or amended standards and interpretations as at December 31, 2011, regardless of effective date. The red book, for example, includes IFRS 9, *Financial Instruments*, which is effective for annual reporting periods beginning on or after January 1, 2015, and includes the requirements necessary for early adoption of standards with effective dates after January 1, 2012. The IFRS narratives and comparisons to U.S. GAAP only refer to standards in the bluebook. Author's Notes provide information about standards and interpretations included in the red book when applicable (for example, to accompany an excerpt illustrating early application of IFRS 9).

Annually, the FASB and the IASB either separately or jointly issue proposals for changes to existing standards or for new standards. In the last year the IASB issued significant exposure drafts that reflect convergence efforts with FASB, including the following:

- In November and December 2011, the IASB issued a revision to its 2010 exposure draft, *Revenue from Contracts with Customers* and *Transition Guidance*, which proposed amendments to IFRS 10, *Consolidated Financial Statements*.
- In 2012, the IASB issued an exposure draft, *Annual Improvements to IFRSs 2010–2012 Cycle*. At the same time, the FASB also issued comparable exposure drafts, which included several Proposed Accounting Standards Updates with respect to *Revenue Recognition (Topic 605): Revenue from Contracts with Customers.*

Brief summaries about proposed changes are provided in Author's Notes throughout this edition where relevant. For easy reference and to avoid potential confusion, comparisons of IFRSs to U.S. GAAP are confined within the U.S. GAAP components of the narratives.

Reporting Trends

Statistical trends tables are easily identified by a shaded background, which distinguishes them from content excerpted from a survey entity's financial statements. These tables show reporting trends across the available choices in recognition, measurement, and presentation in such diverse reporting matters as financial statement format and terminology and the treatment of transactions and events reflected in the financial statements. Additional trends of this nature will be added in future editions.

Indexes

Indexes in this edition include the "Company Index," which alphabetically lists each of the 175 survey entities included in the current edition and identifies where in the text excerpts from their annual reports can be found; the "Pronouncements Index," which provides for easy cross-referencing of the IFRS framework, standards, and interpretations (collectively, IFRSs) to the applicable descriptive narratives; and a detailed "Subject Index," which directs the reader to all significant topics included throughout the narratives.

AUTHORITATIVE SOURCES

Unless otherwise indicated, references to IFRSs throughout this 2012 edition of *IFRS BPPD* refer to the version of those standards and interpretations included in *IFRS 2012* bound volume (the blue book) that are effective for annual reporting periods beginning on or after January 1, 2012. When necessary, Author's Notes provide information about newly issued standards and interpretations that are effective for annual periods beginning on or after a later date.

Unless otherwise indicated, references to U.S. GAAP throughout this 2012 edition of *IFRS BPPD* refer to the FASB *Accounting Standards Codification*™ as at December 31, 2011.

Note that the AICPA *Code of Professional Conduct* has been revised to recognize the IASB in London as an accounting body for purposes of establishing IFRSs, thus granting AICPA members the option to use IFRSs as an alternative to U.S. GAAP.

Also note that the effective dates of recently released guidance affect the timing of its inclusion in the financial statements of the survey entities, thereby affecting the availability of illustrative excerpts for potential inclusion in each edition of *IFRS BPPD*.

INTERNATIONAL FINANCIAL REPORTING STANDARDS

What Is IFRSs?

IFRSs is a set of accounting standards and interpretations developed and issued by the IASB, the London-based independent accounting standard-setting body currently consisting of 15 full-time members. The Trustees voted in 2009 to be expanded to 16 by July 2012, but it has not yet done so. Important elements of member selection include technical competence, recent practical experience, and diversity, including diversity in terms of work experience such as one's background as a financial statement preparer, auditor, and external user, and diversity in terms of a member's country of origin.

IASB began operations in 2001, when it succeeded the International Accounting Standards Committee (IASC). IASC was formed in 1973, soon after the formation of the Financial Accounting Standards Board (FASB). In 2001, when the IASB replaced the IASC, a new, independent oversight body, the IASC Foundation, was created to appoint the members of the IASB and oversee its due process. The IASC Foundation's oversight role is very similar to that of the Financial Accounting Foundation in its capacity as the oversight body of FASB.

The term "IFRSs" has both a narrow and a broad meaning. Narrowly, IFRSs refer to the new numbered series of pronouncements issued by the IASB, as differentiated from International Accounting Standards (IASs) issued by its predecessor, the IASC. More broadly, however, IFRSs refer to the entire body of authoritative IASB pronouncements, including those issued by the IASC and their respective interpretive bodies. Therefore, the authoritative IFRSs literature, in its broadest sense and as applied in *IFRS BPPD*, includes the following:

- Standards, whether labeled IFRSs or IASs
- Interpretations, whether labeled IFRIC (referring to the *International Financial Reporting Interpretations Committee*, the current interpretive body of the IASC Foundation) or SIC (*Standing Interpretations Committee*, the predecessor to IFRIC and former interpretive body of the IASC) IFRS *Conceptual Framework*

The preface to the *IFRS 2012* bound volume states that IFRSs are designed to apply to the general purpose financial statements and other financial reporting of all profit-oriented entities including commercial, industrial, and financial entities regardless of legal form or organization. Included within the scope of profit-oriented entities are mutual insurance companies and other mutual cooperative entities that provide dividends or other economic benefits to their owners, members, or participants. IFRSs are not designed to apply to not-for-profit entities or those in the public sector, but these entities may find IFRSs appropriate in accounting for their activities. In contrast, U.S. GAAP is designed to apply to all nongovernmental entities, including not-for-profit entities, and includes specific guidance for not-for-profit entities, development stage entities, limited liability entities, and personal financial statements.

The IASB's approach to establishing standards and interpretations differs to some degree from that of FASB. In developing an IFRS, the IASB strikes a different balance than FASB in developing U.S. GAAP by expecting preparers to rely on core principles and more limited application guidance with fewer prescriptive rules than found in U.S. GAAP. In contrast, FASB has traditionally leaned more toward providing extensive prescriptive guidance and detailed rules.

The difference in the amount of industry specific guidance is an example of the different approaches. Currently, IFRSs include only three standards (for example, IAS 41, *Agriculture*)[1] that might be regarded as primarily industry-specific guidance. However, the scope of these standards includes all entities to which the scope of IFRSs applies. In contrast, U.S. GAAP has considerable guidance for entities within specific industries. For example, on liability recognition and measurement alone, U.S. GAAP contains specific guidance for entities in the following industries:

- Agriculture
- Health care
- Contractors and construction
- Contractors and the federal government
- Entertainment, with separate guidance for casinos, films, and music
- Financial services, with separate guidance for brokers and dealers, depository and lending, insurance, and investment companies

For nonmonetary transactions, U.S. GAAP provides specific guidance for the airline, software, and entertainment industries. U.S. GAAP also addresses some specific transactions not currently addressed in IFRSs, such as accounting for reorganizations, including quasi-reorganizations, troubled debt restructuring, spinoffs, and reverse spinoffs.

Convergence of U.S. GAAP and IFRSs

Converging the standards of FASB and IASB was the primary focus of both organizations' boards during 2010–2012. The commitment for global convergence gained momentum in 2002, when FASB and the IASB signed what is known as the Norwalk Agreement. At that meeting, FASB and IASB pledged to use their best efforts to (*a*) make their existing financial reporting standards fully compatible as soon as is practicable, and (*b*) to coordinate their future work programs to ensure that, once achieved, compatibility is maintained. That agreement was reaffirmed in a February 2006 Memorandum of Understanding (MoU), which was based on the following three principles:

- Convergence of accounting standards can best be achieved through the development of high quality, common standards over time.
- Trying to eliminate differences between two standards that are in need of significant improvement is not the best use of FASB's and IASB's resources—instead, a new common standard should be developed that improves the financial information reported to investors.
- Serving the needs of investors means that FASB and IASB should seek convergence by replacing standards in need of improvement with jointly developed new standards.

At their joint meeting in April 2008, FASB and the IASB again affirmed their commitment to developing common, high quality standards, and agreed on a path to completing the MoU projects, including projected completion dates. In September 2008, and again in April 2011, the two boards jointly published an update of their 2006 MoU to report the progress they have made since. During 2011, the board regularly updated project completion dates as difficulties in completing projects arose. Some projects (for example, Income Taxes) were removed from the convergence schedules when the boards agreed that convergence was unlikely to be achieved in the short time available, while other projects have reached the exposure draft milestone. Each board believes that these standards, when completed, would improve the quality, consistency, and comparability of financial information for investors and capital markets around the world.

In February 2010, the SEC staff published a work plan that, together with the FASB and IASB's convergence projects, would position the SEC regarding incorporating IFRS into the financial reporting

---

[1] In addition to International Accounting Standards 41, the other International Financial Reporting Standards (IFRSs) that address issues specific to certain industries are IFRS 4, *Insurance Contracts*, and IFRS 6, *Exploration for and Evaluation of Mineral Resources*.

system for U.S. issuers. This work plan contained the following key areas and factors relevant to determining "whether, when, and how the U.S. financial reporting system for U.S. issuers should be transitioned to a system that incorporates IFRSs:"[2]

- development and application of IFRSs,
- independence of standard-setting,
- investor understanding and education regarding IFRSs,
- examination of the U.S. regulatory environment that would be affected by a change in accounting standards,
- impact on both large and small issuers, and
- human capital considerations.

In October 2010, SEC staff issued a progress report on its work plan which addresses each of these issues and describes how the staff is evaluating each of them. For example, with respect to the development and application of IFRSs, the staff is monitoring the development of MoU projects and IFRS projects that are outside the scope of the MoU. SEC staff is also seeking constituent perspectives and researching the experiences of regulators in other jurisdictions, as well as reviewing the financial statements of both SEC and non-SEC registrants to evaluate the application of IFRS in practice.

In May 2011, the SEC staff published a staff paper, *Exploring a Possible Method of Incorporation*, that confirmed that the SEC had not yet made a decision whether or how to incorporate IFRSs of IFRSs into the U.S. financial reporting system. In this paper, the staff proposed a "condorsement" approach, whereby FASB would endorse new IFRSs one at a time as part of a continuing convergence process, rather than a "Big Bang" approach which would specify a mandatory, certain date for adoption of IFRSs. Subsequent to issuing this paper, SEC staff held a roundtable where invited constituents would discuss its proposal. Many of the roundtable participants favored this "condorsement" approach.

In July 2012, the SEC staff published its final staff report, *Work Plan for the Consideration of Incorporating International Financial Reporting Standards into the Financial Reporting System for U.S. Issuers*. In this report, the SEC staff summarizes its observations and analyses in the key areas it had previously identified for study. The following issues emerged from these analyses:

- The perception among U.S. constituents is that, although considered to be of high quality, IFRSs are less well developed than U.S. GAAP in several areas, including accounting for extractive, insurance, and rate-regulated industries.
- Based on its outreach activities, the SEC staff believes that the IASB needs to improve the timeliness of its interpretative process.
- The SEC staff believes that the IASB can and should rely more heavily on the national standard setters in countries that have adopted IFRSs to assist with individual projects, perform outreach activities, and identify areas where it can narrow diversity in practice.
- The SEC staff believes that it is critical that IFRSs are applied and enforced consistently across jurisdictions. Although the results of its review of IFRS financial statements confirmed their general compliance with IFRSs, the SEC staff believes the IASB needs to do more to narrow diversity in practice.
- Although the SEC staff believes that the IASB's governance structure strikes a reasonable balance between oversight and independence, it also believes it may be necessary to retain an active FASB to endorse IFRSs to protect U.S. capital markets.
- The SEC staff is concerned about the IASB's reliance on large public accounting firms as its primary funding source.
- The SEC staff acknowledged receiving helpful input from investors, but generally found investor education on relevant accounting issues to be uneven. The SEC staff believes that, regardless of the final decision by the Commission as to incorporating IFRSs in the U.S. financial reporting process, it needs to consider how to improve investor engagement and education on accounting standards.

Because the original Work Plan did not set out to answer the question of whether transition to or adoption of IFRSs is in the best interests of either the U.S. capital markets or U.S. investors, the Staff Report does not explicitly make a recommendation to the Commission on how to proceed and the Commission has not itself made a policy decision with respect to this question. The SEC staff does believe, however, that "additional analysis and consideration of this threshold policy question is necessary before any decision by the Commission concerning the incorporation of IFRS into the financial reporting system for U.S. issuers can occur."[3]

---

[2] Securities and Exchange Commission Release Nos. 33-9109; 34-61578, *Commission Statements in Support of Convergence and Global Accounting Standards*, Appendix, *Work Plan for the Consideration of Incorporating International Financial Reporting Standards into the Financial Reporting System for U.S. Issuers*, p. 1.

[3] *Work Plan for the Consideration of Incorporating International Financial Reporting Standards into the Financial Reporting System for U.S. Issuers*, Final Staff Report, Office of the Chief Accountant, United States Securities and Exchange Commission, "Introductory Note."

Both IASB and FASB provide extensive information about convergence projects and their other projects on their respective web sites, often with links to the relevant page on the opposite partner's site. The U.S. SEC also has a special section of its website, *Spotlight on Work Plan for Global Accounting Standards*, where the previously cited documents can be found as well as comments from constituents on its proposals.

OTHER AICPA PUBLICATIONS

For the same reasons that you'll find *IFRS BPPD* to be the premier resource for financial reporting under IFRSs, the other publications in the *Accounting Trends & Techniques* series are just as robust and deserving to be your tool of choice for their respective types of financial reporting. A similar publication in this series that focuses exclusively on U.S. GAAP is *U.S. GAAP Financial Statements—Best Practices in Presentation and Disclosure (U.S. GAAP BPPD)* (product code ATTATT12P). Now in its 66th edition, this AICPA bestseller is filled with all new examples of current reporting techniques and methods used by 500 of the top publicly traded U.S. companies across all major industries. See www.cpa2biz.com for ordering information.

The online version of *U.S. GAAP BPPD* also adds XBRL functionality to empower XBRL filers with the analytical tools to inform their own reporting by providing all available XBRL filings from all 500 survey companies and providing full tag information, highlighting company extensions with the click of a button. A subscription to this robust online tool allows you to search, browse, filter, download, and use the data exactly as you need it, and is available at www.cpa2biz.com.

NOTICE

IFRS BPPD is a nonauthoritative practice aid and is not designed to provide a comprehensive understanding of all the requirements contained in U.S. GAAP and IFRSs; it does not identify all possible differences between those aforementioned bases of accounting. *IFRS BPPD* does not include reporting requirements relating to other matters such as internal control or agreed upon procedures.

Authoritative guidance on accounting treatments in accordance with IFRSs can only be made by reference to the IFRSs themselves, which are copyright of the IASC Foundation and can be acquired directly from the IASB.

IFRS BPPD has not been reviewed, approved, disapproved, or otherwise acted on by any senior technical committee of the AICPA and does not represent official positions or pronouncements of the AICPA.

The use of this publication requires the exercise of individual professional judgment. It is not a substitute for the original authoritative pronouncements. Users are urged to refer directly to applicable authoritative pronouncements when appropriate. As an additional resource, users may call the AICPA Technical Hotline at 1-877-242-7212.

FEEDBACK

We hope that you find this third edition of *IFRS BPPD* to be informative and useful. Please let us know! What features do you like? What do you think can be improved or added? We encourage you to give us your comments and questions about all aspects of *IFRS BPPD*. Please direct your feedback to Anjali Patel, using the following contact information. All feedback is greatly appreciated and kept strictly confidential.

Anjali Patel—Accounting & Auditing Publications
AMERICAN INSTITUTE OF CERTIFIED PUBLIC ACCOUNTANTS
220 Leigh Farm Road
Durham, NC 27707-8110
Telephone: 919-402-4580
Email: apatel@aicpa.org

You can also contact the Accounting and Auditing Publications team of the AICPA directly via email:

A&Apublications@aicpa.org

LIST OF ABBREVIATIONS

AICPA	American Institute of Certified Public Accountants
ASC	Accounting Standards Codification™
ASU	Accounting Standards Update
EU	European Union
FASB	Financial Accounting Standards Board
GAAP	Generally Accepted Accounting Principles
IAS	International Accounting Standards
IASB	International Accounting Standards Board
IASC	International Accounting Standards Committee
ICAEW	Institute of Chartered Accountants in England and Wales
IFRIC	International Financial Reporting Interpretations Committee
IFRSs	International Financial Reporting Standards
SEC	U.S. Securities and Exchange Commission
SIC	Standing Interpretations Committee

TABLE OF CONTENTS

LIST OF TABLES

Table **Page**

SECTION 1: GENERAL TOPICS AND RELATED DISCLOSURES[1]

STATISTICAL PROFILE INFORMATION ON SURVEY ENTITIES USED IN THIS EDITION

TABLE 1-1: GENERAL INFORMATION ABOUT SURVEY ENTITIES

Entity Name	Country of Incorporation	Ticker	Stock Exchange[1]	Fiscal Year End	Presentation Currency[2]
Absa Group Limited	South Africa	AMAGB	JSE	December 31 2011	ZAR
Abu Dhabi Aviation PJSC	United Arab Emirates	ADAVIATION	ADX	December 31 2011	AED
Abu Dhabi National Hotels PJSC	United Arab Emirates	ADNH	ADX	December 31 2010	AED
Abu Dhabi Ship Building PJSC	United Arab Emirates	ADSB	ADX	December 31 2011	AED
Adecoagro S.A.	Luxembourg	AGRO	NYSE	December 31 2011	USD
Administradora de Fondos de Pensiones Provida S.A.	Chile	PVD	NYSE	December 31 2011	CLP
AEGON N.V.	The Netherlands	AEG	NYSE	December 31 2011	EUR
AIXTRON SE	Germany	AIXG	NASDAQ-GS	December 31 2011	EUR
Alcatel-Lucent	France	ALU	NYSE	December 31 2011	EUR[5]
Alesco Corporation Limited	Australia	ALS	ASX	May 31 2011	AUD
Allied Irish Bank plc	Ireland	AIB	ISE-ESM	December 31 2011	EUR
Alon Holdings Blue Square—Israel Ltd	Israel	BSI	NYSE	December 31 2011	NIS[5]
Alumina Limited	Australia	AWC	NYSE	December 31 2011	USD
America Movil, S.A.B. de C.V.	Mexico	AMX	NYSE	December 31 2011	MXN[5]
Anheuser-Busch InBev SA/NV	Belgium	BUD	NYSE	December 31 2011	USD
Aquarius Platinum Limited	Bermuda	AQP	ASX	June 30 2011	USD
ArcelorMittal	Luxembourg	MT	NYSE	December 31 2011	USD
Ashtead Group plc	United Kingdom	AHT	LSE	April 30 2011	GBP
Atrium Innovations Inc.	Canada	ATB	TSX	December 31 2011	USD
Banco Bilbao Vizcaya Argentaria, S.A.	Spain	BBVA	NYSE	December 31 2011	EUR
Banco Bradesco S.A.	Brazil	BBDO	NYSE	December 31 2011	BRL
Banco de Chile	Chile	BCH	NYSE	December 31 2011	CLP[5]
Barloworld Limited	South Africa	BAW	JSE	September 30 2011	ZAR
Baytex Energy Corp.	Canada	BTE	TSX	December 31 2011	CAD
BioteQ Environmental Technologies Inc.	Canada	BQE	TSX	December 31 2011	CAD
Braskem S.A.	Brazil	BAK	NYSE	December 31 2011	BRL
BRF—Brasil Foods S.A.	Brazil	BRFS	NYSE	December 31 2011	BRL
British Sky Broadcasting Group plc	United Kingdom	BSY	LSE	June 30 2011	GBP
Brookfield Infrastructure Partners L.P.	Bermuda	BIP	NYSE	December 31 2011	USD
Canadian Natural Resources Limited	Canada	CNQ	TSX	December 31 2011	CAD
Canadian Tire Corporation, Limited	Canada	CTC	TSX	December 31 2011	CAD
Cellcom Israel Ltd	Israel	CEL	NYSE	December 31 2011	NIS[5]
Celtic plc	United Kingdom	CCP	LSE	June 30 2011	GBP
Cementos Pacasmayo S.A.A.	Peru	CPAC	NYSE	December 31 2011	PEN
Cemex, S.A.B. de C.V.	Mexico	CX	NYSE	December 31 2011	MXN

(continued)

---

[1] Unless otherwise indicated, references to International Accounting Standards Board (IASB) standards and interpretations throughout this 2012 edition of *IFRS Financial Statements—Best Practices in Presentation and Disclosure* refer to the version of those standards and interpretations included in the *IFRS 2012* bound volume, the official printed consolidated text of IASB standards and interpretations, including revisions, amendments, and supporting documents, applicable as of 1 January 2012.

TABLE 1-1: GENERAL INFORMATION ABOUT SURVEY ENTITIES—CONTINUED

Entity Name	Country of Incorporation	Ticker	Stock Exchange[1]	Fiscal Year End	Presentation Currency[2]
Cencosud S.A.	Chile	CNCO	NYSE	December 31 2011	CLP
Centum Investment Company Ltd.	Kenya	CENTUM	NSE	March 31 2011	KES
China Eastern Airlines Corporation Limited	China	CEA	NYSE	December 31 2011	CNY
China Mobile Limited	Hong Kong	CHL	NYSE	December 31 2011	CNY
China Telecom Corporation Limited	China	CHA	NYSE	December 31 2011	CNY
China Yuchai International Limited	Bermuda	CYD	NYSE	December 31 2011	CNY
Chocoladefabriken Lindt & Sprüngli AG	Switzerland	LISP	SIX	December 31 2011	CHF
City Telecom (H.K.) Limited	Hong Kong	CTEL	NASDAQ-GS	August 31 2011	HKD
Clicks Group Limited	South Africa	CLS	JSE	August 31 2011	ZAR
CNOOC Limited	Hong Kong	CEO	NYSE	December 31 2011	CNY
Coca-Cola Hellenic Bottling Company S.A.	Greece	CCH	NYSE	December 31 2011	EUR
Compagnie Générale de Géophysique-Veritas, S.A.	France	CGV	NYSE	December 31 2011	EUR
Companhia de Bebidas das Américas (American Beverage Company)—Ambev	Brazil	ABV	NYSE	December 31 2011	BRL
Companhia Siderúrgica Nacional	Brazil	CSN	NYSE	December 31 2011	BRL
Compañía Cervecerías Unidas S.A.	Chile	CCU	NYSE	December 31 2011	CLP
Compañía de Minas Buenaventura S.A.A	Peru	BVN	NYSE	December 31 2011	USD
Copa Holdings, S.A.	Panama	CPA	NYSE	December 31 2011	USD
Counsel Corporation	Canada	CXS	TSX	December 31 2011	CAD
Credicorp Ltd	Bermuda	BAP	NYSE	December 31 2011	USD
CRH Public Limited Company	Ireland	CRH	NYSE	December 31 2011	EUR
CSR plc	United Kingdom	CSR	LSE	December 30[4] 2011	USD
Daimler AG	Germany	DAI	DAX	December 31 2011	EUR
Danubius Hotel and Spa Nyrt.	Hungary	DANUBIUS	BSE	December 31 2011	HUF
Deutsche Bank Aktiengesellschaft	Germany	DBK	NYSE	December 31 2011	EUR
Deutsche Telekom AG	Germany	DTE	DAX	December 31 2011	EUR
DHT Holdings, Inc.	Marshall Islands	DHT	NYSE	December 31 2011	USD
Diploma Group Limited	Australia	DGX	ASX	June 30 2011	AUD
Dr. Reddy's Laboratories Limited	India	DRY	NYSE	March 31 2011	INR[5]
DRDGOLD Limited	South Africa	DRD	NYSE	June 30 2011	ZAR
East Asiatic Company Ltd. A/S	Denmark	EAC	NASDAQ-OMX	December 31 2011	DKK
Elbit Imaging Ltd.	Israel	EMITF	NASDAQ-GS	December 31 2011	NIS[5]
Embraer S.A.	Brazil	ERJ	NYSE	December 31 2011	USD
Empresa Nacional de Electricidad S.A. (Endesa-Chile)	Chile	EOC	NYSE	December 31 2011	CLP
Empresas ICA, S.A.B. de C.V.	Mexico	ICA	NYSE	December 31 2011	MXN[5]
Eni S.p.A.	Italy	E	NYSE	December 31 2011	EUR
Etablissements Delhaize Frères et Cie "Le Lion" (Groupe Delhaize) S.A.	Belgium	DEG	NYSE	December 31 2011	EUR
Fairfax Financial Holdings Limited	Canada	FFH	TSX	December 31 2011	USD
Fibria Cellulose S.A.	Brazil	FBR	NYSE	December 31 2011	BRL
France Telecom	France	FTE	NYSE	December 31 2011	EUR
Gazit-Globe Ltd.	Israel	GZT	NYSE	December 31 2011	NIS[5]
GrainCorp Limited	Australia	GNC	ASX	September 30 2011	AUD
Gruma, S.A.B. de C.V.	Mexico	GMK	NYSE	December 31 2011	MXN
Grupo Radio Centro, S.A.B. de C.V.	Mexico	RC	NYSE	December 31 2011	MXN[5]
Grupo TMM, S.A.B.	Mexico	TMM	NYSE	December 31 2011	USD[6]
Guangshen Railway Company Limited	China	GSH	NYSE	December 31 2011	CNY[5]
Harmony Gold Mining Company Limited	Canada	HMY	NYSE	June 30 2011	USD
Harry Winston Diamond Corporation	Canada	HWD	NYSE	January 31 2012	USD
Hemisphere GPS Inc.	Canada	HEM	TSX	December 31 2011	USD
HGL Limited	Australia	HNG	ASX	September 30 2011	AUD
Huaneng Power International, Inc.	China	HNP	NYSE	December 31 2011	CNY[5]
ING Groep N.V.	The Netherlands	ING	NYSE	December 31 2011	EUR
InterContinental Hotels Group plc	United Kingdom	IHG	NYSE	December 31 2011	USD
JSC Halyk Bank	Kazakhstan	HSBK	KASE	December 31 2011	KZT
Kazakhstan Kagazy PLC	Isle of Man	KAG	LSE	December 31 2011	USD
KB Financial Group Inc.	South Korea	KB	NYSE	December 31 2011	KRW[5]

TABLE 1-1: GENERAL INFORMATION ABOUT SURVEY ENTITIES—CONTINUED

Entity Name	Country of Incorporation	Ticker	Stock Exchange[1]	Fiscal Year End	Presentation Currency[2]
Koninklijke Philips Electronics NV	The Netherlands	PHG	NYSE	December 31 2011	EUR
Korea Electric Power Corporation	South Korea	KEP	NYSE	December 31 2011	KRW
KT Corporation	South Korea	KT	NYSE	December 31 2011	KRW[5]
Lan Airlines S.A.	Chile	LFL	NYSE	December 31 2011	USD
Leisureworld Senior Care Corporaton	Canada	LW	TSX	December 31 2011	CAD
LG Display Co., Ltd.	South Korea	LFL	NYSE	December 31 2011	KRW
Linamar Corporation	Canada	LNR	TSX	December 31 2011	CAD
Lloyds Banking Group plc	United Kingdom	LYG	NYSE	December 31 2011	GBP
Luxottica Group S.p.A	Italy	LUX	NYSE	December 31 2011	EUR
Maple Leaf Foods Inc.	Canada	MFI	TSX	December 31 2011	CAD
Martinrea International Inc.	Canada	MRE	TSX	December 31 2011	CAD
Medical Facilities Corporation	Canada	DR	TSX	December 31 2011	USD
MFC Industrial Ltd.	Canada	MIL	NYSE	December 31 2011	USD
Millicom International Cellular S.A.	Luxembourg	MICC	NYSE	December 31 2011	USD
Mondi Limited and Mondi plc[3]	South Africa and United Kingdom, respectively	MNDI	LSE	December 31 2011	EUR
N Brown Group plc	United Kingdom	BWNG	LSE	February 26[4] 2011	GBP
Nestlé SA	Switzerland	NESN	SIX	December 31 2011	CHF
Newcrest Mining Limited	Australia	NCM	ASX	June 30 2011	AUD
Nokia Corporation	Finland	NOK	NYSE	December 31 2011	EUR
Nortel Inversora S.A.	Argentina	NTL	NYSE	December 31 2011	ARS
Novartis AG	Switzerland	NVS	NYSE	December 31 2011	USD
Novo Nordisk A/S	Denmark	NVO	NYSE	December 31 2011	DKK
OAO Gazprom	Russia	OGZPY	NASDAQ-Other OTC	December 31 2011	RUB
Pargesa Holding AG	Switzerland	PARG	SIX	December 31 2011	CHF
Perusahaan Perseroan (Persero) PT Telekomunikasi Indonesia Tbk	Indonesia	TLK	NYSE	December 31 2011	IDR[5]
PetroChina Company Limited	China	PTR	NYSE	December 31 2011	CNY
Petróleo Brasileiro SGPS, S.A.—Petrobras	Brazil	PBR	NYSE	December 31, 2011	USD
Philippine Long Distance Telephone Company	Philippines	PHI	NYSE	December 31 2011	PHP
Portugal Telecom, SGPS, S.A.	Portugal	PT	NYSE	December 31 2011	EUR
POSCO	South Korea	PKX	NYSE	December 31 2011	KRW
Promotoria de Informaciones, S.A.	Spain	PRIS	NYSE	December 31 2011	EUR
PSP Swiss Property Ltd	Switzerland	PSPN	SIX	December 31 2011	CHF
PT Indosat Tbk	Indonesia	IIT	NYSE	December 31 2011	IDR
REA Vipingo Plantations Limited	Kenya	RPVL	NSE	September 30 2011	KES
Rogers Communications Inc.	Canada	RCI	NYSE	December 31 2011	CAD
Ryanair Holdings plc	Ireland	RYAAY	NASDAQ-GS	March 31 2011	EUR
Sanofi (formerly Sanofi-Aventis)	France	SNY	NYSE	December 31 2011	EUR
SAP AG	Germany	SAP	NYSE	December 31 2011	EUR[5]
Sappi Limited	South Africa	SPP	NYSE	September 30 2011	USD
Sasini Limited	Kenya	SNSI	NSE	September 30 2011	KES
Sasol Limited	South Africa	SSL	NYSE	June 30 2011	ZAR[5]
Scorpio Tankers Inc.	Monaco	STNG	NYSE	December 31 2011	USD
Sequans Communications S.A.	France	SQNS	NYSE	December 31 2011	USD
Shinhan Financial Group	South Korea	SHG	NYSE	December 31 2011	KRW
Siemens Aktiengesellschaft	Germany	SI	NYSE	September 30 2011	EUR
Silver Fern Farms Limited	New Zealand	SFF	Unlisted	September 30 2011	NZD
Sims Metal Management Limited	Australia	SMS	NYSE	June 30 2011	AUD
Sinopec Shanghai Petrochemical Company Limited	China	SHI	NYSE	December 31 2011	CNY
SK Telecom Co., Ltd.	South Korea	SKM	NYSE	December 31 2011	KRW[5]
Smith & Nephew plc	United Kingdom	SNN	NYSE	December 31 2011	USD
Sociedad Quimica y Minera de Chile S.A.	Chile	SQM	NYSE	December 31 2011	USD
Statoil ASA	Norway	STO	NYSE	December 31 2011	NOK
Sterlite Industries (India) Limited	India	SLT	NYSE	March 31 2011	INR[5]

(continued)

TABLE 1-1: GENERAL INFORMATION ABOUT SURVEY ENTITIES—CONTINUED

Entity Name	Country of Incorporation	Ticker	Stock Exchange[1]	Fiscal Year End	Presentation Currency[2]
Sumitomo Mitsui Financial Group, Inc.	Japan	SMFG	NYSE	March 31 2011	JPY
Sun Life Financial, Inc.	Canada	SLF	NYSE	December 31 2011	CAD
Syngenta AG	Switzerland	SYT	NYSE	December 31 2011	USD
Tata Motors Limited	India	TTM	NYSE	March 31 2011	USD
Telecom Argentina	Argentina	TEO	NYSE	December 31 2011	ARS
Telecom Corporation of New Zealand Limited	New Zealand	NZT	NYSE	June 30 2011	NZD
Telecom Italia S.p.A.	Italy	TI	NYSE	December 31 2011	EUR
Telefónica S.A.	Spain	TEF	NYSE	December 31 2011	EUR
Teléfonos de México	Mexico	TMX	NYSE	December 31 2011	MXN
Telecom Austria Aktiengesellschaft	Austria	TKA	VSE	December 31 2011	EUR
Tenaris S.A.	Luxembourg	TS	NYSE	December 31 2011	USD
Ternium S.A.	Luxembourg	TX	NYSE	December 31 2011	USD
The Governor and Company of the Bank of Ireland	Ireland	IRE	NYSE	December 31 2011	EUR
Thomson Reuters Corporation	Canada	TRI	NYSE	December 31 2011	USD
TORM A./S.	Denmark	TRMD	NASDAQ-CM	December 31 2011	USD
TOTAL S.A.	France	TOT	NYSE	December 31 2011	EUR
Tourism Holdings Limited	New Zealand	THL	NZX	June 30 2011	NZD
Trencor Limited	South Africa	TRE	JSE	December 31 2011	ZAR
Trinity Biotech plc	Ireland	TRIB	NASDAQ	December 31 2011	USD
Turkcell Iletisim Hizmetleri AS	Turkey	TKC	NYSE	December 31 2011	USD
UBS AG	Switzerland	UBS	NYSE	December 31 2011	CHF
Ultra Electronics Holdings plc	United Kingdom	ULE	LSE	December 31 2011	GBP
Unilever N.V. and Unilever plc[3]	The Netherlands and United Kingdom, respectively	UN/UL	NYSE	December 31 2011	EUR
Veolia Environnement	France	VE	NYSE	December 31 2011	EUR
VimpelCom Ltd.	Bermuda	VIP	NYSE	December 31 2011	USD
Viña Concha y Toro S.A.	Chile	VCO	NYSE	December 31 2011	CLP
Wipro Limited	India	WIT	NYSE	March 31 2011	INR[5]
WNS (Holdings) Limited	India	WNS	NYSE	March 31 2011	USD
Woori Finance Holdings Co., Ltd.	South Korea	WF	NYSE	December 31 2011	KRW[5]
WPP plc	United Kingdom	WPPGY	NASDAQ	December 31 2011	GBP
Yanzhou Coal Mining Company Limited	China	YZC	NYSE	December 31 2011	CNY
Zouan Fashion Limited	China	ZA	NYSE	December 31 2011	CNY

[1] All but one of the survey entities are listed on stock exchanges. Silver Fern Farms is a cooperative owned by livestock producers. For ease of use, this table uses a code to identify a stock exchange that is either the acronym used by that particular exchange on its website or the common acronym in the International Standards Organization market identifier code list. The name of the stock exchange corresponding to the code in this table and the unique market identifier code assigned by the ISP is shown in table 1-4.

[2] Currency codes used in this table are those established by the International Organization for Standardization:

AED: UAE Dirham
ARS: Argentine Peso
AUD: Australian Dollar
BRL: Brazilian Real
CAD: Canadian Dollar
CHF: Swiss Franc
CLP: Chilean Peso
CNY: Chinese Yuan Renminbi (may also be denoted as RMB)
DKK: Danish Krone
EUR: Euro
GBP: British Pound Sterling
HKD: Hong Kong Dollar
HUF: Hungarian Forint
IDR: Indonesian Rupiah

INR: Indian Rupee
JPY: Japanese Yen
KES: Kenyan Shilling
KRW: South Korean Won
KZT: Kazakhstan Tenge
MXN: Mexican Peso
NIS: New Israeli Sheqel (or Shekel) (may also be denoted as ILS)
NOK: Norwegian Krone
NZD: New Zealand Dollar
PEN: Peruvian Nuevo Sol
PHP: Philippine Peso
RUB: Russian Ruble
USD: U.S. Dollar
ZAR: South African Rand

[3] These entities are dual listed. A *dual listed entity* is a corporate structure in which two listed entities, each with its own shareholders, share one set of assets and liabilities, results of operations, management, and other governance structure. The risks and rewards are shared in proportions laid out in an equalization agreement. These entities issued one set of financial statements applicable to shareholders of both listed entities. See table 1-3.

[4] 52- or 53-week annual fiscal period.

[5] These survey entities provide convenience translations of their financial statements into U.S. dollars.

[6] This survey entity provides a convenience translation of its financial statements into Mexican pesos.

TABLE 1-2: CLASSIFICATION OF SURVEY ENTITIES BY INDUSTRY[1]

Industry	Sectors or Subsectors Included	2011	2010	2009
Automobile & Parts	Automobiles, Tires, Parts	4	1	1
Banks	Banks	15	13	13
Basic Resources	Forestry & Paper, Industrial Metals & Mining, Other Mining (Gold, Gemstones, Coal)	18	23	21
Chemicals	Commodity & Specialty Chemicals	4	4	6
Construction & Materials	Building Materials & Fixtures, Heavy Construction	6	5	5
Financial Services	Asset Managers, Consumer, Specialty & Mortgage Finance Equity Investment Instruments, Non-equity Investment Instruments	4	5	4
Food & Beverage	Beverages, Food Producers	17	16	12
Health Care	Equipment & Services, Pharmaceuticals, Biotechnology	8	13	14
Industrial Goods & Services	Aerospace & Defense, General Industrials, Electronic & Electrical Equipment, Industrial Engineering & Transportation, Support Services (e.g., Business Support, Waste & Disposal)	21	17	16
Insurance	Life & Non-life Insurance	4	5	5
Media	Broadcasting & Entertainment, Media Agencies, Publishing	5	5	5
Oil & Gas	Producers, Equipment Services & Distribution, Alternative Energy	10	9	10
Personal & Household Goods	Household Goods, Home Construction, Leisure Goods, Personal Goods, Tobacco	3	3	3
Real Estate	Real Estate Investment & Services, Real Estate Investment Trusts	4	5	4
Retail	Food & Drug Retailers, General Retailers	4	2	3
Technology	Software & Computer Services, Hardware & Equipment	7	5	6
Telecommunications	Fixed Line & Mobile Telecommunications	26	21	20
Travel and Leisure	Airlines, Gambling, Hotels, Recreational Services, Restaurants & Bars, Travel & Tourism	9	11	8
Utilities	Electricity, Gas, Water & Multi-utilities	6	7	4
Total		**175**	**170**	**160**

[1] The industry classification of the survey entities is determined by the author based on a number of considerations, including a review of the entities' annual reports, regulatory filings, and company profiles available through the following information sources:

a) www.DisclosureNet.com: DisclosureNet[TM] is an online solution that helps users to unlock information in global corporate financial reporting and disclosure filings. Founded in 2002, DisclosureNet[TM] uses an innovative technology that makes it easy to find, store, and share global public disclosure information, while providing a secure platform for l knowledge collaboration.

b) www.NYSE.com: The New York Stock Exchange (NYSE) is a leading global operator of financial markets and provider of innovative trading technologies. NYSE Euronext (NYX) is the holding company and the first cross-border exchange group created by the combination of NYSE Group, Inc. and Euronext N.V., on April 4, 2007.

c) www.alacrastore.com: AlacraStore.com is a service of Alacra, Inc., a leading global provider of business and financial information and proprietary solutions that enable clients to quickly find, analyze, package, and present mission-critical business information.

d) www.corporateinformation.com: CorporateInformation.com is a premier provider of value-added corporate and industry information for competitive analysis and research, and it is a service of Wright Investors' Service. Certain reclassifications have been made to the prior year's data for comparison purposes.

TABLE 1-3: SURVEY ENTITIES' COUNTRY OF INCORPORATION

	2011	2010	2009
Bermuda	6	3	1
Canada	18	12	8
Cayman Islands[1]	0	0	1
Commonwealth of Australia (Australia)	7	6	6
Federal Republic of Germany	6	6	6
Federative Republic of Brazil	8	5	4
French Republic (France)	7	8	8
Grand-Duchy of Luxembourg (Luxembourg)	5	6	5
Hellenic Republic (Greece)	1	0	0
Hong Kong, China	3	3	2
Independent State of Papua New Guinea (Papua New Guinea)	0	1	1
Isle of Man[2]	1	0	0
Italian Republic (Italy)	3	3	2
Japan	1	0	0
Kingdom of Belgium (Belgium)	1	1	1
Kingdom of Denmark (Denmark)	3	3	2
Kingdom of Norway (Norway)	1	0	0
Kingdom of Spain (Spain)	3	2	2
New Zealand	3	3	3
Portuguese Republic (Portugal)	1	1	1
Principality of Monaco (Monaco)	1	0	0
Republic of Argentina (Argentina)	2	1	0
Republic of Austria (Austria)	1	0	0
Republic of Chile (Chile)	8	6	2
Republic of Finland (Finland)	1	1	1
Republic of Hungary (Hungary)	1	1	1
Republic of India (India)	5	1	0
Republic of Indonesia (Indonesia)	2	0	0
Republic of Ireland (Ireland)	5	4	4
Republic of Kazakhstan (Kazakhstan)	1	3	2
Republic of Kenya (Kenya)	3	3	1
Republic of Korea (South Korea)	8	0	0
Republic of Panama (Panama)	1	1	0
Republic of Peru (Peru)	2	0	0
Republic of South Africa (South Africa)	8	6	9
Republic of the Marshall Islands (Marshall Islands)	1	1	1
Republic of the Philippines (Philippines)	1	1	0
Republic of Turkey (Turkey)	1	1	1
Republic of Zimbabwe (Zimbabwe)	0	0	1
Romania	0	0	1
Russian Federation (Russia)	1	1	1
State of Israel (Israel)	4	3	4
Swiss Confederation (Switzerland)	7	21	23
The Netherlands	3	2	3
The People's Republic of China (China)	8	7	6
United Arab Emirates	3	3	2
United Kingdom of Great Britain and Northern Ireland (United Kingdom)	10	36	39
United Mexican States (Mexico)	7	0	0
Dual Listed Companies[2]	2	5	5
Total	**175**	**170**	**160**

[1] Cayman Islands is a non-self-governing British overseas territory.
[2] The Isle of Man is a self-governing British Crown dependency.
[3] The dual listed entities listings are as follows:

    a. United Kingdom and South Africa: Mondi plc and Mondi Limited
    b. United Kingdom and The Netherlands: Unilever plc and Unilever N.V.

TABLE 1-4: STOCK EXCHANGES ON WHICH SURVEY ENTITIES WERE LISTED AS OF DECEMBER 31, 2010

Exchange	International Standards Organization Market Identifier Code	Country	2011	2010	2009
Abu Dhabi Securities Market (ADX)	XASE	United Arab Emirates	3	3	2
Australian Securities Exchange (ASX)	XASX	Australia	7	5	4
BM&FBOVESPA S.A.—Bolsa De Valores, Mercadorias E Futuros (BVMF)	BVMF	Brazil	0	1	1
Budapest Stock Exchange	XBUD	Hungary	1	0	0
Frankfurt Stock Exchange (DAX)	XFRA	Germany	2	2	0
Irish Stock Exchange (ISE)	XDUB	Ireland	1	0	0
JSE Securities Exchange Limited (JSE)	XJSE	South Africa	4	4	6
Kazakhstan Stock Exchange (KASE)	XKAZ	Kazakhstan	1	2	2
London Stock Exchange (LSE)	XLON	United Kingdom	8	20	19
Nairobi Stock Exchange (NSE)	XNAI	Kenya	3	3	1
NASDAQ Stock Market (NASDAQ) (including Global Select and Other OTC markets)	XNAS	United States	9	16	15
NASDAQ OMX Copenhagen	XCSE	Denmark	1	0	0
New York Stock Exchange (NYSE)	XNYS	United States	117	84	78
NYSE Euronext—Euronext: Paris, Paris	XPAR	France	0	1	1
New Zealand Exchange Limited (NZX)	XNZE	New Zealand	1	1	1
SIX Swiss Exchange (SIX)	XVTX	Switzerland	4	18	20
Toronto Stock Exchange (TSX)	XTSE	Canada	11	5	4
TSX Venture Exchange (TSX-V)	XTSX	Canada	0	4	3
Vienna Stock Exchange (VIE)	XVIE	Austria	1	0	0
Zimbabwe Stock Exchange (ZSE)	XZIM	Zimbabwe	0	0	1
Unlisted (See table 1-1)			1	1	2
Total			**175**	**170**	**160**

TABLE 1-5: SURVEY ENTITIES' MONTH OF FISCAL YEAR END

	2011	2010	2009
January	1	1	1
February	0	0	0
March	8	8	9
April	1	2	1
May	1	1	2
June	11	11	9
July	0	1	1
August	2	4	5
September	8	5	3
October	0	0	0
November	0	1	1
December	141	133	124
52–53 week annual fiscal period	2	3	4
Total	**175**	**170**	**160**

TABLE 1-6: SURVEY ENTITIES' AUDIT FIRMS

	2011	2010	2009
KPMG	44	37	37
Deloitte	37	44	40
Ernst & Young	33	27	20
PricewaterhouseCoopers	45	44	44
Grant Thornton	4	3	3
BDO	0	1	1
Audited by two audit firms	10	8	11
Other audit firms	2	6	4
Total	**175**	**170**	**160**

THE CONCEPTUAL FRAMEWORK FOR FINANCIAL REPORTING

IAS 1, *PRESENTATION OF FINANCIAL STATEMENTS*

IAS 8, *ACCOUNTING POLICIES, CHANGES IN ACCOUNTING ESTIMATES AND ERRORS*

Author's Note

Conceptual Framework

The International Accounting Standards Board (IASB) is currently in the process of updating its conceptual framework in stages. As a chapter is finalized, revised paragraphs will replace the relevant paragraphs in the *Framework for the Preparation and Presentation of Financial Statements* (1989). In September 2010, the IASB issued *The Conceptual Framework for Financial Reporting* (International Financial Reporting Standards [IFRS] *Conceptual Framework*), which includes the first two chapters published as a result of this phase of the project:

- Chapter 1, "The Objective of Financial Reporting"
- Chapter 3, "Qualitative Characteristics of Useful Financial Information"

Chapter 2, which is not included in the document published in 2010, will address the reporting entity concept, and the IASB published an exposure draft on this topic in March 2010 with a comment period ending July 2010. After considering the comments received, the board decided it needs more time than originally planned to finalize this chapter.

The board has not yet published discussion papers for Phase B, "Elements," or Phase C, "Measurement." Although the IASB expected to return to development of the IFRS *Conceptual Framework* at the beginning of 2012, it has not yet done so.

Chapter 4 contains the remaining text of the old *Framework* (1989). However, references to the *Framework* (1989) in individual standards have not been revised except that footnotes are provided in individual standards identifying changes. For example, paragraph 25 in International Accounting Standard (IAS) 8, *Accounting Policies, Changes in Accounting Estimates and Errors*, was superseded by Chapter 3 of the IFRS *Conceptual Framework*.

IAS 1, Presentation of Financial Statements

In June 2011, the IASB issued *Presentation of Items of Other Comprehensive Income (Amendments to IAS 1)*. These amendments are effective for annual reporting periods beginning on or after 1 July 2012. Earlier application is permitted. The timing of the effective date of these amendments affects the availability of illustrative excerpts from survey companies' financial statements. Accordingly, the excerpts appearing later

in this section may not reflect some or all of these revisions.

Some of the amendments are cosmetic. For example, the amendments replace the title "income statement" with "statement of profit or loss" and the title "statement of comprehensive income" with "statement of profit or loss and other comprehensive income." However, the standard does not require entities to use the revised titles. See section 3, "Statement of Comprehensive Income and Related Disclosures," for further discussion of these amendments.

IAS 8, Accounting Policies, Changes in Accounting Estimates and Errors

The IASB also amended IAS 8 in the following two new standards:

- IFRS 9, *Financial Instruments* (issued November 2009 and October 2010 with an effective date of 1 January 2015)
- IFRS 13, *Fair Value Measurement* (issued May 2011 with an effective date of 1 January 2013).

IAS 8 states that hindsight should not be used when an entity applies a new accounting policy to, or corrects amounts for, a prior period, either in making assumptions or estimates. The IFRS 9 amendment replaces the example in IAS 8 of the use of hindsight that references IAS 39, *Financial Instruments: Recognition and Measurement*, with one that references IAS 19, *Employee Benefits*.

IFRS 13 amends IAS 8 to clarify the types of estimates that might be impracticable to retrospectively apply a new accounting policy or retrospectively restate. The example provided is "a fair value measurement that uses significant unobservable inputs."

Because these standards and amendments are effective for annual periods beginning on or after 1 January 2012, these amendments are not reflected in the commentary in this section. The timing of the effective dates of these standards and amendments affects the availability of illustrative excerpts from survey companies' financial statements. Accordingly, the excerpts appearing at the end of this section may not reflect all or some of these revisions.

IFRSs Overview and Comparison to U.S. GAAP

1.01 In September 2010, the IASB issued the IFRS *Conceptual Framework*, which supersedes the *Framework for the Preparation and Presentation of Financial Statements*. The IFRS *Conceptual Framework* establishes the concepts that underlie the preparation and presentation of financial statements for external users. Together with the IFRS *Conceptual Framework*, IAS 1, *Presentation of Financial Statements*, and IAS 8, describe the guidance of IFRSs with respect to the necessary characteristics and elements of financial statements; definitions of *assets, liabilities, equity, revenue, and income*; *expenses*; and the general criteria for their recognition.

1.02 The IFRS *Conceptual Framework* establishes the following objective of general purpose financial reporting in accordance with IFRSs:

> To provide financial information about the reporting entity that is useful to existing and potential investors, lenders, and other creditors (financial statement users) in making decisions about providing resources to the entity.

1.03 In making these decisions, such users need information to help them assess the entity's prospects for net cash inflows. This information includes information about the entity's resources, claims against the entity, and how efficiently and effectively the entity's management and governing board of the entity have discharged their responsibilities to use the entity's resources. The IFRS *Conceptual Framework* explains that general purpose financial statements are not designed to show the value of the entity, but to provide information that permits financial statement users to estimate the value of the entity. However, financial statement users would be expected to incorporate information from other sources into this process. Other parties, such as regulators and the general public, may find general purpose financial statements useful, but such statements are not primarily directed to these parties. The IFRS *Conceptual Framework* identifies the following types of information as providing useful information for decisions about providing resources to the entity:

- Economic resources and claims to help assess the entity's financial strengths and weaknesses
- Changes in economic resources and claims to help distinguish changes resulting from financial performance and those from other transactions and events
- Financial performance reflected by accrual accounting to provide a better basis for assessing an entity's past and future performance than only information about cash receipts and payments during the period
- Financial performance reflected by past cash flows to help assess the entity's ability to generate future net cash inflows
- Changes in economic resources and claims not resulting from financial performance to help in understanding the reasons for the change and implications for the entity's future financial performance

1.04 The IFRS *Conceptual Framework* distinguishes between fundamental and enhancing qualitative characteristics:

- The fundamental qualitative characteristics of useful financial information are relevance and faithful representation. Information must have both characteristics, described as follows, to be useful:
  - *Relevance.* Relevant financial information is capable of making a difference in users' decisions. This capability is not dependent on whether users make use of the information or whether they were aware of the information from other sources. To make a difference in decisions, information should have predictive value, confirmatory value, or both. Financial information has predictive value if it can be used to predict future outcomes and has confirmatory value if it provides feedback about previous evaluation. The IFRS *Conceptual Framework* considers *materiality* to be a component of relevance and is defined as influencing decisions about a specific reporting entity if omitted or misstated. Therefore, an entity assesses materiality based on the nature of the infor-

mation, its magnitude, or both, in the context of the entity's financial report.
  - *Faithful representation.* Useful financial information not only represents relevant phenomena, but also faithfully represents the phenomena it purports to represent. A perfectly faithful representation would be complete, neutral, and free from error. Although the IFRS *Conceptual Framework* recognizes that perfection is rarely achieved, the objective is that an entity should maximize these qualities to the extent possible.
- The enhancing qualitative characteristics are comparability, verifiability, timeliness, and understandability, described as follows:
  - *Comparability* helps users to identify and understand similarities and differences among items. Consistency in the use of the same methods for the same items, either in the same period entities or across periods for a single entity, although related to comparability, is not the same. Consistency helps an entity to provide comparable information.
  - *Verifiability* helps users assess whether information faithfully represents the economic phenomena it purports to represent. Verification can be direct (for example, through observation) or indirect (for example, checking inputs to a model). Disclosures that allow verification include underlying assumptions, methods of compiling information, and other factors and circumstances that support the information.
  - *Timeliness* means that the information is available in time to be capable of influencing users' decisions. Some information may continue to be timely after the end of a reporting period (for example, when it helps identify trends).
  - *Understandability* means that information is classified, characterized, and presented clearly and concisely. Although some economic phenomena may be complex and inherently difficult to understand, omitting information about these phenomena would make the financial report incomplete and, therefore, potentially misleading.

1.05 In discussing these characteristics, however, the IFRS *Conceptual Framework* recognizes a cost constraint on useful financial reporting. Therefore, in seeking information about whether the benefits of reporting particular information justify the costs incurred in providing and using it, the IASB considers costs and benefits generally and not just in relation to individual reporting entities.

1.06 The IFRS *Conceptual Framework* presumes that when an entity applies the aforementioned qualitative characteristics and the appropriate IFRSs, an entity's financial statements will convey a fair presentation, or true and fair view, of its financial position and performance. Therefore, although the IFRS *Conceptual Framework* is not an accounting standard and does not create recognition, measurement, or disclosure requirements or override the requirements of any standard, an entity cannot ignore it. IAS 8 requires entities to consider the IFRS *Conceptual Framework* when evaluating an accounting issue not specifically addressed in IFRSs.

Author's Note

See the discussion of IAS 8 under "Recognition and Measurement."

Recognition and Measurement

IFRSs

1.07 The IFRS *Conceptual Framework* defines the elements of financial position: assets, liabilities, and equity. An *asset* is a resource controlled by the entity as a result of past events from which future economic benefits are expected to flow to the entity. A *liability* is a present obligation as a result of past events, the settlement of which is expected to result in an outflow from the entity of resources embodying economic benefits. *Equity* is the residual interest in the assets of the entity after deducting all liabilities (net assets).

1.08 The IFRS *Conceptual Framework* defines the elements of performance: income and expenses. *Income* is increases in economic benefits during the accounting period in the form of inflows or enhancements of assets or decreases in liabilities that result in increases in equity, other than those related to contributions by equity participants. *Expenses* are decreases in economic benefits during the accounting period in the form of outflows or depletion of assets or incurrence of liabilities that result in decreases in equity, other than those related to distributions to equity participants. An entity should only use the term *revenue* to refer to income from ordinary business activities. An entity may use the terms *income* and *expense* to refer to elements from both ordinary business activities and other activities of the entity.

1.09 The IFRS *Conceptual Framework* also describes general recognition criteria, which is frequently reiterated in IFRSs, which prescribe the accounting for particular financial statement elements. An entity should recognize an element of the financial statements if the following two criteria are met:

- It is probable (that is, more likely than not) that any future economic benefit associated with the element will flow to or from the entity (probability criteria).
- The cost or value of the item can be measured reliably (measurement reliability criteria).

Even if an element fails the recognition criteria, an entity may still need to disclose information about the element in the notes.

1.10 IAS 1 establishes the basis for presentation by an entity of general purpose financial statements to ensure comparability with those of other entities and with its own statements from period to period. IAS 1 requires an entity to include the following statements and supplemental information in a complete set of financial statements:

- Statement of financial position
- Statement of comprehensive income
- Statement of cash flows
- Statement of changes in equity
- Note disclosures

Author's Note

As noted previously, an amendment to IAS 1, issued in June 2011, changes the title of the "statement of comprehensive income" to the "statement of profit or loss and other comprehensive income." The amendment is effective for annual periods beginning before or after 1 July 2012. Early application is permitted.

1.11 IAS 1 establishes acceptable formats for the financial statements and their minimum content and line items, the details of which are included among the various sections herein. IAS 1 also requires that each financial statement be presented with the same prominence in a complete set of financial statements.

1.12 An entity should make an explicit, unreserved statement of compliance with IFRSs. However, IAS 1 provides that in extremely rare circumstances, an entity can rebut the presumption that compliance with every IFRS results in a fair presentation and can deviate from an IFRS requirement only when compliance would be so misleading that it would conflict with the objectives of financial statements in the IFRS *Conceptual Framework*. In these circumstances only, an entity should deviate from an IFRS requirement, unless prohibited by its regulatory authority. This deviation is generally referred to as the *true and fair view override*.

1.13 IAS 1 also requires management to assess whether the entity is a going concern, to prepare its financial statements on that basis, and to use the accrual basis of accounting, except for cash flow information.

1.14 IAS 8 establishes the criteria for selecting and changing an accounting policy and the treatment and disclosure of changes in policy (whether voluntary or mandatory), changes in accounting estimates, and corrections of errors in the financial statements of prior periods.

1.15 Among other definitions, IAS 8 includes the following:
Accounting policy. A specific principle, basis, convention, rule, or practice that an entity applies in its financial statements.
Change in accounting estimate. An adjustment of the carrying amount of an asset or liability or the amount of the periodic consumption of an asset that results from a current assessment about the present status or future economic benefits of an asset. Because this change results from new information, it is not an error.
Prior period errors. Omissions or misstatements in the entity's financial statements in one or more prior periods from misuse or failure to use reliable information that either was available or the entity could reasonably have been expected to obtain and taken into account in preparing the financial statements.
Material. Omissions or misstatements of items are material if they could, individually or collectively, influence the economic decisions that users make on the basis of financial statements. An entity should judge materiality based on the nature and size of the omission or misstatement and surrounding circumstances, either alone or in combination.
Impracticable. When the entity cannot apply a requirement of a standard or interpretation even after making every reasonable attempt to do so. IAS 8 provides additional specific guidance for entities in determining whether retrospective application of a change in accounting policy is impracticable.

1.16 IAS 8 requires an entity to determine its accounting policy for a particular issue by applying all relevant IFRSs. In the absence of a relevant IFRS, an entity should use its judgment to develop and use an accounting policy that provides relevant and reliable information, as defined by the qualitative characteristics described in the IFRS *Conceptual Framework*. In making the judgment previously described, IAS 1 requires an entity to refer to and consider the following sources of guidance in IAS 8 in descending order:

- Requirements in IFRSs dealing with similar and related issues
- The definitions, recognition criteria, and measurement concepts for assets, income, and expenses in the IFRS *Conceptual Framework*

An entity may also consider the most recent pronouncements of other standard setters that have a similar conceptual framework, other accounting literature, and accepted industry practices, but only to the extent that these do not conflict with either IFRSs or the IFRS *Conceptual Framework*.

Author's Note

The requirement previously described is generally referred to as the *IFRS hierarchy*.

1.17 IAS 8 requires an entity to apply accounting policies consistently to similar events and circumstances unless a specific IFRS requires or permits categorization of items for which different policies would be appropriate. In the latter case, an entity should apply an accounting policy consistently to each category. IAS 8 permits an entity that is not adopting IFRSs for the first time to change its accounting policy only in one of the following two circumstances:

- IFRSs require a change in policy.
- The new policy provides reliable and more relevant information.

1.18 IAS 8 does not consider an entity's application of a different policy to be a change in accounting policy when the new policy is applied to transactions or events that are substantively different from those occurring before, that did not occur before, or that are immaterial.

1.19 When permitted or required to change an accounting policy, an entity should apply the new policy retrospectively or in accordance with any applicable transitional provisions of an IFRS, except to the extent that it is impracticable to determine the period-specific or cumulative effects of the change. Retrospective application requires the entity to restate its financial statements as if it had always applied the new policy. In addition to restating the relevant assets or liabilities, the entity should adjust the opening balance of each affected component of equity for the earliest period presented. When retrospective application is impracticable for period-specific effects, the entity should apply the new policy retrospectively to the earliest period practicable. When retrospective application is impracticable for the cumulative effect, the entity should apply the new policy prospectively from the earliest period practicable.

1.20 Except to the extent that a change in accounting estimate affects the carrying amounts of assets or liabilities, IAS 8 requires an entity to recognize a change in estimate prospectively by recognizing it in profit or loss in the period of change or future periods, to the extent the change relates to those periods respectively. When the change affects the carrying amount of an asset or liability, the entity should adjust the carrying amount in the period of change. For example, when an entity determines there is a change in the expected pattern of consumption of future benefits over an asset's useful life, it should change its depreciation method to reflect that pattern and treat the change as a change in accounting estimate. An entity will recognize the effects of this change in the amount of depreciation expense recognized both in the current period and in future periods.

1.21 IAS 8 considers a change in measurement basis to be a change in accounting policy, not a change in accounting estimate. However, IAS 8 requires an entity that initially applies a policy of revaluation to applicable assets, either in accordance with IAS 16, *Property, Plant and Equipment*, or IAS 38, *Intangible Assets*, to treat the change from cost to revalued amount as a revaluation in accordance with those standards. When it is difficult to distinguish a change in policy from a change in estimate, an entity should account for the change as a change in estimate.

1.22 With respect to prior period errors, an entity should correct any material errors by retrospective restatement, unless impracticable, in the first set of financial statements authorized for issue after it detects the error by restating

- the comparative amounts for the prior periods affected, when the error occurred during the period covered by the statements or
- the opening affected balance sheet line items of the earliest period presented, when the error occurred prior to the period covered by the statements.

1.23 Retrospective restatement corrects the amounts of financial statement elements as if the error had not occurred. Similar to the impracticability exception for retrospective application, an impracticability exception can apply to an entity's ability to determine both period-specific and cumulative effects. When retrospective restatement is impracticable for period-specific effects, the entity should retrospectively restate in the earliest period for which restatement is practicable. For a cumulative effect, the entity should restate prospectively from the earliest possible date.

U.S. GAAP

1.24 Financial Accounting Standards Board (FASB) *Accounting Standards Codification* (ASC) 105-10-05 explains that if the necessary guidance for a transaction or event is not specified within a source of authoritative U.S. generally accepted accounting principles (GAAP), an entity should first consider accounting principles for similar transactions or events within a source of authoritative U.S GAAP for that entity and then consider nonauthoritative guidance from other sources. When those accounting principles either prohibit the application of the accounting treatment to the particular transaction or event or indicate that the accounting treatment should not be applied by analogy, an entity should not follow those accounting principles. Unlike IFRSs, the concept statements are not considered authoritative sources of U.S GAAP, and FASB ASC does not give preference to the concept statements over other nonauthoritative sources. FASB ASC does not state that consistency with the concept statements in connection with an entity's application of an accounting treatment is necessary. The following items are examples of sources of nonauthoritative accounting and financial reporting practices identified in FASB ASC:

- Practices that are widely recognized and prevalent either generally or in the industry
- FASB Concepts Statements
- AICPA issues papers
- IFRSs

- Pronouncements of professional associations or regulatory agencies
- Technical Information Service Inquiries and Replies included in AICPA *Technical Practice Aids*
- Accounting textbooks, handbooks, and articles (such as *IFRS Accounting Trends & Techniques*).

Author's Note

The AICPA *Code of Professional Conduct and Bylaws* has been revised to recognize the IASB in London as an accounting body for purposes of establishing IFRSs, thus granting AICPA members the option to use IFRSs, including *International Financial Reporting Standard for Small and Medium-sized Entities* (*IFRS for SMEs*), as an alternative to FASB ASC, as applicable. As defined in the standard, *SMEs* are entities that do not have public accountability and publish general purpose financial statements for external users. Therefore, *IFRS for SMEs* is not applicable to Securities and Exchange Commission (SEC) registrants.

1.25 As discussed in FASB ASC 105-10-05-1, unlike IFRSs, U.S. GAAP, as codified in FASB ASC, includes the rules and interpretive releases of the SEC as sources of authoritative U.S. GAAP as a convenience to SEC registrants. In addition to SEC rules and interpretive releases, the SEC staff issues Staff Accounting Bulletins that represent practices that the staff follows when administering SEC disclosure requirements. SEC staff announcements and observer comments made at meetings of the Emerging Issues Task Force publicly announce the staff's views on certain accounting issues for SEC registrants.

Author's Note

SEC rules and interpretative releases may expand, modify, or decrease accounting and disclosure requirements for foreign private issuers, regardless of whether they file their annual financial statements with the SEC in Form 10-K, Form 20-F, or Form 40-F (Canadian issuers). Therefore, it is critical to consider SEC requirements, as well as those of FASB ASC, when reviewing the financial statements of SEC registrants. A general reference to FASB ASC in this publication does not include the SEC materials. When requirements are taken from an SEC rule or regulation, the commentary will cite that rule or regulation directly. However, a reference to U.S. GAAP includes both FASB ASC and SEC requirements.

1.26 Like IFRSs, FASB ASC 250-10-45-1 includes the presumption that, once adopted, an entity should not change an accounting principle (policy) to account for events and transactions of a similar type. Like IFRSs, FASB ASC 250-10-45-2 permits an entity to change an accounting principle in certain circumstances, such as when required to do so by new authoritative accounting guidance that mandates the use of a new accounting principle, interprets an existing principle, expresses a preference for an accounting principle, or rejects a specific principle. Similar to IFRSs, this paragraph also permits an entity to change an accounting principle if it can justify the use of an allowable alternative accounting principle on the basis that it is preferable. However, unlike IFRSs, FASB ASC does not define a preferable policy and,

therefore, does not constrain the choice to one that is more relevant to the users of the financial statements.

1.27 Like IFRSs, FASB ASC 250-10-45-1 does not consider the following to be changes in accounting principle:

- Initial adoption of an accounting principle for new events or transactions
- Initial adoption of an accounting principle for new events or transactions that previously were immaterial in their effect
- Adoption or modification of an accounting principle for substantively different transactions or events from those occurring previously

1.28 Like IFRSs, FASB ASC 250-10-45-5 requires an entity to apply a change in accounting principle retrospectively to all prior periods, unless it is impracticable to do so. Like IFRSs, retrospective application requires cumulative adjustments to the carrying amounts of assets and liabilities at the beginning of the earliest period presented; an adjustment, if any, to the opening balance of retained earnings or other relevant equity account; and adjusted financial statements for each individual prior period presented to reflect the period-specific effects of applying the new accounting principle. FASB ASC 250-10-45-7 provides similar guidance to that in IAS 8 when the impracticability exception applies to period-specific effects or to all periods. However, unlike IFRSs, FASB ASC 250-10-45-8 permits only direct effects of the change to be included in the retrospective adjustment and prohibits an entity from including indirect effects that would have been recognized if the newly adopted accounting principle had been followed in prior periods. An entity should only report indirect effects in the period in which the accounting change is made. In contrast, IFRSs require an entity to adjust the financial statements as if it had always applied the new policy and do not distinguish between the direct and indirect effects of the change.

1.29 Like IFRSs, FASB ASC 250-10-45-17 requires an entity to account for a change in accounting estimate prospectively in the period of change if the change affects that period only or in the period of change and future periods if the change affects both.

1.30 Like IFRSs, paragraphs 18–19 of FASB ASC 250-10-45 recognize that it may be difficult to distinguish between a change in an accounting principle and a change in an accounting estimate. Unlike IFRSs, FASB ASC 250-10-45-18 provides additional guidance for those circumstances when an entity's change in estimate is affected by a change in accounting principle, recognizing that the effect of a change in accounting principle or the method of applying it may be inseparable from the effect of the change in accounting estimate. An example of such change is a change in the method of depreciation, amortization, or depletion for long-lived nonfinancial assets. FASB ASC 250-10-45-19 permits an entity to apply this change prospectively as a change in accounting estimate. The paragraph further states that an entity should only make a change in accounting estimate affected by a change in accounting principle if the entity can justify the new accounting principle on the basis that it is preferable.

1.31 Like IFRSs, paragraphs 23–24 of FASB ASC 250-10-45 require an entity to correct any error in the financial statements of a prior period discovered after the financial statements are issued or available to be issued by restating the prior period financial statements. These paragraphs in FASB ASC require such errors to be reported as an error correction by restating the prior-period financial statements retrospectively with adjustments to the financial statements similar to those required by IFRSs. Unlike IFRSs, FASB ASC 250-10-45 does not provide an impracticability exception related to a correction of an error as FASB ASC 250-10-45-7 addresses with a change in accounting principle.

Presentation

IFRSs

1.32 IAS 1 requires an entity to include, at a minimum, a complete set of prior year comparative financial statements with the financial statements of the current year. When applying a change in an accounting policy retrospectively or making a retrospective restatement for an error correction, the entity should also provide a statement of financial position as of the beginning of the earliest period presented. Individual IFRSs may also require comparative note disclosures.

1.33 IAS 1 requires an entity to present fairly its financial position, financial performance, and cash flows and describes fair presentation in terms of faithful representation in accordance with the definitions and recognition criteria in the IFRS *Conceptual Framework*. An entity should presume that application of all requirements of IFRSs, with additional disclosure when necessary, provides a fair presentation.

1.34 IAS 1 requires an entity to separately present each material class of similar items and to separately present items that are dissimilar by nature or function, unless they are immaterial. An entity should not offset assets and liabilities or income and expense items, unless specifically required or permitted by an IFRS. However, when not material, IAS 1 permits an entity to display gains or losses from similar transactions on a net basis in the statement of comprehensive income.

1.35 IAS 1 requires an entity to present and classify financial statement items consistently, unless the entity finds it apparent that a different presentation or classification is more appropriate or IFRSs require a change in presentation.

U.S. GAAP

1.36 Unlike IFRSs, FASB ASC 205-10-45-2 states only that it is ordinarily desirable for an entity to present the statement of financial position; the income statement; and the statement of changes in equity for one or more preceding years, in addition to those of the current year.

1.37 Like IFRSs, however, Rule 3-01(a) of SEC Regulation S-X requires SEC registrants to present one-year comparative statements of financial position (that is, the current year and prior year). Unlike IFRSs, Rule 3-02(a) of SEC Regulation S-X requires an entity to present two-year comparative income statements and cash flow statements (that is, the current year and the two years immediately preceding the current year). Like IFRSs, paragraphs 3–4 of FASB ASC 205-10-45 require these statements to be comparable and include specific guidance for various changes (for example, changes in accounting principle). An entity is required to repeat, or at least refer to, any notes to financial statements, other expla-

nations, or accountants' reports that contain qualifications for prior years that appeared in the comparative statements when originally issued, to the extent this information remains significant. Multiple rules set forth in SEC Regulation S-X provide guidance to SEC registrants on the form and ordering of financial statements, presentation of amounts, omission of certain items, and requirements for supplemental schedules.

1.38 Unlike IFRSs, FASB ASC 250-10 does not require an entity to present an opening balance sheet of the earliest period presented when an entity retrospectively applies a change in accounting policy or restates to correct an error. FASB ASC 205-10-50-1 only requires an entity to provide an explanation of changes due to reclassifications or for other reasons that affect the manner of, or basis for, presenting corresponding items for two or more periods.

1.39 Like IFRSs, FASB ASC 210-20 permits an entity to offset a liability with an asset only when certain conditions are met. These conditions are similar, but not identical, to those in IFRSs. See section 8, "Financial Instruments and Related Disclosures," for further discussion on offsetting arrangements.

Disclosure

IFRSs

1.40 When an entity applies the true and fair view override in IAS 1, it should disclose the following information:
- Management concludes that the financial statements provide a fair presentation of financial position, financial performance, and cash flows.
- Management has complied with all of the requirements of IFRSs, except for the relevant IFRSs from which it deviated to achieve fair presentation.

The entity should also disclose the title of the relevant IFRSs from which it deviated, the nature of the deviation, an explanation of why the financial statements would be so misleading as to conflict with the objectives in the IFRS *Conceptual Framework* if it complied with the IFRS requirement, and the treatment adopted. In addition, the entity should disclose the financial effect of the deviation on each affected financial statement line item that would have been reported if the entity had complied with the IFRS. When the entity invoked the true and fair view override in a prior period and the current period statements are affected, it should make the same disclosures as required in the period of the deviation.

1.41 When a regulatory authority prohibits an entity from invoking the true and fair view override, it should, to the extent possible, disclose the following information:
- The title of the IFRS in question, the nature of the requirement, and the reason why management concludes that applying the requirement is so misleading that the financial statements conflict with the objectives in the IFRS *Conceptual Framework*
- For each period presented, the adjustments to each affected financial statement line item that would be necessary to achieve fair presentation

1.42 When management is aware of material uncertainties that cast doubt on the entity's ability to continue as a going concern, it should disclose those uncertainties. If the entity has not prepared its financial statements on a going concern basis, it should disclose that fact, the basis on which the statements are prepared, and the reason it is not considered a going concern.

1.43 When an entity changes its reporting year and presents financial statements for a period longer or shorter than one year, it should disclose the reason for the longer or shorter period and the fact that the amounts in the financial statements are not entirely comparable.

1.44 With respect to comparative information, an entity should provide comparative note disclosures, unless IFRSs permit or require otherwise. An entity should also include comparative relevant narrative and descriptive information. When an entity changes the classification of financial statement line items, it should reclassify comparative amounts, unless impracticable. The entity should also disclose the nature of, amount of, and reason for each reclassification by item or class of items. When it is impracticable to reclassify comparative period amounts, it should disclose the reason it was impracticable and the nature of the necessary reclassification adjustments.

1.45 IAS 1 establishes a structure for the note disclosures and requires an entity to provide notes that present information about the basis for preparation of its financial statements and disclose information not presented elsewhere in the financial statements, either because the information is required by another IFRS or is relevant to an understanding of its financial statements. An entity should present the note disclosures in a systematic way and cross-reference each line item in the financial statements to its related note(s). IAS 1 suggests that a useful organization of the notes would be for the entity to start with the required statement of compliance and accounting policies, followed by notes related to financial statement line items, and ending with notes related to off-balance sheet information (such as commitments and contingencies) and any nonfinancial disclosures they provide.

1.46 IAS 1 permits an entity to disclose the basis of preparation and discuss its accounting policies in a section separate from the other note disclosures.

Author's Note

Several survey companies provide accounting policy disclosures in a separate unnumbered section, which are so noted when included in an excerpt.

1.47 In the accounting policy disclosure, IAS 1 requires an entity to disclose the measurement basis (or bases) it uses and any other policy relevant to an understanding of how transactions, events, and conditions are reflected in its financial statements. An entity should also disclose, either in its accounting policy or another note, information about its judgments and decisions that affected the financial statements. The required disclosures take two forms:

- Judgments, other than those involving estimation, that could significantly affect the amounts recognized in the financial statements (for example, classification of financial instruments or whether all risks and rewards have been transferred when financial or leased assets are transferred to another entity)
- Sources of estimation uncertainty that could significantly affect the carrying amounts of assets and liabilities and result in a material adjustment to those amounts within the next fiscal year (for example, fair values of

financial instruments and estimated uncollectible receivables)

With respect to sources of estimation uncertainty, an entity should disclose the nature of the uncertainty and the carrying amount at the end of the reporting period of the related asset or liability.

1.48 IAS 1 requires an entity to disclose qualitative and summary quantitative information about its objectives, policies, and processes for managing its capital. For example, an entity should disclose a description of what constitutes its capital, whether it is subject to externally imposed capital requirements, and how it is meeting its own and externally imposed objectives for managing capital.

1.49 If not disclosed elsewhere, an entity should also disclose similar information about puttable financial instruments that it classifies as equity, including summary quantitative information, its objectives and policies for managing the obligation to repurchase or redeem these instruments, the expected cash outflow on repurchase or redemption, and information about how it determined the expected cash outflow.

1.50 IAS 1 requires an entity to disclose any unrecognized dividends, in total and per share, proposed or declared before the financial statements were authorized for issuance and any unrecognized cumulative preference share dividends.

1.51 If not disclosed elsewhere in the document that includes the financial statements, IAS 1 requires an entity to disclose its domicile and legal form; country of incorporation; and the address of its registered office or principal places of business, if different. An entity should describe the nature of its operations and principal activities, the name of its parent and the ultimate parent of the group to which it belongs, and information about the length of its life if it is an entity with a limited life.

1.52 In the period of the change in accounting policy, IAS 8 requires the following disclosures for changes in accounting policy:

- The nature of the change in accounting policy
- To the extent practicable and for all periods presented, the amount of any adjustments to each affected financial statement line item and, when earnings per share are presented, the effect on basic and diluted earnings per share
- To the extent practicable, the amount of the adjustment related to periods prior to those presented
- If retrospective application was impracticable for a particular prior period or for periods prior to those presented, the circumstances leading to the impracticability and a description of how and when the entity applied the change in policy

1.53 When an IFRS requires an entity to change its accounting policy, the entity should also disclose the title of the relevant IFRS, a description of any available transitional provisions, whether the transitional provisions were applied, and whether there will be any effect from such provisions in future periods. When an entity changes an accounting policy voluntarily, it should also disclose the reasons why the change is reliable and more relevant than its previous policy.

1.54 When a new IFRS has been issued but is not yet effective, an entity should disclose this fact and include the title of the IFRS, the effective date, and the nature of the pending change in policy. An entity should also disclose the date it expects to apply the new IFRS and discuss any known or reasonably estimable information about the expected impact on its financial statements or provide a statement to the effect that the impact is unknown.

1.55 With respect to a change in accounting estimate, an entity should disclose the nature and amount of the change in the current period and, unless impracticable, an estimate of the effect of the change in future periods. In the latter case, an entity should disclose that it was impracticable to estimate the future effect.

1.56 With respect to a prior-period error correction, an entity should disclose the nature of the error and the amount of the correction in the earliest prior period presented. To the extent practicable, an entity should disclose the amount of the error attributable to each prior period presented for each affected financial statement line item and, if earnings per share is presented, the effect on basic and diluted earnings per share. When retrospective restatement is impracticable for particular prior periods or all periods prior to those presented, the entity should disclose the circumstances leading to impracticability and provide a description of how and when the entity corrected the error. IAS 8 does not require these disclosures to be included in subsequent financial statements.

U.S. GAAP

1.57 Unlike IFRSs, FASB ASC does not contain an exception to achieve fair presentation comparable to the true and fair view override in IAS 1.

1.58 Unlike IFRSs, FASB ASC does not currently contain disclosure requirements when there is uncertainty regarding whether the entity will continue as a going concern.

Author's Note

FASB originally undertook a project entitled "Disclosures about Risks and Uncertainties and the Liquidation Basis of Accounting" (formerly "Going Concern") to determine what analysis management should make and the required disclosures in financial statements about risks and uncertainties that cast doubt about an entity's ability to continue as a going concern. At the request of constituents, FASB decided not to require management to assess whether there is substantial doubt about the entity's ability to continue as a going concern and have since shifted its focus to providing guidance on the liquidation basis of accounting. FASB proposed guidance that requires an entity to prepare financial statements on a liquidation basis if liquidation is imminent for that entity. Such financial statements should consist of a "Statement of Net Assets in Liquidation" and a "Statement of Changes in Net Assets in Liquidation." The entity should measure the items in the financial statements to reflect the actual amount of cash that the entity expects to collect or pay during the course of liquidation.

FASB expects to release an exposure draft on this project during the second quarter of 2012.

1.59 Like IFRSs, FASB ASC 205-10-50-1 requires an entity to explain any changes in the manner or basis of presentation of financial statement items, whether because of reclassifications or for other reasons.

1.60 Like IFRSs, FASB ASC 235-10-05 requires disclosure of an entity's accounting policies. Unlike IFRSs, guidance on the specific nature of such disclosures is not contained in a specific standard but dispersed throughout FASB ASC.

Author's Note

Accounting policy disclosure requirements under IFRSs are similar to disclosure requirements of critical accounting estimates or policies disclosed by SEC registrants. However, unlike IFRSs, which requires entities to present such information in note disclosures within the financial statements, SEC registrants generally disclose such information outside the financial statements within management's discussion and analysis (MD&A), in accordance with the SEC Interpretation *Commission Guidance Regarding Management's Discussion and Analysis of Financial Condition and Results of Operations* issued in 2003. This guidance was intended to elicit more meaningful disclosure in MD&A in a number of areas, including the overall presentation and focus of MD&A, with general emphasis on the discussion and analysis of known trends, demands, commitments, events and uncertainties, and specific guidance on disclosures about liquidity, capital resources, and critical accounting estimates.

1.61 Like IFRSs, FASB ASC 275-10-05-2 requires an entity to disclose information about the risks and uncertainties existing as of the date of its financial statements. These requirements are similar in some respects, but not identical, to those required by IAS 1. In accordance with FASB ASC 275-10-50-1, an entity should disclose risks and uncertainties existing as of the date of the financial statements related to the nature of operations, the use of estimates in the preparation of the financial statements, certain significant estimates, and current vulnerability due to certain concentrations. Although both FASB ASC and IFRSs require an entity to disclose risks and uncertainties related to an entity's nature of operations, FASB ASC 275-10-50 provides a more detailed discussion of the type of information that must be disclosed, including an explicit explanation that the preparation of financial statements in conformity with U.S. GAAP requires the use of management's estimates, and criteria for assessing vulnerability due to certain concentrations, as well as the types of concentrations requiring disclosure and their specific disclosure requirements. FASB ASC 275-10-50 also includes more implementation guidance and illustrations than IFRSs.

1.62 Unlike IFRSs, FASB ASC does not include a specific requirement to disclose cash dividends declared after the balance sheet date. Like IFRSs, FASB ASC 505-10-50-5 requires disclosure of the aggregate or per-share amounts at which preferred stock may be called or is subject to redemption through sinking-fund operations or otherwise and the aggregate and per-share amounts of arrearages in cumulative preferred dividends.

Author's Note

See the discussion of adjustments to earnings per share disclosures due to stock dividends and stock splits declared after the balance sheet date in paragraph 1.121.

1.63 Like IFRSs, FASB ASC 505-10-50-11 requires an entity that issues redeemable stock to disclose the amount of redemption requirements, separately by issue or combined, for all issues of capital stock that are redeemable at fixed or determinable prices on fixed or determinable dates in each of the five years following the date of the latest statement of financial position presented.

1.64 With respect to a change in accounting principle, FASB ASC 250-10-50-1 requires an entity to disclose similar information to that required by IFRSs, such as the nature of the change, the method of applying the change, and similar disclosure requirements when retrospective application is impractical. However, unlike IFRSs, FASB ASC does not make a distinction between mandated and voluntary changes in accounting policy. Like IFRSs, FASB ASC 250-10-50-1 does not require an entity to repeat disclosures related to a change in accounting principle in the financial statements of subsequent periods. However, unlike IFRSs, if the change has no material effect in the period of change but is reasonably certain to have a material effect in later periods, an entity should provide the required disclosures whenever the financial statements of the period of change are presented.

Author's Note

IFRSs only require an entity to explain why a voluntary change in accounting policy provides reliable and more relevant information, On the other hand, FASB ASC 250-10-50-1 requires the entity to provide an explanation of why a change in accounting policy is preferable, even when a FASB Accounting Standards Update (ASU) mandates the change.

1.65 Because FASB ASC 250-10-50-1 requires an entity to account for indirect effects of a change in accounting principle differently than direct effects, when an entity recognizes such effects, it should disclose a description of the indirect effects, including the amounts that have been recognized in the current period and the related per share amounts, if applicable. Unless impracticable, the entity should also disclose the amount of the total recognized indirect effects and the related per share amounts, if applicable, that are attributable to each prior period presented. IFRSs make no such distinction between disclosures required for direct or indirect effects of a change in accounting policy.

1.66 Unlike IFRSs, FASB ASC does not require an entity to identify and discuss updates to the authoritative literature and the potential impact on the financial statements. However, SEC *Codification of Staff Accounting Bulletins* topic 11(M), "Miscellaneous Disclosure—Disclosure of the Impact That Recently Issued Accounting Standards Will Have on the Financial Statements of the Registrant When Adopted in a Future Period," states that registrants who have not yet adopted a newly issued accounting standard should discuss the potential effects of adoption in registration statements and reports filed with the SEC. The SEC staff believes that recently issued accounting standards may constitute material matters; therefore, disclosure in the financial statements should also be considered in situations in which the change

to the new accounting standard will be accounted for in financial statements of future periods. This guidance does not require disclosure of the new standard if the entity does not expect the impact on the company's financial position and results of operations to be material. However, it is preferable for the entity to make a statement that the impact of the new standard is not material.

1.67 With respect to changes in accounting estimates and changes in accounting estimates affected by a change in accounting principle, FASB ASC 250-10-50-4 requires an entity to disclose the effect on income from continuing operations, net income (or other performance indicator), and any related per share amounts of the current period. However, unlike IFRSs, FASB ASC does not require this disclosure for estimates made each period in the ordinary course of accounting for items such as uncollectible accounts or inventory obsolescence, unless there has been a change in the estimate and the effect of the change is material. FASB ASC 250-10-50-5 also does not require disclosure of changes in an estimate resulting from a change in a valuation technique or its application. IFRSs do not include comparable exemptions from disclosure.

1.68 Unlike IFRSs, FASB ASC 250-10-50 does not require disclosure of a future effect of a change in accounting estimate; hence, disclosure is not required when it is impracticable to estimate it.

1.69 With respect to error corrections, like IFRSs, paragraphs 7 and 10 of FASB ASC 250-10-50 require an entity to disclose the nature of the error, the fact that the financial statements have been restated, the effect of the correction on each financial statement line item and any per share amounts presented for each prior period presented, and the cumulative effect of the change on the opening balances of retained earnings or other equity accounts for the earliest period presented. Like IFRSs, FASB ASC does not require an entity to include this disclosure in the financial statements of subsequent periods. Unlike IFRSs, FASB ASC does not include an impracticability exemption from retrospective correction of an error.

Presentation and Disclosure Excerpts

Author's Note

Some disclosure requirements of IAS 1 and IAS 8 only apply when an entity makes a change in the way it presents its financial statements or otherwise is not in compliance with the underlying principles of financial reporting established by IAS 1 and the IFRS *Conceptual Framework*. Generally, these requirements are not relevant for the survey companies. Therefore, this section does not include excerpts of all items requiring disclosure (for example, statements not prepared on a going concern basis).

Comprehensive IAS 1 and IAS 8 Disclosures

1.70

Author's Note

The Harry Winston Diamond Corporation disclosure excerpt that follows includes examples of the following disclosures:

- General information about the entity (name, legal form)
- Statement of compliance with IFRSs
- Basis of preparation
- Measurement bases
- Principles of consolidation
- Accounting policies and any changes thereto.
- Use of estimates and judgments, risks and uncertainties
- Discussion of issued but not yet effective IFRSs

Harry Winston Diamond Corporation (Jan 2012)

NOTES TO THE CONSOLIDATED FINANCIAL STATEMENTS

January 31, 2012 with comparative figures
(tabular amounts in thousands of United States dollars, except as otherwise noted)

Note 1: Nature of Operations

Harry Winston Diamond Corporation (the "Company") is a diamond enterprise with assets in the mining and luxury brand segments of the diamond industry.

The Company's mining asset is an ownership interest in the Diavik group of mineral claims. The Diavik Joint Venture (the "Joint Venture") is an unincorporated joint arrangement between Diavik Diamond Mines Inc. ("DDMI") (60%) and Harry Winston Diamond Limited Partnership ("HWDLP") (40%) where HWDLP holds an undivided 40% ownership interest in the assets, liabilities and expenses of the Diavik Diamond Mine. DDMI is the operator of the Diavik Diamond Mine. DDMI and HWDLP are headquartered in Yellowknife, Canada. DDMI is a wholly owned subsidiary of Rio Tinto plc of London, England, and HWDLP is a wholly owned subsidiary of Harry Winston Diamond Corporation of Toronto, Canada.

The Company also owns Harry Winston Inc., the premier fine jewelry and watch retailer with select locations throughout the world. Its head office is located in New York City, United States.

The Company is incorporated and domiciled in Canada and its shares are publicly traded on the Toronto Stock Exchange and the New York Stock Exchange. The address of its registered office is Toronto, Ontario.

These consolidated financial statements have been approved for issue by the Board of Directors on April 4, 2012.

Note 2: Basis of Preparation

(a) Statement of Compliance

These consolidated financial statements have been prepared in accordance with International Financial Reporting Standards ("IFRS"). These are the Company's first annual consolidated financial statements under IFRS for the fiscal year ending January 31, 2012. The accounting policies adopted in these consolidated financial statements are based on IFRS as issued by the International Accounting Standards Board ("IASB") as of January 31, 2012.

(b) Basis of Measurement

These consolidated financial statements have been prepared on the historical cost basis except for the following:

financial instruments through profit and loss are measured at fair value.

liabilities for Restricted Share Unit and Deferred Share Unit Plans are measured at fair value.

(c) Currency of Presentation

These consolidated financial statements are expressed in United States dollars, consistent with the predominant functional currency of the Company's operations. All financial information presented in United States dollars has been rounded to the nearest thousand.

Note 3: Significant Accounting Policies

The accounting policies set out below have been applied consistently to all periods presented in these consolidated financial statements, and have been applied consistently by Company entities.

(a) Basis of Consolidation

The consolidated financial statements comprise the financial statements of the Company and its subsidiaries as at January 31, 2012. Subsidiaries are fully consolidated from the date of acquisition or creation, being the date on which the Company obtains control, and continue to be consolidated until the date that such control ceases. The financial statements of the subsidiaries are prepared for the same reporting period as the parent company, using consistent accounting policies. All intercompany balances, income and expenses, and unrealized gains and losses resulting from intercompany transactions are eliminated in full. For partly owned subsidiaries, the net assets and net earnings attributable to minority shareholders are presented as non-controlling interests on the consolidated balance sheet.

Interest in Diavik Joint Venture

HWDLP owns an undivided 40% ownership interest in the assets, liabilities and expenses of the Joint Venture. The Company records its interest in the assets, liabilities and expenses of the Joint Venture in its consolidated financial statements with a one-month lag. The accounting policies described below include those of the Joint Venture.

(b) Revenue

Sales from the sale of rough diamonds, fine jewelry and watches are recognized when significant risks and rewards of ownership are transferred to the customer, the amount of sales can be measured reliably and the receipt of future economic benefits are probable. Sales are measured at the fair value of the consideration received or receivable, net of value-added taxes, duties and other sales taxes, and after eliminating sales within the Company.

(c) Cash Resources

Cash and cash equivalents consist of cash on hand, balances with banks and short-term money market instruments (with a maturity on acquisition of less than 90 days), and are carried at fair value.

(d) Trade Accounts Receivable

Trade accounts receivable are recorded at the invoiced amount and generally do not bear interest. The allowance for doubtful accounts is the Company's best estimate of the amount of probable credit losses in the existing accounts receivable. The Company reviews its allowance for doubtful accounts monthly. Account balances are written off against the allowance after all means of collection have been exhausted and the potential for recovery is considered remote.

(e) Inventory and Supplies

Luxury brand raw materials and work-in-progress are valued at the lower of cost and net realizable value, with cost determined using either a weighted average or specific item identification basis depending on the nature of the inventory. Work-in-progress costs include an appropriate share of production costs such as material, labour and overhead costs.

Luxury brand merchandise inventory is recorded at the lower of cost or net realizable value and includes jewelry and watches. Cost is determined on a specific item basis for jewelry and the average cost method is used for watches.

Mining rough diamond inventory is recorded at the lower of cost or net realizable value. Cost is determined on an average cost basis including production costs and value-added processing activity.

Mining supplies inventory is recorded at the lower of cost or net realizable value. Supplies inventory includes consumables and spare parts maintained at the Diavik Diamond Mine site and at the Company's sorting and distribution facility locations.

Net realizable value is the estimated selling price in the ordinary course of business, less estimated costs of completion and costs of selling the final product. In order to determine net realizable value, the carrying amount of obsolete and slow moving items is written down on a basis of an estimate of their future use or realization. A provision for obsolescence is made when the carrying amount is higher than net realizable value.

(f) Exploration, Evaluation and Development Expenditures

Exploration and evaluation activities include: acquisition of rights to explore; topographical, geological, geochemical and geophysical studies; exploratory drilling; trenching and sampling; and activities involved in evaluating the technical feasibility and commercial viability of extracting mineral resources. Capitalized exploration and evaluation expenditures are recorded as a component of property, plant and equipment. Exploration and evaluation assets are no longer classified as such when the technical feasibility and commercial viability of extracting a mineral resource are demonstrable. Before reclassification, exploration and evaluation assets are assessed for impairment. Recognized exploration and evaluation assets will be assessed for impairment when the facts and circumstances suggest that the carrying amount may exceed its recoverable amount.

Drilling and related costs are capitalized for an ore body where proven and probable reserves exist and the activities are directed at either (a) obtaining additional information on the ore body that is classified within proven and probable reserves, or (b) converting non- reserve mineralization to proven and probable reserves and the benefit is expected to be realized over an extended period of time. All other drilling and related costs are expensed as incurred.

(g) Property, Plant and Equipment

Items of property, plant and equipment are measured at cost, less accumulated depreciation and accumulated impairment losses. The initial cost of an asset comprises its purchase price and construction cost, any costs directly attributable to bringing the asset into operation, including stripping costs incurred in open pit mining before production commences, the initial estimate of the rehabilitation obligation, and for qualifying assets, borrowing costs. The purchase price or construction cost is the aggregate amount paid and the fair value of any other consideration given to acquire the asset. Also included within property, plant and equipment is the capitalized value of finance leases.

When parts of an item of property, plant and equipment have different useful lives, the parts are accounted for as separate items (major components) of property, plant and equipment.

Gains and losses on disposal of an item of property, plant and equipment are determined by comparing the proceeds from the disposal with the carrying amount of property, plant and equipment and are recognized within cost of sales and selling, general and administrative expenses.

(i) Depreciation

Depreciation commences when the asset is available for use. Depreciation is charged so as to write off the depreciable amount of the asset to its residual value over its estimated useful life, using a method that reflects the pattern in which the asset's future economic benefits are expected to be consumed by the Company. Depreciation methods, useful lives and residual values are reviewed, and adjusted if appropriate, at each reporting date.

The unit-of-production method is applied to a substantial portion of Diavik Diamond Mine property, plant and equipment, and, depending on the asset, is based on carats of diamonds recovered during the period relative to the estimated proven and probable ore reserves of the ore deposit being mined, or to the total ore deposit. Other plant, property and equipment are depreciated using the straight-line method over the estimated useful lives of the related assets, for the current and comparative periods, which are as follows:

Asset	Estimated Useful Life (Years)
Buildings	10–40
Machinery and mobile equipment	3–10
Computer equipment and software	3
Furniture, fixtures and equipment	2–10
Leasehold and building improvements	Up to 20

Amortization for mine related assets was charged to mineral properties during the pre-commercial production stage.

Upon the disposition of an asset, the accumulated depreciation and accumulated impairment losses are deducted from the original cost, and any gain or loss is reflected in current net profit or loss.

Depreciation methods, useful lives and residual values are reviewed at each financial year end and adjusted if appropriate. The impact of changes to the estimated useful lives or residual values is accounted for prospectively.

(ii) Stripping Costs

Mining costs associated with stripping activities in an open pit mine are expensed unless the stripping activity can be shown to represent a betterment to the mineral property, in which case the stripping costs would be capitalized and included in deferred mineral property costs within mining assets. Stripping costs incurred during the production phase of an open pit mine are variable production costs that are included as a component of inventory to be recognized as a component of cost of sales in the same period as the sale of inventory.

(iii) Major Maintenance and Repairs

Expenditure on major maintenance refits or repairs comprises the cost of replacement assets or parts of assets and overhaul costs. When an asset, or part of an asset that was separately depreciated, is replaced and it is probable that future economic benefits associated with the new asset will flow to the Company through an extended life, the expenditure is capitalized. The unamortized value of the existing asset or part of the existing asset that is being replaced is expensed. Where part of the existing asset was not separately considered as a component, the replacement value is used to estimate the carrying amount of the replaced assets, which is immediately written off. All other day-to-day maintenance costs are expensed as incurred.

(h) Intangible Assets

Intangible assets acquired separately are measured on initial recognition at cost, which comprises its purchase price plus any directly attributable cost of preparing the asset for its intended use. The cost of intangible assets acquired in a business combination is measured at fair value as at the date of acquisition.

Intangible assets with indefinite useful lives are not amortized after initial recognition and are tested for impairment annually or more frequently if events or changes in circumstances indicate that the asset is impaired. Harry Winston's trademark and drawings are considered to have an indefinite life because it is expected that these assets will contribute to net cash inflows indefinitely. For purposes of impairment testing, trademark and drawings are tested for recoverability individually. The Company maintains a program to protect its trademark from unauthorized use by third parties. The Harry Winston drawings are very closely related with the brand and have an enduring life expectancy. The archive of drawings reflects unique designs for jewelry and watches that form the basis for newly inspired jewelry and watch designs that are exclusive to Harry Winston and attract its clientele.

Following initial recognition, intangible assets with finite useful lives are carried at cost less any accumulated amortization and any accumulated impairment losses. Intangible assets with finite useful lives are amortized on a straight-line

basis over their useful lives and recognized in profit or loss as follows:

Asset	Estimated Useful Life (Years)
Wholesale distribution network	10

The amortization methods and estimated useful lives of intangible assets are reviewed annually and adjusted if appropriate.

(i) Other Non-Current Assets

Other non-current assets include depreciable assets amortized over a period not exceeding ten years.

(j) Financial Instruments

From time to time, the Company may use a limited number of derivative financial instruments to manage its foreign currency and interest rate exposure. For a derivative to qualify as a hedge at inception and throughout the hedged period, the Company formally documents the nature and relationships between the hedging instruments and hedged items, as well as its risk-management objectives, strategies for undertaking the various hedge transactions and method of assessing hedge effectiveness. Financial instruments qualifying for hedge accounting must maintain a specified level of effectiveness between the hedge instrument and the item being hedged, both at inception and throughout the hedged period. Gains and losses resulting from any ineffectiveness in a hedging relationship must be recognized immediately in net profit or loss.

(k) Provisions

Provisions represent obligations to the Company for which the amount or timing is uncertain. Provisions are recognized when (a) the Company has a present obligation (legal or constructive) as a result of a past event, (b) it is probable that an outflow of resources embodying economic benefits will be required to settle the obligation, and (c) a reliable estimate can be made of the amount of the obligation. The expense relating to any provision is included in net profit or loss. If the effect of the time value of money is material, provisions are discounted using a current pre-tax rate that reflects, where appropriate, the risks specific to the obligation. Where discounting is used, the increase in the provision due to the passage of time is recognized as a finance cost in net profit or loss.

Mine Rehabilitation and Site Restoration Provision:

The Company records the present value of estimated costs of legal and constructive obligations required to restore operating locations in the period in which the obligation is incurred. The nature of these restoration activities includes dismantling and removing structures, rehabilitating mines and tailings dams, dismantling operating facilities, closure of plant and waste sites, and restoration, reclamation and re-vegetation of affected areas.

The obligations generally arise when the asset is installed or the ground/environment is disturbed at the production location. When the liability is initially recognized, the present value of the estimated cost is capitalized by increasing the carrying amount of the related assets. Over time, the discounted liability is increased/decreased for the change in present value based on the discount rates that reflect current market assessments and the risks specific to the liability. Additional disturbances or changes in rehabilitation costs, including remeasurement from changes in the discount rate, are recognized as additions or charges to the corresponding assets and rehabilitation liability when they occur. The periodic unwinding of the discount is recognized in net profit or loss as a finance cost.

(l) Foreign Currency

Foreign Currency Translation

Monetary assets and liabilities denominated in foreign currencies are translated to US dollars at exchange rates in effect at the balance sheet date, and non-monetary assets and liabilities are translated at rates of exchange in effect when the assets were acquired or obligations incurred. Revenues and expenses are translated at rates in effect at the time of the transactions. Foreign exchange gains and losses are included in net profit or loss.

For certain subsidiaries of the Company where the functional currency is not the US dollar, the assets and liabilities of these subsidiaries are translated at the rate of exchange in effect at the reporting date. Sales and expenses are translated at the rate of exchange in effect at the time of the transactions. Foreign exchange gains and losses are accumulated in other comprehensive income under shareholders' equity. When a foreign operation is disposed of, in part or in full, the relevant amount in the foreign exchange reserve account is reclassified to net profit or loss as part of profit or loss on disposal.

(m) Income Taxes

Current and Deferred Taxes

Income tax expense comprises current and deferred tax and is recognized in net profit or loss except to the extent that it relates to items recognized directly in equity, in which case it is recognized in equity or in other comprehensive income.

Current tax expense is the expected tax payable on the taxable income for the year, using tax rates enacted or substantively enacted at the reporting date, and any adjustment to tax payable in respect of previous years. Deferred tax expense is recognized in respect of temporary differences between the carrying amounts of assets and liabilities for financial reporting purposes and the amounts used for taxation purposes. Deferred tax expense is measured at the tax rates that are expected to be applied to temporary differences when they reverse, based on the laws that have been enacted or substantively enacted by the reporting date.

A deferred tax asset is recognized to the extent that it is probable that future taxable profits will be available against which the temporary difference can be utilized. Deferred tax assets are reviewed at each reporting date and are reduced to the extent that it is probable that the related tax benefit will not be realized.

Deferred income and mining tax assets and deferred income and mining tax liabilities are offset, if a legally enforceable right exists to offset current tax assets against current income tax liabilities and the deferred income taxes relate to the same taxable entity and the same taxation authority.

The Company classifies exchange differences on deferred tax assets or liabilities in jurisdictions where the functional currency is different from the currency used for tax purposes as income tax expense.

(n) Stock-Based Payment Transactions

Stock-Based Compensation

The Company applies the fair value method to all grants of stock options. The fair value of options granted is estimated at the date of grant using a Black-Scholes option pricing model incorporating assumptions regarding risk-free interest rates, dividend yield, volatility factor of the expected market price of the Company's stock, and a weighted average expected life of the options. When option awards vest in installments over the vesting period, each installment is accounted for as a separate arrangement. The estimated fair value of the options is recorded as an expense with an offsetting credit to shareholders' equity. Any consideration received on amounts attributable to stock options is credited to share capital.

Restricted and Deferred Share Unit Plans

The Restricted and Deferred Share Unit ("RSU" and "DSU") Plans are full value phantom shares that mirror the value of Harry Winston Diamond Corporation's publicly traded common shares. Grants under the RSU Plan are on a discretionary basis to employees of the Company subject to Board of Directors approval. Under the prior RSU Plan, each RSU grant vests on the third anniversary of the grant date. Under the 2010 RSU Plan, each RSU grant vests equally over a three-year period. Vesting under both RSU Plans is subject to special rules for death, disability and change in control. Grants under the DSU Plan are awarded to non-executive directors of the Company. Each DSU grant vests immediately on the grant date. The expenses related to the RSUs and DSUs are accrued based on fair value. When a share-based payment award vests in installments over the vesting period, each installment is accounted for as a separate arrangement. These awards are accounted for as liabilities with the value of these liabilities being remeasured at each reporting date based on changes in the fair value of the awards, and at settlement date. Any changes in the fair value of the liability are recognized as employee benefit plan expense in net profit or loss.

(o) Employee Benefit Plans

The Company operates defined benefit pension plans, which require contributions to be made to separately administered funds. The cost of providing benefits under the defined benefit plans is determined separately using the projected unit credit valuation method by qualified actuaries. Actuarial gains and losses are recognized immediately in other comprehensive income.

The defined benefit asset or liability comprises the present value of the defined benefit obligation, plus any actuarial gains (less any losses) not recognized as a result of the treatment above, less past service cost not yet recognized and less the fair value of plan assets out of which the obligations are to be settled directly. The value of any asset is restricted to the sum of any past service cost not yet recognized and the present value of any economic benefits available in the form of refunds from the plan or reductions in future contributions to the plan.

Contributions to defined contribution pension plans are expensed as incurred.

(p) Segment Reporting

A segment is a distinguishable component of the Company that is engaged either in providing related products or services (business segment) or in providing products or services within a particular economic environment (geographical segment), which is subject to risks and returns that are different from those of other segments. The Company's primary format for segment reporting is based on business segments. Each operating segment's operations are reviewed regularly by the Company's Chief Executive Officer to make decisions about resources to be allocated to the segment and to assess its performance, and for which discrete financial information is available.

(q) Operating Leases

Minimum rent payments under operating leases, including any rent-free periods and/or construction allowances, are recognized on a straight-line basis over the term of the lease and included in net profit or loss.

(r) Impairment of Non-Financial Assets

The carrying amounts of the Company's non-financial assets other than inventory and deferred taxes are reviewed at each reporting date to determine whether there is any indication of impairment. If any such indication exists, then the asset's recoverable amount is estimated. For an intangible asset that has an indefinite life, the recoverable amount is estimated annually at the same time, or more frequently if events or changes in circumstances indicate that the asset may be impaired.

The recoverable amount of an asset is the greater of its fair value less costs to sell and its value in use. In the absence of a binding sales agreement, fair value is estimated on the basis of values obtained from an active market or from recent transactions or on the basis of the best information available that reflects the amount that the Company could obtain from the disposal of the asset. Value in use is defined as the present value of future pre-tax cash flows expected to be derived from the use of an asset, using a pre-tax discount rate that reflects current market assessments of the time value of money and the risks specific to the asset. For the purpose of impairment testing, assets are grouped together into the smallest group of assets that generates cash inflows from continuing use that are largely independent of the cash inflows of other assets or groups of assets (the "cash-generating unit").

An impairment loss is recognized if the carrying amount of an asset or its cash-generating unit exceeds its estimated recoverable amount. Impairment losses are recognized in the consolidated statement of income in those expense categories consistent with the function of the impaired asset. Impairment losses recognized in respect of cash-generating units would be allocated to reduce the carrying amounts of the assets in the unit (group of units) on a pro rata basis.

For property, plant and equipment, an assessment is made at each reporting date as to whether there is any indication that previously recognized impairment losses may no longer exist or may have decreased. If such indication exists, the Company makes an estimate of the recoverable amount. A previously recognized impairment loss is reversed only if there has been a change in the estimates used to determine the asset's recoverable amount since the last impairment loss was recognized. If this is the case, the carrying amount of the asset is increased to its recoverable amount. The increased amount cannot exceed the carrying amount that would have been determined, net of depreciation, had no impairment loss been recognized for the asset in prior years. Such reversal is recognized in the consolidated statement of income.

(s) Basic and Diluted Earnings Per Share

Basic earnings per share are calculated by dividing net profit or loss by the weighted average number of shares outstanding during the period. Diluted earnings per share are determined using the treasury stock method to calculate the dilutive effect of options and warrants. The treasury stock method assumes that the exercise of any "in-the-money" options with the option proceeds would be used to purchase common shares at the average market value for the period. Options with an exercise price higher than the average market value for the period are not included in the calculation of diluted earnings per share as such options are not dilutive.

(t) Use of Estimates, Judgments and Assumptions

The preparation of the consolidated financial statements in conformity with IFRS requires management to make judgments, estimates and assumptions that affect the application of accounting policies and reported amounts of assets and liabilities and contingent liabilities at the date of the consolidated financial statements, and the reported amounts of sales and expenses during the reporting period. Estimates and assumptions are continually evaluated and are based on management's experience and other factors, including expectations of future events that are believed to be reasonable under the circumstances. However, actual outcomes can differ from these estimates. Revisions to accounting estimates are recognized in the period in which the estimates are revised and in any future periods affected. Information about significant areas of estimation uncertainty and critical judgments in applying accounting policies that have the most significant effect on the amounts recognized in the consolidated financial statements is as follows:

Mineral Reserves, Mineral Properties and Exploration Costs

The estimation of mineral reserves is a subjective process. The Company estimates its mineral reserves based on information compiled by an appropriately qualified person. Forecasts are based on engineering data, projected future rates of production and the timing of future expenditures, all of which are subject to numerous uncertainties and various interpretations. The Company expects that its estimates of reserves will change to reflect updated information. Reserve estimates can be revised upward or downward based on the results of future drilling, testing or production levels, and diamond prices. Changes in reserve estimates may impact the carrying value of exploration and evaluation assets, mineral properties, property, plant and equipment, mine rehabilitation and site restoration provision, recognition of deferred tax assets, and depreciation charges. Estimates and assumptions about future events and circumstances are also used to determine whether economically viable reserves exist that can lead to commercial development of an ore body.

Impairment of Long-Lived Assets

The Company assesses each cash-generating unit at least annually to determine whether any indication of impairment exists. Where an indicator of impairment exists, a formal estimate of the recoverable amount is made, which is considered to be the higher of the fair value of an asset less costs to sell and its value in use. These assessments require the use of estimates and assumptions such as long-term commodity prices, discount rates, future capital requirements, exploration potential and operating performance. Financial results as determined by actual events could differ from those estimated.

Impairment of Intangible Assets With an Indefinite Life

The impairment assessment for trademark and drawings requires the use of estimates and assumptions. Financial results as determined by actual events could differ from those estimated.

Recovery of Deferred Tax Assets

Judgment is required in determining whether deferred tax assets are recognized in the consolidated balance sheet. Deferred tax assets, including those arising from un-utilized tax losses, require management to assess the likelihood that the Company will generate taxable earnings in future periods in order to utilize recognized deferred tax assets. Estimates of future taxable income are based on forecasted income from operations and the application of existing tax laws in each jurisdiction. To the extent that future taxable income differs significantly from estimates, the ability of the Company to realize the deferred tax assets recorded at the consolidated balance sheet date could be impacted. Additionally, future changes in tax laws in the jurisdictions in which the Company operates could limit the ability of the Company to obtain tax deductions in future periods.

Mine Rehabilitation and Site Restoration Provision

The mine rehabilitation and site restoration provision has been provided by management of the Diavik Diamond Mine and is based on internal estimates. Assumptions, based on the current economic environment, have been made which DDMI management believes are a reasonable basis upon which to estimate the future liability. These estimates are reviewed regularly by management of the Diavik Diamond Mine to take into account any material changes to the assumptions. However, actual rehabilitation costs will ultimately depend upon future costs for the necessary decommissioning work required, which will reflect market conditions at the relevant time. Furthermore, the timing of rehabilitation is likely to depend on when the Diavik Diamond Mine ceases to produce at economically viable rates. This, in turn, will depend upon a number of factors including future diamond prices, which are inherently uncertain.

Commitments and Contingencies

The Company has conducted its operations in the ordinary course of business in accordance with its understanding and interpretation of applicable tax legislation in the countries where the Company has operations. The relevant tax authorities could have a different interpretation of those tax laws that could lead to contingencies or additional liabilities for the Company. The Company believes that its tax filing positions as at the balance sheet date are appropriate and supportable. Should the ultimate tax liability materially differ from the provision, the Company's effective tax rate and its profit or loss could be affected positively or negatively in the period in which the matters are resolved.

(u) Standards Issued But Not Yet Effective

The following standards and interpretations have been issued but are not yet effective and have not been early adopted in these financial statements.

The IASB has issued a new standard, IFRS 9, "Financial Instruments" ("IFRS 9"), which will ultimately replace IAS 39, "Financial Instruments: Recognition and Measurement" ("IAS 39"). IFRS 9 provides guidance on the classification and measurement of financial assets and financial liabilities. This standard becomes effective for the Company's fiscal year end beginning February 1, 2015. The Company is currently assessing the impact of the new standard on its consolidated financial statements.

IFRS 10, "Consolidated Financial Statements" ("IFRS 10"), was issued by the IASB on May 12, 2011, and will replace the consolidation requirements in SIC-12, "Consolidation—Special Purpose Entities" and IAS 27, "Consolidated and Separate Financial Statements." The new standard establishes control as the basis for determining which entities are consolidated in the consolidated financial statements and provides guidance to assist in the determination of control where it is difficult to assess. IFRS 10 is effective for the Company's fiscal year end beginning February 1, 2013, with early adoption permitted. The Company is currently assessing the impact of IFRS 10 on its consolidated financial statements.

IFRS 11, "Joint Arrangements" ("IFRS 11"), was issued by the IASB on May 12, 2011 and will replace IAS 31, "Interest in Joint Ventures." The new standard will apply to the accounting for interests in joint arrangements where there is joint control. Under IFRS 11, joint arrangements are classified as either joint ventures or joint operations. The structure of the joint arrangement will no longer be the most significant factor in determining whether a joint arrangement is either a joint venture or a joint operation. Proportionate consolidations will no longer be allowed and will be replaced by equity accounting. IFRS 11 is effective for the Company's fiscal year end beginning February 1, 2013, with early adoption permitted. The Company is currently assessing the impact of IFRS 11 on its results of operations and financial position.

IFRS 13, "Fair Value Measurement" ("IFRS 13"), was also issued by the IASB on May 12, 2011. The new standard makes IFRS consistent with generally accepted accounting principles in the United States ("US GAAP") on measuring fair value and related fair value disclosures. The new standard creates a single source of guidance for fair value measurements. IFRS 13 is effective for the Company's fiscal year end beginning February 1, 2013, with early adoption permitted. The Company is assessing the impact of IFRS 13 on its consolidated financial statements.

General Information, Regulatory Environment

1.71

Administradora de Fondos de Pensiones Provida S.A. (Dec 2011)

NOTES TO THE CONSOLIDATED FINANCIAL STATEMENTS (in part)

Note 1. Legal Aspects of the Administrator

AFP Provida S.A. is an open corporation and legally domiciled at 100 Pedro de Valdivia Avenue, 16th floor, commune of Providencia in Santiago de Chile. The terms "AFP Provida", "Provida" and "Company", refer to the Pension Funds Administrator AFP Provida S.A., unless otherwise stated. References to "AFP" or "AFPs" refer to private pension funds administrators in general.

AFP Provida was constituted by public deed granted by Mr. Patricio Zaldivar Mackenna, Notary of Santiago, on March 3, 1981, and authorized to initiate activities by the Superintendency of Pensions, through Resolution No. E-006/81 of April 1, 1981.

The sole objective of the Company is to administrate Provida's Pension Funds Types A, B, C, D and E, under the terms established in Decree Law 3.500 of 1980 and its amendments, and to provide the services as established therein. From 1994 onward, through Law 19.301, the business of the AFPs was amplified by allowing them to constitute affiliate corporations. Likewise, they were allowed to invest in Corporations constituted as central securities depositories referred to in Law No. 18,876.

On June 13, 1983, AFP Provida was registered in the Securities Registry of the Superintendency of Securities and Insurance (SVS) under number 0211, initiating affiliation activities into the system on May 2, 1981, and collecting contributions from June 1 of the same year.

AFP Provida is a subsidiary of BBVA Inversiones Chile S.A., a Chilean entity controlled by Banco Bilbao Vizcaya Argentaria S.A. (Spanish Entity).

Business activities of AFP Provida are regulated by the Superintendency of Pensions.

Note 2. General Information

a) Regulation of the Pension System

Pension Funds Administrators are corporations whose sole and exclusive objective is to administrate Pension Funds and grant and administrate their benefits and services as required by law. They are subject to the rules and regulations of Decree Law 3,500 of 1980 and, in supplementary form, the provisions of Law No. 18,046 of 1981, its amendments and regulations.

Law No. 20,255, which became effective on July 1, 2009, introduced amendments to DL No. 3,500 in relation to the Pension Reform, as well as Law No. 20,366, which presents the benefits of the Solidarity Pension system.

The Superintendency of Pensions is the agency that regulates the Pension Funds Administrators and supervise the compliance with laws and regulations governing them, and also the instructions that the Superintendency issues. The Superintendency of Pensions also monitors the operations of the Administrators in their legal, administrative and financial aspects; applying sanctions for non-compliance with legal and regulatory provisions, and ensures that Administrators be in compliance with the minimum capital and mandatory investment requirements.

b) Economic Activity

AFP Provida is one of the largest and oldest private pension funds administrators operating in Chile and has occupied a leading position in the industry of private pension funds administrators from the beginning. AFP Provida is the largest AFP among the six operating in Chile in terms of number of participants, contributors, funds under management, total salaries subject to contributions and number of branch offices. The Chilean private pension funds system was created in May 1981, when Decree Law No. 3,500 of November 13, 1980 (the "Pension Law") was implemented to replace the old social security system.

To strengthen its competitive position, Provida, like other large AFPs, merged with smaller AFPs in order to increase its market share and reach scale economies.

On May 2, 1995, through Resolution No. E-107-95, the Superintendency of Pensions authorized the merger with El Libertador Pensions Fund.

On May 28, 1998, Provida acquired a 99.99% ownership interest of AFP Unión S.A. ("AFP Unión") from Inversiones Interamericana S.A. Resolution No. E-146-98 authorized it to merge with AFP Provida and their respective pension funds on June 1, 1998.

On March 18, 1998, Corp Group Pensions acquired an 89.1% ownership interest of AFP Protección S.A. ("AFP Protección"); subsequently, on January 1, 1999, Provida acquired AFP Protección's ownership interest held by Corp Group Pensions and by minority shareholders. Resolution No. E-156-98 authorized the merger of AFP Protección S.A. and AFP Provida and its respective pension funds on January 1, 1999.

These mergers were successful because Provida could sustain the increase in its market share achieved through these acquisitions. In figures, this is reflected by the growth of its market share in terms of participants from 29% before the mergers up to 40% and from 20% up to 29% in terms of funds under management in 2011. AFP Provida continues leading the pension funds industry with funds under management of MUS$39,253 and a portfolio of 3.48 million participants, equivalent to a 29.0% and 38.8% of the market shares, respectively to December 31, 2011.

In addition, starting in 1993, Provida began to participate in private pension funds systems in other Latin American countries. Currently, the Company held ownership interests in AFP Horizonte (Peru), AFP Génesis (Ecuador) and Afore Bancomer (Mexico) through its wholly-owned subsidiary Provida Internacional. Locally, it is an important shareholder of the Centralized Securities Depository ("DCV") and of PreviRed.com, an entity that offers online services for collection of pension fund contributions. Furthermore, in January 2002, after being granted the administration of the Unemployment Insurance on behalf of a consortium comprised of all AFPs, a new company known as the Administradora de Fondos de Cesantia de Chile S.A. ("AFC") was created that started operations on October 1, 2002, and in which AFP Provida holds a 37.8% ownership interest.

The law requires that all AFPs have one single social objective and are authorized to provide the following services:

Collect and administrate contributions made by participants—The collection and administration service that AFPs provide refers to both mandatory and voluntary contributions made by participants.

Invest contributions of participants in pension funds administrated by the AFP—In terms of the general objective of its investing activities, Provida administrates the investment portfolios composed of participants contributions, seeking the higher possible returns based on the risk level and terms for the profile of these participants. For this purpose and according to prevailing regulations, participants can choose from five types of funds that allow them to maximize their expected pension in accordance with their specific risk profile. The types of funds differentiate themselves, as stipulated by law, by the percentage invested in variable income securities. Hence, the funds are classified from Fund Type A, with the highest level of variable income securities, to Fund Type E, which includes a maximum 5% invested in variable income. Regulation establishes a series of restrictions on the investing activities that may be carried out in each fund in order to ensure that this differentiation is maintained among the funds according to the variable income risk permitted in each one.

Manage life and disability benefits for participants—Until June 2009, Provida contracted insurance to cover its obligation to provide life and disability benefits for its participants. The selection of the insurance company was performed through a competitive public bidding process open to all companies with life insurance license in Chile and it was designed to deliver the requested coverage under the best terms possible.

In May 2009, the bidding process for life and disability insurance was carried out, for a 12-month coverage period beginning on July 1, 2009. The cost of the insurance under this new format was 1.87% of the contributable salaries of participants in the AFPs. Therefore, since Provida no longer provided coverage of this insurance, the Company reduced the fees charged to its participants from 2.64% to 1.54% over contributable salaries beginning July 2009.

In May 2010, the second bidding process for life and disability insurance was held by the AFPs for the period July 2010-June 2012. The new rate was reduced to 1.49% of the contributable salaries.

It is important to mention that in the case of dependent workers, the contribution to finance the insurance (additional contribution) is paid by the employer, except for dependent young workers (between 18 and 35 years) who receive pension subsidies. This obligation became effective on July 1, 2009, and a temporary grace period for workers with fewer than 100 employees ended in June 2011.

Provide an old age pension for participants—The service of providing old age pensions stipulates that each AFP must furnish the specific benefits of old age pensions to its participants who meet the legal retirement age requirement of 60 years for women and 65 years for men.

Finally, the last change introduced by the Pension Reform in 2010 refers to the bidding process of all new participants entering to the private pension system over a 24-month period. This change was adopted to motivate price competition so as to obtain lower commissions for the participant; to generate greater price sensitivity to the demand; to ease the entry of new entities into the AFP industry; and to safeguard the participants' pensions.

This bid is awarded to the AFP offering the lowest fee commission rate (lower than to those prevailing at the time of the bid) for a 24-month period, over which such AFP may not modify its commissions and applies them to its current portfolio.

In January 2010, the first bidding process was carried out for the administration of pension accounts of new participants entering the system over the next 24 months. The administrators competing in this process were: AFP Cuprum S.A., AFP Habitat S.A., AFP Planvital S.A. and AFP Modelo S.A. On February 1, 2010, it was informed that AFP Modelo had been awarded the bid since it presented an offer with the lowest fee commission of 1.14%.

In January 2012 the second bidding process was carried out for the administration of pension accounts of new participants for the next 24 months. This time, the administrators competing in such process were: AFP Regional S.A. (legally incorporated, but it has not started operations yet), AFP Planvital S.A. and AFP Modelo. On January 30, 2012 it was informed that AFP Modelo had presented the lowest fee commission of 0,77%, thus it had again been awarded the administration of pension accounts, thus starting August 1, 2012, new participants who will be affiliated to AFP Modelo over the next 24-months.

Provida believes it has the competitive advantages to successfully face the new conditions of the industry, as well as the support of the BBVA Group, a leader in the Latin American pension market. In addition, Provida has implemented all of the processes and developments conducive to fully comply with the amendments of the Pension Reform Law and is continuously training its employees in order to provide the best service to its customers.

Basis of Presentation, Statement of Compliance, Going Concern Assessment

1.72

Diploma Group Limited (Jun 2011)

NOTES TO THE CONSOLIDATED FINANCIAL STATEMENTS (in part)

1. Corporate Information and Basis of Preparation

Diploma Group Limited is a company limited by shares incorporated and domiciled in Australia whose shares are publicly traded on the Australian Securities Exchange.

The address of the registered office is First floor, 140 Abernethy Road, Belmont, Western Australia 6104.

The financial report of Diploma Group Limited for the year ended 30 June 2011 was authorised for issue in accordance with a resolution of the Directors on 28 September 2011.

Basis of Preparation

The financial report is a general-purpose financial report, which has been prepared in accordance with the requirements of the *Corporations Act 2001,* Australian Accounting Standards and other authoritative pronouncements of the Australian Accounting Standards Board. The financial report has been prepared in accordance with the historical cost basis.

The financial report is presented in Australian dollars and all values are rounded to the nearest thousand dollars ($'000) unless otherwise stated under the option available to the

Company under ASIC Class Order 98/0100. The Company is an entity to which the class order applies.

Statement of Compliance

The financial report complies with Australian Accounting Standards as issued by the Australian Accounting Standards Board and International Financial Reporting Standards (IFRS) as issued by the International Accounting Standards Board.

Going Concern

For the year ended 30 June 2011, the Group had a cash deficit at the end of the financial year of $1.806 million, a net operating cash outflow of $8.269 million, and project specific debt totalling $12.490 million due for repayment by September 2011. This amount includes $9.326 million of debt relating to an associate (Zenith), not recognised on the Group's balance sheet. The $9.326 million represents Diploma's share of the total project specific debt of $22.397 million. In addition the Group was in breach of a financial covenant on a corporate facility which had a net drawn down balance at 30 June 2011 of $5.518 million.

Notwithstanding the above, the Directors' are of the opinion that, at the date of signing the financial report, the Group is a going concern having regard to the following pertinent matters:

1. $13.071 million of the $22.397 million of debt associated with the Zenith project was refinanced on 26 September 2011. The balance of this project specific debt totalled $9.326 million which represents Diploma's share. Approval for the refinance of Diploma's share of the project specific debt was received on 28 September 2011. The refinanced facility together with subsequent unit sales in the Zenith project will enable Diploma to repay its share of the Zenith project debt and provide the Group with $1.488 million in working capital along with 30% from each subsequent sale. The settlement profile of the currently contracted apartments will generate further cash inflow to the Group with the refinanced facility expected to be cleared by December 2011.

2. The project specific debt on the Group's Rockingham project (Salt 5) totalling $1.704 million was refinanced on 8 September 2011 and is now due for repayment on 5 April 2012 at which point the facility is expected to be refinanced into a construction facility.

3. Since year end the project specific debt associated with the Cove and Foundry Road projects, totalling $4.618 million has been repaid. The Group has obtained additional funding secured against the remaining unsold stock in these developments totalling $3.1 million.

4. The repayment date on the project specific debt on the Group's iSpire project totalling $1.500 million was extended to February 2012 at which point the facility is expected to be refinanced into a construction facility.

5. The Eleven78 project is due for completion by November 2011. 122 of the 126 apartments in this development have been presold either during or post the GFC. This project is expected to settle quickly once complete and is expected to return in excess of $10 million in cash to the Group.

6. The bank acknowledged the breach at 30 June 2011 and do not intend to take any action. The bank has renewed the facility for a further term until 31 October

2012. The new facility will include a reduction to the measure of the covenant breached and the limit will be reduced to $5.0 million. Furthermore, the same bank has re-affirmed their commitment to the financing of the last stage of the Group's Joondalup (Edge) development due to commence in October 2011.

7. The Group has cash in hand of $2.3 million as at 29 September 2011.

Material Uncertainty that Cast Doubt on the Ability to Continue as a Going Concern

1.73

TORM A/S (Dec 2011)

NOTES TO THE CONSOLIDATED FINANCIAL STATEMENTS (in part)

Note 1—Accounting Policies, Critical Accounting Estimates and Judgements (in part)

TORM A/S is a Danish shipping company founded in 1889 under the Danish Companies Act that is engaged primarily in the ownership and operation of product tankers and dry bulk carriers (hereinafter TORM A/S is referred to as TORM A/S or the Parent Company). TORM A/S and subsidiaries (hereinafter referred to as the Company or TORM) owns product tankers that primarily carry refined products such as naphtha, gasoline, gas oil, jet fuel, and diesel oil. TORM's dry bulk vessels carry commodities such as coal, iron ore and grain. The vessels trade worldwide. TORMS A/S's registered office and principal place of business is at Tuborg Havnevej 18, DK-2900 Hellerup, Denmark.

The Company provides transportation services by utilizing a fleet of vessels that it owns, charter in on short and long-term time charters, or commercially manage as the manager of a pool or through contracts with third-party owners. The Company charters in tankers and bulk vessels as are needed by the pools that it manages.

The annual report has been prepared in accordance with the International Financial Reporting Standards (IFRS).

The annual report has also been prepared in accordance with IFRS as issued by the International Accounting Standards Board (IASB).

The financial statements are prepared in accordance with the historical cost convention except where fair value accounting is specifically required by IFRS.

The functional currency in all major entities within TORM is the USD, and TORM A/S applies the USD as the presentation currency in the preparation of the annual report.

Note 2—Liquidity, Capital Resources, Going Concern and Subsequent Events

Liquidity and Capital Resources

In June 2011, TORM entered an agreement to amend its USD 900 million revolving credit facility agreement that matures with a bullet payment of USD 630 million in June 2013. The agreement was contingent upon completing a rights issue of approximately USD 100 million no later than 16 December

2011. As the rights issue was not completed, the original maturity schedule was not changed.

The continued weak freight markets and the continued uncertainty surrounding the global economy have put TORM's liquidity under significant pressure, and consequently the Company's ability to continue as a going concern is dependent on negotiating a comprehensive financing and restructuring plan with its banks and other stakeholders, which will secure the liquidity throughout 2012 and a long-term, sustainable capital structure.

In December 2011, TORM and the majority of its banks entered installment and covenant standstill agreements valid until 15 January 2012. Subsequently the standstill agreements have been extended latest until April 30, 2012. As of April 23, 2012, installments of USD 67 million have been deferred, and the Company is scheduled to make further loan repayments of USD 132 million during the remainder of 2012.

As of 31 December 2011, TORM's equity ratio was 23.2%, after impairment losses of USD 200 million, resulting in a breach of its financial covenants under the existing loan agreements, and due to this TORM no longer has the unconditional right to defer payments on the loans for more than 12 months. As of 31 December 2011, TORM's mortgage debt and bank loans of USD 1.9 billion were therefore in principle payable on demand and accordingly classified as current liabilities in the balance sheet. In January 2012, TORM also breached the USD 60 million cash covenant. TORM's standstill agreements with its banks do not waive these breaches, but provide for a period of time during which the banks will not take action against TORM in relation to the breaches. As of April 23, 2012, except for the temporary standstill agreements, none of these defaults have been remediated.

TORM entered into a number of charter-in agreements during the cyclical high markets of 2007-2008. The time charter portfolio is significantly misaligned with the current market levels, and consequently TORM and its banks have initiated negotiations with its time charter partners aimed at amending the charter-in rates and agreements. Such a restructuring is a necessary step to reach a financial solution that will ensure financial flexibility and create the resilience needed. The vast majority of the time charter partners have agreed to align the charter-in rates to the current market level until April 30, 2012.

Furthermore, TORM has taken comprehensive measures to address the cost base over the last couple of years, thereby significantly reducing administrative costs by 21% and vessel OPEX per day by 16%. This has been achieved despite underlying inflationary pressure. As part of the plan, TORM will continue its ongoing efficiency program with the target of achieving cumulative cost and cash flow improvements of USD 100 million over the next three years.

To improve the short-term liquidity and reduce the debt, TORM has also eliminated the newbuilding program by cancelling one MR newbuilding and selling two dry bulk newbuilding contracts in 2011. Furthermore, TORM took delivery of one MR newbuilding in January 2012 and one MR newbuilding in March 2012. On 16 March 2012, TORM entered into an agreement to cancel the last MR newbuilding order, which was scheduled for delivery in the second quarter of 2014. TORM does hereafter not have any newbuildings on order.

Despite the efforts to minimize costs and eliminate the newbuilding program, TORM must reach a positive solution with the banks and other important stakeholders as TORM with the current financial position and continuing low freight rate,

levels does not have sufficient liquidity to continue its operations throughout 2012.

On April 4, 2012, TORM announced that it reached a conditional framework agreement in principle with the bank coordination committee and its major time charter partners regarding a financing and restructuring plan. The plan encompasses the following key elements:

- The change in ownership will be implemented through a reduction of the nominal share capital from DKK 5 per share to DKK 0.01 per share and a subsequent capital increase by the banks and time charter partners through conversion of debt and payables.
- The banks will make available a revolving credit facility of USD 100 million to cover working capital requirements. The facility will mature in two years.
- The banks will defer all installments and repayments of loans until December 2016 with simultaneous possibility for rolling up interest the first two years. Should TORM before December 2016 generate liquidity in excess of a pre-defined minimum liquidity threshold, the banks will be entitled to such excess liquidity.
- It is a prerequisite that all time charter partners either align the time charter rates to the market level for the remaining contract periods or agree to cancel the time charters.
- In exchange for the above the banks and the time charter partners will according to the conditional framework agreement in principle receive an ownership interest of 92.5% in TORM A/S, while the existing shareholders will retain an ownership interest of 7.5% after the implementation of the plan.

The solution outlined in the conditional framework agreement in principle will provide TORM with financing and the required liquidity to continue as a going concern at least until the end of 2012.

The majority of the banks support the conditional framework agreement in principle, and acceptance to the agreement has been obtained from the vast majority of the time charter partners.

At the Annual General Meeting on April 23, 2012, TORMs shareholders authorized the Board of Directors to carry out the above-mentioned capital reduction and subsequent capital increase.

The implementation roadmap for the plan is outlined, but it is still subject to:

- finalization of the contractual agreements
- the final approval by the Board of Directors, the banks and time charter partners

The Company expects that the remaining contractual agreements and approvals will be finalized, and accordingly the Annual Report for 2011 is prepared under the assumption that the conditional framework agreement in principle will be successfully finalized.

Going Concern

On the basis of the above the consolidated financial statements have been prepared assuming that the Company will continue as a going concern. Accordingly, the financial statements do not include any adjustments relating to the recoverability and classification of recorded asset amounts, the amounts and classification of liabilities or any other adjustments that might occur in the event the Company is unable to continue as a going concern, except for the current classification of debt discussed in note 17.

If the above plan is not implemented or if the efforts to otherwise reach a comprehensive financing and restructuring plan result in TORM not being able to continue in a substantially unchanged form, the current TORM A/S might not be a going concern. In such a scenario or in a forced sale, the net value of the Company's assets, liabilities and off balance sheet items would be significantly lower than the current carrying amounts as at 31 December 2011, and consequently the financial position of the Company could be impacted (see note 9 for further information).

Subsequent Events

As described above and in note 17, loan covenants have been breached in 2011 and 2012. As the breaches have not been waived or otherwise remediated, the mortgage debt and bank loans of USD 1,579.4 million are reclassified as current liabilities, until new arrangements have been agreed upon with the banks. As outlined above, a comprehensive financing and restructuring plan is under implementation and the standstill agreements with the banks have in 2012 been extended until April 30, 2012.

1.74

Kazakhstan Kagazy PLC (Dec 2011)

NOTES TO THE CONSOLIDATED FINANCIAL STATEMENTS (in part)

1. The Group and Its Operations (in part)

Kazakhstan Kagazy PLC (the "Company") is a public company incorporated and domiciled under the laws of the Isle of Man. Refer to the shareholder Information section of the Annual Report for details of the nature of the Company's listing.

The Company and its subsidiaries (the "Group") operate in three major reportable operating segments, which are:

1) the production and distribution of corrugated product and paperboard packaging, as well as trading other paper products ("Paper Segment");
2) the provision of logistics services through an integrated inland container terminal, supported by Class A and Class B warehousing ("Logistics Segment"); and
3) land held for development and/or future sale ("Property Segment").

2. Significant Accounting Policies (in part)

Basis of preparation. The consolidated financial statements have been prepared in accordance with International Financial Reporting Standards (IFRSs) for Kazakhstan Kagazy PLC ("Company") and its subsidiaries.

These consolidated financial statements have been prepared in accordance with International Financial Reporting Standards ("IFRS") and IFRIC interpretations as applicable to companies reporting under IFRS. The Company's financial statements have been prepared under the historical cost convention, as modified by revaluation of property, plant and equipment and investment property.

Presented below are the significant accounting policies used for preparation of these consolidated financial statements. These accounting policies have been consistently applied to all presented reporting periods, unless stated otherwise.

The preparation of financial statements in compliance with IFRS requires the use of certain critical accounting estimates. It also requires management to exercise its judgement in the process of applying the Group's accounting policies. The areas involving a higher degree of judgement or complexity, or areas where assumptions and estimates are significant to the consolidated financial statements are disclosed in Note 3.

The financial reporting framework that has been applied in their preparation of financial statements is applicable law and International Financial Reporting Standards (IFRSs) as adopted by the European Union and IFRSs issued by the International Accounting Standards Board (IASB). Differences between IFRS and IFRS as adopted by EU did not have a material impact on these financial statements.

Going concern. Management have prepared these financial statements on the basis of going concern. Note 3 discloses the information on uncertainties related to events and conditions which may cast a material uncertainty upon the Group's ability to continue as going concern.

If the Group was unable to continue in operational existence, adjustments would have to be made to reduce the balance sheet values of assets to their recoverable amounts, to provide for further liabilities which might arise and reclassify non-current assets and liabilities as current assets and liabilities, respectively.

3. Critical Accounting Estimates and Judgements (in part)

The Group makes estimates and assumptions that affect the amounts recognised in the financial statements and the carrying amounts of assets and liabilities within the next financial year. Estimates and judgements are continually evaluated and are based on Management's experience and other factors, including expectations of future events that are believed to be reasonable under the circumstances. Management also makes certain judgments, apart from those involving estimations, in the process of applying the accounting policies. Judgments that have the most significant effect on the amounts recognised in the financial statements and estimate that can cause a significant adjustment to the carrying amount of assets and liabilities within the next financial year.

Financial Restructuring and Going Concern

Current Status of Negotiations With the Group's Banks and Bond Holders

In October and November 2009 the Company defaulted on its obligations to DBK and Alliance Bank respectively. During the period from January until April 2010, the Company also defaulted on the EBRD loan and on the coupon payment on all of its bond issues.

Since then, the Company has been conducting a debt restructuring process, which has resulted in the following:

- During 2010, an agreement had been reached with minority Bond Holders of the First issue.
  In the first half of the year 2011 the Group signed restructuring agreements with all of its Bond Holders of the First Issue.

In February and March 2011, amendments to the terms of the prospectus had become effective in respect of the Second, Third and Fourth Bond Issues.

In accordance with the terms of the agreement with the Bond Holders, Kazakhstan Kagazy JSC agreed to raise share capital in an amount not lower than USD 5 million by the end of 2013. Under the principal terms of restructuring signed with EBRD the Group committed to purchase equipment for the Paper business of at least USD 3 million by the end of 2012.

- In November 2010, Alliance Bank agreed to restructure its loan and to refinance the Eurasian Bank loan, for a total of USD 34.4 million. This agreement was further revised in February 2011.
- In June 2011, the Group signed an Agreement on Principal Terms of the Restructuring with DBK and EBRD. As at the date of this report, negotiations with DBK and EBRD to incorporate these terms into legally binding documents.

A summary of the Group's principal amount of outstanding debt is shown below:

In Thousands of USD	31 December 2011		31 December 2010	
	Net of Discount	Principal	Net of Discount	Principal
Bank debt not in default	30,514	33,819	37,806	37,806
Alliance Bank JSC	29,170	32,475	34,763	34,763
Kazkommertsbank JSC	1,150	1,150	3,043	3,043
Raiffeisen Leasing Kazakhstan LLP	194	194	—	—
Bonds not in default[1]	71,832	113,113	9,999	9,677
Total Bank and Bonds not in default	102,346	146,932	47,805	47,483
Bank debt in default	81,990	81,990	95,410	95,410
DBK	55,518	55,518	59,185	59,185
EBRD	26,472	26,472	35,968	35,968
Raiffeisen Leasing Kazakhstan LLP	—	—	257	257
Bonds in default	—	—	90,558	93,529
Total Bank and Bonds in default	81,990	81,990	185,968	188,939
Total debt	184,336	228,922	233,773	236,422

[1] Note: Including unpaid coupon that was capitalised under the terms of amendments to the prospectuses of the Second, Third and Fourth Bond issue.

Alliance Bank

Under the of a restructuring agreement with Alliance Bank general terms were set out as follows: the maturity of the loan was extended to 7 years from August 2013 until December 2020, the interest rate has been reset from 14% to 12.5%, and the loan has been redenominated in KZT, which will reduce future currency risk. Under the new loan conditions, the bank granted a grace period for payment of overdue and accrued interest up to March 2012, as well as repayment of principal until March 2013, subject to repayment of half of the loan refinanced from Eurasian Bank JSC in 2011.

In February 2011, an addendum to the existing loan agreements has been signed with Alliance Bank JSC under which payments of overdue and accrued interest were deferred until March 2014.

In March 2012, the Group sent a request to Alliance Bank to consider a revised repayment schedule. Although operational performance of the Class B warehouses has improved significantly, the current free cash flow cannot further finance the repayment of interest and principal, as some of the investment plans to develop the Class B warehouse site have not materialised. As a result, Alliance Bank agreed to delay repayment of the previously agreed March and April 2012 interest until 15 May 2012 and in the meantime to consider alternatives to extend maturity of the existing repayment schedule. Currently, the Group is in discussions with Alliance Bank.

Bonds

The Group has four issues of bonds ("Bonds")
Terms and conditions before restructuring:

	Nominal Value KZT Million	Nominal Value USD Thousand	Maturity
First Issue (KZ2CKY05B448)	4,000	26,954	2010
Second Issue (KZPC1Y05C020)	3,500	23,585	2011
Third Issue (KZPC2Y07C024)	3,500	23,585	2013
Fourth Issue (KZ2C0Y05D117)	12,000	80,863	2013

Terms and conditions after restructuring:

	Nominal Value KZT Million	Nominal Value USD Thousand	Maturity
First Issue (KZ2CKY05B448)	4,000	26,954	2018, 2020
Second Issue (KZPC1Y05C020)	3,917	26,392	2026
Third Issue (KZPC2Y07C024)	3,964	26,709	2028
Fourth Issue (KZ2C0Y05D117)	14,144	95,310	2028

In the first half of the year 2011 the Group signed restructuring agreements with all of its Bond Holders of the First Issue.

In February and March 2011, revised terms of the prospectuses with Bond Holders of the Second, Third and Fourth Issues were approved by Agency for Financial Regulation and Supervision of the Financial Market and Financial Organisations ("AFN").

The major terms agreed with the Bond Holders of the Second, Third and Fourth Issues, compared with the original terms, are as follows:

	Second Issue		Third Issue		Fourth Issue	
	Original Terms	New Terms	Original Terms	New Terms	Original Terms	New Terms
Maturity	2011	2026	2013	2028	2013	2028
Nominal coupon[1]	CPI* + 1.5%, not more than 12%	13%	CPI* + 1.5%, not more than 12%	13%	12%	13%

* CPI-Consumer price index.
Note (1): No cash coupon is paid in 2011 and 2012, in 2013, the cash coupon is 1%, and further on from 2014 onwards increases by 1% per annum until 2019. The unpaid coupon is accrued and paid on maturity.

Upon completion of the debt restructuring with the Bond Holders of the Second, Third and Fourth Issues the Group must comply with certain covenants and restrictions. These include:
- Prohibition of payment of dividends;
- Gradual reduction of the financial leverage coefficient;
- Capital expenditures shall not exceed twenty-five percent (25%) of the revenue of Kazakhstan Kagazy JSC; and
- Working capital should not increase by more than 35% of revenue of Kazakhstan Kagazy JSC.

The prospectus also introduces the obligation to appoint a representative from the Committee of Creditors (Bond Holders) as an Independent Director with the right to "veto" an acquisition or disposal of assets exceeding 25% or more of the value of total assets of the Group.

Accordingly, Nurlan Amirzhanov was elected as representative of the Committee of Creditors to the Board of Directors of the Kazakhstan Kagazy JSC which took place on the 30 March 2011.

European Bank for Reconstruction and Development ("EBRD")

The Group signed an Agreement on Principal Terms of the Restructuring on 14 June 2011.

On 4 November 2011, the Company held a meeting with representatives of EBRD and presented the financial performance results of the Paper business for the first 9 months of 2011. As a result of the meeting, it was agreed to revise the conditions of restructuring in more favourable terms to the Group.

At the start of 2012 the Board of Directors of Kazakhstan Kagazy JSC approved revised terms and conditions of restructuring. It is expected that final agreement with EBRD will be signed during 2012.

Development Bank of Kazakhstan ("DBK")

On 25 February 2011, DBK sued Astana Contract JSC and Paragon Development LLP. However, as a result of negotiations with representatives of the Bank, both parties agreed to suspend the trial and resolve the matter amicably and on 6 June 2011, the Group signed an Agreement on Principal Terms of the Restructuring.

Under the signed principal terms DBK granted an opportunity to repay the overdue interest before the end of the service period of the loan subject to additional collateral pledge. In addition, a risk manager, as a representative of the bank, was appointed to the Astana Contract group of companies with responsibility for control over the operating and investing activities.

In November 2011, the Group appointed White & Case as a legal adviser for its debt restructuring negotiations with DBK.

Since then it has been conducting negotiations to document the terms agreed, but has not reached a final agreement. Should these negotiations not be successful, the Astana Contract group of companies face the risk of bankruptcy.

Going Concern

Notwithstanding the term sheets signed with EBRD and DBK the terms agreed in them have not yet been incorporated into new legally binding loan agreements and discussions are ongoing.

Therefore Management do not consider that the restructuring with DBK and EBRD is finalised and have concluded that a material uncertainty exists therefore casting doubt on the Group's ability to continue as a going concern. The financial statements do not include the adjustment that would be necessary if the Group was unable to continue as a going concern.

However, Management believes that agreements will be reached with EBRD and DBK on satisfactory terms. Accordingly, based upon this belief the current cash flow projections for the Group, Management have a reasonable expectation that the Group has adequate resources to continue in operational existence for the foreseeable future and therefore the annual financial statements continue to be prepared on a going concern basis.

Offsetting—Taxation

1.75

Fibria Celulose S.A. (Dec 2011)

NOTES TO THE CONSOLIDATED FINANCIAL STATEMENTS (in part)

2. Presentation of Financial Statements and Significant Accounting Practices (in part)

2.10. Income Tax and Social Contribution

The tax expense for the year comprises current and deferred tax. Tax is recognized in the statement of operations, except to the extent that it relates to items recognized in other comprehensive income, directly in shareholders' equity. In this case the tax is also recognized directly in shareholders' equity in other comprehensive income.

The current income tax charge is calculated on the basis of the tax laws enacted or substantively enacted at the balance sheet date in the countries where the Company operates and generates taxable income. Management periodically evaluates positions taken in tax returns with respect to situations in which applicable tax regulation is subject to interpretation. It establishes provisions where appropriate on the basis of amounts expected to be paid to the tax authorities.

Deferred income tax is recognized, using the liability method, on temporary differences arising between the tax bases of assets and liabilities and their carrying amounts in the consolidated financial statements. However, deferred tax liabilities are not recognized if they arise from the initial recognition of goodwill; deferred income tax is not accounted for if it arises from initial recognition of an asset or liability in a transaction other than a business combination that at the time of the transaction affects neither accounting nor taxable profit or loss. Deferred income tax is determined using tax rates (and laws) that have been enacted or substantially enacted by the balance sheet date and are expected to apply when the related deferred income tax asset is realized or the deferred income tax liability is settled.

Deferred income tax assets are recognized only to the extent that it is probable that future taxable profit will be available against which the temporary differences can be utilized.

Deferred income tax is provided on temporary differences arising on investments in subsidiaries, except where the timing of the reversal of the temporary difference is controlled by Fibria and it is probable that the temporary difference will not be reversed in the foreseeable future.

24. Tax Amnesty and Refinancing Program ("REFIS")

In November 2009, the Company joined the REFIS introduced by Law 11941/09, the objective of which is the settlement of fiscal liabilities through a special system for payment of tax and social security debt in installments.

On June 28, 2011 all amounts under the program were consolidated after having complied all formal requirements established in the legislation and the amounts included in the consolidated debt relate mainly to:

- CSLL—judicial measure aiming the exclusion of export earnings of the basis for calculating the social contribution, as established by the constitutional amendment n° 33/2001;
- IRPJ/CSLL—judicial measure aiming the *correção monetária* of the balance sheet without monetary losses generated by the *plano verão*—Economic plan established by the Provisional Measure 32/1989, converted into Law 7.730/89;
- IRRF/CSLL—tax assessments issued due to the offset of income and social contribution tax losses, without compliance the limitation of 30%;
- IPI credit premium—tax credits transferred from KSR to Celpav, related to phase II (April 1, 1981 to April 30, 1985), which were the subject of a tax assessment notice issued by the Brazilian Federal Revenue Secretariat due to supposed noncompliance with accessory tax obligations;
- Economic Domain Intervention Contribution (CIDE)—judicial proceeding regarding CIDE on amounts paid to parties resident abroad as royalties or contractual remuneration, introduced by Law 10168/00 and amended by Law 10332/01—period: as from 2002;
- Tax on Financial Transactions (IOF)—judicial proceeding for declaration of non-existence of legal-tax relationship, in order not to be obliged to pay IOF on foreign exchange contracts entered into for purposes of raising funds abroad through the issue of Euronotes. The IOF amount was deposited in court on February 4, 1994;
- COFINS—rate increase from 2% to 3% as established by Law 9718/98;
- CSLL—tax assessment issued due to the deduction on basis for calculating the social contribution, of expenditure on the monetary correction portion to the difference between the variation of the IPC and of the BTN Fiscal in the year of 1990.

The following is a summary of the final values included in the program, as well as the benefits obtained:

Detail of Amounts	
Total upated debts included in the program	532.734
Benefits for reduction of fines and interest	(78,030)
Fines and interest offset against tax loss and negative basis	(129,397)
Total debt payable	325.307
Payments made	(21,356)
Balance of debt	303.951
Total of judicial deposits updated	349,802
Credit balance	45.851

Considering the legal right to offset judicial deposits related to the debts included in the program and since judicial deposits exceed the remaining debt (after the reductions established by the program) the remaining balance in favor of the Company, updated in December 31, 2011 is R$ 50,096, is presented within non-current assets under other accounts receivable and monthly updated by SELIC.

The benefits for reduction of fines and interest were recorded in financial result in the line "foreign exchange gain(loss) and indexation" and totaled R$ 57,950 in the year ending December 31, 2011 (R$ 61,875 in 2010).

Restatement Due to Change in Accounting Policy and Change in Presentation

1.76

UBS AG (Dec 2011)

CONSOLIDATED STATEMENT OF COMPREHENSIVE INCOME

	For the Year Ended				
	31.12.11			31.12.10	31.12.09
CHF Million	Total	UBS Shareholders	Non-controlling Interests		
Net profit	4,427	4,159	268	7,838	(2,125)
Other Comprehensive Income					
Foreign currency translation					
Foreign currency translation movements, before tax	995	703	292	(951)[2]	(35)
Foreign exchange amounts reclassified to the income statement from equity	8	8		237	(259)
Income tax relating to foreign currency translation movements	(6)	(6)		121	22
Subtotal foreign currency translation movements, net of tax[1]	998	706	292	(593)[2]	(272)
Financial investments available-for-sale					
Net unrealized gains/(losses) on financial investments available-for-sale, before tax	1,458	1,458		(499)	157
Impairment charges reclassified to the income statement from equity	39	39		72	70
Realized gains reclassified to the income statement from equity	(950)	(950)		(357)	(147)
Realized losses reclassified to the income statement from equity	24	24		153	1
Income tax relating to net unrealized gains/(losses) on financial investments available-for-sale	(76)	(76)		13	(54)
Subtotal net unrealized gains/(losses) on financial investments available-for-sale, net of tax[1]	495	495		(618)	27
Cash flow hedges					
Effective portion of changes in fair value of derivative instruments designated as cash flow hedges, before tax	3,093	3,093		927	78
Net (gains)/losses reclassified to the income statement from equity	(1,140)	(1,140)		(1,108)	(756)
Income tax effects relating to cash flow hedges	(417)	(417)		38	257
Subtotal changes in fair value of derivative instruments designated as cash flow hedges[1]	1,537	1,537		(143)	(421)
Total other comprehensive income	3,030	2,737	292	(1,354)[2]	(667)
Total comprehensive income	7,457	6,896	560	6,484[2]	(2,792)
Total comprehensive income attributable to non-controlling interests	560			609[2]	484
Total comprehensive income attributable to UBS shareholders	6,896			5,875	(3,276)

[1] Other comprehensive income attributable to UBS shareholders related to foreign currency translations was negative CHF 909 million in 2010 and negative CHF 136 million in 2009. Other comprehensive income attributable to UBS shareholders related to financial investments available-for-sale was negative CHF 607 million in 2010 and positive CHF 17 million in 2009. Other comprehensive income related to cash flow hedges was attributable to UBS shareholders for all periods presented.

[2] Presentational changes have been made to the prior period related to the redemption of preferred securities; refer to "Note 1b Changes in accounting policies, comparability and other adjustments" for more information.

CONSOLIDATED BALANCE SHEET

CHF Million	Note	31.12.11	31.12.10	31.12.09	% Change From 31.12.10
Assets					
Cash and balances with central banks		40,638	26,939	20,899	51
Due from banks	9a	23,218	17,133	16,804	36
Cash collateral on securities borrowed	10	58,763	62,454	63,507	(6)
Reverse repurchase agreements	10	213,501	142,790	116,689	50
Trading portfolio assets	11	181,525	228,815	232,258	(21)
of which: assets pledged as collateral		39,936	61,352	44,221	(35)
Positive replacement values	23	486,584	401,146	421,694	21
Cash collateral receivables on derivative instruments	10	41,322	38,071	53,774	9
Financial assets designated at fair value	12	10,336	8,504	10,223	22
Loans	9a	266,604	262,877	266,477	1
Financial investments available-for-sale	13	53,174	74,768	81,757	(29)
Accrued income and prepaid expenses		6,327	5,466	5,816	16
Investments in associates	14	795	790	870	1
Property and equipment	15	5,688	5,467	6,212	4
Goodwill and intangible assets	16	9,695	9,822	11,008	(1)
Deferred tax assets	22	8,526	9,522	8,868	(10)
Other assets	17	12,465	22,681	23,682	(45)
Total assets		1,419,162	1,317,247	1,340,538	8
Liabilities					
Due to banks	18	30,201	41,490	31,922	(27)
Cash collateral on securities lent	10	8,136	6,651	7,995	22
Repurchase agreements	10	102,429	74,796	64,175	37
Trading portfolio liabilities	11	39,480	54,975	47,469	(28)
Negative replacement values	23	473,400	393,762	409,943	20
Cash collateral payables on derivative instruments	10	67,114	58,924	66,097	14
Financial liabilities designated at fair value	19	88,982	100,756	112,653	(12)
Due to customers	18	342,409	332,301	339,263	3
Accrued expenses and deferred income		6,850	7,738	8,689	(11)
Debt issued	19	140,617	130,271	131,352	8
Other liabilities	20,21	61,692	63,719	72,344	(3)
Total liabilities		1,361,309	1,265,384	1,291,905	8
Equity					
Share capital		383	383	356	0
Share premium		34,614	34,393	34,824	1
Treasury shares		(1,160)	(654)	(1,040)	77
Equity classified as obligation to purchase own shares		(39)	(54)	(2)	(28)
Retained earnings		23,603	19,444	11,910	21
Cumulative net income recognized directly in equity, net of tax		(3,955)	(6,693)	(5,034)	(41)
Equity attributable to UBS shareholders		53,447	46,820	41,013	14
Equity attributable to non-controlling interests		4,406	5,043	7,620	(13)
Total equity		57,852	51,863	48,633	12
Total liabilities and equity		1,419,162	1,317,247	1,340,538	8

CONSOLIDATED STATEMENT OF CHANGES IN EQUITY

CHF Million	Share Capital	Share Premium	Treasury Shares	Equity Classified as Obligation to Purchase Own Shares	Retained Earnings	Foreign Currency Translation	Financial Investments Available-for-Sale	Cash Flow Hedges	Total Equity Attributable to UBS Shareholders	Non-controlling Interests	Total Equity
Balance as of 1 January 2009	293	25,288	(3,156)	(46)	14,487	(6,309)	347	1,627	32,531	8,002	40,533
Change in accounting policy[1]					159	(159)			0		0
Issuance of share capital	63								63		63
Acquisition of treasury shares			(476)						(476)		(476)
Disposition of treasury shares			2,592						2,592		2,592
Treasury shares gains/(losses) and net premium/(discount) on own equity derivative activity, net of tax		(1,268)							(1,268)		(1,268)
Premium on shares issued and warrants exercised		10,599							10,599		10,599
Employee share and share option plans		291							291		291
Tax benefits from deferred compensation awards		1							1		1
Transaction costs related to share issuances, net of tax		(87)							(87)		(87)
Dividends[2]									0	(849)	(849)
Equity classified as obligation to purchase own shares—movements				44					44		44
Preferred securities									0	(7)	(7)
New consolidations and other increases									0	3	3
Deconsolidations and other decreases									0	(13)	(13)
Total comprehensive income for the year recognized in equity					(2,736)	(136)	17	(421)	(3,276)	484	(2,792)
Balance as of 31 December 2009	356	34,824	(1,040)	(2)	11,910	(6,604)	364	1,206	41,013	7,620	48,633
Issuance of share capital	27								27		27
Acquisition of treasury shares			(1,574)						(1,574)		(1,574)
Disposition of treasury shares			1,960						1,960		1,960
Treasury shares gains/(losses) and net premium/(discount) on own equity derivative activity, net of tax		(43)							(43)		(43)
Premium/(discount) on shares issued and warrants exercised		(27)							(27)		(27)
Employee share and share option plans		(104)							(104)		(104)
Tax benefits from deferred compensation awards		(8)							(8)		(8)
Transaction costs related to share issuances, net of tax		(113)							(113)		(113)
Dividends[2]									0	(305)	(305)
Equity classified as obligation to purchase own shares—movements				(52)					(52)		(52)
Preferred securities									0	(2,622)[3]	(2,622)
New consolidations and other increases		(136)							(136)	6	(130)
Deconsolidations and other decreases									0	(264)	(264)
Total comprehensive income for the year recognized in equity					7,534	(909)	(607)	(143)	5,875	609[3]	6,484
Balance as of 31 December 2010	383	34,393	(654)	(54)	19,444	(7,513)	(243)	1,063	46,820	5,043	51,863

(continued)

CHF Million	Share Capital	Share Premium	Treasury Shares	Equity Classified as Obligation to Purchase Own Shares	Retained Earnings	Foreign Currency Translation	Financial Investments Available-for-Sale	Cash Flow Hedges	Total Equity Attributable to UBS Shareholders	Non-controlling Interests	Total Equity
Issuance of share capital									0		0
Acquisition of treasury shares			(2,455)						(2,455)		(2,455)
Disposition of treasury shares			1,949						1,949		1,949
Treasury shares gains/(losses) and net premium/(discount) on own equity derivative activity, net of tax		188							188		188
Premium on shares issued and warrants exercised		10							10		10
Employee share and share option plans		19							19		19
Tax benefits from deferred compensation awards		9							9		9
Transaction costs related to share issuances, net of tax									0		0
Dividends[2]									0	(269)	(269)
Equity classified as obligation to purchase own shares—movements				15					15		15
Preferred securities									0	(882)	(882)
New consolidations and other increases		(5)							(5)	1	(4)
Deconsolidations and other decreases									0	(47)	(47)
Total comprehensive income for the year recognized in equity					4,159	706	495	1,537	6,896	560	7,457
Balance as of 31 December 2011	383	34,614	(1,160)	(39)	23,603	(6,807)	252	2,600	53,447	4,406	57,852

[1] In 2011, we adjusted the 2009 opening balance of retained earnings by a credit of CHF 159 million and foreign currency translation by a corresponding debit of CHF 159 million to reflect a change in accounting policy. Refer to "Note 1b Changes in accounting policies, comparability and other adjustments" for more information.

[2] Represents dividend payment obligations for preferred securities.

[3] Presentational changes have been made to the prior period related to the redemption of preferred securities; refer to "Note 1b Changes in accounting policies, comparability and other adjustments" for more information.

Equity Attributable to Non-Controlling Interests

CHF Million	For the Year Ended		
	31.12.11	31.12.10	31.12.09
Preferred securities[1]			
Balance at the beginning of the year	4,907	7,254	7,381
Redemptions[2]	(882)	(2,622)[4]	(7)
Foreign currency translation[3]	334	275[4]	(120)
Balance at the end of the year	4,359	4,907	7,254
Other non-controlling interests at the end of the year	47	136	366
Total equity attributable to non-controlling interests	4,406	5,043	7,620

[1] Increases and offsetting decreases due to dividends are excluded from this table.

[2] Represents nominal amount translated at the historical currency exchange rate.

[3] In 2011, foreign currency translation losses of CHF 121 million were offset by the derecognition of cumulative foreign currency translation losses of CHF 455 million related to the redemption of trust preferred securities, which represent the difference between the historical currency exchange rate at issuance and the currency exchange rate prevailing at the redemption date.

[4] Presentational changes have been made to the prior period related to the redemption of preferred securities; refer to "Note 1b) Changes in accounting policies, comparability and other adjustments" for more information.

Number of Shares	For the Year Ended			% Change From
	31.12.11	31.12.10	31.12.09	31.12.10
Shares issued				
Balance at the beginning of the year	3,830,840,513	3,558,112,753	2,932,580,549	8
Issuance of shares	1,281,386	272,727,760	625,532,204	(100)
Balance at the end of the year	3,832,121,899	3,830,840,513	3,558,112,753	0
Treasury shares				
Balance at the beginning of the year	38,892,031	37,553,872	61,903,121	4
Acquisitions	155,636,639	105,824,816	33,566,097	47
Disposals	(109,573,119)	(104,486,657)	(57,915,346)	5
Balance at the end of the year	84,955,551	38,892,031	37,553,872	118

IFRS-BPPD 1.76

Conditional Share Capital

On 31 December 2011, 148,639,326 additional shares could have been issued to fund UBS's employee share option programs. Further conditional capital of up to 100,000,000 shares was available in connection with an arrangement with the Swiss National Bank (SNB). The SNB provided a loan to a fund owned and controlled by the SNB (the SNB Stab-Fund), to which UBS transferred certain illiquid securities and other positions. As part of this arrangement, UBS granted warrants on shares to the SNB and these warrants become exercisable if the SNB incurs a loss on its loan to the SNB StabFund.

On 14 April 2010 the annual general meeting of UBS AG shareholders approved the creation of conditional capital to a maximum amount of 380,000,000 shares for conversion rights/warrants granted in connection with the issuance of bonds or similar financial instruments. These positions are shown as conditional share capital in the UBS AG (Parent Bank) disclosure.

NOTES TO THE CONSOLIDATED FINANCIAL STATEMENTS (in part)

Note 1. Summary of Significant Accounting Policies (in part)

b) Changes in Accounting Policies, Comparability and Other Adjustments (in part)

Effective in 2011

Interests in Consolidated Investment Funds

In 2011, UBS changed its accounting policy for investments in consolidated investment funds that are not considered equity instruments as defined in IAS 32. Effective 2011, foreign currency gains and losses from translation of our investments in such funds are recorded in the income statement on the basis that the investment interests are financial liabilities of the consolidated investment fund. Previously, foreign currency translation gains and losses from these investments were presented in *Foreign currency translation* within *Other comprehensive income* on the basis that the investment interests represented a right to the residual assets and were therefore previously considered non-monetary items.

The revised accounting policy is considered more relevant as it better aligns the treatment of the foreign currency differences arising on the investments in the subsidiaries with the treatment of the investment interests.

This change in accounting policy was applied retrospectively, resulting in an adjustment to the opening balance sheet as of 1 January 2009. *Foreign currency translation* within *Cumulative net income recognized directly in equity, net of tax* was debited by CHF 159 million and *Retained earnings* was credited by CHF 159 million, with a corresponding impact on the statement of changes in equity. There was no impact on the reported net profit of 2009, 2010 and 2011.

Interests in Non-Consolidated Investment Funds

In connection with the above change in accounting policy, the classification of investments in non-consolidated funds in Note 11.

Trading portfolio and Note 13 *Financial investments available-for-sale* has been amended to align to the criteria in IAS 32 *Financial Instruments: Presentation*. The reclas-

sification of these interests from equity instruments to debt instruments has no impact on UBS's income statement and balance sheet. Prior periods in Note 11 and Note 13 have been restated accordingly.

Capitalization of Internally Generated Software

Following the approval of a new long-term IT investment plan, in the third quarter 2011 UBS reviewed the capitalization practice for internally generated computer software. As a result of this review, UBS implemented a process whereby UBS improved the ability to assess how software programs generate future economic benefits for UBS, determine the period over which these economic benefits will accrue to UBS, and track the capitalizable costs associated with the various programs to determine a reliable measurement of an amortizable asset. The change has been applied prospectively and led to capitalizing additional computer software development costs of CHF 106 million in the second half of 2011.

Presentation of Redemption of Preferred Securities

In the third quarter of 2010, UBS redeemed trust preferred securities of USD 1.5 billion classified as non-controlling interests, which had accumulated foreign currency translation (FCT) losses of CHF 1,093 million. At the time of the redemption, the reversal of these accumulated FCT losses was presented as part of the change to *Preferred securities* in non-controlling interests in the Statement of Changes in Equity. This reversal of the FCT loss would have been better presented as a foreign currency translation movement within non-controlling interests within the Statement of Comprehensive Income. The change also impacts the related Preferred securities table. This was only a presentational matter within non-controlling interests on the Statement of Changes in Equity and the Statement of Comprehensive income; balance sheet and income statement lines were not affected and the equity attributable to UBS shareholders was unchanged. Comparative amounts for 2010 have been amended to reflect the improved presentation, as follows:

- In the Statement of comprehensive income, *Foreign currency translation movements during the year, before tax* was changed by CHF 1,093 million to negative CHF 951 million for year ended 31 December 2010. *Total comprehensive income attributable to non-controlling interests* was changed by CHF 1,093 million to positive CHF 609 million for the year ended 31 December 2010.
- In the non-controlling interests component of the Statement of changes in equity for the year ended 31 December 2010, *Preferred securities* were reduced by CHF 1,093 million and *Total comprehensive income for the year recognized in equity* was increased by CHF 1,093 million.
- In the table on preferred securities for the year ended 31 December 2010, *Redemptions* were changed by CHF 1,093 million to negative CHF 2,622 million and *Foreign currency translation* was changed by CHF 1,093 million to positive CHF 275 million.

Definition of Cash and Cash Equivalents

For the purposes of the statement of cash flows, UBS has refined its definition of cash and cash equivalents to restrict it to balances with an original maturity of three months or less including cash, money market paper and balances with central and other banks. This refined definition is considered to result in more relevant and comparable information for the purposes of the statement of cash flows. Cash and cash equivalents have been reduced by CHF 60,888 million at 31 December 2010 and by CHF 92,105 million at 31 December 2009, to CHF 79,934 million and CHF 72,868 million, respectively, with related changes to cash flows from operating activities and investing activities. Nevertheless, the amounts now excluded from cash and cash equivalents in the statement of cash flows continue to be part of our liquidity position.

Transfer of Legacy Portfolio from the Investment Bank to the Corporate Center

On 30 December 2011, a portfolio of legacy assets was transferred from the Investment Bank to the Corporate Center. Together with the option to buy the equity of the SNB StabFund, UBS will report the legacy portfolio as a separate segment in the Corporate Center beginning in the first quarter of 2012, when all necessary internal reporting changes will have been put into place. Restated historical segment information will be provided prior to the publication of our first quarter 2012 financial report.

Personnel Expenses

In 2011, UBS reclassified the costs related to the voluntary employee share ownership plan (Equity Plus) from *Variable compensation—other* to *Other personnel expenses* in order to align the presentation with the FINMA definition of variable compensation. Prior periods in "Note 6 Personnel expenses" have been restated accordingly. As a result, *Other personnel expenses* were increased by CHF 80 million and CHF 132 million for the year ended 31 December 2010 and for the year ended 31 December 2009, respectively, with a corresponding decrease in *Variable compensation—other*. The change in presentation did not affect the total Personnel expenses.

Improvements to IFRS 2010

In May 2010, the IASB issued amendments to seven IFRS standards as part of its annual improvements project. UBS adopted the Improvements to IFRS 2010 on 1 January 2011. The adoption of the amendments resulted only in changes to the disclosure of maximum exposure to credit risk, as shown in Note 28c.

This is the only amendment to accounting standards that significantly impacts UBS effective 2011.

Note 11. Trading Portfolio

CHF Million	31.12.11	31.12.10
Trading Portfolio Assets by Issuer Type		
Debt instruments		
Government and government agencies	62,118	83,952
of which: Switzerland	418	13,292
of which: United States	22,958	19,843
of which: Japan	14,258	25,996
of which: United Kingdom	3,709	2,707
of which: Germany	3,547	3,679
of which: Australia	3,540	4,463
Banks	10,597	14,711
Corporates and other[1]	36,330	48,818
Total debt instruments[1]	109,045	147,481
Equity instruments[1]	37,400	44,335
Financial assets for unit-linked investment contracts	16,376	18,056
Financial assets held for trading	162,821	209,873
Precious metals and other physical commodities	18,704	18,942
Total trading portfolio assets	181,525	228,815
Trading Portfolio Liabilities by Issuer Type		
Debt instruments		
Government and government agencies	18,913	29,628
of which: Switzerland	261	237
of which: United States	5,634	11,729
of which: Japan	3,894	7,699
of which: United Kingdom	1,946	3,103
of which: Germany	2,492	2,350
of which: Australia	756	953
Banks	1,913	3,107
Corporates and other[1]	4,716	5,474
Total debt instruments[1]	25,542	38,209
Equity instruments[1]	13,937	16,765
Total trading portfolio liabilities	39,480	54,975

[1] From 2011 onwards, investment fund units have been classified as Corporates and other debt instruments; previously these investment fund units were classified as equity instruments. The comparative period has been adjusted accordingly; refer to "Note 1b) Changes in accounting policies, comparability and other adjustments" for more information.

CHF Million	31.12.11				31.12.10
	Level 1	Level 2	Level 3	Total	
Trading Portfolio Assets by Product Type					
Debt instruments					
Government bills/bonds	34,449	10,753	95	45,297	66,435
Corporate bonds, municipal bonds, including bonds issued by financial institutions	695	29,699	2,371	32,765	47,237
Loans	0	2,698	1,390	4,088	5,543
Investment fund units[1]	3,779	6,048	33	9,859	13,171
Asset-backed securities	9,513	3,785	3,737	17,035	15,098
of which: mortgage-backed securities	9,513	2,673	1,684	13,868	10,355
Total debt instruments[1]	48,436	52,983	7,625	109,045	147,481
Equity instruments[1]	35,312	1,933	155	37,400	44,335
Financial assets for unit-linked investment contracts	15,616	760	0	16,376	18,056
Financial assets held for trading	99,363	55,677	7,781	162,821	209,873
Precious metals and other physical commodities				18,704	18,942
Total trading portfolio assets				181,525	228,815
Trading Portfolio Liabilities by Product Type					
Debt instruments					
Government bills/bonds	15,418	1,608	0	17,026	26,650
Corporate bonds, municipal bonds, including bonds issued by financial institutions	471	6,315	335	7,122	10,525
Investment fund units[1]	921	161	1	1,083	834
Asset-backed securities	0	17	296	312	200
of which: mortgage-backed securities	0	9	278	287	123
Total debt instruments[1]	16,809	8,101	632	25,542	38,209
Equity instruments[1]	13,621	313	3	13,937	16,765
Total trading portfolio liabilities	30,430	8,414	636	39,480	54,975

[1] From 2011 onwards, investment fund units have been classified as debt instruments; previously these investment fund units were classified as equity instruments. The comparative period has been adjusted accordingly; refer to "Note 1b) Changes in accounting policies, comparability and other adjustments" for more information.

Note 13. Financial Investments Available-for-Sale

CHF Million	31.12.11	31.12.10
Financial Investments Available-for-Sale by Issuer Type		
Debt instruments		
Government and government agencies	47,144	67,552
of which: Switzerland	357	3,206
of which: United States	25,677	38,070
of which: Japan	8,854	6,541
of which: United Kingdom	3,477	8,303
of which: France	2,170	3,005
Banks	4,271	5,091
Corporates and other[1]	1,060	1,206
Total debt instruments[1]	52,475	73,850
Equity instruments[1]	699	918
Total financial investments available-for-sale	53,174	74,768
Unrealized gains—before tax	477	514
Unrealized (losses)—before tax[2]	(55)	(662)
Net unrealized gains/(losses)—before tax	422	(148)
Net unrealized gains/(losses)—after tax	250	(243)

[1] From 2011 onwards, investment fund units have been classified as Corporates and other debt instruments; previously these investment fund units were classified as equity instruments. The comparative period has been adjusted accordingly; refer to "Note 1b) Changes in accounting policies, comparability and other adjustments" for more information.

[2] Includes losses of CHF 28 million with a duration of more than 12 months as of 31 December 2011 (31 December 2010: CHF 31 million).

CHF Million	31.12.11				31.12.10
	Level 1	Level 2	Level 3	Total	
Financial Investments Available-for-Sale by Product					
Debt instruments					
Government bills/bonds	33,999	868	33	34,899	57,642
Corporate bonds, municipal bonds, including bonds issued by financial institutions	632	7,881	77	8,590	11,670
Investment fund units[1]	24	416	5	445	441
Asset-backed securities	0	8,541	0	8,541	4,097
of which: mortgage-backed securities	0	8,541	0	8,541	4,093
Total debt instruments[1]	34,654	17,706	115	52,475	73,850
Equity instruments					
Shares	155	30	296	481	690
Private equity investments	0	1	216	218	227
Total equity instruments[1]	155	32	512	699	918
Total financial investments available-for-sale	34,810	17,738	627	53,174	74,768

[1] From 2011 onwards, investment fund units have been classified as debt instruments; previously these investment fund units were classified as equity instruments. The comparative period has been adjusted accordingly. Refer to "Note 1 Summary of significant accounting policies" for more information.

Note 28. Measurement Categories of Financial Assets and Financial Liabilities (in part)

c) Maximum Exposure to Credit Risk and Credit Quality Information (in part)

The table below represents the Group's maximum exposure to credit risk by class of financial instrument and the respective collateral and other credit enhancements mitigating credit risk for these classes of financial instruments. The maximum exposure to credit risk includes the carrying amounts of financial instruments recognized on the balance sheet subject to credit risk and the notional amounts for off-balance sheet arrangements.

Where available, collateral is presented at fair value; for other collateral such as real estate, a best estimate of fair value is used. Credit enhancements (credit derivative contracts/guarantees) are included at their notional amounts. Both are capped at the maximum exposure to credit risk for which they serve as security.

The section "Risk management and control" describes management's view of credit risk and the related exposures. These differ in certain respects to the requirements of the accounting standard.

Maximum Exposure to Credit Risk

CHF Billion	31.12.11							
	Maximum Exposure to Credit Risk	Collateral				Credit Enhancements		
		Cash Collateral Received	Collateralized by Securities	Secured by Real Estate	Other Collateral[1]	Netting	Credit Derivative Contracts	Guarantees
Financial Assets Measured at Amortized Cost on the Balance Sheet								
Balances with central banks	38.6							
Due from banks	23.2	0.0	2.7		0.5			0.6
Loans[2,3]	266.6	11.4	53.9	148.2	16.4		0.6	2.6
Cash collateral on securities borrowed	58.8		58.8					
Reverse repurchase agreements	213.5		213.5					
Cash collateral receivables on derivative instruments[4]	41.3					28.0		
Accrued income, other assets	10.2		6.2					
Total financial assets measured at amortized cost	652.2	11.5	335.1	148.2	16.9	28.0	0.6	3.2

(continued)

CHF Billion	Maximum Exposure to Credit Risk	Collateral				Credit Enhancements		
		Cash Collateral Received	Collateralized by Securities	Secured by Real Estate	Other Collateral[(1)]	Netting	Credit Derivative Contracts	Guarantees
Financial Assets Measured at Fair Value on the Balance Sheet								
Positive replacement values[(5)]	486.6					428.9		
Trading portfolio assets—debt instruments[(6,7)]	99.2							
Financial assets designated at fair value—debt instruments	9.6		6.7		0.2		1.4	
Financial investments available-for-sale—debt instruments	52.3							
Total financial assets measured at fair value	647.7	0.0	6.7	0.0	0.2	428.9	1.4	0.0
Total maximum exposure to credit risk reflected on the balance sheet	1,299.9	11.5	341.8	148.2	17.1	456.9	2.0	3.2
Guarantees	18.8	1.5	1.9	0.2	1.5		1.8	1.9
Loan commitments	58.2	0.3	0.4	1.1	8.8		18.1	3.0
Forward starting transactions, reverse repurchase and securities borrowing agreements	27.6		27.6					
Total maximum exposure to credit risk not reflected on the balance sheet	104.6	1.8	29.9	1.3	10.3		19.8	5.0
Total at the year-end	1,404.5	13.2	371.7	149.5	27.5	456.9	21.8	8.2

(Header date: 31.12.11)

(1) Includes but not limited to life insurance contracts, inventory, accounts receivable, patents, and copyrights.

(2) Loans include a balance outstanding of USD 4.7 billion to the BlackRock fund. This loan is collateralized by a portfolio of US residential mortgage-backed securities included within "Other collateral." Refer to the "Risk, treasury and capital management" section of this report for more information.

(3) Loans include monoline-protected assets which were reclassified from held-for-trading to loans and receivables in fourth quarter 2008. The remaining carrying value of these assets was CHF 0.8 billion as of 31 December 2011. The fair value of credit default swap protection after credit valuation adjustments related to these assets was CHF 0.2 billion, which is not included in the column "Credit derivative contracts." Refer to the "Risk, treasury and capital management" section of this report for more information.

(4) Included within cash collateral receivables on derivative instruments are margin balances due from exchanges or clearing houses. The amount shown in the netting column represents the netting with related negative replacement values in accordance with Swiss Federal Banking Law.

(5) The amount shown in the netting column represents the netting with related negative replacement values and cash collateral payables in accordance with Swiss Federal Banking Law.

(6) These positions are generally managed under the market risk framework and are included in VaR. For the purpose of this disclosure, collateral and credit enhancements were not considered.

(7) Does not include debt instruments held for unit-linked investment contracts and investment fund units.

CHF Billion	Maximum Exposure to Credit Risk	31.12.10 Collateral				Credit Enhancements		
		Cash Collateral Received	Collateralized by Securities	Secured by Real Estate	Other Collateral[1]	Netting	Credit Derivative Contracts	Guarantees
Financial Assets Measured at Amortized Cost on the Balance Sheet								
Balances with central banks	24.5							
Due from banks	17.1		0.2		0.0			0.3
Loans[2,3]	261.3	8.4	46.3	144.3	17.2		1.1	2.3
Cash collateral on securities borrowed	62.5		62.5					
Reverse repurchase agreements	142.8		142.8					
Cash collateral receivables on derivative instruments[4]	38.1					23.9		
Accrued income, other assets	20.6		16.9					
Total financial assets measured at amortized cost	566.7	8.4	268.7	144.3	17.3	23.9	1.1	2.5
Financial Assets Measured at Fair Value on the Balance Sheet								
Positive replacement values[5]	401.1					338.0		
Trading portfolio assets—debt instruments[6,7]	134.3							
Financial assets designated at fair value—debt instruments	7.6		3.7		0.2		1.7	
Financial investments available-for-sale—debt instruments	73.4							
Total financial assets measured at fair value	616.5	0.0	3.7	0.0	0.2	338.0	1.7	0.0
Total maximum exposure to credit risk reflected on the balance sheet	1,183.3	8.4	272.4	144.3	17.5	361.9	2.8	2.5
Guarantees	16.4	1.5	1.8	0.3	2.3		1.6	1.4
Loan commitments	56.9	0.2	0.2	0.9	8.1		22.5	2.4
Irrevocable commitments to acquire ARS	0.1							
Forward starting transactions, reverse repurchase and securities borrowing agreements	39.5		39.5					
Total maximum exposure to credit risk not reflected on the balance sheet	112.9	1.7	41.4	1.2	10.4		24.1	3.8
Total at the year-end	1,296.1	10.1	313.8	145.5	27.9	361.9	26.9	6.4

[1] Includes but not limited to life insurance contracts, inventory, accounts receivable, patents, and copyrights.

[2] Loans include a balance outstanding of USD 5.7 billion to the BlackRock fund. This loan is collateralized by a portfolio of US residential mortgage-backed securities included within "Other collateral." Refer to the "Risk, treasury and capital management" section of this report for more information.

[3] Loans include monoline-protected assets which were reclassified from held-for-trading to loans and receivables in fourth quarter 2008. The remaining carrying value of these assets was CHF 5.3 billion as of 31 December 2010. The fair value of credit default swap protection after credit valuation adjustments related to these assets was CHF 0.5 billion, which is not included in the column "Credit derivative contracts." Refer to the "Risk, treasury and capital management" section of this report for more information.

[4] Included within cash collateral receivables on derivative instruments are margin balances due from exchanges or clearing houses. The amount shown in the netting column represents the netting with related negative replacement values in accordance with Swiss Federal Banking Law.

[5] The amount shown in the netting column represents the netting with related negative replacement values and cash collateral payables in accordance with Swiss Federal Banking Law.

[6] These positions are generally managed under the market risk framework and are included in VaR. For the purpose of this disclosure, collateral and credit enhancements were not considered.

[7] Does not include debt instruments held for unit-linked investment contracts and investment fund units.

Capital Disclosures

1.77

Embraer S.A. (Dec 2011)

CONSOLIDATED BALANCE SHEET

In millions of US dollars

	Note	12.31.2011	12.31.2010
Shareholders' Equity	28		
Capital		1,438.0	1,438.0
Treasury shares		(183.7)	(183.7)
Revenue reserves		1,740.7	1,759.8
Share-based remuneration		9.7	3.4
Accumulated other comprehensive		2.6	10.9
		3,007.3	3,028.4
Noncontrolling interest		110.5	103.1
Total Shareholders' Equity		3,117.8	3,131.5
Total Liabilities and Shareholders Equity		8,858.3	8,391.0

CONSOLIDATED STATEMENTS OF SHAREHOLDERS' EQUITY (in part)

				Attributable to Owners of Embraer										
				Revenue Reserves					Accumulated Other Comprehensive (Loss) Income					
	Capital	Treasury Shares	Share-Based Remu-neration	Invest-ment Subsidy	Statutory Reserve	Additi-onal Proposed Divi-dends	For Invest-ment and Working Capital	Retained Earnings	Actuarial Gain on Post Employment Benefit Obligations	Cumulative Translation Adjustment	Other Compre-hensive Income	Total	Non-controll-ing Interest	Total Share-holders' Equity
At December 31, 2010	1,438.0	(183.7)	3.4	26.1	127.4	27.2	1,579.1	—	0.7	10.2	—	3,028.4	103.1	3,131.5
Net income for the year	—	—	—	—	—	—	—	111.6	—	—	—	111.6	8.8	120.4
Cumulative translation adjustments—subsidiaries	—	—	—	—	—	—	—	—	—	(7.4)	—	(7.4)	(1.4)	(8.8)
Financial instruments available for sale	—	—	—	—	—	—	—	—	—	—	(0.9)	(0.9)	—	(0.9)
Total comprehensive income	—	—	—	—	—	—	—	111.6	—	(7.4)	(0.9)	103.3	7.4	110.7
Share-based remuneration Stock options grants exercised	—	—	9.7	—	—	—	—	—	—	—	—	9.7	—	9.7
Allocation of profits: Investment subsidy	—	—	—	6.5	—	—	—	(6.5)	—	—	—	—	—	—
Legal reserve	—	—	—	—	4.2	—	—	(4.2)	—	—	—	—	—	—
Interest on own capital (R$ 0.25 per share)	—	—	—	—	—	(27.2)	—	(106.9)	—	—	—	(134.1)	—	(134.1)
Reserve for investments and working capital	—	—	—	—	—	(6.0)	6.0	—	—	—	—	—	—	—
At December 31, 2011	1,438.0	(183.7)	13.1	32.6	131.6	—	1,573.1	—	0.7	2.8	(0.9)	3,007.3	110.5	3,117.8

NOTES TO THE CONSOLIDATED FINANCIAL STATEMENTS (in part)

2. Presentation of the Financial Statements and Accounting Practices (in part)

2.2 Summary of Significant Accounting Policies (in part)

(cc) Dividends and Interest on Own Capital

Proposed distributions of dividends to shareholders are recorded as a liability pursuant to Brazilian Corporate Law and the bylaws. Any amount over and above the minimum mandatory dividends determined under Brazilian Corporate law is only provisioned when declared at the Shareholders' meeting.

Brazilian companies are permitted to pay interest on own capital to shareholders based on shareholders' equity, and treat such payments as a tax deductible expense for Brazilian income tax purposes. This notional interest distribution is treated for accounting purposes as a deduction from shareholders' equity in a manner similar to a dividend. A withholding tax is due and paid upon payments to shareholders. Interest on own capital is treated as a dividend for purposes of the mandatory dividend payable if so approved by the shareholders.

28. Shareholders' Equity

(a) Capital

The authorized capital is divided into 1,000,000,000 common shares. The Company's subscribed and paid up capital at December 31, 2011 is US$ 1,438.0 and comprises 740,465,044 common shares, without par value, of which 16,798,400 shares are held in Treasury.

(b) Brazilian Government Golden Share

The Federal Government holds one "golden share" with the same voting rights as other holders of common shares but which grants it certain additional rights as established in article 9 of the Company's bylaws, including veto rights over decisions pertaining to the following matters:

I   Change of the Company's name or its corporate objective;
II   Alteration and/or application of the Company's logo;
III Creation and/or modification of military programs (whether or not the Federal Republic of Brazil is involved);
IV   Training third parties in technology for military programs;
V   Interruption of the supply of maintenance and spare parts for military aircraft;
VI   Transfer of control of the Company's stock control;
VII Any changes in (i) article 9 of the Company's bylaws, article 4, the main clause of art. 10, articles 11, 14 e 15, sub-item III of art. 18, paragraphs 1 and 2 of art. 27, sub-item X of art. 33, sub-item XII of art. 39 or Chapter VII of the Company's bylaws, or (ii) the rights attributed by the bylaws to the special class share.

(c) Treasury Shares

Treasury shares comprised, as of December 31, 2011, 16,798,400 common shares purchased and held in Treasury during which time their voting and economic rights will be suspended. The activity of Treasury shares is shown below:

	USD	Quantity	Share Value (USD)
In the beginning of the year[i]	183,743	16,800,000	10.94
Used for stock option plan[ii]	(18)	(1,600)	10.94
	—	—	—
At December 31, 2011	183,725	16,798,400	10.94

[i] Relates to 16,800,000 common shares mainly acquired on April 4, 2008, amounting to US$ 183.7, charged to the Reserve for investment and working capital as approved by the Board of Directors on December 7, 2007.

[ii] The beneficiaries of the shares used in the share-based compensation plan include the Statutory Board of Directors, Executive Directors and certain employees (Note 29).

At December 31, 2011 the market value of the shares held in Treasury was US$ 105.3 (2010—US$ 119.0).

(d) Investment Subsidy Reserve

This reserve was formed pursuant to article 195-A of Brazilian Corporate Law (as amended by Law 11,638, of 2007) and corresponds to the appropriation of part of the retained earnings derived from government subsidies received for investments in research and development by the Company and is recognized in the statements of income in the same line item of the realized investments.

These subsidies are not included in the calculation of the minimum mandatory dividends.

(e) Statutory Reserve

The statutory reserve is recorded annually as an appropriation of 5% of the net income for the year. The reserve may not exceed 20% of capital, or 30% of capital and capital reserves.

(f) Interest on Own Capital

According to Brazilian fiscal legislation, interest on own capital, paid or registered as a provision, is recorded in the accounts as a financial expense for tax purposes. However, for purposes of these financial statements, the amount is disclosed as a part of the net income for the year, and reclassified to shareholders' equity; the tax benefits arising from the distributions are included in the net income for the year.

In meetings held in 2011, the Statutory Board of Directors approved the distribution of interest on own capital as follows:

* On March 16, 2011, it approved the payment of interest on capital of US$ 26.7 or US$ 0.04 per share, for the first quarter of 2011, subject to withholding tax of 15%, respecting legal exemptions which was paid from April 19, 2011, without interest;

- On June 9, 2011, it approved the payment of interest on capital of US$ 46.4 or US$ 0.06 per share, for the second quarter of 2011, subject to withholding tax of 15%, respecting legal exemptions which was paid from July 22, 2011, without interest;
- On September 14, 2011, it approved the payment of interest on capital of US$ 35.1 or US$ 0.05 per share, for the third quarter of 2011, subject to withholding tax of 15%, respecting legal exemptions which was paid from October 17, 2011, without interest.

(g) Proposed Dividends

In conformity with the Company's bylaws, the shareholders are entitled to minimum mandatory dividends or interest on own capital equivalent to 25% of annual net income, adjusted by law.

The determination of the annual dividends, subject to the approval of the shareholders at the Annual General Meeting, is presented in Real as Brazilian Corporate Law establishes that all dividends are determined and paid based on Real amounts in the legal books, is shown below:

	12.31.2011	12.31.2010
Net income for the year	156.3	573.6
Investment subsidy	(11.1)	(15.3)
Legal reserve	(7.8)	(28.7)
	137.4	529.6
Minimum mandatory dividend (25%)	34.3	132.4
Dividends:		
Interest on own capital, net of tax	158.6	176.9
Interest on own capital, above minimum mandatory[i]	—	(45.3)
Total stockholder remuneration	158.6	131.6
Payments of the year	(158.5)	(49.6)
Total shareholders remuneration of previous period	0.2	0.2
Total shareholders remuneration—In millions of Brazilian reais	0.2	82.3
Total shareholders remuneration—In millions of US$	0.1	49.4

[1] The excess amount is reclassified from current liabilities to Additional dividends proposed in the Revenue reserve in shareholder's equity and is distributed in the period following the shareholders' approval.

(h) Investment and Working Capital Reserve

The purpose of this reserve is to shield funds which might otherwise be subject to distribution and are earmarked for: (i) investments in property, plant and equipment, without detriment to retained earnings, pursuant to art. 196 of Law 6,404/76;

and (ii) the Company's working capital. The reserve may also be used to (i) redeem, reimburse or purchase shares of the Company and (ii) be distributed to the shareholders.

(i) Other Comprehensive Income

Comprises the following adjustments:

  i Foreign exchange gains/losses resulting from translation of the consolidated financial statements in the functional currency to the presentation currency (Real);
  ii Foreign exchange gains/losses resulting from translation of the foreign subsidiaries' financial statements, measured in the functional currency other than of the Company (dollar), to the functional currency;
  iii Other comprehensive income—these refer to unrealized actuarial gains (losses) resulting from the health-care plans sponsored by the Company and to fair value variation of financial instruments available for sale.

39. Financial Instruments (in part)

(a) Capital Risk Management

The Company uses capital management to ensure the continuity of its investment program and offer a return to its shareholders and benefits to its stakeholders and also to maintain an optimized capital structure in order to reduce costs.

The Company may review its dividends payment policy, pay back capital to the shareholders, issue new shares or sell assets in order to maintain or adjust its capital structure (to reduce the financial indebtedness, for instance).

Liquidity and the leverage level are constantly monitored in order to mitigate refinance risk and to maximize the return to the shareholders. The ratio between the liquidity and the return to the shareholders may be changed pursuant to the assessment of Management.

Accordingly, the Company has been able to maintain cash surpluses over the balance of financial indebtedness and to assure liquidity by establishing and maintaining a standby credit line (Note 19).

The capital management may be changed due to economy scenario alterations or to strategic repositioning of the Company.

At December 31, 2011, cash and cash equivalents exceeded the Company's financial indebtedness by US$ 445.7 (US$ 691.8 in 2010) resulting, on a net basis, in a leverage-free capital structure.

Of the total financial indebtedness at December 31, 2011, 15.2% was short-term (5.1% in 2010) and the average weighted term was equivalent to 4.8 years (6.3 years in 2010). Own capital accounted for 35.2% and 37.3% of the total liabilities at the end of 2011 and 2010, respectively.

Capital Disclosures—Regulatory Capital

1.78

Sumitomo Mitsui Financial Group, Inc. (Mar 2012)

CONSOLIDATED STATEMENT OF FINANCIAL POSITION *(in part)*

(In Millions)	Note	At March 31 2012	2011
Equity:			
Capital stock	24	2,337,896	2,337,896
Capital surplus	24	862,933	1,081,556
Retained earnings	24	2,162,696	1,974,069
Other reserves	24	437,177	280,783
Treasury stock	24	(236,037)	(171,761)
Equity attributable to shareholders of Sumitomo Mitsui Financial Group, Inc.		5,564,665	5,502,543
Non-controlling interests	25	2,050,726	2,048,662
Total equity		7,615,391	7,551,205
Total equity and liabilities		¥141,874,426	¥136,470,927

CONSOLIDATED STATEMENT OF CHANGES IN EQUITY *(in part)*

(In Millions)	Capital Stock	Capital Surplus	Retained Earnings	Available-for-Sale Financial Assets	Exchange Differences on Translating the Foreign Operations	Treasury Stock	Shareholders' Equity	Non-controlling Interests	Total Equity
Balance at March 31, 2011	2,337,896	1,081,556	1,974,069	465,185	(184,402)	(171,761)	5,502,543	2,048,662	7,551,205
Comprehensive income:									
Net profit	—	—	345,430	—	—	—	345,430	112,568	457,998
Other comprehensive income (loss)	—	—	—	184,238	(28,352)	—	155,886	2,344	158,230
Total comprehensive income (loss)	—	—	345,430	184,238	(28,352)	—	501,316	114,912	616,228
Acquisition of subsidiaries	—	—	—	—	—	—	—	2,443	2,443
Transaction with non-controlling interest shareholders	—	(8,368)	(14,792)	508	—	44,127	21,475	(23,270)	(1,795)
Dividends to shareholders	—	—	(142,011)	—	—	—	(142,011)	(92,021)	(234,032)
Purchase of treasury stock	—	—	—	—	—	(111,518)	(111,518)	—	(111,518)
Sale of treasury stock	—	—	—	—	—	3,115	3,115	—	3,115
Loss on sale of treasury stock	—	(679)	—	—	—	—	(679)	—	(679)
Purchase of Type 6 preferred stock	—	—	—	—	—	(210,003)	(210,003)	—	(210,003)
Cancellation of Type 6 preferred stock	—	(210,003)	—	—	—	210,003	—	—	—
Others	—	427	—	—	—	—	427	—	427
Balance at March 31, 2012	¥2,337,896	¥862,933	¥2,162,696	¥649,931	¥(212,754)	¥(236,037)	¥5,564,665	¥2,050,726	¥7,615,391

NOTES TO THE CONSOLIDATED FINANCIAL STATEMENTS (in part)

1. General Information

Sumitomo Mitsui Financial Group, Inc. ("SMFG") was established on December 2, 2002, as a holding company for Sumitomo Mitsui Banking Corporation ("SMBC") and its subsidiaries through a statutory share transfer (*kabushiki-iten*) of all of the outstanding equity securities of SMBC in exchange for SMFG's newly issued securities. SMFG is a joint stock corporation with limited liability (*Kabushiki Kaisha*) incorporated under the Companies Act of Japan ("Companies Act"). Upon the formation of SMFG and the completion of the statutory share transfer, SMBC became a direct, wholly-owned subsidiary of SMFG. SMFG has a primary listing on the Tokyo Stock Exchange (First Section), with further listings on the Osaka Securities Exchange (First Section) and the Nagoya Stock Exchange (First Section). SMFG's American Depositary Shares are listed on the New York Stock Exchange.

SMFG and its subsidiaries (the "SMFG Group") offer a diverse range of financial services, including commercial banking, securities, leasing, credit card and other services.

The accompanying consolidated financial statements have been authorized for issue by the Management Committee on July 23, 2012.

2. Summary of Significant Accounting Policies (in part)

The principal accounting policies applied in the preparation of the consolidated financial statements are set out below. These policies have been consistently applied to all the fiscal years presented, unless otherwise stated.

Basis of Preparation

Compliance with International Financial Reporting Standards

The consolidated financial statements of the SMFG Group have been prepared in accordance with International Financial Reporting Standards ("IFRS") as issued by the International Accounting Standards Board ("IASB").

Basis of Measurement

The consolidated financial statements have been prepared under the historical cost basis except for the following:
- trading assets and liabilities are measured at fair value;
- derivative financial instruments are measured at fair value;
- financial assets at fair value through profit or loss are measured at fair value;

- available-for-sale financial assets are measured at fair value; and
- the liabilities and the assets recognized in the consolidated statement of financial position in respect of defined benefit plans are the present value of the defined benefit obligation less the fair value of plan assets, together with adjustments for unrecognized actuarial gains or losses and past service costs.

4. Segment Analysis (in part)

Business Segments

The SMFG Group's business segment information is prepared based on the internal reporting system utilized by management to assess the performance of its business segments. For the fiscal year ended March 31, 2012, there were no material changes in the organizational structure that affected the composition of the business segments. The SMFG Group has four main business segments: Commercial Banking, Securities, Leasing and Credit Card, with the remaining operations recorded in Others. The business segment information covers SMBC, which accounts for the major portion of the SMFG Group's total assets and revenue, in Commercial Banking, SMBC Nikko Securities Inc. ("SMBC Nikko Securities") and SMBC Friend Securities Co., Ltd. ("SMBC Friend Securities") in Securities, Sumitomo Mitsui Finance and Leasing Company, Limited ("SMFL") in Leasing, and Sumitomo Mitsui Card Company, Limited ("Sumitomo Mitsui Card") and Cedyna Financial Corporation ("Cedyna") in Credit Card.

SMBC's Others

SMBC's Others represents the difference between the aggregate of SMBC's five business units and SMBC as a whole. It mainly consists of administrative expenses related to the headquarters operations and profit or loss on the activities related to capital management. Amounts recorded in SMBC's Others include those related to the Corporate Staff Unit, the Corporate Services Unit, the Compliance Unit, the Risk Management Unit and the Internal Audit Unit, which do not belong to any of the five business units.

In addition, the revenues and expenses of the Investment Banking Unit, which develops and provides investment banking products and services, are in principle allocated to each business unit.

24. Shareholders' Equity

Common Stock

The changes in the number of issued shares of common stock and common stock held by SMFG or its consolidated subsidiaries and associates during the fiscal years ended March 31, 2012, 2011 and 2010 were as follows:

	For the Fiscal Year Ended March 31					
	2012		**2011**		**2010**	
	Outstanding	In Treasury	Outstanding	In Treasury	Outstanding	In Treasury
At beginning of period	1,414,055,625	32,581,914	1,414,055,625	17,070,340	789,080,477	20,049,818
Issuance of common stock	—	—	—	—	588,631,300	—
Conversion of Type 4 preferred stock	—	—	—	—	36,343,848	—
Net change	—	30,357,645[1]	—	15,511,574[2]	—	(2,979,478)
At end of period	1,414,055,625	62,939,559	1,414,055,625	32,581,914	1,414,055,625	17,070,340

[1] Includes an increase of 45,686,368 shares acquired mainly as consideration for the share exchange to make Promise a wholly-owned subsidiary of SMFG, and a decrease of 15,328,723 shares mainly delivered to shareholders of Cedyna by SMFG Card & Credit, a wholly-owned subsidiary of SMFG, as consideration for the share exchange executed on May 1, 2011.

[2] Includes 15,479,400 shares acquired by SMFG Card & Credit in connection with making Cedyna a wholly-owned subsidiary of SMFG Card & Credit through a share exchange.

The total number of authorized shares of common stock was 3,000 million at March 31, 2012 and 2011 with no stated value. All issued shares are fully paid. The details of the stock options outstanding to subscribe for shares of SMFG common stock are described in Note 40 "Share-Based Payment."

Preferred Stock

Preferred stock at March 31, 2012 and 2011 consisted of the following:

	Aggregate Amount	Number of Shares		Liquidation Value per Share
		Authorized	Issued	
	(In Millions)			(In Yen)
At March 31, 2012:				
Type 5 preferred stock	¥ —	167,000	—	¥ —
Type 6 preferred stock[1]	—	70,001	—	—
Type 7 preferred stock	—	167,000	—	—
Type 8 preferred stock	—	115,000	—	—
Type 9 preferred stock	—	115,000	—	—
At March 31, 2011:				
Type 5 preferred stock	¥ —	167,000	—	¥ —
Type 6 preferred stock[1]	210,003	70,001	70,001	3,000,000
Type 7 preferred stock	—	167,000	—	—
Type 8 preferred stock	—	115,000	—	—
Type 9 preferred stock	—	115,000	—	—

[1] SMFG acquired and cancelled all of the Type 6 preferred stocks on April 1, 2011.

The movement of preferred stock for the fiscal years ended March 31, 2012, 2011 and 2010 was as follows:

	Type 4 Preferred Stock		Type 6 Preferred Stock	
	Aggregate Amount	Number of Shares	Aggregate Amount	Number of Shares
	(In Millions)		(In Millions)	
Balance at April 1, 2009	¥ 100,200	33,400	¥ 210,003	70,001
Conversion to common stock	(100,200)	(33,400)	—	—
Balance at March 31, 2010	—	—	210,003	70,001
Balance at March 31, 2011	—	—	210,003	70,001
Acquisition and cancellation	—	—	(210,003)	(70,001)
Balance at March 31, 2012	¥ —	—	¥ —	—

IFRS-BPPD 1.78

All the preferred stocks have no stated value. The numbers in "Aggregate amount" in the table above represent the initial proceeds upon issuance.

Type 4 Preferred Stock

On January 15, 2003, SMFG's Board of Directors resolved to issue an aggregate amount of ¥150.3 billion of Type 4 preferred stock. The face value of each Type 4 preferred stock was ¥3 million. On the same day, SMFG and Goldman Sachs Group, Inc. ("GS") entered into a preferred stock subscription agreement through which GS subscribed for all of the issued Type 4 preferred stock. The Type 4 preferred stock was issued on February 8, 2003.

On April 30, 2008, GS exercised its conversion rights with respect to 16,700 Type 4 preferred stock at a conversion price of ¥3,188. Pursuant to the conversion, SMFG issued 15,715,100 shares of its common stock. GS exercised its conversion rights with respect to the remaining Type 4 preferred stock on January 28, 2010, at a conversion price of ¥2,757. Pursuant to the conversion, SMFG issued 36,343,848 shares of its common stock. None of the Type 4 preferred stock was outstanding at March 31, 2012, 2011, and 2010.

The Type 4 preferred stock had noncumulative and nonparticipating dividend rights. When SMFG paid annual dividends or interim dividends to its common stockholders, SMFG was required to pay to the holders of the Type 4 preferred stock an annual dividend per share of ¥135,000 or an interim dividend per share of ¥67,500 in preference to the common stockholders (any such interim dividend on the Type 4 preferred stock reduced the following annual dividend by the same amount). The holders of the Type 4 preferred stock were not entitled to any other dividends. The holders of the Type 4 preferred stock were not entitled to vote at the general shareholders' meeting unless a proposal to pay dividends to the holders of the Type 4 preferred stock was not submitted to a stockholder vote or was rejected by a stockholder vote.

In the event of SMFG's voluntary or involuntary liquidation, the holders of the Type 4 preferred stock would have been entitled to receive out of SMFG's residual assets a distribution of ¥3 million per share. The holders of the Type 4 preferred stock would have ranked equally with the holders of SMFG's other preferred stocks and in preference to the common stockholders. The holders of the Type 4 preferred stock were not entitled to any further distribution upon SMFG's liquidation.

The Type 4 preferred stock was convertible to common stock at any time from February 7, 2005 up to February 7, 2028. The conversion price was set initially at ¥3,310, the market price at which the Type 4 preferred stock was issued. The conversion price was subject to a downward reset at the time of conversion, if the market price of the common stock was less than the conversion price, as measured by a 30-day moving average. The downward reset was subject to a floor price, which was initially ¥1,092. If any Type 4 preferred stock had remained outstanding on February 7, 2028, it would have been mandatorily converted into common stock on the following day.

The instrument was accounted for in accordance with the substance of the transaction. As such, as required by IAS 32, the Type 4 preferred stock was treated as a compound financial instrument containing a liability component that represented the obligation on SMFG to deliver a variable number of common stock on conversion and an equity component representing the discretionary dividends. The liability component was required to be accounted for under IAS 39, and comprised of an embedded derivative representing the right to exercise the conversion before the maturity and the cap and floor on the number of common stocks to be delivered upon the conversion, and a financial liability representing the obligation to deliver ¥3 million worth of common stocks at maturity. At the contract date, SMFG recognized ¥16.0 billion of financial liability and ¥130.8 billion of embedded derivative, both of which were measured at fair value, and ¥3.5 billion of equity as the residual. The financial liability was subsequently carried at amortized cost and "Interest expense" was recognized in the consolidated income statement using the effective interest rate. The embedded derivative was subsequently carried at fair value and the change in the fair value was recognized in "Net trading income" in the consolidated income statement. At the conversion into common stock, the amount equivalent to the fair value of the common stocks delivered was credited to equity and the difference compared to the carrying amount of the financial liability, and the embedded derivative was recognized as a profit or loss. Dividends on the Type 4 preferred stock were recognized in equity in the period in which they were approved by the shareholders.

Type 6 Preferred Stock

On March 10, 2005, SMFG's Board of Directors resolved at the meeting to issue an aggregate amount of ¥210 billion of Type 6 preferred stock by means of a third-party allocation. On March 29, 2005, SMFG issued Type 6 preferred stock totaling 70,001 stocks to qualified institutional investors as defined in the Financial Instruments and Exchange Act of Japan (Sumitomo Life Insurance Company, Nippon Life Insurance Company and Mitsui Life Insurance Company).

The Type 6 preferred stock had noncumulative and nonparticipating dividend rights. When SMFG paid annual dividends or interim dividends to its common stockholders, SMFG was required to pay to the holders of the Type 6 preferred stock an annual dividend of ¥88,500 or an interim dividend of ¥44,250 in preference to the common stockholders (Any such interim dividend on the Type 6 preferred stock reduced the following annual dividend by the same amount). The holders of the Type 6 preferred stock were not entitled to any other dividends. The holders of the Type 6 preferred stock were not entitled to vote at the general shareholders' meeting unless a proposal to pay dividends to the holders of the Type 6 preferred stock was not submitted to a stockholder vote or was rejected by a stockholder vote.

In the event of SMFG's voluntary or involuntary liquidation, the holders of the Type 6 preferred stock would have been entitled to receive out of SMFG's residual assets a distribution of ¥3 million per share. The holders of the Type 6 preferred stock would have ranked equally with the holders of SMFG's other preferred stocks and in preference to common stockholders in this right. The holders of the Type 6 preferred stock were not entitled to any further distribution upon SMFG's liquidation. The Type 6 preferred stock was not convertible to common stock.

On February 28, 2011, SMFG's Board of Directors resolved at a meeting to acquire and cancel all of the issued Type 6 preferred stock (70,001 shares). Subsequent to the resolution, SMFG acquired and cancelled those preferred stocks on April 1, 2011.

Under IFRS, in accordance with the substance of the contractual arrangement, the Type 6 preferred stock was treated as equity in its entirety because there was no legally binding obligation to pay dividends or principal.

Capital Stock, Capital Surplus and Treasury Stock

"Capital stock" represents share capital under the Companies Act adjusted by the amount corresponding to the preferred stock which is accounted for as a liability under IFRS. Purchases of treasury stock are recognized at cost in "Treasury stock." Any additional paid-in capital, net gains or losses on the sale of treasury stock, and other changes in equity resulting from transactions with shareholders except for dividends are included in "Capital surplus."

Restriction on the Payment of Dividends

The amount of the capital surplus and retained earnings of SMFG that can be paid out as dividends is subject to restrictions under the Companies Act. These amounts are calculated based on SMFG's nonconsolidated statement of financial position prepared in accordance with Japanese GAAP. Therefore, the adjustments made to prepare the IFRS consolidated financial statements have no impact on the calculation.

The total amount that SMFG can pay out as a dividend was ¥630 billion at March 31, 2012.

Other than the restriction by the Companies Act, SMFG is required to maintain a risk-weighted capital ratio above 8% (at least half of which must consist of core capital ("Tier I"), or a risk-weighted core capital ratio of 4%) as per the Banking Act of Japan ("Banking Act"). Therefore, SMFG would not be able to pay a dividend if the ratio were to fall below the minimum amount as a result of the payment of the dividends.

Since SMFG is a holding company, its earnings rely mostly on dividend income from SMBC, and SMFG's other subsidiaries and associates. SMBC is subject to some restrictions on its dividend payment by the Companies Act and the Banking Act, similar to those applied to SMFG.

Other Reserves

Available-for-Sale Financial Assets Reserve

The available-for-sale financial assets reserve includes the accumulated gains and losses of available-for-sale financial assets excluding the amount reclassified to profit or loss when the assets are derecognized or impaired. The movements of the available-for-sale financial assets reserve for the fiscal years ended March 31, 2012, 2011 and 2010 were as follows:

(In Millions)	For the Fiscal Year Ended March 31		
	2012	2011	2010
At beginning of period	¥465,185	¥ 663,907	¥ 349,213
Gains (losses) arising during the period, before tax	253,865	(349,080)	616,762
Income tax (expenses) benefits for changes arising during the period	(50,061)	142,268	(251,308)
Reclassification adjustments for (gains) losses included in net profit, before tax	(21,563)	10,957	(77,339)
Income tax expenses (benefits) for reclassification adjustments	8,867	(5,131)	31,362
Amount attributable to non-controlling interests	(6,167)	2,543	(9,012)
Share of other comprehensive income (loss) of associates and joint ventures	(195)	(279)	4,229
At end of period	¥649,931	¥ 465,185	¥ 663,907

Exchange Differences on Translating the Foreign Operations Reserve

Exchange differences on translating the foreign operations reserve include foreign exchange differences arising from the translation of the net assets of foreign operations from their functional currencies to the SMFG Group's presentation currency, Japanese yen.

The movements of exchange differences on translating the foreign operations reserve for the fiscal years ended March 31, 2012, 2011 and 2010 were as follows:

(In Millions)	For the Fiscal Year Ended March 31		
	2012	2011	2010
At beginning of period	¥(184,402)	¥(108,618)	¥(120,897)
Losses arising during the period, before tax	(34,781)	(121,593)	(15,009)
Income tax (expenses) benefits for losses arising during the period	(503)	9,383	59
Reclassification adjustments for (gains) losses included in net profit, before tax	7,350	(505)	2
Income tax benefits for reclassification adjustments	(2,112)	—	—
Amount attributable to non-controlling interests	4,331	40,877	21,496
Share of other comprehensive income (loss) of associates and joint ventures	(2,637)	(3,946)	5,731
At end of period	¥(212,754)	¥(184,402)	¥(108,618)

25 Non-Controlling Interests

Non-controlling interests at March 31, 2012 and 2011 consisted of the following:

(In Millions)	At March 31	
	2012	2011
Preferred securities issued by subsidiaries	¥1,588,893	¥1,593,619
Others[1]	461,833	455,043
Total non-controlling interests	¥2,050,726	¥2,048,662

[1] For the fiscal year ended March 31, 2012, the SMFG Group recognized the decrease of equity by ¥15 billion from the transactions with non-controlling interests that do not result in a loss of control. Most of the decrease was recognized by the share exchange transaction made in May 2011 to make Cedyna a wholly-owned subsidiary. By this exchange, ¥36 billion of treasury stocks were exchanged with non-controlling interests of Cedyna.

Preferred securities issued by subsidiaries consisted of the following:

(In Millions)	At March 31	
	2012	2011
Issued by SMFG's subsidiaries, other than SMBC:		
SMFG Preferred Capital USD 1 Limited (non-cumulative step-up perpetual preferred securities)	¥ 53,314	¥ 53,976
SMFG Preferred Capital GBP 1 Limited (non-cumulative step-up perpetual preferred securities)	9,657	9,850
SMFG Preferred Capital JPY 1 Limited (non-cumulative perpetual preferred securities)	135,000	135,000
SMFG Preferred Capital USD 2 Limited (non-cumulative perpetual preferred securities)	147,834	149,670
SMFG Preferred Capital USD 3 Limited (non-cumulative step-up perpetual preferred securities)	110,876	112,253
SMFG Preferred Capital GBP 2 Limited (non-cumulative step-up perpetual preferred securities)	32,812	33,470
SMFG Preferred Capital JPY 2 Limited		
Series A (non-cumulative step-up perpetual preferred securities)	113,000	113,000
Series B (non-cumulative perpetual preferred securities)	140,000	140,000
Series C (non-cumulative perpetual preferred securities)	140,000	140,000
Series D (non-cumulative perpetual preferred securities)	145,200	145,200
Series E (non-cumulative perpetual preferred securities)	33,000	33,000
Series F (non-cumulative perpetual preferred securities)	2,000	2,000
Series G (non-cumulative perpetual preferred securities)	125,700	125,700
SMFG Preferred Capital JPY 3 Limited		
Series A (non-cumulative step-up perpetual preferred securities)	99,000	99,000
Series B (non-cumulative perpetual preferred securities)	164,500	164,500
Series C (non-cumulative perpetual preferred securities)	79,500	79,500
Series D (non-cumulative perpetual preferred securities)	45,000	45,000
Issued by a subsidiary of Kansai Urban Banking Corporation:		
KUBC Preferred Capital Cayman Limited (non-cumulative step-up perpetual preferred securities)[1]	12,500	12,500
Preferred securities issued by subsidiaries	¥1,588,893	¥1,593,619

[1] On May 14, 2012, KUBC announced that the preferred securities issued by KUBC Preferred Capital Cayman Limited would be redeemed in full amount on July 25, 2012.

45 Financial Risk Management (in part)

The SMFG Group classifies risks into the following categories: credit risk, market risk, liquidity risk and operational risk (including processing risk and system risk). This note presents information about the SMFG Group's exposure to credit risk, market risk, and liquidity risk, and its policies and processes for measuring and managing these risks.

Risk Management System

The SMFG Group has established a basic approach for risk management. This basic approach includes establishing Group-wide basic policies for risk management, providing all necessary implementation guidance to the SMFG Group companies and monitoring the risk management procedures implemented by all Group companies to ensure their practices meet the relevant standards.

The Group-wide basic policies for risk management are determined by the Management Committee, which consists of designated Board Members, and such policies are authorized by the Board of Directors. The policies include:

- managing risk on a Group-wide basis;
- managing risk using quantification methods;
- ensuring consistency with business strategies;
- setting up a system of checks and balances;
- establishing contingency plans for emergencies and serious situations; and
- verifying preparedness to handle reasonably conceivable risk situations.

The policies also include fundamental principles for each risk category, which each SMFG Group company has to follow when establishing its own risk management system. The Corporate Risk Management Department, in cooperation with the Corporate Planning Department, performs risk management according to the above policies. In addition, the Internal Audit Department is responsible for the independent review of risk management within the SMFG Group.

Risk management systems are in place at the individual SMFG Group companies, and have been established in accordance with the Group-wide basic policies for risk management and implementation guidance provided by SMFG. Based on these policies and guidance, each SMFG Group company implements guidelines and establishes processes for risk management. On an ongoing basis, these processes and risks are monitored by SMFG.

For example, at SMBC, specific departments have been appointed to oversee the handling of the four risk categories listed above, in addition to the risks associated with settlement. Each risk category is managed taking into account, the particular characteristics of that category. In addition, the Risk Management Unit has been established—independent of the business units—and the risk management system has been strengthened by consolidating the functions for managing risks—credit, market, liquidity and operational—into the Risk Management Unit and enhancing SMBC's across-the-board risk monitoring ability. One board member is assigned to oversee the Risk Management Unit comprising the Corporate Risk Management Department and Credit & Investment Planning Department. The Corporate Risk Management Department—the unit's planning department—seeks to manage all categories of risk in cooperation with the Corporate Planning Department. Moreover, the Internal Audit Unit—independent of all business units—conducts periodic audits to ensure that the management system is functioning properly.

The decision-making process for addressing the risks at the operating level is also strengthened by the Credit Risk Management Committee and the Market Risk Management Committee, which are subcommittees of the Management Committee of SMBC.

Risk Capital-Based Management

In order to maintain a balance between risk and return, the SMFG Group employs a risk capital-based management method. The SMFG Group measures "risk capital" based on VaR and other specific measures such as uniform basic measures of credit, market and operational risks, taking into account the special characteristics of each type of risk, and the business activities of each SMFG Group company.

The SMFG Group then allocates risk capital to each unit to keep the total exposure to various risks within the scope of the SMFG Group's resources, i.e., capital. The allocation to each unit is determined by the Management Committee and authorized by the Board of Directors. In this framework, risk capital includes credit concentration risk and interest rate risk in the banking book, which are taken into account under the second pillar of Basel II. In addition, the SMFG Group conducts risk capital management activities on a consolidated basis, including each SMFG Group company.

Capital Management

The SMFG Group manages its capital by taking into consideration regulatory compliance and business development.

The SMFG Group's capital management objectives are to maintain sufficient capital resources to meet the capital adequacy requirements and to maintain a strong capital base to support the development of its business.

External Regulatory Capital Requirement

With regard to capital management, the SMFG Group, SMFG and its principal banking subsidiaries in Japan rigidly abide by the capital adequacy guidelines set by the Financial Services Agency of Japan ("FSA"). Japan's capital adequacy guidelines are based on the Basel Capital Accord, which was proposed by the Basel Committee for uniform application to all banks which have international operations in industrialized countries. Japan's capital adequacy guidelines are different from those of central banks or supervisions of other countries because the FSA designed them to suit the Japanese banking environment. The capital adequacy guidelines mandate that Japanese banks and bank holding companies and banks that have international operations maintain a minimum capital ratio of 8%. The SMFG Group's banking subsidiaries outside of Japan are also subject to the local capital ratio requirements.

The SMFG Group's capital is classified into three tiers, referred to as core capital (Tier I), supplementary capital (Tier II) and junior supplementary capital (Tier III) as follows:

Tier I: Core capital generally consists of stockholders' equity including retained earnings less any recorded goodwill.

Tier II: Supplementary capital generally consists of (1) the general reserve for possible loan losses (subject to a limit of 1.25% of total risk-weighted assets and off-balance sheet exposures), (2) 45% of (a) the unrealized gains on investments in "investment securities" (i.e., investment securities that are not those held for trading purposes, held-to-maturity bonds or shares in subsidiaries, or certain associates), (b) the unrealized appreciation on land, (3) the balance of subordinated perpetual debt and (4) the balance of subordinated term debt with an original maturity of over five years and limited life preferred equity (up to a maximum of 50% of core capital).

Tier III: Junior supplementary capital consists of the balance of subordinated term debt with an original maturity of at least two years. Junior supplementary capital may be counted, subject to certain conditions, according to the amount of market risk or the amount of core capital.

Supplementary capital may be counted up to the amount equivalent to core capital (less junior supplementary capital in case market risk is counted in the capital ratio calculation).

The capital adequacy guidelines permit Japanese banks to choose from the standardized approach, the foundation Internal Ratings-Based ("IRB") approach and the advanced IRB approach as to credit-risk, and the basic indicator approach, the standardized approach ("TSA") and the Advanced Measurement Approach ("AMA") as to operational risk. To be eligible to adopt the foundation IRB approach or the advanced IRB approach as to credit risk, and TSA or AMA as to operational risk, a Japanese bank must have established advanced risk management systems and must receive advance approval from the FSA.

Adopting these approved approaches, the SMFG Group sets a target minimum standard risk-weighted capital ratio of 8.0% (at least half of which must consist of core capital (Tier I), or a risk-weighted core capital ratio of 4.0%) on the SMFG Group's consolidated basis, and both SMBC consolidated and nonconsolidated basis, and has complied with all externally imposed capital requirements throughout the period.

Failure of a Japanese bank, bank holding company or other financial institution to maintain the required risk-weighted capital ratios, may result in administrative actions or sanctions imposed by the FSA.

Regulatory Capital

The table below presents the SMFG Group's total qualifying capital, risk-weighted assets and risk-weighted capital ratios at March 31, 2012 and 2011. Credit risk exposures from balance sheet and off-balance sheet assets under Japanese GAAP are measured based on credit risk quantification parameters, such as PD and LGD. Risk-based capital in the consolidated financial statements prepared under Japanese GAAP is classified into core capital (Tier I capital), supplementary capital (Tier II capital) and junior supplementary capital (Tier III capital).

	At March 31	
(In Millions, Except Percentages)	**2012**	**2011**
Tier I capital:		
Capital stock	¥ 2,337,895	¥ 2,337,895
Capital surplus	759,800	978,851
Retained earnings	2,152,654	1,776,433
Treasury stock	(236,037)	(171,760)
Minority interests	2,030,638	2,029,481
Cash dividends to be paid	(68,230)	(73,612)
Unrealized losses on other securities	—	—
Foreign currency translation adjustments	(141,382)	(122,889)
Stock acquisition rights	692	262
Goodwill and others	(496,434)	(394,343)
Gains on securitization transactions	(38,284)	(36,324)
Amount equivalent to 50% of expected losses in excess of qualifying reserves	(29,052)	—
Deductions of deferred tax assets[1]	—	—
Total Tier I capital	6,272,260	6,323,995
Tier II capital:		
Unrealized gains on other securities after 55% discount	214,611	169,267
Land revaluation excess after 55% discount	35,755	35,739
General reserve for possible loan losses	66,695	100,023
Excess amount of provisions	—	21,742
Subordinated debt	2,454,062	2,210,184
Total Tier II capital	2,771,125	2,536,958
Deductions	(399,634)	(428,082)
Total qualifying capital	¥ 8,643,751	¥ 8,432,871
Risk-weighted assets:		
On-balance sheet items	38,150,731	38,985,243
Off-balance sheet items	7,825,808	7,433,319
Market risk items	1,174,187	584,020
Operational risk	3,892,505	3,691,113
Total risk-weighted assets	¥51,043,232	¥50,693,696
Tier I risk-weighted capital ratio	12.28%	12.47%
Total risk-weighted capital ratio	16.93%	16.63%

[1] The amount of net deferred tax assets was ¥350,182 million and ¥624,219 million at March 31, 2012 and 2011, respectively. Also, the upper limit of the inclusion of deferred tax assets into Tier I capital was ¥1,254,452 million and ¥1,264,799 million at March 31, 2012 and 2011, respectively.

[2] Amounts less than ¥1 million have been omitted in the table of Regulatory Capital. As a result, the totals in Japanese yen shown in the above table do not necessarily agree with the sum of the individual amounts.

The SMFG Group's consolidated capital ratio at March 31, 2012 was 16.93%, 0.30 percentage points higher than 16.63% at March 31, 2011. Total capital, which is the numerator in the capital ratio calculation equation, amounted to ¥8,644 billion at March 31, 2012, which was ¥211 billion higher than ¥8,433 billion at March 31, 2011. This was due primarily to the result of recording of net income for the fiscal year.

Risk-weighted assets, the denominator in the equation, amounted to ¥51,043 billion, which was ¥349 billion higher than ¥50,694 billion at March 31, 2011, due mainly to the increase of market risk items.

Capitalization of Earnings by Distribution of Shares without Nominal Value

1.79

Banco de Chile (Dec 2011)

CONSOLIDATED STATEMENT OF FINANCIAL POSITION *(in part)*

(Expressed in millions of Chilean pesos)

	Notes	2010 MCh$	2011 MCh$	2011 ThUS$
Equity				
Attributable to equity holders of the parent:				
Capital		1,158,752	1,436,083	2,762,761
Reserves		158,282	229,464	441,447
Other comprehensive income		8,210	265	510
Retained earnings:				
Retained earnings from previous periods		65,023	65,311	125,646
Income for the year		417,615	438,186	842,990
Less:				
Provision for minimum dividends		(113,559)	(128,642)	(247,484)
Non-controlling interest		2	2	4
Total equity	27	1,694,325	2,040,669	3,925,874
Total liabilities and equity		18,276,464	21,765,558	41,872,948

CONSOLIDATED STATEMENT OF CHANGES IN EQUITY *(in part)*

	Note	Paid-in Capital MCh$	Reserves		Other Comprehensive Income			Retained Earnings			Attributable to Equity Holders of the Parent MCh$	Non-controlling Interest MCh$	Total Equity MCh$
			Other Reserves MCh$	Reserves from Earnings MCh$	Unrealized Gains (Losses) on Available-for-Sale MCh$	Cumulative Translation Adjustment MCh$	Cash Flow Hedge Adjustment MCh$	Retained Earnings From Previous Periods MCh$	Income for the Year MCh$	Provision for Minimum Dividends MCh$			
Balances as of December 31, 2010		1,158,752	99,293	58,989	8,314*	(104)*	—	65,023	417,615	(113,559)	1,694,323	2	1,694,325
Capitalization of retained earnings	27	67,217	—	—	—	—	—	—	(67,217)	—	—	—	—
Retention (release) earnings		—	—	71,182	—	—	—	—	(71,182)	—	—	—	—
Dividends distributions and paid	27	—	—	—	—	—	—	—	(279,216)	113,559	(165,657)	(1)	(165,658)
Capital increase	27	210,114	—	—	—	—	—	—	—	—	210,114	—	210,114
Cumulative translation adjustment		—	—	—	—	68	—	—	—	—	68	—	68
Valuation adjustment on available-for-sale instruments (net)	11	—	—	—	(7,618)	—	—	—	—	—	(7,618)	—	(7,618)
Cash flow hedge adjustment, net		—	—	—	—	—	(395)	—	—	—	(395)	—	(395)
Equity adjustment in subsidiary		—	—	—	—	—	—	288	—	—	288	—	288
Income for the year		—	—	—	—	—	—	—	438,186	—	438,186	1	438,187
Provision for minimum dividends	27	—	—	—	—	—	—	—	—	(128,642)	(128,642)	—	(128,642)
Balances as of December 31, 2011		1,436,083	99,293	130,171	696*	(36)*	(395)*	65,311	438,186	(128,642)	2,040,667	2	2,040,669

NOTES TO THE CONSOLIDATED FINANCIAL STATEMENTS (in part)

1. Company Information:

Banco de Chile, resulting from the merger of Banco Nacional de Chile, Banco Agrícola and Banco de Valparaíso, was formed on October 28, 1893 in the city of Santiago, in the presence of the Notary Eduardo Reyes Lavalle.

Banco de Chile ("Banco de Chile" or the "Bank") is a Corporation organized under the laws of the Republic of Chile, regulated by the Superintendency of Banks and Financial Institutions ("SBIF"). Since 2001—when the Bank was first listed on the New York Stock Exchange ("NYSE"), in the course of its American Depository Receipt (ADR) program, which is also registered at the London Stock Exchange— Banco de Chile additionally follows the regulations published by the United States Securities and Exchange Commission ("SEC"). Banco de Chile's shares are also listed on the Latin-american securities market of the Madrid Stock Exchange ("LATIBEX").

Banco de Chile offers a broad range of banking services to its customers, ranging from individuals to large corporations. The services are managed in large corporate banking, middle and small corporate banking, personal banking services and retail. Additionally, the Bank offers international as well as treasury banking services. The Bank's subsidiaries provide other services including securities brokerage, mutual fund management, factoring, insurance brokerage, financial advisory and securitization.

Banco de Chile's legal domicile is Ahumada 251, Santiago, Chile and its Web site is www.bancochile.cl.

The consolidated financial statements of the Group for the year ended December 31, 2011 were authorized for issuance in accordance with the directors' resolution on April 18, 2012.

2. Summary of Significant Accounting Principles: (in part)

(y) Equity Reserves:

The equity reserves recorded in the Bank's Statement of Financial Position include:

Reserves from Earnings:

This item includes all the reserves that were originated from earnings and that by legal or statutory dispositions, or agreements of the shareholders' meeting, will not be distributed in the form of future dividends.

Other Reserves:

This item includes all the reserves that do not come from earnings and that do not correspond to those indicated in previous items.

Unrealized Gains (losses) on Available-for-Sale Instruments:

This item comprises changes in the fair value of these instruments.

Cumulative Translation Adjustment:

This item is used to record exchange differences arising from the translation of the net investment in foreign operations.

27. Equity:

i. Authorized, Subscribed and Paid Shares:

As of December 31, 2011, the paid-in capital of Banco de Chile is represented by 86,942,514,973 registered shares (82,551,699,423 in 2010), with no par value, subscribed and fully paid.

ii. Capital Increase:

On January 20th, 2011 the Bank decided to increase its capital in the amount of Ch$240,000,000,000 by means of the issuance of 3,385,049,365 cash shares, "Banco de Chile-S" series, which process concluded in July 2011 in which the subscribed and fully paid was of 3,385,049,365 cash shares, the total amount net of cost associated with the issuance was Ch$ 210,114 million. With this increase the number of shares subscribed and paid grew to 86,942,514,973 shares and the paid capital grew to Ch$1,436,083 millions.

iii. Shares:

(ii.1) On April 15, 2011, the transformation of the shares series "Banco de Chile-S" into ordinary shares "Banco de Chile" has been duly registered in the respective Securities Register as agreed upon the Extraordinary Shareholders Meeting held on March 17, 2011.

Accordingly, the shares in which the capital of the Bank is divided are registered in the Securities Register of the Superintendence of Banks and Financial Institutions and have the name "Banco de Chile."

(ii.2) The following table shows the share movements from December 31, 2009 to December 31, 2011:

	Ordinary Shares	Ordinary S Series Shares	Total Shares
As of December 31, 2009	73,834,890,472	8,716,808,951	82,551,699,423
As of December 31, 2010	73,834,890,472	8,716,808,951	82,551,699,423
Capitalization of retained earnings(**)	1,005,766,185	—	1,005,766,185
Transformation of the shares series "Banco de Chile-S" into ordinary shares "Banco de Chile"	8,716,808,951	(8,716,808,951)	—
Fully paid the share capital increase(*)	3,385,049,365	—	3,385,049,365
Total subscribed and paid shares as of December 31, 2011	86,942,514,973	—	86,942,514,973

(*) During July 2011, the Bank concluded the capital increase process by an amount of Ch$210,114 millions, amount net of cost associated with the issuance.

(**) Capitalization of March 17, 2011.

- The number of authorized shares is the same as for issued shares.

iv. Shareholders' Composition:

- As of December 31, 2011 the shareholder composition was as follows:

Corporate Name or Shareholder's Name	Shares	% of Equity Holding[1]
Sociedad Administradora de la Obligación Subordinada SAOS S.A.	28,593,701,789	32.89
LQ Inversiones Financieras S.A.	27,609,418,295	31.76
Sociedad Matriz del Banco de Chile S.A. SM-Chile S.A.	12,138,525,772	13.96
Other minority shareholders	18,600,869,117	21.39
Total	86,942,514,973	100.00

- As of December 31, 2010 the shareholder composition was as follows:

Corporate Name or Shareholder's Name	Shares	% of Equity Holding[1]
Sociedad Administradora de la Obligación Subordinada SAOS S.A.	28,593,701,789	34.64
LQ Inversiones Financieras S.A.	26,993,155,828	32.70
Sociedad Matriz del Banco de Chile S.A. SM-Chile S.A.	12,138,525,385	14.70
Other minority shareholders	14,826,316,421	17.96
Total	82,551,699,423	100.00

[1] See note 27 letter (ii).

v. Capitalization of Retained Earning:

On March 17, 2011, the Extraordinary Shareholders Meeting approved the capitalization of 30% of the distributable net income obtained during the fiscal year ending as of December 31, 2010 by an amount of Ch$67,217 millions.

vi. Approval and Payment of Dividends:

At the Ordinary Shareholders' Meeting held on March 25, 2010 the Bank's shareholders agreed to distribute and pay dividend N° 198 amounting to Ch$3.496813 per common share of Banco de Chile, with charge to net income for the year ended December 31, 2009.

At the Ordinary Shareholders' Meeting held on March 17, 2011 the Bank's shareholders agreed to distribute and pay dividend N° 199 amounting to Ch$2.937587 per common share of Banco de Chile, with charge to net income for the year ended December 31, 2010.

The following dividends were declared and paid by the Bank for the year ended as of December 31, 2009, 2010 and 2011:

	2009 MCh$	2010 MCh$	2011 MCh$
Dividends on ordinary shares:	220,164	288,669	279,216
Dividends per ordinary share[1]:	Ch$2.72	Ch$3.50	Ch$3.38[*]

[1] Dividends per share are calculated by dividing the amount of the dividend paid during each year by the previous year's number of shares outstanding.

[*] This dividend per share is composed by the dividend paid to Central Bank of Chile and common shareholders for an amount of MCh$122,377 and MCh$156,839, respectively. The Central Bank has 29,161.4 number of shares with a paid of Ch$4.196552 per common share of Banco de Chile and for common shareholders the number of shares are 53,390.2 with a paid of Ch$2.937587 per common share of Banco de Chile.

vii. Provision for Minimum Dividends:

Chilean Corporations Law mandates a minimum distribution of 30% of distributable income. Accordingly, the Bank recorded a liability under the line item "Provisions" for an amount of MCh$128,642 (MCh$113,559 in December 31, 2010) against "Retained earnings."

viii. Other Comprehensive Income:

The cumulative translation adjustment is generated from the Bank's translation of its investments in foreign companies, as it records the effects of foreign currency translation for these items in equity.

In accordance with Note 2 (o), the fair market value adjustment for available-for-sale instruments is generated by fluctuations in the fair value of that portfolio, with a charge or credit to equity, net of deferred taxes.

ix. Earnings per Share:

Earnings per share is calculated by dividing the net profit for the year attributable to the ordinary equity holders of the Bank by the weighted average number of ordinary shares outstanding during the year.

The following table shows the income and share data used in the calculation of EPS:

	As of December 31		
	2009	2010	2011
Basic and diluted earnings per share:			
Net profits attributable to ordinary equity holders of the Bank	261,744	417,615	438,186
Weighted average number of ordinary shares	82,185,276,752	82,551,699,423	86,942,514,973
Earnings per shares	3.18	5.06	5.04

During the periods presented the Bank did not have any instruments that could lead to a dilution of its ordinary shares.

There have been no transactions involving ordinary shares or potential ordinary shares between the reporting date and the date of the completion of these financial statements.

40. Risk Management (in part)

(4) Capital Requirements and Capital Management:

The Bank maintains an actively managed capital base to cover the risks inherent in its business. The adequacy of the Bank's capital is monitored using, among other measures, the rules and ratios established by the Chilean Superintendency of Banks and Financial Institutions. During the past year as well as 2008, the Bank has fully complied with the externally imposed capital requirements.

The primary objectives of the Bank's capital management are to ensure that the Bank complies with externally imposed capital requirements and that the Bank maintains strong credit ratings and healthy capital ratios.

The Bank manages its capital structure and makes adjustments in the light of changes in the economic conditions and the risk characteristics of its activities. In order to maintain or adjust the capital structure the Bank may adjust the amount of dividend payments, return capital to its shareholders or issue capital securities. No changes have been made to the objectives, policies and processes during the years presented.

Regulatory Capital

In accordance with the Chilean General Banking Law, the Bank must maintain a minimum ratio of Effective Equity to Consolidated Risk-Weighted Assets of 8%, net of required provisions, and a minimum ratio of Basic Capital to Total Consolidated Assets of 3%, net of required provisions. However,

due to the 2008 merger of Banco de Chile and Citibank Chile, the Superintendency of Banks and Financial Institutions, in Resolution N° 209 from December 26, 2007, increased the limit on the Bank's ratio of effective equity to risk-weighted assets to 10%. In this context, the SBIF ratified the use of the 10% as minimum fixed in December 2001 when authorizing merge by absorption of Banco Edwards in Banco de Chile.

For this purpose, Effective Equity is determined based on Capital and Reserves or Basic Capital, adjusted by: (a) adding subordinated bonds up to 50% of Basic Capital, (b) adding additional loan provisions, and (c) subtracting the asset balance of goodwill or overpayments and unconsolidated investments in companies.

Assets are weighted using risk categories, which are assigned a risk percentage based on the capital needed to back each asset. There are 5 risk categories (0%, 10%, 20%, 60% and 100%). For example, cash, due from banks and financial instruments issued by the Chilean Central Bank have 0% risk, which means, in accordance with current standards, no capital is required to back these assets. Property and equipment have 100% risk, which means that minimum capital equivalent to 8% of the value of these assets is needed (10% in the case of Banco de Chile).

All derivative instruments traded off-market are taken into account to determine risk assets using conversion factors over notional values, thus calculating the value of the credit risk exposure (or "credit equivalent"). For weighting purposes, "credit equivalent" also considers off-balance sheet contingent loans.

Levels of Basic Capital and Effective Equity as of December 31, 2010 and 2011 are as follows:

	Consolidated Assets		Risk-Weighted Assets	
	2010 MCh$	2011 MCh$	2010 MCh$	2011 MCh$
Balance sheet assets (net of provisions)				
Cash and due from banks	772,329	881,146	767	16,472
Transactions in the course of collection	429,756	373,639	60,922	100,236
Financial assets held-for-trading	279,765	304,912	65,540	78,314
Receivables from repurchase agreements and security borrowing	82,787	47,981	82,787	47,981
Derivative instruments	488,354	381,055	396,511	378,788
Loans and advances to banks	349,588	648,425	338,913	335,562
Loans to customers, net	14,029,968	17,023,756	12,841,904	15,555,760
Financial assets available-for-sale	1,157,105	1,471,120	358,740	488,760
Investments in other companies	11,072	13,196	13,294	15,418
Intangible assets	88,463	81,026	33,992	33,757
Property and equipment	204,352	207,888	206,513	207,887
Investment Properties	17,459	17,079	—	—
Current tax assets	3,363	—	565	141
Deferred tax assets	57,678	60,025	11,120	11,628
Other assets	304,425	254,310	286,021	229,650
Subtotal			14,697,589	17,500,354
Off-balance-sheet assets				
Contingent loans	2,913,689	3,484,007	1,748,106	2,084,517
Total risk-weighted assets			16,445,695	19,584,871

42. Subsequent Events:

a. In an ordinary meeting held on January 26, 2012, our board of directors decided to call an ordinary shareholders meeting to be held on March 22, 2012 with the objective of proposing, among other matters, to increase the Bank's capital through the capitalization of 30% of the Bank's net income

for the fiscal year 2011, by means of the issuance of shares without nominal value, set at the value of $67.48 per share and distributed among shareholders, without charge, at the rate of 0.018956 new shares per each paid for and subscribed share and to adopt all necessary resolutions subject to the options contemplated in Article 31 of Law N°19,396.

In an ordinary meeting held on March 22, 2012, its shareholders' approved the distribution and payment of dividend No.200, in the amount of CLP$2.984740 per Banco de Chile common share, which represents 70% of the Bank's net income for year 2011.

b. On February 16, 2012 and its pursuant to Article 116 of Law No.18,045, Bank of Chile in his capacity as representative of the bondholders Series A, issued by Compañía Sud Americana de Vapores S.A., that because this has occurred the configuration of the disability cause contemplated in the first paragraph of Article 116 of Law No.18,045, that is, being the representative of the bondholders related to the issuer.

Bank of Chile will refrain from further actions as such and will renounce as representative of the bondholders of such issue, for which purpose will proceed to quote in the shortest possible time to a bondholders meeting, to announce the renounce of Bank of Chile as representative and to propose to the assembly the appointment of a new representative.

The said bond issue is in the public deed dated August 29, 2001, executed in Santiago on behalf of the Public Notary

Mr. René Benavente Cash, together with all the amendments and entered in the Registry of Securities of the Chilean Superintendency of Securities and Insurance under No. 274.

c. On March 27, 2012, the Central Bank of Chile communicated to Banco de Chile that in the Extraordinary Session, No.1666E, the Board of the Central Bank of Chile resolved to request its corresponding surplus, from the fiscal year ended on December 31, 2011, including the proportional part of the agreed upon capitalization profits, which will be paid in cash currency.

Change in Accounting Estimate

1.80

Absa Group Limited (Dec 2011)

CONSOLIDATED STATEMENT OF FINANCIAL POSITION (in part)

	Note	Group 2011 Rm	2010[1] RM	2009[1] RM
Liabilities				
Deposits from banks	18	38 339	15 406	36 541
Trading portfolio liabilities	19	55 960	47 454	44 245
Hedging portfolio liabilities	19	2 456	1 881	565
Other liabilities	20	14 695	11 239	12 212
Provisions	21	1 710	1 808	1 684
Current tax liabilities	7	267	965	59
Deposits due to customers	22	440 960	387 598	367 210
Debt securities in issue	23	130 262	164 545	171 376
Liabilities under investment contracts	24	15 233	13 964	12 446
Policyholder liabilities under insurance contracts	25	3 183	3 001	3 136
Borrowed funds	26	14 051	13 649	13 530
Deferred tax liabilities	17	1 198	2 298	2 147
Total liabilities		718 314	663 808	665 151

NOTES TO THE CONSOLIDATED FINANCIAL STATEMENTS (in part)

1. Summary of Signifcant Accounting Policies (in part)

1.10. Deferred Revenue Liability

A deferred revenue liability (DRL) is recognised in respect of fees paid at the inception of an investment management contract by the policyholder, which are directly attributable to a contract. The DRL is then released to revenue as the investment management services are provided over the expected duration of the contract, as a constant percentage of expected gross margins (including investment income) arising from the contract.

The pattern of expected future profit margins is based on historical and expected future experience and is updated at the end of each reporting period. The resulting change to the carrying value of the DRL is recognised in revenue.

Changes in the expected duration of the contract or expected future profit margins are treated as a change in accounting estimate.

1.11 Classification of Insurance and Investment Contracts (in part)

1.11.1 Insurance Contracts (in part)

Life Insurance Contracts

These contracts insure events associated with human life (i.e. death, disability or survival) over a long duration. Premiums are recognised as revenue when they become payable by the contract holder. Premiums are shown before the deduction of commission. Individual life policies, life annuities and single premiums are accounted for in terms of the policy contract. Benefits are recorded as an expense when they are incurred.

A liability for contractual benefits that are expected to be incurred in the future is recorded when the premiums are recognised. The liabilities are valued at each reporting date using the financial soundness valuation (FSV) basis described in Practice Guidance Note 104 (PGN 104) issued by the Actuarial Society of South Africa (ASSA) and the liability is reflected as policyholder liabilities under insurance contracts.

Under the FSV basis, a liability is determined as the sum of the current estimate of the expected discounted value of all the benefit payments and the future administration expenses that are directly related to the contract, less the current estimate of the expected discounted value of the contractual premiums.

The liability is based on assumptions as to mortality, persistency, maintenance expenses and investment income that are established at the time of valuing the contract at each reporting date. Margins for adverse deviations are included in the assumptions.

In respect of outstanding claims, provision is made for the costs of intimated and unintimated claims.

Withdrawals from, and deposits in investment contracts are excluded from the profit and loss component of the statement of comprehensive income.

Intimated claims represent claims where the incident giving rise to a claim has occurred and has been reported to the insurer for settlement but has not yet been finalised and paid by the insurer. The liability is measured at the value assessed for the claim. Unintimated claims represent claims incurred but not yet reported or paid. The liability is estimated by assuming that future trends in reporting of claims will be similar to the past. The profile of claims run-off (over time) is modelled by using historic data of the Group and chain-ladder techniques. The profile is then applied to actual claims data of recent periods for which the run-off is believed not to be complete.

Valuation Methodology

Assumptions used for valuing policy liabilities are based on best estimates of future experience, guided by recent past experience and increased by margins prescribed by the ASSA for prudence and further discretionary margins to ensure that profits are released appropriately over the term of each policy.

Policyholders' reasonable expectations are allowed for by valuing all guaranteed benefits. Maturity guarantee liabilities have been valued in accordance with the requirements of PGN 110 issued by the ASSA. In terms of this guidance, an internationally recognised market-consistent stochastic model is used to perform a range of asset projections from which the maturity guarantee liability is derived. In terms of PGN 110 the projections allow for at least a certain minimum level of market volatility. The liability is equal to the discounted shortfall (of simulated maturity values against minimum guaranteed values) across all projections for the policies concerned.

Liability Adequacy Test

Liabilities are calculated in terms of the FSV basis as described in PGN 104. Since the FSV basis meets the minimum requirement of the liability adequacy test, it is not necessary to perform additional adequacy tests on the liability component. For the liability relating to potential future claims which have already been incurred on the reporting date, but of which the Group has not yet been informed, tests are performed to ensure that the liability is sufficient to cover historical run-off profiles and growth in the volume of business. Refer to the Insurance Risk section in the Risk report for more detail.

Deferred Policy Acquisition Costs

Acquisition costs comprise commissions and other variable costs directly connected with the acquisition or renewal of short-term insurance contracts. The deferred acquisition costs represent the portion of acquisition costs incurred and revenue received which corresponds to the unearned premium reserve.

Deferred acquisition costs are amortised in line with expected future premiums. The amortisation is recognised in the profit and loss component of the statement of comprehensive income.

Philosophy on Release of Profits on the Valuation Basis

The following additional (discretionary) margins are incorporated in the liability calculations:
- Minimum liability equal to the surrender value of a policy and elimination of all negative liabilities to ensure that solvency is maintained if policy cancellations increase. It is not the philosophy of the Group to recognise an asset by (prematurely) recognising the expected future profits of a policy.
- Additional margin on mortality, disability and dreaded disease (equal to compulsory margins for most product lines) to take account of the size of the book, uncertainty surrounding future mortality trends (especially the Aids pandemic), lack of catastrophe reinsurance, and the fact that certain classes of business are not underwritten.
- Reduced lapse assumptions on certain product lines due to the fact that lapses are inherently volatile and as it is not deemed prudent to take credit in advance for future lapses that might not arise.
- No recognition of future investment charges on linked business as the Group's profit recognition policy determines that asset-based fees are more appropriately accounted for as and when they are invoiced.
- A percentage of premiums for certain regular premium business is not taken into account when liabilities are valued. The effect is to increase liabilities. This allows for uncertainty as to whether the premiums will actually be received and is in line with the profit recognition policy whereby profit is not recognised in advance.

Value of Business Acquired (VOBA)

On acquisition of a portfolio of insurance contracts, either directly from another insurer or through the acquisition of a subsidiary company, the Group recognises an intangible asset representing the VOBA.

The VOBA represents the present value of future profits embedded in acquired insurance contracts. The Group amortises the VOBA over the effective life of the acquired contracts. This amortisation is recognised in the profit and loss component of the statement of comprehensive income.

1.11.2 Investment Contracts

Policyholder contracts that do not transfer signifcant insurance risk are classified as investment contracts and are valued at fair value. Acquisition costs directly attributable to investment management contracts are capitalised to a deferred acquisition cost asset and amortised to the profit and loss component of the statement of comprehensive income over the term of the contract.

The Group issues investment contracts with fixed and guaranteed terms. Investment contracts with fixed and guaranteed terms are financial liabilities of which the fair value is dependent on the fair value of the financial assets backing the liabilities. These contracts and the corresponding policy-holder liabilities are designated to be held at fair value though profit or loss at inception. Subsequent changes to fair value are taken to the profit and loss component of the statement of comprehensive income.

Valuation techniques are used to establish the fair value at inception and at each reporting date. The Group's main valuation techniques incorporate all factors that market participants would consider and are based on observable market data. The fair value of a unit-linked investment contract is determined using the current unit values that reflect the fair values of the financial assets contained within the Group's unitised investment funds linked to the financial liability, multiplied by the number of units attributed to the contract holder at the reporting date. The fair value of fixed interest rate products is determined by discounting the maturity value at market rates of interest.

If the investment contract is subject to a put or surrender option held by the customer, the fair value of the financial liability is never less than the amount payable on surrender, discounted for the required notice period, where applicable.

1.12 Cell Arrangements

There are currently two distinct types of cell captive arrangements being:

- 'First party' where the risks that are being insured relate to the cell owner's operations and that of their subsidiaries. Claims within these cells are limited to the funds available in the cell after providing for solvency.
- 'Third party' where the cell owner has the ability to sell branded insurance products into its own customer base. Claims instituted within third party cells are not limited to the funds provided by the cell owner after providing for solvency.

In respect of third party cells, where insurance contracts are issued to third parties directly in the name of the Group, the cell captive is considered to be the reinsurer, as there is insurance risk transfer. The policyholder liabilities and reinsurance assets in respect of these insurance contracts are recognised in the statement of financial position of the Group, in terms of the reinsurance arrangement with the cell captive. Excess assets over policyholder liabilities in the cell captive belong to the cell owner and are not recognised by the Group.

The financial position and performance of first party cells are not included in the financial statements of the Group as no transfer of risks and rewards of assets and liabilities takes place according to the cell agreements.

Each first party cell owner is responsible for the solvency of each cell and the Group therefore does not carry any risk. However, for third party cells, should the cell owner not be able to meet the obligations within the cell, the Group would be required to meet obligations of the cell. The Group therefore carries a credit risk against each cell owner. This risk is limited through the selection process of reputable cell owners.

Monthly financial accounts are prepared and regular actuarial valuations are performed for each cell captive to monitor the financial soundness of the cell.

25. Policyholder Liabilities Under Insurance Contracts

25.1 Reconciliation of Claims Outstanding, Including Claims Incurred But Not Reported

	Group 2011		
	Gross Rm	Reinsurance Rm	Net Rm
Balance at the beginning of the year	729	(208)	521
Cash paid for claims settled during the year	(2 459)	483	(1 976)
Increase in claims arising from current year claims outstanding	2 377	(438)	1 939
Increase in claims arising from prior years' claims outstanding	25	(32)	(7)
Balance at the end of the year (refer to note 25)	672	(195)	477

	Group 2010		
	Gross Rm	Reinsurance Rm	Net Rm
Balance at the beginning of the year	837	(253)	584
Cash paid for claims settled during the year	(2 199)	260	(1 939)
Increase in claims arising from current year claims outstanding	2 073	(210)	1 863
Increase in claims arising from prior years' claims outstanding	18	(5)	13
Balance at the end of the year (refer to note 25)	729	(208)	521

25.2 Reconciliation of Gross Long-Term Insurance Contracts

	Group	
	2011 Rm	2010 Rm
Balance at the beginning of the year	1 463	1 402
Reinsurance liability	(1)	16
Value of in-force acquired for transfer of policies	2	—
Changes in insurance contracts (refer to note 35)	8	45
Change in economic assumptions	27	37
Change in methodology	(14)	(34)
Change in non-economic assumptions	(108)	(154)
Expected cash flow	535	354
Expected release of margins	(572)	(411)
Experience variances	39	(5)
Increase in retrospective liabilities	1	(5)
New business	69	59
Transfer of policies	7	—
Unwind of discount rate	24	34
Balance at the end of the year (refer to note 25)	1 472	1 463
Recoverable from reinsurers	57	58
Net liabilities	1 415	1 405
Unit-linked liabilities	1 106	1 049
Non-linked liabilities	309	356
	1 472	1 463

Change in Accounting Estimate—Policyholder Liabilities Under Insurance Contracts

Policyholder liabilities under insurance contracts are valued using PGN 104, issued by the ASSA. PGN 104 allows for additional margins if the statutory actuary believes that the compulsory margins are insufficient for prudent provisioning and/or to defer the release of profits in line with policy design and company practice. These margins are incorporated into the liability calculations. It is the Group's policy that profit margins contained in the premium basis, which are expected to be released in future as the business runs off, should not be capitalised and recognised prematurely. Such margins should only be released to profits once premiums have been received and the risk cover has been provided.

One of the margins established in terms of the Group's accounting policy, is a discretionary mortality and morbidity margin for certain regular premium business.

Management considered it appropriate to provide for these margins as a result of not having sufficiently large volumes of business and accompanying data. As a result there were random fluctuations in the policyholder liabilities, and the discretionary margins provided to some extent a buffer against these fluctuations. However the volumes of business have shown positive growth over the past financial years and a more credible volume of data has emerged. Management has reconsidered the discretionary mortality and morbidity margin included in the policyholder liabilities and based on the additional data available, set the margins to 0% for both mortality and morbidity (2010: 7,5% mortality and 10% morbidity).

This has resulted in a decrease in policyholder liabilities and an increase in profit before taxation of R72 million (future investment management charges were previously not taken into account, which resulted in a release of R117 million in 2010). This amount is taxed in the corporate fund at 28%, amounting to R20 million, as it represents a transfer from the individual policyholder funds to the corporate fund.

Correction of an Error

1.81

Millicom International Cellular S.A. (Dec 2011)

CONSOLIDATED STATEMENTS OF FINANCIAL POSITIION (in part)

As at December 31, 2011 and 2010

	Notes	2011	2010 (As Restated)[i]
		US$ '000	US$ '000
Assets			
Non-Current Assets			
Intangible assets, net	16	2,170,353	2,282,845
Property, plant and equipment, net	17	2,865,117	2,767,667
Investments in associates	18	62,984	18,120
Pledged deposits	19,27	49,371	49,963
Deferred taxation	14	316,966	23,959
Other non-current assets		37,359	17,754
Total Non-Current Assets		5,502,150	5,160,308
Current Assets			
Inventories		74,593	62,132
Trade receivables, net	20	276,944	253,258
Amounts due from non-controlling interests and joint ventures		158,782	99,497
Prepayments and accrued income		119,362	89,477
Current income tax assets		23,645	10,748
Supplier advances for capital expenditure		32,324	36,189
Other current assets	21	146,615	75,311
Cash and cash equivalents[ii]	22	881,279	1,023,487
Total Current Assets		1,713,544	1,650,099
Assets held for sale	7	66,252	184,710
Total assets		7,281,946	6,995,117
Equity and Liabilities			
Equity			
Share capital and premium	23	662,527	681,559
Treasury shares	23	(378,359)	(300,000)
Put option reserve	25	(737,422)	(737,422)
Other reserves	26	(103,492)	(54,685)
Retained profits		1,886,615	1,134,354
Profit for the year attributable to equity holders		924,515	1,620,277
Parents ownership interests		2,254,384	2,344,083
Non-controlling interests		191,170	45,550
Total equity		2,445,554	2,389,633

(continued)

	Notes	2011	2010 (As Restated)[i]
		US$ '000	US$ '000
Liabilities			
Non-current liabilities			
Debt and financing	27	1,816,852	1,796,572
Derivative financial instruments	35	8,016	18,250
Provisions and other non-current liabilities	28	113,613	79,767
Deferred taxation	14	199,066	195,919
Total non-current liabilities		2,137,547	2,090,508
Current liabilities			
Debt and financing	27	621,426	555,464
Put option liability	28	745,145	769,378
Payables and accruals for capital expenditure		333,551	278,063
Other trade payables		224,089	202,707
Amounts due to joint venture partners		92,677	97,919
Accrued interest and other expenses		263,747	228,360
Current income tax liabilities		105,217	79,861
Provisions and other current liabilities	28	303,335	242,457
Total current liabilities		2,689,187	2,454,209
Liabilities directly associated with assets held for sale	7	9,658	60,767
Total liabilities		4,836,392	4,605,484
Total equity and liabilities		7,281,946	6,995,117

[i] Restatement—see note 4.
[ii] Including $20 million of restricted cash at December 31, 2011.

CONSOLIDATED INCOME STATEMENTS (in part)

For the years ended December 31, 2011, 2010 and 2009

	Notes	2011	2010 (As Restated)[i]	2009
		US$ '000	US$ '000	US$ '000
Revenues	10	4,529,597	3,920,249	3,372,727
Cost of sales		(1,564,401)	(1,330,308)	(1,202,902)
Gross profit		2,965,196	2,589,941	2,169,825
Sales and marketing		(816,715)	(737,691)	(647,009)
General and administrative expenses		(839,423)	(738,779)	(606,213)
Other operating expenses		(95,737)	(74,933)	(65,580)
Other operating income		43,700	3,192	—
Operating profit	10,11	1,257,021	1,041,730	851,023
Interest expense		(186,523)	(214,810)	(173,475)
Interest and other financial income		14,576	14,748	11,573
Revaluation of previously held interests	5	—	1,060,014	32,319
Other non operating expenses, net	13	(4,290)	(61,658)	(32,181)
(Loss) profit from associates	18	(9,591)	(1,817)	2,329
Profit before tax from continuing operations		1,071,193	1,838,207	691,588
Credit (charge) for taxes	14	18,347	(227,096)	(187,998)
Profit for the year from continuing operations		1,089,540	1,611,111	503,590
Profit for the year from discontinued operations, net of tax	7	39,465	11,857	300,342
Net profit for the year		1,129,005	1,622,968	803,932
Attributable to:				
Equity holders of the company		924,515	1,620,277	850,788
Non-controlling interest		204,490	2,691	(46,856)
Earnings per share for the year	15			
(expressed in US$ per common share)				
Basic earnings per share				
—from continuing operations attributable to equity holders		8.50	14.89	5.09
—from discontinued operations attributable to equity holders		0.37	0.08	2.75
—for the year attributable to equity holders		8.87	14.97	7.84
Diluted earnings per share				
—from continuing operations attributable to equity holders		8.49	14.87	5.08
—from discontinued operations attributable to equity holders		0.37	0.08	2.74
—for the year attributable to equity holders		8.86	14.95	7.82

[i] Restatement—see note 4.

CONSOLIDATED STATEMENTS OF COMPREHENSIVE INCOME

	2011	2010 (As Restated)[i]	2009
	US$ '000	US$ '000	US$ '000
Net profit for the year	1,129,005	1,622,968	803,932
Other comprehensive income:			
Exchange differences on translating foreign operations	(46,698)	(5,785)	(14,529)
Cash flow hedges	(3,262)	(1,700)	—
Total comprehensive income for the year	1,079,045	1,615,483	789,403
Attributable to:			
Equity holders of the Company	881,694	1,617,487	837,124
Non-controlling interests	197,351	(2,004)	(47,721)

[i] Restatement—see note 4.

CONSOLIDATED STATEMENTS OF CASH FLOWS

	Notes	2011	2010 (As Restated)[i]	2009
		US$ '000	US$ '000	US$ '000
Profit before tax from continuing operations		1,071,193	1,838,207	691,588
Adjustments for non-operating items:				
Interest expense		186,523	214,810	173,475
Interest and other financial income		(14,576)	(14,748)	(11,573)
Revaluation of previously held interests		—	(1,060,014)	(32,319)
Loss (profit) from associates		9,591	1,817	(2,329)
Other non operating expenses, net		4,290	61,658	32,181
Adjustments for non-cash items:				
Depreciation and amortization	10,11,16,17	738,980	676,986	611,435
Loss (gain) on disposal and impairment of assets	10,11	(21,785)	16,257	7,246
Share-based compensation	24	17,264	30,718	10,175
		1,991,480	1,765,691	1,479,879
Decrease (increase) in trade receivables, prepayments and other current assets		(56,668)	(31,282)	73,380
Decrease (increase) in inventories		(13,143)	(12,606)	8,812
Increase (decrease) in trade and other payables		84,350	44,773	(4,669)
Changes to working capital		14,539	885	77,523
Interest expense paid		(141,138)	(170,604)	(148,038)
Interest received		14,647	14,639	11,316
Taxes paid		(268,071)	(238,723)	(195,851)
Net cash provided by operating activities		1,611,457	1,371,888	1,224,829
Cash flows from investing activities:				
Acquisition of subsidiaries, JV, associates, net of cash acquired	5	(20,369)	(5,284)	(53,086)
Proceeds from disposal of subsidiaries, joint ventures and associates		1,000	5,335	—
Purchase of intangible assets and license renewals	16	(56,473)	(26,238)	(46,004)
Purchase of property, plant and equipment	17	(699,681)	(596,900)	(726,565)
Proceeds from sale of property, plant and equipment		126,832	36,617	3,708
Disposal (purchase) of pledged deposits		8,683	2,462	(45,652)
Disposal (purchase) of time deposits		2,837	46,953	(50,061)
Cash (used) provided by other investing activities		(35,307)	9,334	(12,275)
Net cash used by investing activities		(672,478)	(527,721)	(929,935)
Cash flows from financing activities:				
Proceeds from issuance of shares		1,319	3,276	2,856
Purchase of treasury shares		(498,274)	(300,000)	—
Proceeds from issuance of debt and other financing	27	703,073	1,147,585	627,872
Repayment of debt and financing	27	(791,940)	(1,396,997)	(506,588)
Advance payments to non controlling interests		(27,542)	—	—
Payment of dividends		(493,909)	(788,526)	—
Net cash (used) provided by financing activities		(1,107,273)	(1,334,662)	124,140
Cash provided by discontinued operations	7	53,102	—	416,755
Exchange gains (losses) on cash and cash equivalents		(27,016)	2,820	1,178
Net increase (decrease) in cash and cash equivalents		(142,208)	(487,675)	836,967
Cash and cash equivalents at the beginning of the year		1,023,487	1,511,162	674,195
Cash and cash equivalents at the end of the year		881,279	1,023,487	1,511,162

[i] Restatement—see note 4.

CONSOLIDATED STATEMENTS OF CHANGES IN EQUITY (in part)

For the years ended December 31, 2011, 2010 and 2009

	Number of Shares	Number of Shares Held by the Group	Share Capital(i)	Attributable to Equity Holders					Total Parent's Interests	Non-controlling Interests(vi)	Total Equity
				Share Premium(i)	Treasury Shares	Retained Profits(ii)	Put Option Reserve(iv)	Other Reserves(v)			
	'000	'000	US$ '000	US$ '000	US$ '000	US$ '000	US$ '000	US$ '000	US$ '000	US$ '000	US$ '000
Balance as of January 1, 2011	109,053	(3,254)	163,578	517,981	(300,000)	2,754,631	(737,422)	(54,685)	2,344,083	45,550	2,389,633
Profit for the year	—	—	—	—	—	924,515	—	—	924,515	204,490	1,129,005
Cash flow hedge reserve movement	—	—	—	—	—	—	—	(3,015)	(3,015)	(247)	(3,262)
Currency translation differences	—	—	—	—	—	—	—	(39,806)	(39,806)	(6,892)	(46,698)
Total comprehensive income for the year	—	—	—	—	—	924,515	—	(42,821)	881,694	197,351	1,079,045
Transfer to legal reserve	—	—	—	—	—	(61)	—	61	—	—	—
Dividends(vii)	—	—	—	—	—	(493,909)	—	—	(493,909)	—	(493,909)
Purchase of treasury shares	—	(4,646)	—	—	(498,274)	—	—	—	(498,274)	—	(498,274)
Cancellation of treasury shares	(4,200)	4,200	(6,300)	(20,070)	401,415	(375,045)	—	—	—	—	—
Shares issued via the exercise of stock options	40	6	59	1,184	592	(435)	—	(81)	1,319	—	1,319
Share-based compensation(iii)	—	—	—	—	—	—	—	17,264	17,264	—	17,264
Issuance of shares under the LTIPs(iii)	46	187	70	6,025	17,908	(773)	—	(23,230)	—	—	—
Sale of Amnet Honduras to non-controlling interests	—	—	—	—	—	2,207	—	—	2,207	11,974	14,181
Disposal of Laos	—	—	—	—	—	—	—	—	—	(6,493)	(6,493)
Dividend to non-controlling shareholders	—	—	—	—	—	—	—	—	—	(57,212)	(57,212)
Balance as of December 31, 2011	104,939	(3,507)	157,407	505,120	(378,359)	2,811,130	(737,422)	(103,492)	2,254,384	191,170	2,445,554

(i) Share Capital and Share Premium—see note 23.

(ii) Retained Profits—includes profit for the year attributable to equity holders, of which $94 million (2010: $60 million; 2009: $46 million) are undistributable to equity holders.

(iii) Share based compensation—see note 24.

(iv) Put option reserve—see note 25.

(v) Other reserves—see note 26.

(vi) Non-controlling interests—as at January 1, and December 31, 2009, non controlling interest was negative as the non-controlling shareholders of Colombia Móvil S.A. ESP have a binding obligation to cover their share of the losses of this entity.

(vii) Dividends—see note 29.

(viii) Directors shares—see note 30.

(ix) Change of scope of consolidation—see note 5.

(x) Restatement—see note 4.

NOTES TO THE CONSOLIDATED FINANCIAL STATEMENTS (in part)

4. Restatement of Previously Issued Financial Statements

As previously reported in the Company's press release furnished on Form 6-K filed with the United States Securities and Exchange Commission ("SEC") on January 26, 2012, the board of directors of the Company, based on the recommendation of the audit committee and in consultation with management, concluded that, because of a misstatement in the Company's previously issued financial statements for the year ended December 31, 2010, and for the quarters ending on September 30, 2010 to September 30, 2011, the Company should restate its December 31, 2010 financial statements in this Annual Report on Form 20-F for the fiscal year ended December 31, 2011. Accordingly, the Company has restated its financial statements for these periods.

The restated financial statements as of and for the year ended December 31, 2010 correct the accounting treatment for the Honduras transaction in July 2010 as follows:

Recognition of a liability and corresponding reserve for the put option provided to our partner who holds a non-controlling interest in our Honduran operation.

Following reassessment of the accounting treatment of the put option provided to Millicom's partner who holds a 33.3% non-controlling interest in our Honduran operation, Millicom determined that, as the put option could be exercised under certain change of control events which could be outside the control of Millicom, the option meets the criteria under IAS 32 for recognition as a liability and corresponding equity reserve. Therefore, Millicom has retroactively recorded a liability for the put option at July 1, 2010 of $737 million. As a result of the change in carrying value of the put option between July 1, 2010 and year end, the liability amounted to $769 million at December 31, 2010, representing the redemption value of the option.

Recognition of a loss on revaluation of the put option liability

Recognition for the period between July 1, 2010 to December 31, 2010 of a non operating expense of $32 million, reflecting the change in value of the above mentioned put option liability.

Effects of Restatement

The following table sets forth the effects of the restatement on affected items within Millicom's previously reported Consolidated Statements of Financial Position and Consolidated Income Statements. The adjustments necessary to correct the errors have no effect on reported assets or cash flows or guidance.

(In Thousands of U.S. Dollars, Except per Share Data)		As of and for the Year Ended December 31, 2010
Consolidated Income Statements Data:		
Other non-operating income (expenses), net (including loss from associates)	As previously reported	(31,519)
	Adjustment	(31,956)
	As adjusted	(63,475)
Profit before taxes from continuing operations	As previously reported	1,870,163
	Adjustment	(31,956)
	As adjusted	1,838,207
Net profit for the period	As previously reported	1,652,233
	Adjustment	(31,956)
	As adjusted	1,620,277
Basic earnings per common share	As previously reported	$15.27
	Adjustment	$(0.30)
	As adjusted	$14.97
Diluted earnings per common share	As previously reported	$15.24
	Adjustment	$(0.29)
	As adjusted	$14.95

(In Thousands of U.S. Dollars)		As of and for the Year Ended December 31, 2010
Consolidated Statements of Financial Position Data:		
Accumulated profits brought forward	As previously reported	1,134,354
	Adjustment	—
	As adjusted	1,134,354
Put option reserve	As previously reported	—
	Adjustment	(769,378)
	As adjusted	(769,378)
Total Equity	As previously reported	3,159,011
	Adjustment	(769,378)
	As adjusted	2,389,633
Total Current Liabilities	As previously reported	1,684,831
	Adjustment	769,378
	As adjusted	2,454,209

TABLE 1-7: MANAGEMENT JUDGMENTS AND CRITICAL ACCOUNTING ESTIMATES

	2011	2010	2009
Allowance for uncollectible receivables	70	49	42
Asset retirement obligations and other environmental liabilities	27	29	26
Biological assets	10	6	4
Business combinations	50	30	31
Capitalization of development costs	10	13	12
Classification of financial instruments	12	8	8
Consolidations, including special purpose entities	12	10	9
Derecognition of financial assets	3	3	2
Derivatives and hedging	24	23	25
Liability and equity components of hybrid financial instruments	1	3	3
Mineral and oil and gas resources and reserves	15	13	11
Functional currency	8	6	3
Going concern	5	6	5
Impairment of financial assets	28	2	40
Impairment of goodwill and other intangible assets	139	81	119
Impairment of property, plant, and equipment	89	128	71
Income statement presentation	0	43	3
Insurance contracts and claims	12	14	14
Inventories	39	26	23
Operating segments	1	2	2
Postemployment and other employee benefits	86	82	77
Provisions and contingent liabilities	80	70	67
Residual values and useful lives of property, plant and equipment, intangibles, and natural resources	93	67	58
Revaluation of property, plant and equipment	3	7	4
Revenue recognition	55	48	45
Share-based payments	38	33	33
Taxation	130	116	111
Valuation of financial instruments at fair value	74	39	35
Valuation of investment property at fair value	12	22	20
Survey companies with additional judgments or estimates	59	70	60
Total	**1254**	**1049**	**963**

TABLE 1-8: COMMITMENTS AND CONTINGENCIES

	2011	2010	2009
Commitments			
Business combinations	4	9	9
Capital expenditures	84	107	108
Collaboration and licensing arrangements	6	14	14
Commitments to associates and joint ventures	16	21	19
Commitments to extend credit	19	12	12
Commitments to purchase goods and services	83	45	42
Commitments to purchase investments	12	15	9
Compensation agreements	14	1	1
Environmental matters	24	23	18
Leases	124	142	140
Pensions and other employee benefits	5	10	8
Total	391	399	380
Contingencies			
Contractual disputes, including arbitration	22	10	9
Debt obligations	24	17	14
Guarantees	97	106	104
Letters of credit and other financial facilities	32	25	19
Litigations	123	122	111
Related to government grants	3	3	5
Taxation	44	30	27
Total	349	313	307
Other commitments or contingencies	78	66	62

IAS 27, CONSOLIDATED AND SEPARATE FINANCIAL STATEMENTS

SIC 12, CONSOLIDATION—SPECIAL PURPOSE ENTITIES

IFRSs Overview and Comparison to U.S. GAAP

Author's Note

In May 2011, the IASB issued IFRS 10, *Consolidated Financial Statements*, and a revised IAS 27, *Separate Financial Statements*. IFRS 10 establishes the principles for presentation and preparation of consolidated financial statements and supersedes the requirements of extant IAS 27, *Consolidated and Separate Financial Statements*, and Standing Interpretations Committee (SIC) 12 *Consolidation—Special Purpose Entities*. IFRS 10 and IAS 27 (revised 2011) are effective for annual periods beginning on or after 1 January 2013. Earlier application is permitted.

In addition, IFRS 9 (issued November 2009 and October 2010 with an effective date of 1 January 2015) includes consequential amendments to IAS 27. These amendments remove references to "available for sale" financial instruments and replaces references to IAS 39 with references to IFRS 9.

Because these standards and amendments are effective for annual periods beginning on or after 1 January 2012, these amendments are not reflected in the commentary in this section. The timing of the effective dates of these standards and amendment affects the availability of illustrative excerpts from survey companies' financial statements. Accordingly, the excerpts appearing at the end of this section may not reflect all or some of these revisions.

1.82 IAS 27 (2008) establishes the requirements that an entity should apply in preparing and presenting consolidated financial statements for a group of entities under control of a parent. *Consolidated financial statements* are those of a group of entities presented as those of a single economic entity. A *parent* is an entity with one or more subsidiaries that it controls.

1.83 An entity should also apply IAS 27 in accounting for its investments in associates and joint ventures when preparing separate financial statements, regardless of whether separate statements are required by a regulatory authority or issued voluntarily. *Separate financial statements* are those presented by a parent, an investor in an associate, or an investor in a jointly controlled entity, in which the investments are accounted for on the basis of a direct equity interest rather than on the basis of the investees' reported results and net assets.

Author's Note

In November 2009, the IASB issued IFRS 9 which amends IAS 27 and other IFRSs, and is effective for annual periods beginning on or after 1 January 2013, with early application permitted. Specifically, IFRS 9 applies when an entity is permitted and elects to account for its interest in a subsidiary in accordance with IAS 39 and IFRS 9. An entity is also required to apply IFRS 9 in accounting for any derivatives linked to its interest in a subsidiary, unless the derivative meets the definition of an *equity instrument* in accordance with IAS 32, *Financial Instruments: Presentation*.

Recognition and Measurement

IFRSs

1.84 Unless it meets the criteria for exemption, a parent should present consolidated financial statements that include its investments in subsidiaries (controlled entities) in accordance with the requirements of IAS 27. A parent controls another entity (a subsidiary) when the parent has the power to govern the financial and operating policies of the subsidiary so as to obtain benefits from the subsidiary's activities.

1.85 A parent is only exempt from preparing consolidated financial statements in accordance with IAS 27 if all of the following criteria are met:
- The parent is itself a wholly owned or partially owned subsidiary of another entity and other owners, if any, and all owners, including those not entitled to vote, have been informed and do not object to the parent not preparing consolidated financial statements.

- Neither the parent's debt nor equity instruments are traded in a public market, whether the public market is domestic or foreign, an exchange or over-the-counter, or local or regional.
- The parent has neither filed nor is in the process of filing its financial statements with a regulatory authority for the purpose of listing any class of securities in a public market.
- The ultimate or any intermediate parent of the parent prepares and issues for public use a complete set of consolidated financial statements in compliance with IFRSs.

1.86 If an entity is exempt from preparing consolidated financial statements and elects to present separate financial statements, the entity should prepare the separate statements in accordance with IAS 27.

1.87 An entity should include all subsidiaries in its consolidated financial statements. In order to determine which investments it should consider subsidiaries, an entity should apply the guidance in IAS 27 to determine whether it has control over another entity. An entity should presume that it has control when it owns, directly or indirectly, more than 50 percent of the voting power, unless, in exceptional circumstances, it can clearly demonstrate that such ownership does not constitute control. However, an entity may still have control even if such ownership interests are less than 50 percent. IAS 27 requires an entity to assess the substance of the relationship with the investee to determine whether control exists. IAS 27 does not permit an entity to exclude an investment from consolidation as a subsidiary for any other reason except the absence of control.

1.88 IAS 27 provides guidance to an entity with respect to the consolidation process and requires the entity to eliminate fully any intragroup balances, transactions, income, and expenses in the consolidation process.

1.89 All financial statements, whether of the parent or subsidiaries, included in the consolidated financial statements should be prepared as of the same date. When the financial statements of one or more subsidiaries are prepared as of a different date than the parent's reporting date, these subsidiaries should prepare additional financial statements as of the reporting date of the parent, unless impracticable. When the financial statements of one or more subsidiaries are not prepared as of the same date as the parent's financial statements, the parent should make adjustments for the effects of significant transactions that occurred between the date of the subsidiary's financial statements and its own reporting date. In any event, IAS 27 does not permit a difference in the reporting dates of a parent and its subsidiaries of more than three months.

1.90 IAS 27 requires an entity to apply uniform accounting policies for like transactions and other events in similar circumstances in all financial statements included in the consolidated financial statements. When one or more entities in the group use different accounting policies in their separate financial statements, the parent should make adjustments to conform accounting policies in consolidation.

1.91 A parent should present any noncontrolling interest (that is, other equity owners of subsidiaries) in the equity section of the consolidated balance sheet separate from its own equity accounts.

1.92 A parent accounts for changes in its ownership interest that do not result in loss of control as equity transactions. However, if a parent loses control of a subsidiary, it should account for this event as follows:

  a. Derecognize the carrying amounts of the following:
     i. Subsidiary's assets, including goodwill, and liabilities as of the date the parent lost control
     ii. Noncontrolling interest, including any components of other comprehensive income
  b. Recognize the following when resulting from loss of control:
     i. Fair value of consideration received, if any
     ii. Distribution, if any, of the subsidiary's shares to owners, in their capacity as owners
     iii. Any retained investment in the former subsidiary at fair value as of the date it lost control
  c. Reclassify to profit or loss or transfer directly to retained earnings, if required by an IFRS, all amounts previously recognized in other comprehensive income
  d. Recognize as a gain or loss in profit or loss attributable to the parent, any resulting difference from the required derecognition, recognition, and reclassification of amounts previously recognized in other comprehensive income

1.93 When an entity loses control of a subsidiary and remeasures any retained investment at fair value, it should subsequently account for that retained investment in accordance with other applicable IFRSs. For example, if the entity retained significant influence, it should account for the investment in accordance with IAS 28, *Investments in Associates*.

1.94 In any separate (company- or parent-only) financial statements that it prepares, an entity should account for its investment in a subsidiary, associate, or jointly controlled entity either at cost or in accordance with IAS 39. When an investment is classified as held for sale or discontinued operations, an entity should apply the requirements of IFRS 5, *Non-current Assets Held for Sale and Discontinued Operations*. An entity recognizes any dividends declared by these investees in profit and loss.

1.95 When an entity accounts for its investment in an associate or jointly controlled entity in its consolidated financial statements in accordance with IAS 39 rather than IAS 28 or IAS 31, *Interests in Joint Ventures*, it should also apply IAS 39 in its separate financial statements.

1.96 SIC 12 requires an entity to consolidate another entity that is created for a narrow and well-defined objective (namely a special purpose entity), regardless of its form, when the substance of the relationship between the entity and the special purpose entity indicates that the special purpose entity is controlled by that entity. SIC 12 refers to situations in IAS 27 that indicate an entity controls another entity, even when it has less than 50 percent of the voting power. SIC 12 also provides examples of situations that indicate an entity controls a special purpose entity and, consequently, should consolidate the special purpose entity in its financial statements.

U.S. GAAP

Author's Note

In December 2011, FASB issued ASU No. 2011-10, *Property, Plant, and Equipment (Topic 360): Derecognition of in Substance Real Estate—a Scope Clarification (a consensus of the FASB Emerging Issues Task Force)*. This ASU addresses the accounting for situations in which a parent company ceases to have a controlling financial interest (as described in FASB ASC 810-10) in a subsidiary that is in substance real estate as a result of default on the subsidiary's nonrecourse debt. The amendments in this update state that the parent company should apply the guidance in FASB ASC 360-20 to determine whether it should derecognize the in substance real estate. This guidance is effective for public entities for fiscal years, and interim periods within those years, beginning on or after June 15, 2012, and after December 15, 2013, for nonpublic entities. Early adoption is permitted.

Author's Note

In general, FASB ASC includes considerably more guidance on consolidation than IFRSs. The following discussion only addresses issues directly related to those addressed in IAS 27 or SIC 12.

1.97 Like IFRSs, FASB ASC 810-10-15-8 considers ownership by the reporting entity, directly or indirectly, of more than 50 percent of the outstanding voting shares of another entity to be the usual condition indicating that the reporting entity should consolidate. Also, like IFRSs, this FASB ASC paragraph indicates that the power to control may also exist with a lesser percentage of ownership. However, FASB ASC 810, *Consolidation*, contains considerably more guidance on consolidation and includes exemptions from consolidation not included in IAS 27. For example, paragraphs 10 and 12 of FASB ASC 810-10-15 include the following scope exclusions to consolidation under this topic:

- A majority-owned subsidiary should not be consolidated if control does not rest with the majority owner. For instance, if any of the following are present:
  — The subsidiary is in legal reorganization.
  — The subsidiary is in bankruptcy.
  — The subsidiary operates under foreign exchange restrictions, controls, or other governmentally imposed uncertainties so severe that they cast significant doubt on the parent's ability to control the subsidiary.
  — In some instances, the powers of a shareholder with a majority voting interest to control the operations or assets of the investee are restricted in certain respects by approval or veto rights granted to the noncontrolling shareholder (hereafter referred to as noncontrolling rights). In paragraphs 2–14 of FASB ASC 810-10-25, the term noncontrolling shareholder refers to one or more noncontrolling shareholders. Those noncontrolling rights may have little or no impact on the ability of a shareholder with a majority voting interest to control the investee's operations or assets, or alternatively, those rights may be so restrictive to call into question whether control rests with the majority owner.

—Control exists through means other than through ownership of a majority voting interest.

- A broker-dealer parent within the scope of FASB ASC 940, *Financial Services—Broker and Dealers*, should not consolidate a majority-owned subsidiary in which it has a controlling financial interest if the control is likely to be temporary.
- Except as discussed in FASB ASC 946-810-45-3, an investment company within the scope of FASB ASC 946, *Financial Services—Investment Companies*, should not consolidate a noninvestment company investee.
- An employer should not consolidate an employee benefit plan subject to the provisions of FASB ASC 712, *Compensation—Nonretirement Postemployment Benefits*, or FASB ASC 715, *Compensation—Retirement Benefits*.
- An entity should not consolidate investments accounted for at fair value in accordance with specialized guidance in FASB ASC 946.
- An entity should not consolidate either a governmental entity or a financing entity established by a governmental entity, unless certain conditions are met.

FASB ASC 810-10-15-10 also requires an entity to consider additional guidance to determine whether consolidation is appropriate for a limited partnership, a research and development arrangement, or an entity controlled by contract.

1.98 FASB ASC 810 also includes more specific and detailed guidance than IFRSs for determining when a variable interest entity (VIE) (broadly comparable to a special purpose entity in SIC 12) should be consolidated. FASB ASC 810-10-05-8 explains that a *VIE* is a legal entity in which equity investors do not have the characteristics of a controlling financial interest or sufficient equity at risk for the legal entity to finance its activities without additional subordinated financial support. When applying this guidance, an entity should first determine whether the entity under consideration is a legal entity within the scope of the guidance on consolidation of VIEs, as discussed in FASB ASC 810-10-15-14. The specific design of the legal entity is important for making this determination.

1.99 Like IFRSs, it is preferable under FASB ASC that the subsidiary's financial statements have the same or nearly the same fiscal period as the parent. However, FASB ASC 810-10-45-12 states that for consolidation purposes, it is usually acceptable to use the subsidiary's financial statements if the difference in fiscal period is not more than approximately three months. In addition, when a difference in the fiscal periods exists, FASB ASC does not require adjustments to be made for the effects of significant transactions that occurred between the parents' and subsidiaries' fiscal year-ends. However, FASB ASC 810-10-45-12 requires recognition by disclosure or otherwise of the effect of intervening events that materially affect the financial position or results of operations. FASB ASC does not state what qualifies as an otherwise acceptable means of recognition besides disclosures or adjustments to reported amounts. In contrast, IAS 27 requires both the parents' and subsidiaries' financial statements used in the consolidated financial statements to be prepared as of the same date, unless impracticable. When it is impracticable for a subsidiary to prepare financial statements as of the date of the parent's financial statements, IAS 27 requires an entity

to adjust the financial statements for the effects of significant transactions or events that occurred between the two dates, with the proviso that the difference between the end of the parent's and subsidiary's fiscal year-ends is not more than three months.

1.100 Like IFRSs, FASB ASC 810-10-45-16 requires the entity to present any noncontrolling interest within the "Equity" or "Net Assets" section of the consolidated statement of financial position separately from the parent's equity or net assets.

1.101 Like IFRSs, with some exceptions, FASB ASC 810-10-40-4 requires an entity to deconsolidate a subsidiary or derecognize a group of assets as of the date it ceases to have a controlling financial interest in the subsidiary or group of assets. The process that an entity should follow when it deconsolidates a subsidiary is similar under both IFRSs and FASB ASC, except when an entity deconsolidates a subsidiary through a nonreciprocal transfer to owners (such as a spinoff). According to FASB ASC 810-10-40-5, if a parent deconsolidates a subsidiary through a nonreciprocal transfer to owners, the guidance in FASB ASC 845-10 applies. Otherwise, an entity should recognize a gain or loss in net income measured as the difference between the following amounts:

a. Carrying amount of the assets and liabilities of the former subsidiary or the carrying amount of the group of assets
b. Sum of the following amounts:
   i. Fair value of any consideration received
   ii. Fair value of any retained noncontrolling investment in the former subsidiary or group of assets at the date that the subsidiary is deconsolidated or the group of assets is derecognized
   iii. Carrying amount of any noncontrolling interest in the former subsidiary (including any accumulated other comprehensive income attributable to the noncontrolling interest) at the date the subsidiary is deconsolidated

1.102 Like IFRSs, FASB ASC 810-10-45-11 recognizes that an entity may need to prepare parent-entity (separate) financial statements, in addition to consolidated financial statements. Unlike IFRSs, this paragraph provides guidance on how an entity may choose to present these statements (for example, consolidating financial statements, in which one column is used for the parent and other columns for particular subsidiaries or groups of subsidiaries, which is an effective means of presenting the pertinent information).

Disclosure

IFRSs

1.103 In consolidated financial statements, IAS 27 requires an entity to disclose the following, when applicable:

- Nature of the relationship between the parent and subsidiary if control exists at less than 50 percent of the direct or indirect voting power
- Reasons that control does not exist if the parent has more than 50 percent of the direct or indirect voting power

- Reasons that the parent and subsidiary have different reporting dates
- Nature and extent of significant restrictions on the ability to transfer funds to the parent in the form of dividends, loans, or cash advances
- Schedule of effects of changes in ownership interests that did not result in loss of control
- Gain or loss, if any, recognized in profit or loss when the entity loses control and a disaggregation of the net gain or loss into the following amounts:
  — Portion of gain or loss attributable to recognition of retained investment at fair value
  — Line item(s) in statement of comprehensive income in which the gain or loss is recognized, if not shown separately on the face of the statement

1.104 IAS 27 requires the separate financial statements of a parent, venturer in a jointly controlled entity, or an investor in an associate to include disclosures of the following:

- Statement that the financial statements are separate and the reasons why separate statements are prepared, if not by law
- List of significant investments in subsidiaries, jointly controlled entities, and associates, including the name; country of incorporation or residence; proportion of ownership interest; and, if different, proportion of voting power held
- Description of the method used to account for the investments listed under the previous bullet item

1.105 When a parent prepares separate financial statements because it is exempt from preparing consolidated financial statements in accordance with IAS 27, it should (a) disclose the fact that it is exempt and the name and country of domicile or incorporation of the parent that prepares consolidated financial statements in compliance with IFRSs and (b) address where such statements may be obtained.

1.106 SIC 12 does not include additional disclosure requirements.

U.S. GAAP

1.107 FASB ASC 810-10-50-1 requires an entity to disclose the consolidation policy that is being followed. IFRSs require an entity to disclose whether the financial statements are consolidated or separate.

1.108 Like IFRSs, FASB ASC 810-10-50-1B requires a parent to disclose all of the following when a subsidiary is deconsolidated or a group of assets is derecognized in accordance with in FASB ASC 810-10-40-3A:

- Amount of any gain or loss recognized in accordance with FASB ASC 810-10-40-5
- Portion of any gain or loss related to the remeasurement of any retained investment in the former subsidiary or group of assets to its fair value
- Line item in which the gain or loss is recognized, unless separately presented on the face of the income statement
- In addition, unlike IFRSs, a parent must also disclose the following: A description of the valuation technique(s) used to measure the fair value of any direct or indirect retained investment in the former subsidiary or group of assets
- Information that enables users of the parent's financial statements to assess the inputs used to develop the fair value described previously
- The nature of the continuing involvement with the subsidiary or entity acquiring the group of assets after it has been deconsolidated or derecognized
- Whether the transaction that resulted in the deconsolidation or derecognition was with a related party
- Whether the former subsidiary or entity acquiring a group of assets will be a related party after deconsolidation

Unlike IAS 27, FASB ASC 810-10-50-1A requires additional disclosures about less-than-wholly owned subsidiaries for each reporting period.

1.109 Unlike IFRSs, FASB ASC does not have any specific disclosure requirements for parent-entity-only financial statements.

Presentation and Disclosure Excerpts

Restrictions on Dividend Payments to Shareholders by Subsidiaries

1.110
Grupo TMM, S.A.B. (Dec 2011)

NOTES TO THE CONSOLIDATED FINANCIAL STATEMENTS (in part)

12 Financing:

The total debt as of December 31, 2011 and 2010 is summarized as follows:

	2011	2010
Short term debt:		
DVB Bank America[1]	$ 2,825	$ 4,167
DEG-Deutsche Investition[3]	1,700	1,700
DC Automotriz Servicios[2]	1,305	998
Autofin México[6]	1,157	5,593
Pure Leasing[4]	612	423
Logra Financiamientos[7]	483	—
INPIASA[8]	173	—
Interest payable	9,097	11,086
Transaction costs	(162)	(295)
	$ 17,190	$ 23,672
Long term debt:		
Trust Certificates (CBF) (See note 14)	$ 675,933	$ 775,536
DVB Bank America[1]	24,623	27,486
Bancomext, S.N.C.[5]	14,608	17,743
DC Automotriz Servicios[2]	5,579	7,627
Investors[9]	5,121	—
Autofin México[6]	4,322	2,024
DEG-Deutsche Investition[3]	3,400	5,100
INPIASA[8]	1,023	—
Pure Leasing[4]	702	1,092
	$ 735,311	$ 836,608

[1] In 2007, Grupo TMM Grupo TMM entered into two lines of credit in dollars with DVB Bank to acquire two chemical vessels (Maya and Omega). The first, with a loan facility for US$25.0 million (approximately $348.7 million pesos), with an average interest rate of 7.42%, the senior note with a fixed rate of 6.88%, and the junior note with a fix rate of 11.365%. The second vessel loan facility for the amount of US$27.5 million (approximately $383.6 million pesos), with an average interest rate of 7.78%, the senior note with a fixed rate of 7.21%, and the junior note with a fixed interest rate of 11.7025%.

Both loans are payable in monthly instalments of principal and interest, maturing May 25, 2017, and June 19, 2017, respectively. Both facilities were contracted through the subsidiary TMM Parcel Tankers.

The Company began negotiations with the bank early in 2010 to improve the amortization profile for these loans, and also to reduce the effective rate. On March 30, 2011, the restructuring with DVB Bank was finalized with the signing of two new loans, which were opened April 4, 2011. The first is a "bridge" loan for US$3.5 million (approximately $48.8 million pesos) with draws during the first twenty-four months, and monthly payments on principal starting month twenty-five, quarterly payments of interest at an *AIR* rate (bank available funds interbank rate) plus four hundred basis points, maturing June 2017.

This line of credit will reduce payment on the senior notes by US$150,000 (approximately $2.1 million pesos) during the first eighteen months, and US$133,000 (approximately $1.8 million pesos) during the following six months.

The second is a loan for US$4.0 million (approximately $55.8 million pesos) that was used, together with Company cash, to prepay all the junior notes mentioned previous; this is a single draw loan with payment on principal due June 2017 and quarterly interest payments at an *AIR* rate (bank available funds interbank rate) plus four hundred basis points.

(continued)

(footnote continued)

(2) This loan is comprised of different contracts made with DC Automotriz Servicios as follows:

(a) On July 19, 2007, the Company entered into a loan facility in Mexican pesos as part of the Forced Assignment of Rights Agreement entered into with DC Automotriz Servicios S. de R.L. de C.V. (now Daimler Financial Services México, S. de R.L. de C.V. "Daimler") for the acquisition of automotive transportation assets for approximately US$8.9 million ($123.7 million pesos) at a variable rate of the 91-day TIIE rate plus 200 basis points, through its subsidiary Lacto Comercial Organizada, S.A. de C.V. ("Lacorsa"). Payment of which is made through 84 consecutive monthly payments on the principal plus interests on outstanding balances, commencing January 2008 and maturing in December 2014.

A debt recognition and restructure agreement was signed on this loan on December 1, 2010, for $96.7 million pesos (approximately US$7.8 million) at a variable rate of the 28-day TIIE plus 3.5 percentage points, through Lacorsa. Payment for which is made on 72 consecutive monthly payments on the principal plus interests on outstanding balances starting January 1, 2011 and maturing in December 2016.

(b) On June 4, 2008, the Company entered in a loan facility in Mexican pesos with "Daimler" for the acquisition of 31 transportation units for approximately US$1.4 million ($19.8 million pesos) at a fixed rate of 12.85%, through its subsidiary Lacorsa; payment for which is made on 60 consecutive monthly payments on the principal plus interests on outstanding balances, maturing in June 2013.

On September 26, 2008, the Company entered into a loan facility in Mexican pesos with "Daimler" for the acquisition of 8 transportation units for approximately US$0.4 million ($5.2 million pesos) at a fixed rate of 13.56%, through its subsidiary Lacorsa; payment for which is made on 60 consecutive monthly payments on the principal plus interests on outstanding balances, maturing in September 2013.

In June 2010, the both loans were restructured into a single loan for approximately US$1.6 million ($21.7 million pesos) at a fixed rate of 14.8%, through its subsidiary Lacorsa; payment for which is made on 60 consecutive monthly payments on the principal plus interests on outstanding balances, maturing in May 2015.

(3) On January 11, 2008, Grupo TMM entered into a loan facility listed in dollars to refinance the purchase of "ADEMSA" for US$8.5 million (approximately $118.6 million pesos), at a fixed rate of 8.01%, payment on which is to be made in 14 consecutive semi-annual payments on principal plus interests on outstanding balances, with a two year grace period on the principal and maturing in July 2014.

(4) In September 2009, the Company secured with Pure Leasing, S.A. de C.V. through its subsidiary TMM Logistics, S.A. de C.V., a line of credit in Mexican pesos for working capital and/or current accounts for approximately US$1.9 million ($26.2 million pesos) at a fixed rate of 14.25% with monthly payments on principal and interest on outstanding balances, maturing in September 2014.

(5) In June 2009, the Company secured with Banco Nacional de Comercio Exterior, S.N.C., Institución de Banca de Desarrollo, through its subsidiary TMM División Marítima, S.A. de C.V., a mortgage secured simple line of credit in dollars for working capital for US$25.0 million (approximately $348.7 million pesos) at a variable rate, maturing in June 2015, monthly interest payments on outstanding balances and principal at maturity, drawing both dollars and pesos with the possibility of making prepayments on principal without penalty.

In July 2009, a first draw was made on the line of credit for US $6.9 million (approximately $96.2 million pesos) at a variable rate of the 30-day Libor plus 600 basis points, with monthly interest payments. On July 30, 2010, the principal balance was prepaid in full on this draw and interests.

In November 2009, a second draw was made on the line of credit for approximately US $9.5 million ($132.9 million pesos) at a variable rate of the 28-day TIIE plus 400 basis points, with monthly interest payments. As of December 31, 2011, the effective rate for this draw on the line of credit was 8.7975% with an outstanding balance of $1.3 million (approximately $18.4 million pesos).

In December 2009, a third draw was made on the line of credit for approximately US$0.9 million ($11.9 million pesos) at a variable rate of the 28-day TIIE plus 400 basis points, with monthly interest payments. As of December 31, 2011, the effective rate for this draw on the line of credit was 8.8850% with an outstanding balance of approximately $0.9 million ($11.9 million pesos).

In November 2010, the Company secured with Banco Nacional de Comercio Exterior, S.N.C., Institución de Banca de Desarrollo, through its subsidiary TMM División Marítima, S.A. de C.V., a new line of credit in US dollars for working capital for US$15.0 million (approximately $209.2 million pesos), at a variable rate, maturing in June 2015, with monthly interest payments on outstanding balances and principal on maturity, with the possibility of making prepayments without penalty. The balance on both lines of credit, together, cannot exceed US $25.0 million, or the equivalent in Mexican pesos.

In November 2010, a first draw was made on the new line of credit for approximately US$9.2 million ($115.0 million pesos) at a variable rate of the 28-day TIIE plus 425 basis points, with monthly interest payments. As of December 31, 2011, the effective rate on this draw on the line of credit was 9.0475% with an outstanding balance of approximately US$8.2 million ($115.0 million pesos).

In October 2011, the Company made a second draw on the new line of credit for approximately US $4.7 million ($65.6 million pesos) at a variable rate of the 28-day TIIE plus 425 basis points, with monthly interest payments. The effective rate for this draw on the line of credit as of December 31, 2011 was 9.0475% with an outstanding balance of approximately US$4.7 million ($65.6 million pesos).

(6) In July 2010, the Company secured with Banco Autofin México S.A. Institución de Banca Múltiple ("BAM"), through its subsidiary Proserpec Servicios Administrativos, S.A.P.I. de C.V., a line of credit in Mexican pesos for working capital and treasury obligations for approximately US $7.2 million ($100.0 million pesos), at a variable rate of the 28-day *TIIE* plus 4.5 points, secured with fixed assets and the assignment of collection rights on contracts with some clients; payment for which is made on 24 consecutive monthly payments on the principal plus interest on outstanding balances, starting July 2010 and maturing in June 2012. On September 30, 2011, using the same line of credit, the balance on the principal for this draw and interests was prepaid in full.

In September 2011 and to strengthen the agricultural activities of "ADEMSA" (See Note 24b V), the Company decided to take advantage of the line of credit held by Proserpec Servicios Administrativos, S.A.P.I. de C.V. with BAM, to secure a loan for approximately US $3.1 million ($42.9 million pesos). This amount will be recognized as a capital contribution in the company Comercializadora de Valle Hermoso, S.A. de C.V. ("COVAHESA").

Therefore, considering the prepayment and this new draw on the line of credit, on September 30, 2011 the loans were combined into one for approximately US $5.8 million ($80.4 million pesos) at a variable rate of the 28-day TIIE plus 500 basis points, with monthly payments on principal and interests, and maturing September 2016. The effective rate on this draw on the line of credit as of December 31, 2011 was 9.8000% with an outstanding balance of approximately US $5.5 million ($76.4 million pesos).

(7) In November 2011, the Company decided to secure a line of credit to strength the agricultural activities of "ADEMSA" (See Note 24b V), through its subsidiary Proserpec Servicios Administrativos, S.A.P.I. de C.V. with Logra Financiamientos, S.A. de C.V. SOFOM ENR ("LOGRA"), for approximately US$0.8 million ($10.6 million pesos). This amount will also be recognized as a capital contribution in "COVAHESA." The

(continued)

(footnote continued)

loan accrues interest at a variable rate of the 28-day *TIIE* plus 600 basis points, with monthly interest payments, four capital payments, and maturing December 2012. The effective rate for this draw on the line of credit as of December 31, 2011 was 10.7981% with an outstanding balance of approximately US$0.4 million ($5.6 million pesos).

(8) In November 2011, the Company decided to enter into two loan facilities to strengthen the agricultural activities of "ADEMSA" (See Note 24b V), through its subsidiary Proserpec Servicios Administrativos, S.A.P.I. de C.V. with INPIASA, S.A. de C.V. ("INPIASA"). The first for approximately US$1.1 million ($15.7 million pesos) at a variable rate of the 28-day *TIIE* plus 450 basis points, with monthly payments on principal and interests, and maturing August 2021; the second for approximately US$0.3 million ($4.2 million pesos) at a variable rate of the 28-day *TIIE* plus 450 basis points, with monthly payments on principal and interest, and maturing October 2016. The total amount for both loans will also be recognized as a capital contribution in "COVAHESA." The effective rate for both loans as of December 31, 2011 was 9.2900%, with a total outstanding balance of approximately US$1.4 million ($19.2 million pesos).

(9) In January 2011, the Company decided to enter into two loan facilities to improve the Company's amortization profile and to facilitate the cancellation process for the Obligations from the Sale of Receivables Program (See Note 13), through its subsidiary Transportación Marítima Mexicana, S.A. de C.V. with two private investors ("Investors"), who held "B" certificates, which were also cancelled under the aforementioned restructuring of the Program. Both loans for US$3.0 million (approximately $41.8 million) at a fixed rate of 11.2500%, with semi-annual payments on principal and interests, with a two year grace period on the principal, and maturing January 2016. The total outstanding balance as of December 31, 2011 was US$6.0 million (approximately $83.7 million pesos).

Covenants

The agreements related to the abovementioned loans contain certain covenants including the observance of certain financial ratios, restrictions on dividend payments, and sales of assets, among others. Grupo TMM and its subsidiaries were in compliance with these covenants and restrictions as of December 31, 2011 and 2010.

The interest expense on bank loans was $5.7 million (approximately $79.5 million pesos) and $6.7 million (approximately $93.4 million pesos) for the years ended December 31, 2011 and 2010, respectively.

13 Obligations From the Sale of Receivables

Under its factoring program, the Company and certain of its subsidiaries sold present and future accounts receivable to an independent trust, which in turn issued certificates to investors ("Certificates"). For accounting purposes, the factoring represented the total amount in US dollars for future services provided to customers according to the factoring.

On September 25, 2006, the Company finalized a Factoring program for US $200 million with Deutsche Bank (the "Program"). As of December 31, 2010, the outstanding balance under this Program was US $17.2 million, exclusive of US$6.3 million for the transaction cost and US$0.9 million in interest payable, bearing a fixed interest rate of 12.47% per annum.

This Program contemplated restricted cash to secure any potential payment obligation arising from default. The reserved cash balance as of December 31, 2010 was US$0.7 million.

To improve the amortization profile and the Company's financial expenses, negotiations were opened with Deutsche Bank in mid 2010 to repurchase early the certificates the bank holds. In April 2011, the Company finalized the early repurchase of all the certificates held by Deutsche Bank for a total of US$9.1 million. This amount represents the total value of the certificates at a price of US$0.91, plus the interests earned and unpaid on the date of the repurchase.

The obligations from the sale of receivables as of December 31, 2011 and 2010 had performed as follows:

	2011	2010
2006 Series	$ 200,000	$ 200,000
2006 Series — A Restructuring of certificates — B	—	6,000
Cumulative payments made	(199,462)	(188,849)
Remission of debt	(538)	—
	—	17,151
Interest payable	—	924
Transaction cost	—	(6,302)
Current portion	—	(11,223)
Obligations from the sale of receivables, long term	$ —	$ 550

The maturities of the obligations from the sale of receivables as of December 31, 2009 and 2010 are summarized as follows (carrying value amounts):

	2010
Maturity	
2011	$ 10,299
2012	1,450
2013	2,434
2014 and thereafter	2,968
	$ 17,151

Covenants

The agreements related to the abovementioned loans contemplated certain covenants including the observance of certain financial ratios and restrictions on dividend payments and sale of assets. Grupo TMM and its subsidiaries had fulfilled these Covenants at December 31, 2010.

Additional Parent Company Information Disclosed in a Note to the Consolidated Financial Statements

1.111

KB Financial Group Inc. (Dec 2011)

NOTES TO THE CONSOLIDATED FINANCIAL STATEMENTS (in part)

45. Parent Company Information

The following tables present the Parent Company Only financial information:

Condensed Statements of Financial Position

(In Millions of Korean Won)		2010.01.01		2010.12.31		2011.12.31
Assets						
Cash held at bank subsidiaries	(Won)	845,366	(Won)	759,998	(Won)	32,031
Receivables from nonbanking subsidiaries		170,000		160,000		60,000
Investments in subsidiaries[1]						
Banking subsidiaries		16,774,896		16,774,896		14,821,721
Nonbanking subsidiaries		837,226		898,426		2,951,601
Other assets		36,826		186,592		645,337
Total assets	(Won)	18,664,314	(Won)	18,779,912	(Won)	18,510,690
Liabilities and Shareholders' Equity						
Debts	(Won)	—	(Won)	—	(Won)	130,000
Debentures		798,421		799,353		49,988
Other liabilities		7,450		159,438		614,422
Shareholders' equity		17,858,443		17,821,121		17,716,280
Total liabilities and shareholders' equity	(Won)	18,664,314	(Won)	18,779,912	(Won)	18,510,690

[1] Investments in subsidiaries were accounted at cost method in accordance with IAS 27.

Condensed Statements of Income

(In Millions of Korean Won)		2010		2011
Income				
Dividends from subsidiaries:				
Dividends from banking subsidiaries	(Won)	95,305	(Won)	—
Interest from subsidiaries		36,150		26,999
Other income		831		884
Total income		132,286		27,883
Expense				
Interest expense		53,431		41,571
Noninterest expense		38,177		51,537
Total expense		91,608		93,108
Profit (loss) before tax expense		40,678		(65,225)
Tax income (expense)		897		1,547
Profit (loss) for the year	(Won)	41,575		(63,678)

Condensed Statements of Cash Flows

(In Millions of Korean Won)		2010		2011
Operating Activities				
Net income (loss)	(Won)	41,575	(Won)	(63,678)
Reconciliation of net income (loss) to net cash provided by operating activities:				
Other operating activities, net		11,442		(4,383)
Net cash provided by (used in) operating activities		53,017		(68,061)
Investing Activities				
Net payments from (to) subsidiaries		(51,200)		—
Other investing activities, net		(8,288)		(10,743)
Net cash used in investing activities		(59,488)		(10,743)
Financing Activities				
Increase in debts		—		130,000
Decreases in debentures		—		(750,000)
Cash dividends paid		(78,897)		(41,163)
Net cash provided by (used in) financing activities		(78,897)		(661,163)
Net increase in cash held at bank subsidiaries		(85,368)		(739,967)
Cash held at bank subsidiaries at January 1		845,363		759,995
Cash held at bank subsidiaries at December 31	(Won)	759,995	(Won)	20,028

IAS 10, *EVENTS AFTER THE REPORTING PERIOD*

Author's Note

IFRS 13 includes a consequential amendment to IAS 10, *Events after the Reporting Period,* which replacements the term *market value* with the term *fair value.* The IASB issued IFRS 13 in May 2011 with an effective date of 1 January 2013. Early application is permitted. If an entity early adopts IFRS 13, it should apply this amendment.

Because these standards are effective for annual periods beginning on or after 1 January 2012, this amendment is not reflected in the commentary in this section. However, the amendment would not affect the availability of illustrative excerpts from survey companies' financial statements.

IFRSs Overview and Comparison to U.S. GAAP

1.112 IAS 10 establishes recognition and disclosure requirements for certain events that occur after the balance sheet date. The events within the scope of IAS 10 may be favorable or unfavorable and occur between the balance sheet date and the date the entity authorizes the financial statements for issue.

Recognition and Measurement

IFRSs

1.113 An entity should adjust the financial statements for those events that provide evidence of conditions existing at the balance sheet date (that is, adjusting events) and should not adjust for those events that indicate conditions arising after the balance sheet date (that is, nonadjusting events).

1.114 IAS 10 provides several examples of adjusting events for conditions that existed at the balance sheet date, including the following:
- Settlement of a lawsuit confirming a present obligation
- Confirming information of an asset impairment
- Determination of costs of assets purchased or proceeds of assets sold
- Discovery of fraud or errors

1.115 Examples of nonadjusting events include the following:
- Declines in market values
- Filing of lawsuits
- Issue of new debt or equity securities
- Declaration of dividends

1.116 IAS 10 prohibits an entity from preparing its financial statements on a going concern basis if management determines after the end of the reporting period that it will liquidate the entity or cease operations and has no alternatives to doing so.

U.S. GAAP

1.117 Like IFRSs, FASB ASC 855, *Subsequent Events,* includes general guidance applicable to all entities on accounting for, and disclosure of, events after the reporting period (subsequent events) that are not addressed specifically in other topics within FASB ASC.

1.118 Like IFRSs, paragraphs 1 and 3 of FASB ASC 855-10-25 require an entity to recognize only the effects of events that provide evidence of conditions that existed at the balance sheet date, including accounting estimates, and prohibit an entity from recognizing events that provide evidence about conditions that arose after the balance sheet date. However, unlike IFRS, no exception exists when the going concern assumption is no longer appropriate. Also unlike IFRSs, FASB ASC 855-10-25-1A extends the period over which an SEC filer or a conduit bond obligor for conduit debt securities that are traded in a public market (a domestic or foreign stock exchange or an over-the-counter market, including local or regional markets) should evaluate subsequent events until the date the financial statements are issued, rather than the date of authorization. In addition, FASB ASC 855-10-25-2 requires all other entities that do not meet the criteria outlined in FASB ASC 855-10-25-1A to evaluate such events through the date the financial statements are available to be issued. As defined in the FASB ASC glossary, *financial statements* are considered available to be issued when they are complete in a form and format that complies with U.S. GAAP, and all approvals necessary for issuance have been obtained, for example, from management, the board of directors, or significant shareholders.

1.119 Like IFRSs, FASB ASC 855-10-25-3 prohibits an entity from recognizing subsequent events that provide evidence about conditions that did not exist at the date of the balance sheet but arose after that date and before the financial statements are issued or are available to be issued.

1.120 Unlike IFRSs, FASB ASC 855-10-25-4 also addresses the potential for reissue of the financial statements in reports filed with regulatory agencies. In this circumstance, an entity should not recognize events occurring between the time the financial statements were originally issued or were available to be issued and the time the financial statements were reissued, unless U.S. GAAP or regulatory requirements require the adjustment. Similarly, an entity should not recognize events or transactions occurring after the financial statements were issued or available to be issued in financial statements that are later reissued in comparative form along with financial statements of subsequent periods, unless the adjustment meets the criteria previously stated.

1.121 FASB ASC provides specific guidance on the following:
- Like IFRSs, FASB ASC 740-10-25-15 requires an entity to recognize changes in judgment after the balance sheet date that result in subsequent recognition, derecognition, or a change in measurement of an income tax position taken in a prior annual period as a discrete item when the change occurs.

Author's Note

See the related discussion of income taxes in section 3, "Statement of Comprehensive Income and Related Disclosures."

- Like IFRSs, FASB ASC 260-10-55-12 requires an entity to adjust earnings per share amounts for changes in common stock resulting from stock dividends, stock splits, or reverse stock splits that occur after the close of the period. In addition, if per share computations reflect such changes in the number of shares, that fact should be disclosed. Unlike IFRSs, the period of evaluation for such events is extended to the date before the date that the financial statements are issued or available to be issued, rather than the date of authorization. Also unlike IFRSs, SEC registrants are required to make retroactive adjustments, as previously noted, upon declaration of a stock dividend, stock split, or reverse stock split, even if the actual date of the event is subsequent to financial statement issuance, but the event is declared prior to the issuance of the financial statements.

Author's Note

See the related discussion of earnings per share in section 3, "Statement of Comprehensive Income and Related Disclosures."

- Similar to the treatment of contingent assets in IFRSs, FASB ASC 450-30-25-1 generally prohibits recognition of gain contingencies in the financial statements because to do so might be to recognize revenue before its realization. Comparable to the definition of a *contingent asset* in IFRSs, the FASB ASC glossary defines a *gain contingency* as an existing condition, situation, or set of circumstances involving uncertainty about possible gain to an entity that will ultimately be resolved when one or more future events occur or fail to occur. Unlike IFRSs, FASB ASC does not address recognition when the realization of contingent income is virtually certain.

Author's Note

See the related discussion of provisions, contingent liabilities, and contingent assets in section 2, "Statement of Financial Position and Related Disclosures."

- Like IFRSs, generally, the classification of liabilities as current or noncurrent reflects circumstances at the reporting date. However, unlike IFRSs, paragraphs 14–15 of FASB ASC 470-10-45 address refinancing considerations in determining the classification of debt at the reporting date.

Presentation

IFRSs

1.122 IFRSs do not include specific presentation requirements for events after the reporting date.

U.S GAAP

1.123 Unlike IFRSs, FASB ASC 855-10-50-3 requires an entity to consider supplementing the historical financial statements with pro forma financial data when an unrecognized subsequent event occurs. An entity should present pro forma financial data when an unrecognized subsequent event is sufficiently significant that pro forma information provides the best disclosure. In preparing pro forma data, an entity should include the event as if it had occurred on the balance sheet date. An entity should also consider presenting pro forma statements, usually a statement of financial position only, in columnar form on the face of the historical statements.

Disclosure

IFRSs

1.124 An entity should disclose who authorized the issuance of the financial statements and the authorization date. When applicable, an entity should also disclose the fact that the entity's owners or others have the power to amend the financial statements after issue.

1.125 Even when an entity does not adjust the financial statements for new information about conditions existing at the balance sheet date, it should update disclosures relating to those conditions.

1.126 For material, nonadjusting events, an entity should disclose the following information by category of event:
- Nature of the event
- Estimate of the financial effect or a statement that an estimate cannot be made

U.S. GAAP

1.127 Paragraphs 1 and 4 of FASB ASC 855-10-50 state that an entity, except an SEC registrant, should disclose the date through which subsequent events have been evaluated, as well as whether that date is the date the financial statements were issued or the date the financial statements were available to be issued. An entity, except an SEC registrant, should also disclose in the revised financial statements the date through which subsequent events have been evaluated in both the originally issued financial statements and the reissued financial statements. The aforementioned guidance is similar to IFRSs in that both require disclosure of issuance or authorization, so that the users of the financial statements will know that the financial statements do not reflect events after the date(s) disclosed. Unlike IFRSs, FASB ASC does not explicitly discuss the circumstances when an entity's owners or others have the power to amend financial statements after issue.

1.128 FASB ASC 855-10-S99 provides guidance to SEC registrants on recognition or disclosure, or both, of significant events that occur after the date of the financial statements. FASB ASC 855-10-S99-2 explains that a registrant may widely distribute its financial statements, but before filing them with the SEC, the registrant or its auditor may then become aware of an event or a transaction that existed at the date of the financial statements that causes those financial statements to be materially misleading. If a registrant does not amend those financial statements, so that they are free of material misstatement or omissions when they are filed with the SEC, the registrant will be knowingly filing a false and misleading document. In addition, SEC registrants are reminded of their responsibility to, at a minimum, disclose subsequent events, and independent auditors are reminded of their responsibility to assess subsequent events and evaluate the impact of the events or transactions on their audit report.

1.129 Like IFRSs, FASB ASC 855-10-50-2 requires an entity to disclose the following information about unrecognized subsequent events when failure to disclose would result in misleading financial statements:

- Nature of the event
- Estimate of the event's financial effect or a statement that such an estimate cannot be made

Presentation and Disclosure Excerpts

Downgrade of Credit Rating, Agreement to Acquire Assets, Financial Statement Subject to Approval of Supervisory Board

1.130

Telekom Austria Aktiengesellschaft (Dec 2011)

NOTES TO THE CONSLIDATED FINANCIAL STATEMENTS (in part)

(37) Subsequent Events

On February 13, 2012, the Management Board approved the consolidated financial statements for submission to the Supervisory Board. The Supervisory Board will review the consolidated financial statements and report its decision upon approval.

On January 19, 2012, the rating agency Moody's Investors Service downgraded the long-term rating of Telekom Austria AG from A3 to Baa1 (with stable outlook). Moody's Investor Service confirmed the P-2 short-term rating of Telekom Austria AG.

On January 19, 2012, the RPR private foundation announced that it holds directly and indirectly 20.118% of the shares of Telekom Austria AG.

On February 3, 2012, Telekom Austria Group agreed to acquire assets currently owned by Orange Austria Telecommunication GmbH ("Orange Austria") for a total amount of up to EUR 390,000. Following the acquisition of Orange Austria by Hutchison 3G Austria, Telekom Austria Group will acquire the assets from Hutchison 3G Austria. These assets comprise frequencies, base station sites, the mobile phone oper-

ator YESSS! Telekommunikation GmbH ("YESSS!") as well as certain intangible assets. The acquisition of Orange Austria by Hutchison 3G Austria is conditional on the approval of Telekom Austria Group's acquisition of YESSS! by the relevant regulatory and anti-trust authorities. The transaction is expected to be closed in mid 2012.

Repayment of Convertible Redeemable Preference Share, Offer to Exchange Member Shares, Insurance Claim

1.131

Silver Fern Farms Limited (Sep 2011)

NOTES TO THE CONSOLIDATED FINANCIAL STATEMENTS (in part)

33. Events After the Balance Sheet Date

Repayment of Convertible Redeemable Preference Shares

On 22 September 2011, the Board of Directors resolved to repay in full all convertible redeemable preference shares on issue. The cash was paid to shareholders on 31 October 2011.

Dividend Payable

On 16 November 2011, the Board of Directors resolved to declare a 10c per share dividend on all New ordinary shares on issue. The total dividend payable, cannot be quantified at this stage and will be distributed in December 2011.

Offer to Exchange Member Shares

On 16 November 2011, the Board of Directors resolved to exchange all transacting shareholder Rebate shares and Supplier Investment shares for New Ordinary shares on a 1 for 1 basis. All such shares exchanged under this offer will qualify for the 10c per share dividend to be paid in December 2011.

Insurance Claim—Rena

Silver Fern Farms Limited had 13 containers of finished product on board the Rena when it grounded outside the Port of Tauranga, 5th October 2011. All product on board was fully insured and the claim for insurance relating to this product has been finalised and paid. There was no financial loss as a result of this event.

Adjusting Event: Impairment Charge Recorded due to Planning Closings of Distribution Center and Stores and Abandonment of Investment Properties, Disclosure of Expected Impact on Earnings

1.132

Etablissements Delhaize Frères et Cie "Le Lion" (Groupe Delhaize) S.A. (Dec 2011)

CONSOLIDATED STATEMENT OF CASH FLOWS *(in part)*

(in Millions of EUR)	Note	2011	2010	2009
Operating Activities				
Net profit attributable to equity holders of the Group (Group share in net profit)		475	574	514
Net profit attributable to non-controlling interests		—	1	6
Adjustments for:				
Depreciation and amortization		586	575	515
Impairment	28	135	14	22
Allowance for losses on accounts receivable		11	6	20
Share-based compensation	21.3	13	16	20
Income taxes	22	156	245	227
Finance costs		204	216	209
Income from investments		(23)	(12)	(14)
Other non-cash items		7	(2)	3
Changes in operating assets and liabilities:				
Inventories		(147)	(108)	32
Receivables		(10)	(39)	(8)
Prepaid expenses and other assets		(15)	(10)	3
Accounts payable		(24)	98	58
Accrued expenses and other liabilities		(4)	16	20
Provisions		4	(24)	(13)
Interest paid		(196)	(202)	(199)
Interest received		11	11	9
Income taxes paid		(77)	(58)	(248)
Net cash provided by operating activities		1 106	1 317	1 176

NOTES TO THE CONSOLIDATED FINANCIAL STATEMENTS *(in part)*

28. Other Operating Expenses

Other operating expenses include expenses incurred outside the normal course of operating supermarkets.

(in Millions of EUR)	2011	2010	2009
Store closing and restructuring expenses	8	(2)	36
Impairment	135	14	22
Losses on sale of property, plant and equipment	13	3	9
Other	13	5	2
Total	169	20	69

In 2011, Delhaize Group incurred store closing expenses of EUR 8 million of which EUR 5 million related to the update of estimates for closed store provisions (see Note 20.1). In 2010, the update and revision of the provision for store closing and U.S. organizational restructuring amounted to EUR 3 million income, which, together with incurred store closing expenses of EUR 1 million, resulted in a net gain of EUR 2 million. The 2009 store closing and restructuring expenses mainly represent charges in connection with (i) the U.S. organizational restructuring (EUR 19 million) and store closings, being a result of an operational review (EUR 10 million at Food Lion), both set in motion in December 2009 and (ii) the effect of updating the estimates used for existing store closing provisions (EUR 4 million).

During the fourth quarter of 2011, the Group performed a thorough review of its store portfolio and concluded to impair 126 stores and one distribution center in the U.S. (EUR 115 million, see Note 8) and several of its investment properties (EUR 12 million, see Note 9).

The 2010 impairment charges resulted from the periodic impairment review of underperforming stores for EUR 12 million and investment property for EUR 2 million, mainly located in the U.S. The 2009 impairment losses mainly represent charges relating to (i) the U.S. organizational restructuring (EUR 2 million), (ii) closed stores in the U.S. (EUR 9 million), (iii) early retirement of various software solutions (EUR 5 million) and (iv) other underperforming stores across the Group (EUR 6 million).

"Other" primarily consists of hurricane and other natural disasters related expenses.

35. Subsequent Events

On January 12, 2012, Delhaize Group announced, following a thorough portfolio review of its stores, the decision to close one distribution center and 146 stores across its network: 126 stores in the U.S. (113 Food Lion, 7 Bloom and 6 Bottom Dollar Food) and 20 underperforming Maxi stores (in Serbia, Bulgaria and Bosnia and Herzegovina), and abandon several of its investment properties. As a result, the Group recorded an impairment charge of USD 177 million (EUR 127 million) in the fourth quarter of 2011 (see Note 28). This charge solely relates to the U.S. operations as the underperformance of the stores in Southeastern Europe was already reflected in the fair values of the related assets recorded in the opening balance sheet.

Beginning in the first quarter of 2012, the Group expects earnings to be impacted by approximately EUR 200 million (approximately USD 235 million for the U.S. and EUR 30 million for Southeastern Europe) to reflect store closing liabilities including a reserve for ongoing lease and severance obligations, accelerated depreciation related to store conversions, conversion costs, inventory write-downs and sales price mark downs. This will have an after tax impact of approximately EUR 125 million on the 2012 earnings.

Litigation Settlement Agreement, Court Ordered Compensation for Termination of Rights in Bankruptcy Proceedings, Offer of Voluntary Retirement Scheme to Eligible Employees

1.133

Dr. Reddy's Laboratories Limited (Mar 2011)

NOTES TO THE CONSOLIDATED FINANCIAL STATEMENTS (in part)

37. Contingencies (in part)

Litigations, etc.

The Company is involved in disputes, lawsuits, claims, governmental and/or regulatory inspections, inquiries, investigations and proceedings, including patent and commercial matters that arise from time to time in the ordinary course of business. The more significant matters are discussed below. Most of the claims involve complex issues. Often, these issues are subject to uncertainties and therefore the probability of a loss (if any) being sustained, and an estimate of the amount of any loss, is difficult to ascertain. Consequently, for a majority of these claims, it is not possible to make a reasonable estimate of the expected financial effect, if any, that will result from ultimate resolution of the proceedings. This is due to a number of factors, including: the stage of the proceedings (in many cases trial dates have not been set) and the overall length and extent of pre-trial discovery; the entitlement of the parties to an action to appeal a decision; clarity as to theories of liability; damages and governing law; uncertainties in timing of litigation; and the possible need for further legal proceedings to establish the appropriate amount of damages, if any. In these cases, the Company discloses information with respect to the nature and facts of the case. The Company also believes that disclosure of the amount sought by plaintiffs, if that is known, would not be meaningful with respect to those legal proceedings.

Although there can be no assurance regarding the outcome of any of the legal proceedings or investigations referred to in this Note 37 to the consolidated financial statements, the Company does not expect them to have a materially adverse effect on its financial position. However, if one or more of such proceedings were to result in judgments against the Company, such judgments could be material to its results of operations in a given period.

Product and Patent Related Matters (in part)

Alendronate Sodium, Germany Litigation

In February 2006, MSD Overseas Manufacturing Co. ("MSD"), an entity affiliated with Merck & Co Inc. ("Merck"), initiated infringement proceedings against betapharm before the German Civil Court of Mannheim alleging infringement of the supplementary protection certificate on the basic patent for Fosamax ® (MSD's brand name for alendronate sodium) (the "first MSD patent"). betapharm and some other companies are selling generic versions of this product in Germany. MSD's patent, which expired in April 2008, was nullified in June 2006 by the German Federal Patent Court. However, MSD filed an appeal against this decision at the German Federal Supreme Court. The German Civil Court of Mannheim decided to stay the proceedings against betapharm until the German Federal Supreme Court has decided upon the validity of the patent.

In March 2007, the European Patent Office granted Merck a patent, which will expire on July 17, 2018, covering the use of alendronate sodium for the treatment of osteoporosis (the "second MSD patent"). betapharm filed protective writs to prevent a preliminary injunction without a hearing. betapharm also filed an opposition against this second MSD patent at the European Patent Office, which revoked the second MSD patent on March 18, 2009. Merck filed notice of appeal of such revocation, and a final decision is not expected before 2011. In August 2007, Merck initiated patent infringement proceedings against betapharm before the German civil court of Düsseldorf, which decided to stay the proceedings until a final decision of the European Patent Office is rendered.

There are other jurisdictions within Europe where the second MSD patent has already been revoked. As a result of this, the Company continues selling its generic version of Fosamax. If Merck is ultimately successful in its allegations of patent infringement, the Company could be required to pay damages related to the above product sales made by the Company, and could also be prohibited from selling these products in the future.

On May 9, 2011, betapharm signed a settlement agreement with Merck, MSD's parent, releasing each party from all past, present or future claims arising directly or indirectly with respect to the litigation regarding the first MSD patent and the second MSD patent, without any financial or legal liability. With this settlement, all litigation with respect to these patents and the related products in Germany has ended.

Ceragenix Bankruptcy Litigation

In November 2007, the Company entered into a Distribution and Supply Agreement with Ceragenix Pharmaceuticals, Inc. and Ceragenix Corporation (collectively, "Ceragenix."). Under this agreement, the Company made up-front and milestone payments of U.S.$5 and commenced distribution of the dermatological product EpiCeram, a skin barrier emulsion device, in the United States and its territories. As of March 31, 2011, the Company carried a balance intangible value of U.S.$2.8 relating to these payments.

In June 2010, Ceragenix (both entities) filed voluntary petitions under Chapter 11 of the U.S. Bankruptcy Code. In July 2010, Ceragenix filed a motion for entry of an interim order and, subsequently, filed a motion for entry of a final order authorizing the execution of an asset purchase agreement (executed on November 10, 2010) with PuraCap Pharmaceutical LLC to sell, among other things, the patent rights, certain business assets and intellectual property relating to EpiCeram ® to PuraCap Pharmaceutical LLC and to terminate the Company's rights under the Distribution and Supply Agreement. The Company objected to the proposed sale and termination on various grounds and Ceragenix withdrew the motion.

On June 24, 2011 the United States Bankruptcy Court for the District of Colorado permitted Ceragenix to sell the patent rights, certain business assets and intellectual property relating to EpiCeram ® to PuraCap Pharmaceutical LLC and to terminate the Company's rights under the Distribution and Supply Agreement. However the court had ordered Ceragenix to pay U.S.$2.75 to the Company out of the sales proceeds of the above mentioned assets and intellectual property, as compensation for the termination of the Distribution and Supply Agreement.

39. Subsequent Events

Alendronate Sodium, Germany Litigation

On May 9, 2011, the Company's wholly-owned subsidiary betapharm signed a settlement agreement with Merck & Co. Inc., parent of MSD Overseas Manufacturing Co., releasing each party from all past, present or future claims arising directly or indirectly with respect to the two patents relating to alendronate sodium which had been the subject of litigations between them, without any financial or legal liability. With this settlement, all litigation with respect to these patents and the related products in Germany has ended (refer to Note 37 for additional details).

Ceragenix Bankruptcy Litigation

On June 24, 2011 the United States Bankruptcy Court for the District of Colorado permitted Ceragenix Pharmaceuticals, Inc. and Ceragenix Corporation (collectively, "Ceragenix") to sell the patent rights, certain business assets and intellectual property relating to the dermatological product EpiCeram ® to PuraCap Pharmaceutical LLC and to terminate the Company's rights under its Distribution and Supply Agreement

with Ceragenix. However the court ordered Ceragenix to pay U.S.$2.75 to the Company out of the sales proceeds of the above mentioned assets and intellectual property, as compensation for the termination of the Distribution and Supply Agreement (refer to Note 37 for additional details).

Voluntary retirement scheme

On June 20, 2011, the Company announced a voluntary retirement scheme (i.e., a termination benefit) applicable to certain eligible employees of the parent company. As per the scheme, employees whose voluntary retirement is accepted by the Company will be paid an amount computed based on the methodology mentioned in the scheme, with the maximum amount restricted to ₹0.8 per employee. The financial impact of termination benefits is expected to be approximately ₹135.

Dilution of Ownership of Subsidiary after Share Issue, Loan Repayments, Assessment Letters from Tax Audit, Share Repurchase

1.134

Perusahaan Perseroan (Persero) PT Telekomunikasi Indonesia Tbk (Dec 2011)

NOTES TO THE CONSOLIDATED FINANCIAL STATEMENTS (in part)

42. Subsequent Events

a. Based on notarial deed No. 2 dated January 3, 2012 of Sjaaf De Carya Siregar, S.H., Infomedia's stockholders issued 17,142,857 shares which amounted to Rp.9 billion. Metra, a stockholder of Infomedia, bought all the newly issued shares. As a result the Company's ownership in Infomedia is diluted to 49%.

b. On January 8, 2012, pursuant to the expiry of the agreement with Apple (Note 37 c.iv), Telkomsel and Apple agreed to extend the agreement until March 30, 2012. As of the date of the consolidated financial statement, Telkomsel is in the process of obtaining another extension.

c. On January 20, 2012, Telkomsel repaid US$39 million of loans obtained from ICBC (Note 18 c).

d. On February 2, 2012, Telkomsel repaid Rp.466 billion of loans obtained from OCBC NISP (Note 18 c).

e. On March 12, 2012, Telkomsel received assessment letters as a result of tax audit for fiscal year 2010 by the Tax Authorities. Based on the letters, Telkomsel overpaid the Corporate Income Tax and underpaid the Value Added Tax amounted to Rp.597.4 billion (Note 37) and Rp.302.7 billion (including a penalty of Rp.73.3 billion), respectively. Telkomsel accepted the overpayment of Corporate Income Tax and Rp.12.1 billion of underpayment of Value Added Tax (including a penalty of Rp.6.3 billion). Considering that the amount is insignificant, the accepted portion was charged to the 2012 consolidated statement of comprehensive income. Telkomsel plans to file an objection to the Tax Authorities for underpayment of Value Added Tax of Rp.290.7 billion (including a penalty of Rp.67 billion).

f. As of March 29, 2012, the Company had repurchased 940,125,460 shares equivalent to 4.66% of the issued and outstanding Series B shares, for a repurchase price of Rp.7,474 billion, including broker and custodian fees (Notes 1 c and 22).

Completed and Planned Divestitures, Dividends Declared and Paid

1.135

Thomson Reuters Corporation (Dec 2011)

NOTES TO THE CONSOLIDATED FINANCIAL STATEMENTS (in part)

Note 30: Subsequent Events

Completed Divestitures

In January 2012, the sale of the Trade and Risk Management business was completed. The Company expects to record a gain on this transaction in the first quarter of 2012.

In February 2012, the Company reached agreement to sell its Portia business, a provider of portfolio accounting and reporting applications. The Company expects to record a gain on this transaction, which is expected to close in the second quarter of 2012.

Planned Divestitures

In February 2012, the Company announced its intention to sell the following businesses that are no longer fundamental to its strategy:

Business	Segment	Description
Law School Publishing	Legal	A provider of law school textbooks.
Property Tax Consulting	Tax & Accounting	A provider of property tax outsourcing and compliance services in the U.S.
eXimius	Markets	A provider of software and services to wealth management companies.

These sales are expected to be completed by mid-2012, and will not qualify for discontinued operations classification.

2012 Dividends

In February 2012, the Company's board of directors approved a $0.04 per share increase in the annualized dividend to $1.28 per common share. A quarterly dividend of $0.32 per share was paid on March 15, 2012 to shareholders of record as of February 22, 2012.

Patent Litigation, Tax Litigation, Business Combination

1.136

Compagnie Générale de Géophysique-Veritas, S.A. (Dec 2011)

NOTES TO THE CONSOLIDATED FINANCIAL STATEMENTS (in part)

Note 30—Subsequent Events

ION Litigation

On February 17, 2012, the United States Federal Circuit Court of Appeals affirmed the judgment of the United States District Court for the Eastern District of Texas dated February 16, 2011 with regards to the lawsuit between Sercel and Ion Geophysical (≪ ION ≫) on the US patent N°5 852 242. A provision amounting to €9.2 million (U.S.$12.8 million) was recorded in the consolidated financial statements as of December 31, 2011 to cover the U.S.$10.7 million amount plus pre- and post-judgment interest to be paid to ION. The parties will return to trial court to determine the amount of additional damages related to Sercel SeaRays systems manufactured in Houston.

Acquisition of GRC

On January 17, 2012, Sercel acquired the assets of Geophysical Research Company, LLC ("GRC"). Headquartered in Tulsa, Oklahoma (USA), and established in 1925 by Amerada Petroleum Corporation, GRC is a leading provider of downhole sensors and gauges for the oil and gas industry. The purchase price amounts to U.S.$67 million, including an earn-out of U.S.$17 million.

Indian Tax Litigation

In January 2012, Delhi Income Tax Appelate Tribunal issued an unfavorable decision, based on assumptions which do not fit with the Company's actual situation. The Group intends to challenge the ITAT order through a miscellaneous application and will appeal the same decision to the Nainital High Court. The Group does not expect this claim to have any material impact on the Group's statements

Changes to Stock Compensation Vesting Policy, Share Repurchase for Stock Option Grant Program, Business Combination

1.137

Embraer S.A. (Dec 2011)

NOTES TO THE CONSOLIDATED FINANCIAL STATEMENTS (in part)

43. Events after the Balance Sheet Date

(i) The Extraordinary General Meeting of January 10, 2012 approved changes in the stock compensation vesting policy: (i) from 20% after the first year to 33% after the third year, (ii) from 30% after the second year to 33% after the fourth year and (iii) from 50% after the third year to 34% after the fifth year, always considering the date each stock option was granted.

(ii) On January 23, 2012, the Board of Directors approved the acquisition of 1,065,000 shares of the Company in order to be used for the third and fourth grants of the Stock option grant program. These grants are expected to occur in 2012 and 2013, respectively. These shares represent 0.15% of the total outstanding shares. The deadline for the transaction is 365 days from the approval of the matter, that is, until the day January 23, 2013.

(iii) On March 13th, 2012, Embraer S.A. through its subsidiary Embraer Netherlands B.V. has concluded the acquisition of 30% of Airholding SGPS S.A. from EADS - European Aeronautic, Defence and Space by € 13 million. Airholding SGPS S.A. was founded in 2005 specifically to own stake in OGMA. Considering the acquisition, the Company now owns 100% of Airholding SGPS S.A. capital and through this company, 65% of OGMA, intensifying Embraer presence in the European aerostructures and services market.

Securitization of Receivables, Issue of Bonds, Additional Contribution by Parent, Exercise of Call Option on Shares of Subsidiary

1.138

KT Corporation (Dec 2011)

NOTES TO THE CONSOLIDATED FINANCIAL STATEMENTS (in part)

39. Subsequent Events

Subsequent to December 31, 2011, the Company has issued the unsecured public bonds, as follows:

(In Millions of Korean Won and Thousands of Foreign Currencies)	Issue Date	Face Value of Bond	Interest Rate	Maturity Date	Repayment Method
The 57-1st non-registered unsecured bond	01.05.2012	(Won) 50,000	4.43%	10.05.2014	Lump sum repayment at maturity
The 57-2nd non-registered unsecured bond	01.05.2012	(Won) 20,000	4.44%	10.05.2014	Lump sum repayment at maturity
The 57-3rd non-registered unsecured bond	01.05.2012	(Won) 30,000	4.61%	10.05.2014	Lump sum repayment at maturity
Regulation S.Bond	01.20.2012	USD 350,000	3.875%	01.20.2017	Lump sum repayment at maturity

Subsequent to December 31, 2011, the additional contributions was made by the Controlling Company as follows.

(In Millions of Korean Won)	Date	Number of Shares	Amount	Purpose
KT Capital Co.,Ltd	01.25.2012	4,712,103 common shares	41,000	To strengthen the financial stability

The Company entered into the shareholders' agreement with Vogo-BCC Investment Holdings Co.,Ltd. and KGF-BCC LIMITED on March 25, 2011 for the sustainable control over BC card co., Ltd, which is a subsidiary of the Company. Based on this agreement, the Company has exercised the call option for 1,349,920 common shares of BC Card Co., Ltd, owned by Vogo-BCC Investment Holdings Co.,Ltd. and KGF-BCC LIMITED(30.68% of total shares) for (Won) 28,713,408 million on January 27, 2012.

On April 18, 2012, the Company entered into a contract with Olleh KT First Securitization Specialty Co., Ltd. which is a special purpose entity formed for the securitization of KT's accounts receivable. Based on this contract, the Company sold its accounts receivables with book value of (Won) 529,776 million for a total sales price of (Won) 525,400 million.

IAS 21, THE EFFECTS OF CHANGES IN FOREIGN EXCHANGE RATES

Author's Note

The IASB issued the following standards that include amendments to IAS 21, The Effects of Changes in Foreign Exchange Rates:

- IFRS 9
  This amendment replaces references to IAS 39 with references to IFRS 9.
- IFRS 10
  This amendment replaces references to IAS 27 with references to IFRS 10 and removes the word "venturer" (See amendments to IFRS 11, Joint Arrangements, that follow).
- IFRS 11 (issued May 2011 with an effective date of 1 January 2013)

This amendment removes the word "venturer" and describes an "investor" as one "with joint control of, or significant influence over, an investee." It also removes references to proportionate consolidation as an alternative to applying the equity method. Finally, it rewords the paragraphs describing when a partial disposal of an interest in a foreign operation is accounted for as a disposal.

- IFRS 13
  This amendment replaces the word "determined" with the word "measured."

Early application of these standards is permitted. If an entity early adopts for any of these standards, it should apply the related amendment.

Because these standards are effective for annual periods beginning on or after 1 January 2012, these amendments are not reflected in the commentary in this section. However, these amendments would not affect the availability of illustrative excerpts from survey companies' financial statements.

IFRSs Overview and Comparison to U.S. GAAP

1.139 IAS 21 establishes the accounting for transactions and carrying amounts in foreign currencies, except derivative transactions and carrying amounts within the scope of IAS 39. An entity should also apply IAS 21 in translating the results and financial position of foreign operations that an entity includes in its financial statements by consolidation, proportionate consolidation, or the equity method.

1.140 IAS 21 includes the following definitions relevant to understanding the required accounting:

Functional currency. Currency of the primary economic environment in which an entity operates.

Presentation currency. Currency in which the financial statements are presented. (The presentation currency is sometimes referred to as the *reporting currency*.)

Monetary items. Units of currency that an entity holds or assets or liabilities that an entity expects to receive or pay in fixed or determinable units of currency.

Foreign operation. Subsidiary, associate, jointly controlled entity, or branch of the entity preparing financial statements. The foreign operation bases or conducts its activities in a country or currency different from that of the reporting entity.

Net investment in a foreign operation. Reporting entity's interest in the foreign operation's net assets.

1.141 IAS 21 does not apply to either the presentation of foreign currency transactions in the statement of cash flows or the translation of cash flows of a foreign operation. An entity should apply the requirements of IAS 7, *Statement of Cash Flows*, to these issues.

Recognition and Measurement

IFRSs

1.142 On initial recognition, IAS 21 requires an entity to measure a foreign currency transaction in its functional currency by applying the spot exchange rate between the foreign and functional currencies at the date the transaction qualifies for recognition under IFRSs (transaction date).

1.143 At subsequent balance sheet dates, when the entity keeps its books and records in its functional currency, it should translate any foreign currency monetary items into the functional currency at the closing rate. The method an entity should use to translate nonmonetary items depends on its measurement basis. When the item is carried at historical cost, an entity should translate the carrying value at the exchange rate on the date of the original transaction. When the item is carried at fair value, an entity should translate the carrying value at the date it determined fair value. IAS 21 includes additional guidance for situations in which multiple exchange rates prevailed or no exchange rate is available.

1.144 When an entity keeps its books and records in a currency other than its functional currency, IAS 21 requires the entity to translate all amounts into the functional currency when preparing its financial statements (that is, monetary items are translated at the closing rate and nonmonetary items are translated at either the historical exchange rate at the date of recognition [if measured at historical cost] or the exchange rate at the date when the fair value was determined [if measured at fair value]).

1.145 On translation or settlement of a monetary item, an entity should recognize in profit or loss in the period in which it arises any exchange differences arising from differences in exchange rates from those used previously, except those that form part of the entity's net investment in a foreign operation. An entity should recognize the latter type of foreign exchange difference in its consolidated financial statements in other comprehensive income and then should reclassify these differences to profit and loss on disposal of the net investment. Such differences are recognized either in the separate financial statements of the entity or the individual financial statements of the foreign operation.

1.146 Individual IFRSs may require a gain or loss on a particular nonmonetary item is to be recognized in other comprehensive income rather than profit or loss (for example, revaluations of property, plant, and equipment carried at a revalued amount). In these cases, an entity should also record the effect of any foreign exchange difference in other comprehensive income. However, when an entity recognizes a gain or loss on a nonmonetary item in profit or loss, it should also recognize any foreign exchange difference in profit or loss.

1.147 When an entity's functional currency changes, an entity should apply the requirements of IAS 21 prospectively from the date of change.

1.148 When an entity uses a presentation currency different from its functional currency, IAS 21 requires it to apply the following translation procedures:
  a. Translate all assets and liabilities for each statement of financial position presented (including comparative items) at the closing rate on the balance sheet date.

b. Translate all income and expenses for each statement of comprehensive income or separate income statement presented (including comparatives) at the exchange rate on the transaction date (or a rate that approximates these rates).
c. Recognize resulting exchange differences in other comprehensive income.

An entity that does not apply this translation method to these statements is not in compliance with IFRSs.

1.149 When exchange differences relate to a partially owned foreign operation, the entity should allocate the applicable proportion of these differences to the noncontrolling interest.

1.150 IAS 21 requires different procedures for translating the financial statements of an entity whose functional currency is that of a hyperinflationary economy.

Author's Note

See section 10, "Reporting in Hyperinflationary Economies," for a discussion of the requirements of IAS 21 applicable to hyperinflationary economies, including illustrative examples.

1.151 With respect to acquisition of a foreign operation, an entity should account for any goodwill or fair value adjustments as assets or liabilities of the operation measured in the operation's functional currency. An entity should use the closing rate to translate these assets and liabilities into its presentation currency. On disposal of the foreign operation, an entity should reclassify the cumulative foreign exchange differences from equity to profit or loss at the same time it recognizes any gain or loss on disposal. IAS 21 also requires an entity to account for loss of control; significant influence; and joint control of subsidiaries, associates, and jointly controlled entities, respectively, even when the entity retains an interest, as disposals for the purpose of reclassification of the related cumulative foreign exchange difference.

U.S. GAAP

1.152 Like IFRSs, FASB ASC 830-10-15-3 requires an entity to apply the functional currency approach to all foreign currency transactions in its financial statements and to translate all foreign currency (a currency different from its reporting currency) financial statements that are incorporated in the entity's financial statements, whether by consolidation, combination, or the equity method of accounting.

1.153 Like IFRSs, the FASB ASC glossary defines an entity's *functional currency* as the currency of the primary economic environment in which the entity operates; normally, that is the currency of the environment in which an entity primarily generates and expends cash. Paragraphs 3–6 of FASB ASC 830-10-45 and paragraphs 3–7 of FASB ASC 830-10-55 provide similar guidance as that provided in IFRSs for determining an entity's functional currency.

1.154 For foreign currency transactions, FASB ASC 830-20-30-1, like IFRSs, requires an entity to recognize the assets, liabilities, revenue, expenses, gains, and losses arising from the transaction in the entity's functional currency by translating each transaction into the functional currency at the exchange rate in effect on the recognition date. FASB ASC 830-20-30-2 contains guidance similar to IAS 21 when no

exchange rate exists. FASB ASC 830-10-55 also provides implementation guidance, including the use of averages and methods of approximation. FASB ASC 830-30-S99-1 provides guidance to SEC registrants when multiple foreign currency exchange rates exist.

1.155 Like IFRSs, FASB ASC 830-20-35-1 requires an entity to include a change in exchange rates between the functional currency and the currency in which the transaction is denominated in income for the period of the change. Like IFRSs, FASB ASC 830-10 distinguishes between monetary and nonmonetary items. However, unlike IFRSs, FASB ASC 830-10-45-18 provides specific nonmonetary balance sheet items and related revenue, expenses, gain, and loss accounts that an entity should remeasure at historical rates.

1.156 Like IFRSs, paragraphs 1–2 of FASB ASC 830-20-35 require that an entity adjust the carrying amounts of foreign currency balances to reflect the current exchange rate at the date of the financial statements and should generally recognize these gains or losses in net income. However, FASB ASC 830-20-35-3 denotes that an entity should not recognize in net income gains and losses on foreign currency transactions that are designated and effective hedges of a net investment in a foreign entity or intraentity transactions in which settlement is not planned or anticipated in the foreseeable future (net investment) and the entities that are parties to the transaction are included in the consolidated financial statements of the reporting entity by consolidation, combination, or the equity method.

1.157 Like IFRSs, FASB ASC 830-30-45-3 requires an entity to translate all financial statement items using a current exchange rate, as follows:

- Assets and liabilities should be translated at the exchange rate at the balance sheet date.
- Revenues, expenses, gains, and losses should be translated at the exchange rate at the dates on which those items were recognized.

Like IFRSs, FASB ASC 830-30-45-12 requires an entity to include translation adjustments in other comprehensive income.

1.158 Unlike IFRSs, the guidance in FASB ASC 830-30-45-3 also applies to accounting allocations (for example, depreciation, cost of goods sold) and requires translation at the current exchange rates applicable to the dates those allocations are included in revenues and expenses (that is, not the rates on the dates the related items originated). Like IFRSs, paragraphs 10–11 of FASB ASC 830-10-55 permit the use of an average rate, but provide more guidance than IAS 21 on how an entity should determine the average.

1.159 Like IFRSs, FASB ASC 830-10-45-17 also requires that, when the entity does not maintain its books and records in its functional currency, it should remeasure the transaction in the functional currency before translating to the reporting currency. Although IFRSs do not use the term *remeasure*, both IFRSs and FASB ASC require this process so as to produce financial statements as if the entity had always accounted for its transactions in the functional currency.

1.160 FASB ASC 830-10 has specific guidance for an entity whose functional currency is that of a hyperinflationary economy. However, this guidance is significantly different than that required by IFRSs.

1.161 Like IFRSs, FASB ASC 830-10-15-7 permits the translation of financial statements from one currency to another for purposes other than consolidation, combination, or the equity method but does not provide guidance on the approach an entity should take in preparing such convenience translations.

Disclosure

IFRSs

1.162 An entity should disclose the amount of foreign exchange differences recognized in profit or loss, except those from financial instruments carried at fair value through profit or loss, in accordance with IAS 39, and any net foreign exchange differences recognized in other comprehensive income. An entity should also disclose a reconciliation of the beginning and ending balances in the related component of equity in which such differences are accumulated.

1.163 When an entity's presentation currency is different from its functional currency, it should disclose this fact, its functional currency, and the reason for using a different presentation currency.

1.164 When an entity changes its own functional currency or the functional currency of a significant foreign operation, it should disclose this fact and the reason for the change.

1.165 An entity sometimes chooses to display its financial statements or other financial statement information in a currency that differs from either the presentation or functional currency for the convenience of readers. In this case, an entity should clearly identify that this is supplemental information to distinguish it from the information presented in compliance with IFRSs and should disclose both the display and functional currencies and translation method used to achieve the display amounts.

U.S. GAAP

1.166 Unlike IFRSs, FASB ASC 830-20-45-1 requires an entity to disclose the aggregate transaction gain or loss included in net income, either in the statements or the notes.

1.167 Like IFRSs, paragraphs 18–20 of FASB ASC 830-30-45 require an entity to provide an analysis (reconciliation)

of the changes in the cumulative translation adjustment account (equity), either in a statement or the notes, and provide guidance to the entity on the content of this analysis. Unlike IFRSs, FASB ASC 830-30-45-20 provides a list of the minimum line items that an entity should disclose in this analysis, including the following:

- Beginning and ending amounts of cumulative translation adjustments
- Aggregate adjustment for the period resulting from translation adjustments and gains and losses from certain hedges and intraentity balances
- Amount of income taxes for the period allocated to translation adjustments
- Amounts transferred from cumulative translation adjustments and included in determining net income for the period as a result of the sale or complete or substantially complete liquidation of an investment in a foreign entity

1.168 Unlike IFRSs, FASB ASC 830-20-50-2, with respect to foreign currency transactions, and FASB ASC 830-30-50-2, with respect to foreign currency translation, advise that disclosure of (*a*) a rate change that occurs after the balance sheet date of the reporting entity's financial statements or, after the date of the foreign currency statements of a foreign entity, if consolidated, combined, or accounted for by the equity method in the financial statements of the reporting entity, and (*b*) the effects of the rate change on any unsettled foreign currency transactions may be necessary if these effects are significant. FASB ASC 830-20-50-2 further explains that in some cases, it may not be practicable for the entity to determine the changes to unsettled transactions, and the entity should state that fact. FASB ASC 830-20-50-3 also explicitly encourages entities to supplement the required disclosures with discussion of the potential effects of rate changes on their operating results.

Presentation and Disclosure Excerpts

Author's Note

In the excerpts that follow, the statements of recognized income and expense are comparable to statements of comprehensive income.

Accounting Policy Disclosure, Subsidiary with a Different Functional Currency

1.169

Cementos Pacasmayo S.A.S. (Dec 2011)

CONSOLIDATED INCOME STATEMENT *(in part)*

	Note	2011	2010	2009
		S/.(000)	S/.(000)	S/.(000)
Operating profit		118,896	336,407	226,668
Other income (expenses)				
Finance income	23	2,695	3,277	1,888
Finance costs	24	(19,219)	(15,038)	(18,834)
Gain from exchange difference, net		1,476	2,568	8,856
Total other expenses, net		(15,048)	(9,193)	(8,090)
Profit before income tax		103,848	327,214	218,578
Income tax expense	15	(38,379)	(104,105)	(70,570)
Profit for the year		65,469	223,109	148,008

CONSOLIDATED STATEMENT OF COMPREHENSIVE INCOME

	Note	2011	2010	2009
		S/.(000)	S/.(000)	S/.(000)
Profit for the year		65,469	223,109	148,008
Other comprehensive income				
Change in fair value of available-for-sale financial investments	9(a)	(8,739)	12,517	4,390
Deferred income tax related to component of other comprehensive income	15	2,622	(3,754)	(1,317)
Exchange differences on translation of foreign currency		(274)	(200)	(783)
Other comprehensive income for the year, net of income tax		(6,391)	8,563	2,290
Total comprehensive income for the year, net of income tax		59,078	231,672	150,298
Total comprehensive income attributable to:				
Owners of the parent		61,332	231,782	150,058
Non-controlling interests		(2,254)	(110)	240
		59,078	231,672	150,298

CONSOLIDATED STATEMENT OF CHANGES IN EQUITY *(in part)*

	Attributable to Owners of the Parent							Non-controlling Interests	Total Equity
	Capital Stock	Investment Shares	Legal Reserve	Available-for-Sale Reserve	Foreign Currency Translation Reserve	Retained Earnings	Total		
	S/.(000)	S/.(000)	S/.(000)	S/.(000)	S/.(000)	S/.(000)	S/.(000)	S/.(000)	S/.(000)
Balance as of December 31, 2010	418,777	49,575	74,145	15,374	(983)	435,668	992,556	739	993,295
Profit for the year	—	—	—	—	—	67,694	67,694	(2,225)	65,469
Other comprehensive income	—	—	—	(6,117)	(245)	—	(6,362)	(29)	(6,391)
Total comprehensive income				(6,117)	(245)	67,694	61,332	(2,254)	59,078
Dividends, note 16 (g)	—	—	—	—	—	(91,000)	(91,000)	—	(91,000)
Incorporation of non-controlling interests, note 1	—	—	—	—	—	77,665	77,665	34,547	112,212
Appropriation of legal reserve, note 16 (d)	—	—	16,306	—	—	(16,306)	—	—	—
Balance as of December 31, 2011	418,777	49,575	90,451	9,257	(1,228)	473,721	1,040,553	33,032	1,073,585

CONSOLIDATED STATEMENT OF CASH FLOWS
(in part)

	2011	2010	2009
	S/.(000)	S/.(000)	S/.(000)
Net increase in cash and cash equivalents	209,163	44,761	90,335
Net foreign exchange difference	(377)	(1,928)	(1,010)
Cash and cash equivalents as of January 1	154,493	111,660	22,335
Cash and cash equivalents as of December 31	363,279	154,493	111,660

NOTES TO THE CONSOLIDATED FINANCIAL STATEMENTS (in part)

1. Corporate Information

Cementos Pacasmayo S.A.A. (hereinafter "the Company") was incorporated in 1957 and, under the Peruvian General Corporation Law, is an open stock corporation, with publicly traded shares. The Company is a subsidiary of Inversiones Pacasmayo S.A. (IPSA), which holds 63.92 percent of the Company's common and investment shares and 67.47 of its common shares as of December 31, 2011 and 2010. The registered office is located at Calle La Colonia No.150, Urbanización El Vivero, Santiago de Surco, Lima, Peru.

The Company's main activity is the production and marketing of cement, blocks, concrete and quicklime in Peru's Northern region.

The consolidated financial statements of the Company and its subsidiaries (hereinafter "the Group") for the year ended December 31, 2011 were authorized for issue by the Management on February 14, 2012.

As of December 31, 2011, the consolidated financial statements comprise the financial statements of the Company and the following subsidiaries: Cementos Selva S.A. and subsidiaries, Distribuidora Norte Pacasmayo S.R.L., Empresa de Transmisión Guadalupe S.A.C., Fosfatos del Pacífico S.A., Salmueras Sudamericanas S.A. and Zemex LLC.

The principal activities of the subsidiaries incorporated in the consolidated financial statements are below described:
- Cementos Selva S.A. is engaged in production and marketing of cement and other construction materials in the northeast region of Peru. Also, it holds shares in Dinoselva Iquitos S.A.C. (a cement and construction materials distributor in the north of Peru) and in Acuícola Los Paiches S.A.C. (a fish farm entity).
- Distribuidora Norte Pacasmayo S.R.L. is mainly engaged in selling cement produced by the Company. Additionally, it produces and sells blocks, cement bricks and ready-mix concrete.
- Empresa de Transmision Guadalupe S.A.C. is mainly engaged in providing energy transmission services to the Company.
- Fosfatos del Pacifico S.A., hereinafter "Fosfatos", is mainly engaged in the exploration of phosphate rock deposits and the production of diatomite. In the Board of Directors´ Meeting held on December 21, 2011, the Company agreed to sell 30 percent of the shares of this subsidiary to MCA Phosphates Pte. Ltda.,hereinafter "MCA" (subsidiary of Mitsubishi Corporation, hereinafter "Mitsubishi") for an aggregate purchase price of approximately US$46,100,000. As a consequence of this transaction the Group recognized a net gain of tax, commissions and other minor related costs, for S/.77,665,000

directly in equity. In relation to this sale of shares, on December 29, 2011 Mitsubishi entered into an off-take agreement to purchase the future production of phosphate rock from this subsidiary. The off-take agreement has a term of 20 years, with an option for Mitsubishi to extend the term for additional 5 years upon expiration, see note 27. According to the business plan for the phosphate project, the subsidiary should be able to start production of phosphoric rock early 2016. Additionally the Company and MCA signed a shareholders´ agreement including some clauses about "super-majority decisions" that needs to be agreed between these parties and a call option and put option to be exercised by the Company and MCA, specifically in any deadlock decision or unexpected event defined in such agreement, see note 27. Management considers that the value to be recorded for those options is not significant at the date of the consolidated financial statements.
- Zemex LLC was a diversified corporation, engaged in mining activities in the United States of America and Canada. In 2007, the Company reformulated its growth strategy and decided to discontinue participating in such industrial minerals business. As of December 31, 2011 and 2010, Zemex LLC only holds shares in subsidiaries with no operation activity.
- Salmueras Sudamericanas S.A. ("Salmueras") was incorporated in 2011 as a result of the spin-off of the assets and liabilities of the brine project located in the northern region of Peru. As a result of this spin-off and certain contributions made by Quimpac S.A. a minority partner in the brine project, the Company owns 74.9% of the outstanding shares of Salmueras, and Quimpac S.A. owns the remaining 25.1%. In order to develop this project the Company signed a shareholder´s agreement with Quimpac S.A. including some minority protective rights. The Company also has committed to invest US$100,000,000, see note 27.

2. Summary of Significant Accounting Policies (in part)

2.1 Basis of Preparation—

The consolidated financial statements of the Group have been prepared in accordance with International Financial Reporting Standards (IFRS), as issued by the International Accounting Standards Board (IASB).

The consolidated financial statements have been prepared on a historical cost basis, except for available-for-sale financial investments and certain financial instruments, that have been measured at fair value. The consolidated financial statements are presented in Nuevos Soles and all values are rounded to the nearest thousand (S/.000), except when otherwise indicated.

2.3.3 Foreign Currency Translation—

The Group's consolidated financial statements are presented in Nuevos Soles, which is also the parent company's functional currency. Each subsidiary determines its own functional currency and items included in financial statements of each subsidiary are measured using that functional currency.

Transactions and Balances

Transactions in foreign currencies are initially recorded by the Group at the functional currency rates prevailing at the date of the transaction.

Monetary assets and liabilities denominated in foreign currencies are retranslated at the functional currency spot rate exchange ruling at the reporting date.

All differences are taken to the consolidated income statement or the consolidated statement of comprehensive income, should the specific criteria be met.

Non-monetary items that are measured in terms of historical cost in a foreign currency are translated using the exchange rates as of the dates of the initial transactions.

Translation Differences from Foreign Subsidiaries—

The financial statements of the subsidiary Zemex LLC are expressed in United States dollars (its functional currency), and then translated into Nuevos Soles. The assets and liabilities are translated at the closing rate at the date of the statement of financial position. The income statement is translated at exchange rates at the dates of the transactions; and all resulting exchange differences shall be recognized in other comprehensive income. On disposal of a foreign operation, the component of other comprehensive income related to that particular foreign operation is recognized in the consolidated income statement.

5. Transactions in Foreign Currency

Transactions in foreign currency take place at the open-market exchange rates published by the Superintendent of Banks, Insurance and Pension Funds Administration. As of December 31, 2011, the exchange rates for transactions in United States dollars, published by this institution, were S/.2.695 for purchase and S/.2.697 for sale (S/.2.808 for purchase and S/.2.809 for sale as of December 31, 2010).

As of December 31, 2011 and 2010, the Group had the following assets and liabilities in United States dollars:

	2011	2010
	US$(000)	US$(000)
Assets		
Cash and short-term deposits	50,591	3,335
Trade and other receivables	9,124	6,193
	59,715	9,528
Liabilities		
Trade and other payables	20,092	5,771
Interest-bearing loans and borrowings	22,129	27,611
	42,221	33,382
Net liability position	17,494	(23,854)

As of December 31, 2011 and 2010, the Company had no financial instruments to hedge its foreign exchange risk

16. Equity (in part)

(f) Foreign Currency Translation Reserve—

The foreign currency translation reserve is used to record exchange differences arising from the translation of the financial statements of Zemex LLC.

Prospective Change in Functional Currency

1.170

Ternium S.A. (Dec 2011)

NOTES TO THE CONSOLIDATED FINANCIAL STATEMENTS (in part)

35 Update as of April 25, 2012

(This note was added subsequent to the delivery of these financial statements for their approval by the Annual General Meeting of shareholders of the Company to be held on May 2, 2012.)

(a) Change in Functional Currency of Mexican Subsidiaries

Due to changes in the primary economic environment in which its Mexican subsidiaries operate and in accordance with International Financial Reporting Standards, the Company performed a functional currency review and concluded that the functional currency of its Mexican subsidiaries should change prospectively to the U.S. dollar, effective as of January 1, 2012. The main indicators of such change in economic environment are: an increase of revenues determined and denominated in U.S. dollars (which is expected to continue increasing); the elimination of Mexican import duties on steel products effective 2012; an increase in the weight of raw material costs with U.S. dollar-denominated prices; and a determination that capital expenditures in Mexico (which are made to increase supply capabilities in connection with growing automobile exports to the U.S. market) are mainly incurred in U.S. dollars.

IAS 21 Disclosures with Convenience Translation

1.171

Grupo TMM, S.A.B. (Dec 2010)

Author's Note

Companies that are registrants of the U.S. Securities and Exchange Commission and domiciled outside of the United States most often have the local currency as their functional and presentation currency and present convenience translation in U.S. dollars. In contrast, Grupo TMM's functional and presentation currency is the U.S. dollar and it provides a convenience translation into Mexican pesos.

CONSOLIDATED STATEMENTS OF FINANCIAL POSITION

(Amounts in thousands of dollars ($) and thousands of (Ps))

	2011		2010
	(Dollars)	(Pesos)	(Dollars)
Assets			
Current			
Cash and cash equivalents	$ 36,394	Ps 507,609	$ 89,936
Restricted cash (Notes 13 and 14)	40,729	568,072	52,383
Accounts receivable—Net of allowance for doubtful accounts of $3,494 in 2011 and $3,730 in 2010	38,963	543,440	37,594
Related parties (Note 15)	—	—	408
Tax credits (Note 5)	2,744	38,272	6,775
Other accounts receivable—Net (Note 6)	14,812	206,592	13,687
Materials and supplies	10,342	144,246	9,597
Other current assets (Note 7)	1,226	17,100	1,519
Non-current assets held for sale	—	—	717
Total current assets	145,210	2,025,331	212,616
Concession rights—net (Note 8)	2,577	35,943	2,849
Property, machinery, and equipment—Net (Note 9)	717,880	10,012,703	761,642
Prepaid expenses and other (Note 10)	7,419	103,477	7,617
Intangible assets (Note 11)	11,395	158,933	23,646
Deferred income tax (Note 20)	67,583	942,621	67,492
Total assets	$952,064	Ps13,279,008	$1,075,862
Current Liabilities:			
Current portion of long term debt (Notes 12 and 14)	$ 17,190	Ps 239,759	$ 23,672
Suppliers	21,475	299,525	23,181
Accounts payable and accrued expenses (Note 16)	52,972	738,832	46,988
Related parties (Note 15)	876	12,218	—
Obligations from the sale of receivables (Note13)	—	—	11,223
Total current liabilities	92,513	1,290,334	105,064
Long term debt (Notes 12 and 14)	735,311	10,255,824	836,608
Dividends payable	—	—	14,187
Employee benefits (Note 22)	15,828	220,763	14,583
Obligations from the sale of receivables (Note 13)	—	—	550
Total non-current liabilities	751,139	10,476,587	865,928
Total liabilities	843,652	11,766,921	970,992
Stockholder Equity (Note 17):			
Equity capital, 103,760,541 shares authorized and issued	158,931	1,222,011	158,931
Treasury shares (1,577,700 shares)	(3,354)	(19,387)	(3,754)
Revaluation surplus (Notes 3h and 9)	63,907	790,980	64,097
Statutory reserve	15,554	187,001	15,554
Accrued losses	(96,178)	(1,256,075)	(118,115)
Capital Premium	5,528	54,979	5,528
Initial cumulative translation balance (Note 3)	(17,757)	—	(17,757)
Translation balance (Note 3)	(22,111)	478,294	(8,522)
Controlling interest	104,520	1,457,803	95,962
Non-controlling interest (Note 3r)	3,892	54,284	8,908
Total stockholder equity	108,412	1,512,087	104,870
Total liabilities and stockholder equity	$952,064	Ps13,279,008	$1,075,862

The accompanying notes are an integral part of these consolidated financial statements.

CONSOLIDATED STATEMENTS OF OPERATIONS

	2011		2010	2009
	(Dollars)	(Pesos)	(Dollars)	(Dollars)
Transportation revenues	$269,155	Ps3,754,066	$ 305,398	$ 308,394
Costs and expenses:				
Salaries, wages, and employee benefits	63,822	890,164	67,262	79,470
Leases and other rents	49,634	692,275	57,355	67,431
Purchased services	39,128	545,742	43,820	46,082
Fuel, materials, and supplies	26,193	365,329	25,512	30,441
Other costs and expenses	18,708	260,932	18,872	12,961
Depreciation and amortization	51,541	718,873	57,394	42,493
	249,026	3,473,315	270,215	278,878
Income on transportation	20,129	280,751	35,183	29,516
Other expenses—Net (Note 18)	(14,104)	(196,717)	(5,146)	(5,745)
Operating income	6,025	84,034	30,037	23,771
Interest income	3,606	50,295	8,151	7,410
Interest expense	83,806	1,168,893	78,167	95,051
Gain (loss) on exchange—net (Note 19)	93,701	1,306,905	(38,118)	(30,713)
Comprehensive financing cost	13,501	188,307	(108,134)	(118,354)
Income (loss) before taxes	19,526	272,341	(78,097)	(94,583)
Provision for income taxes (Note 20)	(3,304)	(46,083)	(819)	(1,087)
Net income (loss) for the year	$ 16,222	Ps 226,258	$ (78,916)	$ (95,670)
Attributable to:				
Non-controlling interest	1,009	14,073	1,647	1,380
Grupo TMM, S.A.B. Stockholders	$ 15,213	Ps 212,185	$ (80,563)	$ (97,050)
Net earnings (loss) for the year, per share	$ 0.159	Ps 2.214	$ (0.774)	$ (1.682)
Weighted average of shares outstanding for the period	102,176	102,176	102,007	56,894

CONSOLIDATES STATEMENTS OF COMPREHENSIVE INCOME (LOSS)

	2011		2010	2009
	(Dollars)	(Pesos)	(Dollars)	(Pesos)
Net profit (loss) for the year	$ 16,222	Ps226,258	$(78,916)	Ps(95,670)
Other comprehensive income (loss) entries:				
Stock repurchase	(99)	797	50	—
Translation balance	(13,589)	(14,892)	1,967	2,823
Provision for employee benefits	(3,999)	(55,770)	(2,961)	678
Revaluation surplus	(271)	(3,780)	91,567	—
Cancellation of dividends (Note 17)	9,622	110,916	—	—
Income tax for other comprehensive profit (loss) results	1,281	17,861	(26,582)	(190)
Other comprehensive results for the year, net of taxes	(7,055)	55,132	64,041	3,311
Comprehensive profit (loss) for the year	$ 9,167	Ps281,390	$(14,875)	$(92,359)
Attributable to:				
Non-controlling interest	1,009	14,073	1,647	1,380
Grupo TMM, S.A.B. Stockholders	8,158	267,317	(16,522)	(93,739)
	$ 9,167	Ps281,390	$(14,875)	$(92,359)

CONSOLIDATED STATEMENTS OF CHANGES IN STOCKHOLDER EQUITY *(in part)*

	Number of Shares Issued and Outstanding	Common Stock	Cumulative (Losses) Earnings	Capital Premium	Initial Cumulative Translation Balance	Subtotal	Non-controlling Interest (Formerly, Minority Interest)	Total Stock-holder Equity
Balances as of December 31, 2010	101,994,641	155,177	(46,986)	5,528	(17,757)	95,962	8,908	104,870
Sale of shares repurchased during 2011	188,200	400	(99)	—	—	301	—	301
Revaluation surplus	—	—	(190)	—	—	(190)	—	(190)
Translation adjustment	—	—	(13,589)	—	—	(13,589)	—	(13,589)
Provision for employee benefits	—	—	(2,799)	—	—	(2,799)	—	(2,799)
Cancellation of dividends	—	—	9,622	—	—	9,622	—	9,622
Total year expenses recognized directly in capital			(7,055)					
Reduction of capital in subsidiaries	—	—	—	—	—		(6,025)	(6,025)
Net earnings for the year	—	—	15,213	—	—	15,213	1,009	16,222
Comprehensive earnings for the year			8,158					
Balances as of December 31, 2011	102,182,841	$155,577	$(38,828)	$5,528	$(17,757)	$104,520	$ 3,892	$108,412

	Number of Shares Issued and Outstanding	Common Stock	Cumulative (Losses) Earnings	Capital Premium	Subtotal	Non-controlling Interest (Formerly, Minority Interest)	Total Stockholder Equity
(Supplemental information) Balances as of December 31, 2010	101,994,641	Ps1,200,311	Ps (67,117)	Ps54,979	Ps1,188,173	Ps110,296	Ps1,298,469
Sale of shares repurchased during 2011	188,200	2,313	797	—	3,110	—	3,110
Revaluation surplus	—	—	(2,650)	—	(2,650)	—	(2,650)
Translation adjustment	—	—	(14,892)	—	(14,892)	—	(14,892)
Provision for employee benefits	—	—	(39,039)	—	(39,039)	—	(39,039)
Cancellation of dividends	—	—	110,916	—	110,916	—	110,916
Total year expenses recognized directly in capital			55,132				
Reduction of capital in subsidiaries	—	—	—	—	—	(76,589)	(76,589)
Net earnings for the year	—	—	212,185	—	212,185	20,577	232,762
Comprehensive earnings for the year			267,317	—			
Balances as of December 31, 2011	102,182,841	Ps1,202,624	Ps200,200	Ps54,979	Ps1,457,803	Ps 54,284	Ps1,512,087

CONSOLIDATED STATEMENTS OF CASH FLOW

	2011		2010	2009
	(Dollars)	(Pesos)	(Dollars)	(Dollars)
Cash Flows From Operating Activities:				
Net profit (loss) for the year:	$ 16,222	Ps 226,258	$ (78,916)	$ (95,670)
Adjustments to reconcile net loss (profit) to cash provided by operating activities:				
Depreciation and amortization	51,541	718,873	57,394	42,493
Other amortizations	11,237	156,729	9,614	8,996
Provision for taxes	3,304	46,083	819	1,087
Gain on sale of properties, machinery, and equipment—net	(498)	(6,946)	(335)	(3,267)
Loss on sale of subsidiary shares	—	—	1,014	—
Impairment of long-lived assets	10,426	145,418	—	3,485
Provision for interests on debt	68,870	960,571	66,148	81,542
Exchange (gain) loss—net	(93,216)	(1,300,139)	37,936	27,392
Changes in assets and liabilities:				
Restricted cash	11,654	162,545	11,843	64,314
Accounts receivable	(1,369)	(19,094)	9,959	8,995
Other accounts receivable and related parties	4,190	58,440	10,058	(6,796)
Materials, accessories, and supplies	(745)	(10,391)	(1,019)	(461)
Other current assets	293	4,087	194	841
Other accounts payable and accrued expenses	(23,946)	(333,990)	(40,114)	(6,440)
Other non-current assets	12,449	173,634	8,837	(895)
Employee benefits	1,245	17,365	2,636	(1,354)
Total adjustments	55,435	773,185	174,984	219,932
Cash provided by operating activities	71,657	999,443	96,068	124,262
Cash Flows From Investment Activities:				
Sale of properties, machinery, and equipment	3,823	53,322	5,313	15,784
Acquisition of properties, machinery, and equipment	(15,376)	(214,459)	(32,123)	(73,456)
Sale (purchase) of shares in subsidiaries	—	—	—	(202)
Sale of associate companies	—	—	4,062	—
Reduction of capital in subsidiaries	(6,025)	(84,034)	—	—
Cash used in investment activities	(17,578)	(245,171)	(22,748)	(57,874)
Cash Flows From Financing Activities:				
Proceeds from financial debt	(90,226)	(1,258,436)	982	(35,585)
Cash proceeds from obligations from the sale of receivables—net	(11,902)	(166,004)	(8,787)	(56,388)
Dividends from unconsolidated associates	—	—	—	643
Purchase of capital stock	97	1,353	(13)	—
Cash used in financing activities	(102,031)	(1,423,087)	(7,818)	(91,330)
Effect on cash from currency fluctuation	(5,590)	(77,967)	4,416	5,053
Net (decrease) increase in cash and equivalents	(53,542)	(746,782)	69,918	(19,889)
Cash and cash equivalents at year start	89,936	1,254,391	20,018	39,907
Cash and cash equivalents at year end	$ 36,394	Ps 507,609	$ 89,936	$ 20,018
Supplemental cash disclosures:				
Interest paid	$ 74,108	Ps 1,033,629	$ 29,754	$ 53,192
Income tax and corporate flat tax paid	$ 1,025	Ps 14,296	$ 1,049	$ 3,343

NOTES TO THE CONSOLIDATED FINANCIAL STATEMENTS (in part)

1 Nature of Operations and General Information: (in part)

Grupo TMM, S.A.B. ("Grupo TMM" or the "Company") is a Mexican company whose principal activity is providing multi-modal transportation and logistics services to premium customers throughout Mexico. Grupo TMM provides services related to dedicated trucking, third-party logistics, offshore supply shipping, clean oil and chemical products shipping, tug-boat services, warehouse management, shipping agency, inland and seaport terminal services, container and railcar maintenance and repair, and other activities related to the shipping and land freight transport business.

Due to the geographic location of some of the subsidiaries and the activities in which they are engaged, Grupo TMM and its subsidiaries are subject to the laws and ordinances of other countries, as well as international regulations governing maritime transportation and the observance of safety and environmental regulations.

Grupo TMM's head office is located at Avenida de la Cúspide N° 4755, Colonia Parques del Pedregal, Delegación Tlalpan, C. P. 14010, México, D. F.

3 Summary of Significant Accounting Policies: (in part)

Grupo TMM and its subsidiaries prepare their consolidated financial statements in accordance with International Financial Reporting Standards ("IFRS"), as issued by the International Accounting Standards Board ("IASB"), and these are expressed in US dollars, the Company's primary operating currency and in which a significant portion of the Company's assets and liabilities arose and/or are listed.

The Mexican National Banking and Securities Commission (*Comisión Nacional Bancaria y de Valores*, or *"CNBV"*) approved this method in 1985. The initial effect of conversion to the US dollar is shown as a debit of $17,757 in the accompanying statement of changes in stockholder equity.

In addition, under the *CNBV* authorization mentioned previously, the consolidated statement of financial position, and corresponding statements of operations, comprehensive profit (loss), changes in stockholder equity, and cash flows report supplemental information in Mexican pesos. This supplemental information is obtained by converting the dollar amount reported in the basic financial statements into Mexican pesos, applying the exchange rate corresponding at year close. Equity capital, the premium on convertible obligations, the statutory reserve, and accrued earnings are exempt from this and are expressed in "historic pesos", adding a line titled "Translation", which represents the difference between "historic pesos" and the conversion of dollars to Mexican pesos at the closing exchange rate.

These consolidated financial statements were approved by the Company Board of Directors on February 29, 2012.

IAS 20, *ACCOUNTING FOR GOVERNMENT GRANTS AND DISCLOSURE OF GOVERNMENT ASSISTANCE*

Author's Note

The IASB issued the following standards that include amendments to IAS 20, *Accounting for Government Grants and Disclosure of Government Assistance*:

- IFRS 9
  This amendment replaces references to IAS 39 with references to IFRS 9.

- IFRS 13
  IFRS 13 amended the definition of fair value in IAS 20.

Early application of these standards is permitted. If an entity early adopts for any of these standards, it should apply the related amendment.

Because these standards are effective for annual periods beginning on or after 1 January 2012, these amendments are not reflected in the commentary in this section. However, these amendments would not affect the availability of illustrative excerpts from survey companies' financial statements.

IFRSs Overview and Comparison to U.S. GAAP

1.172 IAS 20 establishes the accounting for government grants and disclosures of government grants and other forms of government assistance. IAS 20 does not address government grants included in the scope of IAS 41, *Agriculture*; government participation in ownership of the entity; government assistance in the form of tax benefits; or special problems associated with changing prices.

1.173 IAS 20 defines a *government grant* to be government assistance in the form of transfers of resources to an entity in return for past or future compliance with certain conditions related to the entity's operating activities, excluding assistance that cannot reasonably be valued and transactions that cannot be distinguished from the entity's ordinary activities. *Government assistance* is defined as actions designed to provide an economic benefit specific to a qualifying entity or entities, excluding benefits provided indirectly through general governmental actions (such as trading constraints on competitors). The term *governments* includes governments, governmental agencies, and similar entities, whether local, regional, national, or international.

Recognition and Measurement

IFRSs

1.174 IAS 20 prohibits an entity from recognizing a government grant, including a nonmonetary grant at fair value, unless the entity is reasonably assured that it will receive the grant and comply with the required conditions.

1.175 An entity should treat a forgivable loan from a government as a government grant when there is reasonable assurance that the entity will meet the terms for forgiveness of the loan.

1.176 An entity should treat the benefit from receiving a government loan at a below market rate as a government grant. An entity should measure the initial carrying value of the loan in accordance with IAS 39 and the benefit received as the difference between the initial carrying value and the loan proceeds. IAS 20 requires the entity to consider any conditions or obligations it has met or should meet in the future when determining costs associated with the benefit received.

1.177 IAS 20 requires an entity to recognize the benefit from a government grant in profit or loss on a systematic basis over the periods that it incurs the expected costs related to the benefits from the grant. IAS 20 states that an entity would usually recognize benefits of grants related to depreciable assets in proportion to the depreciation expense recorded on these assets. An entity would recognize the benefits of other grants when it incurs the costs and meets the grant's conditions.

1.178 IAS 20 requires an entity to recognize in profit or loss a grant related to costs it incurred in the past or to which no conditions are attached when that grant is receivable.

1.179 An entity may recognize a nonmonetary grant at either fair value or a nominal amount.

1.180 SIC 10, *Government Assistance—No Specific Relation to Operating Activities*, clarifies that government assistance can meet the definition of a government grant even when the government does not place conditions on an entity's operations beyond a requirement to operate in specific geographic areas or industry sectors. SIC 10 does not permit an entity to recognize such grants directly in equity.

1.181 If a government grant becomes repayable, an entity should account for the change prospectively as a change in accounting estimate, in accordance with IAS 8. To the extent the repayment exceeds the carrying value of a related liability, or if no liability exists, an entity should recognize the difference in profit or loss immediately. When the repayment relates to a depreciable asset, an entity should increase the carrying value of the asset or the related deferred income by the amount repayable and recognize immediately in profit or loss the cumulative additional depreciation that would have been recognized if it had not received the grant. IAS 20 notes that such repayment may be an indicator of asset impairment.

U.S. GAAP

1.182 Unlike IFRSs, FASB ASC does not include guidance on recognition, measurement, presentation, or disclosure of government grants or assistance, except for those received by not-for-profit entities and entities in regulated industries.

1.183 Without specific guidance to the contrary, FASB ASC would require an entity to treat a loan from the government in the same way as a loan from a private sector entity. Therefore, like IFRSs, an entity would most likely impute interest on loans made at below market rates.

1.184 In the specific implementation guidance on nonreciprocal transfers between an entity and counterparties other than its owners, FASB ASC 845-10-05-5 includes the example of a contribution of land by a governmental unit for construction of productive facilities by an entity. FASB ASC 845-10-30-1 states that for exchanges of nonmonetary assets, an entity should measure the asset received at its fair value, unless the fair value of the asset given up is more clearly evident. In cases of government grants of nonmonetary assets, the asset is transferred in exchange for future services; hence, it is more likely that the fair value of the asset received is more clearly evident. Unlike IFRSs, FASB ASC does not permit an entity to measure a nonmonetary government grant and related asset at nominal amount.

Presentation

IFRSs

1.185 An entity may present government grants in the statement of financial position either as deferred income or a reduction of the carrying value of the related asset.

1.186 IAS 20 suggests that it would be appropriate for an entity to show cash flows from government grants separately in the statement of cash flows even when the grant is presented in the balance sheet as a reduction of the related asset.

1.187 With respect to the statement of comprehensive income, an entity may recognize the income from the grant in the line item "other income" either as part of profit or loss or as a reduction of the related expense.

1.188 IAS 1 does not require an entity to present government grants separately in the financial statements, unless the effect is material to an income or expense item.

U.S. GAAP

1.189 FASB ASC does not include specific presentation requirements for government grants.

Disclosure

IFRSs

1.190 IAS 20 requires an entity to disclose the following information about government grants and, when appropriate, government assistance that does not meet the definition of a grant:
- Accounting policy and presentation methods adopted
- Nature and extent of such grants recognized and an indication of other forms of government assistance that directly benefit the entity
- Unfulfilled conditions and contingencies related to recognized grants

1.191 When a grant is recognized in profit or loss when it is receivable, an entity should disclose the circumstances of the grant so users understand why immediate recognition was appropriate.

U.S. GAAP

1.192 FASB ASC does not include any specific disclosure requirements for government grants.

Presentation and Disclosure Excerpts

Initial Recognition of Non-Monetary Grants at Nominal Amount, Grants Related to Assets Presented as Deferred Income

1.193

China Yuchai International Limited (Dec 2011)

CONSOLIDATED STATEMENT OF FINANCIAL POSITION (in part)

(Rmb and US$ amounts expressed in thousands, except per share data)

	Note	31.12.2010 Rmb'000	31.12.2011 Rmb'000	31.12.2011 US$'000
Equity and Liabilities				
Non-current liabilities				
Interest-bearing loans and borrowings	18[(b)]	201,850	144,883	22,992
Other liabilities	18[(a)]	18,869	830	132
Deferred tax liabilities	9	77,274	100,739	15,986
Deferred grants	19	269,736	318,583	50,556
		567,729	565,035	89,666

CONSOLIDATED STATEMENT OF CASH FLOWS (in part)

(Rmb and US$ amounts expressed in thousands, except per share data)

	31.12.2009 Rmb'000	31.12.2010 Rmb'000	31.12.2011 Rmb'000	31.12.2011 US$'000
Investing Activities				
Acquisition/additional investment in associates and joint ventures	(69,400)	(191,906)	(33,295)	(5,284)
Dividends received from associates	16,931	—	1,656	263
Dividends received from joint ventures	19,122	1,733	10,166	1,613
Interest received	31,578	61,719	53,159	8,436
Purchase of other investments	(82)	—	—	—
Proceeds from disposal of other investments	—	169	—	—
Payment for prepaid operating leases	(205,879)	(66,300)	(16,768)	(2,661)
Proceeds from disposal of prepaid operating leases	—	—	18,800	2,983
Additions of intangible asset	—	(13,389)	(11,365)	(1,804)
Proceeds from disposal of property, plant and equipment	64,745	30,410	150,139	23,826
Purchase of property, plant and equipment	(780,836)	(629,626)	(807,274)	(128,106)
Proceeds from disposal of a subsidiary, net of cash	—	1,902	—	—
Proceeds from disposal of assets classified as held for sale	—	302,655	—	—
Proceeds from disposal of associates	1,906	4,000	—	—
Proceeds from disposal of investment property	—	—	40,528	6,431
Acquisition of non-controlling interests	(29,998)	—	—	—
Proceeds from redemption of preference shares in an associate	551	—	—	—
Proceeds from government grants	150,917	112,592	71,015	11,269
Net cash flows used in investing activities	(800,445)	(386,041)	(523,239)	(83,034)

NOTES TO THE CONSOLIDATED FINANCIAL STATEMENTS (in part)

2. Basis of Preparation and Accounting Policies (in part)

2.3 Summary of Significant Accounting Policies

(h) Government Grants

Government grants are recognised where there is reasonable assurance that the grant will be received and all attached conditions will be complied with. When the grant relates to an expense item, it is recognised as income over the period necessary to match the grant on a systematic basis to the costs that it is intended to compensate. When the grant relates to an asset, it is recognised as deferred income and released to income in equal amounts over the expected useful life of the related asset.

When the Group receives non-monetary grants, the asset and the grant are recorded gross at nominal amounts and released to the income statement over the expected useful life and pattern of consumption of the benefit of the underlying asset by equal annual installments.

8.2 (a) Other Operating Income

	31.12.2009 Rmb'000	31.12.2010 Rmb'000	31.12.2011 Rmb'000	31.12.2011 US$'000
Interest income	31,576	61,719	53,159	8,436
Foreign exchange gain, net	—	19,975	1,599	254
Dividend income from associates	11,162	—	1,656	263
Gain on disposal of associates	1,906	707	—	—
Gain on disposal of subsidiaries	—	2,833	—	—
Gain on disposal of prepaid operating leases	—	—	10,678	1,694
Fair value gain on held for trading investments	—	17,123	—	—
Fair value gain on available-for-sale investment	—	—	10,983	1,743
Gain on disposal of investment properties	—	—	5,908	937
Gain on assignment of debts	5,657	—	—	—
Write-back of impairment of receivables	4,895	—	—	—
Write-back of trade and other payables	23,649	—	—	—
Write-back of impairment of investment in joint ventures	—	10,936	—	—
Government grant income	14,823	11,129	18,420	2,923
Others, net	—	4,653	—	—
	93,668	129,075	102,403	16,250

19. Deferred Grants

	31.12.2010 Rmb'000	31.12.2011 Rmb'000	31.12.2011 US$'000
Balance at beginning of year	179,233	280,696	44,544
Received during the year	112,592	71,015	11,269
Released to consolidated income statement	(11,129)	(18,420)	(2,923)
Balance at end of year	280,696	333,291	52,890
Current (Note 28)	10,960	14,708	2,334
Non-current	269,736	318,583	50,556
	280,696	333,291	52,890

Government grants have been received for the purchase of certain items of property, plant and equipment.

Initial Recognition as Reduction of Carrying Value of Depreciable Assets, Initial Recognition of Grants for Research and Development as Financial Liabilities at Fair Value

1.194

Elbit Imaging Ltd. (Dec 2011)

CONSOLIDATED BALANCE SHEETS (in part)

		December 31		2011
	Note	2011	2010	Convenience Translation (Note 2D)
		(In Thousand NIS)		U.S.$'000
Non-current liabilities				
Borrowings	(19)	5,650,170	5,524,260	1,478,715
Other financial liabilities	(20)	215,752	75,532	56,465
Other liabilities	(21)	12,808	14,005	3,352
Deferred taxes	(22)	108,642	19,773	28,433
		5,987,372	5,633,570	1,566,965

NOTES TO THE CONSOLIDATED FINANCIAL STATEMENTS (in part)

Note 2—Significant Accounting Policies (in part)

N. Property Plant and Equipment: (in part)

(i) Property plant and equipment are stated at cost less accumulated depreciation and accumulated impairment losses. Government grants have been deducted from cost of assets for which they have been granted. Cost of land and building include direct construction and supervision costs incurred in the construction period as well as borrowing costs capitalized in accordance with the Group's accounting policy described in note 2AC. Improvements and renovations are charged to cost of assets. Maintenance and repair costs are charged to the statement of income as incurred.

X. Grants From the Office of Chief Scientist ("OCS"):

Government grants are recognized when reasonable assurance exists about the receipt of the same, and about the Group complying with all the related terms and conditions. Grants received from the OCS for research and development, which the Group is required, under certain conditions, to repay with interest through the payment of royalties to the State of Israel, which are subject to future revenues derived from the sale of products underlying the financed research and development activities, are recognized as a financial liability on the date of their receipt, unless reasonable assurance exists in the opinion of the management of the Group that the grants, in part or in whole, will not be repaid.

The liability associated with government grants is measured at fair value on the date of its initial recognition, based on the present value of the cash flows expected to repay the grants, discounted at a rate reflecting the level of risk of the specific research and development project. The difference between the government grant received and its fair value on the date of its receipt is charged to the statement of income and deducted from research and development expenses. Amounts paid as royalties are recognized as settlement of the government grants liability. At subsequent periods, government grant liabilities are measured at fair value, whereby changes in fair value (those derived from updating the estimated cash flows expected to repay the grants received, as well as those derived from updating the interest rate used for discounting that expected cash flows) are charged to the statement of income.

In the event that reasonable assurance exists that government grants shall not be repaid, in whole or in part, as detailed in the preceding paragraph, the grants are recognized to statement of income on the date on which the Group is entitled thereto, and off-set from research and development expenses.

Note 20—Other Long-Term Financial Liabilities

Composition:

(In Thousand NIS)	December 31 2011	December 31 2010
Grants from the Israeli Office of Chief Science ("OCS")[i]	24,827	23,636
Embedded derivative financial liability carried at fair value through profit and loss	2,417	1,599
Derivative measured at fair value through profit and loss[ii]	24,860	—
Loan from third parties[iii]	163,648	50,297
	215,752	75,532

[i] The balance reflects the the fair value of the total grants received from the OCS by InSightec net of royalties paid up to each balance sheet date discounted at the applicable interest rate for similar loans having the same terms and conditions (2011—27%, 2010—31%). InSightec is obliged to pay royalties to the OCS—in respect of products, the development of which was funded by grants provided by the OCS—at a rate of 3.5% of the revenues from said products as from 2007 and up to the amount of the grants received. InSightec has no obligation to refund the grants if sufficient revenues are not generated. InSightec's technology developed with OCS funding is subject to transfer restrictions, which may apply after InSightec has fully refunded the grants received. In addition, the restrictions may impair InSightec's ability to consummate a merger or similar transaction in which the surviving entity is not an Israeli company. The revenues used in determining the liability to the OCS are to be generated through 2021 as InSightec's management estimates that this is the year in which its obligation towards the OCS will be fully settled.

Grants of Interest-Free Loans, Research Incentives in the Form of Tax Credits

1.195

Sequans Communications S.A. (Dec 2012)

CONSOLIDATED STATEMENTS OF FINANCIAL POSITION (in part)

(In Thousands)	Note	At December 31 2009	At December 31 2010	At December 31 2011
Current assets:				
Inventories	9	1,937	8,768	11,660
Trade receivables	10	7,033	14,163	8,373
Prepaid expenses and other receivables		1,836	3,333	2,571
Recoverable value added tax		337	1,361	2,008
Research tax credit receivable		2,984	2,001	4,423
Cash and cash equivalents	11	7,792	9,739	57,220
Total current assets		21,919	39,365	86,255
Total assets		$28,813	$49,717	$101,030
Equity and Liabilities				
Non-current liabilities:				
Interest-bearing loans and borrowings	14	6,935	—	—
Government grant advances and interest-free loans	15	1,101	1,278	385
Provisions	16	777	184	259
Deferred tax liabilities	5	—	—	55
Other non-current financial liabilities	14	4,925	—	—
Total non-current liabilities		13,738	1,462	699
Current liabilities:				
Trade payables	17	3,384	15,508	8,580
Interest-bearing loans and borrowings	14	3,754	3,564	—
Government grant advances and interest-free loans	15	1,744	1,889	717
Other current financial liabilities	17	3,380	5,270	5,846
Deferred revenue	17	1,651	893	869
Provisions	16	269	432	75
Total current liabilities		14,182	27,556	16,087

NOTES TO THE CONSOLIDATED FINANCIAL STATEMENTS (in part)

1. Corporate Information

Sequans Communications S.A. ("Sequans") is organized as a limited liability company ("*société anonyme*") incorporated and domiciled in the Republic of France, with its principal place of business at 19 Le Parvis, 92073 Paris-La Défense, France. Sequans, together with its subsidiaries (the "Company"), is a leading fabless designer, developer and supplier of 4G semiconductor solutions for wireless broadband applications. The Company's semiconductor solutions incorporate baseband processor and radio frequency transceiver integrated circuits along with our proprietary signal processing techniques, algorithms and software stacks.

2. Summary of Significant Accounting and Reporting Policies (in part)

2.3. Summary of Significant Accounting Policies (in part)

Government Grants, Interest-Free Loans and Research Tax Credits

The Company operates in certain jurisdictions which offer government grants or other incentives based on the qualifying research expense incurred or to be incurred in that jurisdiction. These incentives are recognized as the qualify research expense is incurred if there is reasonable assurance that all related conditions will be complied with and the grant will be received. When the grant relates to an expense item, it is recognized as a reduction of the related expense over the period necessary to match the grant on a systematic basis to the costs that it is intended to compensate. Any cash received in advance of the expenses being incurred is recorded as a liability.

Where loans or similar assistance provided by governments or related institutions are interest-free, the benefit of the below-market rate of interest is recognized as a government grant (see Note 15 to the Consolidated Financial Statements).

The Company also benefits from research incentives in the form of tax credits which are detailed in Note 4.4 to the Consolidated Financial Statements.

Taxation

Current Income Tax

Current income tax assets and liabilities for the current and prior periods are measured at the amount expected to be recovered from or paid to the taxation authorities. The tax rates and tax laws used to compute the amount are those that are enacted or substantively enacted at the reporting date.

The Company operates in certain jurisdictions which offer tax incentives based on the qualifying research expense incurred in those jurisdictions. When the incentive is available only as a reduction of taxes owed, such incentive is accounted for as a reduction of tax expense; otherwise, it is accounted for as a government grant with the benefit recorded as a reduction of research and development expenses.

4. Other Revenues and Expenses (in part)

4.4. Research and Development Expense

All research and development expense was charged directly to expense in the Statement of Operations.

The amount of research tax credit is deducted from research and development costs. In the year ended December 31, 2011, the French tax authorities confirmed that the Company could include certain subsidiary research expenses in the research tax credit calculation.

Government grants have been received in support of certain research programs. Where there are unfulfilled conditions or contingencies relating to the grants, the corresponding amount has been deferred on the Statement of Financial Position until all conditions are fulfilled and contingencies settled at which time amounts earned are recorded as an offset to the corresponding expenses.

The reduction of research and development expense from government grants and research tax credit was as follows:

(In Thousands)	Year Ended December 31		
	2009	2010 Adjusted[1]	2011
Research and development costs	$17,209	$21,394	$30,855
Research tax credit	(2,871)	(1,984)	(4,562)
Government grants	(481)	(1,493)	(1,358)
Total research and development expense	$13,857	$17,917	$24,935

[1] As adjusted to reflect the classification of foreign exchange gains and losses related to hedges of euro-based operating expenses from financial result to operating expenses. The effect on the year ended December 31, 2010 was to reduce Research and development costs by $107,000.

As of December 31, 2009, 2010 and 2011, no development costs were capitalized.

The Company operates in a highly innovative, dynamic and competitive sector. Therefore, the costs incurred from the point when the criteria for capitalization are met to the point when the product is made generally available on the market are not material.

15. Government Grant Advances and Interest-Free Loans

(In Thousands)	December 31		
	2009	2010	2011
Current			
Government grant advances	$ 793	$1,355	$717
Interest-free loans	951	534	—
Total current portion	$1,744	$1,889	$717
Non-current			
Government grant advances	$ 500	$ 654	$385
Interest-free loans	601	624	—
Total non-current portion	$1,101	$1,278	$385

15.1. Government Grant Advances

In 2009, the Company was named as a participant in two projects with combined funding of €300,000 ($415,000), expected to be earned over three years.

In 2010, the Company was named as a participant in four collaborative projects funded by various entities in France and the European Union. The Company's portion of this funding totals €1,554,000 ($2,077,000), which is expected to be released to the Consolidated Statement of Operations over the lives of the projects, generally expected to be between 18 months and three years.

In 2011, the Company was named as a participant in one collaborative project with funding of €355,000 ($481,000), which is expected to be released to the Consolidated Statement of Operations over the life of the project, expected to be approximately three years.

15.2. Interest-Free Loans

The Company has received interest-free loans from Oséo, the French Agency for Innovation. Oséo provides financial incentives to develop new technology in France. In 2006, an amount of €1,300,000 ($1,809,000) was awarded to finance the development of products using WiMAX 802.16e. In January 2010, project financing was awarded for a total of €1,350,000 ($1,973,000) for development of the LTE technology. The financing arrangements called for the loans to be repaid according to a set timeline, but the amount repaid could be reduced if revenue from the products developed did not reach certain minimum amounts.

The €1,300,000 financing for WiMAX 802.16e was received in 2006 and, as the criteria for commercial success of the products was met, repayment was scheduled in four installments in 2008 (€115,000), 2009 (€375,000), 2010 (€410,000) and 2011 (€400,000). The Company repaid €115,000 ($160,000) in 2008 and €125,000 ($178,000) in 2009. Because Oséo agreed to defer the remaining payment scheduled for 2009 until 2010, a total of €660,000 ($913,000) was repaid during the year ended December 31, 2010. In March 2011, the Company repaid €400,000 ($546,000).

Of the €1,350,000 financing for LTE, €540,000 ($789,000) was received in January 2010; the remainder was expected to be received in 2011. In June 2011, the Company decided to repay first installment received (repayment initially scheduled from June 2012 to March 2016), and terminate the financing agreement.

As of December 31, 2011, the Company had no interest-free loans.

18. Information About Financial Instruments (in part)

18.1. Financial Assets And Liabilities (in part)

(In Thousands)	Carrying Amount December 31			Fair Value December 31		
	2009	2010	2011	2009	2010	2011
Financial assets:						
Trade and other receivables	$ 7,045	$14,368	$ 8,387	$ 7,045	$14,368	$ 8,387
Loans and other receivables						
Deposits	398	1,485	531	398	1,485	531
Available for sale instruments						
Long-term investments	463	432	677	463	432	677
Cash and cash equivalents	7,792	9,739	57,220	7,792	9,739	57,220
Total financial assets	$15,698	$26,024	$66,815	$15,698	$26,024	$66,815
Total current	$14,837	$24,107	$65,607	$14,837	$24,107	$65,607
Total non-current	$ 861	$ 1,917	$ 1,208	$ 861	$ 1,917	$ 1,208
Financial liabilities:						
Interest-bearing loans and borrowings:						
Bank convertible notes	3,629	3,392	—	3,629	3,392	—
Category E convertible notes—debt component	7,060	132	—	7,060	132	—
Factoring	—	36	—	—	36	—
Interest-free loans	1,552	1,158	—	1,463	1,149	—
Trade and other payables	3,384	15,508	8,580	3,384	15,508	8,580
Financial instruments at fair value through other comprehensive income:						
Cash flow hedges	21	129	1,007	21	129	1,007
Financial instruments at fair value through profit and loss:						
Category E convertible notes—option component	4,925	—	—	4,925	—	—
Total financial liabilities	$20,571	$20,355	$ 9,587	$20,482	$20,346	$ 9,587
Total current	$ 8,110	$19,731	$ 9,587	$ 8,055	$19,727	$ 9,587
Total non-current	$12,461	$ 624	$ —	$12,426	$ 619	$ —

The carrying values of current financial instruments (cash and cash equivalents, trade receivables and trade and other payables, and factoring) approximate their fair values, due to their short-term nature.

Available for sale long-term investments are primarily related to a bank guarantee issued by the Company in favor of the owners of leased office space to secure annual lease payments by the Company for its office space in Paris and a bank credit line used in connection with the purchase of hedging instruments. This guarantee, which is expected to be renewed annually until the end of the lease in May 2014, is secured by pledges of investments in money market funds. In addition, the Company has pledged money market funds to secure a bank credit line used in connection with the purchase of hedging instruments.

New interest-free loans received from Oséo in 2010 were recorded as financial instruments in compliance with IAS 20 *Accounting for Government Grants and Disclosure of Government Assistance*.

The bank convertible notes bear interest at a variable rate which was reset each quarter; therefore their carrying value was considered to approximate fair value.

The Category E convertible notes were hybrid financial instruments. The fair value of the option component had been revalued at each reporting period.

IAS 24, *RELATED PARTY DISCLOSURES*

Author's Note

The IASB issued the following standards that include amendments to IAS 24, *Related Party Disclosures*:

- IFRS 10
  This amendment replaces references to IAS 27 with references to IFRS 10 and removes the word "venturer" (See amendments to IFRS 11 that follow).
- IFRS 11
  This amendment removes the word "venturer" and describes an "investor" as one "with joint control of, or significant influence over, an investee." It also removes references to proportionate consolidation as an alternative to applying the equity method. Finally, it rewords the paragraphs describing when a partial disposal of an interest in a foreign operation is accounted for as a disposal.
- IFRS 12, *Disclosure of Interests in Other Entities* (issued May 2011 with an effective date of 1 January 2013)
  This amendment clarifies that the disclosures required by IAS 24 are in addition to those required by IFRS 12.

Early application of these standards is permitted. If an entity early adopts for any of these standards, it should apply the related amendment.

Because these standards are effective for annual periods beginning on or after 1 January 2012, these amendments are not reflected in the commentary in this section. However, these amendments would not affect the availability of illustrative excerpts from survey companies' financial statements.

IFRSs Overview and Comparison to U.S. GAAP

1.196 An entity should apply the requirements of IAS 24 when identifying related party relationships and transactions; outstanding balances between the related party and itself; and the circumstances when disclosure about these relationships, transactions, and balances would be required. An entity should also determine the specific disclosures to provide in accordance with IAS 24.

Recognition and Measurement

IFRSs

1.197 For the purposes of IAS 24 disclosures, a *related party* is a person or entity that is related to the entity preparing financial statements (reporting entity). A person or a close member of that person's family is related to a reporting entity if that person

- controls or has joint control over the reporting entity,
- has significant influence over the reporting entity, or

- is a member of the key management personnel of the reporting entity or one of the reporting entity's parents.

An entity is related to the reporting entity if one of the following conditions is met:

- Both are members of the same group.
- One is an associate or joint venture of the other or an associate or joint venture of another member of the group to which the other belongs.
- Both are joint ventures of the same third party.
- One is a joint venture and the other an associate of the same third party.
- One is a postemployment benefit plan for the benefit of employees of the reporting entity or an entity related to the reporting entity.
- Sponsoring employers of a reporting entity that is a postemployment benefit plan.
- The entity is controlled or jointly controlled by a person who is a related party of the reporting entity.
- A person that controls or jointly controls the reporting entity has significant influence over an entity or is a member of the key management personnel of the entity.

1.198 *Key management personnel* are those persons having authority and responsibility for planning, directing, and controlling the activities of the entity, either directly or indirectly. This includes directors of the entity, regardless of whether they are an executive. A *close family member* is one who would be expected to influence or be influenced by the person in the family member's interactions with the entity. Close family members include the following persons:

- Spouse or domestic partners
- Own and spouse or domestic partner's children
- Other dependents of the person or that person's spouse or domestic partner

U.S. GAAP

1.199 The FASB ASC definition of *related parties* is similar, but not identical, to that in IAS 24. In the FASB ASC glossary definition, *related parties* include the following:

- Entity's affiliates (according to the FASB ASC glossary, an *affiliate* is a party that, directly or indirectly through one or more intermediaries, controls, is controlled by, or is under common control with an entity)
- Entities for which investments in their equity securities would be required to be accounted for by the equity method by the investing entity, absent the election of the fair value option under the "Fair Value Option" sections of FASB ASC 825-10-15
- Trusts for the benefit of employees, such as pension and profit-sharing trusts that are managed by or under the trusteeship of management

Author's Note

The requirements of the previous bullet points are likely a lower threshold for meeting the definition of *related parties* than those in IAS 24 included in its guidance related to close family members.

- Principal owners of the entity and members of their immediate families
- Entity's management (according to the FASB ASC glossary, *management* is defined as persons who are responsible for achieving an entity's objectives and who have the authority to establish

policies and make decisions in pursuit of these objectives, regardless of whether those persons have a formal title) and members of their immediate families

Author's Note

Unlike IFRSs, directors are not specifically scoped into the FASB ASC glossary definition of *management*. However, directors have both the responsibility and authority to set and pursue an entity's objectives.

- Other parties with which the entity may deal if one party controls or can significantly influence the management or operating policies of the other to an extent that one of the transacting parties might be prevented from fully pursuing its own separate interests
- Other parties that can significantly influence the management or operating policies of the transacting parties or that have an ownership interest in one of the transacting parties and can significantly influence the other to an extent that one or more of the transacting parties might be prevented from fully pursuing its own separate interests

Presentation

IFRSs

1.200 IAS 24 does not require a particular presentation of related party information. IAS 1 requires separate presentation when the transactions or balances are material. If an entity does not include receivables and payables for key management personnel separately on the balance sheet, it should present in a note disclosure a disaggregation of the balance sheet amounts in which such receivables or payables are included.

U.S. GAAP

1.201 Unlike IFRSs, FASB ASC 850-10-50-2 requires separate presentation of notes or accounts receivable from officers, employees, or affiliated entities on the balance sheet and prohibits an entity from including these accounts with other notes receivable or accounts receivable. IFRSs permit an entity to provide this disaggregation in a note disclosure.

Disclosure

IFRSs

1.202 An entity should disclose relationships between parents and subsidiaries, regardless of whether there are transactions between the related party and the entity, including the name of the entity's parent and, if different, the ultimate controlling party. When neither the parent nor ultimate controlling party prepares publicly available financial statements, an entity should disclose the name of the next most senior parent that does prepare such statements.

1.203 An entity should disclose information about (*a*) the compensation of key management personnel, both in total and separately for each of the categories described in IAS 19 (that is, short-term benefits, postemployment benefits, other long-term employee benefits, and termination benefits), and

(*b*) share-based payments, as described in IFRS 2, *Share-based Payment*.

1.204 In addition, when the entity has transactions with related parties, it should disclose the nature of the related party relationship. At a minimum, an entity should also disclose the following:

- Amounts of transactions
- Amounts of, and other information about, outstanding balances, including the following:
  —Terms and conditions
  —Whether the balances are secured
- Details of any guarantees given or received
- Provision for uncollectible amounts and any bad debt expense recognized during the period

IAS 24 does not require an entity to disclose this information for the comparative periods presented in the financial statements.

1.205 IAS 24 requires an entity to make these disclosures separately for each of the following: parent, entities with joint control or significant influence over the entity, subsidiaries, associates, joint ventures, key management personnel of the entity and its parent, and other related parties. IAS 24 provides examples of transactions that an entity would be expected to disclose, including, for example, purchases or sales of goods; property, plant, and equipment; and financing arrangements.

1.206 IAS 24 permits an entity to aggregate items of a similar nature, unless disaggregation is necessary for understanding the effects of the transactions in the entity's financial statements.

U.S. GAAP

1.207 Like IFRSs, FASB ASC 850-10-50-6 requires an entity to disclose the nature of any control relationship even when there are no transactions between the entities.

1.208 Like IFRSs, FASB ASC 850-10-50-1 requires an entity to disclose material related party transactions. Also like IFRSs, an entity is not required to disclose transactions that are eliminated in consolidation. Unlike IFRSs, FASB ASC 850-10-50-1 exempts compensation arrangements, expense allowances, and other similar items in the ordinary course of business from disclosure requirements. However, Item 402 "Executive Compensation" of SEC Regulation S-K requires SEC registrants to provide compensation information outside the financial statements for specified members of management.

1.209 Like IFRSs, FASB ASC 850-10-50-1 requires an entity to disclose the following:

- Nature of the relationships
- Description of the transactions and other information necessary for understanding of the effects of the transactions on the financial statements
- Amounts of the transactions
- Outstanding balances and, if not otherwise apparent, the terms and manner of settlement

However, unlike IFRS, FASB ASC does not have a requirement for such disclosures to be combined by related party category.

1.210 Unlike IFRSs, FASB ASC 850-10-50-1 requires an entity to disclose the amount of transactions for each period for which the entity presents an income statement and to disclose the effects of any change in the method of establishing the terms from that used in the preceding period. For outstanding balances, an entity should disclose the amount at each balance sheet date presented.

1.211 Unlike IFRSs, FASB ASC 740-10-50-17 also includes guidance for disclosures about the tax effects of transactions between an entity and its affiliates when the entity prepares separate (unconsolidated) financial statements.

1.212 Like IFRSs, FASB ASC 850-10-50-3 permits aggregation of similar transactions by type of related party in certain circumstances.

Presentation and Disclosure Excerpts

Author's Note

None of the excerpts that follow reflect the revisions to IAS 24 that are effective for annual periods beginning on or after 1 January 2011.

Related Party Receivables and Payables

1.213

Coca-Cola Hellenic Bottling Company S.A. (Dec 2011)

CONSOLIDATED BALANCE SHEET (in part)

€ Million	Note	As at 31 December 2011	As at 31 December 2010[(1)]
Assets			
Intangible assets	4	1,947.7	1,966.9
Property, plant and equipment	5	3,051.5	3,122.9
Equity method investments	6	42.9	41.1
Available-for-sale financial assets	7	1.4	1.8
Interest rate swap contracts	8	69.5	73.1
Deferred tax assets	9	35.2	35.0
Other non-current assets	10	36.9	40.4
Total non-current assets		5,185.1	5,281.2
Inventories	11	451.5	481.7
Trade receivables	12	855.2	870.2
Other receivables and assets	13	231.5	233.5
Derivative assets	8	15.7	4.2
Current tax assets		20.0	13.8
Cash and cash equivalents	14	476.1	326.1
Total current assets		2,050.0	1,929.5
Total assets		7,235.1	7,210.7
Liabilities			
Short-term borrowings	15	321.5	535.1
Trade payables	16	423.5	384.7
Other payables	16	1,118.0	1,079.4
Current tax liabilities		58.4	37.2
Total current liabilities		1,921.4	2,036.4
Long-term borrowings	15	1,934.5	1,656.4
Cross-currency swap contracts	8	130.8	136.1
Deferred tax liabilities	9	171.5	162.9
Non-current provisions	17	149.5	144.2
Other non-current liabilities		14.2	13.9
Total non-current liabilities		2,400.5	2,113.5
Total liabilities		4,321.9	4,149.9
Equity			
Share capital	18	549.8	183.1
Share premium	18	569.2	1,119.2
Treasury shares	19	(55.5)	(57.2)
Exchange equalisation reserve	19	(197.9)	(129.2)
Other reserves	19	389.0	375.4
Retained earnings		1,640.7	1,460.8
Equity attributable to owners of the parent		2,895.3	2,952.1
Non-controlling interests	28	17.9	108.7
Total equity		2,913.2	3,060.8
Total equity and liabilities		7,235.1	7,210.7

NOTES TO THE CONSOLIDATED FINANCIAL STATEMENTS (in part)

1. Basis of Preparation and Accounting Policies (in part)

Description of Business

Coca-Cola Hellenic Bottling Company S.A. ('Coca-Cola Hellenic' or 'the Group') is a Société Anonyme (corporation) incorporated in Greece and founded in 1969. It took its current form in August 2000 through the acquisition of the Coca-Cola Beverages plc ('CCB') by Hellenic Bottling Company S.A. ('HBC'). Coca-Cola Hellenic and its subsidiaries (collectively 'the Company' or 'the Group') are principally engaged in the production, sales and distribution of non-alcoholic ready to drink beverages, under franchise from The Coca-Cola Company ('TCCC'). The Company distributes its products in 27 countries in Europe and Nigeria. Information on the Company's operations by segment is included in Note 3.

Coca-Cola Hellenic's shares are listed on the Athens Exchange (symbol: EEEK), with a secondary listing on the London Stock Exchange (symbol: CCB). Coca-Cola Hellenic's American Depositary Receipts (ADRs) are listed on the New York Stock Exchange (symbol: CCH).

These consolidated financial statements were approved for issue by the Board of Directors on 15 March 2012 and are expected to be verified at the Annual General Meeting to be held on 25 June 2012.

Basis of Preparation

The consolidated financial statements included in this document are prepared in accordance with International Financial Reporting Standards ('IFRS') issued by the International Accounting Standards Board ('IASB') and IFRS as adopted by the European Union ('EU').

All IFRS issued by the IASB, which apply to the preparation of these consolidated financial statements, have been adopted by the EU following an approval process undertaken by the European Commission and the European Financial Reporting Advisory Group ('EFRAG').

The consolidated financial statements are prepared under the historical cost convention, as modified by the revaluation of available-for-sale financial assets and derivative financial instruments and the financial statements of certain subsidiaries operating in a hyperinflationary economy which are restated and expressed in terms of the measuring unit currency at the balance sheet date and translated to Euro at the exchange rate of the balance sheet date.

Accounting Pronouncements Adopted in 2011 (in part)

In the current year, the Group has adopted all of the new and revised standards and interpretations issued by the IASB and the International Financial Reporting Interpretations Committee ('IFRIC') of the IASB that are relevant to its operations and effective for accounting periods beginning on 1 January 2011. None of these standards and interpretations had a significant effect on the consolidated financial statements of the Company. The revised standards and interpretations are:

IAS 24, 'Related party disclosures' (revised 2009). The revised standard amends the definition of a related party and modifies certain related-party disclosure requirements for government-related entities. There was no impact to

the Group's consolidated financial statements as a result of adopting the revised standard.

10. Other Non-Current Assets

Other non-current assets consisted of the following at 31 December:

€ Million	2011	2010	2009
Non-current prepayments	32.7	31.3	29.4
Loans to non-related parties	2.4	4.5	7.8
Loans to related parties (refer to Note 34)	0.3	3.0	6.7
Held-to-maturity investments	1.5	1.6	1.6
Total other non-current assets	36.9	40.4	45.5

13. Other Receivables and Assets

Other receivables and assets consisted of the following at 31 December:

€ Million	2011	2010
Prepayments	68.3	100.1
Receivables from related parties (refer to Note 34)	65.1	55.1
VAT and other taxes receivable	19.6	20.1
Collateral for interest rate swap contracts (refer to Note 8)	26.3	11.6
Loans and advances to employees	11.9	8.2
Receivables from sale of property, plant and equipment	0.8	4.0
Assets classified as held for sale	—	1.8
Other receivables	39.5	32.6
Total other receivables and assets	231.5	233.5

The related party receivables, net of the provision for doubtful debts, are as follows:

€ Million	2011	2010
Due within due date	61.0	50.4
Past due	4.1	4.7
Total related party receivables	65.1	55.1
Collateral held against related party receivables	—	0.3

As at 31 December 2011, related party receivables of €4.1m (2010: €4.7m) were past due but not impaired. The ageing analysis of these related party receivables is as follows:

€ Million	2011	2010
Up to 3 months	2.4	3.0
3 to 6 months	0.5	0.5
6 to 9 months	0.4	0.1
More than 9 months	0.8	1.1
Total	4.1	4.7

During 2009, non-current assets with net book value of €1.4m were reclassified from property, plant and equipment to assets held for sale in our developing markets. These assets relate to vehicles and production equipment. As at 31 December 2009, plant and equipment with a net book value of €1.4m remained classified as held for sale. In 2010, €1.0m were reclassified to property, plant and equipment, and the depreciation charge for the year was adjusted for the depreciation that would have been recognized had the assets not been classified as held for sale, because the criteria for continued classification as held for sale were no longer met and €0.4m remained classified as held for sale since we expected that these vehicles would be sold during 2011.

During 2010, non-current assets with a net book value of €1.8m were classified from property, plant and equipment to assets held for sale. The amount of €1.2m concerns land and buildings in our established markets of which €0.4m was sold during 2010 and the amount of €0.6m concerns a plant in our emerging markets.

During 2011 no assets were classified as held for sale. Additionally, non-current assets with a net book value of €1.8m were reclassified to property, plant and equipment, and the depreciation charge for the year was adjusted for the depreciation that would have been recognized had the assets not been classified as held for sale, because the criteria for continued classification as held for sale were no longer met.

15. Borrowings (in part)

The Group held the following borrowings at 31 December:

€ Million	2011	2010
Bank overdrafts	37.5	44.2
Bank loans	9.8	8.9
Current portion of long-term bonds, bills and unsecured notes	—	305.0
Commercial paper	250.0	127.0
Loan payable to related parties (refer to Note 34)	2.3	1.2
	299.6	486.3
Obligations under finance leases falling due within one year	21.9	48.8
Total borrowings falling due within one year	321.5	535.1
Borrowings falling due within one to two years		
Bonds, bills and unsecured notes	411.1	—
Borrowings falling due within two to five years		
Bonds, bills and unsecured notes	1,446.5	1,259.7
Loan payable to related parties (refer to Note 34)	4.3	3.1
Borrowings falling due in more than five years		
Bonds, bills and unsecured notes	—	298.4
	1,861.9	1,561.2
Obligations under finance leases falling due in more than one year	72.6	95.2
Total borrowings falling due after one year	1,934.5	1,656.4
Total borrowings	2,256.0	2,191.5

16. Trade and Other Payables

Trade and other payables consisted of the following at 31 December:

€ Million	2011	2010
Trade payables	423.5	384.7
Accrued liabilities	603.0	594.9
Payables to related parties (refer to Note 34)	188.6	181.4
Deposit liabilities	108.5	107.3
Other tax and social security liabilities	84.2	77.6
Salaries and employee related payable	57.9	62.5
Current portion of provisions (refer to Note 17)	52.0	38.5
Derivative liabilities (refer to Note 8)	4.2	4.1
Deferred income	8.7	2.2
Other payables	10.9	10.9
Total trade and other payables	1,541.5	1,464.1

34. Related Party Transactions

a) The Coca-Cola Company

As at 31 December 2011, TCCC indirectly owned 23.2% (2010: 23.2%, 2009: 23.3%) of the issued share capital of Coca-Cola Hellenic. TCCC considers Coca-Cola Hellenic to be a 'key bottler' and has entered into bottler's agreements with Coca-Cola Hellenic in respect of each of Coca-Cola Hellenic's territories. All the bottler's agreements entered into by TCCC and Coca-Cola Hellenic are Standard International Bottler's ('SIB') agreements. The terms of the bottler's agreements grant Coca-Cola Hellenic the right to produce and the exclusive right to sell and distribute the beverages of TCCC in each of the countries Coca-Cola Hellenic operates. Consequently, Coca-Cola Hellenic is obliged to purchase all concentrate for TCCC's beverages from TCCC, or its designee, in the ordinary course of business. These agreements extend to 2013 and may be renewed at TCCC's discretion until 2023. On 29 December 2008, Kar-Tess Holding and TCCC agreed to extend their existing shareholders' agreement, whereby the combined shareholdings of Kar-Tess Holding and TCCC will not fall below 44% for the period up to January 2014 and not below 40% for the period thereafter until 31 December 2018.

TCCC owns or has applied for the trademarks that identify its beverages in each of the countries Coca-Cola Hellenic operates. TCCC has authorised Coca-Cola Hellenic and certain of its subsidiaries to use the trademark 'Coca-Cola' in their corporate names.

Total purchases of concentrate, finished products and other materials from TCCC and its subsidiaries during 2011 amounted to €1,305.4m (2010: €1,372.9m, 2009: €1,283.6m).

TCCC makes discretionary marketing contributions to Coca-Cola Hellenic's operating subsidiaries. The participation in shared marketing agreements is at TCCC's discretion and, where co-operative arrangements are entered into, marketing expenses are shared. Such arrangements include the development of marketing programmes to promote TCCC's beverages. Total net contributions received from TCCC for marketing and promotional incentives during the year amounted to €76.5m (2010: €60.8m, 2009: €56.9m). Contributions for price support and marketing and promotional campaigns in respect of specific customers are recorded in net sales revenue as an offset to promotional incentives paid to customers. In 2011, such contributions to-talled €49.0m (2010: €48.8m, 2009: €39.9m). Contributions for general marketing programmes are recorded as an off-set to selling expenses. In 2011, such contributions made by TCCC to Coca-Cola Hellenic totalled €21.9m (2010: €19.8m, 2009: €22.5m) and the contributions of Coca-Cola Hellenic to TCCC totalled €9.0m (2010: €7.8m, 2009: €5.5m). TCCC has also customarily made additional payments for market-ing and advertising directly to suppliers as part of the shared marketing arrangements. The proportion of direct and indirect payments, made at TCCC's discretion, will not necessarily be the same from year to year. In addition, support payments re-ceived from TCCC for the placement of cold drink equipment were €14.6m for the year ended 31 December 2011 (2010 and 2009: nil).

In 2011, the Group did not record any gain from the sale of property, plant and equipment to TCCC (2010: nil, 2009: €0.2m).

During the year, the Group sold €32.8m of finished goods and raw materials to TCCC (2010: €19.0m, 2009: €20.5m).

Other income primarily comprises rent, facility and other items of €1.2m (2010: €14.3m, 2009: €4.4m) and a toll-filling relationship in Poland of €13.8m (2010: €17.6m, 2009: €15.0m). Other expenses related to facility costs charged by TCCC and shared costs included in operating expenses amounted to €4.0m (2010: nil, 2009: €1.5m).

During 2011 the Group did not make any purchases of franchise rights (2010: €4.4m, 2009: nil) and did not receive any income from the sale of available-for-sale assets to TCCC (2010: €4.9m, 2009: nil).

As at 31 December 2011, the Group had a total amount due from TCCC of €63.2m (2010: €53.8m, 2009: €64.2m), of which €0.3m (2010: €3.0m, 2009: €6.7m,) related to loans to joint ventures with TCCC, and a total amount due to TCCC of €172.2m of trade payables (2010: €166.0m, 2009: €125.1m) and €7.6m of other liabilities (2010: nil, 2009: nil).

(b) Frigoglass S.A. ('Frigoglass')

Frigoglass, a company listed on the Athens Exchange, is a manufacturer of coolers, glass bottles and crowns. Frigoglass is related to Coca-Cola Hellenic by way of 43.7% ownership by the parent of Kar-Tess Holding (see below). Frigoglass has a controlling interest in Frigoglass Industries Limited, a company in which Coca-Cola Hellenic has a 23.9% effective interest, through its investment in Nigerian Bottling Company plc (refer to Note 6).

Coca-Cola Hellenic entered into a supply agreement with Frigoglass for the purchase of cooling equipment in 1999. The supply agreement was extended in 2004 and, most recently, in 2008, on substantially similar terms. Coca-Cola Hellenic has the status of most favoured customer of Frigoglass, on a non-exclusive basis, provided that it obtains at least 60% (at prices which are negotiated on an annual basis and which must be competitive) of its annual requirements for cooling equipment. The current agreement expires on 31 December 2013.

During 2011, the Group made purchases of €148.0m (2010: €101.0m, 2009: €58.8m) of coolers, glass bottles and crowns from Frigoglass and its subsidiaries and incurred maintenance and other expenses of €6.4m (2010: €5.7m, 2009: €5.3m). In addition the Group recorded other income of €1.0m (2010: €0.5m, 2009: €0.7m). As at 31 Decem-ber 2011, Coca-Cola Hellenic owed €14.4m (2010: €13.9m,

2009: €3.6m) to, and was owed €1.2m (2010: €1.2m, 2009: €4.7m) by Frigoglass.

(c) Directors

Mr George A. David, Mr Haralambos K. Leventis, Mr Anas-tasios P. Leventis and Mr Anastassis G. David have been nominated by Kar-Tess Holding to the board of Coca-Cola Hellenic. Mr Irial Finan and Mr John Hunter have been nom-inated by TCCC to the board of Coca-Cola Hellenic. There have been no transactions between Coca-Cola Hellenic and the directors except for remuneration (refer to Note 33).

(d) Other

Beverage Partners Worldwide ('BPW')

BPW is a 50/50 joint venture between TCCC and Nestlé. Dur-ing 2011, the Group purchased inventory from BPW amount-ing to €99.6m (2010: €89.4m, 2009: €70.0m) and did not record any income (2010: €0.1m, 2009: €0.1m). As at 31 De-cember 2011, Coca-Cola Hellenic owed €4.4m (2010: €4.4m, 2009: €1.7m) to, and was owed €0.1m (2010: nil, 2009: €0.3m) by BPW.

Kar-Tess Holding

As at 31 December 2011, Kar-Tess Holding owned 23.3% (2010: 23.3%, 2009: 29.5%) of the issued share capital of Coca-Cola Hellenic.

On 6 December, 2010 Kar-Tess Holding transferred 22,453,254 of Coca-Cola Hellenic shares and voting rights representing 6.13% of the total number of shares and voting rights of Coca-Cola Hellenic by transferring its 100% owned subsidiaries under the trade names "Sammy LLC", "Lucky 70 LLC", "Zoe 20 LLC", "Kooky LLC", "Utopia Business Com-pany Ltd.", "Harmonia Commercial S.A.", "Ice Cold Holdings Limited" and "Red & White Holdings Limited" to entities and individuals, who were either ultimate beneficial owners of Kar-Tess Holding or have been nominated by them. None of the above persons owns individually more than 2% of the out-standing shares and voting rights of Coca-Cola Hellenic.

Leventis Overseas & AG Leventis (Nigeria) PLC (the 'Leventis Companies')

The Leventis Companies are related to Coca-Cola Hellenic by way of common directors, as a result of which significant influence is considered to exist. During 2011, the Group pur-chased €14.9m (2010: €10.8m, 2009: €10.0m) of finished goods and other materials and had no purchases of fixed as-sets (2010: nil, 2009: €0.4m) from the Leventis Companies. Furthermore the Group did not record any sales of finished goods and raw materials to the Leventis Companies (2010: €0.1m, 2009: nil) and incurred rental expenses of €2.8m (2010: €0.6m, 2009: €2.9m) from the Leventis Companies. In addition during 2011 the Group incurred other expenses of €0.3m (2010: €0.4m, 2009: nil) and recorded other income of €0.3m (2010: €1.0m, 2009: nil) with the Leventis Compa-nies. As at 31 December 2011, the Group owed €3.8m (2010: €1.3m, 2009: €2.2m) to, and was owed €0.2m (2010: €0.8m, 2009: €0.2m) by the Leventis Companies.

Other Coca-Cola Bottlers

The Group sold €1.6m of finished goods (2010: €1.3m, 2009: nil), purchased €2.0m of finished goods (2010: €0.5m, 2009: nil), incurred expenses of €0.1m (2010: €0.1m, 2009: €0.1m) and did not record any income (2010: €0.3m, 2009: €0.4m) from other Coca-Cola bottlers over which TCCC has significant influence. Furthermore during 2011 the Group received reimbursement for direct marketing expenses incurred of €0.1m (2010: €0.8m, 2009: €0.5m) from other Coca-Cola bottlers. At 31 December 2011, the receivables from such Coca-Cola bottlers were €0.3m (2010: €1.5m, 2009: €1.3m).

Other Related Parties

The Group purchased €1.5m (2010: €1.4m, 2009: €2.1m) of raw materials and finished goods and did not perform any purchases of fixed assets from other related parties (2010:

€0.3m, 2009: €0.2m). Further, the Group incurred expenses of €2.6m (2010: €2.1m, 2009: €1.0m) and recorded income of €0.3m (2010: €0.2m, 2009: €0.2m). At 31 December 2011, the Group owed €0.3m (2010: €0.1m, 2009: €0.4m) to, and was owed €0.4m (2010: €0.8m, 2009: nil) by other related parties.

There are no significant transactions with other related parties for the year ended 31 December 2011.

Management Compensation, Employment of Director's Family Member, Employee Discounts

1.214

Alon Holdings Blue Square—Israel Ltd. (Dec 2011)

CONSOLIDATED STATEMENTS OF FINANCIAL POSITION (in part)

In Thousands	Note	December 31 2010	December 31 2011	Convenience Translation (Note 1b) December 31, 2011 U.S. Dollars
		NIS	NIS	U.S. Dollars
Assets				
Current assets:				
Trade receivables	14a	1,731,747	1,576,150	412,497
Other accounts receivable	14b	162,599	295,400	77,310
Inventories	14c	680,296	676,590	177,071
		3,173,013	3,156,918	826,202
Non-current assets:				
Investments in associates	10b	6,012	202,653	53,037
Derivative financial instruments	13	56,078	896	234
Real estate inventories	14d	83,337	100,035	26,180
Payments on account of real estate	11	164,132	191,600	50,144
Investment in securities	12	30,327	33,159	8,678
Loans receivable, net of current maturities	16	176,043	182,654	47,803
Property and equipment, net	7	2,928,515	2,942,487	770,083
Investment property	8	546,870	576,093	150,770
Intangible assets, net	9	1,486,744	1,461,070	382,379
Other long-term receivables	17	47,098	142,331	37,250
Deferred taxes	23	66,018	104,321	27,302
		5,591,174	5,937,299	1,553,860
Total assets		8,764,187	9,094,217	2,380,062

In Thousands	Note	December 31 2010	December 31 2011	Convenience Translation (Note 1b) December 31, 2011
		NIS	NIS	U.S. Dollars
Liabilities and Equity				
Current liabilities:				
Credit and loans from banks and others	21	470,284	1,036,928	271,376
Current maturities of debentures and convertible debentures	21	202,769	212,726	55,673
Current maturities of long-term loans from banks	21	297,771	311,642	81,560
Trade payables		1,342,763	1,243,914	325,547
Other accounts payable and accrued expenses	20	686,447	730,985	191,307
Customers' deposits		30,405	27,733	7,258
Derivative financial instruments	13	7,700	2,814	736
Income taxes payable		7,431	6,311	1,652
Provisions	25	71,870	78,266	20,483
		3,117,440	3,651,319	955,592
Non current liabilities:				
Long-term loans from banks and others, net of current maturities	21	1,399,159	1,240,487	324,650
Convertible debentures, net of current maturities	21	117,801	118,826	31,098
Debentures, net of current maturities	21	2,183,093	2,034,047	532,334
Other liabilities	22	199,983	264,597	69,248
Derivative financial instruments	13	9,151	16,701	4,371
Liabilities in respect of employee benefits, net of amounts funded	24	51,492	62,245	16,290
Deferred taxes	23	103,929	162,795	42,605
		4,064,608	3,899,698	1,020,596
Total liabilities		7,182,048	7,551,017	1,976,188

NOTES TO THE CONSOLIDATED FINANCIAL STATEMENTS (in part)

Note 14—Trade Receivables, Inventories and Other Receivables (in part)

b. Other Receivables

	December 31 2010	December 31 2011
	NIS in Thousands	
Prepayments	13,443	14,776
Related parties, see note 35	33,901	168,642
Government authorities	14,194	8,901
Advances to suppliers and others	22,002	7,476
Current maturities of loans receivable	10,699	8,473
Receivables in respect of gift certificates	16,646	30,159
Other	51,714	56,973
	162,599	295,400

The fair value of other receivables is usually identical or close to their carrying value.

c. Inventories

1) Inventories Presented in Current Assets:

	December 31 2010	December 31 2011
	NIS in Thousands	
Fuel and oil products	102,136	105,338
Consumer (including non-food) products	578,160	571,252
	680,296	676,590

2) Real Estate Inventories (Presented as Non-current Assets)

Representing approximately 240-dunam parcel of property in Point-Wells near Seattle, Washington, USA, acquired by BSRE from a related party (see note 35a.6); BSRE has also signed a development agreement with the related party to initiate and promote a detailed plan for the approval of the building of at least 2,000 residential units on the land. BSRE is operating to change the zoning of the land from heavy industrial use to urban center zoning, and so far has received an "in principal" approval for the zoning change from the Snohomish County (which has the jurisdiction for the area where the land is located; hereinafter—the County) which was statutorily effected in the Urban Centers Code Ordinance. In March 2011, a detailed plan for the construction of residential and public areas and detailed plans for the development of the land were submitted to the County planning committee. Following objections received, the County has been given a year to make certain adjustments to the principal plan. Through December 31, 2011, BSRE invested $ 4.8 million ((NIS 18.3 million) in the development of property rights and capitalized borrowing costs of $ 1.9 million (NIS 7.3 Million) (of which $ 3.3 million and $ 0.68 million, relate to 2010, respectively).

The property serves primarily as a plant for storage and distribution of fuel and oils by the related party, and is rented to the related party for a period of up to 10 years. According to the development agreement, all demolition and contamina- tion cleanups required for the land will be the responsibility of the related party and on its account; the related party will also compensate BSRE for any damages incurred in connection with such activities. In case BSRE was to sell the land the related party will participate in the consideration net of costs as defined in the agreement, see note 35a.b.

Note 16—Loans Receivable

	December 31	
	2010	2011
	NIS in Thousands	
Loans to proportionally jointly controlled companies[1]	53,206	55,908
Loans to the Fuel Administration[2]	29,943	31,091
Loans to others[3][4]	103,593	104,128
	186,742	191,127
Less current maturities	10,699	8,473
	176,043	182,654

[1] Including NIS 31,994 thousand relating to the Wholesale Market project bearing interest of 3%—see also note 11.

[2] The loan to the Fuel Administration is included in accordance with the Control of Commodities and Service Order (Settlements in the Fuel Economy), 1988.

[3] Mainly owners of fueling stations to which the Company supplies fuel. As at December 31, 2011 and 2010 the amount includes a single debtor balance of NIS 19.3 million and 21.8 million respectively.

[4] As of December 31, 2011 and 2010 includes a loan to a related party of NIS 38.3 million and NIS 37.3 million, respectively. The loan is linked to the Israeli CPI, bears interest of 5% and matures in January 2015.

The fair value of these loans at December 31, 2011 is NIS 183 million.

Note 35—Related-Party Disclosures

Key management personnel—includes the members of the board of directors and senior managers in the Company, and CEO's of Dor Alon, BSRE and BEE Group.

The principal related parties of the Company are, among others: Alon Retail Ltd., Alon Israel Oil Company Ltd., Alon USA LP, Bielsol Investments (1987) Ltd., collective acqui- sition entities of kibbutzim in Israel that hold Alon Israel Oil Company Ltd, and other companies, whose interests are con- trolled by the Company's directors among others.

a. Transactions with Related Parties:

	Year Ended December 31		
	2009	2010	2011
	NIS in Thousands		
Fuel sales to related parties[a]	—	59,806	212,902
Fuel sales to joint control entities[a]	—	82,355	380,670
Rental income[b]	—	3,115	6,706
Management fees to parent company[c]	—	1,430	5,956
Directors' fees[d]	1,718	3,070	4,167
Legal consulting[e]	5,051	2,434	5,544
Purchases[f]	840,486	814,583	813,682
Commissions[g]	6,636	4,988	—
Discounts[h]	444	495	—

[a] Relate to transactions that are carried out in the normal course of business in accordance with regular market prices and credit.

[b] Point Wells

During 2010, BSRE signed agreements with subsidiaries of Alon U.S.A, a related party, for the acquisition and development of a property in Point-Wells near Seattle, Washington, USA (presented as real estate inventories—see also note 14c.). The property, which currently serves primarily as a plant for storage and distribution of fuel and oils of the related parties was acquired for U.S. $19.5 million.

According to the development agreement, all demolition and contamination cleanups required for the land will be the responsibility of the related parties and on their own account; the related parties will also compensate BSRE for any damages incurred in connection with such activities. In case the Company was to sell the land the related party may participate in the consideration net of costs as defined in the agreement.

The agreements provide for the lease of the property to the related parties for a period of up to 10 years. Rental income received by BSRE amounts to $1.7 million and $0.8 million for the years 2011 and 2010, respectively (NIS 6.7 million and NIS 3.1 million, respectively)

(continued)

(continued)

(c) In March 2005, Dor Alon and Alon signed a management agreement, whereunder Alon would render Dor Alon management and consulting services; these services were to be provided by the parent company or by its other subsidiaries. During the period of the agreement, the chairman of the Board of Directors of Dor Alon will be appointed based on the parent company's recommendation.

Dor Alon pays quarterly management fees equal to 3% of Dor Alon's EBITDA (income from ordinary operations with the addition of depreciation and amortization) in accordance with Dor Alon's quarterly, consolidated financial statements, but not exceeding NIS 1,250 thousand per quarter, and linked to the CPI of December 2004. The management fees do not include director's fees and such directors (excluding the chairman of the board of directors and the president of the company) would be entitled to receive directors' fees from Dor Alon. This management agreement was in effect until December 31, 2010, and on December 30, 2010 the agreement was renewed with the same terms as stated above, for an additional five year period or a shorter period, subject to approvals required by the Israeli Companies Law.

(d) Commencing November 15, 2005, the Company's Chairman of the board of directors receives compensation for his services of NIS 42,497 per month plus reimbursement of actual expenses incurred in connection with his services to the Company. The compensation amount is linked to the Israeli CPI (base index—November 2005), and is updated every three months. Due to the recent amendment to the Israeli's Companies Law, this arrangement was re-approved by our audit committee, board of directors and shareholders meeting for additional three years commencing on February 2, 2012.

(e) Legal services

The Company receives legal services from S. Biran & Co. a related party of the Company.

(f) Goods purchase from related parties

Mega Retail purchases goods from Tnuva and Dor Alon. These arrangements are in the ordinary course of our business, and the terms and conditions of these arrangements are at "arm's-length". The Company purchases most of its dairy, fresh produce and poultry products from the Tnuva corporation, which holds a leading position in the domestic dairy and poultry markets. To our knowledge, some of the collective acquisition entities of kibbutzim in Israel that hold shares of Alon, our controlling shareholder, hold 21.5% of Tnuva.

(g) Service agreement

In January 2004 the shareholders of Blue Square approved an agreement according to which it provides Dor Alon purchasing and supply services for stores operated by them. In consideration for these services, the Company is entitled to payment equivalent to the cost of the services provided with the addition of a margin as stated in the agreement.

(h) Discounts

On September 13, 2005, the Company's general shareholders meeting approved a discount arrangement for some of the employees of the companies holding directly or indirectly in the Company's shares (some of the employees of Alon Group) (hereinafter—"the entitled employees").

The discounts to be given to the entitled employees will be identical to those given to the Company's employees, which during 2011 were: 12% at the Mega In Town stores, 12% at Mega on-line and 6% at the Zol Beshefa stores and Mega Bool stores.

The discounts are limited to purchases in a total amount of NIS 8,500 a month.

Gift Cards

The Company sells gift certificates for the par value in the certificate less a discount, according to commercial terms negotiated with the clients during the regular course of business.

Employment Agreement With Ms. Moran Wiessman

The Chairman of the Board of Directors' daughter, Ms. Moran Wiessman, is employed in BEE Group as a process engineer since January 2009. Moran Wiessman receives a basic gross monthly wage of NIS 13,000, car maintenance (in the amount of NIS 600 gross per month in addition to fuel expenses) and social benefits as acceptable for an employee of her status. The employment agreement was approved by the audit committee, the board of directors and the general meeting of the Company in July 2009. As part of this approval, the approval procedures in the Company necessary for a pay increase or grants to Ms. Wiessman were determined. Ms. Wiessman holds a B.Sc degree in Industry and Management from Ben Gurion University.

Acquisition of Apartment

During the year 2010 the Company's chairman acquired an apartment from a proportionally consolidated company for NIS 2,330 thousand.

b. Balances With Related Parties

Year-End Balances Arising From Sales/Purchases of Goods/ Services:

	December 31	
	2010	2011
	NIS in Thousands	
Diners credit card customers	—	36,062
Other receivables	33,901	168,642
Loan to related party	37,261	38,291
Loans to joint control entities	53,206	55,908
	124,368	298,903
Trade payables	95,561	52,060
Other payables	327	18,266
Loan from controlling shareholder	129,000	55,000
	224,888	125,326

The receivables from related parties arise mainly from sale transactions and are due two months after the date of the sales. The receivables are unsecured in nature and bear no interest. There are no provisions held against receivables from related parties.

As to a loan from controlling shareholder—see also note 21.

As to a loan receivable from a related party, see note 16.

c. Acquisition of Dor Alon

In connection with the acquisition Alon and the Company obtained a pre-ruling from the Israeli Tax Authority. The pre-ruling is subject to various conditions and provides, among other things, that the cost basis and the purchase date of the shares of Dor Alon for tax purposes in the possession of the Company following the acquisition will be the original price and acquisition date, respectively, as they had been for Alon prior to the acquisition. Alon has clarified to the Company that, in connection with the payment of tax at the time of any future sale by the Company of all or part of its shares in Dor Alon, if any, to a third party, Alon will pay that portion of any applicable tax payable in an amount equal to the amount of tax deferred by the Tax Authority in its pre-ruling (*i.e.,* the amount of tax that would have been payable by Alon in connection with the acquisition had the acquisition not been tax exempt according to the pre-ruling).

d. Dor Alon

1. In May 2005, Dor Alon and Alon signed an agreement, according to which Dor Alon would be allowed to deposit funds with Alon, from time to time, and at the mutual agreement of the parties, and to receive funds from Alon on On-call terms, linked to the prime interest rate less 1.25%, subject to a maximum of NIS 50 million at any time. The agreement is unlimited and either party is entitled to terminate the agreement by providing a three month written notice.

On January 6, 2011 a new overdraft agreement was signed, for a period of five years, under which the funds provided by Dor Alon to Alon as a loan or by Alon as a loan to Dor Alon, will not exceed NIS 150 million at any time linked to the prime interest rate less 1.25%. Against the deposits, the depositor is entitled to require the recipient party to provide her / or third parties bank guarantees, or letters of credit. Each party is entitled to redeem or require redemption of the balance by giving notice of three banking business days. See also note 3.

2. As part of the transfer of assets and operations that took place in 2004, Alon undertook to indemnify Dor Alon for expenses Dor Alon may incur relating to the period through the date of transfer of the assets and Dor Alon undertook to indemnify Alon in case lawsuits would be brought against it in respect of expenses relating to the period subsequent to the transfer of assets to Dor Alon. Also, Dor Alon undertook to indemnify Alon in respect of the tax liability to which Alon would be subject if Dor Alon were to breach the provisions of Section 104A of the Income Tax Ordinance regarding the transferred assets. Alon has undertaken to indemnify Dor Alon in respect of any amount Dor Alon would be required to pay in connection with the period during which 21 employees of Alon that were transferred to Dor Alon as part of the transfer of operations were employed by Alon.

Key Management Compensation

	Year Ended December 31		
	2009	2010	2011
	NIS in Thousands		
Salaries and other short-term employee benefits	22,338	21,825	16,760
Share-based payments	6,172	3,040	1,581
Total	28,510	24,865	18,341

IFRIC 13, *CUSTOMER LOYALTY PROGRAMMES*

IFRSs Overview and Comparison to U.S. GAAP

Author's Note

IFRS 13 amended International Financial Reporting Interpretations Committee (IFRIC) 13, *Customer Loyalty Programmes*, as follows:

- Removed any descriptions or examples of what constitutes fair value with respect to measurement of award credits
- Replaced the terms *estimation technique* with *valuation technique* and *estimate* with *measure*
- Modified the applications guidance paragraphs AG1–AG3 to explain that, if a quoted market price for an identical award credit is not available, the entity should measure fair value using another valuation technique
- Required the entity to take into account nonperformance risk with measuring the fair value of award credits

Early application of IFRS 13 is permitted. If an entity early adopts for this standard, it should apply the related amendment to IFRIC 13.

Because these standards are effective for annual periods beginning on or after 1 January 2012, these amendments are not reflected in the commentary in this section. However, these amendments would not affect the availability of illustrative excerpts from survey companies' financial statements.

In addition, FASB and IASB are working on a joint project on revenue recognition that includes guidance on customer loyalty programs. In November 2011, FASB and IASB jointly published an exposure draft, *Revenue from Contracts with Customers*, which includes requirements on accounting for the issues covered by IFRIC 13. Concurrently, the boards have conducted extensive outreach activities with stakeholders. The boards expect to begin deliberations in the second quarter of 2012 with a target date for issuing a final standard in late 2012 or in 2013.

1.215 IFRIC 13 addresses recognition and measurement of revenues and liabilities related to programs that provide incentives to customers to buy an entity's products or services. Although not formally defined in IFRIC 13, such programs usually grant points or credits (award credits) that a customer can accumulate to become eligible for awards that provide free or discounted products or services. The entity may provide the products or services directly or through a third-party entity. In addition, rather than operating a program itself, an entity may participate in a program operated by another entity. Awards may also be linked to continued purchases or interaction with the company over time or to specific purchases.

1.216 IFRIC 13 applies to award credits that meet the following criteria:
- An entity grants the award credits to the customer as part of a sales transaction.
- Customers, when qualified, can use the award credits in the future to acquire other goods or services.

1.217 IFRIC 13 is effective for annual periods beginning on or after 1 July 2008. Early application is permitted with disclosure of that fact.

Recognition and Measurement

IFRSs

1.218 Paragraph 13 of IAS 18, *Revenue*, requires an entity to apply the revenue recognition criteria separately to identifiable components of a single transaction in order to reflect the substance of the transaction. IFRIC 13 requires an entity to account for award credits as an identifiable component of the sale transaction in which they are awarded to the customer. Therefore, an entity should allocate the consideration received or receivable in these transactions among the award credits and other goods or services received. An entity should measure the amount allocated as the fair value of the amount for which the award credits could be sold.

1.219 When an entity itself provides the awards, it should recognize revenue when the award credits are redeemed and it delivers the products or services awarded. The entity measures the amount of revenue based on the percentage of actual award credits redeemed relative to the total award credits expected to be redeemed.

1.220 When a third party provides the awards, an entity should determine whether, in giving award credits to customers, it is acting on its own account or as an agent for the third party. When the entity collects consideration as an agent for a third party, it should measure revenue only at the net amount it retains, rather than the amount it collects, recognized only when the third party is entitled to the consideration and obligated to provide the awards. The facts and circumstances of the arrangement should determine when this obligating event occurs, and it may not occur until the customer redeems award credits. When an entity receives consideration on its own account, it should recognize revenue when it provides the awards, measured as the amount of consideration allocated to the redeemed award credits.

1.221 Obligations under award credit contracts may lead to an onerous contract—one in which the costs to fulfill the contract exceed the consideration received or receivable. If the contractual obligation under an award credit contract becomes onerous, an entity should recognize a liability for the excess, measured in accordance with IAS 37, *Provisions,*

Contingent Liabilities and Contingent Assets. IFRIC 13 explains that one circumstance in which an entity might need to recognize a liability is when the entity revises its estimate of award credits to be redeemed.

U.S. GAAP

1.222 FASB ASC does not include specific guidance on accounting for the type of award credits or customer loyalty programs covered by IFRIC 13. FASB ASC 605-25-15-2A explicitly scopes out award credits by broad-based loyalty program operators from the guidance on revenue recognition for multiple element arrangements. Therefore, an entity should evaluate other appropriate guidance in FASB ASC to determine the most relevant guidance for its specific situation and apply those requirements by analogy. Some entities may apply the guidance for multiple element arrangements and recognize revenue in a manner similar to that required by IFRIC 13. Unlike IFRIC 13, other entities may apply an incremental cost approach and would recognize and measure revenues differently.

Presentation

IFRSs

1.223 Application of IFRIC 13 does not affect presentation. IAS 1 requires separate presentation or disclosure if the amounts are material.

U.S. GAAP

1.224 FASB ASC does not provide specific presentation guidance on this issue.

Disclosure

IFRSs

1.225 IFRIC 13 does not include disclosure requirements, but it does state that an entity should apply any necessary change in accounting policy retrospectively and to provide the relevant disclosures in accordance with IAS 8.

U.S. GAAP

1.226 Disclosure requirements would depend on the particular section of FASB ASC that an entity uses to recognize and measure revenue for these award credits.

Presentation and Disclosure Excerpts

Customer Loyalty Program

1.227

Canadian Tire Corporation, Limited (Dec 2011)

CONSOLIDATED BALANCE SHEETS *(in part)*

As at (C$ in Millions)	December 31, 2011	January 1, 2011	January 3, 2010
		(Note 44)	(Note 44)
Liabilities			
Bank indebtedness (Note 9)	$ 124.8	$ 118.0	$ 83.7
Deposits (Note 20)	1,182.3	615.6	863.4
Trade and other payables (Note 21)	1,640.9	1,179.9	1,192.9
Provisions (Note 22)	191.9	196.2	220.9
Short-term borrowings (Note 24)	352.6	100.6	163.0
Loans payable (Note 25)	628.7	687.0	757.4
Income taxes payable	3.9	—	—
Current portion of long-term debt (Note 26)	27.9	354.2	690.6
Total current liabilities	4,153.0	3,251.5	3,971.9

CONSOLIDATED STATEMENTS OF INCOME *(in part)*

For the Years Ended (C$ in Millions Except per Share Amounts)	December 31, 2011	January 1, 2011
		(Note 44)
Revenue (Note 32)	$10,387.1	$ 9,213.1
Cost of producing revenue (Note 33)	(7,326.4)	(6,422.1)
Gross margin	3,060.7	2,791.0

NOTES TO THE CONSOLIDATED FINANCIAL STATEMENTS *(in part)*

1. The Company and Its Operations

Canadian Tire Corporation, Limited is a Canadian public company primarily domiciled in Canada. Its registered office is located at 2180 Yonge Street, Toronto, Ontario, M4P 2V8, Canada. It is listed on the Toronto Stock Exchange (TSX-CTC, CTC.A). Canadian Tire Corporation, Limited and entities it controls are together referred to in these consolidated financial statements as "the Company."

The Company is comprised of two main business operations that offer a range of retail goods and services including general merchandise, clothing, sporting goods, petroleum and financial services. Details of its two reportable segments: "Retail" and "Financial Services" are provided in Note 7.

On August 18, 2011 the Company acquired The Forzani Group Ltd. ("FGL Sports"). The operations of FGL Sports are included in the Company's results from operations and financial position commencing August 19, 2011.

The Company's operations are influenced by seasonal trends in the retail environment. The second and fourth quarters of each year are typically when the Company experi-ences stronger revenue and net income due to the seasonal nature of some merchandise in its retail operations and timing of marketing programs.

2. Basis of Preparation *(in part)*

Fiscal Year

The fiscal year of the Company consists of a 52- or 53-week period ending on the Saturday closest to December 31. The fiscal years for the consolidated financial statements and notes presented for 2011 and 2010 are the 52-week period ended December 31, 2011 and the 52-week period ended January 1, 2011, respectively.

Statement of Compliance

These consolidated financial statements have been prepared in accordance with International Financial Reporting Standards ("IFRS") and using the accounting policies described herein.

These are the Company's first annual consolidated financial statements reported under IFRS for the 52-week period ended December 31, 2011 with comparatives for the 52-week period ended January 1, 2011, and IFRS 1—*First-time Adoption of IFRS* ("IFRS 1") has been applied. An explanation of how the transition from previous Canadian Generally Accepted Accounting Principles to IFRS as at January 3, 2010 ("Transition Date") has affected the reported financial position, financial performance and cash flows of the Company, including the mandatory exceptions and optional exemptions under IFRS, is provided in Note 44.

These consolidated financial statements were approved by the Company's Board of Directors on March 15, 2012.

Use of Estimates and Judgments (in part)

The preparation of these consolidated financial statements in accordance with IFRS requires Management to make judgments, estimates and assumptions that affect the application of accounting policies and the reported amounts of assets and liabilities and disclosures of contingent assets and liabilities at the date of these consolidated financial statements, and the reported amounts of revenue and expenses during the reporting period. Actual results may differ from estimates made in these consolidated financial statements.

Estimates are used when estimating the useful lives of property and equipment, investment property and intangible assets for the purposes of depreciation and amortization, when accounting for and measuring items such as inventory allowances, customer loyalty programs, deferred revenue, insurance reserves, assumptions underlying actuarial determination of post-employment defined benefit obligations, income and other taxes, provisions, certain fair value measures including those related to the valuation of business combinations, share-based payments and financial instruments, the testing of goodwill, indefinite useful life intangible assets and other assets for impairment, updating models used in the determination of allowances on loans receivable, purchase price adjustments on business combinations and calculating the pro-forma results as if the acquisition of FGL Sports had occurred at the beginning of the Company's fiscal year.

Provisions (in part)

A provision is recognized if, as a result of a past event, the Company has a present legal or constructive obligation that can be estimated reliably and it is probable that an outflow of economic benefits will be required to settle the obligation. The amount recognized as a provision is the best estimate of the consideration required to settle the present obligation at the end of the reporting period, taking into account risks and uncertainty of cash flow. Where the effect of discounting is material, provisions are determined by discounting the expected future cash flows at a pre-tax rate that reflects current market assessments of the time value of money and the risks specific to the liability. Where the future cash flow estimates have been adjusted for the risks specific to the liability, the discount rate does not reflect the risks specific to the liability. The unwinding of the discount is reflected in finance costs in the Consolidated Statements of Income.

When a portion or all of the economic benefits required to settle a provision are expected to be recovered from a third party, a receivable is recognized as an asset if it is virtually certain that the Company will receive the reimbursement and the amount can be reliably measured.

Customer Loyalty Programs

The Company maintains customer loyalty programs in promoting our interrelated businesses. The Company issues paper-based "Canadian Tire Money" to Dealers and to consumers whenever they make cash or debit card purchases at the Company's Petroleum gas bars. The Company also issues electronic-based "Canadian Tire Money on the Card" whenever consumers make a Canadian Tire Options MasterCard purchase from any location in the World. Both the paper-based and the electronic-based "Canadian Tire Money" can only be redeemed at the Canadian Tire Retail stores for merchandise at the option of the consumer.

An obligation arises from the above customer loyalty program when the Dealers pay the Company to acquire paper-based "Canadian Tire Money," as the Dealers retain the right to return Canadian Tire Money to the Company for refund in cash. An obligation also arises when the Company issues electronic-based "Canadian Tire Money on the Card." These obligations are measured at fair value by reference to the fair value of the awards for which they could be redeemed based on the estimated probability of their redemption and are expensed to sales and marketing expenses in the Consolidated Statements of Income.

Revenue (in part)

The Company recognizes revenue when the amount can be reliably measured, it is probable that future economic benefits will flow to the entity, and when specific criteria have been met for each of the Company's activities as described below.

Customer Loyalty Programs

Loyalty award credits issued as part of a sales transaction relating to the Company's "Gas Advantage" and "Cash Advantage" credit card programs results in revenue being deferred until the loyalty award is redeemed by the customer. The portion of the revenue that is deferred is the fair value of the award. The fair value of the award takes into account the amount for which the award credits could be sold separately, less the proportion of the award credits that are not expected to be redeemed by customers.

22. Provisions (in part)

The following table presents the changes to the Company's provisions:

(C$ in Millions)	Warranties and Returns	Site Restoration and Decommissioning	Onerous Contracts	Customer Loyalty	Other	Total
Balance at January 1, 2011	$109.7	$24.8	$ 6.8	$ 65.3	$ 14.7	$ 221.3
Assumed in a business combination	—	0.1	0.7	—	30.2	31.0
Charges net of reversals	245.1	5.3	1.1	(111.2)	3.1	368.6
Utilizations	(242.9)	(7.5)	(1.5)	114.0	(16.2)	(379.3)
Unwinding of discount	1.2	0.5	—	—	—	1.7
Change in discount rate	0.1	3.6	—	—	—	3.7
Balance at December 31, 2011	$113.2	26.8	7.1	68.1	31.8	$247.0
Less: Current portion	107.9	7.4	2.1	68.1	6.4	191.9
Long-term portion	$ 5.3	$19.4	$ 5.0	$ —	$ 25.4	$ 55.1

(C$ in Millions)	Warranties and Returns	Site Restoration and Decommissioning	Onerous Contracts	Customer Loyalty	Other	Total
Balance at January 3, 2010	$148.9	$24.9	$ 9.2	$ 61.8	$ 2.8	$247.6
Charges net of reversals	181.4	5.8	2.3	118.7	16.7	324.9
Utilizations	(221.7)	(7.8)	(4.8)	(115.2)	(4.8)	(354.3)
Unwinding of discount	1.4	0.5	0.1	—	—	2.0
Change in discount rate	(0.3)	1.4	—	—	—	1.1
Balance at January 1, 2011	$109.7	24.8	6.8	65.3	14.7	$221.3
Less: Current portion	106.1	7.3	3.4	65.3	14.1	196.2
Long-term portion	$ 3.6	$17.5	$ 3.4	$ —	$ 0.6	$ 25.1

Warranties and Returns

The provision for warranties and returns relates to the Company's obligation to stores within its Dealer network for defective goods in their current inventories and defective goods sold to customers throughout its store operations that have yet to be returned, as well as after sales and service for replacement parts. The Company undertakes to make good, by repair, replacement or refund any manufacturing defects that become apparent within one year from the date of sale unless stated otherwise. The provisions are based on estimates made from actual historical experience and data associated with similar products and services. The Company expects to incur substantially all of the liability over the next year.

The Company is reimbursed for defective goods from either the suppliers the products were purchased from or its Dealer network as part of its agreement with its Dealers.

32. Revenue

(C$ in Millions)	2011	2010
Sale of goods	$ 8,997.6	$7,853.8
Interest income on loans receivable	697.2	685.4
Services rendered	354.7	353.7
Royalties and license fees	325.9	310.0
Rental income	11.7	10.2
	$10,387.1	$9,213.1

Major Customers

Revenue is earned from a variety of customers. CTR, Mark's and FGL Sports sell merchandise to a network of over 750 independent Dealers and franchisees. Financial Services and Petroleum provide goods and services to millions of customers. The Company does not have a reliance on any one customer.

Customer Loyalty

The Company maintains a provision related to its loyalty programs, including paper-based "Canadian Tire Money" issued at Petroleum gas bars and issued to Dealers, "Electronic Canadian Tire Money on-the-Card" issued whenever consumers make a Canadian Tire Options MasterCard purchase from any location in the World, and Canadian Tire coins issued to customers at Dealers. The provisions are measured at fair value by reference to the fair value of the awards for which they can be redeemed multiplied by the estimate of the probability of their redemption. The Company expects to discharge substantially all of the liability over the next year.

44. Transition to International Financial Reporting Standards (in part)

The Company has adopted IFRS effective January 2, 2011. Prior to the adoption of IFRS, the Company presented its financial statements in accordance with previous Canadian Generally Accepted Accounting Principles ("previous GAAP"). As a result, the 2010 comparative information has been adjusted from amounts previous reported in the Company's financial statements prepared in accordance with previous GAAP. IFRS 1—*First-time Adoption of International Financial Reporting Standards* ("IFRS 1"), requires first-time adopters to apply IFRS Standards retrospectively as if IFRS had been in effect from the date of the Company's inception. The Company's transition date is January 3, 2010 (the "Transition Date") and an opening Consolidated Balance Sheet has been prepared as at that date. These consolidated financial statements have been presented in accordance with the IFRS accounting policies discussed in Note 3.

D. Reconciliation of Shareholders' Equity From Previous GAAP to IFRS (in part)

The following is a reconciliation of the Company's total Shareholders' Equity reported in accordance with previous GAAP to its Shareholders' Equity reported in accordance with IFRS for the following dates:

(C$ in Millions)	Note	January 1, 2011	January 3, 2010
Total Shareholders' Equity as reported under previous GAAP		$4,066.7	$3,687.9
Transitional adjustments:			
Property and equipment	i	(1.0)	(0.6)
Impairment	ii	(2.5)	(1.3)
Leases	iii	22.8	35.4
Provisions	iv	(24.9)	(24.7)
Loyalty programs	v	(1.2)	(1.6)
Employee benefits	vi	(22.0)	(14.2)
Share-based payments	vii	(6.0)	(6.7)
Consolidation	viii	(0.2)	—
Securitization	ix	(48.0)	(49.2)
Financial instruments	x	0.4	1.1
Foreign exchange translation	xi	4.2	4.2
Income taxes	xii	16.4	12.8
Other		0.2	—
Total transitional adjustments		(61.8)	(44.8)
Total Shareholders' Equity as reported under IFRS		$4,004.9	$3,643.1

The following is an explanation of the adjustments to shareholders' equity:

(v) Loyalty Programs

IFRIC 13—*Customer Loyalty Programmes* requires award credits granted as part of a sales transaction to be accounted for as a separate component of revenue earned on the transaction. Revenue earned on the transaction is allocated to the award credit based on its fair value and deferred until the award credits are redeemed, unless a third party provides the awards, in which case revenue is deferred until the Company fulfills its obligations to the customer in respect of the awards. As a result, the Company has deferred revenue earned on transactions relating to its loyalty programs until the Company has fulfilled its obligation to the customer.

SECTION 2: STATEMENT OF FINANCIAL POSITION AND RELATED DISCLOSURES[1]

INTERNATIONAL ACCOUNTING STANDARDS 1, *PRESENTATION OF FINANCIAL STATEMENTS*

INTERNATIONAL ACCOUNTING STANDARDS 27, *CONSOLIDATED AND SEPARATE FINANCIAL STATEMENTS*

THE CONCEPTUAL FRAMEWORK FOR FINANCIAL REPORTING

Author's Note

Several items that readers may associate with a statement of financial position are covered in other sections within this publication more specific to that topic:

- Government grants and customer loyalty programs (see section 1, "General Topics and Related Disclosures")
- Income, expenses, gains, losses, and changes in fair value associated with balance sheet items (see section 3, "Statement of Comprehensive Income and Related Disclosures")
- Cash and cash equivalents (see section 5, "Statement of Cash Flows and Related Disclosures")
- Construction contracts, assets held for sale, liabilities held for sale, and share-based payments (see section 6, "Noncurrent Assets Held for Sale and Discontinued Operations")
- Financial instruments and related disclosures, loans and receivables, available for sale financial assets, held to maturity investments, financial assets or financial liabilities held for trading, financial assets or financial liabilities designated as fair value through profit or loss, accounts payable, and financial liabilities held at amortized cost (see section 8, "Financial Instruments and Related Disclosures")

Author's Note

In 2010 and 2011, the International Accounting Standards Board (IASB) issued the following standards, which amended International Accounting Standard (IAS) 1, *Presentation of Financial Statements*:

- International Financial Reporting Standard (IFRS) 9, *Financial Instruments* (issued November 2009 and October 2010 with an effective date of 1 January 2015)

This amendment replaces some references to IAS 39, *Financial Instruments: Recognition and Measurement*, with references to IFRS 9

- IFRS 10, *Consolidated Financial Statements* (issued May 2011 with an effective date of 1 January 2013)
- IFRS 12, *Disclosure of Interests in Other Entities* (issued May 2011 with an effective date of 1 January 2013)

Amendments in IFRS 10 and IFRS 12 replace references to IAS 27, *Consolidated and Separate Financial Statements*, with references to IFRS 10 and delete the example of management judgments with respect to special purpose entities. In addition, the amendment in IFRS 12 replaces an example of disclosure related to IAS 31, *Interests in Joint Ventures*, with one related to IAS 40, *Investment Property*, and also adds an example of disclosure of judgment made in determining whether an entity controls another entity required by IFRS 12

- IFRS 13, *Fair Value Measurement* (issued May 2011 with an effective date of 1 January 2013)

These amendments replace a reference to IFRS 7, *Financial Instruments: Disclosures*, with a reference to IFRS 13 in a discussion of other IFRSs that require disclosures of assumptions and replace the phrase "recently observed market prices" with "a quoted price in an active market for an identical asset or liability."

Because these standards are effective for annual reporting periods beginning on or after 1 January 2012, their requirements are not reflected in the commentary in this section. In addition, the timing of the effective dates of these standards affects the availability of illustrative excerpts from survey companies' financial statements. Accordingly, the excerpts appearing later in this section may not reflect all or some of these revisions.

IFRS Overview and Comparison to U.S. GAAP

2.01 IAS 1 requires a statement of financial position (that is, a balance sheet) at the end of the period as part of a complete set of financial statements, but does not prescribe a particular title for the statement. IAS 27 (2011) requires an entity to present a balance sheet that includes all entities (subsidiaries) that it controls, except in certain circumstances.

2.02 A complete set of financial statements should include two balance sheets: one for the end of the current period and one for the comparable previous period, except when IFRSs permit or require otherwise. For example, when an entity applies a change in accounting principle retrospectively, it

---

[1] Unless otherwise indicated, references to International Accounting Standards Board (IASB) standards and interpretations throughout this 2012 edition of *IFRS Financial Statements—Best Practices in Presentation and Disclosure* refer to the version of those standards and interpretations included in the *IFRS 2012* bound volume, the official printed consolidated text of IASB standards and interpretations, including revisions, amendments, and supporting documents, applicable as of 1 January 2012.

should include a restated balance sheet as at the beginning of the earliest period presented.

2.03 When an entity changes the presentation or classification of balance sheet items, it should also reclassify comparative period information, unless it is impracticable to do so.

2.04 *The Conceptual Framework for Financial Reporting* (IFRS *Conceptual Framework*) establishes the concepts that underlie the preparation and presentation of financial statements for external users and contains definitions of the elements of financial statements (that is, assets, liabilities, equity, income, and expenses). Among other purposes, the IFRS *Conceptual Framework* assists preparers of financial statements in applying IFRSs and in dealing with topics that have yet to form the subject of a specific standard or interpretation. IAS 8, *Accounting Policies, Changes in Accounting Estimates and Errors*, states that an entity's management should first refer to, and first consider the applicability of, the requirements in IFRSs dealing with similar and related issues and then to the definitions, recognition criteria, and measurement concepts in the IFRS *Conceptual Framework*. Although the IFRS *Conceptual Framework* is not a standard, the requirements of IAS 8 essentially establish the IFRS *Conceptual Framework* as part of the IFRS hierarchy of accounting and reporting requirements.

Presentation

IFRSs

2.05 At a minimum, IAS 1 requires a balance sheet to include the following line items:
- Financial assets, such as the following:
  — Cash and cash equivalents
  — Trade and other receivables
  — Investments accounted for using the equity method (for example, associates and some joint ventures)
  — Other financial assets (excluding the amounts included in the preceding line items)
- Inventories
- Property, plant, and equipment (PPE)
- Investment property
- Intangible assets
- Biological assets
- Assets and related liabilities classified as held for sale or included in disposal groups classified as held for sale under IFRS 5, *Non-current Assets Held for Sale and Discontinued Operations*, such as the following:
  — Total of assets held for sale and assets included in disposal groups
  — Liabilities included in disposal groups
- Income tax assets and liabilities as defined in IAS 12, *Income Taxes*, such as the following:
  — Assets and liabilities for current tax
  — Deferred tax assets and liabilities
- Financial liabilities, such as the following:
  — Trade and other payables
  — Other financial liabilities (excluding amounts shown in the preceding line items)
- Provisions
- Noncontrolling interest presented within equity
- Issued capital and reserves attributable to owners of the parent

- Additional line items, headings, and subtotals when presentation of these is relevant to understanding the entity's financial position

2.06 IAS 1 requires an entity to present a classified balance sheet, except when a presentation based on liquidity provides reliable, but more relevant information. A classified balance sheet presents current and noncurrent assets and liabilities separately. However, IAS 1 does not prescribe a particular organization of information (for example, either an increasing or a decreasing order of liquidity).

2.07 A *current asset* is one that the entity expects to realize, intends to sell or consume in its normal operating cycle or 12 months after the reporting date, or holds for trading, or is a cash or cash equivalent whose exchange or use is unrestricted for at least 12 months after the reporting date. Similarly, a *current liability* is one that the entity intends to settle within its normal operating cycle or 12 months after the reporting date. In addition, an entity also classifies as current a liability for which it has no unconditional right to defer settlement for at least 12 months after the reporting date, including those with terms that could, at the option of the counterparty, result in settlement by issue of equity instruments. An entity should classify all other assets and liabilities as noncurrent.

2.08 IAS 1 permits a liquidity order balance sheet when it provides more relevant information to users of the financial statements, which may be true for financial institutions (including banks and insurance companies). IAS 1 also permits a mixed presentation (that is, some assets and liabilities in the classified format and others in liquidity order) when it provides more relevant information to users. A mixed presentation may be more relevant when an entity has diverse operations (for example, an entity with both manufacturing and finance subsidiaries).

2.09 Regardless of the method of organization selected, an entity should distinguish amounts it expects to realize or settle within 12 months after the reporting date from those it expects to realize or settle later when combined in a single line item on the balance sheet.

2.10 Specific IFRSs may require additional disclosures about balance sheet items. For example, IAS 39 requires entities to present treasury stock as a contraequity account (reduction) within stockholders' equity.

U.S. GAAP

2.11 The Financial Accounting Standards Board (FASB) *Accounting Standards Codification*™ (ASC) requires an entity to present a balance sheet, although a comparative balance sheet is preferred. U.S. Securities and Exchange Commission (SEC) Regulation S-X, together with Financial Reporting Releases, prescribe the form and content of, and requirements for, financial statements filed with the SEC. Rule 3A-02 of SEC Regulation S-X generally requires consolidated financial statements, although it does allow combined financial statements in some circumstances. Rule 3-01(a) of SEC Regulation S-X also requires an entity to present a consolidated balance sheet for the current period and one comparative period, unless the registrant has been in existence for less than one year. SEC regulations are more prescriptive in terms of formats than IFRSs.

2.12 FASB ASC does not require an entity to present a classified balance sheet or mandate any particular ordering of balance sheet accounts. However, FASB ASC 210-10-05-4 states that companies usually present a classified balance sheet to facilitate calculation of working capital. The FASB ASC glossary includes definitions of *current assets* and *liabilities*, similar to those in IFRSs, if an entity chooses to use this classification. FASB ASC 210-10-45 provides additional guidance for determining these classifications. FASB ASC provides additional guidance with respect to specific assets and liabilities. For example, IFRSs are more prescriptive with respect to required line items.

Disclosure

IFRSs

2.13 As appropriate to its operations, entities should disclose additional subclassifications of the required line items, either on the face of the balance sheet or in the notes. For each class of share capital, however, entities should disclose the following:
- Number of shares authorized
- Number of shares issued and fully paid
- Number of shares issued and not fully paid
- Par value or that shares have no par
- Reconciliation of the number of shares outstanding at the beginning and end of the period
- Rights, preferences, and restrictions, including restrictions on dividend distributions or repayment of capital
- Shares reserved for issue under share-based payment or sale contracts, including terms and amounts

2.14 Entities should also describe the nature and purpose of each reserve. Entities without share capital (for example, trusts) should disclose information similar to the requirements previously mentioned.

2.15 Specific IFRSs may require additional disclosures about balance sheet items.

U.S. GAAP

2.16 FASB ASC also sets forth disclosure guidelines regarding capital structure and other balance sheet items. Depending upon the specific asset, liability, or capital account, FASB ASC may be more or less prescriptive than IFRSs. SEC regulations also contain additional requirements for disclosures that registrants should provide outside the financial statements.

TABLE 2-1: FORMAT OF STATEMENT OF FINANCIAL POSITION

	2011	2010	2009
Classified			
Current assets, noncurrent assets, current liabilities, noncurrent liabilities, equity..........	84	51	43
Noncurrent assets, current assets, equity, noncurrent liabilities, current liabilities........	54	67	64
Noncurrent assets, current assets, current liabilities, noncurrent liabilities, equity..........	16	30	32
Noncurrent assets, current assets, noncurrent liabilities, current liabilities, equity...............	0	5	4
Liquidity Order			
Most current to least current............................	18	14	14
Least current to most current...........................	2	3	3
Most current to least current, except equity appears before liabilities............................	1	0	0
Total..	**175**	**170**	**160**

TABLE 2-2: CAPITAL STRUCTURE

	2011	2010	2009
Companies With One Class of Common Stock and:			
No other equity instrument.............................	117	110	107
One class of preferred stock...........................	16	20	18
Two or more classes of preferred stock...........	7	9	9
Total...	**140**	**139**	**134**
Dual-Listed Companies			
Each Company has one class of common stock..	2	5	5
Other Companies With More Than One Class of Common Stock and:			
No other equity instrument.............................	26	20	18
One class of preferred stock...........................	4	4	3
Two or more classes of preferred stock...........	0	1	0
Total...	**30**	**25**	**21**
Companies With Only Another Equity Instrument (For Example, Units).............	**3**	**1**	**0**
Total Companies..	**175**	**170**	**160**

Presentation and Disclosure Excerpts

Classified Presentation—Decreasing Liquidity

2.17

LG Display Co., Ltd (Dec 2011)

CONSOLIDATED STATEMENTS OF FINANCIAL POSITION

(In Millions of Won)	Note	December 31, 2010	December 31, 2011
Assets			
Cash and cash equivalents	6	(Won) 1,631,009	1,517,977
Deposits in banks	6, 13	1,503,000	815,000
Trade accounts and notes receivable, net	7, 13, 20, 24	3,000,661	2,740,107
Other accounts receivable, net	7, 13	244,662	212,870
Other current financial assets	9, 13	35,370	3,297
Inventories	8	2,215,217	2,317,370
Other current assets	7	210,514	251,444
Total current assets		8,840,433	7,858,065
Investments in equity accounted investees	10	325,532	385,145
Other non-current financial assets	9, 13	83,246	84,548
Deferred tax assets	31	1,074,853	1,424,005
Property, plant and equipment, net	11, 24	12,815,401	14,696,849
Intangible assets, net	12, 24	539,901	535,114
Other non-current assets	7, 13	178,292	179,205
Total non-current assets		15,017,225	17,304,866
Total assets		(Won) 23,857,658	25,162,931
Liabilities			
Trade accounts and notes payable	23	(Won) 2,961,995	3,782,627
Current financial liabilities	13, 14	2,100,979	894,972
Other accounts payable		2,592,527	3,992,671
Accrued expenses		373,717	267,595
Income tax payable		153,890	58,259
Provisions	15	634,815	279,403
Advances received		44,879	616,351
Other current liabilities	19	19,027	19,556
Total current liabilities		8,881,829	9,911,434
Non-current financial liabilities	13, 14	2,542,900	3,722,364
Non-current provisions	15	8,773	5,400
Deferred tax liabilities	31	6,640	240
Employee benefits	18	78,715	146,638
Long-term advances received	20	945,287	668,914
Other non-current liabilities	19	332,547	576,913
Total non-current liabilities		3,914,862	5,120,469
Total liabilities		12,796,691	15,031,903
Equity			
Share capital	22	1,789,079	1,789,079
Share premium		2,251,113	2,251,113
Reserves	22	(35,298)	12,181
Retained earnings		7,031,163	6,063,359
Total equity attributable to equity holders of the Company		11,036,057	10,115,732
Non-controlling interests		24,910	15,296
Total equity		11,060,967	10,131,028
Total liabilities and equity		(Won) 23,857,658	25,162,931

Classified Presentation—Increasing Liquidity

2.18

Promotoria de Informaciones, S.A. (Dec 2011)

CONSOLIDATED BALANCE SHEETS

(Thousands of Euros)

Assets	Notes	12/31/11	12/31/10	Equity and Liabilities	Notes	12/31/11	12/31/10
A) Non-Current Assets		6,178,703	6,293,489	A) Equity	11	2,218,035	2,650,185
I. Property, Plant and Equipment	5	307,441	295,560	I. Share Capital		84,786	84,698
II. Goodwill	6	3,645,077	3,903,514	II. Other Reserves		1,152,640	1,120,539
III. Intangible Assets	7	331,260	360,512	III. Accumulated Profit		380,282	798,876
				—From prior years		831,500	871,746
				—For the year: Profit attributable to the Parent		(451,218)	(72,870)
IV. Non-Current Financial Assets	8	121,688	70,611				
V. Investments Accounted for Using the Equity Method	9	604,082	613,542	IV. Treasury Shares		(2,505)	(4,804)
VI. Deferred Tax Assets	20	1,166,694	1,046,030	V. Exchange Differences		9,755	20,213
VII. Other Non-Current Assets		2,461	3,720	VI. Non-Controlling Interests		593,077	630,663
				B) Non-Current Liabilities		3,882,329	3,526,496
B) Current Assets		1,699,696	1,854,312				
I. Inventories	10	275,403	203,152	I. Non-Current Bank Borrowings	12	3,176,491	2,931,190
				II. Non-Current Financial Liabilities	12-13	302,864	362,754
II. Trade and Other Receivables							
1. Trade receivables for sales and services		940,067	999,237	III. Deferred Tax Liabilities	20	30,409	28,555
2. Receivable from associates		29,500	35,908				
3. Receivable from public authorities	20	61,374	39,733	IV. Long-Term Provisions	14	356,520	185,592
4. Other receivables		309,776	255,492				
5. Allowances		(71,076)	(84,683)	V. Other Non-Current Liabilities		16,045	18,405
		1,269,641	1,245,687				
				C) Current Liabilities		1,778,160	1,974,773
III. Current Financial Assets		56,494	160,260				
				I. Trade Payables		1,180,075	1,234,846
IV. Cash and Cash Equivalents		98,158	244,988				
				II. Payable to Associates		13,870	16,361
V. Other Current Assets		—	225				
				III. Other Non-Trade Payables		115,865	99,583
				IV. Current Bank Borrowings	12	223,625	411,109
				V. Current Financial Liabilities	12-13	88,853	17,788
				VI. Payable to Public Authorities	20	114,814	154,879
				VII. Provisions for Returns		8,686	9,804
				VIII. Other Current Liabilities		32,372	30,403
C) Assets Held for Sale		125	3,653				
Total assets		7,878,524	8,151,454	Total equity and liabilities		7,878,524	8,151,454

Liquidity Order Presentation—Decreasing Liquidity

2.19

Woori Finance Holdings Co., Ltd. (Dec 2011)

Author's Note

Woori Financial Holdings Co., Ltd. implemented IFRSs effective December 31, 2011, with a date of transition of January 1, 2009. The excerpt that follows reflects the initial application of IAS 1.

CONSOLIDATED STATEMENTS OF FINANCIAL POSITION

	Korean Won			U.S. Dollars
	January 1, 2010	December 31, 2010	December 31, 2011	December 31, 2011
		(In Millions)		(In Thousands) (Note 2)
Assets				
Cash and cash equivalents	5,805,996	4,871,109	6,417,123	5,539,165
Financial assets at fair value through profit or loss (Notes 6, 7, 11, 25 and 26)	25,151,525	22,183,761	25,600,231	22,097,739
Available-for-sale financial assets (Notes 8, 11, 17 and 44)	21,337,500	21,997,884	19,671,924	16,980,513
Held-to-maturity financial assets (Notes 9 and 11)	15,953,709	19,885,559	20,036,128	17,294,888
Loans and receivables (Notes 6, 10, 11, 17, 31, 43 and 44)	211,057,174	216,791,805	235,159,956	202,986,583
Investments in jointly controlled entities and associates (Note 12)	655,721	744,844	928,233	801,237
Investment properties (Notes 13 and 16)	746,126	643,271	498,999	430,729
Premises and equipment (Notes 14, 16 and 17)	3,095,029	3,097,378	3,134,472	2,705,630
Intangible assets and goodwill (Notes 15 and 45)	315,187	295,136	447,891	386,613
Current tax assets (Note 40)	28,203	9,568	56,570	48,829
Deferred tax assets (Note 40)	74,101	58,705	79,980	69,038
Derivative assets (Notes 11 and 25)	107,490	131,511	326,840	282,123
Assets held for sale (Note 16)	28,423	87,926	56,243	48,548
Other assets (Notes 16, 18 and 44)	484,822	378,861	377,059	325,472
Total assets	284,841,006	291,177,318	312,791,649	269,997,107
Liabilities				
Financial liabilities at fair value through profit or loss (Notes 11,19, 25 and 26)	10,415,070	8,838,281	9,621,546	8,305,176
Deposits due to customers (Notes 11, 20 and 44)	176,926,868	185,427,625	195,930,482	169,124,283
Borrowings (Notes 11 and 21)	32,455,007	34,265,662	34,666,709	29,923,789
Debentures (Notes 11 and 21)	32,573,979	29,110,640	29,265,833	25,261,833
Provisions (Note 22)	693,521	761,055	892,308	770,227
Retirement benefit obligation (Note 23)	123,011	69,949	119,704	103,327
Current tax liabilities (Note 40)	127,871	173,960	274,257	236,735
Deferred tax liabilities (Note 40)	241,796	212,534	260,431	224,798
Derivative liabilities (Notes 11 and 25)	41,236	5,339	33,493	28,911
Other financial liabilities (Notes 11, 24, 43 and 44)	11,226,749	11,648,328	19,083,709	16,472,774
Other liabilities (Notes 24 and 44)	804,494	399,191	569,783	491,828
Total liabilities	265,629,602	270,912,564	290,718,255	250,943,681
Equity				
Owners' equity:	14,734,993	15,701,540	17,523,998	15,126,455
Capital stock (Note 27)	4,030,077	4,030,077	4,030,077	3,478,703
Hybrid securities (Note 28)	—	—	309,010	266,733
Capital surplus (Note 27)	180,473	180,105	175,768	151,720
Other equity (Note 29)	1,244,096	1,002,019	586,421	506,190
Retained earnings (Note 30)	9,280,347	10,489,339	12,422,722	10,723,109
Non-controlling interests	4,476,411	4,563,214	4,549,396	3,926,971
Total equity	19,211,404	20,264,754	22,073,394	19,053,426
Total liabilities and equity	284,841,006	291,177,318	312,791,649	269,997,107

Liquidity Presentation—Increasing Liquidity

2.20

AEGON N.V. (Dec 2011)

CONSOLIDATED STATEMENTS OF FINANCIAL POSITION

Amounts in EUR Million	Note	2011	2010
Assets			
Intangible assets	21	3,285	4,359
Investments	22	144,079	143,188
Investments for account of policyholders	23	142,529	146,237
Derivatives	24	15,504	6,251
Investments in associates	25	742	733
Reinsurance assets	26	11,517	5,580
Defined benefit assets	41	303	352
Deferred tax assets	43	89	512
Deferred expenses and rebates	27	11,633	11,948
Other assets and receivables	28	7,792	7,831
Cash and cash equivalents	29	8,104	5,231
Total assets		345,577	332,222
Equity and Liabilities			
Shareholders' equity	30	21,000	17,328
Convertible core capital securities	31	—	1,500
Other equity instruments	32	4,720	4,704
Issued capital and reserves attributable to equity holders of AEGON N.V.		25,720	23,532
Non-controlling interests		14	11
Group equity		25,734	23,543
Trust pass-through securities	33	159	143
Subordinated borrowings	34	18	—
Insurance contracts	35	105,175	100,506
Insurance contracts for account of policyholders	36	73,425	77,650
Investment contracts	37	20,847	23,237
Investment contracts for account of policyholders	38	71,433	69,527
Derivatives	24	12,728	5,971
Borrowings	39	10,141	8,518
Provisions	40	444	357
Defined benefit liabilities	41	2,184	2,152
Deferred revenue liabilities	42	104	82
Deferred tax liabilities	43	2,499	1,583
Other liabilities	44	19,501	18,537
Accruals	45	1,185	416
Total liabilities		319,843	308,679
Total equity and liabilities		345,577	332,222

One Class of Share Capital

2.21

Maple Leaf Foods Inc. (Dec 2011)

CONSOLIDATED BALANCE SHEETS *(in part)*

(In Thousands of Canadian Dollars)	As at December 31, 2011	As at December 31, 2010 (See Note 27)	As at January 1, 2010 (See Note 27)
Shareholders' equity			
Share capital (Note 15)	$ 902,810	$ 902,810	$ 869,353
Retained earnings (deficit)	(78,674)	(5,267)	24,076
Contributed surplus	64,327	59,002	57,486
Accumulated other comprehensive loss (Note 15)	(17,042)	(22,585)	(5,055)
Treasury stock	(6,347)	(10,078)	(24,499)
Total shareholders' equity	$ 865,074	$ 923,882	$ 921,361
Non-controlling interest	65,039	62,890	60,442
Total equity	$ 930,113	$ 986,772	$ 981,803
Total liabilities and equity	$2,940,459	$2,834,910	$3,075,039

NOTES TO THE CONSOLIDATED FINANCIAL STATEMENTS *(in part)*

1. The Company

Maple Leaf Foods Inc. ("Maple Leaf Foods" or the "Company") is a leading Canadian-based value-added meat, meals and bakery company, serving wholesale, retail and foodservice customers across North America and internationally. The address of the Company's registered office is Suite 1500, 30 St. Clair Avenue West, Toronto, Ontario, M4V 3A2, Canada. The consolidated financial statements of the Company as at and for the year ended December 31, 2011 include the accounts of the Company and its subsidiaries. The Company's results are organized into three segments: Meat Products Group, Agribusiness Group and Bakery Products Group.

15. Capital and Other Components of Equity

Share Capital

(Thousands of Shares)	Common Shares 2011	Common Shares 2010	Treasury Stock 2011	Treasury Stock 2010
On issue at January 1	139,247	134,859	797	1,915
Issued for cash	—	3,270	—	—
Distributions under stock compensation plans	2,770	1,173	(2,770)	(1,173)
Purchase of treasury stock	(2,500)	(55)	2,500	55
Balance at December 31	139,517	139,247	527	797

Common Shares

The authorized share capital consists of an unlimited number of common shares, an unlimited number of non-voting common shares and an unlimited number of preference shares. These shares have no par value.

The holders of common shares are entitled to receive dividends as declared from time to time, and are entitled to one vote per share at meetings of the Company.

Shareholder Rights Plan

On July 28, 2011, the Company announced a Shareholder Rights Plan (the "Rights Plan"). It follows a previous plan that was allowed to expire on December 29, 2010. The Rights Plan was not adopted in response to any actual or anticipated transaction, but rather to allow the Board of Directors of the Company and its shareholders sufficient time to consider fully any transaction involving the acquisition or proposed acquisition of 20% or more of the outstanding common shares of the Company. The plan allows the Board of Directors time to consider all alternatives and to ensure the fair treatment of shareholders should any such transaction be initiated. One right has been issued with respect to each common share of the Company issued and outstanding as of the close of business on July 27, 2011. Should such an acquisition occur or be announced, each right would, upon exercise, entitle a rights holder, other than the acquiring person and related persons, to purchase common shares of the Company at a 50% discount to the market price at the time. The Rights Plan was approved by shareholders at a special meeting of the shareholders on December 14, 2011.

Treasury Shares

Shares are purchased by a trust in order to satisfy the requirements of the Company's stock compensation plan, as described in Note 21.

Accumulated Other Comprehensive Loss Attributable to Common Shareholders

	Foreign Currency Translation Adjustments	Unrealized Gain (Loss) on Cash Flow Hedges	Change in Actuarial Gains (Losses)	Change in Asset Ceiling and Minimum Funding Requirements	Total Accumulated Other Comprehensive Income (Loss)
Balance at January 1, 2011	$(12,764)	$(9,821)	$ —	$ —	$(22,585)
Other comprehensive income (loss)	5,321	222	(127,336)	12,680	(109,113)
Transfer to retained earnings (deficit)	—	—	127,336	(12,680)	114,656
Balance at December 31, 2011	$ (7,443)	$(9,599)	$ —	$ —	$(17,042)

	Foreign Currency Translation Adjustments	Unrealized Gain (Loss) on Cash Flow Hedges	Change in Actuarial Gains and Losses	Change in Asset Ceiling and Minimum Funding Requirements	Total Accumulated Other Comprehensive Income (Loss)
Balance at January 1, 2010	$ —	$(5,055)	$ —	$ —	$ (5,055)
Other comprehensive income (loss)	(12,764)	(4,766)	(62,643)	29,832	(50,341)
Transferred to retained earnings (deficit)	—	—	62,643	(29,832)	32,811
Balance at December 31, 2010	$(12,764)	$(9,821)	$ —	$ —	$(22,585)

The change in accumulated foreign currency translation adjustments includes tax of $0.1 million for the year ended December 31, 2011 (2010: $0.3 million).

The change in unrealized loss on cash flow hedges includes tax of $0.2 million for the year ended December 31, 2011 (2010: $1.2 million).

The Company estimates that $1.4 million of the unrealized loss included in accumulated other comprehensive loss will be reclassified into net earnings within the next 12 months. The actual amount of this reclassification will be impacted by future changes in the fair value of financial instruments designated as cash flow hedges and the actual amount reclassified could differ from this estimated amount. During the year ended December 31, 2011, a loss of approximately $5.3 million, net of tax of $2.0 million (2010: $2.9 million, net of tax $1.2 million), was released to earnings from accumulated other comprehensive loss and is included in the net change for the period.

Dividends

The following dividends were declared and paid by the Company:

	2011	2010
$0.16 per qualifying common share (2010: $0.16)	$22,386	$21,677

16. Financial Instruments and Risk Management Activities

Capital

The Company's objective is to maintain a cost effective capital structure that supports its long-term growth strategy and maximizes operating flexibility. In allocating capital to investments to support its earnings goals, the Company establishes internal hurdle return rates for capital initiatives. Capital projects are generally financed with senior debt and internal cash flows.

The Company uses leverage in its capital structure to reduce the cost of capital. The Company's goal is to maintain its primary credit ratios and leverage at levels that are designed to provide continued access to investment-grade credit pricing and terms. The Company measures its credit profile using a number of metrics, some of which are non-IFRS measures, primarily net debt to earnings before interest, income taxes, depreciation, amortization, restructuring and other related costs ("EBITDA") and interest coverage.

The following ratios are used by the Company to monitor its capital:

	2011	2010
Interest coverage (EBITDA to net interest expense)	5.5x	5.5x
Leverage ratio (Net debt to EBITDA)	2.5x	2.5x

The Company's various credit facilities, all of which are unsecured, are subject to certain financial covenants. As at December 31, 2011, the Company was in compliance with all of these covenants.

In addition to senior debt and equity, the Company uses operating leases and very limited recourse accounts receivable securitization programs as additional sources of financing.

The Company has maintained a stable dividend distribution that is based on a sustainable net earnings base. From time to time, the Company has purchased shares for cancellation pursuant to normal course issuer bids and to satisfy awards under its Restricted Share Unit plan.

Multiple Classes of Common Share Capital, Restrictions and Limitations on Acquisition of Series AA Shares

2.22

America Movil S.A.B. de C.V. (Dec 2011)

CONSOLIDATED STATEMENTS OF FINANCIAL POSITION (in part)

(In thousands of Mexican pesos)

	At December 31 2010	At December 31 2011	Millions of U.S. Dollars 2011
Equity (Note 19):			
Capital stock	96,433,461	96,419,636	6,892
Retained earnings:			
Prior years	105,009,640	81,198,952	5,804
Profit for the period	91,123,052	82,853,529	5,922
Total retained earnings	196,132,692	164,052,481	11,726
Other comprehensive income items	15,085,830	25,168,067	1,799
Equity attributable to equity holders of the parent	307,651,983	285,640,184	20,417
Non-controlling interests	28,385,187	9,999,511	715
Total equity	336,037,170	295,639,695	21,132
Total liabilities and equity	Ps. 873,515,603	Ps. 945,616,861	US$ 67,590

NOTES TO THE CONSOLIDATED FINANCIAL STATEMENTS (in part)

1. Description of the Business and Relevant Events (in part)

América Móvil, S.A.B. de C.V. and subsidiaries (hereinafter, the "Company or "América Móvil") was incorporated under laws of Mexico on September 25, 2000. The Company provides telecommunications services in 18 countries throughout the United States, Latin America and the Caribbean. These telecommunications services include mobile and fixed voice services, mobile and fixed data services, internet access and paid TV, as well as other related services.

- The voice services provided by the Company, both mobile and fixed, mainly include the following: airtime, local, domestic and international long-distance services, and network interconnection services.
- The data services provided by the Company include the following: value added, corporate networks, data and Internet services.

Paid TV represents basic services, as well as pay per view and additional programming and advertising services.

- Related services mainly include equipment and computer sales, and revenues from advertising in telephone directories, editing services and call center services.

In order to provide these services, América Móvil has the necessary licenses, permits and concessions (collectively referred to herein as "licenses") to build, install, operate and exploit public and/or private telecommunications networks and provide miscellaneous telecommunications services (mostly mobile and fixed telephony services), as well as to operate frequency bands in the radio-electric spectrum to be able to provide fixed wireless telephony and to operate frequency bands in the radio-electric spectrum for point-to-point and

point-to-multipoint microwave links. The Company holds licenses in the 18 countries where it has a presence, and such licenses have different dates of expiration through 2046. In the next two fiscal years there are no contingent liabilities for license expiration and/or termination.

Certain licenses require the payment to the respective governments of a share in sales determined as a percentage of revenues from services under concession. The percentage is set as either a fixed rate or in some cases based on certain size of the infrastructure in operation.

América Móvil is located in Mexico City at Lago Zurich #245, Colonia Ampliación Granada, Miguel Hidalgo, zip code 11529.

The accompanying financial statements were approved for their issuance by the Board of Directors on April 25, 2012. The financial statements must also be approved by the Company's shareholders, who have the authority to modify the Company's financial statements.

19. Shareholders' Equity

Shares

a) At December 31, 2010 and 2011, the Company's capital stock is represented by 80,346,000,000 shares (23,424,632,660 Series AA shares, 785,607,280 Series A shares and 56,135,760,060 registered Series L shares with no par value and limited voting rights ("Series L")) and 76,992,000,000 shares (23,424,632,660 Series AA shares, 756,967,714 Series A shares and 52,810,399,626 Series L shares), respectively. Capital stock includes (i) the retroactive effect of the stock split in June 2011; (ii) the effect of the merger with AMTEL in 2006; (iii) the re-subscription of 8,438,193,725 Series L treasury shares resulting from the public tender offers and share exchange for Carso Global Telecom, S.A.B. de C.V. and Telmex Internacional, S.A.B. de

C.V., which were completed on June 16, 2010; and (iv) the conversions of Series A shares into Series L shares, made by third parties through S.D. Indeval Institución para el Depósito de Valores, S.A. de C.V. These shares represent the outstanding capital stock of the Company as of December 31, 2011.

b) The capital stock of the Company consists of a minimum fixed portion of Ps. 397,873 (nominal amount), represented by a total of 95,489,724,196 shares (including treasury shares available for re-subscription in accordance with the provisions of the Mexican Securities Law), of which (i) 23,424,632,660 are common Series AA shares; (ii) 776,818,130 are common Series A shares; and (iii) 71,288,273,406 are Series L shares. All such shares have been fully subscribed and paid.

c) At December 31, 2010 and 2011, the Company's treasury shares included shares for re-subscription, in accordance with the provisions of the Mexican Securities Law, in the amount of 15,143,724,196 shares (15,142,656,796 Series L shares and 1,067,400 Series A shares), and 18,497,724,196 shares (18,495,699,196 Series L shares and 2,025,000 Series A shares), respectively. The Company's treasury shares include (i) the conversions of Series A shares into Series L shares performed by the Company through S.D. Indeval Institución para el Depósito de Valores, S.A. de C.V. in 2010; and (ii) the re-subscription of 8,438,193,725 Series L shares in the Company's treasury as a result of the public tender offers and share exchange for Carso Global Telecom, S.A.B. de C.V. and Telmex Internacional, S.A.B. de C.V., which was completed on June 16, 2010).

d) The holders of Series AA and Series A shares are entitled to full voting rights. The holders of Series L shares may only vote in certain circumstances, and they are only entitled to appoint two members of the Board of Directors and their respective alternates. The matters in which the shareholders who are entitled to vote are the following: extension of the term of the Company, early dissolution of the Company, change of corporate purpose of the Company, change of nationality of the Company, transformation of the Company, a merger with another company, as well as the cancellation of the registration of the shares issued by the Company in the National Securities Registry and any other foreign stock exchanges where they may be registered, except for quotation systems or other markets not organized as stock exchanges. Within their respective series, all shares confer the same rights to their holders.

The Company's bylaws contain restrictions and limitations related to the subscription and acquisition of Series AA shares by non-Mexican investors.

e) In accordance with the bylaws of the Company, each share of the Series AA or Series A may be exchanged at the option of the holders for one share of Series L. Series AA shares must at all times represent no less than 20% and no more than 51% of the Company's capital stock, and they also must represent at all times no less than 51% of the common shares (entitled to full voting rights, represented by Series AA and Series A shares) representing capital stock.

Series AA shares may only be subscribed to or acquired by Mexican investors, Mexican corporations and/or trusts expressly empowered for such purposes in accordance with the applicable legislation in force. Common Series A shares, which may be freely subscribed, may not represent more than 19.6% of capital stock and may not exceed 49% of the common shares representing such capital. Common shares (entitled to full voting rights, represented by Series AA and Series A shares) may represent no more than 51% of the Company's capital stock.

Lastly, the combined number of Series L shares, which have limited voting rights and may be freely subscribed, and Series A shares may not exceed 80% of the Company's capital stock. For purposes of determining these restrictions, the percentages mentioned above refer only to the number of Company shares outstanding.

Partnership Capital

2.23

Brookfield Infrastructure Partners L.P. (Dec 2011)

CONSOLIDATED STATEMENTS OF FINANCIAL POSITION (in part)

US$ Millions	Notes	As of December 31, 2011	As of December 31, 2010
Limited partners' capital	25	3,539	2,881
General partner capital	25	19	19
Retained earnings		260	297
Reserves		388	174
Non-controlling interest	27	1,683	1,552
Total partnership capital		5,889	4,923
Total liabilities and partnership capital		$13,269	$13,352

NOTES TO THE CONSOLIDATED FINANCIAL STATEMENTS

Note 1. Organization and Description of the Business

Brookfield Infrastructure Partners L.P. (the "partnership") owns and operates utility businesses, transport and energy businesses and timber assets in North and South America, Australasia, and Europe. The partnership was formed as a limited partnership established under the laws of Bermuda, pursuant to a limited partnership agreement dated May 17, 2007, as amended and restated. The partnership is a subsidiary of Brookfield Asset Management Inc. ("Brookfield"). The partnership's limited partnership units are listed on the New York Stock Exchange and the Toronto Stock Exchange under the symbols "BIP" and "BIP.UN", respectively. The registered office is 73 Front Street, Hamilton, Bermuda.

Note 25. Partnership Capital

	General Partnership Units		Limited Partnership Units		Total	
Units Millions	2011	2010	2011	2010	2011	2010
Authorized to issue						
On issue at January 1	1.1	1.1	156.3	105.6	157.4	106.7
Issued for cash	—	—	27.7	50.7	27.7	50.7
Shares repurchased	—	—	—	—	—	—
On issue at December 31	1.1	1.1	184.0	156.3	185.1	157.4

In October 2011, Brookfield Infrastructure issued 27.7 million Limited Partnership units at $24.75 per unit under our shelf registrations in the U.S. and Canada. In total, $677 million of gross proceeds were raised through this issuance and $20 million in equity issuance costs were incurred.

The weighted average number of general partnership units outstanding for the year ended December 31, 2011 was 1.1 million (2010: 1.1 million; 2009: 0.5 million). The weighted average number of limited partnership units outstanding for the year ended December 31, 2011 was 161.4 million (2010: 108.8 million; 2009: 47.2 million).

	General Partnership		Limited Partnership		Total	
US$ Millions	2011	2010	2011	2010	2011	2010
Opening balance	$19	$19	$2,881	$1,807	$2,900	$1,826
Share issuance	—	—	658	1,074	658	1,074
Ending balance	$19	$19	$3,539	$2,881	$3,558	$2,900

Brookfield Infrastructure's capital structure is comprised of two classes of partnership units: general partnership units and limited partnership units.

Limited partnership units entitle the holder to their proportionate share of distributions. The Holding LP has issued 51.7 million redeemable partnership units to Brookfield, which may, at the request of the holder, require the Holding LP to redeem the units at the market price of the partnership. This right is subject to the partnership's right of first refusal which entitles it, at its sole discretion, to elect to acquire any unit so presented to the Holding LP in exchange for one of the partnership's units (subject to certain customary adjustments). Brookfield's aggregate limited partnership interest in the partnership would be approximately 30% if Brookfield exercised its redemption right in full and the partnership fully exercised its right of first refusal. As the partnership, at its sole discretion, has the right to settle the obligation with limited partnership units, the redeemable partnership units are classified as limited partnership units of Brookfield Infrastructure.

General partnership units entitle the holder the right to govern the financial and operating policies of Brookfield Infrastructure. Further, in its capacity as the general partner of the Holding LP, the general partner is entitled to incentive distribution rights which are based on the amount by which quarterly distributions on the limited partnership units exceed specified target levels. To the extent distributions on limited partnership units exceed $0.305 per quarter, the incentive distribution rights are entitled to 15% of incremental distributions above this threshold. To the extent that distributions on limited partnership units exceed $0.33 per unit, the incentive distribution rights are entitled to 25% of incremental distributions above this threshold. During the year, the partnership paid incentive distributions of $4 million (2010: $nil, 2009: $nil).

In June 2010, we implemented a distribution reinvestment plan ("the Plan") that allows eligible holders of the partnership to purchase additional units by reinvesting their cash distributions. Under the Plan, units are acquired at a price per unit calculated by reference to the volume weighted average of the trading price for our units on the New York Stock Exchange for the five trading days immediately preceding the relevant distribution date. During the period, our partnership issued 17,635 units for proceeds of $1 million (2010: 44 units, for proceeds of less than $1 million) under the Plan.

There are no units reserved for issue under options or other contracts.

Redeemable Preference Shares, Convertible Redeemable Preference Shares, Hybrid Bond

2.24

Shinhan Financial Group (Dec 2011)

Author's Note

Shinhan Financial Group implemented IFRSs effective December 31, 2011, with a date of transition of January 1, 2010. The excerpt that follows reflects the initial application of IAS 1.

CONSOLIDATED STATEMENTS OF FINANCIAL POSITION (in part)

(In Millions of Won)	Note	January 1, 2010	December 31, 2010	December 31, 2011
Equity	30			
Capital stock		2,589,553	2,589,553	2,645,053
Other equity instrument		—	—	238,582
Capital surplus		8,834,971	8,834,971	9,886,849
Capital adjustments		(390,866)	(390,853)	(392,654)
Accumulated other comprehensive income		1,437,048	1,629,495	1,188,948
Retained earnings		9,806,764	12,071,221	10,829,723
Total equity attributable to equity holders of Shinhan Financial Group Co., Ltd.		22,277,470	24,734,387	24,396,501
Non-controlling interests	30	2,464,923	2,460,838	2,462,304
Total equity		24,742,393	27,195,225	26,858,805
Total liabilities and equity		(Won) 258,514,489	268,557,407	288,117,481

NOTES TO THE CONSOLIDATED FINANCIAL STATEMENTS (in part)

1. Reporting Entity (in part)

Shinhan Financial Group Co., Ltd., the controlling company, and its subsidiaries included in consolidation (collectively the "Group") are summarized as follows:

(a) Controlling Company

Shinhan Financial Group Co., Ltd. (the "Shinhan Financial Group") was incorporated on September 1, 2001 through a business combination involving the exchange of Shinhan Financial Group's common stock with the former stockholders of Shinhan Bank, Shinhan Investment Corp., Shinhan Capital Co., Ltd. and Shinhan BNP Paribas AMC. Shinhan Financial Group's shares were listed on the Korea Exchange on September 10, 2001 and Shinhan Financial Group's American Depository Shares were listed on the New York Stock Exchange on September 16, 2003.

30. Equity (in part)

(a) Equity as of January 1, 2010 and December 31, 2010 and 2011 were as follows:

	January 1, 2010	December 31, 2010	December 31, 2011
Capital stock:			
Common stock	(Won) 2,370,998	2,370,998	2,370,998
Preferred stock	218,555	218,555	274,055
	2,589,553	2,589,553	2,645,053

(continued)

	January 1, 2010	December 31, 2010	December 31, 2011
Hybrid bond	—	—	238,582
Capital surplus:			
Share premium	8,444,105	8,444,105	9,494,769
Others	390,866	390,866	392,080
	8,834,971	8,834,971	9,886,849
Capital adjustments	(390,866)	(390,853)	(392,654)
Accumulated other comprehensive income, net of tax:			
Valuation gain(loss) on available-for-sale financial assets	1,494,521	1,668,944	1,208,744
Equity in other comprehensive income of associates	(22,075)	(1,313)	1,404
Foreign currency translation adjustments for foreign operations	—	(17,927)	(1,841)
Net loss from cash flow hedges	(35,416)	(21,930)	(20,501)
Other comprehensive income of separate account	18	1,721	1,142
	1,437,048	1,629,495	1,188,948
Retained earnings:			
Legal reserve(*)	1,021,878	1,152,507	1,390,625
Retained earnings	8,784,886	10,918,714	9,439,098
	9,806,764	12,071,221	10,829,723
Non-controlling interest	2,464,923	2,460,838	2,462,304
	(Won) 24,742,393	27,195,225	26,858,805

(*) Legal reserve was restricted for the dividend to stockholders by law or legislation. According to the article 53 of the Financial Holding Companies Act, the controlling company is required to appropriate a legal reserve in an amount equal to at least 10% of cash dividends for each accounting period until the reserve equals 100% of stated capital. The legal reserve may be used to reduce a deficit or may be transferred to common stocks in connection with a free issue of shares.

(b) Capital Stock

i) Capital stock of the Group as of December 31, 2010 and 2011 was as follows:

Number of authorized shares	1,000,000,000
Par value per share in won	(Won) 5,000
Number of issued common stocks outstanding	474,199,587
Number of issued preferred stocks outstanding	
— As of December 31, 2010	43,711,000
— As of December 31, 2011	54,811,000

ii) Preferred stocks issued by the Group as of December 31, 2011 were as follows:

	Number of Shares	Predetermined Dividend Rate (%)(*1)	Redeemable Period
Redeemable preferred stock:			
Series 10(*2)	28,990,000	7.00%	January 25, 2012—January 25, 2027
Convertible redeemable preferred stock:			
Series 11(*3)	14,721,000	3.25%	January 25, 2012—January 25, 2027
Redeemable preferred stock:			
Series 12(*2)	11,100,000	5.58%	April 21, 2016—April 21, 2031
	54,811,000		

(*1) Based on initial issuance price.
(*2) The Group maintains the right to redeem Series 10 and Series 12 redeemable preferred stock in part or in its entirety within the redeemable year. If the preferred shares are not redeemed by the end of the redeemable year, those rights will lapse.
(*3) Details with respect to the conversion right of the Group are as follows:
  Conversion year : January 26, 2008—January 25, 2012
  Conversion ratio : One common stock per one preferred stock
  Conversion price in won : (Won) 57,806

The following redeemable preferred stocks classified as financial liabilities were redeemed as of December 31, 2011. As a result, the amount of capital stock (preferred stock) in accordance with the Commercial Act differs from the total par value of the outstanding capital stock (preferred stock).

Redemption Year	Redeemable Preferred Stock	Number of Shares Redeemed	Par Value
2010	Series 5	9,316,793	(Won) 46,584
	Series 8	66,666	333
2009	Series 4	9,316,792	46,584
2008	Series 3	9,316,792	46,584
	Series 7	2,433,334	12,167
2007	Series 2	9,316,792	46,584
2006	Series 1	9,316,792	46,584
	Series 6	3,500,000	17,500
Preferred stock classified as financial liabilities		52,583,961	(Won) 262,920
Preferred stock classified as an equity instrument			(Won) 274,055
Capital stock (preferred stock) under the Commercial Act			(Won) 536,975

(c) Hybrid Bond

Hybrid bond classified as other equity as of December 31, 2011 is as follows:

	Issue Date	Maturity Date	Amount	Interest Rate (%)
Hybrid bond	(Won) October 24, 2011	October 24, 2041	238,582	5.8%

Hybrid bond could be redeemed early by the Group from 2017 or 5 years after issue date and the maturity could be extended at maturity date on the same terms. In addition, interests are not paid when there are no dividends on common stockholders.

(d) Capital Adjustments

Changes in capital adjustments for the years ended December 31, 2010 and 2011 were as follows:

	2010	2011
Beginning balance	(Won) (390,866)	(390,853)
Changes in a parent's ownership interest in a subsidiary	62	(1,801)
Other transactions with owners	(49)	—
Ending balance	(Won) (390,853)	(392,654)

Multiple Classes of Preference Shares, Treasury Shares, Non-Controlling Interest

2.25

Braskem S.A. (Dec 2011)

Author's Note

See Section 4, *Statement of Changes in Equity and Related Disclosures,* for additional excerpts about Braskem's shareholder's equity.

CONSOLIDATED BALANCE SHEET (in part)

All amounts in thousands of Brazilian reais

Liabilities and Equity	Note	2011	2010
Equity	29		
Capital		8,043,222	8,043,222
Capital reserve		845,998	845,998
Revenue reserves		591,307	1,338,908
Other comprehensive income		315,586	221,350
Treasury shares		(60,217)	(59,271)
Total attributable to the shareholders of the Company		9,735,896	10,390,207
Non-controlling interest	2.2	215,322	18,079
		9,951,218	10,408,286
Total liabilities and equity		37,354,161	34,477,491

NOTES TO THE CONSOLIDATED FINANCIAL STATEMENTS (in part)

1 Operations (in part)

Braskem S.A. together with its subsidiaries and jointly-controlled subsidiaries ("Braskem" or "Company") is a publicly-held corporation headquartered in Camaçari, State of Bahia, which operates 35 industrial units, 28 of which are located in the Brazilian states of Alagoas, Bahia, Rio de Janeiro, Rio Grande do Sul and São Paulo, five are located in the United States, in the states of Pennsylvania, Texas and West Virginia and two are located in Germany. These units produce basic petrochemicals—such as ethylene, propylene butadiene, toluene, xylene and benzene, as well as gasoline and LPG (Liquefied Petroleum Gas)—and thermoplastic resins—polyethylene, polypropylene and polyvinyl chloride ("PVC"). Additionally, Braskem is also engaged in the import and export of chemicals, petrochemicals and fuels, the production, supply and sale of utilities such as steam, water, compressed air, industrial gases, as well as the provision of industrial services and the production, supply and sale of electric energy for its own use and use by other companies. Braskem also invests in other companies, either as a partner or shareholder.

Braskem is controlled by Odebrecht S.A. ("Odebrecht"), which directly and indirectly holds a 50.1% and a 38.1% interest in its voting and total capital, respectively.

2 Summary of Significant Accounting Policies (in part)

2.2 Basis of Consolidation (in part)

2.2.1 Non-Controlling Interest in the Equity and Results of Operations of Subsidiaries

| | Equity | | Profit (Loss) for the Year | |
	2011	2010	2011	2010
Braskem Idesa	93,578	18,079	(4,695)	(5,824)
Cetrel	121,744	—	12,998	—
Total	215,322	18,079	8,303	(5,824)

29 Equity (in part)

(a) Capital

At December 31, 2011, the Company's subscribed and paid up capital amounts to R$ 8,043,222 and comprises 801,665,617 shares with no par value divided into 451,669,063 common shares, 349,402,736 class A preferred shares, and 593,818 class B preferred shares.

The Company's Extraordinary Shareholders' General Meeting held on February 25, 2010 approved a capital increase, regardless of changes in the bylaws, up to the limit of 1,152,937,970 shares, divided into: 535,661,731 common shares, 616,682,421 class A preferred shares and 593,818 class B preferred shares. The amount of preferred shares without voting rights or with restricted voting rights may not exceed the limit of two thirds of the Company's total capital.

On April 14, 2010, the Company's Board of Directors approved a capital increase in the form of private subscription through the issue of 259,904,311 shares, of which: 243,206,530 of which are common shares and 16,697,781 are class A preferred shares with an issue price of R$

14.40 per share, totaling R$ 3,742,622. The amount of R$ 1,363,880 was credited to the capital reserve account and R$ 2,378,742 to the capital account, which increased from R$ 5,473,181 to R$ 7,851,923, comprising 780,832,465 shares divided into 433,668,976 common shares, 346,569,671 class A preferred shares and 593,818 class B preferred shares.

The Extraordinary General Shareholders' Meeting held on June 18, 2010 approved the merger of Quattor shares by Braskem. This merger resulted in the issue of 18,000,087 common shares, amounting to R$ 199,356, R$ 164,744 of which was allocated to the capital account and R$ 34,612 to the capital reserve account. As a result, the Company's capital increased from R$ 7,851,923 to R$ 8,016,667.

The Extraordinary General Shareholders' Meeting held on August 30, 2010 approved the merger of Riopol shares by Braskem. This merger resulted in the issue of 2,434,890 class A preferred shares amounting to R$ 103,087, R$ 22,285 of which was allocated to the capital account and R$ 80,802 to the capital reserve account. As a result, the Company's capital increased from R$ 8,016,667 to R$ 8,038,952.

The Extraordinary General Shareholders' Meeting held on December 27, 2010 approved the merger of Quattor Petroquímica shares by Braskem. This merger resulted in the issue of 398,175 class A preferred shares amounting to R$ 4,270 which was allocated to the capital account. As a result, the Company's capital increased from R$ 8,038,952 to R$ 8,043,222.

(f) Treasury Shares

The breakdown of treasury shares is as follows:

	2011	2010
Quantity		
Common shares	411	411
Preferred shares class "A"[(i)]	2,697,016	2,660,818
	2,697,427	2,661,229
Amount (R$ thousand)	60,217	59,271

[(i)] In the consolidated financial statements as of December 31, 2011 and 2010, the Company recorded the amount of R$ 48,892 within "treasury shares," corresponding to 1,154,758 class A preferred shares issued by Braskem and held by the subsidiary Braskem Petroquímica. These shares were received by Braskem Petroquimica as a result of the merger of Riopol shares by Braskem (Note 1 (b.1 (ix)).

On December 31, 2011, the total amount of treasury shares, calculated based on the closing trading price of BM&FBovespa, is R$34,522 (2010—R$54,201).

In 2010 and 2011, the events that resulted in the increase of the number of treasury shares were the following:

- The Extraordinary General Shareholders' Meeting held on August 30, 2010 approved the merger of Riopol shares by Braskem. As a result, some holders of 411 common shares of Braskem exercised their right to withdraw. The reimbursement of these shares corresponded to the carrying amount of the share in accordance with the balance sheet as of December 31, 2009 of R$ 9.15237722 per share, totaling R$ 3.

- In January 2011, the Company repurchased 36,198 class A preferred shares for the amount of R$ 946 arising from the right of non-controlling shareholders to withdraw from Braskem Petroquímica due to the merger of its shares into Braskem, which was approved by the shareholders on December 27, 2010.

Ordinary and Deferred Shares, Portion of Convertible Preferred Ordinary Shares and Convertible Cumulative Preference Shares Allocated to Debt

2.26

Celtic plc (Jun 2011)

CONSOLIDATED BALANCE SHEET (in part)

	Notes	2011 £000	2010 £000
Equity			
Issued share capital	22	24,264	24,246
Share premium		14,399	14,359
Other reserve		21,222	21,222
Capital reserve		2,629	2,646
Accumulated losses	23	(22,511)	(22,613)
Total equity		40,003	39,860

NOTES TO THE CONSOLIDATED FINANCIAL STATEMENTS (in part)

22 Share Capital

	Authorised 30 June		Allotted, Called Up and Fully Paid 30 June			
Group and Company	2011 No 000	2010 No 000	2011 No 000	2011 £000	2010 No 000	2010 £000
Equity						
Ordinary shares of 1p each	220,096	219,990	90,136	901	89,940	899
Deferred shares of 1p each	495,754	490,609	495,754	4,957	490,638	4,906
Non-equity						
Convertible preferred ordinary shares of £1 each	15,972	16,018	13,984	13,984	14,031	14,031
Convertible cumulative preference shares of 60p each	19,283	19,293	16,783	10,069	16,793	10,076
Less reallocated to debt under IAS 32	—	—	—	(5,647)	—	(5,666)
	751,105	745,910	616,657	24,264	611,402	24,246

On 1 September 2010, 90,255 new Ordinary Shares of 1 p each were issued in respect of mandates received from holders of Convertible Cumulative Preference Shares ("CCP Shares").

From 1 September 2007, the Convertible Preferred Ordinary Shares may be converted into Ordinary Shares and Deferred Shares on the election of the shareholder. The number of Ordinary Shares and Deferred Shares to which a holder of Convertible Preferred Ordinary Shares is entitled on conversion was determined by reference to the middle market price of Ordinary Shares in the three dealing days immediately prior to 1 September 2007. As a result each Convertible Preferred Ordinary Share converts into 2.08 Ordinary Shares and 97.92 Deferred Shares. As at 11 August 2011, the latest practicable date before publication, notices had been received in respect of the conversion of 1,600 Convertible Preferred Ordinary Shares.

Each Convertible Cumulative Preference Share of 60p carries the right, subject to the availability of distributable profits, to the payment of a fixed preference dividend equal to 6% (less tax credit deduction) of its nominal value, cumulative with effect from 1 July 1996. The first dividend was paid on 31 August 1997. Holders of Preference Shares of 60p are entitled to convert each Preference Share into one Ordinary Share of 1p and 59 Deferred Shares of 1p each. During the year ended 30 June 2011, 10,100 Preference Shares were converted in accordance with these provisions. The Ordinary Shares of 1p each, arising on conversion rank pari passu in all respects with the existing Ordinary Shares of 1p each. The Deferred Shares are non-transferable, carry no voting rights, no class rights and have no valuable economic rights. As at 11 August 2011, the latest practicable date before publication no conversion notices had been received in respect of Preference Shares.

Reconciliation of Number of Ordinary Shares in Issue:	2011 No.'000	2010 No.'000
Opening balance	89,940	89,762
Shares issued re scrip dividend scheme	90	126
Shares issued re Convertible Preferred Ordinary Share conversions	96	86
Shares issued re Preference Share Conversion	10	2
Closing Balance	90,136	89,940

Reconciliation of Number of Deferred Shares in Issue:	2011 No.'000	2010 No.'000
Opening balance	490,638	486,460
Convertible Preferred Ordinary Share conversions to Ordinary and Deferred Shares	4,520	100
Shares issued re Preference Share Conversion	596	4,078
Closing Balance	495,754	490,638

Reconciliation of Number of Convertible Preferred Ordinary Shares in Issue:	2011 No.'000	2010 No.'000
Opening balance	14,031	14,072
Convertible Preferred Ordinary Share conversions to Ordinary and Deferred Shares	(47)	(41)
Closing Balance	13,984	14,031

Reconciliation of Number of Cumulative Convertible Preference Shares in Issue:	2011 No.'000	2010 No.'000
Opening balance	16,793	16,794
Convertible Cumulative Preference Share conversions to Ordinary and Deferred Shares	(10)	(1)
Closing Balance	16,783	16,793

23 Reserves

In accordance with Resolution No 8 at the 2002 Annual General Meeting and the Court Order obtained on 9 May 2003, the previous Share Premium Account balance was cancelled and transferred to the Other Reserve. Under the terms of this cancellation, an amount equal to three times the Executive Club loans, currently equal to £390,000 (2010: £408,000) will remain non-distributable from this Other Reserve until such loans are repaid by the Company.

The Capital Reserve has arisen following the reallocation of an element of the Convertible Preferred Ordinary Share capital from equity to debt in line with the capital maintenance requirements of the Companies Act. This reserve increases as debt is repaid but will ultimately be reallocated to equity on the conversion of the Convertible Preferred Ordinary Shares to Ordinary Shares.

The increase in the share premium account reflects the premium on the Ordinary Shares issued in the year.

The profit for the year for the parent company was £0.13m (2010: £1.02m loss).

Current Assets—Prepaid Expenses

2.27

Counsel Corporation (Dec 2011)

Author's Note

Counsel Corporation implemented IFRSs effective December 31, 2011, with a date of transition of January 1, 2010. The excerpt that follows reflects the initial application of IAS 1.

CONSOLIDATED STATEMENT OF FINANCIAL POSITION (in part)

(In thousands of Canadian dollars)

	Notes	December 31, 2011 $	December 31, 2010 $	January 1, 2010 $
Assets				
Current assets				
Cash and cash equivalents		15,212	61,897	8,048
Marketable securities		255	333	1,519
Mortgages, accounts and deferred interest receivable	6	15,643	1,732	4,859
Inventory	7	3,197	4,564	2,852
Prepaid expenses, deposits and deferred charges	8	2,262	1,743	2,347
Assets of discontinued operations	29	180	1,199	1,125
		36,749	71,468	20,750

NOTES TO THE CONSOLIDATED FINANCIAL STATEMENTS (in part)

1. General Information

Counsel Corporation ("Counsel" or "the Company"), founded in 1979, is a financial services company that operates through its individually branded businesses, primarily in mortgage lending, distressed and surplus capital asset transactions, real estate finance and private equity investments. The address of its registered office is 1 Toronto Street, Suite 700, P.O. Box 3, Toronto, Ontario, M5C 2V6.

Counsel currently operates in four business sectors: mortgage lending, asset liquidation, private equity (which includes our case goods business), and real estate.

Counsel carries on its mortgage lending business ("Mortgage Lending") through its subsidiary, Street Capital Financial Corporation ("Street Capital"). Street Capital is a Canadian prime residential mortgage lender. Counsel acquired Street Capital on May 31, 2011.

Counsel's asset liquidation business ("Asset Liquidation") is carried on through a U.S. subsidiary, Counsel RB Capital LLC ("Counsel RB"). Counsel RB specializes in the acquisition and disposition of distressed and surplus assets throughout the United States and Canada, including industrial machinery and equipment, real estate, inventories, accounts receivables and distressed debt.

Counsel carries on its private equity business ("Private Equity") through its wholly-owned subsidiary, Knight's Bridge Capital Partners Inc. ("Knight's Bridge"). Knight's Bridge is responsible for sourcing and managing Counsel's portfolio investment opportunities. Knight's Bridge is an opportunistic and diversified financial service provider with a focus on building portfolio companies into market leaders.

Counsel's case goods business ("Case Goods") is carried on through a Canadian limited partnership, Fleetwood Fine Furniture LP ("Fleetwood"), which was acquired effective April 30, 2006. Fleetwood provides high quality customized case goods for large, upscale hotel chains, primarily in North America, with over 90% of its revenues generated in the United States. Fleetwood serves a focused niche, being the "upscale" and "upper upscale" strata of the hospitality industry.

Counsel's real estate business ("Real Estate") consists of the ownership and development of its own properties as well as the provision of real estate property and asset management services to third parties.

8. Prepaid Expenses, Deposits and Deferred Charges

Deferred charges of $17,014 represent prepaid mortgage portfolio insurance premiums on mortgage pools, which are amortized over the average term of the underlying mortgages. The other prepaid expenses of $1,128 are comprised of prepaid operating expenses including vendor deposits,

insurance, rent, and other miscellaneous items which will be
expensed within the next twelve months.

	December 31, 2011 $	December 31, 2010 $	January 1, 2011 $
Deferred charges	17,014	—	—
Other prepaid expenses.	1,128	1,743	2,347
	18,142	1,743	2,347
Current	2,262	1,743	2,347
Long-term	15,880	—	—
	18,142	1,743	2,347

Current and Non-Current
Assets—Recoverable Taxes

2.28

Fibria Celulose S.A. (Dec 2011)

CONSOLIDATED BALANCE SHEET (in part)

(In thousands of Reais)

	As at December 31, 2011	As at December 31, 2010	As at December 31, 2009
Assets			
Current			
Cash and cash equivalents	381,915	431,463	645,479
Marketable securities	1,677,926	1,640,935	3,251,903
Derivative instruments	—	80,502	5,122
Trade accounts receivable, net	945,362	1,138,176	1,167,151
Inventories	1,178,707	1,013,841	834,371
Recoverable taxes	327,787	282,423	231,294
Assets held for sale	644,166	1,196,149	—
Other assets	108,062	115,165	254,222
	5,263,925	5,898,654	6,389,542
Non-current			
Marketable securities	—	—	65,439
Derivative instruments	—	52,470	—
Related parties receivables	5,469	5,307	—
Deferred taxes	991,768	1,332,025	1,283,544
Recoverable taxes	677,232	590,967	372,509
Advances to suppliers	760,611	693,490	720,127
Judicial deposits	137,060	110,364	—
Other receivables	95,060	145,768	120,644
Investments	7,506	8,301	15,430
Biological assets	3,264,210	3,550,636	3,791,084
Property, plant and equipment	11,841,247	12,979,431	14,037,031
Intangible assets	4,809,448	4,906,443	5,443,354
	22,589,611	24,375,202	25,849,162
Total assets	27,853,536	30,273,856	32,238,704

NOTES TO THE CONSOLIDATED FINANCIAL STATEMENTS (in part)

In thousands of reais, unless otherwise indicated

1 Operations (in part)

(a) General Information (in part)

Fibria Celulose S.A. and its subsidiaries (the "Company", "Fibria", or "we") is a limited liability company constituted in accordance with the laws of the Federative Republic of Brazil and headquartered in São Paulo and after divesting its paper production activities in 2011, operates a single operational segment: producing and selling short fiber pulp.

The Company's business is affected by global pulp prices, which are historically cyclical and subject to significant volatility over short periods, as a result of, among other factors: (a) global demand for products from pulp; (b) global production capacity and strategies adopted by the main producers; (c) availability of substitutes for these products; and (d) exchange rates. All these factors are beyond the control of the Company's management.

14 Recoverable Taxes

	2011	2010
Withholding tax and prepaid income tax (IRPJ) and social contribution (CSLL)	208,993	251,688
Value-added Tax on Sales and Services (ICMS) on purchases of property, plant and equipment	19,520	25,433
Recoverable ICMS and Excise Tax (IPI)	614,274	557,457
Social Integration Program (PIS) and Social Contribution on Revenues (COFINS) Recoverable	669,805	520,339
Provision for impairment on ICMS credits	(507,573)	(481,527)
Other		
	1,005,019	873,390
Non-current	677,232	590,967
Current	327,787	282,423

In the year ended December 31, 2010, the Company accumulated PIS and COFINS credits on the purchase of certain property, plant and equipment assets, in the Três Lagoas, Jacareí and Piracicaba plants, amounting to R$ 309,058 and in the Três Lagos plant and amounting to R$ 47,272 in Jacareí and Piracicaba, which, for accounting purposes, were recorded at the present value of R$ 232,399 and R$ 37,216 respectively, under property, plant and equipment.

Fibria has been accumulating ICMS credits in the States of Espírito Santo, Mato Grosso do Sul and São Paulo since its activities are mostly directed to the exports market. Company management revised the perspectives for the realization of such credits and established an impairment: (i) for the full amount in the case of the Mato Grosso do Sul unit due to the low probability of realization;(ii) a a partial provision for the Espírito Santo unit equivalent to 50% of the total amount; and (iii) a partial provision equivalent to approximately 10% of the balance for the unit in the State of São Paulo. When a partial provision was recorded management has already implanted actions to recover the taxes and they are being recovered through the operations in each of the states.

Based on the budget approved by the Company's management, substantially all the tax credits are expected to be realized by the end of 2016.

	Amount	Percentage
In the next 12 months	327,787	37
In 2013	146,257	16
In 2014	142,676	16
In 2015	118,515	13
In 2016	153,322	18
	888,557	100
PIS and COFINS related to property, plant and equipment[*]	116,462	
	1,005,019	

[*] These credits were not included in the schedule above, since they will be realized over the useful lives of the property, plant and equipment.

Current and Non-Current Assets—Stockpiles and Ore on Leachpads, Other Assets

2.29

Compañía de Minas Buenaventura S.A.A. (Dec 2011)

Author's Note

Compañía de Minas Buonaventura S.A.S implemented IFRSs effective December 31, 2011, with a date of transition of January 1, 2010. The excerpt that follows reflects the initial application of IAS 1.

CONSOLIDATED BALANCE SHEETS (in part)

	At December 31	
(Dollars in Thousands)	2011	2010
Assets		
Cash and cash equivalents	$ 797,991	$ 880,888
Accounts receivable (Note 7)	74,608	25,807
Due from related parties (Note 13)	1,224	1,804
Inventories (Note 8)	63,501	55,941
Stockpiles and ore on leach pads (Note 9)	159,713	166,998
Deferred income tax assets (Note 5)	8,746	8,746
Other current assets (Note 10)	21,643	14,035
Current assets	1,127,426	1,154,219
Property, plant and mine development, net (Note 11)	2,231,212	1,437,300
Stockpiles and ore on leach pads (Note 9)	351,942	328,874
Other long-term assets (Note 10)	76,654	16,601
Total assets	$3,787,234	$2,936,994

NOTES TO THE CONSOLIDATED FINANCIAL STATEMENTS (in part)

(Dollars in thousands unless otherwise stated)

1. Business Activities

Minera Yanacocha S.R.L. (the "Company"), formerly Minera Yanacocha S.A., was incorporated in Peru on January 14, 1992 and commenced operations in 1993. The Company is engaged in the production of gold and exploration and development of gold and copper under the mining concessions it owns or that are owned by S.M.R.L. Chaupiloma Dos de Cajamarca ("Chaupiloma").

The Company is owned 51.35% by Newmont Second Capital Corporation, a 100% indirectly owned subsidiary of Newmont Mining Corporation ("Newmont"), 43.65% owned by Compañía Minera Condesa S.A., which is 100% owned by Compañía de Minas Buenaventura S.A.A. ("Buenaventura") and 5% owned by the International Finance Corporation.

The majority Partners of the Company (or their affiliates) also own the majority interest in Chaupiloma. In accordance with a mining lease, amended effective January 1, 1994, the Company pays Chaupiloma a 3% royalty based on quarterly production sold at current market prices, after deducting refinery and transportation costs. The royalty agreement expires in 2012, but can be extended at the Company's option.

Located in the Cajamarca province of Peru, the Company's operation consists of three major active open pit mines: Cerro Yanacocha, La Quinua and Chaquicocha. However, during the last quarter of 2011 mining operations were reinitiated in sections of the Maqui-Maqui and Carachugo pits. Gold-bearing ores are transported to one of four leach pads for gold recovery using conventional heap-leaching or milling, followed by Merrill-Crowe zinc precipitation and smelting where a final doré product is poured. The doré is then shipped offsite for refining and is sold on the worldwide gold markets.

Gold mining requires the use of specialized facilities and technology. The Company relies heavily on such facilities and technology to maintain production levels. Also, the cash flow and profitability of the Company's operations are significantly affected by the market price of gold. Gold prices can fluctuate widely and are affected by numerous factors beyond the Company's control. During 2011, 2010 and 2009, the Company produced 1.29 million, 1.46 million and 2.07 million ounces of gold, respectively.

The Conga project consists of two gold-copper porphyry deposits located northeast of the Yanacocha operating area in the provinces of Celendin, Cajamarca and Hualgayoc. The project has proven and probable reserves of 12.6 million ounces (unaudited) of contained gold and 3.3 billion pounds (unaudited) of contained copper at December 31, 2011. Construction activity relating to design, procurement and earthworks for the Conga project has begun.

In November 2011, construction activities at Conga were suspended at the request of Peru's central government following increasing protests in Cajamarca by anti-mining activists led by the regional president. At the request of the Peruvian central government, the environmental impact assessment prepared in connection with the project, which was previously approved by the central government in October 2010, will be reviewed by independent experts, in an effort to resolve allegations surrounding the environmental viability of Conga. Construction will remain suspended for the duration of the review, except for sediment control works that are being conducted in the project area, however, progress continues on engineering and procurement work.

Total proven and probable reserves contained in three active open pits, other pits to be developed, stockpiles, ore in process on leach pads and the Conga project are approximately 20.3 million ounces (unaudited) of contained gold and 3.3 billion pounds (unaudited) of contained copper at December 31, 2011.

2. Significant Accounting Policies (in part)

Cash and Cash Equivalents

Cash and cash equivalents consist of all cash balances and highly liquid investments with an original maturity of three months or less. Because of the short maturity of these balances, the carrying amounts approximate their fair value. Restricted cash is excluded from cash and cash equivalents and is included in other current assets or long-term assets depending on restrictions.

Stockpiles, Ore on Leach Pads and Inventories

As described below, costs that are incurred in or benefit the productive process are accumulated as stockpiles, ore on leach pads and inventories. Stockpiles, ore on leach pads and inventories are carried at the lower of average cost or net realizable value. Net realizable value represents the estimated future sales price of the product based on current and long-term metals prices, less the estimated costs to complete production and bring the product to sale. Write-downs of stockpiles, ore on leach pads and inventories to net realizable value are reported as a component of *Costs applicable to sales*. The current portion of stockpiles, ore on leach pads and inventories is determined based on the expected amounts to be processed within the next twelve months. Stockpiles, ore on leach pads and inventories not expected to be processed within the next twelve months are classified as long-term. The major classifications are as follows:

Stockpiles

Stockpiles represent ore that has been extracted from the mine and is available for further processing. Stockpiles are measured by estimating the number of tons added and removed from the stockpile, the number of contained ounces (based on assay data) and the estimated metallurgical recovery rates (based on the expected processing method). Stockpile ore tonnages are verified by periodic surveys. Costs are allocated to stockpiles based on relative values of material stockpiled and processed using current mining costs incurred up to the point of stockpiling the ore, including applicable overhead and amortization relating to mining operations, and removed at each stockpile's average cost per recoverable unit.

Ore on Leach Pads

The recovery of gold from certain gold oxide ores is achieved through the heap leaching process. Under this method, ore is placed on leach pads where it is treated with a chemical solution, which dissolves the gold contained in the ore. The resulting gold-bearing solution is further processed in a plant where the gold is recovered. Costs are added to ore on leach pads based on current mining costs, including applicable overhead and amortization relating to mining operations.

Costs are removed from ore on leach pads as ounces are recovered based on the average cost per recoverable ounce of gold on the leach pad.

The estimates of recoverable gold on the leach pads are calculated from the quantities of ore placed on the pads (measured tons added to the leach pads), the grade of ore placed on the leach pads (based on assay data) and a recovery percentage (based on ore type). In general, the leach pads recover approximately 50% to 95% of the ultimate recoverable ounces in the first year of leaching, declining each year thereafter until the leaching process is complete.

Although the quantities of recoverable gold placed on the leach pads are reconciled by comparing the grades of ore placed on the pads to the quantities of gold actually recovered (metallurgical balancing), the nature of the leaching process inherently limits the ability to precisely monitor inventory levels. As a result, the metallurgical balancing process is constantly monitored and estimates are refined based on actual results over time. Historically, the Company's operating results have not been materially impacted by variations between the estimated and actual recoverable quantities of gold on its leach pads. Variations between actual and estimated quantities resulting from changes in assumptions and estimates that do not result in write-downs to net realizable value are accounted for on a prospective basis.

9. Stockpiles and Ore on Leach Pads

	At December 31	
	2011	2010
Current:		
Stockpiles	$ 36,384	$ 12,333
Ore on leach pads	123,329	154,665
	$159,713	$166,998
Long-term:		
Stockpiles	$ 71,474	$ 56,859
Ore on leach pads	280,468	272,015
	$351,942	$328,874

10. Other Assets

	At December 31	
	2011	2010
Other current assets:		
Prepayments to suppliers and contractors	$11,084	$ 2,972
Claims for tax refunds	4,335	4,038
Restricted cash	943	512
Prepaid expenses and other	5,281	6,513
	$21,643	$14,035
Other long-term assets:		
Intangible assets	$59,748	$ —
San José Reservoir Trust assets	15,502	16,412
Other	1,404	189
	$76,654	$16,601

As of December 31, 2011, *Prepayments to suppliers and contractors* is related to the purchase of equipment of $8,974, supplies of $1,948 and other services $162.

Intangible assets relate to the completion of an alternative road to the coast.

Current Liabilities—Accrued Expenses, Advances From Customers

2.30

Empresas ICA S.A. de C.V. (Dec 2011)

Author's Note

Empresas ICA S.A. de C.V implemented IFRSs effective December 31, 2011, with a date of transition of January 1, 2010. The excerpt that follows reflects the initial application of IAS 1.

CONSOLIDATED STATEMENTS OF FINANCIAL POSITION (in part)

(Thousands of Mexican pesos)

	Millions of U.S. Dollars (Convenience Translation Note 4) December 31, 2011	2011	2010	January 1, 2010 (Transition Date)
Current liabilities:				
Notes payable (Note 16)	$ 418	Ps. 5,826,272	Ps. 4,700,864	Ps. 3,564,187
Current portion of long-term debt (Note 21)	995	13,888,201	1,274,644	657,349
Trade accounts payable	476	6,647,926	5,939,751	4,840,544
Income taxes (Note 23)	30	412,893	378,562	268,536
Accrued expenses and other (Note 17)	484	6,749,015	4,412,010	4,581,263
Provisions (Note 18)	143	1,990,871	1,343,772	894,987
Advances from customers	281	3,921,824	1,907,945	2,917,537
Current liabilities	2,827	39,437,002	19,957,548	17,724,403

NOTES TO THE CONSOLIDATED FINANCIAL STATEMENTS (in part)

(Thousands of Mexican pesos except as otherwise indicated)

1. Activities

Empresas ICA, S.A.B. de C.V. and subsidiaries ("ICA" or, together with its subsidiaries, "the Company") is a holding company incorporated in Mexico with over 64 years experience, the subsidiaries of which are engaged in a wide range of construction and related activities including the construction of infrastructure facilities as well as industrial, urban and housing construction, for both the Mexican public and private sectors. ICA's subsidiaries are also involved in the construction, maintenance and operation of highways, bridges and tunnels granted by the Mexican government and foreign governments under concessions. Through its subsidiaries and affiliates, the Company also manages and operates airports and municipal services under concession arrangements. In addition, some of ICA's subsidiaries are engaged in real estate and housing development. ICA's shares are traded on the Mexican Stock Exchange and the New York Stock Exchange. Its registered address is 36 Boulevard Manuel Avila Camacho, Piso 15, Lomas de Chapultepec, 11000 Mexico, D. F.

4. Basis of Presentation and Consolidation (in part)

a. Statement of Compliance

The consolidated financial statements have been prepared in accordance with IFRS as issued by the IASB. Included in subsection (g) is the Company's policy regarding consolidation and included in Note 5 are the Company's accouting policies and valuation principles applied in preparing the consolidated financial statements.

The accompanying consolidated financial statements include all financial reporting standards and valuation requirements that affect the Company's consolidated financial information, as well as the alternatives allowed by IFRS.

b. Basis of Preparation

The consolidated financial statements have been prepared on the historical cost basis except for the revaluation of certain non-current assets and financial instruments at fair value. Historical cost is generally based on the fair value of the consideration given in exchange for assets. The consolidated financial statements are prepared in pesos, the legal currency of the United Mexican States and are presented in thousands, except where otherwise noted.

5. Significant Accounting Policies (in part)

The consolidated financial statements are prepared in accordance with IFRS. Preparation of financial statements under IFRS requires management of the Company to make certain estimates and use assumptions to value certain of the items in the consolidated financial statements as well as their related disclosures required therein. The areas with a high degree of judgment and complexity or areas where assumptions and estimates are significant in the consolidated financial statements are described in Note 6. The estimates are based on information available at the time the estimates are made, as well as the best knowledge and judgment of management based on experience and current events. However, actual results could differ from those estimates. The Company has implemented control procedures to ensure that its accounting policies are appropriate and are properly applied. Although actual results may differ from those estimates, the Company's management believes that the estimates and assumptions used were adequate under the circumstances.

n. Financial Assets and Liabilities

Financial assets and liabilities are initially measured at fair value. The costs of transaction that are directly attributable to the acquisition or issue of a financial asset or liability (other than financial assets and liabilities that are recognized at fair value through results), are added or deducted from the fair value of the related assets and liabilities upon initial recognition. Transaction costs directly attributable to the acquisition of assets or financial liabilities that are recognized at fair value through profit or loss are recognized immediately in profit or loss for the year.

p. Risk Management Policy

ICA is exposed to risks that are managed through the implementation of systems of identification, measurement, limitation of concentration, and supervision. The Risk Management department in ICA is of a preventative nature, focusing on risks in the medium and long term, taking into account the most likely scenarios of evolution of the variables affecting each risk. Financial risk management pays particular attention to interest rate risk, exchange rate risk, liquidity risk and credit risk (see Note 25).

17. Accrued Expenses and Other

Accrued expenses and other consist of the following:

	December 31, 2011	December 31, 2010	January 1, 2010
Accrued operating expenses	Ps. 5,207,885	Ps. 3,223,039	Ps. 3,600,430
Interest payable	205,113	140,282	110,537
Financial leasing	151,932	26,282	29,169
Derivative financial instruments	140,397	4,741	—
Accounts payable due to related parties	394,521	467,143	334,862
Bonus	321,769	254,412	270,450
Taxes other than income tax	327,398	296,111	235,815
	Ps. 6,749,015	Ps. 4,412,010	Ps. 4,581,263

25. Risk Management (in part)

a. Significant Accounting Policies

The significant accounting policies and adopted methods of recognition, valuation and basis of recognition of related income and expenses for each class of financial asset, financial liability and equity instrument is disclosed in Note 4.

b. Categories of Financial Instruments and Risk Management Policies

The main categories of financial instruments are:

Financial Assets	Classification of Risk	December 31, 2011	December 31, 2010	January 1, 2010
Cash		Ps. 1,913,510	Ps. 813,309	Ps. 889,395
Restricted cash		6,054,749	1,543,578	1,833,086
Cash equivalents	Interest rate	2,931,455	2,162,075	1,788,186
Customers[1]	Credit and Operating	14,721,637	2,306,258	4,143,773
Other receivables	Credit and Operating	3,513,951	2,696,667	2,196,759
Customers—non current[1]	Credit and Operating	6,443,952	12,329,801	7,549,646
Financial assets from concessions	Credit and Interest rate	8,488,478	4,655,476	3,415,788

[1] Cost and estimated earnings in excess of billings on uncompleted contracts is not considered a financial instrument, therefore it is not included.

Financial Liabilities	Classification of Risk	December 31, 2011	December 31, 2010	January 1, 2010
Derivative financial instruments	Interest rate, Foreign exchange and Credit	Ps. 897,626	Ps. 1,116,727	Ps. 1,152,788
Notes payable and current portion of long-term debt	Interest rate, Foreign exchange and Liquidity	19,714,473	5,975,508	4,221,536
Long-term debt	Interest rate, Foreign exchange and Liquidity	30,320,024	26,029,040	18,448,689
Trade accounts payable	Interest rate, Foreign exchange and Liquidity	6,647,926	5,939,751	4,840,544
Accrued expenses and other	Liquidity, Interest rate, Foreign exchange and Credit	2,854,534	1,958,850	2,001,556
Other long-term liabilities	Operating and Liquidity	1,091,723	1,063,744	740,406

Based on the nature of its activities, ICA is exposed to different financial risks, mainly as a result of its ordinary business activities and its debt contracts entered into to finance its operating activities. The principal financial risks to which operating units are exposed are: market risk (interest rates, currency exchange rates and foreign currency pricing), credit risk and liquidity risk.

Periodically, the Company's management assesses risk exposure and reviews the alternatives for managing those risks, seeking to minimize the effects of these risks using financial derivatives to hedge risk exposures. The Board of Directors sets and monitors policies and procedures to measure and manage the risks to which the Company is exposed, which are described below.

e. Liquidity Risk (in part)

Liquidity risk management—This risk is generated by temporary differences between the funding required by the Company to fulfill business investment commitments, debt maturities, current asset requirements, etc., and the origin of funds generated by its regular activities, different types of bank financing and disinvestment. This risk management is intended to maintain a balance between the flexibility, period and conditions of credit facilities contracted to provide short, medium and long-term funding requirements. In this regard, the Company's use of project financing and debt with limited resources, as described in Note 21, and the short-term financing of current assets are particularly noteworthy. The Executive Committee of ICA is ultimately responsible for liquidity management. This Committee has established appropriate liquidity management guidelines. The Company manages its liquidity risk by maintaining reserves, financial facilities and adequate loans, while constantly monitoring projected and actual cash flows and reconciling the maturity profiles of financial assets and liabilities.

The following table shows the remaining contractual maturities of the Company's non-derivative financial liabilities, together with agreed reimbursement periods. This table has been prepared based on the projected non-discounted cash flows of financial assets and liabilities at the date on which ICA must make payments and collect outstanding amounts. The table includes projected interest cash flows such as disbursements required for the financial debt included in the consolidated statement of financial position as well as with interest earned on financial assets. As interest is accrued at variable rates, the non-discounted amount is derived from interest rate curves at the end of the reporting period. Contractual maturity is based on the earliest date when ICA must make the respective payment.

As of December 31, 2011	1 Year	Up to 2 Years	Up to 3 Years	Up to 4 Years	Up to 5 Years	Up to 6 Years and Thereafter	Total
Derivative financial instruments	Ps. 895,174	Ps. 2,452	Ps. —	Ps. —	Ps. —	Ps. —	Ps. 897,626
Notes payable	5,826,272	—	—	—	—	—	5,826,272
Long-term debt[1]	13,888,201	1,194,791	1,245,182	1,835,591	2,634,533	23,409,927	44,208,225
Fixed interest	1,762,971	1,704,264	1,643,093	1,587,653	1,517,556	13,543,703	21,759,240
Variable interest	871,060	688,697	610,210	588,721	543,903	5,225,286	8,527,877
Trade accounts payable	6,647,926	—	—	—	—	—	6,647,926
Accrued expenses and Other	2,854,534	—	—	—	—	—	2,854,534
Other long-term liabilities	—	694,242	49,781	26,849	23,929	296,922	1,091,723
Total	Ps. 32,746,138	Ps. 4,284,446	Ps. 3,548,266	Ps. 4,038,814	Ps. 4,719,921	Ps. 42,475,838	Ps. 91,813,423

Liabilities in Liquidity Order—General Fund and Segregated Insurance and Investment Contract Liabilities

2.31

Sun Life Financial, Inc. (Dec 2011)

Author's Note

Sun Life Financial, Inc., implemented IFRSs effective December 31, 2011, with a date of transition of January 1, 2010. The excerpt that follows reflects the initial application of IAS 1.

CONSOLIDATED STATEMENTS OF FINANCIAL POSITION (in part)

As at (In Millions of Canadian Dollars)	December 31, 2011	December 31, 2010	January 1, 2010
Liabilities			
Insurance contract liabilities (Note 11)	$ 96,374	$ 88,056	$ 86,856
Investment contract liabilities (Note 11)	3,073	4,143	4,915
Derivative liabilities (Notes 5 and 6)	1,059	718	1,294
Deferred tax liabilities (Note 22)	7	39	12
Other liabilities (Note 13)	8,011	6,738	6,693
Senior debentures (Note 14)	2,149	2,151	2,151
Innovative capital instruments (Note 14)	695	1,644	1,644
Subordinated debt (Note 15)	2,746	2,741	3,048
Total general fund liabilities	114,114	106,230	106,613
Insurance contracts for account of segregated fund holders (Note 24)	82,650	81,931	74,293
Investment contracts for account of segregated fund holders (Note 24)	5,533	6,015	6,255
Total liabilities	$202,297	$194,176	$187,161

NOTES TO THE CONSOLIDATED FINANCIAL STATEMENTS (in part)

(Amounts in millions of Canadian dollars except for per share amounts and where otherwise stated)

1. Accounting Policies

1.A Significant Accounting Policies

Description of Business

Sun Life Financial Inc. ("SLF Inc.") is a publicly traded company domiciled in Canada and is the holding company of Sun Life Assurance Company of Canada ("Sun Life Assurance"). Both companies are incorporated under the Insurance Companies Act of Canada, and are regulated by the Office of the Superintendent of Financial Institutions, Canada ("OSFI"). SLF Inc. and its subsidiaries are collectively referred to as "us", "our", "ours", "we" or "the Company." We are an internationally diversified financial services organization providing savings, retirement and pension products, and life and health insurance to individuals and groups through our operations in Canada, the United States, the United Kingdom and Asia. We also operate mutual fund and investment management businesses, primarily in Canada, the United States and Asia.

Statement of Compliance

We prepare our Consolidated Financial Statements using International Financial Reporting Standards as issued by the International Accounting Standards Board ("IASB") and the former International Accounting Standards Committee, which includes International Financial Reporting Standards, International Accounting Standards ("IAS"), and interpretations developed by the International Financial Reporting Interpretations Committee ("IFRIC") and the former Standing Interpretations Committee ("SIC"). These various standards are collectively referred to as "IFRS." Our Consolidated Financial Statements are prepared in accordance with IFRS 1 *First Time Adoption of International Financial Reporting Statements*. The accounting policies have been applied consistently within our Consolidated Financial Statements and our opening Consolidated Statement of Financial Position at the transition date of January 1, 2010 ("the Transition Date") prepared for the purposes of transition to IFRS, which are our first annual financial statements in accordance with IFRS. Note 2 contains the required disclosures with regards to our first time adoption of IFRS and the differences from our previous basis of accounting, Canadian generally accepted accounting principles ("GAAP").

Insurance Contract Liabilities

Insurance contracts are contracts under which we accept significant insurance risk from a policyholder by agreeing to compensate the policyholder if a specified uncertain future event adversely affects the policyholder. The presence of significant insurance risk in individual contracts is assessed by reviewing books of contracts with homogeneous risk features.

As discussed in the Segregated Funds section of this Note, certain insurance contracts under which the policyholder bears the risks associated with the underlying investments are classified as Insurance contracts for account of segregated fund holders in our Consolidated Statements of Financial Position.

Insurance contract liabilities, including policy benefits payable and provisions for policyholder dividends, are determined in accordance with Canadian accepted actuarial practice and any requirements of OSFI. As confirmed by guidance provided by the Canadian Institute of Actuaries ("CIA"), the current Canadian Asset Liability Method ("CALM") of valuation of insurance contract liabilities satisfies the IFRS 4 *Insurance Contracts* requirements for eligibility for use under IFRS. Under CALM, liabilities are set equal to the statement of financial position value of the assets required to support them.

Some insurance contracts contain discretionary participation features ("DPF"), whereby the policyholder has the right to receive potentially significant additional benefits based on the actual investments and other experience on a block of similar contracts. IFRS allows the non-guaranteed, or participating, elements of such contracts to be classified as either a liability or as equity, depending on the nature of our obligation to the policyholder. The contracts issued by us contain constructive obligations to the policyholder with respect to the DPF of the contracts. We have therefore elected to classify these features as a liability, consistent with accounting treatment under CALM, and in accordance with guidance provided by the CIA.

Derivatives embedded in insurance contracts are treated as separate derivatives and measured at fair value with changes in fair value recognized in income, except when the embedded derivative itself meets the definition of an insurance contract under IFRS, or when the risks and characteristics are closely related to those of the host contracts or when the derivative is the policyholder's option to surrender an insurance contract for a fixed amount or an amount based on a fixed amount and an interest rate. The derivatives that have not been separated are accounted for as insurance contract liabilities.

Financial Liabilities (in part)

Investment Contract Liabilities

Contracts issued by us that do not transfer significant insurance risk, but do transfer financial risk from the policyholder to us, are financial liabilities and are accounted for as investment contracts. Service components of investment contracts are treated as service contracts. For further details on how service components of investment contracts are treated, see the Service Contracts accounting policy in this Note.

Liabilities for investment contracts without DPF are measured at FVTPL or amortized cost. Contracts recorded at FVTPL are measured at fair value at inception and each subsequent reporting period. Contracts recorded at amortized cost are initially recognized at fair value, less transaction costs directly attributable to the issue of the contract. These liabilities are derecognized when the obligation of the contract is discharged, cancelled or expired. At each subsequent period, the contracts are measured at amortized cost using the effective interest method. Changes in fair value of investment contract liabilities recorded at FVTPL and amortization on contracts recorded at amortized cost are recorded as an Increase (decrease) in investment contract liabilities in our Consolidated Statements of Operations. Deposits collected from and payments made to contract holders are recorded as an Increase and decrease in investment contract liabilities in our Consolidated Statements of Financial Position.

As discussed in the Segregated Funds section of this Note, certain investment contracts under which the policyholder bears the risks associated with the underlying investments are classified as Investment contracts for account of segregated fund holders in the Consolidated Statements of Financial Position.

The accounting for Investment contracts that contain DPF is described in the Insurance Contract Liabilities section of this Note.

11. Insurance Contract Liabilities and Investment Contract Liabilities

11.A Insurance Contract Liabilities

11.A.i Description of Business

The majority of the products sold by the Company are insurance contracts. These contracts include all forms of life, health and critical illness insurance sold to individuals and groups, life contingent annuities, accumulation annuities, and segregated fund products with guarantees.

11.A.ii Assumptions and Methodology

General

The liabilities for insurance contracts represent the estimated amounts which, together with estimated future premiums and net investment income, will provide for outstanding claims, estimated future benefits, policyholders' dividends, taxes (other than income taxes) and expenses on in-force insurance contracts.

In calculating liabilities for insurance contracts, assumptions must be made about mortality and morbidity rates, lapse and other policyholder behaviour, interest rates, equity market performance, asset default, inflation, expenses and other factors over the life of our products.

We use best estimate assumptions for expected future experience. Most assumptions relate to events that are anticipated to occur many years in the future and require regular review and revision where appropriate. Additional provisions are included in our insurance contract liabilities to provide for possible adverse deviations from the best estimates. If an assumption is more susceptible to change or if there is more uncertainty about an underlying best estimate assumption, a correspondingly larger provision is included in our insurance contract liabilities.

In determining these provisions, we ensure:
- When taken one at a time, each provision is reasonable with respect to the underlying best estimate assumption and the extent of uncertainty present in making that assumption; and
- In total, the cumulative effect of all provisions is reasonable with respect to the total insurance contract liabilities.

In recognition of the long-term nature of insurance contract liabilities, the margin for possible deviations generally increases for contingencies further in the future. The best estimate assumptions and margins for adverse deviations are reviewed annually, and revisions are made where deemed necessary and prudent. With the passage of time and resulting reduction in estimation risk, excess provisions are released into income.

Mortality

Insurance mortality assumptions are generally based on our five-year average experience. Our experience is combined with industry experience where our own experience is insufficient to be statistically valid. Assumed mortality rates for life insurance and annuity contracts include assumptions about future mortality improvement in accordance with CIA standards.

Morbidity

Morbidity refers to both the rates of accident or sickness and the rates of recovery therefrom. Most of our disability insurance is marketed on a group basis. We offer critical illness policies on an individual basis in Canada and Asia, long-term care on an individual basis in Canada and medical stop-loss insurance is offered on a group basis in the United States. In Canada, group morbidity assumptions are based on our five-year average experience, modified to reflect an emerging trend in recovery rates. For long-term care and critical illness insurance, assumptions are developed in collaboration with our reinsurers and are largely based on their experience. In the United States, our experience is used for both medical stop-loss and disability assumptions, with some consideration of industry experience.

Lapse and Other Policyholder Behaviour

Lapse

Policyholders may allow their policies to lapse prior to the end of the contractual coverage period by choosing not to continue to pay premiums or by surrendering their policy for the cash surrender value. Assumptions for lapse experience on life insurance are generally based on our five-year average experience. Lapse rates vary by plan, age at issue, method of premium payment, and policy duration.

Premium Payment Patterns

For universal life contracts, it is necessary to set assumptions about premium payment patterns. Studies prepared by industry or the actuarial profession are used for products where our experience is insufficient to be statistically valid. Premium payment patterns usually vary by plan, age at issue, method of premium payment, and policy duration.

Expense

Insurance contract liabilities provide for future policy-related expenses. These include the costs of premium collection, claims adjudication and processing, actuarial calculations, preparation and mailing of policy statements and related indirect expenses and overheads. Expense assumptions are mainly based on our recent experience using an internal expense allocation methodology. Inflationary increases assumed in future expenses are consistent with the future interest rates used in scenario testing.

Investment Returns

Interest Rates

We generally maintain distinct asset portfolios for each major line of business. Under CALM, the future cash flows from insurance contracts and the assets that support them are projected under a number of interest rate scenarios, some of which are prescribed by Canadian accepted actuarial practice. Reinvestments and disinvestments take place according to the specifications of each scenario, and the liability is set to be at least equal to the assets required to fund the worst prescribed scenario.

Equity Rates of Return

We are exposed to equity markets through our segregated fund and annuity products that provide guarantees linked to underlying fund performance. We have implemented hedging programs involving the use of derivative instruments to mitigate a portion of the equity market risk. As at December 31, 2011, the cost of these hedging programs is reflected in the liabilities.

In addition, the value of our liabilities for insurance products supported by equity assets depends on assumptions about the future level of equity markets. The calculation of insurance contract liabilities for such products includes provisions for moderate changes in rates of equity market return determined in accordance with CIA standards.

Asset Default

Assumptions related to investment returns include expected future credit losses on fixed income investments. Our past experience and industry experience over the long term, as well as specific reviews of the current portfolio, are used to project credit losses.

In addition to the allowances for losses on invested assets outlined in Note 6, the insurance contract liabilities net of reinsurance assets include an amount of $3,376 determined on a pre-tax basis to provide for possible future asset defaults and loss of asset value on current assets and on future purchases. This amount excludes defaults that can be passed through to participating policyholders.

11.A.iii Insurance Contract Liabilities

Insurance contract liabilities consist of the following:

As at December 31, 2011	SLF Canada	SLF U.S.	SLF Asia	Corporate[1]	Total
Individual participating life	$16,973	$ 5,129	$4,194	$2,005	$28,301
Individual non-participating life	5,441	13,261	326	732	19,760
Group life	1,292	1,094	9	—	2,395
Individual annuities	9,505	9,668	—	4,924	24,097
Group annuities	7,197	613	—	—	7,810
Health insurance	7,376	1,255	1	117	8,749
Insurance contract liabilities before other policy liabilities	47,784	31,020	4,530	7,778	91,112
Add: Other policy liabilities[2]	2,630	1,104	1,219	309	5,262
Total insurance contract liabilities	$50,414	$32,124	$5,749	$8,087	$96,374

[1] Primarily business from the U.K. and run-off reinsurance operations. Includes SLF U.K. of $1,929 for Individual participating life; $17 for Individual non-participating life; $4,924 for Individual annuities and $121 for Other policy liabilities.

[2] Consists of amounts on deposit, policy benefits payable, provisions for unreported claims, provisions for policyholder dividends and provisions for experience rating refunds.

As at December 31, 2010	SLF Canada	SLF U.S.	SLF Asia	Corporate[1]	Total
Individual participating life	$16,115	$ 4,978	$3,511	$2,055	$26,659
Individual non-participating life	4,640	11,297	303	608	16,848
Group life	1,270	985	8	—	2,263
Individual annuities	8,628	9,012	—	4,316	21,956
Group annuities	6,489	614	—	—	7,103
Health insurance	6,662	1,124	1	113	7,900
Insurance contract liabilities before other policy liabilities	43,804	28,010	3,823	7,092	82,729
Add: Other policy liabilities[2]	2,832	1,058	1,114	323	5,327
Total insurance contract liabilities	$46,636	$29,068	$4,937	$7,415	$88,056

[1] Primarily business from the U.K. and run-off reinsurance operations. Includes SLF U.K. of $1,976 for Individual participating life; $21 for Individual non-participating life; $4,316 for Individual annuities and $118 for Other policy liabilities.

[2] Consists of amounts on deposit, policy benefits payable, provisions for unreported claims, provisions for policyholder dividends and provisions for experience rating refunds.

As at January 1, 2010	SLF Canada	SLF U.S.	SLF Asia	Corporate[1]	Total
Individual participating life	$15,240	$ 5,162	$3,027	$2,328	$25,757
Individual non-participating life	3,710	9,833	257	1,082	14,882
Group life	1,290	972	8	124	2,394
Individual annuities	8,600	10,690	—	4,380	23,670
Group annuities	6,391	670	—	—	7,061
Health insurance	6,231	1,121	1	115	7,468
Insurance contract liabilities before other policy liabilities	41,462	28,448	3,293	8,029	81,232
Add: Other policy liabilities[2]	2,763	1,142	1,030	689	5,624
Total insurance contract liabilities	$44,225	$29,590	$4,323	$8,718	$86,856

[1] Primarily business from the U.K., life retrocession and run-off reinsurance operations. Includes SLF U.K. of $2,238 for Individual participating life; $24 for Individual non-participating life; $4,380 for Individual annuities and $122 for other policy liabilities.

[2] Consists of amounts on deposit, policy benefits payable, provisions for unreported claims, provisions for policyholder dividends and provisions for experience rating refunds.

11.A.iv Changes in Insurance Contract Liabilities and Reinsurance Assets

Changes in Insurance contract liabilities and Reinsurance assets for the period are as follows:

	For the Year Ended December 31, 2011			For the Year Ended December 31, 2010		
	Insurance Contract Liabilities	Reinsurance Assets	Net	Insurance Contract Liabilities	Reinsurance Assets	Net
Balances, beginning of period	$82,729	$3,652	$79,077	$81,232	$3,133	$78,099
Change in balances on in-force policies	4,515	216	4,299	1,673	589	1,084
Balances arising from new policies	2,486	114	2,372	2,586	153	2,433
Changes in assumptions or methodology	583	(920)	1,503	132	28	104
Increase (decrease) in Insurance contract liabilities and Reinsurance assets	7,584	(590)	8,174	4,391	770	3,621
Balances before the following:	90,313	3,062	87,251	85,623	3,903	81,720
Disposition (Note 3)	—	—	—	(563)	6	(569)
Other[1]	(117)	—	(117)	—	—	—
Foreign exchange rate movements	916	32	884	(2,331)	(257)	(2,074)
Balances before Other policy liabilities and assets	91,112	3,094	88,018	82,729	3,652	79,077
Other policy liabilities and assets	5,262	183	5,079	5,327	203	5,124
Total Insurance contract liabilities and Reinsurance assets	$96,374	$3,277	$93,097	$88,056	$3,855	$84,201

[1] Reduction in liabilities due to Policy loan adjustment.

11.A.v Impact of Changes in Assumptions or Methodology

Impact of Changes in Assumptions or Methodology on Insurance Contract Liabilities Net of Reinsurance Assets—2011.

Assumption or Methodology	Policy Liabilities Increase (Decrease) Before Income Taxes	Description
Mortality/Morbidity	$164	Primarily due to updates to reflect new industry guidance from the CIA related to mortality improvement.
Lapse and other policyholder behaviour	405	Reflects higher lapse rates on term insurance renewals in SLF Canada, as well as updates for premium persistency in Individual Insurance in SLF U.S.
Expense	10	Impact of reflecting recent experience studies across the Company (i.e. higher unit costs).
Investment returns	192	Largely due to updates to a number of investment assumptions including updates to real estate returns and the impact of a lower interest rate environment, partially offset by changes to asset default assumptions.
Model enhancements	(207)	Modelling enhancements to improve the projection of future cash flows across a number of our businesses.

Assumption or Methodology	Policy Liabilities Increase (Decrease) Before Income Taxes	Description
Hedging in the liabilities	939	Reflects a change in methodology to provide for the cost of hedging our existing variable annuity and segregated fund contracts over their remaining lifetime.
Total impact	$1,503	

Impact of Changes in Assumptions or Methodology on Insurance Contract Liabilities Net of Reinsurance Assets—2010

Assumption or Methodology	Policy Liabilities Increase (decrease) Before Income Taxes	Description
Mortality/Morbidity	$(249)	Largely due to favourable changes to the mortality basis in Individual Insurance in SLF U.S., Reinsurance in Corporate and mortality/morbidity in the Company's Group businesses in SLF Canada and SLF U.S.
Lapse and other policyholder behaviour	269	Reflects the impact of higher persistency as a result of low interest rates in Individual insurance in SLF U.S., as well as higher lapse rates on term insurance renewals in SLF Canada.
Expense	54	Impact of reflecting recent experience studies across the Company.
Investment returns	83	Primarily from impact of Company wide revisions to equity and interest rate return assumptions.
Model enhancements	(53)	Modelling enhancements to improve the projection of future cash flows across a number of our businesses.
Total impact	$104	

11.A.vi Gross Claims and Benefits Paid

Gross claims and benefits paid consist of the following:

For the Years Ended December 31	2011	2010
Maturities and surrenders	$ 4,112	$ 4,333
Annuity payments	1,282	1,242
Death and disability benefits	3,075	3,444
Health benefits	3,526	3,360
Policyholder dividends and interest on claims and deposits	901	1,104
Total gross claims and benefits paid	$12,896	$13,483

11.B Investment Contract Liabilities

11.B.i Description of Business

The following are the types of Investment contracts in force:
- Term certain payout annuities in Canada and the U.S.
- Guaranteed Investment Contracts in Canada
- European Medium Term Notes and Medium Term Notes products issued in the U.S.
- Unit-linked products issued in the U.K. and Hong Kong; and
- Non-unit-linked pensions contracts issued in the U.K. and Hong Kong

11.B.ii Assumptions and Methodology

Investment Contracts with Discretionary Participation Features

Investment contracts with DPF are measured using the same approach as insurance contracts.

Investment Contracts without Discretionary Participation Features

Investment contracts without DPF are measured at FVTPL if by doing so a potential accounting mismatch is eliminated or significantly reduced or if the contract is managed on a fair value basis. Other investment contracts without DPF are measured at amortized cost.

The fair value liability is measured through the use of prospective discounted cash-flow techniques. For unit-linked contracts, the fair value liability is equal to the current unit fund value, plus additional non-unit liability amounts on a fair value basis if required. For non-linked contracts, the fair value liability is equal to the present value of expected cash flows.

Amortized cost is measured at the date of initial recognition as the fair value of consideration received, less the net effect of principal payments such as transaction costs and front-end fees. At each reporting date, the amortized cost liability is measured as the value of future best estimate cash flows discounted at the effective interest rate. The effective interest rate is the one that equates the discounted cash payments to the liability at the date of initial recognition.

11.B.iii Investment Contract Liabilities

Investment contract liabilities consist of the following:

As at December 31, 2011	SLF Canada	SLF U.S.	SLF Asia	Corporate	Total
Individual participating life	$ —	$ —	$ —	$19	$ 19
Individual non-participating life	—	—	152	7	159
Individual annuities	1,581	76	—	68	1,725
Group annuities	—	921	249	—	1,170
Total investment contract liabilities	$1,581	$997	$401	$94	$3,073

Included in the Investment contract liabilities of $3,073 are liabilities of $487 for investment contracts with DPF, $1,620 for investment contracts without DPF measured at amortized cost and $966 for investment contracts without DPF measured at fair value.

As at December 31, 2010	SLF Canada	SLF U.S.	SLF Asia	Corporate	Total
Individual participating life	$ —	$ —	$ —	$19	$ 19
Individual non-participating life	—	—	152	7	159
Individual annuities	1,386	78	—	69	1,533
Group annuities	—	2,130	302	—	2,432
Total investment contract liabilities	$1,386	$2,208	$454	$95	$4,143

Included in the Investment contract liabilities of $4,143 are liabilities of $540 for investment contracts with DPF, $1,396 for investment contracts without DPF measured at amortized cost and $2,207 for investment contracts without DPF measured at fair value.

As at January 1, 2010	SLF Canada	SLF U.S.	SLF Asia	Corporate	Total
Individual participating life	$ —	$ —	$ —	$ 23	$ 23
Individual non-participating life	—	—	71	11	82
Individual annuities	1,092	92	—	79	1,263
Group annuities	—	3,174	373	—	3,547
Total investment contract liabilities	$1,092	$3,266	$444	$113	$4,915

Included in the Investment contract liabilities of $4,915 are liabilities of $542 for investment contracts with DPF, $1,149 for investment contracts without DPF measured at amortized cost and $3,224 for investment contracts without DPF measured at fair value.

11.B.iv Changes in Investment Contract Liabilities

Changes in investment contract liabilities without DPF are as follows:

	December 31, 2011		December 31, 2010	
For the Years Ended	Measured at Fair Value	Measured at Amortized Cost	Measured at Fair Value	Measured at Amortized Cost
Balance, beginning of period	$2,207	$1,396	$3,224	$1,149
Deposits	—	395	7	409
Interest	19	40	33	38
Withdrawals	(1,218)	(228)	(984)	(203)
Fees	—	(2)	—	(4)
Change in fair value	(19)	—	40	—
Other	5	17	3	13
Foreign exchange rate movements	(28)	2	(116)	(6)
Balance, end of period	$ 966	$1,620	$2,207	$1,396

Changes in investment contract liabilities with DPF are as follows:

For the Years Ended	December 31, 2011	December 31, 2010
Balance, beginning of period	$540	$542
Change in liabilities on in-force	(74)	(43)
Liabilities arising from new policies	9	75
Changes in assumptions or methodology	—	1
Increase (decrease) in liabilities	(65)	33
Liabilities before the following:	475	575
Foreign exchange rate movements	12	(35)
Balance, end of period	$487	$540

IFRS-BPPD 2.31

11.C Total Assets Supporting Liabilities and Equity

The following tables show the total assets supporting total liabilities for the product lines shown (including insurance contract and investment contract liabilities) and assets supporting equity and other:

As at December 31, 2011

	FVTPL-Debt Securities	AFS-Debt Securities	FVTPL-Equity Securities	AFS-Equity Securities	Mortgages and Loans	Investment Properties	Other	Total
Individual participating life	$15,227	$ —	$2,274	$ —	$ 5,588	$3,658	$ 5,033	$ 31,780
Individual non-participating life	11,247	479	995	9	4,670	699	8,040	26,139
Group life	879	—	8	—	1,293	26	965	3,171
Individual annuities	15,982	382	273	—	6,984	15	3,639	27,275
Group annuities	4,226	169	83	1	4,120	168	650	9,417
Health insurance	3,996	—	98	—	4,694	133	1,144	10,065
Equity and other	70	10,273	—	829	406	614	9,805	21,997
Total assets	$51,627	$11,303	$3,731	$839	$27,755	$5,313	$29,276	$129,844

As at December 31, 2010

	FVTPL-Debt Securities	AFS-Debt Securities	FVTPL-Equity Securities	AFS-Equity Securities	Mortgages and Loans	Investment Properties	Other	Total
Individual participating life	$14,022	$ —	$3,054	$ —	$ 5,295	$3,330	$ 4,321	$ 30,022
Individual non-participating life	9,099	420	1,005	14	3,769	355	6,863	21,525
Group life	848	—	3	—	1,255	25	873	3,004
Individual annuities	15,363	246	274	—	6,957	9	1,596	24,445
Group annuities	4,421	246	76	—	3,921	156	1,265	10,085
Health insurance	3,755	—	35	—	4,242	115	1,201	9,348
Equity and other	474	9,719	2	768	595	554	11,760	23,872
Total assets	$47,982	$10,631	$4,449	$782	$26,034	$4,544	$27,879	$122,301

As at January 1, 2010

	FVTPL-Debt Securities	AFS-Debt Securities	FVTPL-Equity Securities	AFS-Equity Securities	Mortgages and Loans	Investment Properties	Other	Total
Individual participating life	$12,644	$ —	$3,165	$ —	$ 5,488	$3,379	$ 4,335	$ 29,011
Individual non-participating life	7,280	442	847	—	3,639	308	7,231	19,747
Group life	860	—	3	—	1,316	27	960	3,166
Individual annuities	15,054	169	247	—	7,456	—	3,268	26,194
Group annuities	4,737	315	79	—	4,171	155	1,847	11,304
Health insurance	3,337	—	18	—	4,183	138	1,219	8,895
Equity and other	472	8,605	—	610	668	539	12,543	23,437
Total assets	$44,384	$9,531	$4,359	$610	$26,921	$4,546	$31,403	$121,754

11.D Role of the Appointed Actuary

The Appointed Actuary is appointed by the Board and is responsible for ensuring that the assumptions and methods used in the valuation of policy liabilities are in accordance with Canadian accepted actuarial practice, applicable legislation and associated regulations or directives.

The Appointed Actuary is required to provide an opinion regarding the appropriateness of the policy liabilities at the statement dates to meet all obligations to policyholders of the Company. Examination of supporting data for accuracy and completeness and analysis of our assets for their ability to support the amount of policy liabilities are important elements of the work required to form this opinion.

The Appointed Actuary is required each year to analyze the financial condition of the Company and prepare a report for the Board. The 2011 analysis tested our capital adequacy until December 31, 2015, under various adverse economic and business conditions. The Appointed Actuary reviews the calculation of our Canadian capital and surplus requirements. In addition, our foreign operations and foreign subsidiaries must comply with local capital requirements in each of the jurisdictions in which they operate.

IAS 2, *INVENTORIES*

Author's Note

The IASB amended IAS 2, *Inventories*, by issuing several new standards. These amendments are effective for annual periods beginning on or after 1 January 2012 and, therefore, are not discussed in the commentary in this section. Instead, this author's note includes a brief description of the relevant revisions to IAS 2.

The following standards amended IAS 2:

- IFRS 9
  This amendment replaces references to IAS 39 with a reference to IFRS 9.
- IFRS 13
  IFRS 13 replaces the definition of fair value in paragraph 7 of IAS 2 with "Fair value reflects the price at which an orderly transaction to sell the same inventory in the principal or more advantageous market for that inventory would take place between market participants at the measurement date."

Early adoption of these standards is permitted. Because these standards are effective for annual periods beginning on or after 1 January 2012, these amendments are not reflected in the commentary in this section. However, these amendments would not affect the content of illustrative excerpts from survey companies' financial statements.

IFRS Overview and Comparison to U.S. GAAP

2.32 IAS 2 defines *inventories* as assets held for sale in the ordinary course of business, assets in the process of production for such sale, and materials or supplies to be consumed in the production or rendering of services.

Recognition and Measurement

IFRSs

2.33 IAS 2 applies to all inventories, except work in process under construction contracts (IAS 11, *Construction Contracts*); financial instruments (IAS 32, *Financial Instruments: Presentation*, and IAS 39); and biological assets (IAS 41, *Agriculture*).

2.34 IAS 16, *Property, Plant and Equipment*, requires an entity to include spare parts and servicing equipment as inventory, except that the entity may include major spare parts and standby equipment in PPE when it expects to use these items for more than one period or when the parts and equipment can only be used with an item of PPE. Entities should classify intangible assets and investment properties as inventory when these items are developed and held for sale in the ordinary course of business.

2.35 To the extent that inventories are measured according to standard industry practice at net realizable value, IAS 2 exempts the following industries from its measurement requirements: producers of agricultural and forest products, agricultural products after harvest, and minerals and mineral products. Measurement requirements also do not apply to commodity broker-dealers who measure their inventories at fair value less cost to sell. In these cases, an entity should recognize changes in carrying value in profit or loss.

2.36 An entity should recognize items that meet the definition of *inventory* when the items also meet the definition of an *asset* and the *recognition criteria*. To meet the recognition criteria, the asset should be a probable source of future economic benefits (probability criteria), and its cost should be measured reliably (measurement reliability criteria). Cost includes all costs, including purchase, conversion, and other incurred costs, necessary to bring the assets to their present condition and location. An entity should exclude from cost (*a*) abnormal waste, storage, and administrative overheads that do not contribute to bringing inventories to their present location and condition and (*b*) selling costs.

2.37 At initial recognition, an entity should measure inventories at cost of production. Production costs consist mainly of direct labor, including supervisory costs and direct overhead. They also include a systematic allocation of fixed and variable production overheads that are incurred. Unallocated overheads are expensed in the period in which they are incurred. Capitalized costs should not include administrative costs, other nonattributable costs, and profit margins. Entities should measure agricultural produce at fair value less cost to sell at the point of harvest, in accordance with IAS 41. Subsequently, unless an entity is exempt as previously explained, the requirements of IAS 2 apply.

2.38 After initial recognition, an entity should measure inventories at the lower of cost or net realizable value. Convenient techniques for measuring cost, such as standard cost or retail methods, can be used if the results approximate actual cost.

2.39 An entity should use one of the following cost flow assumptions to assign costs to inventories and expense:

- Specific identification for assets that are not interchangeable or segregated and produced for specific projects
- First-in, first-out
- Weighted-average cost

IAS 2 requires an entity to apply the same cost flow assumption to inventories of similar nature and use. IAS 2 prohibits the use of the last-in, first-out (LIFO) cost flow assumption.

2.40 An entity should not carry an asset at an amount exceeding the amount it expects to realize from sale or use. When there are indicators that the cost is not recoverable, such as damage or decline in selling price, an entity should write-down inventories to net realizable value. *Net realizable value* is the estimated selling price in the ordinary course of business less estimated completion costs and costs necessary to make the sale.

2.41 An entity should recognize the carrying amount of inventories sold as an expense in profit or loss in the same period as it recognizes the related revenue.

U.S. GAAP

2.42 As defined in the FASB ASC glossary, *inventory* is the aggregate of those items of tangible personal property that have any of the following characteristics:

- Held for sale in the ordinary course of business
- In process of production for such sale
- To be currently consumed in the production of goods or services to be available for sale

Similar to IFRSs, the term *inventory* applies to goods awaiting sale (the merchandise of a trading concern and the finished goods of a manufacturer), goods in the course of production (work in process), and goods to be consumed directly or indirectly in production (raw materials and supplies). However, this definition specifically excludes from classification as inventory long-term assets subject to depreciation accounting or goods that, when put into use, will be classified as long term. Therefore, under U.S. GAAP, an entity should not classify intangible assets or investment properties held for sale in the normal course of business as inventory, but they could be so classified under IFRSs.

2.43 Two key measurement differences between IFRSs and FASB ASC are the following:

- FASB ASC 330-10-35-1 requires an entity to measure inventories at the lower of cost or market. *Market*, as defined in the FASB ASC glossary, means current replacement cost, with the constraint that market should not exceed net realizable value and should not be lower than net realizable value less an allowance for an approximately normal profit margin.
- FASB ASC 330-10-30-9 permits the use of the LIFO cost flow assumption.

2.44 Unlike IFRSs, FASB ASC 330, *Inventory*, does not permit reversals (or recovery) of write-downs of inventory. A write-down under FASB ASC 330-10-35-14 creates a new cost basis, with the result that no recoveries should be recognized prior to sale or disposal.

Presentation

IFRSs

2.45 An entity should present inventories as a separate line item on the balance sheet, classified as current or noncurrent in accordance with IAS 1.

U.S. GAAP

2.46 Given the scope exclusions noted previously in paragraph 2.42, in accordance with FASB ASC 210-10-45-1, an entity should generally classify inventories as current.

Disclosure

IFRSs

2.47 IAS 2 requires the following disclosures:

- Accounting policies for measuring inventories and the cost flow assumption applied
- Total carrying amount and carrying amounts of classifications appropriate to the entity
- Carrying amount of any inventories held at fair value less cost to sell

- Amount recognized as an expense during the period
- Amounts recognized as write-downs or reversals of write-downs during the period and a recognition of the circumstances that led to the write-down or reversal
- Carrying amount of inventories pledged as security for liabilities

U.S. GAAP

2.48 Required disclosures under FASB ASC are similar to those in IAS 1, except that the SEC requires additional disclosures by entities that use LIFO. Rule 5-02-6(c) of SEC Regulation S-X requires an entity to disclose the excess of replacement or current cost over stated amounts for LIFO inventories, if material. SEC *Codification of Staff Accounting Bulletins* topic 11(F), "LIFO Liquidations," requires disclosures about LIFO liquidations, and topic 5(L), "LIFO Inventory Practices," directs entities to the AICPA issues paper *Identification and Discussion of Certain Financial Accounting and Reporting Issues Concerning LIFO Inventories* for guidance in the absence of authoritative literature.

Presentation and Disclosure Excerpts

First-In, First-Out

2.49

Linamar Corporation (Dec 2011)

Author's Note

Linamar Corporation implemented IFRSs effective December 31, 2011, with a date of transition of January 1, 2010. The excerpt that follows reflects the initial application of IAS 1.

CONSOLIDATED STATEMENT OF FINANCIAL POSITION (in part)

(In thousands of Canadian dollars)

	December 31, 2011 $	December 31, 2010 $	January 1, 2010 $
Assets			
Cash and cash equivalents	99,129	78,907	81,296
Accounts and other receivables (Note 7)	509,416	428,415	310,577
Inventories (Notes 8, 9, 10)	380,274	288,067	259,821
Income taxes recoverable (Note 11)	12,971	16,040	17,786
Current portion of long-term receivables (Notes 7, 8, 9)	5,753	2,406	1,558
Derivative financial instruments (Note 12)	—	735	2,265
Other current assets	7,354	7,632	6,338
Total current assets	1,014,897	822,202	679,641

NOTES TO THE CONSOLIDATED FINANCIAL STATEMENTS (in part)

1 General Information

Linamar Corporation (the "Company") is a diversified global manufacturing Company of highly engineered products. The Company is an Ontario, Canada corporation with common shares listed on the Toronto Stock Exchange. The registered office is located at 287 Speedvale Avenue West, Guelph, Ontario, Canada.

The annual consolidated financial statements of the Company for the year ended December 31, 2011 were authorized for issue in accordance with a resolution of the Company's Board of Directors on March 6, 2012. No changes were made to the consolidated financial statements subsequent to board authorization.

3 Significant Accounting Policies (in part)

The principal accounting policies applied in the preparation of these consolidated financial statements are set out below. These policies have been consistently applied to all the periods presented, unless otherwise stated.

Inventories

Inventories are valued at the lower of cost and net realizable value determined using the first-in, first-out (FIFO) method. Net realizable value is the estimated selling price in the ordinary course of business, less applicable variable selling expenses. The cost of finished goods and work in progress is comprised of material costs, direct labour costs and other direct costs and related production overheads (based on normal operating capacity).

The amount of inventories recognized as an expense during the period is shown as costs of sales. Impairment losses for inventories are recorded when the net realizable value is lower than cost.

Revenue Recognition

Revenue from the sale of products is recognized when the risks and rewards incidental to ownership are transferred. This generally corresponds to when goods are shipped to customers. Revenue from services is recognized when services are rendered. Revenue from the sale of tooling is recognized once the tooling is substantially complete and the customer approves the initial production sample.

Customer tooling costs that are recoverable through the piece price amount of subsequent parts production are generally expensed as incurred. In those instances where the related customer agreement specifically provides a contractual guarantee of reimbursement or of volume levels during the term of the contract, customer tooling costs are classified as inventory and are amortized based on related production volumes.

10 Inventories

	December 31, 2011	December 31, 2010	January 1, 2010
	$	$	$
General stores	59,581	43,363	39,759
Raw materials	141,608	114,899	105,843
Work-in-process	94,642	73,530	63,169
Finished goods	84,443	56,275	51,050
	380,274	288,067	259,821

The cost of inventories recognized as an expense during the year ended December 31, 2011 was $2,170,169 (2010—$1,670,693).

A provision for obsolescence for slow moving inventory items is estimated by management based on historical and expected future sales and is included in cost of goods sold. Lower of cost or net realizable value adjustments are made on a regular basis. In the year ended December 31, 2011 the Company recognized a charge to cost of goods sold for the write-down of slow moving and obsolete inventory, and adjustments to net realizable value aggregating $15,127 (2010—$13,066). In the year ended December 31, 2011 the Company recognized a gain to cost of goods sold for reversal of inventory provisions with a value of $852 (2010—nil). The inventory balance has been reduced by a provision of $31,581 as at December 31, 2011 ($27,297 as at December 31, 2010 and $26,735 as at January 1, 2010).

Weighted Average Cost, Specific Identification for Inventory In-Transit

2.50

KT Corporation (Dec 2011)

Author's Note

KT Corporation implemented IFRSs effective December 31, 2011, with a date of transition of January 1, 2010. The excerpt that follows reflects the initial application of IAS 1.

CONSOLIDATED STATEMENTS OF FINANCIAL POSITION (in part)

(In Millions of Korean Won)	Notes	1.1.2010	12.31.2010	12.31.2011	(In Thousands of U.S. Dollars) 12.31.2011 (Note 2)
Assets					
Current assets					
Cash and cash equivalents	2, 5, 6, 36	(Won) 1,542,872	(Won) 1,161,641	(Won) 1,445,169	$1,253,073
Trade and other receivables, net	2, 5, 7, 35, 36	3,735,368	4,193,377	6,158,914	5,340,253
Short-term loans, net	2, 5, 8, 36	443,722	725,342	698,030	605,246
Current finance lease receivables, net	2, 5, 21, 36	198,987	194,771	248,703	215,645
Other financial assets	2, 5, 9, 36	386,717	269,692	253,625	219,912
Current income tax assets	2	26,664	287	838	727
Inventories, net	2, 10	765,378	710,617	674,727	585,040
Other current assets	11, 35	211,682	263,720	310,653	269,360
Total current assets		7,311,390	7,519,447	9,790,659	8,489,256

NOTES TO THE CONSOLIDATED FINANCIAL STATEMENTS (in part)

1. General Information

The consolidated financial statements include the accounts of KT Corporation, which is the controlling company as defined under IAS 27, *Consolidated and Separate Financial Statements*, and its 51 controlled subsidiaries as described in Note 1.2 (collectively referred to as the "Company").

The Controlling Company

KT Corporation (the "Controlling Company") commenced operations on January 1, 1982, when it spun off from the Korea Communications Commission (formerly the Korean Ministry of Information and Communications) to provide telephone services and to engage in the development of advanced communications services under the Act of Telecommunications of Korea. The headquarters are located in Seongnam-si, Gyeonggi-do, Republic of Korea, and the address of its registered head office is 206, Jungja-dong, Bundang-gu, Seongnam-si, Gyeonggi-do.

On October 1, 1997, upon the announcement of the Government-Investment Enterprises Management Basic Act and the Privatization Law, the Controlling Company became a government-funded institution under the Commercial Code of Korea.

On December 23, 1998, the Controlling Company's shares were listed on the Korea Exchange.

On May 29, 1999, the Controlling Company issued 24,282,195 additional shares and issued American Depository Shares (ADS), representing new shares and government-owned shares, at the New York Stock Exchange and the London Stock Exchange. On July 2, 2001, the additional ADS representing 55,502,161 government-owned shares were issued at the New York Stock Exchange and London Stock Exchange.

In 2002, the Controlling Company acquired 60,294,575 government-owned shares in accordance with the Korean government's privatization plan. As of December 31, 2011, the Korean government does not own any share in the Controlling Company.

On June 1, 2009, the Controlling Company, which is an existing company, was merged with KT Freetel Co., Ltd., which was a subsidiary, to enhance the efficiency of business management.

2. Significant Accounting Policies

The following is a summary of significant accounting policies followed by the Company in the preparation of its financial statements. These policies have been consistently applied to all the periods presented, unless otherwise stated.

2.10 Inventories

Inventories are stated at the lower of cost and net realizable value. Cost is determined using the weighted-average method, except for inventories in-transit which is determined using the specific identification method. Net realizable value is the estimated selling price in the ordinary course of business, less applicable selling expenses.

10. Inventories

Inventories as of January 1, 2010 and December 31, 2010 and 2011, are as follows:

(In Millions of Korean Won)	1.1.2010			12.31.2010			12.31.2011		
	Acquisition Cost	Valuation Allowance[1]	Book Value	Acquisition Cost	Valuation Allowance[1]	Book Value	Acquisition Cost	Valuation Allowance[1]	Book Value
Merchandise	(Won) 635,778	(Won) (45,116)	(Won) 590,662	(Won) 617,919	(Won) (39,695)	(Won) 578,224	(Won) 622,196	(Won) (29,022)	(Won) 593,194
Supplies	31,989	(662)	31,327	29,595	(196)	29,399	20,396	(144)	20,252
Goods in transit	69,250	—	69,250	55,564	—	55,564	—	—	—
Others	77,107	(2,968)	74,139	48,627	(1,197)	47,430	62,274	(993)	61,281
Total	(Won) 814,124	(Won) (48,746)	(Won) 765,378	(Won) 751,705	(Won) (41,088)	(Won) 710,617	(Won) 704,866	(Won) (30,139)	(Won) 674,727

[1] The Company records valuation allowance for inventories when the Company determined that the costs of inventories are not recoverable as these inventories are damaged, as they become wholly or partially obsolete or as the selling prices have declined.

Fair Value Less Cost to Sell—Broker Trader Exemption From IAS 2

2.51

MFC Industrial Ltd. (Dec 2011)

Author's Note

MFC Industrial Ltd. implemented IFRSs effective December 31, 2011, with a date of transition of January 1, 2010. The excerpt that follows reflects the initial application of IAS 1.

CONSOLIDATED STATEMENTS OF FINANCIAL POSITION (in part)

(United States Dollars in Thousands)

	Notes	December 31, 2011	December 31, 2010
Assets			
Current Assets			
Cash and cash equivalents		$387,052	$397,697
Short-term deposits		163	—
Securities	6	13,062	27,894
Restricted cash	7	623	3,464
Loan receivable	8	19,869	5,792
Bills of exchange	9	10,545	—
Trade receivables	9	21,154	13,088
Other receivables	10	9,144	12,107
Inventories	11	81,223	67,102
Real estate held for sale		12,012	12,480
Deposits, prepaid and other	12	9,344	20,847
Total current assets		564,191	560,471

NOTES TO THE CONSOLIDATED FINANCIAL STATEMENTS (in part)

Note 1. Nature of Business and Summary of Significant Accounting Policies (in part)

MFC Industrial Ltd. ("MFC Industrial" or the "Company", formerly Terra Nova Royalty Corporation) is incorporated under the laws of British Columbia, Canada. MFC Industrial is a global commodities supply chain company.

In November and December 2010, MFC Industrial, through a share exchange, acquired all of the issued and outstanding shares of Mass Financial Corp. ("Mass") (see Note 3). Mass and its subsidiaries (collectively, "Mass Group") are primarily in the commodities and resources business, and merchant banking. The Group consolidated the results of the operations of Mass Group since November 16, 2010.

Until the end of March 2010, MFC Industrial also operated in the industrial plant technology, equipment and service business for the cement and mining industries through its former subsidiary KHD Humboldt Wedag International AG in Germany and its subsidiaries and affiliates (collectively "KID"). MFC Industrial ceased to consolidate KID from March 31, 2010 and completed the spin-off of KID by December 31, 2010 (see Note 4). As a result, the results of operations of KID have been presented as discontinued operations. Accordingly, prior period financial statements, including business segment information as disclosed in Note 5, have been reclassified to reflect this change.

B. Significant Accounting Policies (in part)

(viii) Inventories

Inventories consist of raw materials, work-in-progress, and finished goods. Inventories are recorded at the lower of cost or estimated net realizable value. Cost, where appropriate, includes an allocation of manufacturing overheads incurred in bringing inventories to their present location and condition. Net realizable value represents the estimated selling price less all estimated costs of completion and cost to be incurred in marketing, selling and distribution. The amount of any write-down of inventories to net realizable value and all losses of inventories are recognized as an expense in the period the write-down or loss occurs. The amount of a reversal of a write-down of inventories arising from an increase in net realizable value is recognized as a reduction in the amount of inventories recognized as an expense in the period in which the reversal occurs.

Commodities acquired in commodity broker-trader activities with the purpose of selling in the near future and generating a profit from fluctuations in price or broker-traders' margin are measured at fair value less costs to sell.

(xviii) Costs of Sales

Costs of sales include the cost of goods (commodities and resources, real estate properties, medical instruments and supplies) sold. The cost of goods sold includes both the direct cost of materials and indirect costs, freight charges, purchasing and receiving costs, inspection costs, distribution costs, as well as provision for warranty when applicable.

The costs of sales also include the write-downs of inventories and available-for-sale securities, credit losses on loans and receivables, fair value losses on investment property and net losses on securities.

The reversal of write-downs of inventories and allowance for credit losses reduce the costs of sales.

C. Major Sources of Estimation Uncertainty (in part)

The major assumptions and other sources of estimation uncertainty that have a significant risk of resulting in a material adjustment to the carrying amounts of assets and liabilities within the next financial year are discussed below. These items require management's most difficult, subjective or complex judgments.

(ii) Provision for Inventories

The Group had recorded inventories of $81,223 at December 31, 2011. The provision for the inventories is regularly reviewed and general and specific provisions are recognized for balances considered to be irrecoverable. The irrecoverable amounts are estimated based on reviewing the macroeconomic environment and available micro-economic information specific to the product categories.

Note 11. Inventories

	2011	2010
Raw materials	$ 4,741	$ 6,467
Work-in-progress	6,021	10,842
Finished goods	6,846	4,968
Commodity inventories (including goods-in-transit of $42,130 and $30,603 at December 31, 2011 and 2010, respectively)	63,615	44,825
	$81,223	$67,102

The Group entered into sale and repurchase agreements with other commodity broker-traders pursuant to which the Group sold an agreed quantity of commodities at agreed prices and undertakes to buy back the same quantity of the same commodities at the same agreed prices in future periods. These sale and repurchase transactions are accounted for as financing arrangements. The cash received is discounted at the market interest rate and shown as deferred sale liabilities in the consolidated statement of financial position. When the commodities are delivered by the Group to the counterparties, sales transactions are completed and recognized with debits to the deferred sale liabilities. As at December 31, 2011, the Group recognized current and long-term deferred sale liabilities of $14,958 and $25,647, respectively. The long-term deferred liability is due on various dates in 2013. As at December 31, 2010, the Group recognized current and long-term deferred sale liabilities of $23,133 and $39,993, respectively.

As at December 31, 2011 and 2010, there was no inventory pledged as security for liabilities.

Specific Identification—Real Estate Inventories

2.52

Alon Holdings Blue Square—Israel Ltd (Dec 2011)

CONSOLIDATED STATEMENTS OF FINANCIAL POSITION (in part)

In Thousands	Note	December 31 2010	December 31 2011	Convenience Translation (Note 1b) December 31, 2011
		NIS		U.S. Dollars
Assets				
Non-current assets:				
Investments in associates	10b	6,012	202,653	53,037
Derivative financial instruments	13	56,078	896	234
Real estate inventories	14d	83,337	100,035	26,180
Payments on account of real estate	11	164,132	191,600	50,144
Investment in securities	12	30,327	33,159	8,678
Loans receivable, net of current maturities	16	176,043	182,654	47,803
Property and equipment, net	7	2,928,515	2,942,487	770,083
Investment property	8	546,870	576,093	150,770
Intangible assets, net	9	1,486,744	1,461,070	382,379
Other long-term receivables	17	47,098	142,331	37,250
Deferred taxes	23	66,018	104,321	27,302
		5,591,174	5,937,299	1,553,860
Total assets		8,764,187	9,094,217	2,380,062

NOTES TO THE CONSOLIDATED FINANCIAL STATEMENTS (in part)

Note 1—General (in part):

a. Information on the Activities of Alon Holdings Blue Square—Israel Ltd and Its Subsidiaries

Alon Holdings Blue Square—Israel Ltd. (formerly Blue Square—Israel Ltd.) ("Blue Square") is an Israeli corporation, which, directly and through its subsidiaries (together—the Company) mainly operates in Israel. All references to the Company include, unless the context otherwise indicates, Blue-Square and its subsidiaries. Upon completion of the acquisition of Dor Alon in 2010, see note 6, the Company operates in four reportable segments: (1) Supermarkets, (2) Non-food Retail and Wholesale (3) Real Estate and (4) Commercial and fueling sites (see note 5).

Alon Holdings Blue Square—Israel Ltd. is a limited public company incorporated and domiciled in Israel, whose ADSs and shares are listed for trading on the New-York Stock Exchange (the "NYSE") and on the Tel-Aviv Stock Exchange (the "TASE").

The Company is controlled by Alon Israel Oil Company Ltd ("Alon"). The address of its registered office is 2 Amal St., Afek Industrial Zone, Rosh Ha'ayin, Israel. The consolidated financial statements of the Company for the year ended December 31, 2011 were authorized for issue in accordance with a resolution of the directors on April 30, 2012.

The consolidated results for the year 2010 include the results of the subsidiary Dor Alon, acquired in 2010, from October 3, 2010 to December 31, 2010. Dor Alon's shares are listed on the Tel Aviv stock exchange. See also note 6.

Note 2—Summary of Significant Accounting Policies (in part)

j. Borrowing costs

General and specific borrowing costs directly attributable to the acquisition or construction of any qualifying asset (including investment property and real estate inventories) are capitalized during the period of time that is required to complete and prepare the asset for its intended use. Other borrowing costs are expensed in the period they occur. Borrowing costs consist of interest and other costs that an entity incurs in connection with the borrowing of funds.

n. Inventories

Inventories are stated at the lower of cost and net realizable value. Cost, except for real estate inventories, is determined mainly by the "first-in, first-out" (FIFO) method. Net realizable value is the estimated selling price in the ordinary course of business, less applicable selling expenses.

Cost of real estate inventories is specific and includes capitalization of borrowing costs for long term projects.

The Company evaluates inventory shrinkage throughout the year based on the results of periodic stock taking in its stores, and records allowances based on the results of these counts as of the statement of financial position date.

The Company reviews the need for a provision for slow moving inventories, if applicable, by comparing the value of the inventories with the level of sales, the period that passed since the start of distribution and the quality of the goods, on the basis of past experience.

Real estate inventories are stated at the lower of cost and net realizable value. Cost includes the directly identifiable expenses of the acquisition of the inventories and capitalized borrowing costs. Net realizable value is the estimated selling price in the ordinary course of business, less an estimated cost to complete and applicable selling expenses.

5) Revenue From Sales of Residential Apartments and Real Estate Inventories

Revenue from the sale of residential apartment units and real estate inventories is measured at the fair value of the consideration received or receivable. The Company recognizes the revenue when the significant risks and rewards of ownership have passed to the buyer the receipt of the consideration is expected and can be reliably measured. Revenue from the sale of apartments is generally recognized when the apartments have been substantially constructed, accepted by the customer and the full amount resulting from the sale agreement was paid by the buyer.

Note 14—Trade Receivables, Inventories and Other Receivables (in part):

2) Real Estate Inventories (Presented as Non-Current Assets)

Representing approximately 240-dunam parcel of property in Point-Wells near Seattle, Washington, USA, acquired by BSRE from a related party (see note 35a.6); BSRE has also signed a development agreement with the related party to initiate and promote a detailed plan for the approval of the building of at least 2,000 residential units on the land. BSRE is operating to change the zoning of the land from heavy industrial use to urban center zoning, and so far has received an "in principal" approval for the zoning change from the Snohomish County (which has the jurisdiction for the area where the land is located; hereinafter—the County) which was statutorily effected in the Urban Centers Code Ordinance. In March 2011, a detailed plan for the construction of residential and public areas and detailed plans for the development of the land were submitted to the County planning committee. Following objections received, the County has been given a year to make certain adjustments to the principal plan. Through December 31, 2011, BSRE invested $ 4.8 million ((NIS 18.3 million) in the development of property rights and capitalized borrowing costs of $ 1.9 million (NIS 7.3 Million) (of which $ 3.3 million and $ 0.68 million, relate to 2010, respectively).

The property serves primarily as a plant for storage and distribution of fuel and oils by the related party, and is rented to the related party for a period of up to 10 years. According to the development agreement, all demolition and contamination cleanups required for the land will be the responsibility of the related party and on its account; the related party will also compensate BSRE for any damages incurred in connection with such activities. In case BSRE was to sell the land the related party will participate in the consideration net of costs as defined in the agreement, see note 35a.b.

Note 35—Related-Party Disclosures (in part):

a. Relate to Transactions That Are Carried Out in the Normal Course of Business in Accordance With Regular Market Prices and Credit

b. Point Wells

During 2010, BSRE signed agreements with subsidiaries of Alon U.S.A, a related party, for the acquisition and development of a property in Point-Wells near Seattle, Washington, USA (presented as real estate inventories—see also note 14c.). The property, which currently serves primarily as a plant for storage and distribution of fuel and oils of the related parties was acquired for U.S. $19.5 million.

According to the development agreement, all demolition and contamination cleanups required for the land will be the responsibility of the related parties and on their own account; the related parties will also compensate BSRE for any damages incurred in connection with such activities. In case the Company was to sell the land the related party may participate in the consideration net of costs as defined in the agreement.

The agreements provide for the lease of the property to the related parties for a period of up to 10 years. Rental income received by BSRE amounts to $1.7 million and $0.8 million for the years 2011 and 2010, respectively (NIS 6.7 million and NIS 3.1 million, respectively).

TABLE 2-3: CLASSES OF PROPERTY, PLANT, AND EQUIPMENT

	2011	2010	2009
Land and land rights	67	44	33
Buildings	84	59	47
Land and buildings	66	80	84
Production equipment and machinery	112	105	98
Computer and office equipment	55	46	41
Construction in progress	82	86	82
Exploration and evaluation assets	14	5	6
Furniture and fixtures (equipment)	58	57	53
Hardware and parts	8	6	6
Leased assets	29	28	28
Leasehold improvements	35	25	22
Major overhaul (for example, drydocking)	1	1	1
Mineral properties and mining assets	11	12	13
Motor vehicles	54	52	41
Network infrastructure	19	12	10
Other transportation (for example, aircraft or vessels)	23	19	47
Oil and gas properties	5	5	4
Oil depots, storage tanks, and service stations	2	1	1
Other	89	70	61

IAS 16, *PROPERTY, PLANT AND EQUIPMENT*

Author's Note

Issued in May 2011, IFRS 13 amends IAS 16 as follows:
- Changes the terminology by replacing the terms *estimate* and *determine* with the term *measure*.
- For items of PPE carried at revalued amounts, adds the disclosure requirements in IFRS 13 and deletes two specific disclosures in IAS 16.

IFRS 13 is effective for annual reporting periods beginning on or after 1 January 2013. Early adoption is permitted.

Because the effective date is after 1 January 2012, the requirements of IFRS 13 are not discussed in the commentary in this section. The timing of the effective date of this standard affects the availability of illustrative excerpts from survey companies' financial statements. Accordingly, the excerpts appearing later in this section may not reflect all or some of these revisions.

IFRSs Overview and Comparison to U.S. GAAP

2.53 IAS 16 defines items of *PPE* as tangible items held for use in the production or supply of goods or services, items used for rental or administrative purposes, and items expected to be used over more than one period.

Recognition and Measurement

Author's Note

The requirements for depreciation and impairment in IAS 16 are discussed in section 3.

IFRSs

2.54 IAS 16 applies to all items of PPE, unless another standard permits or requires another treatment. For example, IAS 40 prescribes the accounting for land or buildings held for rental, capital appreciation, or both, and provides an alternative measurement option. In addition, the scope of IAS 16 only includes items of PPE used to develop or maintain mineral rights, mineral reserves, and other nonregenerative resources, not the rights, reserves, or resources themselves.

2.55 An entity recognizes an item of PPE when both of the following probability and measurement reliability recognition criteria are met:
- It is probable that future economic benefits will flow to the entity.
- The cost can be measured reliably.

2.56 On initial recognition, an entity should capitalize all directly attributable costs incurred in order to bring the asset to its present location and condition and that are necessary for its intended use. Examples of directly attributable costs include the purchase price, freight, employee benefits, site preparation, installation, assembly, and testing costs. IAS 16 specifically excludes the following costs from being capitalized: costs of opening a new facility, training, general administration, overhead, and selling and marketing costs. As soon as an asset is in the location and condition necessary for it to be capable of operating as intended, the entity should stop capitalizing costs. An entity should not capitalize a cost previously expensed and should not capitalize initial operating losses.

2.57 An entity should include the cost of an asset retirement obligation in the cost of the related item(s) of PPE (or inventory when the obligation is caused by inventory production), with measurement of the obligation determined by reference to IAS 37, *Provisions, Contingent Liabilities and Contingent Assets*. An entity should also record changes in the obligation, except for the effect of unwinding of the discount rate (accretion), as part of the item of PPE. In accordance with International Financial Reporting Interpretations Committee (IFRIC) 1, *Changes in Existing Decommissioning, Restoration and Similar Liabilities*, an entity should recognize the increase in the obligation from accretion as interest expense in profit and loss as incurred.

2.58 IAS 16 offers two models for subsequent measurement: cost and revaluation. An entity should select a model for an entire class of assets. Both models require an entity to record depreciation expense and to test and measure individual assets for impairment.

2.59 Under the cost model, an entity should measure the carrying amount of an item of PPE at its cost less subsequent accumulated depreciation and accumulated impairment losses. Under the revaluation model, an entity should measure the carrying amount of an item of PPE at revalued amount, because its fair value can be measured reliably. The *revalued amount* is the fair value of the asset at the date of revaluation less subsequent accumulated depreciation and accumulated impairment losses.

2.60 If the revaluation model is selected for a class of PPE, an entity should revalue the asset with sufficient regularity that its carrying amount at the reporting date is not materially different from fair value. Although an entity should revalue all items in the class at the same time, it should revalue each item of PPE individually. An entity should recognize increases in carrying amount on revaluation in other comprehensive income (accumulated revaluation surplus), unless the increase reverses a revaluation decrease previously recorded to profit or loss. Similarly, an entity should recognize decreases in carrying amount on revaluation in profit or loss, unless the decrease reduces an existing revaluation surplus.

U.S. GAAP

2.61 The requirements in FASB ASC 360-10 for initial recognition and measurement are essentially the same as those in IAS 16. FASB ASC 410-20-25-5 requires an entity to capitalize an asset retirement cost by increasing the amount of the related long-lived asset by the same amount as the liability for an asset retirement obligation upon initial

recognition of the liability. However, FASB ASC 360, *Property, Plant, and Equipment*, considers mining rights to be a separate component of PPE and land and buildings to be PPE regardless of use, even when held for sale.

2.62 In contrast to IFRSs, FASB ASC 360-10-35 permits only the use of historical cost less accumulated depreciation and impairment losses for subsequent measurement of PPE.

2.63 Like IFRSs, FASB ASC 410-20-35-8 requires an entity to include changes to an asset retirement obligation that result from subsequent revisions of the timing or amount of the original estimate of undiscounted cash flows in the cost of the asset. However, changes to the liability due to the passage of time are expensed and classified as accretion expense. Unlike IFRSs, FASB ASC 835-20-15-7 does not consider accretion to be interest expense in this case.

Presentation

IFRSs

2.64 IAS 1 requires an entity to present PPE as a separate line item on the balance sheet. An entity should classify PPE as noncurrent, unless it has been classified as held for sale or is part of a disposal group classified as held for sale, in accordance with IFRS 5.

U.S. GAAP

2.65 FASB ASC 210-10-45-4 also requires an entity to exclude land and depreciable assets from classification as a current asset. Thus, it can be inferred that PPE should be classified as noncurrent when a classified balance sheet is presented, except when classified as held for sale. As noted previously, FASB ASC 805-20-55-37 identifies mineral rights as tangible assets to be accounted for according to their nature; hence, such rights are to be presented as a separate component of PPE.

Disclosure

IFRSs

2.66 IAS 16 requires the following disclosures for each class of PPE:
- Measurement bases used to determine gross carrying amount
- Depreciation methods and useful lives or depreciation rates
- Reconciliation of the following carrying amounts at the beginning and end of the period:
  — Gross carrying amount
  — Accumulated depreciation and accumulated impairment losses (may be shown combined)

2.67 The reconciliation discussed in the preceding paragraph should show the following line items, if applicable:
- Additions, with separate disclosure of items acquired in a business combination
- Classifications to held for sale or inclusion in a disposal group classified as held for sale
- Increases or decreases from revaluation or impairment losses or reversals recognized in other comprehensive income

- Impairment losses or reversals recognized in profit or loss
- Depreciation
- Foreign exchange differences, net

2.68 IAS 16 requires an entity to provide general disclosures, including the existence and amounts of title restrictions and pledges of collateral; amounts recognized during construction; contractual commitments to acquire; and, if not disclosed separately in the statement of comprehensive income, any compensation from third parties for PPE impaired, lost, or given up.

2.69 An entity that measures a class of PPE using the revaluation model should provide additional disclosures, including the effective date of the revaluation, whether the entity used an independent appraiser, the methods and significant assumptions used to determine fair value, the extent to which fair value came from observable prices in an active market or other arm's–length transactions, and the amount of the revaluation surplus showing the change during the period and any restrictions on distributions to shareholders. In addition, for each class of PPE carried at the revalued amount, an entity should disclose the amount that would have been recognized in the balance sheet if the cost model were used.

2.70 IAS 23, *Borrowing Costs*, requires disclosure of interest capitalized and the capitalization rate used.

U.S. GAAP

2.71 FASB ASC disclosure requirements are essentially the same as IFRSs, except that FASB 360-10-50 does not require the entity to disclose a reconciliation by asset class of the beginning and ending balances of the gross carrying amount, accumulated depreciation, and accumulated impairment losses.

TABLE 2-5: GOODWILL AND CLASSES OF INTANGIBLE ASSETS

	2011	2010	2009
Goodwill	131	131	129
Development costs	37	40	43
Acquired in-process research and development	3	5	5
Software	79	74	72
Information systems	14	12	6
Future servicing rights	1	3	3
Brands	30	37	38
Patents, licenses, trademarks, and similar rights	81	57	51
Distribution rights	11	11	9
Water rights	2	3	2
Customer-related intangibles (for example, customer lists or relationships)	53	40	43
Marketing-related intangibles	5	4	4
Core deposit intangible	2	3	2
Mining interests	8	6	7
Exploration and evaluation expenditures	8	6	6
Concessions	10	9	7
Contract-related intangibles (including favorable leases)	24	20	18
Value of business acquired and acquired in-force insurance policies	4	6	6
Purchased technology	5	7	6
Order backlog	1	1	2
Deferred acquisition costs	0	1	1
Other	99	89	85

TABLE 2-4: ALTERNATIVE MODELS FOR SUBSEQUENT MEASUREMENT OF PROPERTY, PLANT, AND EQUIPMENT

	2011	2010	2009
Cost	172	163	155
Revaluation:			
Land	1	2	3
Buildings	1	1	1
Property (land and buildings)	6	4	4
Other asset class	1	1	1
More than one asset class	1	0	0
All asset classes	3	3	1
Total companies using revaluation for at least one asset class	13	11	10
Companies not disclosing a model	0	3	3
Companies using more than one model	(10)	(7)	(8)
Total Companies	**175**	**170**	**160**

Presentation and Disclosure Excerpts

Cost Model—Buildings and Structures, Production and Other Equipment

2.72

Siemens Aktiengesellschaft (Sep 2011)

CONSOLIDATED STATEMENTS OF FINANCIAL POSITION (in part)

(In millions of €)

	Note	9/30/11	9/30/10
Assets			
Goodwill	16	15,706	15,763
Other intangible assets	17	4,444	4,969
Property, plant and equipment	18	10,477	11,748
Investments accounted for using the equity method	19	4,966	4,724
Other financial assets	20	11,855	10,765
Deferred tax assets	10	3,206	3,940
Other assets		776	739
Total assets		104,243	102,827

NOTES TO THE CONSOLIDATED FINANCIAL STATEMENTS (in part)

1. Basis of Presentation

The accompanying Consolidated Financial Statements present the operations of Siemens AG with registered offices in Berlin and Munich, Germany, and its subsidiaries (the Company or Siemens). They have been prepared in accordance with International Financial Reporting Standards (IFRS), as adopted by the European Union. The financial statements are also in accordance with IFRS as issued by the International Accounting Standards Board (IASB). Certain pronouncements have been early adopted, see Note 2 Summary of significant accounting policies—recently adopted accounting pronouncements.

Siemens prepares and reports its Consolidated Financial Statements in euros (€). Siemens is a German based multinational corporation with a business portfolio of activities predominantly in the field of electronics and electrical engineering, for further information see Note 37 Segment information.

The Consolidated Financial Statements were authorised for issue by the Managing Board on November 23, 2011. The Consolidated Financial Statements are generally prepared on the historical cost basis, except as stated in Note 2 Summary of significant accounting policies.

2. Summary of Significant Accounting Policies (in part)

The accounting policies set out below have been applied consistently to all periods presented in these Consolidated Financial Statements.

Property, plant and equipment—Property, plant and equipment is valued at cost less accumulated depreciation and impairment losses. This also applies to property classified as investment property. Investment property consists of property held either to earn rentals or for capital appreciation or both and not used in production or for administrative purposes. The fair value disclosed for investment property is primarily based on a discounted cash flow approach except for certain cases which are based on appraisal values.

If the costs of certain components of an item of property, plant and equipment are significant in relation to the total cost of the item, they are accounted for and depreciated separately. Depreciation expense is recognized using the straight-line method. Residual values and useful lives are reviewed annually and, if expectations differ from previous estimates, adjusted accordingly. Costs of construction of qualifying assets, i.e. assets that require a substantial period of time to be ready for its intended use, include capitalized interest, which is amortized over the estimated useful life of the related asset. The following useful lives are assumed:

Factory and office buildings	20 to 50 years
Other buildings	5 to 10 years
Technical machinery & equipment	5 to 10 years
Furniture & office equipment	generally 5 years
Equipment leased to others	generally 3 to 5 years

18. Property, Plant and Equipment (in part)

(In Millions of €)	Gross Carrying Amount as of 10/1/2010	Translation Differences	Additions Through Business Combinations	Additions	Reclassifications	Retirements[1]	Gross Carrying Amount as of 9/30/2011	Accumulated Depreciation and Impairment	Net Book Value as of 9/30/2011	Depreciation and Impairment in Fiscal 2011[2]
Land and buildings	8,596	37	17	158	294	(992)	8,110	(3,850)	4,260	(261)
Technical machinery and equipment	9,255	21	10	429	493	(3,619)	6,589	(4,223)	2,366	(460)
Furniture and office equipment	6,797	(8)	26	725	113	(2,446)	5,207	(3,980)	1,227	(619)
Equipment leased to others	3,175	—	2	586	1	(463)	3,301	(1,614)	1,687	(359)
Advances to suppliers and construction in progress	1,114	11	1	911	(901)	(199)	937[3]	—	937	—
Property, plant and equipment	28,937	61	56	2,809	—	(7,719)	24,144	(13,667)	10,477	(1,699)

[1] Includes Property, plant and equipment reclassified to Assets classified as held for disposal and dispositions of those entities, see Note 4 Acquisitions, dispositions and discontinued operations.

[2] Includes impairment expense of €53 million in fiscal 2011, of which €29 million relate to the Energy Sector, as well as €21 million related to SRE.

[3] Includes €804 million expenditures for property, plant and equipment under construction.

As of September 30, 2011 and 2010, contractual commitments for purchases of property, plant and equipment amount to €406 million and €459 million, respectively.

In fiscal 2011 and 2010, government grants awarded for the purchase or the production of property, plant and equipment amounted to €14 million and €23 million, respectively. The award of further government grants of €50 million and €80 million in fiscal 2011 and 2010, respectively, related to costs incurred and future costs.

As of September 30, 2011 and 2010, minimum future lease payments receivable from lessees under operating leases are as follows:

| (In Millions of €) | September 30 | |
	2011	2010
Within one year	426	454
After one year but not more than five years	929	891
More than five years	213	179
	1,568	1,524

Payments from lessees under operating leases primarily relate to buildings, data processing and phone equipment as well as to medical equipment. Total contingent rent recognized in income in fiscal 2011, 2010 and 2009 amounts to €182 million, €233 million and €182 million.

Investment Property

The carrying amount of investment property amounts to €105 million and €130 million compared to a fair value of €283 million and €248 million as of September 30, 2011 and 2010, respectively.

Revaluation Model—Properties, Including Land, Buildings and Facilities, Construction in Progress

2.73

Grupo TMM, S.A.B. (Dec 2011)

CONSOLIDATED STATEMENTS OF FINANCIAL POSITION (in part)

(Amounts in thousands of dollars ($) and thousands of (Ps))

| | 2011 | | 2010 |
	(Dollars)	(Pesos)	(Dollars)
Assets			
Concession rights—net (Note 8)	2,577	35,943	2,849
Property, machinery, and equipment—Net (Note 9)	717,880	10,012,703	761,642
Prepaid expenses and other (Note 10)	7,419	103,477	7,617
Intangible assets (Note 11)	11,395	158,933	23,646
Deferred income tax (Note 20)	67,583	942,621	67,492
Total assets	$952,064	Ps13,279,008	$1,075,862
Stockholder Equity (Note 17):			
Equity capital, 103,760,541 shares authorized and issued	158,931	1,222,011	158,931
Treasury shares (1,577,700 shares)	(3,354)	(19,387)	(3,754)
Revaluation surplus (Notes 3h and 9)	63,907	790,980	64,097
Statutory reserve	15,554	187,001	15,554
Accrued losses	(96,178)	(1,256,075)	(118,115)
Capital Premium	5,528	54,979	5,528
Initial cumulative translation balance (Note 3)	(17,757)	—	(17,757)
Translation balance (Note 3)	(22,111)	478,294	(8,522)
Controlling interest	104,520	1,457,803	95,962
Non-controlling interest (Note 3r)	3,892	54,284	8,908
Total stockholder equity	108,412	1,512,087	104,870
Total liabilities and stockholder equity	$952,064	Ps13,279,008	$1,075,862

NOTES TO THE CONSOLIDATED FINANCIAL STATEMENTS (in part)

3 Summary of Significant Accounting Policies: (in part)

h Properties, Machinery, and Equipment, Net

Property, machinery and equipment are stated at construction or acquisition cost. Acquisitions through capital leases or charter arrangements with an obligation to purchase are capitalized based on the present value of future minimum payments, recognizing the related liability. Depreciation of transportation equipment is computed using the straight-line method based on the useful lives of the assets net of the estimated residual value.

In December 2010, the Company adopted the revaluation model for one class of its assets (Properties) in accordance with IAS 16, recognizing a surplus from revaluation in the fixed assets; this surplus was calculated subtracting the book value from the appraisal value provided by independent appraisers. The increase in value from the revaluation was recognized directly in the stockholder equity as "Revaluation surplus", this item is not susceptible to distribution until the Company releases the asset. A new valuation of these properties was deemed unnecessary for 2011.

v Equity Capital and Reserves—

Common shares are classified as equity. Grupo TMM does not have other equity instruments in addition to its common stock.

Incremental costs directly attributable to the issue of new shares or options are shown in equity as a deduction, net of tax, from the proceeds. Incremental costs directly attributable to the issue of new shares or options, or for the acquisition of a business, are included in the cost of acquisition as part of the purchase consideration.

The surplus from revaluation within the capital includes gains from the revaluation of properties, machinery, and equipment. The variances in the conversion of foreign currency resulting from the conversion of entities whose oper-

ating currency is not the operating currency of the Company are reported in the translation balance.

9 Property, Machinery, and Equipment, Net:

Property, machinery, and equipment as of December 31, 2011 and 2010 are summarized as follows:

	2011						
	Net Balances at Year Start	Additions	Disposals	Transfers and Others	Depreciation/ Impairment	Net Balances at Year End	Estimate Useful Life (Years)
Vessels	$576,568	$ 189	$ —	$ 4,214	$33,598[1]	$547,373	25
Dry-docks:							
Major vessel repairs	5,811	4,919	—	(6)	4,754	5,970	2.5
Building and facilities	15,895	52	52	2,825	916	17,804	20&25
Warehousing equipment	914	—	—	(60)	257	597	10
Computer equipment	600	59	—	2	331	330	3&4
Terminal equipment	738	44	—	89	242	629	10
Ground transportation equipment	26,638	51	2,024	(2,275)	3,480	18,910	4.5&10
Other equipment	1,089	26	12	77	201	979	
	628,253	5,340	2,088	4,866	43,779	592,592	
Lands	106,866	—	312	(7,866)	—	98,688	
Constructions in progress	26,523	10,036	—	(9,959)	—	26,600	
	$761,642	$15,376	$2,400	$(12,959)	$43,779	$717,880	

[1] The Company assessed impairment of $901 for the Vessel Tula.

[2] In 2010 the Company adopted the revaluation method for one class of its assets (properties) in accordance with IAS 16, recognizing a Revaluation Surplus in the fixed assets as follows: Land for $88.9 million, Buildings and facilities for $4.7 million, and Constructions in progress for $(0.2) million, giving a total of $93.4 million (see Note 3h). There were not situations occurring in 2011 that would alter the fair value of the assets, therefore the Company deemed a new valuation unnecessary.

The accumulated depreciation on property, machinery, and equipment as of December 31, 2011 and 2010 is $211.9 million and $183.1 million, respectively.

As of December 31, 2011, 24 offshore vessels, 5 tanker vessels, and 5 tugboats are securing the issue of Trust Certificates. In addition, there are 10 properties, including the "La Moderna" property securing the Bancomext loan. Also, 39 tractor-trailers are securing the financing received from DC Automotriz Servicios.

Revaluation Model—Buildings Not Meeting Criteria for Classification as Investment Property

2.74

Gazit-Globe Ltd (Dec 2011)

CONSOLIDATED STATEMENTS OF FINANCIAL POSITION (in part)

	Note	Convenience Translation into U.S. Dollars (Note 2d(1)) December 31 2011 In Millions	December 31 2011 NIS in Millions	December 31 2010 NIS in Millions
Assets				
Non-Current Assets				
Investments in associates	9	43	166	67
Other investments, loans and receivables	10	107	408	281
Available-for-sale financial assets	11	82	314	218
Financial derivatives	37d	245	937	1,087
Investment property	12	14,297	54,627	43,634
Investment property under development	13	842	3,219	3,296
Non-current inventory	14	14	52	17
Fixed assets, net	15	197	751	633
Goodwill	16	26	101	119
Other intangible assets, net	16	18	69	17
Deferred taxes	25n	44	167	99
		15,915	60,811	49,468

NOTES TO THE CONSOLIDATED FINANCIAL STATEMENTS (in part)

Note 1:—General (in part)

a. The Company and Its Business Activities

The Company, through its investees (collectively, the "Group"), is the owner, operator and developer of income producing properties in North America, Europe, Israel and Brazil and focuses mainly on the supermarket-anchored shopping center sector. In addition, the Group operates in the medical office buildings sector in North America, the senior housing facilities sector in the U.S., as well as in the development and construction of real estate projects in Israel and Eastern Europe. Furthermore, the Group continues to seek and realize business opportunities by acquiring properties and/or companies that operates within its core business or in similar fields, both in regions where it currently operates and also in new regions.

The Company's securities are listed for trading on the Tel Aviv and New York Stock Exchanges.

Note 2:—Significant Accounting Policies (in part)

q. Fixed Assets

Items of fixed assets are measured at cost with the addition of direct acquisition costs, less accumulated depreciation and accumulated impairment losses, if any, and excluding day-to-day servicing expenses.

Depreciation is calculated on a straight-line basis over the useful life of the assets at annual rates as follows:

	%	
Buildings	2–3.33	(mainly 2%)
Building systems	6.67–8.33	(mainly 8.33%)
Motor vehicles	15	
Computers, office furniture and equipment	6–33	
Leasehold improvements	During the lease term	

Leasehold improvements are depreciated on a straight-line basis over the shorter of the lease term (including the extension option held by the Group and intended to be exercised) and the expected useful life of the improvement.

Each part of an item of fixed asset with a cost that is significant in relation to the total cost of the item is depreciated separately using the component method. Depreciation is calculated on a straight line basis over their estimated useful life time.

The useful life and the residual value of an asset are reviewed at least each year-end and the changes, if any, are accounted for prospectively as a change in accounting estimate.

Depreciation of an asset ceases at the earlier of the date that the asset is classified as held for sale and the date that the asset is derecognized. An asset is derecognized on disposal or when no further economic benefits are expected from its use. The gain or loss arising from derecognition of the asset is recognized in profit or loss in the period of derecognition.

Buildings for senior housing facilities are a class of fixed assets that is measured at revalued amount, being their fair value at the date of the revaluation less any subsequent accumulated depreciation and subsequent accumulated impairment losses. Depreciation is recognized in profit or loss on the basis of the revalued amount. Revaluations are performed frequently enough to ensure that the carrying amount does not significantly differ from the value that would have been determined as fair value on the reporting date. Revaluation of fixed assets is carried to other comprehensive income as a revaluation reserve net of tax effect. The revaluation reserve is transferred directly to retained earnings when the asset is being depreciated or derecognized. For further details on buildings for senior housing facilities refer to Note 15b.

Note 15:—Fixed Assets, Net

Fixed assets include mainly buildings, predominantly senior housing facilities in the U.S. and office buildings partly used by the Group, which do not meet the criteria for classification as investment property.

a. Composition and Movement:

	December 31	
	2011	**2010**
	NIS in Millions	
Cost:		
Balance as of January 1	723	791
Acquisitions	36	24
Transfer to investment property	—	(24)
Disposals	(1)	(28)
Initially consolidated companies	83	—
Foreign exchange differences	39	(40)
Balance as of December 31	880	723
Accumulated depreciation:		
Balance as of January 1	197	185
Depreciation	41	38
Disposals	(1)	(7)
Transfer to investment property	—	(2)
Initially consolidated companies	48	—
Foreign exchange differences	10	(17)
Balance as of December 31	295	197
Revaluation reserve (b):		
Balance as of January 1	107	109
Revaluation	59	25
Disposals	—	(27)
Balance as of December 31	166	107
Depreciated cost as of December 31	751	633
Of which senior housing facilities	573	497

b. Revaluation of Senior Housing Facilities:

RSC, a jointly controlled entity, uses the revaluation model to measure senior housing facilities at fair value. The fair value is measured using external independent appraisers with vast experience as to the location and category of the property being valued. A revaluation reserve, with a balance of approximately NIS 166 million as of December 31, 2011 (approximately NIS 98 million net of tax) and approximately NIS 107 million as of December 31, 2010 (approximately NIS 70 million net of tax), arises due to such measurement. In determining fair value of senior housing facilities, the appraisers apply primarily the Income Capitalization approach applying discount rates, which reflects the market conditions of each property at the reporting date with excluding the business value implied in the valuation. Such measurement contains average implied cap rates of 8.0% and 8.2% as of December 31, 2011 and December 31, 2010, respectively.

c. As for Charges, Refer to Note 29.

IAS 38, *INTANGIBLE ASSETS*

IFRS 3, *BUSINESS COMBINATIONS*

Author's Note

In 2011, IASB issued the following standards which amend IAS 38, *Intangible Assets:*

- IFRS 10
- IFRS 11, *Joint Arrangements* (issued May 2011 with an effective date of 1 January 2013)
  These two standards add references to IFRS 10 and adjust the titles of IAS 27 and IAS 28, *Investments in Associates and Joint Ventures* (revised 2011), as the relevant standards for recognition and measurement in the scope exclusion for financial assets
- IFRS 13
  These amendments delete the definitions of *active market* and *fair value* and replace them with those in IFRS 13. IFRS 13 also replaces the term *determine* with the term *measure.*

These standards make similar terminology and reference amendments to IFRS 3, *Business Combinations.* IFRS 9 also amends IFRS 3 by replacing references to IAS 39 with references to IFRS 9.

Because these standards are effective for annual periods beginning on or after 1 January 2012, these amendments are not reflected in the commentary in this section. However, these amendments would not affect the content of illustrative excerpts from survey companies' financial statements.

IFRS Overview and Comparison to U.S. GAAP

2.75 IAS 38 establishes accounting and disclosure requirements for goodwill and other intangible assets. An *intangible asset* is an identifiable, nonmonetary asset without physical substance. An *identifiable asset* is separable or arises from contractual or legal rights. IFRSs require an intangible asset to be identifiable to distinguish it from goodwill. IAS 38 applies to all intangible assets, except those within the scope of another IFRS, financial assets as defined in IAS 32, exploration and evaluation assets, and assets arising from expenditures on development and extraction of minerals, oil, natural gas, and other nonregenerative resources.

2.76 The revisions to IFRS 3 in 2008 amended IAS 38. Entities should apply these amendments prospectively for annual periods beginning on or after July 1, 2009. If an entity adopts IFRS 3 at an earlier date, the amendments to IAS 38 should also be applied for that earlier period. IFRS

3 is discussed more fully in section 9, "Business Combinations." This section includes illustrations of the ongoing general disclosures required for goodwill in reporting periods subsequent to the business combination itself. *Goodwill* recognized in a business combination is an asset representing the future economic benefits arising from other assets acquired in a business combination that are not individually identified and separately recognized.

2.77 The revisions to IAS 1 in 2007 also amended IAS 38. These amendments relate primarily to adjustments to an intangible asset's carrying amount as a result of applying the revaluation model and impairment losses recognized or reversed in other comprehensive income, in accordance with IAS 36, *Impairment of Assets.* An entity should apply those amendments for annual periods beginning on or after 1 January 2009. If an entity applies the amendments to IAS 1 for an earlier period, the amendments to IAS 38 should also be applied for that earlier period.

Recognition and Measurement

IFRSs

2.78 An entity should recognize an intangible asset if, and only if, it is probable that future economic benefits will flow to the entity and the cost of the asset can be measured reliably. Probability is assessed based on reasonable and supportable assumptions representing management's best estimate of the economic conditions expected to exist over the asset's useful life. The probability recognition criteria are always considered to be satisfied when an entity acquires goodwill and other intangible assets in a business combination.

2.79 At initial recognition, an entity should measure intangible assets, acquired separately, at cost (that is, the purchase price, including duties and taxes, and costs that are directly attributable to getting the asset ready for its intended use). Examples of directly attributable costs include employee benefits arising from getting the asset ready for use, professional fees, and the cost of testing. IAS 38 specifically requires expenditures on advertising and promotional activities (including mail order catalogs), training to operate the asset, start-up costs, reorganization and relocation of all or part of the entity, inefficiencies and operation losses, general overhead, and administrative costs to be recognized as an expense. However, IAS 38 does not preclude recognition of a prepayment as an asset when the entity pays for goods or services in advance of obtaining them.

2.80 In accordance with IFRS 3, if an intangible asset is acquired in a business combination, the cost of that intangible asset is its fair value at the acquisition date. IAS 38 permits the acquirer to recognize an intangible asset that is separable but only together with a related contract or liability. In this case, the entity recognizes the intangible separately from goodwill but together with the related item. IAS 38 also permits the acquirer to recognize a group of complementary intangible assets as a single asset, provided that the individual assets in the group have similar useful lives.

2.81 IAS 38 also establishes the accounting treatment for research and development (R&D) costs. An entity can incur R&D costs by acquiring an in-process R&D project, either separately or in a business combination, or by incurring these costs internally, either subsequently for an acquired project or independently. An entity should recognize acquired in-process R&D as an intangible asset if it meets the probability and measurement reliability recognition criteria. An entity should expense costs incurred in a project's research phase (for example, the search for knowledge or the evaluation of alternatives for new or improved products or processes). An entity should recognize an intangible asset when it incurs costs in the development phase only if the entity can demonstrate all of the following:

- Technical feasibility of completing the intangible asset so that it will be available for sale
- Intention and ability to both complete and use or sell the asset
- How the intangible asset will generate probable future economic benefits (for example, demonstrate the existence of a market for the asset's output or the asset's usefulness to the entity if for internal use)
- Availability of adequate resources to complete development and use or sell the asset
- Ability to measure reliably the expenditures directly attributable to the asset during development (for example, cost of materials or services used, employee benefits, fees, and amortization of patents or licenses)

2.82 IAS 38 specifically prohibits recognition of internally generated brands, mastheads, publishing titles, customer lists, and similar items as intangible assets.

2.83 An entity should recognize expenditures on intangible items as an expense in profit and loss, unless the expenditure is a cost of either an intangible asset meeting the recognition criteria or an item acquired in a business combination that is not recognized separately. In the latter case, the cost forms part of the amount recognized as goodwill, in accordance with IFRS 3. An entity should not capitalize an expenditure previously expensed.

2.84 IAS 38 includes two alternative models for subsequent measurement of intangible assets: cost and revaluation. An entity should select a model for an entire class of assets, not for individual assets. However, the revaluation model is only available for those intangible assets that are traded in an active market.

2.85 Under the cost model, an entity should measure the intangible asset at cost less accumulated amortization, if any, and accumulated impairment losses.

2.86 Under the revaluation model, an entity should measure an intangible asset at the *revalued amount*, which is the fair value as of the date of the revaluation, less subsequent accumulated amortization and subsequent accumulated impairment losses. An entity should determine fair value of individual assets by reference to an active market. An entity should conduct revaluations with sufficient regularity so the carrying value of the asset at the reporting date is not materially different from its fair value at that date.

2.87 The revaluation model is only available for intangible assets that are traded in an active market. Therefore, if an active market for an asset is no longer available, an entity should measure the asset at cost less accumulated amortization and impairments. IAS 38 reminds entities that the fact that an active market no longer exists may be an indicator of impairment and that the asset needs to be tested in accordance with IAS 36.

2.88 An entity should recognize increases in the carrying amount from revaluation in other comprehensive income and in equity (accumulated revaluation surplus), but the entity should recognize the increase in profit or loss to the extent that the increase reverses a previous decrease. Similarly, an entity should recognize a decrease in carrying value in profit or loss, but the entity should recognize the decrease in equity to the extent that the decrease reverses a previous increase.

2.89 Standing Interpretations Committee (SIC) 32, *Intangible Assets—Web Site Costs*, specifically addresses costs incurred in developing and maintaining an entity's own website. An entity should treat the development of the website similarly to development costs of an R&D project (that is, an entity only capitalizes expenditures when the criteria for capitalizing development costs are met). However, SIC 32 requires an entity to expense all costs associated with website activities for advertising and promotional purposes.

Author's Note

Amortization and impairment are discussed in section 3.

U.S. GAAP

2.90 The FASB ASC glossary defines an *intangible asset* as an asset (not including a financial asset) without physical substance. Although this definition is similar to that in IAS 38, it does not specifically include the requirement that the asset is identifiable. FASB ASC 350-30-25-1 states that an entity should recognize intangible assets acquired individually or in a group of assets. FASB ASC 805-20-25-10 requires an entity to recognize identifiable intangible assets acquired in a business combination separately from goodwill. The definition in the FASB ASC glossary explains that the term intangible asset is used to refer to intangible assets other than goodwill.

2.91 On initial recognition, FASB ASC 350-30-25-2 requires an entity to allocate cost to intangible assets acquired in a group of assets in a transaction other than through a business combination, based on relative fair values, and not recognize goodwill. However, when an asset is acquired separately, cost and fair value are likely to be the same. As discussed in FASB ASC 820, *Fair Value Measurement*, an entity should determine fair value based on assumptions market participants would use in pricing the asset. FASB ASC 350-30-05-1 refers entities to FASB ASC 805-20 for guidance on recognition and measurement of intangible assets acquired in a business combination.

2.92 Like IFRSs, FASB ASC 805-20-30-1 requires an entity to measure identifiable assets, including intangible assets, acquired in a business combination at their acquisition-date fair value on initial recognition. However, IFRS 3 offers an option to measure the noncontrolling interest at its proportion of the fair value of the net identifiable assets acquired, rather than at fair value. Therefore, an entity could measure goodwill at a different amount under FASB ASC than under IFRSs if it elected this option.

2.93 Unlike IFRSs, FASB ASC 805-10-35-1 states, in general, that an acquirer should subsequently measure and account for assets acquired, liabilities assumed or incurred, and equity instruments issued in a business combination in accordance with other applicable GAAP for those items, depending on their nature. Therefore, as explained by FASB

ASC 350-30-35, an entity should measure an intangible asset at cost less accumulated amortization, if applicable, and accumulated impairment losses. An entity should amortize intangible assets with finite useful lives, including defensive intangible assets acquired to prevent others from obtaining access to the asset, over their expected useful lives. An entity should not amortize an intangible asset with an indefinite useful life or goodwill in accordance with FASB ASC 350-30-35-15 or 350-20-35-1.

2.94 The definition of *R&D* in the FASB ASC glossary differs from that under IFRSs. However, with the exception of certain internally developed software, FASB ASC 350-30-25-3 requires an entity to expense as incurred all internally developing, maintaining, or restoring intangibles that are not specifically identifiable, that have indeterminate lives, or that are inherent in a continuing business activity and related to an entity as a whole, including R&D costs. Like IFRSs, and consistent with the measurement principle in FASB ASC 805-20-30-1, in-process R&D acquired in a business combination is recognized as an intangible asset and measured at the acquisition-date fair value. FASB ASC 350-30-35-17A states that an entity should consider intangible assets acquired in a business combination or an acquisition by a not-for-profit entity that are used in R&D activities to have an indefinite life until the completion or abandonment of the associated R&D efforts. Therefore, such assets are not amortized but are subject to impairment testing annually.

2.95 FASB ASC 985-20 and FASB ASC 350-40 contain specific guidance on the treatment of software developed for sale and internal-use software, respectively, whereas IFRSs do not treat software differently than any other intangible asset. Unlike the treatment in SIC 32, FASB ASC 350-40 and FASB ASC 350-50 have separate guidance regarding costs incurred for software to operate the website, unless the entity has a plan to market the software externally, and other costs, depending upon the stage of development of the website.

2.96 Like IFRSs, FASB ASC 720-15 requires an entity to expense training and start-up costs as incurred. Unlike IFRSs, paragraphs 2–4 of FASB ASC 340-20-25 contain specific criteria that permit capitalization of direct response advertising costs.

Presentation

IFRSs

2.97 An entity should present intangible assets as a separate line item on the balance sheet, classified as current or noncurrent, in accordance with IAS 1. An entity should also present additional line items, headings, and subtotals when they are relevant to an understanding of the entity's financial position.

U.S. GAAP

2.98 FASB ASC 350-30-45-1 states, at a minimum, that all intangible assets should be aggregated and presented as a separate line item in the statement of financial position. Similar to IFRSs, the requirement does not preclude the presentation of individual intangible assets or classes of intangible assets as separate line items.

Disclosure

IFRSs

2.99 An entity should identify major classes of intangible assets and distinguish, at a minimum, between internally generated and other intangible assets. For each identified class of intangible asset, the entity should disclose the following information:
- Whether the assets in the class have a finite or indefinite useful life
- Useful lives or amortization rates and amortization methods for assets with finite lives
- Gross carrying amount and combined accumulated amortization and impairment losses at the beginning and end of the period
- Line items of comprehensive income in which amortization is included
- Reconciliation of the beginning and ending balances in the gross carrying amount and combined accumulated amortization and impairment, identifying reasons for changes in these accounts (for example, additions, classification to held for sale, revaluations, disposals, amortization, impairment losses, and foreign exchange effects)

2.100 For each intangible asset with an indefinite life, an entity should also disclose the asset's carrying amount and reasons that an indefinite life is supported, including factors that made a significant difference in that decision.

2.101 Like indefinite life intangibles, an entity should not amortize goodwill. IFRS 3 requires a reconciliation of the carrying amount of goodwill and accumulated impairment losses showing the following, separately:
- Additional goodwill, except that goodwill related to a disposal group immediately classified as held for sale should be shown separately
- Adjustments due to recognition of deferred tax assets
- Related goodwill derecognized on sale of the disposal group
- Impairment losses
- Foreign exchange adjustments

2.102 An entity should describe any individually material intangible asset and disclose its carrying amount and remaining amortization period. For assets acquired by government grant and initially recognized at fair value, the entity should disclose the fair value initially recognized, the current carrying value, and whether the cost or revaluation model is used subsequently. The entity should also disclose information about carrying amounts of assets with title restrictions or pledged as collateral and information about impaired assets.

2.103 IAS 38 requires additional disclosures about assets measured using the revaluation model.

Author's Note

No survey company selected the revaluation model for a class of intangible assets.

2.104 An entity should disclose the aggregate amount of R&D expenditures recognized as an expense in profit or loss.

2.105 IAS 8 requires an entity to disclose the nature and amount of any change in accounting estimate having a material impact in the current period or expected to have a material impact subsequently.

U.S. GAAP

2.106 FASB ASC requires fewer disclosures than IAS 38. However, FASB ASC 350-30-50-1 does require an entity to identify major classes of intangible assets and specifies required disclosures, including disclosure of any significant residual value, in total, for each class.

2.107 FASB ASC 350-30-50-1 requires an entity to disclose the weighted average amortization period, rather than useful lives or amortization rates, as required by IFRSs, in total and by asset class.

2.108 FASB ASC 350-20-50-2 requires an entity to disclose the gross carrying amount and accumulated amortization and amortization expense for the period, not the compre-hensive reconciliation of these carrying amounts as required by IFRSs.

2.109 FASB ASC 340-20-50 requires specific disclosures related to direct response advertising costs, including the accounting policy (expense or capitalization) selected, a description of any advertising costs recognized as an asset, and the amounts charged to expense for each income statement presented or reported as an asset for each balance sheet presented.

Presentation and Disclosure Excerpts

Goodwill

2.110

Tata Motors Limited (Mar 2011)

CONSOLIDATED BALANCE SHEETS (in part)

(In millions)	Notes	As of March 31 2012	2012	2011
Assets:				
Finance receivables	4	US$ 2,020.7	Rs. 102,802.0	Rs. 81,575.6
Investments	6	142.9	7,269.7	7,616.0
Other financial assets	10	335.9	17,089.9	15,018.2
Property, plant and equipment	11	5,557.1	282,716.1	232,479.0
Goodwill	13	83.6	4,253.0	3,760.8
Intangible assets	14	5,549.8	282,347.4	199,652.6
Investment in equity accounted investees	15	457.3	23,265.9	28,504.3
Non-current income tax assets		97.0	4,933.0	4,573.6
Deferred income taxes	16	809.2	41,170.3	10,640.7
Other non-current assets	17	199.2	10,135.1	9,885.0
Total non-current assets		15,252.7	775,982.4	593,705.8
Total assets		US$ 28,092.5	Rs. 1,429,212.6	Rs. 1,031,526.9

NOTES TO THE CONSOLIDATED FINANCIAL STATEMENTS (in part)

1. Background and Operations

Tata Motors Limited and its subsidiaries, collectively referred to as ("the Company" or "Tata Motors"), designs, manufactures and sells a wide range of automotive vehicles. The Company provides financing for the vehicles sold by dealers of the Company in certain markets. The Company also manufactures engines for industrial and marine applications, aggregates such as axles and transmissions for commercial vehicles and factory automation equipment, and provides information technology services (also refer to note 30 regarding sale of controlling equity interest in Telco Construction Equipment Company Limited (Telcon)—a subsidiary engaged in manufacture and sale of construction equipment).

Tata Motors Limited is a public limited company incorporated and domiciled in India and has its registered office at Mumbai, Maharashtra, India.

The consolidated financial statements were approved by the Board of Directors and authorised for issue on July 30, 2012.

In financial year 2008-09, the Company acquired Jaguar Land Rover businesses (referred to as "JLR") which included three manufacturing facilities and two advanced engineering centers in the UK, and a worldwide sales network.

As on March 31, 2012, Tata Sons Limited (or Tata Sons), together with its subsidiaries, owns 29.02% of the ordinary shares and 3.85% of 'A' ordinary shares of Tata Motors Limited, and has the ability to significantly influence the Company's operations (refer note 25 for voting rights relating to ordinary shares and 'A' ordinary shares).

2. Significant Accounting Policies (in part)

a. Statement of Compliance

These consolidated financial statements have been prepared in accordance with International Financial Reporting Standards (referred to as "IFRS") as issued by the International Accounting Standards Board (referred to as "IASB").

d. Business Combination

Acquisitions of subsidiaries and businesses are accounted for using the acquisition method. Acquisition related costs are recognized in profit or loss as incurred (refer note 2(v)). The acquiree's identifiable assets, liabilities and contingent liabilities that meet the conditions for recognition are recognized at their fair value at the acquisition date, except certain assets and liabilities required to be measured as per the applicable standard.

Purchase consideration in excess of the Company's interest in the acquiree's net fair value of identifiable assets, liabilities and contingent liabilities, is recognized as goodwill. Excess of the Company's interest in the net fair value of the acquiree's identifiable assets, liabilities and contingent liabilities over the purchase consideration is recognized, after reassessment of fair value of net assets acquired, in the income statement

p. Impairment

i) Goodwill

Cash generating unit to which goodwill is allocated are tested for impairment annually at each balance sheet date, or more frequently when there is an indication that the unit may be impaired. If the recoverable amount of the cash generating unit is less than the carrying amount of the unit, the impairment loss is allocated first to reduce the carrying amount of any goodwill allocated to that unit and then to the other assets of the unit pro rata on the basis of carrying amount of each asset in the unit. Goodwill impairment loss recognized is not reversed in subsequent period.

13. Goodwill

	As of March 31		
(In millions)	2012	2012	2011
Balance at the beginning	US$ 73.9	Rs. 3,760.8	Rs. 3,518.3
Goodwill arising on business combination	—	—	83.0
Goodwill impairment	(0.9)	(45.7)	—
Currency translation differences	10.6	537.9	159.5
Balance at the end	US$ 83.6	Rs. 4,253.0	Rs. 3,760.8

In fiscal 2011, the Company acquired Trilix Srl., a subsidiary, for a cash consideration of Rs.119.4 million and acquired net assets of Rs 36.4 million, resulting in goodwill of Rs 83.0 million.

As of March 31, 2012, goodwill of Rs. 229.8 million and Rs. 4,023.2 million relate to the automotive and related activity segment (Tata and other brand vehicles including financing thereof) and 'others' segment, respectively. As of March 31, 2011, goodwill of Rs. 270.9 million and Rs. 3,489.9 million relates to the automotive and related activity segment (Tata and other brand vehicles including financing thereof) and 'others' segment, respectively.

As of March 31, 2012, goodwill of Rs. 4,023.2 million has been allocated to software consultancy and services cash generating unit. The recoverable amount of the cash generating unit has been determined based on value in use. Value in use has been determined based on future cash flows, after considering current economic conditions and trends, estimated future operating results, growth rates and anticipated future economic conditions.

As of March 31, 2012, the estimated cash flows for a period of 5 years were developed using internal forecasts, and a pretax discount rate of 11.92 %. The cash flows beyond 5 years have been extrapolated assuming zero growth rates. The management believes that any reasonably possible change in the key assumptions would not cause the carrying amount to exceed the recoverable amount of the cash generating unit.

Goodwill, Patents and Trademarks, Customer Lists, Non-Compete Agreement, Internal-Use Software, Cash Generating Units

2.111

GRUMA, S.A.B. de C.V. (Dec 2011)

Author's Note

GRUMA implemented IFRSs effective December 31, 2011, with a date of transition of January 1, 2010. The excerpt that follows reflects the initial application of IAS 1, IAS 38, and IFRS 3.

CONSOLIDATED BALANCE SHEETS (in part)

(In thousands of Mexican pesos)
(Notes 1, 2 and 4)

	Note	As of January 1, 2010	As of December 31, 2010	As of December 31, 2011
Assets				
Non-current:				
Long-term notes and accounts receivable	10	543,295	598,961	626,874
Investment in associates	11	4,020,339	4,436,401	143,700
Property, plant and equipment, net	12	20,043,444	17,930,173	20,515,633
Intangible assets, net	13	2,483,254	2,406,437	2,954,359
Deferred tax assets	14	152,292	210,329	314,136
Total non-current assets		27,242,624	25,582,301	24,554,702
Total Assets		Ps. 43,278,444	Ps. 38,927,394	Ps. 44,542,618

NOTES TO THE CONSOLIDATED FINANCIAL STATEMENTS (in part)

1. Entity and Operations

Gruma, S.A.B. de C.V. (GRUMA) is a Mexican company with subsidiaries located in Mexico, the United States of America, Central America, Venezuela, Europe, Asia and Oceania, together referred to as the "Company." The Company's main activities are the production and sale of corn flour, wheat flour, tortillas and related products.

Gruma, S.A.B. de C.V. is a publicly held corporation (*Sociedad Anónima Bursátil de Capital Variable*) organized under the laws of Mexico. The address of its registered office is Rio de la Plata 407 in San Pedro Garza García, Nuevo León, Mexico.

The consolidated financial statements were authorized by the Chief Corporate Office and the Chief Administrative Office of the Company on April 30, 2012.

2. Basis of Preparation (in part)

The consolidated financial statements of Gruma, S.A.B. de C.V. and Subsidiaries as of December 31, 2011 have been prepared for the first time in accordance with the International Financial Reporting Standards (IFRS) as issued by the International Accounting Standards Board (IASB). The IFRS also include the International Accounting Standards (IAS) in force, as well as all the related interpretations issued by the International Financial Reporting Interpretations Committee (IFRIC), including those previously issued by the Standing Interpretations Committee (SIC).

In accordance with the amendments to the Rules for Public Companies and Other Participants in the Mexican Stock Exchange, issued by the Mexican Banking Securities Exchange Commission on January 27, 2009, the Company is required to prepare its financial statements under IFRS starting in 2012.

The Company decided to adopt IFRS earlier, starting January 1, 2011, therefore, these are the Company's first consolidated financial statements prepared in accordance with IFRS as issued by the IASB.

For comparative purposes, the consolidated financial statements as of and for the year ended December 31, 2010 have been prepared in accordance with IFRS, as required by the IFRS 1—First-Time Adoption of International Financial Reporting Standards.

The Company modified its accounting policies from Mexican Financial Reporting Standards (Mexican FRS) in order to comply with IFRS starting January 1, 2011. The transition from Mexican FRS to IFRS was recognized in accordance with IFRS 1, setting January 1, 2010 as the transition date. The reconciliation of the effects of the transition from Mexican FRS to IFRS in equity as of January 1, 2010 and December 31, 2010, in net income and cash flows for the year ended December 31, 2010 are disclosed in Note 28 to these financial statements.

4. Summary of Significant Accounting Policies (in part)

H) Intangible Assets

a. Goodwill

Goodwill represents the excess of the cost of an acquisition over the fair value of the Company's share of the net identifiable assets of the acquired subsidiary at the date of acquisition. Goodwill is tested annually for impairment, or whenever the circumstances indicate that the value of the asset might be impaired. Goodwill is carried at cost less accumulated impairment losses. Gains and losses on the disposal of an entity include the carrying amount of goodwill related to the entity sold.

Goodwill is allocated to cash-generating units for the purpose of impairment testing. The allocation is made to those cash-generating units or groups of cash-generating units that are expected to benefit from the business combination in which the goodwill arose, identified according to operating segment.

b. Intangible Assets with Finite Lives

Intangible assets with finite lives are carried at cost less accumulated amortization and impairment losses. Amortization is calculated using the straight-line method over the estimated useful lives of the assets. Estimated useful lives are as follows:

	Years
Non-compete agreements	20
Patents and trademarks	20
Customer lists	20
Software for internal use	3–7

c. Indefinite-Lived Intangible Assets

Indefinite-lived intangible assets are not amortized, but subject to impairment tests on an annual basis or whenever the circumstances indicate that the value of the asset might be impaired.

d. Research and Development

Research costs are expensed when incurred.

Costs from development activities are recognized as an intangible asset when such costs can be measured reliably, the product or process is technically and commercially feasible, future economic benefits will be obtained, and the Company pretends and has sufficient resources in order to complete the development and use or sell the asset. The amortization is recognized in income based on the straight-line method during the estimated useful life of the asset.

Development costs that do not qualify as intangible assets are recognized in income when incurred.

13. Intangible Assets

Changes in intangible assets for the years ended December 31, 2010 and 2011 were as follows:

	Intangible Assets Acquired					Internally Generated Intangible Assets	Total
	Goodwill	Covenants Not to Compete	Patents and Trademarks	Customer Lists	Software for Internal Use		
At January 1, 2010							
Cost	Ps. 2,169,473	Ps. 461,126	Ps. 107,951	Ps. 100,422	Ps. 735,949	Ps. 105,756	Ps. 3,680,677
Accumulated amortization	—	(306,524)	(61,908)	(48,414)	(687,847)	(92,729)	(1,197,422)
Net book value	2,169,473	154,602	46,043	52,008	48,102	13,027	2,483,255
For the year ended December 31, 2010							
Opening net book value	2,169,473	154,602	46,043	52,008	48,102	13,027	2,483,255
Exchange differences	(111,254)	—	(80)	(3,081)	(11,357)	11,230	(114,542)
Additions	—	—	3,459	—	—	420	3,879
Disposals	—	—	(4)	—	(8)	(2,243)	(2,225)
Amortization	—	(22,631)	(8,158)	(4,345)	(7,429)	(11,817)	(54,380)
Additions through business combinations	90,480	—	—	—	—	—	90,480
Closing net book value	2,148,699	131,971	41,260	44,582	29,308	10,617	2,406,437
At December 31, 2010							
Cost	2,148,699	461,126	107,471	93,719	563,328	67,606	3,441,949
Accumulated amortization	—	(329,155)	(66,211)	(49,137)	(534,020)	(56,989)	(1,035,512)
Net book value	2,148,699	131,971	41,260	44,582	29,308	10,617	2,406,437
For the year ended December 31, 2011							
Opening net book value	2,148,699	131,971	41,260	44,582	29,308	10,617	2,406,437
Exchange differences	214,138	2,587	8,710	12,652	6,829	13,457	258,373
Additions	—	—	18	—	3,841	18,865	22,724
Disposals	—	—	—	—	73	(14,607)	(14,534)
Amortization	—	(24,905)	(8,738)	(8,719)	(6,715)	(7,889)	(56,966)
Additions through business combinations	344,643	16,156	22,458	46,562	292	1,107	431,218
Impairment	(92,893)	—	—	—	—	—	(92,893)
Closing net book value	2,614,587	125,809	63,708	95,077	33,628	21,550	2,954,359
At December 31, 2011							
Cost	2,614,587	480,098	147,577	158,516	640,799	77,166	4,118,743
Accumulated amortization	—	(354,289)	(83,869)	(63,439)	(607,171)	(55,616)	(1,164,384)
Net book value	Ps. 2,614,587	Ps. 125,809	Ps. 63,708	Ps. 95,077	Ps. 33,628	Ps. 21,550	Ps. 2,954,359

At December 31, 2010 and 2011 the Company did not have indefinite-lived intangible assets.

For the years ended December 31, 2010 and 2011, amortization expense of intangible assets amounted to Ps.54,380 and Ps.56,966, respectively, which were recognized in the income statement as selling and administrative expenses.

Research and development costs of Ps.76,604 and Ps.91,011 were recognized in the income statement for the years ended December 31, 2010 and 2011, respectively.

Goodwill acquired in business combinations is allocated at acquisition date to the cash-generating units (CGU) that are expected to benefit from the synergies of the business combinations. The carrying values of goodwill allocated to the CGU or a group of CGU are as follows:

Cash-Generating Unit	At January 1, 2010	At December 31, 2010	At December 31, 2011
Mission Foods Division	Ps. 725,869	Ps. 667,283	Ps. 856,474
Gruma Seaham Ltd.	409,171	360,257	339,222
Gruma Corporation	212,765	212,765	212,765
Rositas Investments Pty, Ltd.	173,403	186,354	209,709
Gruma Holding Netherlands B.V.	149,325	141,099	120,877
Agroindustrias Integradas del Norte, S.A. de C.V.	115,099	115,099	115,099
Altera LLC	—	90,480	99,149
Grupo Industrial Maseca, S.A.B. de C.V.	98,622	98,622	98,622
NDF Azteca Milling Europe SRL	82,720	78,163	93,614
Azteca Milling, L.P.	71,192	67,270	75,986
Gruma Centroamérica	51,207	51,207	51,207
Molinos Azteca de Chiapas, S.A. de C.V.	28,158	28,158	28,158
Harinera de Yucatán, S.A. de C.V.	18,886	18,886	18,886
Harinera de Maíz de Mexicali, S.A. de C.V.	17,424	17,424	17,424
Molinos Azteca, S.A. de C.V.	8,926	8,926	8,926
Harinera de Maíz de Jalisco, S.A. de C.V.	6,706	6,706	6,706
Goodwill not yet allocated	—	—	261,763
	Ps. 2,169,473	Ps. 2,148,699	Ps. 2,614,587

With respect to the determination of the CGU's value in use, the Company's management considered that a reasonably possible change in the key assumptions used, will not cause that the CGU's carrying value to materially exceed their value in use.

At December 31, 2011, goodwill acquired in Semolina A.S. and Solntse Mexico for a total of Ps.261,763 had not been allocated to a CGU since the initial accounting for these businesses had not been completed.

For the year ended December 31, 2011, the Company recognized impairment losses on goodwill by Ps.92,893 within "Other expenses" for Gruma Holding Netherlands B.V. and Gruma Seaham Ltd., which are part of the segment "Corn flour and packaged tortilla division (United States and Europe)." This impairment loss reflected a decrease in the recoverable value of these CGU due to its continued operating losses.

Brands, Supply and Distribution Rights, Software

2.112

Anheuser-Busch Inbev SA/NV (Dec 2011)

CONSOLIDATED STATEMENT OF FINANCIAL POSITION (in part)

As at 31 December Million US Dollar	Notes	2011	2010
Assets			
Non-current assets			
Property, plant and equipment	13	16,022	15,893
Goodwill	14	51,302	52,498
Intangible assets	15	23,818	23,359
Investments in associates	16	6,696	7,295
Investment securities	17	244	243
Deferred tax assets	18	673	744
Employee benefits	24	10	13
Trade and other receivables	20	1,339	1,700
		100,104	101,745

NOTES TO THE CONSOLIDATED FINANCIAL STATEMENTS (in part)

1. Corporate Information

Anheuser-Busch InBev is a publicly traded company (Euronext: ABI) based in Leuven, Belgium, with American Depositary Receipts on the New York Stock Exchange (NYSE: BUD). It is the leading global brewer and one of the world's top five consumer products companies. Beer, the original social network, has been bringing people together for thousands of years and our portfolio of well over 200 beer brands continues to forge strong connections with consumers. We invest the majority of our brand-building resources on our Focus Brands—those with the greatest growth potential such as global brands Budweiser®, Stella Artois® and Beck's®, alongside Leffe®, Hoegaarden®, Bud Light®, Skol®, Brahma®, Antarctica®, Quilmes®, Michelob Ultra®, Harbin®, Sedrin®, Klinskoye®, Sibirskaya Korona®, Chernigivske®, Hasseröder® and Jupiler®. In addition, the company owns a 50 percent equity interest in the operating subsidiary of Grupo Modelo, Mexico's leading brewer and owner of the global Corona® brand. Anheuser-Busch InBev's dedication to heritage and quality originates from the Den Hoorn brewery in Leuven, Belgium dating back to 1366 and the pioneering spirit of the Anheuser & Co brewery, with origins in St. Louis, USA since 1852. Geographically diversified with a balanced exposure to developed and developing markets, Anheuser-Busch InBev leverages the collective strengths of its approximately 116,000 employees based in 23 countries worldwide. In 2011, AB InBev realized 39.0 billion US dollar revenue. The company strives to be the Best Beer Company in a Better World.

The consolidated financial statements of the company for the year ended 31 December 2011 comprise the company and its subsidiaries (together referred to as "AB InBev" or the "company") and the company's interest in associates and jointly controlled entities.

The financial statements were authorized for issue by the Board of Directors on 11 April 2012.

2. Statement of Compliance

The consolidated financial statements are prepared in accordance with International Financial Reporting Standards as issued by the International Accounting Standards Board ("IASB") and in conformity with IFRS as adopted by the European Union up to 31 December 2011 (collectively "IFRS"). AB InBev did not apply any European carve-outs from IFRS. AB InBev has not applied early any new IFRS requirements that are not yet effective in 2011.

3. Summary of Significant Accounting Policies (in part)

The accounting policies set out below have been applied consistently to all periods presented in these consolidated financial statements by the company and its subsidiaries.

(G) Intangible Assets

Research and Development

Expenditure on research activities, undertaken with the prospect of gaining new scientific or technical knowledge and understanding, is recognized in the income statement as an expense as incurred.

Expenditure on development activities, whereby research findings are applied to a plan or design for the production of new or substantially improved products and processes, is capitalized if the product or process is technically and commercially feasible, future economic benefits are probable and the company has sufficient resources to complete development. The expenditure capitalized includes the cost of materials, direct labor and an appropriate proportion of overheads. Other development expenditure is recognized in the income statement as an expense as incurred. Capitalized development expenditure is stated at cost less accumulated amortization (see below) and impairment losses (refer accounting policy P).

Amortization related to research and development intangible assets is included within the cost of sales if production related and in sales and marketing if related to commercial activities.

Borrowing costs directly attributable to the acquisition, construction or production of qualifying assets are capitalized as part of the cost of such assets.

Supply and Distribution Rights

A supply right is the right for AB InBev to supply a customer and the commitment by the customer to purchase from AB InBev. A distribution right is the right to sell specified products in a certain territory.

Acquired customer relationships in a business combination are initially recognized at fair value as supply rights to the extent that they arise from contractual rights. If the IFRS recognition criteria are not met, these relationships are subsumed under goodwill.

Acquired distribution rights are measured initially at cost or fair value when obtained through a business combination.

Amortization related to supply and distribution rights is included within sales and marketing expenses.

Brands

If part of the consideration paid in a business combination relates to trademarks, trade names, formulas, recipes or technological expertise these intangible assets are considered as a group of complementary assets that is referred to as a brand for which one fair value is determined. Expenditure on internally generated brands is expensed as incurred.

Software

Purchased software is measured at cost less accumulated amortization. Expenditure on internally developed software is capitalized when the expenditure qualifies as development activities; otherwise, it is recognized in the income statement when incurred.

Amortization related to software is included in cost of sales, distribution expenses, sales and marketing expenses or administrative expenses based on the activity the software supports.

Other Intangible Assets

Other intangible assets, acquired by the company, are recognized at cost less accumulated amortization and impairment losses.

Other intangible assets also include multi-year sponsorship rights acquired by the company. These are initially recognized at the present value of the future payments and subsequently measured at cost less accumulated amortization and impairment losses.

Subsequent Expenditure

Subsequent expenditure on capitalized intangible assets is capitalized only when it increases the future economic benefits embodied in the specific asset to which it relates. All other expenditures are expensed as incurred.

Amortization

Intangible assets with a finite life are amortized using the straight-line method over their estimated useful lives. Licenses, brewing, supply and distribution rights are amortized over the period in which the rights exist. Brands are considered to have an indefinite life unless plans exist to discontinue the brand. Discontinuance of a brand can be either through sale or termination of marketing support. When AB InBev purchases distribution rights for its own products the life of these rights is considered indefinite, unless the company has a plan to discontinue the related brand or distribution. Software and capitalized development cost related to technology are amortized over 3 to 5 years.

Brands are deemed intangible assets with indefinite useful lives and, therefore, are not amortized but tested for impairment on an annual basis (refer accounting policy P).

Gains and Losses on Sale

Net gains on sale of intangible assets are presented in the income statement as other operating income. Net losses on sale are included as other operating expenses. Net gains and losses are recognized in the income statement when the significant risks and rewards of ownership have been transferred to the buyer, recovery of the consideration is probable, the associated costs can be estimated reliably, and there is no continuing managerial involvement with the intangible assets.

15. Intangible Assets

Million US Dollar	2011					2010
	Brands	Commercial Intangibles	Software	Other	Total	Total
Acquisition cost						
Balance at end of previous year	21,650	1,786	848	169	24,453	24,067
Effect of movements in foreign exchange	14	(76)	(44)	—	(106)	(58)
Acquisitions through business combinations	5	219	—	18	242	15
Acquisitions and expenditures	31	320	50	56	457	428
Disposals	—	(72)	(5)	(1)	(78)	(29)
Transfer (to)/from other asset categories	—	11	35	59	105	30
Balance at end of year	21,700	2,188	884	301	25,073	24,453
Amortization and impairment losses						
Balance at end of previous year	—	(475)	(583)	(36)	(1,094)	(902)
Effect of movements in foreign exchange	—	15	35	—	50	30
Amortization	—	(154)	(128)	(7)	(289)	(248)
Disposals	—	72	5	—	77	25
Impairment losses	—	—	—	—	—	(2)
Transfer to/(from) other asset categories	—	(2)	1	2	1	3
Balance at end of year	—	(544)	(670)	(41)	(1,255)	(1,094)
Carrying value						
at 31 December 2010	21,650	1,311	265	133	23,359	23,359
at 31 December 2011	21,700	1,644	214	260	23,818	—

AB InBev is the owner of some of the world's most valuable brands in the beer industry. As a result, brands and certain distribution rights are expected to generate positive cash flows for as long as the company owns the brands and distribution rights. Given AB InBev's more than 600-year history, brands and certain distribution rights have been assigned indefinite lives.

Acquisitions and expenditures of commercial intangibles mainly represent supply and distribution rights, exclusive multi-year sponsorship rights and other commercial intangibles.

Intangible assets with indefinite useful lives are comprised primarily of brands and certain distribution rights that AB InBev purchases for its own products, and are tested for impairment during the fourth quarter of the year or whenever a triggering event has occurred. As of 31 December 2011, the carrying amount of the intangible assets amounted to 23 818m US dollar (2010: 23 359m US dollar, 2009: 23 165 US dollar) of which 22 462m US dollar was assigned an indefinite useful life (2010: 22 296m US dollar, 2009: 22 265m US

dollar) and 1 356m US dollar a finite life (2010: 1 063m US dollar, 2009: 900m US dollar).

The carrying amount of intangible assets with indefinite useful lives was allocated to the different countries as follows:

Million US Dollar Country	2011	2010
USA	21,248	21,077
Argentina	333	354
China	256	239
Paraguay	193	189
Bolivia	171	169
UK	104	104
Uruguay	50	50
Canada	39	40
Russia	25	27
Chile	24	27
Germany	19	20
	22,462	22,296

Intangible assets with indefinite useful lives have been tested for impairment using the same methodology and assumptions as disclosed in Note 14 *Goodwill*. Based on the assumptions described in that note, AB InBev concluded that no impairment charge is warranted. While a change in the estimates used could have a material impact on the calculation of the fair values and trigger an impairment charge, the company is not aware of any reasonable possible change in a key assumption used that would cause a business unit's carrying amount to exceed its recoverable amount.

Value of In-Force Business, Core Deposit Intangibles, Purchased Credit Card Relationships, Customer-Related Intangibles, Capitalized Software Enhancements

2.113

Lloyds Banking Group plc (Dec 2011)

CONSOLIDATED BALANCE SHEET (in part)

	Note	2011 £ Million	2010 £ Million
Assets			
Cash and balances at central banks		60,722	38,115
Items in the course of collection from banks		1,408	1,368
Trading and other financial assets at fair value through profit or loss	18	139,510	156,191
Derivative financial instruments	19	66,013	50,777
Loans and receivables:			
Loans and advances to banks	20	32,606	30,272
Loans and advances to customers	21	565,638	592,597
Debt securities	24	12,470	25,735
		610,714	648,604
Available-for-sale financial assets	26	37,406	42,955
Held-to-maturity investments	27	8,098	7,905
Investment properties	28	6,122	5,997
Investments in joint ventures and associates	13	334	429
Goodwill	29	2,016	2,016
Value of in-force business	30	6,638	7,367
Other intangible assets	31	3,196	3,496
Tangible fixed assets	32	7,673	8,190
Current tax recoverable		434	621
Deferred tax assets	44	4,496	5,028
Retirement benefit assets	43	1,338	736
Other assets	33	14,428	12,643
Total assets		970,546	992,438

NOTES TO THE CONSOLIDATED FINANCIAL STATEMENTS (in part)

Note 1: Basis of Preparation (in part)

The consolidated financial statements of Lloyds Banking Group plc have been prepared in accordance with International Financial Reporting Standards (IFRS) as adopted by the European Union (EU). IFRS comprises accounting standards prefixed IFRS issued by the International Accounting Standards Board (IASB) and those prefixed IAS issued by the IASB's predecessor body as well as interpretations issued by the International Financial Reporting Interpretations Committee (IFRIC) and its predecessor body. The EU endorsed version of IAS 39 *Financial Instruments: Recognition and Measurement* relaxes some of the hedge accounting requirements; the Group has not taken advantage of this relaxation, and therefore there is no difference in application to the Group between IFRS as adopted by the EU and IFRS as issued by the IASB.

Note 2: Accounting Policies (in part)

The Group's accounting policies are set out below.

(C) Other Intangible Assets

Other intangible assets include brands, core deposit intangibles, purchased credit card relationships, customer-related intangibles and both internally and externally generated capitalised software enhancements. Intangible assets which have been determined to have a finite useful life are amortised on a straight line basis over their estimated useful life as follows:

Capitalised software enhancements	up to 5 years
Brands (which have been assessed as having finite lives)	10–15 years
Customer-related intangibles	up to 10 years
Core deposit intangibles	up to 8 years
Purchased credit card relationships	5 years

Intangible assets with finite useful lives are reviewed at each reporting date to assess whether there is any indication that they are impaired. If any such indication exists the recoverable amount of the asset is determined and in the event that the asset's carrying amount is greater than its recoverable amount, it is written down immediately. Certain brands have been determined to have an indefinite useful life and are not amortised. Such intangible assets are reassessed annually to reconfirm that an indefinite useful life remains appropriate. In the event that an indefinite life is inappropriate a finite life is determined and an impairment review is performed on the asset.

(O) Insurance

The Group undertakes both life insurance and general insurance business. Insurance and participating investment contracts are accounted for under IFRS 4 *Insurance Contracts*, which permits (with certain exceptions) the continuation of accounting practices for measuring insurance and participating investment contracts that applied prior to the adoption of IFRS. The Group, therefore, continues to account for these products using UK GAAP, including FRS 27 *Life Assurance*, and UK established practice.

Products sold by the life insurance business are classified into three categories:

Insurance contracts—these contracts transfer significant insurance risk and may also transfer financial risk. The Group defines significant insurance risk as the possibility of having to pay benefits on the occurrence of an insured event which are significantly more than the benefits payable if the insured event were not to occur. These contracts may or may not include discretionary participation features.

Investment contracts containing a discretionary participation feature (participating investment contracts)—these contracts do not transfer significant insurance risk, but contain a contractual right which gives the holder the right to receive, in addition to the guaranteed benefits, further additional discretionary benefits or bonuses that are likely to be a significant proportion of the total contractual benefits and the amount and timing of which is at the discretion of the Group, within the constraints of the terms and conditions of the instrument and based upon the performance of specified assets.

Non-participating investment contracts—these contracts do not transfer significant insurance risk or contain a discretionary participation feature.

The general insurance business issues only insurance contracts.

(1) Life Insurance Business (in part)

(III) Value of In-Force Business

The Group recognises as an asset the value of in-force business in respect of insurance contracts and participating investment contracts. The asset represents the present value of the shareholders' interest in the profits expected to emerge from those contracts written at the balance sheet date. This is determined after making appropriate assumptions about future economic and operating conditions such as future mortality and persistency rates and includes allowances for both non-market risk and for the realistic value of financial options

and guarantees. Each cash flow is valued using the discount rate consistent with that applied to such a cash flow in the capital markets. The asset in the consolidated balance sheet is presented gross of attributable tax and movements in the asset are reflected within other operating income in the income statement.

The Group's contractual rights to benefits from providing investment management services in relation to non-participating investment contracts acquired in business combinations and portfolio transfers are measured at fair value at the date of acquisition. The resulting asset is amortised over the estimated lives of the contracts. At each reporting date an assessment is made to determine if there is any indication of impairment. Where impairment exists, the carrying value of the asset is reduced to its recoverable amount and the impairment loss recognised in the income statement.

At each balance sheet date liability adequacy tests are performed to ensure the adequacy of insurance and participating investment contract liabilities net of related deferred cost assets and value of in-force business. In performing these tests current best estimates of discounted future contractual cash flows and claims handling and policy administration expenses, as well as investment income from the assets backing such liabilities, are used. Any deficiency is immediately charged to the income statement, initially by writing off the relevant assets and subsequently by establishing a provision for losses arising from liability adequacy tests.

Note 9: Other Operating Income (in part)

	2011 £m	2010 £m	2009 £m
Operating lease rental income	1,268	1,410	1,509
Rental income from investment properties (note 28)	388	337	358
Other rents receivable	34	41	51
Gains less losses on disposal of available-for-sale financial assets (note 49)	343	399	97
Movement in value of in-force business (note 30)	(622)	789	1,169
Liability management gains	599	423	1,498
Other income	758	917	808
Total other operating income	2,768	4,316	5,490

Note 11: Operating Expenses (in part)

	2011 £m	2010 £m[1]	2009 £m
Depreciation and amortisation:			
Depreciation of tangible fixed assets (note 32)	1,434	1,635	1,716
Amortisation of acquired value of in-force non-participating investment contracts (note 30)	78	76	75
Amortisation of other intangible assets (note 31)	663	721	769
	2,175	2,432	2,560
Impairment of tangible fixed assets[3] (note 32)	65	202	—
Goodwill impairment (note 29)	—	—	240

Note 30: Value of In-Force Business

The gross value of in-force business asset in the consolidated balance sheet is as follows:

	2011 £m	2010 £m
Acquired value of in-force non-participating investment contracts	1,391	1,469
Value of in-force insurance and participating investment contracts	5,247	5,898
Total value of in-force business	6,638	7,367

The movement in the acquired value of in-force non-participating investment contracts over the year is as follows:

	2011 £m	2010 £m
At 1 January	1,469	1,545
Amortisation taken to income statement (note 11)	(78)	(76)
At 31 December	1,391	1,469

The acquired value of in-force non-participating investment contracts includes £329 million (2010: £356 million) in relation to OEIC business.

The movement in the value of in-force insurance and participating investment contracts over the year is as follows:

	2011 £m	2010 £m
At 1 January	5,898	5,140
Adjustment on acquisition	—	—
Exchange and other adjustments	(29)	(31)
Movements in the year:		
New business	552	497
Existing business:		
Expected return	(437)	(400)
Experience variances	117	85
Non-economic assumption changes	(576)	306
Economic variance	(278)	301
Movement in the value of in-force business taken to income statement (note 9)	(622)	789
At 31 December	5,247	5,898

This breakdown shows the movement in the value of in-force business only, and does not represent the full contribution that each item in the breakdown contributes to profit before tax. This will also contain changes in the other assets and liabilities, including the effects of changes in assumptions used to value the liabilities, of the relevant businesses. Economic variance is the element of earnings which is generated from changes to economic experience in the period and to economic assumptions over time. The presentation of economic variance includes the impact of financial market conditions being different at the end of the reporting period from those included in assumptions used to calculate new and existing business returns.

The principal features of the methodology and process used for determining key assumptions used in the calculation of the value of in-force business are set out below:

Economic Assumptions

Each cash flow is valued using the discount rate consistent with that applied to such a cash flow in the capital markets. In practice, to achieve the same result, where the cash flows are either independent of or move linearly with market movements, a method has been applied known as the 'certainty equivalent' approach whereby it is assumed that all assets earn a risk-free rate and all cash flows are discounted at a risk-free rate.

A market consistent approach has been adopted for the valuation of financial options and guarantees, using a stochastic option pricing technique calibrated to be consistent with the market price of relevant options at each valuation date. The risk-free rate used for the value of financial options and guarantees is defined as the spot yield derived from the relevant government bond yield curve in line with FSA realistic balance sheet assumptions. Further information on options and guarantees can be found on page 85.

The liabilities in respect of the Group's UK annuity business are matched by a portfolio of fixed interest securities, including a large proportion of corporate bonds. The value of the in-force business asset for UK annuity business has been calculated after taking into account an estimate of the market premium for illiquidity in respect of corporate bond holdings. The illiquidity premium is estimated to be 119 basis points as at 31 December 2011 (31 December 2010: 75 basis points).

The risk-free rate assumed in valuing the non-annuity in-force business is the 15 year government bond yield for the appropriate territory. The risk-free rate assumed in valuing the in-force asset for the UK annuity business is presented as a single risk-free rate to allow a better comparison to the rate used for other business. That single risk-free rate has been derived to give the equivalent value to the UK annuity book, had that book been valued using the UK gilt yield curve increased to reflect the illiquidity premium described above.

The table below shows the resulting range of yields and other key assumptions at 31 December for UK business:

	2011 %	2010 %
Risk-free rate (value of in-force non-annuity business)	2.48	3.99
Risk-free rate (value of in-force annuity business)	3.76	4.66
Risk-free rate (financial options and guarantees)	0.22 to 3.36	0.63 to 4.50
Retail price inflation	3.35	3.56
Expense inflation	4.01	4.20

Non-Market Risk

An allowance for non-market risk is made through the choice of best estimate assumptions based upon experience, which generally will give the mean expected financial outcome for shareholders and hence no further allowance for non-market risk is required. However, in the case of operational risk, reinsurer default and the with-profit funds these can be asymmetric in the range of potential outcomes for which an explicit allowance is made.

Non-Economic Assumptions

Future mortality, morbidity, expenses, lapse and paid-up rate assumptions are reviewed each year and are based on an analysis of past experience and on management's view of future experience.

Mortality and Morbidity

The mortality and morbidity assumptions, including allowances for improvements in longevity, are set with regard to the Group's actual experience where this provides a reliable basis and relevant industry data otherwise. For German business, appropriate industry tables have been considered.

Lapse (Persistency) and Paid-Up Rates

Lapse and paid up rates assumptions are reviewed each year. The most recent experience is considered along with the results of previous analyses and management's views on future experience. In determining this best estimate view, a number of factors are considered, including the credibility of the results (which will be affected by the volume of data available), any exceptional events that have occurred during the period under consideration and any known or expected trends in underlying data.

Maintenance Expenses

Allowance is made for future policy costs explicitly. Expenses are determined by reference to an internal analysis of current and expected future costs. Explicit allowance is made for future expense inflation. For German business appropriate cost assumptions have been set in accordance with the rules of the local regulatory body.

These assumptions are intended to represent a best estimate of future experience, and further information about the effect of changes in key assumptions is given in note 39.

Note 31: Other Intangible Assets

	Brands £m	Core Deposit Intangible £m	Purchased Credit Card Relationships £m	Customer-Related Intangibles £m	Capitalised Software Enhancements £m	Total £m
Cost:						
At 1 January 2010	596	2,770	300	877	487	5,030
Additions	—	—	—	—	153	153
Disposals	—	—	—	—	(30)	(30)
At 31 December 2010	596	2,770	300	877	610	5,153
Exchange and other adjustments	—	—	—	—	5	5
Additions	—	—	—	4	369	373
Disposals	—	—	—	—	(25)	(25)
At 31 December 2011	596	2,770	300	881	959	5,506
Accumulated amortisation:						
At 1 January 2010	21	393	58	237	234	943
Charge for the year	25	400	60	161	75	721
Disposals	—	—	—	—	(7)	(7)
At 31 December 2010	46	793	118	398	302	1,657
Exchange and other adjustments	—	—	—	—	2	2
Charge for the year	19	399	60	88	97	663
Disposals	—	—	—	—	(12)	(12)
At 31 December 2011	65	1,192	178	486	389	2,310
Balance sheet amount at 31 December 2011	531	1,578	122	395	570	3,196
Balance sheet amount at 31 December 2010	550	1,977	182	479	308	3,496

Included within brands above are assets of £380 million (31 December 2010: £380 million) that have been determined to have indefinite useful lives and are not amortised. These brands use the Bank of Scotland name which has been in existence for over 300 years. These brands are well established financial services brands and there are no indications that they should not have an indefinite useful life.

The customer-related intangibles include customer lists and the benefits of customer relationships that generate recurring income. The purchased credit card relationships represent the benefit of recurring income generated from the portfolio of credit cards purchased and the core deposit intangible is the benefit derived from a large stable deposit base that has low interest rates.

Capitalised software enhancements principally comprise identifiable and directly associated internal staff and other costs.

Costs of Acquisition and Retention of Football Personnel

2.114

Celtic plc (Jun 2011)

Author's Note

As described in the Director's Report included in its 2011 Annual Report, the principal activity of Celtic plc Group is "the operation of a professional football club, with related ancillary activities. The principal activity of the [parent] Company is to control and manage the main assets of the business whilst the majority of operating activity is carried out by the subsidiary, Celtic F.C. Limited." Given the nature of its business, Celtic recognizes an intangible asset, often referred to as an "initial player roster," for the direct costs incurred in the acquisition and retention of its football players.

CONSOLIDATED BALANCE SHEETS (in part)

	Notes	2011 £000	2010 £000
Assets			
Non-current assets			
Property, plant and equipment	15	54,357	55,854
Intangible assets	16	10,364	13,769
Investment in subsidiaries	17	—	—
		64,721	69,623
Current assets			
Trade and other receivables	20	14,002	14,224
Cash and cash equivalents	21	10,703	4,913
		24,705	19,137
Total assets		89,426	88,760

NOTES TO THE CONSOLIDATED FINANCIAL STATEMENTS (in part)

2 Accounting Policies (in part)

(c) Intangible Assets

Costs directly attributable to the acquisition and retention of football personnel are capitalised and treated as intangible assets. Subsequent amounts are capitalised only when they become unavoidable due to the elimination of all contingent events relating to their payment and where the value of the asset is enhanced by the underlying event. All of these amounts are amortised to the income statement over the contract period remaining from their capitalisation to nil residual values.

(d) Impairment Policy

The Group and Company tests impairment at each balance sheet date. In determining whether an intangible asset is impaired account is taken of the following:

(i) management's intentions in terms of each specific asset being part of the plans for the coming football season;

(ii) the evidence of this intention such as the level of an asset's participation in the previous football season;

(iii) the level of interest from other clubs in paying a transfer fee for the asset;

(iv) market knowledge of transfer appetite, activity and budgets in the industry through discussion with agents and other clubs;

(v) the financial state of the football industry;

(vi) the level of appetite from clubs for football personnel from Scotland;

(vii) levels of 'cover' for each playing position;

(viii) the football personnel's own career plans and personal intentions for the future, and

(ix) contract terminations.

An impairment loss is recognised for the amount by which the asset's carrying amount exceeds its recoverable amount. Impairment losses are recognised in the Consolidated Statement of Comprehensive Income.

16 Non-Current Assets—Intangible Assets

Group and Company	2011 £000	2010 £000
Cost		
At 1 July	30,283	26,126
Additions	10,294	13,641
Disposals	(10,959)	(9,484)
At 30 June	29,618	30,283
Amortisation		
At 1 July	16,514	13,981
Charge for year	8,155	8,350
Provision for impairment	3,181	1,422
Disposals	(8,596)	(7,239)
At 30 June	19,254	16,514
Net Book Value		
At 30 June	10,364	13,769

	2011 No.	2011 £000	2010 No.	2010 £000
The number of players with a book value in excess of £1m by contract expiry date is as follows:				
Contract expiry within 1 year	—	—	—	—
Contract expiry within 2 years	2	2,522	4	5,853
Contract expiry within 3 years	1	1,113	1	1,084
Contract expiry within 4 years	—	—	2	2,913
	3	3,635	7	9,850

No individual intangible asset included above accounted for more than 14% of the total net book value of the intangible assets (2010: 1 5%). The opening net book value of intangible assets at 1 July 2010 was £13.77m and on 1 July 2009 was £12.14m.

The net gain on sale of intangible assets in the year was £13.23 m (2010: £5.71 m). The impairment provision in 2011 and 2010 within the football segment reflects the Directors' view that the recoverable amount of the intangible asset is lower than the carrying value, as per Note 2(d) above, and recognises a write down to fair value less costs to sell. The valuation of players is based on an independent valuation carried out with reference to the market for player transfers. The impairment charge of £3.18m comprises one player of £0.76m whose contract expired during the year, one player with contract expiring within one year of £0.70m and four players with contracts expiring within two years of £1.72m.

Development Costs, Concessions, Easements, Patents, Registered Trademarks and Other Rights

2.115

Empresa Nacional de Electricidad S.A. (Endesa-Chile) (Dec 2011)

CONSOLIDATED STATEMENTS OF FINANCIAL POSITION (in part)

(In thousands of Chilean pesos)

Assets	Note	12-31-2011 ThCh$	12-31-2010 ThCh$
Non-current assets			
Other non-current financial assets	6	13,598,670	28,295,886
Other non-current non-financial assets	7	1,463,429	10,884,644
Non-current receivables	7	151,608,768	126,461,117
Investments accounted for using the equity method	11	582,198,848	581,743,347
Intangible assets other than goodwill	12	45,679,853	44,354,510
Goodwill	13	106,399,041	100,085,306
Property, plant, and equipment, net	14	4,603,902,502	4,253,906,589
Deferred tax assets	15	97,106,685	96,113,683
Total non-current assets		5,601,957,796	5,241,845,082
Total assets		6,562,013,116	6,034,871,805

NOTES TO THE CONSOLIDATED FINANCIAL STATEMENTS (in part)

1. The Group's Activities and Financial Statements

Empresa Nacional de Electricidad S.A. (hereinafter the Parent Company or the Company) and its subsidiaries comprise the Endesa Group Chile (hereinafter Endesa or the Group).

Endesa Chile is a publicly traded corporation with registered address and head office located at Avenida Santa Rosa, No.76, in Santiago, Chile. The Company is registered in the securities register of the Superintendency of Securities and Insurance of Chile (Superintendencia de Valores y Seguros or SVS) under number 114. In addition, the Company is registered with the Securities and Exchange Commission of the United States of America (hereinafter U.S. SEC), and with Spain's Comisión Nacional del Mercado de Valores. The Company's shares have been listed on the New York Stock Exchange since 1994 and on the Latibex since 2001.

Endesa Chile is a subsidiary of Enersis S.A., a Spanish company controlled by Enel S.p.A. (hereinafter Enel).

The Company was initially created by a public deed dated December 1, 1943. The Treasury Department's Supreme Decree No. 97 of January 3, 1944, authorized the creation of the company and approved its by-laws. For tax purposes, the Company operates under Chilean tax identification number 91,081,000-6.

As of December 31, 2011, the Group had 2,447 employees. During 2011, the Group averaged a total of 2,395 employees. See Note 32 for additional information regarding employee distribution by category and geographic location.

The Company's corporate purpose consists of generating, transporting, producing, and distributing electrical energy. Its corporate purpose also includes investing in financial assets, developing projects, and carrying out activities in the energy industry and in other fields in which electrical energy is essential, and participating in public civil or hyadraulic infrastructure concessions, in which it may participate directly or through subsidiaries or associated companies that are either in Chile or abroad.

The Company's 2010 consolidated financial statements were approved by the Board of Directors at a meeting held on January 26, 2011. The consolidated financial statements were then submitted to the consideration of a General Shareholders Meeting held on April 26, 2011, which gave its final approval on the consolidated financial statements.

These consolidated financial statements are presented in thousands of Chilean pesos (unless expressly stated otherwise), as the Chilean peso is the functional currency of the main economic environment in which Endesa Chile operates. Foreign operations are reported in accordance with the accounting policies stated in Notes 2.6 and 3.k.

2. Basis of Presentation of Consolidated Financial Statements (in part)

2.1 Accounting Principles (in part)

The December 31, 2011 consolidated financial statements of Endesa Chile and its subsidiaries have been prepared in accordance with International Financial Reporting Standards (IFRS), issued by the International Accounting Standards Board (hereinafter "IASB"), and approved by its Board of Directors at its meeting held on January 31, 2012.

3. Accounting Principles Applied (in part)

The main accounting policies used in preparing the accompanying consolidated financial statements were the following:

c) Intangible Assets Other Than Goodwill

c.1) Concessions

IFRIC 12 "Service Concession Agreements" provides accounting guidelines for public-to-private service concession agreements. This accounting interpretation applies if:

(a) The grantor controls or regulates which services the operator should provide with the infrastructure, to whom it must provide them, and at what price; and

(b) The grantor controls—through ownership, beneficial entitlement, or otherwise—any significant residual interest in the infrastructure at the end of the term of the agreement.

If both of the above conditions are met simultaneously, an intangible assets is recognized to the extent that the operator receives the right to charge the users of the public service, provided that these rights are contingent on the degree to which the service is used.

These intangibles are initially recognized at cost, with cost understood to be the fair value of the service provided plus other direct costs that are directly attributable to the operation. They are then amortized over the duration of the concession.

The Group operates administrative concessions in which the counterpart is a government entity. The El Melón Tunnel is the only concession with determining factors leading to the conclusion that the requirements explained above are met simultaneously.

In the concession on the El Melón Tunnel, the Chilean Ministry of Public Works (the "MOP") and our subsidiary Sociedad Concesionaria Túnel El Melón S.A. signed a concession agreement that establishes both the services the operator must provide and the price of these services. The concession right expires in June 2016, at which time the MOP recovers the right to exploit the El Melón Tunnel assets, with no need for the MOP to meet any specific conditions.

The Group has applied the intangibles method established in IFRIC 12. It has not recognized any financial assets in connection with the El Melón Tunnel concession since the agreement signed with the MOP does not provide for guaranteed revenues regardless of circumstances.

The following subsidiary has recognized an intangible asset for its concession agreements:

Concession Holder and Operator	Country	Term	Period Remaining to Expiration
Sociedad Concesionaria Túnel el Melón S.A. (Highway infrastructure)	Chile	23 years	5 years

c.2) Research and Development Expenses

Endesa Chile and its subsidiaries follow the policy of recording the costs incurred in a project's development phase as intangible assets in the statement of financial position as long as the project's technical viability and economic returns are reasonably assured.

Expenditures on research activities are recognized as an expense in the period in which they are incurred. These expenses amounted to ChTh$ 812,917 in 2011. No expenses were recorded for this item in the 2010 and 2009 fiscal years.

c.3) Other Intangible Assets

These intangible assets correspond primarily to computer software, easements, and water rights. They are initially recognized at acquisition or production cost and are subsequently measured at cost less accumulated amortization and impairment losses, if any.

Computer software programs are amortized, on average, over five years. Certain easements and water rights have indefinite useful lives and are therefore not amortized, while others have useful lives ranging from 40 to 60 years, depending on their characteristics, and they are amortized over that term.

The criteria for recognizing the impairment losses of these assets and, if applicable, the impairment loss recoveries recorded in previous fiscal years are explained in letter e) of this Note.

12. Intangible Assets Other Than Goodwill

Intangible assets as of December 31, 2011 and 2010 are detailed as follows:

Intangible Assets, Net	12-31-2011 ThCh$	12-31-2010 ThCh$
Intangible Assets, Net	45,679,853	44,354,510
Development costs	5,386,314	2,262,982
Easements	19,925,736	18,015,386
Concessions	12,152,979	14,200,420
Patents, registered trademarks, and other rights	252,095	23,121
Computer software	4,792,643	5,390,313
Other identifiable intangible assets	3,170,086	4,462,288

Intangible Assets, Gross	12-31-2011 ThCh$	12-31-2010 ThCh$
Intangible Assets, Gross	92,129,085	86,429,809
Development costs	5,669,859	3,875,653
Easements	24,700,484	22,237,811
Concessions	40,156,864	39,461,837
Patents, registered trademarks, and other rights	517,172	25,123
Computer software	14,909,889	13,419,449
Other identifiable intangible assets	6,174,817	7,409,936

Accumulated Amortization and Impairment, Total	12-31-2011 ThCh$	12-31-2010 ThCh$
Accumulated Amortization and Impairment, Total	(46,449,232)	(42,075,299)
Development costs	(283,545)	(1,612,671)
Easements	(4,774,748)	(4,222,425)
Concessions	(28,003,885)	(25,261,417)
Patents, registered trademarks, and other rights	(265,077)	(2,002)
Computer software	(10,117,246)	(8,029,136)
Other identifiable intangible assets	(3,004,731)	(2,947,648)

The reconciliation of the carrying amounts of intangible assets for the 2011 and 2010 fiscal years is as follows:

Year Ended December 31, 2011

Movements in Intangible Assets	Development Costs, Net ThCh$	Easements and Water Rights, Net ThCh$	Concessions, Net ThCh$	Patents, Registered Trademarks, and Other Rights, Net ThCh$	Computer Software, Net ThCh$	Other Identifiable Intangible Assets, Net ThCh$	Intangible Assets, Net ThCh$
Opening balance at 01-01-2011	2,262,982	18,015,386	14,200,420	23,121	5,390,313	4,462,288	44,354,510
Movements in identifiable intangible assets							
Additions	1,844,034	453,174	—	206,661	1,355,938	12,397	3,872,204
Disposals	(464,628)	—	—	—	(130,184)	(20,853)	(615,665)
Amortization(*)	(21,488)	(341,988)	(2,113,018)	(43,460)	(517,197)	(457,716)	(3,494,867)
Foreign currency translation differences	412,888	276,864	1,036,008	52,914	(7,802)	155,993	1,926,865
Other increases (decreases)	1,352,526	1,522,300	(970,431)	12,859	(1,298,425)	(982,023)	(363,194)
Total movements in identifiable intangible assets	3,123,332	1,910,350	(2,047,441)	228,974	(597,670)	(1,292,202)	1,325,343
Closing balance in identifiable intangible assets at 12/31/2011	5,386,314	19,925,736	12,152,979	252,095	4,792,643	3,170,086	45,679,853

(*) See Note 26, Depreciation and Amortization.

Year Ended December 31, 2010

Movements in Intangible Assets	Development Costs, Net ThCh$	Easements and Water Rights, Net ThCh$	Concessions, Net ThCh$	Patents, Registered Trademarks, and Other Rights, Net ThCh$	Computer Software, Net ThCh$	Other Identifiable Intangible Assets, Net ThCh$	Intangible Assets, Net ThCh$
Opening balance at 01-01-2010	12,330	14,935,772	16,641,396	6,837,850	3,549,640	661,587	42,638,575
Movements in identifiable intangible assets							
Additions	854,638	858,513	215,084	—	481,399	3,201,965	5,611,599
Disposals	—	—	—	—	(3,313)	—	(3,313)
Amortization(*)	(1,322)	(350,113)	(2,656,624)	—	(818,506)	(113,431)	(3,939,996)
Foreign currency translation differences	(243,935)	(388,137)	563	(1,932)	(10,070)	254	(643,257)
Other increases (decreases)	1,641,271	2,959,351	1	(6,812,797)	2,191,163	711,913	690,902
Total movements in identifiable intangible assets	2,250,652	3,079,614	(2,440,976)	(6,814,729)	1,840,673	3,800,701	1,715,935
Closing balance in identifiable intangible assets at 12/31/2010	2,262,982	18,015,386	14,200,420	23,121	5,390,313	4,462,288	44,354,510

According to the Group management's estimates and projections, the expected future cash flows attributable to intangible assets allow recovery of the carrying amount of these assets recorded as of December 31, 2011 and 2010 (see Note 3.d). As of December 31, 2011, the Company does not have significant amounts in intangible assets.

IAS 40, *INVESTMENT PROPERTY*

Author's Note

In 2011, IASB issued IFRS 13, which amends IAS 40 as follows:
- Replaces the terms *determine* and *estimate* with the term *measure*
- Requires measurement of fair value in accordance with IFRS 13
- Expands the guidance to be used in deciding whether there is clear evidence of inability to measure fair value reliably

Because these standards are effective for annual periods beginning on or after 1 January 2012, these amendments are not reflected in the commentary in this section. However, these amendments would not affect the content of illustrative excerpts from survey companies' financial statements.

IFRSs Overview and Comparison to U.S. GAAP

2.116 *Investment property*, as defined in IAS 40, is land or buildings (in whole or part) held for rental or capital appreciation, or both, and is a separate asset class. An entity may own an investment property or hold it under a finance (capital) lease. Under certain circumstances, as described subsequently, lessees holding property interests under operating leases may also classify the property interest as an investment property under IAS 40.

2.117 An entity should account for land or buildings held for sale in the ordinary course of business as inventory and account for it in accordance with IAS 2. Land or buildings held for use in the production or supply of goods or services or for administrative purposes is considered *owner occupied* and should be accounted for as PPE, in accordance with IAS 16; otherwise, accounting for those assets should be in accordance with IAS 40.

2.118 The scope of IAS 40 includes investment property under construction and excludes biological assets related to agricultural activity (see IAS 41) and mineral rights and mineral reserves, such as oil, natural gas, and similar nonregenerative resources.

Recognition and Measurement

IFRSs

2.119 On initial recognition, an entity should recognize an investment property as an asset when, and only when
- it is probable that the future economic benefits that are associated with the investment property will flow to the entity, and
- the cost of the investment property can be measured reliably.

Cost should include transaction costs to acquire the investment property and costs incurred subsequently to add to, replace part of, or service the property. An entity should measure the cost of investment property assets held under a finance lease at the lower of the property's fair value and the present value of the minimum lease payments and recognize an equivalent amount as a liability.

2.120 As it would for PPE, an entity should allocate the cost to the components of the property that it expects to replace over the asset's useful life. At the time the component is replaced, an entity should derecognize any remaining carrying amount. Examples of components of investment property are interior walls, elevators, and heating and air conditioning systems.

2.121 IAS 40 has two alternative models for subsequent measurement: cost and fair value. If the entity chooses the cost model, it should account for the asset in accordance with IAS 16 and test the asset for impairment in accordance with IAS 36. However, investment properties that meet the criteria to be classified as held for sale (or are included in a disposal group that is classified as held for sale) should be measured in accordance with IFRS 5.

Author's Note

See paragraph 2.59 for a description of the cost model.

2.122 An entity may choose one of the two alternative models separately for each of the following groups of investment properties:
- All investment property backing liabilities that pay a return linked directly to the fair value of, or returns from, specific assets, including the property
- All other investment property

2.123 Lessees who hold property interests under an operating lease can also classify and account for such interests as an investment property if, and only if, the property would otherwise meet the definition of an *investment property* and the entity chooses the fair value model for subsequent measurement.

2.124 Under the fair value model, an entity should measure all of its investment property at fair value, except in the exceptional case when fair value cannot be determined reliably. IAS 38 states that there is a rebuttable presumption that, if an entity chooses the fair value model, it can reliably determine fair values for its properties. Fair values should reflect market conditions at the end of the reporting period and the entity should report changes in fair value in profit or loss.

2.125 If an entity has previously measured an investment property at fair value, it should continue to measure that investment property at fair value until disposal or transfer to inventory or owner-occupied PPE. For a transfer from investment property carried at fair value to owner-occupied property or inventories, the property's deemed cost for subsequent accounting in accordance with IAS 2 or IAS 16, should be its fair value at the date of change in use. An entity should consider the change in fair value when the asset is transferred from PPE to investment property held at fair value as a revaluation increase or decrease under IAS 16.

2.126 An entity derecognizes an investment property on disposal or when the property is permanently retired (that is, no further economic benefits are expected). An entity should recognize gains or losses on disposal or retirement in profit or loss.

2.127 Entities should recognize compensation from third parties for impairments or losses in profit or loss only when the compensation is receivable.

U.S. GAAP

2.128 FASB ASC does not provide specific guidance on accounting for investment properties. FASB ASC 360 requires an entity to account for land and buildings as PPE, even when held for sale in the ordinary course of business, but the entity should not depreciate a long-lived asset while it is classified as held for sale. Accordingly, the entity should measure the investment property using the cost model. Unlike IFRSs, neither FASB ASC 360 nor FASB ASC 840, *Leases*, discusses whether a property held by a lessee under a lease classified as an operating lease could be accounted for as PPE (effectively, as a capital lease) by the lessee.

Author's Note

FASB ASC does not recognize investment properties as a separate asset class. Such properties are included in PPE. See paragraphs 2.53–.71 for a more comprehensive comparison between FASB ASC and IFRSs related to PPE, including presentation and disclosure.

Presentation

IFRSs

2.129 IAS 1 requires an entity to include a line item for investment properties, and it should present items with different measurement bases separately.

Disclosure

IFRSs

2.130 Regardless of the model chosen, entities should disclose the following:
- Accounting policy (cost or fair value)
- If the fair value model is used, whether and under what circumstances property interests held under operating leases are classified and accounted for as investment property
- When classification is difficult, the criteria used to distinguish investment property from owner-occupied properties and from property held for sale in the ordinary course of business
- Methods and significant assumptions applied in measuring fair values, including a statement regarding the relative weight of market-related evidence and other factors
- Extent to which the fair value of investment property is based on a valuation by independent valuers, with recognized credentials and recent experience, or the fact that no such valuation was done

- Amounts recognized in profit or loss, including rental income, direct operating expenses (generating and not generating rental income), and the cumulative change in fair value recognized in profit or loss when sales occurred between pools of asset under different models

2.131 When an entity applies the fair value model, it should provide a reconciliation of the beginning and ending balance in investment properties, disclosing the following:
- Additions disaggregating individual property acquisitions from expenditures on existing properties
- Additions due to business combinations
- Classification to held for sale or as part of a disposal group classified as held for sale
- Changes in fair value
- Net foreign exchange differences
- Transfers to or from inventory or PPE
- Other changes

2.132 In the exceptional case that fair value can no longer be measured reliably and the cost model is used, an entity should present information about the property separately in the relevant reconciliation disclosure. The entity should also provide a description of the property and the circumstances that led to the determination that fair value was not reliable.

2.133 For investment properties held under the cost model, an entity should provide the same disclosures as required by IAS 16, including the depreciation methods used and useful lives or depreciation rates used. At a minimum, an entity should show investment properties as a separate asset class when the entity includes the required reconciliation with other assets using the cost model. The entity should disclose the aggregated fair value of investment properties measured at cost, except in the rare case when fair value cannot be measured reliably.

TABLE 2-6: ALTERNATIVE MODELS FOR SUBSEQUENT MEASUREMENT OF INVESTMENT PROPERTY

	2011	2010	2009
Cost	26	18	14
Fair Value	18	19	17
Fair value only for investment properties backing liabilities paying a return linked to the fair value of the investment property otherwise, cost model	1	1	1
No model disclosed	2	2	2
Survey companies that do not report investment properties	129	131	126
Companies disclosing both models	(1)	(1)	0
Total Companies	**175**	**170**	**160**

Presentation and Disclosure Excerpts

Investment Property Carried at Cost: Part of a Building

2.134

Sociedad Quimica y Minera de Chile S.A. (Dec 2011)

CONSOLIDATED CLASSIFIED STATEMENTS OF FINANCIAL POSITION (in part)

Assets	Note N°	12.31.2011 ThUS$	12.31.2010 ThUS$
Non-current assets			
Other non-current financial assets	8.1	30,488	92,674
Other non-financial assets, non-current	25	24,651	24,157
Non-current rights receivable	8.2	1,070	1,102
Investments accounted for using the equity method	10.1	60,694	62,271
Intangible assets other than goodwill	12.1	4,316	3,270
Goodwill	12.1	38,605	38,388
Property, plant and equipment	13.1	1,755,042	1,453,973
Investment property	13.4	—	1,373
Deferred tax assets	28	304	365
Total non-current assets		1,915,170	1,677,573
Total assets		3,871,583	3,372,836

NOTES TO THE CONSOLIDATED FINANCIAL STATEMENTS (in part)

Note 2—Basis of Presentation of Consolidated Financial Statements and Summary of Significant Accounting Principles (in part)

2.8 Investment Properties

The Company recognizes as investment properties the net values of land, buildings and other properties held which it intends to commercialize under lease agreements, or to obtain proceeds from their sale as a result of those increases generated in the future in the respective market prices. These assets are not used in the activities and are not destined for the Company's own use.

Investment properties are initially stated at acquisition cost, which includes the acquisition price or production cost plus directly assignable expenses. Subsequently, investment properties are stated at their acquisition cost less accumulated depreciation, and the possible accrued provisions for value impairment.

Note 13—Property, Plant and Epuipment (in part)

13.4 Additional Information (in part)

2) The Investment properties at December 31, 2011 and at December 31, 2010 is as follows:

Description of Assets	12.31.2011 ThUS$	12.31.2010 ThUS$
2 floors of the Las Americas Building, net	—	1,373
Total (net)	—	1,373

Investment Property Carried at Fair Value: Freehold Timberlands No Longer Used for Harvest and Growth of Timber

2.135

Brookfield Infrastructure Partners L.P. (Dec 2011)

Author's Note

Brookfield Infrastructure Partners L.P. implemented IFRSs effective December 31, 2011, with a date of transition of January 1, 2010. The excerpt that follows reflects the initial application of IAS 1 and IAS 40.

CONSOLIDATED STATEMENTS OF FINANCIAL POSITION (in part)

US$ Millions	Notes	As of December 31, 2011	As of December 31, 2010
Assets			
Property, plant and equipment	10	4,073	3,131
Intangible assets	11	2,924	2,903
Standing timber	12	2,890	2,578
Investments in associates	9	1,400	1,089
Goodwill	13	591	591
Investment properties	14	194	175
Financial assets (non-current)	8	114	118
Other assets (non-current)	6	200	132
Deferred income tax asset	24	405	385
Total assets		$13,269	$13,352

NOTES TO THE CONSOLIDATED FINANCIAL STATEMENTS (in part)

Note 1. Organization and Description of the Business

Brookfield Infrastructure Partners L.P. (the "partnership") owns and operates utility businesses, transport and energy businesses and timber assets in North and South America, Australasia, and Europe. The partnership was formed as a limited partnership established under the laws of Bermuda, pursuant to a limited partnership agreement dated May 17, 2007, as amended and restated. The partnership is a subsidiary of Brookfield Asset Management Inc. ("Brookfield"). The partnership's limited partnership units are listed on the New York Stock Exchange and the Toronto Stock Exchange under the symbols "BIP" and "BIP.UN", respectively. The registered office is 73 Front Street, Hamilton, Bermuda.

Note 3. Significant Accounting Policies (in part)

a) Statement of Compliance

These consolidated and combined financial statements have been prepared in accordance with International Financial Reporting Standards ("IFRS") as issued by the International Accounting Standards Board ("IASB").

The financial statements were authorized for issue by the Board of Directors on April 27, 2012.

i) Investment Property

Brookfield Infrastructure uses the fair value method to account for real estate classified as investment property. A property is determined to be an investment property when it is principally held to earn rental income or for capital appreciation, or both. Investment property is initially measured at cost including transaction costs. Subsequent to initial recognition, investment properties are carried at fair value. Gains or losses arising from changes in fair value are included in income.

Land of Brookfield Infrastructure's U.S. and Canadian freehold timberlands, which has been determined to have a higher and better use and which is no longer used for the harvest and growth of timber is classified as investment property.

Fair values are primarily determined by discounting the expected future cash flows of each property, generally over a term of 10 years, using a discount and terminal capitalization rate reflective of the characteristics, location and market of each property. The future cash flows of each property are based upon, among other things, rental income from current leases and assumptions about rental income from future leases reflecting current conditions, less future cash outflows in respect of such current and future leases. Brookfield Infrastructure determines fair value using both internal and external valuations.

r) Critical Accounting Judgments and Key Sources of Estimation Uncertainty (in part)

vi) Valuation of Investment Property

The fair value of investment property is determined with the assistance of an independent valuation expert using recognized valuation techniques, comprising both the discounted cash flow method and the yield method. In some cases, the fair values are determined based on recent real estate transactions with similar characteristics and location to those of Brookfield Infrastructure assets.

The determination of the fair value of investment property requires the use of estimates such as future cash flows from assets (such as lettings, tenants' profiles, future revenue streams, capital values of fixtures and fittings, plant and machinery, any environmental matters and the overall repair and condition of the property) and discount rates applicable to those assets. These estimates are based on local market conditions existing at reporting date.

Note 14. Investment Properties

US$ Millions	U.K. Port Operation	HBU[1]	Total
Gross carrying amount:			
Balance at January 1, 2010	$138	$37	$175
Disposals	—	(2)	(2)
Fair value adjustments	8	—	8
Foreign exchange differences	(6)	—	(6)
Balance at December 31, 2010	$140	$35	$175
Additions	—	4	4
Disposals	(2)	—	(2)
Fair value adjustments	11	4	15
Foreign exchange differences	3	(1)	2
Balance at December 31, 2011	$152	$42	$194

[1] HBU is defined as "higher and better use" lands.

At December 31, 2011, $11 million and $4 million gains were recognized for the U.K. Port operation and HBU properties, respectively (2010: $8 million gain and $nil, respectively). Fair values of investment properties are determined based on valuations prepared by independent appraisers. Fair values are generally determined by calculating the discounted future cash flows of the properties.

Investment Property Carried at Fair Value: Owned and Leased Land

2.136

Alon Holdings Blue Square—Israel Ltd (Dec 2011)

CONSOLIDATED STATEMENTS OF FINANCIAL POSITION (in part)

In Thousands	Note	December 31 2010	December 31 2011	Convenience Translation (Note 1b) December 31, 2011
		NIS	NIS	U.S. Dollars
Assets				
Non-Current Assets:				
Investments in associates	10b	6,012	202,653	53,037
Derivative financial instruments	13	56,078	896	234
Real estate inventories	14d	83,337	100,035	26,180
Payments on account of real estate	11	164,132	191,600	50,144
Investment in securities	12	30,327	33,159	8,678
Loans receivable, net of current maturities	16	176,043	182,654	47,803
Property and equipment, net	7	2,928,515	2,942,487	770,083
Investment property	8	546,870	576,093	150,770
Intangible assets, net	9	1,486,744	1,461,070	382,379
Other long-term receivables	17	47,098	142,331	37,250
Deferred taxes	23	66,018	104,321	27,302
		5,591,174	5,937,299	1,553,860
Total assets		8,764,187	9,094,217	2,380,062

NOTES TO THE CONSOLIDATED FINANCIAL STATEMENTS (in part)

Note 1—General: (in part)

a. Information on the Activities of Alon Holdings Blue Square—Israel Ltd and its Subsidiaries

Alon Holdings Blue Square—Israel Ltd. (formerly Blue Square—Israel Ltd.) ("Blue Square") is an Israeli corporation, which, directly and through its subsidiaries (together—the Company) mainly operates in Israel. All references to the Company include, unless the context otherwise indicates, Blue-Square and its subsidiaries. Upon completion of the acquisition of Dor Alon in 2010, see note 6, the Company operates in four reportable segments: (1) Supermarkets, (2) Non-food Retail and Wholesale (3) Real Estate and (4) Commercial and fueling sites (see note 5).

Alon Holdings Blue Square—Israel Ltd. is a limited public company incorporated and domiciled in Israel, whose ADSs and shares are listed for trading on the New-York Stock Exchange (the "NYSE") and on the Tel-Aviv Stock Exchange (the "TASE").

The Company is controlled by Alon Israel Oil Company Ltd ("Alon"). The address of its registered office is 2 Amal St., Afek Industrial Zone, Rosh Ha'ayin, Israel. The consolidated financial statements of the Company for the year ended December 31, 2011 were authorized for issue in accordance with a resolution of the directors on April 30, 2012.

The consolidated results for the year 2010 include the results of the subsidiary Dor Alon, acquired in 2010, from October 3, 2010 to December 31, 2010. Dor Alon's shares are listed on the Tel Aviv stock exchange. See also note 6.

Note 2—Summary of Significant Accounting Policies: (in part)

The principal accounting policies applied in the preparation of these consolidated financial statements are set out below. These policies have been consistently applied to all the years presented unless otherwise stated.

a. Basis of Presentation

The consolidated financial statements of the Company have been prepared in accordance with International Financial Reporting Standards (hereafter—"IFRS") as issued by the International Accounting Standard Board (hereafter—"IASB").

The accounting policies adopted by the Company are consistent with those of the previous financial year.

The consolidated financial statements have been prepared under the historical cost convention, as modified by actuarial adjustments for defined benefit plan assets and liabilities and financial assets (including derivative instruments) and investment property measured at fair value. The cost of certain nonmonetary assets, investments in associated companies and certain equity items as of the transition date have been determined on the basis of their deemed cost, or historical cost adjusted to inflation in Israel through December 31, 2003, as allowed by the IFRS transition guidance.

The preparation of financial statements in conformity with IFRS requires the use of certain critical accounting estimates. It also requires management to exercise its judgment in the process of applying the Company's accounting policies. The areas involving a higher degree of judgment or complexity, or areas where assumptions and estimates are significant to the consolidated financial statements are disclosed in note 4. Actual results may differ materially from estimates and assumptions used by the Company's management.

f. Investment Property

Investment property is held for long-term rental yields or value appreciation and is not occupied by the Company. Investment property is initially measured at cost, including transaction costs. Subsequent to initial recognition, investment property is stated at fair value, reflecting market conditions, determined at least annually by independent appraisers, "Haushner Civil Eng. & Real Estate Appraisal Ltd." and "Barak Friedman Cohen & Co. Economic & Real Estate Appraisal."

Fair value is based on current prices in an active market, adjusted, if necessary, for any differences in the nature, location or condition of the specific asset. If such information is not available, the Company uses alternative sources such as recent prices on less active markets or discounted cash flow projections.

Gains and losses arising from changes in fair value are recorded in the statement of income under "Changes in fair value of investment property, net" in the period in which they arise.

Land that is held under an operating lease with The Israeli Lands Administration or local authorities, is classified and accounted for as an investment property, provided that the conditions for such classification are met. In such cases, the lease rights are initially recognized as an asset and the lease obligation as a liability, in a manner similar to a finance lease.

Revenue from the sale of investment property, is recognized when the significant risks and rewards of ownership of the property have been transferred to the buyer; such revenue is not recognized where there are significant uncertainties as to the collection of the consideration of the transaction, the costs related thereto, or when the Company has significant continuing involvement in the property that was sold.

j. Borrowing Costs

General and specific borrowing costs directly attributable to the acquisition or construction of any qualifying asset (including investment property and real estate inventories) are capitalized during the period of time that is required to complete and prepare the asset for its intended use. Other borrowing costs are expensed in the period they occur. Borrowing costs consist of interest and other costs that an entity incurs in connection with the borrowing of funds.

aa. Leases

Leases in which a significant portion of the risks and rewards of ownership are retained by the lessor are classified as operating leases. Payments made under operating leases (net of any incentives received from the lessor) are charged to the statement of income on a straight-line basis over the period of the lease.

Land held under an operating lease is classified and accounted for as investment property when the property would otherwise meet the definition of investment property. In such case, the operating lease is accounted for as if it were a finance lease.

Leases of property where the Company has substantially all the risks and rewards of ownership are classified as finance leases. Finance leases are capitalized at the lease's commencement at the lower of the fair value of the leased property and the present value of the minimum lease payments.

Note 3—Financial Risk Management and Financial Instruments (in part)

(c) CPI Risk

As at December 31, 2011, the net excess of financial liabilities over financial assets linked to the CPI was NIS 2,796 million (2010: NIS 3,112 million). As at December 31, 2011 the Company had forward contracts for a notional amount of NIS 502 million in order to partially hedge the CPI risk. These forward contracts are not accounted for using hedge accounting.

At December 31, 2011 if the CPI had increased/decreased by 2% with all other variables held constant, post-tax profit for the year would have decreased/increased by NIS 42.5 million (2010: NIS 48.7 million, 2009: NIS 20.2 million).

In addition, BSRE has several commitments that are index linked: most of its rental agreements are linked to the Israeli CPI, and, following the engagement to acquire the Wholesale Market in Tel Aviv, see note 11, BSRE is committed to a future payment of NIS 345.5 million that is linked to the CPI (relating to the BSRE's share of 50%). As of December 31, 2011, the index adjusted principal amount is NIS 362 million. BSRE has also commitments that are linked to the Israeli Building Index, resulting from engagements with building contractors. Changes in the Building Index affect the costs of construction of investment properties and residential apartment units for sale; as of December 31, 2011, BSRE has NIS 46 million under construction agreements, that are linked to the Building Index. The Company mitigates its exposure to this risk, by linking the apartment purchasing agreements to the Building Index.

As to BSRE's commitments for future minimum payments under non-cancelable operating leases for the years subsequent to the statement of position dates, see note 33a.

(2) Credit Risk (in part)

Credit risk is managed separately by each of the Company's operating units. Credit risk arises from cash and cash equivalents, securities, short term deposits with banks as well as credit exposure to retail and wholesale customers.

BSRE receives current collaterals for third party lease agreements of investment property.

As for the apartment buildings project—the consideration for the sale of apartments is collected during the construction period, commencing with the signing of the purchase agreement and up to the delivery of the apartment to the buyer. In any case, title is not transferred before the apartment is fully paid for.

Balances owed to BSRE by the residence company and the mall company (see note 11) amount to NIS 31,994 thousand and NIS 30,660 thousand, as of December 31 2011 and 2010, respectively; BSRE expects that profits from the wholesale market project will serve to repay this debt. In addition, the other 50% shareholders of these joint venture companies guarantee these loans, and therefore the credit risk of these loans is considered by BSRE as low.

Note 4—Critical Accounting Estimates and Judgements (in part)

2) Change in Fair Value of Investment Property

Investment property is presented at fair value based on assessments of external independent appraisers, who have the appropriate qualifications. In certain cases fair value is determined using discounted cash flows that are based on various assumptions; judgments and estimates are required for cash flows projections that are expected during the remaining economic life of the asset, in accordance with the lease terms during the lease period and, after such period, based on suitable rentals that are determined on the basis of market surveys for similar assets with similar location and terms, using adjustments and discount rates that reflect the current market assessments as to uncertainties prevailing with respect to cash flow amounts and timing.

In some cases, mainly building rights or assets under development, the residual value approach is used to determine fair value. The evaluation of the asset's fair value is based on the value of the completed asset, less estimated constructor's profit and construction costs to complete.

When the rate used for discounting cash flows is different by 0.5% from management estimate the fair value of investment property will be NIS 25 million lower or NIS 28 million higher. When the discount rate is different by 1% from management estimate the fair value of investment property will be NIS 48 million lower or NIS 57 million higher.

Note 8—Investment Property:

The changes in the carrying value of investment property for the years ended December 31, 2011, 2010 and 2009 respectively, are as follows:

NIS in Thousands	2009	2010	2011
At January 1	413,111	421,188	546,870
Transfer to property and equipment (b)	(16,601)	(3,000)	—
Transfer to assets held for sale	—	—	(3,610)
Additions (c)	9,435	38,793	41,520
Disposals (d)	(5,700)	—	(50,600)
Acquisition of subsidiary consolidated for the first time	—	56,972	—
Changes in fair value of investment property, net	20,943	32,917	41,913
At December 31	421,188	546,870	576,093

a) All the Company's investment properties are located in Israel.

b) The property was let to subsidiaries and therefore it was transferred from investment properties to property and equipment.

c) The additions in 2011, totaling NIS 41.5 million, include an amount of approximately NIS 38 million in Kiryat Hasharon, Netanya. The additions in 2010, totaling NIS 38.7 million, include lands in areas used for commercial development. The additions in 2009, totaling NIS 9.4 million, include NIS 1.7 million of rental offices and NIS 7.7 million of land in areas used for commercial development.

d) On July 4, 2011 BSRE and Harel Insurance Company Ltd. (hereafter—Harel) signed an agreement whereby Harel acquired half of the BSRE's rights in an investment property located in Kiryat Hasharon-Netanya (which a commercial center is currently being erected on) in consideration for NIS 50.6 million. In the second quarter of 2011 the company recorded gain from changes in fair value of the said investment property in the amount of NIS 18.1 million to the statement of income.

e) The fair value of the principle investment property items was determined by "O. Haushner Civil Eng. & Real Estate Appraisal Ltd." and "Barak Friedman Cohen & Co. Economic & Real Estate Appraisal", independent qualified appraisers who are members of the Real Estate Appraisers Association in Israel—based on the current prices in an active market for similar property, locations and conditions, and based on the discounted cash flows that are expected to arise from the assets. The range of discount rates used by the appraiser are 7.75%–12% per annum (mainly 7.75%–8.25%) (2010 mainly 7.75%–8.25%).

f) Rental Revenue That has Been Recognized in the Statements of Income Within Revenues:

NIS in Thousands	Year Ended December 31		
	2009	2010	2011
Rental income	21,790	27,012	38,573

g) Break Down of Investment Property at December 31, 2011 and 2010, by Lease Rights and Ownership of Land:

NIS in Thousands	December 31	
	2010	2011
Under ownership	231,177	242,763
Finance lease from the Israeli Land Administration for a period of 999 years	7,070	7,200
Total	238,247	249,963
Finance lease from the Israeli Land Administration are as follows:		
Leases for periods of under 10 years	935	785
Leases for periods between 10–25 years	169,881	178,429
Leases for periods of more than 25 years	138,174	146,916
	308,990	326,130
	547,237	576,093

h) Capitalized Borrowing Costs:

The amount of borrowing costs capitalized during the year ended December 31, 2011 was NIS 5,000 thousand (2010 was NIS 2,900 thousand and 2009 Nil). The rate used to determine the amount of borrowing costs eligible for capitalization was 5.2% in 2011 and 5.2% in 2010 (linked to the Israeli CPI).

Note 33—Commitments (in part):

b. Capital Commitments

Capital expenditure contracted for at the statement of financial position date but not yet incurred is as follows:

NIS in Thousands	December 31	
	2010	2011
Property and equipment	36,043	25,154
Investment property and real estate	35,011	90,634
Inventory	1,376	—

IAS 28, INVESTMENTS IN ASSOCIATES

IFRSs Overview and Comparison to U.S. GAAP

Author's Note

In May 2011, IASB revised IAS 28, *Investments in Associates*, concurrently with issuing IFRS 11 and IFRS 12, renaming it *Investments in Associates and Joint Ventures*. The revised IAS 28 expands the scope of the standard to include investors with joint control, as well as significant influence, over an investee and requires the use of the equity method to account for such investments, unless the entity is exempt from applying the equity method, in accordance with the standard. IAS 28 does not permit use of proportionate consolidation by investors with joint control over an investee. The revised standard is effective for annual periods beginning on or after 1 January 2013, with early application permitted.

The following standards issued in 2011 also amend IAS 28:

- IFRS 9
  These amendments replace references to IAS 39 with references to IFRS 9,
- IFRS 13
  These amendments replace the term *published price quotations* with the term *quoted market prices* and remove the phrase "measured at fair value in accordance with IAS 39." The latter chance is necessary because IAS 39 is amended to require fair value measurement in accordance with IFRS 13.

Because the effective dates of IAS 28, IFRS 9, and IFRS 13 are after 1 January 2012, these revisions are not discussed in the commentary in this section. The timing of the effective dates also affects the availability of illustrative excerpts from survey companies' financial statements. Accordingly, the excerpts appearing later in this section may not reflect all or some of these revisions.

2.137 An *associate*, as defined in IAS 28 (2011), is an entity, including an unincorporated entity (for example, a partnership), over which the investor has significant influence and is neither a subsidiary (controlled entity) nor an interest in a jointly controlled entity (joint venture). An investor has significant influence over its investee when it has the power to participate in the investee's financial and operating policy decisions but does not have control or joint control over those policies.

2.138 IAS 28 applies to investments in which the investor has significant influence. IAS 28 does not apply to the following investments held by

- venture capital entities or
- mutual funds, trusts, and other similar entities (including investment-linked insurance funds)

that, upon initial recognition, are designated as at fair value through profit or loss or are classified as held for trading and accounted for in accordance with IAS 39. IAS 28 states that these entities are to measure such investments at fair value in accordance with IAS 39 and to recognize changes in fair value in profit or loss in the period of the change. However, IAS 28 does not exempt these entities from some disclosures, including the nature and extent of any restrictions on the ability of the associate to transfer funds to the investor in the form of cash dividends, loan repayments, or advances.

Recognition and Measurement

IFRSs

2.139 IFRSs presume that an investor has significant influence if it holds 20 percent or more of the voting or potential voting shares of the associate directly or indirectly and that it does not have significant influence if it holds less. If the investor holds 50 percent or more of the voting or potential voting shares, it must determine whether it has control, in accordance with IAS 27.

2.140 IAS 28 provides guidance to investors in determining whether they have significant influence over an investee and identifies various circumstances that provide evidence that significant influence exists. These circumstances include the following:

- The investor is represented on the board of directors (governing body) of the investee.
- The investor participates in policymaking decisions, including those concerning dividend and other distributions.
- The investor and investee engage in material transactions.
- The investor provides the investee with essential technical information.

2.141 An investor should use the equity method to account for investments in associates, except when the associate is classified as held for sale in accordance with IFRS 5. IAS 27 exempts an entity from preparing consolidated financial statements if certain criteria are met. Similarly, IAS 28 exempts an investor from using the equity method for its investment in an associate if the investor is a parent that is exempt from consolidated financial statements in accordance with IAS 27, or the entity itself meets those same criteria.

2.142 The equity method requires the entity to initially recognize the investment at cost. The investor should include any difference in the cost and the investor's proportionate share of the fair value of the associate's net identifiable assets (referred to as *goodwill*) in the carrying value of the associate. IAS 28 prohibits amortization of this difference. The investor should also include any excess as income in determining the investor's proportionate share of the associate's profit or loss in the period in which the investment is acquired. Subsequently, the investor should adjust the carrying value of the investment for its share in the net profit or loss of the associate and should recognize the same amount in the investor's profit or loss. The investor should also recognize its share of changes in the net assets of the associate recognized in other comprehensive income in its own other comprehensive income.

2.143 An investor should discontinue the equity method when it no longer has significant influence. At that point, the investor should measure any remaining investment at fair value and recognize the change in the carrying value of the investment in profit or loss. Subsequent accounting for the investment should be in accordance with IAS 39.

2.144 An investor should use the most recent financial statements of the associate to apply the equity method. When the investor's and the associate's reporting dates differ, the associate should prepare a set of financial statements as of the investor's fiscal year-end for the investors use, unless it is impracticable. When the associate's financial statements are prepared as of a different date, the investor should make appropriate adjustments for the effect of significant transactions that occur between the two dates. IAS 28 does not permit the difference in reporting dates to be greater than three months.

2.145 The investor should prepare financial statements based on application of the same accounting policies for similar transactions and circumstances. When the associate applies different accounting policies for transactions similar to those of the investor, the investor should make adjustments to the associate's financial statements in order to conform to its own accounting policies.

2.146 An investor's interest in an associate includes the carrying value of the equity method investment plus any other long-term interests that, in substance, form part of the investment (for example, preference shares, unsecured loans, and long-term receivables). The investor should recognize its share of the associate's losses up to the carrying value of its interest. After writing its investment in the associate to zero, the investor should apply any excess losses to the other components in the order of reverse seniority. If the investor's share in losses of the associate exceeds its interest in the associate, the investor should discontinue recognizing further losses. An investor should recognize liabilities only to the extent that it incurs a legal or constructive obligation in accordance with IAS 37.

2.147 After applying the equity method, an investor should test its investment in accordance with the requirements of IAS 39 to determine whether to recognize an impairment loss. When application of IAS 39 indicates that an impairment loss should be recognized, an investor should measure the loss in accordance with IAS 36.

2.148 An investor preparing separate, unconsolidated financial statements (for example, parent-only financial statements), either voluntarily or for regulatory purposes, should account for investments in associates in accordance with IAS 27.

U.S. GAAP

2.149 Like IFRSs, paragraphs 3–5 of FASB ASC 323-10-15 require an investor to use the equity method to account for investments in common stock that give the investor the ability to exercise significant influence over the operating and financial policies of an investee even when the investor holds 50 percent or less of the common stock or in-substance common stock (that is, an investment that gives the entities the same risks and rewards as common stock ownership, as defined in the FASB ASC glossary) of the investee. However, FASB ASC 323, *Investments—Equity Method and Joint Ventures*, includes a number of scope exceptions exceeding those in IAS 28. FASB ASC 323-10-15-4 states that following investments are excluded from the guidance in FASB ASC 323:

- An investment that is accounted for in accordance with guidance on derivatives and hedging in FASB ASC 815-10
- An investment in common stock held by an investment company registered with the SEC under the Investment Company Act of 1940; one that would be registered except that it has limited stockholders and the securities are not offered publicly; or a nonbusiness entity, such as an estate, trust or individual
- An investment in common stock consolidated under FASB ASC 810, *Consolidation*

In addition, unlike IFRSs, FASB ASC 323-10-15-5 provides more targeted guidance to the following investments that are excluded from the overall guidance in FASB ASC 323-10:

- Partnership or unincorporated joint venture (see FASB ASC 323-30)
- Limited liability company that maintains specific ownership accounts for each investor (see FASB ASC 272-10)

2.150 FASB ASC 323-10-15-3 also explicitly includes investments that are in-substance common stock.

2.151 FASB ASC 323-10-15-6 includes indicators similar to those in IAS 28 of an investor's ability to exercise significant influence, including representation on the board of directors, participation in the policymaking processes, material intraentity transactions, the interchange of managerial personnel, technological dependency, and the extent of ownership by an investor in relation to the concentration of other shareholdings.

2.152 Like IFRSs, FASB ASC 323-10-15-8 states that there is a presumption that, in the absence of predominate evidence to the contrary, an investor has the ability to exercise significant influence over an investee if the investment (direct or indirect) in an investee's voting stock is 20 percent or more. FASB ASC 323-10-15-8 also requires an entity to demonstrate its ability to exercise significant influence when its investment is less than 20 percent. Unlike IFRSs, FASB ASC 323-10-15-9 precludes investors taking into account potential voting shares when making their assessment of significant influence.

2.153 FASB ASC 323-10-35-4 explains that under the equity method, an investor should recognize its share of the earnings or losses of the investee in the same period the investee reports earnings or losses, rather than in the period the investee declares a dividend. An investor should adjust the carrying amount of its investment and recognize in income its share of the investee's earnings or losses. Similar to

IFRSs, FASB ASC 323-10-35-18 also requires an investor to recognize its proportionate share of the investee's equity adjustment for other comprehensive income items as an adjustment to the carrying amount of the investment, with a corresponding adjustment in equity. Unlike IFRS, U.S. GAAP does not explicitly constrain the difference in reporting dates of the investor and investee to no more than three months. When there is a lag in reporting by the investee, FASB ASC 323-10-35-6 states that the investor would ordinarily use the investee's most recent financial statements and that the lag in reporting should be consistent from period to period.

2.154 Like IFRSs, FASB ASC 323-10-35-19 states that an investor's share of losses of an investee may equal or exceed the carrying amount of the investment accounted for by the equity method plus advances made by the investor. FASB ASC 323-10-35-19 requires the investor to continue to report losses up to the carrying amount of its investment, including any additional financial support provided or committed by the investor, which may take the form of capital contributions to the investee, investments in additional common stock of the investee, investments in preferred stock or debt securities of the investee, and loans or advances to the investee. See paragraph 3.206 for coverage of impairments of equity method investments under FASB ASC.

Presentation

IFRSs

2.155 IAS 28 requires investors to classify investments in associates as noncurrent assets, unless they are classified as held for sale, in accordance with IFRS 5.

2.156 IAS 1 requires investors to present investments in associates as a separate line item on the balance sheet and the investor's share in the associates' profit or loss as a separate line item on the statement of comprehensive income. An entity should also present additional line items, headings, and subtotals when they are relevant to an understanding of the entity's financial position.

U.S. GAAP

2.157 Like IFRSs, FASB ASC 323-10-45-1 also requires an entity to present its equity method investments as a single amount in a separate line item on the balance sheet and, consistent with FASB ASC 210-10, classify equity method investments as noncurrent when a classified balance sheet is prepared.

2.158 Paragraphs 1–2 of FASB ASC 323-10-45 require an investor to show its share of the associate's profit or loss as a single amount on the income statement, except for the investor's share of extraordinary items and accounting changes reported in the financial statements of the investee, which should be shown separately, in accordance with income statement presentation guidance under FASB ASC 225-20. IFRSs do not permit an entity to present extraordinary items. With respect to the investor's share of an investee's items of other comprehensive income, FASB ASC 323-10-45-3 permits an entity to combine its proportionate share of those amounts with its own other comprehensive income items. In contrast, IFRSs require the investor to present its share of the other comprehensive income of an associate as a separate line item.

Disclosure

IFRSs

2.159 IAS 28 requires investors to provide the following disclosures about its equity method investments in associates:

- Fair value of associates when there are published price quotes
- Summary financial information of associates, including total assets, total liabilities, total revenues, and profit or loss
- Share of profit or loss of each investment, including separate disclosure of its share of discontinued operations, and the investments' carrying amounts
- Investor's share of changes in the net assets of the associate recognized in other comprehensive income
- Unrecognized share of losses of an associate for the period and cumulatively if an investor has discontinued recognition of its share of losses of an associate
- Investor's share of the contingent liabilities of an associate incurred jointly with other investors
- Any contingent liabilities that arise because the investor is severally liable for all or part of the liabilities of the associate

2.160 When an investor does not use the equity method, it should disclose that fact and summary financial information about the investment, including total assets, total liabilities, total revenues, and profit or loss.

2.161 When the presumption of significant influence at 20 percent ownership is rebutted, investors should explain the rationale for overcoming the presumption. When the investor concludes it has significant influence with less than 20 percent ownership, IAS 28 requires a similar disclosure.

2.162 Investors should also disclose the nature and extent of significant restrictions on the associate's ability to transfer funds to the investor and separately disclose any contingent liabilities incurred jointly and those for which it is severally liable.

U.S. GAAP

2.163 The disclosures required by FASB ASC 323 for equity method investments are less comprehensive than those required by IFRSs. Like IFRSs, FASB ASC 323-10-50-3 states that investors should usually disclose the aggregate fair value of equity method investments in common stock when there are published price quotes.

2.164 Unlike IFRSs, FASB ASC 323-10-50-3 explains that, for equity method investments in common stock, investors should disclose, among other things, the name of each investee; the percentage of ownership of common stock; and the difference, if any, between the carrying amount of an investment and the amount of underlying equity in net assets and how the difference is accounted for. Also unlike IFRSs, FASB ASC 323-10-50-3(d) states that conversion of outstanding convertible securities, the exercise of outstanding options and warrants, and other contingent issuances of an investee may have a significant effect on an investor's share of reported earnings or losses and material effects should be included in notes *to the financial statements of an investor.*

Presentation and Disclosure Excerpts

Author's Note

IAS 28 permits an entity to designate on initial recognition investments in associates and account for them in accordance with IAS 39 at fair value through profit and loss. Excerpts illustrating investments in associates accounted for at fair value through profit and loss are provided in section 8.

Significant Influence—More Than 50% Voting Power

2.165

Huaneng Power International, Inc. (Dec 2011)

CONSOLIDATED BALANCE SHEETS (in part)

(Amounts expressed in thousands of RMB or US$)

	Note	As of December 31		
		2011		**2010**
		RMB	**US$**	**RMB**
Assets				
Non-current assets				
Property, plant and equipment	7	177,968,001	28,244,854	155,224,597
Investments in associates/jointly controlled entities	8	13,588,012	2,156,519	11,973,216
Available-for-sale financial assets	10	2,301,167	365,212	2,223,814
Land use rights	11	4,341,574	689,040	4,058,496
Power generation licence	12	3,904,056	619,603	4,105,518
Mining rights	39	1,922,655	305,140	—
Deferred income tax assets	29	526,399	83,543	672,475
Derivative financial assets	13	16,389	2,601	91,478
Goodwill	14	13,890,179	2,204,475	12,640,904
Other non-current assets	15	2,540,104	403,135	5,391,566
Total non-current assets		220,998,536	35,074,122	196,382,064

NOTES TO THE CONSOLIDATED FINANCIAL STATEMENTS (in part)

1. Company Organization and Principal Activities

Huaneng Power International, Inc. (the "Company") was incorporated in the People's Republic of China (the "PRC") as a Sino-foreign joint stock limited company on June 30, 1994. The registered address of the Company is West Wing, Building C, Tianyin Mansion, 2C Fuxingmennan Street, Xicheng District, Beijing, the PRC. The Company and most of its subsidiaries are principally engaged in the generation and sale of electric power to the respective regional or provincial grid companies in the PRC. SinoSing Power Pte. Ltd. ("SinoSing Power") and its subsidiaries, subsidiaries of the Company, are principally engaged in the power generation and sale in the Republic of Singapore ("Singapore").

The directors consider Huaneng International Power Development Corporation ("HIPDC") and China Huaneng Group ("Huaneng Group") as the parent company and ultimate parent company of the Company, respectively. Both HIPDC and Huaneng Group are incorporated in the PRC. Neither Huaneng Group nor HIPDC produced financial statements available for public use.

2. Principal Accounting Policies (in part)

The principal accounting policies adopted in the preparation of these financial statements are set out below. These policies have been consistently applied to all the years presented, unless otherwise stated.

(b) Consolidation (in part)

(iii) Associates and Jointly Controlled Entities

Associates are investees over which the Company and its subsidiaries have significant influence on the financial and operating decisions. Jointly controlled entities are investees over which the Company and its subsidiaries have contractual arrangements to jointly share control with one or more parties and none of the participating parties has unilateral control over the investees.

Investments in associates/jointly controlled entities are initially recognized at cost and are subsequently measured using the equity method of accounting. The excess of the initial investment cost over the proportionate share of the fair value of identifiable net assets of investee acquired is included in the initial investment cost (Note 2(h)). Any shortfall of the initial investment cost to the proportionate share of the fair value of identifiable net assets of investee acquired is recognized in current period profit or loss and long-term investment cost is adjusted accordingly.

When applying equity method, the Company and its subsidiaries adjust net profit or loss of the investees, including the fair value adjustments on the net identifiable assets of the associates/jointly controlled entities and the adjustments to align with the accounting policies of the Company and different financial periods. Current period investment income is then recognized based on the proportionate share of the Company and its subsidiaries in the investees' net profit or loss. Net losses of investees are recognized to the extent of book value of long-term equity investments and any other constituting long-term equity investments in investees in substance. The Company and its subsidiaries will continue to recognize investment losses and provision if they bear additional obligations which meet the recognition criteria under the provision standard.

The Company and its subsidiaries adjust the carrying amount of the investment and directly recognize into related other comprehensive income and equity items based on their proportionate share on other shareholders' other comprehensive income and equity movements of the investees other than net profit or loss, given there is no change in shareholding ratio.

When the investees appropriate profit or declare dividends, the book value of long-term equity investments are reduced correspondingly by the proportionate share of the distribution.

The Company and its subsidiaries determine at each reporting date whether there is any objective evidence that the investment in the associate/jointly controlled entities is impaired. If this is the case, the Company and its subsidiaries calculate the amount of impairment as the difference between the recoverable amount of the associate/jointly controlled entities and its carrying value and recognises the amount adjacent to 'share of profit of associates/jointly controlled entities' in the consolidated statement of comprehensive income.

Profits or losses resulting from transactions between the Company and its subsidiaries and the associates/jointly controlled entities are recognised in the Company and its subsidiaries financial statements only to the extent of interest of unrelated investor's interests in the associates and jointly controlled entities. Loss from transactions between the Company and its subsidiaries and the associates/jointly controlled entities is fully recognized and not eliminated when there is evidence for asset impairment.

Gains and losses arising from dilution of investments in associates/jointly controlled entities are recognized in the consolidated statement of comprehensive income.

8. Investments in Associates/Jointly Controlled Entities (in part)

	2011	2010
Beginning of the year	11,973,216	9,568,576
Additional capital injections in associates	995,805	520,630
Establishments of associates	38,250	13,000
Acquisitions of associates	264,000	531,000
Acquisition of a jointly controlled entity	—	1,058,000
Establishment of a jointly controlled entity	160,000	—
Share of other comprehensive loss	(44,928)	(35,156)
Share of profits before income tax expense	957,843	780,405
Share of income tax expense	(254,282)	(211,611)
Dividends	(501,892)	(251,628)
End of the year	13,588,012	11,973,216

As of December 31, 2011, investments in associates/jointly controlled entities of the Company and its subsidiaries, all of which are unlisted except for Shenzhen Energy Corporation ("SEC") which is listed on the Shenzhen Stock Exchange, were as follows:

Name	Country of Incorporation	Registered Capital	Business Nature and Scope of Operation	Percentage of Equity Interest Held	
				Direct	Indirect
Associates:					
Shandong Rizhao Power Company Ltd. ("Rizhao Power Company")	PRC	RMB1,245,587,900	Power generation	44%	—
Shenzhen Energy Group Co., Ltd. ("SEG")	PRC	RMB230,971,224	Development, production and sale of regular energy, new energy and energy construction project, etc.	25%	—
Shenzhen Energy Management Corporation*	PRC	RMB724,584,330	Management of energy projects	25%	—
SEC**	PRC	RMB2,202,495,332	Energy and investment in related industries	9.08%	—
Hebei Hanfeng Power Generation Limited Liability Company	PRC	RMB1,975,000,000	Power generation	40%	—
Chongqing Huaneng Lime Company Limited ("Lime Company")	PRC	RMB50,000,000	Lime production and sale, construction materials, chemical engineering product	—	25%
Huaneng Finance	PRC	RMB5,000,000,000	Provision for financial service including fund deposit services, lending, finance lease arrangements, notes discounting and entrusted loans and investment arrangement within Huaneng Group	20%	—
Huaneng Sichuan Hydropower Co., Ltd.	PRC	RMB1,469,800,000	Development, investment, construction, operation and management of hydropower	49%	—
Yangquan Coal Industry Group Huaneng Coal-fired Power Investment Co., Ltd.	PRC	RMB1,000,000,000	Investment, development, consulting and management services of coal and power generation projects	49%	—
Huaneng Shidaowan Nuclear Power Development Co., Ltd.	PRC	RMB1,000,000,000	Preparation for construction of pressurized water reactor power plant project	30%	—
Bianhai Railway Co., Ltd.	PRC	RMB389,000,000	Railway construction, freight transportation, materials supplies, agency service, logistics and storage at coastal industrial base in Yingkou, Liaoning	37%	—
Huaneng Shenbei Co-generation Limited Liability Company	PRC	RMB70,000,000	Production and sales of electricity and heat, construction and operation of power plants	40%	—
Hainan Nuclear Power Co., Ltd. ("Hainan Nuclear Power")	PRC	RMB673,076,000	Construction and operation of nuclear power plants, production and sales of electricity	30%	—
Shanxi Luan Group Zuoquan Wulihou Coal Co., Ltd.***	PRC	RMB6,452,910	Coal production and sales	34%	—
Huaneng (Tianjin) Coal Gasification Power Generation Co., Ltd. ("IGCC")	PRC	RMB533,176,000	Power generation, facilities installation, heat supply	35.97%	—
Huaneng Jinling Combined Cycle Co-generation Co., Ltd. ("Jinling CCGT")****	PRC	RMB75,000,000	Construction, operation and management of power generation and related projects	51%	—

*   In 2011, SEG was restructured into two entities, namely, SEG and Shenzhen Energy Management Corporation. After restructuring, the shares of SEC originally held by SEG were transferred to Shenzhen Energy Management Corporation.

**   The Company holds 240 million shares, representing 9.08% shareholding of SEC, which is a subsidiary of Shenzhen Energy Management Corporation, one of the Company's associates. Considered the equity interest effectively held by the Company directly and indirectly through Shenzhen Energy Management Corporation, and directors as well as supervisors appointed by the Company in SEC, the Company exercises significant influence on operations of SEC and classified it as an associate. As of December 31, 2011, the fair value of the Company's shares in SEC were RMB 1,464 million. In 2010, as these shares were still in lock-up period, there was no published price quotation and no price information available for the disclosure purpose.

***   In 2011, Zuoquan Longquan Metallurgy Casting Co., Ltd. was renamed as Shanxi Luan Group Zuoquan Wulihou Coal Co., Ltd.

**** In accordance with relevant terms stipulated in the memorandum and articles of association of Jinling CCGT, since the Company only exercises significant influence, Jinling CCGT is accounted for as an associate.

The gross amounts of operating results, assets and liabilities (excluding goodwill) of the associates of the Company and its subsidiaries were as follows:

	2011	2010
Assets	99,389,071	86,409,821
Liabilities	(59,605,330)	(52,408,864)
Operating revenue	26,291,581	22,932,949
Profit attributable to equity holders of associates	1,662,704	1,490,081

34. Related Party Balances and Transactions (in part)

(a) Related Party Balances (in part)

(iii) Except for a RMB 100 million unsecured short-term loan to one of the associates with annual interest rate of 6.56% as of December 31, 2011, all other balances with Huaneng Group, HIPDC, subsidiaries, associates, jointly controlled entities and other related parties are unsecured, non-interest bearing and receivable/repayable within one year. As of and for the years ended December 31, 2011, 2010 and 2009, no provision is made on receivable balances from these parties.

Other receivables and assets comprised the following balances due from related parties:

	As of December 31	
	2011	2010
Prepayments to associates	321,678	92,487
Prepayments to other related parties	3,266	6,802
Other receivables from subsidiaries	—	—
Other receivables from other related parties	143,402	211,904
Other receivables from Huaneng Group	37	—
Total	468,383	311,193

(iv) Accounts payable and other liabilities comprised the following balances due to related parties:

	As of December 31	
	2011	2010
Due to Huaneng Group	1,445	1,894
Due to HIPDC	27,425	33,844
Due to subsidiaries	—	—
Due to associates	43,271	13,160
Due to a joint controlled entity	209,983	110,012
Due to other related parties	658,477	619,498
Total	940,601	778,408

Significant Influence—Between 20% and 50% Voting Power, Exercised Indirectly With Less Than 20% Voting Power

2.166

Administradora de Fondos de Pensiones Provida S.A. (Dec 2011)

CONSOLIDATED STATEMENTS OF FINANCIAL POSITION (in part)

	Note	12.31.2011 MCh$	12.31.2010 MCh$
Assets			
Non-current assets			
Mandatory investment	6	201,418	204,526
Trade and other receivables, net	8	329	132
Accounts receivable from related parties	11	—	—
Investments accounted for using equity method	14	24,691	21,309
Intangible assets other than goodwill	17	39,838	44,325
Goodwill	18	8,930	8,930
Property, plant and equipment, net	16	27,787	28,660
Deferred tax assets	12	885	995
Prepayments	10	216	366
Other non-current assets	19	76	97
Total non-current assets		304,170	309,340
Total assets		390,348	377,992

NOTES TO THE CONSOLIDATED FINANCIAL STATEMENTS (in part)

Note 1. Legal Aspects of the Administrator

AFP Provida S.A. is an open corporation and legally domiciled at 100 Pedro de Valdivia Avenue, 16th floor, commune of Providencia in Santiago de Chile. The terms "AFP Provida", "Provida" and "Company", refer to the Pension Funds Administrator AFP Provida S.A., unless otherwise stated. References to "AFP" or "AFPs" refer to private pension funds administrators in general.

AFP Provida was constituted by public deed granted by Mr. Patricio Zaldivar Mackenna, Notary of Santiago, on March 3, 1981, and authorized to initiate activities by the Superintendency of Pensions, through Resolution No. E-006/81 of April 1, 1981.

The sole objective of the Company is to administrate Provida's Pension Funds Types A, B, C, D and E, under the terms established in Decree Law 3.500 of 1980 and its amendments, and to provide the services as established therein. From 1994 onward, through Law 19.301, the business of the AFPs was amplified by allowing them to constitute affiliate corporations. Likewise, they were allowed to invest in Corporations constituted as central securities depositories referred to in Law No. 18,876.

On June 13, 1983, AFP Provida was registered in the Securities Registry of the Superintendency of Securities and Insurance (SVS) under number 0211, initiating affiliation activities into the system on May 2, 1981, and collecting contributions from June 1 of the same year.

AFP Provida is a subsidiary of BBVA Inversiones Chile S.A., a Chilean entity controlled by Banco Bilbao Vizcaya Argentaria S.A. (Spanish Entity).

Business activities of AFP Provida are regulated by the Superintendency of Pensions.

Note 4. Accounting Policies (in part)

a. Statement of Compliance With International Financial Reporting Standards (IFRS)

The consolidated financial statements as of December 31, 2011, have been prepared in accordance with International Financial Reporting Standards ("IFRS") as issued by the International Accounting Standards Board (hereinafter "IASB").

These consolidated financial statements presents fairly the financial position of AFP Provida as of December 31, 2011 and December 31, 2010, as well as the results of operations, the changes in equity and cash flows for the years then ended.

The consolidated financial statements of AFP Provida S.A. for fiscal year 2011 were approved by the Board of Directors at meeting held on February 28, 2012, after that the consolidated financial statements will be submitted to a General Shareholders Meeting that will take place on April 27, 2012, to be approved.

Figures on financial statements are expressed in millions of Chilean pesos (MCh$) rounded up. In case of negative figures, they are reported with the minus sign ().

b. Basis of Consolidation

The consolidated financial statements include the financial statements of Provida and its subsidiaries. The subsidiaries' financial statements have been prepared as of the same date as those of Provida, and using uniform accounting policies. When necessary, adjustments are made to uniform any difference between accounting policies that may exist.

All balances and transactions between the subsidiaries and Provida have been eliminated in consolidation. In case of balances and transactions between associated companies and Provida, these are eliminated to the extent of Provida's direct or indirect interest in these companies.

b.3. Associates

An associate is an entity over which Provida has, directly or indirectly, significant influence and that is neither a subsidiary nor an interest in a joint venture. Significant influence is the power to participate in the financial and operating policy decisions of the investee but is not control or joint control over those policies. As a general rule, it is presumed that significant influence is exercised in entities, in which Provida holds either directly or indirectly, 20% to 50% of the ownership interest. The results and assets and liabilities of associates are incorporated in these financial statements using the equity method of accounting.

The following table sets for the associates incorporated in the consolidated financial statements of Provida as of December 31, 2011, 2010 and 2009:

		Ownership Interest %		
Subsidiary	Country	12.31.2011	12.31.2010	12.31.2009
Soc.Adm. de Fondos de Cesantia de Chile S.A.	Chile	37.80%	37.80%	37.80%
Inversiones DCV S.A.	Chile	23.14%	23.14%	23.14%
Servicio de Adm- Previsional S.A.	Chile	37.87%	37.87%	37.87%
AFP Horizonte[1]	Peru	15.87%	15.87%	15.87%

[1] Significant influence is exercised indirectly through entities of the BBVA Group.

Note 14. Investment in Associates Accounted for Using the Equity Method

14.1 Movements in Investments in Associates

The following tables set forth the changes in the equity of the Company's equity method investments during the years ended December 31, 2011 and 2010.

				As of December 31, 2011					
Associate	Country	Functional Currency	Ownership Interest %	Balance as of January 1, 2011	Share of Profit (Loss)	Dividends	Exchange Rate on Translation	Other	Balance as of December 31, 2011
				MCh$	MCh$	MCh$	MCh$	MCh$	MCh$
Sociedad Administradora de Fondos de Cesantía Chile S.A.	Chile	Chilean Peso	37.80%	2,369	1,299	—	—	118	3,786
Inversiones DCV S.A.	Chile	Chilean Peso	23.14%	282	83	(38)	—	—	327
Servicios de Administración Previsional S.A.	Chile	Chilean Peso	37.87%	3,054	2,343	(1,328)	—	(469)	3,600
Afore Bancomer[1]	Mexico	Mexican Peso	7.50%	9,239	3,802	(2,836)	15	—	10,220
AFP Horizonte[1]	Peru	Peruvian Soles	15.87%	6,365	2,184	(2,967)	1,176	—	6,758
Total				21,309	9,711	(7,169)	1,191	(351)	24,691

As of December 31, 2010

Associate	Country	Functional Currency	Ownership Interest %	Balance as of January 1, 2010	Share of Profit (Loss)	Dividends	Exchange Rate on Translation	Other	Balance as of December 31, 2010
				MCh$	MCh$	MCh$	MCh$	MCh$	MCh$
Sociedad Administradora de Fondos de Cesantía Chile S.A.	Chile	Chilean Peso	37.80%	1,332	1,079	—	—	(42)	2,369
Inversiones DCV S.A.	Chile	Chilean Peso	23.14%	248	59	(69)	—	44	282
Servicios de Administración Previsional S.A.	Chile	Chilean Peso	37.87%	2,975	1,787	(1,329)	—	(379)	3,054
Afore Bancomer[1]	Mexico	Mexican Peso	7.50%	7,925	3,616	(2,328)	26	—	9,239
AFP Horizonte[1]	Peru	Peruvian Soles	15.87%	5,101	2,248	(366)	(1,610)	992	6,365
Total				17,581	8,789	(4,092)	(1,584)	615	21,309

[1] Provida exercise significant influence through BBVA Group participation on those companies.

All of our associates do not have published price quotations. There are no restrictions (e.g. resulting from borrowing arrangements or regulatory requirements) on the ability of associates to transfer funds to Provida in the form of cash dividends, or repayment of loans or advances.

For all periods presented no changes in ownership interest in our investment in associates have occurred.

14.2 Summarized Total Financial Information of Investments in Associates

The following tables set forth summarized information of the investment in associates where Provida has significant influence, including the aggregated amounts of assets, liabilities, revenues and profit or loss as of December 31, 2011, and 2010:

As of December 31, 2011

Associate	Ownership Interests %	Current Assets	Non-Current Assets	Current Liabilities	Non-Current Liabilities	Revenues	Expenses	Profit (Loss)
		MCh$	MCh$	MCh$	MCh$	MCh$	MCh$	MCh$
Sociedad Administradora de Fondos de Cesantía Chile S.A.	37.80%	12,233	1,291	2,038	11,486	12,470	(9,034)	3,436
Inversiones DCV S.A.	23.14%	58	1,357	1	1,415	361	(2)	359
Servicios de Administración Previsional S.A.	37.87%	6,924	8,714	6,073	9,563	14,936	(8,749)	6,187
AFORE Bancomer	7.50%	175,491	1,367	40,594	136,264	119,839	(69,140)	50,699
AFP Horizonte	15.87%	18,595	41,509	17,529	42,575	47,137	(33,378)	13,759
Total		213,301	54,238	66,235	201,303	194,743	(120,303)	74,440

As of December 31, 2010

Associate	Ownership Interests %	Current Assets	Non-Current Assets	Current Liabilities	Non-Current Liabilities	Revenues	Expenses	Profit (Loss)
		MCh$	MCh$	MCh$	MCh$	MCh$	MCh$	MCh$
Sociedad Administradora de Fondos de Cesantía Chile S.A.	37.80%	6,822	2,437	1,776	7,483	9,855	(7,000)	2,855
Inversiones DCV S.A.	23.14%	4	1,215	—	1,218	256	(1)	255
Servicios de Administración Previsional S.A.	37.87%	6,609	7,840	6,301	8,149	12,148	(7,430)	4,718
AFORE Bancomer	7.50%	156,663	2,330	35,806	123,187	117,140	(68,923)	48,217
AFP Horizonte	15.87%	18,476	38,396	14,468	42,404	41,490	(27,330)	14,160
Total		188,574	52,218	58,351	182,441	180,889	(110,684)	70,205

IAS 31, *INTERESTS IN JOINT VENTURES*

IFRSs Overview and Comparison to U.S. GAAP

Author's Note

In May 2011, IASB issued IFRS 11 and IFRS 12, concurrently with a revised and renamed IAS 28. IFRS 11 requires all entities that are parties to a joint arrangement to determine the type of joint arrangement in which they are involved by assessing their rights and obligations arising from that arrangement. IFRS 11 defines a *joint arrangement* as an arrangement of which two or more parties have joint control. IFRS 11 defines *joint control* as the contractually agreed sharing of control of an arrangement, which exists only when decisions about the relevant activities (that is, activities that significantly affect the returns of the arrangement) require the unanimous consent of the parties sharing control.

IFRS 11 also requires an entity to classify its joint arrangements into either joint operations or joint ventures. A *joint operation* is one in which the parties that have joint control of the arrangement (joint operators) have rights to the assets and obligations for the liabilities of the arrangement. In contrast, a *joint venture* is one in which the parties that have joint control of the arrangement (joint venturers) have rights to the net assets of the arrangement. Joint operators account for the assets, liabilities, revenue, and expenses of the arrangement in accordance with relevant IFRSs.

IFRS 11 provides guidance on distinguishing joint operations from joint ventures by considering the rights and obligations it has under the arrangement, assessing the arrangement's structure and legal form, the contractual terms of the arrangement, and other relevant facts and circumstances. Joint venturers account for their investment in the joint arrangement using the equity method, in accordance with IAS 28 (2011). IFRS 11 does not permit an entity to use proportionate consolidation to account for jointly controlled entities.

IFRS 12 prescribes the disclosure requirements for all entities that have interests in other entities.

IFRS 11 and IFRS 12 are effective for annual periods beginning on or after 1 January 2013. Early adoption is permitted.

The IASB also issued two additional standards in 2011 which amend IAS 31 as follows:

- IFRS 9
  This amendment replaces references to IAS 39 with references to IFRS 9.
- IFRS 13
  This amendment removes that statement that an entity should measure interests in joint ventures which have been designated as at fair value through profit or loss or classified as held for trading in accordance with IAS 39. IAS 39 as amended by IFRS 13 no longer provides guidance on measurement at fair value, but requires entities to apply the guidance in IFRS 13.

All of the standards in this author's note have effective dates after 1 January 2012 and are not discussed in the commentary in this section. In addition, the timing of the effective dates of these standards affects the availability of illustrative excerpts from survey companies' financial statements. Accordingly, the excerpts appearing later in this section may not reflect all or some of these revisions.

2.167 A *joint venture*, as defined in IAS 31, is a contractual arrangement in which two or more parties undertake an economic activity that is subject to joint control. *Joint control* is the contractually agreed sharing of control over an economic activity among the parties (investors). Joint control exists only when the strategic financing and operating decisions related to the activity require unanimous consent of the parties sharing control.

2.168 IAS 31 identifies three broad forms of joint ventures: jointly controlled operations, jointly controlled assets, and jointly controlled entities. A jointly controlled operation involves the use of the investors' assets and other resources without the venturers forming a separate legal entity or financial structure. A jointly controlled asset involves joint control or ownership of one or more assets acquired or contributed to the joint venture and dedicated to its purpose. Investors share in the output of the asset and obligate themselves to an agreed upon share of the expenses. A *jointly controlled entity* is a separate legal entity (for example, corporation or partnership) in which the investors have an interest. Jointly controlled entities operate in the same way as other entities, except that a contractual arrangement gives the investors joint control.

2.169 IAS 31 establishes the accounting for interests in a joint venture, regardless of form, and the reporting of the joint venture's assets, liabilities, income, and expenses in an investor's financial statements. Investors in joint ventures should account for these investments in accordance with IAS 31. However, IAS 31 makes an exception for venture capital organizations and mutual funds, trusts, and similar entities (including investment-linked insurance funds) whose interests in jointly controlled entities are, upon initial recognition, designated as at fair value through profit or loss or are classified as held for trading and accounted for in accordance with IAS 39. Such entities should measure these investments at fair value in accordance with IAS 39, with changes in fair value recognized in profit or loss in the period of the change. Venturers with such interests should make certain disclosures required by IAS 31. Investors in joint ventures that do not have joint control should recognize their investment in accordance with IAS 28 or IAS 39, as appropriate.

Recognition and Measurement

IFRSs

2.170 IAS 31 requires an investor in jointly controlled operations to recognize only the assets it controls, the liabilities and expenses it incurs, and its share of income it earns from sales of goods or services generated by the operations. An investor in jointly controlled assets should recognize its share of the jointly controlled assets classified by nature, the liabilities and expenses it incurs, its share of liabilities and expenses incurred jointly, and the income from sale or use of its share of the assets' output. For both jointly controlled operations and jointly controlled assets, an investor should recognize only the assets it controls, the liabilities and expenses it incurs, and its share of the income. No adjustments or intercompany eliminations are required in respect of these items when the venturer presents consolidated financial statements.

2.171 An investor in a jointly controlled entity, however, should account for its investment using either the proportionate consolidation or equity method. When it loses joint control, an investor should cease to use the selected method.

Author's Note

See paragraphs 2.137–.164 for a discussion of accounting for investments using the equity method, including a comparison with FASB ASC requirements.

2.172 When an investor applies the proportionate consolidation method, it should include its share of the assets and liabilities of the jointly controlled entity in its balance sheet and its share of income, expenses, and items of other comprehensive income in its statement of comprehensive income. Investors should apply procedures similar to those for full consolidation as described in IAS 27.

2.173 An investor that uses the proportionate consolidation method to account for its interest in a jointly controlled entity should include its share of the assets, liabilities, income, and expenses of the jointly controlled entity in its financial statements using one of two alternative reporting formats:
- Combined on a line-by-line basis with its other assets, liabilities, income, and expenses
- Presented in separate line items

2.174 IAS 31 states that investors should not offset assets and liabilities or income and expenses unless a legal right of offset exists and the net presentation represents the expected realization of the asset or settlement of the liability.

2.175 When the investment in the joint venture is classified as held for sale in accordance with IFRS 5, IAS 31 exempts the investor from using the proportionate consolidation or the equity method. IAS 27 exempts an entity from preparing consolidated financial statements if certain criteria are met. IAS 31 exempts an entity from using the proportionate consolidation method and equity method for its investment in joint ventures if the investor is a parent that is exempt from consolidated financial statements, in accordance with IAS 27, or the investor itself meets those same criteria.

2.176 When an investor ceases to have joint control, it should account for its interest in a jointly controlled entity in accordance with IAS 39. If the jointly controlled entity becomes a subsidiary, an investor should apply both the requirements of IAS 27 and IFRS 3. If the jointly controlled entity becomes an associate, an investor should apply the requirements of IAS 28. At the point the investor in a jointly controlled entity loses joint control, the investor should measure its investment at fair value and recognize the difference between fair value and the joint venture's carrying amount in profit or loss.

U.S. GAAP

2.177 The FASB ASC glossary defines a *corporate joint venture* as a corporation owned and operated by a small group of entities (venturers) as a separate and specific business or project for the mutual benefit of the members of the group. A government may also be a member of the group. Frequently, the purpose of a corporate joint venture is to share risks and rewards in developing a new market, product, or technology; to combine complementary technological knowledge; or to pool resources in developing production or other facilities. A corporate joint venture also usually provides an arrangement under which each joint venture may participate, directly or indirectly, in the overall management of the joint venture. Thus, joint venturers have an interest or relationship other than as passive investors. An entity that is a subsidiary of one of the joint ventures is not itself a corporate joint venture. Although ownership of a corporate joint venture seldom changes, and its stock is usually not traded publicly, FASB ASC does not preclude a corporation from being a corporate joint venture when there is a minority public ownership. The guidance in FASB ASC 323 applies to investments in common or in-substance common stock, or both, including investments in common stock of corporate joint ventures, according to FASB ASC 323-10-15-3. However, in accordance with FASB ASC 323-10-15-4(c), the guidance in FASB ASC 323-10 does not apply to an investment in common stock within the scope of FASB ASC 810, which may include variable interest entities (see paragraphs 13–17 of FASB ASC 810-10-15). In contrast, IAS 31 does not exclude joint ventures in the form of variable interest entities from its scope.

2.178 IAS 31 requires joint ventures to be contractual arrangements in which investors have joint control. As illustrated by the definition of *corporate joint venture* in the FASB ASC glossary, FASB ASC does not require that the agreement among the investors be contractual, but it does include the concept of joint control. In contrast to a passive investment, the definition in the FASB ASC glossary states that investors usually have the ability to participate in the venture's decision-making activities.

2.179 FASB ASC 323-30 also requires the entity to use the equity method to account for partnerships, unincorporated joint ventures, and limited liability companies. However, FASB ASC 810-10-45-14 explains that unincorporated entities in the construction or extractive industries may use a proportionate consolidation method when its use is industry practice (see FASB ASC 932-323-45-1 with respect to the oil and gas industry).

2.180 The FASB ASC glossary does not define *jointly controlled operations* or *assets* but does define a *collaborative arrangement* as a contractual arrangement that involves a joint operating activity involving two (or more) parties that meet both of the following requirements:
- They are active participants in the activity.
- They are exposed to significant risks and rewards dependent on the commercial success of the activity.

FASB ASC 808-10-45 establishes the accounting for such arrangements. Consistent with the requirements of IAS 31 for jointly controlled assets and operations, FASB ASC 808-10-45 explains that participants in such arrangements should account for the costs incurred and revenue generated from third parties (that is, an entity that is not one of the parties to the arrangement) in each entity's respective income statement and should not apply the equity method. FASB ASC 808-10-45 directs entities to FASB ASC 605-45 for additional guidance on whether to report revenue gross (as a principal) or net (as an agent). FASB ASC 970-323 also provides guidance on real estate projects and joint ventures.

2.181 Unlike IAS 31, which contains criteria for exemption from its requirements (similar to the exemption in IAS 27 and IAS 28), FASB ASC does not provide any criteria that could exempt an entity from using the equity method when required.

Presentation

IFRSs

2.182 In accordance with IAS 1, an investor should present investments accounted for under the equity method as a separate line item on the balance sheet and its share of profit or loss from the investment separately on the statement of comprehensive income. In IFRSs, there is no requirement to distinguish between investments in associates and interests in joint ventures. However, an entity should also present additional line items, headings, and subtotals when they are relevant to an understanding of the entity's financial position.

U.S. GAAP

2.183 Investors should apply the same presentation requirements as for other equity method investments, as discussed in FASB ASC 323-10-45.

Disclosure

IFRSs

2.184 An investor should disclose a listing and description of its interests in significant joint ventures, the proportion of its interest in jointly controlled entities, and the method used to account for its interests in jointly controlled entities. If it uses the line-by-line format for proportionate consolidation, the investor should disclose separately the aggregate amounts of current assets, long-term assets, current liabilities, long-term liabilities, income, and expenses related to the proportionately consolidated interests.

2.185 An investor should also disclose information about contingent liabilities and commitments related to its interests in joint ventures separately from its other contingent liabilities and commitments. With respect to contingent liabilities, an investor should disclose not only its contingent liabilities but also those shared jointly with other investors,

its share of contingent liabilities of the venture for which it is contingently liable, and contingent liabilities that arise because it is contingently liable for liabilities of other investors. Similar disclosures are required for commitments.

U.S. GAAP

2.186 IFRSs require more disclosures than FASB ASC about joint ventures, particularly disclosures about contingent liabilities and commitments. When the joint venture is accounted for using the equity method, FASB ASC 323 requires specific equity method disclosures. In particular, FASB ASC 323-10-50-3(c) states that when the equity method investments of a venturer are, in the aggregate, material in relation to its financial position or results of operations, it may be necessary for an investor to disclose summarized information about the joint venture's assets, liabilities, and results of operations in the notes or separate statements.

TABLE 2-7: ACCOUNTING TREATMENT FOR JOINTLY CONTROLLED ENTITIES[1]

	2011	2010	2009
Survey entities using proportionate consolidation	36	40	38
Survey entities using equity method	63	61	58
Survey entities designating an investment "at fair value through profit or loss"	1	1	1
Survey entities with a jointly controlled entity, but no method disclosed	12	13	13
Survey entities with no jointly controlled entities disclosed	64	56	51
Survey entities included in more than one category	(1)	(1)	(1)
Total	**175**	**170**	**160**

[1] IAS 31, *Interests in Joint Ventures*, identifies three broad types of joint ventures: jointly controlled operations, jointly controlled assets, and jointly controlled entities. A jointly controlled entity is a joint venture that involves the establishment of a corporation, partnership, or other entity in which each venturer has an interest. The entity operates in the same way as other entities, except that a contractual arrangement between the venturers establishes joint control over the economic activity of the entity.

Presentation and Disclosure Excerpts

Jointly Controlled Entities—Equity Method

2.187

CNOOC Limited (Dec 2011)

CONSOLIDATED STATEMENTS OF FINANCIAL POSITION (in part)

(All amounts expressed in millions of Renminbi/US$)

	Notes	2010 RMB Million	2011 RMB Million	2011 US$ Million
		Note 2.2		
Non-current assets				
Property, plant and equipment	15	186,678	220,567	35,045
Intangible assets	16	1,148	1,033	164
Investments in associates	17	1,781	2,822	448
Investments in a joint venture	18	20,823	20,175	3,205
Available-for-sale financial assets	19, 33	8,616	7,365	1,170
Other non-current assets		—	379	60
Total non-current assets		219,046	252,341	40,092

NOTES TO THE CONSOLIDATED FINANCIAL STATEMENTS (in part)

1. Corporate Information (in part)

CNOOC Limited (the "Company") was incorporated in the Hong Kong Special Administrative Region ("Hong Kong") of the People's Republic of China (the "PRC") on August 20, 1999 to hold the interests in certain entities thereby creating a group comprising the Company and its subsidiaries (hereinafter collectively referred to as the "Group"). During the year, the Group was principally engaged in the exploration, development, production and sales of crude oil, natural gas and other petroleum products.

The registered office address of the Company is 65/F, Bank of China Tower, 1 Garden Road, Hong Kong.

In the opinion of the directors of the Company (the "Directors"), the parent and the ultimate holding company of the Company is China National Offshore Oil Corporation ("CNOOC"), a company established in the PRC.

2.2 Changes in Accounting Policy and Disclosures (in part)

(a) Standards, revisions and amendments to IFRSs and HK-FRSs which are applicable to the Group, and have been adopted for the first time for the current year's financial statements: (in part)

Early Adopted Before the Mandatory Effective Dates:

IFRS 11/HKFRS 11—Joint Arrangements

IFRS 11/HKFRS 11 replaces IAS 31/HKAS 31 Interests in Joint Ventures and Standing Interpretation Committee-13 Jointly-controlled Entities—Non-monetary Contributions by Venturers. IFRS 11/HKFRS 11 addresses only two forms of joint arrangements (joint operations and joint ventures) where there is joint control. In determining the type of arrangements, IFRS 11/HKFRS 11 requires parties to the arrangement to assess: 1) the legal form of the separate vehicle; 2) the terms of the contractual arrangement; and 3) other facts and circumstances that give them right to the assets and obligations for the liabilities or right to the net assets of the vehicle. A joint arrangement that meets the definition of a joint venture must be accounted for using the equity method. For a joint operation, an entity recognizes its assets, liabilities, revenues and expenses relating to its relative shares thereof.

The application of this new standard impacts the financial position and presentation of statement of income of the Group. This is due to the cessation of proportionate consolidating a joint venture Bridas Corporation and the adoption of equity accounting for this investment.

Bridas Corporation is a separate legal entity that controls its own assets, earns its own income and incurs its own expenses and liabilities. The Group's rights as a shareholder of Bridas Corporation are limited to dividends or distributions of the net assets of Bridas Corporation, rather than having direct rights to any operating assets, production output and obligations for any operating liabilities. Accordingly, the Group has evaluated its interest in Bridas Corporation as an investment in joint venture under IFRS 11/HKFRS 11.

Upon the adoption of IFRS 11/HKFRS 11, the Group changed the accounting for its investment in Bridas Corporation from proportionate consolidation to the equity method. The comparative period has been retrospectively adjusted with the investments in Bridas Corporation being equity accounted since the date of acquisition on May 4, 2010, hence the earlier adoption has no impact on the consolidated statement of financial position as at January 1, 2010. The effect on the consolidated statement of financial position as at December 31, 2010 and the consolidated statement of comprehensive income for the year ended December 31, 2011 and 2010 is summarized below.

IFRS 12/HKFRS 12—Disclosure of Interests in Other Entities

IFRS 12/HKFRS 12 establishes the disclosure objectives for an entity to disclose information concerning its interest in a subsidiary, a joint arrangement, and associate or an unconsolidated structured entity. It also requires an entity to disclose the significant judgments and assumptions it has made in determining the nature of its interest in another entity or arrangement, also in determining the type of joint arrangement in which it has an interest. Additional disclosures are made in the Group's consolidated financial statements.

IAS 27 (Revised)/HKAS 27 (Revised)—Separate Financial Statements

Revisions are made resulting from the issuance of IFRS 10/HKFRS 10 and Consolidated Financial Statements are now addressed by IFRS 10/HKFRS 10. Therefore, IAS 27/HKAS 27 are revised to only address separate financial statements, including how to prepare separate financial statements of an investor and what disclosures should be made in the separate financial statements. The adoption of IAS27 (Revised)/HKAS 27 (Revised) does not have significant impact on the Group's consolidated financial statements.

IAS 28 (Revised)/HKAS 28 (Revised)—Investments in Associates and Joint Ventures

Revisions are made resulting from the issuance of IFRS 11/HKFRS 11. An entity applies IFRS 11/HKFRS 11 to determine the type of a joint arrangement in which it is involved. Once it has determined that it has an interest in a joint venture, the entity recognizes an investment and accounts for it using the equity method.

The five new or revised standards above are required to be adopted for annual periods beginning on or after January 1, 2013 with early application permitted so long as all of the five new or revised standards are applied early. As discussed above, the Group has adopted these five new or revised standards on January 1, 2011.

The following presents the effect of adopting IFRS 11/HKFRS 11 on the consolidated statement of financial position comparing the retrospectively adjusted 2010 balances to the balances previously reported, and the 2011 recorded balances to what would have been reported had the Group continued to proportionately consolidate Bridas Corporation:

Increase/(Decrease)	2010	2011
Assets:		
Property, plant and equipment	(25,653)	(24,440)
Intangible assets and goodwill	(1,874)	(1,783)
Investment in a joint venture	20,823	20,175
Other non-current assets	(1,523)	(1,487)
Trade receivables	(555)	(676)
Cash and cash equivalents	(12,284)	(1,205)
Other current assets	11,570	(73)
	(9,496)	(9,489)
Liabilities:		
Loans and borrowings	(2,294)	(2,206)
Other non-current liabilities	(371)	(477)
Deferred tax liabilities	(6,281)	(5,679)
Trade payables	(494)	(674)
Other current liabilities	(56)	(453)
	(9,496)	(9,489)

The following presents the effect of adopting IFRS 11/HKFRS 11 on the consolidated statement of comprehensive income comparing the retrospectively adjusted 2010 amounts to the amounts previously reported, and the 2011 recorded amounts to what would have been reported had the Group continued to proportionately consolidate Bridas Corporation:

	2010	2011
(Decrease) in revenue	(3,017)	(4,941)
Decrease in operating expenses	557	1,031
Decrease in taxes other than income tax	1,095	1,330
Decrease in depreciation, depletion and amortization	931	1,470
Decrease in other expenses	188	579
Decrease in income tax expense	47	284
Increase in share of profits of a joint venture	199	247
Total increase in net profit	—	—

The adoption of IFRS 11/HKFRS 11 has no material impact on basic and diluted earnings per share for the year ended December 31, 2011 and 2010.

Recognition of the Group's Investment in Bridas Corporation as at December 31, 2010:

	2010
Assets:	
Property, plant and equipment	25,653
Intangible assets and goodwill	1,874
Other non-current assets	1,523
Trade receivables	555
Cash and cash equivalents	12,284
Other current assets	118
Liabilities:	
Loans and borrowings	(2,294)
Other non-current liabilities	(371)
Deferred tax liabilities	(6,281)
Trade payables	(494)
Other current liabilities	(11,744)
Investment in a joint venture	20,823

3. Summary of Significant Accounting Policies (in part)

Joint Arrangements

Certain of the Group's activities are conducted through joint arrangements. Joint arrangements are classified as either a joint operation or joint venture, based on the rights and obligations arising from the contractual obligations between the parties to the arrangement.

Joint Operations

Some arrangements have been assessed by the Group as joint operations as both parties to the contract are responsible for the assets and obligations in proportion to their respective interest, whether or not the arrangement is structured through a separate vehicle. This evaluation applies to both the Group's interests in production sharing arrangements and certain jointly-controlled entities.

The Group entered into numerous production sharing arrangements or similar agreements in China and overseas countries. The Group's participating interest may vary in each arrangement. The Group, as one of the title owners under certain exploration and/or production licenses or permits, is required to bear exploration (with some exceptions in China), development and operating costs together with other co-owners based on each owner's participating interest. Once production occurs, a certain percentage of the annual production or revenue will first be distributed to the local government, which, in most of cases, with the nature of royalty and other taxes or expenses, and the rest of the annual production or revenue will be allocated among the co-owners.

Joint Venture

A joint venture is a joint arrangement whereby the parties that have joint control of the arrangement have rights to the net assets of the arrangement.

The Group's investments in joint ventures are stated in the consolidated statement of financial position at the Group's share of net assets under the equity method of accounting, less any impairment losses. Adjustments are made to bring into line any dissimilar accounting policies that may exist. The Group's share of the post acquisition results and reserves of joint ventures is included in the consolidated statement of comprehensive income and consolidated reserves, respectively. Where the profit sharing ratios is different to the Group's equity interest, the share of post-acquisition results of the joint ventures is determined based on the agreed profit sharing ratio. Unrealized gains and losses resulting from transactions between the Group and its joint ventures are eliminated to the extent of the Groups investments in the joint ventures, except where unrealized losses provide evidence of an impairment of the asset transferred. Goodwill arising from the acquisition of joint ventures is included as part of the Group's investments in joint ventures and is not individually tested for impairment.

The results of joint ventures are included in the Company's comprehensive income statement to the extent of dividend received and receivable. The Company's investments in joint ventures are treated as non-current assets and are stated at cost less any impairment losses.

When an investment in a joint venture is classified as held for sale, it is accounted for in accordance with IFRS 5/HK-FRS 5 Non-current Assets Held for Sale and Discontinued Operations.

4. Acquisitions and Other Ventures (in part)

2011

(i) The Company and Bridas Energy Holdings Ltd. ("BEH"), through Bridas Corporation, a 50% owned joint venture, entered into a share purchase agreement with BP PLC ("BP") on November 28, 2010, pursuant to which Bridas Corporation would acquire a 60% equity interest in Pan America Energy LLC ("PAE") from BP for a consideration of approximately US$7.06 billion. On November 5, 2011, Bridas Corporation sent to BP a letter to terminate the above mentioned transaction to acquire 60% equity interest in PAE from BP.

18. Investment in a Joint Venture

Particulars of the principal joint venture entities are as follows:

Name of Entity	Place and Date of Establishment	Nominal Value of Issued and Paid-Up/Registered Ordinary Share Capital	Percentage of Equity Attributable to the Group	Principal Activities
Bridas Corporation	British Virgin Islands September 15, 1993	US$ 102,325,582	50%	Investment holding

Summarized financial information of the joint venture is disclosed below:

	2010	2011
Cash and cash equivalents	24,568	2,410
Other current assets	1,346	1,585
Total current assets	25,914	3,995
Non-current assets, excluding goodwill	54,352	51,855
Goodwill	3,748	3,566
Total assets	84,014	59,416
Current financial liabilities (excluding trade and other payables and provisions)	(874)	(1,139)
Other current liabilities	(24,476)	(2,254)
Total current liabilities	(25,350)	(3,393)
Non-current financial liabilities	(3,714)	(3,361)
Other non-current liabilities	(13,304)	(12,312)
Total non-current liabilities	(17,018)	(15,673)
Total liabilities	(42,368)	(19,066)
Net assets	41,646	40,350
Net assets, excluding goodwill	37,898	36,784
Revenue	6,034	9,882
Depreciation, depletion and amortization	(1,862)	(2,940)
Interest income	172	50
Finance costs	(200)	(355)
Profit before tax	492	1,062
Income tax expense	(94)	(568)
Profit after tax	398	494
Other comprehensive income	—	—
Total comprehensive income	398	494

Reconciliation of the summarized financial information of the joint venture to the carrying amount of the Group's investment in the joint venture is disclosed below:

	2010	2011
Group share of net assets of joint venture, excluding goodwill	18,949	18,392
Goodwill on acquisition less cumulative impairment	1,874	1,783
Carrying amount of investment in joint venture	20,823	20,175

No dividend received from the joint venture in 2010 and 2011 respectively.

29. Related Party Transactions (in part)

(v) Balances with a Joint Venture

	2010	2011
Amounts due from a joint venture		
—included in held-to-maturity financial assets	—	44
—included in other current assets	11,688	—
	11,688	44

32. Commitments and Contingencies (in part)

(i) Capital Commitments (in part)

Capital commitments of a joint venture:

	2010	2011
Contracted, but not provided for	591	1,384
Authorized, but not contracted for	152	—

As at December 31, 2011, the Group had unutilised banking facilities amounting to approximately RMB160,580 million (2010: RMB179,029 million).

(ii) Operating Lease Commitments

(a) Office Properties (in part)

Office properties commitments of a joint venture:

	2010	2011
Commitments due:		
Within one year	31	7
In the first to second years, inclusive	30	6
After the second but before the fifth years, inclusive	4	11
	65	24

36. Charge of Assets

CNOOC NWS Private Limited, a wholly-owned subsidiary of the Group, together with the other joint venture partners and the operator of the NWS Project, signed a Deed of Cross Charge and an Extended Deed of Cross Charge whereby certain liabilities incurred or to be incurred, if any, by the Company in respect of the NWS Project are secured by its interest in the NWS Project.

Jointly Controlled Operations

2.188

TORM A/S (Dec 2011)

NOTES TO THE CONSOLIDATED FINANCIAL STATEMENTS (in part)

Note 1—Accounting Policies, Critical Accounting Estimates and Judgements

TORM A/S is a Danish shipping company founded in 1889 under the Danish Companies Act that is engaged primarily in the ownership and operation of product tankers and dry bulk carriers (hereinafter TORM A/S is referred to as TORM A/S or the Parent Company). TORM A/S and subsidiaries (hereinafter referred to as the Company or TORM) owns product tankers that primarily carry refined products such as naphtha, gasoline, gas oil, jet fuel, and diesel oil. TORM's dry bulk vessels carry commodities such as coal, iron ore and grain. The vessels trade worldwide. TORMS A/S's registered office and principal place of business is at Tuborg Havnevej 18, DK-2900 Hellerup, Denmark.

The Company provides transportation services by utilizing a fleet of vessels that it owns, charter in on short and long-term time charters, or commercially manage as the manager of a pool or through contracts with third-party owners. The Company charters in tankers and bulk vessels as are needed by the pools that it manages.

The annual report has been prepared in accordance with the International Financial Reporting Standards (IFRS).

The annual report has also been prepared in accordance with IFRS as issued by the International Accounting Standards Board (IASB).

The financial statements are prepared in accordance with the historical cost convention except where fair value accounting is specifically required by IFRS.

The functional currency in all major entities within TORM is the USD, and TORM A/S applies the USD as the presentation currency in the preparation of the annual report.

Key Accounting Policies (in part)

Management considers the following to be the most important accounting policies for TORM.

Participation in Pools

TORM generates its revenue from shipping activities, which to some extent are conducted through pools. Total pool revenue is generated from each vessel participating in the pools in which TORM participates and is based on either voyage or time charter parties. The pool measures net revenues based on the contractual rates and the duration of each voyage, and net revenue is recognized upon delivery of services in accordance with the terms and conditions of the charter parties. The pools are regarded as jointly controlled operations, and the Company's share of the income statement and balance sheet in the respective pools is accounted for by recognizing a proportional share, based on participation in the pool, combining items of a uniform nature. The Company's share of the revenues in the pools is primarily dependent on the number of days the Company's vessels have been available for the pools in relation to the total available pool earning days during the period. In 2011, TORM acted as pool manager of three pools in which the Company is participating with a significant number of vessels. As pool manager TORM receives a chartering commission income to cover the expenses associated with this role. The chartering commission income is calculated as a fixed percentage of the freight income from each charter agreement. If the pool does not earn any freight income, TORM will not receive any commission income. The commission income is recognized in the income statement under "Other operating income" simultaneously with the recognition of the underlying freight income in the pool.

Note 29—Entities in TORM

Parent Company:

TORM A/S		Denmark			

Investments in Subsidiaries*					
TORM Singapore Pte. Ltd.	100%	Singapore	TT Shipowning K/S	100%	Denmark
TORM Norge AS	100%	Norway	Torghatten & TORM Shipowning ApS	100%	Denmark
TORM USA LLC	100%	Delaware	Tiber Shipping LLC	100%	Marshall Islands
Long Range 1 A/S	100%	Denmark	OMI Marine Service Ltd.	100%	Delaware
Medium Range A/S	100%	Denmark	OMI Holding Ltd.	100%	Mauritius
LR1 Management K/S	100%	Denmark	TORM Shipping India Private Limited	100%	India
MR Management K/S	100%	Denmark	OMI Crewing Service Ltd.	100%	Bermuda

Investments in Legal Entitiesc Included as Jointly Controlled Entities*:					
Long Range 2 A/S	50%	Denmark	Ugland & TORM Shipowning ApS	50%	Denmark
LR2 Management K/S	50%	Denmark	FR8 Holdings Pte. Ltd.	50%	Singapore
UT Shipowning K/S	50%	Denmark	TORM SHIPPING (PHILS.) INC.	25%	Philippines

(*) Companies with activities in the financial year.

Furthermore, TORM participates in a number of joint ventures, primarily The MR Pool, The LR1 Pool and The LR2 Pool, which are not legal entities.

The investments in these joint ventures are included as investments in jointly controlled operations.

The following represents the income and expenses and summarized balance sheet data for jointly controlled entities:

USD Million	2009	2010	2011
Total income	70.8	81.6	60.4
Total expenses	(73.1)	(104.6)	(68.8)
Net Profit for the Year	(2.3)	(23.0)	(8.4)
Non-current assets	219.2	288.6	237.0
Current assets	50.2	80.2	62.6
Non-current liabilities	122.9	180.8	163.8
Current liabilities	23.5	42.2	35.2

Net loss for the year reported above excludes the impairment of vessels owned by FR8, a jointly controlled entity. TORM's share of such impairments amounted to USD 13 million in the year ended 31 December 2011 (2010: USD 35 million; 2009: USD 20 million), and were reported separately in the consolidated income statement, in the line item, "Impairment losses on jointly controlled entities."

New Building Contracts and Purchase Options on Vessels in Jointly Controlled Entities

As of 31 December 2011, no purchase options on vessels were exercised (2010: no purchase options) in jointly controlled entities. TORM's share of the total outstanding contractual commitment for the exercised purchase options on vessels amounts to USD 0 million (2010: USD 0 million) as of 31 December 2011.

Jointly Controlled Assets

2.189

Statoil ASA (Dec 2011)

NOTES TO THE CONSOLIDATED FINANCIAL STATEMENTS (in part)

8.1.1 Organisation

Statoil ASA, originally Den Norske Stats Oljeselskap AS, was founded in 1972 and is incorporated and domiciled in Norway.

The address of its registered office is Forusbeen 50, N-4035 Stavanger, Norway.

Statoil's business consists principally of the exploration, production, transportation, refining and marketing of petroleum and petroleum-derived products, and other forms of energy.

Statoil ASA is listed on the Oslo Stock Exchange (Norway) and the New York Stock Exchange (USA).

All Statoil's oil and gas activities and net assets on the Norwegian Continental Shelf (NCS) are owned by Statoil Petroleum AS, a 100% owned operating subsidiary. Statoil Petroleum AS is co-obligor or guarantor of certain debt obligations of Statoil ASA.

Following changes in Statoil's internal organisational structure, the composition of Statoil's reportable segments was changed as of 1 January 2011. For further information see note 4 *Segments* to these financial statements.

The Consolidated financial statements of Statoil for the year ended 31 December 2011 were authorised for issue in accordance with a resolution of the board of directors on 13 March 2012.

8.1.2 Significant Accounting Policies (in part)

Statement of Compliance

The Consolidated financial statements of Statoil ASA and its subsidiaries ("Statoil") have been prepared in accordance with International Financial Reporting Standards (IFRSs) as adopted by the European Union (EU). The accounting policies applied by Statoil also comply with IFRSs as issued by the International Accounting Standards Board (IASB).

Basis of Preparation

The financial statements are prepared on the historical cost basis with some exceptions, as detailed in the accounting policies set out below. These policies have been applied consistently to all periods presented in these consolidated financial statements.

Operating expenses in the Consolidated statement of income are presented as a combination of function and nature in conformity with industry practice. *Purchases [net of inventory variation]* and *Depreciation, amortisation and net impairment losses* are presented in separate lines by their nature, while *Operating expenses* and *Selling, general and administrative expenses* as well as *Exploration expenses* are presented on a functional basis. Significant expenses such as salaries, pensions, etc. are presented by their nature in the notes to the financial statements.

Significant Changes in Accounting Policies in the Current Period

With effect from 2011 Statoil changed its policy for accounting for jointly controlled entities under IAS 31 *Interests in Joint Ventures*, from application of the equity method to proportionate consolidation. The change has been applied retrospectively in these financial statements including the notes and consequently an opening balance sheet as of 31 December 2009 (1 January 2010) has been included. Prior to 2011 Statoil had limited oil and gas development and production activities organised in jointly controlled legal entities. On the basis of increased materiality of such activities, and with a view to ensuring consistency of the accounting for all jointly controlled oil and gas development and production activities, as well as reasonable compatibility with the new IFRS 11 which is further commented upon above, Statoil concluded that reflecting its share of assets, liabilities, revenues and expenses provides more relevant information concerning this type of activity carried out through jointly controlled entities than including it under the equity method.

Basis of Consolidation (in part)

Jointly Controlled Assets, Jointly Controlled Entities and Associates

Interests in jointly controlled assets are recognised by including Statoil's share of assets, liabilities, income and expenses on a line-by-line basis. Interests in jointly controlled entities are accounted for using proportionate consolidation. Investments in companies in which Statoil does not have control or joint control, but has the ability to exercise significant influence over operating and financial policies, are classified as associates and are accounted for using the equity method.

Statoil as Operator of Jointly Controlled Assets

Indirect operating expenses such as personnel expenses are accumulated in cost pools. These costs are allocated to business areas and Statoil operated jointly controlled assets (licences) on an hours incurred basis. Costs allocated to the other partners' share of operated jointly controlled assets reduce the costs in the Consolidated statement of income. Only Statoil's share of the statement of income and balance sheet items related to Statoil operated jointly controlled assets are reflected in the Consolidated statement of income and balance sheet.

IAS 41, *AGRICULTURE*

Author's Note

In 2011, IASB issued the following standards 2011 which amend IAS 41 as follows:
- IFRS 9
  This amendment replaces references to IAS 39 with references to IFRS 9.
- IFRS 13
  This amendment replaces the phrase *market-determined prices or values* with the phrase *quoted market prices* and replaces the terms *estimate* or *determine* with the term *measure*. IFRS 13 also amends the definition of fair value.

All of the standards in this author's note have effective dates after 1 January 2012 and are not discussed in the commentary in this section. In addition, the timing of the effective dates of these standards affects the availability of illustrative excerpts from survey companies' financial statements. Accordingly, the excerpts appearing later in this section may not reflect all or some of these revisions

IFRSs Overview and Comparison to U.S. GAAP

2.190 IAS 41 establishes the accounting for biological assets, agricultural produce at the point of harvest, and certain government grants that relate to agricultural activity. Examples of biological assets include farm animals, trees, grapevines, and other plants. After the point of harvest, IAS 2 or another applicable IFRS is applied. Accordingly, IAS 41 does not apply to the processing of agricultural produce after harvest or to land (found in IAS 16 or IAS 40) or intangible assets (found in IAS 38) related to agricultural activity.

Recognition and Measurement

IFRSs

2.191 IAS 41 states that an entity should recognize *biological assets* (living animal or plant) or *agricultural produce* (harvested product of the biological asset) on the balance sheet only when the following criteria are met:
- The entity controls the biological asset or agricultural produce as a result of past events.
- It is probable that future economic benefits from the asset will flow to the entity.
- The fair value (or cost) of the asset can be measured reliably.

2.192 On initial recognition and at the end of each reporting period, an entity should measure both biological assets and agricultural produce at the point of harvest at fair value less cost to sell. When there is an active market for the agricultural produce or biological asset in its present condition and location, IAS 41 states that the quoted market price in that market is the only appropriate basis for determining fair value. When market-determined prices or values are not available for the asset in its present condition, the entity should use the present value of expected future cash flows discounted at a market-determined rate. In making this calculation, an entity should include the net cash flows that market participants would expect the asset to generate in its most relevant market.

2.193 At initial recognition of a biological asset, an entity can only rebut the presumption that fair value can be measured reliably when there are no market-determined prices or values available and alternative estimates of fair value are clearly unreliable. In this case, an entity should only measure biological assets at cost less accumulated depreciation and impairment losses.

2.194 An entity should recognize gains or losses on initial recognition of biological assets or agricultural produce and changes in fair value of biological assets less cost to sell in profit or loss.

2.195 IAS 41 requires an entity to recognize unconditional government grants related to biological assets that are measured at fair value less cost to sell in profit or loss when the grant becomes receivable. When a government grant is conditional, an entity should recognize the grant only when these conditions are met.

U.S. GAAP

2.196 FASB ASC 905, *Agriculture*, contains industry specific guidance applicable to accounting by agricultural producers and agricultural cooperatives, rather than to accounting for biological assets by all entities. However, FASB ASC 905-10-15-4 excludes the following producers from the scope of this guidance:
- Growers of timber, pineapple, and sugarcane in tropical regions
- Raisers of animals for competitive sports
- Merchants or noncooperative processors of agricultural products that purchase commodities from growers, contract harvesters, or others serving agricultural producers

2.197 However, unlike IFRSs, FASB ASC 905 does not require an entity within the scope of this guidance to account for all types of biological assets in the same way.

2.198 FASB ASC 905-330-25 explains that an entity should account for growing crops (for example, a field, row, tree, bush, or vine crop before harvest) as inventory. For growing crops accounted for as inventory, an entity should capitalize all direct and indirect costs until the time of harvest. An entity should defer and allocate some costs incurred before planting (such as soil preparation) to the cost of the growing crop. Further, an entity should estimate, accrue, and allocate other costs (such as clearing residue of harvest) to the harvested crop (agricultural produce). FASB ASC 905-330-30-1 states that in exceptional cases, it may be impracticable for an entity to determine an appropriate cost basis for these inventories. FASB ASC 905-330 permits an entity to use realizable value, calculated on the basis of quoted market prices, less estimated costs of disposal for these inventories only when all of the following criteria are met:

- The products have immediate marketability at quoted market prices that cannot be influenced by the producer.
- The products have characteristics of unit interchangeability.
- The products have relatively insignificant costs of disposal.

Subsequently, in accordance with FASB ASC 905-330-35-1, an entity should measure inventories of growing crops at the lower of cost or market. FASB ASC 905-330-25-3 explains that an entity is permitted to classify animals with short productive lives (for example, poultry) as inventory. Subsequently, an entity would also measure these animals at the lower of cost or market.

2.199 Unlike IFRSs and in contrast to FASB ASC 905-330 for growing crops, paragraphs 2–3 of FASB ASC 905-360-25 explain that an entity should recognize PPE, such as trees, vines, orchards, groves, and vineyards, as fixed assets. The aforementioned FASB ASC guidance also notes that an entity should capitalize limited-life land development costs and direct and indirect development costs of orchards, groves, vineyards, and *intermediate-life plants* (defined in the FASB ASC glossary as plants having growth and production cycles of more than one year but less than those of trees and vines) during the development period. In accordance with FASB ASC 905-360-25-4, except for animals with short productive lives classified as inventory, an entity should recognize breeding animals, livestock, and production animals as fixed assets. FASB ASC 905-360-35-2 states that when breeding and production animals reach maturity and are transferred to a productive function, an entity should depreciate the accumulated development costs, less any estimated salvage value, over the animals' estimated productive lives. Unlike IFRSs, FASB ASC 905-360-30 also contains additional guidance on other costs to be included as production costs with respect to the end product from these animals.

2.200 Unlike IFRSs, paragraphs 1–2 of FASB ASC 905-360-30 explain that for animals raised for sale, an entity should capitalize all direct and indirect development costs of developing animals and measure them at the lower of cost or market until available for sale. Animals available and held for sale should be measured at the lower of cost or market or sales price, less estimated costs of disposal, when there are reliable, readily determinable, and realizable market prices for the animals; the costs of disposal are relatively insignificant and predictable; and the animals are available for immediate delivery.

Presentation

IFRSs

2.201 An entity should present biological assets as a separate line item on the balance sheet, classified as current or noncurrent, in accordance with IAS 1. An entity should also present additional line items, headings, and subtotals when they are relevant to an understanding of the entity's financial position. This guidance applies to all entities with assets subject to the requirements of IAS 41, not just those in the agriculture industry.

U.S. GAAP

2.202 Unlike IFRSs, FASB ASC 905-205 is applicable only for entities in the agriculture industry and agricultural cooperatives and provides no guidance on the separate presentation in the statement of financial position of biological assets, distinguished from other types of inventory or PPE.

Disclosure

IFRSs

2.203 Entities should disclose a description of each group of biological assets and any aggregate gain or loss from initial recognition or change in fair value, less cost to sell, of biological assets and agricultural produce.

2.204 When not disclosed elsewhere in information published with the financial statements (that is, the information may be outside the audited financial statements), an entity should disclose the following:

- Nature of activities for each group of biological assets
- Nonfinancial measures or estimates of the physical quantities of each group of biological assets at the end of the period and the output of agricultural product during the period

2.205 IAS 41 states that entities should disclose a reconciliation of the beginning and ending balance in biological assets, including the following changes, if applicable:

- Changes in fair value during the period
- Increases from purchases
- Decreases from sales and classification to held for sale, whether alone or as part of a disposal group
- Decreases due to harvest
- Increases from business combinations
- Foreign exchange differences

2.206 IAS 41 also requires an entity to disclose the methods and significant assumptions applied in determining fair value less cost to sell for each group of agricultural produce and biological asset during the period.

2.207 An entity should also disclose the following general information: title restrictions, commitments, and financial risk strategies. Additional disclosures are required for government grants and when the fair value less cost to sell of biological assets cannot be measured reliably.

U.S. GAAP

2.208 FASB ASC does not include special disclosure requirements for biological assets or agricultural produce at the point of harvest. Depending upon the asset category in which the asset appears on the balance sheet (for example, inventory), other U.S. GAAP disclosure requirements apply. However, FASB ASC 905-330-50-1 does state that agricultural cooperatives should disclose the amounts assigned to members' products. In addition, FASB ASC 905-360-50-1 also states that an entity should make financial statement disclosure of the accumulated costs and estimated useful life of intermediate-life plants.

Presentation and Disclosure Excerpts

Current and Non-current Assets— Consumable and Production Animals

2.209

BRF—Brasil Foods S.A. (Dec 2011)

CONSOLIDATED BALANCE SHEETS (in part)

(Amounts expressed in millions of Brazilian reais)

	Note	12.31.11	12.31.10
Assets			
Current assets			
Cash and cash equivalents	7	1,366.8	2,310.6
Marketable securities	8	1,372.7	1,032.4
Trade accounts receivable, net	9	3,207.8	2,565.0
Inventories	10	2,679.2	2,135.8
Biological assets	11	1,156.1	900.7
Recoverable taxes	12	907.9	695.9
Assets held for sale	13	19.0	62.2
Other financial assets	21	23.5	98.6
Other current assets		390.8	219.5
Total current assets		11,123.8	10,020.7
Non-current assets			
Marketable securities	8	153.4	209.1
Trade accounts receivable, net	9	2.4	7.0
Credit notes	9	147.3	93.1
Recoverable taxes	12	744.6	767.4
Deferred income taxes	14	2,628.8	2,487.6
Judicial deposits	15	228.3	234.1
Biological assets	11	387.4	377.7
Other non-current assets		362.6	223.2
Investments	16	20.4	17.5
Property, plant and equipment, net	17	9,798.4	9,066.8
Intangible assets	18	4,386.1	4,247.3
Total non-current assets		18,859.7	17,730.8
Total assets		29,983.5	27,751.5

NOTES TO THE CONSOLIDATED FINANCIAL STATEMENTS (in part)

1. Company's Operations (in part)

The BRF—Brasil Foods S.A. ("BRF") and its subsidiaries (collectively "Company") is one of Brazil's largest companies in the food industry. The Company is a public company, listed on the Brazilian Securities, Commodities & Futures Exchange ("BM&FBOVESPA"), under the ticker BRFS3, and listed on the New York Stock Exchange ("NYSE"), under the ticker BRFS, which headquarters is located at 475, Jorge Tzachel Street in the City of Itajaí, State of Santa Catarina. With a focus on raising, producing and slaughtering of poultry, pork and beef, processing and/or sale of fresh meat, processed products, milk and dairy products, pasta, frozen vegetables and soybean derivatives, among which the following are highlighted:

- Whole chickens and cuts of chicken, turkey, pork and beef cuts;
- Ham products, sausages, bologna, frankfurters and other smoked products;

- Hamburgers, breaded meat products and meatballs;
- Lasagnas, pizzas, vegetables, cheese breads, pies and frozen pastries;
- Milk, dairy products and desserts;
- Juices, soy milk and soy juices;
- Margarine; and
- Soy meal and refined soy flour, as well as animal feed.

During the last quarter of 2011, the Company's activities started to be segregated into 4 operating segments, being: domestic market, foreign market, food service and dairy products.

In the domestic market, the Company operates 45 meat processing plants, 16 milk and dairy products processing plants, 3 margarine processing plants, 4 pasta processing plants, 1 dessert processing plant and 1 soybean crushing plant, all of them located near the Company's raw material suppliers or the main consumer centers.

In the foreign market, the Company operates 3 meat processing plants, 1 margarine and oil processing plant, 1 sauces and mayonnaise processing plant, 1 pasta and pastries processing plant and 1 cheese processing plant, and has subsidiaries or sales offices in the United Kingdom, Italy, Austria, Hungary, Japan, The Netherlands, Russia, Singapore, United Arab Emirates, Portugal, France, Germany, Turkey, China, Cayman Islands, South Africa, Venezuela, Uruguay and Chile.

2. Management's Statement and Basis of Preparation and Presentation of Financial Statements (in part)

The Company's consolidated financial statements for the years ended December 31, 2011, 2010 and 2009 are in accordance with the International Financial Reporting Standards ("IFRS") issued by the International Accounting Standards Board ("IASB").

The Company's consolidated financial statements are expressed in thousands of Brazilian Reais ("R$"), as well as, the amount of other currencies disclosed in the consolidated financial statement, when applicable, were also expressed in thousands.

The Company has an advanced distribution system and uses 38 distribution centers, to deliver its products to supermarkets, retail stores, wholesalers, food service stores and other institutional customers in the domestic market and exports to more than 145 countries.

BRF has a large number of brands, the principal of which are the following: *Batavo, Claybon, Chester*®, *Confiança, Delicata, Doriana, Elegê, Fazenda, Nabrasa, Perdigão, Perdix, Fiesta, Hot Pocket, Miss Daisy, Nuggets, Qualy, Rezende, Sadia, Speciale Sadia, Texas* and *Wilson*, in addition to licensed brands such as *Turma da Mônica*.

3. Summary of Significant Accounting Practices (in part)

3.9. <u>Biological assets:</u> due to the fact that the Company is responsible for managing the biological transformation of poultry, pork and beef, pursuant to IAS 41 "Biological Assets," the Company classified these assets as biological assets.

The Company recognizes biological assets when it controls these assets as a result of a past event and it is probable that future economic benefits associated with these assets will flow to the Company and fair value can be reliably estimated.

Pursuant to IAS 41, the biological assets should be measured at fair value less selling expenses at the time they are initially recognized and at the end of each accrual period, except for cases in which fair value cannot be reliably estimated.

In Management's opinion, the fair value of the biological assets is substantially represented by formation cost, mainly due to the short life cycle of the animals and the fact that a significant share of the profits from our products arises from the manufacturing process rather than from obtaining in natura meat (raw materials at slaughtering point). This opinion is supported by a fair value appraisal report prepared by an independent expert, which presented an immaterial difference between the two methodologies. As a consequence, Management continues to record biological assets at cost.

.30. Accounting judgments, estimates and assumptions: as mentioned in note 2, in the process of applying the Company's accounting policies, Management made the following judgments which have a material impact on the amounts recognized in the consolidated financial statements

- impairment of non-financial assets, see notes 5, 17 and 18;
- share-based payment transactions, see note 23;
- loss on the reduction of recoverable value of taxes, see notes 12 and 14;
- retirement benefits, see note 24;
- measurement at fair value of items related to business combinations, see note 6;
- fair value of financial instruments, see note 4;
- provision for tax, civil and labor risks, see note 25;
- estimated losses on doubtful receivables, see note 9;
- biological assets, see note 11; and
- useful lives of property, plant and equipment, see notes 17 and 18.

The Company reviews estimates and underlying assumptions used in its accounting estimates at least on a quarterly basis. Revisions to accounting estimates are recognized in the consolidated financial statements in the period in each the estimates are revised.

11. Biological Assets

The group of biological assets of the Company comprises living animals which are segregated by the categories: poultry, pork and cattle. In addition, these categories were separated into consumable and for production.

The animals classified in the subgroup of consumables are those intended for slaughtering to produce unprocessed meat and/or manufactured and processed products, and while they do not reach the weight adequate for slaughtering, they are classified as immature. The slaughter and production process occurs sequentially and in a very short time period, and as a consequence, only the living animals transferred for slaughtering in refrigerators are classified as mature.

The animals classified in the subgroup for production (breeding stock) are those that have the function of producing other biological assets. And, while they do not reach the age of reproduction they are classified as immature and when they are able to initiate the reproductive cycle, they are classified as mature.

In the measurement of the biological assets at fair value, the Company adopted the model of discounted cash flow. Firstly, the discount rate used was the Weighted Average Cost of Capital ("WACC"), which was then adjusted to reflect the specific risk of the asset in question, utilizing mathematical model of Weighted Average Return on Assets ("WARA"), as follows:

	12.31.11	12.31.10
Cost of nominal owners' equity	10.31	11.10
Projected inflation rate USA	2.26	1.85
Cost of actual owners' equity	7.88	9.08
Actual WACC	5.80	6.93
WARA discount rate:		
Animals for slaughtering	5.50	6.00
Animals for production	5.75	6.90

In Management's opinion, the fair value of the biological assets is substantially represented by the cost of formation, mainly due to the short life cycle of the animals and to the fact that a significant portion of the profitability of our products derives from the manufacturing process and not from obtaining in natura meat (raw materials at slaughtering point). This opinion is supported by a fair value appraisal report prepared by an independent expert, which presented an immaterial difference between the two methodologies. Therefore, Management maintained the biological assets at formation cost.

The quantities and accounting balances per category of biological assets are presented below:

	12.31.11		12.31.10	
	Quantity	Value	Quantity	Value
Consumable biological assets:				
Immature poultry	209,732.0	485.4	187,584.0	396.3
Immature pork	3,803.0	581.5	4,155.0	479.2
Immature cattle	75.0	89.2	24.0	25.2
Total current	213,610.0	1,156.1	191,763.0	900.7
Production biological assets:				
Immature poultry	7,643.0	97.5	7,372.0	88.2
Mature poultry	12,006.0	132.0	11,559.0	140.5
Immature pork	125.0	18.4	169.0	22.6
Mature pork	409.0	139.5	386.0	126.4
Total non-current	20,183.0	387.4	19,486.0	377.7
	233,793.0	1,543.5	211,249.0	1,278.4

The rollforward of biological assets for the period is set forth below:

	Current				Non-Current		
	Poultry	Pork	Cattle	Total	Poultry	Pork	Total
Balance as of 12.31.10	396.3	479.2	25.2	900.7	228.7	149.0	377.7
Increase due to acquisition	83.1	577.5	244.3	904.9	34.0	57.3	91.3
Increase due to reproduction, consumption of ration, medication and remuneration of partnership	5,417.6	1,787.5	109.3	7,314.4	333.8	67.1	400.9
Business combination[1]	9.8	—	—	9.8	—	—	—
Accumulated depreciation	—	—	—	—	(304.7)	(52.6)	(357.3)
Transfer between current and non-current	62.2	63.0	—	125.2	(62.3)	(62.9)	(125.2)
Reduction due to slaughtering	(5,483.6)	(2,325.7)	(289.6)	(8,098.9)	—	—	—
Balance as of 12.31.11	485.4	581.5	89.2	1,156.1	229.5	157.9	387.4

[1] Business combination of Avex S.A. and Dánica group on October 3, 2011.

The costs of the breeding animals are depreciated using the straight-line method for a period from 15 to 30 months.

The acquisitions of biological assets for production (non-current) occur when there is an expectation that the production plan cannot be met with its own assets and, usually, this acquisition refers to immature animals in the beginning of the life cycle.

The acquisitions of biological assets for slaughtering (poultry and pork) are represented by poultry of one day old and pork of up to 22 kilos, which are subject to the management of a substantial part of the agricultural activity by the Company.

The increase by reproduction of the biological assets classified in the current assets is related to eggs from animals for production.

Non-Current Assets—Forests

2.210

Fibria Celulose S.A. (Dec 2011)

CONSOLIDATED BALANCE SHEETS (in part)

In thousands of reais

	2011	2010
Assets		
Non-current		
Derivative instruments (Note 11)		52,470
Related parties receivables (note 16)	5,469	5,307
Deferred taxes (Note 15)	991,768	1,332,025
Recoverable taxes (Note 14)	677,232	590,967
Advances to suppliers (Note 21)	760,611	693,490
Judicial deposits (Note 23 (d))	137,060	110,364
Other assets	95,060	145,768
Investment in affiliates	7,506	8,301
Biological assets (Note 18)	3,264,210	3,550,636
Property, plant and equipment (Note 17)	11,841,247	12,979,431
Intangible assets (Note 19)	4,809,448	4,906,443
	22,589,611	24,375,202
Total assets	27,853,536	30,273,856

NOTES TO THE CONSOLIDATED FINANCIAL STATEMENTS (in part)

1 Operations

(a) General Information

Fibria Celulose S.A. and its subsidiaries (the "Company", "Fibria", or "we") is a limited liability company constituted in accordance with the laws of the Federative Republic of Brazil and headquartered in SãoPaulo and after divesting its paper production activities in 2011, operates a single operational segment: producing and selling short fiber pulp.

The Company's business is affected by global pulp prices, which are historically cyclical and subject to significant volatility over short periods, as a result of, among other factors: (a) global demand for products from pulp; (b) global production capacity and strategies adopted by the main producers; (c) availability of substitutes for these products; and (d) exchange rates. All these factors are beyond the control of the Company's management.

The company's businesses are operated through the maintenance of its own and third-party forest base, plants for manufacturing bleached pulp and a integrated logistic structure for exporting its production, as detailed in topics (b) and (c) below:

(b) Facilities in Operation and Forest Base

The company operates the following facilities as of December 31, 2010 to produce bleached eucalyptus kraft pulp with a total annual capacity of approximately 5.25 million tons:

Pulp Production Facility	Location (Brazil)	Annual Production Capacity (Tons)
Aracruz	Espírito Santo	2,300,000
Três Lagoas	Mato Grosso do Sul	1,300,000
Jacareí	São Paulo	1,100,000
Veracel[*]	Bahia	550,000
		5,250,000

[*] Represents 50% of the annual production capacity of Veracel's pulp mill consistently with the proportional consolidation of the results of operations of Veracel in our consolidated statement of operations.

The production of bleached pulp is performed only from eucalyptus trees which are a variety of high quality hardwood pulp, with short fibers, generally better suited to manufacturing toilet paper, uncoated and coated paper for printing and writing and coated cardboard for packaging. We use different sources to generate thermal and electric energy for our respective operations, including black liquor, biomass derived from wood debarking, bark and scraps.

Fibria produces only hardwood pulp from planted eucalyptus trees therefore its eucalyptus trees are referred to as forest, which have an average extraction cycle of between six and seven years and are located in six Brazilian States, consisting of approximately 972 thousand hectares as of December 31, 2011, including reforested and protected areas, as follows (in thousand hectares):

State	Area of Forest	Total Area
São Paulo	80,224	147,584
Minas Gerais	13,220	27,213
Rio de Janeiro	1,696	3,413
Mato Grosso do Sul	231,405	350,201
Bahia	145,977	279,055
Espírito Santo	96,242	164,949
	568,764	972,415

The forest base of the Losango project in the state of Rio Grande do Sul is excluded from the table above as their assets qualify as assets held for sale and are being presented as such as detailed in Note 36.

2 Presentation of Financial Statements and Significant Accounting Practices (in part)

2.1 Presentation of Financial Statements (in part)

(a) Consolidated Financial Statements

The company's consolidated financial statements have been prepared and are being presented in accordance with and in compliance with International Financial Reporting Standards (IFRS) as issued by the International Accounting Standards Board (IASB).

The financial statements as of and for the year ended December 31, 2010 were the first financial statements presented in accordance with IFRS prepared by the Company.

The main differences between the accounting practices previously adopted in Brazil (the "BR GAAP") and United States of America and IFRS, including the reconciliation of shareholders' equity and net income as of December 31, 2010 and 2009, are described in Note 39—First-time Adoption of IFRS.

2.9 Inventories

Inventories are stated at the lower of average purchase or production cost and the net realizable value. Finished products and work-in-process consist of raw materials, direct labor, other direct costs and general production expenses.

The raw materials derived from the biological assets are measured based on their fair value less cost to sell at the point of harvest, when transferred from non-current assets to inventories.

Imports in transit are stated at the accumulated cost of each import. The net realizable value is the estimated sales price in the normal course of business, less the applicable variable selling expenses.

2.14 Biological Assets

Biological assets are measured at fair value, net of estimated costs to sell at the time of harvest. Depletion is calculated based on the total volume expected to be harvested.

Biological assets consist of eucalyptus forests exclusively from renewable plantations and intended for the production of bleached pulp. As a result of improvements in forest management techniques, including the genetic improvement of trees, the cycle of harvesting through replanting occurs over approximately six to seven years.

The fair value is determined based on the discounted cash flow method, taking into consideration the cubic volume of wood, segregated by plantation year, and the equivalent sales value of standing timber. The average sales price was estimated based on the local market prices and on transactions researched, adjusted to reflect the forest price. The volumes used in the valuation are consistent with the annual average harvest for each region.

The Company has a policy of carrying out semi-annual appraisals of the fair value of these assets.

3 Critical Accounting Estimates and Assumptions (in part)

Estimates and assumptions are continually evaluated and are based on historical experience and other factors, including expectations of future events that are believed to be reasonable under the circumstances.

The accounting estimates will seldom equal the related actual results. The estimates and assumptions that have a significant risk of causing a material adjustment to the book values of assets and liabilities within the next financial year are addressed below.

(e) Biological Assets

The fair value of biological assets calculation takes into consideration various assumptions with a high degree of judgment, as the sales price, cubic volume of wood and/or the annual average harvest for each region. Any changes in these assumptions used, would change the discounted cash flow result and, consequently cause the appreciation or devaluation of these assets.

18 Biological Assets

The Company's biological assets are substantially comprised of growing forests, intended for the supply of wood for pulp production. Forests in formation are located in the states of São Paulo, Rio Grande do Sul, Espírito Santo and Bahia.

The reconciliation of the book balances at the beginning and at the end of the year is as follows:

	2011	2010	2009
At the beginning of the year	3,550,636	3,791,084	1,890,898
Acquisition of Aracruz			1,849,069
Additions	761,502	642,567	216,300
Harvests in the period			
Historical cost	(569,813)	(440,265)	(127,595)
Fair value	(405,617)	(411,416)	(104,963)
Change in fair value	125,053	92,319	551,604
Reclassification to assets held for sale			
CONPACEL		(160,765)	
Losango	(241,595)		
Sale of the Guaíba unit			(426,303)
Other	44,044	37,112	(57,926)
At the end of the year	3,264,210	3,550,636	3,791,084

In determining the fair value of biological assets, the discounted cash flow model DCF was used, with projections based on a single scenario, with productivity and area of plantation (eucalyptus trees) for a harvest cycle of six to seven years.

The projected cash flows is consistent with area's growing cycle. The volume of production of eucalyptus to be harvested was estimated considering the average productivity in cubic meters of wood from each plantation per hectare at the time of harvest. The average productivity varies according to the genetic material, climate and soil conditions and the forestry management programs. This projected volume is based on the average annual growth (IMA) by region.

The average net sales price was projected based on the estimated price for eucalyptus in the local market, through a market study and research of actual transactions, adjusted to reflect the price of standing timber by region. The average estimated cost contemplates expenses for felling, chemical control of growth, ant and other pest control, composting, road maintenance, inputs and labor services. Tax effects based on current rates, as well as the contribution of other assets, such as property, plant and equipment and land were considered in the estimated based on average rates of return for those assets.

The valuation model considers the net cash flows after taxes on income and the discount rate used also considers the tax benefits.

In the following table we present the main inputs considered in estimating the fair value of biological assets:

	2011	2010
Actual planted area (hectare)	551,959	544,714
Average annual growth (IMA)—m3/hectare	41	42
Net average sale price—R$/m(3)	50,70	49,34
Remuneration of own contributory assets	5.6%	5.6%
Discount rate	7.9%	8.2%

The increase in e fair value of biological assets during the year ended December 31, 2011, when compared to the fair value as of December 31, 2010 is the combined result of the inputs presented above which resulted in a gain of R$125,053.

The estimate of the fair values of biological assets as of December 31, 2011 and 2010 was performed by management with the assistance of valuation specialists.

The company has no biological assets pledged as of December 31, 2011.

Non-Current Assets—Vines and Harvested Grapes

2.211

Compañía Cervecerías Unidas S.A. (Dec 2011)

CONSOLIDATED STATEMENT OF FINANCIAL POSITION (in part)

Assets	Notes	As of December 31, 2011	As of December 31, 2010
Non-current assets			
Other financial assets	6	194,669	15,813
Other non-financial assets	18	2,996,836	8,826,744
Accounts receivable from related companies	16	418,922	444,685
Investment accounted by equity method	19	39,923,677	42,596,043
Intangible assets other than goodwill	20	41,173,260	34,982,221
Goodwill	21	69,441,207	67,761,406
Property, plant and equipment (net)	22	556,949,110	508,162,219
Biological assets	25	18,320,548	16,668,630
Investment property	23	7,720,575	7,403,275
Deferred tax assets	26	18,806,779	18,546,061
Total non-current assets		755,945,583	705,407,097
Total Assets		1,298,491,359	1,151,689,011

NOTES TO THE CONSOLIDATED FINANCIAL STATEMENTS (in part)

Note 1 General Information (in part)

Compañía Cervecerías Unidas S.A. (CCU, or the Company or the Parent Company) was incorporated in Chile as an open stock company, and it is registered in the Securities Record of the Superintendencia de Valores y Seguros de Chile (Local Superintendence of Equity Securities, SVS) under N° 0007, consequently, the Company is subject to Regulation by the SVS. The Company's shares are quoted in Chile on the Santiago Stock Exchange, Electronic Stock Exchange and Valparaíso Stock Exchange. The Company is also registered with the United States of America Securities and Exchange Commission (SEC) and it quotes its American Depositary Shares (ADS) on the New York Stock Exchange (NYSE). One ADS is equivalent to 5 ordinary shares.

Through its subsidiaries, CCU produces, bottles, sells and distributes beverages. It is a multi-category company that participates in businesses such as beer, wine, spirits, cider and non-alcoholic beverages, such as soft drinks, nectars and waters. In the beer business it participates in the Chilean and Argentine markets, as well as in the wine business, where it exports to over 86 countries. Argentina is also involved in the business of cider and in the rest of the businesses the Company participates only in the Chilean market. Additionally, through the joint business Foods Compañía de Alimentos CCU S.A. (Foods) it participates in the ready-to-eat market. CCU, either directly or through its subsidiaries, sells goods or provide services to other business units such as plastic bottles and caps, shared services management, logistics, distribution of finished products and marketing services.

The Company is the largest producer, bottler and distributor of beer in Chile. CCU's beer production and distribution includes a wide range of brands in the super premium, premium, mainstream as well as popular-priced segments, which are marketed under seven proprietary brands (or brand extensions) being the main Cristal, Escudo and Royal Guard. The main brand distributed and/or produced under license is Heineken. Beer manufacturing in Chile is carried out at the Santiago, Temuco and Valdivia plants.

The Company is the second largest beer producer in the Argentine market, with three production facilities in the cities of Salta, Santa Fé and Luján. In Argentina the Company produces and/or distributes Heineken and Budweiser beer under license, as well as proprietary brands, such as: Salta, Santa Fé, Schneider and Palermo. The Company also imports and distributes, among others, beers Negra Modelo, Corona, Guinness and Paulaner.

The Company is also a wine producer in Chile, through its subsidiary Viña San Pedro Tarapacá S.A. ("VSPT"), the second largest wine exporter in Chile, and the third largest winery in the domestic market. VSPT produces and markets ultra-premium, reserve, varietal and popular-priced wines under the brand families Viña San Pedro, Viña Tarapacá, Viña Santa Helena, Viña Misiones de Rengo, Viña Mar, Casa Rivas, Viña Altaïr, Viña Leyda, Tamarí and Finca La Celia, the two latter of Argentine origin.

The Company, through its subsidiary Embotelladora Chilenas Unidas S.A. ("ECUSA") is one of the largest non-alcoholic beverage producers in Chile, including: soft drinks, mineral and purified water, nectars, tea, sports and energetic drink. It is bottler and distributor in Chile under its proprietary brands and of those brands produced under license. The proprietary brands include Bilz and Pap in the category of soft drinks; Cachantún and Porvenir in waters, which are operated by our subsidiary Aguas CCU-Nestlé Chile S.A. The brands under license include PepsiCo (Pepsi, Seven Up, Lipton Tea and Gatorade), Schweppes Holding Limited (Orange Crush and Canada Dry), Nestlé S.A. (Nestlé Pure Life and Perrier) and Promarca (Watts). The Company's soft drinks, purified waters and nectar products are produced at two facilities located in Santiago and Antofagasta; its mineral waters are bottled at two plants in the central region of the country: Coinco and Casablanca.

The Company, through its subsidiary Compañía Pisquera de Chile S.A. ("CPCh"), is one of the largest pisco producers in Chile, and it also participates in the rum and ready-to-drink cocktail businesses. Company-owned brands include: Control C, Mistral and Campanario in pisco and Sierra Morena in rum. CPCh also sells and distributes Bauzá and Pernod Ricard's products including the brands Pisco Bauzá and Havana Club, Chivas Regal and Absolut Vodka, respectively.

Note 2 Summary of Significant Accounting Policies (in part)

Significant accounting policies adopted for the preparation of these consolidated financial statements are described below:

2.1 Basis of Preparation (in part)

The accompanying consolidated financial statements have been prepared and are in compliance with the International Financial Reporting Standards (IFRS), issued by the International Accounting Standard Board (IASB) which have been applied uniformly to the periods presented.

The consolidated financial statements cover the following periods: Statement of Financial Position as of December 31, 2011 and 2010, Statement of changes in Equity, Statement of Income, Statement of Comprehensive Income and Statement of Cash Flow for the years ended December 31, 2011, 2010 and 2009.

The amounts shown in the attached financial statements are expressed in thousands of Chilean pesos, which is the Company's functional currency. All amounts have been rounded to thousand pesos, except when otherwise indicated.

2.13 Biological Assets

Biological assets held by Viña San Pedro Tarapacá S.A. (VSPT or the Company) and its subsidiaries consist in vines under formation and under production. The harvested grapes are used for the later production of wines.

Vines under production are valued at the historic cost, less depreciation and any impairment loss. Agricultural production (grapes) resulting from the vines under production is valued at its cost value when harvested.

Depreciation of under production vines is recorded on a straight-line basis, and it is based on the 25-years estimated production useful life, which is periodically assessed. Vines under formation are not depreciated until they start production.

Costs incurred in acquiring and planting new vines are capitalized.

The Company uses the amortized historical cost to value its biological assets, on that basis management considers that it represents a reasonable approximation of fair value.

Note 3 Estimates and Application of Professional Judgment

Financial statement preparation requires estimates and assumptions from Management affecting the amounts included in the consolidated financial statements and their related notes. The estimates made and the assumptions used by the Company are based on the historical experience, the changes in the industry and the information supplied by external qualified sources. Nevertheless, final results could differ from the estimates under certain conditions.

Significant estimates and accounting policies are defined as those that are important to correctly reflect the Company's financial position and income, and/or those that require a high judgment level by Management.

The main estimates and professional judgments are related to the following concepts:

* The valuation of goodwill acquired to determine the existence of losses due to potential impairment *(Note 2.15 and Note 21)*.
* The valuation of commercial trademarks to determine the existence of potential losses due to potential impairment *(Note 2.14 and Note 20)*.
* The assumptions used in the current calculation of liabilities and obligations to employees *(Note 2.19 and Note 31)*.
* Useful life of property, plant and equipment *(Note 2.10 and Note 22)*, biological assets *(Note 2.13 and Note 25)* and intangibles (software programs) *(Note 2.14 and Note 20)*.
* The assumptions used for the calculation of financial instrument fair value *(Note 2.6 and Note 6)*.
* The occurrence likelihood and the liabilities amount in an uncertain or contingent manner *(Note 2.20, Note 29,)*

Such estimates are based on the best available information on the events analyzed to date of these consolidated financial statements.

However, it is possible that events that may occur in the future result in adjustments to such estimates, which would be done prospectively.

Note 25 Biological Assets

The Company, through its subsidiaries Viña San Pedro Tarapacá S.A., has biological assets corresponding to vines that produce grapes. The vines are segmented into those under formation and those under production, and they are grown both in leased and owned land.

The grapes harvested from these vines are used in the manufacturing of wine under the Company´s own brands, which is marketed both in the domestic market and abroad.

As of December 31, 2011, the Company maintained approximately 4,358, of which 4,226 hectares are for vines in production stage. Of the total hectares mentioned above, 4,043 correspond to own land and 315 to leased land.

The vines under formation are recorded at historic cost, and only start being depreciated when they are transferred to the production phase, which occurs three years after plantation, when they start producing grapes commercially (in volumes that justify their production-oriented handling and later harvest).

During 2011 the production plant vines allowed to harvest a total of approximately 45.7 million kilos of grapes (41.9 million in 2010).

As part of the risk administration activities, the subsidiaries use insurance agreements for the damage caused by nature or other to their biological assets. In addition, either productive or under formation vines are not affected by title restrictions of any kind, nor have they been pledged as a guarantee for financial liabilities.

Under production vines depreciation is carried out on a linear basis and it is based on the 25-years estimated production useful life, which is periodically assessed. Vines under formation are not depreciated until they start production.

The costs incurred for acquiring and planting new vines are capitalized.

The Company uses the amortized historical cost to value its biological assets, the basis that management considers that it represents a reasonable approximation to fair value.

There is no evidence of impairment on the biological assets held by the Company.

The movement of biological assets during the years ended December 31, 2010 and 2011, is as follows:

Biological Assets	Under Production Vines	Training Vines	Total
Book Value	16,030,387	870,248	16,900,635
As of December 31, 2010			
Additions	50,137	758,254	808,391
Depreciation	(935,795)	—	(935,795)
Conversion effect	(104,601)	—	(104,601)
Book Value	15,040,128	1,628,502	16,668,630
As of December 31, 2010			
Historic Cost	25,339,964	1,628,502	26,968,466
Accumulated depreciation	(10,299,836)	—	(10,299,836)
Book Value	15,040,128	1,628,502	16,668,630
As of December 31, 2011			
Additions	—	595,752	595,752
Additions (cost) from business combinations	1,000,156	1,134,892	2,135,048
Additions (depreciation) from business combinations	(30,238)	—	(30,238)
Historic cost conversion effect	27,643	—	27,643
Transfers	831,726	(831,726)	—
Depreciation	(1,066,891)	—	(1,066,891)
Depreciation conversion effect	(9,396)	—	(9,396)
Book Value	15,793,128	2,527,420	18,320,548
As of December 31, 2011			
Historic Cost	27,199,489	2,527,420	29,726,909
Accumulated depreciation	(11,406,361)	—	(11,406,361)
Book Value	15,793,128	2,527,420	18,320,548

IAS 17, *LEASES*

Author's Note

In July 2008, IASB added the project on lease accounting to its agenda as part of its overall convergence activities with FASB. In March 2009, the boards jointly published a discussion paper, *Leases: Preliminary Views*, with a comment deadline of July 2009. In August 2010, the boards jointly published an exposure draft on accounting for leases proposing a "right of use" approach that both lessees and lessors would apply. This approach would require entities to recognize all leases in the statement of financial position and, therefore, provide consistent, more complete, and useful information to the users of financial statements. The comment period on the exposure draft ended December 2011. In January 2011, the boards began to redeliberate these proposals and conducted extensive outreach programs both during and after the comment period.

Some of the early decisions with respect to the scope of the leasing standard are the following:
- The boards unanimously agreed that the following assets would be within the scope of the new standard:
  —Right-of-use assets in a sublease
  —Leases of noncore assets
  —Long-term leases of land
- The boards unanimously agreed on the following scope exclusions:
  —Leases for the right to explore for or use minerals, oil, natural gas, and similar nonregenerative resources
  —Leases of biological assets (IFRSs)
  —Leases of service concession arrangements within the scope of IFRIC 12, *Service Concession Arrangements*
- The boards tentatively agreed to add leases of intangibles to the scope exclusions.

In March 2011, IASB staff published a document showing how the board's tentative decisions to date would affect the proposals in the exposure draft. This document is available on IASB's website.

In July 2011, IASB and FASB announced that their tentative decisions to date were sufficiently different from the proposals in the exposure draft to warrant reexposure of revised proposals. In January 2012, the boards unanimously agreed to reexpose their proposals to provide constituents the opportunity to comment on revisions to the boards' proposals. The boards' tentative decisions at this date include the following:
- An entity would determine whether a contract contains a lease based on the substance of the contract. This determination requires an entity to assess whether contract fulfillment depends on use of a specific asset and whether the contract conveys the right to control use of a specified asset for a period of time.
- A contract conveys the right to control the use of the specified asset if the customer has the ability to direct the use, and receive the benefit from use, throughout the lease term.

- The term *specified asset* refers to an asset that is explicitly or implicitly identifiable.
- A specified asset can be a physically distinct portion of a larger asset of which the customer has exclusive use. However, a portion of capacity of a larger asset is not physically distinct and, therefore, is not a specified asset.
- The boards confirmed the previously described scope inclusions and exclusions and have asked staff to conduct additional research and prepare an analysis of leases of internal-use software as accounted for in accordance with FASB ASC 350-40.
- The boards confirmed their decision to use the right-of-use model for all lease arrangements, with recognition of an asset representing an entity's right to use an underlying asset, and a liability for its obligation to make lease payments, during the lease term.
- With respect to accounting by lessees, the boards tentatively decided that lessees should apply a single approach for all leases consistent with the approach in the exposure draft. In contrast, the boards tentatively decided that a lessor would not use the receivable and residual approach for leases of investment property, but should recognize the underlying asset and lease income over the lease term. Lessors would use the receivable and residual approach for all contracts within the scope of that approach.
- The boards also tentatively decided that a lessee need not recognize leasehold assets and liabilities for a short-term lease, defined to be a lease, that at the date of commencement of the lease, has a maximum possible term, including any renewal options, of 12 months or less. Instead, an entity would recognize lease payments in profit or loss on a straight-line basis over the lease term, unless another systematic and rational basis of allocation is more representative of the time pattern of use of the asset.

The boards continued to discuss accounting by the lessee and amortization of right-to-use assets at their February 2012 meeting. They asked staff to research and assess how operational various amortization methods might be and how useful to users of the financial statements and to will report back to the boards in the second quarter of 2012. Therefore, the boards do not expect to issue a revised exposure draft before the second half of 2012.

Author's Note

In 2011, IASB issued IFRS 13, which amended IAS) 17, *Leases*. This amendment explains that the definition of fair value in IAS 17 is different from that in IFRS 13. Therefore, when applying IAS 17, an entity should measure fair value in accordance with IAS 17 and not IFRS 13.

Because the effective date of this standard is after 1 January 2012, this amendment is not discussed in the commentary in this section. In addition, the timing of the effective date of this amendment affects the availability of illustrative excerpts from survey companies' financial statements. Accordingly, the excerpts appearing later in this section may not reflect all or some of these revisions.

Author's Note

In IFRSs, the term *finance lease* has the same meaning as *capital lease* in FASB ASC. Both terms identify a lease that transfers substantially all significant risks and rewards of ownership of an asset to the lessee. The term *finance lease* is used in the paragraphs that follow when discussing accounting under IFRSs, and the term *capital lease* is used when discussing accounting under U.S. GAAP. Similarly, the term *finance cost or expense* is interchangeable with *interest cost or expense*. IFRSs use both terms.

IFRSs Overview and Comparison to U.S. GAAP

2.212 A *lease*, as defined in IAS 17, *Leases*, is an agreement whereby the lessor conveys to the lessee the right to use an asset for an agreed period of time in return for a payment or series of payments. IAS 17 identifies two types of leases: finance and operating. A finance lease transfers substantially all significant risks and rewards incidental to ownership of the asset to the lessee, although the lessor may or may not eventually transfer title to the lessee. All other leases are considered operating leases.

2.213 IAS 17 establishes the accounting and disclosure requirements for leases for both the lessor and lessee. These recognition and disclosure requirements apply to all leases, except those to explore for and use nonregenerative resources (for example, minerals, oil, and gas) and licensing arrangements for films, video recordings, plays, manuscripts, copyrights, and patents. IAS 17 measurement requirements also apply to all lessees and lessors, except the following:

- Lessees who hold property classified as investment property or lessors who provide investment property under operating leases should account for the investment property in accordance with IAS 40.
- Lessees who hold biological assets under finance leases and lessors who provide biological assets under finance leases should account for the biological assets in accordance with IAS 41.

Although IAS 17 excludes biological assets from the measurement principles of IAS 17, the recognition and disclosure requirements of IAS 17 still apply.

2.214 IFRIC 4, *Determining whether an Arrangement contains a Lease*, establishes criteria that an entity should apply when evaluating whether an arrangement that does not take the legal form of a lease is in substance a lease and should be, in whole or in part, accounted for in accordance with IAS 17. IFRIC 4 identifies two criteria that indicate an arrangement contains a lease: fulfillment of the arrangement depends on the use of one or more specific assets and the arrangement conveys a right of use.

Recognition and Measurement

IFRSs

2.215 IAS 17 requires both lessors and lessees to classify lease arrangements as finance leases or operating leases. When the arrangement transfers substantially all risks and rewards incidental to ownership of the asset, an entity should classify the lease as a finance lease. Otherwise, an entity should classify the lease as an operating lease. Whether the lease is a finance lease should depend on the substance of the arrangement. IAS 17 provides both examples and indicators of circumstances that could lead to classification as a finance lease. However, the standard also states that the identified indicators are not conclusive, and if it is clear from other features of the lease that the risks and rewards of ownership are not borne by the lessee, the lessee should classify the lease as an operating lease. Lessors and lessees should classify leases in the same way.

2.216 IAS 17 provides the following examples of situations that, when considered separately or combined, would normally lead to classifying the lease as a finance lease:
- Agreement transfers ownership of the asset to the lessee at the end of the lease term.
- Lessee has a bargain purchase option to acquire the asset at an amount sufficiently below its fair value that the option's exercise is reasonably certain.
- Lease term is for a major part of the economic life of the asset, even if title is not transferred.
- Present value of the minimum lease payments amounts to at least substantially all of the asset's fair value at the inception of the lease.
- Assets are of such specialized nature that only the lessee can use the assets without major modifications.

2.217 Indicators that the agreement is a finance lease include agreements in which the lessors' losses are borne by the lessee if the lease is cancelled, gains or losses from changes in the fair value of the residual value accrue to the lessee, and the lessee has the ability to renew the lease for a second term at a price substantially below market.

2.218 When a lease is classified as a finance lease, a lessee should recognize a leased asset and a corresponding lease liability at the inception of the lease, measured at the lower of the fair value of the leased asset or the present value of the minimum lease payments. In determining present value, a lessee should use the discount rate implicit in the lease, or when the implicit rate is impracticable to determine, the lessee should use its incremental borrowing rate. The lessee should include incremental direct costs in the cost of the asset.

2.219 Subsequently, a lessee should allocate the minimum lease payments to finance cost (interest expense) and a reduction of the liability using the effective interest method. Lessees should charge any contingent rents to expense in the period they are incurred.

2.220 Lessees should recognize depreciation expense on the leased asset and select an accounting policy consistent with its policy for similar owned assets. An entity should calculate depreciation expense in accordance with IAS 16 or IAS 38, as appropriate. Unless it is reasonably certain that it will obtain ownership by the end of the lease term, a lessee should depreciate the asset fully by the shorter of the lease term or the asset's useful life.

2.221 A lessee recognizes operating lease payments as an expense in profit or loss on a straight-line basis over the lease term, unless another systematic method is more representative of the pattern of benefits received, even when the amounts of the payments and the expense differ.

2.222 A lessor should recognize and present assets held by the lessee under finance leases as receivables in the balance sheet, measured at an amount equal to the net investment in the lease. A lessor should recognize finance income in profit or loss using the effective interest method. A lessor should exclude initial direct costs from the carrying value of the receivable and expense these costs when the profit on sale is recognized, normally at the beginning of the lease term.

2.223 A manufacturer or dealer lessor should recognize the seller's profit or loss in the period, in accordance with its policy for regular sales. If artificially low rates of interest are quoted, IAS 17 restricts the amount of selling profit to an amount that would apply if normal market interest rates are charged. The lessor should expense the costs of negotiating and arranging the lease at the same time as the related profit or loss is recognized.

2.224 In its balance sheet, a lessor should present assets held by lessees under operating leases by their nature. Generally, lessors should recognize lease income on a straight-line basis over the lease term.

2.225 The timing of income recognition by the lessor on a sale and leaseback depends on whether the transaction results in a finance or operating lease. Only when the transaction results in an operating lease and it is clear that the transaction is at fair value should the lessor recognize income immediately. When a sale and leaseback transaction results in a finance lease, IAS 41 establishes criteria for the timing and amount of gain or loss recognition.

U.S. GAAP

2.226 The FASB ASC glossary defines a *lease* as an agreement conveying the right to use PPE (land or depreciable assets, or both), usually for a stated period of time. In contrast, IAS 17 does not restrict to PPE the type of asset that can be the subject of a lease. Both IFRSs and FASB ASC 840 have specific scope exclusions, some of which are the same or produce similar results. For example, FASB ASC 840-10-15-15 excludes lease agreements concerning the rights to explore for or exploit natural resources, such as oil, gas, minerals, precious metals, timber, or other natural resources. Similarly, IFRSs also exclude nonregenerative resources (oil, gas, and minerals). In addition, both IFRSs and FASB ASC 840-10-15-15 exclude licensing agreements for items such as motion picture films, plays, manuscripts, patents, and copyrights.

2.227 Paragraphs 6–15 of FASB ASC 840-10-15 provide more guidance than IFRSs for determining whether the arrangement does or does not qualify as a lease (that is, conveys the right to control the use of the underlying PPE). For example, FASB ASC 840-10-15-10 excludes contracts for services that do not transfer the right to use PPE. This paragraph also states that even when an arrangement identifies a specific item of PPE, an entity should not consider the arrangement a lease unless fulfillment is dependent on the use of that specific item of PPE. This constraint would exclude most arrangements that call for delivery of an asset with quoted market prices available in an active market because these arrangements are generally not dependent on using specific PPE. However, contractual provisions that permit the lessor to substitute other PPE on or after a specified date do not preclude application of lease accounting before substitution occurs.

2.228 Like IFRSs, FASB ASC 840-10-15-9 includes agreements that, although not nominally identified as leases, meet the definition of a *lease* and, therefore, are within the scope of the lease standards.

2.229 Like IFRSs, FASB ASC 840-10-15-3 explains that in determining whether to apply the lease accounting requirements of FASB ASC 840, lessors and lessees should evaluate, at the inception of an arrangement based on the facts and circumstances, whether that arrangement contains a lease. Both IFRSs and FASB ASC include criteria for reassessment after inception.

2.230 Like IFRSs, in accordance with paragraphs 16–19 of FASB ASC 840-10-15, lessors and lessees should evaluate arrangements consisting of separate contracts with the same entity or related parties entered into at or near the same time. FASB ASC presumes that the entity negotiated such arrangements as a package. FASB ASC refers to these arrangements as *multiple element arrangements*. If an arrangement has both lease and nonlease elements, both the lessor and lessee must apply the lease accounting requirements of FASB ASC 840 to that lease.

2.231 Like IFRSs, FASB ASC 840-10-5-2 requires the lessee and lessor to classify a lease as either capital or operating. FASB ASC 840-10-25-1 has specific criteria, similar to those in IFRSs, which an entity should apply in evaluating whether the lease should be accounted for as a capital lease. FASB ASC 840-10-25-29 states that when any one of the four criteria is met, both the lessor and lessee should classify the lease as a capital lease. As described in paragraphs 42–43 of FASB ASC 840-10-25, the lessor should consider all four lease classification criteria and two additional incremental criteria when classifying the lease. However, only the following two criteria are identical to those in IAS 17:

- The lease transfers ownership of the property to the lessee by the end of the lease term.
- The lease contains a bargain purchase option.

In addition, unlike IFRSs, FASB ASC does not address leased assets of a specialized nature.

2.232 Although the concepts underlying the remaining two criteria for capital lease classification are the same in both standards, FASB ASC 840-10-25-1 has explicit quantitative thresholds to be assessed at the inception of the lease and IFRSs do not. These thresholds are the following:

- Lease term is equal to 75 percent or more of the estimated economic life of the leased property.
- Present value of the minimum lease payments, excluding executory costs (including any profit thereon), equals or exceeds 90 percent of the excess of the fair value of the leased property to the lessor at lease inception over any related investment tax credit retained by the lessor.

Neither of these criteria should be applied if the beginning of the lease term falls within the last 25 percent of the total estimated economic life of the leased property.

2.233 Paragraphs 2–27 of FASB ASC 840-10-25 also include specific criteria and guidance for the following issues: fiscal funding clauses, minimum lease payments criterion, guarantees and indemnifications, obligations to retire the leased asset, classification of leases involving real estate or between related parties, and classification of a lease acquired in a business combination.

2.234 Like IFRSs, in accordance with paragraphs 1–4 of FASB ASC 840-30-30, at the inception of a lease classified as a capital lease, lessees should recognize a leased asset and a corresponding lease liability measured at the lower of the present value of the minimum lease payments and the fair value of the asset. FASB ASC 840-10-25 includes more guidance on the payments that should be included in the present value calculation than IAS 17. Both sets of auditing principles establish guidance requiring the calculation to include initial direct costs and exclude indirect (IFRSs) or executory (FASB ASC) costs.

2.235 Both IFRSs and FASB ASC 840 specify the discount rate to be used in the present value calculation. IFRSs specify use of the lessor's implicit interest rate, unless impracticable to determine; otherwise, the lessee's incremental borrowing rate should be used. FASB ASC 840-10-25-31 imposes an additional constraint that the lessee should use the lower of its incremental borrowing rate and the implicit rate, when the latter is known to the lessee.

2.236 Like IFRSs, FASB ASC 840-20-35-3 requires recognized leased assets to be depreciated using the same accounting policy used for owned assets. FASB ASC 840 includes guidance for, and IFRSs do not address, determining residual value when there is a guaranteed residual value and the lessee is entitled to its appreciation.

2.237 In accordance with FASB ASC 840-20-25-1, a lessee should normally recognize operating lease payments as expense on a straight-line basis. However, a lessee is permitted to use another systematic and rational basis if it is more representative of the benefits derived from use.

2.238 Accounting for capital leases by the lessor is more complex under FASB ASC 840 than IFRSs. Lessors should classify leases that do not meet any of the four criteria previously mentioned as operating leases. Although a lessee need only meet one of the four criteria mentioned in FASB 840-10-25-1 for capital lease classification, paragraphs 42–43 of FASB ASC 840-10-25 require the lessor to meet two additional criteria to determine whether it should classify the capital lease as a sales type, direct financing, or leveraged lease. These lessor criteria are the following:

- The lessor can reasonably predict collectability of the minimum lease payments (that is, can estimate uncollectable accounts).
- No important uncertainties surround the amount of unreimbursable costs yet to be incurred by the lessor under the lease.

If the lessor meets both of these additional criteria, FASB ASC 840-10-25-43 provides additional guidance for selecting among the lessor capital lease classifications. The specific lessor classification determines whether a sale or financing transaction has occurred and the timing and amounts of revenue and gains (losses) from sales. Otherwise, FASB ASC 840-10-25-43(d) explains that the lessor should classify the lease as an operating lease. Therefore, under FASB ASC 840, unlike IFRSs, a lessor and lessee may have different classifications for the same lease.

Presentation

IFRSs

2.239 IAS 1 does not require an entity to present leased assets, lease liabilities, or related revenues or expenses as separate line items in the relevant financial statement. However, lessees and lessors should apply the other requirements of IAS 1 (for example, classify amounts as current or noncurrent on the balance sheet). An entity should also present additional line items, headings, and subtotals when they are relevant to an understanding of the entity's financial position.

U.S. GAAP

2.240 Paragraphs 1–2 of FASB ASC 840-30-45 require lessees to separately identify assets held under capital leases and the related accumulated depreciation and obligations under capital leases within the balance sheet or footnotes. FASB ASC further states that capital lease obligations are subject to the same considerations as other obligations in classifying them with current and noncurrent liabilities.

2.241 Paragraphs 2–3 of FASB 840-20-45 require lessors to include leased property classified as an operating lease within or near PPE in the balance sheet and to deduct accumulated depreciation from their investment in the property. FASB ASC 840-30-45-4 states that, in sales-type and direct financing leases, lessors should present lease receivables at the net investment in the lease and allocate these receivables, utilizing the same considerations as other assets, between current and noncurrent classifications when preparing a classified balance sheet. FASB ASC 840-30-45-5 states that in a leveraged lease, lessors should present deferred taxes related to the investment separately from the remainder of the net investment.

Disclosure

IFRSs

2.242 Whether leases are classified as finance or operating, IAS 17 requires a lessee to disclose a general description of the lessee's material leasing arrangements, including the basis for contingent rent payments, the existence and terms of renewal or purchase options or escalation clauses, and any restrictions imposed by the leasing arrangements (for example, restrictions on dividends, additional debts, or further leasing).

2.243 For finance leases, in addition to disclosures required by IFRS 7, a lessee should disclose the following:
- Net carrying amount at the end of the reporting period by class of asset
- Reconciliation of the total and present value of future minimum lease payments at the end of the reporting period and for each of the following periods: not later than one year, later than one year but not later than five years, and later than five years

- Contingent rents recognized as expense
- Total future minimum sublease payments expected to be received under noncancellable leases at the end of the reporting period

2.244 Depending on the nature of the leased asset, IAS 17 explains that lessees should disclose all information required by the related standard for owned assets (for example, IAS 16 for a leased building).

2.245 For operating leases, a lessee should disclose the following:
- Total future minimum lease payments at the end of the reporting period and for each of the following periods: not later than one year, later than one year but not later than five years, and later than five years
- Total future minimum sublease payments expected to be received under noncancellable leases at the end of the reporting period
- Lease and sublease payment recognized as expense during the period, separately reporting minimum lease payments, sublease payments, and contingent rents

2.246 All lessors, in addition to providing required IFRS 7 disclosures, should disclose a general description of material leasing arrangements and contingent rents recognized as income. Lessors recognizing receivables in respect of a finance lease should disclose a reconciliation of gross investment in the lease and the present value of the future minimum lease payments receivable (similar to that required for lessees), unearned finance income, the amounts of unguaranteed residual values accruing to the lessor, and the amount of the accumulated allowance for uncollectible receivables. Lessors with assets held by lessees under operating leases should disclose the future minimum lease payments for the same periods as the lessee.

2.247 IAS 17 requires the same disclosures for lessees and lessors in sale and leaseback transactions. Sale and leasebacks may require separate disclosure under IAS 1.

U.S. GAAP

2.248 Unlike IFRSs, FASB ASC 840 does not address whether entities should also provide any additional disclosures required by FASB ASC about financial instruments for any recognized lease receivables.

2.249 Like IFRSs, paragraphs 2–3 of FASB ASC 840-10-50 require a lessee to disclose, either in the financial statements or notes, a description of its leasing arrangements, including, but not limited to, the basis on which contingent rental payments are determined; the existence and terms of renewal and purchase options and escalation clauses; and restrictions imposed by lease agreements, such as those on dividend payments, additional debt, and further leasing. FASB ASC 460, *Guarantees*, also requires disclosures about guarantees.

2.250 FASB ASC 840-30-50-1 states that lessees should disclose the gross carrying amount of assets recorded under capital leases separately either on the balance sheet or in the notes. Lessees should separately report related lease liabilities on the balance sheet. FASB ASC 840-30-45-3 explains that depreciation expense on leased assets is not required to be shown separately, but if it is not included with other depreciation and amortization expense, the charge should be disclosed either on the face of the income statement or in the notes.

2.251 Like IFRSs, FASB ASC 840-30-50-1 requires lessees to disclose the following, either in the financial statements or notes:

- Gross amount of assets held under capital leases by major classes (according to nature or function), which may be combined with the comparable information for owned assets
- Future minimum lease payments as of the date of the current balance sheet both in the aggregate and for each of the five succeeding fiscal years
- Contingent rent expense incurred for each period for which an income statement is presented

FASB ASC 840-30-50-1 also requires lessees to disclose separately deductions for executory costs included in the minimum lease payments, imputed interest, and total future minimum lease payments from noncancelable subleases.

2.252 In accordance with paragraphs 4–5 of FASB ASC 840-10-50, exclusive of leveraged leasing, lessors should disclose a description of their leasing arrangements when leasing is a significant portion of their business activities. Lessors should also disclose their accounting policy for contingent rental income. If a lessor accrues contingent rental income before the lessee's achievement of the specified target (provided that achievement of that target is probable), lessors should disclose the impact on rental income.

2.253 For leases classified as operating, FASB ASC 840-20-50-4 requires lessors to provide disclosures similar to IFRSs. Lessors should disclose the following:

- Cost and carrying amount, if different, of property on lease or held for leasing by major classes of property according to nature or function and the total amount of accumulated depreciation as of the current balance sheet date
- Minimum future lease payments on noncancelable leases as of the balance sheet date, both in the aggregate and for each of the five succeeding fiscal years
- Total contingent rents included in income for each period presented

2.254 Unlike IFRSs, FASB ASC 840-30-50-4 requires specific disclosures by lessors for sales-type and direct financing leases, including the components of the net investment in the lease, minimum lease payments, and contingent rents. Paragraphs 5–6 of FASB ASC 840-30-50 require disclosure by lessors of the net investment in leveraged leases when such leasing is a significant part of the lessor's business activities.

2.255 With respect to sale and leaseback transactions, FASB ASC 840-40-50-1 requires similar disclosures to IAS 17 for the seller-lessee to describe the contract terms, including future commitments, obligations, provisions, or other circumstances that would require its continuing involvement. These disclosures are in addition to general lease disclosures addressed in FASB ASC 840-10-50, as well as disclosure requirements addressed under real estate sales in FASB ASC 360-20-50.

Presentation and Disclosure Excerpts

Author's Note

See paragraphs 3.238–.239 in section 3 for excerpts of disclosures required by lessees holding assets under operating leases.

Lessee—Operating and Finance Leases for Forests and Land

2.256

Mondi Limited and Mondi plc (Dec 2011)

COMBINED AND CONSOLIDATED STATEMENT OF FINANCIAL POSITION (in part)

As at 31 December 2011

€ Million	Notes	2011	2010
Intangible assets	13	238	312
Property, plant and equipment	14	3,377	3,976
Forestry assets	15	297	320
Investments in associates	16	10	16
Financial asset investments	18	33	34
Deferred tax assets	25	5	21
Retirement benefits surplus	26	8	11
Derivative financial instruments	23	3	3
Total non-current assets		3,971	4,693

NOTES TO THE CONSOLIDATED FINANCIAL STATEMENTS (in part)

1 Accounting Policies (in part)

Basis of Preparation

The Group's combined and consolidated financial statements have been prepared in accordance with International Financial Reporting Standards (IFRS) as issued by the International Accounting Standards Board (IASB). The Group has also complied with South African Statements and Interpretations of Statements of Generally Accepted Accounting Practice. There are no differences for the Group in applying IFRS as issued by the IASB and IFRS as adopted by the European Union (EU) and therefore the Group also complies with Article 4 of the EU IAS Regulation. The combined and consolidated financial statements have been prepared on a going concern basis as discussed in the business review, under the heading 'Going concern'.

Comparative information has been restated where appropriate to reflect the discontinued operation of Mpact (formerly Mondi Packaging South Africa) as described in note 9.

The financial statements have been prepared on the historical cost basis, except for the revaluation of certain properties and financial instruments. Historical cost is generally based on the fair value of the consideration given in exchange for assets. The principal accounting policies adopted are set out below.

Basis of Consolidation

Dual Listed Structure

The Group has two separate legal parent entities, Mondi Limited and Mondi plc, which operate under a dual listed company (DLC) structure. The substance of the DLC structure is such that Mondi Limited and its subsidiaries, and Mondi plc and its subsidiaries, operate together as a single economic entity through a sharing agreement, with neither parent entity assuming a dominant role. Accordingly, Mondi Limited and Mondi plc are reported on a combined and consolidated basis as a single reporting entity.

Non-Current Non-Financial Assets Excluding Goodwill, Deferred Tax and Retirement Benefits Surplus (in part)

Property, Plant and Equipment (in part)

Property, plant and equipment comprise land and buildings, property, plant and equipment and assets in the course of construction.

Property, plant and equipment is stated at cost less accumulated depreciation and impairment losses. Cost includes all costs incurred in bringing the assets to the location and condition for their intended use and includes borrowing costs incurred to the extent that the asset is a qualifying asset.

Depreciation is charged so as to write off the cost of assets, other than land, and assets in the course of construction, over their estimated useful lives to their estimated residual values. Residual values and useful lives are reviewed at least annually.

Assets in the course of construction are carried at cost, less any recognised impairment. Depreciation commences when the assets are ready for their intended use. Buildings and plant and equipment are depreciated to their residual values at varying rates, on a straight-line basis over their estimated useful lives. Estimated useful lives range from three years to 20 years for items of plant and equipment and to a maximum of 50 years for buildings.

Assets held under finance leases are capitalised at the lower of cash cost and the present value of minimum lease payments at the inception of the lease. These assets are depreciated over the shorter of the lease term and the expected useful lives of the assets.

Leases

Leases are classified as finance leases whenever the terms of the lease transfer substantially all the risks and rewards of ownership to the lessee. All other leases are classified as operating leases.

Operating Leases

Rental costs under operating leases are charged to the combined and consolidated income statement in equal annual amounts over the lease term unless another systematic basis is more representative of the pattern of use.

Finance Leases

Assets held under finance leases are recognised as assets of the Group at inception of the lease at the lower of fair value or the present value of the minimum lease payments derived by discounting using the interest rate implicit in the lease. The interest element of the rental is recognised as a finance charge in the combined and consolidated income statement, unless it is directly attributable to qualifying assets, in which case it is capitalised in accordance with the Group's policy on borrowing costs.

2 Operating Segments (in part)

€ Million	Operating Lease Charges 2011	Operating Lease Charges (Restated) 2010	Green Energy Sales and Disposal of Emissions Credits 2011	Green Energy Sales and Disposal of Emissions Credits (Restated) 2010
Europe & International				
Uncoated Fine Paper	7	8	5	6
Corrugated	32	27	43	38
Bags & Coatings	10	9	36	36
Total Europe & International	49	44	84	80
South Africa Division	5	5	—	—
Newsprint businesses	1	6	—	—
Corporate & other businesses	1	2	—	—
Group and segments total from continuing operations	56	57	84	80

3 Operating Profit From Continuing Operations Before Special Items (in part)

Operating profit from continuing operations before special items for the year has been arrived at after (charging)/crediting:

€ Million	2011	(Restated) 2010
Depreciation of property, plant and equipment	(332)	(331)
Amortisation of intangible assets	(10)	(9)
Operating lease charges (see note 2)	(56)	(57)
Research and development expenditure	(12)	(9)
Restructuring and closure costs (excluding special items)	(1)	—
Net foreign currency (losses)/gains (see note 7)	(4)	6
Green energy sales and disposal of emissions credits (see note 2)	84	80
Fair value gains on forestry assets (see note 15)	49	36
Felling costs (see note 15)	(65)	(65)
Profit on disposal of tangible and intangible assets	—	1

6 Net Finance Costs (in part)

Net finance costs and related foreign exchange gains/(losses) from continuing operations are presented below:

€ Million	2011	(Restated) 2010
Investment Income		
Interest income		
Bank deposits, loan receivables and other	9	8
Available-for-sale investments	—	—
Total interest income	9	8
Dividend income	—	1
Expected return on defined benefit arrangements (see note 26)	21	22
Total investment income	30	31
Foreign Currency Gains		
Foreign currency gains	—	8
Less: foreign currency gains capitalised (see note 14)	—	(1)
Total foreign currency gains (see note 7)	—	7
Financing Costs		
Interest expense		
Interest on bank overdrafts and loans	(108)	(120)
Interest on obligations under finance leases	—	(1)
Interest on defined benefit arrangements (see note 26)	(33)	(31)
Total interest expense	(141)	(152)
Less: interest capitalised (see note 14)	—	8
Total financing costs	(141)	(144)
Net finance costs from continuing operations	(111)	(106)

There was no interest capitalised for the year ended 31 December 2011. The weighted average interest rate applicable to interest on general borrowings capitalised for the year ended 31 December 2010 was 3.9%.

14 Property, Plant and Equipment

2011/€ Million	Land and Buildings	Plant and Equipment	Other[1]	Total
Cost				
At 1 January	1,565	6,330	505	8,400
Acquired through business combinations (see note 30)	1	3	—	4
Additions	8	50	191	249
Disposal of assets	(6)	(56)	(12)	(74)
Disposal of discontinued operation (see note 9)	(24)	(264)	(44)	(332)
Disposal of businesses (see note 31)	(16)	(31)	(3)	(50)
Reclassification	61	61	(204)	(82)
Currency movements	(59)	(299)	(19)	(377)
At 31 December	1,530	5,794	414	7,738
Accumulated Depreciation and Impairments				
At 1 January	613	3,556	255	4,424
Charge for the year	34	296	18	348
Impairments[2]	10	39	—	49
Disposal of assets	(4)	(50)	(10)	(64)
Disposal of discontinued operation (see note 9)	(7)	(113)	(17)	(137)
Disposal of businesses (see note 31)	(2)	(15)	(2)	(19)
Reclassification	—	(69)	(10)	(79)
Currency movements	(13)	(138)	(10)	(161)
At 31 December	631	3,506	224	4,361
Net book value as at 31 December	899	2,288	190	3,377

(continued)

2010/€ Million	Land and Buildings	Plant and Equipment	Other[1]	Total
Cost				
At 1 January	1,475	5,590	874	7,939
Acquired through business combinations (see note 30)	5	8	1	14
Additions	15	79	270	364
Disposal of assets	(20)	(55)	(12)	(87)
Disposal of businesses (see note 31)	(53)	(163)	(22)	(238)
Reclassification	82	505	(639)	(52)
Currency movements	61	366	33	460
At 31 December	1,565	6,330	505	8,400
Accumulated Depreciation and Impairments				
At 1 January	577	3,229	286	4,092
Charge for the year	38	302	20	360
Impairments[2]	16	32	5	53
Impairments reversed[2]	(1)	(5)	(3)	(9)
Disposal of assets	(15)	(50)	(11)	(76)
Disposal of businesses (see note 31)	(24)	(113)	(20)	(157)
Reclassification	—	(16)	(33)	(49)
Currency movements	22	177	11	210
At 31 December	613	3,556	255	4,424
Net book value as at 31 December	952	2,774	250	3,976

Notes:

[1] Other includes €139 million (2010: €190 million) of assets in the course of construction, which are not yet being depreciated in accordance with the accounting policy set out in note 1.

[2] Impairments include €48 million (2010: €32 million) of asset impairments reflected in special items, €nil (2010: €14 million) of asset impairments as a result of being classified as held for sale reflected in special items, €nil (2010: €1 million) of asset impairments reflected in profit from discontinued operation, and €1 million (2010: €6 million) of other impairments. Impairments reversed consist of €nil (2010: €9 million) of reversals of asset impairments reflected in special items.

Included in the cost above is €nil of interest (2010: €8 million) and €nil of foreign exchange gains (2010: €1 million of foreign exchange losses) incurred on qualifying assets which has been capitalised during the year. Tax relief on interest and foreign exchange gains/(losses) capitalised is based on the tax rates prevailing in the jurisdiction in which these items are incurred.

The net book value and depreciation charges relating to assets held under finance leases amount to €8 million (2010: €20 million) and €2 million (2010: €3 million) respectively.

The residual values and useful lives were reviewed during the current year and there were no material changes from previous years.

The net book value of land and buildings comprises:

€ Million	2011	2010
Freehold	893	944
Leasehold—long	—	1
Leasehold—short (less than 50 years)	6	7
Total land and buildings	899	952

15 Forestry Assets

€ Million	2011	2010
At 1 January	320	251
Capitalised expenditure	39	44
Acquisition of assets	3	2
Fair value gains[1]	49	36
Felling costs	(65)	(65)
Currency movements	(49)	52
At 31 December	297	320

Note:

[1] Forestry assets are revalued to fair value less estimated costs to sell each reporting year in accordance with the accounting policy set out in note 1. The fair value is calculated on the basis of future expected cash flows discounted using a discount rate relevant in the local country, based on a pre tax real yield on long-term bonds over the last five years. All fair value gains/(losses) originate from South Africa.

Forestry assets comprise forests with the maturity profile disclosed in the table below.

€ Million	2011	2010
Mature	166	169
Immature	131	151
Total forestry assets	297	320

Mature forestry assets are those plantations that are harvestable, while immature forestry assets have not yet reached that stage of growth. Plantations are considered harvestable after a specific age depending on the species planted and regional considerations.

22 Borrowings (in part)

€ Million	2011			2010		
	Current	Non-Current	Total	Current	Non-Current	Total
Secured						
Bank loans and overdrafts	9	1	10	26	127	153
Obligations under finance leases	2	10	12	4	14	18
Total secured	11	11	22	30	141	171
Unsecured						
Bank loans and overdrafts	253	155	408	363	282	645
Bonds	—	492	492	—	491	491
Other loans	22	79	101	17	123	140
Total unsecured	275	726	1,001	380	896	1,276
Total borrowings	286	737	1,023	410	1,037	1,447

The maturity analysis of the Group's borrowings, presented on an undiscounted future cash flow basis, is included as part of a review of the Group's liquidity risk within note 38.

Obligations Under Finance Leases

The maturity of obligations under finance leases is:

€ Million	2011	2010
Not later than one year	3	4
Later than one year but not later than five years	10	15
Later than five years	—	2
Future value of finance lease liabilities	13	21
Future finance charges	(1)	(3)
Present value of finance lease liabilities	12	18

The Group does not have any individual finance lease arrangements which are considered material.

€ Million	2011	2010
Assets Held Under Finance Leases		
Property, plant and equipment	9	20
Assets Pledged as Collateral for Other Borrowings		
Property, plant and equipment	21	230
Inventories	5	79
Financial assets	17	166
Other	17	20
Total value of assets pledged as collateral	69	515

The Group is entitled to receive all cash flows from these pledged assets. Further, there is no obligation to remit these cash flows to another entity.

36 Operating Leases

Lease Agreements

The principal operating lease agreements in place include the following:

Polish Plant Lease

The heat and power plant lease agreement was entered into by the Group on 29 April 2002 for a total term of 20 years. The lease is renewable by the lessee 18 months prior to the end of the initial lease term. Rental escalates on an annual basis by 1.9%. An option to purchase the plant during the lease term is included in the lease agreement. The lease does not contain any clauses with regard to contingent rent and does not impose any significant restrictions on the lessee.

Russian Forestry Leases

The forestry lease agreements were entered into by the Group on 1 November 2007 for a total term of 47 years and on 30 June 2008 for a total term of 49 years. The leases are not renewable. Rental escalates on an annual basis by CPI of the local jurisdiction. The leases do not contain any clauses with regard to contingent rent or options to purchase the forestry assets at the end of the lease term, and do not impose any significant restrictions on the lessee.

South African Land Lease

The Group entered into a land lease agreement on 1 January 2001 for a total term of 70 years. The operating lease commitment and annual escalation rate are renegotiated every five years. The operating lease charge recorded in the combined and consolidated income statement amounted to €1 million (2010: €1 million). The lease does not contain any clauses with regard to contingent rent or an option to purchase the land at the end of the lease term, and does not impose any significant restrictions on the lessee. There are 59 years remaining on the lease. The operating lease commitments of this lease are not included in the table below.

As at 31 December, the Group had the following outstanding commitments under non-cancellable operating leases:

€ Million	2011		2010	
	Forestry Assets	Land, Buildings and Other Assets	Forestry Assets	Land, Buildings and Other Assets
Expiry Date				
Within one year	5	48	6	51
One to two years	5	37	11	49
Two to five years	16	73	16	128
After five years	99	66	118	94
Total operating leases	125	224	151	322

38 Financial Risk Management (in part)

Liquidity Risk

Liquidity risk is the risk that the Group could experience difficulties in meeting its commitments to creditors as financial liabilities fall due for payment. The Group manages its liquidity risk by using reasonable and retrospectively-assessed assumptions to forecast the future cash-generative capabilities and working capital requirements of the businesses it operates and by maintaining sufficient reserves, committed borrowing facilities and other credit lines as appropriate.

Contractual Maturity Analysis

Trade receivables, the principal class of non-derivative financial asset held by the Group, are settled gross by customers.

The Group's financial investments, which are not held for trading and therefore do not comprise part of the Group's liquidity planning arrangements, make up the remainder of the non-derivative financial assets held.

The following table presents the Group's outstanding contractual maturity profile for its non-derivative financial liabilities. The analysis presented is based on the undiscounted contractual maturities of the Group's financial liabilities, including any interest that will accrue, except where the Group is entitled and intends to repay a financial liability, or part of a financial liability, before its contractual maturity. Non-interest bearing financial liabilities which are due to be settled in less than 12 months from maturity equal their carrying values, since the impact of the time value of money is immaterial over such a short duration.

Maturity Profile of Outstanding Financial Liabilities

2011 /€ Million	<1 Year	1–2 Years	2–5 Years	5 + Years	Total
Bank loans and overdrafts	262	24	72	60	418
Bonds	—	—	—	492	492
Other borrowings	21	18	53	9	101
Finance leases	3	1	8	—	12
Total borrowings	286	43	133	561	1,023
Interest on borrowings	33	40	103	46	222
Trade and other payables (excluding tax and social security) (see note 21)	833	—	—	—	833
Total undiscounted cash flows	1,152	83	236	607	2,078

Lessee and Lessor—Operating and Finance Leases

2.257

Etablissements Delhaize Frères et Cie "le Lion" (Groupe Delhaize) S.A. (Dec 2011)

CONSOLIDATED BALANCE SHEET (in part)

(In Millions of EUR)	Note	2011	2010	2009
Goodwill	6	3,373	2,828	2,640
Intangible assets	7	855	634	574
Property, plant and equipment	8	4,555	4,075	3,785
Investment property	9	85	60	50
Investment in securities	11	13	125	126
Other financial assets	12	18	17	16
Deferred tax assets	22	96	95	23
Derivative instruments	19	57	61	96
Other non-current assets		23	19	19
Total non-current assets		9,075	7,914	7,329
Total assets		12,242	10,902	9,748
Long-term debt	18.1	2,325	1,966	1,904
Obligations under finance leases	18.3	689	684	643
Deferred tax liabilities	22	625	543	227
Derivative instruments	19	20	16	38
Provisions	20, 21	253	233	228
Other non-current liabilities		73	68	57
Total non-current liabilities		3,985	3,510	3,097
Short-term borrowings	18.2	60	16	63
Long-term debt—current portion	18.1	88	40	42
Obligations under finance leases	18.3	61	57	44
Derivative instruments	19	—	—	2
Provisions	20, 21	82	52	52
Income taxes payable		56	17	65
Accounts payable		1,844	1,574	1,436
Accrued expenses	23	442	393	397
Other current liabilities		194	174	141
Total current liabilities		2,827	2,323	2,242
Total liabilities		6,812	5,833	5,339
Total liabilities and equity		12,242	10,902	9,748

NOTES TO THE CONSOLIDATED FINANCIAL STATEMENTS (in part)

1. General Information

The principal activity of Delhaize Group (also referred to, with its consolidated and associated companies, except where the context otherwise requires, as "we," "us," "our," "the Group" and "the Company") is the operation of food supermarkets in eleven countries on three continents. The Group's sales network also includes other store formats such as proximity stores. In addition to food retailing, Delhaize Group engages in food wholesaling to affiliated stores in its sales network and independent wholesale customers and in retailing of non-food products such as pet products.

The Company is a limited liability company incorporated and domiciled in Belgium, with its shares listed on NYSE Euronext Brussels and on the New York Stock Exchange ("NYSE"), under the symbols "DELB" and "DEG", respectively.

The consolidated financial statements for the year ended December 31, 2011 as presented in this annual report were prepared under the responsibility of the Board of Directors and authorized for issue by the Board of Directors on March 7, 2012 subject to approval of the statutory non-consolidated financial statements by the shareholders at the Ordinary General Meeting to be held on May 24, 2012. In compliance with Belgian law, the consolidated accounts will be presented for informational purposes to the shareholders of Delhaize Group at the same meeting. The consolidated financial statements are not subject to amendment except conforming changes to reflect decisions, if any, of the shareholders with respect to the statutory non-consolidated financial statements affecting the consolidated financial statements.

2. Significant Accounting Policies (in part)

2.1 Basis of Preparation

The consolidated financial statements comprise the financial statements of Delhaize Group and its subsidiaries as of December 31, 2011 except for the Delhaize Group's U.S. subsidiaries for which the fiscal year ends the Saturday closest to December 31. Consequently, the consolidated results of Delhaize Group for 2011, 2010, and 2009 include the results of operations of its U.S. subsidiaries for the 52 weeks ended December 31, 2011, 52 weeks ended January 1, 2011 and 52 weeks ended January 2, 2010, respectively.

Delhaize Group's consolidated financial statements are prepared in accordance with International Financial Reporting Standards (IFRS) as issued by the International Accounting Standards Board (IASB), and as adopted by the European Union (EU). The only difference between the effective IFRS as issued by the IASB and as adopted by the EU relates to certain paragraphs of IAS 39 *Financial Instruments: Recognition and Measurement*, which are not mandatory applicable in the EU (so-called "carve-out"). Delhaize Group is not affected by the carve-out and therefore for the Group there is no difference between the effective IFRS as issued by the IASB and adopted by the EU. We further refer to the comments made in connection with the Initial Application of New, Revised or Amended IASB Pronouncements in Note 2.2 and Standards and Interpretations Issued but not yet Effective in Note 2.5.

These financial statements have been prepared under the historical cost convention except for derivative financial instruments, available-for-sale financial assets and financial liabilities being part of a designated fair value hedge relationship that have been measured at their relevant fair values, as disclosed in the corresponding notes. Assets and disposal groups classified as held for sale have been measured at the lower of carrying value and fair value less costs to sell.

The preparation of financial statements in conformity with IFRS requires the use of certain critical accounting estimates. It also requires management to exercise its judgment in the process of applying the Group's accounting policies. The areas involving a higher degree of judgment or complexity, or area

2.3. Summary of Significant Accounting Policies (in part)

The principle accounting policies applied in the preparation of these consolidated financial statements are described below. These policies have been consistently applied to all financial years presented except as explained in Note 2.2.

Intangible Assets (in part).

Intangible assets include trade names, customer relationships and favorable lease rights that have been acquired in business combinations (unfavorable lease rights are recognized as "Other liabilities" and released in analogy with SIC 15 *Operating Leases—Incentives*), computer software, various licenses and prescription files separately acquired. Separately acquired intangible assets are initially recognized at cost, while intangible assets acquired as part of a business

combination are measured initially at fair value (see "Business Combinations and Goodwill"). Intangible assets acquired as part of a business combination that are held to prevent others from using them ("defensive assets")—often being brands with no intended future usage—are recognized separately from goodwill.

Leases

The determination of whether an agreement is, or contains a lease, is based on the substance of the agreement at inception date. Leases are classified as finance leases when the terms of the lease agreement transfer substantially all the risks and rewards incidental to ownership to the Group. All other leases are classified as operating leases.

Assets held under finance leases are recognized as assets at the lower of fair value or present value of the minimum lease payments at the inception of the lease. The corresponding liability to the lessor is included in the balance sheet as a finance lease obligation. Lease payments are allocated between finance costs and a reduction of the lease obligation to achieve a constant rate of interest over the lease term. Finance lease assets and leasehold improvements are depreciated over the shorter of the expected useful life of similar owned assets or the relevant lease term.

Rents paid on operating leases are charged to income on a straight-line basis over the lease term. Benefits received and receivable as an incentive to enter into an operating lease are spread over the relevant lease term on a straight-line basis as a reduction of rent expense.

In connection with investment property, where the Group is the lessor, leases where the Group does not transfer substantially all the risk and rewards incident to the ownership of the investment property are classified as operating leases and are generating rental income. Contingent rents are recognized as other operating income (see Note 27) in the period in which they are earned.

2.4 Significant Use of Estimates, Assumptions and Judgment (in part)

The preparation of financial statements in conformity with IFRS requires Delhaize Group to make judgments, estimates and assumptions that affect the application of accounting policies and the reported amounts of assets, liabilities and income and expenses, which inherently contain some degree of uncertainty. These estimates are based on experience and assumptions Delhaize Group believes to be reasonable under the circumstances. By definition, actual results could and will often differ from these estimates. In the past, the Group's estimates generally have not deviated materially from actual results. Revisions to accounting estimates are recognized in the period in which the estimates are revised and in any future periods affected.

Information about significant areas of estimation uncertainty and critical judgments in applying accounting policies that have the most significant effect on the amounts in the consolidated financial statements is included in, but not limited to, the following notes:

* Note 18.3—Classification of leases;

8. Property, Plant and Equipment (in part)

(In Millions of EUR)	Land and Buildings	Leasehold Improvements	Furniture, Fixtures, Equipment and Vehicles	Construction in Progress and Advance Payments	Property Under Finance Leases	Total Property, Plant and Equipment
Cost at January 1, 2011	1,930	1,861	3,217	94	930	8 032
Additions	112	92	265	204	35	708
Sales and disposals	(8)	(22)	(96)	(5)	(18)	(149)
Acquisitions through business combinations	323	21	81	7		432
Transfers (to) from other accounts	138	(90)	76	(211)	(6)	(93)
Currency translation effect	41	40	85	2	28	196
Balance at December 31, 2011	2,536	1,902	3,628	91	969	9,126
Accumulated depreciation at January 1, 2011	(587)	(1,055)	(1,881)	—	(380)	(3,903)
Accumulated impairment at January 1, 2011	—	(12)	(23)	—	(19)	(54)
Depreciation expense	(74)	(126)	(264)	—	(49)	(513)
Impairment loss	(17)	(24)	(39)	—	(35)	(115)
Sales and disposals	4	20	89	—	19	132
Transfers to (from) other accounts	(60)	65	(3)	—	3	5
Currency translation effect	(20)	(29)	(58)	—	(16)	(123)
Accumulated depreciation at December 31, 2011	(735)	(1,126)	(2,117)	—	(422)	(4,400)
Accumulated impairment at December 31, 2011	(19)	(35)	(62)	—	(55)	(171)
Net carrying amount at December 31, 2011	1,782	741	1,449	91	492	4,555

The impairment charges can be summarized by property, plant and equipment categories as follows:

(In Millions of EUR)	December 31 2011	December 31 2010	December 31 2009
Land and buildings	17	—	1
Leasehold improvements	24	2	5
Furniture, fixtures, equipment and vehicles	39	5	7
Property under finance leases	35	5	—
Total	115	12	13

In 2011, EUR 31 million related to property in the United States was reclassified to investment property (see Note 9). In accordance with the Group's policy, closed stores held under finance lease agreements are reclassified to investment property. In addition, the Group transferred EUR 41 million of assets acquired from Delta Maxi to "Assets classified as held for sale" (see Note 5).

Property under finance leases consists mainly of buildings. The number of owned versus leased stores by segment at December 31, 2011 is as follows:

	Owned	Finance Leases	Operating Leases	Affiliated and Franchised Stores Owned by Their Operators or Directly Leased by Their Operators From a Third Party	Total
United States	221	666	763	—	1,650
Belgium	151	33	198	439	821
Southeastern Europe & Asia	323	—	570	44	937
Total	695	699	1,531	483	3,408

10.2 Financial Liabilities (in part)

Financial Liabilities by Class and Measurement Category

				December 31, 2011		
		Financial Liabilities Measured at Fair Value		**Financial Liabilities Being Part of a Fair**		
(In Millions of EUR)	**Note**	**Derivatives-Through Profit or Loss**	**Derivatives-Through Equity**	**Value Hedge Relationship**	**Financial Liabilities at Amortized Cost**	**Total**
Non-Current						
Long-term debt	18.1	—	—	541	1,784	2,325
Obligations under finance lease	18.3	—	—	—	689	689
Derivative instruments	19	9	11	—	—	20
Current						
Short-term borrowings	18.2	—	—	—	60	60
Long-term debt—current portion	18.1	—	—	—	88	88
Obligations under finance leases	18.3	—	—	—	61	61
Derivative instruments	19	—	—	—	—	—
Accounts payable	—	—	—	—	1,844	1,844
Total financial liabilities		9	11	541	4,526	5,087

18.3 Leases

As described in Note 2.3, the classification of a lease agreement depends on the allocation of risk and rewards incidental to the ownership of the leased item. When assessing the classification of a lease agreement, certain estimates and assumptions need to be made and applied, which include, but are not limited to, the determination of the expected lease term and minimum lease payments, the assessment of the likelihood of exercising options and estimation of the fair value of the lease property.

Delhaize Group as Lessee—Finance and Operating Lease Commitments

As detailed in Note 8, Delhaize Group operates a significant number of its stores under finance and operating lease arrangements. Various properties leased are (partially or fully) subleased to third parties, where the Group is therefore acting as a lessor (see further below). Lease terms (including reasonably certain renewal options) generally range from 1 to 40 years with renewal options ranging from 3 to 36 years.

The schedule below provides the future minimum lease payments, which have not been reduced by expected minimum sublease income of EUR 34 million, due over the term of non-cancellable subleases, as of December 31, 2011:

(In Millions of EUR)	2012	2013	2014	2015	2016	Thereafter	Total
Finance Leases							
Future minimum lease payments	139	127	121	116	107	915	1525
Less amount representing interest	(78)	(76)	(69)	(62)	(57)	(433)	(775)
Present value of minimum lease payments	61	51	52	54	50	482	750
Of which related to closed store lease obligations	3	3	3	3	2	13	27
Operating Leases							
Future minimum lease payments (for non-cancellable leases)	317	275	248	215	185	907	2147
Of which related to closed store lease obligations	12	11	9	8	6	20	66

The average effective interest rate for finance leases was 11.8%, 12.0% and 11.8% at December 31, 2011, 2010 and 2009, respectively. The fair value of the Group's finance lease obligations using an average market rate of 4.5% at December 31, 2011 was EUR 1,016 million (2010: 5.1%, EUR 994 million; 2009: 6.1%, EUR 887 million).

The Group's obligation under finance leases is secured by the lessors' title to the leased assets.

Rent payments, including scheduled rent increases, are recognized on a straight-line basis over the minimum lease term. Total rent expense under operating leases was EUR 311 million, EUR 295 million and EUR 270 million in 2011, 2010 and 2009, respectively, being included predominately in "Selling, general and administrative expenses."

Certain lease agreements also include contingent rent requirements which are generally based on store sales and were insignificant in 2011, 2010 and 2009.

Sublease payments received and recognized into income for 2011, 2010 and 2009 were EUR 17 million, EUR 16 million and EUR 16 million, respectively.

Delhaize Group signed lease agreements for additional store facilities under construction at December 31, 2011. The corresponding lease terms as well as the renewal options generally range from 10 to 30 years. Total future minimum lease payments for these agreements relating to stores under construction were approximately EUR 71 million.

Provisions for EUR 46 million, EUR 44 million and EUR 54 million at December 31, 2011, 2010 and 2009, respectively, representing the discounted value of remaining lease payments, net of expected sublease income, for closed stores, were included in "Closed Store Provisions" (see Note 20.1). The discount rate is based on the incremental borrowing rate for debt with similar terms to the lease at the time of the store closing.

Delhaize Group as Lessor—Expected Finance and Operating Lease Income

As noted above, occasionally, Delhaize Group acts as a lessor for certain owned or leased property, mainly in connection with closed stores that have been sub-leased to other parties, retail units in Delhaize Group shopping centers or within a Delhaize Group store. Currently, the Group did not enter into any lease arrangements with independent third party lessees that would qualify as finance leases. Rental income is included in "Other Operating Income" in the income statement.

The undiscounted expected future minimum lease payments to be received under non-cancellable operating leases as at December 31, 2011 can be summarized as follows:

(In Millions of EUR)	2012	2013	2014	2015	2016	Thereafter	Total
Future minimum lease payments to be received	35	30	17	5	3	16	106
Of which related to sub-lease agreements	14	10	5	2	2	1	34

The total amount of EUR 106 million represents expected future lease income to be recognized as such in the income statement and excludes expected future sub-lease payments to receive in relation to stores being part of the "Closed Store Provision" (see Note 20.1).

Contracts including contingent rent clauses are insignificant to the Group.

IAS 37, *PROVISIONS, CONTINGENT LIABILITIES AND CONTINGENT ASSETS*

Author's Note

As evidenced by the findings from a review of the survey companies, diversity in practice exists in the use of the term *provision*. Almost all survey companies used the term *provision* to refer not only to liabilities that meet the IAS 37 definition, but also to such items as valuation allowances (for example, provision for estimated uncollectible receivables) and expenses (for example, provision for income taxes). IASB recognizes this diversity in practice exists and, in response, addressed this issue in two exposure drafts, in 2005 and January 2010. Among other significant proposed changes, the January 2010 exposure draft does not use *provision* as a defined term; instead, it proposes to use the term *nonfinancial liability*, which includes items previously described as provisions, as well as other liabilities. It would also clarify that IAS 37, except in specified cases, should be applied to all nonfinancial liabilities that are not within the scope of other standards. In November 2010, the IASB and FASB decided to amend the timetable for some projects that are important but less urgent than others to allow the boards to focus on the projects they aim to complete in the FASB convergence project. Therefore, IASB has placed on hold the project to revise IAS 37, now titled *Liabilities*, and intends to revisit the timing of completion of the project as part of the 2012 agenda consultation.

Author's Note

IFRS 9 amended IAS 37 by replacing the reference to IAS 39 with a reference to IFRS 9 in the scope exclusion for financial instruments. Because the effective date of IFRS 9 is after 1 January 2012, this amendment is not discussed in the commentary in this section. In addition, the timing of the effective date of this amendment affects the availability of illustrative excerpts from survey companies' financial statements. Accordingly, the excerpts appearing later in this section may not reflect all or some of these revisions.

IFRSs Overview and Comparison to U.S. GAAP

2.258 IAS 37 establishes the accounting for most liabilities. A *provision*, as stated in IAS 37, is a liability of uncertain timing or amount. To be recognized as a provision, an obligation must meet the definition of a *liability* (that is, be a present obligation resulting from past transactions or events, settlement of which is probable, and resulting in an outflow of resources embodying economic benefits) and the entity should estimate the amount of the obligation reliably. In IAS 37, *probable* means more likely than not.

2.259 A *contingent liability* is defined as either a possible obligation only confirmed by the occurrence or nonoccurrence of a future event not wholly in the control of the entity or a present obligation that fails to meet either the probability or measurement reliability criteria. A *contingent asset* is a possible asset only confirmed by the occurrence or nonoccurrence of a future event not wholly in the control of the entity.

2.260 IAS 37 also establishes the accounting for onerous contracts and restructuring programs. An *onerous contract* is defined as a contract in which the unavoidable costs of fulfilling the contract terms exceed the expected benefits to be received. A *restructuring program* is a program planned and controlled by management that materially changes either the scope of an entity's business activities or the manner in which it conducts that business.

2.261 Provisions, contingent liabilities, and contingent assets resulting from executory contracts that are not onerous and those covered by another standard are excluded from the scope of IAS 37. Examples of provisions covered by another standard are deferred tax liabilities (IAS 12), postemployment benefits (IAS 19, *Employee Benefits*), construction contracts (IAS 11), and leases (see IAS 17, with the exception of operating leases that have become onerous).

2.262 IFRSs require an entity to recognize the cost of a decommissioning, environmental remediation, and similar liability as a liability in accordance with IAS 37 and to include this cost in the cost of the related asset.

2.263 Accounting and disclosure requirements for financial liabilities are covered in IAS 32, IAS 39, and IFRS 7.

Recognition and Measurement

IFRSs

2.264 An entity should recognize a provision (liability) only when it has a present obligation, either legal or constructive, as a result of a past transaction or event, and the probability and measurement reliability recognition criteria are met. IAS 37 acknowledges that there may be rare cases when it is unclear whether a present obligation exists. In these cases, the entity should recognize a liability if, taking all of the evidence into account, the existence of a present obligation is more likely than not.

2.265 An entity should not recognize contingent liabilities or contingent assets. Once the relevant probability and measurement reliability recognition criteria are met, the asset or liability is no longer considered contingent.

2.266 In some circumstances (for example, warranty obligations), an entity should evaluate the probability recognition criterion with respect to a class of, rather than individual, obligations. IAS 37 states that the use of estimates is known to be an essential part of financial statement preparation; therefore, an entity's use of estimates does not invalidate measurement reliability. However, when an entity concludes that a liability should not be recognized, it should disclose the obligation as a contingent liability, unless the possibility of an outflow of resources is remote.

2.267 An entity should measure provisions at the best pretax estimate of the expenditure required to settle the liability at the balance sheet date, taking into account the risks and uncertainties incorporated into that estimate. When no estimate in a range is better than another, an entity should use the midpoint in the range.

2.268 IAS 37 also requires an entity to calculate the present value of the liability when this would result in a material difference from the sum of the gross outflows. An entity should use a pretax interest rate(s) incorporating current market expectations of the time value of money and risks associated with this liability. An entity should adjust either future cash flows or the interest rate for a specific risk, but not both.

2.269 An entity should reflect the effects of expected events only when there is sufficient evidence that these events will occur. For example, an entity should only incorporate possible changes in legislation when it is virtually certain that the legislation will be passed. An entity should not include any expected gains from asset disposals in measuring a provision.

2.270 An entity should recognize a reimbursement as a separate asset, and not a reduction of the liability, only when receipt of the reimbursement is probable and the amount can be measured reliably. An entity should not measure a reimbursement for more than the amount of the related liability. However, on the statement of comprehensive income, an entity may show the expense related to the liability net of the reimbursement income. An entity should review its provisions at each balance sheet date and adjust them to its current best estimate of the settlement amount. When it is no longer probable that a settlement will occur, the entity should reverse the provision.

2.271 An entity should not use a provision for expenditures, other than those originally intended.

2.272 IAS 37 includes specific requirements for future operating losses and onerous contracts. An entity should not recognize a liability for future operating losses. When a contract becomes onerous, an entity should recognize a liability and measure it in accordance with this standard. However, before recognizing this liability, the entity should test any assets related to the contract for impairment and recognize an impairment loss when necessary.

2.273 IAS 37 requires an entity to satisfy additional criteria before recognizing provisions for a restructuring program. An entity should have a detailed formal plan, and the plan must include, at a minimum, the business concerned, affected locations, location, function, approximate number of employees to receive compensation under the plan, planned expenditures, and timing of implementation. The entity should also have created a valid expectation in the employees affected either by announcing the plan or starting implementation. An entity should not consider management or board decisions that occurred before the balance sheet date to be sufficient by themselves to create a constructive obligation and, therefore, should not recognize restructuring provisions under those circumstances.

2.274 Only when there is a binding sales agreement should an entity recognize a provision for the sale of an operation. In addition, an entity should recognize provisions only for direct expenditures required by the restructuring and not those connected to continuing operations. For example, an entity should not recognize provisions for retraining employees for other positions in the entity, for marketing, or for acquisition or development of new systems or technology.

U.S. GAAP

2.275 Unlike IFRSs, FASB ASC does not consolidate its guidance on accounting for a wide variety of liabilities in one topic. Recognition, measurement, and disclosure requirements are dispersed across many topics. In addition, unlike IFRSs, FASB ASC provides transaction-specific guidance on accounting for noncash payments, restructurings, foreclosures, unclaimed wages, deposits on returnable containers, advance sales, dealer reserves, coupons and similar promotions, and energy trading contracts.

2.276 FASB ASC 405-20-40-1 prescribes the following criteria for derecognition (extinguishment) of a liability:
- Debtor pays the creditor and is relieved of its obligation.
- Debtor is legally released as the primary obligor under the liability, either judicially or by the creditor.

Therefore, it can be inferred that like IFRSs, an entity can only charge against the liability (provision) expenditures related to its original nature. Netting expenditures against a liability (provision) that was originally recognized for another purpose would conceal the impact of two different liabilities.

2.277 Although the accounting results may be similar, the FASB ASC glossary and IFRSs definitions of, and approaches to, a contingency are different. IFRSs address the issue from the perspective of asset or liability recognition on the balance sheet, and FASB ASC 450, *Contingencies*, addresses the issue from the perspective of gain or loss recognition in the income statement. As defined by the FASB ASC glossary, a *contingency* is an existing condition, situation, or set of circumstances involving uncertainty concerning possible gain (gain contingency) or loss (loss contingency) to an entity that will ultimately be resolved when one or more future events occur or fail to occur.

2.278 FASB ASC 450-20-25-2 requires an entity to recognize an estimated loss from a loss contingency in income only when the following two conditions are met:

- Information is available before the financial statements are issued or are available to be issued indicating it is probable (that is, the future event[s] are likely to occur, as defined in the FASB ASC glossary) that an asset has been impaired or liability incurred as of the balance sheet date, with the implicit understanding that it is probable that a future event(s) will occur to confirm the loss.
- The amount of the loss can be reasonably estimated.

Despite the similarity in these conditions to those in IAS 37, IFRSs recognize that financial statements deal with the financial position of an entity at the end of its reporting period and not its possible position in the future. Therefore, under IFRSs, a liability should not be recognized for costs that an entity needs to incur to operate in the future. The only liabilities that an entity should recognize in its statement of financial position are those that exist at the end of the reporting period.

2.279 FASB ASC 450-20-50-5 also expresses a preference for disclosure when the amount cannot be reasonably estimated (see discussion of disclosure requirements starting with paragraph 2.295).

2.280 In accordance with FASB ASC 450-20-30-1, when one estimate within a range is better than others, an entity should measure the loss and liability at that amount. When no estimate is better than another, an entity should use the minimum in the range, whereas IFRSs require the entity to use the midpoint.

2.281 Unlike IFRSs, FASB ASC 460-10-25-5 considers warranties a contingency. Therefore, an entity should meet the two conditions described in paragraph 2.278 before recognizing a loss and related liability. FASB ASC 460-10 contains additional guidance concerning the items that an entity should consider in order to meet the probability recognition criteria, including references to the entity's own and others' experience. FASB ASC also provides more specific guidance for extended warranties and product maintenance contracts, which are not discussed in IFRSs.

2.282 FASB ASC 450-30-25-1 usually does not permit recognition of gain contingencies because to do so might be to recognize revenue before its realization. Unlike IFRSs, FASB ASC 450-30-50-1 does not contain a probability threshold that an entity should meet before disclosure.

2.283 FASB ASC 410, *Asset Retirement and Environmental Obligations*, contains extensive guidance on accounting for asset retirement obligations, including scope, recognition and measurement rules, and disclosures that far exceed those in IFRSs.

2.284 IAS 37 includes specific conditions that must be met before an entity can recognize restructuring liabilities. FASB ASC refers to these liabilities as *exit and disposal activities*, and with the exception of one-time liabilities for employee termination benefits, FASB ASC 420-10-25-1 requires an entity to recognize a liability for a cost associated with these activities in the period that the liability is incurred, measured at fair value. When fair value cannot be reasonably estimated, an entity should defer recognition until it can make a reasonable estimate. Paragraphs 2–3 of FASB ASC 420-10-30 express a preference for quoted market prices followed by present value techniques to make the estimate; however, it does not preclude the use of other techniques and computational shortcuts when consistent with fair value measurements.

2.285 However, in the case of one-time employee termination benefits, paragraphs 4–10 of FASB ASC 420-10-25 explain that such an arrangement exists only when the entity has communicated the arrangement to the affected employees and the date of the termination plan meets several conditions, including management approval. Many are similar to the conditions in IAS 37. However, FASB ASC 420-10-25 contains additional conditions that affect the timing of measurement of the termination benefit liability, including a minimum retention period not exceeding the legal notification period or, in its absence, 60 days. For example, FASB ASC 420-10-25-9 explains that when an entity requires employees to render services until termination in order to receive benefits and the retention period exceeds the minimum, it recognizes the liability at the communication date but measures fair value as of the termination date. The entity should then recognize the termination benefits ratably over the future service period. In all other cases, the entity recognizes and measures the fair value of the liability at the communication date. IFRSs do not include this specific guidance.

2.286 Like IFRSs, FASB ASC 420-10-25-3 does not permit recognition of anticipated future operating losses because such losses do not meet the definition of a *liability*. An entity should recognize such losses only in the period in which they occur.

Presentation

IFRSs

2.287 IAS 1 requires entities to present trade and other payables and provisions as a separate line item on the balance sheet, disaggregated into their current and noncurrent components. An entity should also present additional line items, headings, and subtotals when they are relevant to an understanding of the entity's financial position.

2.288 IFRS 5 requires an entity to present separately liabilities associated with disposal groups classified as held for sale and discontinued operations.

U.S. GAAP

2.289 U.S. GAAP has more specific guidance than IFRSs on presentation of current liabilities. SEC guidance in Regulation S-X permits aggregation on the financial statements and requires more disaggregated disclosures either on the face of the financial statements or in the notes. (See, for example, sections 210.5-01 through 210.5-04 of SEC Regulation S-X for guidance relevant to commercial and industrial companies.)

2.290 FASB ASC 210-20 contains similar criteria to IFRSs permitting offsetting of assets and liabilities only when the entity has both a legal right to settle net and the intention to do so. See section 8 for further discussion on offsetting arrangements.

Disclosure

IFRSs

2.291 For each class of provision, IAS 37 requires an entity to disclose a description of the nature of the provision and the expected timing of settlements. An entity should also discuss any uncertainties in these estimates, including major assumptions about future events. An entity should disclose the amount of expected reimbursements, including any amount recognized as an asset.

2.292 An entity should also provide reconciliations of the beginning and ending balance for each class of provision. Changes in the provision should include the following changes to the accounts: additions to, and increases in, provisions; charges against the provision; reversals; and unwinding of the discount rate when provisions have been measured at present value. Comparative information is not required.

2.293 Unless the possibility of an outflow is remote, an entity should disclose a brief description of each class of contingent liability. When practicable, this disclosure should include an estimate of financial impact, a discussion of uncertainties relating to possible outflows, and the possibility of reimbursement. Only when the probability of an inflow of benefits is probable should an entity disclose information about contingent assets and, when practicable, an estimate of the expected financial impact. When the impracticability exception is used, an entity should disclose that fact.

2.294 Finally, IAS 37 recognizes that disclosure of some of the required information on contingent liabilities can have a prejudicial effect on litigation or other disputes. In those cases, the entity need not disclose all of the required information. However, the general nature of the contingency should be disclosed and described, together with the reason that the entity has not provided the remaining information.

U.S. GAAP

2.295 FASB ASC 210-10-45-5 requires an entity to present the total amounts of current liabilities on a classified balance sheet. An entity has considerable discretion concerning how much disaggregation to present on the face of the statement or in the notes. Regulation S-X contains requirements for disaggregating different types of obligations and classification as current or noncurrent. As previously noted, Regulation S-X requires specific disaggregation of balance sheet line items either on the face of the relevant financial statements or in the notes.

2.296 Several FASB ASC topics discuss asset retirement costs and obligations: FASB ASC 360, 410-20, and 450. With respect to asset retirement obligations, see disclosure guidance within FASB ASC 410-20-50 and SEC *Codification of Staff Accounting Bulletins* topic 5(Y), "Accounting and Disclosures Related to Loss Contingencies." For example, an entity should disclose whether the liability has been measured at present value and, if so, it should disclose information about the present value technique used, in accordance with FASB ASC 820-10-50.

2.297 When the asset retirement obligation is a loss contingency, an entity should disclose the same information that it would disclose for all loss contingencies, including the nature of the contingency, the amount of any accruals, and the reasons that an accrual has not been made, as described in FASB ASC 450-20-50. As noted previously, FASB ASC 450-30-50-1 does not prohibit disclosure of a contingency that might result in a gain, but it does state that an entity should exercise caution so as not to be misleading about the likelihood of realization.

2.298 Like IFRSs, FASB ASC 420-10-50-1 requires an entity to disclose a description of exit and disposal activities. However, although it is likely that a restructuring would constitute a major class of provision, unlike FASB ASC, IFRSs do not specifically require separate reconciliations of the major costs in a restructuring. FASB ASC 420-10-50-1 also requires disclosure of information about these activities by reportable operating segment and the line item(s) on the income statement that contains these costs.

Author's Note

See also the discussion in paragraph 2.346 of the requirement to disclose a reconciliation of liabilities recognized for termination benefits that are a major part of exit and disposal activities.

Presentation and Disclosure Excerpts

Accident Future Costs, Livestock Procurement, Employee Entitlements, Restructuring

2.299

Silver Fern Farms Limited (Sep 2011)

CONSOLIDATED BALANCE SHEETS (in part)

		Parent		Consolidated	
NZD in Thousands ($000)	Notes	As at 30 Sept 11	As at 30 Sept 10	As at 30 Sept 11	As at 30 Sept 10
Liabilities—Current liabilities					
Bank overdraft	24, 19	7,283	860	9,807	2,847
Derivative financial instruments	26	5,956	705	5,956	705
Trade and other payables	18	118,786	95,145	102,556	77,263
Provisions	21	18,113	13,722	18,402	13,820
Advances from subsidiaries		8,543	8,543	—	—
Tax provision	9	—	—	494	26
Interest bearing loans and borrowings	19	111,057	397	111,057	397
Bonds payable	20	—	75,052	—	75,052
Total current liabilities		269,738	194,424	248,272	170,110
Liabilities—Non-current Liabilities					
Provisions	21	9,683	8,633	9,683	8,633
Interest bearing loans and borrowings	19	550	41,832	550	41,832
Bonds payable	20	—	—	—	—
Deferred income tax	9	20,724	11,265	21,225	11,895
Total non-current liabilities excluding members' shares		30,957	61,730	31,458	62,360
Total liabilities excluding members' shares		300,695	256,154	279,730	232,470
Net assets excluding members' shares		406,838	378,004	394,767	367,771
Convertible redeemable preference shares	19, 22	1,584	1,595	1,584	1,595
Supplier investment shares	22	7,155	7,203	7,155	7,203
Members' ordinary shares	22	19,601	20,360	19,601	20,360
Total Members' Shares		28,340	29,158	28,340	29,158
Net assets		378,498	348,846	366,427	338,613

NOTES TO THE CONSOLIDATED FINANCIAL STATEMENTS (in part)

1 Corporate Information

The financial statements of Silver Fern Farms Limited for the 12 months ended 30 September 2011 were authorised for issue in accordance with a resolution of the directors on 18 November 2011.

Silver Fern Farms Limited (the Parent) is registered under the Companies Act 1993 and the Co-operative Companies Act 1996. Silver Fern Farms Limited is an issuer for the purposes of the Financial Reporting Act 1993.

On 29 April 2010, Silver Fern Farms Limited announced a change of balance date to 30 September. The later 30 September balance date better reflects Silver Fern Farm Limited's financial performance from the sales of meat and associated products supplied in the season. Financial statements for the Parent and Group have been prepared for the 12 months ended 30 September 2011. The comparative period is for the 13 months ended 30 September 2010 and therefore the comparative amounts shown in the statement of comprehensive income, statement of changes in equity, balance sheet, the cash fow statement and related notes may not be directly comparable.

The nature of the operations and principal activities of the Group are described in note 4.

2 Summary of Significant Accounting Policies (in part)

A Basis of Preparation

The financial statements have been prepared in accordance with generally accepted accounting practice in New Zealand (NZ GAAP) and the requirements of the Companies Act 1993 and the Financial Reporting Act 1993.

The financial statements have also been prepared on a historical cost basis, except for operational land and buildings which are measured at fair value. Derivative financial instruments and available for sale financial assets have been measured at fair value.

The financial statements are presented in New Zealand dollars and all values are rounded to the nearest thousand dollars ($'000).

B Statement of Compliance

The financial statements have been prepared in accordance with NZ GAAP. They comply with New Zealand equivalents to International Financial Reporting Standards (NZ IFRS) and other applicable Financial Reporting Standards, as appropriate for proft-oriented entities. These financial statements comply with International Financial Reporting Standards (IFRS).

U Provisions and Employee Leave Benefits

Provisions are recognised when the Group has a present obligation (legal or constructive) as a result of a past event, it is probable that an outflow of resources embodying economic benefits will be required to settle the obligation and a reliable estimate can be made of the amount of the obligation.

Wages, Salaries, Annual Leave and Sick Leave

Liabilities for wages and salaries, annual leave and accumulating sick leave expected to be settled within 12 months of the reporting date are recognised in respect of employee's services up to the reporting date. They are measured at the amounts expected to be paid when liabilities are settled. Liabilities for non-accumulating sick leave are recognised when the leave is taken and are measured at the rates paid or payable.

Long Service Leave

The liability for long service leave is recognised and measured in the balance sheet at the present value of expected future payments to be made in respect of services provided by employees up to the reporting date. Consideration is given to the expected future wage and salary levels, experience of employee departures, and periods of service.

3 Significant Accounting Judgements, Estimates and Assumptions (in part)

In applying the Group's accounting policies, management continually evaluates judgements, estimates and assumptions based on experience and other factors, including expectations of future events that may have an impact on the Group. All judgements, estimates and assumptions made are believed to be reasonable based on the most current set of circumstances available to management. Actual results may differ from the judgements, estimates and assumptions. Significant judgements, estimates and assumptions made by management in the preparation of these financial statements are outlined below:

ii. Significant Accounting Estimates and Assumptions

Long Service Leave Provision

As discussed in note 2(u), the liability for the long service leave is recognised and measured at the present value of the estimated future cash flows to be made in respect of all ^employees at balance date. In determining the present value of the liability, attrition rates and pay increases through promotion and inflation have been taken into account.

ACC Provision

The liability for the future costs of ACC claims outstanding is recognised and measured at the present value of the estimated future cash flows to be made in respect of all claims outstanding at balance date. In determining the present value of the liability, historical accident rates and average costs per accident and cost inflation assumptions have been taken into account.

21 Provisions

Parent NZD in Thousands ($000)	Accident Future Costs	Livestock Procurement Provision	Employee Entitlements	Restructuring	Total
At 1 October 2010	3,529	294	18,271	261	22,355
Arising during the year	533	1,916	26,080	1,695	30,224
Utilised	(450)	(294)	(23,746)	(261)	(24,751)
Excess provision released	—	—	(32)	—	(32)
At 30 September 2011	3,612	1,916	20,573	1,695	27,796
Current 2011	2,156	1,916	12,346	1,695	18,113
Non-Current 2011	1,456	—	8,227	—	9,683
	3,612	1,916	20,573	1,695	27,796
Current 2010	2,329	294	10,838	261	13,722
Non-Current 2010	1,200	—	7,433	—	8,633
	3,529	294	18,271	261	22,355

Consolidated NZD in Thousands ($000)	Accident Future Costs	Livestock Procurement Provision	Employee Entitlements	Restructuring	Total
At 1 October 2010	3,529	294	18,369	261	22,453
Arising during the year	533	1,916	26,269	1,696	30,414
Utilised	(450)	(294)	(23,745)	(261)	(24,750)
Excess provision released	—	—	(32)	—	(32)
At 30 September 2011	3,612	1,916	20,861	1,696	28,085
Current 2011	2,156	1,916	12,634	1,696	18,402
Non-Current 2011	1,456	—	8,227	—	9,683
	3,612	1,916	20,861	1,696	28,085
Current 2010	2,329	294	10,936	261	13,820
Non-Current 2010	1,200	—	7,433	—	8,633
	3,529	294	18,369	261	22,453

a Accident Future Cost Provision

The group participates in the ACC Partnership Programme, Full Self Cover Plan. The provision for the future cost of accidents related to the estimated future cost of accidents incurred by employees that the Group will have to bear. These payments are ongoing throughout the lifetime of the rehabilitation period.

ACC Partnership Programme: Overview

Responsibilities and Accountabilities

The General Manager Human Resources is responsible for the development and ongoing review of injury management policy and procedures in consultation with relevant parties. This includes the establishment and monitoring of the partnership programme contract with ACC and notification to them of changes in the Silver Fern Farms Limited injury management operations or personnel.

Risks are managed by ensuring the manager has a working knowledge of the relevant legislation and information and communication requirements. Rehabilitation is managed as soon as practicable through liaising with treatment providers, claims administrators and the claimant.

Assumptions and Methodology Used

The chain ladder is used to project the ultimate number of claims expected from each accident period using historic cumulative ratios of claims. An approach called the Payments Per Claim Incurred (PPCI) Method has been used to determine suitable expected claim payment patterns for the average claim.

In the development of Claim Payment Patterns and projecting claim payment liabilities the following economic assumptions have been made:
- Pre valuation date claim inflation has been taken as 50% (2010: 50%) of movements in the Consumer Price Index (CPI) and 50% (2010: 50%) of the movements in the Average Weekly Earnings (AWE) Index. This assumes that increases in claim costs are equally affected by general price increases and by wage increases.
- Post valuation date claim inflation has been taken as 4% (2010: 4%) pa. Most claims are of a short to medium term duration and we are currently in an environment where inflation and wage increases are likely to run above the norm in the short to medium term.
- The Discount Rate used is 3.8% (2010: 4.5%) pa. This is approximately the average gross yield on Government Bonds of short to medium term duration consistent with the duration of the liabilities.
- The actuarial assessment of the provision for future claims was prepared by Marcelo Lardies (BSc Hons) of AON New Zealand Limited, effective 30 September 2011. The assessment is dated 19 September 2011 (2010: 14 September 2010).

b Employee Entitlements

Included in employee entitlements is wages and salaries payable, annual leave due and long service leave payable. Wages, salaries and annual leave are measured at the amounts expected to be paid when liabilities are settled. Long service leave is recognised at the present value of expected future payments to be made in respect of services provided by employees up to the reporting date. These provisions will reduce as the entitlements fall due.

An independent actuarial valuation was undertaken as at 30 September 2011 to estimate the present value of long service leave.

The present value of the long service leave obligations depends on a number of factors that are determined on an actuarial basis using a number of assumptions. Two key assumptions used in calculating the liability include the discount rate and the salary inflation factor. Any changes in these assumptions will impact on the carrying amount of the liability.

The weighted average yields on NZ Government stock with terms of maturity that match closely to the estimated future cash outflows have been used in determining the discount rate. The discount rates applied to the anticipated annual future cashflows range from 3.0% to 5.4% (2010: 3.6% to 6.0%).

The historical salary and wage growth patterns have been used in determining the salary and wage inflation factor after obtaining advice from an independent actuary. The growth rates applied to salary and wages costs range from 1.5% to 3.0% (2010: 1.5% to 3.0%).

The actuarial assessment of the provision for the long service leave liability was prepared by Marcelo Lardies (BSc Hons) of AON New Zealand Limited, effective 30 September 2011. The assessment is dated 27 October 2011.

c Other Provisions

The livestock procurement provision relates to incentive payments made in addition to schedule payments for certain classes of livestock. Payments are made on a six monthly basis and annual basis. The restructuring provision was established for obligations at year end relating to the reconfiguration of operations. The residual in the restructuring provision will be utilised during the 2011/2012 financial year.

Onerous Contract, Onerous Lease, Returns and Warranty, Litigation, Restructuring

2.300

CSR plc (Dec 2011)

CONSOLIDATED BALANCE SHEET (in part)

	Notes	30 December 2011 $'000	31 December 2010 $'000
Current liabilities			
Trade and other payables	25	180,621	125,223
Current tax liabilities		9,613	2,852
Obligations under finance leases	24	16	51
Derivative financial instruments	22	1,585	899
Provisions	27	29,495	5,602
		221,330	134,627
Net current assets		312,615	505,312
Non-current liabilities			
Trade and other payables	25	49,590	45,694
Contingent consideration	26	—	1,567
Long-term provisions	27	1,926	1,483
Obligations under finance leases	24	143	195
Defined benefit pension scheme deficit	35	117	—
		51,776	48,939
Total liabilities		273,106	183,566
Net assets		877,907	774,564

NOTES TO THE CONSOLIDATED FINANCIAL STATEMENTS (in part)

1. General Information

CSR plc is a company incorporated in the United Kingdom under the Companies Act 2006. The address of the registered office is Churchill House, Cambridge Business Park, Cowley Road, Cambridge, CB4 0WZ, United Kingdom. CSR is a leading provider of multifunction connectivity, audio, video and imaging and location platforms.

These financial statements are presented in US dollars because that is the currency of the primary economic environment in which the Group operates. Foreign operations are included in accordance with the policies set out in note 3.

Going Concern

The financial statements have been prepared on the going concern basis. The directors have considered future cash forecasts and revenue projections, based on prudent market data, in their consideration of going concern. The issues surrounding going concern are discussed regularly by the Board and were evaluated as part of the Group's budget for the next financial year and the Group's longer term plans.

Note 36 includes the Group's objectives, policies and processes for managing its capital; its financial risk management objectives; details of the financial instruments and hedging activities; and its exposure to credit risk. Management is currently of the opinion that the Group has adequate financial resources and a robust policy towards treasury risk and cash flow management. The Group has $277.8 million of cash and cash equivalents, including treasury deposits and investments, as at 30 December 2011 and no debt liabilities. Further, the Group's portfolio of investments is not exposed to material credit risk as a consequence of holdings of European sovereign debt.

In 2011, management prepared a working capital report for the Group in anticipation of the acquisition of Zoran.

The directors believe that the Group is securely placed to manage its business risks successfully despite the current uncertain economic outlook and challenging macro economic conditions.

After considering the above factors, the directors have a reasonable expectation that the Company and the Group have adequate resources to continue in operational existence for the foreseeable future. Accordingly, they continue to adopt the going concern basis in preparing the financial statements.

3. Accounting Policies (in part)

Basis of Accounting

The financial statements have been prepared in accordance with International Financial Reporting Standards (IFRSs) as issued by the International Accounting Standards Board (IASB) and as adopted by the European Union (EU).

The financial statements have been prepared on the historical cost basis, except for the revaluation of financial instruments. The principal accounting policies adopted are set out below. The financial statements cover the 52 week period from 1 January 2011 to 30 December 2011; the comparatives are presented for the 52 week period from 2 January 2010 to 31 December 2010 and income statement comparatives for the 52 week period from 3 January 2009 to 1 January 2010. The financial statements are reported on a 52 or 53 week basis to be consistent with the Group's internal reporting.

Provisions

Provisions are recognised when the Group has a present obligation (legal or constructive) as a result of a past event, it is probable that the Group will be required to settle that obligation and a reliable estimate can be made of the amount of the obligation.

Provisions for warranty and returns costs are recognised at the date of sale of the relevant products, at the directors' best estimate of the expenditure required to settle the Group's liability.

Provision is made for onerous contracts at the fair value of the minimum unavoidable payments, net of any amounts recoverable. Where amounts are known and timings certain, onerous amounts are accrued instead.

A restructuring provision is recognised when the Group has developed a detailed formal plan for the restructuring and has raised a valid expectation in those affected that it will carry out the restructuring by starting to implement the plan or announcing its main features to those affected by it. The measurement of a restructuring provision includes only the direct expenditures arising from the restructuring, which are those amounts that are both necessarily entailed by the restructuring and not associated with the ongoing activities of the entity.

12. Finance Costs

	52 Weeks Ended 30 December 2011 $'000	52 Weeks Ended 31 December 2010 $'000	52 Weeks Ended 1 January 2010 $'000
Interest expense and similar charges	418	493	795
Unwinding of discount on contingent consideration	53	15	—
Unwinding of discount on onerous lease provision	252	210	459
Unwinding of discount on litigation accrual	2,525	—	—
Unwinding of discount on intangible asset accrual	438	—	—
Unwinding of discount on defined benefit pension deficit	274	—	—
Loss on purchase of treasury shares	338	—	—
	4,298	718	1,254

27. Provisions

	Onerous Contract Provision $'000	Onerous Lease Provision $'000	Returns and Warranty Provision $'000	Litigation Provision $'000	Restructuring Provision $'000	Total $'000
At 1 January 2010	2,990	4,529	3,319	—	—	10,838
Additional provision in the period	—	—	3,139	—	—	3,139
Unwinding of discount	—	210	—	—	—	210
Utilised in period	(2,990)	(1,649)	(2,463)	—	—	(7,102)
At 31 December 2010	—	3,090	3,995	—	—	7,085
Additional provision in the period	—	72	3,219	—	21,683	24,974
Unwinding of discount	—	252	—	—	—	252
On acquisition of subsidiary	—	1,337	—	11,986	10,951	24,274
Utilised in period	—	(1,533)	(2,674)	(686)	(20,271)	(25,164)
At 30 December 2011	—	3,218	4,540	11,300	12,363	31,421

	30 December 2011 $'000	31 December 2010 $'000
Amounts included within current liabilities	29,495	5,602
Amounts included within non-current liabilities	1,926	1,483
	31,421	7,085

Onerous Lease Provision

The Group has provided for the discounted anticipated costs of satisfying the terms of any onerous leases, less any anticipated income from subletting the buildings. It is anticipated that the provision will be used over the remaining lease terms (5 years). There has been no change in the discount rate applied in the period (2010: no change). The onerous lease acquired with Zoran has been calculated with reference to the interest rate on 10 year Eurobonds and accordingly a discount rate of 1.83% has been applied. It is anticipated that the provision over the acquired onerous lease will be used over the remaining lease term of 10 years.

Returns and Warranty Provision

The Group provides for the anticipated costs associated with contractual liabilities under standard warranty terms. It is anticipated that the provision will be utilised within one year (see note 3).

Litigation Provision

Through the acquisition of Zoran, the group assumed the obligation to meet any liabilities that may arise as a consequence of continuing SEC investigations of former executives of Microtunes Inc., a subsidiary undertaking. The investigations were still ongoing at the balance sheet date and it is uncertain when the provision will be utilised.

Restructuring Provision

A restructuring programme was implemented following the acquisition of Zoran Corporation. In December 2011, a decision was taken to discontinue investment in the digital television and silicon tuners business lines which had been acquired with Zoran and a further restructuring programme commenced.

As at 30 December 2011, approximately 30% of the 800 affected employees had left the Group's employment with a further 20% leaving the day after the year end. The remainder of the affected employees are expected to leave the group during 2012 (see note 33).

33. Integration and Restructuring

In Q3 2011, a restructuring programme was implemented following the acquisition of Zoran Corporation. Headcount and other reductions were implemented with the aim of achieving cost synergies and rightsizing savings, lowering the cost base of the enlarged Group through all functions. This was planned prior to the acquisition of Zoran with input from management teams in CSR and Zoran.

In December 2011, a decision was taken to discontinue investment in the digital television and silicon tuners business lines which had been acquired with Zoran. This is an additional restructuring programme to that commenced in Q3 2011. This decision was made so that the Group can concentrate its resources on areas of the business in which it has market leadership positions and the ability to deliver differentiated platforms and products.

These restructuring programmes are expected to result in around 800 employees leaving the group across all functions and locations, approximately 160 people left the group the day after the end of the reporting period and 250 left during 2011.

A charge of $33.7 million has been recorded in relation to these integration and restructuring programmes. The main components of this charge were $21.7 million of severance costs, $9.6 million of consultancy and legal costs and $1.9 million of fixed asset impairments. There was a provision of $11.0 million in the Zoran opening balance sheet related to change of control provisions and Zoran's restructuring programmes which they had operated prior to the acquisition. At 30 December 2011 a provision of $12.4 million in respect of these severance payments was held.

In 2010, a decision was taken to close the NordNav Technologies AB office in Stockholm, Sweden. This led to approximately 10 employees leaving the Group. A charge of $1.1 million was recorded in relation to the closure with the main component being $0.6 million of severance costs. At 31 December 2010, $1.1 million of accruals in respect of these payments was held. The remaining payments were made during the course of 2011.

A restructuring programme was implemented at the end of Q2 2009, following the acquisition of SiRF Technology Holdings Inc. This led to approximately 100 employees leaving the Group. The headcount reductions were implemented following careful consideration of the long-term strategic objectives and shorter term targets for 2009 and 2010. This planning commenced prior to the acquisition date to ensure that once the Group was able to operate as a single business, the Group could integrate and restructure as quickly as possible and ensure that the core projects of the enlarged Group were adequately resourced.

The main components of the $12.2 million charge were onerous lease charges of $2.2 million, severance costs of $4.3 million, consultancy and legal costs of $4.5 million and $1.2 million of other integration related costs. Approximately 100 employees left the Group as part of the 2009 combined integration and restructuring programme spread through all functions mostly, in the UK and US. There were no further payments or charges outstanding as a result of this restructuring programme as at 30 December 2011.

36. Financial Instruments (in part)

Financial Risk Management

The Group has exposure to the following risks from its use of financial instruments:
- Credit risk
- Market risk
- Liquidity risk

This note presents information about the Group's exposure to each of the above risks, the Group's objectives, policies and processes for measuring and managing risk, and the Group's management of capital. Further quantitative disclosures are included throughout these consolidated financial statements.

Liquidity Risk (in part)

Liquidity Risk Management (in part)

The Group manages liquidity risk by maintaining adequate cash reserves and by continuously monitoring forecast and actual cash flows and matching the maturity of financial assets and liabilities. The Group has no significant borrowings from third parties and therefore liquidity risk is not considered a significant risk at this time. The table below details the Group's remaining contractual maturity for its non-derivative financial liabilities with agreed repayment periods. The tables have been prepared based on undiscounted cash flows of financial liabilities based on the earliest date on which the Group can be required to pay.

30 December 2011	Weighted Average Effective Interest Rate %	Less Than One Month $'000	1–2 Months $'000	2–3 Months $'000	3–6 Months $'000	More Than 6 Months $'000	Total $'000
Obligations under finance leases	—	—	—	—	—	159	159
Litigation accrual (undiscounted)	—	3,125	—	—	3,125	46,875	53,125
Other payables	—	2,080	—	2,319	775	16,969	22,143
Onerous lease provision (undiscounted)	—	10	10	10	29	3,385	3,444
		5,215	10	2,329	3,929	67,388	78,871

Environmental and Litigation Provisions

2.301

Korea Electric Power Corporation (Dec 2011)

Author's Note

Korea Electric Power Corporation implemented IFRSs effective December 31, 2011, with a date of transition of January 1, 2010. The excerpt that follows reflects the initial application of IAS 1 and IAS 37.

CONSOLIDATED STATEMENTS OF FINANCIAL POSITION (in part)

(KRW in Millions)	Notes	Dec. 31, 2011	Dec. 31, 2010	Jan. 1, 2010
Liabilities				
Current liabilities:				
Accounts and other payables, net	6, 23, 25, 39, 44, 46	6,576,158	4,571,145	4,166,228
Short-term borrowings	6, 24, 39, 44	1,173,568	457,931	592,875
Current financial liabilities, net	6, 12, 24, 39, 44, 46	5,852,342	6,324,952	5,631,972
Income tax payables	40	505,154	257,563	83,487
Current non-financial liabilities	28, 29	3,541,562	2,383,303	1,828,701
Current provisions	27, 44	92,383	77,279	65,758
		17,741,167	14,072,173	12,369,021
Non-current liabilities:				
Non-current accounts and other payables, net	6, 23, 25, 39, 44, 46	4,178,137	5,280,924	5,245,490
Non-current financial liabilities, net	6, 12, 24, 39, 44, 46	39,403,578	33,052,466	28,034,241
Non-current non-financial liabilities	28, 29	5,611,010	5,221,856	5,251,182
Employee benefits obligations, net	26, 44	1,942,994	1,964,155	1,985,131
Deferred tax liabilities, net	40	6,786,779	6,307,322	6,463,994
Non-current provisions	27, 44	7,000,235	6,342,361	5,981,636
		64,922,733	58,169,084	52,961,674
Total liabilities	5	82,663,900	72,241,257	65,330,695

NOTES TO THE CONSOLIDATED FINANCIAL STATEMENTS (in part)

1. Generals:

Korea Electric Power Corporation ("KEPCO") was incorporated on January 1, 1982 in accordance with the Korea Electric Power Corporation Act (the "KEPCO Act") to engage in the generation, transmission and distribution of electricity and development of electric power resources in the Republic of Korea. The Company's stock was listed on the Korea Stock Exchange on August 10, 1989 and the Company listed its Depository Receipts (DR) on the New York Stock Exchange on October 27, 1994.

As of December 31, 2011, the Government of the Republic of Korea (Government), Korea Finance Corporation ("KoFC") which is wholly owned by the Government, and foreign investors held 21.17%, 29.94%, and 23.38%, respectively, of the Company's shares.

On January 21, 1999, in accordance with the restructuring plan by the Ministry of Knowledge Economy (the "MKE") (the "Restructuring Plan"), on April 2, 2001 KEPCO spun off its power generation divisions, resulting in the establishment of six power generation subsidiaries.

In addition, the Government established a Tripartite Commission consisting of representatives of the Government, leading businesses and labor unions in Korea to deliberate on ways to introduce competition in electricity distribution, such as by forming and privatizing new distribution subsidiaries. Meanwhile, on June 30, 2004, the privatization initiatives were discontinued, instead independent business divisions for distribution within the Company were created to improve operational efficiency through internal competition. These business divisions have separate management structures, financial accounting systems and performance evaluation systems, but with a common focus on maximizing profitability.

2. Significant Accounting Policies: (in part)

(1) Basis of Preparation

The Company maintains its official accounting records in Republic of Korean won ("Won") and prepares consolidated financial statements in conformity with International Financial Reporting Standards ("IFRS") as issued by International Accounting Standard Board ("IASB"). The Company has adopted IFRS as issued by IASB for the annual period beginning on January 1, 2011. In accordance with IFRS 1 First-time adoption of IFRS, the Company's transition date to IFRS is

January 1, 2010. Refer to Note 4, for transition adjustments to IFRS.

The significant accounting policies under IFRS followed by the Company in the preparation of its consolidated financial statements are summarized below. Unless stated otherwise, these accounting policies have been applied consistently to the financial statements for the current period and accompanying comparative period.

The consolidated financial statements have been prepared on the historical cost basis except for certain non-current assets and financial instruments that are measured at revalued amounts or fair values, as explained in the accounting policies below. Historical cost is based on the fair value of the consideration given in exchange for assets.

(19) Provisions

Provisions are recognized when the Company has a present obligation (legal or constructive) as a result of a past event, it is probable that the Company will be required to settle the obligation, and a reliable estimate can be made of the amount of the obligation.

The amount recognized as a provision is the best estimate of the consideration required to settle the present obligation at the end of the reporting period, taking into account the risks and uncertainties surrounding the obligation. When a provision is measured using the cash flows estimated to settle the present obligation, its carrying amount is the present value of those cash flows (where the effect of the time value of money is material).

When some or all of the economic benefits required to settle a provision are expected to be recovered from a third party, a receivable is recognized as an asset if it is virtually certain that reimbursement will be received and the amount of the receivable can be measured reliably.

Increase in provisions due to passage of time is recognized as finance expense during the period. At the end of each reporting period, the remaining provision balance is reviewed and assessed to determine if the current best estimate is being recognized. If the existence of an obligation to transfer economic benefit is no longer probable, the related provision is reversed during the period.

Provisions for estimated future costs are discounted to present value, based on a discount rate which reflects the current market assessment of the time value of money, risks specific to the liability and pre-tax.

(a) Provision for Decommissioning Costs

The Company records the fair value of estimated decommissioning costs as a liability in the period in which we incur a legal obligation associated with retirement of long-lived assets that result from acquisition, construction, development and/or normal use of the assets. The Company also recognizes a corresponding asset that is depreciated over the life of the asset. Accretion expense consists of period-to-period changes in the liability for decommissioning costs resulting from the passage of time and revisions to either the timing or the amount of the original estimate of undiscounted cash flows. Depreciation and accretion expenses are included in cost of sales of goods in the accompanying consolidated statements of comprehensive income.

Under the Korean Electricity Business Act (EBA) Article 94, the Company is required to record a liability for the dis-

mantling (demolition) of nuclear power plants and disposal of spent fuel and low & intermediate radioactive wastes.

(b) Provision for Polychlorinated Biphenyls ("PCB")

Under the regulation of Persistent Organic Pollutants Management Act, enacted in 2007, the Company is required to remove polychlorinated biphenyls (PCBs), a toxin, from the insulating oil of its transformers by 2025. As a result of the enactments, the Company is required to inspect the PCBs contents of transformers and dispose of PCBs in excess of safety standards under the legally settled procedures. The Company's estimates and assumptions used to determine fair value can be affected by many factors, such as the estimated costs of inspection and disposal, inflation rate, discount rate, regulations and the general economy.

(c) Provisions for Power Plant Regional Support Program

In accordance with regulations on nuclear and hydro-electric power plants' social responsibility to support the surrounding communities of the power plants sites; KHNP, the Company's nuclear generation subsidiary, accrues 0.25won per KWH of KHNP's generation volume from two periods prior, as a provision for power plant regional support program during the year. Power plant regional support programs consist of scholarship programs to local students, local economy support programs, local culture support programs, environment development programs, and local welfare programs.

(21) Financial Liabilities and Equity Instruments Issued by the Company (in part)

(e) Financial Guarantee Contract Liabilities

Financial guarantee contract liabilities are initially measured at their fair values and, if not designated as at FVTPL, are subsequently measured at the higher of: (a) the amount of the obligation under the contract, as determined in accordance with IAS 37 *Provisions, Contingent Liabilities and Contingent Assets*; or (b) the amount initially recognized less, cumulative amortization recognized in accordance with the IAS 18 *Revenue*.

27. Provisions:

Litigation

The Company is involved in legal proceedings regarding matters arising in the ordinary course of business. Related to these matters, as of December 31, 2011, the Company was engaged in 429 lawsuits as a defendant and 103 lawsuits as a plaintiff. The total amount claimed against the Company was (Won) 138,498 million and the total amount claimed by the Company was (Won) 21,403 million as of December 31, 2011. As of December 31, 2011, the Company had an accrual for loss contingencies of (Won) 44,409 million. The Company records liabilities for estimated loss contingencies when the Company assesses that a loss is probable and the amount of the loss can be reasonably estimated. The determination for a loss contingency is based on management judgment and estimates with respect to the likely outcome of the matter, including the analysis of different scenarios. Liabilities are recorded or adjusted when events or circumstances cause these judgments or estimates to change. In assessing whether a loss is a reasonable possibility, the Company may consider the following factors: the nature of the litigation, claim or assessment, available information, opinions or views of legal counsel and other advisors, and the experience gained from similar cases. The Company provides disclosures for material contingencies when there is a reasonable possibility that a loss or an additional loss may be incurred.

As new developments occur or more information becomes available, our assumptions and estimates of these liabilities may change. Revisions to contingent liabilities are generally reflected in income when new or different facts or information become known or circumstances change that affect previous assumptions with respect to the likelihood or amount of loss. If changes in these or other assumptions or the anticipated outcomes the Company uses to estimate contingencies cause a loss to become more likely, it could materially affect future results of operations for any particular quarterly or annual period.

Actual amounts realized upon settlement of contingencies may be different than amounts recorded and disclosed and could have a significant impact on the liabilities and expenses recorded on the consolidated financial statements.

Provision for Decommissioning Cost

Under the Korean Electricity Business Act (EBA) Article 94, the Company is required to record a liability for the dismantling of nuclear power plants and disposal of spent fuel and low & intermediate radioactive wastes. In addition, under the Korean Atomic Energy Act (AEA), an entity which constructs and operates a nuclear power reactor and related facilities must obtain permission from the Ministry of Education, Science and Technology (the "MEST", formerly the Ministry of Science and Technology).

Accretion expense consists of period-to-period changes in the liability for decommissioning costs resulting from passage of time and changes in estimate related to either the timing or the amount of the initial estimate of undiscounted cash flows. This cost is included in cost of electric power in the accompanying statements of operations.

Provisions of Decontanmination of Transfomer—PCBs

Under the regulation of Persistent Organic Pollutants Management Act, enacted in 2007, the Company is required to remove polychlorinated biphenyls (PCBs), a toxin, from the insulating oil of its transformers by 2025. As a result of the enactments, the Company is required to inspect the PCBs contents of transformers and dispose of PCBs in excess of safety standards under the legally settled procedures. The Company's estimates and assumptions used to determine fair value can be affected by many factors, such as the estimated costs of inspection and disposal, inflation rate, discount rate, regulations and the general economy.

(1) Provisions as of December 31, 2011, December 31, 2010 and January 1, 2010 are as follows (KRW in millions):

	Dec. 31, 2011		Dec. 31, 2010		Jan. 1, 2010	
	Current	Non-current	Current	Non-current	Current	Non-current
Litigation						
Litigation provision	(Won) —	(Won) 44,409	(Won) —	(Won) 79,116	(Won) —	(Won) 45,317
Decommissioning cost						
Nuclear plants	—	5,061,265	—	4,694,607	—	4,498,716
Spent fuel	—	869,549	—	834,247	—	743,103
Waste	—	796,521	—	447,473	—	453,404
PCBs	—	215,082	—	278,011	—	231,470
Other recovery provisions	—	—	—	—	—	—
Others						
Power plant regional support program	91,987	—	76,955	—	65,360	—
Provision for tax	—	2,013	—	8,219	—	8,119
Provision for financial guarantee	—	11,300	—	—	—	—
Others	396	96	324	688	398	1,507
	(Won) 92,383	(Won) 7,000,235	(Won) 77,279	(Won) 6,342,361	(Won) 65,758	(Won) 5,981,636

(2) Changes in provisions for the years ended December 31, 2011 and 2010 are as follows (KRW in millions):

	2011						
	Jan. 1, 2011	Liabilities Incurred	Accretion Expense	Payment	Reversal	Other	Dec. 31, 2011
Litigation							
Litigation provision	(Won) 79,116	(Won) 40,144	(Won) 628	(Won) (7,373)	(Won) (39,124)	(Won) (28,982)	(Won) 44,409
Decommissioning cost							
Nuclear plants	4,694,607	155,718	210,940	—	—	—	5,061,265
Spent fuel	834,247	197,596	122,004	(284,298)	—	—	869,549

(continued)

2011

	Jan. 1, 2011	Liabilities Incurred	Accretion Expense	Payment	Reversal	Other	Dec. 31, 2011
Waste[*1]	447,473	—	279,330	(13,026)	—	82,744	796,521
PCBs	278,011	22,153	16,351	(16,276)	(85,157)	—	215,082
Others							
Power plant regional support program	76,955	—	39,437	(42,299)	—	17,895	91,987
Provision for tax	8,219	205	—	—	(6,411)	—	2,013
Provision for financial guarantee	—	11,300	—	—	—	—	11,300
Others	1,012	211	—	(70)	(53)	(609)	492
	(Won) 6,419,640	(Won) 427,327	(Won) 668,690	(Won) (363,342)	(Won) (130,746)	(Won) 71,049	(Won) 7,092,618

[*1] For the year ended December 31, 2011, the Company recorded a change in estimate related to the KHNP's, a subsidiary, asset retirement obligation related to its low and intermediate radioactive waste disposal.

2010

	Jan. 1, 2010	Liabilities Incurred	Accretion Expense	Payment	Reversal	Other	Dec. 31, 2010
Litigation							
Litigation provision	(Won) 45,317	(Won) 52,594	(Won) 1,271	(Won) (5,307)	(Won) (14,759)	(Won) —	(Won) 79,116
Decommissioning cost							
Nuclear plants	4,498,716	—	196,164	(273)	—	—	4,694,607
Spent fuel	743,103	247,248	95,568	(251,671)	—	—	834,248
Waste	453,404	—	17,361	(23,294)	—	—	447,472
PCBs	231,470	69,969	15,022	(38,450)	—	—	278,011
Others							
Power plant regional support program	65,360	—	38,536	(45,443)	—	18,502	76,955
Provision for tax	8,119	101	—	—	—	—	8,220
Provision for financial guarantee	—	—	—	—	—	—	—
Others	1,905	105	616	(66)	(1,443)	(105)	1,012
	(Won) 6,047,394	(Won) 370,017	(Won) 364,538	(Won) (364,504)	(Won) (16,202)	(Won) 18,397	(Won) 6,419,640

36. Other Operating Income and Expense

(1) Other operating income for the years ended December 31, 2011 and 2010 are as follows (KRW in millions):

	2011	2010
Reversal of other provisions	(Won) 110	(Won) 14,754
Reversal of allowance for doubtful accounts	460	6,952
Gains on assets contributed	4,392	1,390
Gains on liabilities exempted	4,578	5,679
Compensation and reparations revenue	30,350	12,501
Electricity infrastructure development fund	48,154	41,189
Revenue from research contracts	6,124	542
Revenue related to transfer of assets from customers	280,458	257,505
Rental income	180,563	168,386
Others	43,114	28,017
	(Won) 598,303	(Won) 536,915

(2) Other operating expense for the years ended December 31, 2011, December 31, 2010 and January 1, 2010 are as follows (KRW in millions):

	2011	2010
Compensation and reparations expense	(Won) 2,000	(Won) —
Transfer to other provisions	238	22,004
Depreciation expenses on investment properties	927	1,129
Depreciation expenses on assets not in use	6,619	6,723
Other bad debt expense	867	471
Donations	100,352	30,874
Others	36,592	8,586
	(Won) 147,595	(Won) 69,787

Disclosure—Contingent Asset and Contingent Liabilities

2.302

Empresas ICA S.A. de C.V.

Author's Note

Empresas ICA S.A. de C.V. implemented IFRSs effective December 31, 2011, with a date of transition of January 1, 2010. The excerpt that follows reflects the initial application of IAS 1 and IAS 37.

NOTES TO THE CONSOLIDATED FINANCIAL STATEMENTS (in part)

3. Significant Events (in part)

Sale of the Service Provision Project ("PPS") of Irapuato La Piedad y Querétaro Irapuato to RCO—In September 2011, the Company executed a contract for the disposal of shares (the "Transaction") with Red de Carreteras de Occidente, S.A.P.I.B, de C.V. ("RCO") (affiliate company) to transfer to RCO all of the Company's shareholdings in its subsidiaries Concesionaria Irapuato La Piedad, S.A. de C.V. ("CONIPSA") and Concesionaria de Vías Irapuato Queretaro, S.A. de C.V. ("COVIQSA").

The total cost of the Transaction was Ps.2,150 million, liquidated through Ps.1,550 million in additional shares issued by RCO and Ps.250 million in cash, as well as an additional payment, in-kind with stock, for Ps.350 million (the "Additional Payment"), the latter subject to the satisfaction of certain conditions. As of December 31, 2011, the Additional Payment represents a contingent asset which is not recognized in the consolidated statement of financial position. As a result of this transaction, ICA increased its share capital in RCO to 18.73%. In the instance that the requirements for the Additional Payment are fulfilled, the shareholding of ICA in RCO will increase in proportion to such payment. The price of the Transaction was determined based on discounted cash flows. The main effects of the Transaction are described in Note 4.g.

4. Basis of Presentation and Consolidation (in part)

a. Statement of Compliance

The consolidated financial statements have been prepared in accordance with IFRS as issued by the IASB. Included in subsection (g) is the Company's policy regarding consolidation and included in Note 5 are the Company's accounting policies and valuation principles applied in preparing the consolidated financial statements.

The accompanying consolidated financial statements include all financial reporting standards and valuation requirements that affect the Company's consolidated financial information, as well as the alternatives allowed by IFRS.

b. Basis of Preparation

The consolidated financial statements have been prepared on the historical cost basis except for the revaluation of certain non-current assets and financial instruments at fair value. Historical cost is generally based on the fair value of the consideration given in exchange for assets. The consolidated financial statements are prepared in pesos, the legal currency of the United Mexican States and are presented in thousands, except where otherwise noted.

g. Principles of Consolidation

Financial statements of those companies in which ICA owns more than 50% of the capital stock or owns less than 50% of such capital stock but effectively controls such entity are consolidated within the financial statements. Control is achieved where the Company has the power to govern the financial and operating policies of an entity so as to obtain benefits from its activities.

Joint venture—The assets, liabilities, revenues, costs and expenses of companies or associations subject to contractually agreed joint control are included in the consolidated financial statements using proportionate consolidation in accordance with International Accounting Standard ("IAS") No. 31, Interests in Joint Ventures. The principal subsidiaries that are proportionately consolidated are: ICA Fluor Daniel, S. de R.L de C.V. and subsidiaries ("ICAFD"), Grupo Rodio Kronsa, S.A.; Suministro de Agua de Querétaro, S.A. de C.V., Constructora Nuevo Necaxa Tihuatlán, S.A. de C.V., Autovía Nuevo Necaxa Tihuatlán, S.A. de C.V. and Los Portales, S.A.

The financial statements of companies that are included in the consolidation are prepared as of December 31 of each year.

All intra-group transactions, balances, income and expenses are eliminated in full on consolidation. However, the balances and transactions related to construction contracts performed by companies in the construction segment for the benefit of the concessions segment were not eliminated in the consolidation process, as those construction revenues require recognition while the works are being executed. This principle, implemented by ICA, is established in the International Financial Reporting Interpretations Committee ("IFRIC") Interpretation No. 12, *Service Concession Arrangements*.

The non-controlling interests in equity of subsidiaries are presented separately as non-controlling interests in the consolidated statements of financial position, within the stockholders' equity section, and the consolidated statements of comprehensive income.

Note 39 includes the subsidiaries consolidated by ICA as well as information related thereto.

The results of subsidiaries acquired or divested during the year are included in the consolidated statement of comprehensive income from the acquisition date or the date of divestiture, as applicable.

24. Contingencies

a. *Esmeralda Resort Project*—In 2010, an arbitration proceeding was filed against ICA by the companies Proyecto Esmeralda Resort, S.A. de C.V. ("PER") and Marina Esmeralda Resort, S.A. de C.V. ("MER"), whereby these entities intended to rescind the two contracts for services provided by ICA for the construction of five buildings, the urbanization and electrification contract, and the contract for the construction of the Proyecto Esmeralda Resort marina in the State of Campeche. These claimants also requested a payment of Ps.268 million for alleged penalties, plus U.S.$439 million for alleged contractual, extra-contractual and non-pecuniary damages.

After several actions taken, as of December 31, 2010, the plaintiffs had dismissed the arbitration proceeding. Although there is a discrepancy with respect to the final representations of the claimants, the ultimate outcome of the proceeding is expected to occur in the near future.

As a result of the suspension of services under the aforementioned contracts, in July 2010, ICA legally convened a General Stockholders' Meeting with the stockholders of PER, MER and Campeche Golf, S.A. de C.V. ("GOLF") (together, the "companies"), which was held on August 18, 2010. During this meeting, the stockholders approved the revocation of the then current Board of Directors of the companies and in its place, appointed a Sole Administrator for the companies. This Sole Administrator recognized the validity of the amounts owed by the companies to ICA as a result of noncompliance under the aforementioned contracts. In August 2010, ICA filed a trust foreclosure procedure as provided in the trust agreement (such trust established as part of the original project).The trust assets guarantee the amounts loaned by ICA to the companies for Ps.920 million, as well as previous amounts owed to ICA for services performed of Ps.361 million, plus interest and other matters. During this process, the Sole Administrator of the companies recognized: (i) the existence of events of default of the companies and (ii) the legal basis of the execution procedure for the amounts being requested by ICA.

In December 2010, the trust foreclosure concluded. As a result, the pledged assets were transferred to ICA as a partial payment of the amounts still owed to ICA by the companies. As of December 31, 2010, the remaining amount owed by PER, MER and GOLF was approximately Ps.553 million, which is guaranteed. On October 20, 2011, ICA received an additional payment in the amount of Ps.151.5 million, paid in-kind with land, thus reducing the receivable owed to ICA from PER.

b. *Malla Vial Colombia*—In April 2002, an Arbitratral Court ordered ICA to pay all damages to the Instituto de Desarrollo Urbano del Distrito Capital de Bogotá, Colombia ("IDU") for noncompliance with the work contract of the "Malla Vial" project in Bogotá, of approximately US$2.2 million and set the criteria for the settlement of such contract. This ruling was recognized by the Mexican judicial authorities in January 2009 and ICA paid the required amount. At the same time, in a separate but related proceess, the IDU and ICA filed counter law suits against each other which in December 2004 were recognized by an administrative court.

Through a separate proceeding related to the same project, IDU filed a lawsuit against ICA with a Colombian court for damages resulting from contractual noncompliance for the approximate amount of US$4.72 million. Likewise, IDU filed legal proceedings against the bonding company to obtain the refund of the unapplied advance payment.

ICA filed a counterclaim requesting compensation and damages for the amount of US$ 17.8 million. The court ordered that the claim filed against the bonding company be suspended until the counterclaim filed by ICA is resolved. In June 2011, the suspension order issued by the judge regarding the executory action filed against the bonding company ended, thereby creating the possibility whereby, despite the reciprocal claims filed by the parties, the execution of bonds for the amount of US$ 17 million could be requested, although certain legal instances could be used to challenge a ruling in this regard.

Since April 2010, ICA and IDU have been engaged in negotiations. In December 2011, the parties jointly filed a request with the court for a conciliation hearing. On February 23, 2012, the court scheduled this hearing for May 29, 2012.

Company management considers that the conciliation agreement will have an approximate value of US$6 million, for which a provision has already been created.

c. *Airports*—A lawsuit was filed against Aeropuerto de Ciudad Juárez, S. A. de C. V., a subsidiary of the Company, on November 15, 1995, claiming a portion of plots of land (240 hectares) where the Ciudad Juárez International Airport is located, because such plots were claimed to have been incorrectly transferred to the Mexican government. The plaintiff sought a payment of US$120 million (approximately Ps.1,486 million) as an alternative to recovery of the land. In May 2005, an appeals court ruled that Aeropuerto de Ciudad Juárez, S. A. de C. V., had to return this land. The airport filed an amparo (constitutional claim), which was granted requiring the appellate court to re-analyze the case and the related evidence. On November 8, 2007, the Appeals Court issued a ruling declaring the previous sentence null, after which the plaintiffs filed an amparo, which was granted to them permitting them to continue the trial with the Mexican federal government as a party. The SCT filed an appearance in the case, responded to the complaint and requested removal to federal court due to lack of jurisdiction by the current court. On May 11, 2010, the court ruled in favor of the SCT´s motion and remanded the case to federal court. On June 2, 2010, the plaintiffs filed another amparo (constitutional claim) with the First District Court of the State of Chihuahua, which on November 10, 2010 confirmed the ruling removing the case from state court.On November 29, 2010, the plaintiffs filed a motion for review of the November 10, 2010 ruling, which will be heard by a Circuit Court, and is still pending.

As of the date of these consolidated financial statements, the Company reports this matter as a contingency due to the fact that the substance of the claim has not been definitively ruled upon even though the SCT has now appeared in the case. The Company believes that in the event of an unfavorable ruling, the economic repercussions of the lawsuit will be borne by the Federal government, as established in the concession title. Accordingly, the Company has not recorded any provisions for this matter.

There are several administrative-law enforcement actions against the airports of Ciudad Juárez, Culiacán, Zihuatanejo, and Reynosa. In November 2009, the Municipality of Ciudad Juárez once again requested payment from the Ciudad Juárez airport, stating the existence of a debt of Ps.8 million. A new proceeding for annulment was filed by the Company and is still unresolved. In June 2010, the Municipality of Culiacán requested payment of property taxes from by the Company (Aeropuerto de Culiacán, S. A. de C. V.) for Ps.4 million. An action for annulment was filed against this request with the Administrative-Law Court of the State of Sinaloa, and is still unresolved. In October 2010, the Municipality of Zihuatanejo requested payment of Ps.2 million from the Zihuatanejo airport. An action for annulment was filed with the Tax Court of the State of Guerrero by the airport, which is still unresolved. In February 2011, the Municipality of Reynosa once again requested payment of property taxes of Ps.118 million from the Reynosa Airport (Aeropuerto de Reynosa, S.A. de C.V.). An action for annulment will again be filed by the airport. The Company does not believe that an unfavorable outcome is probable and thus, has not recognized any provisions related to these contingencies.

d. *Tren Urbano in Puerto Rico*—In 2005, the Highway and Transportation Authority of Puerto Rico ("HTA"), (the client of ICA Miramar), filed a lawsuit against ICA Miramar for the indemnification in a lawsuit between the HTA and its main contractor in the Puerto Rico Urban Train project. The main contractor filed the lawsuit on December 24, 2003, and the HTA filed a counterclaim on November 23, 2004. ICA Miramar estimates that the lawsuit could result in a liability for the Company of approximately U.S.$ 4 million.

After a lengthy suspension, the court appointed a special judge given the complexity of the lawsuits against ICA Miramar. The main contractor subsequently modified its lawsuit against the HTA and in 2009, the HTA modified its lawsuit against ICA Miramar. The court ordered the parties to negotiate the appointment of an arbitrator. The lawsuit is currently in the information gathering stage. On April 9, 2010, the HTA and the main contractor notified the courts of a transaction regarding the lawsuits against each other. The Company does not believe that a significant loss is probable.

e. *Performance guarantees*—In the ordinary course of business, the Company is required to secure construction obligations, mainly related to the completion of construction contracts or the quality of its work, by granting letters of credit or bonds. At December 31, 2011, the Company had granted bonds to its customers for Ps.20,401 million and U.S.$277 million, respectively.

Additionally, the Company has issued letters of credit to guarantee its performance obligations under certain concession arrangements and construction contracts, in the amount of Ps.2,835 million, U.S.$143 million dollars and $10 million euros.

Tax Contingencies, Tax Amnesty, Legal Right to Offset Judicial Deposits against Tax Liability

2.303

Fibria Celulose S.A. (Dec 2011)

CONSOLIDATED BALANCE SHEETS *(in part)*

In thousands of reais

	2011	2010
Assets		
Non-current		
Derivative instruments (Note 11)		52,470
Related parties receivables (note 16)	5,469	5,307
Deferred taxes (Note 15)	991,768	1,332,025
Recoverable taxes (Note 14)	677,232	590,967
Advances to suppliers (Note 21)	760,611	693,490
Judicial deposits (Note 23 (d))	137,060	110,364
Other assets	95,060	145,768
Investment in affiliates	7,506	8,301
Biological assets (Note 18)	3,264,210	3,550,636
Property, plant and equipment (Note 17)	11,841,247	12,979,431
Intangible assets (Note 19)	4,809,448	4,906,443
	22,589,611	24,375,202
Total assets	27,853,536	30,273,856

NOTES TO THE CONSOLIDATED FINANCIAL STATEMENTS *(in part)*

In thousands of reais, unless otherwise indicated

1 Operations

(a) General Information

Fibria Celulose S.A. and its subsidiaries (the "Company", "Fibria", or "we") is a limited liability company constituted in accordance with the laws of the Federative Republic of Brazil and headquartered in São Paulo and after divesting its paper production activities in 2011, operates a single operational segment: producing and selling short fiber pulp.

The Company's business is affected by global pulp prices, which are historically cyclical and subject to significant volatility over short periods, as a result of, among other factors: (a) global demand for products from pulp; (b) global production capacity and strategies adopted by the main producers; (c) availability of substitutes for these products; and (d) exchange rates. All these factors are beyond the control of the Company's management.

2 Presentation of Financial Statements and Significant Accounting Practices *(in part)*

(a) Consolidated Financial Statements

The company's consolidated financial statements have been prepared and are being presented in accordance with and in compliance with International Financial Reporting Standards (IFRS) as issued by the International Accounting Standards Board (IASB).

The financial statements as of and for the year ended December 31, 2010 were the first financial statements presented in accordance with IFRS prepared by the Company. The main differences between the accounting practices previously adopted in Brazil (the "BR GAAP") and United States of America and IFRS, including the reconciliation of shareholders' equity and net income as of December 31, 2010 and 2009, are described in Note 39—First-time Adoption of IFRS.

(b) Approval of the Financial Statements

The financial statements were approved by the Board of Directors in on January 30, 2012.

2.21 Contingent Assets and Contingent Liabilities and Legal Obligations

The accounting practices for the accounting and disclosure of contingent assets and contingent liabilities and legal obligations are as follows: (a) contingent assets are recognized only when there is evidence that realization is virtually certain, or favorable, final and unappealable court decisions have been obtained. Contingent assets with probable success are only disclosed in the notes to the financial statements; (b) contingent liabilities are provided to the extent that the Company expects that is probable that will disburse cash. Tax and civil proceedings are accrued when losses are assessed as probable and the amounts involved can be reliably measured.

When the expectation of loss in these processes is possible, a description of the processes and amounts involved is disclosed in explanatory notes. Labor proceedings are provisioned based on the historical percentage of disbursements. Contingent liabilities assessed as remote losses are neither accrued nor disclosed; and (c) legal obligations are accounted for as payables.

23 Contingencies

The Company is party to labor, civil and tax lawsuits at various court levels. The provisions for contingencies against probable unfavorable outcome of claims in progress are established and updated based on management evaluation, as supported by external legal counsel. Provisions and corresponding judicial deposits are as follows:

	2011			2010		
	Judicial Deposits	Provision	Net	Judicial Deposits	Provision	Net
Nature of claims						
Tax	119,572	173,823	54,251	59,128	273,335	214,207
Labor	47,819	88,834	41,015	39,266	80,457	41,191
Civil	821	7,149	6,328	311	10,305	9,994
	168,212	269,806	101,594	98,705	364,097	265,392

The Company has tax and civil claims arising in the normal course of business that are assessed as possible (but not probable) losses by management, as supported by outside legal counsel. No provision has been recorded to cover possible unfavorable outcomes from these claims. At December 31, 2011, these claims amount to: tax R$ 3,352,635 and civil R$ 56,692.

The change in the provision for contingencies is as follows:

	2011	2010	2009
At the beginning of the year	364,097	712,873	443,252
Reversal(*)	(123,624)	(396,696)	(212,745)
New litigation		13,934	24,004
Merger of Aracruz			429,688
Accrual of financial charges	29,333	33,986	28,674
At the end of the year	269,806	364,097	712,873

(*) The reversal in 2010 was due to the REFIS (R$ 215,181—item (viii) below) and the reversal of the provision for CSLL taxes on export revenue in 2003 (R$ 156,331—item (iii) below) among others.

(a) Comments Regarding Probable Tax Contingencies

The tax processes with probable loss are represented by discussions related to federal, State and municipal taxes, for which, substantially, there are judicial deposits as collateral, so there is no material exposure to the company. The remaining balance, not deposited, refers to the discussion regarding ICMS on Interstate transfers and social contribution over the export sales in approximated amount of R$ 26 million of each discussion.

(b) Comments Regarding Possible Tax Contingencies

We present below comments on possible tax contingencies for which the Company has not recognized any provision. In the table below we present a detail of the amounts of these contingencies:

	Amount
Income tax assessment—Normus[i]	1,433,502
Tax incentive—agency for the development[ii]	76,207
IRPJ/CSL—partial approval[iii]	139,980
IRPJ/CSLL—Newark[iv]	88,842
IPI-BEFIEX[v]	167,802
Other tax liabilities[vi]	1,446,302
Total possible tax contingencies	3,352,635

[i] Income Tax Assessment—Normus

On December 2007, Fibria's subsidiary Normus Empreendimentos e Participaço'es Ltda. received an income tax assessment from the Brazilian Federal Revenue Service (Receita Federal do Brasil) charging Income Tax (Imposto de Renda) and Social Contribution (Contribuição Social sobre o Lucro Líquido) over earnings of its foreign subsidiarires, during the period from 2002 to 2006. The amount of the assessment was R$ 1,294 million updated through December 31, 2011.

On October 2011, the assessment was revised by the Tax Federal Administrative Court (Conselho Administrativo de Recursos Fiscais) which decided to maintain the assessment through a casting vote after a tie of 3 votes favourable to Fibria and 3 votes against Fibria by the 6 members of the court. Fibria can file a new appeal challenging the ruling, but the Company is waiting for the formal notification in order to appeal.

On September 2010, Normus Empreendimentos e Participaço'es Ltda. received a new tax assessment charging Income Tax (Imposto de Renda) and Social Contribution (Contribuição Social sobre o Lucro Líquido), but this time for the year 2007. The amount of the assessment was R$ 140 million updated through December 31, 2011.

The subsidiary in question, domiciled in Hungary, sells pulp and paper in the global market.

Based on the position of outside legal counsel, management understands that this Hungarian subsidiary is subject to taxation in its country of incorporation and the position taken by the tax authorities violates prevision of Brazilian tax law, in particular the Brazilian-Hungarian treaty to avoid double taxation, which precludes double taxation by Brazilian taxes of net income of a Brazilian company for operations in Hungary.

In 2011 a Inconstitutional Process (ADI-Ação Direta de Inconstitucionalidade) was filed by the National Industry Association (CNI-Confederação Nacional da Industria) with the Supreme Federal Court (STF-Supremo Tribunal Federal) challenging the constitutionality of article 74 of Provisional Measure 2,158 which establishes the taxation for income tax and social contribution purposes of income earned by subsidiaries and affiliates incorporated outside Brazil irrespective of whether such income was made available to the shareholder in Brazil. On its session of August 17, 2011 the STF considered the ADI with 5 members voting for the constitutionality of article 74 and 4 members voting for the unconstitutionality of such article. The session was suspended until Justice Joaquim Barbosa to cast its vote which is the only vote not yet casted.

Considering the outcome of the session of the STF indicated above internal and external legal counsel have reviewed their probability assessment which previously was of a remote loss and currently consider the loss as reasonably possible.

[ii] Tax incentives—Agency for the Development of Northeastern Brazil (ADENE)

The Company has business units located within the regional development area of ADENE. As the paper and pulp industry is deemed to be a priority for regional development (Decree 4213, of April 16, 2002), in December 2002, the Company requested and was granted by the Brazilian Federal Revenue Service (Receita Federal do Brasil) the right to benefit from reductions in corporate income tax and non-refundable surcharges calculated on operating profits (as defined) for Aracruz plants A and B (period from 2003 to 2013) and plant C (period from 2003 to 2012), when the qualification reports for the tax reductions are approved by ADENE.

On January 9, 2004, the Company was served Official Notice 1406/03 by the liquidator of the former Superintendence for the Development of the Northeast (SUDENE), who reported that, "based on the review carried out by the Legal Advisory Office of the Ministry of Integration as regards the special extent of the incentive, the right to use the benefit previously granted is unfounded and will be cancelled."

During 2004 and 2005, various ADENE determinations were issued to cancel the tax benefits. Such determinations were challenged and/or refuted by the Company, but no final court decision has been announced in relation to the merits of the case.

Nevertheless, the Brazilian Federal Revenue Service (Receita Federal do Brasil) served the Company an assessment notice in December 2005 requiring the payment of the amounts of the tax incentive used, plus interest, but without imposing any fine, amounting to R$ 316,355. The Company challenged such assessment notice, which was deemed to be valid at the administrative level. The Company filed an appeal against that assessment and in August 2011, the Tax Federal Administrative Court (Conselho Administrativo de Recursos Fiscais) considered that part of the assessment needed to be upheld. Therefore, the portion of the assessment related with 2003 benefits was canceled and the portion related with 2004 was upheld. Because this ruling, the amount of the assessment was reduced to R$ 76 million updated through December 31, 2011.

Company's management, supported by its legal counsel, believes that the decision to cancel the tax benefits is erroneous and should not prevail, whether with respect to benefits already used, or with respect to future periods.

With respect to the benefits obtained through 2004, based on the position of its legal counsel, management believes that the tax payment demanded is not justified, since the Company used the benefits strictly in accordance with the legal requirements and in conformity with the Brazilian Federal Revenue Service (Receita Federal do Brasil) determinations and ADENE's qualifying reports.

Considering that the CARF maintained the assessment with respect to the benefits used during 2004 amounting to R$ 73,100 the Company offered to provide a bank guarantee for the amount being challenged and expects for the collection phase of the legal process where it will challenge the amount of the assessment.

With respect to the remaining incentive period, extending to 2012 (plant C) and 2013 (plants A and B), based on the opinion of its legal counsel, management believes that it is illegal revoke the tax benefits, because the benefits granted were conditional to achieving certain pre-established requirements (implementation, expansion or modernization of industrial enterprise) and the benefits were granted through the end of the term established in the Law and related regulations.

Although the Company is confident that it will prevail, considering the facts that occurred in 2004 and 2005, which indicate that ADENE and the Brazilian Federal Revenue Service (Receita Federal do Brasil) intend to cancel the tax benefits, the Company decided to cease the use of tax benefits as from 2005, until a final court decision is obtained on the matter.

Since the benefits used through 2003 were maintained by the decision of CARF they are currently under discussion the benefits for the year 2004 and those after 2005 for which the Company has not used the benefits. The tax contingency is considered as of possible loss and therefore no provision has been recorded.

[iii] IRPJ/CSLL—partial approval

The Company has three requests for the approval of income tax (Imposto de Renda) credits with the Brazilian Federal Revenue Service (Receita Federal do Brasil), referring to 1997, 1999 and the fourth quarter of 2000, totaling R$ 134 million, of which only R$ 83 million was approved, creating a contingency of R$ 139 million updated through December 31, 2011. The Company timely appealed the rejection of the tax credits.

With respect to the year 1997, the claim is pending a decision from the first trial court (Delegacia Regional de Julgamento). With respect to the fourth quarter of 2000, the Company is awaiting a decision from Tax Federal Administrative Court (Conselho Administrativo de Recursos Fiscais), and with respect to 1999 it awaits a decision on an appeal to the High Court of Justice.

Based on the position of legal counsel, management understands that the likelihood of an unfavorable outcome for these trials is possible and therefore no provision has been recorded.

[iv] IRPJ/CSLL—Newark

Fibria received, in December 2007 and December 2010, two tax assessments in the amount, together, of R$ 219 million where Brazilian Federal Revenue Service (Receita Federal do Brasil) charged Income Tax (Imposto de Renda) and Social Contribution (Contribuição Social sobre o Lucro Líquido) of Newark Financial Inc., an offshore company controlled by VCP Exportadora e Participaço'es Ltda. (succeeded by Fibria) with respect to the fiscal year 2005. Based on advice from internal and external counsel we tha the probability of loss for the first tax assessment (December 2007—R$ 130 million) as remote and the probability of loss for the second tax assesment (December 2010- R$ 89 million) as possible and and, accordingly, no provision has been recorded with respect thereto.

[v] IRPJ—BEFIEX

Fibria has received a tax assessment because of allegedly using tax losses, consolidated during the BEFIEX program, six years after it was consolidated. The amount involved in this assessment is R$ 168 million. Based on our in house and external legal counsel, Fibria has recorded no provision with respect thereto.

[vi] Other Tax liabilities

Fibria has more than 334 trials for individual amounts of less than R$ 80 million. The amount involved in all of those trials is R$ 1.446.302. The average value of each trial is R$ 4,3 million.

(c) Comments on Labor/Civil Proceedings

The Company is a party to approximately 3,629 labor lawsuits filed by former employees, third parties and unions, claiming the payment of severance pay, health and safety premiums, overtime, commuting time, occupational illnesses and workers' compensation, tangible and moral damages, understated indexation on the fine of 40% of the Government Severance Indemnity Fund for Employees (FGTS), and 883 civil lawsuits, most of which refer to claims for compensation by former employees or third parties for alleged occupational illnesses and workers' compensation, collection lawsuits and bankruptcy situations, reimbursement of funds claimed from delinquent landowners and possessory actions filed in order to protect the Company's equity. The Company has insurance for public liability that covers, within the limits set in the policy, unfavorable sentences in the civil courts for claims for compensation of losses.

Class Action

In November 2008, a securities class action was filed against the Company (ex-Aracruz) and certain of its current and former officers and directors on behalf of purchasers of the Company's ADRs between April 7 and October 2, 2008. The complaint asserts alleged violations of the U.S. Securities Exchange Act, alleging that the Company failed to disclose information in connection with, and losses arising from, certain derivative transactions. The indemnity claimed by the plaintiffs has not yet been specified and will depend, if the action continues, on expert proof and determination of damages. Due to the unpredictability of the likelihood of an unfavorable outcome and no basis on which to estimate the amount or range of potential loss, no provision has been recognized.

(d) Remaining Judicial Deposits

The company has at December 31, 2011 the amount of R$ 137,060 (R$ 110,364 in December 31, 2010) deposited judicially in cases classified by external legal advisors as of remote or possible loss, for which no provision has been recorded. The contingencies refer to PIS, COFINS, IRPJ taxes and to contributions to the INSS, among others of smaller amount. Additionally, it includes the amount of R$ 50,096 of the credit balance of REFIS, as detailed in Note 25.

(e) Obligations to Dismantle and Remove Items of Property, Plant and Equipment and Restore the Site

The Company has no long-term assets expected to be abandoned or sold, or that would require a provision for obligations due to the decommissioning of assets as requested in the IAS 16 "Obligations to Dismantle and Remove Items of Property, Plant and Equipment and Restore the Site."

24 Tax Amnesty and Refinancing Program ("REFIS")

In November 2009, the Company joined the REFIS introduced by Law 11941/09, the objective of which is the settlement of fiscal liabilities through a special system for payment of tax and social security debt in installments.

On June 28, 2011 all amounts under the program were consolidated after having complied with all formal requirements established in the legislation and the amounts included in the consolidated debt relate mainly to:

- CSLL—judicial measure aiming the exclusion of export earnings of the basis for calculating the social contribution, as established by the constitutional amendment n° 33/2001;
- IRPJ/CSLL—judicial measure aiming the *correção monetária* of the balance sheet without monetary losses generated by the *plano verão*—Economic plan established by the Provisional Measure 32/1989, converted into Law 7.730/89;
- IRRF/CSLL—tax assessments issued due to the offset of income and social contribution tax losses, without compliance with the limitation of 30%;
- IPI credit premium—tax credits transferred from KSR to Celpav, related to phase II (April 1, 1981 to April 30, 1985), which were the subject of a tax assessment notice issued by the Brazilian Federal Revenue Secretariat due to supposed noncompliance with accessory tax obligations;
- Economic Domain Intervention Contribution (CIDE)—judicial proceeding regarding CIDE on amounts paid to parties resident abroad as royalties or contractual remuneration, introduced by Law 10168/00 and amended by Law 10332/01—period: as from 2002;
- Tax on Financial Transactions (IOF)—judicial proceeding for declaration of non-existence of legal-tax relationship, in order not to be obliged to pay IOF on foreign exchange contracts entered into for purposes of raising funds abroad through the issue of Euronotes. The IOF amount was deposited in court on February 4, 1994;
- COFINS—rate increase from 2% to 3% as established by Law 9718/98;
- CSLL—tax assessment issued due to the deduction on basis for calculating the social contribution, of expenditure on the monetary correction portion to the difference between the variation of the IPC and of the BTN Fiscal in the year of 1990.

The following is a summary of the final values included in the program, as well as the benefits obtained:

Detail of Amounts	
Total upated debts included in the program	532.734
Benefits for reduction of fines and interest	(78,030)
Fines and interest offset against tax loss and negative basis	(129,397)
Total debt payable	325.307
Payments made	(21,356)
Balance of debt	303.951
Total of judicial deposits updated	349,802
Credit balance	45.851

Considering the legal right to offset judicial deposits related to the debts included in the program and since judicial deposits exceed the remaining debt (after the reductions established by the program) the remaining balance in favor of the Company, updated on December 31, 2011 is R$ 50,096, is presented within non-current assets under other accounts receivable and monthly updated by SELIC.

The benefits for reduction of fines and interest were recorded in financial result in the line "foreign exchange gain(loss) and indexation" and totaled R$ 57,950 in the year ending December 31, 2011 (R$ 61,875 in 2010).

IAS 19, *EMPLOYEE BENEFITS*

IFRIC 14, *IAS 19—THE LIMIT ON A DEFINED BENEFIT ASSET, MINIMUM FUNDING REQUIREMENTS AND THEIR INTERACTION*

IFRSs Overview and Comparison to U.S. GAAP

Author's Note

In June 2011, the IASB issued a revised IAS 19, which is effective for annual reporting periods beginning on or after 1 January 2013, with early application permitted. The amendments to IAS 19 finalize proposals related to the accounting for termination benefits and include a revised definition and recognition and measurement requirements. The key changes are the following:

- *Termination benefits* are employee benefits provided in exchange for the termination of an employee's employment as a result of either of the following:
  - An entity's decision to terminate an employee's employment before the normal retirement date
  - An employee's decision to accept an offer of benefits in exchange for the termination of employment
- An entity should recognize a liability and expense for termination benefits at the earlier of the following dates:
  - When the entity can no longer withdraw the offer of those benefits
  - When the entity recognizes costs for a restructuring that is within the scope of IAS 37 and that involves the payment of termination benefits
- An entity should measure the liability for termination benefits, both initially and subsequently, according to the nature of the employee benefit, provided that if the benefit is an enhancement of a postemployment benefit, the liability is measured in accordance with the requirements of IAS 19 for those benefits.

IAS 19 does not require specific disclosures related to termination benefits, but reminds entities that other IFRSs may require disclosures, such as IAS 24, *Related Party Disclosures*.

In 2011, the IASB issued IFRS 13, which amended IAS 19. Early adoption is permitted. IFRS 13 amended the definition of fair value and replaced the term *determine* with the term *measure*.

Because the effective dates of the revisions to IAS 19 and IFRS 13 are after 1 January 2012, these revisions are not discussed in the commentary in this section. In addition, the timing of the effective date of this standard affects the availability of illustrative excerpts from survey companies' financial statements. Accordingly, the excerpts appearing later in this section may not reflect all or some of these revisions.

2.304 *Employee benefits*, as defined in IAS 19, are all forms of consideration given by an entity for services rendered by its employees. An entity should account for all employee benefits in accordance with IAS 19, except those to which IFRS 2, *Share-based Payment*, applies.

2.305 IAS 19 recognizes that an entity can provide employee benefits under agreements with individual or groups of employees, legislative requirements or industry arrangements, or informal arrangements that give rise to constructive obligations. *Constructive obligations* are defined as those in which an entity indicates to other parties by its past actions, published policy, or current statements that it will accept certain responsibilities and, hence, creates a valid expectation in affected parties that those responsibilities will be discharged. For example, an entity can have a constructive obligation for an employee benefit when it has always given its employees a set amount of money as a holiday bonus, even though it has no legal or contractual obligation to do so.

2.306 IAS 19 establishes separate requirements for four types of employee benefits: short-term, long-term, postemployment, and termination. Employee benefits include those provided directly to employees, their spouses or dependents, or others (for example, insurance companies). Employees include personnel providing services to an entity on a full-time, part-time, permanent, casual, or temporary basis and also include directors and other management personnel.

Recognition and Measurement

IFRSs

2.307 Unless another IFRS permits an amount to be included in the cost of an asset, IAS 19 requires an entity to recognize a liability for the undiscounted amount of short-term benefits it expects to pay for employee services, after deducting amounts already paid, and a corresponding expense in profit or loss. When amounts already paid exceed the undiscounted amount of the benefits, the entity should recognize an asset (prepaid expense). Short-term benefits include salaries and wages; Social Security contributions; paid sick leave or vacation leave (short-term compensating absences); profit sharing and bonuses payable within 12 months after the end of the period that the employee rendered service; and nonmonetary benefits, such as medical care, cars, and free or subsidized goods.

2.308 With respect to short-term compensating absences, an entity should recognize a liability for the expected cost. When compensating absences can be accumulated (that is, the employee's entitlement can be carried forward to future periods), the entity recognizes the expected cost when service increases the employee's entitlement to the benefit. Otherwise, the entity should recognize the expected cost when the absence occurs. An entity should measure the expected cost of accumulating compensating absences as the additional amount it expects to pay as a result of the entitlement carried forward to the next period.

2.309 An entity should recognize the expected cost of profit sharing and bonus plans when it has a present legal or constructive obligation to make payments as a result of past events and it can make a reliable estimate of its liability. An entity has a present obligation when it has no realistic alternative but to make the payments. Estimates should take into account the fact that some employees may leave without receiving a bonus. An entity should include any payments due beyond 12 months with long-term employee benefits.

2.310 Postemployment benefits include pensions and other benefits, such as insurance and medical care. IAS 19 establishes the requirements for accounting for both defined contribution and defined benefit postemployment benefit plans. *Defined contribution plans* are defined as those in which the entity's legal or constructive obligation is limited to the agreed contributions to the plan; therefore, the employee bears the actuarial risk that benefits will be less than expected and investment risk that the assets will be insufficient to meet the expected benefits. All other plans are considered defined benefit plans for the purposes of accounting in accordance with IAS 19.

2.311 For defined contribution plans, an entity should recognize liabilities for contributions payable in exchange for employee service and a corresponding expense in profit or loss, unless appropriately included in the cost of another asset. When payments exceed the liability, an entity should recognize an asset (prepaid expense) for the excess. An entity should discount contributions payable beyond 12 months and, in most circumstances, should use a discount rate determined by reference to market yields on high-quality corporate bonds, with consistent currency and estimated maturity.

2.312 Accounting for defined benefit plans under IAS 19 is more complex than that for defined contribution plans. To determine the amount of a liability and the associated expense to recognize in the current period, an entity should take the following steps, separately, for each defined benefit plan:
   a. Use actuarial techniques to reliably estimate the amount of the benefit earned.
   b. Discount the benefit using the projected unit credit method to determine the present value of the defined benefit obligation.
   c. Determine the fair value of any plan assets.
   d. Determine the total amount of actuarial gains and losses and the amount to be recognized in the current period.
   e. Determine any past service cost resulting from the introduction of a new plan or change to an existing plan.
   f. Determine the resulting gain or loss from a plan curtailment or settlement.

2.313 An entity should apply the requirements of IAS 19 not only to its legal obligations but also to its constructive obligations, with the understanding that a constructive obligation exists when failure to pay benefits would result in unacceptable damage to an entity's relationship with employees.

2.314 An entity should recognize a net defined benefit obligation as the present value of the defined benefit obligation (calculated as described previously) adjusted by the following amounts:
   • Net unrecognized actuarial gains (or losses)
   • Unrecognized past service cost
   • Fair value of the plan assets available to settle the liability

2.315 An entity should determine the present value of the defined benefit obligation and fair value of the plan assets with sufficient regularity so that amounts recognized are not materially different from those that it would determine at the balance sheet date.

2.316 An entity should not recognize a defined benefit asset at an amount more than the present value of economic benefits available in the form of refunds or reductions in future contributions (asset ceiling). IAS 19 includes specific requirements for recognition of any gains or losses that might result from application of this constraint. IFRIC 14, *IAS 19— The Limit on a Defined Benefit Asset, Minimum Funding Requirements and their Interaction*, provides guidance on the recognition of an entity's right to a refund or contribution reduction, as well as how a minimum funding requirement affects the availability of reductions in future contributions and might give rise to a liability.

2.317 Except to the extent that it may be included in the cost of an asset, an entity should recognize the net total of the following amounts as an expense in profit or loss:
   • Service cost
   • Interest cost
   • Expected return on plan assets and any reimbursement rights
   • Actuarial gains or losses, if any (subsequently described)
   • Past service cost
   • Effect of any curtailments or settlements
   • Effect of the asset ceiling

2.318 IAS 19 gives an entity two alternatives for recognizing the effects of actuarial gains and losses in profit or loss. An entity may recognize only a portion of actuarial gains and losses in profit or loss using the corridor method. An entity should apply the corridor method separately to each plan to amortize unrecognized actuarial gains or losses to profit or loss. To determine the amount to be included in expense using the corridor method, an entity takes the following steps:
   a. Determine the amount by which the net cumulative unrecognized actuarial gains and losses exceed the greater of 10 percent of the present value of the defined benefit obligation and 10 percent of the fair value of the plan assets. (If this amount is zero or negative, no expense is recognized.)
   b. Divide the excess, if any, by the expected average remaining working lives of plan participants and recognize this amount as an expense. (If there is no excess, no expense is recognized.)

2.319 Alternatively, an entity may use another systematic method of amortizing unrecognized actuarial gains and losses as long as the selected method recognizes these gains and losses faster than the corridor method. When an entity chooses to recognize all actuarial gains and losses on all its defined benefit plans in the period in which they occur, it should recognize them in other comprehensive income. When so recognized, these actuarial gains and losses will never affect profit or loss in the future.

2.320 Multiemployer plans (that is, asset pools from contributions by entities that are not under common control to be used to provide benefits to employees of more than one entity) can be either defined contribution or defined benefit plans. When these plans are defined benefit plans, an entity should apply defined benefit plan accounting in accordance with IAS 19, unless insufficient information is available. In the latter case, the entity should apply defined contribution accounting and make additional disclosures. An entity should account for state plans (established by legislation for all entities or all entities in a particular category) as if the plans were multiemployer plans.

2.321 When the risks of a defined benefit plan are shared among entities under common control, the plan is not considered to be a multiemployer plan. An entity participating in such a plan should not claim it does not have sufficient information to apply defined benefit plan accounting. IAS 19 provides guidance about how the individual entity should account for its participation in these plans in its separate financial statements. In addition, participation in these plans is considered a related party transaction and additional disclosures are required, in accordance with IAS 24.

2.322 An entity should treat insured benefits as defined contribution plans, unless it has a remaining legal or constructive obligation to pay benefits or further amounts if the insurer does not pay. An entity should account for any remaining legal or constructive obligation as a defined benefit plan.

2.323 An entity might offer other types of long-term employee benefits, such as sabbaticals, housing, disability benefits, or deferred compensation. An entity should recognize and measure the liability and related expense for these benefits in a manner similar to that for postemployment benefit obligations except that it recognizes any actuarial gains and losses and past service cost immediately in profit or loss.

2.324 An entity should recognize termination benefits as a liability and expense when the entity is demonstrably committed to terminate employment before normal retirement or to provide such benefits due to an offer encouraging voluntary termination. IAS 19 states that an entity is only demonstrably committed when it has a detailed formal plan for termination, with no realistic possibility of withdrawing. IAS 19 requires an entity to include specific items in such a plan (for example, termination benefits by job category). An entity should measure termination benefits due within 12 months at the amount payable and those due beyond 12 months at present value using a similar interest rate as that required for defined contribution plans.

U.S. GAAP

2.325 Accounting for short-term and long-term employee benefits is similar under FASB ASC and IFRSs, especially with respect to compensating absences. Consistent with FASB ASC 710-10-25-1, obligations and corresponding expenses are generally recognized when the settlement of the obligation is probable and the amount can be measured reasonably (reliably in IFRSs). However, FASB ASC 710-10-25-4 makes a distinction for certain sabbatical leaves by explaining that when the purpose of a sabbatical leave is solely for research or public service expected to enhance the reputation or otherwise benefit the entity in the future, an entity should not consider the sabbatical a benefit related to the employee's past service. Therefore, an entity should not accrue the liability in advance.

2.326 The FASB ASC glossary defines *defined contribution plan* more directly than IFRSs. Such a plan is one that provides an individual account for each participant and provides benefits based on amounts contributed to the participant's account by the employer or employee, investment experience, and any forfeitures allocated to the account less any administrative expenses charged to the plan. The accounting for such plans is similar to IAS 19, except FASB ASC 715-70-35-1 states that when a plan requires an entity to make contributions after the employee terminates or retires, the en-tity should accrue the estimated cost during the employee's service period.

2.327 Like IFRSs, when a plan does not meet the definition of *defined contribution plan*, an entity should account for it as a defined benefit plan.

2.328 Although the accounting for postemployment benefit plans is similar under both FASB ASC and IFRSs, several important differences exist, including the following:

- The FASB ASC glossary defines the following two obligations:
  - *Projected benefit obligation* (PBO) is the actuarial present value of all benefits attributed by the pension benefit formula to employee service rendered up to the date the PBO is calculated. An entity should measure the PBO using assumptions about future compensation levels if the pension benefit formula is based on those future compensation levels (for example, career-average-pay plans).
  - *Accumulated postretirement benefit obligation* (APBO) is the actuarial present value of all future benefits attributed to an employee's service rendered to the date the APBO is calculated, based on the assumption that the plan will continue in effect and that all assumptions about future events are fulfilled. The APBO generally reflects a pro rata allocation of expected future benefits to employee service already rendered in the attribution period. Before an employee's full eligibility date, that employee's APBO as of a particular date is the portion of the expected postretirement benefit obligation attributed to that employee's service rendered to that date. On and after the full eligibility date, the accumulated and expected postretirement benefit obligations for an employee are the same.
- FASB ASC 715-60-35-79 requires an entity to select a discount rate to compute the present value of the defined benefit obligation based on either of the following:
  - Interest rate inherent in the amount at which the postretirement benefit obligation could be settled, if it is possible to settle the obligation with third-party insurers
  - Yields currently available on high-quality, fixed-rate investments whose cash flows match the timing and amount of expected benefit payments (FASB ASC 715-60-35-80 requires the use of rates on high-quality, fixed-rate investments for other postretirement obligations)
- FASB ASC 715-30-35-36 states that an entity should use the projected unit credit method to determine the obligation for pay-related plans, such as final-pay and career-average-pay plans. Unlike IFRSs, this paragraph further states that entities should use the benefit-years-of-service approach when the benefit formula defines benefits similarly for all years of service.
- An entity should calculate the expected return on plan assets based on the *market-related value of plan assets*, defined in the FASB ASC glossary as either the fair value or a calculated value that recognizes changes in fair value in a systematic and rational manner over a period not longer than five years.
- An entity should accumulate in other comprehensive income (*a*) gains and losses not included in pension expense, including gains and losses resulting from

changes in experience (for example, the difference between the actual and expected return on plan assets) and assumptions (for example, actuarial assumptions), as stated by FASB ASC 715-60-35-25, and (*b*) prior service costs, as stated by FASB ASC 715-60-35-16. (FASB ASC 715-60-35-31 permits an entity to use the same corridor method used in IAS 19 or another method that recognizes gains and losses more quickly if the method is used consistently and treats gains and losses in the same way. However, the entity should recognize the minimum amortization in any period in which it is greater [reduces the net gain or loss balance by more] than the amount that the entity would recognize under the method used.)

2.329 The FASB ASC glossary defines *multiemployer plans* similarly to IFRSs. However, FASB ASC 715-80-35-1 explains that an entity should recognize as net pension cost or net periodic postretirement benefit cost the required contributions to multiemployer plans, rather than use defined benefit accounting, as would generally be required under IFRSs.

2.330 Under FASB ASC, an entity should account for termination benefits depending upon the type of arrangement. As noted by FASB ASC 715-30-25-10, when the benefits are contractual, an entity should recognize a liability and expense loss when it is probable that employees will be entitled to benefits and it can reasonably estimate the liability. These conditions may not be met until the entity acts. When an employer offers special termination benefits to employees, the entity recognizes a liability and loss when the employees accept the offer and it can reasonably estimate the amounts to be paid. As stated by FASB ASC 715-30-55-189, a plan that provides termination benefits for virtually all employees is considered a pension plan. Such plans are either defined contribution or defined benefits plans and should be accounted for accordingly.

2.331 Under FASB ASC 420-10, an entity that provides involuntary termination benefits associated with exit or disposal activities (one-time termination benefits) is subject to similar conditions to those in IFRSs and should account for these benefits in a similar manner.

Presentation

IFRSs

2.332 IAS 1 does not require assets and liabilities associated with postemployment benefit plans to be shown as separate line items. However, IAS 19 prohibits an entity from offsetting assets and liabilities related to different plans in the balance sheet, unless it has a legal right to use a surplus in one plan to settle a liability in another and it intends to do so. IAS 19 does not provide guidance on whether an entity should disaggregate these assets and liabilities into current and noncurrent portions.

U.S. GAAP

2.333 Paragraphs 2–3 of FASB ASC 715-20-45 contain guidance for classification of defined benefit retirement plans on the balance sheet. Otherwise, FASB ASC does not prescribe any particular presentation for employee benefits in the financial statements.

Disclosure

IFRSs

2.334 IAS 24 requires disclosure of key management personnel compensation and, together with the general guidance of IAS 1, specific disclosures of employee benefits. Although IAS 19 does not require specific disclosures about short-term or long-term employee benefits, other than the subsequently discussed disclosures required for defined benefit and defined contribution plans, the requirements of IAS 1 and IAS 24 still apply.

2.335 With respect to defined contribution benefit plans, an entity should disclose the amount recognized as an expense during the period.

2.336 With respect to defined benefit plans, an entity should disclose descriptions of the type(s) of plans and its accounting policy choice for recognition of actuarial gains and losses. An entity should disclose a reconciliation of the beginning and ending balances of the following:
- Present value of the defined benefit obligation
- Fair value of the plan assets
- Reimbursement rights, if any

2.337 In these reconciliations, an entity should disclose, when applicable, the separate components of expense (for example, service cost, interest cost, and so on); contributions to the plan and payments to beneficiaries; effects of business combinations and disposals; and any foreign currency adjustments. An entity should also reconcile the balances in the net benefit obligation, plan assets, and amounts recognized in the balance sheet, including any unrecognized amounts (past service cost, actuarial gains and losses, asset due to the asset ceiling, and so on), and discuss any links between reimbursement rights and related obligation.

2.338 An entity should disclose an analysis of its defined benefit obligation into fully or partially funded and unfunded amounts.

2.339 An entity should disclose the amounts recognized in the statement of comprehensive income. For the expense recognized in profit or loss, an entity should disclose the components of the expense (for example, service cost and interest cost). For the amount recognized in other comprehensive income, an entity should separately disclose actuarial gains and losses and the effect of the asset ceiling. When the entity has opted to report all actuarial gains and losses of the period directly in other comprehensive income, the entity should disclose the cumulative amount recognized.

2.340 An entity should disclose the following with respect to defined benefit plans:
- Major categories of plan assets
- Percentage or amount of each major category of the fair value of plan assets
- Any property occupied or assets used by the entity
- Rate of return on plan assets, including a narrative describing the method used to determine the expected return and the effects of major categories
- Actual return on plan assets and recognized reimbursement rights

2.341 An entity should also disclose the following with respect to defined benefit plans:

- Information about actuarial assumptions used (for example, discount rates, salary increases, and health care cost trends)
- Effect of one percentage point change in health care cost trend on the aggregate of service and interest cost of net postemployment medical costs and net postemployment benefit obligation
- Historical information about the net benefit obligation and fair value of plan assets, including experience adjustments
- Best estimate of expected contributions to the plan in the next reporting period

2.342 IAS 19 does not require specific disclosure of termination benefits. However, the requirements of IAS 1 and IAS 24 both apply. In addition, uncertainty about whether, or how many, employees will accept an offer of voluntary termination may give rise to a contingent liability. In this case and with respect to restructuring activities, an entity should recognize and disclose such a contingency in accordance with IAS 37.

U.S. GAAP

2.343 Although the principal required disclosures are the same as those required under IFRSs, FASB ASC 715-20-50 disclosure requirements are more extensive and, for example, include the following:
- Description of how the entity makes investment allocation decisions
- Inputs and valuation techniques used to measure the fair value of plan assets
- Effect of fair value measurements using significant unobservable inputs (level 3) on changes in plan assets for the period
- Significant concentrations of risk within plan assets
- Accumulated benefit obligation for defined benefit plan
- Benefits expected to be paid in each of the next five fiscal years and in the aggregate for the five fiscal years thereafter

FASB ASC 715-70-50 and 715-80-50 include specific disclosure requirements for defined contribution plans and multiemployer plans, respectively.

Authors' Note

In September 2011, FASB issued FASB Accounting Standard Update (ASU) No. 2011-09, *Compensation—*

Retirement Benefits—Multiemployer Plans (Subtopic 715-80): Disclosures about an Employer's Participation in a Multiemployer Plan, to improve transparency about such plans by requiring employers to provide additional disclosures. An entity should include additional details in these disclosures including plan names and identifying numbers for significant multiemployer plans, the level of employers' participation in the plans, the financial health of the plans, and the nature of the employer commitments to the plans. The amendments in ASU No. 2011-09 are effective for public and nonpublic entities for fiscal years ending after December 15, 2011, and December 15, 2012, respectively.

2.344 Paragraphs 2–4 of FASB ASC 715-20-50 also include conditions under which disclosures about plans in different jurisdictions or plans with different funding statuses can be combined or should be shown separately.

2.345 With respect to other postemployment benefits, FASB ASC 715-60-50 requires additional disclosures on the impact of subsidies from the Medicare Prescription Drug, Improvement, and Modernization Act of 2003.

2.346 Unlike IFRSs, when termination benefits are a major cost of an exit and disposal activity, FASB ASC 420-10-50-1 requires an entity to disclose the total expected amount, amount incurred in the period, and cumulative amount incurred to date. An entity should also provide a reconciliation of beginning and ending balances in the liability showing adjustments to the liability, amounts incurred and charged to expense, and costs paid or otherwise settled and should explain why the entity made such adjustments.

Presentation and Disclosure Excerpts

Current and Non-Current Liabilities: Payroll and Social Liabilities

2.347

Adecoagro S.A (Dec 2011)

CONSOLIDATED STATEMENTS OF FINANCIAL POSITION (in part)

	Note	2011	2010 (As Revised) (Note 2.3)	2009 (As Revised) (Note 2.3)
Assets				
Liabilities				
Non-current liabilities				
Trade and other payables	11, 19	8,418	11,785	6,822
Borrowings	11, 20	203,409	250,672	203,134
Derivative financial instruments		—	—	280
Deferred income tax liabilities	21	92,989	91,088	77,588
Payroll and social liabilities	22	1,431	1,178	1,106
Provisions for other liabilities	23	3,358	4,606	3,326
Total non-current liabilities		309,605	359,329	292,256

(continued)

	Note	2011	2010	2009
			(As Revised) (Note 2.3)	(As Revised) (Note 2.3)
Current liabilities				
Trade and other payables	11, 19	114,020	69,236	62,098
Current income tax liabilities		872	978	222
Payroll and social liabilities	22	17,010	15,478	10,079
Borrowings	11, 20	157,296	138,800	103,647
Derivative financial instruments	11	6,054	8,920	12,607
Provisions for other liabilities	23	969	4,601	1,652
Total current liabilities		296,221	238,013	190,305
Total liabilities		605,826	597,342	482,561

NOTES TO THE CONSOLIDATED FINANCIAL STATEMENTS (in part)

1. General Information and Reorganization (in part)

Adecoagro S.A. (the "Company" or "Adecoagro") is a holding company primarily engaged through its operating subsidiaries in agricultural and agro-industrial activities. The Company and its operating subsidiaries are collectively referred to hereinafter as the "Group". These activities are carried out through three major lines of business, namely, Farming; Sugar, Ethanol and Energy; and Land Transformation. Farming is further comprised of five reportable segments, which are described in detail in Note 5 to these consolidated financial statements.

The Group was established in 2002 and has subsequently grown significantly both organically and through acquisitions. The Group currently has operations in Argentina, Brazil and Uruguay. See Note 32 for a description of the Group companies.

The Company is the Group's ultimate parent company and is a Societe Anonyme corporation incorporated and domiciled in the Grand Duchy of Luxembourg. The address of its registered office is 13-15 Avenue de la Liberté, L-1931, Luxembourg.

These consolidated financial statements have been approved for issue by the Board of Directors on March 27, 2012.

2. Summary of Significant Accounting Policies

The principal accounting policies applied in the preparation of these consolidated financial statements are set out below. These policies have been consistently applied to all the years presented, unless otherwise stated.

2.1. Basis of Preparation (in part)

The consolidated financial statements of the Group have been prepared in accordance with International Financial Reporting Standards (IFRS) of the International Accounting Standards Board (IASB) and the Interpretations of the International Financial Reporting Interpretations Committee (IFRIC). All IFRS issued by the IASB, effective at the time of preparing these consolidated financial statements have been applied.

The financial year corresponds to the calendar year. The consolidated statements of income, of changes in shareholders´ equity, of comprehensive income and of cash flows include two comparative years.

Presentation in the consolidated statement of financial position differentiates between current and non-current assets and liabilities. Assets and liabilities are regarded as current if they mature within one year or are held for sale. The consolidated financial statements are presented in United States Dollars.

The consolidated financial statements have been prepared under the historical cost convention as modified by financial assets and financial liabilities (including derivative instruments) at fair value through profit or loss and biological assets and agricultural produce at the point of harvest measured at fair value.

The preparation of consolidated financial statements in conformity with IFRS requires the use of certain critical accounting estimates. It also requires management to exercise its judgment in the process of applying the Group's accounting policies. The areas involving a higher degree of judgment or complexity, or areas where assumptions and estimates are significant to the consolidated financial statements are disclosed in Note 4.

22. Payroll and Social Security Liabilities

	2011	2010
Non-current		
Social security payable	1,431	1,178
	1,431	1,178
Current		
Salaries payable	3,174	3,471
Social security payable	2,758	2,223
Provision for vacations	7,100	6,155
Provision for bonuses	3,978	3,629
	17,010	15,478
Total payroll and social security liabilities	18,441	16,656

Defined Contribution Benefit Plans, Unfunded Defined Benefit Plans Using the Corridor Method for Recognition of Actuarial Gains and Losses, Non-Current Liabilities for Service Awards With Immediate Recognition of Actuarial Gains and Losses

2.348

Telekom Austria Aktiengesellschaft (Dec 2011)

CONSOLIDATED STATEMENT OF FINANCIAL POSITION (in part)

Notes		December 31, 2011	December 31, 2010
	Non-current liabilities		
(25)	Long-term debt	−2,934,929	−3,077,240
(26)	Lease obligations and Cross Border Lease	−124	−13,879
(27)	Employee benefit obligations	−128,976	−131,576
(22)	Non-current provisions	−888,208	−761,771
(30)	Deferred tax liabilities	−127,260	−125,402
(28)	Other non-current liabilities and deferred income	−74,178	−86,063
	Total non-current liabilities	−4,153,675	−4,195,929

NOTES TO THE CONSOLIDATED FINANCIAL STATEMENTS (in part)

(1) The Company and Significant Accounting Policies (in part)

Description of Business, Organization and Relationship with the Federal Republic of Austria

Telekom Austria AG is incorporated as a joint stock corporation ("Aktiengesellschaft") under the laws of the Republic of Austria and is located in Austria, Lassallestrasse 9, 1020 Vienna. Telekom Austria AG and its subsidiaries ("Telekom Austria Group") are engaged as full service telecommunications providers of long distance, local and wireless services, corporate data communications services as well as internet services and television broadcasting. Telekom Austria Group also supplies telephones and technical equipment for telephone communications. These activities are conducted primarily in Austria, Croatia, Slovenia, Bulgaria, Serbia, Macedonia and Belarus.

The Federal Republic of Austria, through Österreichische Industrieholding AG ("ÖIAG"), is a significant shareholder of Telekom Austria Group. ÖIAG's stake in Telekom Austria Group is disclosed in Note (29).

In addition to the related party transactions described in Note (10), the Federal Republic of Austria authorizes and supervises the Rundfunk und Telekom Regulierungs—GmbH ("RTR"), which regulates certain activities of Telekom Austria Group. In addition, the government holds the taxing authority for the Austrian operations of Telekom Austria Group and imposes taxes such as corporate income tax and value-added taxes on Telekom Austria Group.

The use of automated calculation systems may give rise to rounding differences.

Basis of Presentation

Telekom Austria Group prepared the accompanying consolidated financial statements as of December 31, 2011 in compliance with the provisions of the International Financial Reporting Standards ("IFRS/IAS"), issued by the International Accounting Standards Board ("IASB"), the interpretations of the International Financial Reporting Interpretation Committee ("IFRIC") and the interpretation of the Standards Interpretation Committee ("SIC"), effective as of December 31, 2011 and as endorsed by the European Union.

Provisions

A provision is recorded when an obligation to a third party exists, the payment is probable and the amount can be reasonably estimated. Long-term provisions relating to personnel and social costs, restructuring provisions and asset retirement obligation are recorded at their net present value. Provisions for restructuring are recorded if there is a detailed formal plan for the restructuring and if a valid expectation has been raised in those affected that the restructuring will be carried out by starting to implement that plan or announcing its main features to those affected by it.

Employee Benefit Obligations

Telekom Austria Group provides retirement benefits under defined contribution and defined benefit plans.

In the case of defined contribution plans, Telekom Austria Group pays contributions to publicly or privately administered pension or severance insurance plans on a mandatory or contractual basis. Once the contributions have been paid, Telekom Austria Group has no further payment obligations. The regular contributions constitute net periodic costs for the year in which they are due.

All other employee benefit obligations are unfunded defined benefit plans for which Telekom Austria Group records provisions which are calculated using the projected unit credit method in accordance with IAS 19. The future benefit obligations are measured using actuarial methods on the basis of an appropriate assessment of the discount rate, rate of compensation increase, rate of employee turnover and rate of increase of pensions. For severance and pension obligations, Telekom Austria Group recognizes actuarial gains and losses in accordance with the corridor method and not directly comprehensive income. Actuarial gains and losses are recorded using the corridor method and are therefore not recognized directly in other comprehensive income (OCI). For severance and pensions, Telekom Austria Group recognizes a portion of its actuarial gains and losses as income or expense if the net cumulative unrecognized actuarial gains and losses at the end of the reporting period exceed the corridor of 10% of the projected benefit obligation. The excess is amortized over the expected remaining service period. Prior service costs are recognized over the remaining service period. For service awards, actuarial gains and losses are recognized immediately.

According to IAS 19.118, entities may distinguish between current and non-current assets and liabilities arising from post-employment benefits. Telekom Austria Group applies this distinction in its financial statements.

Interest cost related to employee benefit obligations is reported in the financial result, while service cost is reported in employee expenses.

Use of Estimates

The preparation of the consolidated financial statements requires Management to make estimates and assumptions that affect the assets, liabilities and contingent liabilities reported at the end of any given period, and revenues and expenses for that reported period. Actual results may differ from these estimates.

Management has made judgments in the process of applying Telekom Austria Group's accounting policies. Additionally, at the reporting date, Management has made the following key assumptions concerning the future and has identified other key sources of estimation uncertainty at the reporting date which bear a significant risk of causing a material adjust-

ment to the carrying amounts of assets and liabilities within the next financial year:

(a) Employee benefit plans: The measurement of the various pension and other post-employment benefit plans as well as service awards is based on a method that uses various parameters, such as the expected discount rate, rate of compensation increase, rate of employee turnover and pension and salary increase. Changes in these parameters could result in higher or lower expenses (see Note (27)).

(22) Provisions and Accrued Liabilities (in part)

Provisions and accrued liabilities consist of the following:

	Restructuring	Employees	Customer Allowances	Asset Retirement Obligation	Legal	Interconnection/ Roaming	Other	Total
Balance at January 1, 2011	711,108	77,906	55,679	120,911	15,954	18,803	19,423	1,019,784
Additions	254,950	41,717	37,443	3,404	5,332	7,154	12,226	362,226
Changes in estimate	0	0	0	2,358	0	0	0	2,358
Used	−57,896	−41,553	−37,596	−693	−3,071	−741	−10,897	−152,447
Released	−55,674	−2,973	−6,162	−646	−823	0	−2,620	−68,898
Accretion expense	29,892	0	0	7,039	0	0	0	36,931
Reclassifications*	−7,098	9,940	0	0	40	0	−40	2,842
Translation adjustment	0	−683	0	−6,002	−17	−18	−112	−6,831
Changes in reporting entities	0	432	0	0	−333	295	3,422	3,817
Balance at December 31, 2011	875,283	84,786	49,364	126,371	17,082	25,493	21,402	1,199,781
Thereof long-term								
December 31, 2011	761,837	0	0	126,371	0	0	0	888,208
December 31, 2010	640,860	0	0	120,911	0	0	0	761,771

* Reclassification to short-term liabilities and short-term portion of employee benefit obligations.

In establishing provisions, Management assesses different scenarios of reasonably estimated outcomes to determine the amount that Telekom Austria Group is expected to pay upon the resolution of a contingency. Telekom Austria Group records provisions based on the best estimate of the expenditure required to settle the present obligation.

Telekom Austria Group expects that approximately 60% of the provisions and accrued liabilities, with the exception of the asset retirement obligation and the provision for restructuring, will be utilized during the following financial year. Even if Telekom Austria Group does not expect an outflow of funds in the following financial year, provisions and accrued liabilities are reported as short-term if the timing of such outflow cannot be controlled by Telekom Austria Group.

Employees

The provisions for employees contain unused vacation days, bonuses, overtime and the short-term portion of employee benefit obligations for severance, service awards and pensions (see also Note (27)).

(27) Employee Benefit Obligations

Long-term employee benefit obligations consist of the following:

At December 31	2011	2010
Service awards	61,694	63,425
Severance	61,750	59,441
Pensions	5,420	5,851
Other	112	2,859
Long-term employee benefit obligations	128,976	131,576

Actuarial Assumptions

The actuarial assumptions used in the measurement of obligations for service awards, severance payments and pensions are set out in the following table:

At December 31	2011	2010
Discount rate	4.5%	4.5%
Rate of compensation increase—civil servants	5.5%	5.5%
Rate of compensation increase—other employees	3.1%	3.1%
Rate of increase of pensions	1.6%	1.6%
Employee turnover rate[*]	0.0%–4.5%	0.0%–4.1%

[*] depending on years of service.

Interest expense related to employee benefit obligations is recorded in interest expense; service cost is recorded in employee costs.

Service Awards

Civil servants and certain employees (together "employees") in Austria are eligible to receive service awards. Under these plans, eligible employees receive a cash bonus of two months salary after 25 years of service and four months' salary after 40 years of service. Employees with at least 35 years of service when retiring (at the age of 65) or who are retiring based on a specific legal regulation are eligible to receive to monthly salaries. The compensation is accrued as earned over the period of service, taking into account estimates of employees whose employment will be terminated or who will retire prior to completion of the required service period. All actuarial gains and losses are recognized in profit or loss in the period they are realized or incurred.

The following table provides the components and a reconciliation of the changes in the provision for service awards for the years ended December 31, 2011 and 2010:

	2011	2010
Obligation at the beginning of the year	67,119	60,178
Service cost	2,482	2,283
Interest cost	2,949	3,234
Actuarial losses (gains)	−3,082	4,351
Benefits paid	−3,118	−2,941
Past service cost	1	14
Obligation at the end of the year	66,351	67,119
Less short-term portion	−4,657	−3,694
Non-current obligation	61,694	63,425

Of the defined benefit obligations for service awards, less than 1% related to foreign subsidiaries as of December 31, 2011 and 2010, respectively.

The experience adjustments and the defined benefit obligation as of December 31 amount to:

	2011	2010	2009	2008	2007
Defined benefit obligation	66,351	67,119	60,178	55,480	52,599
Experience adjustments	3,075	1,281	360	−3,115	−343

Severance

Obligations for employees starting to work for Telekom Austria Group in Austria on or after January 1, 2003 are covered by a defined contribution plan. Telekom Austria Group paid EUR 1,474 and EUR 1,316 (1.53% of the salary) into this defined contribution plan (BAWAG Allianz Mitarbeitervorsorgekasse AG) in 2011 and 2010, respectively.

Severance benefit obligations for employees hired before January 1, 2003 are covered by defined benefit plans. Upon termination by Telekom Austria Group or retirement, eligible employees receive severance payments equal to a multiple of their monthly compensation which comprises fixed compensation plus variable elements such as overtime or bonuses. Maximum severance is equal to a multiple of twelve times the eligible monthly compensation. Up to three months of bene-

fits are paid upon termination, with any benefit in excess of that amount being paid in monthly installments over a period not exceeding ten months. In case of death, the heirs of an eligible employee receive 50% of the severance benefits.

The following table provides the components of the net periodic benefit cost for the years ended December 31, 2011 and 2010:

	2011	2010
Service cost	4,469	3,696
Interest cost	2,984	2,882
Amortization of actuarial losses (gains)	−11	−1,174
Net periodic benefit cost	7,443	5,403

The following table provides a reconciliation of the changes in severance benefit obligations for the years ended December 31, 2011 and 2010:

	2011	2010
Defined benefit obligation at the beginning of the year	67,093	54,565
Foreign currency adjustments	2	−6
Change in reporting units	20	25
Service cost	4,469	3,696
Interest cost	2,984	2,882
Benefits paid	−5,133	−4,762
Past service cost	0	3
Actuarial losses (gains)	39	10,690
Defined benefit obligation at the end of the year	69,521	67,093
Unrecognized actuarial gain (loss)	−6,278	−6,228
Obligation at the end of the year	63,243	60,865
Less short-term portion	−1,493	−1,424
Non-current obligation	61,750	59,441

Of the defined benefit obligations for severance, approximately 3% related to foreign subsidiaries as of December 31, 2011 and 2010, respectively.

The experience adjustments and the defined benefit obligation at December 31 amount to:

	2011	2010	2009	2008	2007
Defined benefit obligation	69,521	67,093	54,565	45,759	52,425
Experience adjustments	−352	−1,256	−2,388	−3,904	−20,714

Pensions

Defined Contribution Pension Plans

In Austria, pension benefits generally are provided by the social security system for employees and by the government for civil servants. Telekom Austria Group is required to assist in funding the Austrian government's pension and health care obligations to Telekom Austria Group's current and former civil servants and their surviving dependents. In 2011 and 2010, the rate of contribution for active civil servants amounted to a maximum of 28.3% depending on the age of the civil servant. 15.75% are borne by Telekom Austria Group and the remaining portion is contributed by the civil servants.

Contributions to the government, net of the share contributed by civil servants, amounted to EUR 40,037 and EUR 40,816 in 2011 and 2010, respectively.

Additionally, Telekom Austria Group sponsors a defined contribution plan for employees of some of its Austrian subsidiaries. Telekom Austria Group's contributions to this plan are based on a percentage of the compensation not exceeding 5%. The annual cost of this plan amounted to EUR 12,658 and EUR 13,006 in 2011 and 2010, respectively.

Defined Benefit Pension Plans

Telekom Austria Group provides defined benefits for certain former employees. All such employees are retired and were employed prior to January 1, 1975. This unfunded plan provides benefits based on a percentage of salary and years employed, not exceeding 80% of the salary before retirement, and taking into consideration the pension provided by the social security system.

Telekom Austria Group uses the projected unit credit method to determine pension cost for financial reporting purposes. Under this method, Telekom Austria Group amortizes actuarial gains and losses using the corridor method.

The pension cost for 2011 and 2010 is set out in the following table:

	2011	2010
Interest cost	303	372
Amortization of actuarial losses (gains)	0	0
Net periodic pension cost	303	372

The following table provides a reconciliation of the changes of benefit obligations for the years ended December 31, 2011 and 2010:

	2011	2010
Defined benefit obligation at the beginning of the year	7,133	7,186
Interest cost	303	372
Benefits paid	−801	−774
Past service cost	90	0
Actuarial losses (gains)	394	349
Defined benefit obligation at the end of the year	7,120	7,133
Unrecognized actuarial gain (loss)	−934	−539
Obligation at the end of the year	6,186	6,593
Less short-term portion	−766	−742
Non-current obligation	5,420	5,851

Past service cost relates to an increase in pension payments for prior periods due to an unfavorable change in estimate, which could not be deferred to future periods. The experience adjustments and the defined benefit obligation at December 31 amounted to:

	2011	2010	2009	2008	2007
Defined benefit obligation	7,120	7,133	7,186	6,773	7,489
Experience adjustments	−394	179	−610	−419	−303

Any changes to the major underlying actuarial assumptions used in the calculation of employee benefit obligations could have a material effect on such obligations and on the net employee costs, as well as on interest expense of Telekom Austria Group. A change in the discount rate of one percentage point would lead to the following defined benefit obligations:

At December 31, 2011	3.5%	4.5%	5.5%
Service awards	71,785	66,351	61,522
Severance	82,955	69,521	58,698
Pensions	7,720	7,120	6,686

Defined Benefit Plans, Recognition of Actuarial Gains and Losses in Other Comprehensive Income, Settlement of Defined Benefit Plans

2.349

Rogers Communications Inc. (Dec 2011)

Author's Note

Rogers Communications Inc. implemented IFRSs effective December 31, 2011, with a date of transition of January 1, 2010. The excerpt that follows reflects the initial application of IAS 1 and IAS 12.

CONSOLIDATED STATEMENTS OF FINANCIAL POSITION (in part)

(In millions of Canadian dollars)

	December 31, 2011	December 31, 2010	January 1, 2010
Liabilities and Shareholders' Equity			
Current liabilities:			
Bank advances	$ 57	$ 45	$ —
Accounts payable and accrued liabilities	2,085	2,133	2,066
Income tax payable	—	238	147
Current portion of provisions (note 16)	35	21	14
Current portion of long-term debt (note 17)	—	—	1
Current portion of derivative instruments (note 18)	37	67	80
Unearned revenue	335	329	335
	2,549	2,833	2,643
Provisions (note 16)	38	62	58
Long-term debt (note 17)	10,034	8,654	8,396
Derivative instruments (note 18)	503	840	1,004
Other long-term liabilities (note 19)	276	229	177
Deferred tax liabilities (note 9)	1,390	655	291
	14,790	13,273	12,569

NOTES TO THE CONSOLIDATED FINANCIAL STATEMENTS (in part)

(Tabular amounts in millions of Canadian dollars, except per share amounts)

1. Nature of the Business:

Rogers Communications Inc. ("RCI") is a diversified Canadian communications and media company, incorporated in Canada, with substantially all of its operations and sales in Canada. Through its Wireless segment ("Wireless"), RCI is engaged in wireless voice and data communications services. RCI's Cable segment ("Cable") consists of Cable Operations, Rogers Business Solutions ("RBS") and Rogers Video ("Video"). Through Cable Operations, RCI provides television, high-speed Internet and telephony products primarily to residential customers; RBS provides local and long-distance telephone, enhanced voice and data networking services, and IP access to medium and large Canadian businesses and governments; and Video offers digital video disc ("DVD") and video game sales and rentals. RCI is engaged in radio and television broadcasting, televised shopping, consumer, trade and professional publications, sports entertainment, and digital media properties through its Media segment ("Media"). RCI and its subsidiary companies are collectively referred to herein as the "Company".

The Company's registered office is located at 333 Bloor Street East, 10th Floor, Toronto, Ontario, M4W 1G9.

RCI Class A Voting and Class B Non-Voting shares are traded in Canada on the Toronto Stock Exchange ("TSX") and its Class B Non-Voting shares are also traded on the New York Stock Exchange ("NYSE").

2. Significant Accounting Policies: (in part)

(a) Statement of Compliance:

These consolidated financial statements have been prepared in accordance with International Financial Reporting Standards ("IFRS") as issued by the International Accounting Standards Board ("IASB"). These are the Company's first annual consolidated financial statements prepared in accordance with IFRS, and the Company has elected January 1, 2010 as the date of transition to IFRS (the "Transition Date"). IFRS 1, First-time Adoption of IFRS ("IFRS 1"), has been applied. An explanation of how the transition to IFRS has affected the consolidated financial statements is included in note 3.

The consolidated financial statements of the Company for the years ended December 31, 2011 and 2010 and as at January 1, 2010 were approved by the Board of Directors on February 21, 2012.

(n) Employee Benefits:

(i) Pension Benefits:

The Company provides both contributory and non-contributory defined benefit pension plans, which provide employees with a lifetime monthly pension upon retirement. The Company's net obligation in respect of defined benefit pension plans is calculated separately for each plan by estimating the amount of future benefits that employees have earned in return for their service in the current and prior years; that benefit is discounted to determine its present value. The Company accrues its pension plan obligations as employees render the services necessary to earn the pension. The Company uses a discount rate determined by reference to market yields at the measurement date on high quality corporate bonds to measure the accrued pension benefit obligation. Actuarial gains and losses are determined at the end of the year in connection with the valuation of the plans and are recognized in OCI and retained earnings.

The Company uses the following methods and assumptions for pension accounting associated with its defined benefit plans:

    (a) the cost of pensions is actuarially determined using the projected unit credit method. The projected unit credit method takes into account the expected rates of salary increases, for instance, as the basis for future benefit increases.

    (b) for the purpose of calculating the expected return on plan assets, those assets are valued at fair value.

    (c) past service costs from plan amendments are expensed immediately in the consolidated statements of income to the extent that they are already vested. Unvested past service costs are deferred and amortized on a straight-line basis over the average remaining vesting period.

Contributions to defined contribution plans are recognized as an employee benefit expense in the consolidated statements of income in the periods during which related services are rendered by employees.

(ii) Termination Benefits:

Termination benefits are recognized as an expense when the Company is committed without realistic possibility of withdrawal, to a formal detailed plan to terminate employment before the normal retirement date.

(s) Use of Estimates: (in part)

The preparation of financial statements requires management to make judgements, estimates and assumptions that affect the application of accounting policies and the reported amounts of assets, liabilities, revenue and expenses. Actual results could differ from these estimates.

Key areas of estimation, where management has made difficult, complex or subjective judgements, often as a result of matters that are inherently uncertain are as follows:

(vii) Pensions:

Pension benefit costs are determined in accordance with actuarial valuations, which rely on assumptions including discount rates, life expectancies and expected return on plan assets. In the event that changes in assumptions are required with respect to discount rates and expected returns on invested assets, the future amounts of the pension benefit cost may be affected materially.

20. Pensions:

The Company maintains both contributory and non-contributory defined benefit pension plans that cover most of its employees. The plans provide pensions based on years of service, years of contributions and earnings. The Company does not provide any non-pension post retirement benefits. The Company also provides supplemental unfunded pension benefits to certain executives.

Actuarial estimates are based on projections of employees' compensation levels at the time of retirement. Maximum retirement benefits are primarily based upon career average earnings, subject to certain adjustments. The most recent actuarial valuations were completed as at January 1, 2011 for three of the plans and January 1, 2009 for one of the other plans. The next actuarial valuation for funding purposes must be of a date no later than January 1, 2012 for these plans.

The estimated present value of accrued plan benefits and the estimated market value of the net assets available to provide for these benefits at December 31, 2011 and 2010 and January 1, 2010 are as follows:

	December 31, 2011	December 31, 2010	January 1, 2010
Plan assets, at fair value	$ 684	$652	$541
Accrued benefit obligations	817	728	569
Deficiency of plan assets over accrued benefit obligations	(133)	(76)	(28)
Effect of asset ceiling limit	(1)	(4)	(8)
Net deferred pension liability	$(134)	$(80)	$(36)
Consists of:			
Deferred pension asset	$ 33	$ 26	$ 13
Deferred pension liability	(167)	(106)	(49)
Net deferred pension liability	$(134)	$(80)	$(36)

The following information is provided on pension fund assets measured at December 31, 2011 and 2010 for the years then ended:

Years Ended December 31	2011	2010
Plan assets, January 1	$ 652	$541
Expected return on plan assets	44	40
Actuarial gain (loss) recognized in equity	(17)	21
Contributions by employees	20	21
Contributions by employer	80	60
Benefits paid	(27)	(31)
Plan settlements	(68)	—
Plan assets, December 31	$684	$652

The following information is provided on pension fund assets measured at January 1, 2010, including the adjustments from the previously disclosed September 30, 2009 measurement date under Canadian GAAP:

	January 1, 2010
Plan assets, measured at September 30, 2009	$518
Actuarial gain recognized in equity	10
Contributions by employees	6
Contributions by employer	15
Benefits paid	(8)
Plan assets, January 1, 2010	$541

Accrued benefit obligations arising from funded obligations are outlined below for the years ended December 31, 2011 and 2010:

Years Ended December 31	2011	2010
Accrued benefit obligations, January 1	$728	$569
Service cost	36	25
Interest cost	44	40
Benefits paid	(27)	(31)
Contributions by employees	20	22
Actuarial loss recognized in equity	73	103
Plan settlements	(57)	—
Accrued benefit obligations, December 31	$817	$728

The following information is provided on accrued benefit obligations measured at January 1, 2010 related to funded obligations including the adjustments from the previously disclosed September 30, 2009 measurement date under Canadian GAAP:

	January 1, 2010
Accrued benefit obligations, September 30, 2009	$526
Service cost	4
Interest cost	10
Benefits paid	(9)
Contributions by employees	6
Actuarial loss recognized in equity	32
Accrued benefit obligations, January 1, 2010	$569

Net pension expense, which is included in employee salaries and benefits expense, is outlined below:

Years Ended December 31	2011	2010
Plan cost:		
Service cost	$36	$25
Interest cost	44	40
Expected return on plan assets	(44)	(40)
Net pension expense	36	25
Plan settlements	11	—
Total pension cost recognized in the consolidated statements of income	$47	$25

The Company also provides supplemental unfunded pension benefits to certain executives. The accrued benefit obligations relating to these supplemental plans amounted to approximately $39 million at December 31, 2011 (December 31, 2010—$36 million; January 1, 2010—$32 million), and the related expense for 2011 was $4 million (2010—$4 million). In connection with these plans, $1 million (2010—$2 million) of actuarial losses were recorded directly to OCI and retained earnings.

Certain subsidiaries have defined contribution plans with total pension expense of $2 million in 2011 (2010—$2 million).

(a) Actuarial Assumptions:

	December 31, 2011	December 31, 2010	January 1, 2010
Weighted average discount rate used to determine accrued benefit obligations	5.5%	5.9%	6.9%
Weighted average discount rate used to determine pension expense	6.0%	6.9%	N/A
Weighted average rate of compensation increase used to determine accrued benefit obligations	3.0%	3.0%	3.0%
Weighted average rate of compensation increase used to determine pension expense	3.0%	3.0%	N/A
Weighted average expected long-term rate of return on plan assets	6.8%	7.0%	7.0%

Expected return on assets represents management's best estimate of the long-term rate of return on plan assets applied to the fair value of the plan assets. The Company establishes its estimate of the expected rate of return on plan assets based on the fund's target asset allocation and estimated rate of return for each asset class. Estimated rates of return are based on expected returns from fixed income securities which take into account bond yields. An equity risk premium is then applied to estimate equity returns. Differences between expected and actual return are included in actuarial gains and losses.

The estimated average remaining service periods for the plans range from 8 to 11 years.

(b) Allocation of Plan Assets:

	Percentage of Plan Assets			
Asset Category	December 31, 2011	December 31, 2010	January 1, 2010	Target Asset Allocation Percentage
Equity securities:				
Domestic	19.0%	18.6%	18.6%	10% to 29%
International	37.7%	40.3%	39.9%	29% to 48%
Debt securities	42.4%	40.5%	40.1%	38% to 47%
Other—cash	0.9%	0.6%	1.4%	0% to 2%
	100.0%	100.0%	100.0%	

Plan assets are comprised primarily of pooled funds that invest in common stocks and bonds. The pooled Canadian equity fund has investments in the Company's equity securities comprising approximately 1% of the pooled fund. This results in approximately $1 million (December 31, 2010—$1 million; January 1, 2010—$1 million) of the plans' assets being indirectly invested in the Company's equity securities.

The Company makes contributions to the plans to secure the benefits of plan members and invests in permitted investments using the target ranges established by the Pension Committee of the Company. The Pension Committee reviews actuarial assumptions on an annual basis.

(c) Actual Contributions to the Plans for the Years Ended December 31 are as Follows:

	Employer	Employee	Total
2011	$80	$20	$100
2010	60	21	81

Expected contributions by the Company in 2012 are estimated to be $73 million.

Employee contributions for 2012 are assumed to be at levels similar to 2011 on the assumption staffing levels in the Company will remain the same on a year-over-year basis.

(d) Settlement of Pension Obligations:

During 2011, the Company made a lump-sum contribution of $18 million to its pension plans, following which the pension plans purchased annuities from insurance companies for all employees who had retired during the period from January 1, 2009 to January 1, 2011. The purchase of the annuities relieves the Company of primary responsibility for, and eliminates significant risk associated with, the accrued benefit obligations for the retired employees. This transaction resulted in a non-cash loss from the settlement of pension obligations of approximately $11 million recorded in operating costs on the consolidated statement of income.

(e) Historical Information:

History of Annual Experience (Gains) and Losses:

	December 31, 2011	December 31, 2010
Funded plan:		
Actuarial loss on plan liabilities	$90	$82
Effect of asset ceiling limit	(2)	(4)
Total loss recognized in OCI	88	78
Unfunded plan:		
Total loss recognized in OCI	1	2
Cumulative loss recognized in OCI	$89	$80

Actual return on plan assets was $27 million in 2011 (2010—$61 million).

The Company's experience loss (gain) on funded plan liabilities was $16 million in 2011 (2010—$(24) million), and the Company's experience loss (gain) on unfunded plan liabilities was $1 million in 2011 (2010—$(1) million).

History of Obligation and Assets:

	December 31, 2011	December 31, 2010	January 1, 2010
Funded plan:			
Benefit obligation	$817	$728	$569
Fair value of plan assets	684	652	541
Deficit	$(133)	$(76)	$(28)
Unfunded plan:			
Benefit obligation	$ 39	$ 36	$ 32
Fair value of plan assets	—	—	—
Deficit	$(39)	$(36)	$(32)

As the Company is a first-time adopter of IFRS, the Company is disclosing the history of obligation and assets prospectively from the Transition Date.

Liability for Employment Termination Indemnities

2.350

Luxottica Group S.p.A (Dec 2011)

CONSOLIDATED STATEMENTS OF FINANCIAL POSITION (in part)

(Amounts in Thousands of Euro)	Note Reference	2011	2010
Liabilities and Stockholders' Equity			
Non-current liabilities:			
Long-term debt	20	2,244,583	2,435,071
Liability for termination indemnities	21	45,286	45,363
Deferred tax liabilities	22	456,375	429,848
Other liabilities	23	299,545	310,590
Total non-current liabilities		3,045,789	3,220,872
Total liabilities and stockholders' equity		8,644,156	7,993,579

NOTES TO THE CONSOLIDATED FINANCIAL STATEMENTS (in part)

General Information

Luxottica Group S.p.A. (the "Company") is a corporation with a registered office in Milan, Italy, at Via C. Cantù 2.

The Company and its subsidiaries (collectively, the "Group") operate in two industry segments: (1) manufacturing and wholesale distribution; and (2) retail distribution.

Through its manufacturing and wholesale distribution operations, the Group is engaged in the design, manufacturing, wholesale distribution and marketing of house brand and designer lines of mid- to premium-priced prescription frames and sunglasses, as well as of performance optics products.

Through its retail operations, as of December 31, 2011, the Company owned and operated approximately 6,511 retail locations worldwide and franchised an additional 531 locations principally through its subsidiaries Luxottica Retail North America, Inc., Sunglass Hut Trading, LLC, OPSM Group Limited, Oakley, Inc. ("Oakley") and Multiopticas Internacional S.L.

The retail division's fiscal year is a 52- or 53-week period ending on the Saturday nearest December 31. The accompanying consolidated financial statements include the operations of the North America retail division for the 52-week periods for fiscal years 2011, 2010 and 2009. The fiscal years for the retail distribution divisions in Asia Pacific and South Africa included a 52-week period for 2011 and 2010 and a 53-week period for 2009.

The Company is controlled by Delfin S.à r.l., a company subject to Luxembourg law.

These consolidated financial statements were authorized to be issued by the Board of Directors of the Company at its meeting on February 28, 2012.

Basis of Preparation (in part)

The consolidated financial statements as of December 31, 2011 have been prepared in accordance with the International Financial Reporting Standards ("IFRS") as issued by the International Accounting Standards Board ("IASB") as of the date of approval of these consolidated financial statements by the Board of Directors of the Company.

IFRS are all the international accounting standards ("IAS") and all the interpretations of the International Financial Reporting Interpretations Committee ("IFRIC").

The principles and standards utilized in preparing these consolidated financial statements have been consistently applied through all periods presented.

1. Consolidation Principles, Consolidation Area and Significant Accounting Policies (in part)

Significant Accounting Policies (in part)

Employee Benefits

The Group has both defined benefit and defined contribution plans.

A defined contribution plan is a pension plan under which the Group pays fixed contributions into a separate entity. The Group has no legal or constructive obligations to pay further contributions if the fund does not hold sufficient assets to pay all employees the benefits relating to employee service in the current and prior periods.

A defined benefit plan is a pension plan that is not a defined contribution plan. Typically, defined benefit plans define an amount of pension benefit that an employee will receive upon retirement, usually dependent on one or more factors such as age, years of service and compensation. The liability recognized in the consolidated statement of financial position in respect of defined benefit pension plans is the present value of the defined benefit obligation at the end of the reporting period less the fair value of plan assets, together with adjustments for unrecognized past-service costs. The defined benefit obligation is calculated annually by independent actuaries using the projected unit credit method. The present value of the defined benefit obligation is determined by discounting the estimated future cash outflows using interest rates of high-quality corporate bonds that are denominated in the currency in which the benefits will be paid and that have terms to maturity approximating the terms of the related pension obligation.

Actuarial gains and losses due to changes in actuarial assumptions or to changes in the plan's conditions are recognized as incurred in the consolidated statement of comprehensive income.

For defined contribution plans, the Group pays contributions to publicly or privately administered pension insurance plans on a mandatory, contractual or voluntary basis. The Group has no further payment obligations once the contributions have been paid. The contributions are recognized as employee benefits expenses when they are due. Prepaid contributions are recognized as an asset to the extent that a cash refund or a reduction in future payments is available.

Use of Accounting Estimates (in part)

The preparation of financial statements in conformity with IFRS requires the use of certain critical accounting estimates and assumptions which influence the value of assets and liabilities as well as revenues and costs reported in the consolidated statement of financial position and in the consolidated statement of income, respectively or the disclosures included in the notes to the consolidated financial statements in relation to potential assets and liabilities existing as of the date the consolidated financial statements were authorized for issue.

Estimates are based on historical experience and other factors. The resulting accounting estimates could differ from the related actual results. Estimates are periodically reviewed and the effects of each change are reflected in the consolidated statement of income in the period in which the change occurs.

The current economic and financial crisis has resulted in the need to make assumptions on future trends that are characterized by a significant degree of uncertainty and, therefore, the actual results in future years may significantly differ from the estimate.

The most significant accounting principles which require a higher degree of judgment from management are illustrated below.

(f) Benefit plans. The Group participates in benefit plans in various countries. The present value of pension liabilities is determined using actuarial techniques and certain assumptions. These assumptions include the discount rate, the expected return on plan assets, the rates of future compensation increases and rates relative to mortality and resignations. Any change in the abovementioned assumptions could result in significant effects on the employee benefit liabilities.

21. Liability for Termination Indemnities

Liabilities for termination indemnity were equal to Euro 45.3 million (Euro 45.4 million as of December 31, 2010).

This item primarily includes the liabilities related to the post-employment benefits of the Italian companies' employees (hereinafter "TFR"), accounted for in accordance with Article 2120 of the Italian Civil Code.

Effective January 1, 2007, the TFR system was reformed, and under the new law, employees are given the ability to choose where the TFR compensation is invested, whereas such compensation otherwise would be directed to the National Social Security Institute or Pension Funds. As a result, contributions under the reformed TFR system are accounted for as a defined contribution plan. The liability accrued until December 31, 2006 continues to be considered a defined benefit plan. Therefore, each year, the Group adjusts its accrual based upon headcount and inflation, excluding changes in compensation level.

This liability as of December 31, 2011 represents the estimated future payments required to settle the obligation resulting from employee service, excluding the component related to the future salary increases.

The liabilities as of December 31, 2011 amounted to Euro 36.3 million (Euro 37.8 million as of December 31, 2010).

Contribution expense was Euro 17.1 million, Euro 16.2 million and Euro 15.0 million for the years 2011, 2010 and 2009, respectively.

In application of IAS 19, the valuation of TFR liability accrued as of December 31, 2006 was based on the Projected Unit Credit Cost method. The main assumptions utilized are reported below:

	2011	2010	2009
Economic Assumptions			
Discount rate	4.60%	4.60%	5.10%
Annual TFR increase rate	3.00%	3.00%	3.00%
Death probability:	Those determined by the General Accounting Department of the Italian Government, named RG48	Those determined by the General Accounting Department of the Italian Government, named RG48	Those determined by the General Accounting Department of the Italian Government, named RG48
Retirement probability:	Assuming the attainment of the first of the retirement requirements applicable for the Assicurazione Generale Obbligatoria (General Mandatory Insurance)	Assuming the attainment of the first of the retirement requirements applicable for the Assicurazione Generale Obbligatoria (General Mandatory Insurance)	Assuming the attainment of the first of the retirement requirements applicable for the Assicurazione Generale Obbligatoria (General Mandatory Insurance)

Movements in liabilities during the course of the year are detailed in the following table:

(Amounts in Thousands of Euro)	2011	2010	2009
Liabilities at the beginning of the period	37,838	37,829	39,712
Expenses for interests	1,685	1,929	2,090
Actuarial loss (income)	(840)	1,575	(819)
Benefits paid	(2,426)	(3,495)	(3,154)
Liabilities at the end of the period	36,257	37,838	37,829

Key Management Compensation

2.351

Medical Facilities Corporation (Dec 2011)

Author's Note

Medical Facilities Corporation implemented IFRSs effective December 31, 2011, with a date of transition of January 1, 2010. The excerpt that follows reflects the initial application of IAS 1 and IAS 19.

NOTES TO THE CONSOLIDATED FINANCIAL STATEMENTS (in part)

1. Reporting Entity

Medical Facilities Corporation (the "Company"), is a British Columbia corporation and a public company listed on the Toronto Stock Exchange under the ticker symbol DR. The Company owns indirect controlling interests in five limited liability entities (the "Centers" and collectively with the Company, the "Corporation"), each of which owns a specialty hospital or an ambulatory surgery center located in the United States. The Centers, their locations and the Corporation's ownership interest in each are as follows:

Centers	Location	Ownership Interest December 31 2011	2010
Black Hills Surgical Hospital, LLP ("BHSH")	Rapid City, South Dakota	54.2%	54.2%
Sioux Falls Specialty Hospital, LLP ("SFSH")[(1)]	Sioux Falls, South Dakota	51.0%	51.0%
Dakota Plains Surgical Center, LLP ("DPSC")	Aberdeen, South Dakota	64.6%	64.6%
Oklahoma Spine Hospital, LLC ("OSH")	Oklahoma City, Oklahoma	57.8%	56.1%
The Surgery Center of Newport Coast, LLC ("Newport Coast")	Newport Beach, California	51.0%	51.0%

[(1)] Sioux Falls Surgical Hospital changed its name to Sioux Falls Specialty Hospital effective August 22, 2011.

These consolidated financial statements include the results of operations of Barranca Surgery Center, LLC ("Barranca"), a second ambulatory surgery center in California, until August 13, 2010 at which time the Corporation's indirect 51% interest in this Center was redeemed by the holders of the non-controlling interest (note 6).

The Corporation previously issued income participating securities ("IPS") units pursuant to an initial public offering on March 29, 2004. Each IPS unit was comprised of Cdn$5.90 aggregate principal value of 12.5% subordinated notes payable and one common share of the Corporation. On May 31, 2011, the Corporation completed a conversion to a traditional common share structure (the "Conversion") which was approved by common shareholders at the annual and special meeting on May 13, 2011. Subsequently, at a special meeting held on May 13, 2011, the subordinated noteholders agreed to exchange their subordinated notes for new common shares. Pursuant to the Conversion, each existing common share of the Corporation was exchanged for approximately 0.54 of a new common share of the Corporation and each Cdn$5.90 aggregate principal amount of 12.5% subordinated note payable was exchanged for approximately 0.46 of a new common share of the Corporation (note 13).

Concurrently with the Conversion, the Corporation undertook a restructuring of its U.S. corporate entities (the "Restructuring"). Medical Facilities Holdings (USA), LLC, the Corporation's wholly-owned subsidiary that holds interests in the Centers, converted to a Delaware corporation and was renamed Medical Facilities (USA) Holdings, Inc. ("MFH"). The Corporation incorporated a new wholly-owned subsidiary, Medical Facilities America, Inc. ("MFA") under the laws of the State of Delaware. The Corporation transferred the shares of MFH to MFA in exchange for common shares and a promissory note of MFA.

2. Basis of Preparation

2.1 Statement of Compliance

These consolidated financial statements have been prepared in accordance with International Financial Reporting Standards ("IFRS") issued by the International Accounting Standards Board ("IASB") and Interpretations of the International Financial Reporting Interpretations Committee. These are the Corporation's first consolidated annual financial statements in accordance with IFRS and IFRS 1, *First-time Adoption of International Financial Reporting Standards* ("IFRS 1") has been applied. The Corporation's accounting policies presented in note 3 have been applied in preparing these consolidated financial statements and the comparative information, including the balance sheet at the date of transition.

Previously, the Corporation prepared its annual consolidated financial statements in accordance with Canadian generally accepted accounting principles ("GAAP"). An explanation of how the transition to IFRS has affected the reported financial position, financial performance and cash flows of the Corporation is provided in note 4. The comparative figures presented in these consolidated financial statements are in accordance with IFRS.

These consolidated financial statements were approved by the Corporation's board of directors on March 21, 2012.

16. Employee Future Benefits

Benefits programs at the Centers include qualified 401(k) retirement plans which cover all employees who meet eligibility requirements. Each participating Center makes matching contributions subject to certain limits. In 2011, contributions made by the five Centers to such plans were $1,083 (in 2010: $994).

20. Related Party Transactions and Balances (in part)

The Corporation and the Centers routinely enter into transactions with certain related parties. These parties are considered related through ownership in them by the holders of non-controlling interests in the respective Centers. Such transactions are in the normal course of operations and are at the exchange amounts agreed upon by the parties involved.

20.3 Key Management Compensation

Key management personnel are comprised of three executive officers, namely the President, the Chief Executive Officer and Chief Financial Officer, and the directors of the Corporation. Key management compensation for the years ended December 31, 2011 and December 31, 2010 was as follows:

	2011 $	2010 $
Salaries and other short-term employee benefits for executive officers	1,052,761	1,504,964
Director compensation	709,235	706,095
Total key management compensation	1,761,996	2,211,059

Salaries and other short-term employee benefits for executive officers include cash payments to executive officers for their base salaries, bonuses, social security payments, medical insurance payments and payments under the Corporation's long-term incentive plan. Director compensation consists of retainer and meeting fees.

IFRS 2, *SHARE-BASED PAYMENT*

Author's Note

The IASB has issued the following standards, which have amended IFRS 2:
- IFRS 10
- IFRS 11
  These amendments replace the references to IAS 27 with IFRS 10 and IFRS 11, respectively.
- IFRS 13
  This amendment explains that the definition of *fair value* used in IFRS 2 differs from that in IFRS 13. When an entity applies IFRS 2, it should measure fair value in accordance with IFRS 2, not IFRS 13.

Because the effective dates of these standards are after January 1, 2012, these amendments are not discussed in the commentary in this section. In addition, the timing of the effective dates affects the availability of illustrative excerpts from survey companies' financial statements. Accordingly, the excerpts appearing later in this section may not reflect all or some of these revisions.

IFRSs Overview and Comparison to U.S. GAAP

Author's Note

See section 3, beginning with paragraph 3.155, for an additional discussion of employee share-based pay-

ment transactions (such as, employee stock option plans) and a comparison to U.S. GAAP recognition and measurement requirements. Excerpts for equity-settled employee share-based payment compensation schemes are also provided in that section.

2.352 The objective of IFRS 2 is to reflect the effects of share-based payment transactions, whether with employees or others, on an entity's profit or loss and financial position of the reporting period. A *share-based payment transaction*, as defined in appendix A of IFRS 2, is a transaction in which an entity receives goods or services as consideration for the entity's equity instruments (including shares or share options) or acquires goods or services by incurring liabilities to the supplier of those goods and services for amounts that are based on the price of the entity's shares or other equity instruments. An entity may grant share options or other equity instruments (for example, contracts giving the holder the right, but not the obligation, to subscribe to an entity's shares at a fixed or determinable price for a specific period of time) to employees as part of their compensation for services rendered to the entity.

2.353 Transfers of an entity's equity instruments by its shareholders in exchange for supplying goods and services to the entity are also considered share-based payments within the scope of IFRS 2, unless the transfer is clearly for some other purpose than the supply of goods or services to the entity. Also included within the scope of IFRS 2 are transfers of equity instruments of the entity's parent, or equity instruments of another entity in the same group as the entity, to parties that have supplied goods or services to the entity. Goods include inventories, consumables, PPE, intangible assets, and other nonfinancial assets.

2.354 The revisions to IFRS 3 in 2008 amended the guidance in IFRS 2 related to share-based payments in a business combination. An entity should apply those amendments to annual periods beginning on or after July 1, 2009. If an entity applies IFRS 3, as revised in 2008, in an earlier period, the amendments to IFRS 2 should also be applied in that earlier period.

Recognition and Measurement

IFRS

2.355 Under IFRS 2, an entity should recognize goods and services at the time they are received and either a corresponding decrease in equity for equity-settled transactions or a liability for cash-settled transactions.

2.356 In the case when the supplier chooses the settlement option, IFRS 2 considers the entity to have issued a compound financial instrument. This compound financial instrument includes both a *debt component* (that is, the supplier's right to demand payment in cash) and an *equity component* (that is, the supplier's right to demand settlement in equity instruments rather than cash). When the fair value of the goods or services is measured directly, an entity should first measure the debt component at fair value. Then, the entity measures the equity component as the difference between the fair values of the goods and services and the debt component. This approach is usually referred to as the *incremental approach*.

2.357 In the case when the entity chooses the settlement option, the entity should still recognize a liability if the option to issue equity has no commercial substance (for example, the entity is prohibited from issuing equity) or it has a past practice of always settling in cash. Only if no present obligation exists should the entity account for the transaction as equity-settled. An example of a cash-settled share-based payment is a stock appreciation right.

U.S. GAAP

2.358 Like IFRSs, FASB ASC 718, *Compensation—Stock Compensation*, requires an entity to determine whether to classify a share-based payment transaction as cash settled or equity settled. Paragraphs 6–19 of FASB ASC 718-10-25 provide guidance for determining whether certain financial instruments awarded in share-based payment transactions are liabilities. FASB ASC 718-10-25-6 further states that in determining whether instruments not specifically discussed in the preceding paragraphs are classified as a liability or equity, an entity should apply U.S. GAAP applicable to financial instruments issued in transactions not involving share-based payment.

Presentation

2.359 Neither IFRSs nor FASB ASC 718-30 require separate presentation of share-based payment liabilities, unless they are material to the financial statements.

Disclosure

Author's Note

See section 3, beginning at paragraph 3.177, for a comparison of disclosure requirements for share-based payments classified as equity.

IFRSs

2.360 When the entity has recognized liabilities from share-based payment transactions, IFRS 2 requires the entity to disclose the following amounts:
- Total carrying amount at the end of the period
- Total intrinsic value at the end of the period of liabilities for which the counterparty's right to cash or other assets had vested by the end of the period (for example, vested share appreciation rights)

U.S. GAAP

2.361 FASB ASC 718-30 does not prescribe specific disclosures related to share-based payments recognized as liabilities.

Presentation and Disclosure Excerpts

Phantom Stock Plan for Granting Cash-Settled Share Appreciation Rights

2.362

Thomson Reuters Corporation (Dec 2011)

CONSOLIDATED STATEMENT OF FINANCIAL POSITION (in part)

(Millions of U.S. Dollars)	Notes	December 31 2011	2010
Liabilities and Equity			
Liabilities			
Current indebtedness	18	434	645
Payables, accruals and provisions	20	2,675	2,924
Deferred revenue		1,379	1,300
Other financial liabilities	18	81	142
Current liabilities excluding liabilities associated with assets held for sale		4,569	5,011
Liabilities associated with assets held for sale	13	35	—
Current liabilities		4,604	5,011
Long-term indebtedness	18	7,160	6,873
Provisions and other non-current liabilities	21	2,513	2,217
Other financial liabilities	18	27	71
Deferred tax	22	1,422	1,684
Total liabilities		15,726	15,856

NOTES TO THE CONSOLIDATED FINANCIAL STATEMENTS (in part)

(Unless otherwise stated, all amounts are in millions of U.S. dollars)

Note 1: Summary of Business and Significant Accounting Policies

General Business Description

Thomson Reuters Corporation (the "Company" or "Thomson Reuters") is an Ontario, Canada corporation with common shares listed on the Toronto Stock Exchange ("TSX") and the New York Stock Exchange ("NYSE") and Series II preference shares listed on the TSX. The Company provides intelligent information to businesses and professionals. Its offerings combine industry expertise with innovative technology to deliver critical information to decision makers.

These financial statements were approved by the Company's board of directors on March 7, 2012.

Basis of Preparation

These consolidated financial statements were prepared in accordance with International Financial Reporting Standards ("IFRS"), as issued by the International Accounting Standards Board ("IASB"), on an going concern basis, under the historical cost convention, as modified by the revaluation of financial assets and financial liabilities (including derivative instruments) at fair value.

The preparation of financial statements in accordance with IFRS requires the use of certain critical accounting estimates. It also requires management to exercise judgment in applying the Company's accounting policies. The areas involving a higher degree of judgment or complexity, or areas where assumptions and estimates are significant to the financial statements are disclosed in note 2.

Employee Future Benefits

For defined benefit pension plans and other post-employment benefits, the net periodic pension expense is actuarially determined on an annual basis by independent actuaries using the projected unit credit method. The determination of benefit expense requires assumptions such as the expected return on assets available to fund pension obligations, the discount rate to measure obligations, expected mortality, the expected rate of future compensation and the expected healthcare cost trend rate. For the purpose of calculating the expected return on plan assets, the assets are valued at fair value. Actual results will differ from results which are estimated based on assumptions. The vested portion of past service cost arising from plan amendments is recognized immediately in the income statement. The unvested portion is amortized on a straight-line basis over the average remaining period until the benefits become vested.

The asset or liability recognized in the statement of financial position is the present value of the defined benefit obligation at the end of the reporting period less the fair value of plan assets, together with adjustments for unrecognized past service costs. The present value of the defined benefit obligation is determined by discounting the estimated future cash outflows using interest rates of high-quality corporate bonds that are denominated in the currency in which the benefits will be paid and that have terms to maturity approximating the terms of the related pension liability. All actuarial gains and losses that arise in calculating the present value of the defined benefit obligation and the fair value of plan assets are recognized immediately in retained earnings and included in the statement of comprehensive income. For funded plans, surpluses are recognized only to the extent that the surplus is considered recoverable. Recoverability is primarily based on the extent to which the Company can unilaterally reduce future contributions to the plan.

Payments to defined contribution plans are expensed as incurred, which is as the related employee service is rendered.

Share-Based Compensation Plans

The Company operates a number of equity-settled and cash-settled share-based compensation plans under which it receives services from employees as consideration for equity instruments of the Company or cash payments based on the value of equity instruments of the Company.

For equity-settled share-based compensation, expense is based on the grant date fair value of the awards expected to vest over the vesting period. For cash-settled share-based compensation, the expense is determined based on the fair value of the liability at the end of the reporting period until the award is settled. The expense is recognized over the vesting period, which is the period over which all of the specified vesting conditions are satisfied. For awards with graded vesting, the fair value of each tranche is recognized over its respective vesting period. At the end of each reporting period, the Company re-assesses its estimates of the number of awards that are expected to vest and recognizes the impact of the revisions in the income statement.

Profit Sharing and Bonus Plans

Liabilities for bonuses and profit-sharing are recognized based on a formula that takes into consideration various financial metrics after certain adjustments. The Company recognizes a provision where contractually obliged or where there is a past practice that has created a constructive obligation to make such compensation payments.

Note 5: Operating Expenses (in part)

The components of operating expenses include the following:

	Year Ended December 31	
	2011	2010
Salaries, commissions and allowances	5,132	4,852
Share-based payments	87	92
Post-employment benefits	242	229
Total staff costs	5,461	5,173
Goods and services[1]	2,487	2,637
Data	1,044	1,006
Telecommunications	628	635
Real estate	526	493
Fair value adjustments[2]	(149)	117
Total operating expenses	9,997	10,061

[1] Goods and services include professional fees, consulting services, contractors, technology-related expenses, selling and marketing, and other general and administrative costs.

[2] Fair value adjustments primarily represent mark-to-market impacts on embedded derivatives and certain share-based awards.

Operating expenses include costs incurred in the ordinary course of business as well as costs associated with the Company's integration program that commenced in April 2008 in conjunction with the acquisition of Reuters Group PLC ("Reuters"), and other legacy efficiency initiatives. The Company incurred restructuring costs, including severance and losses on lease terminations in connection with the initiatives. The integration program was completed in 2011. Because the integration and legacy efficiency programs were corporate initiatives, the related expenses are excluded from segment operating profit and are reported separately in the segment information disclosures in note 4.

Operating expenses in 2011 also include a $50 million charge primarily related to a reorganization of the Markets division.

The chart below summarizes the aggregate integration and reorganization costs:

	Year Ended December 31	
	2011	2010
Integration programs expenses	215	463
Reorganization charge	50	—

Employee termination benefits associated with the above programs, including severance and equity-based compensation are reported within "Salaries, commissions and allowances" and "Share-based payments", respectively. In addition, consulting and technology-related expenses associated with the integration programs are reported within "Goods and services." See note 21.

	Integration & Restructuring	Other Provisions	Total Provisions
Balance at December 31, 2009	185	236	421
Charges	126	22	148
Utilization	(149)	(41)	(190)
Translation and other	(16)	21	5
Balance at December 31, 2010	146	238	384
Less: short-term provisions	121	82	203
Long-term provisions	25	156	181
Balance at December 31, 2010	146	238	384
Charges	214	28	242
Utilization	(189)	(32)	(221)
Translation and other	1	2	3
Balance at December 31, 2011	172	236	408
Less: short-term provisions	149	83	232
Long-term provisions	23	153	176

Integration and restructuring provisions relate to the integration program initiated by the Company in conjunction with the Reuters acquisition in 2008, legacy savings programs pursued prior to the acquisition and the 2011 reorganization of the Markets division. These provisions primarily provide for severance obligations and remaining rental payments on vacated leases. At December 31, 2011, severance provisions are expected to be utilized in 2012 or slightly longer and lease-related provisions will be primarily utilized over the next four years. See note 5.

Other provisions include lease retirement obligations, which arise when the Company agrees to restore a leased property to a specified condition at the completion of the lease period. These lease retirement provisions relate primarily to leases which expire over the next nine years.

Note 21: Provisions and Other Non-Current Liabilities

	December 31	
	2011	2010
Net defined benefit plan obligations (see note 25)	1,438	1,026
Deferred compensation and employee incentives	218	239
Provisions	176	181
Unfavorable contract liability	147	208
Uncertain tax positions	446	459
Other non-current liabilities	88	104
Total provisions and other non-current liabilities	2,513	2,217

The following table presents the movement in provisions for the years ended December 31, 2011 and 2010:

Note 24: Share-Based Compensation (in part)

The Company operates a number of equity-settled and cash-settled share-based compensation plans under which it receives services from employees as consideration for equity instruments of the Company or cash payments. Each plan is described below:

Stock Incentive Plan

Under its stock incentive plan, the Company may grant stock options, TRSUs, PRSUs and other awards to certain employees for a maximum of up to 50 million common shares. As of December 31, 2011, there were 19,292,115 awards available for grant (2010—20,265,608).

The following table summarizes the methods used to measure fair value for each type of award and the related vesting period over which compensation expense is recognized:

Type of Award	Vesting Period	Fair Value Measure	Equity Settled	Cash Settled[1]
			Compensation Expense Based On:	
Stock options	Up to four years	Black-Scholes option pricing model	Fair value on business day prior to grant date	Fair value at reporting date
TRSUs	Up to seven years	Closing common share price	Fair value on business day prior to grant date	Fair value at reporting date
PRSUs	Three year performance period	Closing common share price	Fair value on business day prior to grant date	Fair value at reporting date

[1] Cash settled awards represent the portion of share-based compensation relating to withholding tax.

Additional information on each type of award is as follows:

Share Appreciation Rights (SARs)

The Company has a phantom stock plan that provides for the granting of stock appreciation rights ("SARs") and other cash-based awards to certain employees. SARs provide the opportunity to receive a cash payment equal to the fair market value of the Company's common shares less the grant price. SARs vest over a four year period and expire four to ten years after the grant date. Compensation expense is recognized based on the fair value of the awards that are expected to vest and remain outstanding at the end of the reporting period using a Black-Scholes option pricing model. There were no SAR grants in 2011 and 2010.

The movement in the number of awards outstanding and their related weighted average exercise prices are as follows:

	Stock Options	TRSUs	PRSUs	SAYE	SARs	Total	Weighted Average Exercise Price ($)
Awards Outstanding in Thousands:							
Outstanding at December 31, 2009	16,798	2,768	4,523	1,155	589	25,833	25.46
Granted	1,925	433	2,068	—	—	4,426	15.32
Exercised	(1,933)	(484)	(646)	(17)	—	(3,080)	19.58
Forfeited	(1,516)	(12)	(325)	(132)	(106)	(2,091)	34.64
Expired	(2,004)	—	—	—	(58)	(2,062)	45.14
Outstanding at December 31, 2010	13,270	2,705	5,620	1,006	425	23,026	21.89
Exercisable at December 31, 2010	8,129	—	—	1	394	8,524	37.74
Granted	1,902	862	1,791	—	—	4,555	16.24
Exercised	(2,339)	(1,785)	(999)	(28)	(13)	(5,164)	15.21
Forfeited	(639)	(69)	(1,248)	(57)	(48)	(2,061)	11.87
Expired	(1,623)	—	—	(51)	(57)	(1,731)	46.24
Outstanding at December 31, 2011	10,571	1,713	5,164	870	307	18,625	21.10
Exercisable at December 31, 2011	6,367	—	—	689	300	7,356	33.53

The weighted average share price at the time of exercise was $37.06 per share (2010—$36.20).

Share-based compensation expense included in the income statement for years ended December 31, 2011 and 2010 was as follows:

	Stock Options	TRSUs	PRSUs	Others[2]	Total
December 31, 2011[1]	(6)	19	26	5	44
December 31, 2010[1]	27	32	37	9	105

[1] Includes gain of $43 million at December 31, 2011 (2010—loss of $13 million) relating to the revaluation of withholding taxes on stock based compensation awards, which is included within fair value adjustments in the presentation of "Operating expenses" in note 5.
[2] Principally comprised of expense related to ESPP, SAYE and SARs.

The Company recorded a liability for cash-settled share incentive awards of $55 million at December 31, 2011 (2010: $98 million). The intrinsic value of the liability for vested awards was $14 million (2010: $22 million).

The following table summarizes additional information relating to the awards outstanding at December 31, 2011:

Range of Exercise Prices	Number Outstanding (In Thousands)	Weighted Average Remaining Contractual Life (Years)	Weighted Average Exercise Price for Plans Outstanding	Number Exercisable (In Thousands)	Weighted Average Exercise Price for Plans Exercisable
0.00–30.00	10,042	2.23	$ 7.07	1,966	$22.28
30.01–35.00	890	2.65	$33.61	881	$33.64
35.01–40.00	6,314	6.57	$36.91	3,130	$36.48
40.01–45.00	1,359	3.52	$42.74	1,359	$42.74
45.01–50.00	20	0.09	$47.50	20	$47.50
Total	18,625			7,356	

Phantom Shares

2.363

Harry Winston Diamond Corporation (Jan 2012)

Author's Note

Harry Winston Diamond Corporation implemented IFRSs effective December 31, 2011, with a date of transition of January 1, 2010. The excerpt that follows reflects the initial application of IAS 1 and IFRS 2.

CONSOLIDATED BALANCE SHEETS (in part)

(Expressed in thousands of United States dollars)

As at January 31	2012	2011	February 1, 2010
Liabilities and Equity			
Current liabilities			
Trade and other payables (note 12)	$104,681	$139,551	$75,893
Employee benefit plans (note 13)	6,026	4,317	11,284
Income taxes payable (note 14)	29,450	6,660	46,297
Promissory note (note 15)	—	70,000	—
Current portion of interest-bearing loans and borrowings (note 15)	29,238	24,215	23,831
	169,395	244,743	157,305
Interest-bearing loans and borrowings (note 15)	270,485	235,516	161,691
Deferred income tax liabilities (note 14)	325,035	309,868	246,398
Employee benefit plans (note 13)	9,463	7,287	6,898
Provisions (note 16)	65,245	50,130	43,691
Total liabilities	839,623	847,544	615,983

NOTES TO THE CONSOLIDATED FINANCIAL STATEMENTS (in part)

January 31, 2012 with comparative figures
(tabular amounts in thousands of United States dollars, except as otherwise noted)

Note 1: Nature of Operations

Harry Winston Diamond Corporation (the "Company") is a diamond enterprise with assets in the mining and luxury brand segments of the diamond industry.

The Company's mining asset is an ownership interest in the Diavik group of mineral claims. The Diavik Joint Venture (the "Joint Venture") is an unincorporated joint arrangement between Diavik Diamond Mines Inc. ("DDMI") (60%) and Harry Winston Diamond Limited Partnership ("HWDLP") (40%) where HWDLP holds an undivided 40% ownership interest in the assets, liabilities and expenses of the Diavik Diamond Mine. DDMI is the operator of the Diavik Diamond Mine. DDMI and HWDLP are headquartered in Yellowknife, Canada. DDMI is a wholly owned subsidiary of Rio Tinto plc of London, England, and HWDLP is a wholly owned subsidiary of Harry Winston Diamond Corporation of Toronto, Canada.

The Company also owns Harry Winston Inc., the premier fine jewelry and watch retailer with select locations throughout the world. Its head office is located in New York City, United States.

The Company is incorporated and domiciled in Canada and its shares are publicly traded on the Toronto Stock Exchange and the New York Stock Exchange. The address of its registered office is Toronto, Ontario.

These consolidated financial statements have been approved for issue by the Board of Directors on April 4, 2012.

Note 2: Basis of Preparation (in part)

(a) Statement of Compliance

These consolidated financial statements have been prepared in accordance with International Financial Reporting Standards ("IFRS"). These are the Company's first annual consolidated financial statements under IFRS for the fiscal year ending January 31, 2012. The accounting policies adopted in these consolidated financial statements are based on IFRS as issued by the International Accounting Standards Board ("IASB") as of January 31, 2012.

(b) Basis of Measurement

These consolidated financial statements have been prepared on the historical cost basis except for the following:
- financial instruments through profit and loss are measured at fair value.
- liabilities for Restricted Share Unit and Deferred Share Unit Plans are measured at fair value.

Note 3: Significant Accounting Policies (in part)

The accounting policies set out below have been applied consistently to all periods presented in these consolidated financial statements, and have been applied consistently by Company entities.

(n) Stock-Based Payment Transactions

Stock-Based Compensation

The Company applies the fair value method to all grants of stock options. The fair value of options granted is estimated at the date of grant using a Black-Scholes option pricing model incorporating assumptions regarding risk-free interest rates, dividend yield, volatility factor of the expected market price of the Company's stock, and a weighted average expected life of the options. When option awards vest in installments over the vesting period, each installment is accounted for as a separate arrangement. The estimated fair value of the options is recorded as an expense with an offsetting credit to shareholders' equity. Any consideration received on amounts attributable to stock options is credited to share capital.

Restricted and Deferred Share Unit Plans

The Restricted and Deferred Share Unit ("RSU" and "DSU") Plans are full value phantom shares that mirror the value of Harry Winston Diamond Corporation's publicly traded common shares. Grants under the RSU Plan are on a discretionary basis to employees of the Company subject to Board of Directors approval. Under the prior RSU Plan, each RSU grant vests on the third anniversary of the grant date. Under the 2010 RSU Plan, each RSU grant vests equally over a three-year period. Vesting under both RSU Plans is subject to special rules for death, disability and change in control. Grants under the DSU Plan are awarded to non-executive directors of the Company. Each DSU grant vests immediately on the grant date. The expenses related to the RSUs and DSUs are accrued based on fair value. When a share-based payment award vests in installments over the vesting period, each installment is accounted for as a separate arrangement. These awards are accounted for as liabilities with the value of these liabilities being remeasured at each reporting date based on changes in the fair value of the awards, and at settlement date. Any changes in the fair value of the liability are recognized as employee benefit plan expense in net profit or loss.

Note 13: Employee Benefit Plans (in part)

The employee benefit obligation reflected in the consolidated balance sheet is as follows:

	February 1		
	2012	2011	2010
Defined benefit plan obligation—Harry Winston luxury brand segment (a)	$11,381	$ 9,009	$ 7,104
Defined contribution plan obligation—Harry Winston luxury brand segment (b)	88	80	70
Deferred compensation plan obligation—Harry Winston luxury brand segment (b)	—	—	9,207
Post-retirement benefit plan—Diavik Diamond Mine (c)	289	—	—
RSU and DSU plans (note 17)	3,731	2,515	1,801
Total employee benefit plan obligation	$15,489	$11,604	$18,182

	February 1		
	2012	2011	2010
Non-current	$ 9,463	$ 7,287	$ 6,898
Current	6,026	4,317	11,284
Total employee benefit plan obligation	$15,489	$11,604	$18,182

The amounts recognized in the consolidated income statement in respect of employee benefit plans are as follows:

	2012	2011
Defined benefit pension plan—Harry Winston luxury brand segment (a)	$2,074	$1,907
Defined contribution plan—Harry Winston luxury brand segment (b)	1,065	783
Defined contribution plan—Harry Winston mining segment (b)	207	218
Defined contribution plan—Diavik Diamond Mine (b)	2,081	1,061
Post-retirement benefit plan—Diavik Diamond Mine (c)	299	—
RSU and DSU plans (note 17)	2,169	936
	$7,895	$4,905
Share-based payments	2,091	1,338
Total employee benefit plan expense	$9,986	$6,243

Employee benefit plan expense has been included in the consolidated income statement as follows:

	2012	2011
Cost of sales	$3,135	$1,717
Selling, general and administrative expenses	6,851	4,526
	$9,986	$6,243

Note 17: Share Capital (in part)

(e) RSU and DSU Plans

RSU	Number of Units
Balance, January 31, 2010	45,880
Awards and payouts during the year (net)	
RSU awards	145,880
RSU payouts	(35,814)
Balance, January 31, 2011	155,946
Awards and payouts during the year (net)	
RSU awards	66,991
RSU payouts	(46,963)
Balance, January 31, 2012	175,974

DSU	Number of Units
Balance, January 31, 2010	159,475
Awards and payouts during the year (net)	
DSU awards	33,739
DSU payouts	—
Balance, January 31, 2011	193,214
Awards and payouts during the year (net)	
DSU awards	38,781
DSU payouts	(17,127)
Balance, January 31, 2012	214,868

During the fiscal year, the Company granted 66,931 RSUs (net of forfeitures) and 38,781 DSUs under an employee and director incentive compensation program, respectively. The RSU and DSU Plans are full value phantom shares that mirror the value of Harry Winston Diamond Corporation's publicly traded common shares.

Grants under the RSU Plan are on a discretionary basis to employees of the Company subject to Board of Directors approval. The RSUs granted vest one-third on March 31 and one-third on each anniversary thereafter. The vesting of grants of RSUs is subject to special rules for a change in control, death and disability. The Company shall pay out cash on the respective vesting dates of RSUs and redemption dates of DSUs.

Only non-executive directors of the Company are eligible for grants under the DSU Plan. Each DSU grant vests immediately on the grant date.

The expenses related to the RSUs and DSUs are accrued based on fair value. This expense is recognized on a straight-line basis over each vesting period. The Company recognized an expense of $2.2 million (2011—$0.9 million) for the year ended January 31, 2012. The total carrying amount of liabilities for cash settled share-based payment arrangements is $3.7 million (2011—$2.5 million). The amounts for obligations and expense (recovery) for cash settled share-based payment arrangements have been grouped with Employee Benefit Plans in Note 13 for presentation purposes.

IAS 12, *INCOME TAXES*

SIC 21, *INCOME TAXES—RECOVERY OF REVALUED NON-DEPRECIABLE ASSETS*

Author's Note

Accounting for income taxes is significantly different between IFRSs and FASB ASC. Therefore, revising IAS 12 was originally part of a convergence project with FASB. However, in 2009, the two boards determined that revising their respective standards on accounting for income taxes was a larger project than originally anticipated, and they removed it from that agenda. In March 2010, the IASB determined to proceed with more limited amendments to IAS 12 and planned to issue an exposure draft in late 2010 and a revised standard in the first half of 2011. The IASB proposed including the following in a revised standard:

- An initial step in which the entity would consider whether the recovery of an asset or settlement of liability will affect taxable profit
- Recognition of a deferred tax asset in full and an offsetting valuation allowance to the extent necessary, which is similar to that required in U.S. GAAP
- Guidance on assessing the need for a valuation allowance
- Guidance on substantive enactment
- Allocation of current and deferred taxes within a group that files a consolidated tax return

The IASB is also considering proposals on the following issues:

- Treatment of the tax effect of dividends paid by entities such as real estate investment trusts and cooperatives

- Uncertain tax positions, after finalizing the revision of IAS 37
- Deferred tax on property remeasured at fair value

In December 2010, IASB issued *Deferred Tax: Recovery of Underlying Assets: Amendments to IAS 12*, which only addressed the last item in the preceding list: deferred tax on property remeasured at fair value. IAS 12 requires an entity to measure the deferred tax relating to an asset depending on whether the entity expects to recover the carrying amount of the asset through use or sale. When the asset is measured using the fair value model in IAS 40, an entity might find it difficult and subjective to assess whether recovery will be through use or sale. This amendment provides a practical solution to the problem by introducing a presumption that recovery of the carrying amount will normally be through sale. As a result of these amendments, SIC 21, *Income Taxes—Recovery of Revalued Non-Depreciable Assets*, would no longer apply to investment properties carried at fair value. The amendments also incorporate into IAS 12 the remaining guidance previously contained in SIC 21, which is accordingly withdrawn. The amendments are effective for annual periods beginning on or after 1 January 2012, with early application permitted. Given the issue and effective dates, no survey companies would have applied these amendments to their 2010 financial statements.

The IASB may consider a fundamental review of accounting for income taxes as part of its 2012 agenda consultation process.

In 2011, the IASB amended IAS 12 by issuing new standards. These amendments are effective for annual periods beginning on or after 1 January 2012 and, therefore, are not discussed in the commentary in this section. Instead, this author's note includes a brief description of the relevant revisions to IAS 2.

The following standards amended IAS 2:

- IFRS 9, *Financial Instruments* (issued November 2009 and October 2010 with an effective date of 1 January 2015)
  This amendment replaces references to IAS 39 with a reference to IFRS 9.
- IFRS 11, *Joint Arrangements* (issued May 2011 with an effective date of 1 January 2013)
  Among other terminology changes, IFRS 11 replaces the term *joint venture* with the term *joint arrangement* and adds the terms *joint venturer* and *joint operator* to the list of entities able to control the timing of the reversal of a timing difference.

Early adoption of these standards is permitted. However, because the effective dates of these standards are after January 1, 2012, these amendments are not discussed in the commentary in this section. In addition, the timing of the effective dates affects the availability of illustrative excerpts from survey companies' financial statements. Accordingly, the excerpts appearing later in this section may not reflect all or some of these revisions.

IFRSs Overview and Comparison to U.S. GAAP

2.364 IAS 12 establishes the accounting for the current and future tax consequences of taxes levied on an entity's income by taxation authorities. Because the accounting for financial reporting and tax purposes may be different, an entity can have current and future tax consequences from the future recovery of the carrying amount of assets, the future settlement of its liabilities, and transactions and other events in the current period recognized in its financial statements.

2.365 In IAS 12, income taxes include all domestic and foreign taxes that are based on taxable profits and also include taxes, such as withholding taxes, which are payable by a subsidiary, associate, or joint venture on distributions to the reporting entity. IAS 12 does not address the accounting for government grants but does address the accounting for temporary differences that may arise from such grants or investment tax credits.

Recognition and Measurement

IFRSs

2.366 Accounting for income taxes in accordance with IAS 12 relies on the following two essential differences between financial reporting and tax reporting:

- Difference between profit or loss on the statement of comprehensive income and taxable profit determined by the rules of the relevant taxation authorities
- Difference between the carrying value of an asset or a liability in the balance sheet and its *tax base*, which is the amount that is attributable to the asset or liability for tax purposes (temporary difference)

2.367 Temporary differences may be either taxable or deductible. A taxable or deductible temporary difference results in taxable amounts or deductible amounts, respectively, in a future period when the carrying amount of the asset is recovered or the liability is settled. Deferred tax assets and deferred tax liabilities are amounts that are recoverable or taxable, respectively, in future periods as a result of these temporary differences. Deferred tax liabilities result from taxable temporary differences. Deferred tax assets can result not only from deductible temporary differences but also an unused tax loss or unused tax credit carryforward.

2.368 *Tax expense* (or *income*) is defined as the aggregate amount included in profit or loss for the period in respect of current and deferred tax. *Current tax expense* is the amount of income taxes payable (or recoverable) in respect of taxable profit (or loss) during the period. Although not explicitly defined, measurement of deferred tax assets and liabilities in accordance with IAS 12 determines the measurement of deferred tax expense.

2.369 An entity should recognize as a liability current tax and any current tax from prior periods that remains unpaid. Taxes paid in advance or payments in excess of tax payable in prior periods are recognized as an asset. When the benefits of a tax loss can be carried back to prior periods to recover current tax paid in prior periods, an entity should also recognize an asset.

2.370 An entity should recognize a deferred tax liability for all taxable temporary differences, except when the difference arises on initial recognition of either goodwill or an asset or a liability from a transaction that was not a business combination and at the time of the transaction did not affect either accounting or taxable profit (or loss). An entity should recognize a deferred tax asset for all deductible temporary differences to the extent that future taxable profit will be available, except when the difference arises on initial recognition of an asset or a liability from a transaction that was not a business combination and at the time of the transaction did not affect either accounting or taxable profit (or loss).

2.371 In accordance with the recognition and measurement requirements of IFRS 3, an entity should measure goodwill arising in a business combination as either the excess of the sum of the consideration transferred or the amount of the noncontrolling interest and the fair value of any previously held equity interest over the net identifiable assets acquired. However, many taxation authorities do not permit reductions in the carrying amount of goodwill to be deductible for tax purposes; hence, the tax base of goodwill is nil. Although the difference between the tax base and its carrying value is a taxable temporary difference, IAS 12 does not permit recognition of the deferred tax liability because goodwill is measured as a residual and its recognition would result in an increase in the carrying value of goodwill. In contrast, if the carrying value of goodwill is less than its tax base, the entity should recognize a deferred tax asset to the extent that future taxable profit would be available against which the deduction could be used.

2.372 An entity should recognize a deferred tax asset for unused tax losses and unused tax credits that can be carried forward to future years to the extent that future taxable profit would be available against which the loss or credit could be used. At the end of each reporting period, an entity should reassess any unrecognized deferred tax assets. To the extent that it is probable that future taxable profit would be available, an entity should recognize a deferred tax asset. An entity should review the carrying value of deferred tax assets and liabilities at the end of each reporting period and reduce deferred tax assets to the extent future taxable profit will not be available against which to use the asset. This reduction can be reversed in the future if taxable profit becomes available. *Probable* is not specifically defined in IAS 12.

2.373 An entity should not recognize a deferred tax asset or liability in respect of its investments in subsidiaries, associates, and joint ventures when it is probable that the temporary difference will not reverse in the foreseeable future and with respect to the following:
- *Deferred tax asset.* The entity expects future taxable profit to be available against which to use the deductible temporary difference.
- *Deferred tax liability.* The entity can control the timing of the reversal of the taxable temporary difference.

2.374 Using enacted or substantially enacted tax rates or laws, an entity should measure current tax liabilities or assets for the current period at the amount they expect to pay or recover, respectively. An entity should measure deferred tax assets and liabilities at enacted or substantially enacted tax rates that are expected to apply in the period of recovery or payment. Measurement of deferred tax assets or liabilities should reflect that manner in which the entity expects to recover the asset or settle the liability. For example, when there are differential tax rates for income generated by operating activities and income from sales of assets and the entity intends to recover the asset by its use in operations, the entity should use the rate on operating income to measure the liability.

2.375 An entity should not discount future cash inflows and outflows to measure a deferred tax asset or liability.

2.376 IAS 12 notes that a revaluation of an asset may not always affect taxable profit or loss in the period of the revaluation; consequently, the entity should not adjust the tax base of the asset as a result of the revaluation. However, if the future recovery of the asset's carrying amount will be taxable, an entity should recognize any difference between the carrying amount of the revalued asset and its tax base as a deferred tax liability or asset in respect of the temporary difference. SIC 21 requires an entity to recognize the deferred tax consequences of revaluation of a nondepreciable asset, such as land, based on its recovery through sale and use of the tax rate that would apply in that circumstance.

U.S. GAAP

2.377 FASB ASC 740, *Income Taxes*, provides more extensive requirements and guidance on recognition and measurement of income taxes.

2.378 Like IFRSs, the FASB ASC glossary defines *income taxes* as domestic and foreign federal (national), state, and local (including franchise) taxes based on income. To accomplish the objectives of recognizing income tax, FASB ASC 740-10-05-5 explains that an entity should recognize the following in its financial statements:
- Amount of estimated taxes payable or refundable on tax returns for the current year as a tax liability or asset
- Deferred tax liabilities and assets for the estimated future tax effects attributable to temporary differences and carryforwards

2.379 Like IFRSs, FASB ASC 740-10-05-7 applies the concept of temporary differences to incorporate in the financial statements the differences that exist between financial reporting standards and jurisdiction-specific tax regulations or law. Both sets of principles confront these differences with an asset-liability approach and, therefore, focus on the difference between the carrying value of an asset or a liability in the entity's financial statements and its tax basis for tax reporting.

2.380 However, unlike IFRSs, FASB ASC 740-10-10-1 recognizes that some events do not have tax consequences. Certain income is not taxable, and certain expenses or losses are not deductible. For example, in the United States, municipal bond interest income is generally not taxable but would be reported as income in the company's income statements.

2.381 Unlike IFRSs, which permit the use of substantially enacted tax rates, FASB ASC 740-10-10-3 only permits the use of enacted tax rates that are expected to apply to taxable income in the period in which the deferred tax asset or liability is expected to be recovered or settled, respectively.

2.382 Like IFRSs, FASB ASC 740-10-05-5 requires an entity to recognize deferred tax assets and liabilities at amounts recoverable or taxable, respectively, in future periods as a result of temporary differences. Both deferred tax assets and liabilities can result from temporary differences and carry-forwards. FASB ASC 740-10-25-29 explains that an entity should recognize a deferred tax liability or asset for all temporary differences and operating loss and tax credit carryforwards, in accordance with FASB ASC 740-10-30-5. However, FASB ASC 740-10-25-3 includes certain exemptions from these requirements, unless the temporary differences are expected to reverse in the foreseeable future.

2.383 Although different criteria apply, neither FASB ASC nor IFRSs requires deferred tax to be recognized on temporary differences arising from investments in foreign subsidiaries or corporate joint ventures until it becomes apparent that those temporary differences will reverse in the foreseeable future, as discussed in FASB ASC 740-10-25-3. IFRSs also exempt temporary differences from investments in associates. FASB ASC 740-10-25-3 includes some exemptions for events that occurred before specific dates (for example, bad debt reserves for tax purposes of U.S. savings and loans that arose in tax years beginning before December 31, 1987). Unlike IFRSs, FASB ASC 740-10-25-3 also prohibits recognition of deferred tax assets or liabilities for the following:
- Leveraged leases
- Goodwill when amortization is not tax deductible (similar to the IFRSs exception)
- Differences due to the intraentity difference between the tax basis of the assets in the buyer's tax jurisdiction and their cost as reported in the consolidated financial statements
- Differences due to remeasurement of assets and liabilities from the local currency into the functional currency, using historical exchange rates, and differences that result from changes in exchange rates or indexing for tax purposes

2.384 Measurement requirements for deferred tax assets and liabilities under U.S. GAAP are similar to those under IFRSs. In contrast with the net approach to recognizing deferred tax assets under IFRSs, the FASB ASC glossary definition of *deferred tax asset* explains that an entity is required to reduce the deferred tax asset balance by a valuation allowance if, based on the weight of available evidence, it is more likely than not that some or all of the deferred tax asset will not be realized. An entity should measure the valuation allowance at an amount that reduces the carrying value of the net deferred tax asset to the amount more likely than not to be recovered. FASB ASC 740-10-25-6 clarifies that for purposes of applying the more likely than not threshold in evaluating the potential realization of deferred tax assets, *more likely than not* is defined as a likelihood of more than 50 percent.

2.385 Unlike IFRSs, U.S. GAAP includes requirements regarding uncertain tax positions. The FASB ASC glossary defines a *tax position* as a position in a previously filed tax return, or a position expected to be taken in a future tax return, that is reflected in measuring current or deferred income tax assets and liabilities for interim or annual periods. A tax position can result in a permanent reduction in income taxes payable, a deferral of income taxes otherwise currently payable to future years, or a change in the expected realizability of deferred tax assets. The term *tax position* also encompasses, but is not limited to, a decision not to file a tax return; an allocation or a shift of income between jurisdictions; the characterization of income or a decision to exclude reporting taxable income in a tax return; a decision to classify a transaction, entity, or other position in a tax return as tax exempt; and an entity's status, including its status as a pass-through entity or a tax-exempt not-for-profit entity. FASB ASC 740-10 includes detailed procedures for recognition, measurement, and disclosure of uncertain tax positions.

2.386 Unlike IFRSs, FASB ASC 740-20 also includes requirements for intraperiod tax allocation, including computation of tax expense and treatment of tax carryforwards.

Presentation

IFRSs

2.387 IFRSs require deferred tax assets and liabilities to be presented separately from current tax receivable and payable and classified as noncurrent in a classified balance sheet. IAS 12 prohibits the offsetting of tax assets and liabilities, unless they relate to the same tax authority and the entity has a legal right and intends to recover or settle net.

U.S. GAAP

2.388 Rule 5-02 of SEC Regulation S-X requires SEC registrants to present deferred credits in the balance, with separate amounts for deferred income taxes and deferred tax credits, and also other assets (for example, deferred tax assets) when they exceed 5 percent of total assets. However, unlike IFRSs, in a classified statement of financial position, FASB ASC 740-10-45-4 requires deferred tax assets and liabilities to be classified as either current or noncurrent based on the classification of the related asset or liability. For example, deferred tax assets due to temporary differences related to accounts receivable would be classified as current. Similarly, deferred tax liabilities due to temporary differences related to PPE would be classified as noncurrent. FASB ASC 740-10-45-11 requires an entity that presents a classified balance sheet to classify a liability associated with an unrecognized tax benefit (or the amount of a net operating loss carryforward or amount refundable that is reduced) as a current liability, to the extent that the entity expects to pay or receive cash within the next 12 months (or current operating cycle if longer). FASB ASC 740-10-45-5 requires an entity to allocate any valuation allowances for the same tax jurisdictions on a pro rata basis between current and noncurrent.

2.389 Like IFRSs, FASB ASC 740-10-45-6 prohibits offsetting deferred tax assets and liabilities attributable to different tax-paying components of the entity or different tax jurisdictions. However, an entity should present current deferred tax assets and liabilities as a single amount and all noncurrent deferred tax assets and liabilities as a single amount only for a particular tax-paying component of the entity and within a particular tax jurisdiction. FASB ASC 740-10-45-13 prohibits the offset of cash or other assets against the tax liability, unless the general criteria for offsetting, in accordance with FASB ASC 210-20-45-6, are met.

Disclosure

Author's Note

Both IAS 12 and FASB ASC 740 require significant additional disclosures about the effects of accounting for income taxes on the statement of comprehensive income. These disclosures are described, and excerpts are provided, beginning with paragraph 3.317 of section 3.

IFRSs

2.390 Under IAS 12, an entity should disclose the amount of deferred tax assets and liabilities due to each type of temporary difference, unused tax loss, and unused tax credit. An entity should also disclose the aggregate amount of temporary differences associated with investments in subsidiaries, associates, and joint ventures for which deferred tax liabilities have not been recognized. For unused tax losses and tax credits, an entity should disclose the amount and expiration date (if any) of deductible temporary differences.

2.391 An entity should disclose the amount of any deferred tax asset and the nature of the evidence supporting recognition when the following two conditions are met:

- Recovery of the asset relies on future taxable profit in excess of that arising from reversal of existing taxable temporary differences.
- Entity reported a loss in the current or preceding period in the relevant tax jurisdiction.

U.S. GAAP

2.392 FASB ASC 740-10-50-2 requires an entity to disclose the aggregate of all deferred tax liabilities, the aggregate of all deferred tax assets, and the valuation allowance recognized for deferred tax assets.

2.393 Like IFRSs, for unrecognized tax loss and tax credit carryforwards, FASB ASC 740-10-50-3 states that an entity should disclose the amounts of these carryforwards and their expiration dates for tax purposes. Unlike IFRSs, an entity should also disclose the portion of any valuation allowance for deferred tax assets for which subsequently recognized tax benefits will be credited directly to contributed capital rather than income. FASB ASC 740-10-50-6 requires public entities also to disclose the approximate tax effect of each type of temporary difference and carryforward that gives rise to a significant portion of deferred tax assets and deferred tax liabilities (before allocation of valuation allowances).

Presentation and Disclosure Excerpts

Current and Non-current Tax Payables, Deferred Tax Liabilities, and Tax Loss Carryforwards

2.394

Telecom Argentina (Dec 2011)

CONSOLIDATED STATEMENTS OF FINANCIAL POSITION (in part)

(In millions of Argentine pesos)

	Note	As of December 31 2011	2010
Liabilities			
Current liabilities			
Trade payables	10	3,407	2,736
Deferred revenues	11	292	225
Financial debt	12	19	42
Salaries and social security payables	13	536	390
Income tax payables	14	605	491
Other taxes payables	15	457	531
Other liabilities	16	30	31
Provisions	17	173	64
Total current liabilities		5,519	4,510
Non-current liabilities			
Deferred revenues	11	307	190
Financial debt	12	115	121
Salaries and social security payables	13	136	110
Deferred income tax liabilities	14	210	247
Income tax payables	14	13	14
Other liabilities	16	72	39
Provisions	17	782	581
Total non-current liabilities		1,635	1,302

NOTES TO THE CONSOLIDATED FINANCIAL STATEMENTS (in part)

Note 1—Description of Business and Basis of Preparation of the Consolidated Financial Statements (in part)

a) The Company and Its Operations (in part)

Telecom Argentina was created by a decree of the Argentine Government in January 1990 and organized as a *sociedad anónima* under the name "Sociedad Licenciataria Norte S.A." in April 1990.

Telecom Argentina commenced operations on November 8, 1990, upon the transfer to the Company of the telecommunications network of the northern region of Argentina previously owned and operated by the state-owned company, Empresa Nacional de Telecomunicaciones ("ENTel").

Telecom Argentina's license, as originally granted, was exclusive to provide telephone services in the northern region of Argentina through October 10, 1999. As from such date, the Company also began providing telephone services in the southern region of Argentina and competing in the previously exclusive northern region.

The Company provides fixed-line public telecommunication services, international long-distance service, data transmission and Internet services in Argentina and through its subsidiaries, mobile telecommunications services in Argentina and Paraguay and international wholesale services in the United States of America. Information on the Telecom Group's licenses and the regulatory framework is described in Note 2.

c) Basis of Preparation (in part)

These consolidated financial statements have been prepared in accordance with IFRS as issued by the International Accounting Standards Board. IFRS comprises all effective IAS together with all the SIC and all interpretations issued by the IFRIC.

The preparation of financial statements in conformity with IFRS requires the use of certain critical accounting estimates. It also requires Management to exercise its judgment in the process of applying the Telecom Group's accounting policies. The areas involving a higher degree of judgment or complexity, or areas where assumptions and estimates are significant to the consolidated financial statements are disclosed in Note 3.

Note 3—Significant Accounting Policies (in part)

o) Taxes Payables

The Company is subject to different taxes and levies such as municipal taxes, tax on deposits to and withdrawals from bank accounts, turnover taxes, regulatory fees (including SU) and income taxes, among others, that represent an expense for the Group. It is also subject to other taxes over its activities that generally do not represent an expense (internal taxes, VAT, ENARD tax).

The principal taxes that represent an expense for the Company are the following:

Income Taxes

Income taxes are recognized in the consolidated income statement, except to the extent that they relate to items directly recognized in Other comprehensive income or directly in equity. In this case, the tax is also recognized in Other comprehensive income or directly in equity, respectively. The tax expense for the period comprises current and deferred tax.

As per Argentinean Tax Law, income taxes payables have been computed on a separate return basis (i.e., the Company is not allowed to prepare a consolidated income tax return). All income tax payments are made by each of the subsidiaries as required by the tax laws of the countries in which they operate. The Company records income taxes in accordance with IAS 12.

Deferred taxes are recognized using the "liability method." Temporary differences arise when the tax base of an asset or liability differs from their carrying amounts in the consolidated financial statements. A deferred income tax asset or liability is recognized on those differences, except for those differences related to investments in subsidiaries where the timing of the reversal of the temporary difference is controlled by the Group and it is probable that the temporary difference will not reverse in the foreseeable future.

Deferred tax assets relating to unused tax loss carryforwards are recognized to the extent that it is probable that future taxable income will be available against which they can be utilized. Current and deferred tax assets and liabilities are offset when the income taxes are levied by the same tax authority and there is a legally enforceable right of offset. Deferred tax assets and liabilities are determined based on enacted tax rates in the respective jurisdictions in which the Group operates that are expected to apply to taxable income in the years in which those temporary differences are expected to be recovered or settled.

The statutory income tax rate in Argentina was 35% for all years presented. Cash dividends received from a foreign subsidiary are computed on the statutory income tax rate. As per Argentinean Tax Law, income taxes paid abroad may be recognized as tax credits.

The statutory income tax rate in Paraguay was 10% for all years presented. As per Paraguayan Tax Law, dividends paid are computed with an additional income tax rate of 5% (this is the criterion used by Núcleo for the recording of its deferred tax assets and liabilities, representing an effective tax rate of 14.75%). However, the effect of the additional income tax rate according to the Argentine tax law in force on the undistributed profits of Núcleo is fully recognized as it is considered probable that those results will flow to Personal in the form of dividends.

t) Use of Estimates (in part)

The preparation of consolidated financial statements and related disclosures in conformity with IFRS requires Management to make estimates and assumptions based also on subjective judgments, past experience and hypotheses considered reasonable and realistic in relation to the information known at the time of the estimate.

Such estimates have an effect on the reported amount of assets and liabilities and disclosure of contingent assets and liabilities at the date of the financial statements as well as the amount of revenues and costs during the year. Actual results could differ, even significantly, from those estimates owing to possible changes in the factors considered in the determination of such estimates. Estimates are reviewed periodically.

The most important accounting estimates which require a high degree of subjective assumptions and judgments are addressed below:

Financial Statement Item/Area	Accounting Estimates
Income taxes and recoverability assessment of deferred tax assets	Income taxes (current and deferred) are calculated in each company of the Telecom Group according to a reasonable interpretation of the tax laws in effect in each jurisdiction where the companies operate. The recoverability assessment of deferred tax assets sometimes involves complex estimates to determine taxable income and deductible and taxable temporary differences between the carrying amounts and the taxable amounts. In particular, deferred tax assets are recognized to the extent that future taxable income will be available against which they can be utilized. The measurement of the recoverability of deferred tax assets takes into account the estimate of future taxable income based on the Company's projections and on conservative tax planning.

Note 4—Cash and Cash Equivalents and Investments. Additional Information on the Consolidated Statements of Cash Flows (in part)

Changes in Assets/Liabilities Components:

	Years Ended December 31		
	2011	2010	2009
Net (increase) decrease in assets			
Investments not considered as cash or cash equivalents	3	1	(33)
Trade receivables, net	(516)	(476)	(314)
Other receivables, net	(100	(116)	(39)
Inventories, net	(101)	(236)	(37)
	(714)	(827)	(423)
Net (decrease) increase in liabilities			
Trade payables	376	503	241
Deferred revenues	184	37	29
Salaries and social security payables	172	91	55
Other taxes payables	38	193	(17)
Other liabilities	16	9	(5)
Provisions	(56)	(36)	(16)
	730	797	287

Income tax paid consists of the following:

	Years Ended December 31		
	2011	2010	2009
Income tax returns	(529)	(451)	(321)
Payments in advance	(703)	(494)	(231)
Other payments	(84)	(62)	(78)
Total payments of income tax	(1,316)	(1,007)	(630)

Main Non-Cash Operating Transactions:

	Years Ended December 31		
	2011	2010	2009
SU receivables offset with taxes payable	112	—	—
Government bonds received in exchange for trade receivables	—	2	—
Credit on minimum presumed income tax offset with income taxes	—	—	7
Legal fee from Tax Regularization Regime (Note 3.l)	—	—	14

Note 6—Other Receivables, Net (in part)

Other receivables, net consist of the following:

	As of December 31	
	2011	2010
Current other receivables, net		
Prepaid expenses	164	114
SU credits (Note 2.d)	—	112
Tax credits	56	52
Restricted funds	23	15
Related parties (Note 27.c)	1	—
Other	74	42
Subtotal	318	335
Allowance for doubtful accounts	(12)	(13)
	306	322
Non-current other receivables, net		
Credit on SC Resolution No. 41/07 and IDC (Note 2.e and f)	90	90
Restricted funds	23	31
Tax credits	17	17
Prepaid expenses	68	55
Credit on minimum presumed income tax	5	6
Other	7	8
Subtotal	210	207
Allowance for regulatory matters (Note 2 e. and f)	(90)	(90)
Allowance for doubtful accounts	(17)	(17)
	103	100
Total other receivables, net	409	422

Movements in the allowances are as follows:

	Years Ended December 31	
	2011	2010
Current allowance for regulatory matters		
At January 1	—	(4)
Reclassifications[*]	—	4
At December 31	—	—
Non-current allowance for regulatory matters		
At January 1	(90)	(75)
Additions[**]	—	(13)
Reclassifications[*]	—	(2)
At December 31	(90)	(90)

[*] In 2010, includes reclassifications of $2 to Provisions.
[**] Included in Provisions in the consolidated income statements.

| | Years Ended December 31 | |
	2011	2010
Current allowance for doubtful accounts		
At January 1	(13)	(12)
Additions(***)	—	(1)
Reversals(***)	1	—
At December 31	(12)	(13)
Non-current allowance for doubtful accounts		
At January 1	(17)	(21)
Reversals(***)	—	4
At December 31	(17)	(17)

(***) Included in Taxes and fees with the Regulatory Authority in the consolidated income statements.

Note 14—Income Tax Payables and Deferred Income Tax

Income tax payables as of December 31, 2011 and 2010 consist of the following:

| | As of December 31, 2011 | | | | | As of December 31, 2010 |
	Telecom Argentina	Personal	Núcleo	Telecom USA	Total	
Income tax payables	376	1,033	16	—	1,425	1,071
Payments in advance of income taxes	(317)	(501)	(5)	—	(823)	(584)
Law No. 26,476 Tax Regularization Regime	3	—	—	—	3	3
Current income tax payables	62	532	11	—	605	(*)490
Deferred income tax liabilities	2	206	1	1	210	247
Law No. 26,476 Tax Regularization Regime	13	—	—	—	13	14
Non-current Income tax payables	15	206	1	1	223	261

(*) Includes (1) from Núcleo's receivable which is included in Current other receivables, net—Tax credits.

The tax effects of temporary differences that give rise to significant portions of the Company's deferred tax assets and liabilities are presented below:

| | As of December 31, 2011 | | | | | As of December 31, 2010 |
	Telecom Argentina	Personal	Núcleo	Telecom USA	Total	
Tax loss carryforwards	—	2	—	—	2	1
Allowance for doubtful accounts	35	35	1	—	71	49
Provisions	243	101	—	—	344	241
Inventory	—	14	—	—	14	8
Termination benefits	66	—	—	—	66	54
Deferred revenues on connection fees	33	6	—	—	39	35
Other deferred tax assets	36	11	—	—	47	52
Total deferred tax assets	413	169	1	—	583	440
PP&E and intangible assets	(116)	(322)	(3)	(1)	(442)	(330)
Inflation adjustments(i)	(299)	(4)	1	—	(302)	(336)
Other deferred tax liabilities	—	(28)	—	—	(28)	(5)
Total deferred tax liabilities	(415)	(354)	(2)	(1)	(772)	(671)
Subtotal net deferred tax liabilities	(2)	(185)	(1)	(1)	(189)	(231)
—Valuation allowance	—	(ii) (21)	—	—	(21)	(16)
Net deferred tax liabilities	(2)	(206)	(1)	(1)	(210)	(247)

(i) Mainly related to inflation adjustment on PP&E and intangible assets for financial reporting purposes booked prior to the adoption of IFRS and included in the deemed cost of long lived assets.

(ii) Includes (1) corresponding to Springville.

As of December 31, 2011, the Company had tax loss carry-forward of $2 expiring in 2011.

	Year Ended December 31, 2011				
	Telecom Argentina	Personal	Núcleo	Telecom USA	Total
Current tax expense	(379)	(1,039)	(16)	—	(1,434)
Deferred tax benefit (expense)	99	(58)	2	1	44
Valuation allowance	—	(5)	—	—	(5)
Income tax expense	(280)	(1,102)	(14)	1	(1,395)

	Year Ended December 31, 2010				
	Telecom Argentina	Personal	Núcleo	Telecom USA	Total
Current tax expense	(408)	(655)	(4)	—	(1,067)
Deferred tax benefit (expense)	79	(79)	(6)	—	(6)
Valuation allowance	—	(3)	—	—	(3)
Income tax expense	(329)	(737)	(10)	—	(1,076)

	Year Ended December 31, 2009				
	Telecom Argentina	Personal	Núcleo	Telecom USA	Total
Current tax expense	(301)	(511)	(6)	—	(818)
Deferred tax benefit (expense)	29	(6)	—	(1)	22
Valuation allowance	—	(2)	—	—	(2)
Income tax expense	(272)	(519)	(6)	(1)	(798)

Income tax expense for the years ended December 31, 2011, 2010 and 2009 consists of the following:

Income tax expense for the years ended December 31, 2011, 2010 and 2009 differed from the amounts computed by applying the Company's statutory income tax rate to pre-tax income as a result of the following:

	For the Years Ended December 31		
	2011	2010	2009
Pre-tax income	3,937	3,025	2,215
Non taxable items—Other income from investments	—	—	(13)
Non taxable items—Other	17	42	44
Subtotal	3,954	3,067	2,246
Weighted statutory income tax rate[*]	34.7%	34.4%	34.3%
Income tax expense at weighted statutory tax rate	(1,373)	(1,054)	(771)
Other changes in tax assets and liabilities	(17)	(19)	(6)
Law No. 26,476 Tax Regularization Regime	—	—	(19)
Changes in valuation allowance	(5)	(3)	(2)
	(1,395)	(1,076)	(798)

[*] Effective income tax rate based on weighted statutory income tax rate in the different countries where the Company has operations. The statutory tax rate in Argentina was 35% for all the years presented, in Paraguay was 10% plus an additional rate of 5% in case of payment of dividends for all the years presented, in Uruguay the statutory tax rate was 25% for all the years presented and in the USA the effective tax rate was 40%, 34% and 21%, respectively.

Note 15—Other Taxes Payables

Other taxes payables consist of the following:

	As of December 31	
	2011	2010
Current		
VAT, net	129	126
Tax on SU (Note 2.d)	85	206
Tax withholdings	85	69
Internal taxes	50	40
Turnover tax	40	40
Regulatory fees	40	31
Municipal taxes	13	8
Retention Decree No. 583/10 ENARD	8	5
Other	7	6
	457	531

Current Tax Receivables and Payables, Deferred Tax Assets and Liabilities

2.395

ING Groep N.V. (Dec 2011)

CONSOLIDATED BALANCE SHEET (in part)

As at December 31

Amounts in Millions of Euros	2011	2010
Assets		
Cash and balances with central banks 1	31,194	13,072
Amounts due from banks 2	45,323	51,828
Financial assets at fair value through profit and loss 3		
—trading assets	123,688	125,675
—investments for risk of policyholders	116,438	120,481
—non-trading derivatives	17,159	11,722
—designated as at fair value through profit and loss	5,437	6,016
Investments 4		
—available-for-sale	208,539	222,547
—held-to-maturity	8,868	11,693
Loans and advances to customers 5	596,877	608,938
Reinsurance contracts 17	5,870	5,789
Investments in associates 6	2,370	3,925
Real estate investments 7	1,670	1,900
Property and equipment 8	2,886	6,132
Intangible assets 9	3,558	5,372
Deferred acquisition costs 10	10,204	10,499
Assets held for sale 11	62,483	681
Other assets 12	31,016	36,469
Total assets	1,273,580	1,242,739
Liabilities		
Subordinated loans 14	8,858	10,645
Debt securities in issue 15	139,861	135,604
Other borrowed funds 16	19,684	22,291
Insurance and investment contracts 17	278,833	271,128
Amounts due to banks 18	72,233	72,852
Customer deposits and other funds on deposit 19	467,547	511,362
Financial liabilities at fair value through profit and loss 20		
—trading liabilities	107,682	108,050
—non-trading derivatives	22,165	17,782
—designated as at fair value through profit and loss	13,021	12,707
Liabilities held for sale 11	64,265	424
Other liabilities 21	33,202	36,446
Total liabilities	1,227,351	1,199,291

2.1 NOTES TO THE CONSOLIDATED FINANCIAL STATEMENTS (in part)

2.1.1 Accounting Policies for the Consolidated Annual Accounts of ING Group

Authorization of Annual Accounts

The consolidated annual accounts of ING Groep N.V. ('ING Group') for the year ended December 31, 2011 were authorized for issue in accordance with a resolution of the Executive Board on March 12, 2012. The Executive Board may decide to amend the annual accounts as long as these are not adopted by the General Meeting of Shareholders. The General Meeting of Shareholders may decide not to adopt the annual accounts, but may not amend these. ING Groep N.V. is incorporated and domiciled in Amsterdam, the Netherlands. The principal activities of ING Group are described in Item 4 'Information on the Company'.

Basis of Presentation (in part)

ING Group prepares financial information in accordance with International Financial Reporting Standards as issued by the International Accounting Standards Board ('IFRS-IASB') for purposes of reporting with the U.S. Securities and Exchange Commission ('SEC'), including financial information contained in this Annual Report on Form 20-F. ING Group's accounting policies and its use of various options under IFRS-IASB are described under 'Principles of valuation and determination of results' in the consolidated financial statements. In this document the term 'IFRS-IASB' is used to refer to IFRS-IASB as applied by ING Group.

Taxation

Income tax on the result for the year comprises current and deferred tax. Income tax is recognised in the profit and loss account but it is recognised directly in equity if the tax relates to items that are recognised directly in equity.

Deferred Income Tax

Deferred income tax is provided in full, using the liability method, on temporary differences arising between the tax bases of assets and liabilities and their carrying amounts in the consolidated financial statements. Deferred income tax is determined using tax rates (and laws) that have been enacted or substantially enacted by the balance sheet date and are expected to apply when the related deferred income tax asset is realised or the deferred income tax liability is settled. Deferred tax assets and liabilities are not discounted.

Deferred tax assets are recognised where it is probable that future taxable profit will be available against which the temporary differences can be utilised. Deferred income tax is provided on temporary differences arising from investments in subsidiaries and associates, except where the timing of the reversal of the temporary difference is controlled by the Group and it is probable that the difference will not reverse in the foreseeable future. The tax effects of income tax losses available for carry forward are recognised as an asset where it is probable that future taxable profits will be available against which these losses can be utilised.

Deferred tax related to fair value remeasurement of available-for-sale investments and cash flow hedges, which are recognised directly in equity, is also recognised directly in equity and is subsequently recognised in the profit and loss account together with the deferred gain or loss.

12 Other Assets (in part)

Other Assets by Type

	2011	2010
Reinsurance and insurance receivables	1,971	2,201
Deferred tax assets	2,801	3,425
Property development and obtained from foreclosures	1,584	2,153
Income tax receivable	542	527
Accrued interest and rents	14,387	16,194
Other accrued assets	2,200	2,888
Pension assets	3,762	3,458
Other	3,769	5,623
	31,016	36,469

Other includes EUR 1,840 million (2010: EUR 1,875 million) related to transactions still to be settled at balance sheet date.

Disclosures in respect of deferred tax assets and pension assets are provided in Note 21 'Other liabilities'.

21 Other Liabilities

Other Liabilities by Type

	2011	2010
Deferred tax liabilities	2,242	1,537
Income tax payable	858	1,210
Pension benefits	378	543
Post-employment benefits	179	172
Other staff-related liabilities	1,111	1,248
Other taxation and social security contributions	898	885
Deposits from reinsurers	1,015	1,007
Accrued interest	11,698	13,220
Costs payable	2,400	2,873
Amounts payable to brokers	72	111
Amounts payable to policyholders	2,173	2,130
Reorganisation provision	599	434
Other provisions	638	533
Share-based payment plan liabilities	39	40
Prepayments received under property under development	83	173
Amounts to be settled	5,442	5,553
Dividend payable		
Other	3,377	4,777
	33,202	36,446

Other mainly relates to year-end accruals in the normal course of business.

Other staff-related liabilities include vacation leave provisions, bonus provisions, jubilee provisions and disability/illness provisions.

Deferred taxes are calculated on all temporary differences under the liability method using tax rates applicable in the jurisdictions in which the Group is liable to taxation.

Changes in Deferred Tax

	Net Liability 2010	Change Through Equity	Change Through Net Result	Changes in the Composition of the Group	Exchange Rate Differences	Other	Net Liability 2011
Investments	(296)	1,188	452	(58)	74	265	1,625
Real estate investments	383		(10)	7	1		381
Financial assets and liabilities at fair value through profit and loss	(527)		(175)	(9)	6	(20)	(725)
Deferred acquisition costs and VOBA	3,111	(272)	(194)	(57)	131	12	2,731
Fiscal reserve	1		(1)				
Depreciation	4	1	24	9	2		40
Insurance provisions	(1,866)	(572)	(773)	(7)	(130)	(2)	(3,350)
Cash flow hedges	263	373	4				640
Pension and post-employment benefits	503	1	68	(12)	(10)	2	552
Other provisions	(655)		379	25	16	(21)	(256)
Receivables	(51)		(8)	(12)	(1)	(2)	(74)
Loans and advances to customers	(608)	97	(143)		6	96	(552)
Unused tax losses carried forward	(1,851)	(1)	305	34	20	195	(1,298)
Other	(299)	(65)	27	(4)	(17)	85	(273)
	(1,888)	750	(45)	(84)	98	610	(559)
Comprising:							
—Deferred tax liabilities	1,537						2,242
—Deferred tax assets	(3,425)						(2,801)
	(1,888)						(559)

In 2011, Investments-Other, Loans and advances to customers-Other and Unused tax losses carried forward-Other relates mainly to the classification of ING Direct USA as a disposal group held for sale. Reference is made to Note 11 'Assets and liabilities held for sale'.

Changes in Deferred Tax

	Net Liability 2009	Change Through Equity	Change Through Net Result	Changes in the Composition of the Group	Exchange Rate Differences	Other	Net Liability 2010
Investments	209	1,205	(1,359)	(2)	73	(39)	87
Financial assets and liabilities at fair value through profit and loss	(312)	(18)	(185)	(2)	5	(15)	(527)
Deferred acquisition costs and VOBA	2,849	(368)	301		326	3	3,111
Fiscal reserve			1				1
Depreciation	12		9	(10)	(1)	(6)	4
Insurance provisions	(1,446)	(389)	109		(135)	(5)	(1,866)
Cash flow hedges	69	210			(14)	(2)	263
Pension and post-employment benefits	700		(183)		7	(21)	503
Other provisions	(1,012)	(13)	476	5	(127)	16	(655)
Receivables	(149)	(1)	82	6	2	9	(51)
Loans and advances to customers	(215)		(353)	(5)	(15)	(20)	(608)
Unused tax losses carried forward	(2,508)	1	801	(3)	(152)	10	(1,851)
Other	(814)	29	419	11	(32)	88	(299)
	(2,617)	656	118	0	(63)	18	(1,888)
Comprising:							
—deferred tax liabilities	1,352						1,537
—deferred tax assets	(3,969)						(3,425)
	(2,617)						(1,888)

Deferred tax in connection with unused tax losses carried forward.

	2011	2010
Total unused tax losses carried forward	9,093	9,335
Unused tax losses carried forward not recognised as a deferred tax asset	(4,529)	(2,862)
Unused tax losses carried forward recognised as a deferred tax asset	4,564	6,473
Average tax rate	28.4%	28.6%
Deferred tax asset	1,298	1,851

The following tax loss carry forwards and tax credits will expire as follows as at December 31,:

Total Unused Tax Losses Carried Forward Analysed by Expiry Terms

	No Deferred Tax Asset Recognised		Deferred Tax Tax Asset Recognised	
	2011	2010	2011	2010
Within 1 year	30	14	49	67
More than 1 year but less than 5 years	378	406	539	461
More than 5 years but less than 10 years	774	243	1,971	3,768
More than 10 years but less than 20 years	3,185	2,093	192	1,285
Unlimited	162	106	1,813	892
	4,529	2,862	4,564	6,473

Deferred tax assets are recognised for temporary deductible differences, for tax loss carry forwards and unused tax credits only to the extent that realisation of the related tax benefit is probable.

The deferred tax asset includes balances for which the utilisation is dependent on future taxable profits whilst the related entities have incurred losses in either the current year or the preceding year. The aggregate amount for the most significant entities where this applies is EUR 490 million (2010: EUR 1,102 million).

This can be specified by jurisdiction as follows:

Breakdown by Jurisdiction

	Banking Operations		Insurance Operations		Total	
	2011	2010	2011	2010	2011	2010
The Netherlands		190				190
United States		508	120	232	120	740
Great Britain	116	89			116	89
Belgium			70	13	70	13
Australia	36	40			36	40
Spain		11	19		19	11
Germany	5	19			5	19
France	66				66	
Mexico	32				32	
Italy	26				26	
	281	857	209	245	490	1,102

In 2011 the deferred tax assets for banking operations for which the utilisation is dependent on future taxable profits, as disclosed above, decreased significantly compared to 2010, as a result of the announced sale of ING Direct USA. Reference is made to Note 30 'Companies acquired and companies disposed'.

In 2011, ING Group has reconsidered its method of determining the breakdown by jurisdiction. The recoverability is now determined at the level of the fiscal unity within that jurisdiction and not at the level of the individual company. Also the offsetting of deferred tax assets with deferred tax liabilities was revised. The comparatives provided in this table have been adjusted accordingly.

Recognition is based on the fact that it is probable that the entity will have taxable profits and/or can utilise tax planning opportunities before expiration of the deferred tax assets. Changes in circumstances in future periods may adversely impact the assessment of the recoverability. The uncertainty of the recoverability is taken into account in establishing the deferred tax assets.

As of December 31, 2011 and December 31, 2010, ING Group had no significant temporary differences associated with the parent company's investments in subsidiaries, branches and associates and interest in joint ventures as any economic benefit from those investments will not be taxable at parent company level.

48 Taxation

Profit and Loss Account

Taxation on Continuing Operations by Type

	Netherlands			International			Total		
	2011	2010	2009	2011	2010	2009	2011	2010	2009
Current taxation	48	168	159	1,006	790	416	1,054	958	575
Deferred taxation	167	(104)	(1,218)	(212)	222	(137)	(45)	118	(1,355)
	215	64	(1,059)	794	1,012	279	1,009	1,076	(780)

Reconciliation of the weighted average statutory income tax rate to ING Group's effective income tax rate

	2011	2010	2009
Result before tax from continuing operations	4,727	3,333	(2,492)
Weighted average statutory tax rate	26.2%	24.2%	32.9%
Weighted average statutory tax amount	1,238	806	(819)
Associates exemption	(329)	(403)	(166)
Other income not subject to tax	(263)	(125)	(227)
Expenses not deductible for tax purposes	122	102	47
Impact on deferred tax from change in tax rates	(56)	8	
Deferred tax benefit from previously unrecognised amounts			(32)
Current tax benefit from previously unrecognised amounts	4		
Write down/reversal of deferred tax assets	284	740	535
Adjustment to prior periods	9	(52)	(118)
Effective tax amount	1,009	1,076	(780)
Effective tax rate	21.3%	32.3%	31.3%

The weighted average statutory tax rate in 2011 compared to 2010 does not differ significantly.

The weighted average statutory tax rate decreased significantly in 2010 compared to 2009. This is caused by the fact that in 2010 profits were realised in a significant part of the tax jurisdictions that incurred losses in 2009.

The effective tax rate in 2011 was lower than the weighted average statutory tax. This is mainly caused by exempt income, which was only partly offset by non deductible expenses and write down of deferred tax assets.

The effective tax rate in 2010 was higher than the weighted average statutory tax. This is caused by an off-setting effect of the write-down of deferred tax assets (mainly in the United States) and the non-deductable expenses which exceeded tax exempt income and prior year adjustments.

The effective tax rate in 2009 was lower than the weighted average statutory tax rate. This is caused by the fact that a write-down of the carrying value of deferred tax assets and non-deductible expenses exceeded tax exempt income.

Adjustment to prior periods in 2011 relates to final tax assessments and other marginal corrections.

Adjustment to prior periods in 2010 relates mainly to a tax settlement.

Comprehensive Income

Income Tax Related to Components of Other Comprehensive Income

	2011	2010	2009
Unrealised revaluations	(873)	(1,216)	(4,712)
Realised gains/losses transferred to profit and loss (reclassifications from equity to profit and loss)	(291)	8	(494)
Changes in cash flow hedge reserve	(373)	(194)	203
Transfer to insurance liabilities/DAC	847	719	1,017
Exchange rate differences	(39)	8	13
Total income tax related to components of other comprehensive income	(729)	(675)	(3,973)

SECTION 3: STATEMENT OF COMPREHENSIVE INCOME AND RELATED DISCLOSURES[1]

IAS 1, *PRESENTATION OF FINANCIAL STATEMENTS*

IAS 27, *CONSOLIDATED AND SEPARATE FINANCIAL STATEMENTS*

THE CONCEPTUAL FRAMEWORK FOR FINANCIAL REPORTING

Author's Note

The following items are covered in the indicated sections within this publication more specific to that topic:
- Assets and liabilities associated with certain income and expense items (see section 2, "Statement of Financial Position and Related Disclosures")
- Assets held for sale and discontinued operations (see section 6, "Non-current Assets Held for Sale and Discontinued Operations")
- Financial instruments (see section 8, "Financial Instruments and Related Disclosures")

Author's Note

In May 2011, the International Accounting Standards Board (IASB) issued International Financial Reporting Standard (IFRS) 10, *Consolidated Financial Statements*, which supersedes the requirements of International Accounting Standard (IAS) 27, *Consolidated and Separate Financial Statements*, with respect to consolidation, and Standing Interpretations Committee (SIC) 12, *Consolidation—Special Purpose Entities*. IFRS 10 requires an entity to consolidate all entities that it controls. IFRS 10 defines the principle of control and establishes control as the basis for determining which entities an entity should consolidate. IFRS 10 also prescribes the accounting requirements for the preparation of consolidated financial statements. Therefore, IAS 27, *Separate Financial Statements* (as amended in 2011), retains only the requirements for accounting and disclosure of investments in subsidiaries, joint ventures, and associates when an entity prepares separate (or company-only) financial statements. IAS 27 (2011) requires an entity preparing separate financial statements to account for those investments at cost or in accordance with IFRS 9, *Financial Instruments*.

Both IFRS 10 and IAS 27 (2011) are effective for annual reporting periods beginning on or after 1 January 2013. IFRS 9 is effective for annual periods beginning on or after 1 January 2015. These standards permit early adoption.

In June 2011, IASB issued *Presentation of Other Comprehensive Income* (Amendments to IAS 1) to improve consistency and clarity of presentation of items of other comprehensive income (OCI). These amendments are effective for annual reporting periods beginning on or after 1 July 2012 and modify IAS 1, *Presentation of Financial Statements*, as follows:
- Change the statement title: *Statement of Profit or Loss and Other Comprehensive Income* replaces *Statement of Comprehensive Income*
- Permit an entity to prepare the statement of profit or loss and OCI in
  —a single statement with two sections, profit or loss section and OCI section, or
  —two statements, statement of profit or loss and statement of OCI, presented sequentially
- Require the profit or loss section of the statement of profit or loss and OCI or the statement of profit or loss to include the following line items, at a minimum:
  —Revenues
  —Finance costs (interest expense)
  —Share of profit or loss of equity-method investments (for example, associates and joint ventures)
  —Tax expense
  —Discontinued operations as a total single amount in accordance with IFRS 5, *Noncurrent Assets Held for Sale and Discontinued Operations*
- Require the OCI section of the statement of profit or loss and OCI or the statement of OCI to include line items for amounts of OCI in the period as follows:
  —Classified by these items by nature, including the share of OCI of associates and joint ventures accounted for using the equity method
  —Grouped into the following categories:
    o Items that will not be reclassified subsequently to profit or loss
    o Items that will be reclassified subsequently to profit or loss when specific conditions are met (reclassification adjustments)

IAS 1 does not address which items an entity presents in OCI and did not change the option to present these items either gross or net of tax. However, when an entity presents items of OCI net of tax, these amendments require an entity to present the tax amount for items subject to reclassification adjustments separately from the tax amount for those that are not.

These amendments also require an entity to provide separate allocations of profit or loss and OCI attributable to the noncontrolling interest and owners of

---

[1] Unless otherwise indicated, references to International Accounting Standards Board (IASB) standards and interpretations throughout this 2012 edition of *IFRS Financial Statements—Best Practices in Presentation and Disclosure* refer to the version of those standards and interpretations included in the *IFRS 2012* bound volume, the official printed consolidated text of IASB standards and interpretations, including revisions, amendments, and supporting documents, applicable as of 1 January 2012.

the parent entity. When the entity presents profit or loss in a separate statement, it should present this allocation of profit or loss in that statement.

In 2010 and 2011, IASB also issued the following standards, which amended IAS 1:

- IFRS 9 (issued November 2009 and October 2010 with an effective date of 1 January 2015)

  This amendment replaces some references to IAS 39, *Financial Instruments: Recognition and Measurement*, with references to IFRS 9

- IFRS 10 (issued May 2011 with an effective date of 1 January 2013)

- IFRS 12, *Disclosure of Interests in Other Entities* (issued May 2011 with an effective date of 1 January 2013)

  Amendments in IFRS 10 and IFRS 12 replace references to IAS 27 with references to IFRS 10 and delete the example of management judgments with respect to special purpose entities. In addition, the amendment in IFRS 12 replaces an example of disclosure related to IAS 31, *Interests in Joint Ventures*, with one related to IAS 40, *Investment Property*; it also adds an example of disclosure of judgment made in determining whether an entity controls another entity required by IFRS 12.

- IFRS 13, *Fair Value Measurement* (issued May 2011 with an effective date of 1 January 2013)

These amendments replace a reference to IFRS 7, *Financial Instruments: Disclosures*, with a reference to IFRS 13, in a discussion of other IFRSs that require disclosures of assumptions and replace the phrase "recently observed market prices" with a quoted price in an active market for an identical asset or liability.

Because all of these standards and amendments are effective after 1 January 2012, they are not discussed in the commentary in this section. In addition, the timing of the effective dates of these standards affects the availability of illustrative excerpts from survey companies' financial statements. Accordingly, the excerpts appearing later in this section may not reflect all or some of these revisions.

IFRS Overview and Comparison to U.S. GAAP

3.01 IAS 1 requires an entity to include in a complete set of financial statements a statement of comprehensive income for the period. A statement of comprehensive income should present all income and expense items recognized in the period. An entity can choose to present the required income, expense, and OCI items in either a single statement of comprehensive income or in two statements presented sequentially. When an entity chooses the two-statement format, it should prepare a separate income statement that displays the components of profit or loss followed by a second statement that begins with profit or loss and displays the components of OCI.

3.02 IAS 27 requires a statement of comprehensive income to include the results of all entities (subsidiaries) that the reporting entity controls, except in certain circumstances, eliminating intragroup income, expenses, and dividends.

3.03 A complete set of financial statements should include two statements of comprehensive income, one for the current period and one for the comparable previous period, except when IFRSs permit or require otherwise.

3.04 When an entity changes the presentation or classification of items in the statement of comprehensive income, it should also reclassify comparative period information, unless it is impracticable to do so.

3.05 *The Conceptual Framework for Financial Reporting* (IFRS *Conceptual Framework*) establishes the concepts that underlie the preparation and presentation of financial statements for external users and contains definitions of the elements of financial statements (that is, *assets*, *liabilities*, *equity*, *income*, and *expenses*). Among other purposes, the IFRS *Conceptual Framework* assists preparers of financial statements in applying IFRSs and in dealing with topics that have yet to form the subject of a specific standard or interpretation.

3.06 IAS 8, *Accounting Policies, Changes in Accounting Estimates and Errors*, states that when making judgments about an issue not specifically addressed in IFRSs, an entity's management should first refer to and consider the applicability of the requirements in IFRSs dealing with similar and related issues and then refer to the definitions, recognition criteria, and measurement concepts in the IFRS *Conceptual Framework*. Although the IFRS *Conceptual Framework* is not a standard, the requirements of IAS 8 essentially establish the IFRS *Conceptual Framework* as part of the IFRS hierarchy of accounting and reporting requirements.

3.07 The IFRS *Conceptual Framework* defines *income* as increases in economic benefits during the accounting period in the form of inflows or enhancements of assets or decreases in liabilities that result in increases in equity, other than those increases relating to contributions from the entity's owners. This definition includes both revenue and gains. *Revenue* is defined as income that arises in the course of an entity's ordinary activities. *Gains*, on the other hand, may or may not arise from ordinary activities of the entity, and IFRSs do not consider gains to be a separate element of the financial statements. An entity should recognize income when an increase in future economic benefits related to an increase in an asset or a decrease in a liability can be measured reliably. However, an entity should only recognize an increase in an asset when it is probable that future economic benefits will flow to the entity.

3.08 The IFRS *Conceptual Framework* defines an *expense* as outflows or depletions of assets or an incurrence of liabilities that result in a decrease in equity, other than those relating to distributions to the entity's owners. Expenses, which include the concept of losses, may or may not arise in the course of the ordinary activities of the entity. IFRSs also do not consider a loss to be a separate element of the financial statements. An entity should recognize an expense when a decrease in economic benefits related to a decrease in an asset or an increase in a liability can be measured reliably. However, an entity should recognize an increase in a liability only when it is probable that an outflow of economic benefits will occur.

Author's Note

Although not specifically discussed in the IFRS *Conceptual Framework*, changes in fair value meet the definition of *income* or *expense* when recognized in either profit or loss or OCI.

3.09 The IFRS *Conceptual Framework* also notes that expenses usually are recognized in profit and loss when directly associated with a specific item of income, often referred to as the "matching concept." However, the IFRS *Conceptual Framework* explicitly states that application of this concept does not permit recognition of items on the balance sheet that do not meet the definition of an *asset* or a *liability*. An entity should recognize an expense immediately for an expenditure that does not produce future benefits or to the extent that the expenditure does not qualify for recognition as an asset. An entity also recognizes an expense when it incurs a liability without the recognition of an asset (for example, product warranty liabilities). Expenses related to the use of assets over several accounting periods should be allocated to profit or loss on a rational, systematic basis.

Presentation

IFRSs

3.10 At a minimum, IAS 1 requires the statement of comprehensive income to include the following line items:
- Revenues
- Finance costs (interest expense)
- Share of profit or loss of equity-method investments (for example, associates and jointly controlled entities)
- Tax expense
- Discontinued operations as a single amount consisting of the sum of any profit or loss from the discontinued operations and any gain or loss on disposal of related assets or disposal groups
- Profit or loss (net income)
- Share of the OCI of equity-method investments
- Each component of OCI classified by nature
- Total comprehensive income

3.11 An entity should also provide separate allocations of profit or loss and total comprehensive income attributable to the following:
- Noncontrolling interest
- Owners of the parent entity

3.12 An entity should also present additional line items, headings, and subtotals when these items would be relevant for understanding its financial performance during the period. IAS 1 also suggests that an entity should amend descriptions of line items and consider factors such as materiality and the nature or function of line items when making these decisions.

3.13 An entity should not offset income and expense items unless required or permitted by an IFRS.

3.14 IAS 1 prohibits the presentation of any line item as an extraordinary item in the statement of comprehensive income, a separate income statement (if presented), or in the notes.

Author's Note

Despite the prohibition against the presentation of an extraordinary item (that is, presenting the item net of income taxes and outside of continuing operations), IAS 1 does not define *exceptional* or *unusual* items. Except for discontinued operations, all other income statement income and expense items are considered to be operating items, regardless of the titles an entity uses for subtotals it provides in the income statement. Several survey companies use the terms *exceptional* or *unusual* to differentiate among line items included in the income statement before income taxes. An entity may also define and disclose its own non-U.S. generally accepted accounting principles (U.S. GAAP) performance metric (for example, underlying earnings is not measured in accordance with U.S. GAAP) as long as it also provides a reconciliation of that metric to profit or loss measured in accordance with IFRSs.

3.15 An entity should present all items of income and expense in profit or loss, unless IFRSs require or permit otherwise, and should disclose reclassification adjustments related to components of OCI. An entity should disclose the amount of income tax related to components of OCI and may either show each component net of related tax or each component at its pretax amount, with an aggregated amount of tax related to total OCI items.

U.S. GAAP

3.16 Financial Accounting Standards Board (FASB) *Accounting Standards Codification* (ASC) 220-10-45-5 requires an entity to report all components of comprehensive income in its financial statements in the period in which the components are recognized and to display a total amount for comprehensive income in the financial statement where the components of OCI are reported. When the entity has a noncontrolling interest in a subsidiary, it should present separate amounts for both comprehensive income attributable to the parent and attributable to the noncontrolling interest in the subsidiary on the face of the relevant financial statement, in addition to presenting total consolidated comprehensive income. FASB ASC 220-10-45-13 explains that an entity should classify components of comprehensive income based on their nature.

3.17 Like IFRSs, FASB ASC 220-10-45-8 does not require one format for the statement in which an entity presents comprehensive income and its components, as long as the financial statement is displayed with the same prominence as its other financial statements and net income is shown as a component of comprehensive income in that financial statement. Additionally, like IFRSs, FASB ASC 220-10-45-9 permits an entity to include the components of comprehensive income in the income statement or in a separate statement that begins with net income and encourages an entity to use one of these formats. Although FASB ASC 220-10-45-10 states that presenting items of OCI in an income statement-like form is superior to presenting these items in a statement of changes in equity, unlike IFRSs, FASB ASC 220-10-45-14 permits an entity to present the components of comprehensive income in a statement of changes in equity.

Author's Note

In June 2011, FASB issued FASB Accounting Standards Update (ASU) No. 2011-05, *Comprehensive Income (Topic 220): Presentation of Comprehensive Income*, which amends FASB ASC by eliminating the option to present the components of OCI as part of the statement of changes in stockholders' equity. Going forward, an entity will present the total of comprehensive income, the components of net income, and the components of OCI either in a single continuous statement of comprehensive income or in two separate but consecutive statements. In either option, an entity should present each component of net income together with total net income, each component of OCI together with a total for OCI, and a total amount for comprehensive income. The amendments to FASB ASC 220, *Comprehensive Income*, in ASU No. 2011-05 do not change which items an entity should present in OCI or when an entity should reclassify an item of OCI to net income. ASU No. 2011-05 is effective for fiscal years, and interim periods within those years, beginning after December 15, 2011. For nonpublic entities, the amendments are effective for fiscal years ending after December 15, 2012, and interim and annual periods thereafter. Early adoption is permitted because the remaining options are already permitted by FASB ASC 220. The amendments do not require any transition disclosures.

ASU No. 2011-05 is the result of a joint project with IASB to improve presentation of comprehensive income.

In December 2011, FASB issued ASU No. 2011-12, *Comprehensive Income (Topic 220): Deferral of the Effective Date for Amendments to the Presentation of Reclassifications of Items Out of Accumulated Other Comprehensive Income in ASU No. 2011-05*. ASU No. 2011-12 defers the changes in ASU No. 2011-05 related only to the presentation of reclassification adjustments. Preparers had argued that these reclassification adjustments would be difficult for preparers and might add unnecessary complexity to the financial statements. FASB issued ASU No. 2011-12 to allow sufficient time for it to redeliberate whether an entity should present the effects of reclassification adjustments on the face of the financial statements for all periods presented. While FASB is considering preparers' concerns, entities should continue to report reclassification adjustments in accordance with the requirements of FASB ASC 220 in effect before issuance of ASU No. 2011-05. The amendments in ASU No. 2011-12 are effective at the same time as the amendments in ASU No. 2011-05.

3.18 Like IFRSs, FASB ASC 220-10-45-12 requires an entity to disclose the amount of income tax expense or benefit allocated to each component of OCI, including reclassification adjustments, either on the face of the relevant statement or in the notes to the financial statements.

3.19 Rule 5-03, "Income Statements," of Securities and Exchange Commission (SEC) Regulation S-X prescribes the format of the income statement for issuers and requires an issuer to display net sales and gross revenues, separately disclosing the following classes, which are different from those required by IFRSs:

- Net sales of tangible products (gross sales less discounts, returns, and allowances)
- Operating revenues of public utilities or others
- Income from rentals
- Revenues from services
- Other revenues

3.20 The aforementioned SEC rule permits an entity to combine classes of net sales and gross revenue derived from a particular class with another class if each is not more than 10 percent of the sum of the classes. When such classes of income are combined, an entity should also combine the related costs and expenses. IFRSs do not include a quantitative threshold for aggregating the prescribed line items on the statement of comprehensive income.

3.21 Unlike IFRSs, FASB ASC 225-20 provides for the presentation of extraordinary items in the income statement when the required conditions are met. *Extraordinary items*, as defined in the FASB ASC glossary, are events and transactions that are distinguished by both their unusual nature and infrequency of occurrence. Additionally, extraordinary items should be material in relation to income before extraordinary items, to the trend of annual earnings before extraordinary items, or material by other appropriate criteria in order to be classified separately in the income statement in accordance with FASB ASC 225-20-45-3. Unlike IFRSs, Rule 5-03 of SEC Regulation S-X includes a long list of cost and expense line items that an entity should show separately, including extraordinary items, net of tax. Some of these line items may be provided in note disclosures. Like IFRSs, an entity should show material amounts of the preceding items separately.

Disclosure

IFRSs

3.22 IAS 1 requires an entity to present the following additional information either in the statement or in the notes:

- Nature and amount of material items of income or expense (for example, inventory write-downs, restructuring activities, disposals of investments, and so on).
- Analysis of expenses by nature or by function (for example, cost of sales), whichever provides reliable and more relevant information, with subclassifications to highlight differences in components (such as frequency and potential for gain or loss). When an entity classifies expenses by function, it should also disclose information about the nature of expenses, particularly depreciation and amortization expense and employee benefit expense.

Author's Note

IAS 1 encourages entities to provide the analysis of expenses in the statement of comprehensive income or the income statement, rather than in the notes. However, some companies present one line item, "operating expenses," in the statement with the disaggregation in a note disclosure.

U.S. GAAP

3.23 FASB ASC 225-10 does not contain a disclosure requirement comparable to the analysis of expenses. However, Rule 5-03 of SEC Regulation S-X effectively requires SEC registrants to provide this analysis by its list of required cost and expense line items. Paragraphs 9 and 12 of FASB ASC 225-20-45 explain that extraordinary items should be segregated from the results of ordinary operations and shown separately in the income statement, with disclosure of the nature and amounts thereof, including earnings per share data, presented either on the face of the income statement or in the related notes.

TABLE 3-1: ANALYSIS OF EXPENSES RECOGNIZED IN PROFIT AND LOSS

	2011	2010	2009
Survey entities reporting expenses by function	96	92	86
Survey entities reporting expenses by nature			
Financial institutions	17	11	12
Insurance entities	5	8	8
Entities in other industries	57	59	54
Total	175	170	160

TABLE 3-2: ITEMS OF OTHER COMPREHENSIVE INCOME

	2011	2010	2009
Foreign currency translation	144	136	129
Change in fair value of available for sale financial instrument	100	106	102
Change in fair value of property plant and equipment held at revalued amount	16	15	13
Change in fair value of intangible assets held at revalued amount	0	0	0
Cash flow hedges	96	101	94
Hedge of net investment in a foreign operation	15	11	11
Other derivatives and hedging transactions	14	11	20
Actuarial gains and losses on defined benefit plans	60	61	62
Share of other comprehensive income of associates and joint ventures	36	35	32
Share-based payments	1	2	4
Revaluation of equity interest	6	8	9
Other	27	31	20
Disclosure of Income Tax Recognized Directly in Equity			
Tax effect shown in statement	78	94	87
Items shown net of tax	87	65	64
No items of other comprehensive income	10	11	9
Total Companies	175	170	160

Presentation and Disclosure Excerpts

Single Statement—Statement of Comprehensive Income, Expenses by Nature

3.24

Woori Finance Holdings Co., Ltd. (Dec 2011)

CONSOLIDATED STATEMENTS OF COMPREHENSIVE INCOME

For the years ended December 31, 2010 and 2011

	Korean Won		U.S. Dollars
	2010	2011	2011
	(In Millions, Except per Share Data)		(In Thousands, Except per Share Data) (Note 2)
Net interest income (Notes 33 and 44)	6,423,145	7,262,045	6,268,490
Interest income	14,057,227	15,044,846	12,986,488
Interest expense	7,634,082	7,782,801	6,717,998

(continued)

	Korean Won		U.S. Dollars
	2010	2011	2011
	(In Millions, Except per Share Data)		(In Thousands, Except per Share Data) (Note 2)
Net fees and commissions income (Notes 34 and 44)	1,115,774	1,195,492	1,031,931
Fees and commissions income	1,688,039	1,774,434	1,531,665
Fees and commissions expense	572,265	578,942	499,734
Dividends (Note 35)	200,780	203,005	175,231
Gain on financial assets at FVTPL (Note 36)	39,074	119,403	103,067
Gain on available-for-sale financial assets (Note 37)	1,073,469	1,072,877	926,091
Gain on held-to-maturity financial assets	21	82	71
Impairment loss on credit loss (Note 38)	2,872,943	2,268,927	1,958,504
Other net operating expenses (Notes 39 and 44)	(3,910,451)	(4,423,304)	(3,818,131)
Operating income (Note 46)	2,068,869	3,160,673	2,728,246
Share of profits of jointly controlled entities and associates (Note 12)	29,926	16,700	14,415
Net income before income tax expense	2,098,795	3,177,373	2,742,661
Income tax expense (Note 40)	498,121	744,093	642,290
Net income	1,600,674	2,433,280	2,100,371
Net income attributable to owners	1,288,856	2,136,828	1,844,478
Net income attributable to non-controlling interests	311,818	296,452	255,893
Other comprehensive income (loss), net of tax	(235,991)	(385,374)	(332,649)
Loss on available-for-sale financial assets	(205,332)	(374,877)	(323,589)
Share of other comprehensive loss of jointly controlled entities and associates	(20,546)	(37,602)	(32,457)
Gain (loss) on overseas business translation	(18,826)	24,591	21,227
Gain on valuation of cashflow hedge	8,713	2,514	2,170
Total comprehensive income	1,364,683	2,047,906	1,767,722
Comprehensive income attributable to owners	1,051,725	1,729,658	1,493,015
Comprehensive income attributable to non-controlling interests	312,958	318,248	274,707
Basic and diluted earnings per share (Note 41)	1,599	2,649	2.29

NOTES TO THE CONSOLIDATED FINANCIAL STATEMENTS (in part)

1. General

(1) Woori Finance Holdings Co., Ltd.

Woori Finance Holdings Co., Ltd. (hereinafter referred to "Woori Finance Holdings" or "Parent" or the "Company") was incorporated under the laws of the Republic of Korea on March 27, 2001, to manage the following five financial institutions: Woori Bank, Kyongnam Bank, Kwangju Bank, Woori Credit Card Co., Ltd. (formerly known as Peace Bank of Korea which merged into Woori Bank on March 31, 2004) and Woori Investment Bank (which merged into Woori Bank on July 31, 2003), whose shares were contributed to the Company by the Korea Deposit Insurance Corporation (the "KDIC") in accordance with the provisions of the Financial Holding Company Act. As of December 31, 2011, the Company controls the following entities: three commercial banks, which include Woori Bank (formerly known as Hanvit Bank), Kyongnam Bank and Kwangju Bank (collectively referred to as the "Bank Subsidiaries"); Woori FIS Co., Ltd. (formerly known as Woori Finance Information System Co., Ltd., "Woori FIS"); Woori F&I Co., Ltd. ("Woori F&I"); Woori Investment & Securities Co., Ltd. ("Woori Investment & Securities"); Woori Asset Management Co., Ltd. ("Woori Asset Management", formerly known

as Woori Credit Suisse Asset Management Co., Ltd.); Woori Private Equity Co., Ltd. ("Woori PE"); Woori Financial Co., Ltd. ("Woori Financial", formerly known as Hanmi Capital Co., Ltd.) and Woori FG Savings Bank; all collectively referred to as "Woori Subsidiaries." Several of the Woori Subsidiaries also have other subsidiaries of which the Company is now the ultimate financial holding company. As a result of its functional restructuring, as of December 31, 2011, the Company consolidates Woori Bank, nine other subsidiaries, and 133 2nd-tier subsidiaries including Woori Credit Information Co., Ltd.

Upon incorporation, the Company's stock amounted to 3,637,293 million Won, consisting of 727,458,609 common shares (5,000 Won per share). As a result of several capital increases, exercise of warrants and conversion rights since incorporation, as of December 31, 2011, the Company's stock amounted to 4,030,077 million Won, consisting of 806,015,340 common shares issued and outstanding of which KDIC owns 459,198,609 shares (56.97% ownership).

On June 24, 2002, the Company listed its common shares on the Korea Exchange. On September 29, 2003, the Company registered with the Securities and Exchange Commission in the United States of America and listed its American Depositary Shares on the New York Stock Exchange.

Two Statements—Income Statement and Statement of Other Comprehensive Income, Expenses by Function, Disaggregation of Expenses by Nature in Note Disclosure

3.25

Braskem S.A. (Dec 2011)

CONSOLIDATED STATEMENT OF OPERATIONS

Years ended December 31
All amounts in thousands of Brazilian reais, except for earnings (loss) per share

	Note	2011	2010	2009
Net sales revenue	31	33,176,160	25,494,817	16,136,070
Cost of products sold		(29,317,951)	(21,411,775)	(13,529,696)
Gross profit		3,858,209	4,083,042	2,606,374
Income (expenses)				
Selling		(343,655)	(383,454)	(298,847)
Distribution		(480,532)	(335,510)	(300,735)
General and administrative		(1,025,668)	(969,929)	(648,310)
Research and development		(99,083)	(78,778)	(63,119)
Results from equity investments	15 (c)	(1,419)	20,302	3,188
Results from business combinations	5		975,283	102,051
Other operating income (expenses), net	33	22,053	(95,995)	3,705
Operating profit		1,929,905	3,214,961	1,404,307
Financial results	34			
Financial expenses		(3,574,240)	(1,696,949)	685,439
Financial income		769,341	369,426	(331,330)
		(2,804,899)	(1,327,523)	354,109
Profit (loss) before income tax and social contribution		(874,994)	1,887,438	1,758,416
Current income tax and social contribution	23.1	(18,981)	(61,536)	(353,551)
Deferred income tax and social contribution	23.1	377,136	63,583	(1,006,374)
		358,155	2,047	(1,359,925)
Profit (loss) for the year		(516,839)	1,889,485	398,491
Attributable to:				
Company's shareholders		(525,142)	1,895,309	398,491
Non-controlling interest	2.2	8,303	(5,824)	—
		(516,839)	1,889,485	398,491
Earnings (loss) per share attributable to the shareholders of the Company at the end of the year (R$)	30			
Basic earnings (loss) per share—common		(0.6580)	2.7037	0.7551
Basic earnings (loss) per share—preferred		(0.6580)	2.5904	0.7842
Diluted earnings (loss) per share—common		(0.6577)	2.7031	0.7554
Diluted earnings (loss) per share—preferred		(0.6577)	2.5898	0.7845

CONSOLIDATED STATEMENT OF COMPREHENSIVE INCOME

Years ended December 31
   All amounts in thousands of Brazilian reais

	Note	2011	2010	2009
Profit (loss) for the year		(516,839)	1,889,485	398,491
Other comprehensive income or loss:				
Available for sale financial assets			58	(10,722)
Cash flow hedge	21.2.2	45,034	6,032	42,794
Foreign currency translation adjustment		56,809	(79,346)	
Income tax and social contribution related to components of comprehensive income	21.2.2	(2,458)	6,793	3,851
Total other comprehensive income or loss		99,385	(66,463)	35,923
Total comprehensive income or loss for the year		(417,454)	1,823,022	434,414
Attributable to:				
Company's shareholders		(427,935)	1,829,057	434,414
Non-controlling interest		10,481	(6,035)	
		(417,454)	1,823,022	434,414

NOTES TO THE CONSOLIDATED FINANCIAL STATEMENTS (in part)

1 Operations

Braskem S.A. together with its subsidiaries and jointly-controlled subsidiaries ("Braskem" or "Company") is a publicly-held corporation headquartered in Camaçari, State of Bahia, which operates 35 industrial units, 28 of which are located in the Brazilian states of Alagoas, Bahia, Rio de Janeiro, Rio Grande do Sul and São Paulo, five are located in the United States, in the states of Pennsylvania, Texas and West Virginia and two are located in Germany. These units produce basic petrochemicals—such as ethylene, propylene butadiene, toluene, xylene and benzene, as well as gasoline and LPG (Liquefied Petroleum Gas)—and thermoplastic resins—polyethylene, polypropylene and polyvinyl chloride ("PVC"). Additionally, Braskem is also engaged in the import and export of chemicals, petrochemicals and fuels, the production, supply and sale of utilities such as steam, water, compressed air, industrial gases, as well as the provision of industrial services and the production, supply and sale of electric energy for its own use and use by other companies. Braskem also invests in other companies, either as a partner or shareholder.

Braskem is controlled by Odebrecht S.A. ("Odebrecht"), which directly and indirectly holds a 50.1% and a 38.1% interest in its voting and total capital, respectively.

35 Expenses by Nature

The Company chose to present its expenses by function in the income statement. As required by IAS 1, the breakdown of expenses by nature is presented below:

	2011	2010	2009
Classification by nature:			
Raw materials other inputs	(25,198,575)	(18,059,704)	(10,900,495)
Personnel expenses	(1,576,192)	(1,273,617)	(1,007,702)
Outsourced services	(838,652)	(694,487)	(534,351)
Tax expenses	(54,775)	(60,222)	(23,005)
Depreciation, amortization and depletion	(1,683,175)	(1,606,354)	(1,038,061)
Variable selling expenses	(508,065)	(449,459)	(377,800)
Freights	(993,428)	(786,353)	(710,604)
Other expenses	(414,027)	(249,250)	(248,689)
Total	(31,266,889)	(23,179,446)	(14,840,707)
Classification by function:			
Cost of products sold	(29,317,951)	(21,411,775)	(13,529,696)
Selling	(343,655)	(383,454)	(298,847)
Distribution	(480,532)	(335,510)	(300,735)
General and administrative	(1,025,668)	(969,929)	(648,310)
Research and development	(99,083)	(78,778)	(63,119)
Total	(31,266,889)	(23,179,446)	(14,840,707)

Analysis of Expenses by Function, Expenses by Function and Additional Disaggregation of Operating Expenses in Note Disclosure

3.26

Telecom Argentina (Dec 2011)

CONSOLIDATED INCOME STATEMENTS

(In millions of Argentine pesos)

	Note	For the Years Ended December 31		
		2011	**2010**	**2009**
Revenues	21	18,498	14,627	12,170
Other income	21	55	32	34
Total revenues		18,553	14,659	12,204
Employee benefit expenses and severance payments	22	(2,609)	(1,975)	(1,572)
Interconnection costs and other telecommunication charges	22	(1,503)	(1,377)	(1,361)
Fees for services, maintenance, materials and supplies	22	(1,702)	(1,326)	(1,071)
Taxes and fees with the Regulatory Authority	22	(1,595)	(1,254)	(1,011)
Commissions	22	(1,515)	(1,141)	(942)
Cost of equipments and handsets	7	(1,657)	(1,207)	(906)
Advertising	22	(599)	(441)	(357)
Provisions	17	(225)	(130)	(48)
Bad debt expenses	5	(169)	(119)	(131)
Other operating expenses	22	(964)	(815)	(644)
Depreciation and amortization	22	(2,158)	(1,712)	(1,545)
Operating income	23	3,857	3,162	2,616
Other income from investments	27.d	—	—	13
Finance income	24	310	192	256
Finance expenses	24	(230)	(329)	(670)
Net income before income tax expense		3,937	3,025	2,215
Income tax expense	14	(1,395)	(1,076)	(798)
Net income for the year		2,542	1,949	1,417
Attributable to:				
Owners of the Parent		2,513	1,935	1,405
Non-controlling interest		29	14	12
		2,542	1,949	1,417
Earnings per share attributable to owners of the Parent				
Basic and diluted	25	2.55	1.97	1.43

(In millions of Argentine pesos)

	For the Years Ended December 31		
	2011	**2010**	**2009**
Net income for the year	2,542	1,949	1,417
Other components of the Statements of Comprehensive Income			
Currency translation adjustments (non-taxable)[i]	27	18	28
Cash flow hedges	—	—	(13)
Income tax effect on cash flow hedges	—	—	5
Other components of the comprehensive income, net of tax	27	18	20
Total comprehensive income for the year	2,569	1,967	1,437
Attributable to:			
Owners of the Parent	2,532	1,948	1,411
Non-controlling interest	37	19	26
	2,569	1,967	1,437

[i] In 2009, net of a gain of $13 realized on capital reimbursement of Núcleo (Note 27.d).

The accompanying notes are an integral part of these consolidated financial statements.

The movements of the components of the Statements of Comprehensive Income for the years ended December 31, 2011, 2010 and 2009 and the corresponding tax effect are the following:

| | Cash Flow Hedges | | | Currency Translation Adjustment |
	Gross Amount	Income Tax	Total	
At January 1, 2009	13	(5)	8	—
Increase	—	—	—	41
Reclassification to income statement	(13)	5	(8)	(13)
At December 31, 2009	—	—	—	28
Increase	—	—	—	18
At December 31, 2010	—	—	—	46
Increase	—	—	—	27
At December 31, 2011	—	—	—	73

NOTES TO THE CONSOLIDATED FINANCIAL STATEMENTS (in part)

Note 1—Description of Business and Basis of Preparation of the Consolidated Financial Statements (in part)

a) The Company and Its Operations

Telecom Argentina was created by a decree of the Argentine Government in January 1990 and organized as a *sociedad anónima* under the name "Sociedad Licenciataria Norte S.A." in April 1990.

Telecom Argentina commenced operations on November 8, 1990, upon the transfer to the Company of the telecommunications network of the northern region of Argentina pre-viously owned and operated by the state-owned company, Empresa Nacional de Telecomunicaciones ("ENTel").

Telecom Argentina's license, as originally granted, was exclusive to provide telephone services in the northern region of Argentina through October 10, 1999. As from such date, the Company also began providing telephone services in the southern region of Argentina and competing in the previously exclusive northern region.

The Company provides fixed-line public telecommunication services, international long-distance service, data transmission and Internet services in Argentina and through its subsidiaries, mobile telecommunications services in Argentina and Paraguay and international wholesale services in the United States of America. Information on the Telecom Group's licenses and the regulatory framework is described in Note 2.

Entities included in consolidation and the respective equity interest owned by Telecom Argentina is presented as follows:

Subsidiaries	Percentage of Capital Stock Owned and Voting Rights[i]	Indirect Control Through	Date of Acquisition
Telecom USA	100.00%		09.12.00
Micro Sistemas[ii]	99.99%		12.31.97
Personal	99.99%		07.06.94
Springville[ii]	100.00%	Personal	04.07.09
Núcleo[iii]	67.50%	Personal	02.03.98

[i] Percentage of equity interest owned has been rounded.
[ii] Dormant entity at December 31, 2011, 2010 and 2009.
[iii] Non-controlling interest of 32.50% is owned by the Paraguayan company ABC Telecomunicaciones S.A.

Note 22—Operating Expenses

Operating expenses disclosed by nature of expense amounted to $14,696, $11,497 and $9,588 for the years ended December 31, 2011, 2010 and 2009, respectively.

The main components of the operating expenses are the following:

Employee Benefit Expenses and Severance Payments

	Years Ended December 31		
	2011	**2010**	**2009**
Wages and salaries	(1,857)	(1,429)	(1,153)
Social security expenses	(538)	(417)	(327)
Severance indemnities and termination benefits	(153)	(94)	(65)
Training costs	(8)	(9)	(10)
Other employee benefits	(53)	(26)	(17)
	(2,609)	(1,975)	(1,572)

Interconnection Costs and Other Telecommunication Charges

	Years Ended December 31		
	2011	**2010**	**2009**
Fixed telephony interconnection costs	(190)	(196)	(180)
Cost of international outbound calls	(150)	(134)	(152)
Lease of circuits	(169)	(143)	(139)
Mobile services—charges for roaming	(241)	(199)	(167)
Mobile services—charges for TLRD	(753)	(705)	(723)
	(1,503)	(1,377)	(1,361)

Fees for Services, Maintenance, Materials and Supplies

	Years Ended December 31		
	2011	**2010**	**2009**
Maintenance of hardware and software	(235)	(157)	(110)
Technical maintenance	(101)	(94)	(99)
Maintenance of buildings, vehicles and other assets	(178)	(126)	(97)
Service connection fees for fixed lines and Internet lines	(116)	(106)	(113)
Service connection fees capitalized as SAC (Note 3.i)	5	5	9
Service connection fees capitalized as Intangible assets (Note 3.i)	22	18	19
Other maintenance costs	(232)	(242)	(190)
Call center fees	(477)	(318)	(224)
Call center fees capitalized as SAC (Note 3.i)	6	4	4
Fees for IT services	(92)	(93)	(76)
Cleaning and security fees	(118)	(96)	(81)
Other fees for services	(173)	(111)	(105)
Directors and Supervisory Committee's fees	(13)	(10)	(8)
	(1,702)	(1,326)	(1,071)

Taxes and Fees With the Regulatory Authority

	Years Ended December 31		
	2011	**2010**	**2009**
Turnover tax	(823)	(657)	(519)
Taxes with the Regulatory Authority	(425)	(330)	(260)
Tax on deposits to and withdrawals from bank accounts	(166)	(135)	(107)
Municipal taxes	(98)	(76)	(68)
Other taxes	(83)	(56)	(57)
	(1,595)	(1,254)	(1,011)

Commissions

	Years Ended December 31		
	2011	**2010**	**2009**
Agent commissions	(1,019)	(705)	(600)
Agent commissions capitalized as SAC (Note 3.i)	248	137	121
Distribution of prepaid cards commissions	(458)	(338)	(274)
Collection commissions	(220)	(171)	(142)
Other commissions	(66)	(64)	(47)
	(1,515)	(1,141)	(942)

Advertising

	Years Ended December 31		
	2011	**2010**	**2009**
Media advertising	(377)	(272)	(223)
Fairs and exhibitions	(108)	(77)	(65)
Customer rewards	(24)	(23)	(14)
Market research and other costs	(32)	(22)	(20)
Other advertising costs	(58)	(47)	(35)
	(599)	(441)	(357)

Other Operating Expenses

	Years Ended December 31		
	2011	**2010**	**2009**
Transportation, freight and travel expenses	(299)	(239)	(210)
Delivery costs capitalized as SAC (Note 3.i)	17	13	13
Rental expense	(170)	(146)	(109)
Cost of mobile value added services	(178)	(142)	(94)
Energy, water and others	(160)	(131)	(111)
International and satellite connectivity	(109)	(97)	(81)
Other	(65)	(73)	(52)
	(964)	(815)	(644)

D&A

	Years Ended December 31		
	2011	**2010**	**2009**
Depreciation of PP&E	(1,538)	(1,302)	(1,098)
Amortization of SAC and service connection costs	(602)	(387)	(428)
Amortization of other intangible assets	(18)	(23)	(19)
	(2,158)	(1,712)	(1,545)

As required by the Argentine Corporations Law, the operating expenses disclosed by function are as follows:

	Years Ended December 31		
	2011	**2010**	**2009**
Cost of sales and services	(9,110)	(7,352)	(6,243)
General and administrative expenses	(695)	(530)	(466)
Selling expenses	(4,666)	(3,485)	(2,831)
Provisions	(225)	(130)	(48)
	(14,696)	(11,497)	(9,588)

Operating Leases

Future minimum lease payments as of December 31, 2011, 2010 and 2009 are as follows:

	Less Than 1 Year	1–5 Years	More Than 5 Years	Total
2009	86	185	4	275
2010	193	259	23	475
2011	214	409	90	713

IAS 18, *REVENUE*

SIC 31, *REVENUE—BARTER TRANSACTIONS INVOLVING ADVERTISING SERVICES*

Author's Note

In 2002, IASB and FASB jointly initiated a project on revenue recognition with the objective of developing a single coherent asset and liability model for revenue recognition. In such a model, revenue is a function of changes in assets and liabilities and is not based on the notions of realization and the completion of an earnings process. Currently, significant differences exist between IFRSs and U.S. GAAP in how and when an entity recognizes revenue. In the course of this project, the boards issued the following due process documents:

- In December 2008, the boards published for public comment a discussion paper, *Preliminary Views on Revenue Recognition in Contracts with Customers*, which set out a joint approach for revenue recognition. Comments were due by June 2009.

- In January 2010, the boards published for public comment an exposure draft, *Revenue from Contracts with Customers*. The proposed standard would replace IAS 18, *Revenue*; IAS 11, *Construction Contracts*; and related interpretations. In U.S. GAAP, it would supersede most of the guidance on revenue recognition in FASB ASC 605, *Revenue Recognition*. Comments were due by October 2010.

The core principle in the exposure draft is to recognize revenue so as "to depict the *transfer* of goods or services in an amount that reflects the consideration expected to be received in exchange for those goods or services." An entity would take five steps to apply this principle:

1. Identify the customer contract(s).
2. Identify the separate performance obligations.
3. Determine the transaction price for the contract(s).
4. Allocate the transaction price to the performance obligations.
5. Recognize revenue when the entity settles the performance obligations.

Overall, comment letters supported the project's objective to create a single revenue recognition standard to be used across industries and capital markets. However, other comments resulted in the boards redeliberating a number of issues including determining when transfer occurs for services, clarifying what constitutes a "distinct" performance obligation, handling of contract modifications, reducing complexity of proposed approach to segmenting contracts, determining whether an entity should expense all contract acquisition costs, accruing "statutory" warranty costs, determining how to account for licenses, reducing complexity of measurements, and determining when to apply a test for an onerous contract.

Because of the extent of the changes to the proposed standard, in November 2011, the boards reexposed their revised proposals. Some of the changes to the original exposure draft include the boards' decisions to do the following:

- Add risks and rewards of ownership as an indicator of transfer of control of a good or service and eliminate customer-specific design or function as an indicator of control.
- Revise the criteria for identifying separate performance obligations in three ways:
  —The criteria specify when an entity should account for a bundle of highly interrelated goods or services as a single performance obligation.
  —The criteria require an entity to consider only whether it sells the good or service separately and not consider whether the good or service is sold by other entities.
  —The "distinct profit margin" criterion is eliminated.
- Require an entity to recognize revenue at the amount of consideration to which it is entitled without including expectations of collectability in that measurement.
- Require an entity to present impairment losses related to contracts with customers as a separate line item adjacent to the revenue line item so that users can easily compare revenues and reductions of revenue arising from credit risk.

- Amend the revenue recognition constraint to be "reasonably assured" and applied when consideration is variable and only to the cumulative amount of revenue. (The boards clarified that this constraint is not quantitative but considers the quality of information used to estimate the amount of variable consideration to which the entity is entitled.)
- Refine how an entity would apply the onerous performance obligation test by limiting the test to those performance obligations satisfied over a period of time longer than one year, and clarifying the measurement.
- Affirm the disclosure requirements while acknowledging both their volume and usefulness to users of financial statements.

During the first half of 2012, the boards began to deliberate these proposals based on the comments received on this exposure draft with a target date for issuing an IFRS in late 2012, or early 2013.

Author's Note

IASB issued the following standards which amended IAS 18:

- IFRS 9
  This amendment replaced references to IAS 39 with references to IFRS 9 in the paragraph on scope exclusions.
- IFRS 11, *Joint Arrangements* (issued May 2011 with an effective date of 1 January 2013)
  This amendment replaced references to IAS 28, *Investments in Associates*, with references to IFRS 11 in the paragraph on scope exclusions.
- IFRS 13
  This amendment changed the definition of fair value to agree with the definition in IFRS 13 in the paragraph on scope exclusions.

Early adoption of these standards is permitted. Because the effective date of these standards is after 1 January 2012, these amendments are not reflected in the commentary in this section. However, these amendments would not affect the availability of illustrative excerpts from survey companies' financial statements.

IFRS Overview and Comparison to U.S. GAAP

3.27 The IFRS *Conceptual Framework* defines *income* as increases in economic benefits during the period in the form of inflows or enhancements of assets or reductions of liabilities that result in an increase in equity other than an increase from contributions by equity participants. Income includes both revenues and gains. The IFRS *Conceptual Framework* defines *revenue* as income that results from the entity's ordinary business activities. Gains also meet the definition of *income* but may or may not result from the entity's ordinary business activities. Because gains represent increases in economic benefits, they are no different in nature from revenue. Whereas the IFRS *Conceptual Framework* considers revenue to be a separate element of the financial statements, a gain is not considered a separate element.

Recognition and Measurement

IFRSs

3.28 IAS 18 establishes the accounting and disclosure requirements for revenue from the sale of goods, rendering of services, and the use by others of an entity's assets that yield interest, dividends, or royalties. IAS 18 does not address the accounting for revenue or income generated by the extraction of mineral ores, changes in value of current assets, or assets covered by another IFRS. For example, IAS 18 does not apply to revenue arising from leases, dividends from equity-method investments, insurance contracts, change in fair value or disposal of financial instruments, agricultural produce, and biological assets because other IFRSs address these issues.

3.29 Revenue includes only gross inflows received or receivable by an entity on its own account. When amounts are collected on behalf of third parties (for example, fees and commissions), an entity should only recognize revenue for its fee or commission, not the amount collected. Similarly, amounts collected on behalf of third parties, such as sales taxes, goods and services taxes, and value-added taxes, are not economic benefits that flow to the entity and do not result in increases in equity; therefore, these items are excluded from revenue.

3.30 IAS 18 requires an entity to segment or combine transactions to arrive at the substance of the arrangement for revenue recognition purposes. Because IAS 18 provides limited guidance on segmenting and combining, the entity should refer to and consider the applicability of the guidance on segmenting and combining transactions included in IAS 11.

Author's Note

For more information on IAS 11, see paragraph 3.63 in this section.

3.31 Revenue is measured at the fair value of the consideration received or receivable. The fair value should take into account any trade discounts or volume rebates. When a transaction is effectively a financing arrangement, IAS 18 requires an entity to determine the fair value by discounting future cash flows using an imputed interest rate. The *imputed rate of interest* is the more clearly determinable of either the prevailing rate on similar instruments by issuers with similar credit ratings or the rate that discounts the nominal amount of the instrument to the current cash sales price of the goods or services provided. An entity should recognize the difference between the present value and the nominal amount as interest revenue, in accordance with IAS 39.

3.32 When goods and services are exchanged, an entity should not recognize revenue when the goods or services are similar. An entity should only recognize revenue when it exchanges dissimilar goods or services. In an exchange, an entity should measure revenue at the fair value of the goods or services received. Only when this fair value cannot be measured reliably should the entity recognize revenue at the fair value of the goods or services given up, adjusted by any cash or cash equivalent transferred.

3.33 SIC 31, *Revenue—Barter Transactions Involving Advertising Services*, states that when entering into a barter transaction, an entity should recognize revenue only when the fair value is determined by reference to nonbarter transactions with certain characteristics.

3.34 IAS 18 requires an entity to meet two conditions before recognizing revenue on the sale of goods. The entity should
- transfer the significant risks and rewards of ownership of the goods to the buyer and
- retain neither continuing management involvement associated with ownership nor effective control over the goods sold.

3.35 An entity should determine that the economic benefits from the transfer of the goods are probable and should measure reliably both the revenue and the costs associated with the transaction. An entity should recognize a sale when it retains only an insignificant amount of the risk and rewards of ownership.

3.36 To meet the probability criteria when an entity does not receive consideration at the time the goods are transferred and is uncertain about the consideration's future collectability, the entity should measure revenue at the amount expected to be collected.

3.37 With respect to revenue generated by providing services, an entity should recognize revenue using the percentage-of-completion method; that is, the entity recognizes revenue when it is probable that future economic benefits will be received and it can reliably measure all of the following:
- Amount of revenue
- Stage of completion
- Costs incurred
- Costs to complete the project

IAS 18 does not require an entity to use a particular method for measuring the stage of completion. Use of surveys of work performed, services performed to date, and the percentage of costs incurred are all acceptable measurement methodologies.

3.38 When the outcome of a transaction for services cannot be measured reliably, an entity should recognize revenue only up to the amount of recoverable costs incurred.

3.39 An entity should recognize revenue from the use of assets generating interest, dividends, or royalties only when receipt of the expected economic benefits is probable and it can measure the amount reliably. IAS 18 requires an entity to recognize these types of revenue as follows:
- Recognize interest revenue using the effective interest method
- Recognize royalty revenue using the accrual basis, in accordance with the substance of the relevant agreement
- Recognize dividend revenue when an entity's shareholder rights to dividends are established

U.S. GAAP

3.40 FASB ASC 605 includes extensive requirements and guidance for revenue recognition and measurement, which exceed that provided in IAS 18. Revenue guidance is contained in both FASB ASC and rules of the SEC.

3.41 FASB ASC 605-10-25-1 generally permits an entity to recognize revenue only in the following circumstances:
- The revenue is realized or realizable (that is, when the goods or services are exchanged for cash or claims to cash).
- The revenue is being earned (that is, when the entity has substantially accomplished what it must do to be entitled to the benefits represented by the revenues).

3.42 However, FASB ASC 605-10-25-4 permits revenue and gain recognition using the installment or cost-recovery methods under exceptional circumstances. The cost-recovery method yields essentially the same results as the requirements of IAS 18 in circumstances when the outcome of a transaction cannot be measured reliably. IFRSs do not permit entities to use the installment method. Unlike IFRSs, for transactions involving the rendering of services, FASB ASC 605 does not require an entity to use the percentage-of-completion method of revenue recognition.

3.43 SEC *Codification of Staff Accounting Bulletins* topic 13, "Revenue Recognition," states that revenue generally is realized or realizable and earned when all of the following criteria are met:
- Persuasive evidence of an arrangement exists.
- Delivery of the goods has occurred or services have been rendered.
- The seller's price to the buyer is fixed or determinable.
- Collectability is reasonably assured.

3.44 In addition, unlike IFRSs, FASB ASC and SEC sources contain detailed transaction-specific guidance. For example, these sources provide guidance on revenue recognition for sales when the title is retained, bill and hold sales, goods are shipped but not billable or are subject to conditions, consignment sales, layaway sales, options to buy, special orders and drop shipments, sale and repurchase agreements, subscriptions, and points and other items redeemable for goods or services.

3.45 Despite the detailed guidance on the timing of recognition, FASB ASC and SEC sources contain little guidance on measurement, other than the previously noted requirement for the seller's price to be fixed or determinable. Additional guidance about this condition exists for extended payment terms, reseller arrangements, customer cancellation privileges, fiscal funding clauses, and software arrangements. If the fee is not fixed or determinable, an entity should recognize revenue as payments are received.

3.46 FASB ASC 605-25 contains more guidance on segmenting of transactions, referred to as *multiple element arrangements*, for both recognition and measurement. FASB ASC 605-25-25-2 requires that an entity should divide revenue arrangements with multiple deliverables into separate units of accounting if both the delivered item(s) have value to the customer on a standalone basis and, if the arrangement includes a general right of return, delivery and performance of the undelivered item(s) is probable and substantially in the vendor's control. FASB ASC 605-25-30-2 requires an entity to allocate the arrangement consideration at the inception of the arrangement to all deliverables based on their relative selling price (relative selling price method), except when another topic in FASB ASC requires a unit of accounting in the arrangement to be recorded at fair value or the amount that can be allocated to a unit of accounting is limited to an amount that is not contingent on delivery of additional deliverables or specified performance conditions. When a vendor applies the relative selling price method, an entity should determine the selling price using vendor-specific objective evidence of selling price, if it exists; otherwise, the vendor should use its best estimate of selling price for that deliverable. Vendors should not ignore information that is reasonably available without undue cost or effort.

3.47 Like IFRSs, FASB ASC 605-45 requires entities to recognize revenue at the net amount retained when acting as an agent.

Presentation

IFRSs

3.48 IAS 1 requires an entity to present total revenue separately on the statement of comprehensive income. Use of the term *revenue* is not required.

Author's Note

Companies domiciled in the United Kingdom commonly use the term "turnover" in place of revenue.

U.S. GAAP

3.49 Rule 5-03 of SEC Regulation S-X requires SEC registrants to present revenues on a separate line item on the income statement.

3.50 Unlike IFRSs, FASB ASC 605-45-50-3 explains that an entity may present taxes collected from customers and remitted to governmental authorities on either a gross basis (included in both revenues and costs) or net basis (excluded from revenues). The method that an entity chooses is an accounting policy decision.

Disclosure

IFRSs

3.51 An entity should disclose its accounting policies for revenue recognition separately for the following categories: sales of goods, services, interest, dividends, and royalties. The policies should appear either on the face of the statement of comprehensive income or in the notes. Entities should also disclose the amount of revenue recognized from the exchange of goods or services in each of those categories.

U.S. GAAP

3.52 FASB ASC 235-10-50-3 also requires entities to disclose the accounting policy for revenue recognition. FASB ASC 235 does not require disclosures comparable to those required by IAS 18 for each type of revenue.

3.53 FASB ASC 605 includes extensive disclosure requirements, including those pertaining to multiple element arrangements and specific industry requirements. For example, FASB ASC 605-25-50-1 requires an entity to provide specific disclosures regarding multiple element arrangements, including the accounting policy for such arrangements (for example, whether deliverables are separable into units of accounting) and the nature of such arrangements (for example, provisions for performance, termination, or cancellation of the agreement). FASB ASC 605-25-50-1 explains that the objective of the disclosure guidance is to provide both qualitative and quantitative information about a vendor's revenue arrangements and the significant judgments made about the

application of FASB ASC 605-25, changes in those judgments, or the application of FASB ASC 605-25 that may significantly affect the timing or amount of revenue recognition. Therefore, in addition to the required disclosures, a vendor shall also disclose other qualitative and quantitative information as necessary to comply with this objective. FASB ASC 605-25-50-2 requires a vendor to disclose specific information by similar arrangements including the nature of multiple deliverable arrangements; significant deliverables and the general timing of delivery or performance of service; contract provisions including performance, termination, and refund-type; discussion of significant factors, inputs, assumptions, and methods used to determine selling price; information about whether significant deliverables qualify as separate units of accounting, general timing of revenue recognition for significant deliverables, and effects of changes in selling price or methods for determining selling price.

3.54 For SEC registrants, SEC *Codification of Staff Accounting Bulletins* topic 13(B), "Disclosures," provides SEC staff views on disclosures pertaining to revenue recognition.

Presentation and Disclosure Excerpts

Revenue—Sales of Goods, Construction and Real Estate Sales, and Concessions

3.55

Empresas ICA S.A. de C.V. (Dec 2011)

CONSOLIDATED STATEMENTS OF COMPREHENSIVE INCOME (in part)

(Thousands of Mexican pesos, except per share data)

	Millions of U.S. Dollars (Convenience Translation Note 4) December 31, 2011	2011	2010
Continuing operations:			
Revenues:			
Construction	$2,431	Ps. 33,920,383	Ps. 27,849,781
Concessions	224	3,129,808	2,102,123
Sales of goods and other	410	5,718,594	4,524,158
Total revenues	3,065	42,768,785	34,476,062
Costs:			
Construction	2,204	30,741,641	24,940,301
Concessions	160	2,236,438	1,533,548
Sales of goods and other	229	3,201,299	3,019,269
Total costs (Note 29)	2,593	36,179,378	29,493,118
Gross profit	472	6,589,407	4,982,944

NOTES TO THE CONSOLIDATED FINANCIAL STATEMENTS (in part)

For the years ended December 31, 2011 and 2010 and at January 1, 2010

(Thousands of Mexican pesos except as otherwise indicated)

1. Activities

Empresas ICA, S.A.B. de C.V. and subsidiaries ("ICA" or, together with its subsidiaries, "the Company") is a holding company incorporated in Mexico with over 64 years experience, the subsidiaries of which are engaged in a wide range of construction and related activities including the construction of infrastructure facilities as well as industrial, urban and housing construction, for both the Mexican public and private sectors. ICA's subsidiaries are also involved in the construction, maintenance and operation of highways, bridges and tunnels granted by the Mexican government and foreign governments under concessions. Through its subsidiaries and affiliates, the Company also manages and operates airports and municipal services under concession arrangements. In addition, some of ICA's subsidiaries are engaged in real estate and housing development. ICA's shares are traded on the Mexican Stock Exchange and the New York Stock Exchange. Its registered address is 36 Boulevard Manuel Avila Camacho, Piso 15, Lomas de Chapultepec, 11000 Mexico, D. F.

4. Basis of Presentation and Consolidation (in part)

a. Statement of Compliance

The consolidated financial statements have been prepared in accordance with IFRS as issued by the IASB. Included in subsection (g) is the Company's policy regarding consolidation and included in Note 5 are the Company's accouting policies and valuation principles applied in preparing the consolidated financial statements.

The accompanying consolidated financial statements include all financial reporting standards and valuation requirements that affect the Company's consolidated financial information, as well as the alternatives allowed by IFRS.

5. Significant Accounting Policies (in part)

The consolidated financial statements are prepared in accordance with IFRS. Preparation of financial statements under IFRS requires management of the Company to make certain estimates and use assumptions to value certain of the items in the consolidated financial statements as well as their related disclosures required therein. The areas with a high degree of judgment and complexity or areas where assumptions and estimates are significant in the consolidated financial statements are described in Note 6. The estimates are based on information available at the time the estimates are made, as well as the best knowledge and judgment of management based on experience and current events. However, actual results could differ from those estimates. The Company has implemented control procedures to ensure that its accounting policies are appropriate and are properly applied. Although actual results may differ from those estimates, the Company's management believes that the estimates and assumptions used were adequate under the circumstances.

w. Revenue Recognition

Revenues are recognized when it is likely that the Company will receive the economic benefits associated with the transaction. Revenue is measured at the fair value of the consideration received or receivable and represents the amounts receivable for goods and services provided in the normal course of activities. Revenues are reduced for estimated customer returns, rebates and other similar allowances.

By type of activity, revenue is recognized based on the following criteria.

Construction Contracts

Revenues from construction contracts are recognized using the percentage-of-completion method based on the costs incurred method or the units of work method, considering total costs and revenues estimated at the end of the project, in accordance with IAS 11, *Construction Contracts*. The percentage-of-completion method provides an understanding of the performance of the project in a timely manner, and appropriately presents the legal and economic substance of the contracts. Under this method, revenues are determined based on the contract costs incurred in comparison to total contract costs, representing the profits that can be attributed to the portion of work completed.

The base revenue utilized to calculate the amount of revenue to recognize as work progresses includes the following: (i) the initial amount established in the contract, (ii) additional work orders requested by the customer, (iii) changes in the considered yields, (iv) the value of any adjustments (for inflation, exchange rates or changes in prices, for example) agreed to in the contract, (v) the decrease in the original contract value and agreements in contracts, (vi) claims and conventional penalties, and (vii) completion or performance bonuses, as of the date on which any revision takes place and is effectively approved by the customers.

Under the terms of various contracts, revenues that are recognized are not necessarily related to the amounts billable to customers. Management periodically assesses the reasonableness of the accounts receivable. When there is evidence of difficulty in the recovery of the receivables, reserves are recorded for doubtful accounts affecting the results of the year in which the impairment occurs. The estimation of this reserve is based on the best judgment of the Company under the circumstances prevailing at the time of its determination.

Contract costs include all direct costs such as materials, labor, subcontracting costs, manufacturing and supply costs of equipment, start-up costs and indirect costs. Periodically, the Company evaluates the reasonableness of the estimates used in the determination of the percentage-of-completion. If, as a result of this evaluation, there are modifications to the revenue or cost previously estimated, or if the total estimated cost of the project exceeds expected revenues, an adjustment is made in order to reflect the effect in results of the period in which the adjustment or loss is incurred. For projects financed by the Company in which the amount of the contract included project revenue and the related financing, the financing cost, which also includes changes in the fair value of derivative financial instruments, is considered part of the contract cost which is recognized in results in accordance with progresses of project. In these types of contracts, the collection of the contract amount from the client may take place at the end of the project. However, periodic progress reports are presented to and approved by the customer, which form the basis for the Company to obtain where appropriate, financing for the project in question.

The item of "Cost and Estimated Earnings in Excess of Billings on Uncompleted Contracts" included in the heading of "Customers", originates from construction contracts and represents the costs incurred plus recognized profit (or less any recognized losses) for all contracts in progress over the amount of the certificates of work performed and invoiced.

Infrastructure Concessions

In accordance with IFRIC 12, both for the financial assets and intangible assets, the revenues and costs related to construction or improvements during the construction phase are recognized in revenues and construction costs.

Revenues stemming from the financing of concessions are recorded in the income statement as they accrue and are recorded within finance income from continuing operations.

Revenues from the operation of concession projects are recognized as concession revenues, as they accrue, which is generally at the time vehicles make use of the highway and pay the respective toll in cash or electronically at toll collection booths. Revenues are derived directly from users of the concession, or at times, from the grantor of the concession. Aeronautical services revenues consist of the right of use of airports. These revenues are recognized when services are provided. Prices for the services rendered are regulated by the grantor. In concessions involving toll revenues, tariff revisions do not apply until their effective date of application.

Real Estate Sales

According to IFRIC 15, *Agreements for the Construction of Real Estate* and IAS 18, *Revenue*, revenues derived from sales of low- and medium-income housing and real estate are recognized as revenue once the house or real estate development is completed and the rights, benefits and obligations related to the property have transferred to the buyer, which occurs upon formalization of the deed.

Real estate inventories are divided into two large segments: land held for development and inventories in-progress (which include both houses under construction and unsold finished houses).

Dividend and Interest Revenue

Dividend revenue from investments is recognized when the stockholders' right to receive payment has been established.

Interest income is recorded on a periodic basis, with reference to capital and the effective interest rate applicable.

Revenue—Sales of Services and Barter Transactions

3.56

Grupo Radio Centro, S.A.B. De C.V. (Dec 2011)

CONSOLIDATED STATEMENTS OF COMPREHENSIVE INCOME (in part)

For the years ended December 31, 2011 and 2010
(In thousands of Mexican pesos (Ps.) and in thousands of U. S. dollars (US $), except per share data)

	Notes	31/12/2011 (Convenience Translation; See Note 3)	31/12/2011	31/12/2010
Revenues:				
Broadcasting revenue		US $ 70,722	Ps. 988,598	Ps. 907,925
Expenses:				
Broadcasting expenses, excluding depreciation and amortization	19	51,456	719,294	691,434
Depreciation and amortization		1,786	24,967	23,861
Corporate expenses	19	1,069	14,939	14,939
Other expenses, net	20	4,298	60,077	57,661

NOTES TO THE CONSOLIDATED FINANCIAL STATEMENTS (in part)

As of December 31, 2011and 2010 and January 1, 2010 and for the years ended December 31, 2011 and 2010
((In thousands of Mexican pesos (Ps.) and in thousands of U. S. dollars (US $), unless otherwise indicated)

1. General Information

Grupo Radio Centro, S. A. B. de C. V. ("Grupo Radio Centro") and subsidiaries (collectively, the "Company") is a corporation organized under the laws of Mexico and incorporated on June 8, 1971. The address of its registered office and principal place of business is Constituyentes 1154, 7th floor, Mexico City, México.

The Company is a Mexican commercial broadcasting company whose principal line of business is the production and radio broadcasting of musical programs, news and special events. Its revenues are derived primarily from the sale of commercial air time to advertising agencies and business. The Company also operates a radio network in Mexico, under the trade name OIR (*Organización Impulsora de Radio*).

3. Significant Accounting Policies (in part)

The principal accounting policies followed by the Company in the preparation of its financial consolidated statements are summarized below:

3.14 Revenue Recognition

Broadcasting revenues are recognized when the corresponding airtime is broadcast.

3.15 Barter Transactions

The Company, from time to time, receives products and services in exchange for advertising airtime. Revenues from barter transactions are generally measured at the fair value of the goods or serviced received. However, when that amount cannot be measured reliably, revenues from barter transactions are measured based on reference to the fair value of advertising services provided in non-barter transactions.

Revenues from advertising airtime exchanged is recognized when the advertisement is aired.

Services or goods received in exchange are expensed when consumed by the Company.

15. Non-Cash Transactions

During the years ended December 31, 2011 and 2010, the Company entered into the following non-cash barter transactions, in which airtime was exchanged for the following services, for which reason such transactions are not reflected in the consolidated statements of cash flows:

	31/12/2011	31/12/2010
Publicity	Ps. 17,882	Ps. 17,300
Air fare	6,739	7,741
Insurance	3,307	2,451
Vehicles	3,280	1,278
Other	1,169	2,248
	Ps. 32,377	Ps. 31,018

23. Related Party Transactions (in part)

23.1 During the Year, the Company Entered Into the Following Transactions With Related Parties:

	31/12/2011	31/12/2010
Grupo Radio México, S. A. de C. V.—other related party:		
Commissions paid for sales of broadcasting services[b]	Ps. (30,330)	Ps. (20,861)
Gains on sale of equipment	1,043	762
Aguirre Family:		
Recovery of expenses and gains on sales of equipment[a]	4,305	3,797

[a] Relates to the personal use of goods and services that the Company acquired in barter transactions and for which they paid the Company.

[b] On January 5, 2000, Grupo Radio Centro entered into a contract with an entity owned by Francisco Aguirre G., chairman of the board of directors of the Company, for an indefinite term pursuant to which this entity is compensated for consulting services and the sale of airtime provided to the Company by Mr. Aguirre. The Company incurred expenses under this contract totaling Ps. 4.7 million in 2011 and Ps. 4.0 million in 2010.

Revenue—Bill and Hold Transactions

3.57

Tenaris S.A. (Dec 2011)

CONSOLIDATED INCOME STATEMENT (in part)

(All Amounts in Thousands of U.S. Dollars, Unless Otherwise Stated)	Notes	Year Ended December 31		
		2011	2010	2009
Continuing Operations				
Net sales	1	9,972,478	7,711,598	8,149,320
Cost of sales	1 & 2	(6,229,526)	(4,700,810)	(4,864,922)
Gross profit		3,742,952	3,010,788	3,284,398

NOTES TO THE CONSOLIDATED FINANCIAL STATEMENTS (in part)

I. General Information

Tenaris S.A. (the "Company") was established as a public limited liability company (Societé Anonyme) under the laws of the Grand-Duchy of Luxembourg on December 17, 2001. The Company holds, either directly or indirectly, controlling interests in various subsidiaries in the steel pipe manufacturing and distribution businesses. References in these Consolidated Financial Statements to "Tenaris" refer to Tenaris S.A. and its consolidated subsidiaries.

The Company's shares trade on the Buenos Aires Stock Exchange, the Italian Stock Exchange and the Mexico City Stock Exchange; the Company's American Depositary Securities ("ADS") trade on the New York Stock Exchange.

These Consolidated Financial Statements were approved for issue by the Company's Board of Directors on February 23, 2012.

II. Accounting Policies (in part)

The principal accounting policies applied in the preparation of these Consolidated Financial Statements are set out below. These policies have been consistently applied to all the years presented, unless otherwise stated.

S Revenue Recognition

Revenue comprises the fair value of the consideration received or receivable for the sale of goods and services in the ordinary course of Tenaris' activities. Revenue is shown net of value-added tax, returns, rebates and discounts and after eliminating sales within the group.

Tenaris' products and services are sold based upon purchase orders, contracts or upon other persuasive evidence of an arrangement with customers, including that the sales price is known or determinable. Sales are recognized as revenue upon delivery, when neither continuing managerial involvement nor effective control over the products is retained by Tenaris and when collection is reasonably assured. Delivery is defined by the transfer of risk, provision of sales contracts and may include delivery to a storage facility located at one of the Company's subsidiaries. For bill and hold transactions revenue is recognized only to the extent (a) it is probable delivery will be made; (b) the products have been specifically identified and are ready for delivery; (c) the sales contract specifically acknowledges the deferred delivery instructions; (d) the usual payment terms apply.

The percentage of total sales that were generated from bill and hold arrangements for products located in Tenaris's storage facilities that have not been shipped to customers amounted to 1.3%, 1.2% and 0.7% as of December 31, 2011, 2010 and 2009, respectively. The Company has not experienced any material claims requesting the cancellation of bill and hold transactions.

Other revenues earned by Tenaris are recognized on the following bases:
- Interest income: on the effective yield basis.
- Dividend income from investments in other companies: when Tenaris' right to receive payment is established.

Revenue—Sales of Aircraft and Parts, Exchange Pool Program, Multiple Element Arrangements

3.58

Embraer S.A. (Dec 2011)

CONSOLIDATED STATEMENTS OF INCOME (in part)

Years Ended
In millions of US dollars, except earnings per share

	Note	12.31.2011	12.31.2010	12.31.2009
Revenue		5,803.0	5,364.1	5,497.8
Cost of sales and services		(4,495.9)	(4,338.1)	(4,428.4)
Gross profit		1,307.1	1,026.0	1,069.4

NOTES TO THE CONSOLIDATED FINANCIAL STATEMENTS (in part)

In millions of US dollars, unless otherwise stated

1. Operations

Embraer S.A. (the "Company" or "Embraer") is a publicly-held company incorporated under the laws of the Federative Republic of Brazil with headquarters in São José dos Campos, State of São Paulo, Brazil. The corporate purpose of the Company is:
- The development, production and sale of jet and turboprop aircraft for civil and defense aviation, aircraft for agricultural use, structural components, mechanical and hydraulic systems, aviation services and technical activities related to the production and maintenance of aerospace material;
- The design, construction and sale of equipment, materials, systems, software, accessories and components to the defense, security and energy industries and the promotion or performance of technical activities related to

production and maintenance, keeping the highest technological and quality standards;
- The performance of other technological, industrial, commercial and service activities related to the defense, security and energy industries; and
- Contribution to the formation of technical professionals necessary to the aerospace industry.

The Company's shares are listed on the enhanced corporate governance segment of the Stock Exchange in Brazil ("BM&FBOVESPA"), known as the New Market ("Novo Mercado"). The Company also has American Depositary Shares (evidenced by American Depositary Receipts-ADRs) which are registered with the Securities and Exchange Commission ("SEC") and are listed on the New York Stock Exchange ("NYSE"). The Company has no controlling group and its capital comprises only common shares.

The Company has consolidated wholly-owned and jointly controlled entities and/or commercial representation offices which are located in Brazil, the United States of America ("United States"), France, Spain, Portugal, China and Singapore. Their activities comprise sales, marketing, and after sales and maintenance services.

The presented Financial Statements were approved by the Board of Directors of the Company on March 15, 2012.

2. Presentation of the Financial Statements and Accounting Practices (in part)

2.2 Summary of Significant Accounting Policies (in part)

(ii) Revenue Recognition

Revenue comprises the fair value of the remuneration received or to be received for the sale of products and services in the normal course of business. Revenue is presented net of taxes, returns, reductions and discounts, and in the consolidated financial statements, after eliminating intercompany sales.

(i) Revenue From Aircrafts, Spare Parts and Services

Revenues from sales of commercial, executive and other aircraft, spare parts and services are generally recognized at the time of delivery or shipment, when the risks and benefits are transferred to the customer. When the sale of aircraft does not meet the contractual obligations at the time of the delivery related revenue is deferred and accounted for as Unearned income until the obligations are met.

(ii) Revenue With Multiple Element

Revenue from aircraft sales contracts involving the supply of spare parts, training and technical representation is recognized when effectively realized.

(iii) Revenue From Exchange Pool Program

Revenue from the Exchange Pool Program is recognized during the period of the contract and consists of a fixed charge and a variable charge directly related to the hours effectively flown by the aircraft under the program.

(iv) Revenue From Construction Contracts

In the defense and government segment, a significant portion of revenues is derived from long-term development contracts, for which the Company recognizes revenues under the percentage of completion ("POC") method. Such contracts contain provisions for price escalation based on a mix of indices related to raw material and labor cost. From time to time, the Company reassesses the expected margins of certain long-term contracts, adjusting revenue recognition based upon projected costs to completion.

(v) Revenue From Operating Leases

The Company also recognizes the revenue from aircraft rental as operating leases, proportional to the lease period, and records such revenues as income by segment. Revenues are allocated to their respective segments (commercial, executive and defense and security).

3. Critical Accounting Estimates

The preparation of the financial statements in conformity with generally accepted accounting principles requires management to make estimates and adopt assumptions that affect the reported amounts of assets and liabilities, disclosure of contingent assets and liabilities and the fair value of financial instruments and guarantees on the balance sheet dates and the reported amounts of revenues and expenses during the reporting period. Actual results may differ from such estimates.

In order to provide an understanding about how Management forms its judgments about future events, including the variables and assumptions underlying the estimates, and the sensitivity of those judgments to different variables and conditions, the estimates and assumptions that may cause a risk of material adjustment to the carrying amounts of assets and liabilities are addressed below:

a) Sales and Other Operating Revenues

The Company recognizes revenues from sales made by the commercial, executive, aviation services and Defense and security business when benefits and risk of ownership are transferred to customers, which, in the case of aircraft, occurs when delivery is made, and, in the case of aviation services, when the service is rendered.

The Company also recognizes rental revenue for leased aircraft, classified as operating leases on a straight-line basis over the lease term and, when presenting information by operating segment, rental revenue is recorded in Other related businesses line of the segment reporting.

In the Defense and security segment, a significant portion of revenues is derived from long-term development contracts with the Brazilian and foreign governments accounted for on the POC method. These contracts contain provisions for price escalation based on a mix of indices related to raw material and labor cost. From time to time, the Company reassesses the expected margins of certain long-term contracts, adjusting revenue recognition based upon projected costs to completion. Use of the POC method requires the Company to estimate the total costs to be incurred on the contracts. Were the total costs to be incurred to come in 10% below Management's estimates, the amount of revenue recognized in the year of 2011 would increase by US$ 72.7 and if the total costs were to come in by 10% above the estimate, the amount of revenue recognized would decrease by US$ 77.7.

Revenue under Exchange Pool Programs is recognized monthly over the contract term and consists in part of a fixed fee and in part a variable fee directly related to aircraft flying hours.

The Company enters into transactions that represent multiple-element arrangements, such as training, technical assistance, spare parts and others concessions, which are included in the aircraft purchase price. Multiple-element arrangements are assessed to determine whether they can be separated into more than one unit of accounting when all of the following criteria are met:

- the delivered item has value to the client on a stand-alone basis;
- there is objective and reliable evidence of the fair value of the undelivered item; and
- if the arrangement includes a general right of return relative to the delivered item, delivery or performance of the undelivered item is considered probable and substantially under the Company's control.

If these criteria are not met, the arrangement is accounted for as a single unit of accounting, which results in revenue being deferred until the earlier of when such criteria are met or when the last completed element is delivered. If these criteria are met for each element and there is objective and reliable evidence of fair value for all units of accounting in an arrangement, the arrangement consideration is allocated to the separate units of accounting based on each unit's relative fair value.

33. Revenue and (Expenses) by Nature

The Company opted to present the statements of income by function. The table shows the detailed costs and expenses by nature:

	12.31.2011	12.31.2010	12.31.2009
As Presented as Statements of Income:			
Revenue	5,803.0	5,364.1	5,497.8
Cost of sales and services	(4,483.2)	(4,338.1)	(4,428.4)
Administrative	(259.0)	(197.5)	(191.3)
Selling	(415.1)	(374.1)	(304.6)
Research	(85.3)	(72.1)	(55.6)
Other income (expenses), net	(337.5)	9.4	(138.5)
Equity	(0.3)	—	—
Operating profit before financial income (expense)	222.6	391.7	379.4
Revenue (Expenses) by Nature:			
Revenue from sales of goods	5,193.0	4,977.0	5,190.3
Revenue from sales of services	688.0	448.6	372.7
Sales deductions and tax on revenue	(78.0)	(61.5)	(65.2)
Material cost	(4,244.4)	(4,118.9)	(4,197.1)
Depreciation	(109.3)	(103.0)	(115.2)
Amortization	(129.5)	(116.2)	(114.1)
Personnel expenses	(335.0)	(282.8)	(251.7)
Selling expenses	(97.0)	(99.8)	(86.8)
Other operating (expense) income	(665.2)	(251.7)	(353.5)
Operating profit before financial income (expense)	222.6	391.7	379.4

Revenue—Sales of Concentrates, Gold, Silver, Royalty Income

3.59

Compañía de Minas Buenaventura S.A.A. (Dec 2011)

CONSOLIDATED INCOME STATEMENT (in part)

For the years ended December 31, 2011 and 2010

	Note	2011	2010
		US$(000)	US$(000)
Operating Income			
Net sales	19	1,493,882	1,047,885
Royalty income	32(a)	62,742	55,883
Total income		1,556,624	1,103,768
Operating Costs			
Cost of sales, without considering depreciation and amortization	20	(446,163)	(347,129)
Exploration in units in operation	21	(109,355)	(91,441)
Depreciation and amortization		(96,381)	(74,864)
Royalties	22	(60,262)	(52,270)
Total operating costs		(712,161)	(565,704)
Gross income		844,463	538,064

NOTES TO THE CONSOLIDATED FINANCIAL STATEMENTS (in part)

As of December 31, 2011, 2010 and January 1, 2010

1. Identification and Business Activity (in part)

(a) Identification—

Compañía de Minas Buenaventura S.A.A. (hereafter "Buenaventura" or "the Company") is a publicly traded corporation incorporated in 1953. Buenaventura's stock is traded on the Lima and New York Stock Exchanges through American Depositary Receipts (ADRs), which represent Company shares deposited in the Bank of New York. Buenaventura's legal domicile is at Carlos Villaran Avenue 790, Santa Catalina, Lima, Peru.

(b) Business Activity—

Buenaventura (individually and in association with third parties) is engaged in the exploration, extraction, concentration, smelting and commercialization of polymetallic ores and metals.

Buenaventura directly operates eight mining units located in Peru: Uchucchacua, Orcopampa, Poracota, Julcani, Recuperada, Antapite and Ishihuinca. In addition, the Company has a controlling interest in Sociedad Minera El Brocal S.A.A. (hereinafter "El Brocal"), which operates the Colquijirca mining unit, Minera La Zanja S.R.L. (hereinafter "La Zanja"), which operates La Zanja mining unit and Compañía de Exploraciones, Desarrollo e Inversiones Mineras S.A.C. (hereinafter "Cedimin"), which operates the Shila—Paula mining unit. The Company also holds interests in a number of other

mining companies. The Company also owns an electric power distribution company, an electric power generation company (construction stage), a mining engineering services company and another company which will provide chemical processing to treat concentrates from Uchucchacua. See note 1(d).

2. Significant Accounting Principles (in part)

2.2 Significant Accounting Judgments, Estimates and Assumptions—(in part)

The preparation of consolidated financial statements in conformity with IFRS requires Management to make judgments, estimates and assumptions that affect the reported amounts of assets, liabilities and the disclosure of contingent assets and liabilities at the date of consolidated financial statements, and reported amounts of revenues and expenses to be reported for the years ended December 31, 2011 and 2010. In Management's opinion, these estimates were made on the basis of their best knowledge of the relevant facts and circumstances at the date of preparation of consolidated financial statements; however, the actual outcomes can differ from these estimates. The Company's Management does not expect that these changes would have a significant effect on the consolidated financial statements.

2.3 Summary of Significant Accounting Principles and Policies—(in part)

(p) Revenue Recognition—

Revenue is recognized to the extent that it is probable that the economic benefits will flow to the Company. Revenue is measured at the fair value of the consideration received, excluding discounts. The following specific recognition criteria must also be met before revenue is recognized:

Sales of Concentrates, Gold and Silver—

Revenues from sales of concentrates, gold and silver are recognized when the significant risks and rewards of ownership are transferred to the buyer, and selling price are known or can be reasonably estimated.

As far as the measurement of revenues from the sale of concentrate, the Company assigns a provisional value to these sales, since they are subject to a final price adjustment at the end of a contractually-set period, which normally ranges between 30 and 180 days after delivery of the concentrate to the customer. Exposure to changes in metals price generates an embedded derivative that must be separated from the commercial contract. At the close of each period, the sale price used initially is adjusted in accordance with the future price for the quotation period stipulated in the contract. Adjustment of the provisional sale value is posted as an increase or decrease in net sales.

Interest Received—

Financial income is recognized as interest accrues.

Income for Engineering Service Rendered—

Income for engineering service rendered by Buenaventura Ingenieros S.A., a subsidiary of the Company, is recognized based on the progress of the current service contracts.

19. Net Sales

The Company's revenues are mostly from sales of gold and precious metals in the form of concentrates, including silver-lead, silver-gold, zinc and lead-gold-copper concentrates and ounces of gold. The table below presents the net sales to customers by geographic region and product type:

	2011	2010
	US$(000)	US$(000)
Net sales by geographic region		
America	710,729	504,648
Peru	600,147	479,126
Europe	132,662	35,937
Asia	8,321	7,944
	1,451,859	1,027,655
Services rendered		
Peru	41,225	20,230
Asia	710	—
America	82	—
Europe	6	—
	1,493,882	1,047,885

	2011	2010
	US$(000)	US$(000)
Net sales by product		
Gold	791,387	578,582
Silver	526,380	274,624
Copper	193,215	129,444
Zinc	72,095	92,884
Lead	36,880	46,913
	1,619,957	1,122,447
Deductions	(127,957)	(112,254)
Prior-period settlements	2,429	(4,922)
	1,494,429	1,005,271
Adjustment to open provisional liquidations	(22,679)	6,630
Embedded derivatives from sale of concentrate (a)	(11,210)	13,870
Hedging operations	(8,681)	1,884
	1,451,859	1,027,655
Sale of services, power and other minor items	42,023	20,230
	1,493,882	1,047,885

(a) Embedded Derivative—

The terms of metal in concentrate sales contracts with third parties contain provisional pricing arrangements whereby the selling price for metal in concentrate is based on prevailing spot prices on a specified future date. The Company's sales based on a provisional sales price contain an embedded derivative, which is required to be bifurcated from the host contract. The host contract is the sale of the metals contained in the concentrates at the current spot LME price. The embedded derivative, which does not qualify for hedge accounting, is marked-to-market through earnings each period. At December 31, 2011 and 2010, the Company had consolidated embedded derivatives based on forward prices for the expected settlement dates. Final prices on these sales will be established over the next several months pursuant to terms of sales contracts. The impact of fluctuations in the forward prices used for these derivatives through the settlement date is reflected as derivative gains and losses in revenues.

Concentrate sales include adjustments to the provisional sale value resulting from changes in the fair value of the embedded derivative. These adjustments resulted in lower sales by US$11,210,000 and higher sales by US$13,870,000 in 2011, and 2010, respectively, as a result of the future behavior of metal prices trade by the Company at the cutoff date. See note 19 and 28(c).

(b) Concentration of Sales—

In 2011, the three most important customers represented 58%, 21% and 6% of total sales (49%, 0% and 2% of total sales in 2010). As of December 31, 2011, 86% of the accounts receivable are related to these customers (34% as of December 31, 2010). The Company's sales of gold and concentrates are delivered to investment banks and national and international well known companies. See note 29(b). Some have sales contracts that guarantee supplying them the production from the Company's mines at prices that are based on market quotations.

32. Transactions With Associates Companies

(a) The Company has carried out the following transactions with its associates in the years 2011 and 2010:

	2011	2010
	US$(000)	US$(000)
Minera Yanacocha S.R.L.:		
Paid royalties to:		
S.M.R.L. Chaupiloma Dos de Cajamarca	62,742	55,883
Services received by:		
Buenaventura Ingenieros S.A. (Implementation of specific work orders)	11,579	1,575
Consorcio Energético de Huancavelica S.A. (Electric power transmission)	4,279	4,788
Sociedad Minera Cerro Verde S.A.A.:		
Granted dividends to:		
Compañía de Minas Buenaventura S.A.A.	—	182,955
Compañía Minera Coimolache S.A.:		
Income for:		
Compañía de Minas Buenaventura S.A.A. (Expenses recovery of exploration projects)	—	15,013

Revenue—Mortgage Lending, Asset Liquidation, Management and Leasing Fees, Case Goods, Rental Revenue

3.60

Counsel Corporation (Dec 2011)

CONSOLIDATED STATEMENT OF OPERATIONS (in part)

For the year ended December 31
(In thousands of Canadian dollars, except per share data)

	Notes	2011 $	2010 $
Revenues			
Operating revenue		77,659	13,719
Earnings from equity-accounted joint ventures and investments		2,151	7,830
		79,810	21,549

NOTES TO THE CONSOLIDATED FINANCIAL STATEMENTS (in part)

December 31, 2011
(In thousands of Canadian dollars, except per share data)

1. General Information

Counsel Corporation ("Counsel" or "the Company"), founded in 1979, is a financial services company that operates through its individually branded businesses, primarily in mortgage lending, distressed and surplus capital asset transactions, real estate finance and private equity investments. The address of its registered office is 1 Toronto Street, Suite 700, P.O. Box 3, Toronto, Ontario, M5C 2V6.

Counsel currently operates in four business sectors: mortgage lending, asset liquidation, private equity (which includes our case goods business), and real estate.

Counsel carries on its mortgage lending business ("Mortgage Lending") through its subsidiary, Street Capital Financial Corporation ("Street Capital"). Street Capital is a Canadian prime residential mortgage lender. Counsel acquired Street Capital on May 31, 2011.

Counsel's asset liquidation business ("Asset Liquidation") is carried on through a U.S. subsidiary, Counsel RB Capital LLC ("Counsel RB"). Counsel RB specializes in the acquisition and disposition of distressed and surplus assets throughout the United States and Canada, including industrial machinery and equipment, real estate, inventories, accounts receivables and distressed debt.

Counsel carries on its private equity business ("Private Equity") through its wholly-owned subsidiary, Knight's Bridge Capital Partners Inc. ("Knight's Bridge"). Knight's Bridge is responsible for sourcing and managing Counsel's portfolio investment opportunities. Knight's Bridge is an opportunistic and diversified financial service provider with a focus on building portfolio companies into market leaders.

Counsel's case goods business ("Case Goods") is carried on through a Canadian limited partnership, Fleetwood Fine Furniture LP ("Fleetwood"), which was acquired effective April 30, 2006. Fleetwood provides high quality cus-tomized case goods for large, upscale hotel chains, primarily in North America, with over 90% of its revenues generated in the United States. Fleetwood serves a focused niche, being the "upscale" and "upper upscale" strata of the hospitality industry.

Counsel's real estate business ("Real Estate") consists of the ownership and development of its own properties as well as the provision of real estate property and asset management services to third parties.

3. Significant Accounting Policies (in part)

The significant accounting policies used in the preparation of these consolidated financial statements are described below.

Revenue

The Mortgage Lending division earns revenue from the placement and servicing activities related to the mortgage business. The majority of originated mortgages are sold to institutional investors. When mortgages are placed with institutional investors, the Company transfers the contractual right to receive mortgage cash flows to the investor. Since the Company has transferred substantially all the risks and rewards of ownership of these mortgages, it has derecognized these financial assets. Upon the placement of the mortgage, the Company receives the following compensation: a cash premium and in some cases, an excess interest rate spread over the remaining life of the mortgage, which are recognized in income upon placement. Mortgage life insurance premiums are recorded as revenue when received.

Asset Liquidation revenue consists of the proceeds from asset sales through auctions, liquidations and negotiated sales. Revenue is recognized when the significant risks and rewards of ownership have been transferred to the buyer, the amount of revenue can be measured reliably and it is probable that the Company will receive the consideration. Asset Liquidation commission and fee revenue is recognized as earned.

The Company earns management fees for the management of Private Equity funds. The Company recognizes management fees as earned.

Revenue from Case Goods is recognized when the significant risks and rewards of ownership have been transferred to the buyer, the amount of revenue can be measured reliably and it is probable that the Company will receive the consideration.

The Company is entitled to management fees and leasing fees on the management of investment properties for third parties. The Company recognizes management fees and leasing fees as earned.

The Company accounts for leases with tenants of its investment properties as operating leases as substantially all of the risks and benefits of ownership have been retained by the Company. Revenue recognition under a lease commences when the tenant has a right to use the leased assets. Generally, this occurs on the lease inception date or, where the Company is required to make additions to the property in the form of tenant improvements which enhance the value of the property, upon substantial completion of those improvements. The total amount of contractual rent to be received from operating leases is recognized on a straight-line basis over the term of the lease; a straight-line rent receivable, which is included in the carrying amount of investment property, is recorded for the difference between the rental revenue recorded and the contractual amount received.

Rental revenue also includes percentage rents and recoveries of operating expenses, including property and capital taxes. Percentage participating rents are recognized in the period that recoverable costs are chargeable to tenants.

31. Segment Information (in part)

The Company's reportable segments are: Mortgage Lending, Asset Liquidation, Case Goods, Private Equity, Real Estate, and Corporate and Patent Licensing.

The Mortgage Lending business is carried on through Street Capital. Street Capital is a Canadian prime residential mortgage lender with two major institutional clients who contributed over 80% of the Company's top line revenues in 2011. Counsel acquired Street Capital on May 31, 2011.

The Asset Liquidation business is carried on through Counsel RB. Counsel RB specializes in the acquisition and disposition of distressed and surplus assets throughout the United States and Canada, including industrial machinery and equipment, real estate, inventories, accounts receivables and distressed debt.

The Private Equity business is carried on through Knight's Bridge. Knight's Bridge is responsible for sourcing and managing Counsel's portfolio investment opportunities.

The Case Goods business is carried on through Fleetwood. Fleetwood provides high quality customized case goods for large, upscale hotel chains, primarily in North America, with over 90% of its revenues generated in the United States. Fleetwood serves a focused niche, being the "upscale" and "upper upscale" strata of the hospitality industry.

Counsel's Real Estate business encompasses the ownership and development of its own properties as well as the provision of real estate property and asset management services to third parties.

Corporate and Patent Licensing includes the corporate overheads of Counsel and CRBCI and the costs associated with maintaining the intellectual property of CRBCI. In prior years, Patent Licensing was considered a reportable segment by the Company; however, management has now determined that it no longer meets the criteria for separate disclosure. Patent Licensing operations have been consolidated in the Corporate reportable segment, and the prior year's information has been restated to reflect the change.

Each segment operates as a strategic business unit. The Company assesses performance based on operating income. The accounting policies for the segments are the same as those described in Note 3 to these financial statements.

| | | | | | | 2011 | |
	Mortgage Lending (a) $	Asset Liquidation (b) $	Private Equity (c) $	Case Goods $	Real Estate $	Corporate & Patent Licensing $	Total $
Revenues							
Canada	51,792	7	10	504	1,188	138	53,639
United States	—	18,910	660	6,601	—	—	26,171
	51,792	18,917	670	7,105	1,188	138	79,810

(a) The composition of Mortgage Lending revenue is as follows:

	2011 $	2010 $
Gain on sale of mortgages	51,677	—
Other	115	—
	51,792	—

(b) The composition of Asset Liquidation revenue is as follows:

	2011 $	2010 $
Asset sales	14,264	2,852
Earnings from equity-accounted joint ventures	2,146	7,806
Commission and fees	2,507	551
	18,917	11,209

(c) The composition of Private Equity revenue is as follows:

	2011 $	2010 $
Earnings from equity-accounted associates	5	24
Gain on sale of portfolio investments	—	336
Other	17	159
Interest earned on investment	422	—
Management fees	1,576	1,548
Deduct: management fees eliminated due to consolidation[i]	(1,350)	(1,362)
	670	705

[i] Knight's Bridge earns a 2% management fee on all committed capital of KBCP Fund I. However, since Counsel controls and consolidates KBCP Fund I, the management fees are eliminated from the revenue of Knight's Bridge and the expenses of KBCP Fund I, and the third party management fees earned are recovered as a reduction of non-controlling interest.

Interest Income, Fees and Commissions, Net Insurance Loss, Dividend Income, Net Trading Income

3.61

Shinhan Financial Group Co., Ltd. (Dec 2011)

CONSOLIDATED STATEMENTS OF
COMPREHENSIVE INCOME (in part)

For the years ended December 31, 2010 and 2011

(In Millions of Won)	Note	2010	2011
Interest income		(Won) 12,908,734	13,780,714
Interest expense		(6,436,118)	(6,700,743)
Net interest income	32	6,472,616	7,079,971
Fees and commission income		3,397,247	3,557,132
Fees and commission expense		(1,639,409)	(1,797,961)
Net fees and commission income	33	1,757,838	1,759,171
Net insurance loss	28	(75,569)	(119,201)
Dividend income	34	217,451	208,860
Net trading income (loss)	35	332,536	(131,848)
Net foreign currency transaction gain		117,417	13,874
Net gain (loss) on financial instruments designated at fair value through profit or loss	36	(124,757)	171,911
Net gain on sale of available-for-sale financial assets	13	652,188	846,345
Impairment loss on financial assets	37	(1,416,047)	(987,309)
General and administrative expenses	38	(3,847,674)	(4,135,357)
Net other operating expenses	40	(671,516)	(571,645)
Operating income	43	3,414,483	4,134,772

NOTES TO THE CONSOLIDATED FINANCIAL
STATEMENTS (in part)

For the years ended December 31, 2010 and 2011

1. Reporting Entity

Shinhan Financial Group Co., Ltd., the controlling company, and its subsidiaries included in consolidation (collectively the "Group") are summarized as follows:

(a) Controlling Company

Shinhan Financial Group Co., Ltd. (the "Shinhan Financial Group") was incorporated on September 1, 2001 through a business combination involving the exchange of Shinhan Financial Group's common stock with the former stockholders of Shinhan Bank, Shinhan Investment Corp., Shinhan Capital Co., Ltd. and Shinhan BNP Paribas AMC. Shinhan Financial Group's shares were listed on the Korea Exchange on September 10, 2001 and Shinhan Financial Group's American Depository Shares were listed on the New York Stock Exchange on September 16, 2003.

3. Significant Accounting Policies

The significant accounting policies applied by the Group in preparation of its consolidated financial statements are included below. The accounting policies set out below have been applied consistently to all periods presented in these consolidated financial statements and in preparing the opening IFRS statement of financial position at January 1, 2010 for the purpose of the transition to IFRS, unless otherwise indicated.

(w) Financial Income and Expense

i) Interest

Interest income and expense are recognized in profit or loss using the effective interest method. The effective interest rate is the rate that exactly discounts the estimated future cash payments and receipts through the expected life of the financial asset or liability (or, where appropriate, a shorter year) to the carrying amount of the financial asset or liability. When calculating the effective interest rate, the Group estimates future cash flows considering all contractual terms of the financial instrument, but not future credit losses.

The calculation of the effective interest rate includes all fees and points paid or received that are an integral part of the effective interest rate. Transaction costs include incremental costs that are directly attributable to the acquisition or issue of a financial asset or liability.

Once an impairment loss has been recognized on a loan, although the accrual of interest in accordance with the contractual terms of the instrument is discontinued, interest income is recognized on the rate of interest that was used to discount future cash flow for the purpose of measuring the impairment loss.

ii) Fees and Commission

Fees and commission income and expense that are integral to the effective interest rate on a financial asset or liability are included in the measurement of the effective interest rate.

Fees and commission income, including account servicing fees, investment management fees, sales commission, placement fees and syndication fees, are recognized as the related services are performed. When a loan commitment is not expected to result in the draw-down of a loan, the related loan commitment fees are recognized on a straight-line basis over the commitment period.

Fees and commission expense relate mainly to transaction and service fees, which are expensed as the services are received.

iii) Dividends

Dividend income is recognized when the right to receive income is established.

(z) Accounting for Trust Accounts

The Group accounts for trust accounts separately from its group accounts under the Financial Investment Services and Capital Markets Act and thus the trust accounts are not included in the consolidated financial statements except Guaranteed Fixed Rate Money Trusts controlled by the Group, based on an evaluation of the substance of its relationship with the Group and the SPE's risks and rewards. Funds transferred between Group account and trust accounts are recognized as borrowings from trust accounts in other liabilities with fees for managing the accounts recognized as non-interest income by the Group.

28. Liability Under Insurance Contracts (in part)

(e) Income or expenses on insurance for the years ended December 31, 2010 and 2011 were as follows:

	2010	2011
Insurance Income		
Premium income	(Won) 3,109,610	3,553,537
Reinsurance income	99,329	7,528
Separate account income	69,888	22,008
	3,278,827	3,583,073
Insurance Expenses		
Claims paid	1,255,901	1,329,067
Reinsurance premium expenses	99,451	6,733
Provision for policy reserves	1,510,472	1,882,436
Separate account expenses	69,888	22,008
Discount charge	361	332
Acquisition costs	508,805	656,236
Collection expenses	11,498	12,373
Deferred acquisition costs (−)	(470,579)	(622,198)
Amortization of deferred acquisition costs	368,599	415,287
	3,354,396	3,702,274
Net loss on insurance	(Won) (75,569)	(119,201)

32. Net Interest Income

Net interest income for the years ended December 31, 2010 and 2011 were as follows:

	2010	2011
Interest Income		
Cash and due from banks	(Won) 168,530	248,571
Trading assets	346,387	394,296
Financial assets designated at fair value through profit or loss	11,943	19,743
Available-for-sale financial assets	961,865	1,025,523
Held-to-maturity financial assets	687,373	642,931
Loans	10,570,658	11,281,606
Others	161,978	168,044
	12,908,734	13,780,714
Interest Expense		
Deposits	3,935,630	4,181,049
Borrowings	390,271	485,253
Debt securities issued	2,041,212	1,942,850
Others	69,005	91,591
	6,436,118	6,700,743
Net interest income	(Won) 6,472,616	7,079,971

Accrued interest recognized on impaired financial assets for the years ended December 31, 2010 and 2011 were (Won) 82,220 million and (Won) 86,853 million, respectively.

33. Net Fees and Commission Income

Net fees and commission income for the years ended December 31, 2010 and 2011 were as follows:

	2010	2011
Fees and commission income		
Credit placement fees	(Won) 48,226	50,440
Commission received as electronic charge receipt	141,767	145,449
Brokerage fees	510,115	495,082
Commission received as agency	111,951	114,970
Investment banking fees	84,475	68,856
Commission received in foreign exchange activities	158,345	161,887
Asset management fees	68,396	68,289
Credit card fees	1,894,986	2,020,010
Others	378,986	432,149
	3,397,247	3,557,132
Fees and commission expense		
Credit-related fee	13,591	25,148
Credit card fees	1,387,506	1,544,291
Others	238,312	228,522
	1,639,409	1,797,961
Net fees and commission income	(Won) 1,757,838	1,759,171

34. Dividend Income

Dividend income for the years ended December 31, 2010 and 2011 were as follows:

	2010	2011
Trading assets	(Won) 2,701	2,290
Available-for-sale financial assets	214,750	206,570
	(Won) 217,451	208,860

35. Net Trading Income

Net trading income (loss) for the years ended December 31, 2010 and 2011 were as follows:

	2010	2011
Trading assets		
Gain on valuation of debt securities	(Won) 50,523	1,731
Gain on sale of debt securities	27,954	4,603
Gain (loss) on valuation of equity securities	24,385	(3,304)
Gain (loss) on sale of equity securities	52,345	(36,315)
Gain on valuation of other trading assets	54,010	23,939
	209,217	(9,346)
Trading liabilities		
Gain (loss) on valuation of securities sold	325	(251)
Loss on disposition of securities sold	(19,911)	(22,284)
Loss on valuation of other trading liabilities	(67,261)	(29,670)
Gain (loss) on disposition of other trading liabilities	(117)	5,308
	(86,964)	(46,897)
Derivatives		
Gain (loss) on valuation of derivatives	100,136	(93,403)
Gain on transaction of derivatives	110,147	17,798
	210,283	(75,605)
	(Won) 332,536	(131,848)

Income—Alternative Fuel Credits

3.62

Sappi Limited (Sep 2011)

Author's Note

In the absence of specific guidance in IFRSs with respect to emissions rights and similar credits, different companies elect different accounting policies. Some companies recognize emissions rights as intangible assets at cost (usually nil) and others at fair value, in accordance with the alternative treatments for government grants. Some companies record sales of such credits in income and others as a reduction of cost of goods sold or selling, general and administrative expenses. These accounting policy choices may also be a function of the nature of the credits and the nature of

the company's obligation to the granting government or governmental agency.

GROUP INCOME STATEMENTS (in part)

For the year ended September 2011

(US$ Million)	Note	2011	2010	2009
Sales		7,286	6,572	5,369
Cost of sales	4	6,454	5,786	5,029
Gross profit		832	786	340
Selling, general and administrative expenses	4	454	448	385
Other operating expenses	4	298	10	39
Share of profit from associates and joint ventures	13	(6)	(13)	(11)
Operating profit (loss)	4	86	341	(73)
Net finance costs	5	307	255	145
Finance costs		348	309	198
Finance revenue		(12)	(16)	(61)
Net foreign exchange gains		(13)	(17)	(17)
Net fair value (gain) loss on financial instruments		(16)	(21)	25
(Loss) profit before taxation		(221)	86	(218)

NOTES TO THE CONSOLIDATED FINANCIAL STATEMENTS (in part)

For the year ended September 2011

1. Business

Sappi Limited, a corporation organised under the laws of the Republic of South Africa (the "company" and, together with its consolidated subsidiaries, "Sappi" or the "group"), was formed in 1936 and is a global company focused on providing chemical cellulose, paper-pulp and paper based solutions to its direct and indirect customer base across more than 100 countries. Our chemical cellulose products are used worldwide by converters to create viscose fibre for clothing and textiles, acetate tow, pharmaceutical products as well as a wide range of consumer products. Our market-leading range of paper products includes: coated fine papers used by printers, publishers and corporate end-users in the production of books, brochures, magazines, catalogues, direct mail and many other print applications; casting release papers used by suppliers to the fashion, textiles, automobile and household industries; and in the Southern Africa region newsprint, uncoated graphic and business papers and premium quality packaging papers and tissue products.

The group is comprised of Sappi Fine Paper North America, Sappi Fine Paper Europe and Sappi Southern Africa reportable segments. Sappi Fine Paper which comprises Sappi Fine Paper Europe and Sappi Fine Paper North America, has manufacturing and marketing facilities in North America, Europe and Asia and produces mainly high quality branded coated fine paper. The group operates a trading network called Sappi Trading for the international marketing and distribution of chemical cellulose and market pulp throughout the world and of the group's other products in areas outside its core operating regions of North America, Europe and southern Africa. The financial results and position associated with Sappi Trading are allocated to our reportable segments.

2. Accounting Policies (in part)

The following principal accounting policies have been consistently applied in dealing with items that are considered material in relation to the Sappi Limited group financial statements.

2.2.12 Emission Trading

The group recognises grants, when allocated by governments for emission rights, as an intangible asset at cost with an equal liability at the time of the grant.

The group does not recognise a liability for emissions to the extent that it has sufficient allowances to satisfy emission liabilities. Where there is a shortfall of allowances that the group would have to deliver for emissions, a liability is recognised at the current market value of the shortfall.

Where the group sells allowances to parties outside the group at amounts greater than carrying value, a gain is recognised in selling, general and administrative expenses in profit or loss for the period.

2.2.13 Alternative Fuel Mixture Credits

Up until 31 December 2009, the U.S. Internal Revenue Code allowed an excise tax credit for alternative fuel mixtures produced by a taxpayer for sale, or for use as a fuel in a taxpayer's trade or business.

The group qualified for the alternative fuel mixtures tax credit through its North American operations because it used a bio-fuel known as black liquor, which is a by-product of its wood pulping process, to power its mills.

The group recognises income for the alternative fuel mixture credits when its right to receive the credit is established. This occurs when the group has complied with the requirements of the Internal Revenue Code and has submitted a claim for the credits due. This is recorded in profit and loss under other operating income. The group considers the tax credits earned in fiscal 2010 and fiscal 2009 as fully taxable and have treated them as such in the calculation of its tax provision in the consolidated financial statements.

4. Operating Profit

4.2 Other Operating Expenses (income)

(US$ million)	2011	2010	2009
Included in other operating expenses are the following:			
Impairments (reversals) of assets and investments	167	(10)	79
Profit on sale and write-off of property, plant and equipment	(1)	(5)	(1)
Restructuring provisions raised and closure costs	135	46	34
Alternative fuel mixture credits	—	(51)	(87)
Black Economic Empowerment (BEE) charge:	5	23	—
—Unwinding of the 2006 Black Economic Empowerment transaction	—	19	—
—IFRS 2 costs on management and employee share option plans	5	4	—

IAS 11, *CONSTRUCTION CONTRACTS*

IFRIC 15, *AGREEMENTS FOR THE CONSTRUCTION OF REAL ESTATE*

IFRS Overview and Comparison to U.S. GAAP

3.63 A *construction contract* is a contract specifically negotiated for the construction of an asset or combination of assets that are closely interrelated or interdependent in terms of their design, technology, and function or their ultimate purpose or use. IAS 11 establishes the accounting by contractors for these contracts. In addition to contracts for the construction of tangible assets, IAS 11 includes contracts for rendering of services directly related to the construction of an asset, destruction or restoration of an asset, or restoration of the environment after destruction of the asset. International Financial Reporting Interpretations Committee (IFRIC) 15, *Agreements for the Construction of Real Estate*, provides guidance for determining whether an agreement for the construction of real estate is a construction contract within the scope of IAS 11 or is a contract for the sale of goods within the scope of IAS 18. IFRIC 15 was issued in July 2008 and is effective for annual periods beginning on or after 1 January 2009. Earlier application is permitted.

3.64 IAS 11 includes the definitions of two types of contracts: cost plus and fixed price. A *cost-plus contract* is one in which the contractor is reimbursed for allowable or otherwise defined costs plus either a percentage of these costs or a fixed fee. A *fixed-price contract* is one in which the contractor agrees to a fixed contract price or a fixed rate per unit of output, which in some cases is subject to escalation clauses.

Recognition and Measurement

IFRSs

3.65 The requirements of IAS 11 generally apply separately to each construction contract. However, the standard recognizes that contracts can be written so that there are separately identifiable components covering the construction of multiple assets. Multiple contracts can be so interrelated that they are, in effect, part of a single project with an overall profit margin. Therefore, contractors should assess whether to segment a particular contract into components or whether to combine a group of contracts. If the criteria for combining or segmenting are met, the contracts should be combined or segmented, as appropriate.

3.66 The guidance in IAS 11 states that contractors should treat individual assets as separate contracts when the customer submitted separate proposals and separately negotiated for each asset so the customer or contractor, or both, could accept or reject the parts of the contract relating to each asset and the contractor is able to identify each asset's costs and revenues. In contrast, contractors should combine contracts when the customer and contractor negotiated a group of assets as a package and the contracts are so interrelated that they, in substance, form one project with an overall profit margin and the contractor will perform the contracts either concurrently or in sequence.

3.67 IAS 11 also specifies that contractors should treat construction of an additional asset as a separate contract when the asset differs in design, technology, or function from other assets covered by the original contract or the price for the additional asset is negotiated independent of the original contract price.

3.68 IAS 11 defines *contract revenue* as the sum of the following amounts:
- Initial amount of revenue agreed in the contract
- Variations in contract work, claims, and incentive payments to the extent that it is probable that these items will result in revenue and can be measured reliably

Contractors should measure contract revenue at fair value of the consideration received or receivable.

3.69 IAS 11 defines *contract costs* as the sum of the following amounts:
- Costs that relate directly to the specific contract
- Costs that are attributable to contract activity in general and can be allocated to the specific contract
- Other costs specifically chargeable to the customer under the terms of the contract

In addition to providing guidance on cost that can or may be attributable to the contract, IAS 11 does not permit an entity to include general administration costs or research and development costs in contract costs, unless the contract specifies reimbursement, selling costs, and depreciation of idle plant and equipment not used on that contract.

3.70 When the outcome of the contract can be estimated reliably, the contractor should recognize contract revenue and costs according to the percentage-of-completion method, with reference to the stage of completion at the end of the reporting period. When it is probable that total contract costs will exceed total contract revenues, contractors should immediately recognize expected losses as an expense.

3.71 IAS 11 provides that costs directly related to securing a contract and other precontract costs are included as part of contract costs only when it is probable that the contract will be obtained and the costs can be identified separately and measured reliably. An entity should not capitalize costs previously expensed.

3.72 For fixed-price contracts, IAS 11 states that the contractor can estimate the contract outcome reliably when all of the following criteria are met:
- The contractor can measure reliably the total contract revenue, the costs to complete the contract, and the stage of completion at the end of the reporting period.
- It is probable that future economic benefits will flow to the contractor from the contract.
- Attributable contract costs can be clearly identified and measured reliably so that accrued costs can be compared with prior estimates.

3.73 For cost-plus contracts, IAS 11 states that the contractor can estimate the contract outcome reliably when it is probable that future economic benefits will flow to the contractor from the contract and attributable contract costs can be clearly identified and measured reliably, regardless of whether they are specifically reimbursable, so that accrued costs can be compared with prior estimates. Because the percentage-of-completion method is applied on a cumulative basis, changes in the required estimates are accounted for prospectively as a change in accounting estimate, in accordance with IAS 8.

3.74 When the contract outcome cannot be estimated reliably, the contractor should recognize contract costs as an expense in the period incurred and contract revenue only to the extent that contract costs were incurred and cost recovery is probable.

Author's Note

The method used when the contract outcome cannot be measured reliably is commonly referred to as either the *cost-recovery-first* or *zero-profit method*, although IAS 11 does not use these terms.

U.S. GAAP

3.75 FASB ASC 605-35 also includes guidance that an entity may use for combining contracts for revenue recognition and loss determination. FASB ASC 605-35-25-5 states that the presumption in combining contracts is that revenue and profit are earned and should be reported uniformly over the performance of the combined contracts. In addition to the criteria established under IFRSs for combining contracts, FASB ASC 605-35-25-8 includes the following additional indicators that a group of contracts may be combined:
- Contracts are, in essence, an agreement to complete a single project.
- Contracts are, in substance, an agreement with a single customer.

3.76 Unlike IFRSs, FASB ASC 605-35-25-12 permits an entity to segment a construction contract if all of the following steps were taken and are documented and verifiable:
- (a) The contractor submitted bona fide proposals on the separate components of the project and the entire project.
- (b) The customer had the right to accept the proposals on either basis.
- (c) The aggregate amount of the proposals on the separate components approximated the amount of the proposal on the entire project.

When these restrictive conditions are not met, contractors may segment contracts only if seven other conditions, discussed in FASB ASC 605-35-25-13, are met.

3.77 FASB ASC 605-35-25 includes significantly more guidance than IAS 11 for determining total contract revenue and contract costs. With respect to revenues, paragraphs 16–31 of FASB ASC 605-35-25 include specific requirements for determining the basic contract price for cost-type (cost-plus) and fixed-price contracts, for incorporating customer-furnished materials, priced and unpriced change orders, contract options and additions, and for claims.

3.78 With respect to costs, paragraphs 32–44 of FASB ASC 605-35-25 include specific guidance on the costs that contractors should include in construction-in-progress accounts. Although the accounting for costs incurred to secure a contract and other precontract costs is similar to IFRSs, FASB ASC 605-35-25 provides more extensive guidance and, unlike IFRSs, allows for deferral of such costs until receipt of the anticipated contract in certain circumstances. Paragraphs 42–43 of FASB ASC 605-35-25 specify the accounting treatment for back charges, requiring both adjustments to receivables and payables for back charges to and from others.

3.79 Like IFRSs, FASB ASC 605-35-25-45 requires an entity to recognize a loss immediately when estimated contract costs exceed contract revenues. However, unlike IFRSs, paragraphs 45–50 of FASB ASC 605-35-25 provide considerable guidance on how contractors should estimate the loss.

3.80 FASB ASC 605-35-05-5 identifies the percentage-of-completion method and the completed-contract method as the two accounting methods commonly followed by contractors. An entity should use one of the two methods in specified circumstances and should not consider the methods acceptable alternatives for the same circumstances.

3.81 Paragraphs 56–61 of FASB ASC 605-35-25 describe the circumstances under which use of the percentage-of-completion method would be appropriate. Specifically, the use of the percentage-of-completion method requires an entity to make reasonably dependable estimates of the extent of progress toward completion, contract revenues, and contract costs. FASB ASC 605-35-25-60 states that normally, a contractor will be able to estimate total contract revenue and total contract cost in single amounts. Those amounts should normally be used as the basis for accounting for contracts under the percentage-of-completion method. Unlike IFRSs, guidance on how an entity should apply this method and allowed alternatives is extensive.

3.82 Paragraphs 88–89 of FASB ASC 605-35-25 state that under the completed-contract method, an entity recognizes income only when a contract is completed or substantially completed. However, in accordance with paragraphs 45–50 of FASB ASC 605-35-25, an entity should recognize expected contract losses as soon as they become evident. Paragraphs 90–93 of FASB ASC 605-35-25 identify appropriate circumstances under which an entity should apply the completed-contract method. Contractors may use the completed-contract method as their accounting policy either when their financial position and operating results would not be materially different from that which would result from using the percentage-of-completion method or inherent hazards and undependable estimates would make the necessary forecasts required by the percentage-of-completion method unreliable. For example, a contractor with primarily short-term contracts could use the completed-contract method. In contrast, IFRSs do not permit contractors to use the completed-contract method in any circumstances.

Presentation

IFRSs

3.83 IFRSs contain limited presentation guidance for contract revenues, expenses, or the related assets and liabilities. Although not required to present these as separate line items on the balance sheet, an entity should present the following amounts:

- Gross amount due from customers for contract work as an asset
- Gross amount due to customers for contract work as a liability

The *gross amount due from customers* for contract work is the net amount of costs incurred plus recognized profits (less the sum of recognized losses and progress billings) for all contracts in progress for which costs incurred plus recognized profits (less recognized losses) exceed progress billings.

The *gross amount due to customers* for contract work is the net amount of costs incurred plus recognized profits (less the sum of recognized losses and progress billings) for all contracts in progress for which progress billings exceed costs incurred plus recognized profits (less recognized losses).

U.S. GAAP

3.84 Like IFRSs, FASB ASC 605-35 contains limited presentation guidance for contract revenues and expenses, and related assets and liabilities. FASB ASC 605-35-45-3 states that, when an entity applies the percentage-of-completion method, current assets may include costs and recognized income not yet billed, with respect to certain contracts. Liabilities—in most cases, current liabilities—may include billings in excess of costs and recognized income, with respect to other contracts.

3.85 FASB ASC 605-35-45-4 explains that when the completed-contract method is used, an excess of accumulated costs over related billings should be shown in the balance sheet as a current asset, and an excess of accumulated billings over related costs should be shown among the liabilities, in most cases as a current liability. Similar to IFRSs, if costs exceed billings on some contracts and billings exceed costs on others, the contracts should ordinarily be segregated so that the amounts shown as assets include only those contracts on which costs exceed billings and those shown as liabilities include only those on which billings exceed costs. FASC 605-35-45-5 recommends that an entity describe the asset as costs of uncompleted contracts in excess of related billings, rather than as inventory or work in process. The entity should describe the liability as billings on uncompleted contracts in excess of related costs.

3.86 Paragraphs 1–2 of FASB ASC 605-35-45 require an entity to recognize expected contract losses in the income statement as additional contract costs, not a reduction of contract revenues. Unless the loss is material in amount or unusual or infrequent in nature, an entity should not show the loss contract cost separately in the income statement. If the loss is shown separately, an entity should present it as a component of the cost included in the computation of gross profit.

Disclosure

IFRSs

3.87 Contractors should disclose the amount of revenue recognized during the period and the methods used to determine the contract revenue and stage of completion. For contracts in progress, contractors should disclose the aggregate amount of costs incurred and recognized net profits, amount of advances received, and amount of retentions. They should also disclose any contingencies in accordance with IAS 37, *Provisions, Contingent Liabilities and Contingent Assets* (for example, warranty costs, claims, penalties, and possible losses).

U.S. GAAP

3.88 FASB ASC 605-35-50 requires fewer disclosures than IFRSs. According to FASB ASC 605-35-50-1, contractors should disclose their accounting policy (for example, percentage of completion or completed contract). In addition, the guidance in FASB ASC 605-35-50-3 states that if a contractor departs from the percentage-of-completion method as its basic accounting policy for a single contract or group of contracts for which the entity cannot make reasonably dependable estimates or for which inherent hazards make estimates doubtful, the entity should disclose that fact and the reason. Similarly, in accordance with FASB ASC 605-35-50-5, if an entity departs from the completed-contract method as its basic accounting policy, it should disclose and explain that departure.

Presentation and Disclosure Excerpts

Construction Contracts

3.89

Gazit-Globe Ltd (Dec 2011)

CONSOLIDATED STATEMENTS OF INCOME (in part)

	Note	Convenience Translation Into U.S. Dollars (Note 2d(1)) Year Ended December 31, 2011 In Millions	Year Ended December 31 2011	2010	2009
			NIS in Millions (Except for Per Share Data)		
Rental income	30	1,371	5,239	4,596	4,084
Revenues from sale of buildings, land and contractual works performed	31	329	1,257	691	596
Total revenues		1,700	6,496	5,287	4,680
Property operating expenses	32	455	1,740	1,551	1,369
Cost of buildings sold, land and contractual works performed	31	314	1,199	622	554
Total cost of revenues		769	2,939	2,173	1,923
Gross profit		931	3,557	3,114	2,757

NOTES TO THE CONSOLIDATED FINANCIAL STATEMENTS (in part)

Note 1: General (in part)

a. The Company and Its Business Activities

The Company, through its investees (collectively, the "Group"), is the owner, operator and developer of income producing properties in North America, Europe, Israel and Brazil and focuses mainly on the supermarket-anchored shopping center sector. In addition, the Group operates in the medical office buildings sector in North America, the senior housing facilities sector in the U.S., as well as in the development and construction of real estate projects in Israel and Eastern Europe. Furthermore, the Group continues to seek and realize business opportunities by acquiring properties and/or companies that operates within its core business or in similar fields, both in regions where it currently operates and also in new regions.

The Company's securities are listed for trading on the Tel Aviv and New York Stock Exchanges.

Note 2: Significant Accounting Policies (in part)

j. Receivables From Construction Contracts

Income receivable from construction contracts is separately calculated for each construction contract and presented in the statement of financial position at the aggregate amount of total costs incurred and total recognized profits less total recognized losses and progress billings. Progress billings are amounts billed for work performed up to the reporting date, whether settled or not settled. If the amount is due from the customer, it is recorded in the statement of financial position as an asset under receivables for construction contracts presented under Trade receivables. If the amount is due to the customer, it is recorded in the statement of financial position as a liability for construction contracts. The financial asset, receivables for construction contracts, is reviewed for impairment and derecognition as discussed below regarding impairment of financial assets presented at amortized cost and the derecognition of financial assets, respectively.

Costs of projects based on construction contracts are recognized at cost that includes identifiable direct costs and shared indirect costs. Shared indirect costs are allocated between the projects using a relevant basis.

y. Revenue Recognition (in part)

Revenues are recognized in the income statement when the revenues can be measured reliably, it is probable that the economic benefits associated with the transaction will flow to the Group and the costs incurred or to be incurred in respect of the transaction can be measured reliably.

Revenues From Construction Contracts

Revenues from construction contracts are recognized by the percentage of completion method when all the following conditions are satisfied: the revenues are known or can be estimated reliably, collection is probable, costs related to performing the work are determinable or can be reasonably determined, there is no substantial uncertainty regarding the Group's ability (as the contractor) to complete the contract and meet the contractual terms and the percentage of completion can be estimated reliably. The percentage of completion is determined based on the proportion of costs incurred to date to the estimated total costs.

If not all the criteria for recognition of revenue from construction contracts are met, then revenue is recognized only to the extent of costs whose recoverability is probable ("zero profit margin" presentation).

An expected loss on a contract is recognized immediately irrespective of the stage of completion and classified within cost of revenues.

Note 5: Trade Receivables

a. Composition:

	December 31	
	2011	2010
	NIS in Millions	
Open accounts (1)	263	176
Checks receivable	22	9
Receivables for construction contracts (2)	429	159
Total	714	344
(1) Net of allowance for doubtful accounts (see e below)	58	57
(2) Receivables for construction contracts		
Costs incurred plus recognized profits	4,364	1,396
Less—progress billings	3,935	1,237
	429	159

b. Trade receivables are non-interest bearing. As for the linkage basis of trade receivables, refer to Note 37.

c. In 2011 and 2010, the Group had no major tenant who contributed more than 10% to total rental income.

d. There are no significant past due and impaired receivables except those that have been included in the provision for doubtful accounts. The balances of receivables for construction contracts represent amounts not yet due as of the balance sheet dates.

e. Movement in allowance for doubtful accounts:

	2011	2010
	NIS in Millions	
At the beginning of the year	57	60
Charge for the year	30	35
Release for the year	(8)	(5)
Write down of accounts	(25)	(28)
Initially consolidated company	2	—
Exchange differences	2	(5)
At the end of the year	58	57

Note 9: Investments in Investees (in part)

m. Investment in Acad Building and Investments Ltd. ("Acad")

In September 2007, a wholly-owned subsidiary of the Company acquired 50% of the share capital and voting rights of Acad, thus obtaining joint control over Acad, for a consideration of approximately NIS 184 million. Since the acquisition date, Acad has been accounted for as a jointly controlled entity, using proportionate consolidation.

Acad's primary activity is the direct and indirect holding of the share capital and voting rights of U. Dori Ltd. ("Dori Group"), a public company listed on the Tel-Aviv Stock Exchange which is primarily engaged in the development and construction (both as an initiator and as a contractor for third

parties) of residential and commercial buildings and as a contractor performing construction contracts in the field of infrastructure. Dori Group operates in Israel and in Eastern Europe. Dori Group is also operating (along with others) to build a power station in Israel for the production of electricity. Besides the holdings in Dori Group, Acad had a construction contracts activity in Nigeria (50%) that was sold after the reporting date with estimated gain of NIS 10 million, and owns 26% interest in an income producing property in Israel (26%).

On March 10, 2011 the other shareholders of Acad at that time (the "Partners") submitted an offer to the Company, to buy or sell 50% of Acad's share capital, according to the Buy and Sell ("BMBY") mechanism set out in Acad's shareholders agreement. On April 3, 2011 the Company notified the Partners that it would purchase their 50% interest in Acad at the price indicated in their offer (NIS 82 million (the "transaction price") reflecting a total value of NIS 164 million for Acad). On April 17, 2011 the transaction closed and commencing on that date Acad is fully consolidated in the Company's financial statements.

The acquisition was accounted for as a business combination achieved in stages under IFRS 3, with the previously owned interest in Acad revalued to its fair value at the acquisition date according to the transaction price. As a result of such revaluation, the Company recognized a NIS 31 million loss (including the currency translation reserve realization amounted to NIS 12 million) charged to profit or loss.

Note 31: Revenues and Costs From Sale of Buildings, Land and Contractual Works Performed

	Year Ended December 31		
	2011	2010	2009
	NIS in Millions		
a. Revenues			
Revenues from sale of buildings and land	64	155	154
Revenues from construction contracts	1,193	536	442
	1,257	691	596
b. Cost of revenues by revenue sources			
Cost of sale of buildings and land	60	126	141
Cost of revenues from construction contracts	1,139	496	413
	1,199	622	554
c. Cost of revenues by expense components			
Land	21	36	39
Materials	274	110	96
Subcontractors	745	399	345
Salaries and related expenses	78	35	28
Others	76	39	43
Depreciation	5	3	3
	1,199	622	554

IAS 2, *INVENTORIES*

TABLE 3-3: INVENTORY COST DETERMINATION

	2011	2010	2009
First-in first-out (FIFO)	50	52	51
(Weighted) average cost	96	88	78
Specific identification	13	10	9
Fair value less cost to sell (broker-dealer exemption)	7	8	4
Other	4	3	4
No valuation method disclosed	18	14	16
No inventory or not-material	21	28	27
Total	**209**	**203**	**189**
Less: Companies disclosing at least two valuation methods	(30)	(30)	(27)
Companies disclosing at least three valuation methods	(4)	(3)	(2)
Total Companies in Sample	**175**	**170**	**160**

Author's Note

IASB amended IAS 2, *Inventories*, by issuing the following standards:
- IFRS 9
  This amendment replaces references to IAS 39 with a reference to IFRS 9.
- IFRS 13
  IFRS 13 replaces the definition of fair value in paragraph 7 of IAS 2 with the following:
  > Fair value reflects the price at which an orderly transaction to sell the same inventory in the principal or more advantageous market for that inventory would take place between market participants at the measurement date.

Early adoption of these standards is permitted. Because these standards are effective for annual periods beginning on or after 1 January 2012, these amendments are not reflected in the commentary in this section. However, these amendments would not affect the availability of illustrative excerpts from survey companies' financial statements.

IFRS Overview and Comparison to U.S. GAAP

3.90 IAS 2 establishes the requirements for recognition and measurement of cost of sales, write-downs, and reversals of write-downs of inventory. IAS 1 establishes the requirements for presentation of this information in the statement of comprehensive income and note disclosures.

Author's Note

See paragraphs 2.32–.41 in section 2 for coverage of accounting for inventories under IFRSs. The discussion that follows focuses only on the expenses and losses addressed in IAS 2 that are recognized in the statement of comprehensive income.

3.91 IAS 2 applies to all inventories except work in process arising under construction contracts, financial instruments, biological assets related to agricultural activity, and agricultural produce at the point of harvest.

Recognition and Measurement

IFRSs

3.92 An entity should use one of the following cost flow assumptions to assign costs to inventories and cost of sales:
- Specific identification for inventory items that are not interchangeable or segregated and produced for specific projects
- First in, first out (FIFO)
- Weighted average cost

IAS 2 requires an entity to apply the same cost flow assumption to inventories of similar nature and use. IAS 2 prohibits the use of the last in, first out (LIFO) cost flow assumption.

3.93 An entity should recognize the carrying amount of inventories sold as an expense in the same period as the related revenue is recognized.

3.94 An entity should not carry inventories on the balance sheet at amounts exceeding those it expects to realize from sale or use. When there are indicators that the cost is not recoverable, such as damage or decline in selling price, an entity should write down inventories to net realizable value. An entity normally should write down inventories on an item-by-item basis. However, IAS 2 recognizes that when an entity tests its inventory for impairment, there may be circumstances when it is more appropriate to group similar or related items (for example, items in the same product line that cannot be evaluated separately).

3.95 *Net realizable value* is the estimated selling price in the ordinary course of business less the sum of estimated costs to complete and costs necessary to make the sale. An entity should recognize a write-down of inventory in profit or loss in the period recognized. IAS 2 permits reversals of inventory write-downs.

U.S. GAAP

3.96 Relative to IFRSs, FASB ASC 330, *Inventory*, establishes a more complex process for determining the circumstances for, and the amount by, which an entity should record inventory write-downs and provides considerably more guidance for applying this process. FASB ASC 330-10-35-1 requires an entity to value inventories at the lower of cost or market, in contrast to the IAS 2 requirement to value inventories at the lower of cost or net realizable value. *Market*, as defined in the FASB ASC glossary, is generally considered to be replacement cost not to exceed net realizable value (the ceiling) and not to be less than net realizable value less an allowance for an approximately normal profit margin (the floor). The FASB ASC glossary defines *net realizable value* similarly to IFRSs.

3.97 FASB ASC 330-10 explains that the lower of cost or market rule applies to all inventory cost flow assumptions (for example, FIFO, weighted average cost, and LIFO). However,

FASB ASC 330-10-35-7 explains that the concept of "market" is intended as a guide, not a literal rule, and discusses application of this concept in the context of the retail inventory method. Because the retail method already incorporates the concept of lower of cost or market when adequate markdowns are taken, FASB ASC explains that an entity is not required to make additional adjustments because the inventory method applied already meets the objectives of the lower of cost or market rule. IFRSs do not discuss the retail method in the same detail as FASB ASC 330-10 but permit use of either the standard cost or retail inventory method if the result approximates cost.

3.98 Both paragraphs 8–10 of FASB ASC 330-10-35 and IFRSs provide guidance on testing inventory for impairments. Both conclude that an entity should generally test individual items but recognize that there may be circumstances when performing the test on groups of items is more appropriate.

3.99 Unlike IFRSs, FASB ASC 330-10 does not permit reversals of inventory write-downs, with the rationale that inventory written down acquires a new cost basis and recovery of the original cost is only permitted on sale or disposal. However, as noted in paragraphs 15–16 of FASB ASC 330-10-35, in exceptional circumstances, certain inventories (for example, precious metals with a fixed monetary value and no substantial marketing costs) may be stated above cost.

Presentation

IFRSs

3.100 IAS 1 does not require an entity to present cost of sales or cost of inventory as a separate line item on the statement of comprehensive income. IAS 1 does require an entity to provide an analysis of expenses either on the face of the income statement or in the notes. An entity may choose from two formats for this analysis: by function or by nature. The by function format is often referred to as the *cost of sales* format. Unless an entity uses the by function format, an entity should disclose cost of sales in the notes.

U.S. GAAP

3.101 Rule 5-03 of SEC Regulation S-X states that SEC registrants should disclose cost of sales or cost of revenues as a separate line item on the income statement. However, unlike IFRSs, neither FASB ASC nor SEC rules require a particular presentation format for this disclosure.

3.102 Unlike IFRSs, paragraphs 2 and 5 of FASB ASC 330-10-50 respectively require an entity to present substantial and unusual write-downs and net losses on firm purchase commitments separately from cost of goods sold.

Disclosure

IFRSs

3.103 IAS 2 requires an entity to disclose the accounting policies adopted to measure inventories, the cost flow assumptions (formula) used (for example, FIFO), the amount of inventories recognized as an expense during the period, and the amounts of any write-downs or reversals of write-

downs recognized in profit or loss. An entity should also discuss the circumstances or events that led to the reversal of a write-down of inventories.

U.S. GAAP

3.104 FASB ASC 330-10-50-1 requires an entity reporting under U.S. GAAP to disclose whether inventories are stated at the lower of cost or market or another basis and the relevant cost flow assumption (for example, LIFO).

3.105 When an SEC registrant using the LIFO method liquidates a substantial portion of its LIFO inventory and, as a result, includes a material amount of income in its income statement due to the liquidation, the registrant should disclose the amount of income realized as a result of the liquidation, either in a note or parenthetically on the face of the income statement, in accordance with SEC *Codification of Staff Accounting Bulletins* topic 11(F), "LIFO Liquidations."

3.106 Unlike IFRSs, when entities recognize inventory write-downs, FASB ASC 330-10-50-2 only requires disclosure of the amount of any substantial and unusual write-downs.

Presentation and Disclosure Excerpts

Analysis of Expenses by Function (Cost of Sales)—First-In, First-Out Cost Flow Assumption, Write-Downs and Reversal of Write-Downs of Inventory

3.107

East Asiatic Company Ltd. A/S (Dec 2011)

Author's Note

East Asiatic Company has a subsidiary, Plumrose, mentioned in this excerpt. Plumrose manufactures branded, processed meat products in Venezuela, which is considered a hyperinflationary economy. Plumrose markets its products under the brands Plumrose and Oscar Mayer through a wide product portfolio. See Section 10, *Reporting in Hyperinflationary Economies*, for additional information about the effects of hyperinflation on East Asiatic's financial statements.

CONSOLIDATED INCOME STATEMENT *(in part)*

DKK Million	Note	2011	2010
Revenue	4	6,274	3,858
Cost of sales		4,367	2,740
Gross profit		1,907	1,118
Selling and distribution expenses		1,067	633
Administrative expenses		434	272
Other operating income	5	5	4
Other operating expenses	6	24	12
Other taxes		57	19
Operating profit		330	186

NOTES TO THE CONSOLIDATED FINANCIAL STATEMENTS (in part)

1. Accounting Policies for the Consolidated Financial Statements (in part)

General Information

The East Asiatic Company Ltd. A/S (the Company) and its subsidiaries (together the EAC Group or the Group) have the following two lines of business:
- Santa Fe Group provides moving, value-added relocation and records management services to corporate and individual clients.
- Plumrose is an integrated manufacturer and distributor of processed meat products in Venezuela.

The Company is a limited liability company incorporated and domiciled in Denmark. The address of its registered office is 20 Indiakaj, DK-2100 Copenhagen Ø, Denmark.

The annual report comprises both consolidated financial statements and separate Parent Company financial statements.

The Company has its listing on NASDAQ OMX Copenhagen A/S.

On 23 February 2012, the Supervisory Board approved this annual report for publication and approval by the shareholders at the annual general meeting to be held on 27 March 2012.

The financial statements are presented in DKK million unless otherwise stated.

Refer to page 37 for further details about the EAC Group and page 83 for details about the Parent Company.

Income Statement (in part)

Cost of sales comprises costs incurred to achieve sales for the year, including raw materials, consumables, direct labour costs and production overheads such as maintenance and depreciation, etc. as well as operation, administration and management of factories.

Assets (in part)

Inventories are measured at the lower of cost and net realisable value. Cost is determined using the first-in, first-out (FIFO) methods. The cost of finished goods and work in progress comprises raw materials, direct labour, other direct costs and related production overheads (based on normal operating capacity). Net realisable value is the estimated selling price in the ordinary course of business, less applicable variable selling expenses.

2. Significant Accounting Estimates and Judgements (in part)

In connection with the preparation of the consolidated financial statements, Management has made accounting estimates and judgements that affect the assets and liabilities reported at the balance sheet date as well as the income and expenses reported for the financial period. Management continuously reassesses these estimates and judgements based on a number of other factors in the given circumstances.

The following accounting estimates are considered significant for the financial reporting.
- The measurement of inventories is subject to some uncertainty in relation to the fair value of livestock. More-

over, the need for impairment write-down is estimated at net realisable value based on Management's assessment of the selling price anticipated at the balance sheet date under normal business conditions. The carrying amount of inventories at the balance sheet date is DKK 1,036m (2010: DKK 514m). See note 21.

21. Inventories

DKK Million	2011	2010
Raw materials	632	271
Work in progress	93	65
Finished goods	311	178
Total	1,036	514
Inventories recognised as an expense during the year	2,770	1,926
Amounts of write-down of inventory recognised as expense during the year	36	3
Amount of reversal of write-down of inventories during the year	31	3
Carrying amount of inventory carried at fair value less cost to sell	9	9

Change in write-down of inventories during 2011 were attributable to Plumrose.

Analysis of Expenses by Function (Cost of Sales)—Weighted Average Cost, Inventories Stated at Net Realizable Value, Costs Include Gains and Losses on Qualifying Cash Flow Hedges for Purchases of Raw Materials

3.108

GRUMA, S.A.B. de C.V. (Dec 2011)

CONSOLIDATED INCOME STATEMENTS (in part)

(In thousands of Mexican pesos, except per-share data) (Notes 1, 2 and 4)

	Note	2010	2011
Net sales		Ps. 46,232,454	Ps. 57,644,749
Cost of sales		(31,563,342)	(40,117,952)
Gross profit		14,669,112	17,526,797

NOTES TO THE CONSOLIDATED FINANCIAL STATEMENTS (in part)

(In thousands of Mexican pesos, except where otherwise indicated)

1. Entity and Operations

Gruma, S.A.B. de C.V. (GRUMA) is a Mexican company with subsidiaries located in Mexico, the United States of America, Central America, Venezuela, Europe, Asia and Oceania, together referred to as the "Company." The Company's main activities are the production and sale of corn flour, wheat flour, tortillas and related products.

Gruma, S.A.B. de C.V. is a publicly held corporation (*Sociedad Anónima Bursátil de Capital Variable*) organized under the laws of Mexico. The address of its registered office is Rio de la Plata 407 in San Pedro Garza García, Nuevo León, Mexico.

The consolidated financial statements were authorized by the Chief Corporate Office and the Chief Administrative Office of the Company on April 30, 2012.

2. Basis of Preparation (in part)

The consolidated financial statements of Gruma, S.A.B. de C.V. and Subsidiaries as of December 31, 2011 have been prepared for the first time in accordance with the International Financial Reporting Standards (IFRS) as issued by the International Accounting Standards Board (IASB). The IFRS also include the International Accounting Standards (IAS) in force, as well as all the related interpretations issued by the International Financial Reporting Interpretations Committee (IFRIC), including those previously issued by the Standing Interpretations Committee (SIC).

In accordance with the amendments to the Rules for Public Companies and Other Participants in the Mexican Stock Exchange, issued by the Mexican Banking Securities Exchange Commission on January 27, 2009, the Company is required to prepare its financial statements under IFRS starting in 2012.

The Company decided to adopt IFRS earlier, starting January 1, 2011, therefore, these are the Company's first consolidated financial statements prepared in accordance with IFRS as issued by the IASB.

For comparative purposes, the consolidated financial statements as of and for the year ended December 31, 2010 have been prepared in accordance with IFRS, as required by the IFRS 1—First-Time Adoption of International Financial Reporting Standards.

The Company modified its accounting policies from Mexican Financial Reporting Standards (Mexican FRS) in order to comply with IFRS starting January 1, 2011. The transition from Mexican FRS to IFRS was recognized in accordance with IFRS 1, setting January 1, 2010 as the transition date. The reconciliation of the effects of the transition from Mexican FRS to IFRS in equity as of January 1, 2010 and December 31, 2010, in net income and cash flows for the year ended December 31, 2010 are disclosed in Note 28 to these financial statements.

4. Summary of Significant Accounting Policies (in part)

E) Inventories

Inventories are measured at the lower of cost and net realizable value. Cost is determined using the average cost method. The net realizable value is the estimated selling price of inventory in the normal course of business, less applicable variable selling expenses. The cost of finished goods and production in process comprises raw materials, direct labor, other direct costs and related production overheads. Cost of inventories may also include the transfer from equity of any gains or losses on qualifying cash flow hedges for purchases of raw materials.

6. Risk and Capital Management (in part)

Commodity Price Risk and Derivatives

The availability and price of corn, wheat and other agricultural commodities and fuels are subject to wide fluctuations due to factors outside of the Company's control, such as weather, plantings, government (domestic and foreign) farm programs and policies, changes in global demand/supply and global production of similar and competitive crops. The Company hedges a portion of its production requirements through commodity futures and options contracts in order to reduce the risk created by price fluctuations and supply of corn, wheat, natural gas, diesel and soy oils which exist as part of ongoing business operations. The open positions for hedges of purchases do not exceed the maximum production requirements for a period no longer than 18 months.

During 2011, the Company entered into short-term hedge transactions through commodity futures and options to hedge a portion of its requirements. All derivative financial instruments are recorded at their fair value as either assets or liabilities. Changes in the fair value of derivatives are recorded each period in earnings or accumulated other comprehensive income in equity, depending on whether the derivative qualifies for hedge accounting and is effective as part of a hedge transaction. Ineffectiveness results when the change in the fair value of the hedge instruments differs from the change in the fair value of the position.

For hedge transactions that qualify and are effective, gains and losses are deferred until the underlying asset or liability is settled, and then are recognized as part of that transaction.

Gains and losses which represent hedge ineffectiveness and derivative transactions that do not qualify for hedge accounting are recognized in the income statement.

At December 31, 2011, financial instruments that qualify as hedge accounting represented a favorable effect of Ps. 14,876, which was recognized as comprehensive income in equity.

From time to time the Company hedges commodity price risks utilizing futures and options strategies that do not qualify for hedge accounting. As a result of non-qualification, these derivative financial instruments are recognized at their fair values and the associated effect is recorded in current period earnings. For the years ended December 31, 2010 and 2011, the Company recognized an unfavorable effect of Ps. 13,228 and Ps. 40,207, respectively, from not-settled financial instruments that did not qualify as hedge accounting. Additionally, as of December 31, 2010 and 2011, the Company realized Ps. 42,970 and Ps. 52,626, respectively, in net losses on commodity price risk hedges that did not qualify for hedge accounting.

During 2010, the Company entered into hedge contracts for corn purchases, which were designated as fair value hedges. Therefore, the derivative financial instruments, as well as the assets and liabilities being hedged, are recognized at fair value at the trade date. Changes in the fair value of the derivative financial instruments and the assets and liabilities being hedged are recognized in income for the year. All contracts were settled in November 2010. As a result of the valuation at fair value, as of December 31, 2010, the balance of Inventories included Ps. 162,254 for these contracts.

Based on the Company's overall commodity exposure at December 31, 2011, a hypothetical 10 percent decline in market prices applied to the fair value of these instruments would result in an effect to the income statement of Ps. 40,431 (for non-qualifying contracts).

In Mexico, to support the commercialization of corn for Mexican corn growers, Mexico's Secretary of Agriculture, Livestock, Rural Development, Fisheries and Food Ministry (Secretaría de Agricultura, Ganadería, Desarrollo Rural, Pesca y Alimentación, or SAGARPA), through the Agricultural Incentives and Services Agency (Apoyos y Servicios a la Comercialización Agropecuaria, or ASERCA), a government agency founded in 1991, implemented a program designed to promote corn sales in Mexico. The program includes the following objectives:

- Ensure that the corn harvest is brought to market, providing certainty to farmers concerning the sale of their crops and supply security for the buyer.

- Establish a minimum price for the farmer, and a maximum price for the buyer, which are determined based on international market prices, plus a basic formula specific for each region.
- Implement a corn hedging program to allow both farmers and buyers to minimize their exposure to price fluctuations in the international markets.

To the extent that this or other similar programs are canceled by the Mexican government, we may be required to incur additional costs in purchasing corn for our operations, and therefore we may need to increase the prices of our products to reflect such additional costs.

9. Inventories

Inventories consisted of the following:

	At January 1, 2010	At December 31, 2010	At December 31, 2011
Raw materials, mainly corn and wheat	Ps. 5,815,253	Ps. 5,641,754	Ps. 8,633,094
Finished products	845,178	724,516	917,014
Materials and spare parts	433,148	389,352	639,307
Production in process	217,841	160,239	149,714
Advances to suppliers	153,383	256,829	194,297
Inventory in transit	71,785	91,544	167,405
	Ps. 7,536,588	Ps. 7,264,234	Ps. 10,700,831

For the years ended December 31, 2010 and 2011, the cost of raw materials consumed and the changes in the inventories of production in process and finished goods, recognized as cost of sales amounted to Ps. 26,697,273 and Ps. 34,374,608, respectively.

For the years ended December 31, 2010 and 2011, the Company recognized Ps. 62,964 and Ps. 76,086, respectively, for inventory that was damaged, slow-moving and obsolete.

Analysis of Expenses by Nature—Multiple Cost Flow Assumptions, Provision for Inventory Obsolescence

3.109

Perusahaan Perseroan (Persero) PT Telekomunikasi Indonesia Tbk (Dec 2011)

CONSOLIDATED STATEMENTS OF COMPREHENSIVE INCOME (in part)

(Figures in tables are presented in billions of Rupiah and millions of United States Dollars, except per share and per ADS data)

	Notes	2010 Rp.	2011 Rp.	2011 US$ (Note 3)
Revenues	25	68,529	71,238	7,856
Other Income		548	666	73
Expenses				
Operations, maintenance and telecommunication services	28	(16,046)	(16,453)	(1,815)
Depreciation and amortization	11, 12, 13	(14,580)	(14,823)	(1,635)
Personnel	15, 27, 32, 33	(7,447)	(8,671)	(956)
Interconnection	30	(3,086)	(3,555)	(392)
Marketing		(2,525)	(3,278)	(362)
General and administrative	7, 29	(2,537)	(2,935)	(324)
Gain (loss) on foreign exchange—net		43	(210)	(23)
Share of loss of associated companies	10	(14)	(10)	(1)
Others		(145)	(192)	(21)
Total expenses		(46,337)	(50,127)	(5,529)
Profit before finance (costs)/income and income tax		22,740	21,777	2,400

NOTES TO THE CONSOLIDATED FINANCIAL STATEMENTS (in part)

1. General (in part)

a. Establishment and General Information (in part)

Perusahaan Perseroan (Persero) P.T. Telekomunikasi Indonesia Tbk (the "Company") was originally part of "Post en Telegraafdienst", which was established in 1884 under the framework of Decree No. 7 dated March 27, 1884 of the Governor General of the Dutch Indies and was published in State Gazette No. 52 dated April 3, 1884.

In 1991, the status of the Company was changed into a state-owned limited liability corporation ("Persero") based on Government Regulation No. 25/1991.

The Company was established based on notarial deed No. 128 dated September 24, 1991 of Imas Fatimah, S.H. The deed of establishment was approved by the Minister of Justice of the Republic of Indonesia in his Decision Letter No. C2-6870.HT.01.01.Th.1991 dated November 19, 1991, and was published in State Gazette No. 5 dated January 17, 1992, Supplement No. 210. The Articles of Association have been amended several times, the latest amendments were to comply with Badan Pengawas Pasar Modal and Lembaga Keuangan Indonesia ("BAPEPAM-LK") Regulation No. IX.J.1 of Main Provisions of the Articles of Association of Company that Make an Equity Public Offering and Public Company and BAPEPAM-LK Regulation No. IX.E.2 of Material Transaction and Changes of the Core Business Activities, and to add the Company's purposes and objectives, based on notarial deed No. 37 dated June 24, 2010 of A. Partomuan Pohan, S.H., LLM. The changes were accepted and approved by the Minister of Justice and Human Rights of the Republic of Indonesia ("MoJHR") as in his Letter No.AHU-AH.01.10-18476 dated July 22, 2010 and Letter No.AHU-35876.AH.01.02/2010 dated July 19, 2010 and was published in State Gazette of the Republic of Indonesia No. 63 dated August 9, 2011, Supplement of the Republic of Indonesia No. 23552.

In accordance with Article 3 of the Company's Articles of Association, the scope of its activities is to provide telecommunication network and services, informatics and optimization of the Company's resources in accordance with prevailing regulations. To achieve this objective, the Company is involved in the following activities:

a. Main Business:

i. Planning, building, providing, developing, operating, marketing or selling, leasing and maintaining telecommunications and information networks in accordance with prevailing regulations.
ii. Planning, developing, providing, marketing or selling and improving telecommunications and information services in accordance with prevailing regulations.

b. Supporting Business:

i. Providing payment transactions and money transferring services through telecommunications and information networks.
ii. Performing activities and other undertakings in connection with optimization of the Company's resources, which among others includes the utilization of the Company's property, plant and equipment and moving assets, information systems, education and training, and repairs and maintenance facilities.

The Company's head office is located at Jalan Japati No. 1, Bandung, West Java.

The Company was granted several telecommunications licenses which are valid for an unlimited period of time as long as the Company complies with prevailing laws and telecommunications regulations and fulfills the obligations stated in those permits. For every license, an evaluation is performed annually and an overall evaluation is performed every 5 (five) years. The Company is obliged to submit reports of services to the Indonesian Directorate General of Post and Telecommunications ("DGPT") annually. The reports comprise information such as network development progress, service quality standard achievement, total customer, license payment and universal service contribution, while for internet telephone services for public purpose ("ITKP") there are additional information required such as operational performance, customer segmentation, traffic, and gross revenue.

2. Summary of Significant Accounting Policies (in part)

h. Inventories

Inventories consist of components and modules, which are subsequently expensed or transferred to property, plant and equipment upon use. Components and modules represent telephone terminals, cables, transmission installation spare parts and other spare parts. Inventories also include Subscriber Identification Module ("SIM") cards, Removable User Identity Module ("RUIM") cards, handsets, set top box, wireless broadband modem and prepaid voucher blanks, which are expensed upon sale. The costs of inventories comprise of the purchase price, import duties, other taxes, transport, handling and other costs directly attributable to the acquisition. Inventories are stated at the lower of cost and net realizable value. Net realizable value is the estimate of selling price less the costs to sell.

Cost is determined using the weighted average method for components, SIM cards, RUIM cards, handsets, set top box, wireless broadband modem and prepaid voucher blanks, and the specific-identification method for modules.

The amount of any write-down of inventories below cost to net realizable value and all losses of inventories shall be recognized as an expense in the period in which the write-down or loss occurs. The amount of any reversal of any write-down of inventories, arising from an increase in net realizable value, shall be recognized as a reduction in the amount of general and administrative expense in the period in which the reversal occurs.

Provision for obsolescence is primarily based on the estimated forecast of future usage of these items.

l. Property, Plant and Equipment—Direct Acquisitions (in part)

The Company and its subsidiaries periodically evaluate its property, plant and equipment for impairment, whenever events and circumstances indicate that the carrying amount of the assets may not be recoverable. When the carrying amount of an asset exceeds its estimated recoverable amount, the asset is written-down to its estimated recoverable amount, which is determined based upon the greater of its fair value less cost to sell or value in use.

Spare parts and servicing equipment are carried as inventory and recognized in profit or loss as consumed. Major spare parts and stand-by equipment that are expected to be used for more than 12 months are recorded as part of property, plant and equipment.

7. Inventories

	January 1, 2010	December 31, 2010	December 31, 2011
Modules	234	292	297
Components	162	159	329
SIM cards, RUIM cards, set top box and prepaid voucher blanks	111	147	238
Total	507	598	864
Provision for obsolescence			
Modules	(65)	(76)	(91)
Components	(7)	(7)	(15)
SIM cards, RUIM cards, set top box and prepaid voucher blanks	(—)	(—)	(—)
Total	(72)	(83)	(106)
Net	435	515	758

Movements in the provision for impairment are as follows:

	December 31, 2010	December 31, 2011
Beginning balance	72	83
Provision of inventory recognized during the year (Note 29)	15	27
Inventories write-off	(4)	(4)
Ending balance	83	106

The cost of inventories recognized as expense and included in operations, maintenance, and telecommunication services expenses (Note 28) as of December 31, 2010 and 2011 amounted to Rp. 1,022 billion and Rp. 818 billion, respectively.

Management believes that the provision is adequate to cover losses from declines in inventory value due to obsolescence.

Certain inventories of the Company's subsidiaries have been pledged as collateral for lending agreements (Notes 17 and 18).

As of December 31, 2010 and 2011, modules and components held by the Company and its subsidiaries have been insured against fire, theft, all industrial risks, loss risk during delivery and other specific risks with the total sum insured as of December 31, 2010 and 2011 is amounting to Rp. 144 billion and Rp. 235 billion, respectively.

Management believes that the insurance coverage is adequate to cover potential losses of the insured inventories.

29. General and Administrative Expenses

	2010	2011
Provision for impairment of receivables and inventory obsolescence (Notes 6d and 7)	525	883
Collection expenses	401	327
General	301	326
Social contribution	171	290
Traveling	260	256
Professional fees	163	235
Training, education and recruitment	216	229
Security and screening	215	97
Meetings	80	86
Stationery and printing	64	53
Vehicle rental	51	43
Others	90	110
Total	2,537	2,935

Refer to Note 34 for details of related party transactions.

Analysis of Expenses by Function—Multiple Cost Flow Assumptions, Broker-Dealer Exemption

3.110

MFC Industrial Ltd. (Dec 2011)

CONSOLIDATED STATEMENTS OF OPERATIONS
(in part)

(United States Dollars in Thousands, Except per Share Amounts)

	Notes	2011	2010	2009
Net sales	5&25	$514,797	$84,476	$14,718
Equity income	5&25	5,912	954	—
Gross revenues		520,709	85,430	14,718
Costs and Expenses:				
Costs of sales	25	435,392	51,362	8,525
Impairment of available-for-sale securities		12,408	—	—
Selling, general and administrative		40,378	18,316	16,474
Share-based compensation (recovery)—selling, general and administrative	24	7,219	72	(2,713)
Finance costs		7,198	974	477
		502,595	70,724	22,763
Income (loss) from operations		18,114	14,706	(8,045)

NOTES TO THE CONSOLIDATED FINANCIAL STATEMENTS (in part)

Note 1. Nature of Business and Summary of Significant Accounting Policies (in part)

MFC Industrial Ltd. ("MFC Industrial" or the "Company", formerly Terra Nova Royalty Corporation) is incorporated under the laws of British Columbia, Canada. MFC Industrial is a global commodities supply chain company.

In November and December 2010, MFC Industrial, through a share exchange, acquired all of the issued and outstanding shares of Mass Financial Corp. ("Mass") (see Note 3). Mass and its subsidiaries (collectively, "Mass Group") are primarily in the commodities and resources business, and merchant banking. The Group consolidated the results of the operations of Mass Group since November 16, 2010.

Until the end of March 2010, MFC Industrial also operated in the industrial plant technology, equipment and service business for the cement and mining industries through its former subsidiary KHD Humboldt Wedag International AG in Germany and its subsidiaries and affiliates (collectively "KID"). MFC Industrial ceased to consolidate KID from March 31, 2010 and completed the spin-off of KID by December 31, 2010 (see Note 4). As a result, the results of operations of KID have been presented as discontinued operations. Accordingly, prior period financial statements, including business segment information as disclosed in Note 5, have been reclassified to reflect this change.

A. Basis of Presentation (in part)

Basis of Accounting

These consolidated financial statements have been prepared in accordance with the English language version of International Financial Reporting Standards ("IFRS") which include International Accounting Standards ("IAS") and Interpretations ("IFRIC" and "SIC") as issued by the International Accounting Standards Board (the "IASB").

These consolidated financial statements were prepared on going concern and accrual bases (except for cash flow information), under the historical cost convention, as modified by the revaluation of investment property and certain financial assets and financial liabilities at fair value through profit or loss.

The presentation currency of these consolidated financial statements is the United States of America (the "US") dollar ($), as rounded to the nearest thousand (except per share amounts).

B. Significant Accounting Policies (in part)

(viii) Inventories

Inventories consist of raw materials, work-in-progress, and finished goods. Inventories are recorded at the lower of cost or estimated net realizable value. Cost, where appropriate, includes an allocation of manufacturing overheads incurred in bringing inventories to their present location and condition. Net realizable value represents the estimated selling price less all estimated costs of completion and cost to be incurred in marketing, selling and distribution. The amount of any write-down of inventories to net realizable value and all losses of inventories are recognized as an expense in the period the write-down or loss occurs. The amount of a reversal of a write-down of inventories arising from an increase in net realizable value is recognized as a reduction in the amount of inventories recognized as an expense in the period in which the reversal occurs.

Commodities acquired in commodity broker-trader activities with the purpose of selling in the near future and generating a profit from fluctuations in price or broker-traders' margin are measured at fair value less costs to sell.

(ix) Real Estate Held for Sale

Real estate held for sale are real estate intended for sale in the ordinary course of business or in the process of construction or development for such sale.

Real estate held for sale are accounted for as inventories at the lower of cost (on a specific item basis) and net realizable value. Net realizable value is determined by reference to sale proceeds of properties sold in the ordinary course of business less all estimated selling expenses around the reporting date, or by management estimates based on prevailing market conditions. The amount of any write-down of properties to net realizable value is recognized as an expense in the period the write-down occurs. The amount of a reversal of a write-down arising from an increase in net realizable value is recognized in the period in which the reversal occurs.

(xviii) Costs of Sales

Costs of sales include the cost of goods (commodities and resources, real estate properties, medical instruments and supplies) sold. The cost of goods sold includes both the direct cost of materials and indirect costs, freight charges, purchasing and receiving costs, inspection costs, distribution costs, as well as provision for warranty when applicable.

The costs of sales also include the write-downs of inventories and available-for-sale securities, credit losses on loans and receivables, fair value losses on investment property and net losses on securities.

The reversal of write-downs of inventories and allowance for credit losses reduce the costs of sales.

C. Major Sources of Estimation Uncertainty (in part)

The major assumptions and other sources of estimation uncertainty that have a significant risk of resulting in a material adjustment to the carrying amounts of assets and liabilities within the next financial year are discussed below. These items require management's most difficult, subjective or complex judgments.

(ii) Provision for Inventories

The Group had recorded inventories of $81,223 at December 31, 2011. The provision for the inventories is regularly reviewed and general and specific provisions are recognized for balances considered to be irrecoverable. The irrecoverable amounts are estimated based on reviewing the macroeconomic environment and available micro-economic information specific to the product categories.

Note 11. Inventories

	2011	2010
Raw materials	$ 4,741	$ 6,467
Work-in-progress	6,021	10,842
Finished goods	6,846	4,968
Commodity inventories (including goods-in-transit of $42,130 and $30,603 at December 31, 2011 and 2010, respectively)	63,615	44,825
	$81,223	$67,102

The Group entered into sale and repurchase agreements with other commodity broker-traders pursuant to which the Group sold an agreed quantity of commodities at agreed prices and undertakes to buy back the same quantity of the same commodities at the same agreed prices in future periods. These sale and repurchase transactions are accounted for as financing arrangements. The cash received is discounted at the market interest rate and shown as deferred sale liabilities in the consolidated statement of financial position. When the commodities are delivered by the Group to the counterparties, sales transactions are completed and recognized with debits to the deferred sale liabilities. As at December 31, 2011, the Group recognized current and long-term deferred sale liabilities of $14,958 and $25,647, respectively. The long-term deferred liability is due on various dates in 2013. As at December 31, 2010, the Group recognized current and long-term deferred sale liabilities of $23,133 and $39,993, respectively.

As at December 31, 2011 and 2010, there was no inventory pledged as security for liabilities.

Note 25. Consolidated Statements of Operations (in part)

Expenses

The Group's costs of sales comprised:

	2011	2010	2009
Commodities and resources	$414,745	$45,994	$8,512
Loss on securities, net	4,314	834	—
Credit losses (recovery) on loans and receivables	(530)	795	—
Change in fair value of investment property	56	294	—
Write-down on real estate held for sale	—	241	—
Market value decrease on commodities	4,422	—	—
Loss on derivative contracts, net	—	2,010	—
Other	12,385	1,194	13
Total cost of sales	$435,392	$51,362	$8,525

The Group's net loss on securities comprised:

	2011	2010	2009
Trading securities	$6,507	$ —	$—
Available-for-sale securities	(1,721)	—	—
Subsidiaries	(405)	834	—
Short-sale	(67)	—	—
Total cost of sales	$4,314	$834	$—

The Group included the following items in its costs of sales:

	2011	2010	2009
Inventories as costs of goods sold (including depreciation, amortization and depletion expenses allocated to costs of goods sold)	$373,048	$46,147	$8,512
(Recovery of) write-down of inventories	(29)	88	—

The Group collected a reimbursement of legal costs from an arbitration of $1,503, $nil and $nil in 2011, 2010 and 2009, respectively. The aforesaid reimbursement was shown as a reduction in the selling, general and administrative expenses.

Additional Information on the Nature of Expenses

	2011	2010	2009
Depreciation, amortization and depletion	$13,204	$11,766	$8,563
Employee benefits expenses	19,687	3,758	2,759

DEPRECIATION AND AMORTIZATION

Author's Note

The commentary that follows addresses depreciation and amortization of assets covered by the following IFRSs:

- IAS 16, *Property, Plant and Equipment*
- IAS 17, *Leases*
- IAS 38, *Intangible Assets*
- IAS 40, *Investment Property*

IASB issued several standards in 2010 and 2011 that amended these standards, including IFRS 9, IFRS 10, IFRS 11, and IFRS 13. The amendments are discussed in an author's note in section 2 at the relevant standard. None of these amendments affect accounting for depreciation and amortization and would have no effect on the content or availability of illustrative excerpts from survey companies' financial statements.

TABLE 3-4: DEPRECIATION AND AMORTIZATION METHODS

	2011	2010	2009
Property, Plant, and Equipment Investment Properties Held at Cost			
Straight line	170	157	148
Declining balance	11	3	3
Units of production	18	17	16
Other (for example, proportion of proven reserves)	8	9	8
No property, plant and equipment or depreciation method disclosed	3	6	5
Total	**210**	**192**	**180**
Less: Companies disclosing at least two depreciation methods	(28)	(19)	(18)
Companies disclosing at least three depreciation methods	(7)	(3)	(2)
Total Companies	**175**	**170**	**160**
Intangible Assets With Finite Life			
Straight line	133	124	118
Units of production	6	8	18
Other (for example, pattern of consumption)	23	28	29
Assets not yet available for use	1	1	0
No finite-life intangible assets or amortization method disclosed	32	31	26
Total	**195**	**192**	**181**
Less: Companies disclosing at least one amortization method	(19)	(20)	(19)
Companies disclosing at least three amortization methods	(1)	(2)	(2)
Total Companies	**175**	**170**	**160**

IFRS Overview and Comparison to U.S. GAAP

3.111 Depreciation and amortization are terms describing the systematic allocation of an asset's carrying amount less estimated residual value (depreciable or amortizable amount) over the asset's estimated useful life. IFRSs require an entity to record depreciation or amortization on the following asset classes for all assets in the class with finite useful lives:

- Property, plant, and equipment (PPE) (measured under either the cost or revaluation model)
- Intangible assets (measured under the cost or revaluation model)
- Investment property (measured under the cost model)
- Assets held under a finance (capital) lease (those previously listed)

Author's Note

Section 2 provides the general recognition and measurement requirements applicable to these asset classes.

Recognition and Measurement

IFRSs

3.112 IAS 16 requires an entity to measure items of PPE initially at cost and to allocate that cost to the item's significant component parts. This allocation of cost is often referred to as *componentization* or *component accounting*. One such part, or component, to which an entity should allocate cost is major inspection and overhaul costs. An entity should depreciate all significant components separately. To calculate depreciation, an entity should determine the depreciable base of assets with finite lives by estimating the asset's useful life and residual value. IAS 16 also requires an entity to depreciate separately each component part with an individual cost that is significant in relation to the total cost of the item.

3.113 IAS 16 requires an entity to begin to depreciate an asset when it is available for use (that is, when the asset is in the location and condition necessary for it to be capable of operating in the manner intended by management). Depreciation of an asset should cease at the earlier of the date that the asset is classified as held for sale (or included in a disposal group that is classified as held for sale), in accordance with IFRS 5 or the date that the asset is derecognized. Therefore, an entity does not stop recognizing depreciation when the asset becomes idle or is retired from active use, unless the asset is fully depreciated. However, under methods of depreciation based on usage or units of production, the depreciation charge can be zero while there is no production.

3.114 To allocate the asset's depreciable base over its useful life on a reasonable and systematic basis, an entity should select a depreciation method that most closely reflects the pattern in which economic benefits from the asset will flow to the entity. Specific methods mentioned in the standard are straight line, declining balance, and units of production, but no methods are specifically required or prohibited.

3.115 Depreciation expense should be recognized in profit or loss in each reporting period, unless included in the carrying value of another asset (for example, inventory, assets under construction, and capitalized development costs). An entity should annually review depreciation methods and estimates of useful lives and residual values. Changes in estimated useful lives, residual values, and depreciation methods should be considered a change in accounting estimate, and the change should be applied prospectively, in accordance with IAS 8.

3.116 When using the revaluation model for subsequent measurement, an entity continues to recognize depreciation expense. At each revaluation, the revalued amount becomes the new cost basis for the asset. At the same time, the entity should reassess the asset's useful life and residual value, if any, and calculate depreciation expense going forward based on the new cost basis and these estimates. The *carrying value* of the asset is the revalued amount less any subsequent accumulated depreciation and impairment losses.

3.117 An entity should measure depreciation in accordance with IAS 16 for investment property measured under the cost model.

3.118 IFRSs require an entity to measure a decommissioning or restoration obligation (that is, asset retirement obligation) in accordance with IAS 37 and include the amount in the cost of the asset that gives rise to the obligation. When that asset is PPE, including land, an entity should depreciate over the useful life of the asset the amount of a decommissioning or restoration obligation capitalized. Generally, land is considered to have an indefinite life; therefore, an entity that capitalizes the obligation as a component of the cost of land should depreciate the amount over the period that benefits are expected to flow to the entity, unless the land itself is determined to have a finite life. In the latter case, depreciation should be recorded over the useful life of the land.

3.119 IAS 38 requires an entity to assess whether an intangible asset's useful life is indefinite (that is, no foreseeable limit to the asset's ability to generate net future cash inflows) or finite. If the asset's useful life is determined to be finite, the entity should determine the length of the life in time or units of production. The useful life of an asset that arises from contractual or other legal rights (for example, a patent) should not exceed the period of those rights. If the contracts contain renewal clauses, these clauses should be taken into account if the entity has the ability to renew without significant cost. An assessment of the useful life of reacquired rights in a business combination only considers the remaining original contract period; renewals are not considered.

3.120 For intangible assets with finite useful lives, the entity should allocate the asset's depreciable base (original cost less residual value) over its useful life to profit or loss. Amortization begins when the asset is available for use and stops at the earlier of the date that it is classified as held for sale or derecognized. The residual value of an intangible asset is assumed to be zero, unless the entity has a commitment from a third party to purchase the asset at the end of its useful life or there is an active market for the asset that the entity expects to exist at the end of the asset's useful life and from which it expects to determine a reliable residual value.

3.121 Like PPE, when measuring an intangible asset using the revaluation model, an entity records amortization based on the revalued amount less any residual value over the estimated useful life of the asset. The carrying value of the asset is the revalued amount less subsequent accumulated amortization and impairment losses.

3.122 Amortization should reflect the pattern of benefits to be received from the asset's use. If it cannot determine the pattern reliably, an entity should use the straight-line method. An entity should review both the amortization period and method annually. Changes to either should be considered changes in accounting estimate and applied prospectively, in accordance with IAS 8.

3.123 Goodwill acquired in a business combination (see section 9, "Business Combinations") and intangible assets with indefinite lives should not be amortized. Instead, IAS 38 requires an entity to test goodwill and indefinite-life intangibles for impairment annually.

3.124 An entity should account for leased assets in accordance with IAS 17. IAS 17 requires leased items of PPE, investment properties, and intangible assets that an entity accounts for as a finance lease to be depreciated in a manner consistent with the depreciation policy on similar assets owned by the entity.

U.S. GAAP

3.125 FASB ASC 350, *Intangibles—Goodwill and Other*, and FASB ASC 360, *Property, Plant, and Equipment*, establish essentially the same requirements for depreciation and amortization of PPE and intangible assets owned or held under a capital (finance) lease. FASB ASC 360 does not consider investment property to be a separate asset class. FASB ASC 360 requires an entity to classify as PPE those land and buildings classified as investment property under IFRSs.

3.126 Consistent with IFRSs and subject to the same conditions, FASB ASC 350-30-35-8 explains that an entity should assume the residual value of an intangible asset is zero. FASB ASC 350-30-35-9 states that an entity should review estimates of useful lives of intangible assets each reporting period and amortize these assets prospectively over their remaining useful lives.

3.127 In contrast, measuring depreciation of PPE or investment properties under FASB ASC 360 requires an entity to estimate both useful lives and residual values (salvage values). Unlike IFRSs, FASB ASC 360 does not require an entity to review estimates of the useful lives of these assets each reporting period. Instead, such a review is required, in accordance with FASB ASC 360-10-35-22, only when events or changes in circumstances indicate that the current estimates are no longer appropriate, as is also the case with depreciation methods.

Author's Note

In the process of determining appropriate FASB ASC references for U.S. GAAP requirements, we found that FASB ASC 360-10-35-3 states that depreciation expense in financial statements for an asset shall be determined based on the asset's useful life. Neither FASB ASC 360 nor other sections of FASB ASC include the requirement to estimate residual values for items of PPE in determining depreciation expense. The FASB ASC glossary does not include definitions of *depreciation*, *depreciable base*, or *residual value of PPE*. The existing definition of residual value applies to an intangible asset. FASB ASC briefly discusses residual value in the context of leased assets. Notwithstanding the absence of specific guidance in FASB ASC, it is generally accepted that an entity should include estimates of useful or depreciable lives and residual or salvage values in calculating depreciation expense.

3.128 Like IFRSs, an entity should select a depreciation method. Paragraphs 9–10 of FASB ASC 360-10-35 specify two methods that are unacceptable for financial reporting: the accelerated cost recovery system if the number of years specified by that system does not fall within a reasonable range of the asset's useful life (used for tax reporting in the United States) and the annuity method. Unlike IFRSs, changes in depreciation method should be considered to be a change in accounting estimate affected by a change in accounting principle, in accordance with FASB ASC 250-10-45-18. Although accounted for prospectively, as stated by FASB ASC 250-10-45-19, an entity should make this change only if it is justifiable on the basis that it is preferable.

3.129 Consistent with FASB ASC 360-10-35-4, FASB ASC 410-20-35-2 states that an entity should depreciate the costs of asset retirement obligations included in the cost of the related asset over the useful life of that asset using a rational and systematic basis.

Presentation

IFRSs

3.130 IAS 1 does not require separate presentation of depreciation or amortization expense in the statement of comprehensive income.

U.S. GAAP

3.131 FASB ASC 350-30-45 permits an entity to present amortization expense and impairment losses for intangible assets in income statement line items within continuing operations, as the entity deems appropriate. However, FASB ASC 360 does not address the presentation of depreciation expense for PPE.

Disclosure

Author's Note

Required disclosures about the relevant balance sheet accounts are discussed in section 2.

IFRSs

3.132 Both IAS 16 and IAS 38 require disclosure of depreciation and amortization methods used and estimates of useful lives (when the intangible asset has a finite life) or depreciation and amortization rates by asset class are necessary. Both standards require an entity to disclose depreciation and amortization as line items in the relevant reconciliation of the beginning and ending balances in the accumulated depreciation and impairment loss account.

3.133 IAS 1 requires an entity classifying expenses by function to disclose total depreciation and amortization expense in the notes. Entities classifying expenses by nature should present total depreciation and amortization expense on the face of the statement of comprehensive income.

U.S. GAAP

3.134 FASB ASC does not require an entity to provide reconciliation disclosures. For PPE, FASB ASC 360-10-50-1 does require disclosure of depreciation expense for the period, account balances by major classes of depreciable assets, accumulated depreciation either by major depreciable asset classes or in total, and a general description of the depreciation method(s) used.

3.135 For intangible assets subject to amortization, FASB ASC 350-30-50-2 requires an entity to disclose the gross carrying amount and accumulated amortization, in total and by major intangible asset class; aggregate amortization expense for the period; and estimated aggregate amortization expense for each of the five succeeding fiscal years.

Presentation and Disclosure Excerpts

Property, Plant, and Equipment and Investment Property—Cost Model, Straight Line Method and Declining Balance Methods

3.136

KB Financial Group Inc. (Dec 2011)

CONSOLIDATED STATEMENTS OF COMPREHENSIVE INCOME (in part)

	2010	2011	2011
	(In Millions of Korean Won, Except per Share Amounts)		Translation Into U.S. Dollars (Note 3) (In Thousands, Except per Share Amounts)
Interest income	(Won) 13,051,936	(Won) 13,956,257	US$ 12,046,834
Interest expense	(6,878,132)	(6,851,745)	(5,914,325)
Net interest income	6,173,804	7,104,512	6,132,509
Fee and commission income	2,481,451	2,829,754	2,442,602
Fee and commission expense	(776,737)	(1,035,004)	(893,401)
Net fee and commission income	1,704,714	1,794,750	1,549,201

(continued)

	2010	2011	2011
	(In Millions of Korean Won, Except per Share Amounts)		**Translation Into U.S. Dollars (Note 3) (In Thousands, Except per Share Amounts)**
Net gains (losses) on financial assets/liabilities at fair value through profit and loss	814,808	1,035,867	894,145
Net other operating income (expenses)	(1,067,343)	(1,092,009)	(942,606)
Employee compensation and benefits	(2,406,852)	(1,870,864)	(1,614,901)
Depreciation and amortization	(347,692)	(342,493)	(295,634)
Other general and administrative expenses	(1,612,085)	(1,718,451)	(1,483,342)
General and administrative expenses	(4,366,629)	(3,931,808)	(3,393,877)
Operating profit before provision for credit losses	3,259,354	4,911,312	4,239,372

NOTES TO THE CONSOLIDATED FINANCIAL STATEMENTS (in part)

1. The Parent Company

KB Financial Group Inc. (the "Parent Company") was incorporated on September 29, 2008, under the Financial Holding Companies Act of Korea. KB Financial Group Inc. and its subsidiaries (the "Group") derive substantially all of their revenue and income from providing a broad range of banking and related financial services to consumers and corporations primarily in Korea and in selected international markets. The Parent Company's principal business includes ownership and management of subsidiaries and associated companies that are engaged in financial services or activities. In 2011, Kookmin Bank spun off its credit card business segment and established a new separate credit card company, KB Kookmin Card Co., Ltd., and KB Investment & Securities Co., Ltd. merged with KB Futures Co., Ltd.

The Parent Company's paid in capital as of December 31, 2011 is (Won) 1,931,758 million. The Parent Company is authorized to issue up to 1,000 million shares. The Parent Company has been listed on the Korea Exchange ("KRX") since October 10, 2008, and listed on the New York Stock Exchange ("NYSE") for its American Depositary Shares ("ADS") since September 29, 2008.

2. Basis of Preparation (in part)

2.1 Application of IFRS (in part)

The Group's financial statements for the annual period beginning on January 1, 2011, have been prepared in accordance with the International Financial Reporting Standards ("IFRS") as issued by the International Accounting Standards Board ("IASB") and the application of IFRS 1, First-time Adoption of International Financial Reporting Standards, is required for the consolidated financial statements.

3. Significant Accounting Policies

The significant accounting policies applied in the preparation of these consolidated financial statements are set out below. These policies have been consistently applied to all periods presented, unless otherwise stated.

3.8 Property and Equipment

3.8.1 Recognition and Measurement

All property and equipment that qualify for recognition as an asset are measured at its cost and subsequently carried at its cost less any accumulated depreciation and any accumulated impairment losses.

The cost of property and equipment includes any costs directly attributable to bringing the asset to the location and condition necessary for it to be capable of operating in the manner intended by management and the initial estimate of the costs of dismantling and removing the item and restoring the site on which it is located.

Subsequent expenditures are capitalized only when they prolong the useful life or enhance values of the assets but the costs of the day-to-day servicing of the assets such as repair and maintenance costs are recognized in profit or loss as incurred. When part of an item of an asset has a useful life different from that of the entire asset, it is recognized as a separate asset.

3.8.2 Depreciation

Land is not depreciated, whereas other property and equipment are depreciated using the method that reflects the pattern in which the asset's future economic benefits are expected to be consumed by the Group. The depreciable amount of an asset is determined after deducting its residual value. As for leased assets, if there is no reasonable certainty that the Group will obtain ownership by the end of the lease term, the asset is fully depreciated over the shorter of the lease term and its useful life.

Each part of an item of property and equipment with a cost that is significant in relation to the total cost of the item is depreciated separately.

The depreciation method and estimated useful lives of the assets are as follows:

Property and Equipment	Depreciation Method	Estimated Useful Lives
Buildings and structures	Straight-line	40 years
Leasehold improvements	Declining-balance	4 years
Equipment and vehicles	Declining-balance	3–5 years

The residual value, the useful life and the depreciation method applied to an asset are reviewed at least at each financial year end and, if expectations differ from previous estimates or if there has been a significant change in the expected pattern of consumption of the future economic benefits embodied in the asset, the changes are accounted for as a change in an accounting estimate.

3.9 Investment Properties

Properties held to earn rentals or for capital appreciation or both are classified as investment properties. Investment properties are measured initially at their cost and subsequently the cost model is used.

14. Property and Equipment, and Investment Property

The details of property and equipment as of January 1, 2010, and December 31, 2010 and 2011, are as follows:

As of January 1, 2010

(In Millions of Korean Won)	Acquisition Cost	Accumulated Depreciation	Accumulated Impairment Losses	Carrying Amount
Land	(Won) 2,010,300	(Won) —	(Won) (586)	(Won) 2,009,714
Buildings	1,138,390	(245,309)	(3,498)	889,583
Leasehold improvements	397,499	(335,781)	—	61,718
Equipment and vehicles	1,781,709	(1,507,631)	—	274,078
Construction in-progress	350	—	—	350
Financial lease assets	33,045	(10,577)	—	22,468
Total	(Won) 5,361,293	(Won) (2,099,298)	(Won) (4,084)	(Won) 3,257,911

As of December 31, 2010

(In Millions of Korean Won)	Acquisition Cost	Accumulated Depreciation	Accumulated Impairment Losses	Carrying Amount
Land	(Won) 2,023,447	(Won) —	(Won) (583)	(Won) 2,022,864
Buildings	1,168,155	(274,267)	(2,668)	891,220
Leasehold improvements	429,790	(379,156)	—	50,634
Equipment and vehicles	1,640,867	(1,466,049)	—	174,818
Construction in-progress	119	—	—	119
Financial lease assets	33,045	(22,440)	—	10,605
Total	(Won) 5,295,423	(Won) (2,141,912)	(Won) (3,251)	(Won) 3,150,260

As of December 31, 2011

(In Millions of Korean Won)	Acquisition Cost	Accumulated Depreciation	Accumulated Impairment Losses	Carrying Amount
Land	(Won) 2,022,943	(Won) —	(Won) (581)	(Won) 2,022,362
Buildings	1,200,813	(301,947)	(2,661)	896,205
Leasehold improvements	484,328	(424,742)	—	59,586
Equipment and vehicles	1,710,477	(1,513,746)	—	196,731
Construction in-progress	1,075	—	—	1,075
Financial lease assets	43,756	(33,695)	—	10,061
Total	(Won) 5,463,392	(Won) (2,274,130)	(Won) (3,242)	(Won) 3,186,020

The changes in property and equipment for the years ended
December 31, 2010 and 2011, are as follows:

(In Millions of Korean Won)	For the Year Ended December 31, 2010						
	Beginning	Acquisition	Transfers[1]	Disposal	Depreciation[2]	Others	Ending
Land	(Won) 2,009,714	(Won) —	(Won) 12,475	(Won) (1,437)	(Won) —	(Won) 2,112	(Won) 2,022,864
Buildings	889,583	40	28,622	(1,022)	(27,395)	1,392	891,220
Leasehold Improvements	61,718	1,366	27,346	(169)	(44,887)	5,260	50,634
Equipment and vehicles	274,078	67,066	—	(379)	(166,011)	64	174,818
Construction in-progress	350	52,307	(52,538)	—	—	—	119
Financial lease assets	22,468	—	—	—	(11,863)	—	10,605
Total	(Won) 3,257,911	(Won) 120,779	(Won) 15,905	(Won) (3,007)	(Won) (250,156)	(Won) 8,828	(Won) 3,150,260

[1] Including transfers with investment property and assets held for sale.
[2] Including (Won) 96 million recorded in other operating expenses in the statement of comprehensive income.

(In Millions of Korean Won)	For the Year Ended December 31, 2011						
	Beginning	Acquisition	Transfers[1]	Disposal	Depreciation[2]	Others	Ending
Land	(Won) 2,022,864	(Won) 195	(Won) (706)	(Won) (18)	(Won) —	(Won) 27	(Won) 2,022,362
Buildings	891,220	3,019	30,207	(26)	(28,307)	92	896,205
Leasehold Improvements	50,634	11,414	39,195	(423)	(47,447)	6,213	59,586
Equipment and vehicles	174,818	160,319	—	(847)	(137,559)	—	196,731
Construction in-progress	119	76,258	(75,302)	—	—	—	1,075
Financial lease assets	10,605	10,700	—	—	(11,244)	—	10,061
Total	(Won) 3,150,260	(Won) 261,905	(Won) (6,606)	(Won) (1,314)	(Won) (224,557)	(Won) 6,332	(Won) 3,186,020

[1] Including transfers with investment property and assets held for sale.
[2] Including (Won) 122 million recorded in other operating expenses in the statement of comprehensive income.

The changes in accumulated impairment losses of property
and equipment for the years ended December 31, 2010 and
2011, are as follows:

(In Millions of Korean Won)	For the Year Ended December 31, 2010			
Beginning	Impairment	Reversal	Others	Ending
(Won) (4,084)	(Won) —	(Won) —	(Won) 833	(Won) (3,251)

(In Millions of Korean Won)	For the Year Ended December 31, 2011			
Beginning	Impairment	Reversal	Others	Ending
(Won) (3,251)	(Won) —	(Won) —	(Won) 9	(Won) (3,242)

The details of investment property as of January 1, 2010, and
December 31, 2010 and 2011, are as follows:

(In Millions of Korean Won)	As of January 1, 2010		
	Acquisition Cost	Accumulated Depreciation	Carrying Amount
Land	(Won) 50,037	(Won) —	(Won) 50,037
Buildings	23,524	(5,584)	17,940
Total	(Won) 73,561	(Won) (5,584)	(Won) 67,977

| (In Millions of Korean Won) | As of December 31, 2010 | | |
	Acquisition Cost	Accumulated Depreciation	Carrying Amount
Land	(Won) 38,633	(Won) —	(Won) 38,633
Buildings	18,941	(4,653)	14,288
Total	(Won) 57,574	(Won) (4,653)	(Won) 52,921

| (In Millions of Korean Won) | As of December 31, 2011 | | |
	Acquisition Cost	Accumulated Depreciation	Carrying Amount
Land	(Won) 37,451	(Won) —	(Won) 37,451
Buildings	18,961	(4,860)	14,101
Total	(Won) 56,412	(Won) (4,860)	(Won) 51,552

As of January 1, 2010 and December 31, 2010 and 2011, fair values of the investment properties amount to (Won) 67,471 million, (Won) 52,740 million and, (Won) 48,996 million, respectively. The investment properties were valued by qualified independent appraisers with experience in valuing similar properties in the same location.

Rental income from the above investment properties for the years ended December 31, 2010 and 2011, amounts to (Won) 1,122 million and (Won) 683 million, respectively.

The changes in investment property for the year ended December 31, 2010 and 2011, are as follows:

| (In Millions of Korean Won) | For the Year Ended December 31, 2010 | | | |
	Beginning	Transfers	Depreciation	Ending
Land	(Won) 50,037	(Won) (11,404)	(Won) —	(Won) 38,633
Buildings	17,940	(3,205)	(447)	14,288
Total	(Won) 67,977	(Won) (14,609)	(Won) (447)	(Won) 52,921

| (In Millions of Korean Won) | For the Year Ended December 31, 2011 | | | |
	Beginning	Transfers	Depreciation	Ending
Land	(Won) 38,633	(Won) (1,182)	(Won) —	(Won) 37,451
Buildings	14,288	264	(451)	14,101
Total	(Won) 52,921	(Won) (918)	(Won) (451)	(Won) 51,552

Property and equipment insured as of January 1, 2010, and December 31, 2010 and 2011, are as follows:

| Type | Assets Insured | Insurance Coverage | | | Insurance Company |
| | | As of January 1, 2010 | As of December 31, 2010 | 2011 | |
		(In Millions of Korean Won)			
General property insurance	Buildings[1]	(Won) 965,269	(Won) 986,576	(Won) 1,061,097	Samsung Fire & Marine Insurance Co., Ltd. and others
	Leasehold improvements	172,467	144,267	134,595	
	Equipment and vehicles and others	342,144	168,920	179,804	
	Total	(Won) 1,479,880	(Won) 1,299,763	(Won) 1,375,496	

[1] Buildings include office buildings, investment properties and assets held for sale.

Property, Plant, and Equipment—Cost Model, Straight Line and Units of Production Methods

3.137

Statoil ASA (Dec 2011)

CONSOLIDATED STATEMENT OF INCOME (in part)

(In NOK Million)	Note	2011	For the Year Ended 31 December 2010 (Restated)	2009 (Restated)
Revenues and Other Income				
Revenues		645,599	526,950	462,519
Net income from associated companies	15	1,264	1,168	1,457
Other income		23,342	1,797	1,374
Total revenues and other income	4	670,205	529,915	465,350
Operating Expenses				
Purchases [net of inventory variation]		(319,605)	(257,436)	(205,870)
Operating expenses		(60,419)	(57,670)	(56,974)
Selling, general and administrative expenses		(13,208)	(11,081)	(10,321)
Depreciation, amortisation and net impairment losses	13,14	(51,350)	(50,694)	(53,830)
Exploration expenses	14	(13,839)	(15,773)	(16,686)
Total operating expenses		(458,421)	(392,654)	(343,681)
Net operating income	4	211,784	137,261	121,669

NOTES TO THE CONSOLIDATED FINANCIAL STATEMENTS (in part)

8.1.1 Organisation

Statoil ASA, originally Den Norske Stats Oljeselskap AS, was founded in 1972 and is incorporated and domiciled in Norway.

The address of its registered office is Forusbeen 50, N-4035 Stavanger, Norway.

Statoil's business consists principally of the exploration, production, transportation, refining and marketing of petroleum and petroleum-derived products, and other forms of energy.

Statoil ASA is listed on the Oslo Stock Exchange (Norway) and the New York Stock Exchange (USA).

All Statoil's oil and gas activities and net assets on the Norwegian Continental Shelf (NCS) are owned by Statoil Petroleum AS, a 100% owned operating subsidiary. Statoil Petroleum AS is co-obligor or guarantor of certain debt obligations of Statoil ASA.

Following changes in Statoil's internal organisational structure, the composition of Statoil's reportable segments was changed as of 1 January 2011. For further information see note 4 *Segments* to these financial statements.

The Consolidated financial statements of Statoil for the year ended 31 December 2011 were authorised for issue in accordance with a resolution of the board of directors on 13 March 2012.

8.1.2 Significant Accounting Policies (in part)

Statement of Compliance

The Consolidated financial statements of Statoil ASA and its subsidiaries ("Statoil") have been prepared in accordance with International Financial Reporting Standards (IFRSs) as adopted by the European Union (EU). The accounting policies applied by Statoil also comply with IFRSs as issued by the International Accounting Standards Board (IASB).

Basis of Preparation

The financial statements are prepared on the historical cost basis with some exceptions, as detailed in the accounting policies set out below. These policies have been applied consistently to all periods presented in these consolidated financial statements.

Operating expenses in the Consolidated statement of income are presented as a combination of function and nature in conformity with industry practice. *Purchases [net of inventory variation]* and *Depreciation, amortisation and net impairment losses* are presented in separate lines by their nature, while *Operating expenses* and *Selling, general and administrative expenses* as well as *Exploration expenses* are presented on a functional basis. Significant expenses such as salaries, pensions, etc. are presented by their nature in the notes to the financial statements.

Oil and Gas Exploration and Development Expenditure

Statoil uses the "successful efforts" method of accounting for oil and gas exploration costs. Expenditures to acquire mineral interests in oil and gas properties and to drill and equip exploratory wells are capitalised as exploration and evaluation expenditure within intangible assets until the well is complete and the results have been evaluated. If, following evaluation, the exploratory well has not found proved reserves, the previously capitalised costs are evaluated for de-recognition or tested for impairment. Geological and geophysical costs and other exploration expenditures are expensed as incurred.

For exploration and evaluation asset acquisitions (farm-in arrangements) in which Statoil has made arrangements to fund a portion of the selling partner's (farmor's) exploration and/or future development expenditures (carried interests), these expenditures are reflected in the financial statements as and when the exploration and development work progresses. Statoil reflects exploration and evaluation asset dispositions (farm-out arrangements), when the farmee correspondingly undertakes to fund carried interests as part of the consideration, on a historical cost basis with no gain or loss recognition.

A gain or loss related to a post-tax based disposition of assets on the NCS includes the release of tax liabilities previously computed and recognised related to the assets in question. The resulting gross gain or loss is recognised in full in the line item *Other income* in the Consolidated statement of income.

Exchanges (swaps) of exploration and evaluation assets are accounted for at the carrying amounts of the assets given up with no gain or loss recognition.

Unproved oil and gas properties are assessed for impairment when facts and circumstances suggest that the carrying amount of the asset may exceed its recoverable amount, and at least once a year. Exploratory wells that have found reserves, but where classification of those reserves as proved depends on whether major capital expenditure can be justified or where the economic viability of that major capital expenditure depends on the successful completion of further exploration work, will remain capitalised during the evaluation phase for the exploratory finds. Thereafter it will be considered a trigger for impairment evaluation of the well if no development decision is planned for the near future, and there are no concrete plans for future drilling in the licence. Impairment of unsuccessful wells is reversed, as applicable, to the extent that conditions for impairment are no longer present. Impairment and reversals of impairment of exploration and evaluation assets are charged to *Exploration expenses* in the Consolidated statement of income.

Capitalised exploration and evaluation expenditure, including expenditures to acquire mineral interests in oil and gas properties, related to wells that find proved reserves are transferred from Exploration expenditure (*Intangible assets*) to Assets under development (*Property, plant and equipment*) at the time of sanctioning of the development project.

Property, Plant and Equipment

Property, plant and equipment is reflected at cost, less accumulated depreciation and accumulated impairment losses. The initial cost of an asset comprises its purchase price or construction cost, any costs directly attributable to bringing the asset into operation, the initial estimate of an asset retirement obligation, if any, and, for qualifying assets, borrowing costs. Property, plant and equipment also include assets acquired under the terms of profit sharing agreements (PSAs) in certain countries, and which qualify for recognition as assets of the group. State-owned entities in the respective countries however normally hold the legal title to such PSA-based property, plant and equipment.

Exchanges of assets are measured at the fair value of the asset given up, unless the fair value of neither the asset received nor the asset given up is reliably measurable.

Expenditure on major maintenance refits or repairs comprises the cost of replacement assets or parts of assets, inspection costs and overhaul costs. Where an asset or part of an asset is replaced and it is probable that future economic benefits associated with the item will flow to the group, the expenditure is capitalised. Inspection and overhaul costs associated with major maintenance programs are capitalised and amortised over the period to the next inspection. All other maintenance costs are expensed as incurred.

Capitalised exploration and evaluation expenditure, development expenditure on the construction, installation or completion of infrastructure facilities such as platforms, pipelines and the drilling of development wells, and field-dedicated transport systems for oil and gas are capitalised as producing oil and gas properties within *Property, plant and equipment*. Such capitalised cost is depreciated using the unit of production method based on proved developed reserves expected to be recovered from the area during the concession or contract period. Capitalised acquisition costs of proved properties are depreciated using the unit of production method based on total proved reserves. Depreciation of other assets and transport systems used by several fields is calculated on the basis of their estimated useful lives, normally using the straight-line method. Each part of an item of property, plant and equipment with a cost that is significant in relation to the total cost of the item is depreciated separately. For exploration and production (E&P) assets Statoil has established separate depreciation categories which as a minimum distinguish between platforms, pipelines, and wells.

The estimated useful lives of property, plant and equipment are reviewed on an annual basis and changes in useful lives are accounted for prospectively. An item of property, plant and equipment is derecognised upon disposal or when no future economic benefits are expected to arise from the continued use of the asset. Any gain or loss arising on derecognition of the asset (calculated as the difference between the net disposal proceeds and the carrying amount of the item) is included in other income or operating expenses, respectively, in the period the item is derecognised.

8.1.13 Property, Plant and Equipment

(In NOK Million)	Machinery, Equipment and Transportation Equipment	Production Plants Oil and Gas, Incl. Pipelines	Refining and Manufacturing Plants	Buildings and Land	Vessels	Assets Under Development	Total
Cost at 31 December 2010	17,705	678,216	55,476	16,533	4,434	76,118	848,482
Transfered from assets classified as held for sale**	0	0	0	0	0	32,515	32,515
Additions and transfers	1,930	98,413	1,267	812	0	1,953	104,375
Addition from business combination***	68	6,266	0	4	0	1,176	7,514
Disposals assets at cost	(1,246)	(38,653)	(3,400)	(135)	0	(13,537)	(56,971)
Effect of movements in foreign exchange—assets	209	7,131	294	(305)	102	(544)	6,887
Cost at 31 December 2011	18,666	751,373	53,637	16,909	4,536	97,681	942,802
Accumulated depreciation and impairment losses at 31 December 2010	(12,959)	(437,610)	(36,746)	(6,648)	(1,305)	(1,636)	(496,904)
Additions and transfers	0	0	0	0	0	(2,155)	(2,155)
Depreciation and net impairment losses for the year	(1,747)	(45,427)	(5,741)	(786)	(228)	1,817	(52,112)
Accumulated depreciation and impairment disposed assets	944	16,435	1,935	127	0	38	19,479
Effect of movements in foreign exchange—depreciation and impairment losses	(182)	(3,431)	(156)	113	(45)	176	(3,525)
Accumulated depreciation and impairment losses at 31 December 2011	(13,944)	(470,033)	(40,708)	(7,194)	(1,578)	(1,760)	(535,217)
Carrying amount at 31 December 2011	4,722	281,340	12,929	9,715	2,958	95,921	407,585
Estimated useful lives (years)	3–10	*	15–20	20–33	20–25		

(In NOK Million)	Machinery, Equipment and Transportation Equipment	Production Plants Oil and Gas, Incl. Pipelines	Refining and Manufacturing Plants	Buildings and Land	Vessels	Assets Under Development	Total
Cost at 31 December 2009	18,549	618,487	44,098	15,735	4,079	90,250	791,198
Additions and transfers	(267)	61,026	11,642	1,086	195	18,780	92,462
Disposals assets at cost	(721)	(2,894)	(418)	(291)	(11)	(1,426)	(5,761)
Assets classified as held for sale	0	0	0	0	0	(32,515)	(32,515)
Effect of movements in foreign exchange—assets	144	1,597	154	3	171	1,029	3,098
Cost at 31 December 2010	17,705	678,216	55,476	16,533	4,434	76,118	848,482
Accumulated depreciation and impairment losses at 31 December 2009	(12,205)	(397,591)	(31,794)	(6,003)	(1,018)	(67)	(448,678)
Depreciation and net impairment for the year	(1,252)	(41,570)	(5,074)	(671)	(286)	(1,655)	(50,508)
Accumulated depreciation and impairment disposed assets	531	2,681	266	144	11	0	3,633
Effect of movements in foreign exchange—depreciation and impairment losses	(33)	(1,130)	(144)	(118)	(12)	86	(1,351)
Accumulated depreciation and impairment losses at 31 December 2010	(12,959)	(437,610)	(36,746)	(6,648)	(1,305)	(1,636)	(496,904)
Carrying amount at 31 December 2010	4,746	240,606	18,730	9,885	3,129	74,482	351,578
Estimated useful lives (years)	3–10	*	15–20	20–33	20–25		

(In NOK Million)	Machinery, Equipment and Transportation Equipment	Production Plants Oil and Gas, Incl. Pipelines	Refining and Manufacturing Plants	Buildings and Land	Vessels	Assets Under Development	Total
Cost at 1 January 2009	18,231	582,066	42,224	16,528	5,604	77,883	742,536
Additions and transfers	4,379	58,269	2,532	1,431	(788)	21,097	86,920
Disposals assets at cost	(1,411)	(514)	(223)	(348)	0	0	(2,496)
Effect of movements in foreign exchange—assets	(2,650)	(21,334)	(435)	(1,876)	(737)	(8,730)	(35,762)
Cost at 31 December 2009	18,549	618,487	44,098	15,735	4,079	90,250	791,198
Accumulated depreciation and impairment losses at 1 January 2009	(10,856)	(365,575)	(27,140)	(6,311)	(869)	(1,521)	(412,272)
Depreciation and net impairment losses for the year	(3,468)	(43,570)	(5,001)	(617)	(333)	319	(52,670)
Accumulated depreciation and impairment disposed assets	867	513	139	214	0	0	1,733
Effect of movements in foreign exchange—depreciation and impairment losses	1,252	11,041	208	711	184	1,135	14,531
Accumulated depreciation and impairment losses at 31 December 2009	(12,205)	(397,591)	(31,794)	(6,003)	(1,018)	(67)	(448,678)
Carrying amount at 31 December 2009	6,344	220,896	12,304	9,732	3,061	90,183	342,520
Estimated useful lives (years)	3–10	*	15–20	20–33	20–25		

*   Depreciation according to Unit of production method, see note 2 *Significant accounting policies*.
**   Reflects a reversal of previous period's assets classified as held for sale for which the portion sold during the period is included as Disposals.
***   For information on assets from business combination, see note 5 *Business development*.

In 2011, 2010 and 2009 capitalised borrowing cost amounted to NOK 0.9 billion, NOK 1.0 billion and NOK 1.4 billion, respectively.

The carrying amount of transfer of assets to *Property, plant and equipment* from *Intangible assets* in 2011, 2010 and 2009 amounted to NOK 3.7 billion, NOK 11.0 billion and NOK 4.9 billion, respectively.

(In NOK Million)	For the Year Ended 31 December		
	2011	2010	2009
Impairment losses	(4,718)	(4,820)	(8,176)
Reversal of impairment losses	2,692	280	1,743
Net impairment losses	(2,026)	(4,540)	(6,433)

In 2011 Statoil recognised impairment losses of NOK 3,8 billion related to refinery assets in the MPR segment. The basis for the impairment losses is value in use estimates triggered by decreasing expectations on refining margins. The impairment losses have been presented as *Depreciation, amortisation and net impairment losses*.

In 2011 Statoil recognised a reversal of impairment losses in the DPI segment of NOK 2.6 billion related to assets in the Gulf of Mexico. The basis for the impairment losses are value in use estimates triggered by changes in cost estimates and market conditions.

In 2010 Statoil recognised impairment losses of NOK 2.9 billion related to refinery assets in the MPR segment. The basis for the impairment losses were value in use estimates triggered by decreasing expectations on refining margins. In 2010 Statoil also recognised an impairment loss of NOK 1.6 billion related to a gas development project in the DPI segment. The basis for the impairment loss were reduced value in use estimate mainly driven by project delays, changes in certain cost estimates and market conditions.

In 2009 Statoil recognised impairment losses in the MPR segment related to machinery equipment and refinery assets of NOK 2.2 billion and NOK 3.2 billion, respectively.

In assessing the need for impairment of the carrying amount of a potentially impaired asset, the asset's carrying amount is compared to its recoverable amount. The recoverable amount is the higher of fair value less costs to sell and estimated value in use. When preparing a value in use calculation the estimated future cash flows are adjusted for risks specific to the asset and discounted using a real post-tax discount rate adjusted for asset specific differences. The base discount rate used is 6.5% real after tax. The discount rate is derived from Statoil's weighted average cost of capital. A derived pre-tax discount rate would generally be in the range of 8-12%, depending on asset specific characteristics, such as specific tax treatments, cash flow profiles and economic life. For certain assets a pre-tax discount rate could be outside this range, mainly due to special tax elements (for example permanent differences) affecting the pre-tax equivalent. The use of post-tax discount rates in determining value in use does not result in a materially different determination of the need for, or the amount of, impairment that would be required if pre-tax discount rates had been used.

Property, Plant, and Equipment—Cost Model, Straight Line Method, Capitalization of Drydock Expenditures

3.138

Scorpio Tankers Inc. (Dec 2011)

CONSOLIDATED STATEMENTS OF PROFIT OR LOSS (in part)

For the years ended December 31, 2011, 2010 and 2009

	Notes	For the Year Ended December 31		
		2011	2010	2009
Revenue:				
Vessel revenue	16	$ 82,109,691	$38,797,913	$27,619,041
Operating Expenses:				
Vessel operating costs	18	(31,369,646)	(18,440,492)	(8,562,118)
Voyage expenses		(6,881,019)	(2,542,298)	—
Charterhire	17	(22,750,257)	(275,532)	(3,072,916)
Impairment	7	(66,610,544)	—	(4,511,877)
Depreciation		(18,460,117)	(10,178,908)	(6,834,742)
General and administrative expenses	19	(11,636,713)	(6,200,094)	(416,908)
Total operating expenses		(157,708,296)	(37,637,324)	(23,398,561)
Operating (loss)/income		(75,598,605)	1,160,589	4,220,480

NOTES TO THE CONSOLIDATED FINANCIAL STATEMENTS (in part)

1. General Information and Significant Accounting Policies (in part)

Company

Scorpio Tankers Inc. and its subsidiaries (together "we", "our" or the "Company") are engaged in seaborne transportation of crude oil and refined petroleum products in the international shipping markets. Scorpio Tankers Inc. was incorporated in the Republic of the Marshall Islands on July 1, 2009.

On October 1, 2009, Simon Financial Limited ("Simon") transferred to Scorpio Tankers Inc. three operating subsidiary companies, as described further below. Simon is owned by the Lolli-Ghetti family of which, Emanuele Lauro, our founder, Chairman and Chief Executive Officer is a member.

On April 6, 2010, we closed on the initial public offering of 12,500,000 shares of common stock at $13.00 per share. The stock trades on the New York Stock Exchange under the symbol STNG. Further details of the initial public offering and certain follow-on offerings are provided in Note 14.

Prior to the initial public offering, a subsidiary of Simon owned 100% of our shares (or 5,589,147 shares). As of December 31, 2011 and after completion of both the initial public offering and subsequent follow-on offerings, the Lolli-Ghetti family no longer maintains a controlling interest in the Company.

Business

Our owned fleet at December 31, 2011 consisted of one LR2 product tanker, four LR1 product tankers, two MR product tankers, four Handymax tankers and one post-Panamax tanker engaged in seaborne transportation of crude oil and refined petroleum products in the international shipping markets. We had one LR2 and six Handymax product tankers time chartered-in as of December 31, 2011. Additionally, we had contracted for six newbuilding MR tankers under construction at Hyundai Mipo Dockyard Co. Ltd. of South Korea ("Hyundai") as of December 31, 2011.

Our vessels are commercially managed by Scorpio Commercial Management S.A.M. ("SCM"), which is currently owned by the Lolli-Ghetti family. SCM's services include securing employment, in pools, in the spot market and on time charters.

Our vessels are technically managed by Scorpio Ship Management S.A.M. ("SSM"), which is also owned by the Lolli-Ghetti family. SSM facilitates vessel support such as crew, provisions, deck and engine stores, insurance, maintenance and repairs, and other services as necessary to operate the vessels such as drydocks and vetting/inspection under a technical management agreement.

During 2011, we had an administrative services agreement with Liberty Holding Company ("Liberty"), which is a subsidiary of Simon. On March 13, 2012, the agreement was assigned to Scorpio Services Holding Ltd or SSH. The administrative services provided under the agreement primarily include accounting, legal compliance, financial, information technology services, and the provision of administrative staff and office space. Liberty has contracted these services to SCM. We pay our managers fees for these services and reimburse them for direct or indirect expenses that they incur in providing these services.

Basis of Accounting (in part)

The consolidated financial statements have been presented in United States dollars (USD or $), which is the functional currency of Scorpio Tankers Inc. and all its subsidiaries. The financial statements have been prepared in accordance with

International Financial Reporting Standards (IFRSs) as issued by the International Accounting Standards Board and on a historical cost basis, except for the revaluation of certain financial instruments.

Significant Accounting Policies (in part)

Vessels and Drydock

Our fleet is measured at cost, which includes directly attributable financing costs and the cost of work undertaken to enhance the capabilities of the vessels, less accumulated depreciation and impairment losses.

Depreciation is calculated on a straight-line basis to the estimated residual value over the anticipated useful life of the vessel from date of delivery. Vessels under construction are not depreciated until such time as they are ready for use. The residual value is estimated as the lightweight tonnage of each vessel multiplied by scrap value per ton. The scrap value per ton is estimated taking into consideration the historical four year scrap market rates at the balance sheet date with changes accounted for in the period of change and in future periods.

The vessels are required to undergo planned drydocks for replacement of certain components, major repairs and maintenance of other components, which cannot be carried out while the vessels are operating, approximately every 30 months or 60 months depending on the nature of work and external requirements. These drydock costs are capitalized and depreciated on a straight-line basis over the estimated period until the next drydock. We only include in deferred drydocking costs those direct costs that are incurred as part of the drydocking to meet regulatory requirements, or are expenditures that add economic life to the vessel, increase the vessel's earnings capacity or improve the vessel's efficiency. Direct costs include shipyard costs as well as the costs of placing the vessel in the shipyard. Expenditures for normal maintenance and repairs, whether incurred as part of the drydocking or not, are expensed as incurred.

For an acquired or newly built vessel, a notional drydock is allocated from the vessel's cost. The notional drydock cost is estimated by us, based on the expected costs related to the next drydock, which is based on experience and past history of similar vessels, and carried separately from the cost of the vessel. Subsequent drydocks are recorded at actual cost incurred. The drydock asset is amortized on a straight-line basis to the next estimated drydock. The estimated amortization period for a drydock is based on the estimated period between drydocks. We estimate the period between drydocks to be 30 months to 60 months. When the drydock expenditure is incurred prior to the expiry of the period, the remaining balance is expensed.

Critical Accounting Judgements and Key Sources of Estimation Uncertainty (in part)

In the application of the accounting policies, we are required to make judgements, estimates and assumptions about the carrying amounts of assets and liabilities that are not readily apparent from other sources. The estimates and associated assumptions are based on historical experience and other factors that are considered to be relevant. Actual results may differ from these estimates.

The estimates and underlying assumptions are reviewed on an ongoing basis. Revisions to accounting estimates are recognized in the period in which the estimate is revised if the revision affects only that period, or in the period of the revision and future periods if the revision affects both current and future periods.

The significant judgements and estimates are as follows: (in part)

Vessel Lives and Residual Value

The carrying value of each of our vessels represents its original cost at the time it was delivered or purchased less depreciation and impairment. We depreciate our vessels to their residual value on a straight-line basis over their estimated useful lives. Effective April 1, 2010, we revised the estimated useful life of our vessels from 20 years to 25 years from the date of initial delivery from the shipyard. The estimated useful life of 25 years is management's best estimate and is also consistent with industry practice for similar vessels. The residual value is estimated as the lightweight tonnage of each vessel multiplied by a forecast scrap value per ton. The scrap value per ton is estimated taking into consideration the historical four year scrap market rate average at the balance sheet date.

An increase in the estimated useful life of a vessel or in its scrap value would have the effect of decreasing the annual depreciation charge and extending it into later periods. A decrease in the useful life of a vessel or scrap value would have the effect of increasing the annual depreciation charge.

When regulations place significant limitations over the ability of a vessel to trade on a worldwide basis, the vessel's useful life is adjusted to end at the date such regulations become effective. The estimated salvage value of the vessels may not represent the fair market value at any one time since market prices of scrap values tend to fluctuate.

Deferred Drydock Cost

We recognize drydock costs as a separate component of each vessel's carrying amount and amortize the drydock cost on a straight-line basis over the estimated period until the next drydock. We use judgment when estimating the period between drydocks performed, which can result in adjustments to the estimated amortization of the drydock expense. If the vessel is disposed of before the next drydock, the remaining balance of the deferred drydock is written-off and forms part of the gain or loss recognized upon disposal of vessels in the period when contracted. We expect that our vessels will be required to be drydocked approximately every 30 to 60 months for major repairs and maintenance that cannot be performed while the vessels are operating. Costs capitalized as part of the drydock include actual costs incurred at the drydock yard and parts and supplies used in making such repairs.

6. Vessels

Operating Vessels and Drydock

	Vessels	Drydock	Total
Cost			
As of January 1, 2011	$379,723,400	$4,589,021	$384,312,421
Additions[3]	70,934,675	3,168,355	74,103,030
Write off[1]	—	(620,055)	(620,055)
As of December 31, 2011	450,658,075	7,137,321	457,795,396
Accumulated depreciation and impairment			
As of January 1, 2011	(49,501,513)	(1,385,522)	(50,887,035)
Charge for the period	(15,906,544)	(2,291,978)	(18,198,522)
Impairment[2]	(66,610,544)	—	(66,610,544)
Write off[1]	—	358,460	358,460
As of December 31, 2011	(132,018,601)	(3,319,040)	(135,337,641)
Net Book Value			
As of December 31, 2011	$318,639,474	$3,818,281	$322,457,755
Cost			
As of January 1, 2010	$138,713,588	$1,680,784	$140,394,372
Additions[3]	241,009,812	2,997,820	244,007,632
Write off[1]	—	(89,583)	(89,583)
As of December 31, 2010	379,723,400	4,589,021	384,312,421
Accumulated Depreciation			
As of January 1, 2010	(40,499,502)	(300,603)	(40,800,105)
Charge for the period	(9,002,011)	(1,174,502)	(10,176,513)
Write off[1]	—	89,583	89,583
As of December 31, 2010	(49,501,513)	(1,385,522)	(50,887,035)
Net Book Value			
As of December 31, 2010	330,221,887	3,203,499	333,425,386

[1] Represents the write off of the net book value of drydock costs for the *STI Harmony* of $223,726, which was drydocked in August 2011 and *STI Highlander* of $37,869 which was drydocked in October 2011. *STI Conqueror* and *STI Heritage* were also drydocked in 2010 and the residual costs written off.

[2] See Note 7 for impairment discussion.

[3] Venice, *STI Harmony* and *STI Highlander* were drydocked during the year ended December 31, 2011 for a total cost of $2.6 million. The remaining additions to drydock of $0.5 million during the year ended December 31, 2011 resulted from the notional drydock calculated on our vessel purchases of *STI Coral* and *STI Diamond* in May 2011. The additions in 2010 relate to costs incurred of $0.9 million during the drydock of the *STI Conqueror* and *STI Heritage* as well as $2.0 million arising from vessel purchases.

Delivery of STI Coral and STI Diamond

On May 10, 2011, we took delivery of two MR product tankers that we previously agreed to acquire for an aggregate purchase price of $70.0 million. The ships were built in 2008 at the STX shipyard in Korea and were charter free at delivery.

Vessels Under Construction

On June 6, 2011, we signed contracts with Hyundai Mipo Dockyard Co. Ltd. of South Korea to construct five MR product tankers for approximately $37.4 million each. The vessels are scheduled to be delivered to the Company July 2012 and September 2012.

On December 21, 2011, we signed another contract with Hyundai Mipo Dockyard Co. Ltd. of South Korea to construct an additional MR product tanker for approximately $36.4 million. This vessel is scheduled to be delivered to the Company in January 2013.

We have made payments of $50.5 million on all six new-building vessels as of December 31, 2011. Furthermore, on December 28, 2011 the keels were laid on the first five new-building vessels. We made a related progress payment of $9.4 million in January 2012 which was accrued at December 31, 2011. In accordance with IAS 23 "Borrowing Costs", applicable interest costs are also capitalized during the period that vessels are under construction. As of December 31, 2011, we capitalized $0.6 million (2010: $0) of interest expense attributable to the aforementioned vessels under construction, bringing the total amount capitalized at December 31, 2011 to $60.3 million. The interest capitalized was calculated by applying a rate of 4.4% to expenditure on such assets.

The following table is a timeline of future expected payments and dates as of December 31, 2011*:

Q1 2012	$ 18.7 million
Q2 2012	18.6 million
Q3 2012	110.2 million
Q4 2012	3.6 million
Q1 2013	21.8 million
	$172.9 million

* These are estimates only and are subject to change as construction progresses. The Q1 2012 includes the $9.4 million accrued at December 31, 2011.

IFRS-BPPD 3.138

Collateral Agreements

Noemi, Senatore, Venice, STI Harmony, STI Heritage, STI Conqueror, STI Matador, STI Gladiator and *STI Highlander,* with an aggregated net book value of $228.2 million as of December 31, 2011 were provided as collateral under a loan agreement dated June 2, 2010 and amended on July 13, 2011 (the "2010 Revolving Credit Facility", See Note 11).

STI Spirit, with a net book value of $37.7 million as of December 31, 2011, was provided as collateral under a loan agreement dated March 9, 2011 (the "STI Spirit Credit Facility", See Note 11).

STI Coral and *STI Diamond,* with a net book value of $56.5 million as of December 31, 2011, were provided as collateral

under a loan agreement dated May 3, 2011 (the "2011 Credit Facility", See Note 11).

The vessels which collateralize the 2011 Credit Facility and 2010 Revolving Credit Facility also serve as collateral for the designated interest rate swap agreements (as described in Note 12), subordinated to the outstanding borrowings under each credit facility.

Property, Plant, and Equipment—Revaluation Model Applied to Multiple Asset Classes

3.139

Kazakhstan Kagazy PLC (Dec 2011)

CONSOLIDATED STATEMENT OF COMPREHENSIVE INCOME (in part)

In Thousands of US$	Note	2011 Results Before Exceptional Items	2011 Exceptional Items (Note 5)	2011 Total	2010 Results Before Exceptional Items	2010 Exceptional Items (Note 5)	2010 Total
Revenue	6	79,989	—	79,989	69,376	—	69,376
Cost of sales	7	(45,010)	—	(45,010)	(46,448)	—	(46,448)
Gross profit		34,979	—	34,979	22,928	—	22,928
Loss from the revaluation of property, plant and equipment and investment property	9	—	(21,913)	(21,913)	—	(47,490)	(47,490)
Administrative expenses	10	(13,947)	(1,182)	(15,129)	(15,278)	(1,032)	(16,310)
Distribution costs	11	(4,512)	—	(4,512)	(5,870)	—	(5,870)
Other operating expenses	12	(1,633)	(142)	(1,775)	(1,753)	—	(1,753)
Loss from disposal of subsidiary		—	—	—	(234)	—	(234)
Operating profit/(loss)		14,887	(23,237)	(8,350)	(207)	(48,522)	(48,729)
Finance income	13	141	39,025	39,166	5,259	—	5,259
Finance expense	13	(19,806)	(6,594)	(26,400)	(21,514)	(937)	(22,451)
Profit/(loss) before income tax		(4,778)	9,194	4,416	(16,462)	(49,459)	(65,921)
Income tax (expense)/benefit	14	—	(2,392)	(2,392)	—	9,920	9,920
Profit/(loss) for the financial year from continuing operations		(4,778)	6,802	2,024	(16,462)	(39,539)	(56,001)
Other comprehensive income/(loss)							
Profit/(loss) from revaluation of property, plant and equipment and investment property	9			792			(286)
Exchange differences on translation to presentation currency				479			415
Exchange differences arising on net investment in foreign operations				(1,042)			269
Income tax recorded directly in other comprehensive income	14			(139)			(1,238)
Other comprehensive income/(expense) for the year				90			(840)
Total comprehensive income/(expense) for the year				2,114			(56,841)

NOTES TO THE CONSOLIDATED FINANCIAL STATEMENTS (in part)

1 The Group and Its Operations

Kazakhstan Kagazy PLC (the "Company") is a public company incorporated and domiciled under the law of the Isle of Man. Refer to the shareholder Information section of the Annual Report for details of the nature of the Company's listing.

The Company and its subsidiaries (the "Group") operate in three major reportable operating segments, which are:

(1) the production and distribution of corrugated product and paperboard packaging, as well as trading other paper products ("Paper Segment");

(2) the provision of logistics services through an integrated inland container terminal, supported by Class A and Class B warehousing ("Logistics Segment"); and

(3) land held for development and/or future sale ("Property Segment").

2 Significant Accounting Policies (in part)

Basis of preparation. The consolidated financial statements have been prepared in accordance with International Financial Reporting Standards (IFRSs) for Kazakhstan Kagazy PLC ("Company") and its subsidiaries.

These consolidated financial statements have been prepared in accordance with International Financial Reporting Standards ("IFRS") and IFRIC interpretations as applicable to companies reporting under IFRS. The Company's financial statements have been prepared under the historical cost convention, as modified by revaluation of property, plant and equipment and investment property.

Presented below are the significant accounting policies used for preparation of these consolidated financial statements. These accounting policies have been consistently applied to all presented reporting periods, unless stated otherwise.

The preparation of financial statements in compliance with IFRS requires the use of certain critical accounting estimates. It also requires management to exercise its judgement in the process of applying the Group's accounting policies. The areas involving a higher degree of judgement or complexity, or areas where assumptions and estimates are significant to the consolidated financial statements are disclosed in Note 3.

The financial reporting framework that has been applied in their preparation of financial statements is applicable law and International Financial Reporting Standards (IFRSs) as adopted by the European Union and IFRSs issued by the International Accounting Standards Board (IASB). Differences between IFRS and IFRS as adopted by EU did not have a material impact on these financial statements.

Property, plant and equipment. Property, plant and equipment, excluding transport and other immaterial property are stated at cost less depreciation, adjusted to the market price at the end of the reporting period. Costs include the original purchase price of the asset and the costs attributable to bringing the asset to its working condition for its intended use.

Property, plant and equipment are subject to revaluation at market value with sufficient regularity to ensure that the carrying amount does not differ materially from that which would be determined using fair value at the end of the reporting period.

Increases in the carrying amount arising on revaluation of land and buildings are credited to other reserves in owners' equity. Decreases that offset previous increases of the same asset are recognised in other comprehensive income and decrease the previously recognised revaluation surplus in equity; all other decreases are charged to profit or loss account for the year. The revaluation reserve for property, plant and equipment included in equity is transferred directly to accumulated deficit when the revaluation surplus is realised on the retirement or disposal of the asset.

For the purposes of the Group's property, plant and equipment, market value is determined on the basis of the reports of independent appraisers with an appropriate professional qualification as well as recent experience of the property valuation of the same nature and the same territory.

Accounting policies in terms of valuation are presented in Note 3.

Costs of minor repairs and maintenance are expensed when incurred. Cost of replacing major parts or components of property, plant and equipment items are capitalised and the replaced part is retired.

At each end of each reporting period Management assess whether there is any indication of impairment of property, plant and equipment. If any such indication exists, Management estimates the recoverable amount, which is determined as the higher of an asset's fair value less costs to sell and its value in use. The carrying amount is reduced to the recoverable amount and the impairment loss is recognised in profit or loss for the year to the extent it exceeds the previous revaluation surplus in equity. An impairment loss recognised for an asset in prior years is reversed where appropriate if there has been a change in the estimates used to determine the asset's value in use or fair value less costs to sell.

Gains and losses on disposal of property, plant and equipment are determined by comparing proceeds with carrying amount and are recognised in profit or loss for the year within other operating income or costs.

Construction in progress intended for use as property, plant and equipment. Property, plant and equipment under construction is initially recognised at cost, and is subsequently carried at fair value, based on valuations by independent professionally qualified appraisers. During construction revaluation difference is recognised in other comprehensive income. After completion construction in progress gets revalued as at completion date, and any resulting adjustment is recognised in a revaluation reserve in respect to the asset.

Construction in progress comprises costs directly related to construction of the asset including an appropriate allocation of directly attributable variable overheads that are incurred in construction and qualifying borrowing costs.

Construction in progress is not depreciated until commissioning. When the assets are ready for their intended use, their fair value is transferred to the appropriate classification within property, plant and equipment.

Depreciation. Land and construction in progress are not depreciated. Depreciation on other items of property, plant and equipment is calculated using the straight-line method to allocate their cost or revalued amounts to their residual values over their estimated useful lives:

	Useful Life Years	Annual Rate of Depreciation %
Buildings and construction	33–50	2–3
Machinery and equipment	13–33	3–8
Transport	10–14	7–10
Other		10–20

The residual value of an asset is the estimated amount that the Group would currently obtain from disposal of the asset less the estimated costs of disposal, if the asset were already of the age and in the condition expected at the end of its useful life. The assets' residual values and useful lives are reviewed, and adjusted if appropriate, at the end of each reporting period.

3 Critical Accounting Estimates and Judgements (in part)

Valuation of property, plant and equipment, investment property. The Group has used the report of independent appraisers to determine the fair value of its investment property. Valuation of land is based on comparable sales, while valuation of investment property is based both on comparable sales and discounted future cash flows.

Estimation of discounted future cash flows is based on different assumptions, including future rental income, expected maintenance costs, future costs for development and respective discount rates.

The fair value of the property is the price at which the property could be exchanged between knowledgeable, willing parties in an arm's length transaction. A "willing seller" is not a forced seller prepared to sell at any price. The best evidence of fair value is given by current prices in an active market for similar property in the same location and condition. In the absence of current prices in an active market, the Group considers information from a variety of sources, including:

(a) current prices in an active market for properties of different nature, condition or location, adjusted to reflect those differences;

(b) recent prices of similar properties on less active markets, with adjustments to reflect any change in economic conditions since the date of the transactions that occurred at those prices; and

(c) discounted cash flow projections based on reliable estimates of future cash flows, supported by the terms of any existing lease and other contracts and (when possible) by external evidence such as current market rents for similar properties in the same location and condition, and using discount rates that reflect current market assessments of the uncertainty in the amount and timing of the cash flows.

Market value of the Group's property is determined based on reports of independent appraisers, who hold a recognised and relevant professional qualification and who have recent experience in the valuation of property in similar locations and categories.

Disclosure on the valuation of land and buildings is provided in Note 9.

Useful lives of property, plant and equipment. The estimation of the useful lives of items of property, plant and equipment is a matter of judgment based on the experience with similar assets. The future economic benefits embodied in the assets are consumed principally through use. However, other factors, such as technical or commercial obsolescence and wear and tear, often result in the diminution of the economic benefits embodied in the assets. Management assesses the remaining useful lives annually in accordance with the current technical conditions of the assets and estimated period during which the assets are expected to earn benefits for the Group.

The following primary factors are considered: (a) expected usage of the assets; (b) expected physical wear and tear, which depends on operational factors and maintenance programme; and (c) technical or commercial obsolescence arising from changes in market conditions.

7 Cost of Sales

In Thousands of US$	2011	2010
Purchased paper	12,734	11,359
Waste paper	7,732	6,548
Staff costs	7,531	6,137
Depreciation of property, plant and equipment	3,993	4,343
Chemicals	3,142	2,651
Maintenance expenses	2,219	1,793
Utilities	2,092	1,915
Natural gas	1,597	1,582
Rail road expenses	1,179	726
Fuel	838	754
Transport expenses	778	454
Security services	513	308
Goods for resale (Kagazy Trading)	333	6,210
Rent expenses	302	210
Insurance	100	152
Other	495	886
Total	45,578	46,028
Change in finished goods and work in progress	(568)	420
Total cost of sales	45,010	46,448

9 Revaluation of Property, Plant and Equipment and Investment Property

The impact of revaluation property, plant and equipment and investment property is as follows:

In Thousands of US$	Profit and Loss		Other Comprehensive Loss		Total	
	2011	2010	2011	2010	2011	2010
Property, plant and equipment (Note 15)	(846)	(41,816)	792	502	(54)	(41,314)
Land	—	(17,594)	—	(8,306)	—	(25,900)
Buildings and construction	771	(3,970)	246	8,925	1,017	4,955
Machinery and equipment	(1,617)	(11,782)	540	(186)	(1,077)	(11,968)
Transport and other property, plant and equipment	—	—	6	—	6	—
Construction in progress	—	(8,470)	—	69	—	(8,401)
Investment property (Note 16)	(21,067)	(5,674)	—	(788)	(21,067)	(6,462)
Land	(14,623)	5,617	—	(788)	(14,623)	4,829
Buildings and construction	2,363	(5,747)	—	—	2,363	(5,747)
Construction in progress	(8,807)	(5,544)	—	—	(8,807)	(5,544)
Total	(21,913)	(47,490)	792	(286)	(21,121)	(47,776)

In November 2011, the Group revalued its investment properties. However, the property, plant and equipment has not been revalued as last revaluation was performed as of 31 December 2010 and according to the Group's accounting policy, property, plant and equipment is revalued every 3–5 years. Management tested property, plant and equipment for impairment as of 31 December 2011 and identified no impairment (see Note 15).

The Group has determined the value of the Group's investment properties by reference to independent valuation reports conducted in accordance with Kazakh legislation, the Valuation Standards of the International Valuation Standards Committee by a qualified expert "Grant Thornton Appraisal" LLP.

In reaching their conclusions, the Valuers have used the following methods:

Land

All land has been valued using the comparative market approach.

Buildings, Machinery and Equipment

Buildings, machinery and equipment have been valued on the depreciated replacement cost approach cross checked by reference to the income approach, which considers the net present value of expected future cash flows from the relevant operating assets and comparative approach based on analysis of the market situation and completed transactions or offer to sell similar assets.

Construction in Progress

Construction in progress is valued on the basis of depreciated replacement cost provided that there is a reasonable expectation that the construction will be completed.

As a result of the valuation of investment property performed in 2011 the Group recorded the amount of revaluation of investment property on the basis of assessment reports made by the end of January 2011.

10 Administrative Expenses

In Thousands of US$	2011	2010
Staff costs	5,345	6,132
Professional fees	2,589	2,189
Provision against doubtful debts	2,287	2,499
Property tax and other taxes, than income tax	1,397	1,463
Audit remuneration	350	350
Business trip costs	324	347
Depreciation of property, plant and equipment	292	295
Property and vehicle rental costs	254	200
Security costs	252	382
Banking costs	247	206
Property, plant and equipment servicing and maintenance costs	220	84
Insurance costs	208	421
Procurement costs	137	201
Communication costs	133	151
Utilities	104	94
Transportation costs	50	138
Penalties and fines	33	65
Amortisation of intangible assets	6	6
Other administrative expenses	901	1,087
Total administrative expenses	15,129	16,310
Including exceptional item	1,182	1,032

Exceptional item—Included in the total administrative expenses are costs incurred solely in relation to restructuring and represents consulting services and legal services.

11 Distribution Costs

In Thousands of US$	2011	2010
Delivery costs	2,346	2,647
Staff costs	1,557	1,831
Raw materials procurement costs	183	208
Property, plant and equipment servicing and maintenance costs	90	247
Depreciation of property, plant and equipment	2	100
Marketing and advertising costs	75	63
Rent of transport and other property	26	361
Cargo handling and forwarding costs	22	222
Utilities	2	5
Other distribution costs	129	186
Total distribution costs	4,512	5,870

15 Property, Plant and Equipment

In Thousands of US$	Land	Buildings and Construction	Machinery and Equipment	Transport	Other	Construction in Progress	Total
Cost or Valuation							
Balance as at 1 January 2010	56,534	75,022	78,332	1,621	3,404	20,355	235,268
Additions	—	590	926	68	246	6,151	7,981
Transferred from construction in progress	—	2	1,204	—	—	(1,206)	—
Reclassification with investment property	71	(552)	—	—	—	—	(481)
Reclassification from assets held for sale	—	—	1,332	—	—	—	1,332
Reclassification from intangible assets	—	—	—	—	1	—	1
Reclassification into between property, plant and equipment groups	—	301	(306)	(3)	7	—	(1)
Revaluation through other comprehensive loss	(8,306)	9,977	(824)	—	—	69	916
Revaluation through the statement of comprehensive income	(17,594)	(4,211)	(13,464)	—	—	(8,470)	(43,739)
Disposals	—	(2)	(817)	52	(311)	—	(1,078)
Translation differences	412	532	565	2	21	148	1,680
Balance as at 31 December 2010	31,117	81,659	66,948	1,740	3,368	17,047	201,879
Additions	137	675	1,914	73	637	327	3,763
Transferred from construction in progress	—	356	56	—	3	(414)	1
Reclassification into between property, plant and equipment groups	—	53	3	—	(56)	—	—
Revaluation through other comprehensive loss	—	392	641	8	1	—	1,042
Revaluation through the statement of comprehensive income	—	834	(1,902)	—	—	—	(1,068)
Disposals	(821)	(2,808)	(186)	—	(157)	(2)	(3,974)
Translation differences	(202)	(542)	(467)	(25)	(31)	(115)	(1,382)
Balance as at 31 December 2011	30,231	80,619	67,007	1,796	3,765	16,843	200,261

In Thousands of US$	Land	Buildings and Construction	Machinery and Equipment	Transport	Other	Construction in Progress	Total
Accumulated Depreciation							
Balance as at 1 January 2010	—	10,866	19,255	406	469	—	30,996
Charges per year	—	1,369	3,138	129	349	—	4,985
Reclassification between property, plant and equipment groups	—	4	(3)	2	(3)	—	—
Revaluation through other comprehensive loss	—	1,052	(638)	—	—	—	414
Revaluation through the statement of comprehensive income	—	(241)	(1,682)	—	—	—	(1,923)
Disposals	—	(2)	(135)	(15)	(124)	—	(276)
Translation differences	—	79	136	—	—	—	217
Balance as at 31 December 2010	—	13,127	20,071	524	691	—	34,413
Charges per year	—	1,302	2,740	131	364	—	4,537
Reclassification between property, plant and equipment groups	—	10	—	—	(10)	—	—
Revaluation through other comprehensive loss	—	146	101	2	—	—	249
Revaluation through the statement of comprehensive income	—	63	(285)	—	—	—	(222)
Disposals	—	(422)	(47)	—	(46)	—	(515)
Translation differences	—	(101)	(171)	(10)	(12)	—	(294)
Balance as at 31 December 2011	—	14,125	22,409	647	987	—	38,168
Carrying Value							
As at 1 January 2010	56,534	64,156	59,077	1,215	2,935	20,355	204,272
As at 31 December 2010	31,117	68,532	46,877	1,216	2,677	17,047	167,466
As at 31 December 2011	30,231	66,494	44,598	1,149	2,778	16,843	162,093
Historical Cost							
As at 1 January 2010	135,227	91,324	52,753	1,152	2,908	22,476	305,840
As at 31 December 2010	109,810	98,373	37,957	1,152	2,648	19,168	269,108
As at 31 December 2011	108,924	95,733	37,814	1,087	2,749	18,964	265,271

The Group has the legal right of ownership in respect of all its property, plant and equipment. Assets under finance leases are disclosed in Note 27 d. Refer to Note 27 f for details of the assets pledged as security for bank loans.

Construction in progress is comprised of the Astana City Project. This construction is financed by DBK loans and therefore was suspended in 2009 due to the ongoing debt restructuring discussions with DBK (see Note 3 and Note 13).

In July 2011, the Group acquired the warehousing equipment, shelving, forklifts and software, which forms an integral part of the warehousing complex (Class A warehouses) in the amount of USD 1,477 thousand excluding VAT, previously pledged to ATF Bank JSC (Note 31).

In addition, during 2011, the Group made the following major capital investments: repairing the roof of the industrial building of the Paper Plant in the amount of USD 588 thousands and land use changes of paper business in the amount of USD 137 thousand. In the Logistics business a ramp was constructed for USD 91 thousand, the warehouse was renovated for USD 34 thousand and shelving equipment was purchased for an amount of USD 63 thousand.

In January 2011, the Group sold its production base and land plot of Kazupack, whose residual value to be written-off comprised USD 3,272 thousand (Note 12).

Impairment Test for Property, Plant and Equipment

Property, plant and equipment was not revalued at the end of the year as it was revalued in the prior year end; according to the Group's accounting policy, property, plant and equipment is revalued every 3–5 years.

Management reviewed property, plant and equipment for impairment based on each cash generating unit (CGU). The CGUs are individual businesses in Paper and Logistics operating segments—Paper Plant, Class A, Class B and Container Terminal. Property segment contains investment property only, which was revalued at the year end—see Note 9 and Note 16. The carrying value of these businesses was compared to the recoverable amount of the CGUs, which was based predominantly on value-in-use. Value-in-use calculations use pre-tax cash flow projections based on financial budgets approved by management covering a 5-year period. Cash flows beyond the 5-year period are extrapolated using the estimated growth rates which do not exceed the long-term average growth rates for the businesses. Other key assumptions applied in the impairment tests include the expected product or service price, demand for the products and services, product and service cost, related expenses and applicable exchange rate. Management determined these key assumptions based on past performance and its expectations of market development. Further, management adopted a pre-tax weighted average cost of capital of 11.25% (2010: not applicable as property was externally revalued) that reflects specific risks related to CGUs as discount rates. The assumptions above are used in analysing recoverable amounts of CGUs within Paper and Logistics operating segments.

Based on Management's impairment assessment, there was no impairment to other property, land and equipment of the Group as of December 31, 2011. Management's conclusion on impairment assessment is predominantly dependent upon its judgements used in arriving at projected disposal values, future growth rates and the discount rate applied to cash flow projections. The estimates and judgment used in the assessment represent management's best estimate based on current experience and information available, which may be different from the actual result in the future due to changes in the Group's business and other external environment.

Intangible Assets—Straight Line and Declining Balance Methods

3.140

VimpelCom Ltd (Dec 2011)

CONSOLIDATED INCOME STATEMENT (in part)

(In Millions of US Dollars, Except per Share Amounts)	Note	Years Ended December 31		
		2011	2010	2009
Service revenues		19,579	10,291	8,691
Sale of equipment and accessories		516	194	110
Other revenues	10	167	37	12
Total operating revenues		20,262	10,522	8,813
Operating expenses				
Service costs		4,962	2,251	1,895
Cost of equipment and accessories		663	217	111
Selling, general and administrative expenses	27	6,381	3,198	2,482
Depreciation		2,726	1,403	1,190
Amortization		2,059	610	440
Impairment loss	15	527	—	—
Loss on disposals of non-current assets		90	49	77
Total operating expenses		17,408	7,728	6,195
Operating profit		2,854	2,794	2,618

NOTES TO THE CONSOLIDATED FINANCIAL STATEMENTS (in part)

1 General Information

VimpelCom Ltd. ("VimpelCom", the "Company", and together with its consolidated subsidiaries the "Group" or "we") was incorporated in Bermuda on 5 June 2009, as an exempted company under the name New Spring Company Ltd., which was subsequently changed to VimpelCom Ltd. on 1 October 2009. VimpelCom Ltd. was formed to recapitalize Open Joint Stock Company "Vimpel-Communications" ("OJSC Vimpel-Com") and acquire CJSC "Kyivstar G.S.M." ("Kyivstar")(Note 7). Altimo Holdings & Investments Limited ("Altimo") and Telenor ASA ("Telenor") together with certain of their respective affiliates were the two major shareholders in each of the companies. The registered office of VimpelCom Ltd. Is Victoria Place, 31 Victoria Street, Hamilton HM 10, Bermuda. Vimpel-Com Ltd.'s headquarters and principal place of business are located at Claude Debussylaan 88, 1082 MD Amsterdam.

In these notes U.S. dollar amounts are presented in millions, except for share and per share (or ADS) amounts and as otherwise indicated.

On 21 April 2010, VimpelCom Ltd. successfully completed an exchange offer ("Exchange Offer") for OJSC VimpelCom shares (including shares represented by American Depositary Shares ("ADSs")), and acquired approximately 98% of OJSC VimpelCom's outstanding shares (including shares represented by ADSs). Therefore, effective 21 April 2010, OJSC VimpelCom is a subsidiary of VimpelCom Ltd. As the continuation of the existing Group, VimpelCom Ltd. is the accounting successor to OJSC VimpelCom, and therefore accounting data and disclosures related to the period prior to 21 April 2010 represent accounting data and disclosures of OJSC VimpelCom. Information about the number of shares prior to 21 April 2010 has been adjusted to reflect the effect of the recapitalization due to the Exchange Offer.

On 25 May 2010, VimpelCom Ltd. served a squeeze-out demand notice to OJSC VimpelCom demanding that the remaining shareholders of OJSC VimpelCom sell their shares to VimpelCom Ltd. The squeeze-out process was completed on 6 August 2010. As a result, VimpelCom Ltd. became the sole shareholder of OJSC VimpelCom. The increase in capital surplus of USD 31 represents the difference between the amount recorded as liability to noncontrolling interest in OJSC VimpelCom on 21 April 2010 in the amount of USD 501 and the amount recorded on 25 May 2010 when a squeeze-out demand notice was served (effectively this transaction represented a purchase of own shares legally affected through purchase of non-controlling interest in OJSC VimpelCom).

VimpelCom Ltd. ADS began trading on the New York Stock Exchange ("NYSE") on 22 April 2010 while OJSC VimpelCom ADS were delisted from the NYSE on 14 May 2010.

On 4 October 2010, the Company and Weather Investments S.p.A ("Weather") signed an agreement to combine their two groups (the "Transaction"). The Transaction terms provided that at the closing of the Transaction, the Company will own, through Weather, 51.7% of Orascom Telecom Holding S.A.E. ("Orascom Telecom", or "OTH") and 100% of Wind Telecomunicazioni S.p.A. ("Wind Italy").

At its meeting on 16 January 2011, the Supervisory Board approved new terms of the Transaction, under which shareholders of Wind Telecom S.p.A. ("Wind Telecom", formerly Weather) would contribute to VimpelCom their shares in Wind Telecom in exchange for consideration consisting of 325,639,827 newly-issued VimpelCom common shares, 305,000,000 newly-issued VimpelCom convertible preferred shares and USD1,495 in cash. The newly-issued convertible preferred shares have the same rights as the existing convertible preferred shares. In addition, pursuant to the terms of the Transaction, at or shortly after the closing of the Transaction, certain assets were spun off from the Wind Telecom group and transferred back to Weather Investments II S.a r.l., the 72.65% shareholder of Wind Telecom ("Weather II") prior to completion of the Transaction. These assets included certain assets from OTH, which VimpelCom committed to transfer back to Weather II, or in the event the assets could not be transferred, VimpelCom would have had to pay up to USD 770. These assets were transferred to Weather II in February 2012.

On 17 March 2011, the shareholders of the Company approved the issuance of common and convertible preferred shares to Wind Telecom's shareholders and the related increase in the Company's share capital.

On 15 April 2011, VimpelCom successfully completed the Transaction and obtained control over Wind Telecom. As a result of the Transaction, VimpelCom owns, through Wind Telecom, 51.9% of Orascom Telecom and 100% of Wind Italy (Note 7).

VimpelCom earns revenues by providing voice, data and other telecommunication services through a range of wireless, fixed and broadband internet services, as well as selling equipment and accessories. As of 31 December 2011, the Company operated telecommunications services in Russia, Italy, Algeria, Kazakhstan, Ukraine, Pakistan, Bangladesh, Armenia, Tajikistan, Uzbekistan, Georgia, Kyrgyzstan, Laos, Central African Republic, Burundi, Canada, Zimbabwe, Vietnam and Cambodia.

The consolidated financial statements of the Company for the year ended 31 December 2011 were authorized for issue in accordance with a resolution of the directors on 24 April 2012.

2 Basis of the Consolidated Financial Statements

2.1 Basis of Preparation

These consolidated financial statements of the Company have been prepared in accordance with International Financial Reporting Standards ("IFRS") as issued by the International Accounting Standards Board ("IASB"), effective at the time of preparing the consolidated financial statements and applied by VimpelCom.

For all periods up to and including the year ended 31 December 2010, VimpelCom Ltd. and OJSC VimpelCom, the accounting predecessor of the Company, prepared its consolidated financial statements in accordance with generally accepted accounting principles in the United States ("US GAAP"). VimpelCom is a formal foreign company in the Netherlands which falls under the Formal Foreign Companies Act ("FFCA") and is therefore subject to certain parts of the Dutch Civil Code. VimpelCom was considered a first-time adopter of IFRS for the 2010 financial statements filed for the Dutch statutory purposes. Therefore in the first VimpelCom group consolidated IFRS financial statements as of 31 December 2010, VimpelCom stated that the consolidated financial statements have been prepared in accordance with IFRS as adopted by the European Commission and also comply with the IFRS as issued by the IASB. These financial statements include certain supplemental disclosures in the form of reconciliations from US GAAP to IFRS as issued by the IASB to disclose the changes in the basis of presentation from US GAAP basis-financial statements. Refer to Note 4 for information on the Company's adoption of IFRS.

The consolidated financial statements have been prepared on a historical cost basis, unless disclosed otherwise.

3 Significant Accounting Policies (in part)

Intangible Assets (Excluding Goodwill)

Intangible assets acquired separately are measured initially at cost. Following initial recognition, intangible assets are carried at cost less accumulated amortization and accumulated impairment losses, if any. Internally generated intangible assets (excluding eligible development costs) are not capitalized and expenditure is reflected in the income statement in the year when the expenditure is incurred. The costs of the intangible assets acquired as part of a business combination is their fair value at acquisition date.

Intangible assets with an indefinite useful life and also intangible assets not yet available for their intended use, are tested for impairment at least annually as of October 1 to determine whether events and circumstances continue to support an indefinite useful life assessment for that asset. Change in the useful life of an intangible asset from indefinite to finite life is treated on a prospective basis. Any impairment to the asset is charged to the income statement in the year in which it arises.

Intangible assets with a finite useful life are amortized over that life on a systematic basis. The amortization method used reflects the pattern in which the asset's future economic benefits are expected to be consumed by the Group. If that pattern cannot be determined reliably, the straight-line method is used. For intangible assets associated with customer relationships the Company uses declining balance amortization pattern based on value contribution the customers bring. For other intangible assets the straight-line method is used. The amortization charge for each period is recognized in profit or loss. The amortization period and the amortization method for an intangible asset with a finite useful life is reviewed at least at each financial year-end.

Gains or losses arising from derecognition of an intangible asset are measured as the difference between the net disposal proceeds and the carrying amount of the asset and are recognized in the income statement when the asset is derecognized, if any.

Reclassifications (in part)

The Company changed the presentation of certain items in the consolidated statement of financial position and consolidated income statement as compared to the presentation used under US GAAP.

The most significant reclassifications related to the presentation of:
- software including annual updates which is an integral part of telecommunication equipment in property and equipment instead of a separate item in the statement of financial position and prepayments with respect to annual updates of software which were included in other current assets;
- other software and frequency permissions as part of intangible assets instead of a separate line item for software and other non-current assets for frequency permissions;

Critical Accounting Estimates (in part)

A critical accounting estimate is one which is both important to the presentation of the Group's financial position and results and requires management's most difficult, subjective or complex judgements, often as a result of the need to make important estimates based on assumptions about the outcome of matters that are inherently uncertain. Management evaluates such estimates on an ongoing basis, based upon historical results and experience, consultations with experts, trends and other methods which management considers reasonable under the circumstances, as well as forecasts as to how these might change in the future.

Depreciation and Amortization of Non-Current Assets

Depreciation and amortization expenses are based on management estimates of residual value, amortization method and the useful life of property and equipment and intangible assets. Estimates may change due to technological developments, competition, changes in market conditions and other factors and may result in changes in the estimated useful life and in the amortization or depreciation charges. Technological developments are difficult to predict and our views on the trends and pace of development may change over time. Some of the assets and technologies, in which the Group invested several years ago, are still in use and provide the basis for the new technologies. Critical estimates in the evaluations of useful lives for intangible assets include, but are not limited to, estimated average customer relationship based on churn, remaining license or concession period and expected developments in technology and markets. The useful lives of property and equipment and intangible assets are reviewed at least annually taking into consideration the factors mentioned above and all other important relevant factors. Estimated useful lives for similar types of assets may vary between different entities in the Group due to local factors such as growth rate, maturity of the market, history and expectations for replacements or transfer of assets, climate and quality of components used. The actual economic lives of intangible assets may be different than our estimated useful lives, thereby resulting in a different carrying value of our intangible assets with finite lives. We continue to evaluate the amortization period for intangible assets with finite lives to determine whether events or circumstances warrant revised amortization periods. A change in estimated useful lives is a change in accounting estimate, and depreciation and amortization charges are adjusted for prospectively.

14 Intangible Assets

The total gross carrying value and accumulated amortization of VimpelCom's intangible assets consisted of the following at 31 December:

	Telecommunications Licenses, Frequencies and Permissions	Goodwill	Software	Brands and Trademarks	Customer Relation-ships	Telephone Line Capacity	Other Intangible Assets	Total
Cost								
At 1 January 2009	1,513	3,481	878	37	467	167	426	6,969
Additions	24	—	95	—	1	3	4	128
Disposals	(1)	—	(43)	(16)	—	—	—	(60)
Transfer	—	—	3	(1)	25	—	(27)	—
Other	1	—	(58)	(2)	35	(2)	(32)	(58)
Translation adjustment	(116)	(189)	(45)	(1)	(9)	(13)	(32)	(405)
At 31 December 2009	1,421	3,292	830	17	519	155	339	6,573
Additions	55	—	123	—	—	12	7	197
Acquisition of a subsidiary (Note 7)	130	3,477	182	177	816	—	—	4,782
Disposals	—	—	(31)	—	—	—	—	(31)
Transfer	1	—	42	—	86	—	(90)	39
Other	(1)	—	8	—	3	(7)	18	21
Translation adjustment	(6)	(47)	(6)	(1)	6	(1)	(13)	(68)
At 31 December 2010	1,600	6,722	1,148	193	1,430	159	261	11,513
Additions	331	—	137	—	1	10	1,891	2,370
Acquisition of a subsidiary (Note 7)	3,330	11,331	9	2,308	2,937	1	1,390	21,306
Disposals	(80)	—	(33)	—	—	(1)	(28)	(142)
Transfer	2	—	3	—	(14)	(10)	12	(7)
Other	10	—	15	(4)	(25)	(14)	47	29
Translation adjustment	(277)	(1,151)	(43)	(174)	(242)	(2)	(261)	(2,150)
At 31 December 2011	4,916	16,902	1,236	2,323	4,087	143	3,312	32,919
Amortization and Impairment								
At 1 January 2009	(638)	—	(510)	(28)	(56)	(52)	(202)	(1,486)
Amortization charge for the year	(172)	—	(137)	(4)	(27)	(13)	(86)	(439)
Disposals	—	—	37	15	—	12	—	64
Other	(2)	—	44	4	(44)	4	57	63
Translation adjustment	40	—	19	2	(4)	3	8	68
At 31 December 2009	(772)	—	(547)	(11)	(131)	(46)	(223)	(1,730)
Amortization charge for the year	(175)	—	(206)	(8)	(182)	(10)	(29)	(610)
Disposals	—	—	28	—	—	—	—	28
Other	2	—	(5)	—	(37)	—	37	(3)
Translation adjustment	12	—	4	—	4	—	(1)	19
At 31 December, 2010	(933)	—	(726)	(19)	(346)	(56)	(216)	(2,296)
Amortization charge for the year	(387)	—	(183)	(118)	(1,083)	(43)	(246)	(2,060)
Disposals	71	—	30	5	—	—	25	131
Impairment (Note 15)	(128)	(126)	(4)	—	—	—	—	(258)
Other	(1)	—	(9)	2	11	8	(7)	4
Translation adjustment	7	—	35	7	83	3	26	161
At 31 December, 2011	(1,371)	(126)	(857)	(123)	(1,335)	(88)	(418)	(4,318)
Net Book Value								
At 31 December 2009	649	3,292	283	6	388	109	116	4,843
At 31 December 2010	667	6,722	422	174	1,084	103	45	9,217
At 31 December 2011	3,545	16,776	379	2,200	2,752	55	2,894	28,601

Telecommunication licenses not in use mainly comprise of the LTE licenses in Italy and Uzbekistan, for which the business operations have not yet been started, in the amount of USD 1,513 as of 31 December 2011.

Oil and Gas Producing Properties—Depreciation, Depletion and Amortization, Straight Line and Units of Production Methods

3.141

Petróleo Brasileiro S.A.—Petrobras (Dec 2011)

CONSOLIDATED STATEMENT OF INCOME (in part)

(In millions of Dollars, except income per share)

	Note	Year Ended December 31		
		2011	2010	2009
Sales revenues	24	145,915	120,452	91,146
Cost of sales	25	(99,595)	(77,145)	(54,023)
Gross profit		46,320	43,307	37,123
Income (expenses)				
Selling expenses	25	(5,346)	(4,863)	(3,693)
Administrative and general expenses	25	(5,161)	(4,441)	(3,662)
Exploration costs		(2,630)	(2,168)	(2,061)
Research and development expenses		(1,454)	(989)	(685)
Other taxes		(460)	(509)	(327)
Other operating income and expenses, net	26	(3,984)	(3,965)	(3,772)
		(19,035)	(16,935)	(14,200)
Net income before financial results, profit sharing and income taxes		27,285	26,372	22,923

NOTES TO THE CONSOLIDATED FINANCIAL STATEMENTS (in part)

(In millions of Dollars)

1. The Company and Its Operations

Petróleo Brasileiro S.A.—Petrobras is a Brazilian petroleum company which, directly or through its subsidiaries (referred to jointly as "Petrobras" or "the Company") is dedicated to prospecting, drilling, refining, processing, trading and transporting petroleum originating from wells, shale or other rocks, and oil products, natural gas and other liquid hydrocarbons, in addition to activities connected with energy and it may carry out research, development, production, transport, distribution and trading of all forms of energy, as well as any other correlated or similar activities. The Company's head office is located in Rio de Janeiro—RJ.

2. Basis of Preparation (in part)

2.1 Statement of Compliance

The consolidated financial statements are being presented in accordance with the international financial reporting standards (IFRS) issued by the International Accounting Standards Board (IASB) in U.S. dollar.

The consolidated financial statements were authorized for issue by the Board of Directors on February 28, 2012.

2.4 Use of Estimates and Judgments

In the preparation of the consolidated financial statements it is necessary to use estimates and assumptions for certain assets, liabilities and other transactions. These estimates include: oil and gas reserves, pension and health plans liabilities, depreciation, depletion and amortization, decommissioning costs, provisions for contingencies, fair value of financial instruments, present value adjustments of accounts receivable and payable of relevant transactions, income tax. Although Management uses its best estimates and judgments that are reviewed periodically, the actual results could differ from these estimates.

4. Summary of Significant Accounting Policies (in part)

4.6 Property, Plant and Equipment, Net

Valuation

Property, plant and equipment, net is stated at the cost of acquisition or construction, which represents the costs incurred for bringing the asset to the condition for operation, adjusted during hyperinflationary periods, less accumulated depreciation and impairment losses.

The costs incurred in connection with the exploration, development and production of oil and gas are accounted for in accordance with the successful efforts method. This method requires that capitalization of costs incurred in connection with the development of proved reserve areas and successful exploratory wells. In addition, costs related to geological and geophysical activities are expensed when incurred and exploratory wells drilled in areas of unproved reserves are expensed when determined to be dry or non-economical.

Expenditures on major maintenance of industrial units and ships are capitalized if certain recognition criteria of IAS 16 are met. Such maintenance occurs, on average, every four years.

Borrowing costs directly attributable to the acquisition or construction of qualifying assets are capitalized as part of the costs of these assets. Borrowing costs of funds borrowed generally are capitalized based on the Company's weighted average cost of borrowings, excluding borrowing costs directly attributable.

Depreciation

Depreciation, depletion and amortization of proved oil and gas producing properties, except for signature bonus, is accounted for according to the unit-of-production method, applied on a field by field basis, based on the ratio of reserves produced.

Reserves are estimated by the Company's technical experts according to the criteria established by the U.S. Securities and Exchange Commission—SEC. Estimates are revised for depreciation, depletion and amortization purposes at least once a year or on interim basis, if material changes occur.

The straight-line method is used for assets with a useful life shorter than the life of the field.

Except for land, which is not depreciated, other property, plant and equipment are depreciated on a straight line basis, in accordance with the following estimated useful lives:

Class of Assets	Useful Life Weighted Average
Buildings and improvements	25 years (25–40 years)
Equipment and other assets	20 years (3–31 years)

The stoppages for maintenance occur in programmed intervals, on average, of 4 years, and the respective expenses are depreciated as a production cost until the beginning of the following stoppage.

4.7 Intangible Assets

Intangible assets are stated at the cost, less accumulated amortization and impairment losses. It comprise rights and concessions that include: the signature bonus paid for obtaining concessions for exploration of oil and natural gas, including assignment agreement in blocks of the pre-salt area ("Cessão Onerosa"); public service concessions; trademarks; patents; software and goodwill.

Amortization of signature bonus costs of producing properties is recorded using the unit-of-production method, applied on a field by field basis, based on the ratio of reserves produced. Other intangible assets with definite useful life are amortized on a straight line basis.

12. Property, Plant and Equipment, Net

12.1 By Type of Asset

	Land, Buildings and Improvements	Equipment and Other Assets	Assets Under Construction[*]	Oil and Gas Producing Properties	Total
Balance at December 31, 2009	4,169	39,766	66,863	17,954	128,752
Additions	126	2,950	32,727	1,784	37,587
Capitalized interest			3,141		3,141
Business combination	49	56	14		119
Write-offs	(81)	(51)	(863)	(635)	(1,630)
Transfers	1,068	19,829	(22,459)	4,478	2,916
Depreciation, amortization and depletion	(331)	(4,368)		(3,259)	(7,958)
Impairment—provision		(104)		(156)	(260)
Impairment—reversal		77		240	317
Accumulated translation adjustment	256	166	3,747	951	5,120
Balance at December 31, 2010	5,256	58,321	83,170	21,357	168,104
Cost	7,450	96,353	83,170	46,545	233,518
Accumulated depreciation, amortization and depletion	(2,194)	(38,032)		(25,188)	(65,414)
Balance at December 31, 2010	5,256	58,321	83,170	21,357	168,104
Additions	101	1,570	31,840	2,059	35,570
Capitalized interest			4,382		4,382
Business combination			12		12
Write-offs	(25)	(262)	(1,296)	(326)	(1,909)
Transfers	2,413	18,406	(23,598)	8,401	5,622
Depreciation, amortization and depletion	(473)	(5,800)		(3,904)	(10,177)
Impairment—provision		(50)	(150)	(213)	(413)
Impairment—reversal	1	15		36	52
Accumulated translation adjustment	(685)	(5,838)	(9,831)	(2,424)	(18,778)
Balance at December 31, 2011	6,588	66,362	84,529	24,986	182,465
Cost	8,990	104,477	84,529	52,272	250,268
Accumulated depreciation, amortization and depletion	(2,402)	(38,115)		(27,286)	(67,803)
Balance at December 31, 2011	6,588	66,362	84,529	24,986	182,465
Weighted average of useful life in years	25 to 40 (except land)	3 to 31		Units of production method	

[*] It includes oil and gas exploration and development assets.

12.2 Estimated Useful Life

Buildings and Improvements, Equipments and Other Assets

Estimated Useful Life	Cost	Accumulated Depreciation	As of December 31, 2011
Up to 5 years	4,312	(2,521)	1,791
6–10 years	17,595	(8,610)	8,985
11–15 years	1,784	(843)	941
16–20 years	21,146	(8,499)	12,647
21–25 years	23,897	(5,885)	18,012
25–30 years	21,896	(3,085)	18,811
More than 30 years	2,711	(1,779)	932
Unit-of Production Method	19,274	(9,296)	9,978
	112,615	(40,518)	72,097
Buildings and improvements	8,138	(2,403)	5,735
Equipments and other assets	104,477	(38,115)	66,362

12.3 Depreciation

The depreciation for the years ended December 31, 2011 and 2010 is presented as follows:

	Year Ended December 31	
	2011	2010
Recognized in inventories regarding:		
Property, plant and equipment	4,886	4,279
Exploration and production expenditures	3,266	3,207
Decommissioning	235	232
	8,387	7,718
Recognized in results of operations	748	683
	9,135	8,401

13. Intangible Assets

13.1 By Type of Asset

		Software			
	Rights and Concessions	Acquired	Developed In-House	Goodwill	Total
Balance at December 31, 2010	47,386	191	816	544	48,937
Addition	496	64	198	11	769
Acquisition through business combination	—	—	—	2	2
Capitalized interest	—	—	21	—	21
Write-off	(167)	(3)	(7)	—	(177)
Transfers	5	12	(22)	(4)	(9)
Amortization	(87)	(67)	(204)	—	(358)
Impairment—provision	(1)	—	—	—	(1)
Accumulated translation adjustment	(5,165)	(17)	(87)	(49)	(5,318)
Balance at December 31, 2011	42,467	180	715	504	43,866
Estimated useful life—years	25	5	5	Undefined	

13.2 Oil Exploration Rights—Assignment Agreement ("Cessão Onerosa")

At December 31, 2011, the Company's intangible assets include an agreement with the Brazilian federal government and National Agency of Petroleum, Natural Gas and Biofuels (ANP)—(Assignment Agreement), under which the government assigned to the Company the right to conduct research activities and the exploration and production of fluid hydrocarbons in specified pre-salt areas (Franco, Florim, Nordeste de Tupi, Entorno de Iara, Sul de Guará e Sul de Tupi), subject to a maximum production of five billion barrels of oil equivalent up to 40 years renewable for more five years upon certain conditions.

On February 8, 2012, the Company concluded the drilling of the first well of the onerous assignment, the results of which proved the extent of the oil reserves located at the Northwest of the discovery well of the Franco area. Immediately afterwards Petrobras will conduct a formation test to assess the productivity and will continue with the activities and investments established in the contract.

The Assignment Agreement provides for a subsequent revision of the volume and the price, based on an independent third party assessment. If revision determines that the value of the rights acquired is higher than the initial purchase price, the Company may either pay the difference to the Brazilian federal government, in which case is expected the recog-

nition of the difference in Intangible Assets, or reduce the total volume acquired under the contract, in which case there would be no impact on the balance sheet. If revision determines that the value of the rights acquired is lower than the initial purchase price, the Brazilian federal government will pay for the difference in cash and/or bonds, depending on Government Budget conditions and it is expected a reduction of the amount originally recorded in Intangible Assets by the amount received from the Brazilian federal government.

When the effects of the revision become probable and measurable, the Company will make the respective adjustments to the acquisition cost.

The agreement also establishes minimum commitments with respect to local acquisition of goods and services from Brazilian suppliers in the exploration stage and in the development stage of production which will be subject to ANP analysis. In the event of non-compliance, ANP will be able to apply administrative and pecuniary sanctions established in the contract.

13.3 Exploration Rights Returned to National Agency of Petroleum, Natural Gas and Biofuels (ANP)

In 2011, the Company returned the following blocks, amounting to US$ 84, to ANP:
- Blocks—Exclusive concession of Petrobras: Rio do Peixe basin: RIOP-T-41.

Santos basin: S-M-613, S-M-1356 and S-M-1480.
Pelotas Sea basin: P-M-1267 and P-M-1349.
Potiguar basin: POT-T-706
- Blocks in partnership (devolved by Petrobras or by its operators):
Santos basin: S-M-1227, S-M-792, S-M-791, S-M-1162, S-M-320, S-M-1163 and S-M-731.
Espírito Santo Terra basin: ES-T-401.

13.4 Fields Returned to the National Agency of Petroleum, Natural Gas and Biofuels (ANP)

In 2011, the Company returned to ANP the Mutum field, located in Sergipe/Alagoas basin.

13.5 Concession of Services for Distribution of Piped Natural Gas

At December 31, 2011, the intangible assets include concession agreements for the distribution of piped natural gas in Brazil amounting to US$ 243, with maturities between 2029 and 2043, which may be extended. The concessions establish distribution to the industrial, residential, commercial, vehicular, air conditioning, transport and other sectors.

The remuneration for providing services consists, basically, of the combination of operating costs and expenses, and return on invested capital. The fees charged for the volume of gas distributed are subject to periodic reviews and adjustments by the state regulatory agency.

Based on appraisals, concession agreements determine indemnification to the Company regarding assets subject to return at the end of the concession.

25. Expenses by Nature

| | Year Ended December 31 | | |
	2011	2010	2009
Raw material/products purchased	(57,274)	(43,952)	(29,677)
Contracted services, freight, rents and general charges	(14,771)	(13,133)	(7,805)
Government interest	(16,228)	(11,547)	(9,787)
Personnel expenses and benefits	(11,294)	(9,509)	(6,980)
Depreciation, depletion and amortization	(10,535)	(8,308)	(7,129)
	(110,102)	(86,449)	(61,378)
Cost of sales	(99,595)	(77,145)	(54,023)
Selling expenses	(5,346)	(4,863)	(3,693)
Administrative and general expenses	(5,161)	(4,441)	(3,662)
	(110,102)	(86,449)	(61,378)

IAS 19, *EMPLOYEE BENEFITS*

Author's Note

In 2011, IASB issued a revised IAS 19, *Employee Benefits*, which is effective for annual reporting periods beginning on or after 1 January 2013, with early application permitted. See the author's note preceding

paragraph 2.304 in section 2 for a discussion of the amendments to this standard.

The IASB also issued IFRS 13, which amended IAS 19. Early adoption is permitted. IFRS 13 amended the definition of fair value and replaced the term *determine* with the term *measure*.

Because these standards are effective for annual periods beginning on or after 1 January 2012, these amendments are not reflected in the commentary in this section. However, these amendments would not affect the availability of illustrative excerpts from survey companies' financial statements.

IFRS Overview and Comparison to U.S. GAAP

3.142 *Employee benefits* are all forms of consideration given by an entity for services rendered by its employees. IAS 19 establishes the requirement of accounting for four general categories of employee benefits within its scope: short term (for example, wages and compensating absences); postemployment (for example, pensions); other long term (for example, long-term disability); and termination benefits (for example, severance pay). An entity should account for all employee benefits, except those to which IFRS 2, *Share-based Payment*, applies, in accordance with IAS 19.

Author's Note

See section 2, beginning with paragraph 2.304, for a more comprehensive discussion of recognition, measurement, presentation, and disclosure requirements set forth in IAS 19. This subsection only provides a brief overview of the effects of IAS 19 on the statement of comprehensive income.

Recognition and Measurement

IFRSs

3.143 For most employee benefits, IAS 19 requires an entity to recognize both a liability and related expense in profit or loss when it is probable that settlement of the obligation will result in an outflow of economic benefits and the cost can be estimated reliably, except to the extent that the cost may be included in the cost of an asset.

3.144 An entity should recognize termination benefits as a liability and expense when the entity is demonstrably committed to terminate employment before normal retirement or provide such benefits due to an offer encouraging voluntary termination.

3.145 With respect to postemployment benefits, IAS 19 requires an entity to recognize the net total of the following amounts as an expense in profit or loss, except as otherwise required or permitted to be included in the cost of an asset:
- Service costs
- Interest costs
- Expected returns on plan assets and any reimbursement rights
- Actuarial gains or losses, if any (see the following paragraph)

- Past service costs
- Effect of any curtailments or settlements
- Effect of the limit on recognition of a defined benefit asset, unless recognized in OCI

3.146 For defined benefit plans, IAS 19 provides an entity with alternatives for recognizing the effects of actuarial gains and losses. An entity can recognize only a portion of actuarial gains and losses in profit or loss using the corridor method. An entity should apply the corridor method to each defined benefit plan separately. An entity using the corridor method should determine the amount, if any, of unrecognized actuarial gains or losses to be recognized in profit or loss as follows:

(a) Determine the amount by which the net cumulative unrecognized actuarial gains and losses exceed the greater of 10 percent of the present value of the defined benefit obligation and 10 percent of the fair value of the plan assets. (If this amount is zero or negative, no expense is recognized.)

(b) Divide the excess, if any, by the expected average remaining working lives of plan participants and recognize this amount as an expense. (If there is no excess, no expense is recognized.)

Alternatively, IAS 19 states that an entity may use a systematic method that recognizes actuarial gains or losses more quickly, as long as the method treats gains and losses the same and is applied consistently from period to period. If the entity chooses to recognize all actuarial gains and losses on all its defined benefit plans in the period in which they occur, it can recognize them in OCI, rather than profit or loss.

U.S. GAAP

3.147 Like IFRSs, U.S. GAAP requires an entity to recognize obligations and corresponding expenses when settlement of the obligation is probable and the amount can be measured reasonably. FASB ASC 710, *Compensation—General*, addresses general employee compensation (such as salaries, wages, and compensating absences); deferred compensation; and lump sum payments under union contracts. FASB ASC 712, *Compensation—Nonretirement Postemployment Benefits*, FASB ASC 715, *Compensation—Retirement Benefits*, and FASB ASC 718, *Compensation—Stock Compensation*, address postemployment nonretirement benefits; pensions and other retirement benefits; and stock compensation respectively.

3.148 With respect to defined benefit postemployment benefit plans, FASB ASC 715 requires an entity to recognize essentially the same components on the income statement as IAS 19, except that FASB ASC 220-10-55-2(h)–(j) requires an entity to report in OCI the following items associated with pensions and other postretirement benefits:

- Gains and losses and transition assets or obligations to the extent these items are not recognized immediately as a component of net periodic pension cost
- Prior service costs or credits

Presentation

3.149 Neither IAS 19 nor FASB ASC requires an entity to present employee benefits as a separate line item(s) in the statement of comprehensive income. An entity may disaggregate information either on the statement or in the notes.

However, it is common in practice for actuarial gains and losses to be shown as a separate line item in OCI.

Disclosure

IFRSs

3.150 IAS 19 requires an entity to disclose amounts recognized in the statement of comprehensive income. For the expense recognized in profit or loss, an entity should disclose the components of the expense (for example, service cost and interest cost). For the amount recognized in OCI, an entity should separately disclose actuarial gains and losses and the effect of the asset ceiling. When the entity has opted to report all actuarial gains and losses of the period directly in OCI, the entity should disclose the cumulative amount recognized.

U.S. GAAP

3.151 FASB ASC 715 requires similar disclosures for items reported on the income statement and in OCI.

Presentation and Disclosure Excerpts

Short-Term and Postemployment Benefits—Actuarial Gains and Losses Recognized Immediately in Equity, Effect of the Asset Ceiling, Termination Benefits

3.152

Siemens Aktiengesellschaft (Sep 2011)

CONSOLIDATED STATEMENTS OF INCOME
(in part)

(In millions of €, per share amounts in €)

	Note	2011	2010	2009
Revenue		73,515	68,978	70,053
Cost of goods sold and services rendered		(51,388)	(48,977)	(50,933)
Gross profit		22,127	20,001	19,120
Research and development expenses		(3,925)	(3,558)	(3,597)
Marketing, selling and general administrative expenses		(10,297)	(9,666)	(9,525)
Other operating income	6	555	839	719
Other operating expense	7	(502)	(1,554)	(582)
Income (loss) from investments accounted for using the equity method, net	8	147	9	(1,620)
Interest income	9	2,207	2,045	2,028
Interest expense	9	(1,716)	(1,759)	(2,074)
Other financial income (expense), net	9	646	(383)	(434)
Income from continuing operations before income taxes		9,242	5,974	4,035

NOTES TO THE CONSOLIDATED FINANCIAL STATEMENTS (in part)

1. Basis of Presentation

The accompanying Consolidated Financial Statements present the operations of Siemens AG with registered offices in Berlin and Munich, Germany, and its subsidiaries (the Company or Siemens). They have been prepared in accordance with International Financial Reporting Standards (IFRS), as adopted by the European Union. The financial statements are also in accordance with IFRS as issued by the International Accounting Standards Board (IASB). Certain pronouncements have been early adopted, see Note 2 Summary of significant accounting policies—recently adopted accounting pronouncements.

Siemens prepares and reports its Consolidated Financial Statements in euros (€). Siemens is a German based multinational corporation with a business portfolio of activities predominantly in the field of electronics and electrical engineering, for further information see Note 37 Segment information.

The Consolidated Financial Statements were authorised for issue by the Managing Board on November 23, 2011. The Consolidated Financial Statements are generally prepared on the historical cost basis, except as stated in Note 2 Summary of significant accounting policies.

2. Summary of Significant Accounting Policies (in part)

The accounting policies set out below have been applied consistently to all periods presented in these Consolidated Financial Statements.

Functional costs—In general, operating expenses by types are assigned to the functions following the functional area of the corresponding profit and cost centers. Expenses relating to cross-functional initiatives or projects are assigned to the respective functional costs based on an appropriate allocation principle. For additional information on amortization see Note 17 Other intangible assets, on depreciation see Note 18 Property, plant and equipment and on employee benefit expense see Note 35 Personnel costs.

Defined benefit plans—Siemens measures the entitlements of the defined benefit plans by applying the projected unit credit method. The approach reflects an actuarially calculated net present value of the future benefit entitlement for services already rendered. In determining the net present value of the future benefit entitlement for service already rendered (Defined Benefit Obligation (DBO)), Siemens considers future compensation and benefit increases, because the employee's final benefit entitlement at regular retirement age depends on future compensation or benefit increases. For post-employment healthcare benefits, Siemens considers health care trends in the actuarial valuations.

For unfunded plans, Siemens recognizes a pension liability equal to the DBO adjusted by unrecognized past service cost. For funded plans, Siemens offsets the fair value of the plan assets with the benefit obligations. Siemens recognizes the net amount, after adjustments for effects relating to unrecognized past service cost and any asset ceiling, in line item Pension plans and similar commitments or in line item Other current assets.

Actuarial gains and losses, resulting for example from an adjustment of the discount rate or from a difference between actual and expected return on plan assets, are recognized by Siemens in the Consolidated Statements of Comprehensive Income in the year in which they occur. Those effects are recorded in full directly in equity, net of tax

Termination benefits—Termination benefits are recognized in the period incurred and when the amount is reasonably estimable. Termination benefits in accordance with IAS 19, Employee Benefits, are recognized as a liability and an expense when the entity has demonstrably committed itself, through a formal termination plan or otherwise created a valid expectation, to either provide termination benefits as a result of an offer made in order to encourage voluntary redundancy or terminate employment before the normal retirement date.

3. Critical Accounting Estimates (in part)

Siemens' Consolidated Financial Statements are prepared in accordance with IFRS as issued by the IASB and as adopted by the EU. Siemens' significant accounting policies, as described in Note 2 Summary of significant accounting policies are essential to understanding the Company's results of operations, financial positions and cash flows. Certain of these accounting policies require critical accounting estimates that involve complex and subjective judgments and the use of assumptions, some of which may be for matters that are inherently uncertain and susceptible to change. Such critical accounting estimates could change from period to period and have a material impact on the Company's results of operations, financial positions and cash flows. Critical accounting estimates could also involve estimates where management reasonably could have used a different estimate in the current accounting period. Management cautions that future events often vary from forecasts and that estimates routinely require adjustment.

Employee benefit accounting—Pension plans and similar commitments—Obligations for pension and other post-employment benefits and related net periodic benefit costs are determined in accordance with actuarial valuations. These valuations rely on key assumptions including discount rates, expected return on plan assets, expected salary increases, mortality rates and health care trend rates. The discount rate assumptions are determined by reference to yields on high-quality corporate bonds of appropriate duration and currency at the end of the reporting period. In case such yields are not available discount rates are based on government bonds yields. Expected returns on plan assets assumptions are determined on a uniform methodology, considering long-term historical returns and asset allocations. Due to changing market and economic conditions the underlying key assumptions may differ from actual developments and may lead to significant changes in pension and other post-employment benefit obligations. Such differences are recognized in full directly in equity in the period in which they occur without affecting profit or loss. See Note 24 Pension plans and similar commitments for further information.

Termination benefits—Siemens runs restructuring projects on an individual basis. Costs in conjunction with terminating employees and other exit costs are subject to significant estimates and assumptions. See Note 5 Restructuring expense for further information.

5. Restructuring Expense

Siemens has implemented and will continue to run various restructuring measures. In fiscal 2011, the three Sectors Industry, Energy and Healthcare, in total, incurred personnel-related termination benefits of €120 million. In fiscal 2010, the

Industry Sector reported personnel-related expenses of €185 million from continuing operations for a number of restructuring projects.

The SG&A program was initiated in fiscal 2008, which aimed at reducing marketing, selling, general and administrative expense (SG&A) by approximately €1.2 billion by the year 2010. In fiscal 2009, net expenses under the SG&A program of €235 million were reported in Corporate items which include termination benefits resulting from the SG&A program and other ongoing personnel-related restructuring measures of €337 million. They also include a gain of €102 million attributable to the reversal of accrued termination benefits recognized as of September 30, 2008 for the German part of SG&A and related programs which is due to a change in estimate on the respective program measures, i.e. more intensive use of the early retirement arrangements as compared to severance payments in conjunction with transfer companies.

Restructuring costs are recorded in line item Income from continuing operations before income taxes. Line item Other current liabilities include the majority of the termination benefits.

The Siemens IT Solutions and Services restructuring program is disclosed at discontinued operations, see Note 4 Acquisitions, dispositions and discontinued operations.

22. Other Current Liabilities

(In Millions of €)	September 30, 2011	2010
Billings in excess of costs and estimated earnings on uncompleted contracts and related advances	12,488	12,180
Other employee related costs	2,127	2,265
Payroll obligations and social security taxes	1,718	2,121
Bonus obligations	1,144	1,582
Accruals for outstanding invoices	1,033	987
Miscellaneous tax liabilities	694	657
Deferred income	993	940
Deferred reservation fees received	68	77
Other	755	985
	21,020	21,794

Item Other employee related costs primarily includes vacation payments, accrued overtime and service anniversary awards, severance payments, as well as liabilities related to termination benefits.

24. Pension Plans and Similar Commitments

Pension benefits provided by Siemens are currently organized primarily through defined benefit pension plans which cover almost all of the Company's domestic employees and many of the Company's foreign employees. To reduce the risk exposure to Siemens arising from its pension plans, the Company performed a redesign of some major pension plans during the last several years towards benefit schemes which are predominantly based on contributions made by the Company. In order to fund Siemens' pension obligations, the Company's major pension plans are funded with assets in segregated pension entities.

Furthermore, the Company provides other post-employment benefits, which primarily consist of transition payments to German employees after retirement as well as post-employment health care and life insurance benefits to employees in the U.S. and Canada. These predominantly unfunded other post-employment benefit plans qualify as defined benefit plans under IFRS.

The Consolidated Statements of Financial Position include the following significant components related to pension plans and similar commitments as of September 30, 2011 and 2010:

(In Millions of €)	September 30, 2011	2010
Pension benefit plans	6,552	7,640
Other post-employment benefit plans	754	824
Liabilities for pension plans and similar commitments	7,306	8,464
Prepaid costs for post-employment benefits	149	37
Actuarial (losses)/gains	(5,670)	(6,023)
Effects in connection with asset ceiling	(163)	(145)
Income tax effect	1,007	1,259
Net amount recognized in the Consolidated Statements of Changes in Equity, net of tax	(4,826)	(4,909)

In addition to the above, the Company has foreign defined contribution plans for pensions and other post-employment benefits or makes contributions to social pension funds based on legal regulations (State plans). The recognition of a liability is not required because the obligation of the Company is limited to the payment of the contributions into these plans or funds.

Pension Benefits

Beginning with fiscal 2011, figures presented cover both principal and non-principal pension benefits provided by Siemens. The presentation of prior-year information has been adjusted to conform to the current-year presentation.

The pension benefit plans cover 481,000 participants, including 197,000 active employees, 91,000 former employees with vested benefits and 193,000 retirees and surviving dependents. Individual benefits are generally based on eligible compensation levels and/or ranking within the Company hierarchy and years of service. Retirement benefits under these plans vary depending on legal, fiscal and economic requirements in each country. The majority of Siemens' active employees in Germany participate in a pension scheme introduced in fiscal 2004, the BSAV (Beitragsorientierte Siemens Altersversorgung). The BSAV is a funded defined benefit pension plan whose benefits are predominantly based on contributions made by the Company and returns earned on such contributions, subject to a minimum return guaranteed by the Company. The BSAV is funded via the BSAV Trust. In connection with the implementation of the BSAV, benefits provided under defined benefit pension plans funded via the Siemens German Pension Trust were modified to substantially eliminate the effects of compensation increases by freezing the accrual of benefits under the majority of these plans.

The Company's pension benefit plans are explicitly explained in the subsequent sections with regard to:
- Pension obligations, plan assets and funded status,
- Components of NPBC,
- Amounts recognized in the Consolidated Statements of Comprehensive Income,

- Assumptions used for the calculation of the DBO and NPBC,
- Sensitivity analysis,
- Plan assets, and
- Pension benefit payments.

Pension Benefits: Pension Obligations, Plan Assets and Funded Status

A reconciliation of the funded status of the pension benefit plans to the amounts recognized in the Consolidated Statements of Financial Position is as follows:

(In Millions of €)	September 30, 2011			September 30, 2010		
	Total	Domestic	Foreign	Total	Domestic	Foreign
Fair value of plan assets	20,965	12,309	8,656	24,107	14,059	10,048
Total defined benefit obligation	27,121	16,624	10,497	31,475	18,897	12,578
Defined benefit obligation (funded)	26,189	16,406	9,783	30,375	18,620	11,755
Defined benefit obligation (unfunded)	932	218	714	1,100	277	823
Funded status	(6,156)	(4,315)	(1,841)	(7,368)	(4,838)	(2,530)
Germany	(4,315)	(4,315)		(4,838)	(4,838)	
U.S.	(1,083)		(1,083)	(1,091)		(1,091)
U.K.	148		148	(329)		(329)
Other	(906)		(906)	(1,110)		(1,110)
Unrecognized past service cost (benefits)	(84)	—	(84)	(90)	—	(90)
Effects due to asset ceiling	(163)	—	(163)	(145)	—	(145)
Net amount recognized	(6,403)	(4,315)	(2,088)	(7,603)	(4,838)	(2,765)
Amounts recognized in the Consolidated Statements of Financial Position consist of:						
Pension asset	149	—	149	37	—	37
Pension liability	(6,552)	(4,315)	(2,237)	(7,640)	(4,838)	(2,802)

The fair value of plan assets, DBO and funded status as of September 30, 2009 amounted to €21,990 million, €26,944 million and €(4,954) million, respectively. As of September 30, 2008, the fair value of plan assets, DBO and funded status were €21,002 million, €24,261 million and €(3,259) million.

As of September 30, 2007, the fair value of plan assets, DBO and funded status were €24,974 million, €26,829 million and €(1,855) million.

A detailed reconciliation of the changes in the DBO and in plan assets for fiscal 2011 and 2010 as well as additional information by country is provided in the following tables:

(In Millions of €)	September 30, 2011			September 30, 2010		
	Total	Domestic	Foreign	Total	Domestic	Foreign
Change in defined benefit obligations:						
Defined benefit obligation at beginning of year	31,475	18,897	12,578	26,944	16,163	10,781
Foreign currency exchange rate changes	234	—	234	714	—	714
Service cost	491	316	175	538	305	233
Interest cost	1,292	768	524	1,417	844	573
Settlements and curtailments	(970)	(18)	(952)	(422)	(1)	(421)
Plan participants' contributions	137	81	56	137	78	59
Amendments and other	98	20	78	32	(2)	34
Actuarial (gains) losses	(1,766)	(1,611)	(155)	3,704	2,499	1,205
Acquisitions	46	25	21	4	3	1
Benefits paid	(1,553)	(1,005)	(548)	(1,512)	(986)	(526)
Divestments	(763)	(326)	(437)	(81)	(6)	(75)
Reclassification to assets and to liabilities associated with assets classified as held for disposal for OSRAM	(1,600)	(523)	(1,077)	—	—	—
Defined benefit obligation at end of year	27,121	16,624	10,497	31,475	18,897	12,578
Germany	16,624	16,624		18,897	18,897	
U.S.	3,429		3,429	4,043		4,043
U.K.	3,053		3,053	3,585		3,585
Other	4,015		4,015	4,950		4,950

(In Millions of €)	September 30, 2011			September 30, 2010		
	Total	Domestic	Foreign	Total	Domestic	Foreign
Change in plan assets:						
Fair value of plan assets at beginning of year	24,107	14,059	10,048	21,990	13,290	8,700
Foreign currency exchange rate changes	208	—	208	618	—	618
Expected return on plan assets	1,475	886	589	1,395	841	554
Actuarial gains (losses) on plan assets	(1,653)	(1,357)	(296)	941	559	382
Acquisitions and other	79	1	78	77	—	77
Settlements	(773)	—	(773)	(172)	—	(172)
Employer contributions	849	276	573	658	245	413
Plan participants' contributions	137	81	56	137	78	59
Benefits paid	(1,470)	(973)	(497)	(1,445)	(953)	(492)
Divestments and other	(766)	(273)	(493)	(92)	(1)	(91)
Reclassification to assets and to liabilities associated with assets classified as held for disposal for OSRAM	(1,228)	(391)	(837)	—	—	—
Fair value of plan assets at end of year	20,965	12,309	8,656	24,107	14,059	10,048
Germany	12,309	12,309		14,059	14,059	
U.S.	2,346		2,346	2,952		2,952
U.K.	3,201		3,201	3,256		3,256
Other	3,109		3,109	3,840		3,840

The total defined benefit obligation at the end of the fiscal year includes €8,443 million for active employees, €3,446 million for former employees with vested benefits and €15,232 million for retirees and surviving dependents.

In fiscal 2011, the DBO decreased due to an increase in discount rate for the domestic and some foreign pension plans. Also in fiscal 2011, the DBO and the fair value of plan assets decreased by €741 million and €735 million due to the disposal of Siemens IT Solutions and Services pension liabilities and plan assets. These effects are included in line items Divestments and Divestments and other in the tables above. Furthermore, in fiscal 2011, Siemens transferred pension liabilities and plan assets of its major pension plan in the Netherlands to the industry pension fund PME. The PME will be accounted for as a defined contribution plan with a resulting decrease in DBO and plan assets. The DBO and plan asset transfer amounted to both €753 million and is included in line items Settlements and curtailments and Settlements in the tables above. In addition, a settlement gain of €68 million was recognized in equity and is included in line item Actuarial (gains) losses in the first table above. Further-

more, line item Settlements and curtailments in fiscal 2011, includes €(122) million resulting from the disposal of pension liabilities of Siemens IT Solutions and Services. In fiscal 2010, the DBO increased due to a decrease in discount rate for the domestic and foreign pension plans. Line item Settlements and curtailments in fiscal 2010, in the table above, includes €(193) million resulting from a curtailment of two defined benefit pension plans in the U.S. and €(109) million due to a partial settlement of pension plans in Canada.

Employer contributions expected to be paid to the funded pension plans during fiscal 2012 are €650 million, therein €276 million to the domestic pension plans and €374 million to the foreign pension plans. Line item Employer contributions in fiscal 2010, includes supplemental employer contributions in the U.K. The amount of €(93) million in line item Settlements in fiscal 2010, is due to the partial settlement of pension plans in Canada.

Pension Benefits: Components of NPBC

The components of the NPBC for the fiscal years ended September 30, 2011, 2010 and 2009 are as follows:

(In Millions of €)	Year Ended September 30, 2011			Year Ended September 30, 2010			Year Ended September 30, 2009		
	Total	Domestic	Foreign	Total	Domestic	Foreign	Total	Domestic	Foreign
Service Cost	431	283	148	481	287	194	461	260	201
Interest Cost	1,189	733	456	1,293	802	491	1,356	834	522
Expected return on plan assets	(1,364)	(847)	(517)	(1,281)	(801)	(480)	(1,197)	(738)	(459)
Amortization of past service cost (benefits)	12	20	(8)	20	—	20	19	18	1
Loss (gain) due to settlements and curtailments	(8)	—	(8)	(203)	—	(203)	(26)	(9)	(17)
Net periodic benefit cost	260	189	71	310	288	22	613	365	248
Germany	189	189		288	288		365	365	
U.S.	20		20	(48)		(48)	139		139
U.K.	(2)		(2)	13		13	22		22
Other	53		53	57		57	87		87

In addition to net periodic benefit cost for continuing operations presented in the table above, €(70) million, €44 million and €65 million were recognized for Siemens IT Solutions and Services and for OSRAM for the years ended September 30, 2011, 2010 and 2009. The amount of €(70) million for the year ended September 30, 2011, includes €122 million settlement gain resulting from the disposal of pension liabilities of Siemens IT Solutions and Services.

Line item Net periodic benefit cost in fiscal 2010, in the table above, includes a €193 million curtailment gain resulting from a freeze of two defined benefit pension plans in the

U.S. Employees will keep benefits earned, however, will not earn future benefits under these plans. Instead, employer contributions will be made to existing defined contribution plans.

Pension Benefits: Amounts Recognized in the Consolidated Statements of Comprehensive Income

The actuarial gains and losses on defined benefit pension plans recognized in the Consolidated Statements of Comprehensive Income for the fiscal years ended September 30, 2011, 2010 and 2009, were as follows:

(In Millions of €)	Year Ended September 30, 2011			Year Ended September 30, 2010			Year Ended September 30, 2009		
	Total	Domestic	Foreign	Total	Domestic	Foreign	Total	Domestic	Foreign
Actuarial losses (gains)	(113)	(254)	141	2,763	1,940	823	1,517	910	607
Effects in connection with asset ceiling	18	—	18	6	—	6	125	—	125
Income tax effect	146	227	(81)	(824)	(594)	(230)	(436)	(197)	(239)
Net amount recognized in the Consolidated Statements of Comprehensive Income, net of tax	51	(27)	78	1,945	1,346	599	1,206	713	493
Germany	(27)	(27)		1,346	1,346		713	713	
U.S.	228		228	138		138	130		130
U.K.	(208)		(208)	71		71	268		268
Other	58		58	390		390	95		95

For the year ended September 30, 2011, cumulative income or expense of €(6) million is recognized in line item Net amount recognized in the Consolidated Statements of Comprehensive Income, net of tax which relates to OSRAM.

Pension Benefits: Assumptions for the Calculation of the DBO and NPBC

Assumed discount rates, compensation increase rates and pension progression rates used in calculating the DBO together with long-term rates of return on plan assets vary according to the economic conditions of the country in which the retirement plans are situated or where plan assets are invested as well as capital market expectations.

The weighted-average discount rate used for the actuarial valuation of the DBO at period-end and the expected return on plan assets for the fiscal year ending at period-end were as follows:

	Year Ended September 30, 2011			Year Ended September 30, 2010			Year Ended September 30, 2009		
	Total	Domestic	Foreign	Total	Domestic	Foreign	Total	Domestic	Foreign
Discount rate	4.5%	4.7%	4.3%	4.2%	4.0%	4.4%	5.3%	5.3%	5.2%
Germany	4.7%	4.7%		4.0%	4.0%		5.3%	5.3%	
U.S.	4.10%		4.10%	4.80%		4.80%	5.69%		5.69%
U.K.	5.7%		5.7%	5.3%		5.3%	5.7%		5.7%
Expected return on plan assets	6.3%	6.5%	6.1%	6.4%	6.5%	6.2%	6.5%	6.5%	6.4%
Germany	6.5%	6.5%		6.5%	6.5%		6.5%	6.5%	
U.S.	6.95%		6.95%	6.95%		6.95%	6.97%		6.97%
U.K.	6.0%		6.0%	6.0%		6.0%	6.5%		6.5%

The rates of compensation increase for countries with significant effects with regard to this assumption were as follows for the years ended September 30, 2011, 2010 and 2009: U.S.: 3.50%, 3.52% and 3.76%, U.K.: 5.00%, 5.00% and 4.9%, Switzerland: 1.5%, 1.5% and 1.5%, Netherlands: 2.95%, 2.95% and 2.95%. The compensation increase rate for the domestic pension plans for the year ended September 30, 2011, was 2.25% (2010: 2.25%, 2009: 2.25%). However, due to the implementation of the BSAV, the effect of the compensation increase on the domestic pension plans is

substantially eliminated. The rates of pension progression for countries with significant effects with regard to this assumption were as follows for the years ended September 30, 2011, 2010 and 2009: Germany: 1.75%, 1.75% and 1.75%, U.K.: 3.1%, 3.1% and 3.0% and for the Netherlands for the years ended September 30, 2010 and 2009, 1.61% and 1.5%.

The assumptions used for the calculation of the DBO as of the period-end of the preceding fiscal year are used to determine the calculation of interest cost and service cost of the following year. The total expected return for the fiscal year will be based on the expected rates of return for the respective year multiplied by the fair value of plan assets at the preceding fiscal years period-end date. The fair value and thus the expected return on plan assets are adjusted for significant events after the fiscal year end, such as a supplemental funding.

The discount rate assumptions reflect the rates available on high-quality corporate bonds or government bonds of consistent duration and currency at the period-end date. The expected return on plan assets is determined on a uniform basis, considering long-term historical returns, asset allocation, and future estimates of long-term investment returns. In fiscal 2011 and fiscal 2010, the expected return on plan assets remained primarily unchanged. Changes of other actuarial assumptions not mentioned above, such as employee turnover, mortality, disability, etc., had an only minor effect on the overall DBO as of September 30, 2011.

Experience adjustments, which result from differences between the actuarial assumptions and the actual occurrence, decreased the DBO by 0.6% in fiscal 2011, did not affect the DBO in fiscal 2010, decreased the DBO by 0.5% in fiscal 2009, increased the DBO by 0.4% in fiscal 2008 and did not affect the DBO in fiscal 2007.

Pension Benefits: Sensitivity Analysis

A one-percentage-point change of the established assumptions mentioned above, used for the calculation of the NPBC for fiscal 2012, or a change in the fair value of plan assets of €500 million, as of September 30, 2011, respectively, would result in the following increase (decrease) of the fiscal 2012 NPBC:

| | Effect on NPBC 2012 Due to a | |
| | --- | --- |
(In Millions of €)	One-Percentage-Point/€500 Increase	One-Percentage-Point/€500 Decrease
Discount rate	57	(72)
Expected return on plan assets	(189)	189
Rate of compensation increase	18	(15)
Rate of pension progression	124	(96)
Fair value of plan assets	(32)	32

Increases and decreases in the discount rate, rate of compensation increase and rate of pension progression which are used in determining the DBO do not have a symmetrical effect on NPBC primarily due to the compound interest effect created when determining the net present value of the future pension benefit. If more than one of the assumptions were changed simultaneously, the cumulative impact would not necessarily be the same as if only one assumption was changed in isolation.

Pension Benefits: Plan Assets

The asset allocation of the plan assets of the pension benefit plans as of the period-end date in fiscal 2011 and 2010, as well as the target asset allocation for fiscal year 2012, are as follows:

| | | Asset Allocation | | | | | |
| | Target Asset Allocation | September 30, 2011 | | | September 30, 2010 | | |
Asset Class	September 30, 2012	Total	Domestic	Foreign	Total	Domestic	Foreign
Equity	20–50%	28%	29%	27%	27%	27%	28%
Fixed income	40–70%	62%	63%	62%	62%	62%	61%
Real estate	5–15%	7%	6%	8%	7%	6%	9%
Cash and other assets	0–15%	3%	2%	3%	4%	5%	2%
		100%	100%	100%	100%	100%	100%

Derivatives are reported under the asset class whose risk is hedged. Current asset allocation is composed of high quality government and selected corporate bonds. Siemens constantly reviews the asset allocation in light of the duration of its pension liabilities and analyzes trends and events that may affect asset values in order to initiate appropriate measures at a very early stage.

The plan assets include own shares and debt instruments of the Company with a fair value of €78 million and €68 million as of September 30, 2011 and 2010.

The following table shows the actual return on plan assets in fiscal 2011, 2010 and 2009:

| | Year Ended September 30, 2011 | | | Year Ended September 30, 2010 | | | Year Ended September 30, 2009 | | |
(In Millions of €)	Total	Domestic	Foreign	Total	Domestic	Foreign	Total	Domestic	Foreign
Actual return on plan assets	(178)	(471)	293	2,336	1,400	936	1,949	1,546	403

Line item Actual return on plan assets for the year ended September 30, 2011, includes €10 million related to OSRAM.

The actual return over the last twelve months amounted to a negative 0.8% or €(178) million compared to an expected return of 6.4% or €1,475 million. The experience adjustment arising on plan assets was (7.2)% in fiscal 2011 (fiscal 2010: 4.4%; fiscal 2009: 3.5%; fiscal 2008: (16.2)%; fiscal 2007: (0.9)%). For the domestic pension plans, €(471) million or (3.5)% was realized, as compared to an expected return on plan assets of 6.5% or an amount of €886 million that was included in the NPBC. For the foreign pension plans, €293 million or 3.1% was realized, as compared to an expected return on plan assets of 6.1% or an amount of €589 million that was included in the NPBC.

Pension Benefits: Pension Benefit Payments

The following overview comprises pension benefits paid out of the pension benefit plans during the years ended September 30, 2011 and 2010, and expected pension payments for the next five years and in the aggregate for the five years thereafter (undiscounted):

(In Millions of €)	Total	Domestic	Foreign
Pension benefits paid			
2010	1,512	986	526
2011	1,553	1,005	548
Expected pension payments			
2012	1,482	997	485
2013	1,516	986	530
2014	1,535	991	544
2015	1,559	1,007	552
2016	1,577	1,004	573
2017–2021	8,240	5,192	3,048

Amounts presented for the years ended September 30, 2011 and 2010 in the table above include amounts related to Siemens IT Solutions and Services and OSRAM.

As pension benefit payments for Siemens' funded pension benefit plans reduce the DBO and plan assets by the same amount, there is no impact on the funded status of such plans.

Other Post-Employment Benefits

Beginning with fiscal 2011, figures presented cover both principal and non-principal pension benefits provided by Siemens.

In Germany, employees who entered into the Company's employment on or before September 30, 1983, are entitled to transition payments for the first six months after retirement equal to the difference between their final compensation and the retirement benefits payable under the corporate pension plan. Certain foreign companies, primarily in the U.S. and Canada, provide other post-employment benefits in the form of medical, dental and life insurance. The amount of obligations for other post-employment benefits in the form of medical and dental benefits specifically depends on the expected cost trend in the healthcare sector. To be entitled to such healthcare benefits, participants must contribute to the insurance premiums. Participant contributions are based on specific regulations of cost sharing which are defined in the benefit plans. The Company has the right to adjust the cost allocation at any time, generally this is done on an annual basis. Premiums for life insurance benefits are paid solely by the Company.

The Company's other post-employment benefits are illustrated in detail in the subsequent sections with regard to:
- Obligations, plan assets and funded status,
- Components of NPBC,
- Amounts recognized in the Consolidated Statements of Comprehensive Income,
- Assumptions used in the calculation of the DBO and the NPBC,
- Sensitivity analysis, and
- Benefit payments.

Other Post-Employment Benefits: Obligations, Plan Assets and Funded Status

The funded status of plan assets and a reconciliation of the funded status to the amounts recognized in the Consolidated Statements of Financial Position are as follows:

(In Millions of €)	September 30, 2011			September 30, 2010		
	Total	Domestic	Foreign	Total	Domestic	Foreign
Fair value of plan assets	4	—	4	4	—	4
Total defined benefit obligation	764	307	457	838	350	488
Defined benefit obligation (funded)	286	—	286	278	—	278
Defined benefit obligation (unfunded)	478	307	171	560	350	210
Funded status	(760)	(307)	(453)	(834)	(350)	(484)
Unrecognized past service cost (benefits)	6	—	6	8	—	8
Net amount recognized	(754)	(307)	(447)	(826)	(350)	(476)

The following tables show a detailed reconciliation of the changes in the benefit obligation and in plan assets for other post-employment benefits for the years ended September 30, 2011 and 2010:

(In Millions of €)	September 30, 2011			September 30, 2010		
	Total	Domestic	Foreign	Total	Domestic	Foreign
Change in benefit obligations:						
Defined benefit obligation at beginning of year	838	350	488	742	333	409
Foreign currency exchange rate changes	2	—	2	25	—	25
Service cost	22	10	12	25	10	15
Interest cost	38	14	24	43	17	26
Settlements and curtailments	(11)	(2)	(9)	(7)	(5)	(2)
Plan amendments and other	2	—	2	(6)	—	(6)
Actuarial (gains) losses	(24)	(18)	(6)	77	25	52
Acquisitions	3	3	—	—	—	—
Benefits paid	(56)	(28)	(28)	(61)	(30)	(31)
Divestments	(12)	(11)	(1)	—	—	—
Reclassification to assets and to liabilities associated with assets classified as held for disposal for OSRAM	(38)	(11)	(27)	—	—	—
Defined benefit obligation at end of year	764	307	457	838	350	488

IFRS-BPPD 3.152

(In Millions of €)	September 30, 2011			September 30, 2010		
	Total	Domestic	Foreign	Total	Domestic	Foreign
Change in plan assets:						
Fair value of plan assets at beginning of year	4	—	4	3	—	3
Actual return on plan assets	—	—	—	1	—	1
Employer contributions	24	—	24	27	—	27
Benefits paid	(24)	—	(24)	(27)	—	(27)
Fair value of plan assets at end of year	4	—	4	4	—	4

Other Post-Employment Benefits: Components of NPBC

The components of the NPBC for other post-employment benefits for the years ended September 30, 2011, 2010 and 2009, are as follows:

(In Millions of €)	Year Ended September 30, 2011			Year Ended September 30, 2010			Year Ended September 30, 2009		
	Total	Domestic	Foreign	Total	Domestic	Foreign	Total	Domestic	Foreign
Service cost	21	10	11	24	10	14	17	10	7
Interest cost	36	13	23	41	17	24	45	18	27
Amortization of unrecognized past service cost (benefits)	4	—	4	2	—	2	(29)	—	(29)
Loss (gain) due to settlements and curtailments	(10)	—	(10)	(5)	—	(5)	(13)	(9)	(4)
Net periodic benefit cost	51	23	28	62	27	35	20	19	1

In addition to net periodic benefit cost for continuing operations presented in the table above, less than a million €, €(2) million and €3 million were recognized for Siemens IT Solutions and Services and for OSRAM for the years ended September 30, 2011, 2010 and 2009.

Other Post-Employment Benefits: Amounts Recognized in the Consolidated Statements of Comprehensive Income

The actuarial gains and losses on other post-employment benefit plans recognized in the Consolidated Statements of Comprehensive Income for the fiscal years ended September 30, 2011, 2010 and 2009 were as follows:

(In Millions of €)	Year Ended September 30, 2011			Year Ended September 30, 2010			Year Ended September 30, 2009		
	Total	Domestic	Foreign	Total	Domestic	Foreign	Total	Domestic	Foreign
Actuarial losses (gains)	(24)	(18)	(6)	77	25	52	54	37	17
Income tax effect	7	5	2	(27)	(8)	(19)	(17)	(11)	(6)
Net amount recognized in the Consolidated Statements of Comprehensive Income, net of tax	(17)	(13)	(4)	50	17	33	37	26	11
Germany	(13)	(13)		17	17		26	26	
U.S.	—		—	21		21	8		8
Canada	(1)		(1)	7		7	1		1
Other	(3)		(3)	5		5	2		2

For the year ended September 30, 2011, cumulative income or expense of less than a million € is recognized in line item Net amount recognized in the Consolidated Statements of Comprehensive Income, net of tax which relates to OSRAM.

Other Post-Employment Benefits: Assumptions Used in the Calculation of the DBO and NPBC

Discount rates and other key assumptions used for transition payments in Germany are the same as those utilized for domestic pension benefit plans.

The weighted-average assumptions used in calculating the actuarial values for the post-employment healthcare and life insurance benefits are as follows:

	Year Ended September 30, 2011	Year Ended September 30, 2010	Year Ended September 30, 2009
Discount rate	4.57%	5.18%	5.98%
U.S.:			
Medical trend rates (initial/ultimate/year):			
Medicare ineligible pre-65	9%/5%/2020	8%/5%/2017	8.5%/5%/2017
Medicare eligible post-65	8.5%/5%/2019	8.5%/5%/2018	9%/5%/2018
Dental trend rates (initial/ultimate/year)	6%/5%/2021	6%/5%/2021	6%/5%/2021
Canada:			
Medical trend rates (initial/ultimate/year)	9%/5%/2019	5%	5%
Drug trend rates (initial/ultimate/year)	9%/5%/2019	5%	7%/5%/2010
Dental trend rates	4%	4%	4%

Experience adjustments, which result from differences between the actuarial assumptions and the actual occurrence, decreased the DBO by 3.0% in fiscal 2011, increased the DBO by 0.5% in fiscal 2010 and decreased the DBO by 1.6%, 0.9% and 0.3% in fiscal 2009, 2008 and 2007, respectively.

Other Post-Employment Benefits: Sensitivity Analysis

The health care assumptions may be significantly influenced by the expected progression in health care expense. A one-percentage-point change in the healthcare trend rates would have resulted in the following increase (decrease) of the defined benefit obligation and the service and interest cost as of and for the year ended September 30, 2011:

	September 30, 2011 One-Percentage-Point	
(In Millions of €)	Increase	Decrease
Effect on defined benefit obligation	20	(14)
Effect on total of service and interest cost components	2	(1)

Other Post-Employment Benefits: Benefit Payments

The following overview comprises benefit payments for other post-employment benefits paid out of the other defined benefit post-employment plans during the years ended September 30, 2011 and 2010, and expected pension payments for the next five years and in the aggregate for the five years thereafter (undiscounted):

(In Millions of €)	Total	Domestic	Foreign
Payments for other post-employment benefits			
2010	61	30	31
2011	56	28	28
Expected payments for other post-employment benefits			
2012	69	39	30
2013	51	24	27
2014	56	28	28
2015	62	33	29
2016	63	34	29
2017–2021	332	182	150

Amounts presented for the years ended September 30, 2011 and 2010 in the table above include amounts related to Siemens IT Solutions and Services and OSRAM.

Since the benefit obligations for other post-employment benefits are generally not funded, such payments will impact the current operating cash flow of the Company.

Defined Contribution Plans and State Plans

The amount recognized as an expense for defined contribution plans amounted to €437 million in fiscal 2011, €334 million in fiscal 2010, and €362 million in fiscal 2009, respectively. Contributions to state plans amounted to €1,528 million in fiscal 2011, €1,453 million in fiscal 2010, and €1,519 million in fiscal 2009, respectively.

26. Other Liabilities

	September 30	
(In Millions of €)	2011	2010
Employee related liabilities	461	685
Deferred income	237	274
Other	1,169	1,321
	1,867	2,280

35. Personnel Costs

	Year Ended September 30		
(In Millions of €)	2011	2010	2009
Wages and salaries	19,167	18,311	17,397
Statutory social welfare contributions and expenses for optional support payments	3,093	2,894	2,883
Expenses relating to pension plans and employee benefits	938	681	870
	23,198	21,886	21,150

Item Expenses relating to pension plans and employee benefits includes service costs for the period. Expected return on plan assets and interest cost are included in pension related interest income (expense), see Note 9 Interest income, interest expense and other financial income (expense), net.

Included in fiscal 2010, are expenses of €0.3 billion related to special remuneration for non-management employees, see Note 37 Segment information.

IFRS-BPPD 3.152

Wages and salaries, statutory social welfare contributions and expenses for optional support payments and expenses relating to pension plans and employee benefits for continuing and discontinued operations amounts to €26,239 million, €25,709 million and €24,774 million in fiscal 2011, 2010 and 2009.

The average number of employees in fiscal years 2011, 2010 and 2009 was 350.5 thousand, 332.6 thousand and 339.7 thousand, respectively (based on continuing operations). Part-time employees are included on a proportionate basis. The employees were engaged in the following activities:

(In Thousands)	Year Ended September 30	
	2011	2010
Manufacturing and services	214.5	204.6
Sales and marketing	73.8	70.5
Research and development	27.8	27.2
Administration and general services	34.4	30.3
	350.5	332.6

The average number of employees in fiscal years 2011 and 2010 was 412.0 thousand and 403.0 thousand, respectively (based on continuing and discontinued operations). Thereof, in fiscal 2011 and 2010, 264.1 thousand and 262.1 thousand employees were engaged in manufacturing and services, 80.4 thousand and 78.0 thousand employees were engaged in sales and marketing, 30.4 thousand and 30.1 thousand employees were in research and development and 37.1 thousand and 32.8 thousand employees were in administration and general services in fiscal 2011 and 2010, respectively.

Postemployment Benefits—Corridor Method

3.153

AEGON N.V. (Dec 2011)

CONSOLIDATED INCOME STATEMENTS (in part)

Amounts in EUR Million (Except per Share Data)	Note	2011	2010	2009
Premium income	6	19,521	21,097	19,473
Investment income	7	8,167	8,762	8,681
Fee and commission income	8	1,465	1,744	1,593
Other revenues		6	5	4
Total revenues		29,159	31,608	29,751
Income from reinsurance ceded	9	2,775	1,869	1,721
Results from financial transactions	10	(187)	15,662	14,937
Other income	11	39	40	—
Total income		31,786	49,179	46,409
Premiums to reinsurers	6	3,407	1,859	1,727
Policyholder claims and benefits	12	20,191	38,081	36,899
Profit sharing and rebates	13	94	83	117
Commissions and expenses	14	6,164	6,034	5,983
Impairment charges/(reversals)	15	483	701	1,369
Interest charges and related fees	16	491	426	412
Other charges	17	69	122	389
Total charges		30,899	47,306	46,896
Income before share in profit/(loss) of associates and tax		887	1,873	(487)

NOTES TO THE CONSOLIDATED FINANCIAL STATEMENTS (in part)

Amounts in EUR million, unless otherwise stated

1 General Information

AEGON N.V., incorporated and domiciled in the Netherlands, is a public limited liability share company organized under Dutch law and recorded in the Commercial Register of The Hague under its registered address at AEGONplein 50, 2591 TV The Hague. AEGON N.V. serves as the holding company for the AEGON Group and has listings of its common shares in Amsterdam, New York and London.

AEGON N.V. (or "the Company"), its subsidiaries and its proportionally consolidated joint ventures (AEGON or "the Group") have life insurance and pensions operations in over twenty countries in the Americas, Europe and Asia and are also active in savings and asset management operations, accident and health insurance, general insurance and limited banking operations. Headquarters are located in The Hague, the Netherlands. The Group employs approximately 25,000 people worldwide.

2 Summary of Significant Accounting Policies (in part)

2.1 Basis of Presentation (in part)

The consolidated financial statements have been prepared in accordance with International Financial Reporting Standards (IFRS), as adopted by the European Union (EU), with IFRS as issued by the International Accounting Standards Board (IASB) and with Part 9 of Book 2 of the Netherlands Civil Code. The consolidated financial statements have been prepared in accordance with the historical cost convention as modified by the revaluation of investment properties and those financial instruments (including derivatives) and financial liabilities that have been measured at fair value. Information on the standards and interpretations that were adopted in 2011 is provided below in paragraph 2.1.1.

With regard to the income statement of AEGON N.V., article 402, Part 9 of Book 2 of the Netherlands Civil Code has been applied, allowing a simplified format.

The preparation of financial statements in conformity with IFRS requires management to make estimates and assumptions affecting the reported amounts of assets and liabilities as of the date of the financial statements and the reported amounts of revenues and expenses for the reporting period. Those estimates are inherently subject to change and actual results could differ from those estimates. Included among the material (or potentially material) reported amounts and disclosures that require extensive use of estimates are: fair value of certain invested assets and derivatives, deferred acquisition costs, value of business acquired and other purchased intangible assets, goodwill, policyholder claims and benefits, insurance guarantees, pension plans, income taxes and the potential effects of resolving litigated matters.

The consolidated financial statements of AEGON N.V. were approved by the Executive Board and by the Supervisory Board on March 21, 2012. The financial statements are put to the Annual General Meeting of Shareholders on May 16, 2012 for adoption. The shareholders' meeting can decide not to adopt the financial statements but cannot amend them.

2.1.2 Future Adoption of New IFRS Accounting Standards (in part)

The following standards, amendments to existing standards and interpretations, published prior to January 1, 2012, were not early adopted by the Group, but will be applied in future years:

- IAS 19 Employee Benefits[1].

IAS 19 Employee Benefits

The amended standard applies to financial years beginning on or after January 1, 2013. The amendments eliminate the option to defer the recognition of actuarial gains and losses, known as the "corridor method". The amendments streamline the presentation of changes in assets and liabilities arising from defined benefit plans, including requiring remeasurements to be presented in other comprehensive income. And furthermore, they enhance the disclosure requirements for defined benefit plans, providing information about the characteristics of defined benefit plans and the risks that entities are exposed to through participation in those plans. Based on the consolidated figures as per December 31, 2011, AEGON estimates the adverse impact on equity to be approximately EUR 1 billion (post tax).

2.22 Assets and Liabilities Relating to Employee Benefits (in part)

A. Short-Term Employee Benefits

A liability is recognized for the undiscounted amount of short-term employee absences benefits expected to be paid within one year after the end of the period in which the service was rendered. Accumulating short-term absences are recognized over the period in which the service is provided. Benefits that are not service-related are recognized when the event that gives rise to the obligation occurs.

B. Post-Employment Benefits

The Group has issued defined contribution plans and defined benefit plans. A plan is classified as a defined contribution plan when the Group has no further obligation than the payment of a fixed contribution. All other plans are classified as defined benefit plans.

Defined Contribution Plans

The contribution payable to a defined contribution plan for services provided is recognized as an expense in the income statement. An asset is recognized to the extent that the contribution paid exceeds the amount due for services provided.

Defined Benefit Plans

The defined benefit obligation is based on the terms and conditions of the plan applicable on the balance sheet date. Plan improvements are charged directly to the income statement, unless they are conditional on the continuation of employment. In this case the related cost is deducted from the liability as past service cost and amortized over the vesting period. In measuring the defined benefit obligation the Group uses the projected unit credit method and actuarial assumptions that represent the best estimate of future variables. The benefits are discounted using an interest rate based on the market yields for high-quality corporate bonds on the balance sheet date.

Plan assets are qualifying insurance policies and assets held by long-term employee benefit funds that can only be used to pay the employee benefits under the plan and are not available to the Group's creditors. They are measured at fair value and are deducted in determining the amount recognized on the statement of financial position.

The cost of the plans is determined at the beginning of the year, based on the prevalent actuarial assumptions, discount rate and expected return on plan assets. Changes in assumptions, discount rate and experience adjustments are not charged to the income statement in the period in which they occur, but are deferred.

The unrecognized actuarial gains and losses are amortized in a straight line over the average remaining working life of the employees covered by the plan, to the extent that the gains or losses exceed the corridor limits. The corridor is defined as ten percent of the greater of the defined benefit obligation or the plan assets. The amortization charge is reassessed at the beginning of each year. The corridor approach described above was not applied retrospectively to periods prior to the transition to IFRS (January 1, 2004).

AEGON recognizes gains or losses on the curtailment or settlement of a defined benefit plan when the curtailment or settlement occurs. The gain or loss on a curtailment or settlement comprise:

- Any resulting change in the present value of the defined benefit obligation.
- Any resulting change in the fair value of the plan assets.
- Any related actuarial gains and losses and past service cost that had not previously been recognized.

Where only part of an obligation is settled and in respect of closure to future accrual, the gain or loss includes a proportionate share of the previously unrecognized past service cost and actuarial gains and losses. The proportionate share is determined on the basis of the present value of the obligations before and after the curtailment or settlement.

3 Critical Accounting Estimates and Judgment in Applying Accounting Policies (in part)

Application of the accounting policies in the preparation of the financial statements requires management to apply judgment involving assumptions and estimates concerning future results or other developments, including the likelihood, timing or amount of future transactions or events. There can be no assurance that actual results will not differ materially from those estimates. Accounting policies that are critical to the financial statement presentation and that require complex estimates or significant judgment are described in the following sections.

Actuarial Assumptions

The main assumptions used in measuring DPAC, VOBA and the liabilities for life insurance contracts with fixed or guaranteed terms relate to mortality, morbidity, investment return and future expenses. Depending on local accounting principles, surrender rates may be considered.

Mortality tables applied are generally developed based on a blend of company experience and industry wide studies, taking into consideration product characteristics, own risk selection criteria, target market and past experience. Mortality experience is monitored through regular studies, the results of which are fed into the pricing cycle for new products and reflected in the liability calculation when appropriate. For contracts insuring survivorship, allowance may be made for further longevity improvements. Morbidity assumptions are based on own claims severity and frequency experience, adjusted where appropriate for industry information.

Investment assumptions are either prescribed by the local regulator or based on management's future expectations. In the latter case, the anticipated future investment returns are set by management on a countrywide basis, considering available market information and economic indicators. A significant assumption related to estimated gross profits on variable annuities and variable life insurance products in the United States and some of the smaller country units, is the annual long-term growth rate of the underlying assets. The reconsideration of this assumption may affect the original DPAC or VOBA amortization schedule, referred to as DPAC or VOBA unlocking. The difference between the original DPAC or VOBA amortization schedule and the revised schedule, which is based on estimates of actual and future gross profits, is recognized in the income statement as an expense or a benefit in the period of determination.

For 2011, AEGON kept its long-term equity market return assumption for the estimated gross profits on variable life and variable annuity products in the Americas at 9% (2010: 9%). On a quarterly basis, the difference between the estimated equity market return and the actual market return is unlocked.

In the third quarter of 2011, to reflect the low interest rate environment, AEGON has lowered its long-term assumption for 10-year US Treasury yields by 50 basis points to 4.75% (graded uniformly from 2011 yields over the next five years) and lowered the 90-day treasury yield to 0.2% for the next two years followed by a three year grade to 3% (2010: 3.5%). No change has been made to the long-term credit spread or default assumptions. In addition, AEGON has lowered its assumed return for US separate account bond fund returns by 200 basis points to 4% over the next five years, followed by a return of 6% thereafter (2010: 6% and 6% respectively).

The bond fund return is a gross assumption from which asset management and policy fees are deducted to determine the policyholder return. In total, these assumption changes led to a charge of USD 237 million in the third quarter of 2011.

A 1% decrease in the expected long-term equity growth rate with regards to AEGON's variable annuities and variable life insurance products in the United States and Canada would result in a decrease in DPAC and VOBA balances and reserve strengthening of approximately EUR 159 million. The DPAC and VOBA balances for these products in the United States and Canada amounted to EUR 2 billion at December 31, 2011.

For the fixed annuities and fixed universal life insurance products, the estimated gross profits ("EGP") calculations include a net interest rate margin, which AEGON assumes will remain practically stable under any reasonably likely interest-rate scenario.

Applying a reasonably possible increase to the mortality assumption, which varies by block of business, would reduce net income by approximately EUR 93 million. A 20% increase in the lapse assumption would increase net income by approximately EUR 44 million.

A reasonably possible increase in the assumption on maintenance expenses AEGON uses to determine EGP margins would reduce net income by approximately EUR 57 million.

Assumptions on future expenses are based on the current level of expenses, adjusted for expected expense inflation if appropriate.

Surrender rates depend on product features, policy duration and external circumstances such as the interest rate environment and competitor and policyholder behavior. Credible own experience, as well as industry published data, are used in establishing assumptions. Lapse experience is correlated to mortality and morbidity levels, as higher or lower levels of surrenders may indicate future claims will be higher or lower than anticipated. Such correlations are accounted for in the mortality and morbidity assumptions based on the emerging analysis of experience.

41 Defined Benefit Plans

	2011	2010
Retirement benefit plans	1,634	1,566
Other post-employment benefit plans	247	234
Total defined benefit plans	1,881	1,800
Retirement benefit plans in deficit	303	352
Retirement benefit plans in surplus	—	—
Total defined benefit assets	303	352
Retirement benefit plans in deficit	1,937	1,918
Other post-employment benefit plans in deficit	247	234
Total defined benefit liabilities	2,184	2,152

	2011			2010		
Movements During the Year in Defined Benefit Plans	Retirement Benefit Plans	Other Post-Employment Benefit Plans	Total	Retirement Benefit Plans	Other Post-Employment Benefit Plans	Total
At January 1	1,566	234	1,800	1,533	215	1,748
Defined benefit expenses	174	21	195	210	21	231
Contributions paid	(33)	—	(33)	(42)	—	(42)
Benefits paid	(91)	(16)	(107)	(131)	(16)	(147)
Net exchange differences	(1)	6	5	(12)	13	1
Other	19	2	21	8	1	9
At December 31	1,634	247	1,881	1,566	234	1,800

The amounts recognized in the statement of financial position are determined as follows:

Retirement Benefit Plans	2011	2010	2009	2008	2007
Present value of wholly or partly funded obligations	3,309	2,925	2,545	2,144	2,357
Fair value of plan assets	(2,543)	(2,507)	(2,092)	(1,786)	(2,541)
	766	418	453	358	(184)
Present value of wholly unfunded obligations[1]	2,272	1,952	1,831	1,644	1,622
Unrecognized actuarial gains/(losses)	(1,404)	(804)	(751)	(586)	110
Unrecognized past service cost	—	—	—	—	2
At December 31	1,634	1,566	1,533	1,416	1,550

Other Post-Employment Benefit Plans	2011	2010	2009	2008	2007
Present value of wholly or partly funded obligations	3	3	3	4	4
Fair value of plan assets	—	—	—	—	—
	3	3	3	4	4
Present value of wholly unfunded obligations	271	256	224	231	224
Unrecognized actuarial gains/(losses)	(27)	(25)	(12)	(19)	(29)
Unrecognized past service cost	—	—	—	—	—
At December 31	247	234	215	216	199

Defined Benefit Plans	2011	2010	2009	2008	2007
Present value of wholly or partly funded obligations	3,312	2,928	2,548	2,148	2,361
Fair value of plan assets	(2,543)	(2,507)	(2,092)	(1,786)	(2,541)
	769	421	456	362	(180)
Present value of wholly unfunded obligations[1]	2,543	2,208	2,055	1,875	1,846
Unrecognized actuarial gains/(losses)	(1,431)	(829)	(763)	(605)	81
Unrecognized past service cost	—	—	—	—	2
At December 31	1,881	1,800	1,748	1,632	1,749

[1] Assets held by AEGON The Netherlands backing retirement benefits of EUR 2,039 million (2010: EUR 1,747 million) do not meet the definition of plan assets and as such were not deducted in calculating this amount. Instead, these assets are recognized as general account assets. Consequently, the return on these assets also does not form part of the calculation of defined benefit expenses.

The fair value of AEGON's own financial instruments included in plan assets and the fair value of other assets used by AEGON included in planned assets was nil in both 2011 and 2010.

Defined Benefit Expenses	2011			2010		
	Retirement Benefit Plans	Other Post-Employment Benefit Plans	Total	Retirement Benefit Plans	Other Post-Employment Benefit Plans	Total
Current year service costs	87	8	95	93	6	99
Interest cost	253	12	265	259	13	272
Expected return on plan assets	(160)	—	(160)	(162)	—	(162)
Actuarial (gains)/losses recognized	47	—	47	51	—	51
(Gains)/losses on curtailment	(56)	—	(56)	(29)	—	(29)
Past service cost	3	1	4	1	2	3
Other	—	—	—	(3)	—	(3)
Total defined benefit expenses	174	21	195	210	21	231

Defined Benefit Expenses	2009		
	Retirement Benefit Plans	Other Post- Employment Benefit Plans	Total
Current year service costs	79	6	85
Interest cost	231	14	245
Expected return on plan assets	(133)	—	(133)
Actuarial (gains)/losses recognized	59	—	59
Past service cost	1	(2)	(1)
Total defined benefit expenses	237	18	255

Defined benefit expenses are included in "Commissions and expenses" in the income statement.

	2011			2010		
	Retirement Benefit Plans	Other Post-Employment Benefit Plans	Total	Retirement Benefit Plans	Other Post-Employment Benefit Plans	Total
Actual return on plan assets and reimbursement rights	50	—	50	337	—	337

Movements During the Year of the Present Value of the Defined Benefit Obligations	2011	2010
At January 1	5,136	4,603
Current year service costs	95	99
Interest cost	265	272
Contributions by plan participants	12	11
Actuarial (gains)/losses	511	258
Benefits paid	(235)	(256)
Settlements and curtailments	(69)	(40)
Past service cost	4	3
Net exchange differences	119	183
Other	17	3
At December 31	5,855	5,136

Movements During the Year in Plan Assets for Retirement Benefit Plans	2011	2010
At January 1	2,507	2,092
Expected return on plan assets	160	162
Actuarial gains/(losses)	(110)	175
Contributions by employer	44	53
Benefits paid	(128)	(109)
Net exchange differences	70	134
At December 31	2,543	2,507

Breakdown of Plan Assets for Retirement Benefit Plans	2011	2010
Equity instruments	1,335	1,418
Debt instruments	1,004	933
Other	204	156
At December 31	2,543	2,507

All other post-employment benefit plans are unfunded.

Sensitivity of Assumed Medical Cost Trend Rates

Assumed medical cost trend rates have an effect on the amounts reported for the health care plans. A one-percentage change in assumed medical cost trend rates would have the following effects:

	2011		2010	
	+1%	−1%	+1%	−1%
Aggregate of current service cost and interest cost components of net periodic post-employment medical costs	2	(1)	2	(1)
Accumulated post-employment benefit obligation for medical cost	18	(17)	18	(16)

Experience Adjustments Arising on	2011	2010	2009	2008	2007
Plan liabilities	14	59	(11)	(3)	(37)
Plan assets	(110)	175	241	(882)	64

An experience adjustment on plan liabilities is the difference between the actuarial assumptions underlying the scheme and the actual experience during the period. This excludes the effect of changes in the actuarial assumptions that would also qualify as actuarial gains and losses. Experience adjustments on plan assets are the difference between expected and actual return on assets.

Best estimate of contributions expected for the next annual period	103

Estimated Future Benefits	Pension Benefits	Other Benefits	Total
2012	250	18	268
2013	246	19	265
2014	252	20	272
2015	257	21	278
2016	264	21	285
2017–2021	1,393	116	1,509

Defined benefit plans are mainly operated by AEGON USA, AEGON The Netherlands and AEGON UK. The following sections contain a general description of the plans in each of these subsidiaries, a summary of the principal actuarial assumptions applied in determining the value of defined benefit plans and a description of the basis used to determine the overall expected rate of return on plan assets.

AEGON USA

AEGON USA has defined benefit plans covering substantially all its employees that are qualified under the Internal Revenue Service Code. The benefits are based on years of service and the employee's eligible annual compensation. The defined benefit plans were unfunded by EUR 524 million at December 31, 2011 (2010: EUR 171 million unfunded).

AEGON USA also sponsors supplemental retirement plans to provide senior management with benefits in excess of normal pension benefits. These plans are unfunded and non-qualified under the Internal Revenue Service Code. The unfunded amount related to these plans, for which a liability has been recorded, is EUR 208 million (2010 EUR 184 million).

	2011	2010
Assumptions Used to Determine Benefit Obligations at Year-End:		
Discount rate	4.50%	5.25%
Rate of increase in compensation levels	3.91%	4.59%
Assumptions Used to Determine Net Periodic Benefit Cost for the Year Ended December 31:		
Discount rate	5.25%	6.00%
Rates of increase in compensation levels	4.59%	4.59%
Expected long-term rate of return on assets	7.05%	7.65%

The expected return on plan assets is set at the long-term rate expected to be earned based on the long-term investment strategy and the various classes of the invested funds. For each asset class, a long-term asset return assumption is developed taking into account the long-term level of risk of the asset and historical returns of the asset class. A weighted average expected long-term rate was developed based on long-term returns for each asset class and the target asset allocation of the plan.

AEGON USA provides health care benefits to retired employees, which are predominantly unfunded. The post-retirement health benefit liability amounts to EUR 197 million (2010: EUR 185 million).

The principal actuarial assumptions that apply for the year ended December 31, 2011 are as follows:

	2011	2010
Assumed Health Care Trend Rates:		
Health care cost trend rate assumed for next year	7.25%	7.50%
Rate that the cost trend rate gradually declines to	5.00%	5.00%
Year that the rate reaches the rate that it is assumed to remain at	2020	2020
Target Allocation of Plan Assets for Retirement Benefit Plans for the Next Annual Period Is:		
Equity instruments	53–73%	53–73%
Debt instruments	15–35%	15–35%
Other	0–15%	0–15%

The overall goal of the plans is to maximize total investment returns to provide sufficient funding for the present and anticipated future benefit obligations within the constraints of a prudent level of portfolio risk and diversification. AEGON believes that the asset allocation is an important factor in determining the long-term performance of the plans. From time to time the actual asset allocation may deviate from the desired asset allocation ranges due to different market performance among the various asset categories. If it is determined that rebalancing is required, future additions and withdrawals will be used to bring the allocation to the desired level.

Pension plan contributions were not required for AEGON USA in 2011 or 2010.

AEGON The Netherlands

AEGON The Netherlands has a number of defined benefit plans and a small defined contribution plan. The contributions to the retirement benefit plan of AEGON The Netherlands are paid by both the employees and the employer, with the employer contribution being variable. The benefits covered are retirement benefits, disability, death and survivor pension and are based on an average salary system. Employees earning more than EUR 45,749 per year (as at January 1, 2011) have an option to contribute to a defined contribution plan for the excess salary. However, the cost for the company remains the same. The defined benefit plans were unfunded by EUR 2,050 million at December 31, 2011 (2010: EUR 1,756 million). Assets held by AEGON The Netherlands for retirement benefits do not meet the definition of plan assets and as such were not deducted in calculating this amount. Instead, these assets are recognized as general account assets. Consequently, the return on these assets do not form part of the calculation of defined benefit expenses.

AEGON The Netherlands also has a post-retirement medical plan that contributes to the health care coverage of employees and beneficiaries after retirement. The liability related to this plan amounted to EUR 46 million at December 31, 2011 (2010: EUR 46 million).

Assumptions Used to Determine Benefit Obligations at Year-End:

	2011	2010
Discount rate	4.60%	5.25%
Salary increase rate	2.50%	2.50%
Social security increase rate	2.00%	2.50%
Pension increase rate	2.00%	2.00%

Assumptions Used to Determine Net Periodic Benefits Costs for the Year Ended December 31:

	2011	2010
Discount rate	5.25%	5.30%
Salary increase rate	2.50%	2.50%
Social security increase rate	2.50%	2.50%
Pension increase rate	2.00%	2.00%
Health care cost trend rate assumed for next year	2.00%	0.00–2.00%
Rate that the cost trend rate gradually declines to	2.00%	0.00–2.00%
Year that the rate reaches the rate it is assumed to remain at	N.A.	N.A.

AEGON UK

AEGON UK operates a defined benefit pension scheme providing benefits for staff based on final pensionable salary. The assets of the scheme are held under trust separately from those of the Group. The assets of the scheme are held in policies affected with Scottish Equitable plc. In 2011, the scheme was closed to new entrants. This resulted in a curtailment gain of EUR 56 million. The remaining unrealized actuarial losses amount to EUR 177 million. Under IAS 19, the defined benefit plan has a deficit of EUR 242 million at December 31, 2011 (2010: EUR 247 million).

For each asset class, a long-term return assumption is derived taking into account market conditions, historical returns (both absolute returns and returns relative to other asset classes) and general forecasts for future returns. Government bonds are taken as providing the return with the least risk. The expected long-term rate of return is calculated as a weighted average of these assumed rates, taking account of the long-term strategic allocation of funds across the different classes adopted by the trustees of the scheme.

Assumptions Used to Determine Benefit Obligations at Year-End:

	2011	2010
Discount rate	4.70%	5.40%
Salary increase rate	2.00–4.00%	4.40%
Pension increase rate	2.20–3.00%	2.60–3.30%
Price inflation	2.20–3.00%	3.40%
Expected long-term return on assets	4.70%	6.00%

Assumptions Used to Determine Net Periodic Benefit Costs for the Year Ended December 31, 2011:

	2011	2010
Discount rate	5.40%	5.70%
Salary increase rate	4.40%	4.90%
Pension increase rate	2.60–3.30%	3.60%
Price inflation	3.40%	3.60%
Expected long-term return on assets	6.00%	6.40%
Target allocation of plan assets for retirement benefit plans for the next annual period is:		
Equity instruments	40%	50%
Debt instruments	60%	50%

New Markets

New Markets mostly operate defined contribution plans.

Post-Employment Benefits—Retrospective Application of Change in Accounting Policy to Recognize Actuarial Gains and Losses in Other Comprehensive Income

3.154

Coca-Cola Hellenic Bottling Company S.A. (Dec 2011)

CONSOLIDATED INCOME STATEMENT (in part)

		Year Ended 31 December		
	Note	2011 € Million	2010[1] € Million	2009[1] € Million
Net sales revenue	3	6,854.3	6,793.6	6,543.6
Cost of goods sold		(4,258.8)	(4,048.6)	(3,904.7)
Gross profit		2,595.5	2,745.0	2,638.9
Operating expenses	20	(2,055.6)	(2,058.4)	(1,984.2)
Restructuring costs	20	(71.5)	(36.7)	(44.9)
Other items	20	—	—	32.8
Operating profit	3	468.4	649.9	642.6
Finance income		9.8	7.4	9.4
Finance costs		(96.1)	(83.1)	(82.2)
Loss on net monetary position	21	(7.8)	—	—
Total finance costs, net	21	(94.1)	(75.7)	(72.8)
Share of results of equity method investments	6	1.2	2.5	(1.9)
Profit before tax		375.5	576.7	567.9
Tax	3,22	(102.7)	(138.0)	(142.9)
Profit after tax		272.8	438.7	425.0

[1] Comparative figures have been restated where necessary to reflect changes in accounting policy as detailed in Note 1.

CONSOLIDATED STATEMENT OF COMPREHENSIVE INCOME (in part)

	Year Ended 31 December		
	2011 € Million	2010[1] € Million	2009[1] € Million
Profit after tax	272.8	438.7	425.0
Other comprehensive income:			
Actuarial (losses)/gains	(31.8)	2.7	4.4
Income tax relating to components of other comprehensive income (refer to Note 24)	3.9	(0.3)	2.8
Other comprehensive income for the year, net of tax (refer to Note 24)	(74.9)	173.7	(82.7)
Total comprehensive income for the year	197.9	612.4	342.3

[1] Comparative figures have been restated where necessary to reflect changes in accounting policy as detailed in Note 1.

NOTES TO THE CONSOLIDATED FINANCIAL STATEMENTS (in part)

1. Basis of Preparation and Accounting Policies

Description of Business

Coca-Cola Hellenic Bottling Company S.A. ('Coca-Cola Hellenic' or 'the Group') is a Société Anonyme (corporation) incorporated in Greece and founded in 1969. It took its current form in August 2000 through the acquisition of the Coca-Cola Beverages plc ('CCB') by Hellenic Bottling Company S.A. ('HBC'). Coca-Cola Hellenic and its subsidiaries (collectively 'the Company' or 'the Group') are principally engaged in the production, sales and distribution of non-alcoholic ready to drink beverages, under franchise from The Coca-Cola Company ('TCCC'). The Company distributes its products in 27 countries in Europe and Nigeria. Information on the Company's operations by segment is included in Note 3.

Coca-Cola Hellenic's shares are listed on the Athens Exchange (symbol: EEEK), with a secondary listing on the London Stock Exchange (symbol: CCB). Coca-Cola Hellenic's American Depositary Receipts (ADRs) are listed on the New York Stock Exchange (symbol: CCH).

These consolidated financial statements were approved for issue by the Board of Directors on 15 March 2012 and are expected to be verified at the Annual General Meeting to be held on 25 June 2012.

Basis of Preparation

The consolidated financial statements included in this document are prepared in accordance with International Financial Reporting Standards ('IFRS') issued by the International Accounting Standards Board ('IASB') and IFRS as adopted by the European Union ('EU').

All IFRS issued by the IASB, which apply to the preparation of these consolidated financial statements, have been adopted by the EU following an approval process undertaken by the European Commission and the European Financial Reporting Advisory Group ('EFRAG').

The consolidated financial statements are prepared under the historical cost convention, as modified by the revaluation of available-for-sale financial assets and derivative financial instruments and the financial statements of certain subsidiaries operating in a hyperinflationary economy which are restated and expressed in terms of the measuring unit currency at the balance sheet date and translated to Euro at the exchange rate of the balance sheet date.

Employee Benefits

The Group operates a number of defined benefit and defined contribution pension plans in its territories.

The defined benefit plans are made up of both funded and unfunded pension plans and employee leaving indemnities. The assets of funded plans are generally held in separate trustee-administered funds and are financed by payments from employees and/or the relevant Group companies.

The liability recognised in the balance sheet in respect of defined benefit plans is the present value of the defined benefit obligation at the balance sheet date less the fair value of the plan assets, together with adjustments for unrecognised past service costs. The value of any defined benefit asset recognised is restricted to the sum of any past service costs and the present value of any economic benefits available in the form of refunds from the plan or reductions in the future contributions to the plan.

For defined benefit pension plans, pension costs are assessed using the projected unit credit method. Actuarial gains and losses are recognised in full in the period in which they occur in other comprehensive income. Such actuarial gains and losses are also immediately recognised in retained earnings and are not reclassified to the income statement in subsequent periods. The defined benefit obligations are measured at the present value of the estimated future cash outflows using interest rates of corporate or government bonds, depending on whether or not there is a deep market for corporate bonds in the relevant country, which have terms to maturity approximating the terms of the related liability. Past service cost is recognised immediately to the extent that the benefits are already vested and otherwise are amortised over the remaining vesting period.

A number of the Group's operations have other long service benefits in the form of jubilee plans. These plans are measured at the present value of the estimated future cash outflows with immediate recognition of actuarial gains and losses.

The Group's contributions to the defined contribution pension plans are charged to the income statement in the period to which the contributions relate.

Changes in Accounting Policy

Coca-Cola Hellenic has assessed its accounting policy with regard to IAS 19 *Employee Benefits* and the recognition of actuarial gains and losses arising from its post employment defined benefit plans. The Group previously recognised these actuarial gains and losses based on the corridor method (i.e. only the net cumulative unrecognised actuarial gains and losses of the previous period which exceeded 10% of the higher of the defined benefit obligation and the fair value of the plan assets were recognised) in accordance with IAS 19. As a consequence, its balance sheet did not reflect a significant part of the net actuarial assets and liabilities.

As of 1 January 2011, the Group determined that it would change its accounting policy to recognise actuarial gains and losses, in the period in which they occur, in other comprehensive income (OCI) as it believes this policy provides reliable and more relevant information about the effects of employee benefits on the Group's financial position and financial performance. Changes have to apply retrospectively in accordance with IAS 8 *Accounting Policies, Changes in Accounting Estimates and Errors*, resulting in the restatement of prior year financial information.

As a result of the voluntary accounting policy change, the following adjustments were made to the consolidated financial statements:

	Year Ended 31 December 2010 € Million	Year Ended 31 December 2009 € Million
Profit after tax		
Profit before change in accounting policy	434.9	421.6
Reversal of actuarial losses	4.9	3.8
Change in deferred tax	(1.1)	(0.4)
Profit after change in accounting policy	438.7	425.0

	Year Ended 31 December 2010 € Million	Year Ended 31 December 2009 € Million
Total comprehensive income		
Total comprehensive income before change in accounting policy	606.5	334.9
Net change to profit after tax	3.8	3.4
Reversal of actuarial losses in other comprehensive income	2.7	4.4
Change in deferred tax	(0.6)	(0.4)
Total comprehensive income after change in accounting policy	612.4	342.3

Earnings per share for the twelve months ended 31 December 2010 and 2009 as a result of the restatement increased from €1.16 to €1.17 and from €1.09 to €1.10 respectively.

If the accounting policy had not been changed, the profit after tax for the twelve months ended 31 December 2011 would have been €1.0 million lower and the actuarial gains and losses recognised in other comprehensive income and pension liability would have remained to a large extent un-recognised.

	As at 31 December 2010 € Million	As at 31 December 2009 € Million	As at 1 January 2009 € Million
Consolidated statement of changes in equity			
Equity before change in accounting policy	3,095.9	2,595.9	2,930.8
Allocation of unrecognised net losses to retained earnings	(34.0)	(39.5)	(47.3)
Allocation of unrecognised net losses to non-controlling interests	(1.1)	(1.5)	(1.1)
Equity after change in accounting policy	3,060.8	2,554.9	2,882.4

	As at 31 December 2010 € Million	As at 31 December 2009 € Million
Non-current provisions		
Non-current provisions before change in accounting policy	119.9	129.6
Recognition of actuarial losses	24.3	40.8
Non-current provisions after change in accounting policy	144.2	170.4

	As at 31 December 2010 € Million	As at 31 December 2009 € Million
Deferred tax liabilities		
Deferred tax liabilities before change in accounting policy	172.8	142.3
Change in deferred tax	(9.9)	(8.8)
Deferred tax liabilities after change in accounting policy	162.9	133.5

	As at 31 December 2010 € Million	As at 31 December 2009 € Million
Other non-current assets		
Other non-current assets before change in accounting policy	61.3	57.5
Recognition of actuarial losses	(20.9)	(12.0)
Other non-current assets after change in accounting policy	40.4	45.5

	As at 31 December 2010 € Million	As at 31 December 2009 € Million
Deferred tax assets		
Deferred tax assets before change in accounting policy	34.8	29.6
Change in deferred tax	0.2	3.0
Deferred tax assets after change in accounting policy	35.0	32.6

17. Provisions (in part)

Provisions consisted of the following at 31 December:

	2011 € Million	2010 € Million	2009 € Million
Current			
Employee benefits	23.9	22.4	22.5
Restructuring and other	28.1	16.1	18.6
Total current provisions	52.0	38.5	41.1
Non-current			
Employee benefits	146.5	130.5	151.1
Other	3.0	13.7	19.3
Total non-current provisions	149.5	144.2	170.4
Total provisions	201.5	182.7	211.5

Employee Benefits

Employee benefits consisted of the following at 31 December:

	2011 € Million	2010 € Million	2009 € Million
Defined benefit plans			
Employee leaving indemnities	94.6	99.4	113.4
Pension plans	41.4	19.5	25.0
Long service benefits—jubilee plans	7.9	7.7	7.0
Total defined benefits plans	143.9	126.6	145.4
Other employee benefits			
Annual leave	9.2	9.6	6.7
Stock appreciation rights	—	0.1	1.2
Other employee benefits	17.3	16.6	20.3
Total other employee benefits	26.5	26.3	28.2
Total employee benefits obligations	170.4	152.9	173.6

Employee benefit obligations at 31 December were split between current and non-current as follows:

	2011 € Million	2010 € Million	2009 € Million
Current	23.9	22.4	22.5
Non-current	146.5	130.5	151.1
Total employee benefits obligations	170.4	152.9	173.6

20. Total Operating Costs (in part)

(e) Staff Costs

Staff costs included in the income statement in operating expenses and in the cost of goods sold lines are analysed as follows:

	2011 € Million	2010 € Million	2009 € Million
Wages and salaries	828.4	840.0	779.0
Social security costs	175.7	161.0	151.0
Pension and other employee benefits	131.1	124.6	159.6
Termination benefits	48.6	32.8	35.2
Total staff costs	1,183.8	1,158.4	1,124.8

Staff costs included in operating expenses amounted to €934.3m in 2011 (2010: €913.0m, 2009: €892.3m).

Staff costs included in cost of goods sold amounted to €249.5m in 2011 (2010: €245.4m, 2009: €232.5m).

The average number of full-time equivalent employees in 2011 was 41,715 (2010: 42,505, 2009: 44,231).

IFRS 2, *SHARE-BASED PAYMENT*

Author's Note

IASB amended IFRS 2 by issuing the following new standards.

- IFRS 9
  This amendment replaces references to IAS 39, with references to IFRS 9.
- IFRS 10
  This amendment replaces references to IAS 27 with references to IFRS 10.
- IFRS 11
  This amendment replaces references to IAS 31 with references to IFRS 11.
- IFRS 13
  This amendment explains that IFRS 2 uses the term *fair value* in a way that differs from the definition of fair value in IFRS 13. An entity should use the definition of fair value in IFRS 2 when applying this standard.

Because these standards are effective for annual periods beginning on or after 1 January 2012, these amendments are not reflected in the commentary in this section. However, these amendments would not affect the content or availability of illustrative excerpts from survey companies' financial statements.

IFRS Overview and Comparison to U.S. GAAP

3.155 The objective of IFRS 2 is to reflect the effects of share-based payment transactions, whether with employees or others, in an entity's profit or loss and financial position for the reporting period. IFRS 2 defines *share-based payment transactions* as transfers of an entity's equity instruments by its shareholders to parties that have supplied goods or services to the entity, including employees, unless the transfer is clearly for a purpose other than payment for goods or services supplied to the entity. Included in this definition are transfers of equity instruments of the entity's parent, or equity instruments of another entity in the same group as the reporting entity, to parties that have supplied goods or services to the entity. The term *goods* includes inventories, consumables, PPE, intangible assets, and other nonfinancial assets.

3.156 Also within the scope of IFRS 2 are share options (for example, contracts giving the holder the right, but not the obligation, to subscribe to an entity's shares at a fixed or determinable price for a specific period of time) and other equity instruments granted to employees as part of their compensation for services rendered to the entity.

3.157 The revisions to IFRS 3, *Business Combinations*, in 2008 amended the guidance in IFRS 2 related to business combinations. An entity should apply those amendments for annual periods beginning on or after 1 July 2009. If an entity applies IFRS 3 (revised 2008) in an earlier period, the entity should apply the amendments to IFRS 2 from that earlier period.

Author's Note

See section 2, beginning with paragraph 2.352, for further discussion of accounting for share-based payments and comparison to U.S. GAAP.

Recognition and Measurement

IFRSs

3.158 An entity should apply the accounting for share-based payments in IFRS 2 to equity-settled, cash-settled, and other transactions in which it receives or acquires goods or services in exchange for its equity instruments (equity-settled), amounts based on the price or value of these instruments (cash settled), or when either the entity can settle with or the supplier (employee) can choose to receive the entity's equity instruments.

3.159 In the case in which the supplier chooses the settlement option, IFRS 2 considers the entity to have issued a compound financial instrument. This compound instrument includes both a debt component (that is, the supplier's right to demand payment in cash) and an equity component (that is, the supplier's right to demand settlement in equity instruments rather than in cash). When the fair value of the goods or services is measured directly, the entity should measure the debt component (that is, the right to receive cash) first and then measure the equity component as the difference between the fair values of the goods and services and the debt component. In the case the entity chooses the settlement option, the entity may still recognize a liability if the option to issue equity has no commercial substance (for example, the entity is prohibited from issuing equity) or it has a past practice of always settling in cash. Only if no present obligation exists should the entity account for the transaction as equity-settled.

3.160 Under IFRS 2, at the time the entity receives goods or services, it should recognize the goods and services received and either a corresponding decrease in equity for equity-settled transactions or a liability for cash-settled transactions. When such transactions do not result in recognition of an asset, the entity recognizes an expense in profit or loss.

3.161 The entity should measure equity-settled transactions at the fair value of the goods and services received, unless the fair value cannot be measured reliably. Otherwise, the entity measures the transaction at the fair value of the equity instruments granted. The latter measurement is generally the case for services received from employees. In contrast, when goods or services are received from nonemployees, IFRS 2 states that there is a rebuttable presumption that transactions with others can be measured directly by reference to the fair value of the goods or services received.

3.162 An important issue with respect to share-based payments is whether the supplier is vested (entitled to the payment) at the time of the grant. When suppliers are vested immediately, the entity recognizes the transaction as if the services have been received in full. When the entity requires suppliers to complete an additional period of service before vesting, it should recognize the services received over the vesting period.

3.163 When share-based payment transactions are measured by reference to the fair value of the equity instruments granted, IFRS 2 requires an entity to measure the transaction at the grant date for transactions with employees and at the date the entity receives the goods or services for other suppliers. Only when market prices are not available should the entity estimate the fair value of the equity instruments using a valuation technique consistent with generally accepted valuation methodologies for financial instruments. An entity should incorporate in the formula the factors and assumptions that knowledgeable and willing parties to the transaction would incorporate.

3.164 An entity should incorporate market-vesting and non-vesting conditions into the fair value estimation process but not performance-vesting conditions or reload features.

3.165 An entity should not make subsequent adjustments to either the goods or services rendered or equity after the vesting date, even when employees forfeit the instruments granted.

3.166 In the rare case that the fair value of neither the goods and services nor the equity instruments can be measured reliably, the entity should measure the equity instruments at intrinsic value at the date the entity receives the goods or services. Subsequently, the entity should remeasure the intrinsic value of the equity instruments at each reporting date and the final settlement date and recognize the change in intrinsic value in profit or loss. The entity should also recognize the goods or services received based on the number of equity instruments that ultimately vest or are exercised.

3.167 An entity should only recognize the effects of modifications to the terms or conditions on which equity instruments are granted when the modifications increase the total fair value of the share-based payment transaction. When a grant is cancelled or settled during the vesting period, other than by forfeiture, the entity should consider this action to be an acceleration of vesting and recognize the remaining amount immediately. An entity should account for any payments to employees from such cancellation or modification as a return of equity. An entity should consider grants of new equity instruments as replacements of those cancelled and account for them as if they were modifications.

3.168 An entity should measure cash-settled transactions (for example, share appreciation rights) at the fair value of the liability incurred. Until the liability is settled, the entity remeasures the liability at the end of each reporting period and at settlement and recognizes the change in the liability in profit or loss for the period.

U.S. GAAP

3.169 FASB ASC provides guidance on equity-based payments in different sections. FASB ASC 718 includes guidance on share-based payments to employees, whether classified as equity or liabilities, and FASB ASC 505, *Equity*, includes guidance on equity-based payments to nonemployees. The guidance in these sections differs in some respects. FASB ASC 505-50-30-6 requires measurement of share-based payments to nonemployees at either the fair value of the goods or services received or the fair value of the equity instruments, whichever is more reliably measurable. In contrast, when the fair value of the goods or services can be measured reliably, IFRS 2 requires an entity to use that measure. However, as expressed in SEC *Codification of Staff Accounting Bulletins* topic 14(A), "Share-Based Payment Transactions with Nonemployees," the SEC staff believes that, generally, an entity should apply by analogy the U.S. guidance for employee share-based payments to share-based payment transactions with nonemployees, unless other authoritative accounting literature more clearly addresses the appropriate accounting or the application of this guidance would be inconsistent with the terms of the instrument issued. Therefore, the remainder of this section only compares IFRS 2 with the requirements for employee share-based payments in FASB ASC 718.

3.170 Like IFRS 2, FASB ASC 718 prescribes different accounting treatments for equity-settled and cash-settled share-based payment transactions because this classification determines whether the entity recognizes a change in equity or a liability. Paragraphs 6–19 of FASB ASC 718-10-25 provide more extensive guidance to an entity in making this classification and address the following instruments specifically:

- Puttable or callable shares that do not meet certain conditions
- Options or similar instruments related to shares that the entity either has recognized as a liability or could be required to settle in cash or other assets
- Awards indexed to another factor besides the entity's share price
- Awards with substantive terms that differ from the written terms
- Awards with a provision permitting broker-assisted cashless exercise
- Awards with a provision related to the entity's minimum statutory withholding requirements

For all other instruments, FASB ASC 718-10-25-6 directs the entity to the general requirements of GAAP for distinguishing liabilities from equity. IFRS 2 does not specifically address the preceding instruments.

3.171 For employee share-based payments, FASB ASC 718-10-30-2 generally requires an entity to measure the transaction at the fair value of the equity instruments at the grant date, except as previously noted in FASB ASC 718-10-30-4 when a reasonable estimate of fair value is not possible. As stated by paragraphs 6–7 of FASB ASC 718-10-30, an entity should measure these instruments based on observable market prices for options or other instruments with similar features and conditions and include factors such as volatility.

3.172 Like IFRSs, FASB ASC 718-10-30 includes specific requirements for whether and how to incorporate vesting conditions, nontransferability, performance or services conditions, market conditions, and reload and contingency features, among others, into the measurement of the transaction.

3.173 Like IFRSs, FASB ASC 718-10-30-22 requires an entity to use intrinsic value when the entity cannot reasonably estimate the fair value of the equity instrument, and FASB ASC 718-10-55-9 requires an entity to remeasure liabilities to their fair values at each reporting date until the liability is settled.

3.174 FASB ASC 718-40 and 718-50 also provide separate guidance on accounting for employee stock ownership plans and employee share purchase plans.

Presentation

IFRSs

3.175 For each class of share capital, IAS 1 requires an entity to present shares reserved for share issue under options and contracts for the sale of shares, including terms and amounts, either in the balance sheet, statement of changes in equity, or in the notes.

U.S. GAAP

3.176 FASB ASC 718 does not provide specific guidance on stock compensation presentation. Like other compensation, stock compensation could be included in cost of goods sold or administrative expenses as appropriate. See the discussion over presentation of related liabilities in paragraph 2.359 of section 2. However, for SEC registrants, SEC *Codification of Staff Accounting Bulletins* topic 14(F), "Classification of Compensation Expense Associated with Share-Based Payment Arrangements," requires this expense to be included in the same line item as cash compensation to the same employee. The SEC staff believes that SEC registrants should consider disclosing the portion of the expense related to the share-based payment, with appropriate disclosure, in a parenthetical note to the respective income statement line item, on the cash flow statement, in the notes to the financial statements, or in the management discussion and analysis.

Disclosure

IFRSs

3.177 IFRS 2 requires an entity to disclose information that enables users of its financial statements to understand the effect of share-based payments on the financial statements. At a minimum, IFRS 2 requires disclosures about the various share-based payment arrangements in existence during the period, including the following:

- Detailed descriptions, including general terms and conditions
- Number and weighted average exercise prices of share options outstanding at the beginning of the period; options granted, exercised, forfeited, and expired during the period; and options exercisable and outstanding at the end of the period
- For options exercised, weighted average share price on exercise dates
- For options outstanding at the end of the period, range of exercise prices and weighted average remaining lives

3.178 IFRS 2 also requires disclosures about the methods used to determine the fair value of the goods or services or the equity instruments granted. For share options, these disclosures include option pricing models used, inputs to those models, assumptions required, information about volatility, and how other features of the arrangement have been incorporated into the model. For other instruments, these disclosures include whether the entity used observable market data, how that data was determined, and whether the model took dividends into account. An entity should also disclose information about any modifications made to these arrangements.

3.179 With respect to the effects of share-based payment transactions on profit or loss, an entity should disclose the total expense recognized immediately in profit or loss during the period, with separate disclosure of the amount associated with equity-settled transactions. When the entity has recognized liabilities, the entity should disclose end of period amounts of the total carrying amount and total intrinsic value of liabilities for which the suppliers' rights are vested.

3.180 IAS 24, *Related Party Disclosures*, also requires disclosures about share-based payments.

U.S. GAAP

3.181 U.S. GAAP disclosure requirements are very similar to those in IFRS 2. IFRSs rely more heavily on the principle that an entity should disclose information that enables users to understand the effects of share-based payment transactions on the balance sheet and the statement of comprehensive income. In contrast, FASB ASC 718-10-50 specifies more items that an entity should disclose (for example, cash flow effects and amount capitalized as part of the cost of an asset).

Presentation and Disclosure Excerpts

Author's Note

For completeness, related excerpts from the statement of changes in equity are provided for each of the provided disclosure excerpts.

Stock Option Plan—Cash Settled and Equity Settled

3.182

Thomson Reuters Corporation (Dec 2011)

CONSOLIDATED INCOME STATEMENT (in part)

(Millions of U.S. Dollars, Except per Share Amounts)	Notes	Year Ended December 31 2011	2010
Revenues		13,807	13,070
Operating expenses	5	(9,997)	(10,061)
Depreciation		(438)	(457)
Amortization of computer software		(659)	(572)
Amortization of other identifiable intangible assets		(612)	(545)
Goodwill impairment	17	(3,010)	—
Other operating gains (losses), net	6	204	(16)
Operating (loss) profit		(705)	1,419

NOTES TO THE CONSOLIDATED FINANCIAL STATEMENTS (in part)

(Unless otherwise stated, all amounts are in millions of U.S. dollars)

Note 1: Summary of Business and Significant Accounting Policies (in part)

General Business Description

Thomson Reuters Corporation (the "Company" or "Thomson Reuters") is an Ontario, Canada corporation with common shares listed on the Toronto Stock Exchange ("TSX") and the New York Stock Exchange ("NYSE") and Series II preference shares listed on the TSX. The Company provides intelligent information to businesses and professionals. Its offerings combine industry expertise with innovative technology to deliver critical information to decision makers.

These financial statements were approved by the Company's board of directors on March 7, 2012.

Basis of Preparation (in part)

These consolidated financial statements were prepared in accordance with International Financial Reporting Standards ("IFRS"), as issued by the International Accounting Standards

Board ("IASB"), on a going concern basis, under the historical cost convention, as modified by the revaluation of financial assets and financial liabilities (including derivative instruments) at fair value.

The preparation of financial statements in accordance with IFRS requires the use of certain critical accounting estimates. It also requires management to exercise judgment in applying the Company's accounting policies. The areas involving a higher degree of judgment or complexity, or areas where assumptions and estimates are significant to the financial statements are disclosed in note 2.

Share-Based Compensation Plans (in part)

The Company operates a number of equity-settled and cash-settled share-based compensation plans under which it receives services from employees as consideration for equity instruments of the Company or cash payments based on the value of equity instruments of the Company.

For equity-settled share-based compensation, expense is based on the grant date fair value of the awards expected to vest over the vesting period. For cash-settled share-based compensation, the expense is determined based on the fair value of the liability at the end of the reporting period until the award is settled. The expense is recognized over the vesting period, which is the period over which all of the specified vesting conditions are satisfied. For awards with graded vesting, the fair value of each tranche is recognized over its respective vesting period. At the end of each reporting period, the Company re-assesses its estimates of the number of awards that are expected to vest and recognizes the impact of the revisions in the income statement.

Note 5: Operating Expenses

The components of operating expenses include the following:

	Year Ended December 31 2011	2010
Salaries, commissions and allowances	5,132	4,852
Share-based payments	87	92
Post-employment benefits	242	229
Total staff costs	5,461	5,173
Goods and services[1]	2,487	2,637
Data	1,044	1,006
Telecommunications	628	635
Real estate	526	493
Fair value adjustments[2]	(149)	117
Total operating expenses	9,997	10,061

[1] Goods and services include professional fees, consulting services, contractors, technology-related expenses, selling and marketing, and other general and administrative costs.

[2] Fair value adjustments primarily represent mark-to-market impacts on embedded derivatives and certain share-based awards.

Note 24: Share-Based Compensation

The Company operates a number of equity-settled and cash-settled share-based compensation plans under which it receives services from employees as consideration for equity instruments of the Company or cash payments. Each plan is described below:

Stock Incentive Plan

Under its stock incentive plan, the Company may grant stock options, TRSUs, PRSUs and other awards to certain employees for a maximum of up to 50 million common shares. As of December 31, 2011, there were 19,292,115 awards available for grant (2010—20,265,608).

The following table summarizes the methods used to measure fair value for each type of award and the related vesting period over which compensation expense is recognized:

Type of Award	Vesting Period	Fair Value Measure	Equity Settled Compensation Expense Based on	Cash Settled[1] Compensation Expense Based on
Stock options	Up to four years	Black-Scholes option pricing model	Fair value on business day prior to grant date	Fair value at reporting date
TRSUs	Up to seven years	Closing common share price	Fair value on business day prior to grant date	Fair value at reporting date
PRSUs	Three year performance period	Closing common share price	Fair value on business day prior to grant date	Fair value at reporting date

[1] Cash settled awards represent the portion of share-based compensation relating to withholding tax.

Additional information on each type of award is as follows:

Stock Options

The maximum term of an option is 10 years from the date of grant. Under the plan, options may be granted by reference to the Company's common share price on the NYSE or TSX.

The weighted-average fair value of options granted for the years ended December 31, 2011 and 2010 and principal assumptions used in applying the Black-Scholes option pricing model were as follows:

	2011	2010
Weighted average fair value ($)	8.39	8.92
Weighted average of key assumptions:		
Share price ($)	38.90	35.22
Exercise price ($)	38.90	35.22
Risk-free interest rate	2.6%	2.8%
Dividend yield	3.3%	3.1%
Volatility factor	29%	33%
Expected life (in years)	6	6

The Black-Scholes model was developed for use in estimating the fair value of traded options that have no vesting restrictions. The model requires the use of subjective assumptions, including expected stock-price volatility. Historical data has been considered in setting the assumptions.

Time-Based Restricted Share Units (TRSUs)

TRSUs give the holder the right to receive one common share for each unit that vests on the vesting date. The holders of TRSUs have no voting rights and accumulate additional units based on notional dividends paid by the Company on its common shares on each dividend payment date, which are reinvested as additional TRSUs. The weighted-average fair value of TRSUs granted was $35.31 and $36.55 for the years ended December 31, 2011 and 2010, respectively.

Performance Restricted Share Units (PRSUs)

PRSUs give the holder the right to receive one common share for each unit that vests on the vesting date. The holders of PRSUs have no voting rights and accumulate additional units based on notional dividends paid by the Company on its common shares on each dividend payment date, which are reinvested as additional PRSUs. The percentage of PRSUs initially granted that vests depends upon the Company's performance over a three-year period against pre-established performance goals. Between 0% and 200% of the initial amounts may vest for grants made from 2009 through 2011.

The weighted-average fair value of PRSUs granted was $38.92 and $35.40 for the years ended December 31, 2011 and 2010, respectively.

Employee Stock Purchase Plan (ESPP)

The Company maintains an ESPP whereby eligible employees can purchase common shares at a 15% discount to the closing share price on the NYSE on the last business day of each quarter. Each quarter, employees may elect to authorize payroll deductions from their eligible compensation, up to a maximum of $21,250 per year (or a comparable amount in foreign currency for the global ESPP). The discount is expensed as incurred. A maximum of 14 million common shares can be purchased through the ESPP. The maximum number of shares currently issuable for the U.S. ESPP is 8 million and for the global ESPP is 6 million.

The Company previously offered a Sharesave or "Save-as-you-earn" ("SAYE") plan, as a subset of the global ESPP, whereby eligible employees were given the option to acquire depositary interests representing common shares of the Company. The Company ceased offering the SAYE in 2010, replacing it with participation in the ESPP. Existing options under the SAYE were unaffected.

Share Appreciation Rights (SARs)

The Company has a phantom stock plan that provides for the granting of stock appreciation rights ("SARs") and other cash-based awards to certain employees. SARs provide the opportunity to receive a cash payment equal to the fair market value of the Company's common shares less the grant price. SARs vest over a four year period and expire four to ten years after the grant date. Compensation expense is recognized based on the fair value of the awards that are expected to vest and remain outstanding at the end of the reporting period using a Black-Scholes option pricing model. There were no SAR grants in 2011 and 2010.

The movement in the number of awards outstanding and their related weighted average exercise prices are as follows:

Awards Outstanding in Thousands:	Stock Options	TRSUs	PRSUs	SAYE	SARs	Total	Weighted Average Exercise Price ($)
Outstanding at December 31, 2009	16,798	2,768	4,523	1,155	589	25,833	25.46
Granted	1,925	433	2,068	—	—	4,426	15.32
Exercised	(1,933)	(484)	(646)	(17)	—	(3,080)	19.58
Forfeited	(1,516)	(12)	(325)	(132)	(106)	(2,091)	34.64
Expired	(2,004)	—	—	—	(58)	(2,062)	45.14
Outstanding at December 31, 2010	13,270	2,705	5,620	1,006	425	23,026	21.89
Exercisable at December 31, 2010	8,129	—	—	1	394	8,524	37.74
Granted	1,902	862	1,791	—	—	4,555	16.24
Exercised	(2,339)	(1,785)	(999)	(28)	(13)	(5,164)	15.21
Forfeited	(639)	(69)	(1,248)	(57)	(48)	(2,061)	11.87
Expired	(1,623)	—	—	(51)	(57)	(1,731)	46.24
Outstanding at December 31, 2011	10,571	1,713	5,164	870	307	18,625	21.10
Exercisable at December 31, 2011	6,367	—	—	689	300	7,356	33.53

The weighted average share price at the time of exercise was $37.06 per share (2010—$36.20).

Share-based compensation expense included in the income statement for years ended December 31, 2011 and 2010 was as follows:

	Stock Options	TRSUs	PRSUs	Others[2]	Total
December 31, 2011[1]	(6)	19	26	5	44
December 31, 2010[1]	27	32	37	9	105

[1] Includes gain of $43 million at December 31, 2011 (2010—loss of $13 million) relating to the revaluation of withholding taxes on stock based compensation awards, which is included within fair value adjustments in the presentation of "Operating expenses" in note 5.

[2] Principally comprised of expense related to ESPP, SAYE and SARs.

The Company recorded a liability for cash-settled share incentive awards of $55 million at December 31, 2011 (2010: $98 million). The intrinsic value of the liability for vested awards was $14 million (2010: $22 million).

The following table summarizes additional information relating to the awards outstanding at December 31, 2011:

Range of Exercise Prices	Number Outstanding (In Thousands)	Weighted Average Remaining Contractual Life (Years)	Weighted Average Exercise Price for Plans Outstanding	Number Exercisable (In Thousands)	Weighted Average Exercise Price for Plans Exercisable
0.00–30.00	10,042	2.23	$ 7.07	1,966	$22.28
30.01–35.00	890	2.65	$33.61	881	$33.64
35.01–40.00	6,314	6.57	$36.91	3,130	$36.48
40.01–45.00	1,359	3.52	$42.74	1,359	$42.74
45.01–50.00	20	0.09	$47.50	20	$47.50
Total	18,625			7,356	

IAS 23, *BORROWING COSTS*

IFRS Overview and Comparison to U.S. GAAP

3.183 IAS 23, *Borrowing Costs* (revised 2007), establishes the accounting for interest and other costs that an entity incurs in borrowing funds. It does not cover the actual or imputed cost of equity, including the cost of preferred capital that is not classified as a liability. IAS 23 is also not applicable to borrowing costs in connection with an asset measured at fair value or inventories that are manufactured, or otherwise produced, in large quantities on a repetitive basis. The revised IAS 23 is effective for annual periods beginning on or after 1 January 2009. The 2007 revision to IAS 23 removed the option to expense all borrowing costs, and given the cost and difficulties associated with retrospective application in this case, IAS 23 requires prospective application. Early adoption is permitted.

Recognition and Measurement

IFRSs

3.184 IAS 23 requires an entity to account for borrowing costs as follows:
  (a) Capitalize borrowing costs that are directly attributable to the acquisition, construction, or production of a qualifying asset (that is, an asset that necessarily takes a substantial period of time to get ready for its intended use or sale)
  (b) Expense all other borrowing costs incurred during the period

3.185 Borrowing costs include interest cost measured using the effective interest method, finance charges related to finance leases, and foreign exchange differences from foreign currency borrowings to the extent they are interest cost adjustments.

3.186 Qualifying assets may be inventories, except as previously described (for example, investment properties held for trading), PPE, intangibles assets, or investment properties.

3.187 An entity should calculate the amount of borrowing costs to be capitalized as follows:
  (a) To the extent that the entity borrowed funds specifically for the qualifying asset, it should capitalize the actual borrowing costs incurred less any investment income on any amount of the borrowing that it temporarily invested.
  (b) To the extent that the entity borrows funds generally and uses these funds to obtain the qualifying asset, it should apply a capitalization rate to its expenditures on the asset to determine the amount of borrowing costs to be capitalized.

3.188 An entity determines the capitalization rate as the weighted average interest rate applicable to borrowings outstanding during the period, not including any borrowings specifically for the qualifying asset.

3.189 An entity should not capitalize more than the actual amount of borrowing costs incurred during the period. An entity should continue to capitalize borrowing costs even when there are indicators that the qualifying asset is impaired. Depending upon the nature of the qualifying asset, an entity then should test that asset for impairment in accordance with the relevant standard. For example, an entity should test and measure any impairment losses for inventory in accordance with IAS 2 and for an item of PPE in accordance with IAS 36, *Impairment of Assets*.

3.190 IAS 23 requires an entity to begin capitalization when the following three conditions are met:
  • The entity incurs expenditures for the asset.
  • The entity incurs borrowing costs.
  • The entity has begun activities necessary to get the asset ready for its intended use or sale.
An entity should suspend capitalization during extended periods of inactivity on development of the asset and stop capitalization when it completes substantially all of the activities necessary to get the asset ready for its intended use or sale.

U.S. GAAP

3.191 Despite the fact that IAS 23 and the corresponding U.S. GAAP guidance resulted from a convergence project, several differences between FASB ASC 835, *Interest*, and IFRSs remain.

3.192 U.S. GAAP uses the term *interest cost*, rather than the broader term *borrowing costs* used in IAS 23, which encompasses other costs such as foreign exchange differences considered interest cost adjustments. FASB ASC 835-20-30-7 explains that gains and losses on the effective portion of a fair value hedge are part of capitalized interest cost. IAS 23 does not discuss the treatment of gains and losses on hedging transactions.

3.193 A comparison of IFRSs to paragraphs 5–6 of FASB ASC 835-20-15 reveals the following differences in the types of assets (qualifying assets) for which interest can be capitalized:
  • FASB ASC 835 only requires the asset to take a period of time for the activities necessary to get it ready for use or sale, not the substantial period of time required by IAS 23.
  • FASB ASC 835 does not address assets held at fair value, which are excluded from the scope of IAS 23.
  • FASB ASC 835 permits equity-method investments to be qualifying assets (while the investee has activities in progress necessary to begin its planned principal operations, and the investee's activities include the use of funds to acquire qualifying assets for its operations), but IAS 23 does not.
  • FASB ASC 835 does not permit interest to be capitalized on assets acquired with gifts or grants. IAS 23 does not address such circumstances.

3.194 Rather than requiring an entity to capitalize the actual interest less investment income on temporarily invested funds, FASB ASC 835-20-30-3 requires an entity to determine the amount capitalized in an accounting period by applying a capitalization rate to the average amount of accumulated expenditures for the asset during the period. An entity should base the capitalization rates it uses on the rates applicable to borrowings outstanding during the period. If an entity's financing plans associate a specific new borrowing with a qualifying asset, this paragraph permits the entity to use the rate on that borrowing as the capitalization rate to be applied to that portion of the average accumulated expenditures for the asset up to the amount of that borrowing. If average accumulated expenditures for the asset exceed the amounts of specific new borrowings associated with the asset, the entity should determine the weighted average of the rates applicable to other borrowings of the entity and use that rate as the capitalization rate. In contrast to IAS 23, FASB ASC 835 does not permit an entity to reduce the amount of interest capitalized for investment income on temporary investment of the borrowed funds.

Presentation

IFRSs

3.195 IAS 1 requires an entity to present a separate line item for finance costs. IFRSs do not explicitly define *finance costs*, but they are generally understood to be interest costs and other finance charges that are included in the term *borrowing* *costs.* An entity should present separate line items for finance cost and finance income.

U.S. GAAP

3.196 Rule 5-03(b) of Regulation S-X requires SEC registrants to present interest expense, including amortization of debt premiums or discounts, as a separate line item on the income statement.

Author's Note

Companies reporting under U.S. GAAP generally offset interest income and interest expense on the face of the income statement.

Disclosure

IFRSs

3.197 IAS 1 requires disclosure of total finance costs during the period. IAS 23 requires an entity to disclose the amount

of borrowing costs capitalized and the capitalization rate used.

U.S. GAAP

3.198 FASB ASC 835-20-50 does not require disclosure of the capitalization rate. However, FASB ASC 835-20-50-1 states that an entity should disclose total interest costs incurred, the amount capitalized, and the amount expensed during the period.

Presentation and Disclosure Excerpts

Finance Costs

3.199

SK Telecom Co., Ltd. (Dec 2011)

CONSOLIDATED STATEMENTS OF INCOME
(in part)

	Notes	Korean Won 2010	Korean Won 2011	Translation into U.S. Dollars (Note 2) 2011
		(In Millions Except for per Share Data)		(In Thousands Except for per Share Data)
Operating income	27	2,285,911	2,131,458	1,839,844
Financial income	23	477,217	442,325	381,808
Financial costs	23	(441,623)	(343,776)	(296,742)
Equity in earnings of affiliates	8	41,828	39,131	33,777
Equity in losses of affiliates	8	(45,242)	(86,280)	(74,476)
Income From Continuing Operation Before Income Tax		2,318,091	2,182,858	1,884,211

NOTES TO THE CONSOLIDATED FINANCIAL STATEMENTS (in part)

1. General

SK Telecom Co., Ltd. ("SK Telecom") was incorporated in March 1984 under the laws of Korea to engage in providing cellular telephone communication services in the Republic of Korea. SK Telecom Co., Ltd. and its subsidiaries (the "Company") mainly provide wireless telecommunications in the Republic of Korea. The Company's common shares and depositary receipts (DRs) are listed on the Stock Market of Korea Exchange, the New York Stock Exchange and the London Stock Exchange. As of December 31, 2011, the Company's total issued shares are held by the following:

	Number of Shares	Percentage of Total Shares Issued (%)
SK Holdings, Co., Ltd.	20,363,452	25.22
Tradewinds Global Investors, LLC	4,050,518	5.02
POSCO Corp.	2,341,569	2.90
Institutional investors and other minority stockholders	42,939,460	53.17
Treasury stock	11,050,712	13.69
	80,745,711	100.00

2. Summary of Significant Accounting Policies (in part)

The Company maintains its official accounting records in Republic of Korean won ("Won") and prepares consolidated financial statements in conformity with International Financial Reporting Standards ("IFRS") as issued by International Accounting Standard Board ("IASB"). The Company has adopted IFRS as issued by IASB for the annual period beginning on January 1, 2011. In accordance with IFRS 1 First-time adoption of IFRS, the Company's transition date to IFRS is January 1, 2010. Refer to Note 3, for transition adjustments to IFRS.

The accompanying consolidated financial statements are stated in Korean won, the currency of the country in which the Company is incorporated and operates. The translation of Korean won amounts into U.S. dollar amounts is included solely for the convenience of readers of financial statements and has been made at the rate of (Won)1,158.50 to US$1.00, the Noon Buying Rate in the City of New York for cable transfers in Korean won as certified for customs purposes by the Federal Reserve Bank of New York on the last business day of the year ended December 30, 2011.

The consolidated financial statements have been prepared on a historical cost basis except for certain non-current assets and financial instruments that are measured at revalued amounts or at fair values. Major accounting policies used for the preparation of the consolidated financial statements are stated below and these accounting policies have been applied consistently to the financial statements for the current period and comparative periods. Historical cost is generally based on the fair value of the consideration paid in exchange for assets. The consolidated financial statements were approved by the board of directors on February 9, 2012.

o. Borrowing Costs

Borrowing costs directly attributable to the acquisition, construction or production of qualifying assets, which are assets that necessarily take a substantial period of time to get ready for their intended use or sale, are added to the cost of those assets, until such time as the assets are substantially ready for their intended use or sale. Investment income earned on the temporary investment of specific borrowings pending their expenditure on qualifying assets is deducted from the borrowing costs eligible for capitalization. All other borrowing costs are recognized in net income in the period in which they are incurred.

23. Finance Income and Costs

Details of finance income and costs for the years ended December 31, 2011 and 2010 are as follows (in millions of Korean won):

	For the Year Ended	
	December 31, 2011	December 31, 2010
Finance Income:		
Interest income	(Won) 168,148	(Won) 237,392
Dividends	26,433	28,680
Gain on foreign currency transactions	11,135	10,163
Gain on foreign currency translation	1,984	16,950
Gain on valuation of financial asset at FVTPL	2,617	—
Gain on disposal of long-term investment securities	164,454	174,801
Reversal of loss on impairment of investment securities	—	39
Gain on valuation of derivatives	3,785	1,241
Gain on derivative settlement	—	7,951
Gain on valuation of financial liability at FVTPL	63,769	—
	(Won) 442,325	(Won) 477,217
Finance Costs:		
Gain on derivative settlement	(Won) 297,172	(Won) 379,289
Loss on foreign currency transactions	10,382	14,471
Loss on foreign currency translation	6,409	1,788
Loss on disposal of short-term investment securities	—	1,866
Loss on disposal of long-term investment securities	447	2,368
Loss on impairment of investment securities	12,846	3,404
Loss on valuation of derivatives	943	19,198
Loss on derivative settlement	15,577	—
Loss on disposal of accounts receivable	—	6
Loss on valuation of financial liability at FVTPL	—	19,233
	(Won) 343,776	(Won) 441,623

Details of interest income included in finance income for the years ended December 31, 2011 and 2010 are as follows (in millions of Korean won):

	For the Years Ended	
	December 31, 2011	December 31, 2010
Interest income on cash equivalents and deposits	(Won) 61,577	(Won) 27,987
Interest income on installment receivables and other interest income	106,571	209,405
	(Won) 168,148	(Won) 237,392

Details of interest expenses included in finance for the years ended December 31, 2011 and 2010 are as follows (in millions of Korean won):

	For the Years Ended	
	December 31, 2011	December 31, 2010
Interest expense on bank overdrafts and borrowings	(Won) 60,271	(Won) 89,178
Interest on finance lease liabilities	4,422	8,383
Interest on bonds	208,403	252,646
Other interest expenses	24,076	29,082
	(Won) 297,172	(Won) 379,289

Details of income and costs by type of financial assets or financial liabilities for the years ended December 31, 2011 and 2010 are as follows (in millions of Korean won):

| | For the Year Ended | | | |
| | December 31, 2011 | | December 31, 2010 | |
	Financial Income	Financial Costs	Financial Income	Financial Costs
Financial Assets:				
Financial assets designated as at FVTPL	(Won) 3,013	(Won) 943	(Won) 1,991	(Won) 21,064
Available-for-sale financial assets	198,547	13,293	223,425	5,772
Loans and receivables	173,498	12,603	228,909	16,221
Derivatives designated as hedging instruments	—	8,088	505	—
Sub-total	375,058	34,927	454,830	43,057
Financial Liabilities:				
Financial liabilities designated as at FVTPL	67,158	2,353	—	19,233
Financial liabilities at amortized cost	109	301,360	15,691	379,333
Derivatives designated as hedging instruments	—	5,136	6,696	—
Sub-total	67,267	308,849	22,387	398,566
Total	(Won) 442,325	(Won) 343,776	(Won) 477,217	(Won) 441,623

Details of impairment losses for each class of financial assets for the years ended December 31, 2011 and December 31, 2010 are as follows (in millions of Korean won):

| | For the Years Ended | |
	December 31, 2011	December 31, 2010
Impairment loss on long-term investment securities	(Won) 12,846	(Won) 3,404
Bad debt	83,748	77,780
Other bad debt	12,847	12,293
	(Won) 109,441	(Won) 93,477

Capitalized Borrowing Costs

3.200

Companhia Siderúrgica Nacional (Dec 2011)

CONSOLIDATED STATEMENTS OF INCOME (in part)

| | Note | Thousands of Brazilian Reais | | |
		2011	2010	2009
Profit before finance income (costs) and taxes		5.756.922	4.998.346	3.561.232
Finance income	26	717.450	643.140	586.025
Finance costs	26	−2.723.253	−2.554.598	−832.460
Profit before income taxes		3.751.119	3.086.888	3.314.797

NOTES TO THE CONSOLIDATED FINANCIAL STATEMENTS (in part)

(Expressed In thousands of reais—R$, unless otherwise stated)

1. Description of Business

Companhia Siderúrgica Nacional is a publicly-held company incorporated on April 9, 1941, under the laws of the Federative Republic of Brazil (Companhia Siderúrgica Nacional, its subsidiaries and jointly controlled entities collectively referred to herein as "CSN" or the "Company").The Company's registered office social is located at Avenida Brigadeiro Faria Lima, 3400—São Paulo, SP.

CSN is a Company with shares listed on the São Paulo Stock Exchange (BOVESPA) and the New York Stock Exchange (NYSE). Accordingly, it reports its information to the Brazilian Securities Commission (CVM) and the U.S. Securities and Exchange Commission (SEC).

The main operating activities of CSN are divided into 5 (five) segments as follows:
• Steel:
The Company's main industrial facility is the Presidente Vargas Steel Mill ("UPV"), located in the city of Volta Redonda, State of Rio de Janeiro. This segment consolidates the operations related to the production, distribution and sale of flat steel, metallic packaging and galvanized steel. In addition to the facilities in Brazil, CSN has operations in the United States and Portugal aimed at gaining markets and performing excellent services for final consumers. Its steels are used in the home appliances, civil construction and automobile industries.
• Mining:
The production of iron ore is developed in the city of Congonhas, in the State of Minas Gerais. It further mines tin in the State of Rondônia to supply the needs of UPV, with the excess of these raw materials being sold to subsidiaries and third parties.CSN holds a concession to operate TECAR, a solid bulk maritime terminal, of the 4 (four) terminals that form the Itaguaí Port, located in Rio de Janeiro. Importations of coal and coke are carried out through this terminal.

- Cement:

The Company entered the cement market boosted by the synergy between this new activity and its already existing businesses. Next to the Presidente Vargas Steel Mill in Volta Redonda (RJ), it installed a new business unit: CSN Cimentos, which produces CP-III type cement by using slag produced by the UPV blast furnaces in Volta Redonda. Explores also limestone and dolomito Arches drive in the State of Minas Gerais, to feed the needs of UPV and CSN Cement, and the surplus of such raw materials is sold to subsidiaries and third parties.

During 2011, the Clinker used in the manufacture of cement was purchased from third parties, however, by the end of 2011, with the completion of the first stage of the Clinker plant in Arcos (MG), this has already filled the needs of grinding of CSN Cimentos located in Volta Redonda.

- Logistics:

Railroads:

CSN has equity interests in two railroad companies: MRS Logística, which manages the former Southeast Network of Rede Ferroviária Federal S.A. (RFFSA), and Transnordestina Logística, which operates the former Northeast Network of the RFFSA in the states of Maranhão, Piauí, Ceará, Rio Grande do Norte, Paraíba, Pernambuco and Alagoas.

Ports:

In the State of Rio de Janeiro, the Company operates the Container Terminal known as Sepetiba Tecon at the Itaguaí Port. Located in the Bay of Sepetiba, this port has privileged highway, railroad and maritime access.

Tecon handles the shipments of CSN steel products, movement of containers, as well as storage, consolidation and deconsolidation of cargo.

- Energy:

As energy is fundamental in its production process, the Company has invested in assets for generation of electric power to guarantee its self-sufficiency.

For further details on strategic investments in the Company's segments, see Note 27—Segment Information.

2. Summary of Significant Accounting Policies (in part)

(a) Basis of Preparation

The consolidated financial statements have been prepared and are being presented in accordance with International Financial Reporting Standards (IFRS) issued by the International Accounting Standards Board (IASB).

The preparation of financial statements in conformity with IFRS requires the use of certain critical accounting estimates. It also requires management to exercise its judgment in the process of applying the Company's accounting policies. The areas involving a higher degree of judgment or complexity, or areas where assumptions and estimates are significant to the consolidated financial statements, are disclosed in the notes to this report and refer to the allowance for doubtful debts, provision for inventory losses, provision for labor, civil, tax, environmental and social security risks, depreciation, amortization, depletion, provision for impairment, deferred taxes,

financial instruments and employee benefits. Actual results may differ from these estimates.

The financial statements are presented in thousands of reais (R$). Depending on the applicable IFRS standard, the measurement criterion used in preparing the financial statements considers the historical cost, net realizable value, fair value or recoverable amount.

Some balances for the financial years 2009 and 2010 were reclassified to permit a better comparability with 2011.

The consolidated financial statements were approved by the Board of Directors and authorized for issue on April 26, 2012.

(i) Property, Plant and Equipment (in part)

Property, plant and equipment are carried at cost of acquisition, formation or construction, less accumulated depreciation or depletion and any impairment loss. Depreciation is calculated under the straight-line method based on the remaining economic useful economic lives of assets, as mentioned in note 12. The depletion of mines is calculated based on the quantity of ore mined. Land is not depreciated since its useful life is considered indefinite. However, if the tangible assets are mine-specific, they are depreciated over the economic useful lives for such assets. The Company recognizes in the carrying amount of property, plant and equipment the cost of replacement, reducing the carrying amount of the part that it is replacing if it is probable that future economic benefits embodied therein will revert to the Company, and if the cost of the asset can be reliably measured. All other disbursements are expensed as incurred. Borrowing costs related to funds obtained for construction in progress are capitalized until these projects are completed.

(q) Finance Income and Finance Costs

Finance income includes interest income from funds invested (including available-for-sale financial assets), dividend income (except for dividends received from investees accounted for under the equity method in Company), gains on disposal of available-for-sale financial assets, changes in the fair value of financial assets measured at fair value through profit or loss, and gains on hedging instruments that are recognized in profit or loss. Interest income is recognized in profit or loss under the effective interest method. Dividend income is recognized in profit or loss when the Company's right to receive payment has been established. Distributions received from investees accounted for by the equity method reduce the investment value.

Finance costs comprise interest expenses on borrowings, net of the discount to present value of the provisions, dividends on preferred shares classified as liabilities, losses in the fair value of financial instruments measured at fair value through profit or loss, impairment losses recognized in financial assets, and losses on hedging instruments that are recognized in profit or loss. Borrowing costs that are not directly attributable to the acquisition, construction or production of a qualifying asset are measured through profit or loss under the effective interest method.

Foreign exchange gains and losses are reported on a net basis.

12. Property, Plant and Equipment (in part)

The breakdown of the projects comprising construction in progress is as follows:

Project Objective	Start Date	Scheduled Completion	12/31/2010	12/31/2011
Construction in Progress—Main Projects				
Logistics			1,889,411	3,795,760
Expansion of Transnordestina railroad around 1,728 km to boost the transportation of varied products as iron ore, limestone, soybeans, cotton, sugarcane, fertilizers, oil and fuels.	2009	2014	1,774,875	3,489,871
Expansion of MRS's capacity and current investments for maintenance of current operations			111,763	290,410
Current investments for maintenance of current operations			2,773	15,479
Mining			1,364,733	1,931,047
Expansion of Casa de Pedra Mine capacity production to 42 Mtpa	2007	2012/13[1]	1,101,234	1,322,433
Expansion of TECAR to permit an annual exportation of 60 Mtpa	2009	2013	167,163	425,134
Expansion of Namisa capacity production to 39 Mtpa	2008	2015/16	81,172	137,059
Current investments for maintenance of current operations			15,164	46,421
Steel			803,798	1,164,239
Implementation of the long steel mill in the states of Rio de Janeiro, Minas Gerais and São Paulo for production of rebar and wire rod.	2008	2013[1]	618,832	907,521
Current investments for maintenance of current operations				
Expansion of TECAR to allow annual exports of 45 mtpy			184,966	256,718
Expansion of Namisa production capacity to 39 mpty				
Cement			457,864	165,273
Construcion of Cement plant in the Northeast and Southern region of Brazil and in the city of Arcos, Minas Gerais	2011	2013[3]	98,258	132,986
Construcion of clinquer plant in the city of Arcos, Minas Gerais	2007	2011[4]	357,981	27,536
Current investments for maintenance of current operations			1,625	4,751
Total construction in progress			4,515,806	7,056,319

[1] Expected date for completion of the 40 Mtpa and 42 Mtpa Stages.
[2] Expected date for completion of the Rio de Janeiro unity.
[3] Expected date for completion of new grinding on Arcos—MG.
[4] Manufacturing plant in operation, in "ramp-up".

The costs classified in construction in progress comprise basically the acquisition of services, purchase of parts to be used as investments for improvement of performance, upgrading of technology, enlargement, expansion and acquisition of assets that will be transferred to the relevant line items and depreciated as from the time they are available for use.

a) The Company capitalized borrowing costs amounting to R$353,156 (R$215,624 as of December 31, 2010) (see note 26).These costs are basically calculated for mining, cement, long steel and Transnordestina projects, mainly relating to: (i) Casa de Pedra Mine expansion; (ii) construction of the cement plant in Volta Redonda, RJ, and the clinker plant in the city of Arcos, MG; (iii) construction of the long steel

mill in the city of Volta Redonda, RJ; and (iv) extension of Transnordestina railroad, which will connect the countryside of the northeast region to the Suape, State of Pernambuco, and Pecém, State of Ceará, ports.

The rates used to capitalize borrowing costs are as follows:

	Fees	
Specific Projects	**Non-Specific Projects**
TJLP + 1.3% to 3.2%	10.56%
UM006 + 2.7%	

26. Finance Income (Costs)

	12/31/2011	12/31/2010	12/31/2009
Finance Costs:			
Borrowings and financing—foreign currency	(639,197)	(641,632)	(598,849)
Borrowings and financing—local currency	(1,622,365)	(791,926)	(277,699)
Related parties	(389,059)	(374,929)	(365,150)
Capitalized interest	353,156	215,624	85,260
PIS/COFINS on other revenues	(1,230)	(1,079)	(1,072)
Losses on derivatives[*]	(20,594)	(27,252)	(152,102)
Net effect of REFIS—Law 11941/09 and MP 470/09	(77,335)	(33,921)	2,336
Interest, fines and late payment charges	(264,359)	(283,768)	(281,190)
Other finance costs	(222,938)	(261,570)	(304,049)
	(2,883,921)	(2,200,453)	(1,892,515)

(continued)

	12/31/2011	12/31/2010	12/31/2009
Finance Income:			
Related parties	29,300	53,491	55,750
Income from short-term investments	538,882	394,183	276,177
Other income	149,268	195,466	254,098
	717,450	643,140	586,025
Inflation Adjustments:			
— Assets	6,330	271	8,465
— Liabilites	(43,781)	(8,714)	69,266
	(37,451)	(8,443)	77,731
Exchange Gains (Losses):			
— On assets	1,041,200	(585,719)	(295,526)
— On liabilities	(753,666)	398,527	995,064
— Exchange gains (losses) on derivatives[*]	(89,415)	(158,510)	282,786
	198,119	(345,702)	982,324
Inflation adjustment and exchange gains (losses), net	160,668	(354,145)	1,060,055
Finance costs, net	(2,005,803)	(1,911,458)	(246,435)
(*) Statement of Gains and Losses on Derivative Transactions			
CDI to USD swap	(115,490)	(231,673)	(581,523)
EUR to USD swap	9,574	(6,763)	
Future US dollar		79,926	(231,563)
Total return equity swap			1,026,463
Other	16,501	(8,388)	(65,248)
	(89,415)	(166,898)	148,129
Libor to CDI swap	(20,594)	(18,864)	(17,445)
	(20,594)	(18,864)	(17,445)
	(110,009)	(185,762)	130,684

IAS 28, *INVESTMENTS IN ASSOCIATES*

IAS 31, *INTERESTS IN JOINT VENTURES*

Author's Note

In May 2011, IASB revised IAS 28, *Investments in Associates*, concurrently with issuing IFRS 11, and IFRS 12, and retitled it as *Investments in Associates and Joint Ventures*. The revised IAS 28 expands the scope of the standard to include investors with joint control, as well as significant influence, over an investee and requires the use of the equity method to account for such investments, unless the entity is exempt from applying the equity method, in accordance with the standard. IAS 28 does not permit use of proportionate consolidation by investors with joint control over an investee. The revised standard is effective for annual periods beginning on or after 1 January 2013, with early application permitted. See the author's note preceding paragraphs 2.137 and 2.167 in section 2 for a discussion of these new standards.

The following standards issued in 2011 also amend IAS 28:
- IFRS 9
  These amendments replace references to IAS 39 with references to IFRS 9.
- IFRS 13
  These amendments replace the term *published price quotations* with the term *quoted market prices* and remove the phrase "measured at fair value in accordance with IAS 39." The latter change is necessary because IAS 39 is amended to require fair value measurement in accordance with IFRS 13.

Because the effective dates of IAS 28, IFRS 9, and IFRS 13 are after 1 January 2012, the requirements of these standards are not reflected in the commentary in this section. The timing of the effective dates also affects the availability of illustrative excerpts from survey companies' financial statements. Accordingly, the excerpts appearing later in this section may not reflect all or some of these revisions.

IFRS Overview and Comparison to U.S. GAAP

3.201 When accounting for its investments in either associates or jointly controlled entities using the equity method, in accordance with IAS 28 or IAS 31, an investor-entity should recognize all of the following items in profit and loss:

- Investor's share of the profit or loss of the investee
- Impairment loss or reversal of an impairment loss on the equity-method investment
- Difference between the carrying value of the investment and the fair value of any retained investment when it discontinues the equity method (which may be a gain or loss on disposal)

3.202 An investor-entity should recognize in OCI its share of items recognized by the investee in OCI.

Author's Note

The requirements of these standards with respect to recognition, measurement, presentation, and disclosure on the balance sheet are discussed in section 2, beginning with paragraph 2.137.

Recognition and Measurement

IFRSs

3.203 IAS 28 and IAS 31 require an entity that accounts for its investments in associates and joint ventures using the equity method to recognize in profit or loss its share of the profit or loss of its investee and to recognize in OCI its share of the investee's items of OCI.

3.204 In addition, IAS 28 requires an entity to stop applying the equity method when it no longer has significant influence. An entity should remeasure any retained investment at fair value and recognize in profit or loss the difference between this fair value and the carrying value before remeasurement.

3.205 With respect to impairment, IAS 28 requires an entity to recognize its share of the associate's losses and then apply the requirements of IAS 39 to determine whether it should recognize an additional impairment loss with respect to its net investment. If an entity recognizes this impairment loss, it should also assess whether an additional impairment loss is necessary for its interest in the associate that may exceed the carrying value of its net investment. Whenever application of the requirements of IAS 39 indicates that the investment may be impaired, an entity should then measure the impairment loss in accordance with IAS 36 in order to recognize any impairment on goodwill embedded in the carrying amount of the investment.

Author's Note

The requirements of IAS 36 are discussed in detail in this section, beginning with paragraph 3.240.

U.S. GAAP

3.206 Like IFRSs, FASB ASC 323-10-35-4 requires an entity to recognize in income its share of the earnings or losses of an equity-method investee in the same period the investee reports them in its financial statements. As stated by FASB ASC 323-10-35-5, the amount recognized in income should reflect adjustments similar to those for consolidation, including adjustments to

- eliminate intra-entity profits and losses.
- amortize, if appropriate, any difference between investor cost and underlying equity in net assets of the investee at the date of investment.
- reflect the investor's share of changes in the investee's capital.
- OCI.

3.207 With respect to recognition of the investees' losses, like IFRSs, FASB ASC 323-10-35-4 requires an entity to recognize its share of losses of an investee. As explained in FASB ASC 323-10-35-19, when these losses equal or exceed the carrying amount of an investment accounted for by the equity method plus advances by the entity, the entity should continue to report losses up to the carrying amount of the entity's investment, including any additional financial support, which may include capital contributions to the investee, investments in additional common stock or preferred stock, and loans or debt securities.

3.208 Like IFRSs, FASB ASC 323-10-35-35 requires an entity to recognize gains and losses on the sales of stock of an investee equal to the difference at the time of sale between the selling price and the carrying amount of the stock sold.

3.209 As discussed in FASB ASC 323-10-35-36, when an entity no longer has significant influence over its investee, it should discontinue use of the equity method. Unlike IFRSs, an entity is not required to immediately remeasure the investment to fair value. An entity is required to include any earnings or losses that relate to a retained investment as part of its carrying amount. Unlike IFRSs, an entity must reduce the carrying value of the retained investment by any dividends it receives in a subsequent period that exceed its share of the investee's earnings, rather than recognize these dividends as income. FASB ASC 323-10-35-37 also provides guidance on the treatment of items recognized in OCI when an entity discontinues use of the equity method. Unless it elects the fair value option, in accordance with FASB ASC 320, *Investments—Debt and Equity Securities*, the entity should classify an investment with a readily determinable fair value as either trading or available for sale, as appropriate, with subsequent measurement based on the selected classification.

3.210 Paragraphs 31–32 A of FASB ASC 323-10-35 also provide guidance to an entity when a series of operating losses or other factors may indicate that there has been an other than temporary decline in the investment exceeding that required by the equity method and the entity should recognize this additional impairment loss. Several factors are provided that the entity should consider when making this determination, including the absence of an ability to recover the investment's carrying amount, the inability of the investee to sustain an earnings capacity to justify the carrying amount, or a current fair value that is less than the carrying amount. However, an entity is required to evaluate all factors in making this determination. An equity method investor should not separately test an investee's underlying asset(s) for impairment. However, an equity investor should recognize its share of any impairment charge recorded by an investee and consider the effect, if any, of the impairment on the investor's basis difference in the assets that give rise to the investee's impairment charge.

Presentation

IFRSs

3.211 IAS 1 requires an entity to present its share of the profit or loss of an associate or jointly controlled entity as a separate line item in the income statement and its share of the associate's or jointly controlled entity's OCI in OCI.

U.S. GAAP

3.212 Like IFRSs, paragraphs 1–2 of FASB ASC 323-10-45 require an entity to show its share of earnings or losses from its investment in its income statement as a single amount. Unlike IFRSs, an entity should separately show its share of extraordinary items and its share of accounting changes reported in the financial statements of the investee.

3.213 Like IFRSs, FASB ASC 323-10-45-3 states that an entity may combine its proportionate share of the amounts of the investee's OCI items with its own OCI items and display the aggregate of those amounts.

Disclosure

IFRSs

3.214 IAS 28 requires an entity to disclose the amount of any unrecognized share of losses of an associate, both for the

reporting period and cumulatively, if it has discontinued loss recognition. IAS 36 disclosures would also apply when an entity recognizes an impairment loss. However, IAS 31 does not include this requirement.

U.S. GAAP

3.215 Unlike IFRSs, FASB ASC 323-10 does not require additional disclosure about the effect of items recognized in the statement of comprehensive income. FASB ASC 323-10-50-3 requires disclosure of the difference between the carrying value of the investment and its share of the underlying net assets of the investee. Although not specifically stated, this disclosure requirement appears to require disclosure of unrecognized losses, if any.

Presentation and Disclosure Excerpts

Share of Post-Tax Profit or Loss of Associates and Joint Ventures Included in Pre-Tax Profit, Venture Capital Associates and Joint Ventures Designated at Fair Value through Profit or Loss, Impairment Losses

3.216

Lloyds Banking Group plc (Dec 2011)

CONSOLIDATED INCOME STATEMENT (in part)

	Note	2011 £ Million	2010 £ Million	2009 £ Million
Interest and similar income		26,316	29,340	28,238
Interest and similar expense		(13,618)	(16,794)	(19,212)
Net interest income	5	12,698	12,546	9,026
Fee and commission income		4,935	4,992	4,728
Fee and commission expense		(1,391)	(1,682)	(1,517)
Net fee and commission income(1)	6	3,544	3,310	3,211
Net trading income	7	(368)	15,724	19,098
Insurance premium income	8	8,170	8,148	8,946
Other operating income	9	2,768	4,316	5,490
Other income		14,114	31,498	36,745
Total income		26,812	44,044	45,771
Insurance claims(1)	10	(6,041)	(19,088)	(22,493)
Total income, net of insurance claims		20,771	24,956	23,278
Government Asset Protection Scheme fee		—	—	(2,500)
Payment protection insurance provision		—	(3,200)	—
Other operating expenses		(13,050)	(13,270)	(13,484)
Total operating expenses	11	(13,050)	(16,470)	(15,984)
Trading surplus		7,721	8,486	7,294
Impairment	12	(8,094)	(10,952)	(16,673)
Share of results of joint ventures and associates	13	31	(88)	(752)
Gain on acquisition	14	—	—	11,173
Loss on disposal of businesses	15	—	(365)	—
(Loss) profit before tax		(342)	(2,919)	1,042

NOTES TO THE CONSOLIDATED FINANCIAL STATEMENTS (in part)

Note 1: Basis of Preparation (in part)

The consolidated financial statements of Lloyds Banking Group plc have been prepared in accordance with International Financial Reporting Standards (IFRS) as adopted by the European Union (EU). IFRS comprises accounting standards prefixed IFRS issued by the International Accounting Standards Board (IASB) and those prefixed IAS issued by the IASB's predecessor body as well as interpretations issued by the International Financial Reporting Interpretations Committee (IFRIC) and its predecessor body. The EU endorsed version of IAS 39 *Financial Instruments: Recognition and Measurement* relaxes some of the hedge accounting requirements; the Group has not taken advantage of this relaxation, and therefore there is no difference in application to the Group between IFRS as adopted by the EU and IFRS as issued by the IASB.

The financial information has been prepared under the historical cost convention, as modified by the revaluation of investment properties, available-for-sale financial assets, trading securities and certain other financial assets and liabilities at fair value through profit or loss and all derivative contracts. As stated on page 166, the directors consider that it is appropriate to continue to adopt the going concern basis in preparing the accounts.

Certain disclosures required under IFRS in relation to financial instruments have been included within the Risk Management section of this annual report on Form 20-F on pages 58 through 131, and identified therein as 'audited'.

In previous years the Group has included annual management charges on non-participating investment contracts within insurance claims. In light of developing industry practice, these amounts (2011: £606 million; 2010: £577 million; 2009: £474 million) are now included within net fee and commission income.

Note 2: Accounting Policies (in part)

The Group's accounting policies are set out below.

(A) Consolidation (in part)

The assets, liabilities and results of Group undertakings (including special purpose entities) are included in the financial statements on the basis of accounts made up to the reporting date. Group undertakings include subsidiaries, associates and joint ventures.

(2) Joint Ventures and Associates

Joint ventures are entities over which the Group has joint control under a contractual arrangement with other parties. Associates are entities over which the Group has significant influence, but not control or joint control, over the financial and operating policies. Significant influence is the power to participate in the financial and operating policy decisions of the entity and is normally achieved through holding between 20 per cent and 50 per cent of the voting share capital of the entity.

The Group utilises the venture capital exemption for investments where significant influence or joint control is present and the business unit operates as a venture capital business. These investments are designated at initial recognition at fair value through profit or loss. Otherwise, the Group's investments in joint ventures and associates are accounted for by the equity method of accounting and are initially recorded at cost and adjusted each year to reflect the Group's share of the post-acquisition results of the joint venture or associate based on audited accounts which are coterminous with the Group or made up to a date which is not more than three months before the Group's reporting date. The share of any losses is restricted to a level that reflects an obligation to fund such losses.

(B) Goodwill

Goodwill arises on business combinations, including the acquisition of subsidiaries, and on the acquisition of interests in joint ventures and associates; goodwill represents the excess of the cost of an acquisition over the fair value of the Group's share of the identifiable assets, liabilities and contingent liabilities acquired. Where the fair value of the Group's share of the identifiable assets, liabilities and contingent liabilities of the acquired entity is greater than the cost of acquisition, the excess is recognised immediately in the income statement.

Goodwill is recognised as an asset at cost and is tested at least annually for impairment. If an impairment is identified the carrying value of the goodwill is written down immediately through the income statement and is not subsequently reversed. Goodwill arising on acquisitions of associates and joint ventures is included in the Group's investment in joint ventures and associates. At the date of disposal of a subsidiary, the carrying value of attributable goodwill is included in the calculation of the profit or loss on disposal except where it has been written off directly to reserves in the past.

(E) Financial Assets and Liabilities (in part)

On initial recognition, financial assets are classified into fair value through profit or loss, available-for-sale financial assets, held-to-maturity investments or loans and receivables. Financial liabilities are measured at amortised cost, except for trading liabilities and other financial liabilities designated at fair value through profit or loss on initial recognition which are held at fair value. Purchases and sales of securities and other financial assets and trading liabilities are recognised on trade date, being the date that the Group is committed to purchase or sell an asset.

Financial assets are derecognised when the contractual right to receive cash flows from those assets has expired or when the Group has transferred its contractual right to receive the cash flows from the assets and either:
- substantially all of the risks and rewards of ownership have been transferred; or
- the Group has neither retained nor transferred substantially all of the risks and rewards, but has transferred control.

Financial liabilities are derecognised when they are extinguished (ie when the obligation is discharged), cancelled or expire.

(1) Financial Instruments at Fair Value Through Profit or Loss

Financial instruments are classified at fair value through profit or loss where they are trading securities or where they are designated at fair value through profit or loss by management. Derivatives are carried at fair value (see (F) below).

Trading securities are debt securities and equity shares acquired principally for the purpose of selling in the short term or which are part of a portfolio which is managed for short-term gains. Such securities are classified as trading securities and recognised in the balance sheet at their fair value. Gains and losses arising from changes in their fair value together with interest coupons and dividend income are recognised in the income statement within net trading income in the period in which they occur.

Other financial assets and liabilities at fair value through profit or loss are designated as such by management upon initial recognition. Such assets and liabilities are carried in the balance sheet at their fair value and gains and losses arising from changes in fair value together with interest coupons and dividend income are recognised in the income statement within net trading income in the period in which they occur. Financial assets and liabilities are designated at fair value through profit or loss on acquisition in the following circumstances:

- it eliminates or significantly reduces the inconsistent treatment that would otherwise arise from measuring the assets and liabilities or recognising gains or losses on different bases. The main type of financial assets designated by the Group at fair value through profit or loss are assets backing insurance contracts and investment contracts issued by the Group's life insurance businesses. Fair value designation allows changes in the fair value of these assets to be recorded in the income statement along with the changes in the value of the associated liabilities, thereby significantly reducing the measurement inconsistency had the assets been classified as available-for-sale financial assets.
- the assets and liabilities are part of a group which is managed, and its performance evaluated, on a fair value basis in accordance with a documented risk management or investment strategy, with management information also prepared on this basis. As noted in (A)(2)

above certain of the Group's investments are managed as venture capital investments and evaluated on the basis of their fair value and these assets are designated at fair value through profit or loss.
- where the assets and liabilities contain one or more embedded derivatives that significantly modify the cash flows arising under the contract and would otherwise need to be separately accounted for.

The fair values of assets and liabilities traded in active markets are based on current bid and offer prices respectively. If the market is not active the Group establishes a fair value by using valuation techniques. These include the use of recent arm's length transactions, reference to other instruments that are substantially the same, discounted cash flow analysis, option pricing models and other valuation techniques commonly used by market participants. Refer to note 3 (Critical accounting estimates and judgements: Fair value of financial instruments) and note 55(3) (Financial instruments: Fair values of financial assets and liabilities) for details of valuation techniques and significant inputs to valuation models.

The Group is permitted to reclassify, at fair value at the date of transfer, non-derivative financial assets (other than those designated at fair value through profit or loss by the entity upon initial recognition) out of the trading category if they are no longer held for the purpose of being sold or repurchased in the near term, as follows:

- if the financial assets would have met the definition of loans and receivables (but for the fact that they had to be classified as held for trading at initial recognition), they may be reclassified into loans and receivables where the Group has the intention and ability to hold the assets for the foreseeable future or until maturity;
- if the financial assets would not have met the definition of loans and receivables, they may be reclassified out of the held for trading category into available-for-sale financial assets in 'rare circumstances'.

Note 4: Segmental Analysis (in part)

	Retail £m	Wholesale £m	Commercial £m	Wealth and International £m	Insurance £m	Other £m	Reported Basis Total £m
Year ended 31 December 2011							
Net interest income	7,497	2,139	1,251	828	(67)	585	12,233
Other income (net of fee and commission expense)	1,649	3,335	446	1,197	2,687	(7)	9,307
Effects of liability management, volatile items and asset sales	48	(1,415)	—	—	—	1,293	(74)
Total income	9,194	4,059	1,697	2,025	2,620	1,871	21,466
Insurance claims	—	—	—	—	(343)	—	(343)
Total income, net of insurance claims	9,194	4,059	1,697	2,025	2,277	1,871	21,123
Operating expenses	(4,438)	(2,518)	(948)	(1,548)	(812)	(357)	(10,621)
Trading surplus	4,756	1,541	749	477	1,465	1,514	10,502
Impairment	(1,970)	(2,901)	(303)	(4,610)	—	(3)	(9,787)
Share of results of joint ventures and associates	11	14	—	3	—	(1)	27
Profit (loss) before tax and fair value unwind	2,797	(1,346)	446	(4,130)	1,465	1,510	742
Fair value unwind	839	2,174	53	194	(43)	(1,274)	1,943
Profit (loss) before tax	3,636	828	499	(3,936)	1,422	236	2,685
External revenue	12,267	2,895	1,263	2,144	3,253	(356)	21,466
Inter-segment revenue	(3,073)	1,164	434	(119)	(633)	2,227	—

(continued)

IFRS-BPPD 3.216

	Retail £m	Wholesale £m	Commercial £m	Wealth and International £m	Insurance £m	Other £m	Reported Basis Total £m
Segment revenue	9,194	4,059	1,697	2,025	2,620	1,871	21,466
Segment external assets	356,295	320,435	28,998	74,623	140,754	49,441	970,546
Segment customer deposits	247,088	91,357	32,107	42,019	—	1,335	413,906
Segment external liabilities	279,162	259,209	32,723	75,791	129,350	147,717	923,952
Other segment items reflected in income statement above:							
Depreciation and amortisation	364	967	53	60	91	67	1,602
Increase (decrease) in value of in-force business	—	—	—	3	(625)	—	(622)
Defined benefit scheme charges	121	33	33	25	23	(36)	199
Other segment items:							
Additions to tangible fixed assets	189	1,435	2	212	451	806	3,095
Investments in joint ventures and associates at end of year	147	80	—	104	—	3	334

Note 13: Investments in Joint Ventures and Associates

The Group's share of results of and investments in joint ventures and associates comprises:

	Joint Ventures			Associates			Total		
	2011 £m	2010 £m	2009 £m	2011 £m	2010 £m	2009 £m	2011 £m	2010 £m	2009 £m
Share of income statement amounts:									
Income	316	318	708	160	135	5	476	453	713
Expenses	(261)	(209)	(544)	(161)	(91)	(96)	(422)	(300)	(640)
Impairment	(20)	(126)	(272)	1	(92)	(114)	(19)	(218)	(386)
Insurance claims	—	—	(465)	—	—	—	—	—	(465)
Profit (loss) before tax	35	(17)	(573)	—	(48)	(205)	35	(65)	(778)
Tax	(4)	(22)	24	—	(1)	2	(4)	(23)	26
Share of post-tax results	31	(39)	(549)	—	(49)	(203)	31	(88)	(752)
Share of balance sheet amounts:									
Current assets	3,346	3,370	2,754	246	378	605	3,592	3,748	3,359
Non-current assets	2,148	2,868	4,662	976	1,184	1,611	3,124	4,052	6,273
Current liabilities	(714)	(588)	(2,175)	(293)	(433)	(494)	(1,007)	(1,021)	(2,669)
Non-current liabilities	(4,471)	(5,324)	(4,871)	(904)	(1,026)	(1,613)	(5,375)	(6,350)	(6,484)
Share of net assets at 31 December	309	326	370	25	103	109	334	429	479
Movement in investments over the year:									
At 1 January	326	370	55	103	109	—	429	479	55
Exchange and other adjustments	(3)	(8)	(15)	(1)	40	60	(4)	32	45
Adjustment on acquisition	—	—	956	—	—	219	—	—	1,175
Additional investments	7	71	140	3	6	12	10	77	152
Acquisitions	—	—	3	—	—	60	—	—	63
Disposals	(47)	(68)	(199)	(79)	(2)	(39)	(126)	(70)	(238)
Share of post-tax results	31	(39)	(549)	—	(49)	(203)	31	(88)	(752)
Dividends paid	(5)	—	(21)	(1)	(1)	—	(6)	(1)	(21)
Share of net assets at 31 December	309	326	370	25	103	109	334	429	479

During 2011, the Group recognised a net £8 million of losses of associates not previously recognised. The Group's unrecognised share of losses of associates during 2010 was £8 million (2009: £64 million) and of joint ventures is £85 million in 2011 (2010: £180 million; 2009: £424 million). For entities making losses, subsequent profits earned are not recognised until previously unrecognised losses are extinguished. The Group's unrecognised share of losses net of unrecognised profits on a cumulative basis of associates is £56 million (2010: £104 million; 2009: £64 million) and of joint ventures is £299 million (2010: £339 million; 2009: £424 million).

The Group's principal joint venture investment at 31 December 2011 was in Sainsbury's Bank plc; the Group owns 50 per cent of the ordinary share capital of Sainsbury's Bank plc, whose business is banking and principal area of operation is the UK. Sainsbury's Bank plc is incorporated in the UK and the Group's interest is held by a subsidiary.

Where entities have statutory accounts drawn up to a date other than 31 December management accounts are used when accounting for them by the Group.

Note 53: Related Party Transactions (in part)

Other Related Party Transactions (in part)

Joint Ventures and Associates

The Group provides both administration and processing services to its principal joint venture, Sainsbury's Bank plc. The amounts receivable by the Group during the year were £21 million (2010: £31 million), of which £10 million was outstanding at 31 December 2011 (2010: £8 million). At 31 December 2011, Sainsbury's Bank plc also had balances with the Group that were included in loans and advances to banks of £1,173 million (2010: £1,277 million), deposits by banks of £780 million (2010: £1,358 million) and trading liabilities of £340 million (2010: nil).

At 31 December 2011 there were loans and advances to customers of £5,185 million (2010: £5,660 million) outstanding and balances within customer deposits of £88 million (2010: £151 million) relating to other joint ventures and associates.

In addition to the above balances, the Group has a number of other associates held by its venture capital business that it accounts for at fair value through profit or loss. At 31 December 2011, these companies had total assets of approximately £11,500 million (2010: £12,216 million), total liabilities of approximately £10,807 million (2010: £11,937 million) and for the year ended 31 December 2011 had turnover of approximately £7,376 million (2010: £3,829 million) and made a net loss of approximately £83 million (2010: net profit of £182 million). In addition, the Group has provided £5,767 million (2010: £3,316 million) of financing to these companies on which it received £106 million (2010: £93 million) of interest income in the year.

Note 55: Financial Instruments (in part)

Valuation of Financial Instruments Carried at Fair Value

The valuations of financial instruments have been classified into three levels according to the quality and reliability of information used to determine the fair values.

Level 1 Portfolios

Level 1 fair value measurements are those derived from unadjusted quoted prices in active markets for identical assets or liabilities. Products classified as level 1 predominantly comprise equity shares, treasury bills and other government securities.

Level 2 Portfolios

Level 2 valuations are those where quoted market prices are not available, for example where the instrument is traded in a market that is not considered to be active or valuation techniques are used to determine fair value and where these techniques use inputs that are based significantly on observable market data. Examples of such financial instruments include most over-the-counter derivatives, financial institution issued securities, certificates of deposit and certain asset-backed securities.

Level 3 Portfolios

Level 3 portfolios are those where at least one input which could have a significant effect on the instrument's valuation is not based on observable market data. Such instruments would include the Group's venture capital and unlisted equity investments which are valued using various valuation techniques that require significant management judgement in determining appropriate assumptions, including earnings multiples and estimated future cash flows. Certain of the Group's asset-backed securities and derivatives, principally where there is no trading activity in such securities, are also classified as level 3.

Valuation Hierarchy (in part)

	Level 1 £m	Level 2 £m	Level 3 £m	Total £m
At 31 December 2011				
Trading and other financial assets at fair value through profit or loss				
Loans and advances to customers	—	9,766	—	9,766
Loans and advances to banks	—	1,355	—	1,355
Debt securities:				
Government securities	21,326	2,041	—	23,367
Other public sector securities	375	808	—	1,183
Bank and building society certificates of deposit	—	3,248	—	3,248
Asset-backed securities:				
Mortgage-backed securities	187	524	—	711
Other asset-backed securities	178	1,605	203	1,986
Corporate and other debt securities	5,098	15,337	1,423	21,858
	27,164	23,563	1,626	52,353
Equity shares	74,381	41	1,315	75,737
Treasury and other bills	299	—	—	299
Total trading and other financial assets at fair value through profit or loss	101,844	34,725	2,941	139,510

(continued)

	Level 1 £m	Level 2 £m	Level 3 £m	Total £m
Available-for-sale financial assets				
Debt securities:				
Government securities	25,143	93	—	25,236
Other public sector securities	27	—	—	27
Bank and building society certificates of deposit	323	43	—	366
Asset-backed securities:				
Mortgage-backed securities	—	1,803	—	1,803
Other asset-backed securities	—	807	257	1,064
Corporate and other debt securities	41	5,192	12	5,245
	25,534	7,938	269	33,741
Equity shares	55	96	1,787	1,938
Treasury and other bills	972	755	—	1,727
Total available-for-sale financial assets	26,561	8,789	2,056	37,406
Derivative financial instruments	204	63,160	2,649	66,013
Total financial assets carried at fair value	128,609	106,674	7,646	242,929
Trading and other financial liabilities at fair value through profit or loss				
Liabilities held at fair value through profit or loss (debt securities)	—	5,339	—	5,339
Trading liabilities:				
Liabilities in respect of securities sold under repurchase agreements	—	12,378	—	12,378
Short positions in securities	3,168	533	—	3,701
Other	—	3,537	—	3,537
	3,168	16,448	—	19,616
Total trading and other financial liabilities at fair value through profit or loss	3,168	21,787	—	24,955
Derivative financial instruments	35	57,436	741	58,212
Financial guarantees	—	—	49	49
Total financial liabilities carried at fair value	3,203	79,223	790	83,216

There were no significant transfers between level 1 and level 2 during the year.

Valuation Methodology (in part)

Equity Investments (Including Venture Capital)

Unlisted equities and fund investments are accounted for as trading and other financial assets at fair value through profit or loss or as available-for-sale financial assets. These investments are valued using different techniques as a result of the variety of investments across the portfolio in accordance with the Group's valuation policy and are calculated using International Private Equity and Venture Capital Guidelines.

Included within the gains (losses) recognised in other comprehensive income are losses of £132 million (2010: gains of £269 million) related to financial instruments that are held in the level 3 portfolio at the year end.

	Valuation Basis/Technique	Main Assumptions	At 31 December 2011 Carrying Value £m	Effect of Reasonably Possible Alternative Assumptions Favourable Changes £m	Unfavourable Changes £m	At 31 December 2010 Carrying Value £m	Effect of Reasonably Possible Alternative Assumptions Favourable Changes £m	Unfavourable Changes £m
Trading and Other Financial Assets at Fair Value Through Profit or Loss								
Asset-backed securities	Lead manager or broker quote/ consensus pricing from market data provider	Use of single pricing source	203	1	(1)	283	8	(8)
Equity and venture capital investments	Various valuation techniques	Earnings, net asset value and earnings multiples, forecast cash flows	1,823	56	(59)	2,072	135	(111)
Unlisted equities and property partnerships in the life funds			915	—	—	481	—	—
			2,941			2,836		

Venture Capital and Equity Investments

Third party valuers have been used to determine the value of unlisted equities and property partnerships included in the Group's life insurance funds.

The valuation techniques used for unlisted equities and venture capital investments vary depending on the nature of the investment, as described in the valuation methodology section above. Reasonably possible alternative valuations for these investments have been calculated by reference to the relevant approach taken as appropriate to the business sector and investment circumstances and as such the following inputs have been considered:

- for valuations derived from earnings multiples, consideration is given to the risk attributes, growth prospects and financial gearing of comparable businesses when selecting an appropriate multiple;
- the discount rates used in discounted cash flow valuations; and

- in line with International Private Equity and Venture Capital Guidelines, the values of underlying investments in fund investments portfolios.

Share of Income and Other Comprehensive Income From Associates and Jointly-Controlled Entities Excluded From Operating Profit

3.217

Coca-Cola Hellenic Bottling Company S.A. (Dec 2011)

CONSOLIDATED INCOME STATEMENT (in part)

	Note	Year Ended 31 December		
		2011 € Million	2010[1] € Million	2009[1] € Million
Operating profit	3	468.4	649.9	642.6
Finance income		9.8	7.4	9.4
Finance costs		(96.1)	(83.1)	(82.2)
Loss on net monetary position	21	(7.8)	—	—
Total finance costs, net	21	(94.1)	(75.7)	(72.8)
Share of results of equity method investments	6	1.2	2.5	(1.9)
Profit before tax		375.5	576.7	567.9

CONSOLIDATED STATEMENT OF COMPREHENSIVE INCOME (in part)

	Year Ended 31 December		
	2011 € Million	2010[1] € Million	2009[1] € Million
Other comprehensive income:			
Share of other comprehensive income of equity method investments	(0.8)	1.4	(0.7)
Other comprehensive income for the year, net of tax (refer to Note 24)	(74.9)	173.7	(82.7)
Total comprehensive income for the year	197.9	612.4	342.3

NOTES TO THE CONSOLIDATED FINANCIAL STATEMENTS (in part)

1. Basis of Preparation and Accounting Policies (in part)

Description of Business

Coca-Cola Hellenic Bottling Company S.A. ('Coca-Cola Hellenic' or 'the Group') is a Société Anonyme (corporation) incorporated in Greece and founded in 1969. It took its current form in August 2000 through the acquisition of the Coca-Cola Beverages plc ('CCB') by Hellenic Bottling Company S.A. ('HBC'). Coca-Cola Hellenic and its subsidiaries (collectively 'the Company' or 'the Group') are principally engaged in the production, sales and distribution of non-alcoholic ready to drink beverages, under franchise from The Coca-Cola Company ('TCCC'). The Company distributes its products in 27 countries in Europe and Nigeria. Information on the Company's operations by segment is included in Note 3.

Coca-Cola Hellenic's shares are listed on the Athens Exchange (symbol: EEEK), with a secondary listing on the London Stock Exchange (symbol: CCB). Coca-Cola Hellenic's American Depositary Receipts (ADRs) are listed on the New York Stock Exchange (symbol: CCH).

These consolidated financial statements were approved for issue by the Board of Directors on 15 March 2012 and are expected to be verified at the Annual General Meeting to be held on 25 June 2012.

Basis of Preparation

The consolidated financial statements included in this document are prepared in accordance with International Financial Reporting Standards ('IFRS') issued by the International Accounting Standards Board ('IASB') and IFRS as adopted by the European Union ('EU').

All IFRS issued by the IASB, which apply to the preparation of these consolidated financial statements, have been adopted by the EU following an approval process undertaken by the European Commission and the European Financial Reporting Advisory Group ('EFRAG').

The consolidated financial statements are prepared under the historical cost convention, as modified by the revaluation of available-for-sale financial assets and derivative financial instruments and the financial statements of certain subsidiaries operating in a hyperinflationary economy which are restated and expressed in terms of the measuring unit currency at the balance sheet date and translated to Euro at the exchange rate of the balance sheet date.

Investments in Associates

Investments in associated undertakings are accounted for by the equity method of accounting. Associated undertakings are all entities over which the Group has significant influence but not control, generally accompanying a shareholding of between 20% to 50% of the voting rights.

The equity method of accounting involves recognising the Group's share of the associates' post acquisition profit or loss

for the period in the income statement and its share of the post-acquisition movement in other comprehensive income is recognised in other comprehensive income. The Group's interest in each associate is carried in the balance sheet at an amount that reflects its share of the net assets of the associate and includes goodwill on acquisition. When the Group's share of losses in an associate equals or exceeds its interest in the associate, the Group does not recognise further losses, unless the Group has incurred obligations or made payments on behalf of the associate.

Investment in Joint Ventures

The Group's interests in its jointly controlled entities are accounted for using the equity method of accounting. In respect of its interests in jointly controlled operations and jointly controlled assets the Group recognises its proportional share of related assets, liabilities, income and expenses.

6. Equity Method Investments

(a) Investments in Associates

The effective interest held in and the carrying value of the investments in associates at 31 December are:

	Country of Incorporation	Effective Interest Held 2011	Effective Interest Held 2010	Carrying Value 2011 € Million	Carrying Value 2010 € Million
Frigoglass Industries Limited	Nigeria	24%	16%	15.6	14.5
PET to PET Recycling Österreich GmbH	Austria	20%	20%	0.9	0.9
Total investments in associates				16.5	15.4

The Group holds an effective interest in Frigoglass Industries Limited through a 23.9% (2010: 23.9%) holding held by Nigerian Bottling Company plc in which the Group has a 100%

(2010: 66.4%) interest since September 2011. There are restrictive controls on the movement of funds out of Nigeria.

Summarised financial information of the associates, concerning our effective interest held, is as follows:

	Frigoglass Industries Limited 2011 € Million	2010 € Million	2009 € Million	PET to PET Recycling Österreich GmbH 2011 € Million	2010 € Million	2009 € Million
Assets	35.4	19.9	14.5	3.3	3.4	3.2
Liabilities	12.1	6.4	3.9	2.4	2.6	2.4
Revenues	23.9	14.8	12.5	2.6	2.0	1.5
Total profit and loss for the year	2.9	2.0	1.3	0.1	0.1	0.1

(b) Jointly Controlled Entities

The effective interest held in and the carrying value of the Group's jointly controlled entities, which are accounted for using the equity method of accounting, as at 31 December are:

	Country of Incorporation	Effective Interest Held 2011	Effective Interest Held 2010	Carrying Value 2011 € Million	Carrying Value 2010 € Million
Fonti Del Vulture S.r.l	Italy	50%	50%	21.0	20.8
Ilko Hellenic Partners GmbH	Austria	0%	33%	—	0.9
Multivita Sp. z o.o.	Poland	50%	50%	3.0	1.7
Valser Mineralquellen GmbH	Switzerland	50%	50%	2.4	2.3
Total investments in jointly controlled entities				26.4	25.7

Apart from the companies mentioned above, the Group holds 50% effective interest (2010: 50%) in two additional jointly controlled entities, Dorna Apemin S.A. in Romania and Vlasinka d.o.o., in Serbia, whose carrying values are not significant.

On 27 March 2008 the Group together with TCCC and Illycaffe S.p.A. formed a three-party joint venture, Ilko Hellenic Partners GmbH, for the manufacture, marketing, selling and distribution of premium ready-to-drink coffee under the "illy" brand across Coca-Cola Hellenic's territories. In 2011, the Group disposed its interest in the joint venture, which had no significant effect on the Group's financial statements (loss of €0.6 m). The Group continues to sell and distribute ready-to-drink coffee under the "illy" brand across its territories.

Changes in the carrying amounts of equity method investments are as follows:

	2011 € Million	2010 € Million	2009 € Million
As at 1 January	41.1	36.2	38.8
Capital increase	1.7	2.9	—
Disposals	(0.3)	—	—
Share of results of equity method investments	1.2	2.5	(1.9)
Return of capital from associates	—	(1.9)	—
Foreign currency translation	(0.8)	1.4	(0.7)
As at 31 December	42.9	41.1	36.2

IAS 17, *LEASES*

IFRS Overview and Comparison to U.S. GAAP

Author's Note

In August 2010, IASB and FASB published an exposure draft on accounting for leases as part of their convergence agenda. An author's note in section 2 in section titled "IAS 17, *Leases*" provides brief update on the status of this project.

The discussion in this subsection addresses only the effect of IAS 17 on the statement of comprehensive income. Recognition, measurement, presentation, and disclosures related to leasehold assets and liabilities shown on the balance sheet are discussed in section 2.

Author's Note

In 2011, IASB issued IFRS 13, which amended IAS 17. This amendment explains that the definition of fair value in IAS 17 is different from that in IFRS 13. Therefore, when applying IAS 17, an entity should measure fair value in accordance with IAS 17 and not IFRS 13.

Because this standard is effective for annual periods beginning on or after 1 January 2012, these amendments are not reflected in the commentary in this section. However, these amendments would not affect the availability of illustrative excerpts from survey companies' financial statements.

3.218 IAS 17 establishes the criteria for revenue and expense recognition for both lessees and lessors, regardless of whether the entity accounts for the lease as an operating or finance lease. A *finance lease* is one that transfers substantially all of the risks and rewards of ownership to the lessee. Classification as a finance lease requires a lessee to recognize an asset and related liability on its balance sheet and a lessor to remove the leased asset from its balance sheet and recognize a receivable for the lease payments. When a lease does not meet the criteria for classification as a finance lease, both the lessee and lessor should classify it as an operating lease.

Recognition and Measurement

IFRSs

3.219 Lessees holding assets under finance leases should recognize depreciation expense on the leasehold asset and a finance charge (interest expense) on the leasehold liability using the effective interest method of amortization. A lessee should recognize contingent rents as an expense of the period in which they are incurred.

3.220 A lessee should test and measure impairment losses on leased assets in accordance with IAS 36.

3.221 A lessee holding leased assets under operating leases should recognize expense on a straight-line basis over the lease term, unless another systematic basis better represents the pattern of benefits it expects to receive from the asset's use.

3.222 At the inception of a finance lease, a lessor should recognize a receivable measured at its net investment in the leased asset. A lessor should treat the lease payment as a return of principal and finance income and recognize the latter based on the effective interest method. A manufacturer or dealer lessor should recognize selling profit or loss during the period in accordance with its policy for regular sales. However, if artificially low rates of interest are quoted, the entity should restrict its selling profit to what would be earned if it charged a market rate of interest. Manufacturer and dealer lessors should recognize costs incurred to negotiate or conclude the lease as an expense in the same period as they recognize selling profit or loss.

3.223 A lessor should recognize lease income on operating leases on a straight-line basis over the lease term, unless another systematic basis better represents the pattern of benefits it expects to receive from the asset's use. A lessor should recognize other costs, such as depreciation expense on the leased asset, as an expense. A lessor should add any initial indirect costs of negotiating and concluding the lease agreement to the carrying value of the asset and recognize an expense over the lease term on the same basis as it recognizes income.

U.S. GAAP

3.224 Like IFRSs, FASB ASC 840-10-25 contains guidance for assessing whether a lessee holds an asset under an operating lease or a capital (finance) lease. These criteria are similar to those in IFRSs. Like IFRSs, when the lessee holds an asset under an operating lease, FASB ASC 840-20-25-1 requires the lessee to recognize operating lease payments as expense on a straight-line basis over the lease term, unless another systematic and rational basis is more representative of the time pattern in which use benefit is derived from the leased property. In the latter case, the entity should use that basis.

3.225 Like IFRSs, FASB ASC 840-30-25-1 requires a lessee that holds an asset under a capital lease to record a leased asset and a corresponding lease liability. In accordance with paragraphs 1 and 6 of FASB ASC 840-30-35, when the asset is depreciable, the lessee should recognize depreciation expense on the asset and recognize interest expense on the liability using the effective interest method.

3.226 Unlike IFRSs, when the lessee recognizes a capital lease, paragraphs 41–45 of FASB ASC 840-10-25 provide additional criteria that lessors should meet before recognizing a capital lease and removing the asset from their balance sheet. Once a lessor meets those criteria, like IFRSs, FASB ASC 840-30 requires the entity to recognize a receivable measured at its net investment in the lease. The lessor should then recognize interest income using the effective interest method. Similar to the requirements for lessee recognition of rent expense, FASB ASC 840-20-25-1 explains that if the lessor has an operating lease, it should recognize lease income on a straight-line basis over the lease term, unless another systematic and rational basis is more representative of the time pattern in which use benefit is derived from the leased property. In the latter case, the entity should use that basis.

Presentation

IFRSs

3.227 Unless an item of income or expense is material, neither IAS 1 nor IAS 17 require an entity to present income or expense items associated with lease agreements separately in the statement of comprehensive income.

U.S. GAAP

3.228 FASB ASC 840-30-45-3 does not require a lessee to classify interest expense or amortization of leased assets as separate items in the income statement. However, when the lessee includes amortization of assets held under capital leases in depreciation expense and discloses that fact, the lessee should separately disclose the amount of the amortization in either the financial statements or notes. FASB ASC 840-30-45 does not address any lessor income statement presentation matters.

3.229 FASB ASC 840-20-45-1 states that lessees should include rental costs associated with an operating lease in income from continuing operations. However, like IFRSs, this paragraph does not require rental costs to be identified separately on the income statement. FASB ASC 840-20-45 does not address income statement presentation by a lessor.

Disclosure

IFRSs

3.230 A lessee holding assets under finance leases should disclose any contingent rents recognized as an expense dur-

ing the period. A lessee holding assets under operating leases should disclose lease and sublease payments recognized as an expense during the period, separately disclosing the amounts of minimum lease payments, sublease payments, and contingent rents.

3.231 If an impairment loss is recognized or reversed with respect to leased assets, an entity should make the required disclosures, in accordance with IAS 36.

3.232 Leases are included within the scope of IFRS 7, *Financial Instruments: Disclosures*, the requirements of which are applicable to lessors. In addition, for a finance lease, a lessor should disclose a reconciliation of its gross investment in the lease and present value of the lease receivable and any unearned finance income and contingent rents recognized as income during the period. For an operating lease, a lessor should disclose the amounts of future minimum lease payments and contingent rents recognized as income during the period.

U.S. GAAP

3.233 Like IFRSs, FASB ASC 840-20-50-1 requires a lessee holding assets under an operating lease to disclose rental expense for each period for which an income statement is presented, with separate amounts for minimum rentals, contingent rentals, and sublease rentals. An entity need not include rental payments under leases with terms of one month or less that were not renewed. For operating leases having initial or remaining noncancelable lease terms of more than one year, FASB ASC 840-20-50-2 requires a lessee to disclose the following, as of the date of the latest balance sheet presented:
- Required future minimum rental payments (in the aggregate and for each of the five succeeding fiscal years)
- Total future minimum rentals to be received under noncancelable subleases

3.234 Like IFRSs, FASB ASC 840-30-50-1 requires a lessee holding assets under a capital lease to disclose the following:
- As of the date of the latest balance sheet presented, future minimum lease payments (in the aggregate and for each of the five succeeding fiscal years) and total future minimum sublease rentals to be received
- For each period for which an income statement is presented, contingent rentals payments actually incurred

3.235 Like IFRSs, FASB ASC 235-10-50-1 requires disclosures of accounting policies. However, paragraphs 4–5 of FASB ASC 840-10-50 include more specific guidance with respect to accounting policy disclosures when leasing is a significant part of the lessor's income; they also require disclosure of its policy on contingent rents. See paragraph 2.252 in section 2 for a discussion of lessors' disclosure requirements.

3.236 Like IFRSs, FASB ASC 840-20-50-4 requires lessors with operating leases to disclose future minimum lease payments and contingent rental income recognized during the period.

3.237 Unlike IFRSs, U.S. GAAP does not generally require reconciliation disclosures previously explained. Also, FASB ASC 840-30 does not direct an entity to the guidance on financial liabilities as IAS 17 directs lessees that are contractually obligated under finance leases to IFRS 7. FASB

ASC 825-10-50-8 exempts an entity from providing the required fair value disclosures for its lease contracts. However, like IFRSs, paragraphs 20–23 of FASB ASC 825-10-50 require an entity to provide the required disclosures about concentrations of credit risk and market risk for its lease liabilities.

Presentation and Disclosure Excerpts

Lessee—Finance and Operating Leases, Lessor—Operating Leases

3.238

Embraer S.A. (Dec 2011)

CONSOLIDATED STATEMENTS OF INCOME
(in part)

In millions of US dollars, except earnings per share

	Note	12.31.2011	12.31.2010	12.31.2009
Revenue		5,803.0	5,364.1	5,497.8
Cost of sales and services		(4,495.9)	(4,338.1)	(4,428.4)
Gross Profit		1,307.1	1,026.0	1,069.4
Operating Income (Expense)				
Administrative		(262.5)	(197.5)	(191.3)
Selling		(419.3)	(374.1)	(304.6)
Research		(85.3)	(72.1)	(55.6)
Other operating (expense) income, net	32	(221.5)	9.4	(138.5)
Equity		(0.3)	—	—
Operating profit before financial income (expense)		318.2	391.7	379.4
Financial income (expense), net	34	(90.7)	17.5	10.2
Foreign exchange gain (loss), net	35	20.0	(1.1)	(68.8)
Profit before taxes on income		247.5	408.1	320.8

NOTES TO THE CONSOLIDATED FINANCIAL STATEMENTS (in part)

In millions of US dollars, unless otherwise stated

1. Operations

Embraer S.A. (the "Company" or "Embraer") is a publicly-held company incorporated under the laws of the Federative Republic of Brazil with headquarters in São José dos Campos, State of São Paulo, Brazil. The corporate purpose of the Company is:

- The development, production and sale of jet and turboprop aircraft for civil and defense aviation, aircraft for agricultural use, structural components, mechanical and hydraulic systems, aviation services and technical activities related to the production and maintenance of aerospace material;
- The design, construction and sale of equipment, materials, systems, software, accessories and components to the defense, security and energy industries and the promotion or performance of technical activities related to production and maintenance, keeping the highest technological and quality standards;
- The performance of other technological, industrial, commercial and service activities related to the defense, security and energy industries; and
- Contribution to the formation of technical professionals necessary to the aerospace industry.

The Company's shares are listed on the enhanced corporate governance segment of the Stock Exchange in Brazil ("BM&FBOVESPA"), known as the New Market ("Novo Mercado"). The Company also has American Depositary Shares (evidenced by American Depositary Receipts-ADRs) which are registered with the Securities and Exchange Commission ("SEC") and are listed on the New York Stock Exchange ("NYSE"). The Company has no controlling group and its capital comprises only common shares.

The Company has consolidated wholly-owned and jointly controlled entities and/or commercial representation offices which are located in Brazil, the United States of America ("United States"), France, Spain, Portugal, China and Singapore. Their activities comprise sales, marketing, and after sales and maintenance services.

The presented Financial Statements were approved by the Board of Directors of the Company on March 15, 2012.

2. Presentation of the Financial Statements and Accounting Practices (in part)

2.1 Presentation of the Financial Statements

Basis of Preparation

The consolidated financial statements have been prepared in conformity with International Financial Reporting Standards ("IFRS") issued by the International Accounting Standards Board ("IASB") which comprise (i) IFRS, (ii) the International Accounting Standard ("IAS"), and (iii) the International Financial Reporting Interpretations Committee ("IFRIC") or its predecessor the Standing Interpretations Committee ("SIC"). For the purposes of these consolidated financial statements presented in accordance with IFRS there are no differences in relation to the current accounting practices adopted in Brazil ("Brazilian GAAP") for the periods presented.

These consolidated financial statements were prepared under the historical cost convention and adjusted to reflect assets and liabilities measured at fair value through profit or loss or marked to market when available for sale.

The preparation of financial statements in conformity with IFRS requires the use of certain critical accounting estimates. It also requires management of the Company ("Management") to exercise its judgment in the process of applying the Company's accounting policies. The areas which involve a higher degree of judgment or complexity, or assumptions and estimates significant to the consolidated financial statements are disclosed in Note 3. The actual results may differ from these estimates and assumptions.

(p) Property, Plant and Equipment

Property, plant and equipment are recorded at purchase, formation or construction cost, less accumulated depreciation and impairment losses.

Depreciation is calculated on the straight-line method (except spare parts held in the Exchange Pool Program) based on their estimated useful lives. (Note 16) This considers the time over which the asset will provide a financial return for the Company, and is reviewed annually. Land is not depreciated.

The Company estimates the residual value for certain aircraft and spare parts included in the Exchange Pool Program. Other items of property, plant and equipment do not have residual value attributed by the Company since, due to the characteristics and use of these assets, it is unusual to dispose of large quantities of these assets and, when this occurs, they are realized at insignificant values.

Subsequent costs are included in the book value of the asset or recorded as a separate asset, as appropriate, only when it is likely that the item will yield future economic benefits and the cost of the item can be reliably measured. The book value of replacement items or parts is written off. All other repairs and maintenance costs incurred are recorded in the statement of income.

Materials allocated to specific projects are capitalized in property, plant and equipment in progress and subsequently transferred to the final property, plant and equipment accounts.

The cost of charges on loans obtained to finance construction of property, plant and equipment are capitalized during the period required to build and prepare the asset for its intended use.

The gains and losses on disposals are determined by comparing the amount received with the book value and are reported under Other operating income (expenses), net in the statement of income.

The items comprising property, plant and equipment are summarized below:
- Land—mainly comprises areas on which the industrial, engineering and administrative buildings are located.
- Buildings and land improvements—buildings are mainly plants, engineering departments and offices, and land improvements include parking lots, road systems and water and sewage networks.
- Facilities—comprise auxiliary industrial facilities that directly or indirectly support the Company's industrial operations, as well as facilities of the engineering and administrative departments.
- Machinery and equipment—comprise the machinery and other equipment directly or indirectly used in the manufacturing process.
- Furniture and fixtures—comprise furniture and fixtures used in the production, engineering and administrative departments.
- Vehicles—comprise mainly industrial vehicles and automobiles.
- Aircraft—comprise mainly aircraft leased to airlines, and those used by the parent company to assist in testing new projects.
- Computers and peripherals—comprise technology equipment used mainly in the production process, engineering and administration.
- Property, plant and equipment in progress—comprise construction works to expand the manufacturing plants and aircraft maintenance centers.
- Spare parts pool—comprises a spare parts pool for the exclusive use of customers who are included in the Exchange Pool Program. This program allows these customers to exchange a damaged component for one in working condition, as defined in the contract. These items are depreciated based on estimated useful lives of seven to ten years and an average residual value of 35%, which the Company believes to be the approximate utilization time and realizable amount, respectively.

(u) Leases

The classification of a lease depends on whether an agreement is or contains a lease, is based on the essence of the agreement and includes a determination as to whether (i) the fulfillment of the agreement depends on the use of one or more specific assets and (ii) the agreement assigns the right to use the asset.

(i) Aircraft Leases

Aircraft leases classified as operating leases are recorded on the balance sheet as property, plant and equipment, and depreciated over their estimated useful lives. The rental income (net of any subsidy granted to the lessee) is recorded by the straight-line method over the lease period. Aircraft leases classified as finance leases are derecognized as Company's assets once the lease commences; the income and respective cost of sales are recorded at inception.

(ii) Other Leases

Other leases in which the Company holds substantially all the risks and benefits of ownership are classified as finance leases. Finance leases are recorded as a financed purchase, initially by recording a property, plant and equipment asset and a financial liability (lease). Property, plant and equipment assets purchased classified as finance leases are depreciated at the rates in Note 16.

Other leases in which a significant part of the risks and benefits of ownership are assumed by the lessor are classified as operating leases. Payments made for operating leases are appropriated to the statement of income on the straight-line method over the contract period.

(gg) Unearned Income

This refers to commitments to supply spare parts, training, technical representatives and other commitments established in sales contracts for aircraft already delivered, the income from which will be appropriated when the service or product is delivered to the customer.

This account also includes the unearned income on the sale of certain aircraft that, because of contractual obligations, are accounted for as operating leases.

(ii) Revenue Recognition (in part)

(v) Revenue from Operating Leases

The Company also recognizes the revenue from aircraft rental as operating leases, proportional to the lease period, and records such revenues as income by segment. Revenues are allocated to their respective segments (commercial, executive and defense and security).

(jj) Cost of Sales and Services

Cost of sales and services consist of the cost of the aircraft, spare parts and services rendered, comprising:
  (i) Material—substantially all material costs are covered by contracts with suppliers. Prices under these contracts are generally adjusted based on escalation formula which reflect, in part, inflation in the United States.
  (ii) Labor—comprises salaries and related charges, primarily in Brazilian Real.
  (iii) Depreciation—property, plant and equipment are depreciated over their useful lives, on a straight-line basis, from five to 48 years.

  Depreciation of aircraft classified as operating leases is recorded in Cost of sales and services, from lease inception using the straight-line method over the estimated asset useful lives less a residual value at the end of the lease term.
  (iv) Amortization—Internally generated intangible assets are amortized in accordance with the estimated sales of the series of aircraft. Intangible assets acquired from third parties are amortized on straight-line bases over their estimated useful lives.
  (v) Product warranties—The Company estimates and records a liability for guarantees obligations related to its products on the date of delivery of the aircraft, based on historical experience.
  (vi) Multiple elements arrangements—The Company enters into transactions that represent multiple-element arrangements, such as for providing training, technical assistance, spare parts and other concessions. These costs are recognized when the product or service is provided to the customer.

3. Critical Accounting Estimates (in part)

The preparation of the financial statements in conformity with generally accepted accounting principles requires management to make estimates and adopt assumptions that affect the reported amounts of assets and liabilities, disclosure of contingent assets and liabilities and the fair value of financial instruments and guarantees on the balance sheet dates and the reported amounts of revenues and expenses during the reporting period. Actual results may differ from such estimates.

In order to provide an understanding about how Management forms its judgments about future events, including the variables and assumptions underlying the estimates, and the sensitivity of those judgments to different variables and conditions, the estimates and assumptions that may cause a risk of material adjustment to the carrying amounts of assets and liabilities are addressed below:

a) Sales and Other Operating Revenues

The Company recognizes revenues from sales made by the commercial, executive, aviation services and Defense and security business when benefits and risk of ownership are transferred to customers, which, in the case of aircraft, occurs when delivery is made, and, in the case of aviation services, when the service is rendered.

The Company also recognizes rental revenue for leased aircraft, classified as operating leases on a straight-line basis over the lease term and, when presenting information by operating segment, rental revenue is recorded in Other related businesses line of the segment reporting.

In the Defense and security segment, a significant portion of revenues is derived from long-term development contracts with the Brazilian and foreign governments accounted for on the POC method. These contracts contain provisions for price escalation based on a mix of indices related to raw material and labor cost. From time to time, the Company reassesses the expected margins of certain long-term contracts, adjusting revenue recognition based upon projected costs to completion. Use of the POC method requires the Company to estimate the total costs to be incurred on the contracts. Were the total costs to be incurred to come in 10% below Management's estimates, the amount of revenue recognized in the year of 2011 would increase by US$ 72.7 and if the total costs were to come in by 10% above the estimate, the amount of revenue recognized would decrease by US$ 77.7.

Revenue under Exchange Pool Programs is recognized monthly over the contract term and consists in part of a fixed fee and in part a variable fee directly related to aircraft flying hours.

The Company enters into transactions that represent multiple-element arrangements, such as training, technical assistance, spare parts and others concessions, which are included in the aircraft purchase price. Multiple-element arrangements are assessed to determine whether they can be separated into more than one unit of accounting when all of the following criteria are met:
  • the delivered item has value to the client on a stand-alone basis;
  • there is objective and reliable evidence of the fair value of the undelivered item; and
  • if the arrangement includes a general right of return relative to the delivered item, delivery or performance of the undelivered item is considered probable and substantially under the Company's control.
If these criteria are not met, the arrangement is accounted for as a single unit of accounting, which results in revenue being deferred until the earlier of when such criteria are met or when the last completed element is delivered. If these criteria are met for each element and there is objective and reliable evidence of fair value for all units of accounting in an arrangement, the arrangement consideration is allocated to the separate units of accounting based on each unit's relative fair value.

c) Guarantees and Residual Value

The Company may offer financial and residual value guarantees. The Company reviews the value of these commitments relative to the aircraft's anticipated future fair value and, in the case of financial guarantees, the creditworthiness of the obligor. Provisions and losses are recorded when and if payments become probable and are reasonably estimable. The Company estimates future fair value using third-party appraisals of aircraft valuations, including information developed from the sale or lease of similar aircraft in the secondary market. The Company evaluates the creditworthiness of obligors for which it provides credit guarantees by analyzing a number of factors, including third-party credit ratings and the estimated obligors' borrowing costs.

d) Residual Interests in Aircraft

In structured financing arrangements, an entity purchases an aircraft from the Company, pays the full purchase price on delivery or at the conclusion of the sales financing structure, and leases the related aircraft to the ultimate customer. A third-party financial institution facilitates the financing of the aircraft and a portion of the credit risk remains with that third party.

Although it has no equity investee interests, the Company controls the SPEs operations or takes a majority share of their risks and rewards. When the Company no longer holds control, the assets and liabilities related to the aircraft are deconsolidated from the Company's balance sheet.

The Company evaluates control characteristics over the SPE principally based on a qualitative assessment. This includes a review of the SPE's capital structure, contractual relationships and terms, nature of the SPE's operations and purpose, nature of the SPE's interests issued, and the Company's interests in the entity which either create or absorb variability. The Company evaluates the design of the SPE and the related risks the entity and the variable interest holders are exposed to in evaluating consolidation. In a few cases, when it is unclear from a qualitative standpoint if the Company has control over the SPE, it uses a quantitative analysis to calculate the probability-weighted expected losses and probability-weighted expected residual returns using cash flow and statistical risk measurement modeling.

10. Collateralized Accounts Receivable and Recourse and Non-Recourse Debt (In part)

(a) Collateralized Accounts Receivable

	12.31.2011	12.31.2010
Minimum lease payments receivable	366.9	455.3
Estimated residual value of leased assets	458.4	458.4
Unearned income	(337.7)	(375.5)
Investment in sales-type lease	487.6	538.2
Less-current portion	14.9	11.6
Long-term portion	472.7	526.6

19. Loans and Financing (in part)

	Currency	Contractual Interest Rate—%	Effective Interest Rate—%	Maturity	12.31.2011	12.31.2010
Other currencies:						
		1.00% to 6.38%	1.00% to 6.72%			
Working Capital	US$	LIBOR 1M + 0.50% to 1.10%	LIBOR 1M + 0.50% to 1.10%		933.8	949.3
	Euro	Euribor 6M + 1.75%	Euribor 6M + 1.75%	2020	29.6	10.1
		1.5% to 2.68%	1.5% to 2.68%			
Project development	US$	6.87%	6.87%	2015	1.1	1.4
		2.62%	2.62%			
Property, plant and equipment	US$	LIBOR 1M + 2.44%	LIBOR 1M + 2.44%	2035	70.8	71.3
		6.16% to 7.95%	6.16% to 7.95%			
Finance leasing	US$	LIBOR 12M + 2.54% to 3.40%	LIBOR 12M + 2.54% to 3.40%	2014	1.8	2.2
In local currency:					1,037.1	1,034.3
Export Financing	R$	4.5% to 9.0%	4.5% to 9.0%	2013	405.1	331.4
		TJLP + 1.92% to 5.0%	TJLP + 1.92% to 5.0%			
Project development	R$	3.5% to 4.5%	3.5% to 4.5%	2018	214.8	67.6
Finance leasing	R$	CDI + 0.49% to 2.46%	CDI + 0.49% to 2.46%	2015	1.1	1.5
					621.0	400.5
					1,658.1	1,434.8
Less-current portion					251.8	72.6
Long-term portion					1,406.3	1,362.2

(b) Capital Lease Obligations

The leasing operations are guaranteed by the assets under lease and their breakdown by maturity is shown below:

	12.31.2011	12.31.2010
Less than one year	1.4	1.7
More than one year and less than five years	1.8	2.6
	3.2	4.3
Less-Implicit interest	(0.3)	(0.6)
Capital lease obligation	2.9	3.7
The present value of capital lease obligations, following:		
Less than one year	1.3	1.6
More than one year and less than five years	1.6	2.1
	2.9	3.7

IFRS-BPPD 3.238

21. Other Payables

	12.31.2011	12.31.2010
Other accounts payable[i]	45.5	39.3
Contractual obligations[ii]	29.6	29.2
Security deposit	6.9	10.1
Insurance	6.4	6.4
Commercial incentives	3.9	12.9
Accrued materials[iii]	1.5	1.6
Financial credit[iv]	1.4	2.0
Brazilian Air Force[v]	—	2.7
Related party[vi]	—	7.8
	95.2	112.0
Less—current portion	81.2	84.4
Long—term portion	14.0	27.6

[i] Expenses incurred in December, for payment in the following month;
[ii] Represents mainly amounts provided to cover maintenance costs of aircraft under operating under lease agreements;
[iii] Accessories or components to be installed in aircraft already delivered, in accordance with the contracts;
[iv] Amounts provided to compensate customers for certain financing costs;
[v] The Brazilian Air Force is a related party; and
[vi] Refers mainly to the intercompany loan between OGMA and EMPORDEF, an OGMA shareholder.

39. Financial Instruments (in part)

(c) Liquidity Risk (in part)

This is the risk of the Company not having sufficient liquid funds to honor its financial commitments as a result of a mismatch of terms or volumes of estimated receipts and payments.

To manage the liquidity of cash in Dollar and Real, Management has established projections and assumptions based on contracts for future disbursements and receipts, which are monitored daily by the Company, aiming to detect possible mismatches well in advance allowing the Company to adopt mitigation measures in advance, always trying to reduce the risk and financial cost.

The following table provides additional information related to undiscounted contractual obligations and commercial commitments and their respective maturities.

	Total	Less Than One Year	One to Three Years	Three to Five Years	More Than Five Years
At December 31, 2011					
Loans	2,113.9	313.7	464.9	213.3	1,122.0
Suppliers	829.9	829.9	—	—	—
Recourse and Non Recourse Debt	462.6	312.8	31.8	44.6	73.4
Financial Guarantees	494.9	317.3	85.2	69.7	22.7
Other Liabilities	161.4	5.9	37.5	70.9	47.1
Capital Lease	3.2	1.4	1.6	0.2	—
Total	4,065.9	1,781.0	621.0	398.7	1,265.2

40. Responsibilities and Commitments (in part)

(a) Trade-In

The Company has offered one trade-in aircraft option agreement. Trade-in transactions are directly tied to contractual obligations with the customer and the purchase of new aircraft. The exercise of the trade-in option is dependent on the customer complying with all the contractual clauses. These options establish that the price of the asset given in payment may be put towards the purchase price of a new and more up-to-date aircraft model produced by the Company. The trade-in is priced based on a percentage of the original purchase price of the aircraft. The Company continuously monitors all trade-in commitments in order to anticipate any adverse economic impact. Based on the current evaluation of the Company and third-party independent appraisals, the Company believes that any aircraft accepted under trade-in may be sold or leased in the market without significant losses.

(b) Leases

In the parent company's statements the operating leases refer to telephone and computer equipment and in the subsidiary EAH they relate to non-cancelable operating leases of land and equipment. These leases expire at various dates through 2020.

The Company has, at December 31, 2011, operating leases with payments scheduled as follows:

Year	
2012	2.9
2013	2.0
2014	1.7
2015	0.8
2016	0.6
After 2016	9.5
Total	17.5

Lessor—Finance and Operating Leases, Lessee—Operating Leases

3.239

Shinhan Financial Group Co., Ltd. (Dec 2011)

CONSOLIDATED STATEMENTS OF COMPREHENSIVE INCOME (in part)

(In Millions of Won)	Note	2010	2011
Interest income		(Won) 12,908,734	13,780,714
Interest expense		(6,436,118)	(6,700,743)
Net interest income	32	6,472,616	7,079,971
Fees and commission income		3,397,247	3,557,132
Fees and commission expense		(1,639,409)	(1,797,961)
Net fees and commission income	33	1,757,838	1,759,171
Net insurance loss	28	(75,569)	(119,201)
Dividend income	34	217,451	208,860
Net trading income (loss)	35	332,536	(131,848)
Net foreign currency transaction gain		117,417	13,874
Net gain (loss) on financial instruments designated at fair value through profit or loss	36	(124,757)	171,911
Net gain on sale of available-for-sale financial assets	13	652,188	846,345
Impairment loss on financial assets	37	(1,416,047)	(987,309)
General and administrative expenses	38	(3,847,674)	(4,135,357)
Net other operating expenses	40	(671,516)	(571,645)
Operating income	43	3,414,483	4,134,772

NOTES TO THE CONSOLIDATED FINANCIAL STATEMENTS (in part)

1. Reporting Entity (in part)

Shinhan Financial Group Co., Ltd., the controlling company, and its subsidiaries included in consolidation (collectively the "Group") are summarized as follows:

(a) Controlling Company

Shinhan Financial Group Co., Ltd. (the "Shinhan Financial Group") was incorporated on September 1, 2001 through a business combination involving the exchange of Shinhan Financial Group's common stock with the former stockholders of Shinhan Bank, Shinhan Investment Corp., Shinhan Capital Co., Ltd. and Shinhan BNP Paribas AMC. Shinhan Financial Group's shares were listed on the Korea Exchange on September 10, 2001 and Shinhan Financial Group's American Depository Shares were listed on the New York Stock Exchange on September 16, 2003.

2. Basis of Preparation (in part)

(a) Statement of Compliance

The consolidated financial statements have been prepared in accordance with International Financial Reporting Standards as issued by the International Accounting Standards Board. ("IFRS").

These are the Group's first consolidated financial statements prepared in accordance with IFRS and IFRS 1 *First-time Adoption of International Financial Reporting Standards ("IFRS 1")* has been applied. The Group's date of transition to IFRS is January 1, 2010, and the effect of the transition from Korean Generally Accepted Accounting Principles ("K-GAAP") to IFRS on the Group's reported financial position and financial performance is explained in note 50.

3. Significant Accounting Policies (in part)

The significant accounting policies applied by the Group in preparation of its consolidated financial statements are included below. The accounting policies set out below have been applied consistently to all periods presented in these consolidated financial statements and in preparing the opening IFRS statement of financial position at January 1, 2010 for the purpose of the transition to IFRS, unless otherwise indicated.

(i) Property and Equipment

Property and equipment are initially measured at cost and after initial recognition, are carried at cost less accumulated depreciation and accumulated impairment losses. The cost of property and equipment includes expenditures arising directly from the construction or acquisition of the asset, any costs directly attributable to bringing the asset to the location and condition necessary for it to be capable of operating in the manner intended by management and the initial estimate of the costs of dismantling and removing the item and restoring the site on which it is located.

In addition, in the preparation of the opening IFRS consolidated statement of financial position on the date of transition to IFRS, the Group measures land and buildings at fair value at the date of transition, which is deemed cost, in accordance with IFRS 1.

Items of property and equipment are measured at cost less accumulated depreciation and accumulated impairment losses.

The cost of replacing a part of an item of property or equipment is recognized in the carrying amount of the item if it is probable that the future economic benefits embodied within the part will flow to the Group and its cost can be measured reliably. The carrying amount of the replaced cost is derecognized. The cost of the day to day servicing of property and equipment are recognized in profit or loss as incurred.

Property and equipment are depreciated on a straight-line basis over the estimated useful lives, which most closely reflect the expected pattern of consumption of the future economic benefits embodied in the asset. Leased assets under finance lease are depreciated over the shorter of the lease term and their useful lives.

The estimated useful lives for the current and comparative years are as follows:

Descriptions	Depreciation Method	Useful Lives
Buildings	Straight-line	40 years
Other properties	Straight-line	4–5 years

Depreciation methods, useful lives and residual value are reassessed at each fiscal year-end and any adjustment is accounted for as a change in accounting estimate.

(l) Leased Assets

i) Classification of a Lease

The Group classifies and accounts for leases as either a finance or operating lease, depending on the terms. Leases where the lessee assumes substantially all of the risks and rewards of ownership are classified as finance leases. All other leases are classified as operating leases.

ii) Lessee

Under a finance lease, the lessee recognizes the leased asset and a liability for future lease payments. Upon initial recognition the leased asset is measured at an amount equal to the lower of its fair value and the present value of the minimum lease payments. Subsequent to initial recognition, the asset is accounted for in accordance with the accounting policy applicable to that asset.

Under an operating lease, the lessee recognizes the lease payments as expense over the lease term and does not recognize the leased asset in its statement of financial position.

iii) Lessor

Under a finance lease, the lessor recognizes a finance lease receivable. Over the lease term the lessor accrues interest income on the net investment. The receipts under the lease are allocated between reducing the net investment and recognizing finance income, so as to produce a constant rate of return on the net investment.

Under an operating lease, the lessor recognizes the lease payments as income over the lease term and the leased asset in its statement of financial position.

19. Lease

(a) Finance lease receivables of the Group as lessor as of January 1, 2010 and December 31, 2010 and 2011 were as follows:

January 1, 2010

	Gross Investment	Unearned Finance Income	Present Value of Minimum Lease Payment	Unguaranteed Residual Value
Not later than 1 year	(Won) 654,231	67,967	586,264	—
1–5 years	1,023,196	100,403	904,365	18,427
Later than 5 years	72,645	15,884	56,761	—
	(Won) 1,750,072	184,254	1,547,390	18,427

December 31, 2010

	Gross Investment	Unearned Finance Income	Present Value of Minimum Lease Payment	Unguaranteed Residual Value
Not later than 1 year	(Won) 703,559	78,660	624,899	—
1–5 years	960,364	79,265	870,173	10,926
Later than 5 years	54,696	5,582	49,114	—
	(Won) 1,718,619	163,507	1,544,186	10,926

December 31, 2011

	Gross Investment	Unearned Finance Income	Present Value of Minimum Lease Payment	Unguaranteed Residual Value
Not later than 1 year	(Won) 784,923	86,082	686,907	11,933
1–5 years	970,068	91,958	878,109	—
Later than 5 years	67,905	5,370	62,535	—
	(Won) 1,822,896	183,410	1,627,551	11,933

(b) The scheduled maturities of minimum lease payments of the Group as lessor as of December 31, 2011 are as follows:

i) Finance Leases

	December 31, 2011		
	Minimum Lease Payment	Unearned Finance Income	Present Value of Minimum Lease Payment
Not later than 1 year	(Won) 772,989	86,082	686,907
1–5 years	970,067	91,958	878,109
Later than 5 years	67,905	5,370	62,535
	(Won) 1,810,961	183,410	1,627,551

ii) Operating Leases

	December 31, 2011
	Minimum Lease Payment
Not later than 1 year	(Won) 6,281
1–5 years	7,078
Later than 5 years	—
	(Won) 13,359

(c) Future minimum lease payments under non-cancellable operating lease of the Group as lessee as of December 31, 2011 are as follows:

	December 31, 2011
	Minimum Lease Payment
Not later than 1 year	(Won) 70,712
1–5 years	81,945
Later than 5 years	1,289
	(Won) 153,946

27. Provisions (in part)

(a) Provisions as of January 1, 2010 and December 31, 2010 and 2011 were as follows:

	January 1, 2010	December 31, 2010	December 31, 2011
Asset retirement obligation	(Won) 31,818	33,693	35,727
Expected loss related to litigation	109,223	101,132	215,808
Unused credit commitments	464,980	462,478	444,770
Bonus card points program	27,407	25,203	24,439
Financial guarantee contracts issued	106,068	170,982	85,778
Others	42,138	65,869	63,070
	(Won) 781,634	859,357	869,592

(b) Changes in provisions for the years ended December 31, 2010 and 2011 were as follows:

		2011					
	Asset Retirement	Litigation	Unused Credit	Card Point	Guarantee	Other	Total
Beginning balance	(Won) 33,693	101,132	462,477	25,203	170,983	65,870	859,358
Provision/reversal	297	124,551	(18,570)	17,265	(70,860)	(1,407)	51,276
Provision used	(526)	(9,875)	—	(18,029)	—	(4,751)	(33,181)
Foreign exchange translation	—	—	863	—	1,227	—	2,090
Others	2,263	—	—	—	(15,572)	3,358	(9,951)
Ending balance	(Won) 35,727	215,808	444,770	24,439	85,778	63,070	869,592

* Provisions for card point were classified as fees and commission expense.

(c) Asset retirement obligation liabilities represent the estimated cost to restore the existing leased properties which is discounted to the present value using the appropriate discount rate at the end of the reporting period. Disbursements of such costs are expected to incur at the end of lease contract. Such costs are reasonably estimated using the average lease year and the average restoration expenses. The average lease year is calculated based on the past ten-year historical data of the expired leases. The average restoration expense is calculated based on the actual costs incurred for the past three years using the three-year average inflation rate.

40. Net Other Operating Expenses (in part)

Other operating income and other operating expense for the years ended December 31, 2010 and 2011 were as follows:

Other Operating Expense

Loss on sale of assets:		
Loans	46,047	57,806
Property and equipment	7,867	1,910
Investment property	5	—
Non-current assets held-for-sale	—	1,531
Others	256	107
	54,175	61,354
Others:		
Loss on hedge activity	541,781	276,088
Loss on allowance for acceptances and guarantee	41,023	—
Loss on other allowance	27,454	100,589
Contribution to fund	229,908	239,841
Donations	126,643	117,887
Depreciation of investment properties	8,352	9,245
Impairment loss on Intangible asset	—	39,674
Others[*]	462,205	514,119
	1,437,366	1,297,443
	1,491,541	1,358,797

IAS 36, *IMPAIRMENT OF ASSETS*

Author's Note

IASB amended IAS 2 by issuing the following standards:
- IFRS 9
  This amendment replaces references to IAS 39 with a reference to IFRS 9.
- IFRS 13
  IFRS 13 replaces the definition of fair value in paragraph 7 of IAS 2 with the following:
    Fair value is the price that would be received to sell an asset or paid to transfer a liability in an orderly transaction between market participants at the measurement date.

Because these standards are effective for annual periods beginning on or after 1 January 2012, these amendments are not reflected in the commentary in this section. However, these amendments would not affect the availability of illustrative excerpts from survey companies' financial statements.

IFRS Overview and Comparison to U.S. GAAP

3.240 IAS 36 establishes the procedures that an entity applies to ensure that an asset is carried at no more than its recoverable amount. *Recoverable amount* is the higher of fair value less costs to sell and value in use. An entity should apply IAS 36 in testing and measuring impairment losses, or reversals of such losses, for all assets, except the following:
- Inventories
- Assets arising from construction contracts
- Deferred tax assets
- Assets arising from employee benefits
- Financial assets within the scope of IAS 39
- Investment property measured at fair value
- Biological assets related to agricultural activity measured at fair value
- Deferred acquisition costs and intangible assets arising from insurance contracts
- Noncurrent assets or disposal groups classified as held for sale within the scope of IFRS 5

3.241 Financial assets classified as subsidiaries, associates, and jointly controlled entities are included in the scope of IAS 36. IAS 36 also applies to assets held at revalued amount in accordance with IAS 16 and IAS 38.

3.242 IAS 36 also applies to cash generating units (CGU). A *CGU* is the smallest identifiable group of assets that generates cash inflows that are largely independent of the cash inflows of other assets or groups of assets.

Recognition and Measurement

IFRSs

3.243 At the end of each reporting period, an entity should assess whether there is any indication that an asset may be impaired. If any indication exists, the entity should test the asset for impairment in accordance with the procedures in IAS 36. IAS 36 provides examples of both internal and external indicators of impairment. An entity should test assets individually, unless the recoverable amount cannot be determined without other assets. In that case, an entity should test the CGU to which the asset belongs. An entity should only include a liability in a CGU when a recoverable amount cannot be determined without including that liability.

3.244 However, an entity should test the following assets annually for impairment even when no indicator exists:
- Goodwill
- Indefinite-life intangible asset
- Intangible asset not yet available for use (for example, development costs)

3.245 An entity can perform the impairment test on these assets at any time during the year, but it should perform the test at the same time each year. Different intangible assets may be tested at different times during the year. Even when an entity acquired an intangible asset during the year, it should test the asset for impairment before the end of the reporting period.

3.246 To perform an impairment test, an entity should determine the following amounts:
- Fair value less cost to sell (FVLCS)
- Value in use (VIU)

3.247 IAS 36 includes a hierarchical procedure for determining FVLCS. IAS 36 states that the best evidence of FVLCS is a price in a binding sales agreement in an arm's-length transaction, adjusted for any incremental costs directly attributable to the asset's disposal. When there is no binding sales agreement, an entity should use a price determined in an active market reduced by costs to sell. When no binding sales agreement or active market exists, an entity should base its determination of FVLCS on the best available information of what the entity would obtain at the end of the reporting period in an arm's-length transaction between knowledgeable and willing parties.

3.248 An entity calculates an asset's VIU on the basis of the following information:
- Estimates of future cash flows it expects to receive from the asset
- Expectations about variations in the amounts or timing of these cash flows
- Current market risk-free interest rate
- Price for bearing the risk inherent in the asset
- Other factors, such as lack of liquidity, which market participants would use in determining a price for the asset

An entity then calculates the present value of the estimated future cash flows, making the adjustment for risk to either the cash flows or the discount rate.

3.249 An entity should base its estimates of future cash flows on reasonable and supportable assumptions representing management's best estimates of the range of economic conditions that will exist over the asset's life. An entity should give greater weight to external evidence, rather than internal evidence. An entity should use management cash flow projections, up to a maximum of five years. Cash flows should relate to the asset in its current condition and exclude any cash flows resulting from future restructurings or other actions to improve the asset's performance. Cash flows should include cash flows from continuing use of the asset, other cash flows necessary to the continued use of the asset that the entity can directly attribute or allocate on a reasonable and supportable basis, and net cash flows from the asset's disposal. IAS 36 explicitly prohibits an entity from including cash flows relating to financing activities and income tax receipts or payments. An entity should extrapolate cash flows beyond the five-year limit for specific projections using a steady or declining growth rate. This growth rate should not exceed the long-term growth rate on similar products, industries, or countries, unless the entity can justify a higher rate.

3.250 An entity should use a pretax discount rate that reflects current market assessments of both the time value of money and the risks inherent in the asset itself. An entity may use surrogates when a market interest rate is not available.

3.251 The recoverable amount is determined as the higher of FVLCS and VIU. To test for an impairment loss, an entity should compare the recoverable amount with the asset's carrying value. Except for assets carried at a revalued amount, an entity should record an impairment loss, measured as the difference between the carrying value and the recoverable amount, in profit or loss when the recoverable amount is lower than the carrying value. An entity should recognize an impairment loss on an asset carried at a revalued amount as a revaluation decrease, in accordance with the relevant standard.

3.252 When the amount estimated for an impairment loss is greater than the carrying amount of the asset(s) to which it relates, an entity should recognize a liability if, and only if, recognition is required by another IFRS.

3.253 When an impairment loss is recognized on a depreciable asset, an entity should assess its remaining useful life and residual value and adjust depreciation or amortization expense prospectively.

3.254 An entity should test and measure a reversal of an impairment loss in the same manner as the original impairment test, based on internal and external indicators that the impairment no longer exists. An entity should reverse an impairment up to the amount that the carrying value would have been had an impairment loss not been recorded.

3.255 If it is not possible to test an individual asset for impairment, an entity identifies the smallest CGU to which the asset belongs and tests the CGU for impairment by calculating the recoverable amount of the CGU and comparing that amount with its carrying value. An entity should not include a liability in a CGU unless the recoverable amount cannot be calculated otherwise. When an active market exists for the output of an asset or group of assets, an entity should consider that asset or group of assets to be a CGU, even if some or all of the output is used internally. An entity should base its estimates of cash flows on external prices, not transfer prices. An entity should define its CGUs consistently from period to period and determine the carrying amount in a manner consistent with the determination of the recoverable amount.

3.256 An entity should allocate goodwill to the CGUs to which the goodwill relates. An entity should allocate goodwill acquired in a business combination to CGUs at the acquisition date. This allocation should be at the lowest CGU

expected to benefit from the business combination but should be no larger than an operating segment defined in accordance with IFRS 8, *Operating Segments*. An entity should allocate goodwill no later than the end of the reporting period following the acquisition.

3.257 When an entity changes its reporting structure and, in consequence, the CGUs to which it had allocated goodwill, it should reallocate goodwill to the CGUs affected.

3.258 Similar to allocating goodwill, an entity should allocate to CGUs other corporate assets (for example, IT, headquarters building, and so on) that do not generate cash flows in order to test these assets for impairment.

3.259 When either goodwill or corporate assets cannot be allocated to CGUs to which the goodwill or corporate assets relate, an entity should first test the CGU for impairment, excluding the goodwill or corporate asset, and recognize any impairment loss. The entity should then identify the smallest CGU that includes the CGU under review and to which the entity can allocate goodwill or the corporate asset and then test this new CGU for impairment and recognize any impairment loss.

3.260 When an entity recognizes an impairment loss on a CGU to which it allocated goodwill, the impairment loss is attributed first to goodwill and then proportionately to the other assets in the CGU based on their carrying values. In attributing the impairment loss to the other assets in the CGU, an entity should not decrease their carrying values below the highest of FVLCS, VIU, or zero. Any remaining impairment loss that would otherwise have been allocated to the asset should be allocated pro rata to the other assets of the CGU (or group of CGUs).

3.261 An entity should record a reversal of an impairment loss on a CGU by allocating that reversal on a pro rata basis to the assets in the CGU. An entity should not recognize a reversal of an impairment loss for any asset in the CGU above its recoverable amount or the carrying value that would have been determined if no impairment loss had been recorded. An entity should not reverse impairment losses recognized for goodwill.

U.S. GAAP

3.262 FASB ASC 350 and 360 include guidance on impairment testing and recognition for the same long-lived assets covered by IAS 36 (that is, PPE, intangible assets, and goodwill), and that guidance applies both to individual assets and asset groups. Unlike IFRSs, this guidance also applies to assets held for disposal. Like IFRSs, FASB ASC 350 recognizes that an entity cannot test goodwill for impairment as a separate asset.

3.263 The FASB ASC glossary defines an *asset group* as a unit of accounting for a long-lived asset or assets to be held and used, which represents the lowest level for which identifiable cash flows are largely independent of the cash flows of other groups of assets and liabilities. Although an asset group is similar to a CGU, unlike IFRSs, FASB ASC 360-10-35-25, in limited circumstances, permits an entity to include liabilities in an asset group without the constraint in IFRSs that an entity should only include liabilities necessary for conducting the impairment test. Therefore, an asset group may include all the assets and liabilities of the entity. For example, a corporate headquarters facility may not have identifiable cash flows that are largely independent of the cash flows of other assets and liabilities and other asset groups, and the entity would only test it for impairment at the reporting entity level.

3.264 FASB ASC 350-20-35-1 requires an entity to test goodwill for impairment at a level of reporting referred to as a reporting unit. As defined in the FASB ASC glossary, a *reporting unit* is an operating segment or one level below an operating segment (also known as a component). However, IFRSs do not permit a CGU to be larger than a reportable operating segment, and an entity should allocate corporate assets, such as a headquarters facility, to the CGUs to which these assets relate.

3.265 In contrast, like IFRSs, FASB ASC 360-10-35-21 requires an entity to test for recoverability an individual long-lived asset or asset group that does not include goodwill whenever events or changes in circumstances indicate that its carrying amount may not be recoverable. However, IFRSs specifically require an entity to assess at each reporting date whether such events or circumstances exist, whereas FASB ASC 360 does not require this assessment.

3.266 Unlike IFRSs, FASB ASC 360-10-35-17 requires an entity to determine recoverability by comparing the carrying amount of a long-lived asset or asset group that does not include goodwill with the sum of the undiscounted cash flows expected to result from the use and eventual disposition of the asset or asset group. When the asset or asset group's carrying value exceeds the sum of the undiscounted cash flows, an entity should recognize an impairment loss as the amount by which the carrying amount exceeds its fair value.

3.267 Like IFRSs, FASB ASC 360-10-35-20 requires an entity to recognize the impairment loss by adjusting the asset's carrying amount by the loss, with the adjusted carrying amount becoming the new cost basis. When the asset is subject to depreciation or amortization, an entity should depreciate or amortize the new cost basis over the remaining useful life of the asset. Like IFRSs, FASB ASC 360-10-35-22 suggests that when an asset or asset group is tested for recoverability, an entity may also need to review its depreciation estimates and method or the amortization period.

3.268 Unlike IFRSs, for assets other than goodwill, FASB ASC 360-10-35-20 prohibits an entity from reversing a previously recognized impairment loss.

3.269 To test goodwill for impairment, IFRSs require an entity to allocate goodwill to the CGUs or groups of CGUs expected to benefit from the synergies from the business combination. An entity should allocate the goodwill to the lowest level at which goodwill is monitored, which should not be larger than an operating segment. In contrast, FASB ASC 360-10-35-26 requires an entity to include goodwill in an asset group only if the asset group is or includes a reporting unit and does not permit an entity to include goodwill in a lower-level asset group that includes only part of a reporting unit.

3.270 IFRSs require an entity to test a CGU with allocated goodwill by comparing the carrying amount of the unit, including the goodwill, with the recoverable amount of the CGU. An entity should only record an impairment loss when the carrying amount of the unit exceeds the recoverable amount. Paragraphs 4–19 of FASB ASC 350-20-35

delineate a more complicated, two-step approach to impairment testing of a reporting unit that includes goodwill. First, the goodwill impairment test compares the fair value of a reporting unit with its carrying amount, including goodwill, with the following consequences:

- When the carrying amount is greater than zero and its fair value exceeds its carrying amount, the entity should not consider the goodwill impaired and the second step is unnecessary.
- When the carrying amount of the reporting unit exceeds its fair value, an entity should proceed to step two to measure the loss by comparing the implied fair value of the goodwill with its carrying value.
- When the carrying amount of the reporting unit is zero or negative, an entity should proceed to step two to measure an impairment loss, if any, when it is more likely than not that a goodwill impairment exists. An entity should evaluate whether there are adverse qualitative factors in making that "more likely than not" assessment. FASB ASC 350-20-35-30(a)–(g) provides examples of such qualitative factors.

An entity should determine implied fair value in the same way goodwill is measured in a business combination by assigning the fair value of a reporting unit to all the assets and liabilities of that unit (including any unrecognized intangible assets). An entity should then recognize the impairment loss by reducing the carrying value of goodwill.

Author's Note

The guidance in FASB ASC 350-20-35 with respect to assessing a goodwill impairment for reporting units with negative or zero carrying values is still shown as pending content because nonpublic entities would apply this guidance for annual periods beginning after December 15, 2011. Public entities would apply this guidance for annual periods beginning after December 15, 2010.

3.271 Like IFRSs, FASB ASC 360-10-35-28 requires an entity to reduce only the carrying amounts of a long-lived asset or assets of the group on a pro rata basis using the relative carrying amounts of those assets, except that the loss allocated to an individual long-lived asset of the group shall not reduce the carrying amount of that asset below its fair value whenever that fair value is determinable without undue cost and effort. However, unlike IFRSs, there is no need to allocate an impairment loss for a CGU first to goodwill because an entity recognizes an impairment loss on goodwill directly (as previously described).

Presentation

IFRSs

3.272 IAS 36 has no specific requirements for presentation of impairment losses. IAS 1 requires material items of expense to be presented separately. Otherwise, impairment losses can be included in various line items in profit or loss on the statement of comprehensive income.

U.S. GAAP

3.273 Paragraphs 2–3 of FASB ASC 350-20-45 require an entity to present the aggregate amount of goodwill impairment losses as a separate line item in the income statement within continuing operations, except when the goodwill impairment loss is associated with a discontinued operation. A goodwill impairment loss associated with a discontinued operation should be included (net of tax) within the results of discontinued operations. FASB ASC 350 and 360 allow for other impairment losses, including impairment losses on PPE and other intangibles, to be included in other line items on the income statement that the entity deems appropriate. SEC registrants should comply with the requirements of Rule 5-03 of Regulation S-X, which also does not include separate presentation of other impairment losses.

Disclosure

IFRSs

3.274 For each class of assets, an entity should disclose the amount of impairment losses recognized in profit or loss and the amount of reversals of impairment losses. An entity should also disclose the line item on the statement of comprehensive income in which the loss or reversal is presented. For revalued assets, an entity should disclose the amounts recorded in OCI either as an impairment loss or a reversal. An entity usually discloses these amounts in the reconciliation disclosure for the asset class to which the asset(s) belongs.

3.275 An entity should also disclose impairment losses and reversals in its operating segment disclosures in accordance with IFRS 8.

3.276 For each material impairment loss or reversal recognized during the period, an entity should discuss the facts and circumstances that led to the loss or reversal, including whether the recoverable amount was determined to be FVLCS or VIU, and disclose the amount of the reversal. When the recoverable amount is FVLCS or VIU, an entity should disclose the basis it used to determine FVLCS or the discount rates used in the current and previous estimate of VIU, respectively.

3.277 If the loss or reversal is related to an individual asset, an entity should disclose the nature of the asset and, if appropriate, the reportable segment to which the asset belongs. If the loss or reversal is related to a CGU, an entity should disclose a description of the CGU, the amount, and a description of any changes to the composition of the CGU since the entity's previous estimate of the recoverable amount.

3.278 For the aggregate impairment losses or reversals recognized during the period, excluding individually material losses or reversals, an entity should disclose the main asset classes affected by losses and reversals, respectively, and the main events or circumstances that led to their recognition.

3.279 For each CGU or group of CGUs with significant allocations of goodwill or indefinite-life intangible assets in comparison with the total amount of an entity's goodwill and indefinite-life intangible assets, an entity should disclose the following:
- Carrying amount of allocated goodwill
- Carrying amount of allocated indefinite-life intangible assets
- Basis for the recoverable amount

3.280 If the basis for the recoverable amount is VIU, the disclosures should include descriptions of key assumptions

in the entity's cash flow projections, identifying those to which the recoverable amount is most sensitive. If the basis for the recoverable amount is FVLCS, the disclosures should include descriptions of key assumptions in the entity's estimate of FVLCS, identifying those to which the recoverable amount is most sensitive. In both cases, an entity should disclose management's approach to determining the values assigned to these assumptions (for example, past experience and external sources), the period over which management has projected cash flows based on the financial budgets or forecasts, the growth rate used for extrapolating beyond the forecast, and the discount rate used to calculate present value. If FVLCS is determined based on discounted cash flows, an entity should disclose the period over which cash flow projections were made, the growth rate used to extrapolate the cash flows, and discount rate used to calculate present value. Additional disclosure is required so that users of the financial statements understand the effects of reasonably possible changes in these key assumptions.

3.281 Similar disclosures are required, in the aggregate, for allocated goodwill or intangible assets with indefinite useful lives when the amount allocated to a CGU or group of CGUs is not significant in comparison with the entity's total carrying amount of goodwill or intangible assets with indefinite useful lives.

U.S. GAAP

3.282 U.S. GAAP disclosures are less extensive than those required by IFRSs. FASB ASC 360-10-50-2 requires an entity to disclose all of the following information in the period when an impairment loss is recognized for PPE classified as held and used:
- Description of the impaired long-lived asset or asset group and the facts and circumstances leading to the impairment
- Amount of the impairment loss and the income statement line item that includes the loss, if not separately presented on the face of the statement
- Method or methods for determining fair value (for example, whether based on a quoted market price, prices for similar assets, or another valuation technique)
- Segment in which the impaired long-lived asset (asset group) is reported, if applicable

3.283 Similarly, for each impairment loss recognized related to an intangible asset, FASB ASC 350-30-50-3 requires an entity to disclose the following in the notes to financial statements that include the period in which the impairment loss is recognized:
- Description of the impaired intangible asset and the facts and circumstances leading to the impairment
- Amount of the impairment loss and the method for determining fair value
- Caption in the income statement or the statement of activities in which the impairment loss is aggregated
- Segment in which the impaired intangible asset is reported, if applicable

3.284 FASB ASC 350-20-50-1 requires an entity to disclose a reconciliation of goodwill showing a separate line item for impairment losses. FASB ASC 350-20-50-2 requires that for each goodwill impairment loss recognized during the period, an entity should also disclose all of the following:

- Description of the facts and circumstances leading to the impairment.
- Amount of the impairment loss and the method used to determine the fair value of the associated reporting unit (for example, whether the fair value was based on quoted market prices, prices of comparable businesses or nonprofit activities, a present value or other valuation technique, or a combination of methods).
- If the recognized impairment loss was an initial estimate, an entity should disclose the fact and reasons that the amount is not final and, in subsequent periods, the nature and amount of any significant adjustments made to the initial estimate of the impairment loss.

Presentation and Disclosure Excerpts

Impairment—Losses on Land, Buildings, and Structures in Leased Office, Investment Properties Held at Cost

3.285

Woori Finance Holdings Co., Ltd. (Dec 2011)

CONSOLIDATED STATEMENTS OF COMPREHENSIVE INCOME (in part)

	Korean Won		U.S. Dollars
	2010	**2011**	**2011**
			(In Thousands, Except per Share Data) (Note 2)
	(In Millions, Except per Share Data)		
Net interest income (Notes 33 and 44)	6,423,145	7,262,045	6,268,490
Interest income	14,057,227	15,044,846	12,986,488
Interest expense	7,634,082	7,782,801	6,717,998
Net fees and commissions income (Notes 34 and 44)	1,115,774	1,195,492	1,031,931
Fees and commissions income	1,688,039	1,774,434	1,531,665
Fees and commissions expense	572,265	578,942	499,734
Dividends (Note 35)	200,780	203,005	175,231
Gain on financial assets at FVTPL (Note 36)	39,074	119,403	103,067
Gain on available-for-sale financial assets (Note 37)	1,073,469	1,072,877	926,091
Gain on held-to-maturity financial assets	21	82	71
Impairment loss on credit loss (Note 38)	2,872,943	2,268,927	1,958,504
Other net operating expenses (Notes 39 and 44)	(3,910,451)	(4,423,304)	(3,818,131)
Operating income (Note 46)	2,068,869	3,160,673	2,728,246

NOTES TO THE CONSOLIDATED FINANCIAL STATEMENTS (in part)

1. General

(1) Woori Finance Holdings Co., Ltd.

Woori Finance Holdings Co., Ltd. (hereinafter referred to "Woori Finance Holdings" or "Parent" or the "Company") was incorporated under the laws of the Republic of Korea on March 27, 2001, to manage the following five financial institutions: Woori Bank, Kyongnam Bank, Kwangju Bank, Woori Credit Card Co., Ltd. (formerly known as Peace Bank of Korea which merged into Woori Bank on March 31, 2004) and Woori Investment Bank (which merged into Woori Bank on July 31, 2003), whose shares were contributed to the Company by the Korea Deposit Insurance Corporation (the "KDIC") in accordance with the provisions of the Financial Holding Company Act. As of December 31, 2011, the Company controls the following entities: three commercial banks, which include Woori Bank (formerly known as Hanvit Bank), Kyongnam Bank and Kwangju Bank (collectively referred to as the "Bank Subsidiaries"); Woori FIS Co., Ltd. (formerly known as Woori Finance Information System Co., Ltd., "Woori FIS"); Woori F&I Co., Ltd. ("Woori F&I"); Woori Investment & Securities Co., Ltd. ("Woori Investment & Securities"); Woori Asset Management Co., Ltd. ("Woori Asset Management", formerly known as Woori Credit Suisse Asset Management Co., Ltd.); Woori Private Equity Co., Ltd. ("Woori PE"); Woori Financial Co., Ltd. ("Woori Financial", formerly known as Hanmi Capital Co., Ltd.) and Woori FG Savings Bank; all collectively referred to

as "Woori Subsidiaries." Several of the Woori Subsidiaries also have other subsidiaries of which the Company is now the ultimate financial holding company. As a result of its functional restructuring, as of December 31, 2011, the Company consolidates Woori Bank, nine other subsidiaries, and 133 2nd-tier subsidiaries including Woori Credit Information Co., Ltd.

Upon incorporation, the Company's stock amounted to 3,637,293 million Won, consisting of 727,458,609 common shares (5,000 Won per share). As a result of several capital increases, exercise of warrants and conversion rights since incorporation, as of December 31, 2011, the Company's stock amounted to 4,030,077 million Won, consisting of 806,015,340 common shares issued and outstanding of which KDIC owns 459,198,609 shares (56.97% ownership).

On June 24, 2002, the Company listed its common shares on the Korea Exchange. On September 29, 2003, the Company registered with the Securities and Exchange Commission in the United States of America and listed its American Depositary Shares on the New York Stock Exchange.

2. Significant Basis of Preparation and Accounting Policies (in part)

(1) Basis of Presentation

The Group has adopted International Financial Reporting Standards ("IFRS") as issued by the International Accounting Standards Board ("IASB") for the annual periods beginning on January 1, 2011. In accordance with IFRS 1 *First-time adoption of International Financial Reporting Standards*, the transition date to IFRS is January 1, 2010. An explanation of how the transition to IFRS has affected the consolidated statements of financial position as of January 1, 2010 (date of transition) and December 31, 2010, and the consolidated statements of comprehensive income for the year ended December 31, 2010 of the Group are provided in Note 47 "Transition to IFRSs."

The Group operates primarily in Korea and its official accounting records are maintained in Korean Won. The United States dollar ("U.S. dollar" or "US$" or "USD") amounts are provided herein as supplementary information solely for the convenience of readers outside Korea. Korean Won amounts are expressed in U.S. Dollars at the rate of 1,158.5 Korean Won to US$1.00, the noon buying exchange rate in effect on December 30, 2011, as quoted by the Federal Reserve Bank of New York in the United States. Such convenience translation into U.S. Dollars should not be construed as representations that Korean Won amounts have been, could have been, or could in the future be, converted at this or any other rate of exchange.

The Group's consolidated financial statements have been prepared based on the historical cost method except for specific non-current assets and certain financial assets or liabilities reported at fair value.

(11) Investment Properties

The Group classifies a property held to earn rentals and/or for capital appreciation as an investment property. Investment properties are measured initially at cost, including transaction costs, less subsequent depreciation and impairment.

While land is not depreciated, all other investment properties are depreciated based on the respective assets' estimated useful lives using the straight-line method. The estimated useful lives, residual values and depreciation method are reviewed at the end of each reporting period, with the effect of any change in estimate accounted for on a prospective basis.

(12) Premises and Equipment

Premises and equipment are stated at cost less subsequent accumulated depreciation and accumulated impairment losses. The cost of an item of premises and equipment is directly attributable to their purchase or construction, which includes any costs directly attributable to bringing the asset to the location and condition necessary for it to be capable of operating in the manner intended by management. It also includes the initial estimate of the costs of dismantling and removing the item and restoring the site on which it is located. However, under IFRS 1 *First-time adoption of International Financial Reporting Standard,* certain premises and equipment such as land and buildings were re-evaluated at fair value, which is regarded as deemed cost, at the date of transition to IFRS.

Subsequent costs to replace part of the premises and equipment are recognized in carrying amount of an asset or as an asset if it is probable that the future economic benefits associated with the assets will flow into the Group and the cost of an asset can be measured reliably. Routine maintenance and repairs are expensed as incurred.

Depreciation is charged to net income on a straight-line basis on the estimated economic useful lives as follows:

	Useful Life
Buildings used for business purpose	35 to 57 years
Structures in leased office	4 to 5 years
Properties for business purpose	4 to 5 years
Leased assets	Useful lives of the same kind or similar other promises and equipment

The Group assesses the depreciation method, the estimated useful lives and residual values of premises and equipment at the end of each reporting period. If expectations differ from previous estimates, the changes are accounted for as a change in an accounting estimate. When the carrying amount of a fixed asset exceeds the estimated recoverable amount, the carrying amount of such asset is reduced to the recoverable amount.

(14) Impairment of Non-Monetary Assets

Intangible assets with indefinite useful lives or intangible assets that are not yet available for use are tested for impairment annually, regardless of whether or not there is any indication of impairment. All other assets are tested for impairment when there is an objective indication that the carrying amount may not be recoverable, and if the indication exists. The Group estimates the recoverable amount. Recoverable amount is the higher of value in use and net fair value less costs to sell. If the recoverable amount of an asset is estimated to be less than its carrying amount, the carrying amount of the asset is reduced to its recoverable amount and such impairment loss is recognized immediately in net income.

13. Investment Properties

(1) Investment properties are as follows (Unit: Korean Won in millions):

	January 1, 2010	December 31, 2010	December 31, 2011
Acquisition cost	751,210	657,240	514,819
Accumulated depreciation	(5,084)	(13,969)	(15,820)
Net carrying value	746,126	643,271	498,999

(2) Changes in investment properties are as follows (Unit: Korean Won in millions):

	For the Year Ended December 31	
	2010	2011
Beginning balance	746,126	643,271
Acquisition	—	1,356
Disposition	(985)	(144,097)
Depreciation	(9,576)	(6,462)
Impairment loss	(3,911)	(2,212)
Reclassified to assets held for sale	(42,239)	—
Transfer to properties for business use	(38,193)	(6,464)
Foreign currencies translation adjustments	(25)	11
Others	(7,926)	13,596
Ending balance	643,271	498,999

(3) Fair value of investment properties is 554,722 million Won as of December 31, 2011.

(4) Rental fees earned from investment properties are 13,598 million Won and 13,508 million Won as of December 31, 2010 and December 31, 2011, respectively.

14. Premises and Equipment (in part)

(1) Premises and equipment are as follows (Unit: Korean Won in millions):

				December 31, 2011			
	Land	Building	Properties for Business Use	Structures in Leased Office	Construction in Progress	Structures	Total
Acquisition cost	1,828,009	990,772	1,392,065	331,517	4,433	20	4,546,816
Accumulated depreciation	—	(60,434)	(1,075,775)	(276,122)	—	(13)	(1,412,344)
Net carrying value	1,828,009	930,338	316,290	55,395	4,433	7	3,134,472

(2) Changes in premises and equipment are as follows (Unit: Korean Won in millions):

				For the Year Ended December 31, 2011			
	Land	Building	Properties for Business Use	Structures in Leased Office	Construction in Progress	Structures	Total
Beginning balance	1,815,070	931,419	298,686	49,792	2,404	7	3,097,378
Acquisition	7,261	33,575	159,367	30,224	20,958	—	251,385
Disposition (transfer)	(21,491)	(6,284)	(5,861)	(791)	(18,929)	—	(53,356)
Depreciation	—	(29,141)	(119,017)	(23,813)	—	—	(171,971)
Impairment loss	—	(59)	—	—	—	—	(59)
Classified to assets held for sale	(1,482)	(1,123)	—	—	—	—	(2,605)
Foreign currencies translation adjustment	15	(81)	336	178	—	—	448
Others	28,636	2,032	(17,221)	(195)	—	—	13,252
Ending balance	1,828,009	930,338	316,290	55,395	4,433	7	3,134,472

39. Other Net Operating Income (Expense)

(1) Other operating incomes recognized are as follows (Unit: Korean Won in millions):

	For the Years Ended December 31	
	2010	2011
Gain on transaction of FX	7,585,168	8,292,591
Gain on translation of FX	41,073	46,882
Rental fee income	18,511	16,520
Gain on transactions of loans and receivables	173,231	62,157
Gain on disposal of investment in jointly controlled entities and associates	175	61,071
Gain on disposal of premises and equipment and other assets	12,145	74,140
Reversal of impairment loss of premises and equipment and other assets	3,146	791
Gain on transactions of derivatives	7,684	233
Gain on valuations of derivatives	121,434	187,038
Gain on fair value hedged items	36,691	3,876
Reversal of other provisions	30,185	8,350
Others	75,646	101,343
Total	8,105,089	8,854,992

Impairment—Goodwill

3.286

Empresa Nacional de Electricidad S.A. (Endesa-Chile) (Dec 2011)

CONSOLIDATED STATEMENTS OF COMPREHENSIVE INCOME (in part)

(In thousands of Chilean pesos)

Statement of Comprehensive Income	Note	2011 ThCh$	2010 ThCh$	2009 ThCh$
Net Income				
Sales	23	2,387,451,263	2,397,944,527	2,406,367,778
Other operating income	23	17,038,942	37,437,927	12,551,577
Total Revenues		2,404,490,205	2,435,382,454	2,418,919,355
Raw materials and consumables used	24	(1,217,260,077)	(1,191,327,819)	(976,145,889)
Contribution Margin		1,187,230,128	1,244,054,635	1,442,773,466
Other work performed by the entity and capitalized		10,597,856	10,126,628	731,901
Employee benefits expenses	25	(80,389,456)	(80,066,349)	(75,564,322)
Depreciation and amortization expense	26	(176,447,100)	(179,007,900)	(196,142,075)
Reversal of impairment loss (impairment loss) recognized in the year's profit or loss	26	(9,472,766)	(706,125)	(43,999,600)
Other expenses	27	(143,548,052)	(103,677,256)	(110,868,779)
Operating Income		787,970,610	890,723,633	1,016,930,591

NOTES TO THE CONSOLIDATED FINANCIAL STATEMENTS (in part)

(In thousands of Chilean pesos)

1. The Group's Activities and Financial Statements

Empresa Nacional de Electricidad S.A. (hereinafter the Parent Company or the Company) and its subsidiaries comprise the Endesa Group Chile (hereinafter Endesa or the Group).

Endesa Chile is a publicly traded corporation with registered address and head office located at Avenida Santa Rosa, No.76, in Santiago, Chile. The Company is registered in the securities register of the Superintendency of Securities and Insurance of Chile (Superintendencia de Valores y Seguros or SVS) under number 114. In addition, the Company is registered with the Securities and Exchange Commission of the United States of America (hereinafter U.S. SEC), and with Spain's Comisión Nacional del Mercado de Valores. The Company's shares have been listed on the New York Stock Exchange since 1994 and on the Latibex since 2001.

Endesa Chile is a subsidiary of Enersis S.A., a Spanish company controlled by Enel S.p.A. (hereinafter Enel).

The Company was initially created by a public deed dated December 1, 1943. The Treasury Department's Supreme Decree No. 97 of January 3, 1944, authorized the creation of the company and approved its by-laws. For tax purposes, the Company operates under Chilean tax identification number 91,081,000-6.

As of December 31, 2011, the Group had 2,447 employees. During 2011, the Group averaged a total of 2,395 employees. See Note 32 for additional information regarding employee distribution by category and geographic location.

The Company's corporate purpose consists of generating, transporting, producing, and distributing electrical energy. Its corporate purpose also includes investing in financial assets, developing projects, and carrying out activities in the energy industry and in other fields in which electrical energy is essential, and participating in public civil or hyadraulic infrastructure concessions, in which it may participate directly or through subsidiaries or associated companies that are either in Chile or abroad.

The Company's 2010 consolidated financial statements were approved by the Board of Directors at a meeting held on January 26, 2011. The consolidated financial statements were then submitted to the consideration of a General Shareholders Meeting held on April 26, 2011, which gave its final approval on the consolidated financial statements.

These consolidated financial statements are presented in thousands of Chilean pesos (unless expressly stated otherwise), as the Chilean peso is the functional currency of the main economic environment in which Endesa Chile operates. Foreign operations are reported in accordance with the accounting policies stated in Notes 2.6 and 3.k.

2. Basis of Presentation of Consolidated Financial Statements (in part)

2.1 Accounting Principles (in part)

The December 31, 2011 consolidated financial statements of Endesa Chile and its subsidiaries have been prepared in accordance with International Financial Reporting Standards (IFRS), issued by the International Accounting Standards Board (hereinafter "IASB"), and approved by its Board of Directors at its meeting held on January 31, 2012.

These consolidated financial statements present fairly the financial position of Endesa Chile and its subsidiaries as of

December 31, 2011 and 2010, as well as the results of operations, the changes in equity, and the cash flows for the years ending December 31, 2011, 2010 and 2009.

These consolidated financial statements voluntarily present the figures for the 2009 fiscal year consolidated statement of comprehensive income, consolidated statement of cash flow, and consolidated statement of changes in equity, along with their corresponding notes.

These consolidated financial statements have been prepared using cost method accounting applied to the business in operation principle except, in accordance with IFRS, those assets and liabilities that are reported at a fair value and those non-current assets and groups that are available for sale, which are recorded at the book value or the fair value minus sales costs, whichever is lower (see Note 3).

The consolidated financial statements have been prepared from accounting records maintained by the Company and its subsidiaries. Each entity prepares its financial statements according to the accounting principles and standards in force in each country, so the necessary adjustments and reclassifications have been made in the consolidation process in order to present the consolidated financial statements in accordance with IFRS and the criteria of the IFRS Interpretation Committee, (hereinafter IFRIC).

2.3 Responsibility for the Information Given and the Estimates Made (in part)

The Company's Board of Directors is responsible for the information contained in these consolidated financial statements and expressly states that all IFRS principles and standards that are applicable to the Group have been fully implemented.

In preparing the consolidated financial statements, certain estimates made by the Company's Management have been used to quantify some of the assets, liabilities, income, expenses, and commitments recorded in the statements.

These estimates basically refer to:

- The valuation of assets and goodwill to determine the existence of impairment losses (see Note 3.d).

2.6 Basis of Consolidation and Business Combinations (in part)

The subsidiaries are consolidated and all their assets, liabilities, income, expenses, and cash flows are included in the consolidated financial statements once the adjustments and eliminations from intra-Group transactions have been made.

Jointly controlled entities are consolidated using the proportional consolidation method. Endesa Chile recognizes, line by line, its share of the assets, liabilities, income, and expenses of such entities, so the adding of balances and subsequent eliminations take place only in proportion to Endesa Chile's ownership interest in them.

The comprehensive income of subsidiaries and jointly controlled entities is included in the consolidated comprehensive income statement from the effective date of acquisition until the effective date of disposal or termination of joint control, as applicable.

The parent company's and its subsidiaries' operations, as well as those of jointly controlled entities, have been consolidated under the following basic principles:

1. At the date of acquisition, the assets, liabilities, and contingent liabilities of the subsidiary or jointly controlled entity are recorded at market value. If, in the parent company's stake, there is a positive difference between the acquisition cost and the fair value of the assets and liabilities of the company acquired, including contingent liabilities, this difference is recorded as goodwill. If the difference is negative, it is recorded as a credit to income.

3. Accounting Principles Applied (in part)

The main accounting policies used in preparing the accompanying consolidated financial statements were the following:

b) Goodwill

Goodwill generated upon consolidation represents the difference between the acquisition cost and the Group's share of the fair value of assets and liabilities, including identifiable contingent assets and liabilities of a subsidiary at the acquisition date.

Acquired assets and liabilities are temporarily valued as of the date the company takes control and reviewed within no more than a year after the acquisition date. Until the fair value of assets and liabilities is ultimately determined, the difference between the acquisition price and the book value of the acquired company is temporarily recorded as goodwill.

If goodwill is finally determined as existing in the financial statements the year following the acquisition, the prior year's accounts, which are presented for comparison purposes, are modified to include the value of the acquired assets and liabilities and of the definitive goodwill from the acquisition date.

Goodwill generated from acquiring companies with functional currencies other than the Chilean peso is valued in the functional currency of the acquired company and converted to Chilean pesos using the exchange rate in effect as of the date of the statement of financial position.

Goodwill generated before the date of transition to IFRS, on January 1, 2004, is maintained at its net value recorded as of that date, while goodwill originated afterwards is valued at acquisition cost (see Notes 13 and 22.5.l).

Goodwill is not amortized; instead, at each period end the Company estimates whether any impairment has reduced its recoverable value to an amount less than the net recorded cost and, if so, it immediately adjusts for impairment (see Note 3.d).

d) Asset Impairment (in part)

During the period, and principally at period end, the Company evaluates whether there is any indication that an asset has been impaired. Should any such indication exist, the company estimates the recoverable amount of that asset to determine the amount of impairment in each case. In the case of identifiable assets that do not generate cash flows independently, the company estimates the recoverability of the Cash Generating Unit to which the asset belongs, which is understood to be the smallest identifiable group of assets that generates independent cash inflows.

Notwithstanding the preceding paragraph, in the case of Cash Generating Units to which goodwill or intangible assets with an indefinite useful life have been allocated, a recoverability analysis is performed routinely at each period end.

The recoverable amount is the greater amount between the fair value less the cost needed to sell and the value in use, which is defined as the present value of the estimated future cash flows. In order to calculate the recoverable value of Property, plant, and equipment, goodwill and intangible assets, the Group uses value in use criteria in practically all cases.

To estimate the value in use, the Group prepares future cash flow projections, before tax, based on the most recent budgets available. These budgets incorporate management's best estimates of Cash Generating Units' revenue and costs using sector projections, past experience, and future expectations.

In general, these projections cover the next ten years, estimating cash flows for subsequent years by applying reasonable growth rates, between 3.2% and 7.0%, which, in no case,

are increasing nor exceed the average long-term growth rates for the particular sector and country.

These cash flows are discounted at a given pre-tax rate in order to calculate their present value. This rate reflects the cost of capital of the business and the geographical area in which the business is conducted. The discount rate is calculated taking into account the current value of money and the risk premiums generally used by analysts for the specific business activity and country involved.

The following discount rates, before tax and expressed in nominal terms, were applied in 2011 and 2010:

| Country | Currency | 2011 | | 2010 | |
		Minimum	Maximum	Minimum	Maximum
Chile	Chilean peso	9.2%	10.1%	7.5%	8.7%
Argentina	Argentine peso		17.1%	16.8%	16.9%
Brazil	Brazilian real	9.5%	11.6%	9.6%	10.8%
Peru	Peruvian sol		9.3%		7.9%
Colombia	Colombian peso		10.9%		9.6%

If the recoverable amount is less than the net carrying amount of the asset, the corresponding provision for impairment loss is recorded for the difference, and charged to "Reversal of impairment loss (impairment loss) recognized in profit or loss" in the consolidated statement of comprehensive income.

Impairment losses recognized for an asset in prior periods are reversed when its estimated recoverable amount

changes, increasing the asset's value with a credit to earnings, limited to the asset's carrying amount if no adjustment had occurred. In the case of goodwill, adjustments that would have been made are not reversible.

13. Goodwill

The following table shows goodwill by the Cash-Generating Unit or group of Cash-Generating Units to which it belongs and movements for the 2011 and 2010 fiscal years:

Company	Opening Balance at 01-01-2011 ThCh$	Impairment Loss Accounted for in Income Statement ThCh$	Foreign Currency Translation ThCh$	Closing Balance at 12-31-2011 ThCh$
Empresa Eléctrica Pangue S.A.	3,139,337	—	—	3,139,337
Endesa Costanera S.A.(*)	5,315,282	(5,448,372)	133,090	—
Hidroeléctrica El Chocón S.A.	12,509,433	—	313,226	12,822,659
Compañía Eléctrica San Isidro S.A.	1,516,768	—	—	1,516,768
Edegel S.A.A.	72,931,068	—	10,848,528	83,779,596
Emgesa S.A. E.S.P.	4,660,782	—	465,875	5,126,657
GasAtacama S.A.	12,636	—	1,388	14,024
Total	100,085,306	(5,448,372)	11,762,107	106,399,041

(*) See Note 31.3.

Company	Opening Balance at 01-01-2010 ThCh$	Impairment Loss Accounted for in Income Statement ThCh$	Foreign Currency Translation ThCh$	Closing Balance at 12-31-2010 ThCh$
Pangue S.A.	3,139,337	—	—	3,139,337
Endesa Costanera S.A.	6,023,583	—	(708,301)	5,315,282
Hidroeléctrica El Chocón S.A.	14,176,409	—	(1,666,976)	12,509,433
San Isidro S.A.	1,516,768	—	—	1,516,768
Edegel S.A.	75,920,260	—	(2,989,192)	72,931,068
Emgesa S.A. E.S.P.	4,755,333	—	(94,551)	4,660,782
GasAtacama S.A.	13,692	—	(1,056)	12,636
Total	105,545,382	—	(5,460,076)	100,085,306

According to the Endesa Chile management's estimates and projections, the expected future cash flows projections attributable to the Cash-Generating Units or groups of Cash-

Generating Units to which the acquired goodwill has been allocated allow recovery of its carrying value as of December 31, 2011 and 2010 (see Note 3.b).

26. Depreciation, Amortization, and Impairment Losses

Depreciation, amortization, and impairment losses recognized in profit or loss as of December 31, 2011, 2010, and 2009 can be broken down as follows:

	Balance at		
	12-31-2011 ThCh$	12-31-2010 ThCh$	12-31-2009 ThCh$
Depreciation	(172,952,233)	(175,067,904)	(192,772,740)
Amortization	(3,494,867)	(3,939,996)	(3,369,335)
Reversal (Losses) from impairment of financial assets (see Note 7)	(4,024,394)	(308,268)	—
(Loss) from impairment of goodwill (see Note 13)	(5,448,372)	—	—
(Loss) from impairment of fixed assets	—	(397,857)	(43,999,600)
Total	(185,919,866)	(179,714,025)	(240,141,675)

Impairment—Investment in Associate

3.287

Sasol Limited (Jun 2011)

INCOME STATEMENT (in part)

	Note	2011	2011	2010	2009
		Unaudited US$m*	Rm	Rm	Rm
Turnover	30	17,585	142,436	122,256	137,836
Cost of sales and services rendered	31	(11,169)	(90,467)	(79,183)	(88,508)
Gross profit		6,416	51,969	43,073	49,328
Other operating income	32	134	1,088	854	1,021
Marketing and distribution expenditure		(839)	(6,796)	(6,496)	(7,583)
Administrative expenditure		(1,221)	(9,887)	(9,451)	(10,063)
Other operating expenditure		(793)	(6,424)	(4,043)	(8,037)
Other expenses		(668)	(5,408)	(3,036)	(7,871)
Translation losses	33	(125)	(1,016)	(1,007)	(166)
Operating profit	34	3,697	29,950	23,937	24,666
Finance income	38	122	991	1,332	1,790
Share of profit of associates (net of tax)	39	36	292	217	270
Finance expenses	40	(224)	(1,817)	(2,114)	(2,531)
Profit before tax		3,631	29,416	23,372	24,195

NOTES TO THE CONSOLIDATED FINANCIAL STATEMENTS (in part)

A. Accounting Policies and Financial Reporting Terms (in part)

Sasol Limited is the holding company of the Sasol group (the group) and is domiciled in the Republic of South Africa. The following principal accounting policies were applied by the group for the financial year ended 30 June 2011. Except as otherwise disclosed, these policies are consistent in all material respects with those applied in previous years.

2. Basis of Consolidation of Financial Results (in part)

The consolidated financial statements reflect the financial results of the group. All financial results are consolidated with similar items on a line by line basis except for investments in associates, which are included in the group's results as set out below.

Inter-company transactions, balances and unrealised gains and losses between entities are eliminated on consolidation. To the extent that a loss on a transaction provides evidence of a reduction in the net realisable value of current assets or an impairment loss of a non-current asset, that loss is charged to the income statement.

In respect of joint ventures and associates, unrealised gains and losses are eliminated to the extent of the group's

IFRS-BPPD 3.287

interest in these entities. Unrealised gains and losses arising from transactions with associates are eliminated against the investment in the associate.

Associates

The financial results of associates are included in the group's results according to the equity method from acquisition date until the disposal date.

Under this method, investments in associates are recognised initially at cost. Subsequent to the acquisition date, the group's share of profits or losses of associates is charged to the income statement as equity accounted earnings and its share of movements in equity reserves is recognised as other comprehensive income. All cumulative post-acquisition movements in the equity of associates are adjusted against the cost of the investment. When the group's share of losses in associates equals or exceeds its interest in those associates, the carrying amount of the investment is reduced to zero, and the group does not recognise further losses, unless the group has incurred a legal or constructive obligation or made payments on behalf of those associates.

Goodwill relating to associates forms part of the carrying amount of those associates.

The total carrying amount of each associate is evaluated annually, as a single asset, for impairment or when conditions indicate that a decline in fair value below the carrying amount is other than temporary. If impaired, the carrying amount of the group's share of the underlying assets of associates is written down to its estimated recoverable amount in accordance with the accounting policy on impairment and charged to the income statement. A previously recognised impairment loss will be reversed, insofar as estimates change as a result of an event occurring after the impairment loss was recognised.

Associates whose financial year ends are within three months of 30 June are included in the consolidated financial statements using their most recently audited financial results. Adjustments are made to the associates' financial results for material transactions and events in the intervening period.

7 Investments in Associates

	Note	2011	2010	2009
		Rm	Rm	Rm
Balance at beginning of year		3,573	2,170	830
Acquisition of associates		—	—	1,310
Additional investments in associates		91	1,248	524
Share of profit of associates, net of dividends received		(105)	164	(210)
Impairment of investment in associate	42	(123)	—	—
Effect of translation of foreign operations		(365)	(9)	(284)
Balance at end of year		3,071	3,573	2,170
Comprising				
Investments at cost (net of impairment)		3,306	3,365	2,105
Share of post-acquisition reserves		(235)	208	65
		3,071	3,573	2,170

Fair Value of Investments in Associates

The fair value of investments in associates is determined using a discounted cash flow method using market related rates at 30 June. The market related rates used to discount estimated cash flows were between 9,10% and 9,72% (2010—9,96% and 15,50%).

	Note	2011	2010	2009
		Rm	Rm	Rm
Estimated fair value of investments in associates		6,439	6,301	6,050
Dividends received from associates	52	397	53	480
Business segmentation				
Synfuels		8	8	9
Synfuels International		2,351	2,701	1,507
Polymers		678	830	611
Other chemical businesses		2	2	3
Other businesses		32	32	40
Total operations		3,071	3,573	2,170
Key financial information of associates*				
Non-current assets		44,645	39,886	29,616
Property, plant and equipment		3,279	3,546	3,452
Assets under construction		41,325	36,041	26,020
Other non-current assets		41	299	144
Current assets		5,006	9,644	4,931
Total assets		49,651	49,530	34,547
Shareholders' equity		20,852	23,382	12,551
Long-term debt (interest bearing)		5	5	109
Long-term provisions		—	—	2
Other non-current liabilities		27,002	24,299	19,595
Interest bearing current liabilities		860	815	1,248
Non-interest bearing current liabilities		932	1,029	1,042
Total equity and liabilities		49,651	49,530	34,547
Total turnover		6,886	5,827	7,496
Operating profit		3,071	2,295	3,139
Finance income		61	2	3
Finance expenses		(80)	(33)	(50)
Profit before tax		3,052	2,264	3,092
Taxation		(771)	(571)	(794)
Profit		2,281	1,693	2,298

* The financial information provided represents the full financial position and results of the associates.

There were no contingent liabilities at 30 June 2011 relating to associates other than disclosed in note 57.

In 2011, an amount of R148 million (2010—R1, 266 million, 2009—R2, 468 million) has been committed by the group for further development of the Escravos GTL (EGTL) project.

Impairment testing in respect of investments in associates is performed at each reporting date by comparing the recoverable amount based on the value-in-use of the cash generating unit to the carrying amount as described in note 42.

At 30 June, the group's associates, interest in those associates and the total carrying value were:

Name	Country of Incorporation	Nature of Business	Interest	Carrying Value		
				2011	2010	2009
			%	Rm	Rm	Rm
Escravos GTL (EGTL)*	Nigeria	GTL plant	10	2,351	2,702	1,507
Optimal Olefins Malaysia Sdn Bhd**	Malaysia	Ethane and propane gas cracker	12	538	676	484
Wesco China Limited	Hong Kong	Trading and distribution of plastic raw materials	40	140	154	128
Other			various	42	41	51
				3,071	3,573	2,170

* In December 2008, Sasol reduced its interest in EGTL from 37,5% to 10%. The 10% interest retained by Sasol in the EGTL project has been recognised as an investment in an associate at its fair value at the date of disposal. Although the group holds less than 20% of the voting power of EGTL, the group exercises significant influence as a member of Sasol's senior management serves on the executive committee of the project and Sasol is responsible for providing essential technical support to the project.

**Although the group holds less than 20% of the voting power of Optimal Olefins Malaysia Sdn Bhd, the group exercises significant influence as a member of Sasol's senior management serves on the board of directors of the company.

Associates whose financial year ends are within three months of 30 June are included in the consolidated financial statements using their most recently audited financial results. Adjustments are made to the associates' financial results for material transactions and events in the intervening period.

None of the group's investments in associates are publicly traded and therefore no quoted market prices are available. The fair value of investments in associates is determined using a discounted cash flow method using market related rates at 30 June.

There are no significant restrictions on the ability of the associates to transfer funds to Sasol Limited in the form of cash dividends or repayment of loans or advances.

39 Share of Profit of Associates (Net of Tax)

	2011	2010	2009
	Rm	Rm	Rm
Profit before tax	388	289	365
Taxation	(96)	(72)	(95)
Share of profit of associates (net of tax)	292	217	270
Dividends received from associates	397	53	480
Business segmentation			
Synfuels	5	4	3
Polymers	286	220	273
Olefins & Surfactants	(1)	(1)	(9)
Other chemical businesses	2	(6)	3
Total operations	292	217	270

42 Remeasurement Items Affecting Operating Profit

	Note	2011	2010	2009
		Rm	Rm	Rm
Impairment of		(190)	(110)	(458)
property, plant and equipment	2	(49)	(47)	(294)
assets under construction	3	(2)	(61)	(19)
other intangible assets	5	(16)	(1)	(137)
investments in associate	7	(123)	—	
investments in securities	6	—	(1)	(8)
Reversal of impairment of		535	365	—
property, plant and equipment	2	529	348	—
assets under construction	3	2	2	—
other intangible assets	5	4	15	—
Profit/(loss) on disposal of		29	5	(761)
property, plant and equipment		14	4	11
other intangible assets		—	(1)	(2)
investment in associate	56	6	7	—
investments in businesses	56	9	(5)	(770)
Scrapping of property, plant and equipment		(267)	(124)	(133)
Scrapping of assets under construction		(92)	(32)	(101)
Write off of unsuccessful exploration wells	3	(441)	(58)	(16)
		(426)	46	(1,469)
Tax effect thereon		(106)	19	(35)
		(532)	65	(1,504)
Business segmentation				
South African energy cluster		(223)	(69)	(141)
Mining		(3)	(1)	(3)
Gas		(6)	—	(4)
Synfuels		(197)	(58)	(137)
Oil		(17)	(10)	3
International energy cluster		(568)	(112)	(794)
Synfuels International		(126)	(4)	(777)
Petroleum International		(442)	(108)	(17)
Chemical cluster		402	251	(510)
Polymers		(46)	(14)	1
Solvents		(63)	(58)	(158)
Olefins & Surfactants		500	344	(106)
Other		11	(21)	(247)
Other businesses		(37)	(24)	(24)
Total operations		(426)	46	(1,469)

	Gross 2011	Tax 2011	Non-Controlling Interest 2011	Net 2011
	Rm	Rm	Rm	Rm
Impairment of	(190)	12	—	(178)
property, plant and equipment	(49)	8	—	(41)
assets under construction	(2)	—	—	(2)
other intangible assets	(16)	4	—	(12)
investment in associate	(123)	—	—	(123)
Reversal of impairment of	535	(160)	—	375
property, plant and equipment	529	(159)	—	370
assets under construction	2	(1)	—	1
other intangible assets	4	—	—	4
Profit/(loss) on disposal of	29	(3)	—	26
property, plant and equipment	14	—	—	14
investment in associate	6	—	—	6
investments in businesses	9	(3)	—	6
Scrapping of property, plant and equipment	(267)	34	—	(233)
Scrapping of assets under construction	(92)	11	—	(81)
Write off of unsuccessful exploration wells	(441)	—	—	(441)
	(426)	(106)	—	(532)

Impairment/Reversal of Impairments

The group's non-financial assets, other than inventories and deferred tax assets, are reviewed for impairment at each reporting date or whenever events or changes in circumstances indicate that the carrying value may not be recoverable. Recoverable amounts are estimated for individual assets or, where an individual asset cannot generate cash inflows independently, the recoverable amount is determined for the larger cash generating unit to which it belongs.

Value-in-Use Calculations

The recoverable amount of the assets reviewed for impairment is determined based on value-in-use calculations. Key assumptions relating to this valuation include the discount rate and cash flows used to determine the value in use. Future cash flows are estimated based on financial budgets approved by management covering a three, five and ten year period and are extrapolated over the useful life of the assets to reflect the long-term plans for the group using the estimated growth rate for the specific business or project. The estimated future cash flows and discount rates used are post-tax, based on an assessment of the current risks applicable to the specific entity and country in which it operates. Discounting post-tax cash flows at a post-tax discount rate yields the same result as discounting pre-tax cash flows at a pre-tax discount rate.

Management determines the expected performance of the assets based on past performance and its expectations of market development. The weighted average growth rates used are consistent with the increase in the geographic segment long-term Producer Price Index. Estimations are based on a number of key assumptions such as volume, price and product mix which will create a basis for future growth and gross margin. These assumptions are set in relation to historic figures and external reports on market growth. If necessary, these cash flows are then adjusted to take into account any changes in assumptions or operating conditions that have been identified subsequent to the preparation of the budgets.

The weighted average cost of capital rate (WACC) is derived from a pricing model based on credit risk and the cost of the debt. The variables used in the model are established on the basis of management judgement and current market conditions. Management judgement is also applied in estimating the future cash flows of the cash generating units. These values are sensitive to the cash flows projected for the periods for which detailed forecasts are not available and to the assumptions regarding the long-term sustainability of the cash flows thereafter.

Main Assumptions Used for Value-In-Use Calculations

		South Africa	North America	Europe
		%	%	%
Growth rate—long-term Producer Price Index (PPI)	2011	4,80	1,50	1,50
Discount rate—weighted average cost of capital (WACC)	2011	12,95	8,00	8,00 to 8,70
Growth rate—long-term Producer Price Index (PPI)	2010	4,80	1,50	1,50
Discount rate—weighted average cost of capital (WACC)	2010	13,25	7,75	7,75

Sensitivity to Changes in Assumptions

Management has considered the sensitivity of the values in use determined above to various key assumptions such as crude oil prices, commodity prices and exchange rates. These sensitivities have been taken into consideration in determining the required impairments and reversals of impairments.

Significant Reversal/(Impairments) of Assets

	Business Unit	Property, Plant and Equipment 2011	Assets Under Construction 2011	Other Intangible Assets 2011	Investment in Associate 2011	Total 2011
		Rm	Rm	Rm	Rm	Rm
Sasol Italy Organics business	Olefins & Surfactants	485	2	4	—	491
Sasol Germany Organics business	Olefins & Surfactants	29	—	—	—	29
Emission rights	Olefins & Surfactants	—	—	(5)	—	(5)
Emission rights	Solvents	—	—	(4)	—	(4)
Solvents Germany (Herne site)	Solvents	(31)	(2)	(1)	—	(34)
Solvents Germany—Methyl Ethyl Ketone business	Solvents	9	—	—	—	9
Exploration assets in Nigeria	Petroleum International	—	(1)	—	—	(1)
Investment in associate—Escravos GTL	Synfuels International	—	—	—	(123)	(123)
Sasol Nitro—Fertiliser downstream business	Other chemical businesses	(8)	—	—	—	(8)
Emission rights	Other businesses	—	—	(4)	—	(4)
Other	Various	(4)	1	(2)	—	(5)
		480	—	(12)	(123)	345

Reversal of Impairment of the Sasol Italy Organics Business

During 2007, the Sasol Italy Organics business was fully impaired due to a decline in the economics of the business. In 2008, management commenced with the implementation of a rigorous turnaround strategy regarding this business, which was focused on the reduction of cash fixed costs, improved asset utilisation and a reduction in headcount. The restructuring plan was successfully implemented by the end of 2010 and the turnaround interventions have increased the robustness and profitability of this cash generating unit. Based on the successful implementation of the restructuring plan at the end of 2010 and the increased robustness of the cash generating unit, management has concluded that the results of the turnaround plan are sustainable to the extent that a reversal of R491 million (2010—R350 million) of the previous impairment was recognised during 2011.

Reversal of Impairment of the Sasol Germany Organics Business

During 2007, the Cumol Sulfonate and Butyl Glycol Ether businesses within the Sasol Germany Organics cash generating unit were impaired as these assets were not performing. In 2008, management implemented a restructuring plan which was focused on the reduction of cash fixed costs and improved asset utilisation. Based on the current indicators from the turnaround process, management has concluded that these businesses are showing signs of sustainable improvement and has recorded a reversal of R29 million of the previous impairment recognised during 2011.

Impairment of the Solvents Germany (Herne site)

In 2008, due to the significant increase of feedstock prices into the ethanol business at the Herne site in Germany and a decline in the economics of the business, the site was fully impaired. In 2011, further capital expenditure incurred to meet environmental and legal requirements was also impaired as the economics of the site has not improved.

Impairment of Investment in Associate

In December 2008, Sasol reduced its interest in the Escravos GTL project from 37,5% to 10%. The 10% interest retained by Sasol has been recognised as an investment in associate. Due to the delay in the project and the increasing costs for completion of the project, an impairment review was performed based on the current project economics. The results of the impairment review indicated that the value in use was lower than the carrying value of the investment resulting in an impairment of R123 million.

Reversal of Impairment—Investment in Joint Ventures

3.288

China Yuchai International Limited (Dec 2011)

CONSOLIDATED INCOME STATEMENT (in part)

(Rmb and US$ amounts expressed in thousands, except per share data)

	Note	31.12.2009 Rmb'000	31.12.2010 Rmb'000	31.12.2011 Rmb'000	31.12.2011 Rmb'000
Continuing Operations					
Sales of goods	7	13,139,578	16,138,580	15,378,190	2,440,363
Rendering of services	7	36,325	69,604	66,238	10,511
Revenue	7	13,175,903	16,208,184	15,444,428	2,450,874
Cost of sales (goods)		(10,612,260)	(12,112,215)	(11,966,496)	(1,898,962)
Cost of sales (services)		(17,825)	(87,038)	(35,653)	(5,658)
Gross profit		2,545,818	4,008,931	3,442,279	546,254
Other operating income	8.2a	93,668	129,075	102,403	16,250
Other operating expenses	8.2b	(16,113)	(41,447)	(29,325)	(4,654)
Research and development costs	8.1, 8.3	(297,259)	(324,123)	(328,140)	(52,072)
Selling, distribution and administrative costs	8.1	(1,471,857)	(1,822,764)	(1,652,129)	(262,175)
Operating profit		854,257	1,949,672	1,535,088	243,603
Finance costs	8.4	(77,493)	(130,446)	(156,174)	(24,783)
Share of profit/(loss) of associates	5	2,954	(121)	1,519	241
Share of results of joint ventures	6	(16,000)	(53,902)	(81,151)	(12,878)
Gain on acquisition of Guangxi Yulin Hotel Company in settlement of past loan	30	202,950	—	—	—
Profit before tax from continuing operations		966,668	1,765,203	1,299,282	206,183

NOTES TO THE CONSOLIDATED FINANCIAL STATEMENTS (in part)

(Rmb and US$ amounts expressed in thousands, except per share data)

1. Corporate Information (in part)

1.1 Incorporation

The consolidated financial statements of China Yuchai International Limited and its subsidiaries (the "Group") for the year ended December 31, 2011 were authorised for issue in accordance with a resolution of the directors on April 19, 2012. China Yuchai International Limited is a limited company incorporated under the laws of Bermuda whose shares are publicly traded. The registered office is located at 16 Raffles Quay #26-00, Hong Leong Building, Singapore 048581.

1.2 Investment in Guangxi Yuchai Machinery Company Limited

China Yuchai International Limited (the "Company") was incorporated under the laws of Bermuda on April 29, 1993. The Company was established to acquire a controlling financial interest in Guangxi Yuchai Machinery Company Limited ("Yuchai"), a Sino-foreign joint stock company which manufactures, assembles and sells diesel engines in the People's Republic of China (the "PRC"). The principal markets for Yuchai's diesel engines are truck manufacturers in the PRC.

The Company owns, through six wholly-owned subsidiaries, 361,420,150 shares or 76.41% of the issued share capital of Yuchai ("Foreign Shares of Yuchai"). Guangxi Yuchai Machinery Group Company Limited ("State Holding Company"), a state-owned enterprise, owns 22.09% of the issued share capital of Yuchai ("State Shares of Yuchai").

In December 1994, the Company issued a special share (the "Special Share") at par value of US$0.10 to Diesel Machinery (BVI) Limited ("DML"), a company controlled by Hong Leong Corporation Limited, now known as Hong Leong (China) Limited ("HLC"). The Special Share entitles its holder to designate the majority of the Company's Board of Directors (six of eleven). The Special Share is not transferable except to Hong Leong Asia Ltd. ("HLA"), the holding company of HLC, or any of its affiliates. During 2002, DML transferred the Special Share to HL Technology Systems Pte Ltd. ("HLT"), a subsidiary of HLC.

Yuchai established three direct subsidiaries, Yuchai Machinery Monopoly Company Limited ("YMMC"), Guangxi Yulin Yuchai Accessories Manufacturing Company Limited ("YAMC") (previously known Guangxi Yulin Yuchai Machinery Spare Parts Manufacturing Company Limited) and Yuchai Express Guarantee Co., Ltd. ("YEGCL"). YMMC and YAMC were established in 2000, and are involved in the manufacture and sale of spare parts and components for diesel engines in the PRC. YEGCL was established in 2004, and is involved in the provision of financial guarantees to mortgage loan applicants in favor of banks in connection with the applicants' purchase of automobiles equipped with diesel engines produced by Yuchai. In 2006, YEGCL ceased granting new guarantees with the aim of servicing the remaining outstanding guarantee commitments to completion. YEGCL has no more guarantee commitments remaining at the end of 2011. As at December 31, 2011, Yuchai held an equity interest of 71.83%, 97.14% and 100.0% respectively in these companies. As at December 31, 2011, YMMC had direct controlling interests in twenty nine subsidiaries (2010: 31 subsidiaries) which are involved in the trading and distribution of spare parts of diesel engines and automobiles, all of which are established in the PRC.

In December 2006, Yuchai established a wholly-owned subsidiary called Xiamen Yuchai Diesel Engines Co., Ltd. This new subsidiary was established to facilitate the construction of a new diesel engine assembly factory in Xiamen, Fujian province in China.

In December 2007, Yuchai purchased a subsidiary, Guangxi Yulin Hotel Company Limited ("Yulin Hotel Company").

(a) Cooperation with Zhejiang Geely Holding Group Co. Ltd

On April 10, 2007, Yuchai signed a Cooperation Framework Agreement with Zhejiang Geely Holding Group Co., Ltd. or Geely and Zhejiang Yinlun Machinery Company Limited or Yinlun to consider establishing a proposed company to develop diesel engines for passenger cars in China. Yuchai was to be the largest shareholder followed by Geely as the second largest shareholder.

In December 2007, further to the Cooperation Framework Agreement, Yuchai entered into an Equity Joint Venture Agreement with Geely and Yinlun, to form two joint entities in Tiantai, Zhejiang province and Jining, Shandong province. The entities will be primarily engaged in the development, production and sales of a proprietary diesel engine including the engines of 4D20 series and its parts for passenger vehicles. Yuchai is the controlling shareholder with 52% with Geely and Yinlun holding 30% and 18% shareholding respectively in both entities. These two entities have been duly incorporated.

(b) Cooperation with Caterpillar (China) Investment Co., Ltd

On December 11, 2009, Yuchai, pursuant to a Joint-Venture Agreement entered into with Caterpillar (China) Investment Co., Ltd. ("Caterpillar"), incorporated Yuchai Remanufacturing Services Co., Ltd. ("Yuchai Remanufacturing") in Suzhou, Jiangsu province to provide remanufacturing services for and relating to Yuchai's diesel engines and components and certain Caterpillar's diesel engines and components. The registered capital of the Yuchai Remanufacturing is US$ 200,000,000. Yuchai holds 51% and Caterpillar holds the remaining 49% in the joint venture. Yuchai and Caterpillar holds joint control in governing the financial and operating policies of the Company and Caterpillar has veto rights in relation to certain key decisions despite having only 49% voting rights. As such, Yuchai continued to account for Yuchai Remanufacturing as a Joint Venture.

(c) Cooperation with Chery Automobile Co., Ltd

On August 11, 2009, Yuchai, pursuant to a Framework Agreement entered into with Jirui United Heavy Industry Co., Ltd. ("Jirui United"), a company jointly established by China International Marine Containers Group Ltd. ("CIMC") and Chery Automobile Co., Ltd. ("Chery") (collectively referred to as "CIMC-Chery"), and Shenzhen City Jiusi Investment Management Co., Ltd. ("Jiusi") incorporated Y & C Engine Co.,

Ltd. ("Y & C") in Wuhu, Anhui province to produce heavy-duty vehicle engines with the displacement range from 10.5L to 14L including the engines of YC6K series. The registered capital of the Y & C is Rmb 500,000,000. Yuchai and Jirui United each hold 45% in the joint venture with Jiusi holding the remaining 10%.

1.3 Investment in Thakral Corporation Ltd.

In March 2005, the Company through Venture Delta Limited ("Venture Delta") and Grace Star Services Ltd. ("Grace Star") held 14.99% of the ordinary shares of Thakral Corporation Ltd. ("TCL"). TCL is a company listed on the main board of the Singapore Exchange Securities Trading Limited (the "Singapore Exchange") and is involved in the manufacture, assembly and distribution of high-end consumer electronic products and home entertainment products in the PRC. Three directors out of eleven directors on the board of TCL were appointed by the Company. Based on the Company's shareholdings and representation in the board of directors of TCL, management concluded that the Company had the ability to exercise significant influence over the operating and financial policies of TCL. Consequently, the Company's consolidated financial statements include the Company's share of the results of TCL, accounted for under the equity method. The Company acquired an additional 1% of the ordinary shares of TCL in September 2005. As a result of the rights issue of 87,260,288 rights shares on February 16, 2006, the Company's equity interest in TCL increased to 19.4%.

On August 15, 2006, the Company exercised its right to convert all of its 52,933,440 convertible bonds into 529,334,400 new ordinary shares in the capital of TCL. Upon the issue of the new shares, the Company's interest in TCL has increased to 36.6% of the total issued and outstanding ordinary shares. During the year ended December 31, 2007, the Company did not acquire new shares in TCL. However, as a result of conversion of convertible bonds into new ordinary shares by TCL's third party bondholders, the Company's interest in TCL was diluted to 34.4%. On September 2, 2008, Venture Delta transferred 1,000,000 ordinary shares, representing 0.04% interest in TCL to Grace Star.

On December 1, 2009, TCL announced its plan to return surplus capital of approximately S$130.6 million to shareholders by way of the Capital Reduction Exercise. Concurrently with the Capital Reduction Exercise, Venture Delta and Grace Star intend to appoint a broker to sell 550,000,000 shares out of their 898,990,352 shares in TCL at a price of S$0.03 per share on an ex-distribution basis ("Placement"). As of December 1, 2009, from the date that an associate is classified as held for sale, the Group ceased to apply the equity method and the investment in TCL is measured at the lower of the carrying amount and fair value less cost to sell and classified as held-for-sale.

On July 7, 2010, TCL made payment of cash distribution to shareholders pursuant to the Capital Reduction Exercise. Subsequent to the cash distribution, the Company began to sell its shares in TCL in the market. As of December 31, 2010, 580,253,000 shares in TCL had been disposed of and the Company's shareholding interest in TCL had reduced from 34.4% to 12.2%. In line with the decrease of the Company's shareholding interest in TCL, the Company's representation in the board of directors of TCL also reduced to one out of eight directors on the board of TCL. As of December 31, 2010, the Company did not exercise significant influence over the operating and financial policies of TCL. The Company's investment in TCL was classified as held for trading as they were held for the purpose of selling in the near term. The Company's investment in TCL was measured at fair value with changes in fair value recognised in other income in the income statement.

As of December 31, 2011, the Company's shareholding interest in TCL remained at 12.2%. The Company's investment in TCL was classified as held for trading, and was measured at fair value with changes in fair value recognised in other income in the income statement.

1.4 Investment in HL Global Enterprises Limited

On February 7, 2006, the Company acquired 29.1% of the ordinary shares of HL Global Enterprises Limited ("HLGE"). HLGE is a public company listed on the main board of the Singapore Exchange. HLGE is primarily engaged in investment holding, and through its group companies, invests in rental property, hospitality and property developments in Asia. On November 15, 2006, the Company exercised its right to convert all of its 196,201,374 non-redeemable convertible cumulative preference shares ("NCCPS") into 196,201,374 new ordinary shares in the capital of HLGE. Upon the issue of the new shares, the Company's equity interest in HLGE has increased to 45.4% of the enlarged total number of ordinary shares in issue. During the year ended December 31, 2007, the Company did not acquire new shares in HLGE. However, new ordinary shares were issued by HLGE arising from the third party's conversion of non-redeemable convertible cumulative preference shares, and the Company's interest in HLGE was diluted to 45.4%.

On March 26, 2010, the Company converted 17,300,000 of RCPS B shares into HLGE ordinary shares. On September 24, 2010, the Company further converted 16,591,000 of RCPS B shares into HLGE ordinary shares. Meanwhile, 154,758 of new ordinary shares were issued by HLGE arising from third parties' conversion of NCCPS. As of December 31, 2010, the Company's interest in HLGE increased from 45.4% to 47.4%.

On March 24, 2011, the Company converted 17,234,000 of RCPS B shares into HLGE ordinary shares. On September 23, 2011, the Company further converted 17,915,000 of RCPS B shares into HLGE ordinary shares. As of December 31, 2011, the Company's interest in HLGE increased from 47.4% to 49.4%.

The Company considers its ability to exercise the potential voting privileges in the RCPS instruments in HLGE when assessing the entity's power to govern the financial and operating policies of HLGE and concluded that the Company has the ability to control HLGE. Consequently, the Company consolidated HLGE with effect from November 15, 2006.

As at December 31, 2010, three directors out of seven directors on the board of HLGE were appointed by the Company. As at December 31, 2011, four directors, including the chairman, out of eight directors on the board of HLGE were appointed by the Company.

2. Basis of Preparation and Accounting Policies (in part)

2.1 Basis of Preparation

The consolidated financial statements of the Group have been prepared in accordance with International Financial Reporting Standards as issued by the International Accounting Standards Board ("IFRS").

The consolidated financial statements have been prepared on a historical cost basis, except for derivative financial instruments and available-for-sale financial assets that have been measured at fair value. The consolidated financial statements are presented in Renminbi (Rmb) and all values are rounded to the nearest thousand (Rmb'000) except when otherwise indicated.

2.3 Summary of Significant Accounting Policies

(c) Investments in Joint Ventures

The Group has an interest in joint ventures, which are jointly controlled entities, whereby the venturers have a contractual arrangement that establishes joint control over the economic activities of the entity. The agreement requires unanimous agreement for financial and operating decisions among the venturers. The Group recognises its interest in the joint venture using the equity method.

Under the equity method, the investment in the joint venture is carried on the statement of financial position at cost plus post acquisition changes in the Group's share of net assets of the joint venture. Goodwill relating to the joint venture is included in the carrying amount of the investment and is neither amortised nor individually tested for impairment.

The income statement reflects the Group's share of the results of operations of the joint venture. When there has been a change recognised directly in the equity of the joint venture, the Group recognises its share of any changes and discloses this, when applicable, in the statement of changes in equity. Unrealised gains and losses resulting from transactions between the Group and the joint venture are eliminated to the extent of the interest in the joint ventures.

The Group's share of profit of joint ventures is shown on the face of the income statement. This is the profit attributable to equity holders of the joint venture and, therefore, is profit after tax and non-controlling interests in the subsidiaries of the joint venture.

The financial statements of the joint venture are prepared for the same reporting period as the Group. When necessary, adjustments are made to bring the accounting policies in line with those of the Group.

After application of the equity method, the Group determines whether it is necessary to recognise an additional impairment loss on its investment in its joint ventures. The Group determines at each reporting date whether there is any objective evidence that the investment in the joint venture is impaired. If this is the case, the Group calculates the amount of impairment as the difference between the recoverable amount of the joint venture and its carrying value and recognises the amount in the "share of results of joint ventures" in the income statement.

Upon loss of joint control and provided the former jointly controlled entity does not become a subsidiary or associate, the Group measures and recognises any retaining investment at its fair value. Any differences between the carrying amount of the former jointly controlled entity upon loss of joint control and the fair value of the retained investment and proceeds from disposal are recognised in profit or loss. When the retaining investment constitutes significant influence, it is accounted for as investment in an associate.

6. Investment in Joint Ventures

Movement in the Group's share of the joint ventures' post acquisition retained earnings is as follows:

	31.12.2010 Rmb'000	31.12.2011 Rmb'000	31.12.2011 US$'000
Unquoted equity shares, at cost	650,454	683,749	108,504
At January 1	(83,580)	(133,143)	(21,128)
Share of results after tax[1]	(53,902)	(81,151)	(12,878)
Dividend received	(1,733)	(10,166)	(1,613)
Write-back of impairment	10,936	—	—
Others	—	(2,305)	(366)
Translation adjustment	(4,864)	1,354	215
At January 1/December 31	(133,143)	(225,411)	(35,770)
Share of post acquisition retained earnings	(2,998)	(1,593)	(253)
Investment in joint ventures	514,313	456,745	72,481

[1] Share of results after tax is composed of:

	31.12.2010 Rmb'000	31.12.2011 Rmb'000	31.12.2011 US$'000
Share of joint venture losses	(11,375)	(12,639)	(2,006)
Impairment of investment in joint ventures	(2,117)	(53,540)	(8,496)
Fair value adjustments arising from purchase price allocation for PPEs in joint ventures	(40,410)	(14,972)	(2,376)
Share of results after tax	(53,902)	(81,151)	(12,878)

In 2011, the Group made additional investment of Rmb 33,295 in Yuchai Remanufacturing. The Group's percentage of interest in Yuchai Remanufacturing remains unchanged.

The Group has interests in the following joint ventures:

	Percentage of Interest		
Name of Company	31.12.2010 %	31.12.2011 %	Principal Activities
Held by Subsidiaries:			
Augustland Hotel Sdn Bhd	45	45	Hotel development and operation
Copthorne Hotel Qingdao Co., Ltd.	60	60	Owns and operates a hotel in Qingdao, PRC
Shanghai Equatorial Hotel Management Co., Ltd.	49	49	Hotel management and hotel consultancy
Shanghai International Equatorial Hotel Co., Ltd.	50	50	Owns and operates a hotel and club in Shanghai, PRC
Y&C Engine Co., Ltd.	45	45	Heavy duty diesel engine
Yuchai Remanufacturing Services Co., Ltd.	51	51	Remanufacture and sale of automobile parts, diesel engines and components

The Group has included in its consolidated financial statements its share of assets and liabilities incurred by the joint ventures and its share of the results of the joint ventures using equity method.

The summarised financial information on the Group's share is as follows:

	31.12.2010 Rmb'000	31.12.2011 Rmb'000	31.12.2011 US$'000
Assets and liabilities			
Current assets	197,526	269,293	42,734
Non-current assets	406,166	497,520	78,951
Current liabilities	145,808	152,237	24,158
Non-current liabilities	78,803	226,192	35,893
Net assets	379,081	388,384	61,634

	31.12.2009 Rmb'000	31.12.2010 Rmb'000	31.12.2011 Rmb'000	31.12.2011 US$'000
Results				
Revenue	110,886	150,161	212,401	33,706
Expenses	(118,353)	(158,130)	(223,811)	(35,517)
Taxation	(471)	(3,406)	(1,229)	(195)
Loss after taxation	(7,938)	(11,375)	(12,639)	(2,006)

8.2 (a) Other Operating Income

	31.12.2009 Rmb'000	31.12.2010 Rmb'000	31.12.2011 Rmb'000	31.12.2011 US$'000
Interest income	31,576	61,719	53,159	8,436
Foreign exchange gain, net	—	19,975	1,599	254
Dividend income from associates	11,162	—	1,656	263
Gain on disposal of associates	1,906	707	—	—
Gain on disposal of subsidiaries	—	2,833	—	—
Gain on disposal of prepaid operating leases	—	—	10,678	1,694
Fair value gain on held for trading investments	—	17,123	—	—
Fair value gain on available-for-sale investment	—	—	10,983	1,743
Gain on disposal of investment properties	—	—	5,908	937
Gain on assignment of debts	5,657	—	—	—
Write-back of impairment of receivables	4,895	—	—	—
Write-back of trade and other payables	23,649	—	—	—
Write-back of impairment of investment in joint ventures	—	10,936	—	—
Government grant income	14,823	11,129	18,420	2,923
Others, net	—	4,653	—	—
	93,668	129,075	102,403	16,250

GAINS AND LOSSES ON DERECOGNITION OF NONCURRENT ASSETS

IFRS Overview and Comparison to U.S. GAAP

3.289 This subsection addresses recognition of gains or losses on derecognition of noncurrent assets accounted for in accordance with IAS 16, IAS 17, IAS 38, and IAS 40. The requirements of these standards with respect to recognition, measurement, presentation, and disclosure on the statement of financial position are discussed in section 2. The requirements of these standards with respect to depreciation, amortization, and impairment testing and recognition are discussed elsewhere in this section.

Recognition and Measurement

IFRSs

3.290 IAS 16 and IAS 38 require an entity to derecognize an item of PPE on disposal or when no future economic benefits are expected to flow to the entity from use or disposal. IAS 40 also adds the condition that the property be permanently withdrawn from use.

3.291 In all cases, an entity should recognize gains or losses in profit or loss as the difference between the net proceeds from disposal, if any, and the carrying value of the asset in the period in which the retirement or disposal occurs, unless the asset is the subject of a sale and leaseback transaction under IAS 17.

3.292 In accordance with IAS 17, an entity should recognize profit or loss immediately when the sale and leaseback results in an operating lease and either
- it is clear that the transaction occurred at fair value, or
- the transaction occurred at less than fair value and the loss is not compensated by future lease payments at below market price.

Otherwise, an entity defers and amortizes any gain or loss over the period in which the entity expects to use the asset.

3.293 Both IAS 16 and IAS 38 prohibit an entity from recognizing gains on disposal or retirement as revenue.

3.294 When an asset is held at revalued amount, an entity transfers any remaining revaluation surplus account to retained earnings when the asset is derecognized. For the purpose of transferring the revaluation surplus to retained earnings, an entity may transfer either part of the revaluation surplus as the asset is depreciated or the entire revaluation surplus when it disposes of or retires the asset.

U.S. GAAP

3.295 FASB ASC 360-10-40 provides very little guidance on derecognition of long-lived assets on disposal or retirement. General guidance states that an entity should derecognize long-lived assets when it no longer has rights to the asset. An entity should recognize a gain or loss on the date of the sale, in accordance with FASB ASC 360-10-40-5.

3.296 However, FASB ASC 360-10-40 contains more guidance and conditions than IFRSs that must be met before an entity recognizes gains or losses on sale and leaseback transactions, referencing FASB ASC 840, *Leases*. Specifically, paragraphs 1–3 of FASB ASC 840-40-35 contain guidance on the recognition of profit or loss on sale-leaseback transactions.

Presentation

IFRSs

3.297 IAS 1 does not require separate presentation of gains and losses from disposals of noncurrent assets on the income statement.

U.S. GAAP

3.298 Like IFRSs, FASB ASC 360-10-45-5 does not require separate presentation of these transactions. However, this paragraph further states that if a subtotal, such as income from operations, is presented, an entity should include the amounts of gains or losses recognized on the sale of the noncurrent asset in that subtotal.

Disclosure

IFRSs

3.299 Unless a gain or loss on derecognition is material, IFRSs do not require an entity to disclose this information.

U.S. GAAP

3.300 Unlike IFRSs, when an entity does not separately present gains or losses on the sale of a long-lived asset on the face of the income statement, FASB 205-20-50-1 requires the entity to disclose in the notes to the relevant financial statements the caption of the income statement item that contains that gain or loss.

Presentation and Disclosure Excerpts

Gain (Loss) on Disposal of Property, Plant, and Equipment and Intangible Assets

3.301

LG Display Co., Ltd (Dec 2011)

CONSOLIDATED STATEMENTS OF COMPREHENSIVE INCOME (LOSS) (in part)

(In Millions of Won, Except Earnings per Share)	Note	2009	2010	2011
Revenue	23, 24, 25	(Won) 20,037,701	25,511,535	24,291,289
Cost of sales	8, 23	(17,476,995)	(21,780,880)	(23,081,322)
Gross profit		2,560,706	3,730,655	1,209,967
Other income	26	1,365,554	1,483,443	1,223,545
Selling expenses	17	(712,580)	(846,376)	(728,419)
Administrative expenses	17	(325,325)	(521,035)	(564,337)
Research and development expenses		(407,857)	(674,684)	(681,228)
Other expenses	26	(1,470,146)	(1,861,531)	(1,383,864)
Results from operating activities		1,010,352	1,310,472	(924,336)
Finance income	29	332,721	240,988	207,266
Finance costs	29	(343,855)	(288,472)	(363,309)
Other non-operating loss, net		(6,475)	(15,611)	(16,627)
Equity income on investments, net		20,217	18,192	16,047
Profit (loss) before income tax		1,012,960	1,265,569	(1,080,959)

CONSOLIDATED STATEMENTS OF CASH FLOWS (in part)

(In Millions of Won)	Note	2009	2010	2011
Cash flows from operating activities:				
Profit (loss) for the year		(Won) 1,117,778	1,159,234	(787,895)
Adjustments for:				
Income tax expense (benefit)	30	(104,818)	106,335	(293,064)
Depreciation	11	2,778,727	2,756,532	3,413,450
Amortization of intangible assets	12	63,339	168,846	237,996
Gain on foreign currency translation		(159,293)	(119,880)	(85,804)
Loss on foreign currency translation		31,844	85,263	132,295

(continued)

(In Millions of Won)	Note	2009	2010	2011
Gain on disposal of property, plant and equipment		(486)	(1,387)	(740)
Loss on disposal of property, plant and equipment		234	415	862
Impairment loss on property, plant and equipment		664	—	3,589
Gain on disposal of intangible assets		(9)	—	—
Loss on disposal of intangible assets		—	—	1,588
Impairment loss on intangible assets		—	—	5,574

NOTES TO THE CONSOLIDATED FINANCIAL STATEMENTS (in part)

1. Reporting Entity (in part)

(a) Description of the Controlling Company

LG Display Co., Ltd. (the "Controlling Company") was incorporated in February 1985 under its original name of LG Soft, Ltd. as a wholly owned subsidiary of LG Electronics Inc. In 1998, LG Electronics Inc. and LG Semicon Co., Ltd. transferred their respective Thin Film Transistor Liquid Crystal Display ("TFT-LCD") related business to the Controlling Company. The main business of the Controlling Company and its subsidiaries is to manufacture and sell TFT-LCD panels. The Controlling Company is a stock company ("Jusikhoesa") domiciled in the Republic of Korea with its address at 128, Yeouidae-ro, Yeongdeungpo-gu, Seoul, the Republic of Korea, to which the Controlling Company moved in December 2011. In July 1999, LG Electronics Inc. and Koninklijke Philips Electronics N.V. ("Philips") entered into a joint venture agreement. Pursuant to the agreement, the Controlling Company changed its name to LG.Philips LCD Co., Ltd. However, on February 29, 2008, the Controlling Company changed its name to LG Display Co., Ltd. based upon the approval of shareholders at the general shareholders' meeting on the same date as a result of the decrease in Philips's share interest in the Controlling Company and the possibility of its business expansion to Organic Light Emitting Diode ("OLED") and Flexible Display products. As of December 31, 2011, LG Electronics Inc. owns 37.9% (135,625,000 shares) of the Controlling Company's common shares.

As of December 31, 2011, the Controlling Company has its TFT-LCD manufacturing plants, OLED manufacturing plant and LCD Research & Development Center in Paju and TFT-LCD manufacturing plants and OLED manufacturing plant in Gumi. The Controlling Company has overseas subsidiaries located in the United States of America, Europe and Asia.

The Controlling Company's common stock is listed on the Korea Exchange under the identifying code 034220. As of December 31, 2011, there are 357,815,700 shares of common stock outstanding. The Controlling Company's common stock is also listed on the New York Stock Exchange in the form of American Depository Shares ("ADSs") under the symbol "LPL." One ADS represents one-half of one share of common stock. As of December 31, 2011, there are 20,924,578 ADSs outstanding.

2. Basis of Presenting Financial Statements (in part)

(a) Statement of Compliance

These consolidated financial statements have been prepared in accordance with International Financial Reporting Standards ("IFRSs") as issued by the International Accounting Standards Board.

The consolidated financial statements were authorized for issuance by the Board of Directors on January 26, 2012.

3. Summary of Significant Accounting Policies (in part)

(e) Property, Plant and Equipment

(i) Recognition and Measurement

Items of property, plant and equipment are measured at cost less accumulated depreciation and accumulated impairment losses. Cost includes an expenditure that is directly attributable to the acquisition of the asset. The cost of self-constructed assets includes the cost of materials and direct labor, any costs directly attributable to bringing the assets to a working condition for their intended use, the costs of dismantling and removing the items and restoring the site on which they are located and borrowing costs on qualifying assets.

The gain or loss arising from the derecognition of an item of property, plant and equipment shall be determined as the difference between the net disposal proceeds, if any, and the carrying amount of the item and recognized in other income and expenses.

11. Property, Plant and Equipment

Changes in property, plant and equipment for the year ended December 31, 2011 are as follows:

(In Millions of Won)	Land	Buildings and Structures	Machinery and Equipment	Furniture and Fixtures	Construction-In-Progress(*1)	Others	Total
Acquisition cost as of January 1, 2011	(Won) 442,962	3,879,677	24,099,414	672,508	2,703,860	242,687	32,041,108
Accumulated depreciation as of January 1, 2011	—	(876,361)	(17,626,751)	(529,303)	—	(193,292)	(19,225,707)
Book value as of January 1, 2011	442,962	3,003,316	6,472,663	143,205	2,703,860	49,395	12,815,401
Additions	—	—	—	—	5,264,019	—	5,264,019
Depreciation	—	(193,120)	(3,141,295)	(61,324)		(17,712)	(3,413,451)
Impairment loss	—	—	(138)	(3,222)	—	(229)	(3,589)
Disposals	—	(166)	(563)	(366)	—	(15)	(1,110)

(continued)

(In Millions of Won)	Land	Buildings and Structures	Machinery and Equipment	Furniture and Fixtures	Construction-In-Progress[*1]	Others	Total
Others[*2]	1,290	278,471	4,091,712	74,323	(4,478,639)	32,843	—
Effect of movements in exchange rates	—	9,843	18,757	2,163	5,537	884	37,184
Subsidy decrease (increase)	—	(22)	(1,583)	—	—	—	(1,605)
Book value as of December 31, 2011	(Won) 444,252	3,098,322	7,439,553	154,779	3,494,777	65,166	14,696,849
Acquisition cost as of December 31, 2011	(Won) 444,252	4,170,768	28,028,986	720,716	3,494,778	261,526	37,121,025
Accumulated depreciation as of December 31, 2011	(Won) —	(1,072,446)	(20,589,295)	(562,715)	—	(196,131)	(22,420,587)
Accumulated impairment loss as of December 31, 2011	(Won) —	—	(138)	(3,222)	—	(229)	(3,589)

[*1] As of December 31, 2011, construction-in-progress relates to construction of plants, including their machinery and equipment.

[*2] Others are mainly amounts transferred from construction-in-progress.

12. Intangible Assets, Continued

Changes in intangible assets for the year ended December 31, 2011 are as follows:

(In Millions of Won)	Intellectual Property Rights	Software	Member-ships	Development Costs	Construction-In-Progress (Software)	Customer Relation-ships	Technology	Goodwill	Others[*2]	Total
Acquisition cost as of January 1, 2011	(Won) 507,862	317,807	47,147	265,092	11,463	24,011	11,074	23,912	13,084	1,221,452
Accumulated amortization as of January 1, 2011	(436,151)	(119,179)	—	(113,395)	—	(2,300)	(742)	—	(9,784)	(681,551)
Book value as of January 1, 2011	71,711	198,628	47,147	151,697	11,463	21,711	10,332	23,912	3,300	539,901
Additions-internally developed	—	—	—	127,381	—	—	—	—	—	127,381
Other additions	21,890	—	2,931	—	87,346	—	—	—	7	112,174
Amortization[*1]	(11,501)	(86,021)	—	(134,867)	—	(3,424)	(1,110)	—	(1,073)	(237,996)
Disposals	(1,588)	—	—	—	—	—	—	—	—	(1,588)
Impairment loss	—	(1,039)	(4,535)	—	—	—	—	—	—	(5,574)
Transfer from construction-in-progress	—	87,990	—	—	(87,990)	—	—	—	—	—
Effect of movements in exchange rates	18	801	—	—	—	—	—	—	(3)	816
Book value as of December 31, 2011	(Won) 80,530	200,359	45,543	144,211	10,819	18,287	9,222	23,912	2,231	535,114
Acquisition cost as of December 31, 2011	(Won) 523,873	407,832	50,078	392,473	10,819	24,011	11,074	23,912	13,090	1,456,162
Accumulated amortization as of December 31, 2011	(Won) (443,343)	(206,434)	—	(248,262)	—	(5,724)	(1,852)	—	(10,859)	(916,474)
Accumulated impairment loss as of December 31, 2011	(Won) —	(1,039)	(4,535)	—	—	—	—	—	—	(5,574)
Remaining amortization period (year)	7.46	2.49	N/A	0.55	N/A	5.33	8.33	N/A	2.60	

[*1] The Group has classified the amortization as manufacturing overhead costs, selling expenses and administrative expenses.

[*2] Others mainly consist of rights to use of electricity and gas supply facilities.

26. Other Income and Other Expenses

(a) Details of other income for the years ended December 31, 2009, 2010 and 2011 are as follows:

(In Millions of Won)	2009	2010	2011
Rental income	(Won) 4,116	4,305	6,325
Foreign currency gain	1,336,721	1,465,830	1,190,793
Gain on disposal of property, plant and equipment	486	1,387	740
Gain on disposal of investments	11	—	—
Reversal of stock compensation cost	—	—	469
Commission earned	—	5,555	8,630
Gain on disposal of intangible assets	9	—	—
Reversal of allowance for doubtful accounts for other receivables	548	—	—
Others	23,663	6,366	16,588
	(Won) 1,365,554	1,483,443	1,223,545

(b) Details of other expenses for the years ended December 31, 2009, 2010 and 2011 are as follows:

(In Millions of Won)	2009	2010	2011
Other bad debt expenses	(Won) 2	65	849
Foreign currency loss	1,172,296	1,550,909	1,220,143
Loss on disposal of property, plant and equipment	234	415	862
Impairment loss on property, plant, and equipment	664	—	3,589
Loss on disposal of intangible assets	—	—	1,588
Impairment loss on intangible assets	—	—	5,574
Expenses related to legal proceedings or claims and others	296,950	310,142	151,259
	(Won) 1,470,146	1,861,531	1,383,864

Loss on Disposal of Property, Plant and Equipment and Investment Property

3.302

POSCO (Dec 2011)

CONSOLIDATED STATEMENTS OF COMPREHENSIVE INCOME (in part)

(In Millions of Won Except per Share Information)	Notes	December 31, 2011	December 31, 2010
Revenue	26, 36	(Won) 68,938,725	47,887,255
Cost of sales	29	(59,823,850)	(39,722,461)
Gross profit		9,114,875	8,164,794
Selling and administrative expenses	27, 29		
Administrative expenses		(2,048,264)	(1,500,370)
Selling expenses		(1,612,128)	(1,120,340)
		(3,660,392)	(2,620,710)
Other operating income	28	337,078	231,387
Other operating expenses	29	(383,459)	(341,951)
Operating profit		5,408,102	5,433,520

CONSOLIDATED STATEMENTS OF CASH FLOWS
(in part)

(In Millions of Won)	Note	December 31, 2011	December 31, 2010
Cash flows from operating activities			
Profit for the period		(Won) 3,714,286	4,185,650
Adjustments for:			
Depreciation		2,118,626	2,942,137
Amortization		133,289	75,344
Impairment loss of property, plant and equipment and others		99,072	128,083
Loss on disposal of property, plant and equipment		60,550	83,494
Finance income		(1,734,280)	(879,110)
Finance costs		2,245,957	1,278,630
Income tax expense		1,068,109	1,081,472
Share of profit or loss of equity-accounted investees		(50,569)	(182,657)
Accrual of severance benefits		236,999	173,971
Bad debt expenses		45,477	60,266
Others		41,136	(143,715)

NOTES TO THE CONSOLIDATED FINANCIAL STATEMENTS *(in part)*

1. General Information *(in part)*

General information about POSCO, its 58 domestic subsidiaries ("the Company") including POSCO Engineering & Construction Co., Ltd., 161 foreign subsidiaries including POSCO America Corporation and its 91 associates are as follows:

(a) The Controlling Company

POSCO, the controlling company, was incorporated on April 1, 1968, under the Commercial Code of the Republic of Korea to manufacture and sell steel rolled products and plates in the domestic and foreign markets.

The shares of POSCO have been listed on the Korea Exchange since 1988. POSCO owns and operates two steel plants (Pohang and Gwangyang) and one office in Korea and it also operates internationally through ten of its overseas liaison offices.

As of December 31, 2011, POSCO's shareholders are as follows:

Shareholder's Name	Number of Shares	Ownership (%)
National Pension Service	5,937,323	6.81%
Nippon Steel Corporation[*1]	4,394,712	5.04%
SK Telecom Co., Ltd.	2,481,310	2.85%
Pohang University of Science and Technology	1,905,000	2.18%
Shinhan Financial Group Inc.[*2]	1,870,879	2.15%
Others	70,597,611	80.97%
	87,186,835	100.00%

[*1] Nippon Steel Corporation has American Depository Receipts (ADRs), each of which represents 0.25 share of POSCO's common share which has par value of (Won) 5,000 per share.

[*2] Includes number of shares subsidiaries hold at the end of the reporting period under commercial law.

As of December 31, 2011, the shares of POSCO are listed on the Korea Exchange, while its depository receipts are listed on the New York, Tokyo and London Stock Exchanges.

2. Statement of Compliance *(in part)*

Statement of Compliance

The consolidated financial statements have been prepared in accordance with International Financial Reporting Standards ("IFRSs") as issued by the International Accounting Standards Board. These are the Company's first consolidated financial statements prepared in accordance with IFRSs and IFRS No. 1 *"First-time adoption of* International Financial Reporting Standards" ("IFRS No. 1") has been applied.

The Company's date of transition to IFRSs in accordance with IFRS 1 is January 1, 2010. Prior to the adoption of IFRSs, the Company prepared consolidated financial statements in accordance with Korean Generally Accepted Accounting Principles ("K-GAAP"). An explanation of how the transition to IFRSs has affected the Company's reported financial position, financial performance and cash flows is provided in note 38.

Non-Current Assets Held for Sale

Non-current assets or disposal groups comprising assets and liabilities, that are expected to be recovered primarily through sale rather than through continuing use, are classified as held for sale. In order to be classified as held for sale, the assets or disposal groups must be available for immediate sale in their present condition and their sale must be highly probable. The assets or disposal groups that are classified as non-current assets held for sale are measured at the lower of their carrying amount and fair value less cost to sell.

The Company recognizes an impairment loss for any initial or subsequent write-down of disposal group to fair value less costs to sell, and a gain for any subsequent increase in fair value less costs to sell, up to the cumulative impairment loss previously recognized in accordance with IAS No. 36 *"Impairment of Assets"*.

A non-current asset that is classified as held for sale or part of a disposal group classified as held for sale is not depreciated (or amortized).

11. Investment Property, Net

(a) Investment property as of December 31, 2011, 2010 and January 1, 2010 are as follows:

(In Millions of Won)	December 31, 2011	December 31, 2010	January 1, 2010
Cost	(Won) 766,905	701,005	629,357
Less: Accumulated depreciation and accumulated impairment loss	(239,372)	(207,640)	(71,150)
Carrying value	(Won) 527,533	493,365	558,207

As of December 31, 2011, the fair value of investment property is (Won) 837,511 million, among which the Company evaluated investment property of 7 subsidiaries including International Business Center Corporation as its book value amounted to (Won) 82,396 million since it is believed that fair value is approximately same as book value.

(b) Changes in the carrying value of investment property for the years ended December 31, 2011 and 2010 are as follows:

1) For the Year Ended December 31, 2011

(In Millions of Won)	Beginning	Acquisition	Business Combination	Disposal	Depreciation[*1]	Others[*2]	Ending
Land	(Won) 211,464	41,243	94	(57,905)	(14,010)	38,591	219,477
Buildings	278,361	109,757	—	(56,953)	(22,783)	(6,649)	301,733
Structures	3,540	6,072	—	—	(640)	(2,649)	6,323
Total	(Won) 493,365	157,072	94	(114,858)	(37,433)	29,293	527,533

[*1] Impairment losses of investment property amounted to (Won) 23,048 million are included.
[*2] Includes reclassification resulting from changing purpose of use, adjustment of foreign currency translation difference and others.

12. Property, Plant and Equipment, Net

(a) Property, plant and equipment as of December 31, 2011, 2010 and January 1, 2010 are as follows:

(In Millions of Won)	2011	2010	January 1, 2010
Cost	(Won) 51,653,789	46,992,804	41,210,602
Less: Accumulated depreciation	(23,134,937)	(21,523,736)	(18,866,625)
Less: Government grants	(65,668)	(31,328)	(1,230)
Book value	(Won) 28,453,184	25,437,740	22,342,747

(b) The changes in carrying value of property, plant and equipment as for the years ended December 31, 2011 and 2010 are as follows:

1) For the Year Ended December 31, 2011

(In Millions of Won)	Beginning	Acquisition[*1]	Business Combination	Disposal	Depreciation[*2]	Others[*3]	Ending
Land	(Won) 2,011,851	450,151	92,806	(55,751)	—	50,121	2,549,178
Buildings	3,551,163	701,166	38,382	(38,755)	(278,097)	45,970	4,019,829
Structures	2,070,189	289,524	8,961	(10,775)	(163,072)	65,610	2,260,437
Machinery and equipment	13,777,382	2,892,960	204,871	(45,950)	(1,605,342)	955,463	16,179,384
Vehicles	64,173	21,041	1,981	(1,795)	(17,894)	(763)	66,743
Tools	75,437	38,477	2,259	(1,477)	(37,743)	3,924	80,877
Furniture and fixtures	124,677	66,297	1,995	(1,657)	(28,249)	6,626	169,689
Capital Lease Assets	43,106	8,029	20	(145)	(14,081)	1,613	38,542
Construction-in-progress	3,719,762	4,593,524	10,536	—	—	(5,235,317)	3,088,505
Total	(Won) 25,437,740	9,061,169	361,811	(156,305)	(2,144,478)	(4,106,753)	28,453,184

[*1] Acquisition includes assets transferred from construction-in-progress.
[*2] Impairment losses of property, plant and equipment amounted to (Won) 25,852 million are included.
[*3] Includes reclassification for changing purpose of use, adjustment of foreign currency translation difference and others.

28. Other Operating Income and Expenses

(a) Other Operating Income

Details of other operating income for the years ended December 31, 2011 and 2010 are as follows:

(In Millions of Won)	December 31, 2011	December 31, 2010
Gain on disposal of property, plant and equipment	(Won) 13,812	26,366
Gain on disposal of investment of equity-accounted investees	2,247	2,942
Reversal of allowance for doubtful accounts	86,451	3,796
Outsourcing income	42,136	11,055
Gain on disposal of wastes	9,641	2,997
Gain from claim compensation	33,103	58,200
Penalty income from early termination of contracts	38,570	14,081
Others	111,118	111,950
	(Won) 337,078	231,387

(b) Other Operating Expenses

Details of other operating expenses for the years ended December 31, 2011 and 2010 are as follows:

(In Millions of Won)	December 31, 2011	December 31, 2010
Loss on disposal of property, plant and equipment	(Won) 60,550	83,494
Loss on disposal of investment property	8,826	11,896
Cost of idle assets	16,881	795
Other bad debt expenses	28,081	12,877
Contributions	66,558	74,343
Loss on disposal of wastes	17,648	15,245
Impairment loss of property, plant and equipment and others	99,072	128,083
Others	85,843	15,218
	(Won) 383,459	341,951

29. Expenses by Nature

Expenses by nature in the statements of comprehensive income for the years ended December 31, 2011 and 2010 are as follows:

(In Millions of Won)	December 31, 2011	December 31, 2010
Changes in inventories	(Won) 40,166,313	19,496,278
Employee benefits expenses	2,639,966	2,363,727
Depreciation(*1)	2,133,011	2,960,550
Amortization	133,288	75,344
Outsourcing fee	7,823,815	7,270,872
Electricity and water expenses	692,544	504,308
Research and development expenses	592,649	537,025
Freight and custody expenses	1,406,268	948,891
Losses on disposition	60,550	83,494
Donation	66,559	74,344
Other operating expenses	256,350	184,114
Other expenses	7,896,389	8,186,175
	(Won) 63,867,702	42,685,122

(*1) Includes depreciation expense of investment properties.

CHANGE IN FAIR VALUE OF NONFINANCIAL ASSETS

IFRS Overview and Comparison to U.S. GAAP

3.303 When permitted or required by IFRSs, an entity may measure a nonfinancial asset at fair value subsequent to initial recognition. When an entity applies this accounting policy, by electing to apply a fair value model or revaluation model, as appropriate, the subsequent measurement of these assets affects its statement of comprehensive income. The following standards permit or require these models and are addressed in this subsection:

- IAS 16—revaluation model
- IAS 38—revaluation model
- IAS 40—fair value model
- IAS 41, *Agriculture*—fair value model

Author's Note

Recognition, measurement, presentation, and disclosure requirements for the assets within the scope of these standards are discussed in section 2. This subsection only addresses the effects on the statement of comprehensive income.

Recognition and Measurement

IFRSs

3.304 IAS 16 permits an entity to remeasure the carrying value of items of PPE to *revalued amount*, which is fair value on the date of revaluation. An entity should revalue all assets in the relevant class of PPE with sufficient regularity such that the carrying value of the class is not materially different from fair value at the balance sheet date. An entity should recognize an increase in carrying value from revaluation in OCI (revaluation surplus), except that the entity should recognize the increase to profit and loss to the extent that the increase reverses accumulated prior decreases. Similarly, an entity should recognize a decrease in carrying value in profit or loss, except that the entity should recognize the decrease in OCI to the extent it reverses an existing revaluation surplus.

3.305 IAS 38 permits an entity to select the revaluation model only if the class of intangible assets has an active market. The effect of a change in carrying value revaluation on the statement of comprehensive income is the same as IAS 16.

3.306 IAS 40 permits an entity to remeasure the carrying value of all investment properties to fair value at the reporting date. When the fair value model is selected, an entity should recognize the change in fair value in profit or loss.

3.307 IAS 41 requires an entity to recognize biological assets initially and in subsequent reporting periods and agricultural produce initially and at the point of harvest at FVLCS and recognize the change in fair value in profit or loss. An entity should recognize any gains or losses on initial recognition at FVLCS and on remeasurement in profit or loss.

U.S. GAAP

3.308 Unlike IFRSs, FASB ASC does not permit an entity to remeasure nonfinancial assets to fair value, revalued amount, or FVLCS, subsequent to initial recognition, except in rare circumstances. For example, when an entity recognizes an impairment loss, it remeasures the asset to fair value. (See the guidance related to the recognition and measurement of asset impairments starting with paragraph 3.240)

Presentation

IFRSs

3.309 Changes in fair value, revalued amount, or FVLCS are, by nature, different from other income and expense items. In contrast to the alternative to present expenses by nature or function in profit or loss, IAS 1 requires an entity to present information of OCI by nature. When an entity presents information recognized in profit or loss by function, it should disclose an analysis of expenses by nature in a note disclosure.

U.S. GAAP

3.310 Because FASB ASC does not permit nonfinancial assets to be remeasured to fair value, revalued amount, or FVLCS, there is no guidance to reference here.

Disclosure

IFRSs

3.311 IAS 16 and IAS 38 require an entity to disclose revaluation increases or decreases as a separate line in the reconciliation of the gross carrying amount of the relevant asset class.

3.312 IAS 40 requires an entity to disclose the net gains or losses from fair value adjustments of investment properties.

3.313 IAS 41 requires an entity to disclose any gains or losses from changes in FVLCS.

U.S. GAAP

3.314 Because FASB ASC does not permit nonfinancial assets to be remeasured to fair value, revalued amount, or FVLCS, there is no guidance to reference here.

Presentation and Disclosure Excerpts

Author's Note

None of the survey companies selected for this edition elected the revaluation model for intangible assets. Therefore, no disclosure excerpts were available for inclusion.

Changes in Fair Value of Biological Assets Recognized in Profit and Loss
3.315
Fibria Celulose S.A. (Dec 2011)

CONSOLIDATED STATEMENTS OF OPERATIONS AND COMPREHENSIVE INCOME (LOSS) (in part)

In thousand of reais, except for the income per shares

	2011	2010	2009
Continuing Operations			
Net revenues (Note 29)	5,854,300	6,283,387	5,292,972
Cost of sales (Note 31)	(5,124,269)	(4,694,659)	(4,555,729)
Gross profit	730,031	1,588,728	737,243
Operating income (expenses)			
Selling expenses (Note 31)	(294,928)	(281,428)	(296,974)
General and administrative (Note 31)	(310,425)	(312,316)	(296,123)
Equity in losses of affiliate	(414)	(7,328)	(1,133)
Other operating income (expenses), net (Note 31)	253,395	(7,499)	1,609,016
	(352,372)	(608,571)	1,014,786
Income before financial income and expenses	377,659	980,157	1,752,029

CONSOLIDATED STATEMENTS OF CASH FLOWS
(in part)

	2011	2010	2009
Income (loss) from continuing operations before taxes on income	(1,491,012)	615,939	3,323,564
Adjusted by			
Income before taxes on income from discontinued operations (Note 36)	364,629	112,897	141,053
Depreciation, depletion and amortization	1,838,827	1,616,705	1,650,820
Depletion of wood from forestry partnership programs	45,368	49,686	25,092
Unrealized foreign exchange (gains) losses, net	935,922	(301,677)	(2,626,572)
Change in fair value of derivative financial instruments	276,877	(152,284)	(148,403)
Equity in losses of affiliate	414	7,328	1,133
Gain on sale of investments (CONPACEL, KSR and Piracicaba)	(532,850)		(33,414)
Accretion of present value—Payable for Aracruz acquisition	40,893	289,830	474,536
Loss (gain) on disposal of property, plant and equipment	(25,361)	17,472	(3,177)
Interest and gain and losses in marketable securities	(178,895)	(199,000)	(172,730)
Interest expense	660,084	743,417	753,658
Change in fair value of biological assets	(145,884)	(92,319)	(551,604)
Gain on remeasurement of the initial interest on Aracruz			(1,378,924)
Provisions and other	124,632	53,282	(41,445)

NOTES TO THE CONSOLIDATED FINANCIAL STATEMENTS *(in part)*

In thousands of reais, unless otherwise indicated

1 Operations (in part)

(a) General Information

Fibria Celulose S.A. and its subsidiaries (the "Company", "Fibria", or "we") is a limited liability company constituted in accordance with the laws of the Federative Republic of Brazil and headquartered in São Paulo and after divesting its paper production activities in 2011, operates a single operational segment: producing and selling short fiber pulp.

The Company's business is affected by global pulp prices, which are historically cyclical and subject to significant volatility over short periods, as a result of, among other factors: (a) global demand for products from pulp; (b) global production capacity and strategies adopted by the main producers; (c) availability of substitutes for these products; and (d) exchange rates. All these factors are beyond the control of the Company's management.

The company's businesses are operated through the maintenance its own and third-party forest base, plants for manufacturing bleached pulp and an integrated logistic structure for exporting its production, as detailed in topics (b) and (c) below:

(b) Facilities in Operation and Forest Base

The company operates the following facilities as of December 31, 2010 to produce bleached eucalyptus kraft pulp with a total annual capacity of approximately 5.25 million tons:

Pulp Production Facility	Location (Brazil)	Annual Production Capacity (Tons)
Aracruz	Espírito Santo	2,300,000
Três Lagoas	Mato Grosso do Sul	1,300,000
Jacareí	São Paulo	1,100,000
Veracel(*)	Bahia	550,000
		5,250,000

(*) Represents 50% of the annual production capacity of Veracel's pulp mill consistently with the proportional consolidation of the results of operations of Veracel in our consolidated statement of operations.

The production of bleached pulp is performed only from eucalyptus trees which are a variety of high quality hardwood pulp, with short fibers, generally better suited to manufacturing toilet paper, uncoated and coated paper for printing and writing and coated cardboard for packaging. We use different sources to generate thermal and electric energy for our respective operations, including black liquor, biomass derived from wood debarking, bark and scraps.

Fibria produces only hardwood pulp from planted eucalyptus trees therefore its eucalyptus trees are referred as forest, which have an average extraction cycle of between six and seven years and are located in six Brazilian States, consisting of approximately 972 thousand hectares as of December 31, 2011, including reforested and protected areas, as follows (in thousand hectares):

	Area of Forest	Total Area
State		
São Paulo	80,224	147,584
Minas Gerais	13,220	27,213
Rio de Janeiro	1,696	3,413
Mato Grosso do Sul	231,405	350,201
Bahia	145,977	279,055
Espírito Santo	96,242	164,949
	568,764	972,415

The forest base of the Losango project in the state Rio Grande do Sul is excluded from the table above as their assets qualify as assets held for sale and are being presented as such as detailed in Note 36.

2 Presentation of Financial Statements and Significant Accounting Practices (in part)

2.1 Presentation of Financial Statements (in part)

(a) Consolidated Financial Statements

The company's consolidated financial statements have been prepared and are being presented in accordance with and in compliance with International Financial Reporting Standards (IFRS) as issued by the International Accounting Standards Board (IASB).

The financial statements as of and for the year ended December 31, 2010 were the first financial statements presented in accordance with IFRS prepared by the Company. The main differences between the accounting practices previously adopted in Brazil (the "BR GAAP") and United States of America and IFRS, including the reconciliation of shareholders' equity and net income as of December 31, 2010 and 2009, are described in Note 39—First-time Adoption of IFRS.

2.14 Biological Assets

Biological assets are measured at fair value, net of estimated costs to sell at the time of harvest. Depletion is calculated based on the total volume expected to be harvested.

Biological assets consist of eucalyptus forests exclusively from renewable plantations and intended for the production of bleached pulp. As a result of improvements in forest management techniques, including the genetic improvement of trees, the cycle of harvesting through replanting occurs over approximately six to seven years.

The fair value is determined based on the discounted cash flow method, taking into consideration the cubic volume of wood, segregated by plantation year, and the equivalent sales value of standing timber. The average sales price was estimated based on the local market prices and on transactions researched, adjusted to reflect the forest price. The volumes used in the valuation are consistent with the annual average harvest for each region.

The Company has a policy of carrying out semi-annual appraisals of the fair value of these assets.

3 Critical Accounting Estimates and Assumptions (in part)

Estimates and assumptions are continually evaluated and are based on historical experience and other factors, including expectations of future events that are believed to be reasonable under the circumstances.

The accounting estimates will seldom equal the related actual results. The estimates and assumptions that have a significant risk of causing a material adjustment to the book values of assets and liabilities within the next financial year are addressed below.

(e) Biological Assets

The fair value of biological assets calculation takes into consideration various assumptions with a high degree of judgment, as the sales price, cubic volume of wood and/or the annual average harvest for each region. Any changes in these assumptions used, would change the discounted cash flow result and, consequently cause the appreciation or devaluation of these assets.

4 Risk Management (in part)

During 2011 following the commitment of Fibria with good governance practices the Governance, Risks and Compliance area was established which accumulates the activities of the risk management, internal controls, internal audit and ombudsman areas. The objective was to promote the synergy between the areas, to contribute with value creation for the business and mainly, to strengthen governance of the company. The new area reports directly to the CEO and its processes are monitored by the Audit and Risks Committee, an advisory body of the Board of Directors.

The risk management process of Fibria classifies the risks inherent to its business in the following categories:

(a) Market risk—a detail of the policies for managing market risk is included in Note 4.2.1 (a).

(b) Credit risk—a detail of the policies for managing credit risk is included in Note 4.2.1 (b).

(c) Compliance risk: corresponds to legal or regulatory penalties, financial losses or reputational damage that the Company may face due to a regulatory noncompliance. In order to manage this risk, the Company continually monitors compliance with laws, standards and regulations, implements contingency plans and segregation of duties in order to avoid conflicts of interest and to facilitate the assessment of risk and the related internal controls of the Company. These assessments includes assessment of environmental, labor and tax risks. The monitoring process if documents and reported to senior management.

(d) Operational risk: results from the lack of consistency or adequacy of information systems, of processing and operational control, from failures in the management of assets or in the internal controls fund management, or from frauds that affect the activities of the Company.

One of the steps in the process of managing the operational risk of Fibria, which is managed through matrixes, is a materiality analysis and an analysis of the strategies of the Company in order to design controls and specific monitoring actions for the most significant accounts and processes. The Company has improved risk management with a control assessment tool which facilitates assessing the effectiveness of the control, generating reports and correcting deviations identified in the processes.

The area responsible for compliance operates along with the corresponding business areas in order to comply with internal controls through the monitoring of processes which results in a mitigating factor for operational risk.

(e) Event risk: results from internal and external events that affect the reputation and sustainability of the Company, such as those caused by climate change, social movements or trade unions, shutdown of facilities, layoffs, leak of sensitive information, etc. The Company continually monitors its relationships in an effort to anticipate potential risks. Fibria has a workstream to manage all strategic risks of which the Company is exposed. The ERM (Enterprise Risk Management) project was launched in 2010 and currently comprises the analysis, evaluation, monitoring and treatment of strategic risks. For those risks defined as a priority (high level of potential impacts and of probability of occurrence) different workstreams have been put in place by the Company for which action plans and indicators (KRI's—key risk indicators) have been developed.

18 Biological Assets

The Company's biological assets are substantially comprised of growing forests, intended for the supply of wood for pulp production. Forests in formation are located in the states of São Paulo, Rio Grande do Sul, Espírito Santo and Bahia.

The reconciliation of the book balances at the beginning and at the end of the year is as follows:

	2011	2010	2009
At the beginning of the year	3,550,636	3,791,084	1,890,898
Acquisition of Aracruz			1,849,069
Additions	761,502	642,567	216,300
Harvests in the period			
Historical cost	(569,813)	(440,265)	(127,595)
Fair value	(405,617)	(411,416)	(104,963)
Change in fair value	125,053	92,319	551,604
Reclassification to assets held for sale			
CONPACEL		(160,765)	
Losango	(241,595)		
Sale of the Guaíba unit			(426,303)
Other	44,044	37,112	(57,926)
At the end of the year	3,264,210	3,550,636	3,791,084

In determining the fair value of biological assets, the discounted cash flow model DCF was used, with projections based on a single scenario, with productivity and area of plantation (eucalyptus trees) for a harvest cycle of six to seven years.

The projected cash flows is consistent with area's growing cycle. The volume of production of eucalyptus to be harvested was estimated considering the average productivity in cubic meters of wood from each plantation per hectare at the time of harvest. The average productivity varies according to the genetic material, climate and soil conditions and the forestry management programs. This projected volume is based on the average annual growth (IMA) by region.

The average net sales price was projected based on the estimated price for eucalyptus in the local market, through a market study and research of actual transactions, adjusted to reflect the price of standing timber by region. The average estimated cost contemplates expenses for felling, chemical control of growth, ant and other pest control, composting, road maintenance, inputs and labor services. Tax effects based on current rates, as well as the contribution of other assets, such as property, plant and equipment and land were considered in the estimate based on average rates of return for those assets.

The valuation model considers the net cash flows after taxes on income and the discount rate used also considers the tax benefits.

In the following table we present the main inputs considered in estimating the fair value of biological assets:

	2011	2010
Actual planted area (hectare)	551,959	544,714
Average annual growth (IMA)—m3/hectare	41	42
Net average sale price—R$/m(3)	50,70	49,34
Remuneration of own contributory assets	5.6%	5.6%
Discount rate	7.9%	8.2%

The increase in e fair value of biological assets during the year ended December 31, 2011, when compared to the fair value as of December 31, 2010 is the combined result of the inputs presented above which resulted in a gain of R$ 125,053.

The estimate of the fair values of biological assets as of December 31, 2011 and 2010 was performed by management with the assistance of valuation specialists.

The company has no biological assets pledged as of December 31, 2011.

31 Expenses by Nature (in part)

	2011	2010	2009
Other operating expenses, net			
Fair value amortization (including the gain on investment sold—Guaíba unit)	(23,197)	(83,123)	(242,868)
Gain related to the remeasurement of equity interest held prior to the acquisition of controlling equity interest in Aracruz			1,378,924
Gain on disposal—Piracicaba	175,654		
Provision for loss—sale of investment	(30,844)		
Change in fair value of biological assets	145,884	92,319	551,604
Others	(14,102)	(16,695)	(78,644)
	253,395	(7,499)	1,609,016

(*) Includes handling expenses, storage and transportation expenses and sales commissions, among others.

Change in Fair Value Recognized in Profit and Loss—Investment Property, Change in Revalued Amount Recognized in Other Comprehensive Income—Property, Plant and Equipment

3.316

The Governor and Company of the Bank of Ireland (Dec 2011)

CONSOLIDATED INCOME STATEMENT (in part)

	Note	Year Ended 31 December 2011 €m	Year Ended 31 December 2010 €m	9 Months Ended 31 December 2009 €m
Interest income	3	4,618	5,179	4,188
Interest expense	4	(3,084)	(2,960)	(2,009)
Net interest income		1,534	2,219	2,179
Net insurance premium income	5	929	969	665
Fee and commission income	6	612	633	474
Fee and commission expense	6	(192)	(257)	(255)
Net trading income/(expense)	7	19	225	(28)
Life assurance investment income, gains and losses	8	(38)	474	958
Gain on liability management exercises	9	1,789	1,402	1,037
Other operating income	10	12	199	31
Total operating income		4,665	5,864	5,061

CONSOLIDATED STATEMENT OF OTHER COMPREHENSIVE INCOME (in part)

	Year Ended 31 December 2011 €m	Year Ended 31 December 2010 €m	9 Months Ended 31 December 2009 €m
Profit/(loss) for the period			
Other comprehensive income, net of tax:	40	(609)	(1,469)

CONSOLIDATED CASH FLOW STATEMENT (in part)

	Year Ended 31 December 2011 €m	Year Ended 31 December 2010 €m	9 Months Ended 31 December 2009 €m
Cash Flows From Operating Activities			
Loss before taxation	(190)	(950)	(1,813)
Share of results of associates and joint ventures	(39)	(49)	(35)
(Profit)/loss on disposal of business activities	(34)	(15)	3
Depreciation and amortisation	136	147	107
Impairment charges on financial assets (excluding assets sold to NAMA)	1,960	2,027	2,335
Impairment charges assets sold to NAMA	44	257	1,722
(Gain)/loss on sale of assets to NAMA including associated costs	(33)	2,241	—
Loss on deleveraging of financial assets	565	—	—
Decline in value of property below cost	15	10	6
Revaluation of investment property	10	(49)	98
Interest expense on subordinated liabilities and other capital instruments	171	312	163
Charge for retirement benefit obligation	88	174	149
Impact of amendments to defined benefit pension schemes	(2)	(733)	—
Gain on subordinated liability management exercises	(1,789)	(1,402)	(1,037)
(Gains)/Charges arising on the movement in credit spreads on the Group's own debt and deposits accounted for at 'fair value through profit or loss'	(56)	(360)	6
Other non-cash items	45	144	(86)

NOTES TO THE CONSOLIDATED FINANCIAL STATEMENTS (in part)

Accounting Policies (in part)

The following are Bank of Ireland Group's principal accounting policies.

Basis of Preparation

The financial statements comprise the Consolidated income statement, the Consolidated statement of other comprehensive income, the Consolidated balance sheet, the Consolidated statement of changes in equity, the Consolidated cash flow statement, the Group accounting policies and the notes to the Consolidated financial statements. The notes include the information contained in those parts of the Risk Management Report in Item 11 'Quantitative and Qualitative Disclosures about Market Risk' that are described as being an integral part of the financial statements.

The financial statements are prepared in accordance with International Financial Reporting Standards (IFRS) and International Financial Reporting Interpretations Committee (IFRIC) interpretations as adopted by the European Union (EU) and with those parts of the Companies Acts, 1963 to 2009 applicable to companies reporting under IFRS, with the European Communities (Credit Institutions: Accounts) Regulations, 1992 and with the Asset Covered Securities Acts, 2001 to 2007. The EU adopted version of IAS 39 currently relaxes some of the hedge accounting rules in IAS 39 'Financial Instruments—Recognition and Measurement'. The Group has not availed of this, hence these financial statements comply with both IFRS as adopted by the EU and IFRS as issued by the IASB.

The financial statements have been prepared under the historical cost convention as modified to include the fair valuation of certain financial instruments and land and buildings.

The preparation of the financial statements in conformity with IFRS requires the use of estimates and assumptions that affect the reported amounts of assets and liabilities at the date of the financial statements and the reported amounts of revenues and expenses during the reporting period. Although these estimates are based on management's best knowledge of the amount, event or actions, actual results ultimately may differ from those estimates. A description of the critical estimates and judgements is set out on pages F-41 to F-44.

References to 'the State' throughout this document should be taken to refer to the Republic of Ireland, its Government and, where and if relevant, Government departments, agencies and local Government bodies.

Property, Plant and Equipment

Freehold land and buildings are initially recognised at cost, and subsequently are revalued annually to open market value by independent external valuers. Revaluations are made with sufficient regularity to ensure that the carrying amount does not differ materially from the open market value at the balance sheet date.

All other property, plant and equipment, including freehold and leasehold adaptations, are stated at historical cost less accumulated depreciation. Cost includes expenditure that is directly attributable to the acquisition of the items. Subsequent costs are included in the asset's carrying amount or are recognised as a separate asset, as appropriate, only when it is probable that future economic benefits associated with the item will flow to the Group and the cost of the item can be measured reliably. All other repairs and maintenance are charged to the income statement during the financial year in which they are incurred.

Increases in the carrying amount arising on the revaluation of land and buildings are recognised in other comprehensive income. Decreases that offset previous increases on the same asset are recognised in other comprehensive income: all other decreases are charged to the income statement.

The Directors consider that residual values of freehold and long leasehold property based on prices prevailing at the time of acquisition or subsequent valuation are such that depreciation is not material.

Depreciation is calculated on the straight line method to write down the carrying value of other items of property, plant and equipment to their residual values over their estimated useful lives as follows:

- Adaptation works on freehold and leasehold property—Fifteen years, or the remaining period of the lease
- Computer and other equipment—Maximum of ten years

The assets' residual values and useful lives are reviewed, and adjusted if appropriate, at each balance sheet date. Property, plant and equipment are reviewed for impairment whenever events or changes in circumstances indicate that the carrying amount may not be recoverable. An asset's carrying amount is written down immediately to its recoverable amount if its carrying amount is greater than its estimated recoverable amount. The estimated recoverable amount is the higher of the asset's fair value less costs to sell or its value in use.

Gains and losses on the disposal of property, plant and equipment are determined by reference to their carrying amount and are taken into account in determining profit before tax. If the asset being disposed of had previously been revalued then any amount in other comprehensive income relating to that asset is reclassified to retained earnings on disposal.

Investment Property

Property held for long term rental yields and capital appreciation is classified as investment property. Investment property comprises freehold and long leasehold land and buildings. It is carried at fair value in the balance sheet based on annual revaluations at open market value and is not depreciated. Changes in fair values are recorded in the income statement. Rental income from investment properties is recognised as it becomes receivable over the term of the lease.

Capital Stock and Reserves (in part)

(6) Revaluation Reserve

The revaluation reserve represents the cumulative gains and losses on the revaluation of property occupied by Group businesses, included within property, plant and equipment and non-financial assets classified as held for sale.

35 Investment Properties

	31 December 2011 €m	31 December 2010 €m
At beginning of year	1,304	1,265
Exchange adjustment	7	11
Revaluation	(10)	49
Reclassifications	(44)	(14)
Disposals	(53)	(7)
At end of year	1,204	1,304

Of the €1,204 million (31 December 2010: €1,304 million) €875 million (31 December 2010: €980 million) is held on behalf of Bank of Ireland Life policyholders.

Investment properties are carried at fair value as determined by external qualified property surveyors appropriate to the variety of properties held. Fair values have been calculated using both current trends in the market and recent transactions for similar properties. The downward revaluation in the current year is primarily driven by a decrease in the fair value of Irish and international investment property.

Rental income from investment property amounted to €94 million for the year ended 31 December 2011 (year ended 31 December 2010: €97 million). Expenses directly attributable to investment property generating rental income amounted to €18 million for the year ended 31 December 2011 (year ended 31 December 2010: €18 million). There were no expenses directly attributable to investment property not generating rental income for the year ended 31 December 2011 or the year ended 31 December 2010.

36 Property, Plant and Equipment (in part)

	Freehold Land and Buildings and Long Leaseholds (Held at Fair Value) €m	Adaptations (At Cost) €m	Computer and Other Equipment (At Cost) €m	Finance Lease Assets (At Cost) €m	Payments on Accounts and Assets in the Course of Construction (At Cost) €m	Total €m
Cost or Valuation						
At 1 January 2011	177	151	543	7	18	896
Exchange adjustments	1	1	3	—	—	5
Additions	—	1	4	3	23	31
Disposals	(4)	(3)	(35)	(5)	—	(47)
Revaluation						
—Recognised in the income statement	(15)	—	—	—	—	(15)
—Recognised in other comprehensive income	(8)	—	—	—	—	(8)
Reclassifications	—	14	7	—	(25)	(4)
At 31 December 2011	151	164	522	5	16	858
Accumulated Depreciation						
At 1 January 2011	—	(83)	(434)	(7)	—	(524)
Exchange adjustments	—	(1)	(2)	—	—	(3)
Disposals	—	3	34	5	—	42
Reclassifications	—	(2)	2	—	—	
Charge for the year (note 12)	—	(12)	(24)	(1)	—	(37)
At 31 December 2011	—	(95)	(424)	(3)	—	(522)
Net book value at 31 December 2011	151	69	98	2	16	336

Property, plant and equipment at 31 December 2011 held at fair value was €151 million (31 December 2010: €177 million). The historical cost of property, plant and equipment held at fair value at 31 December 2011 was €92 million (31 December 2010: €91 million). The net book value of property, plant and equipment at 31 December 2011 held at cost less accumulated depreciation and impairment amounted to €185 million (31 December 2010: €195 million).

Property

A revaluation of Group property was carried out as at 31 December 2011. All freehold and long leasehold (50 years or more unexpired) commercial properties were valued by Lisney as external valuers, who also reviewed the valuation of all other property carried out by the Bank's professionally qualified staff. Valuations were made on the basis of open market value.

IAS 12, *INCOME TAXES*

Author's Note

In December 2010, IASB issued *Deferred Tax: Recovery of Underlying Assets: Proposed Amendments to IAS 12*. The amendments are effective for annual periods beginning on or after 1 January 2012, with early application permitted. Given the issue and effective dates, no survey companies would have applied these amendments to their 2010 financial statements. See the author's note preceding paragraph 2.364 in section 2 for a discussion of these amendments and the remaining issues in this project. IASB may consider a fundamental review of accounting for income taxes as part of its 2012 agenda consultation process.

In 2011, the IASB amended IAS 12, *Income Taxes,* by issuing new standards. These amendments are effective for annual periods beginning on or after 1 January 2012 and, therefore, are not discussed in the commentary in this section. See the author's note preceding paragraph 2.364 in section 2 for a discussion of the terminology changes that result from these amendments.

Because these standards are effective for annual periods beginning on or after 1 January 2012, these amendments are not reflected in the commentary in this section. However, these amendments would not affect the availability of illustrative excerpts from survey companies' financial statements.

IFRS Overview and Comparison to U.S. GAAP

3.317 The objective of IAS 12 is to establish accounting for the current and future tax consequences of taxes levied on income by taxation authorities. Because accounting for financial reporting and accounting for tax purposes may be different, an entity should recognize in its financial statements the current and future tax consequences from the future recovery of the carrying amount of assets, the future settlement of its liabilities, transactions, and other events in the current period.

Author's Note

Both IAS 12 and GAAP use the asset-liability approach to measuring current and deferred tax expense and the carrying amounts of current and deferred tax assets and liabilities. Issues associated with income taxes not directly related to the effects of these requirements on the statement of comprehensive income are addressed in the section titled "IAS 12" in section 2.

Recognition and Measurement

IFRSs

3.318 IAS 12 generally requires an entity to recognize current and deferred tax income or expense in profit or loss for the period. However, to the extent that the temporary difference arises from a business combination or a transaction or an event recognized in OCI or directly in equity, an entity should recognize the current or deferred tax income or expense in OCI or directly in equity, respectively.

3.319 An entity should recognize current or deferred tax income or expense in OCI when it relates to items recognized in OCI and directly in equity when it relates to items recognized directly in equity. Examples of items recognized in OCI are changes in the carrying amount of PPE held under the revaluation method or changes in fair value of financial assets classified as available for sale. Examples of items recognized directly in equity include adjustments to retained earnings from a change in accounting policy and amounts arising on initial recognition of the equity component of a compound financial instrument.

3.320 IAS 12 provides additional specific guidance to entities in accounting for deferred tax arising in a business combination and share-based payment transactions.

U.S. GAAP

3.321 FASB ASC 740, *Income Taxes*, establishes standards for accounting and reporting for income taxes that are currently payable and for the tax consequences of all of the following:
- Revenues, expenses, gains, or losses that are included in taxable income in an earlier or later year than the year in which they are recognized in financial income
- Other events that create differences between the tax bases of assets and liabilities and their amounts for financial reporting
- Operating loss or tax credit carrybacks for refunds of taxes paid in prior years and carryforwards to reduce taxes payable in future years

3.322 Like IFRSs, FASB ASC 740-10-30-3 requires an entity to measure the total income tax expense (or benefit) for the year as the sum of deferred tax expense (or benefit) and income taxes currently payable or refundable. The measurement of the expense is dependent on an entity's measurement of the carrying values of related assets and liabilities. FASB ASC 740-10-30-2 requires entities to measure current and deferred tax expense in the following manner:
- Unlike IFRSs, an entity should measure current and deferred tax liabilities and assets based on provisions of the enacted tax law. The effects of future changes in tax laws or rates are not anticipated. IFRSs permit the use of substantially enacted tax laws.
- Like IFRSs, an entity should reduce the carrying value of deferred tax assets, if necessary, by the amount of any tax benefits that, based on available evidence, the entity does not expect to realize.

FASB ASC glossary defines *deferred tax expense (or benefit)* as the change during the year in an entity's deferred tax liabilities and assets.

3.323 FASB ASC 740 includes extensive guidance on accounting for income taxes that far exceeds the guidance in IAS 12 on measurement of current and deferred tax assets and liabilities and the resultant benefit or expense.

Presentation

IFRSs

3.324 An entity should present tax expense or income from ordinary activities in the statement of comprehensive income. When using the two-statement format and presenting the components of profit and loss in a separate statement, it should also present tax expense or income from ordinary activities in that statement.

3.325 IAS 1 permits an entity to show items of OCI either net of related tax effects or before tax effects, with one amount presented for the total tax effect of these items.

3.326 IAS 1 requires an entity to disclose separately the amount of income tax relating to each component of OCI. However, IAS 1 allows two alternative presentations of income tax effects in the statement of comprehensive income. An entity may present either
- each component of comprehensive income net of related tax or
- each component of comprehensive income pretax, with one line item for the aggregate amount of income tax on all components.

U.S. GAAP

3.327 Paragraphs 14 and 25 of FASB ASC 740-10-45 provide limited guidance to nonpublic entities on presentation in the income statement of interest and penalties and the effects of changes in deferred tax accounts caused by the following changes:
- In tax laws or rates
- In the tax status of an entity (for example, an entity's change from a corporation to a partnership)
- Affecting the valuation allowance for deferred tax assets related to the realizability of the deferred tax asset in future years
- Related to assets acquired outside of a business combination

3.328 For public entities, SEC Regulation S-X and various SEC Staff Accounting Bulletin topics establish presentation requirements, including the requirement to separately present income tax expense on the face of the income statement.

Disclosure

IFRSs

3.329 IAS 12 requires entities to disclose the following major components of income tax expense:
- Current tax income or expense
- Adjustments in the period for current tax of other periods
- Deferred tax income or expense from origination or reversal of temporary differences
- Deferred tax income or expense from changes in tax rates or laws
- Benefits from previously unrecognized tax loss or tax credit carryforwards
- Deferred tax expense (income) from write-downs (or reversals) of deferred tax assets

- Tax income or expense resulting from a change in accounting policy or errors (when included in profit and loss because they cannot be accounted for retrospectively)

3.330 Entities should separately disclose the aggregate amount of current and deferred income tax income or expense relating to items charged to OCI or directly to equity.

3.331 Entities should explain the relationship between tax income or expense and accounting profit by disclosing either or both of the following reconciliations:
- The amount of reported income tax income or expense to the expected amount based on applicable tax rate(s)
- The average effective tax rate to the applicable tax rate(s)

3.332 In both cases, entities should disclose the basis on which the applicable tax rate was computed. Entities should explain any differences in the applicable tax rate(s) from the previous period.

3.333 When an entity prepares the reconciliation disclosure, it should use an applicable tax rate that provides the most meaningful information to financial statement users. This tax rate is often the domestic tax rate of the country in which the entity is domiciled, taking into account both national and local tax rates. However, when an entity operates in multiple jurisdictions, it may determine that aggregating separate reconciliations prepared using the domestic rate in each individual jurisdiction is more meaningful.

3.334 With respect to discontinued operations, entities should disclose the tax expense or income from gains or losses on discontinuance and profit or loss of the discontinued operation for all periods presented.

U.S. GAAP

3.335 Like IFRSs, FASB ASC 740-10-50-9 requires entities to disclose the significant components of income tax expense, with the following additions:
- Government grants (to the extent recognized as a reduction of income tax expense)
- Benefits of operating loss carryforwards
- The tax expense from allocating certain tax benefits directly to contributed capital
- Adjustments to the deferred tax assets or liabilities as a result of enacted changes in tax laws or a change in the entity's tax status
- Adjustments to the beginning of a valuation allowance as a result of a change to the assessment of the ability of the entity to recover the deferred tax asset (IFRSs do not currently use valuation allowances)

3.336 FASB ASC 740-10-50-10 also requires an entity to disclose the amount of income tax benefit or expense allocated to continuing operations and the amounts separately allocated to other items (in accordance with the requirements for intraperiod tax allocation) for each year these items are presented. IAS 12 has no requirements or guidance on intraperiod tax allocation.

3.337 Like IFRSs, FASB ASC 740-10-50 requires reconciliations from reported to statutory amounts. As required by FASB ASC 740-10-50-12, a public entity should disclose a reconciliation of reported income tax benefit or expense to the expected amount using percentages or dollar amounts of the reported income tax income or expense attributable to continuing operations to the amount that would result from applying domestic federal statutory tax rates to pretax income from continuing operations. The entity should use the regular statutory tax rates even if alternatives exist. An entity should disclose both the estimated amount and the nature of each significant reconciling item. FASB ASC 740-10-50-13 states that a nonpublic entity should disclose the nature of significant reconciling items but may omit a numerical reconciliation.

Author's Note

Rule 4.08(h)(2) of SEC Regulation S-X requires SEC registrants applying U.S. GAAP to provide a reconciliation between the amount of reported total income tax expense (benefit) and the amount computed by multiplying the income (loss) before tax by the applicable statutory federal income tax rate, showing the estimated dollar amount of each of the underlying causes for the difference. However, when the reporting person is a foreign entity (foreign private issuer), the entity should normally use the income tax rate in that entity's country of domicile when making the preceding computation. Different rates should not be used for subsidiaries or other segments of a reporting entity. When the rate used by a reporting person is other than the United States federal corporate income tax rate, an

entity should disclose the rate used and the basis for using such rate. When such foreign private issuers prepare their financial statements in accordance with U.S. GAAP, rather than IFRSs, they prepare this reconciliation based on the statutory rate in their country of domicile, whether they file their financial statements on Form 10-K or Form 20-F. In contrast, IAS 12 permits an entity to reconcile tax expense reported on the income statement to tax expense computed at either the statutory tax rate in the country of domicile or a weighted average tax rate.

Presentation and Disclosure Excerpts

Effects of Change in Tax Rate, Tax Effects of Items Recognized in Other Comprehensive Income Shown as a Single Amount

3.338

Cellcom Israel Ltd (Dec 2011)

CONSOLIDATED STATEMENTS OF INCOME *(in part)*

	Note	Year Ended December 31, 2009 NIS Millions	Year Ended December 31, 2010 NIS Millions	Year Ended December 31, 2011 NIS Millions	Convenience Translation Into US Dollars (Note US$ 2D) Year Ended December 31, 2011 NIS Millions
Profit before taxes on income		1,549	1,708	1,129	296
Taxes on income	28	(367)	(417)	(304)	(80)
Profit for the year		1,182	1,291	825	216

CONSOLIDATED STATEMENTS OF COMPREHENSIVE INCOME *(in part)*

	Year Ended December 31, 2009 NIS Millions	Year Ended December 31, 2010 NIS Millions	Year Ended December 31, 2011 NIS Millions	Convenience Translation Into US Dollars (Note US$ 2D) Year Ended December 31, 2011 NIS Millions
Profit for the year	1,182	1,291	825	216
Net change in fair value of cash flow hedges transferred to profit or loss	(14)	(10)	20	5
Changes in fair value of cash flow hedges, net of income tax	(2)	9	13	3
Income tax on other comprehensive income	4	3	(5)	(1)
Other comprehensive income for the year, net of income tax	(12)	2	28	7

NOTES TO THE CONSOLIDATED FINANCIAL STATEMENTS *(in part)*

Note 1—Reporting Entity

Cellcom Israel Ltd. ("the Company") is a company incorporated and domiciled in Israel and its official address is 10 Hagavish Street, Netanya 42140, Israel. These consolidated financial statements of the Company as at December 31,

2011 are comprised of the Company and its subsidiaries ("the Group"). The Group operates and maintains a cellular mobile telephone system and provides cellular and landline telecommunications services in Israel. As of September 1, 2011, following the completion of the acquisition of Netvision Ltd. ("Netvision", see note 7, regarding acquisition of subsidiary), the Group also provides internet services (ISP) and international calls services. The Company is a consolidated subsidiary of Discount Investment Corporation (the parent company "DIC"). The Company's ultimate parent company is Ganden Holdings Ltd., and Mr. Nochi Dankner is the ultimate controlling shareholder.

Note 2—Basis of Preparation (in part)

A. Statement of Compliance

The consolidated financial statements have been prepared in accordance with International Financial Reporting Standards (IFRSs), as issued by the International Accounting Standards Board (IASB). The Company adopted IFRSs for the first time in 2008, with the date of transition to IFRSs being January 1, 2007 (hereinafter—"the date of transition").

These consolidated financial statements were approved by the Board of Directors on March 6, 2012.

O. Income Tax Expense

Income tax comprises current and deferred tax. Current tax and deferred tax are recognized in profit or loss except to the extent that it relates to a business combination, or are recognized directly in equity or in other comprehensive income to the extent they relate to items recognized directly in equity or in other comprehensive income.

Current tax is the expected tax payable on the taxable income for the year, using tax rates enacted or substantially enacted at the reporting date, and any adjustment to tax payable in respect of previous years.

Deferred tax is recognized using the balance sheet method, providing for temporary differences between the carrying amounts of assets and liabilities for financial reporting purposes and the amounts used for taxation purposes. Deferred tax is measured at the tax rates that are expected to be applied to the temporary differences when they reverse, based on the laws that have been enacted at the reporting date. Deferred tax assets and liabilities are offset if there is a legally enforceable right to offset current tax liabilities and assets, and they relate to income taxes levied by the same tax authority on the same taxable entity, or on different tax entities, but they intend to settle current tax liabilities and assets on a net basis or their tax assets and liabilities will be realized simultaneously.

A deferred tax asset is recognized to the extent that it is probable that future taxable profits will be available against which the temporary difference can be utilized. Deferred tax assets are reviewed at each reporting date and are reduced to the extent that it is no longer probable that the related tax benefit will be realized.

Note 28—Income Tax (in part)

A. Details Regarding the Tax Environment of the Group

(1) Amendments to the Income Tax Ordinance and the Land Appreciation Tax Law

(a) On July 14, 2009, the Israeli parliament passed the Economic Efficiency Law (Legislation Amendments for Implementation of the 2009 and 2010 Economic Plan)—2009,

which provided, inter alia, an additional gradual reduction in the company tax rate to 18% as from the 2016 tax year. In accordance with the aforementioned amendments, the company tax rates applicable as from the 2009 tax year are as follows: In the 2009 tax year—26%, in the 2010 tax year—25%, in the 2011 tax year—24%, in the 2012 tax year—23%, in the 2013 tax year—22%, in the 2014 tax year—21%, in the 2015 tax year—20% and as from the 2016 tax year the company tax rate will be 18%.

On December 5, 2011 the Israeli parliament approved the Law to Change the Tax Burden (Legislative Amendments)—2011. According to the law the tax reduction that was provided in the Economic Efficiency Law, as aforementioned, will be cancelled and the company tax rate will be 25% as from 2012.

Current taxes for the periods reported in these financial statements are calculated according to the tax rates specified in the Economic Efficiency Law.

Deferred tax balances as at December 31, 2011 are calculated in accordance with the tax rates specified in the Law to Change the Tax Burden, at the tax rate expected on the date of reversal. The effect of the change in the tax rate on the financial statements as at December 31, 2011 is reflected in an increase of NIS 33 million in the deferred tax liability against deferred tax expenses of NIS 33 million.

(b) On February 4, 2010 Amendment 174 to the Income Tax Ordinance—Temporary Order for Tax Years 2007, 2008 and 2009 was published in the Official Gazette (hereinafter—"the Temporary Order"). In accordance with the Temporary Order, Israeli Accounting Standard No. 29 regarding the adoption of International Financial Reporting Standards (IFRS) (hereinafter—"Standard 29") shall not apply when determining the taxable income for the 2007–2009 tax years even if it was applied when preparing the financial statements. On January 12, 2012 Amendment 188 to the Income Tax Ordinance was published, which amended the Temporary Order, in a manner that Standard 29 shall not apply also when determining the taxable income for 2010 and 2011.

(2) Taxation Under Inflation

The Income Tax Law (Adjustments for Inflation)—1985 (hereinafter—the Law) is effective as from the 1985 tax year. The Law introduced the concept of measurement of results for tax purposes on a real (net of inflation) basis.

On February 26, 2008 the Israeli parliament enacted the Income Tax Law (Adjustments for Inflation) (Amendment No. 20) (Restriction of Effective Period)—2008 (hereinafter—the Amendment). In accordance with the Amendment, the effective period of the Adjustments Law terminated at the end of the 2007 tax year and as from the 2008 tax year the provisions of the law no longer apply, other than the transitional provisions intended at preventing distortions in the tax calculations.

In accordance with the Amendment, as from the 2008 tax year, income for tax purposes is no longer adjusted to a real (net of inflation) measurement basis. Furthermore, the depreciation of inflation immune assets and carried forward tax losses are no longer linked to the CPI, so that these amounts are adjusted until the end of the 2007 tax year after which they ceased to be linked to the CPI. The effect of the Amendment to the Adjustments Law is reflected in the calculation of current and deferred taxes as from 2008.

B. Composition of Income Tax Expense (Income)

	Year Ended December 31		
	2009 NIS Millions	2010 NIS Millions	2011 NIS Millions
Current tax expense (income)			
Current year	423	462	288
Adjustments for prior years, net	6	(18)	—
Changes in accounting policy	(1)	—	—
Total current tax expenses	428	444	288
Deferred tax expense (income)			
Creation and reversal of temporary differences	(20)	(27)	(17)
Change in tax rate	(41)	—	33
Total deferred tax expenses (income)	(61)	(27)	16
Income tax expense	367	417	304

C. Income Tax Recognized Directly in Equity

	Year Ended December 31, 2011		
	Before Tax NIS Millions	Tax Expenses NIS Millions	Net of Tax NIS Millions
Hedging transactions— equity component	37	(9)	28

	Year Ended December 31, 2010		
	Before Tax NIS Millions	Tax Expenses NIS Millions	Net of Tax NIS Millions
Hedging transactions— equity component	3	(1)	2

	Year Ended December 31, 2009		
	Before Tax NIS Millions	Tax Benefit NIS Millions	Net of Tax NIS Millions
Hedging transactions— equity component	(16)	4	(12)

D. Reconciliation Between the Theoretical Tax on the Pre-Tax Profit and the Tax Expense:

	Year Ended December 31		
	2009 NIS Millions	2010 NIS Millions	2011 NIS Millions
Profit before taxes on income	1,549	1,708	1,129
Primary tax rate of the Group	26%	25%	24%
Tax calculated according to the Group's primary tax rate	403	427	271
Additional tax (tax saving) in respect of:			
Non-deductible expenses	3	2	4
Taxes in respect of previous years	6	(18)	—
Effect of changes in tax rate	(41)	—	33
Other differences, including inflation differences	(4)	6	(4)
Income tax expense	367	417	304

E. Deferred Tax Assets and Liabilities

(1) Recognized Deferred Tax Assets and Liabilities

Deferred taxes are calculated according to the tax rate anticipated to be in effect on the date of reversal as stated above.

The movement in deferred tax assets and liabilities is attributable to the following items:

	Allowance for Doubtful Debts NIS Millions	Property, Plant and Equipment and Intangible Assets NIS Millions	Hedging Transactions NIS Millions	Carry Forward Tax Deductions and Losses NIS Millions	Other NIS Millions	Total NIS Millions
Balance of deferred tax asset (liability) as at January 1, 2011	64	(164)	7	—	28	(65)
Changes recognized in profit or loss	(9)	17	—	(5)	14	17
Changes recognized in equity	—	—	(9)	—	—	(9)
Effect of change in tax rate	10	(55)	—	4	8	(33)
Business combinations (see note 7)	13	(80)	—	23	—	(44)
Deferred tax asset (liability) as at December 31, 2011	78	(282)	(2)	22	50	(134)
Deferred tax asset	78	18	—	22	50	168
Offset of balances						128
Deferred tax asset in statement of financial position as at December 31, 2011						40
Deferred tax liability	—	(300)	(2)	—	—	(302)
Offset of balances						(128)
Deferred tax liability in statement of financial position as at December 31, 2011						(174)

IFRS-BPPD 3.338

(2) Unrecognized Deferred Tax Liability

As at December 31, 2011 a deferred tax liability for temporary differences related to an investment in subsidiaries was not recognized because the decision as to whether to incur the liability rests with the Group and it is satisfied that it will not be incurred in the foreseeable future.

F. Tax Loss Carryforwards and Other Temporary Differences

As of December 31, 2011 Netvision and its subsidiaries have tax loss carryforwards and capital loss carryforwards in a total amount of NIS 145 million. In respect of these losses and in respect of other temporary deductible differences, the Group recorded in the consolidated financial statement deferred tax asset, net, in the amount of NIS 40 million.

G. Tax Assessments

The Company has received final tax assessments up to and including the year ended December 31, 2008 (the 2008 tax year).

Tax Effects of Discontinued Operations, Used and Unused Tax Loss Carryforwards, Tax Effects of Items Recognized in Other Comprehensive Income Shown as a Single Amount

3.339

Alcatel-Lucent (Dec 2011)

CONSOLIDATED INCOME STATEMENTS (in part)

(In Millions Except per Share Information)	Notes	2011[1]	2011	2010[5]	2009[5]
Income (loss) before income tax and discontinued operations		241	186	(311)	(743)
Income tax (expense) benefit	(9)	706	544	(14)	77
Income (loss) from continuing operations		947	730	(325)	(666)
Income (loss) from discontinued operations	(10)	537	414	33	162
Net income (loss)		1,484	1,144	(292)	(504)

[1] Translation of amounts from euros into U.S. dollars has been made merely for the convenience of the reader at Noon Buying Rate of € 1 = U.S. dollar 1.2973 on December 30, 2011.

CONSOLIDATED STATEMENTS OF COMPREHENSIVE INCOME (in part)

(In Millions)	Notes	2011[1]	2011	2010	2009
Net income (loss) for the year		U.S.$1,484	€ 1,144	€ (292)	€ (504)
Items to be subsequently reclassified to Income Statement		344	265	233	64
Financial assets available for sale	(17)	(14)	(11)	(22)	13
Cumulative translation adjustments		367	283	262	39
Cash flow hedging	(29)	(9)	(7)	(12)	11
Tax on items recognized directly in equity	(9)	—	—	5	1
Items that will not be subsequently reclassified to Income Statement		(1,342)	(1,034)	(75)	(637)
Unrecognized actuarial gains and losses	(26)	(1,470)	(1,133)	(70)	(582)
Tax on items recognized directly in equity	(9)	128	99	15	(2)
Other adjustments		—	—	(20)	(53)
Other comprehensive income (loss) for the period		(998)	(769)	158	(573)
Total comprehensive income (loss) for the period		486	375	(134)	(1,077)
Attributable to:					
• Equity owners of the parent		358	276	(226)	(1,079)
• Non-controlling interests		128	99	92	2

[1] Translation of amounts from euros into U.S. dollars has been made merely for the convenience of the reader at Noon Buying Rate of € 1 = U.S. dollar 1.2973 on December 30, 2011.

NOTES TO THE CONSOLIDATED FINANCIAL STATEMENTS (in part)

Alcatel-Lucent (formerly called Alcatel) is a French public limited liability company that is subject to the French Commercial Code and to all the legal requirements governing commercial companies in France. On November 30, 2006, Alcatel changed its name to Alcatel-Lucent on completion of the business combination with Lucent Technologies Inc. Alcatel-Lucent was incorporated on June 18, 1898 and will be dissolved on June 30, 2086, unless its existence is extended or shortened by shareholder vote. Alcatel-Lucent's headquarters are located at 3, avenue Octave Gréard, 75007, Paris, France. Alcatel-Lucent is listed principally on the Paris and New York stock exchanges.

The consolidated financial statements reflect the results and financial position of Alcatel-Lucent and its subsidiaries (the "Group") as well as its investments in associates ("equity affiliates") and joint ventures. They are presented in Euros rounded to the nearest million.

The Group develops and integrates technologies, applications and services to offer innovative global communications solutions.

On February 8, 2012, Alcatel-Lucent's Board of Directors authorized for issuance these consolidated financial statements at December 31, 2011. The consolidated financial statements will be final once approved at the Annual Shareholders' Meeting to be held on June 8, 2012.

Note 1 Summary of Accounting Policies

Due to the listing of Alcatel-Lucent's securities on the Euronext Paris and in accordance with the European Union's regulation No. 1606/2002 of July 19, 2002, the consolidated financial statements of the Group are prepared in accordance with IFRSs (International Financial Reporting Standards), as adopted by the European Union ("EU"), as of the date when our Board of Directors authorized these consolidated financial statements for issuance.

IFRSs can be found at: www.ec.europa.eu/internal_market/accounting/ias/index_en.htm.

IFRSs include the standards approved by the International Accounting Standards Board ("IASB"), that is, International Accounting Standards ("IASs") and accounting interpretations issued by the IFRS Interpretations Committee ("IFRIC") or the former Standing Interpretations Committee ("SIC").

As of December 31, 2011, all IFRSs that the IASB had published and that are mandatory are the same as those endorsed by the EU and mandatory in the EU, with the exception of:

- IAS 39, which the EU only partially adopted. The part not adopted by the EU has no impact on Alcatel-Lucent's financial statements.

As a result, the Group's consolidated financial statements comply with International Financial Reporting Standards as published by the IASB.

l/ Deferred Taxation and Penalties on Tax Claims

Deferred taxes are computed in accordance with the liability method for all temporary differences arising between the tax basis of assets and liabilities and their carrying amounts, including the reversal of entries recorded in individual accounts of subsidiaries solely for tax purposes. All amounts resulting from changes in tax rates are recorded in equity or in net income (loss) for the year in which the tax rate change is enacted.

Deferred tax assets are recorded in the consolidated statement of financial position when it is probable that the tax benefit will be realized in the future. Deferred tax assets and liabilities are not discounted.

To assess the ability of the Group to recover deferred tax assets, the following factors are taken into account:

- existence of deferred tax liabilities that are expected to generate taxable income, or limit tax deductions upon reversal;
- forecasts of future tax results;
- the impact of non-recurring costs included in income or loss in recent years that are not expected to be repeated in the future;
- historical data concerning recent years' tax results, and
- if required, tax planning strategy, such as the planned disposal of undervalued assets.

As a result of a business combination, an acquirer may consider it probable that it will recover its own deferred tax assets that were not recognized before the business combination. For example, an acquirer may be able to utilize the benefit of its unused tax losses against the future taxable profit of the acquiree. In such cases, the acquirer recognizes a deferred tax asset, but does not include it as part of the accounting for the business combination, and therefore does not take it into account in determining the goodwill or the amount of any excess of the acquirer's interest in the net fair value of the acquiree's identifiable assets, liabilities and contingent liabilities over the cost of the combination.

If the potential benefit of the acquiree's income tax loss carry-forwards or other deferred tax assets do not satisfy the criteria in IFRS 3 Revised for separate recognition when a business combination is initially accounted for, but are subsequently realized, the acquirer will recognize the resulting deferred tax income in profit or loss. If any deferred tax assets related to the business combination with Lucent are recognized in future financial statements of the combined company, the impact will be accounted for in the income statement (for the tax losses not yet recognized related to both historical Alcatel and Lucent entities).

Amounts of reduction of goodwill already accounted for in the purchase price allocation related to the acquisition of Lucent are disclosed in Note 9.

Penalties recognized on tax claims are accounted for in the "income tax" line item in the income statement.

o/ Finance Costs and Other Financial Income (Loss)

Finance costs include interest charges relating to net consolidated debt, which consists of bonds, the liability component of compound financial instruments such as OCEANE and other convertible bonds, other long-term debt (including finance lease obligations) and interest income on all cash and similar items (cash, cash equivalents and marketable securities) and the changes in fair values of marketable securities accounted for at fair value through profit or loss.

Borrowing costs that are directly attributable to the acquisition, construction or production of an asset are capitalized as part of the cost of that asset.

When tax law requires interest to be paid (received) on an underpayment (overpayment) of income taxes, this interest is accounted for in the "other financial income (loss)" line item in the income statement.

t/ Assets Held for Sale and Discontinued Operations

A non-current asset or disposal group (group of assets or a cash generating unit) to be sold is considered as held for sale if its carrying amount will be recovered through a sale transaction rather than through continuing use. For this to be the case, the asset must be available for sale and its sale must be highly probable. These assets or disposal groups classified as held for sale are measured at the lower of carrying amount and fair value less costs to sell.

A discontinued operation is a separate major line of business or geographical area of operations for the Group that is either being sold or is being held for sale. The net income (loss) and statement of cash flow elements relating to such discontinued operations are presented in specific captions in the consolidated financial statements for all periods presented.

Note 9 Income Tax

a/ Analysis of Income Tax Benefit (Expense)

(In Millions of Euros)	2011	2010	2009
Current income tax (expense) benefit	(42)	(78)	(57)
Deferred taxes related to the purchase price allocation for the Lucent business combination[1]	114	124	115
Deferred tax (charge) related to the post-retirement benefit plan amendments[2]	—	(12)	—
Deferred taxes related to Lucent's post-retirement benefit plans[3] [4]	(87)	(136)	(35)
Deferred taxes related to Lucent's 2.875% Series A convertible debentures[5]	—	(9)	65
Other deferred income tax (expense) benefit, net[6]	559	97	(13)
Deferred income tax benefit (expense), net	586	64	134
Income tax benefit (expense)	544	(14)	77

[1] Related to the reversal of deferred tax liabilities accounted for in the purchase price allocation of Lucent.

[2] Related to the post-retirement plan amendments described in Note 26.

[3] Tax impact of the pension credit and changes in deferred tax assets and liabilities recognized on temporary differences related to pension and other post-employment benefits, other than those recognized directly in equity as prescribed by the option of IAS 19 that the Group applies (see Note 1j and Note 26).

[4] The 2010 impact is mainly due to consequences of the recent Healthcare laws enacted in the U.S. These laws have one significant provision that impacted the Group involving the Medicare Part D tax free subsidy of about US$34 million annually that we receive from Medicare for continuing to provide our prescription drug benefits to Medicare-eligible active represented employees and formerly union-represented retirees. This legislation eliminates the deduction for expense allocable to the subsidy beginning in 2013, resulting in a reduction in our deferred tax asset and a corresponding income statement charge of about US$101 million (€ 76 million) in 2010.

[5] Reversal of deferred tax liabilities related to Lucent's 2.875 % Series A convertible debentures (see Notes 8, 25 & 27).

[6] The 2011 and 2010 impacts are mainly due to the re-assessment of the recoverability of certain deferred tax assets mainly in connection with the 2011 and 2010 impairment tests of goodwill performed in the second and fourth quarters of 2011 and second quarter of 2010, respectively.

    2009 impact is mainly due to the re-assessment of the recoverability of deferred tax assets recognized in connection with the 2009 annual impairment test of goodwill performed in the second quarter.

b/ Disclosure of Tax Effects Relating to Each Component of Other Comprehensive Income

(In Millions of Euros)	2011 Value Before Taxes	2011 Tax (Expense) Benefit	2011 Value Net of Tax	2010 Value Before Taxes	2010 Tax (Expense) Benefit	2010 Value Net of Tax	2009 Value Before Taxes	2009 Tax (Expense) Benefit	2009 Value Net of Tax Amount
Financial assets available for sale	(11)	—	(11)	(22)	5	(17)	13	1	14
Cumulative translation adjustments	283	—	283	262	—	262	39	—	39
Cash flow hedging	(7)	—	(7)	(12)	—	(12)	11	—	11
Actuarial gains (losses)	(1,133)	99	(1,034)	(70)	15	(55)	(582)	(3)	(585)
Other	—	—	—	(20)	—	(20)	(53)	1	(52)
Other comprehensive income	(868)	99	(769)	138	20	158	(572)	(1)	(573)

c/ Effective Income Tax Rate

The effective tax rate can be analyzed as follows:

(In Millions of Euros Except for Percentage)	2011	2010	2009
Income (loss) before income tax and discontinued operations	186	(311)	(743)
Average income tax rate	32.9%	23.9%	32.9%
Expected tax (charge) benefit	(60)	74	244
Impact on tax (charge) benefit of:			
• reduced taxation of certain revenues	12	41	—
• permanent differences and utilization of previously unrecognized tax losses	546	203	49
• adjustment to prior years' current tax charge	(4)	—	9
• recognition of previously unrecognized deferred tax assets	1,052[1]	95	198
• deferred tax assets no longer recognized	(488)[2]	(17)	(127)
• non-recognition of tax losses	(532)[2]	(417)	(332)
• tax credits	20	16	29
• other	(2)	(9)	1
Actual income tax (charge) benefit	544	(14)	77
Effective tax rate	(292.5)%	(4.5)%	10.3%

[1] Mainly related to the United States (see note 2f).
[2] Mainly related to the French tax group.

Average income tax rate is the sum of income (loss) before taxes of each subsidiary, multiplied by the local statutory rate for each subsidiary, divided by consolidated income (loss) before taxes from continuing operations.

Changes in average income tax rate are due to differences in the contribution of each tax entity to income (loss) before tax and to the fact that some entities have a positive contribution and others have a negative one.

d/ Deferred Tax Balances

(In Millions of Euros) Balances	2011	2010	2009
Deferred tax assets:			
• deferred tax assets recognizable	12,973	12,706	11,958
• of which not recognized	(11,019)	(11,758)	(11,122)
Net deferred tax assets recognized	1,954	948	836
Deferred tax liabilities	(1,017)	(1,126)	(1,058)
Net deferred tax assets (liabilities)	937	(178)	(222)

Analysis of Deferred Tax Assets and Liabilities by Temporary Differences

(In Millions of Euros)	December 31, 2010	Impact on Net Income (Loss)	Translation Adjustments	Reclassification and Other	December 31, 2011
Fair value adjustments of tax assets and liabilities resulting from business combinations	(677)	124	(13)	(1)	(567)
Provisions	338	(72)	—	4	270
Pension reserves	1,555	77	53	6	1,691
Prepaid pensions	(954)	(302)	(21)	318	(959)
Property, plant and equipment and intangible assets	1,144	(107)	26	8	1,071
Temporary differences arising from other statement of financial position captions	257	5	5	106	379
Tax loss carry-forwards and tax credits	9,917	315	151	(307)	10,077
Deferred tax assets (liabilities), gross	11,580	40	201	135	11,956
Deferred tax assets not recognized	(11,758)	884	(107)	(38)	(11,019)
Net deferred tax assets (liabilities)	(178)	924	94	97	937

Change During the Period

		Impact on Net Income (Loss)				
(In Millions of Euros)	December 31, 2010	Income Tax Benefit (Expense)	Income Loss From Discontinued Operations	Translation Adjustments	Other	December 31, 2011
Deferred tax assets recognized	948	570	338	111	(13)	1,954
Deferred tax liabilities	(1,126)	16	—	(17)	110	(1,017)
Net deferred tax assets (liabilities)	(178)	586	338	94	97	937

Deferred taxes not recognized relating to temporary differences on investments in subsidiaries, equity affiliates and joint ventures were zero at December 31, 2011, December 31, 2010 and December 31, 2009.

As the Board of Directors does not intend to propose a dividend for 2011 at the Annual Shareholders' Meeting (see Note 23), there will be no tax consequences.

e/ Tax Losses Carried Forward and Temporary Differences

Total tax losses carried forward represent a potential tax saving of €10,056 million at December 31, 2011 (€9,917 million at December 31, 2010 and €9,274 million at December 31, 2009). The increase in tax losses carried forward between 2010 and 2011 includes a foreign exchange impact of € 349 million related to the United States. The potential tax savings relate to tax losses carried forward that expire as follows:

(In Millions of Euros)

Years	Recognized	Unrecognized	Total
2012	60	1	61
2013	41	1	42
2014	45	6	51
2015	59	3	62
2016	36	13	49
2017 and thereafter	147	4,701	4,848
Indefinite	73	4,891	4,964
Total	461	9,616	10,077

In addition, temporary differences were € 1,879 million at December 31, 2011 (€ 1,663 million at December 31, 2010 and € 1,626 million at December 31, 2009), of which € 476 million have been recognized and € 1,403 million have not been recognized (€ (398) million and € 2,061 million, respectively, at December 31, 2010 and € (687) million and € 2,313 million, respectively, at December 31, 2009).

Recognized negative temporary differences mainly correspond to deferred tax liabilities that have been recorded resulting from the Lucent purchase accounting entries (in particular intangible assets).

Note 10 Discontinued Operations, Assets Held for Sale and Liabilities Related to Disposal Groups Held for Sale (in part)

Discontinued operations for 2011, 2010 and 2009 were as follows:

- in 2011: On October 19, 2011, Alcatel-Lucent announced that it had received a binding offer of U.S. $1.5 billion from a company owned by the Permira funds for the acquisition of its Genesys business. The closing of the deal was completed on February 1, 2012. The Genesys business is presented in discontinued operations in the consolidated income statements and statements of cash flows for all periods presented. Assets and liabilities related to this business as of December 31, 2011 are classified in "assets held for sale and assets included in disposal groups held for sale" and "liabilities related to disposal groups held for sale" in the statement of financial position;
- in 2010: settlements of litigations related to businesses disposed of in prior periods; and
- in 2009: adjustment of the selling price related to the disposal of the space business to Thales that was sold in 2007.

Other assets held for sale concern real estate property sales in progress at December 31, 2011, December 31, 2010 and December 31, 2009.

(In Millions of Euros) Income Statement of Discontinued Operations	2011	2010	2009
Revenues	369	338	316
Cost of sales	(83)	(69)	(60)
Gross profit	286	(269)	256
Administrative and selling expenses	(142)	(138)	(137)
Research and development costs	(53)	(59)	(59)
Restructuring costs	—	(4)	(7)
Net capital gain (loss) on disposal of discontinued operations[1]	(4)	(12)	132
Income (loss) from operations	87	56	184
Financial income (loss)	2	—	(5)
Income tax (expense) benefit	325[2]	(23)	(17)
Income (loss) from discontinued operations	414	33	162

[1] The 2009 impact includes € 132 million from an adjustment of the purchase price related to the contribution of our interests in two joint ventures in the space sector to Thales in 2007.

[2] Including € 338 million of deferred tax assets recognized in relation with the coming disposal of Genesys in 2012 (see Notes 2f and 9d).

Offsetting of Assets and Liabilities From the Same Tax Authority, Income Tax on Items Recognized in Other Comprehensive Income Shown Separately for Items That Will or Will Not Be Reclassified to Profit or Loss

3.340

Syngenta AG (Dec 2011)

CONSOLIDATED INCOME STATEMENTS (in part)

(US$ Million, Except Share and per Share Amounts)	Notes	2011	2010	2009
Operating income		2,051	1,793	1,819
Income/(loss) from associates and joint ventures		15	25	(3)
Interest income	28	93	90	88
Interest expense	28	(152)	(172)	(163)
Other financial expense		(20)	(22)	(17)
Currency gains/(losses), net	28	(86)	(37)	(30)
Financial expense, net		(165)	(141)	(122)
Income before taxes		1,901	1,677	1,694
Income tax expense	7	(301)	(275)	(283)
Net income		1,600	1,402	1,411

CONSOLIDATED STATEMENT OF COMPREHENSIVE INCOME (in part)

(US$ Million)	Notes	2011	2010	2009
Net income		1,600	1,402	1,411
Components of other comprehensive income (OCI) items that will not be reclassified to profit or loss:				
Actuarial gains/(losses) of defined benefit post-employment plans	22	(252)	50	(98)
Income tax relating to items that will not be reclassified to profit or loss	7	71	(17)	32
		(181)	33	(66)
Items that may be reclassified subsequently to profit or loss: Unrealized gains/(losses) on available-for-sale financial assets	28	3	4	(18)
Gains/(losses) on derivatives designated as cash flow and net investment hedges	29	(150)	120	72
Currency translation effects		(186)	146	260
Income tax relating to items that may be reclassified subsequently to profit or loss	7	(14)	(20)	34
		(347)	250	348
Total comprehensive income		1,072	1,685	1,693

NOTES TO THE CONSOLIDATED FINANCIAL STATEMENTS (in part)

1. Basis of Preparation of the Consolidated Financial Statements

These consolidated financial statements have been prepared in accordance with International Financial Reporting Standards (IFRSs) as issued by the International Accounting Standards Board (IASB). The consolidated financial statements have been prepared on an historical cost basis, except for items that are required by IFRSs to be measured at fair value, principally derivative financial instruments, available-for-sale financial assets and biological assets, which are valued at fair value less costs to sell.

The consolidated financial statements incorporate the financial statements of Syngenta AG, a company domiciled and incorporated in Switzerland, and all of its subsidiaries (together referred to as "Syngenta") and Syngenta's interests in associates and joint ventures. Syngenta AG's principal executive offices are at Schwarzwaldallee 215, 4058 Basel, Switzerland.

The consolidated financial statements are presented in United States dollars ("US$") as this is the major currency in which revenues are denominated. The functional currency of Syngenta AG is the Swiss franc ("CHF").

Syngenta has global, integrated risk management processes. Within the scope of these processes, the Board of Directors of Syngenta AG evaluates the risks once a year in accordance with article 663b paragraph 12 of the Swiss Code of Obligations and discusses if any corresponding actions are necessary.

The preparation of financial statements requires management to exercise judgment when applying accounting policies and to make estimates and assumptions that affect the reported amounts of assets and liabilities, the disclosure of contingent assets and liabilities at the date of the financial statements and the reported amounts of revenues and expenses during the reporting period. Actual results could differ from those estimated. Note 2 below includes further discussion of certain critical accounting estimates.

2. Accounting Policies (in part)

Income Taxes

Income taxes for the year comprise current and deferred taxes, calculated using rates enacted or substantively enacted at the balance sheet date.

Current tax is the expected tax payable on taxable income for the year and any adjustments to tax payable in respect of previous years. Deferred tax is recognized using the liability method and thus is calculated on temporary differences between the tax bases of assets and liabilities and their respective carrying amounts in the consolidated balance sheet.

Deferred tax is provided on temporary differences arising on investments in subsidiaries, associates and joint ventures, except where the timing of the reversal of the temporary difference can be controlled and it is probable that the difference will not reverse in the foreseeable future. Deferred tax liabilities are not recognized on the initial recognition of goodwill if the carrying amount of goodwill exceeds its tax base. Deferred tax assets, including those related to unused tax losses, are recognized to the extent that it is probable that future taxable profit will be available against which the assets can be utilized.

Income tax expense, current and deferred, is recognized in profit or loss unless it relates to items recognized in OCI or in equity in which case the tax expense is also recognized in OCI or equity respectively.

Syngenta's policy is to comply fully with applicable tax regulations in all jurisdictions in which Syngenta's operations are subject to income taxes. Syngenta's estimates of current income tax expense and liabilities are calculated assuming that all tax computations filed by Syngenta's subsidiaries will be subject to review or audit by the relevant tax authorities. Syngenta and the relevant tax authorities may have different interpretations of how regulations should be applied to actual transactions. Syngenta records provisions for taxes it estimates will ultimately be payable when the reviews or audits have been completed, including allowances for any interest and penalties which may become payable. Syngenta releases these provisions when the tax audit of the applicable year is completed or an Advance Pricing Agreement (APA) settlement is reached that impacts previous years' tax payments, or otherwise when the statute of limitations for the applicable year expires, unless there is evident reason for earlier release.

Deferred tax on share based compensation awards is based on the tax deduction, if any, that would be obtained if the Syngenta AG share price at the period end was the tax base for the award. Deferred tax on unvested awards is recognized ratably over the vesting period. Deferred tax on awards already vested is recognized immediately. Any income tax benefits recorded in the income statement are limited to the tax effect of the related cumulative pre-tax compensation expense recorded. The total tax benefit on an award may exceed this amount in some circumstances. The excess tax benefit is considered by IFRS to be the result of a transaction with shareholders rather than with employees, and is recorded within shareholders' equity.

Deferred Tax Assets

At December 31, 2011, Syngenta's deferred tax assets are US$930 million (2010: US$824 million). Included in this balance are deferred tax assets for unused tax losses of US$34 million (2010: US$46 million). The ultimate realization of deferred tax assets is dependent upon the generation of future taxable income during the periods in which those temporary differences become deductible or in which tax losses can be utilized. The tax effect of unused tax losses is recognized as a deferred tax asset when it becomes probable that the tax losses will be utilized. In making assessments regarding deferred tax assets, management considers the scheduled reversal of deferred tax liabilities, projected future taxable income and tax planning strategies. At December 31, 2011, based upon the level of historical taxable income and projections for future taxable income over the periods in which deferred tax assets are deductible, management believes that it is more likely than not that Syngenta will realize the benefits of these deductible differences. The amount of deferred tax assets considered realizable could however be reduced in subsequent years if estimates of future taxable income during their carry forward periods are reduced, or rulings by the tax authorities are unfavorable. Estimates are therefore subject to change due to both market related and government related uncertainties, as well as Syngenta's own future decisions on restructuring and other matters. Syngenta is unable to accurately quantify the future adjustments to deferred income tax expense that may occur as a result of these uncertainties.

The principal jurisdictions where deferred tax assets have not been recognized are Brazil, Argentina, Colombia and Russia. For Argentina, Colombia and Russia, no net deferred tax assets have been recognized at December 31, 2011 or 2010. At December 31, 2011, the carrying amount of deferred tax assets recognized in the consolidated balance sheet of one major Syngenta subsidiary in Brazil is US$152 million (2010: US$84 million) and the amount not recognized is US$10 million (US$38 million). Syngenta has restricted the amount of deferred tax asset recognized for this subsidiary to the amount recoverable from the forecast taxable profits in the five years (2010: three years) following the balance sheet date. Deferred income tax expense for 2011 was reduced by US$40 million (2010: US$77 million) because the continued generation of actual taxable profits by this subsidiary in recent years indicates that an increased proportion of its deferred tax asset is more likely than not to be utilized against its estimated future taxable profits.

Uncertain Tax Positions

Syngenta's Crop Protection supply chain, and to a lesser extent its Seeds supply chain, are international, and intellectual property rights owned by Syngenta are used internationally within the Group. Transfer prices for the delivery of goods and charges for the provision of products and services by one Syngenta subsidiary to another, and arrangements to share research and development costs, may be subject to challenge by the national tax authorities in any of the countries in which Syngenta operates. Interpretation of taxation rules relating to financing arrangements between Syngenta entities and to foreign currency translation differences may also give rise to uncertain tax positions.

Several prior years' tax computations are generally still open for review or audit for most Syngenta subsidiaries at the balance sheet date. Syngenta estimates and accrues taxes that will ultimately be payable when reviews or audits by tax authorities of tax returns are completed.

These estimates include significant management judgments about the eventual outcome of the reviews and audits of all open years based on the latest information available about the positions expected to be taken by each tax authority. Actual outcomes and settlements may differ significantly from the estimates recorded in these consolidated financial statements. This may affect income tax expense reported in future years' consolidated income statements. At December 31, 2011, Syngenta's balance sheet includes assets of US$79 million (2010: US$70 million) included within Other accounts receivable, and liabilities of US$547 million (2010: US$406 million) shown separately on the face of the balance sheet, for current income taxes. These liabilities include US$274 million in respect of the uncertain tax positions described above (2010: US$225 million), which reflects increased exposures at December 31, 2011 due to underlying business growth and the integration of Syngenta's Crop Protection and Seeds commercial organisations. The liability for uncertain income tax positions which Syngenta expects to be resolved in 2012 is less than 10 percent of total recognized current income tax liabilities.

7. Income Taxes

Income before taxes from continuing operations for the years ended December 31, 2011, 2010 and 2009 consists of the following:

(US$ Million)	2011	2010	2009
Switzerland	779	587	1,113
Foreign	1,122	1,090	581
Total income before taxes	1,901	1,677	1,694

Income tax (expense)/benefit on income from continuing operations for the years ended December 31, 2011, 2010 and 2009 consists of the following:

(US$ Million)	2011	2010	2009
Current income tax (expense):			
Switzerland	(138)	(87)	(32)
Foreign	(347)	(200)	(160)
Total current income tax (expense)	(485)	(287)	(192)
Deferred income tax (expense)/benefit:			
Switzerland	1	(38)	(173)
Foreign	183	50	82
Total deferred income tax (expense)/benefit	184	12	(91)
Total income tax (expense):			
Switzerland	(137)	(125)	(205)
Foreign	(164)	(150)	(78)
Total income tax (expense)	(301)	(275)	(283)

The components of current income tax (expense) on income from continuing operations for the years ended December 31, 2011, 2010 and 2009 are:

(US$ Million)	2011	2010	2009
Current tax (expense) relating to current years	(491)	(275)	(209)
Adjustments to current tax for prior periods	2	(19)	3
Benefit of previously unrecognized tax losses	4	7	14
Total current income tax (expense)	(485)	(287)	(192)

The components of deferred income tax (expense)/benefit on income from continuing operations for the years ended December 31, 2011, 2010 and 2009 are:

(US$ Million)	2011	2010	2009
Origination and reversal of temporary differences	130	(67)	(137)
Changes in tax rates or legislation	21	20	2
Benefit of previously unrecognized deferred tax assets	43	88	44
Non recognition of deferred tax assets	(10)	(29)	—
Total deferred income tax (expense)/benefit	184	12	(91)

Income tax expense for 2011 includes US$61 million resulting from a change in prior year estimates related to the taxation of certain licensing transactions.

Income tax relating to OCI for the years ended December 31, 2011, 2010 and 2009 is as follows:

(US$ Million)	2011			2010			2009		
	Pre-Tax	Tax	Post-Tax	Pre-Tax	Tax	Post-Tax	Pre-Tax	Tax	Post-Tax
Items that will not be reclassified to profit or loss:									
Actuarial gains/(losses)	(252)	71	(181)	50	(17)	33	(98)	32	(66)
Items that may be reclassified to profit or loss:									
Available-for-sale financial assets	3	—	3	4	(1)	3	(18)	1	(17)
Cash flow and net investment hedges	(150)	34	(116)	120	(46)	74	72	(16)	56
Foreign currency translation effects	(186)	(48)	(234)	146	27	173	260	49	309
Total	(585)	57	(528)	320	(37)	283	216	66	282

The following tax was (charged)/credited to shareholders' equity for the years ended December 31, 2011, 2010 and 2009:

(US$ Million)	2011	2010	2009
Current tax[1]	7	—	6
Deferred tax[1]	3	(1)	10
Total income tax (charged)/credited to equity	10	(1)	16

[1] Current and deferred tax related to share based payments.

Analysis of Tax Rate

The table below represents the main elements causing Syngenta's effective tax rate to differ from the statutory tax rate for the years ended December 31, 2011, 2010 and 2009. Syngenta's statutory rate consists of the domestic Swiss tax rate. Syngenta applies the domestic Swiss tax rate as it is more meaningful than using the weighted average tax rate. The domestic Swiss tax rate consists of the Swiss federal income tax rate (8.50 percent) and the income tax rate of the canton Basel (21.00 percent). Federal and canton tax rates are deductible from the tax basis, therefore the Swiss domestic tax rate is 22.78 percent.

	2011 %	2010 %	2009 %
Statutory tax rate	23	23	23
Effect of income taxed at different rates	(5)	(3)	(4)
Tax on share based payments	—	1	1
Effect of other disallowed expenditures and income not subject to tax	(2)	(1)	(3)
Effect of changes in tax rates and laws on previously recognized deferred tax assets	(1)	(1)	—
Effect of recognition of previously unrecognized tax losses	—	(1)	(3)
Effect of recognition of other previously unrecognized deferred tax assets	(2)	(5)	—
Effect of non-recognition of deferred tax assets on tax losses in current year	1	—	—
Changes in prior year estimates and other items	2	2	2
Effect of non-recognition of deferred tax assets	—	1	1
Effective tax rate	16	16	17

IFRS-BPPD 3.340

The movements in deferred tax assets and liabilities during
the year ended December 31, 2011 are as follows:

2011 (US$ Million)	January 1	Recognized in Net Income	Recognized in Equity & OCI	Currency Translation Effects	Other Movements & Acquisitions	December 31
Assets associated with:						
Inventories	449	22	(31)	(3)	(3)	434
Accounts receivable	146	58	—	(20)	—	184
Pensions and employee costs	127	(22)	73	(2)	(1)	175
Provisions	234	85	—	(10)	—	309
Unused tax losses	46	(8)	—	(1)	(4)	33
Financial instruments, including derivatives	19	1	4	(1)	(3)	20
Other	74	16	(19)	3	4	78
Deferred tax assets	1,095	152	27	(34)	(7)	1,233
Liabilities associated with:						
Property, plant and equipment	(302)	(9)	—	3	1	(307)
Intangible assets	(266)	(23)	—	1	(17)	(305)
Inventories	(133)	34	—	11	—	(88)
Financial instruments, including derivatives	(56)	(2)	(5)	—	3	(60)
Other provisions and accruals	(255)	31	—	1	—	(223)
Other	(72)	1	—	(2)	—	(73)
Deferred tax liabilities	(1,084)	32	(5)	14	(13)	(1,056)
Net deferred tax asset/(liability)	11	184	22	(20)	(20)	177

The movements in deferred tax assets and liabilities during
the year ended December 31, 2010 were as follows:

2010 (US$ Million)	January 1	Recognized in Net Income	Recognized in Equity & OCI	Currency Translation Effects	Other Movements & Acquisitions	December 31
Assets associated with:						
Inventories	375	45	2	—	27	449
Accounts receivable	107	(10)	—	5	44	146
Pensions and employee costs	202	(55)	(15)	(5)	—	127
Provisions	221	(13)	—	2	24	234
Unused tax losses	42	(7)	—	3	8	46
Financial instruments, including derivatives	33	(7)	(12)	—	5	19
Other	59	7	—	3	5	74
Deferred tax assets	1,039	(40)	(25)	8	113	1,095
Liabilities associated with:						
Property, plant and equipment	(284)	(13)	—	(4)	(1)	(302)
Intangible assets	(262)	(8)	—	(11)	15	(266)
Inventories	(141)	18	—	(9)	(1)	(133)
Financial instruments, including derivatives	(64)	17	(3)	(2)	(4)	(56)
Other provisions and accruals	(188)	(13)	—	(16)	(38)	(255)
Other	(41)	51	13	—	(95)	(72)
Deferred tax liabilities	(980)	52	10	(42)	(124)	(1,084)
Net deferred tax asset/(liability)	59	12	(15)	(34)	(11)	11

The deferred tax assets and liabilities at December 31, 2011
and 2010 reconcile to the amounts presented in the consolidated balance sheet as follows:

(US$ Million)	2011	2010
Deferred tax assets	1,233	1,095
Adjustment to offset deferred tax assets and liabilities[1]	(303)	(271)
Adjusted deferred tax assets	930	824
Deferred tax liabilities	(1,056)	(1,084)
Adjustment to offset deferred tax assets and liabilities[1]	303	271
Adjusted deferred tax liabilities	(753)	(813)

[1] Deferred tax assets and liabilities relating to income taxes levied by the same taxation authority on the same taxable entity or on entities which intend to settle current tax assets and liabilities on a net basis or to realize the assets and settle the liabilities simultaneously are offset for presentation on the face of the consolidated balance sheet where a legal right of set-off exists.

The gross value at December 31, 2011 and 2010 of unused tax loss carry forwards for which no deferred tax asset has been recognized, by expiration date, is as follows:

(US$ Million)	2011	2010
One year	6	7
Two years	—	—
Three years	7	2
Four years	2	14
Five years	11	23
More than five years	481	407
No expiry	3	8
Total	510	461

The above losses consist mainly of US state tax loss carry forwards. The applicable tax rate for these US state tax carry forwards is 5.00 percent of the gross amounts.

Deferred tax assets, other than those related to unused tax losses, are not subject to expiry.

A deferred tax asset or liability has not been recognized at December 31, 2011 and 2010 on the following items:

(US$ Million)	2011	2010
Temporary differences for which no deferred tax assets have been recognized	259	238
Temporary differences associated with investments in subsidiaries for which deferred tax liabilities have not been recognized	612	620

There are no income tax consequences for Syngenta of paying a dividend to its shareholders.

Tax Expense Reconciliation Disclosure—Use of Single Domestic Statutory Tax Rate, Disclosure of Tax Effects of Items Recognized in Other Comprehensive Income

3.341

Sinopec Shanghai Petrochemical Company Limited (Dec 2011)

CONSOLIDATED STATEMENTS OF INCOME
(in part)

(Amounts in thousands, except per share data)

| | Note | Years Ended December 31 | | |
		2009 Renminbi (Restated)*	2010 Renminbi (Restated)*	2011 Renminbi
Earnings before income tax		2,163,011	3,529,878	1,296,706
Income tax	9 (a)	(510,175)	(735,497)	(310,184)
Net income		1,652,836	2,794,381	986,522

NOTES TO THE CONSOLIDATED INCOME STATEMENTS (in part)

(All Renminbi amounts in thousands, except per share data and except otherwise stated)

1. Organization, Principal Activities and Basis of Preparation (in part)

Sinopec Shanghai Petrochemical Company Limited ("the Company"), formerly Shanghai Petrochemical Company Limited, was established in the People's Republic of China ("the PRC" or "the State") on June 29, 1993 as a joint stock limited company to hold the assets and liabilities of the production divisions and certain other units of the Shanghai Petrochemical Complex ("SPC"). SPC was established in 1972 and owned and managed the production divisions as well as the related housing, stores, schools, hotels, transportation, hospitals and other municipal services in the community of Jinshanwei.

The Company's former controlling shareholder, China Petrochemical Corporation ("CPC") completed its reorgani-

zation on February 25, 2000 in which its interests in the Company were transferred to its subsidiary, China Petroleum & Chemical Corporation ("Sinopec Corp"). In connection with the reorganization, CPC transferred the ownership of its 4,000,000,000 of the Company's state owned legal shares, which represented 55.56 percent of the issued share capital of the Company, to Sinopec Corp. On October 12, 2000, the Company changed its name to Sinopec Shanghai Petrochemical Company Limited.

The principal activity of the Company and its subsidiaries (the "Group") is the processing of crude oil into petrochemical products for sale. The Group is one of the largest petrochemical enterprises in the PRC, with a highly integrated petrochemical complex which processes crude oil into a broad range of synthetic fibres, resins and plastics, intermediate petrochemicals and petroleum products. Substantially all of its products are sold in the PRC domestic market.

These financial statements have been approved by the Board of Directors on March 29, 2012.

2. Principal Accounting Policies (in part)

(v) Income Tax

Income tax expense comprises current and deferred tax. Income tax expense is recognized in profit or loss except to the extent that it relates to items recognized in other comprehensive income or directly in equity, in which case the relevant amounts of tax are recognized in other comprehensive income or directly in equity, respectively.

Current tax is the expected tax payable on the taxable income for the year, using tax rates enacted or substantially enacted at the balance sheet date, and any adjustment to tax payable in respect of previous years.

Deferred tax is provided using the balance sheet liability method, providing for temporary differences between the carrying amounts of assets and liabilities for financial reporting purposes and the amounts used for taxation purposes, except differences relating to goodwill not deductible for tax purposes and the initial recognition of assets or liabilities which affect neither accounting nor taxable income. The amount of deferred tax provided is based on the expected manner of realization or settlement of the carrying amount of assets and liabilities, using tax rates enacted or substantially enacted at the balance sheet date. The effect on deferred tax of any changes in tax rates is charged or credited to the profit or loss, except for the effect of a change in tax rate on the carrying amount of deferred tax assets and liabilities which were previously charged or credited directly to equity upon initial recognition, in such case the effect of a change in tax rate is also charged or credited to equity.

A deferred tax asset is recognized only to the extent that it is probable that future taxable income will be available against the assets which can be realized or utilized. Deferred tax assets are reduced to the extent that it is no longer probable that the related tax benefit will be realized.

9. Income Tax

(a) Taxation in the Consolidated Statements of Income Represents:

	Years Ended December 31		
	2009	2010	2011
	(Restated)*	(Restated)*	
Current tax			
—Provision for PRC income tax for the year	58,410	22,523	30,280
—Under/(over)-provision in respect of prior years	843	3,453	(436)
Deferred taxation	450,922	709,521	280,340
Total income tax expense	510,175	735,497	310,184

A reconciliation of the expected income tax expense calculated at the applicable tax rate with the actual income tax expense is as follows:

	Years Ended December 31		
	2009	2010	2011
	(Restated)*	(Restated)*	
Earnings before income tax	2,163,011	3,529,878	1,296,706
Expected PRC income tax expense at the statutory tax rate of 25% (2010: 25%; 2009: 25%)	540,752	882,469	324,177
Tax effect of non-deductible expenses	5,932	6,240	22,604
Tax effect of non-taxable income	(472)	(225)	(3,957)
Under/(over)-provision in prior years	843	3,453	(436)
Tax effect of share of profit recognized under the equity method	(60,343)	(165,322)	(38,164)
Tax effect of unused tax losses not recognized	26,823	12,324	10,582
Tax effect of unrecognized deferred tax assets	18,755	—	—
Utilization of unrecognized deferred tax assets	(17,176)	—	—
Others	(4,939)	(3,442)	(4,622)
Actual income tax expense	510,175	735,497	310,184

* See note 3.

The Group did not carry out business overseas and therefore does not incur overseas income taxes.

(b) Deferred Taxation:

(i) Deferred tax assets and deferred tax liabilities are attributable to items detailed in the tables below:

	Assets		Liabilities		Net balance	
	December 31		December 31		December 31	
	2010	2011	2010	2011	2010	2011
	(Restated)*				(Restated)*	
Current						
Provisions	21,539	42,123	—	—	21,539	42,123
Non-current						
Provisions for impairment losses	139,379	112,297	—	—	139,379	112,297
Capitalization of borrowing costs	—	—	(23,448)	(20,395)	(23,448)	(20,395)
Tax losses carry forward	651,529	374,186	—	—	651,529	374,186
Others	10,610	11,058	—	—	10,610	11,058
Deferred tax assets/(liabilities)	823,057	539,664	(23,448)	(20,395)	799,609	519,269

(ii) Movements in deferred tax assets and liabilities are as follows:

	The Group			
	Restated Balance at January 1, 2009	Recognized in Consolidated Statements of Income	Recognized in Reserve	Restated Balance at December 31, 2009
Current				
Provisions	203,974	(167,196)	—	36,778
Forward exchange contracts	(24,411)	24,411	—	—
Non-current				
Provision for impairment losses	98,156	(13,044)	—	85,112
Capitalization of borrowing costs	(29,196)	2,874	—	(26,322)
Available-for-sale financial assets	(27,634)	—	27,634	—
Tax losses carry forward	1,701,453	(299,475)	—	1,401,978
Others	10,076	1,508	—	11,584
Net deferred tax assets	1,932,418	(450,922)	27,634	1,509,130

* See note 3.

	The Group		
	Restated Balance at January 1, 2010	Recognized in Consolidated Statements of Income	Restated Balance at December 31, 2010
Current			
Provisions	36,778	(15,239)	21,539
Non-current			
Provision for impairment losses	85,112	54,267	139,379
Capitalization of borrowing costs	(26,322)	2,874	(23,448)
Tax losses carry forward	1,401,978	(750,449)	651,529
Others	11,584	(974)	10,610
Net deferred tax assets	1,509,130	(709,521)	799,609

	The Group		
	Balance at January 1, 2011	Recognized in Consolidated Statements of Income	Balance at December 31, 2011
Current			
Provisions	21,539	20,584	42,123
Non-current			
Provision for impairment losses	139,379	(27,082)	112,297
Capitalization of borrowing costs	(23,448)	3,053	(20,395)
Tax losses carry forward	651,529	(277,343)	374,186
Others	10,610	448	11,058
Net deferred tax assets	799,609	(280,340)	519,269

The Group recognizes deferred tax assets only to the extent that it is probable that future taxable income will be available against which the assets can be utilized. Based on the level of historical taxable income and projections for future taxable income over the periods which the deferred tax assets will be utilized, management believes that it is probable the Group will realize the benefits of these temporary differences.

(iii) Deferred Tax Assets Not Recognized:

As at December 31, 2011, a subsidiary of the Company did not recognize the deferred tax assets in respect of the impairment losses on property, plant and equipment amounting to RMB 432,579 (2010: RMB 432,579; 2009: RMB 432,579) and the unused tax losses carried forward for PRC income tax purposes amounting to RMB 465,414 (2010: RMB 452,443; 2009: RMB 417,688), because it was not probable that the related tax benefit will be realized. The unused tax losses carried forward of RMB 68,548, RMB 197,952, RMB 107,292, RMB 49,294 and RMB 42,328 will expire in 2012, 2013, 2014, 2015 and 2016, respectively.

12. Other Comprehensive Income

(a) Tax Effects Relating to Each Component of Other Comprehensive Income

	2009		
	Before-Tax Amount	Tax Expense	Net-of Tax Amount
Available-for-sale financial assets:			
Net movement in fair value reserve	(110,537)	27,634	(82,903)

	2010		
	Before-Tax Amount	Tax Benefit	Net-of Tax Amount
Available-for-sale financial assets:			
Net movement in fair value reserve	—	—	—

	2011		
	Before-Tax Amount	Tax Benefit	Net-of Tax Amount
Available-for-sale financial assets:			
Net movement in fair value reserve	—	—	—

(b) Reclassification Adjustments Relating to Components of Other Comprehensive Income

	Years Ended December 31		
	2009	2010	2011
Available-for-sale financial assets:			
Changes in fair value recognized during the year	112,273	215	685
Reclassification adjustments for amounts transferred to profit or loss—gain on disposal	(222,810)	(215)	(685)
Income tax on other comprehensive income	27,634	—	—
Net movement in fair value reserve during the year recognized in other comprehensive income	(82,903)	—	—

Effective Tax Rate Reconciliation Disclosure—Use of Weighted Average Statutory Tax Rate

3.342

Millicom International Cellular S.A. (Dec 2011)

CONSOLIDATED INCOME STATEMENTS (in part)

	Notes	2011 US$ '000	2010 (As Restated)[i] US$ '000	2009 US$ '000
Profit before tax from continuing operations		1,071,193	1,838,207	691,588
Credit (charge) for taxes	14	18,347	(227,096)	(187,998)
Profit for the year from continuing operations		1,089,540	1,611,111	503,590
Profit for the year from discontinued operations, net of tax	7	39,465	11,857	300,342
Net profit for the year		1,129,005	1,622,968	803,932

[i] Restatement—see note 4.

NOTES TO THE CONSOLIDATED FINANCIAL STATEMENTS (in part)

1. Corporate Information

Millicom International Cellular S.A. (the "Company"), a Luxembourg Société Anonyme, and its subsidiaries, joint ventures and associates (the "Group" or "Millicom") is a global group providing communications, information, entertainment, solutions and financial services in emerging markets. We operate various combinations of mobile and fixed telephony, cable and broadband businesses in 15 countries in Central America, South America and Africa. The Group was formed in December 1990 when Investment AB Kinnevik ("Kinnevik"), formerly named Industriförvaltnings AB Kinnevik, a company established in Sweden, and Millicom Incorporated ("Millicom Inc."), a corporation established in the United States of America, contributed their respective interests in international mobile telephony joint ventures to form the Group.

Millicom operates its mobile businesses in El Salvador, Guatemala and Honduras in Central America; in Bolivia, Colombia and Paraguay in South America; in Chad, the Democratic Republic of Congo, Ghana, Mauritius, Rwanda, Senegal and Tanzania in Africa. Millicom's operations in Laos were sold in March 2011, in Sierra Leone and Cambodia in November 2009; and in Sri Lanka in October 2009 (see notes 6, 7).

In 2008, Millicom acquired 100% of Amnet Telecommunications Holding Limited, a provider of broadband and cable television services in Costa Rica, Honduras and El Salvador, of fixed telephony in El Salvador and Honduras, and of corporate data services in the above countries as well as Guatemala and Nicaragua. In addition, in December 2008, Millicom was successful in the tender for the third national mobile license in Rwanda. Services in Rwanda were launched in early December 2009.

The Company's shares are traded on the Stockholm stock exchange under the symbol MIC and over the counter in the US under the symbol MICC. The Company has its registered office at 15, Rue Léon Laval, L-3372, Leudelange, Grand Duchy of Luxembourg and is registered with the Luxembourg Register of Commerce under the number RCS B 40 630.

The Board of Directors ("Board") approved these consolidated financial statements on March 1, 2012. The approval of the consolidated financial statements will be submitted for ratification by the shareholders at the Annual General Meeting on May 29, 2012.

2. Summary of Consolidation and Accounting Policies (in part)

2.1 Basis of Preparation

The consolidated financial statements of the Group are presented in US dollars and all values are rounded to the nearest thousand (US$ '000) except when otherwise indicated. The consolidated financial statements have been prepared on a historical cost basis except for certain financial assets and liabilities that have been measured at fair value.

In accordance with Regulation (EC) No 1606/2002 of the European Parliament and of the Council of 19 July 2002 on the application of international accounting standards, the consolidated financial statements for the year ended December 31, 2011 have been prepared in accordance with International Financial Reporting Standards as adopted by the European Union ("IFRS").

As of December 31, 2011, International Financial Reporting Standards as adopted by the European Union are similar to those published by the International Accounting Standards Board ("IASB"), except for IAS 39—Financial Instruments that has been partially adopted by the European Union and for new standards and interpretations not yet endorsed but effective in future periods. Since the provisions that have not been adopted by the European Union are not applicable to the Group, the consolidated financial statements comply with both International Financial Reporting Standards as issued by the IASB and as adopted by the European Union.

The preparation of financial statements in conformity with IFRS requires management to exercise its judgment in the process of applying the Group's accounting policies. It also requires the use of certain critical accounting estimates and assumptions that affect the reported amounts of assets and liabilities and disclosure of contingent assets and liabilities at the date of the financial statements and the reported amounts of revenues and expenses during the reporting period. Although these estimates are based on management's best knowledge of current events and actions, actual results may ultimately differ from these estimates. Areas involving a higher degree of judgment or complexity, or areas where assumptions and estimates are significant to the consolidated financial statements are disclosed in note 3.

2.26 Taxation

Current Tax

Current tax assets and liabilities for current and prior periods are measured at the amount expected to be recovered from or paid to the taxation authorities. The tax rate and tax laws used to compute the amount are those enacted or substantively enacted by the statement of financial position date.

Deferred Tax

Deferred income tax is provided using the liability method and calculated from temporary differences at the statement of financial position date between the tax base of assets and liabilities and their carrying amount for financial reporting purposes. Deferred tax liabilities are recognized for all taxable temporary differences, except where the deferred tax liability arises from the initial recognition of goodwill or of an asset or liability in a transaction that is not a business combination and, at the time of the transaction, affects neither accounting, nor taxable, profit or loss.

Deferred income tax assets are recognized for all deductible temporary differences and carry-forward of unused tax credits and unused tax losses, to the extent that it is probable that taxable profit will be available against which the deductible temporary difference and the carry-forward of unused tax credits and unused tax losses can be utilized, except where the deferred tax assets relate to deductible temporary differences from initial recognition of an asset or liability in a transaction that is not a business combination, and, at the time of the transaction, affects neither accounting, nor taxable, profit or loss.

The carrying amount of deferred income tax assets is reviewed at each statement of financial position date and reduced to the extent that it is no longer probable that sufficient taxable profit will be available to utilize the deferred income tax asset. Unrecognized deferred income tax assets are reassessed at each statement of financial position date and are recognized to the extent it is probable that future taxable profit will enable the deferred tax asset to be recovered.

Deferred income tax assets and liabilities are measured at the tax rate expected to apply in the year when the assets are realized or liabilities settled, based on tax rates and tax laws that have been enacted or substantively enacted at the statement of financial position date. Income tax relating to items recognized directly in equity is recognized in equity and not in the consolidated income statement. Deferred tax assets and deferred tax liabilities are offset where legally enforceable set off rights exist and the deferred taxes relate to the same taxable entity and the same taxation authority.

14. Taxes

Group taxes mainly comprise income taxes of subsidiaries and joint ventures. As a Luxembourg commercial company, the Company is subject to all taxes applicable to a Luxembourg Société Anonyme. Due to losses incurred and brought forward, no taxes based on Luxembourg-only income have been computed for 2011, 2010 and 2009.

The effective tax rate on continuing operations is (2%) (2010: 12%, 2009: 27%). Currently Millicom operations are in jurisdictions with income tax rates of 10% to 40% (2010 and 2009: 10% to 40%).

The reconciliation between the weighted average statutory tax rate and the effective average tax rate is as follows:

	2011 %	2010 %	2009 %
Weighted average statutory tax rate[i]	24	23	23
Recognition of previously unrecorded tax losses	(29)	—	—
Unrecognized current year tax losses[ii]	1	7	9
Non taxable income and non deductible expenses, net	1	—	(1)
Taxes based on revenue	(6)	(7)	(8)
Income taxes at other than statutory tax rates	4	2	3
Withholding taxes on transfers between operating and non operating entities	3	3	3
Non-taxable gain arising from revaluation of previously held interests	—	(16)	(2)
Effective tax rate	(2)	12	27

[i] The weighted average statutory tax rate has been determined by dividing the aggregate statutory tax charge of each subsidiary and joint venture, which was obtained by applying the statutory tax rate to the profit or loss before tax, by the aggregate profit before tax excluding the impact of the revaluation of Honduras in 2010 (see note 5).

[ii] Unrecognized current year tax losses mainly consist of tax losses at the Company level and tax losses recorded in the Group's operations in the Democratic Republic of Congo and Rwanda (2010: DRC, Rwanda and Colombia; 2009: DRC and Colombia).

The credit (charge) for income taxes from continuing operations is shown in the following table and recognizes that revenue and expense items may affect the financial statements and tax returns in different periods (temporary differences):

	2011 US$ '000	2010 US$ '000	2009 US$ '000
Current income tax credit (charge)	(278,502)	(223,077)	(201,230)
Net deferred income tax benefit (expense)	296,849	(4,019)	13,232
Credit/(charge) for taxes	18,347	(227,096)	(187,998)

The tax effects of significant items comprising the Group's net deferred income tax asset and liability as of December 31, 2011 and 2010 are as follows:

	Consolidated Balance Sheets		Consolidated Income Statements		
	2011 US$ '000	2010 US$ '000	2011 US$ '000	2010 US$ '000	2009 US$ '000
Loss carry-forwards	182,562	—	182,562	(5,877)	(1,945)
Provision for doubtful debtors	9,124	4,206	4,918	602	408
Temporary differences between book and tax basis of intangible assets and property, plant and equipment	4,993	(45,456)	50,449	(2,398)	(2,411)
Deferred tax liabilities recognized as part of the acquisition of Celtel (see note 5)	(94,390)	(105,392)	11,002	8,460	—
Deferred tax liabilities recognized as part of the acquisition of Amnet (see note 5)	(19,413)	(25,805)	6,392	6,237	9,485
Deferred tax liabilities recognized as part of the acquisition of Navega (see note 5)	(2,358)	(3,126)	768	936	540
Other temporary and translation differences	37,382	3,613	40,758	(11,979)	7,155
Deferred tax benefit (expense)			296,849	(4,019)	13,232
Deferred tax assets (liabilities), net	117,900	(171,960)			
Reflected in the statements of financial position as:					
Deferred tax assets	316,966	23,959			
Deferred tax liabilities	(199,066)	(195,919)			

Deferred income tax assets and liabilities reflect temporary differences between the carrying amounts of assets and liabilities for financial reporting purposes and the amounts used for income tax purposes.

No deferred tax liability was recognized in respect of $3,352 million (2010: $3,659 million) of unremitted earnings of subsidiaries and joint ventures, because the Group was in a position to control the timing of the reversal of the temporary differences and it was unlikely that such differences would reverse in a foreseeable future. Furthermore, it was not practicable to estimate the amount of unrecognized deferred tax liabilities in respect of these unremitted earnings.

During 2011, a tax credit of $308 million was recognized in our Colombian operation relating to expected utilization of tax loss carry-forwards and other temporary differences related mainly to property, plant and equipment and intangible assets. The expected utilisation of tax loss carryforwards was based on an assessment by management that sufficient taxable profit will be available to allow the benefit of the deferred tax asset to be utilised.

Unrecognized net operating losses and other tax loss carryforwards relating to continuing operations amounted to $169 million as at December 31, 2011 (2010: $775 million, 2009: $885 million) with expiry periods of between 1 and 5 years. In addition the Company has unrecognized net operating losses of $1,742 million (2010: $1,833 million) which do not expire.

IAS 33, *EARNINGS PER SHARE*

Author's Note

IASB amended IAS 33, *Earnings per Share*, by issuing the following new standards.
- IFRS 10
- IFRS 11
  These amendments delete the term *venturer* and amend the term *investor* to include those with "joint control of, or significant influence over, the investee."
- IFRS 13
  This amendment explains that terms defined in IAS 32, *Financial Instruments: Presentation*, are used in IAS 33 and that IFRS 13 defines fair value and sets out the requirements for applying that definition, except with respect to share options and other share-based payment arrangements to which IFRS 2 applies. In the latter case, an entity measures fair value in accordance with IFRS 2, not IFRS 13.

Because these standards are effective for annual periods beginning on or after 1 January 2012, these amendments are not reflected in the commentary in this section. However, these amendments would not affect the content or availability of illustrative excerpts from survey companies' financial statements.

IFRS Overview and Comparison to U.S. GAAP

3.343 IAS 33 establishes the requirements for calculating and presenting earnings per share (EPS), including basic EPS and diluted EPS. IAS 33 applies to separate, individual, and consolidated financial statements of an entity whose ordinary or potential ordinary shares are traded in a public market or who files, or is in the process of filing, with a securities commission or other regulatory authority for the purpose of issuing such securities in a public market. However, any entity that discloses EPS should do so only in accordance with IAS 33.

Recognition and Measurement

IFRSs

3.344 IAS 33 requires an entity to calculate basic and diluted EPS, attributable to equity holders of the parent entity, for profit or loss from continuing operations, if presented, and profit or loss.

3.345 Basic EPS is calculated by dividing the relevant profit or loss amount attributable to the equity holders of the parent by the weighted average number of ordinary shares outstanding during the period. An entity should adjust reported earnings and earnings from continuing operations by subtracting any posttax dividends declared, and similar effects, on preference shares (classified as equity) to arrive at the relevant amounts attributable to the equity holders of the parent.

3.346 An entity should calculate diluted EPS by adjusting earnings and earnings from continuing operations, if presented, attributable to the equity holders of the parent for the posttax effects of the following:
- Dividends or other items related to dilutive potential ordinary shares deducted in arriving at earnings attributable to equity holders of the parent
- Any interest expense recognized in respect to dilutive potential ordinary shares
- Any other changes that would result from conversion of dilutive potential ordinary shares

3.347 An entity should also adjust the weighted average ordinary shares outstanding for the weighted average ordinary shares that would be issued on conversion of dilutive potential ordinary shares into ordinary shares. An entity should make these adjustments as if conversion of the dilutive potential ordinary shares occurred at the beginning of the reporting period or the issue date, if later.

3.348 An entity should consider a potential ordinary share to be dilutive only if its conversion will decrease EPS or EPS from continuing operations.

3.349 IAS 33 discusses the dilutive nature of the following potential ordinary shares: options, warrants and their equivalents, convertible instruments, contingently issuable shares, contracts that may be settled in ordinary shares or cash, purchased options, and written put options.

3.350 With respect to options, warrants, and similar instruments, an entity should assume exercise. The entity should regard the assumed proceeds of these shares to have been received from the issue of shares at the average market price. Therefore, the assumed proceeds divided by the average market price of ordinary shares during the period will be the number of shares that would have been issued. The difference between the number of shares issued on exercise and the number of shares that would have been issued is the additional shares to be added to the weighted average number of shares outstanding in the diluted EPS calculation. Accordingly, these securities are dilutive when they are issued for less than the average market price of ordinary shares during the period and antidilutive if issued for more than the average price.

3.351 When dilutive, an entity should adjust both earnings and the weighted average ordinary shares outstanding for the effects of convertible securities. If the convertible securities are preferred shares, the entity should no longer deduct preferred share dividends from earnings and should increase the weighted average common shares outstanding for the additional number of ordinary shares issued on conversion. If the convertible securities are debt securities, the entity should adjust earnings for the posttax effect of interest expense and increase the weighted average ordinary shares outstanding by the additional shares issued on conversion.

3.352 An entity should treat any contingently issuable shares as outstanding when the specified conditions are satisfied (that is, the events have occurred on which issuance depends) and should make the necessary adjustments to the diluted EPS calculation as of the beginning of the period or the date of the contingent share agreement, whichever is later. If the conditions are not satisfied, an entity should base the adjustment to the diluted EPS calculation on the number of shares that would be issued if the end of the period were the end of the contingency period.

3.353 For contracts that may be settled in equity or cash at the entity's option, an entity should presume settlement would be in equity. For those contracts that may be settled at the holder's option, the entity should assume the more dilutive of the two cases.

3.354 An entity should not include contracts such as purchased options in the calculation of diluted EPS because exercise would be antidilutive.

3.355 An entity should include in the calculation of diluted EPS contracts that require it to repurchase its own shares when the effect is dilutive. If such contracts are "in the money" during the period, the entity should calculate the potential dilutive effect as follows:
   (a) Assume that sufficient ordinary shares will be issued at the beginning of the period at the average market price to raise the proceeds to fulfill the contract.
   (b) Assume the proceeds are used to repurchase shares under the contract.
   (c) Adjust the weighted average number of ordinary shares outstanding for any incremental number of ordinary shares issued over the number of shares repurchased.

3.356 When the number of ordinary shares increases due to capitalizations, bonuses, stock splits, or dividends that occur after the balance sheet date but before the financial statements are issued, the entity should recalculate EPS for these changes.

U.S. GAAP

3.357 Like IFRSs, paragraphs 10–11 of FASB ASC 260-10-45 specify that an entity should calculate basic EPS by dividing income available to common stockholders (the numerator) by the weighted average number of common shares outstanding (the denominator) during the period. An entity should compute income available to common stockholders by deducting both the dividends declared in the period on preferred stock (regardless of whether they are paid) and the dividends accumulated for the period on cumulative preferred stock (regardless of whether they are earned) from income from continuing operations (if that amount appears in the income statement) and from net income. If there is a loss from continuing operations or a net loss, the amount of the loss should be increased by those preferred dividends.

3.358 Both IFRSs and FASB ASC 260-10-45-11A require that, when computing EPS in consolidated financial statements, income from continuing operations and net income exclude income attributable to any noncontrolling interests.

3.359 Both IFRSs and FASB ASC 260-10-45-12A state that an entity should include contingently issuable shares in the EPS calculation only when there is no circumstance under which those shares would not be issued (that is, the necessary conditions upon which issuance is predicated have been met). However, paragraphs 12A–14 of FASB ASC 260-10-45 provide more guidance on what constitutes a contingently issuable share.

3.360 Like IFRSs, FASB ASC 260-10-45-16 requires an entity to adjust the numerator for any convertible preferred dividends and the posttax amount of interest recognized in the period associated with any convertible debt in computing the dilutive effect of convertible securities. An entity should also adjust the numerator for any other changes in income or loss that would result from the assumed conversion of these potential common shares. FASB ASC 260-10-55-38 also provides an illustration of similar adjustments when a contract provides the issuer or holder with a choice between settlement methods.

3.361 Like IFRSs, FASB ASC 260-10-45-17 states that an entity should not include the conversion, exercise, or contingent issuance of any security that would be antidilutive in the calculation of EPS. An entity should determine whether potential common shares are dilutive or antidilutive separately for each issue or series of issues of potential common shares.

3.362 Like IFRSs, FASB ASC 260-10-45-21 requires an entity to base the calculation of diluted EPS on the most advantageous conversion rate or exercise price from the standpoint of the security holder when there is more than one basis for conversion.

3.363 Like IFRSs, FASB ASC 260-10-45-16 requires an entity to include in the denominator of the calculation the number of additional common shares that would have been outstanding if the dilutive potential common shares had been issued when calculating diluted EPS. As described in FASB ASC 260-10-45, calculation of the number of additional common shares to be included depends upon the type of potentially dilutive security. FASB ASC 260-10-45 specifies that an entity should use the treasury stock method for options, warrants, and similar instruments; reverse treasury stock method for written put options or forward purchase contracts; and the if-converted method for convertible securities to determine the additional amounts.

3.364 Although the requirements are described differently than in IFRSs, paragraphs 22–27 of FASB ASC 260-10-45 requires an entity to apply what is known as the treasury stock method to determine the effect of an exercise of options, warrants, or similar instruments (for example, stock purchase contracts) on diluted EPS. This method assumes that the entity would take the entire proceeds from exercise and repurchase shares at the average market price for the period. Therefore, the entity should only include any excess shares issued over those repurchased in the diluted EPS calculation. Like IFRSs, FASB ASC 260-10-45-37 does not permit an entity to include purchased put or call options in the calculation because they are antidilutive. Paragraphs 28–32 of FASB ASC 260-10-45 provide more guidance than IAS 33 on including share-based compensation arrangements in the calculation, including guidance on how to account for excess tax benefits associated with these arrangements. IFRSs and FASB ASC 260-10-45-35 are also consistent in their treatment of written put options and forward purchase contracts, if dilutive, by assuming that the entity would issue sufficient shares and use the proceeds to satisfy the contract.

3.365 To determine the effect of convertible securities on diluted EPS, paragraphs 40–41 of FASB ASC 260-10-45 require an entity to use the if-converted method, which produces adjustments that are essentially the same as those required by IFRSs. An entity should adjust the numerator for the posttax consequences of reversing dividend declarations on preferred shares and interest expense on debt instruments with a corresponding increase in weighted average common shares outstanding. An entity should not include an antidilutive security in the calculation.

3.366 With respect to contracts with a settlement option, in contrast to IFRSs, paragraphs 45–47 of FASB ASC 260-10-45 require an entity to presume the most dilutive option, regardless of whether the entity or holder can select the method of settlement, unless past experience or a stated policy provides a reasonable basis to believe that the contract will be paid partially or wholly in cash.

3.367 Both IFRSs and paragraphs 59A–70 of FASB ASC 260-10-45 use the two-class method for calculating the effect of participating securities and two-class ordinary shares.

Presentation

IFRSs

3.368 For each class of ordinary shares and each period presented in the statement of comprehensive income, an entity should present basic and diluted EPS for profit or loss from continuing operations and profit or loss for the period, attributable to equity holders of the parent, in the statement of comprehensive income. An entity should present basic and diluted EPS with equal prominence.

3.369 An entity should disclose basic and diluted EPS even when the amount is negative. An entity should disclose EPS from discontinued operations either on the face of the statement or in the notes.

3.370 IAS 33 also constrains the location where EPS can be presented when the entity presents both separate and consolidated financial statements.

3.371 IAS 33 permits an entity to disclose EPS effects for additional components of the statement of comprehensive income with the caveat that it should calculate these per share amounts based on the weighted average ordinary shares outstanding, determined in accordance with IAS 33, and they are shown with equal prominence as the required EPS amounts. An entity should disclose the basis for the numerator and whether the amounts are before or after tax.

U.S. GAAP

3.372 Like IFRSs, FASB ASC 260-10-45-2 requires an entity to present EPS for income from continuing operations and net income on the face of the income statement. Unlike IFRSs, U.S. GAAP requires an entity with a simple capital structure (that is, only common stock outstanding) to present only basic EPS. Like IFRSs, U.S. GAAP requires all other entities to present basic and diluted EPS for income from continuing operations and net income on the face of the income statement with equal prominence.

3.373 Like IFRSs, FASB ASC 260-10-45-3 requires an entity that reports a discontinued operation to present basic and diluted EPS for this line item either on the face of the income statement or in the notes to the financial statements. However, U.S. GAAP requires an entity to also report basic and diluted EPS for a reported extraordinary item.

3.374 Like IFRSs, FASB ASC 260-10-45-5 permits an entity to present additional EPS amounts as long as they are calculated in accordance with FASB ASC 260-10 and only allows disclosure of these additional EPS amounts in the notes to financial statements. An entity should also disclose whether these amounts are calculated before or after tax.

3.375 Like IFRSs, FASB ASC 260-10-45-7 requires EPS data to be presented for all periods for which an income statement or summary of earnings is presented. If diluted EPS is reported for at least one period, an entity should report diluted EPS data for all periods presented, even if they are the same amounts as basic EPS. When basic and diluted EPS are the same amount, this paragraph permits a dual presentation in one line on the income statement.

Disclosure

IFRSs

3.376 IAS 33 requires an entity to disclose all of the following:
- Amounts used as the numerator in the basic and diluted EPS calculations and a reconciliation of the numerator to the amount reported in profit or loss attributed to the equity holders of the parent, with separate disclosure of the effects of each class of instrument included
- Weighted average number of ordinary shares used as the denominator in the basic and diluted EPS calculations, a reconciliation of the amounts used for basic and diluted EPS, and a reconciliation showing the effects of each class of instrument included
- Instruments that could potentially dilute EPS but were not included in the calculation because they were antidilutive, including any contingently issuable shares
- Description of any transaction (for example, issue of shares for cash), other than those for which an entity is required to adjust EPS, that occurred after the balance sheet date and would have changed significantly the number of shares or potential shares outstanding if the shares had been issued before the balance sheet date

3.377 If, in addition to the required basic and diluted EPS, an entity discloses amounts per share based on a component of the statement of comprehensive income (or a separate income statement) that is different from that required for IAS 33 (a non-IFRS EPS), IAS 33 requires the entity to calculate that non-IFRS EPS using the weighted average common shares outstanding, determined in accordance with IAS 33. In addition, an entity should do the following:
- Indicate the basis on which the numerator of the non-IFRS EPS was determined, including whether the amounts are pretax or posttax.

- Disclose the non-IFRS EPS with equal prominence to basic and diluted EPS presented in the notes.
- Reconcile the component used, if it is not a separate line item in the statement of comprehensive income (or separate income statement), with the relevant reported line item.

U.S. GAAP

3.378 Like IFRSs, FASB ASC 260-10-50-1 requires an entity to disclose all of the following for each income statement presented in the financial statements:

- A reconciliation of the numerators and denominators of the basic and diluted per-share computations for income from continuing operations, including individual income and share amounts for the effects of all securities that affect EPS (the entity is encouraged to refer readers to pertinent information about securities included in EPS computations addressed in other sections of the financial statements)
- The effect of preferred dividends on basic EPS
- Information about securities (including those contingently issuable shares) that could potentially dilute basic EPS in the future and were not included in the computation of diluted EPS because they were antidilutive, with disclosure of the terms and conditions of the securities, regardless of their exclusion from the calculation of diluted EPS in the current period

3.379 FASB ASC 260-10-50-2 also requires the same disclosure as IFRSs for any transaction that occurs after the end of the most recent period but before the financial statements are issued or are available for issue that would have changed materially the number of common shares or potential common shares outstanding at the end of the period if the transaction had occurred before the end of the period.

Presentation and Disclosure Excerpts

Basic and Diluted EPS Reported on One Line—No Dilutive Potential Shares

3.380

Telecom Argentina (Dec 2011)

CONSOLIDATED INCOME STATEMENTS (in part)

(In millions of Argentine pesos)

	Note	For the Years Ended December 31		
		2011	2010	2009
Net income for the year		2,542	1,949	1,417
Attributable to:				
Owners of the parent		2,513	1,935	1,405
Non-controlling interest		29	14	12
		2,542	1,949	1,417
Earnings per share attributable to owners of the parent				
Basic and diluted	25	2.55	1.97	1.43

NOTES TO THE CONSOLIDATED FINANCIAL STATEMENTS (in part)

Note 1—Description of Business and Basis of Preparation of the Consolidated Financial Statements (in part)

a) The Company and Its Operations

Telecom Argentina was created by a decree of the Argentine Government in January 1990 and organized as a *sociedad anónima* under the name "Sociedad Licenciataria Norte S.A." in April 1990.

Telecom Argentina commenced operations on November 8, 1990, upon the transfer to the Company of the telecommunications network of the northern region of Argentina previously owned and operated by the state-owned company, Empresa Nacional de Telecomunicaciones ("ENTel").

Telecom Argentina's license, as originally granted, was exclusive to provide telephone services in the northern region of Argentina through October 10, 1999. As from such date, the Company also began providing telephone services in the southern region of Argentina and competing in the previously exclusive northern region.

The Company provides fixed-line public telecommunication services, international long-distance service, data transmission and Internet services in Argentina and through its subsidiaries, mobile telecommunications services in Argentina and Paraguay and international wholesale services in the United States of America. Information on the Telecom Group's licenses and the regulatory framework is described in Note 2.

Entities included in consolidation and the respective equity interest owned by Telecom Argentina is presented as follows:

Subsidiaries	Percentage of Capital Stock Owned and Voting Rights[i]	Indirect Control Through	Date of Acquisition
Telecom USA	100.00%		09.12.00
Micro Sistemas[ii]	99.99%		12.31.97
Personal	99.99%		07.06.94
Springville[ii]	100.00%	Personal	04.07.09
Núcleo[iii]	67.50%	Personal	02.03.98

[i]   Percentage of equity interest owned has been rounded.
[ii]   Dormant entity at December 31, 2011, 2010 and 2009.
[iii]   Non-controlling interest of 32.50% is owned by the Paraguayan company ABC Telecomunicaciones S.A.

c) Basis of Preparation

These consolidated financial statements have been prepared in accordance with IFRS as issued by the International Accounting Standards Board. IFRS comprises all effective IAS together with all the SIC and all interpretations issued by the IFRIC.

The preparation of financial statements in conformity with IFRS requires the use of certain critical accounting estimates. It also requires Management to exercise its judgment in the process of applying the Telecom Group's accounting policies. The areas involving a higher degree of judgment or complexity, or areas where assumptions and estimates are significant to the consolidated financial statements are disclosed in Note 3.

The Company has split certain items in the current and noncurrent liabilities of the statement of financial position in order to enable users of the financial statements to better understand the information contained therein. As a result a new item "Deferred revenues" was added in the statement of financial position. In addition asset retirement obligation liabilities previously reported under "Other liabilities" were classified under the "Provisions" item line. Information for year 2010 was also reclassified to conform to the current year presentation.

The financial statements (except for cash flow information) are prepared on an accrual basis of accounting. Under this basis, the effects of transactions and other events are recognized when they occur. Therefore income and expenses are recognized at fair value on an accrual basis regardless of when they are perceived or paid. When significant, the difference between the fair value and the nominal amount of income and expenses is recognized as finance income or expense using the effective interest method over the relevant period.

The accompanying consolidated financial statements have also been prepared on a going concern basis (further details are provided in Note 3).

Publication of these consolidated financial statements for the year ended December 31, 2011 was approved by resolution of the Board of Directors' meeting held on March 22, 2012.

s) Earnings per Share

Basic earnings per share are calculated by dividing the net income or loss attributable to owners of the Parent by the weighted average number of ordinary shares outstanding during the year (see Note 25).

Note 25—Earnings per Share

The Company computes net income per common share by dividing net income for the year attributable to owners of the Parent by the weighted average number of common shares outstanding during the year. Diluted net income per share is computed by dividing the net income for the year by the weighted average number of common and dilutive potential common shares then outstanding during the year. Since the Company has no dilutive potential common stock outstanding, there are no dilutive earnings per share amounts.

For financial years 2011, 2010 and 2009, the weighted average of shares outstanding totaled 984,380,978 shares.

Basic and Diluted EPS—Stock Options and Multiple Convertible Securities Anti-Dilutive

3.381

Alcatel-Lucent (Dec 2011)

CONSOLIDATED INCOME STATEMENTS (in part)

(In Millions Except per Share Information)	Notes	2011[1]	2011	2010[5]	2009[5]
Net Income (Loss)		1,484	1,144	(292)	(504)
Attributable to:					
● Equity owners of the parent		1,421	1,095	(334)	(524)
● Non-controlling interests		63	49	42	20
Net income (loss) attributable to the equity owners of the parent per share (in euros and U.S.$)					
● Basic earnings per share	(11) U.S.$	0.62€	0.48€	(0.15)€	(0.23)
● Diluted earnings per share	(11) U.S.$	0.54€	0.42€	(0.15)€	(0.23)
Net income (loss) before discontinued operations attributable to the equity owners of the parent per share (in euros and U.S.$)					
● Basic earnings per share	U.S.$	0.39€	0.30€	(0.16)€	(0.30)
● Diluted earnings per share	U.S.$	0.36€	0.28€	(0.16)€	(0.30)
Net income (loss) of discontinued operations per share (in euros and U.S.$)					
● Basic earnings per share	U.S.$	0.23€	0.18€	0.01€	0.07
● Diluted earnings per share	U.S.$	0.18€	0.14€	0.01€	0.07

[1] Translation of amounts from euros into U.S. dollars has been made merely for the convenience of the reader at Noon Buying Rate of €1 = U.S. dollar 1.2973 on December 30, 2011.

[5] 2009 and 2010 consolidated income statements are re-presented to reflect the impacts of discontinued operations (see Note 10).

NOTES TO THE CONSOLIDATED FINANCIAL STATEMENTS (in part)

Alcatel-Lucent (formerly called Alcatel) is a French public limited liability company that is subject to the French Commercial Code and to all the legal requirements governing commercial companies in France. On November 30, 2006, Alcatel changed its name to Alcatel-Lucent on completion of the business combination with Lucent Technologies Inc. Alcatel-Lucent was incorporated on June 18, 1898 and will be dissolved on June 30, 2086, unless its existence is extended or shortened by shareholder vote. Alcatel-Lucent's headquarters are located at 3, avenue Octave Gréard, 75007, Paris, France. Alcatel-Lucent is listed principally on the Paris and New York stock exchanges.

The consolidated financial statements reflect the results and financial position of Alcatel-Lucent and its subsidiaries (the "Group") as well as its investments in associates ("equity affiliates") and joint ventures. They are presented in Euros rounded to the nearest million.

The Group develops and integrates technologies, applications and services to offer innovative global communications solutions.

On February 8, 2012, Alcatel-Lucent's Board of Directors authorized for issuance these consolidated financial statements at December 31, 2011. The consolidated financial statements will be final once approved at the Annual Shareholders' Meeting to be held on June 8, 2012.

Note 1 Summary of Accounting Policies (in part)

Due to the listing of Alcatel-Lucent's securities on the Euronext Paris and in accordance with the European Union's regulation No. 1606/2002 of July 19, 2002, the consolidated financial statements of the Group are prepared in accordance with IFRSs (International Financial Reporting Standards), as adopted by the European Union ("EU"), as of the date when our Board of Directors authorized these consolidated financial statements for issuance.

IFRSs can be found at: www.ec.europa.eu/internal_market/accounting/ias/index_en.htm.

IFRSs include the standards approved by the International Accounting Standards Board ("IASB"), that is, International Accounting Standards ("IASs") and accounting interpretations issued by the IFRS Interpretations Committee ("IFRIC") or the former Standing Interpretations Committee ("SIC").

As of December 31, 2011, all IFRSs that the IASB had published and that are mandatory are the same as those endorsed by the EU and mandatory in the EU, with the exception of:

- IAS 39, which the EU only partially adopted. The part not adopted by the EU has no impact on Alcatel-Lucent's financial statements.

As a result, the Group's consolidated financial statements comply with International Financial Reporting Standards as published by the IASB.

Note 11 Earnings Per Share

Basic earnings per share is computed using the number of shares issued, after deduction of the weighted average number of shares owned by consolidated subsidiaries and the weighting effect of shares issued during the year.

In accordance with IAS 33 revised (paragraph 23), the weighted average number of shares to be issued upon conversion of bonds redeemable for shares is included in the calculation of basic earnings per share.

Diluted earnings per share takes into account share equivalents having a dilutive effect, after deducting the weighted average number of share equivalents owned by consolidated subsidiaries, but not share equivalents that do not have a dilutive effect. Net income (loss) is adjusted for after-tax interest expense relating to convertible bonds.

The dilutive effects of stock option and stock purchase plans are calculated using the "treasury stock method", which provides that proceeds to be received from the exercise of options or purchase of stock are assumed to be used first to purchase shares at market price. The dilutive effects of convertible bonds are calculated on the assumption that the bonds and notes will be systematically redeemed for shares (the "if converted method").

The tables below reconcile basic earnings per share to diluted earnings per share for the periods presented:

(In Millions of Euros) Net Income (Loss)	2011	2010	2009
Net income (loss) attributable to the equity owners of the parent—basic	1,095	(334)	(524)
Adjustment for dilutive securities on net income: Interest expense related to convertible securities	119	—	—
Net income (loss)—diluted	1,214	(334)	(524)

Number of Shares	2011	2010	2009
Weighted average number of shares—basic	2,265,024,193	2,259,877,263	2,259,696,863
Dilutive effects:			
• Equity plans (stock options, RSU)	35,686,744	—	—
• Alcatel-Lucent's convertible bonds (Oceane) issued on June 12, 2003 and on September 10, 2009	309,597,523	—	—
• 7.75% convertible securities	—	—	—
• 2.875% Series A convertible securities	24,886,871	—	—
• 2.875% Series B convertible securities	230,735,668	—	—
Weighted average number of shares—diluted	2,865,930,999	2,259,877,263	2,259,696,863

Earnings per Share, Attributable to the Owners of the Parent (in Euros)	2011	2010	2009
Basic	0.48	(0.15)	(0.23)
Diluted	0.42	(0.15)	(0.23)

Ordinary Shares

Ordinary Shares Owned by Consolidated Subsidiaries of the Group	2011	2010	2009
Number of Alcatel-Lucent ordinary shares (weighted average number)	58,220,040	58,281,560	58,351,371
Number of Alcatel-Lucent share equivalents	—	—	—

Shares Subject to Future Issuance

	December 31, 2011	December 31, 2010	December 31, 2009
Number of stock options not exercised	175,729,780	196,702,252	212,292,704

The following table summarizes the number of potential ordinary shares that were excluded from the diluted per share calculation, because the effect of including these potential shares was anti-dilutive:

	2011	2010	2009
Equity plans (stock options, RSU)	—	14,023,726	7,624,288
Alcatel-Lucent's convertible bonds (Oceane) issued on June 12, 2003 and on September 10, 2009	—	360,161,154	360,162,302
7.75% convertible securities	37,557,287	37,557,287	37,557,287
2.875% Series A convertible securities	—	32,895,828	196,117,249
2.875% Series B convertible securities	—	304,989,763	325,813,655

Note 24 Equity (in part)

a/ Number of Shares Comprising the Capital Stock

Number of Shares	2011	2010	2009
Number of ordinary shares issued (share capital)	2,325,383,328	2,318,385,548	2,318,060,818
Treasury shares	(58,219,944)	(58,202,419)	(58,320,394)
Number of shares in circulation	2,267,163,384	2,260,183,129	2,259,740,424
Weighting effect of share issues (of which stock options exercised)	(2,139,095)	(226,725)	(12,584)
Weighting effect of treasury shares	(96)	(79,141)	(30,977)
Number of shares used for calculating basic earnings per share	2,265,024,193	2,259,877,263	2,259,696,863

Basic and Diluted EPS—Continuing Operations, Discontinued Operations

3.382

KT Corporation (Dec 2011)

CONSOLIDATED STATEMENTS OF INCOME
(in part)

(In Millions of Korean Won, Except per Share Amounts)	Notes	2010	2011	(In Thousands of U.S. Dollars) 2011
Profit for the period from the continuing operations		1,284,904	1,281,151	1,110,856
Discontinued Operations:				
Profit from discontinued operations		29,980	170,868	148,156
Profit for the period	38	(Won) 1,314,884	(Won) 1,452,019	$1,259,012
Profit for the period attributable to:				
Equity holders of the Parent Company		(Won) 1,295,841	(Won) 1,446,551	$1,254,271
Profit from continuing operations		1,273,191	1,276,512	1,106,834
Profit from discontinued operations		22,650	170,039	147,437
Non-controlling interest		(Won) 19,043	(Won) 5,468	$4,741
Profit from continuing operations		11,713	4,639	4,022
Profit from discontinued operations		7,330	829	719
Earnings per share attributable to the equity holders of the Parent Company during the period (in won):				
Basic earnings per share	31	(Won) 5,328	(Won) 5,946	$ 5,156
From continuing operations		5,235	5,247	4,550
From discontinued operations		93	699	0,606
Diluted earnings per share		(Won) 5,328	(Won) 5,946	$ 5,156
From continuing operations		5,235	5,247	4,550
From discontinued operations		93	699	0,606

NOTES TO THE CONSOLIDATED FINANCIAL STATEMENTS *(in part)*

1. General Information *(in part)*

The consolidated financial statements include the accounts of KT Corporation, which is the controlling company as defined under IAS 27, *Consolidated and Separate Financial Statements*, and its 51 controlled subsidiaries as described in Note 1.2 (collectively referred to as the "Company").

The Controlling Company

KT Corporation (the "Controlling Company") commenced operations on January 1, 1982, when it spun off from the Korea Communications Commission (formerly the Korean Ministry of Information and Communications) to provide telephone services and to engage in the development of advanced communications services under the Act of Telecommunications of Korea. The headquarters are located in Seongnam-si, Gyeonggi-do, Republic of Korea, and the address of its registered head office is 206, Jungja-dong, Bundang-gu, Seongnam-si, Gyeonggi-do.

On October 1, 1997, upon the announcement of the Government-Investment Enterprises Management Basic Act and the Privatization Law, the Controlling Company became a government-funded institution under the Commercial Code of Korea.

On December 23, 1998, the Controlling Company's shares were listed on the Korea Exchange.

On May 29, 1999, the Controlling Company issued 24,282,195 additional shares and issued American Depository Shares (ADS), representing new shares and government-owned shares, at the New York Stock Exchange and the London Stock Exchange. On July 2, 2001, the additional ADS representing 55,502,161 government-owned shares were issued at the New York Stock Exchange and London Stock Exchange.

In 2002, the Controlling Company acquired 60,294,575 government-owned shares in accordance with the Korean government's privatization plan. As of December 31, 2011, the Korean government does not own any share in the Controlling Company.

On June 1, 2009, the Controlling Company, which is an existing company, was merged with KT Freetel Co., Ltd., which was a subsidiary, to enhance the efficiency of business management.

2. Significant Accounting Policies

The following is a summary of significant accounting policies followed by the Company in the preparation of its financial statements. These policies have been consistently applied to all the periods presented, unless otherwise stated.

2.1 Basis of Preparation

The Company determined to adopt International Financial Reporting Standards ("IFRS") as issued by the International Accounting Standards Board ("IASB") for the annual periods beginning on or after January 1, 2011.

The Company's IFRS transition date from accounting principles generally accepted in the Republic of Korea ("Korean GAAP") to IFRS according to IFRS 1, *First-time Adoption of IFRS*, is January 1, 2010, and reconciliations and descriptions of the effect of the transition from Korean GAAP to IFRS on the Company's assets, liabilities, equity, and comprehensive income are provided in Note 4.

The preparation of financial statements in accordance with IFRS requires the use of certain critical accounting estimates. It also requires management to exercise judgment in the process of applying the Company's accounting policies. The areas involving a higher degree of judgment and complexity, or the areas where assumptions and estimates are significant to these financial statements are disclosed in Note 3.

31. Earnings per Share

Calculation of earnings per share for the years ended December 31, 2010 and 2011, are as follows:

1) Basic Earnings per Share From Continuing Operations

Basic earnings per share from continuing operations is calculated by dividing the profit from continuing operations attributable to equity holders of the Company by the weighted average number of common stocks outstanding during the period, excluding common stocks purchased by the Company and held as treasury stock (Note 24).

Basic earnings per share from continuing operations for the years ended December 31, 2010 and 2011, are calculated as follows:

	2010	2011
Profit from continuing operations attributable to common stock (In millions of Korean won)	(Won) 1,273,191	(Won) 1,276,512
Weighted average number of common stock outstanding	243,207,149	243,268,052
Basic earnings per share from continuing operations (In Korean won)	(Won) 5,235	(Won) 5,247

2) Basic Earnings per Share From Discontinued Operations

Basic earnings per share from discontinued operations is calculated by dividing the profit from discontinued operations attributable to equity holders of the Company by the weighted average number of common stocks outstanding during the period, excluding common stocks purchased by the Company and held as treasury stock (Note 24).

Basic earnings per share from discontinued operations for the years ended December 31, 2010 and 2011, are calculated as follows:

	2010	2011
Profit from discontinued operations attributable to common stock (in millions of Korean won)	(Won) 22,650	(Won) 170,039
Weighted average number of common stock outstanding	243,207,149	243,268,052
Basic earnings per share from discontinued operations (in Korean won)	(Won) 93	(Won) 699

3) Basic Earnings per Share

Basic earnings per share is calculated by dividing the profit attributable to equity holders of the Company by the weighted average number of common stocks outstanding during the year, excluding common stocks purchased by the Company and held as treasury stock (Note 24).

Basic earnings per share for the years ended December 31, 2010 and 2011, are calculated as follows:

	2010	2011
Net income attributable to common stock (In millions of Korean won)	(Won) 1,295,841	(Won) 1,446,551
Weighted average number of common stock outstanding	243,207,149	243,268,052
Basic earnings per share (In Korean won)	(Won) 5,328	(Won) 5,946

4) Diluted Earnings per Share From Continuing Operations

Diluted earnings per share from continuing operations is calculated by adjusting the weighted average number of common stocks outstanding to assume conversion of all dilutive potential common stocks. The Company has dilutive potential common stocks from stock options.

Diluted earnings per share from continuing operations for the years ended December 31, 2010 and 2011, are calculated as follows:

	2010	2011
Profit from continuing operations attributable to common stock (In millions of Korean won)	(Won) 1,273,191	(Won) 1,276,512
Adjusted Profit from continuing operations attributable to common stock (In millions of Korean won)	1,273,191	1,276,512
Number of dilutive potential common shares outstanding	18,081	32,960
Weighted-average number of common shares outstanding and dilutive common shares	243,225,230	243,301,012
Diluted earnings per share from continuing operations (In Korean won)	(Won) 5,235	(Won) 5,247

Diluted earnings per share from continuing operations is calculated by dividing adjusted profit from continuing operations attributable to equity holders of the Company by the sum of the number of common stocks and dilutive potential common stocks. Certain stock options and other share-based payments have no dilutive effect and are excluded from the calculation of diluted earnings per share from continuing operations.

5) Diluted Earnings per Share From Discontinued Operations

Diluted earnings per share from discontinued operations is calculated by adjusting the weighted average number of common stocks outstanding to assume conversion of all dilutive potential common stocks. The Company has dilutive potential common stocks from stock options.

Diluted earnings per share from discontinued operations for the years ended December 31, 2010 and 2011, are calculated as follows:

	2010	2011
Profit from discontinued operations attributable to common stock (in millions of Korean won)	(Won) 22,650	(Won) 170,039
Adjusted profit from discontinued operations attributable to common stock (in millions of Korean won)	22,650	170,039
Number of dilutive potential common shares outstanding	18,081	32,960
Weighted-average number of common shares outstanding and dilutive common shares	243,225,230	243,301,012
Diluted earnings per share from discontinued operations (in Korean won)	(Won) 93	(Won) 699

Diluted earnings per share from discontinued operations is calculated by dividing adjusted profit from discontinued operations attributable to equity holders of the Company by the sum of the number of common stocks and dilutive potential common stocks. Certain stock options and other share-based payments have no dilutive effect and are excluded from the calculation of diluted earnings per share from discontinued operations.

6) Diluted Earnings per Share

Diluted earnings per share is calculated by adjusting the weighted average number of common stocks outstanding to assume conversion of all dilutive potential common stocks. The Company has dilutive potential common stocks from stock options.

Diluted earnings per share for the years ended December 31, 2010 and 2011, are calculated as follows:

	2010	2011
Net income attributable to common stock (in millions of Korean won)	(Won) 1,295,841	(Won) 1,446,551
Adjusted net income attributable to common stock (in millions of Korean won)	1,295,841	1,446,551
Number of dilutive potential common shares outstanding	18,081	32,960
Weighted-average number of common shares outstanding and dilutive common shares	243,225,230	243,301,012
Diluted earnings per share (in Korean won)	(Won) 5,328	(Won) 5,946

Diluted earnings per share is calculated by dividing adjusted net income attributable to equity holders of the Company by the sum of the number of common stocks and dilutive potential common stocks. Certain stock options and other share-based payments have no dilutive effect and are excluded from the calculation of diluted earnings per share.

Basic and Diluted EPS—Common and Preferred Shares

3.383

Companhia de Bebidas das Américas (American Beverage Company)—Ambev (Dec 2011)

CONSOLIDATED INCOME STATEMENTS (in part)

(Expressed in millions of Brazilian Reais)

	Note	2011	2010	2009
Net income		8,719.8	7,619.2	5,988.4
Attributable to:				
Equity holders of Ambev		8,641.0	7,561.4	5,986.1
Non-controlling interests		78.8	57.8	2.3
Basic earnings per share—preferred		2.93	2.58	2.05
Diluted earnings per share—preferred		2.91	2.57	2.05
Basic earnings per share—common		2.66	2.34	1.86
Diluted earnings per share—common		2.65	2.33	1.86

NOTES TO THE CONSOLIDATED FINANCIAL STATEMENTS (in part)

1. Corporate Information (in part)

Companhia de Bebidas das Américas—Ambev (referred to as "we", the "Company" or "Ambev"), headquartered in São Paulo, Brazil; produces and sells beer, draft beer, soft drinks, other non-alcoholic beverages, malt and food in general, either directly or by participating in other Brazilian-domiciled companies and elsewhere in the Americas.

The Company has an agreement with PepsiCo International, Inc. ("PepsiCo") to bottle, sell and distribute Pepsi products in Brazil and in other Latin American countries, including Pepsi Cola, 7Up, Lipton Ice Tea, Gatorade and H2OH!.

The Company has a licensing agreement with Anheuser-Busch, Inc., to produce, bottle, sell and distribute Budweiser products in Brazil, Canada and Paraguay. The Company and certain of its subsidiaries produce and distribute Stella Artois under license to Anheuser-Busch InBev S.A./N.V. ("AB InBev") in Brazil, Canada, Argentina and other countries and, by means of a license granted to AB InBev, it also distributes Brahma's product in parts of Europe, Asia and Africa.

The Company's shares are traded on the Brazilian Stock Exchange—BM&FBOVESPA Bolsa de Valores S.A., Mercados e Futuros and on the New York Stock Exchange—NYSE, in the form of American Depositary Receipts—ADRs.

2. Statement of Compliance

The consolidated financial statements have been prepared in accordance with International Financial Reporting Standards ("IFRS") as issued by the International Accounting Standards Board ("IASB").

Ambev has not applied early any new IFRS requirements.

3. Summary of Significant Accounting Policies (in part)

(a) Basis of Preparation and Measurement (in part)

The consolidated financial statements were prepared in accordance with IFRS requirements and the interpretations of the International Financial Reporting Interpretations Committee ("IFRIC") that were in force on December 31, 2011.

The consolidated financial statements are presented in millions of Brazilian Reais (R$), rounded to the nearest million indicated. Depending on the applicable IFRS requirement, the measurement basis used in preparing the financial statements is cost, net realizable value, fair value or recoverable amount. Whenever IFRS provides an option between cost and another measurement basis (e.g., systematic remeasurement), the cost approach is applied.

21. Changes in Equity (in part)

(i) Earnings per Share

Basic Earnings per Share

The calculation of basic earnings per share is based on the net income attributable to equity holders of Ambev of R$8,641.0 (R$7,561.4 and R$5,986.1 in 2010 and 2009 respectively) and the weighted average number of shares outstanding during the year, calculated as follows:

Thousand Shares	2011		
	Preferred	Common	Total
Issued shares at January 1	1,360,472	1,743,889	3,104,361
Treasury shares	(608)	(524)	(1,132)
Effect of shares issued/repurchased	3,926	4,223	8,149
Weighted average number of shares at December 31	1,363,790	1,747,588	3,111,378

Thousand Shares	2010		
	Preferred	Common	Total
Issued shares at January 1	1,351,965	1,732,975	3,084,940
Treasury shares	(2,155)	(605)	(2,760)
Effect of shares issued/repurchased	5,448	4,868	10,316
Weighted average number of shares at December 31	1,355,260	1,737,236	3,092,496

Thousand Shares	2009		
	Preferred	Common	Total
Issued shares at January 1	1,347,140	1,727,540	3,074,680
Treasury shares	(4,135)	(525)	(4,660)
Effect of shares issued/repurchased	3,695	3,765	7,460
Weighted average number of shares at December 31	1,346,700	1,730,780	3,077,480

Diluted Earnings per Share

Diluted earnings per share is calculated by adjusting the weighted average number of shares outstanding to assume conversion of all potentially dilutive shares comprising the net income attributable to equity holders of Ambev of R$8,641.0 (R$7,561.4 and R$5,986.1 in 2010 and 2009 respectively) and the weighted average number of shares outstanding during the year, as follows:

Thousand Shares	2011		
	Preferred	Common	Total
Issued shares at December 31, net of treasury shares	1,363,790	1,747,588	3,111,378
Effect of shares issued/repurchased	12,590	—	12,590
Weighted average number of shares (diluted) at December 31	1,376,380	1,747,588	3,123,968

Thousand Shares	2010		
	Preferred	Common	Total
Issued shares at December 31, net of treasury shares	1,355,260	1,737,236	3,092,496
Effect of shares issued/repurchased	9,971	—	9,971
Weighted average number of shares (diluted) at December 31	1,365,231	1,737,236	3,102,467

Thousand Shares	2009		
	Preferred	Common	Total
Issued shares at December 31, net of treasury shares	1,346,700	1,730,780	3,077,480
Effect of shares issued/repurchased	4,305	275	4,580
Weighted average number of shares (diluted) at December 31	1,351,005	1,731,055	3,082,060

Basic Earnings per Share Before Special Items

The calculation of earnings per share before special items (basic) is based on the net income before special items, attributable to equity holders of Ambev, calculated as follows:

(Expressed in Millions of Brazilian Reais)	2011		
	Preferred	Common	Total
Income attributable to equity holders of Ambev	3,991.4	4,649.6	8,641.0
Special items, after taxes, attributable to equity holders of Ambev	(19.0)	(22.1)	(41.1)
Income before special items (basic), attributable to equity holders of Ambev	4,010.4	4,671.7	8,682.1

(Expressed in millions of Brazilian Reais)	2010		
	Preferred	Common	Total
Income attributable to equity holders of Ambev	3,492.0	4,069.3	7,561.4
Special items, after taxes, attributable to equity holders of Ambev	(56.3)	(65.6)	(121.9)
Income before special items (basic), attributable to equity holders of Ambev	3,548.3	4,134.9	7,683.3

(Expressed in Millions of Brazilian Reais	2009		
	Preferred	Common	Total
Income attributable to equity holders of Ambev	2,760.6	3,225.4	5,986.1
Special items, after taxes, attributable to equity holders of Ambev	89.7	104.8	194.5
Income before special items (basic), attributable to equity holders of Ambev	2,670.9	3,120.6	5,791.6

Diluted Earnings per Share Before Special Items

The calculation of earnings per share before special items (diluted) is based on the net income before special items, attributable to equity holders of Ambev, calculated as follows:

(Expressed in Millions of Brazilian Reais)	2011		
	Preferred	Common	Total
Income attributable to equity holders of Ambev	4,011.1	4,629.9	8,641.0
Special items, after taxes, attributable to equity holders of Ambev	(19.0)	(22.1)	(41.1)
Income before special items (diluted), attributable to equity holders of Ambev	4,030.1	4,652.0	8,682.1

(Expressed in Millions of Brazilian Reais)	2010		
	Preferred	Common	Total
Income attributable to equity holders of Ambev	3,505.8	4,055.6	7,561.4
Special items, after taxes, attributable to equity holders of Ambev	(56.5)	(65.3)	(121.8)
Income before special items (diluted), attributable to equity holders of Ambev	3,562.3	4,120.9	7,683.2

(Expressed in Millions of Brazilian Reais)	2009		
	Preferred	Common	Total
Income attributable to equity holders of Ambev	2,765.1	3,220.9	5,986.1
Special items, after taxes, attributable to equity holders of Ambev	89.8	104.6	194.5
Income before special items (diluted), attributable to equity holders of Ambev	2,675.3	3,116.3	5,791.6

The tables below present the calculation of earnings per share ("EPS"):

(Expressed in Millions of Brazilian Reais)	2011		
	Preferred	Common	Total
Income attributable to equity holders of Ambev	3,991.4	4,649.6	8,641.0
Weighted average numbers of shares	1,363,790.0	1,747,588.0	3,111,378.0
Basic EPS	2.93	2.66	
Income before special items, attributable to equity holders of Ambev	4,010.4	4,671.7	8,682.1
Weighted average numbers of shares	1,363,790.0	1,747,588.0	3,111,378.0
Basic EPS before special items	2.94	2.67	
Income attributable to equity holders of Ambev	4,011.1	4,629.9	8,641.0
Weighted average numbers of shares (diluted)	1,376,380.0	1,747,588.0	3,123,968.0
Diluted EPS	2.91	2.65	
Income before special items, attributable to equity holders of Ambev	4,030.1	4,652.0	8,682.1
Weighted average numbers of shares (diluted)	1,376,380.0	1,747,588.0	3,123,968.0
Diluted EPS before special items	2.93	2.66	

(Expressed in Millions of Brazilian Reais)	2010		
	Preferred	Common	Total
Income attributable to equity holders of Ambev	3,492.0	4,069.3	7,561.4
Weighted average numbers of shares	1,355,260.0	1,737,236.5	3,092,496.5
Basic EPS	2.58	2.34	
Income before special items, attributable to equity holders of Ambev	3,548.3	4,134.9	7,683.2
Weighted average numbers of shares	1,355,260.0	1,737,236.5	3,092,496.5
Basic EPS before special items	2.62	2.38	
Income attributable to equity holders of Ambev	3,505.8	4,055.6	7,561.4
Weighted average numbers of shares (diluted)	1,365,231.0	1,737,237.0	3,102,468.0
Diluted EPS	2.57	2.33	
Income before special items, attributable to equity holders of Ambev	3,562.3	4,120.9	7,683.2
Weighted average numbers of shares (diluted)	1,365,231.0	1,737,237.0	3,102,468.0
Diluted EPS before special items	2.61	2.37	

SECTION 4: STATEMENT OF CHANGES IN EQUITY AND RELATED DISCLOSURES[1]

IAS 1, *PRESENTATION OF FINANCIAL STATEMENTS*

IFRIC 17, *DISTRIBUTIONS OF NON-CASH ASSETS TO OWNERS*

Author's Note

The International Accounting Standards Board has issued several new standards which amend International Accounting Standard (IAS) 1, *Presentation of Financial Statements*. These standards are effective for annual reporting periods after 1 January 2012. Therefore, the requirements of these standards are discussed briefly in author's notes and are not included in the commentary. The effect of these amendments on the Statements of Financial Position, Comprehensive Income, and Cash Flows is discussed in author's notes in section 2, "Statement of Financial Position and Related Disclosures;" section 3, "Statement of Comprehensive Income and Related Disclosures;" and section 5, "Statement of Cash Flows and Related Disclosures;" respectively.

Because these standards are effective for annual periods beginning on or after 1 January 2012, these amendments are not reflected in the commentary in this section. However, these amendments would not affect the availability of illustrative excerpts from survey companies' financial statements.

IFRSs Overview and Comparison to U.S. GAAP

4.01 IAS 1 establishes the basis for presentation of general purpose financial statements to ensure comparability both with the entity's financial statements of previous periods and the financial statements of other entities. This standard establishes overall requirements for the presentation of financial statements, guidelines for their structure, and minimum requirements for their content. IAS 1 requires the presentation of both a statement of comprehensive income and a statement of changes in equity as part of a complete set of financial statements (See section 3.). All changes related to owners in their capacity as owners are shown separately

from nonowner changes. Effective for fiscal years beginning on or after 1 January 2009, an entity should allocate total comprehensive income to the components of equity. IAS 1 no longer permits components of comprehensive income to be presented in the statement of changes in equity.

4.02 IAS 1 also requires disclosures about an entity's capital and dividends, including dividends per share.

4.03 *General purpose financial statements* are those intended to meet the needs of users who are not in a position to require an entity to prepare reports tailored to their particular information needs. Although referred to numerous times in U.S. generally accepted accounting principles (U.S. GAAP), general purpose financial statements are not explicitly defined in Financial Accounting Standards Board (FASB) *Accounting Standards Codification*™ (ASC).

Presentation

IFRSs

4.04 IAS 1 requires an entity to present a *statement of changes in equity*. This statement includes total comprehensive income for the period, showing separately the total amounts attributable to owners of the parent and to noncontrolling interests. IAS 1 requires the components of other comprehensive income (OCI) to be shown in either a single statement of comprehensive income or in a statement of OCI accompanying a statement of income. IAS 1 does not permit an entity to avoid preparing the statement of OCI by presenting these components in the statement of changes in equity. IAS 1 now requires an entity to allocate total comprehensive income to the separate components of equity.

4.05 In addition, for each component of equity, the statement should provide a reconciliation of the carrying amount at the beginning and end of the period. This reconciliation should disclose separately changes resulting from profit or loss, each item of OCI, and transactions with owners in their capacity as owners. Contributions from and distributions to owners and changes in ownership interests in subsidiaries that do not result in a loss of control also should be shown separately. International Financial Reporting Interpretations Committee (IFRIC) 17, *Distributions of Non-cash Assets to Owners*, provides additional guidance for the following two types of nonreciprocal distributions of assets by an entity to its owners acting in their capacity as owners:
- Distributions of noncash assets (for example, items of property, plant, and equipment and businesses as defined in International Financial Reporting Standards (IFRS) 3, *Business Combinations*, and ownership interests in another entity or disposal groups as defined in IFRS 5, *Non-current Assets Held for Sale and Discontinued Operations*)
- Distributions that give owners a choice of receiving either noncash assets or a cash alternative

[1] Unless otherwise indicated, references to International Accounting Standards Board (IASB) standards and interpretations throughout this 2012 edition of *IFRS Financial Statements—Best Practices in Presentation and Disclosure* refer to the version of those standards and interpretations included in the *IFRS 2012* bound volume, the official printed consolidated text of IASB standards and interpretations, including revisions, amendments, and supporting documents, issued as of 1 January 2012.

IFRIC 17 was issued in October 2008 and is effective for annual periods beginning on or after 1 July 2009. Earlier application is permitted.

4.06 An entity should also show separately changes from retrospective application of a change in accounting policy or a retrospective restatement due to an error correction.

4.07 IAS 1 permits the following items to be presented either on the face of the statement of changes in equity or in the notes:
- Amount of dividends recognized as distributions to owners during the period
- Related dividends per share

U.S. GAAP

Author's Note

Under the amendments to FASB Accounting Standards Update (ASU) No. 2011-05, *Comprehensive Income (Topic 220): Presentation of Comprehensive Income*, an entity has the option to present the total of comprehensive income, the components of net income, and the components of OCI either in a single continuous statement of comprehensive income or in two separate but consecutive statements. In both choices, an entity is required to present each component of net income along with total net income, each component of OCI along with a total for OCI, and a total amount for comprehensive income. ASU No. 2011-05 eliminates the option to present the components of OCI as part of the statement of changes in stockholders' equity. The amendments in ASU No. 2011-05 do not change the items that must be reported in OCI or when an item of OCI must be reclassified to net income.

ASU No. 2011-05 is effective for fiscal years, and interim periods within those years, beginning after December 31, 2011, for public companies and December 31, 2012, for nonpublic companies.

In December 2011, FASB issued ASU No. 2011-12, *Comprehensive Income (Topic 220): Deferral of the Effective Date for Amendments to the Presentation of Reclassifications of Items Out of Accumulated Other Comprehensive Income in ASU No. 2011-05*. ASU No. 2011-12 defers specific changes in ASU No. 2011-05 related only to the presentation of reclassification of items out of accumulated OCI to allow the board time to redeliberate whether to present on the face of the financial statements the effects of these reclassifications on the components of net income and OCI for all periods presented. In order to avoid delaying the effective date of ASU No. 2011-05, with this amendment the board instructs entities to continue to report these reclassification adjustments consistent with the presentation requirements in effect before ASU No. 2011-05. It should be noted that the effective dates of ASU No. 2011-12 and the amendments to IAS 1 described previously in this section are different. Until FASB resolves the issues regarding presentation of reclassification adjustments, it is unclear when IFRS or U.S GAAP reporting entities will first present items of OCI in accordance with these amendments.

4.08 As described in the preceding author's note, like IFRS, FASB ASC 220-10-451 requires an entity to present components of comprehensive income either in a single, continuous statement or in two separate but consecutive statements. However, unlike IFRS, in accordance with FASB 505-10-50-2, an entity may present changes in equity in either the basic financial statements or notes thereto or a separate statement. Under Rule 3-04 of Securities and Exchange Commission (SEC) Regulation S-X, an entity should provide an analysis of the changes in each caption of stockholders' equity and noncontrolling interests presented in the balance sheets either in a note or separate statement. FASB ASC 220-10-45-14 provides guidance for reporting OCI in the "Equity" section of a statement of financial position.

4.09 Under FASB ASC 220-10-45-3, financial statements should reflect both comprehensive income (total nonowner changes in equity) and investments by, and distributions to, owners during the period. Thus, it can be inferred, like IFRSs, that an entity should present owner-related changes separately from nonowner-related changes in the statement of changes in equity.

Disclosure

IFRSs

4.10 IAS 1 requires disclosure of information to enable users of the financial statements to evaluate the entity's objectives, policies, and processes for managing capital. This disclosure should include the following:
- (a) Qualitative information about its objectives, policies, and processes for managing capital, including the following:
  - (i) A description of what the entity manages as capital
  - (ii) When an entity is subject to externally imposed capital requirements, the nature of those requirements, and how an entity incorporates those requirements into its capital management policies and procedures
  - (iii) How the entity meets its objectives for managing capital
- (b) Summary quantitative data about what the entity manages as capital, that is, whether certain financial liabilities (for example, some forms of subordinated debt) are considered part of capital or some components are considered part of equity (for example, components arising from cash flow hedges)
- (c) Any changes in (a) and (b) from the previous period
- (d) Whether, during the period, the entity complied with any externally imposed capital requirements to which it was subject
- (e) When the entity has not complied with such externally imposed capital requirements, the consequences of such noncompliance

The entity should base these disclosures on the information provided internally to key management personnel.

4.11 Additional dividend disclosures include the following:
- Amount of dividends proposed or declared before the financial statements were authorized for issue, but not recognized as a distribution to owners during the period, and the related amount per share

- Amount of any cumulative preference dividends not recognized

U.S. GAAP

4.12 Rule 3-04 of SEC Regulation S-X requires an SEC registrant to disclose an analysis of the changes in each caption of other stockholders' equity and noncontrolling interests presented in the balance sheets in a note or separate statement (see also FASB ASC 505-10-S99-1). With respect to any dividends, the entity should state the amount per share and in the aggregate for each class of shares. The entity is not constrained to provide dividend information in either the notes or statement of changes in shareholders' equity but could provide this information in the statement of financial position. The latter is an additional option not available in IFRSs.

4.13 FASB ASC 810-10-50-1A (d) requires an entity to provide in a note disclosure a separate schedule that shows the effects of any changes in a parent's ownership interest in a subsidiary on the equity attributable to the parent.

TABLE 4-1: COMPONENTS OF SHAREHOLDERS' EQUITY

Components Included in the Statement of Shareholders' Equity:	2011	2010	2009[1]
Number of shares of common (ordinary) shares...	49	31	30
Number of shares of treasury (own) shares..........	3	6	6
Common (ordinary) share capital (stock)..............	175	163	140
Preference (preferred) share capital (stock)..........	12	8	5
Share premium (additional paid-in capital, paid-in capital in excess of nominal (par) value)............	119	117	99
Convertible securities	7	21	25
Other equity instruments	13	3	2
Treasury (own) shares.....................................	65	75	66
Shares held by employee benefit trusts (for example, employee stock ownership plans and so on)...	8	6	4
Foreign currency translation reserve.....................	91	90	78
Revaluation reserve (surplus) (related to revaluation of tangible assets).....................	15	16	8
Investment valuation reserve (change in fair value of available for sale financial assets).................	53	61	57
Hedging reserve (cash flow and net investment hedges)...	59	62	52
Share-based compensation reserve.....................	23	29	24
Actuarial gains and losses on pensions................	7	6	5
Retained earnings or deficit (undistributed profits)...	175	170	140
Noncontrolling (minority) interest...........................	120	115	98
Other reserves...	114	106	85

[1] Prior to 1 January 2009, International Accounting Standard 1, *Presentation of Financial Statements*, did not require entities to present changes in equity in a separate statement. Of the 160 survey companies in the 2009 edition of *IFRS Accounting Trends & Techniques*, only 140 companies presented a statement of changes in equity. The remaining 20 companies included this information in a note disclosure. All survey companies in the 2010 and later editions present a statement of changes in equity.

TABLE 4-2: TYPES OF CHANGES IN SHAREHOLDERS' EQUITY

Companies Presenting a Statement of Changes in Shareholders' Equity	2011	2010	2009[1]
Allocation of total comprehensive income only......	54	57	58
Separate allocation of net income and comprehensive income or allocation of one or more components of other comprehensive income..	121	113	82
Total Companies...	**175**	**170**	**140**

Changes Resulting From Transactions With Owners Presented			
Cash dividends..	134	126	99
Preference share dividends.................................	8	8	5
Other dividends and shares issued in lieu of dividends..	9	8	16
Issue of common shares....................................	69	72	57
Issue of preference shares.................................	5	6	6
Rights issues...	6	3	4
Treasury share transactions................................	82	86	76
Share-based compensation.................................	76	115	89
Shares acquired by employee benefit trusts..........	11	17	20
Exercise of stock options..................................	44	38	27
Transfers from reserves to retained earnings........	19	33	30
Share issuance costs.......................................	14	4	11
Changes to the scope of consolidation.................	22	15	34
Acquisition and disposal of noncontrolling (minority) interest..	68	47	54
Dividends paid to noncontrolling (minority) interests...	28	19	19
Government contributions or returns of assets to government..	1	2	3
Adjustment for hyperinflation (with respect to hyperinflation in subsidiaries)...........................	5	2	2
Adjustment to beginning balance due to change in accounting policy.....................................	9	5	8
Adjustment to beginning balances due to error correction...	1	0	1
Other...	90	102	83

[1] Prior to 1 January 2009, International Accounting Standard 1, *Presentation of Financial Statements*, did not require entities to present changes in equity in a separate statement. Of the 160 survey companies in the 2009 edition of *IFRS Accounting Trends & Techniques*, only 140 companies presented a statement of changes in equity. The remaining 20 companies included this information in a note disclosure. All survey companies in the 2010 and later editions present a statement of changes in equity.

Presentation and Disclosure Excerpts

Issue of Common Shares to Non-Controlling Interests and under Dividend Reinvestment and Share Purchase Plans, Issue of Preferred Shares, Issuance Costs, Dividends on Common and Preferred Shares, Disclosure of Changes in Non-Controlling Interests

4.14

Sun Life Financial, Inc. (Dec 2011)

CONSOLIDATED STATEMENTS OF CHANGES IN EQUITY (in part)

For the Years Ended December 31, (In Millions of Canadian Dollars)	2011	2010
Shareholders:		
Preferred shares (Note 16)		
Balance, beginning of year	$ 2,015	$ 1,741
Issued	500	280
Issuance cost, net of taxes	(12)	(6)
Balance, end of year	2,503	2,015
Common shares		
Balance, beginning of year	7,407	7,126
Stock options exercised (Note 20)	48	18
Issued to non-controlling interests (Note 17)	37	—
Issued under dividend reinvestment and share purchase plan (Note 16)	243	263
Balance, end of year	7,735	7,407
Contributed surplus (Note 20)		
Balance, beginning of year	95	81
Share-based payments	13	17
Stock options exercised	(6)	(3)
Balance, end of year	102	95
Retained earnings		
Balance, beginning of year	6,489	5,898
Net Income (loss)	(200)	1,499
Dividends on common shares	(829)	(811)
Dividends on preferred shares	(100)	(93)
Change due to transactions with non-controlling interests (Note 17)	(141)	(4)
Balance, end of year	5,219	6,489
Accumulated other comprehensive income (loss), net of taxes		
Unrealized gains (losses) on available-for-sale assets	387	107
Unrealized cumulative translation differences, net of hedging activities	(505)	—
Unrealized gains (losses) on transfers to investment properties	6	—
Unrealized gains on derivatives designated as cash flow hedges	38	55
Balance, beginning of year	(74)	162
Total other comprehensive income (loss) for the year	122	(236)
Balance, end of year	48	(74)
Total shareholders' equity, end of year	$15,607	$15,932
Participating policyholders:		
Retained earnings		
Balance, beginning of year	$ 117	$ 109
Net Income (loss)	7	8
Balance, end of year	124	117
Accumulated other comprehensive income (loss), net of taxes		
Unrealized cumulative translation differences, net of hedging activities	(2)	—
Balance, beginning of year	(2)	—
Total other comprehensive income (loss) for the year	1	(2)
Balance, end of year	(1)	(2)
Total participating policyholders' equity, end of year	$ 123	$ 115
Non-controlling interests: (Note 17)		
Balance, beginning of year	$ 24	$ 24
Net income (loss)	9	11
Other changes in non-controlling interests	(33)	(11)
Total non-controlling interests, end of year	$ —	$ 24
Total equity	$15,730	$16,071

NOTES TO THE CONSOLIDATED FINANCIAL STATEMENTS (in part)

(Amounts in millions of Canadian dollars except for per share amounts and where otherwise stated)

1. Accounting Policies (in part)

1.A Significant Accounting Policies (in part)

Description of Business

Sun Life Financial Inc. ("SLF Inc.") is a publicly traded company domiciled in Canada and is the holding company of Sun Life Assurance Company of Canada ("Sun Life Assurance"). Both companies are incorporated under the Insurance Companies Act of Canada, and are regulated by the Office of the Superintendent of Financial Institutions, Canada ("OSFI"). SLF Inc. and its subsidiaries are collectively referred to as "us," "our," "ours," "we" or "the Company." We are an internationally diversified financial services organization providing savings, retirement and pension products, and life and health insurance to individuals and groups through our operations in Canada, the United States, the United Kingdom and Asia. We also operate mutual fund and investment management businesses, primarily in Canada, the United States and Asia.

Statement of Compliance

We prepare our Consolidated Financial Statements using International Financial Reporting Standards as issued by the International Accounting Standards Board ("IASB") and the former International Accounting Standards Committee, which includes International Financial Reporting Standards, International Accounting Standards ("IAS"), and interpretations developed by the International Financial Reporting Interpretations Committee ("IFRIC") and the former Standing Interpretations Committee ("SIC"). These various standards are collectively referred to as "IFRS." Our Consolidated Financial Statements are prepared in accordance with IFRS 1 *First Time Adoption of International Financial Reporting Statements*. The accounting policies have been applied consistently within our Consolidated Financial Statements and our opening Consolidated Statement of Financial Position at the transition date of January 1, 2010 ("the Transition Date") prepared for the purposes of transition to IFRS, which are our first annual financial statements in accordance with IFRS. Note 2 contains the required disclosures with regards to our first time adoption of IFRS and the differences from our previous basis of accounting, Canadian generally accepted accounting principles ("GAAP").

Dividends

Dividends payable to holders of shares of SLF Inc. are recognized in the period in which they are authorized or approved. Dividends that have been reinvested in additional common shares under the Dividend Reinvestment and Share Purchase Plan ("DRIP") are also reflected as dividends within retained earnings. Where SLF Inc. has issued common shares from treasury under the DRIP, the additional shares have been reflected in common shares.

16. Share Capital

The authorized share capital of SLF Inc. consists of the following:

- An unlimited number of common shares without nominal or par value. Each common share is entitled to one vote at meetings of the shareholders of SLF Inc. There are no pre-emptive, redemption, purchase or conversion rights attached to the common shares.
- An unlimited number of Class A and Class B non-voting preferred shares, issuable in series. The Board is authorized before issuing the shares, to fix the number, the consideration per share, the designation of, and the rights and restrictions of the Class A and Class B shares of each series, subject to the special rights and restrictions attached to all the Class A and Class B shares. The Board has authorized thirteen series of Class A non-voting preferred shares ("Preferred Shares"), nine of which are outstanding.

The common and preferred shares qualify as capital for Canadian regulatory purposes, and are included in Note 23.

Dividends and Restrictions on the Payment of Dividends

Under provisions of the Insurance Companies Act that apply to each of SLF Inc. and Sun Life Assurance, we are prohibited from declaring or paying a dividend on preferred or common shares if there are reasonable grounds for believing we are, or by paying the dividend would be, in contravention of the requirement that we maintain adequate capital and adequate and appropriate forms of liquidity, that we comply with any regulations in relation to capital and liquidity that are made under the Insurance Companies Act, and that we comply with any order by which OSFI directs us to increase our capital or provide additional liquidity.

We have covenanted that, if a distribution is not paid when due on any outstanding SLEECS issued by Sun Life Capital Trust and Sun Life Capital Trust II, then (i) Sun Life Assurance will not pay dividends on its Public Preferred Shares, if any are outstanding, and (ii) if Sun Life Assurance does not have any Public Preferred Shares outstanding, then SLF Inc. will not pay dividends on its preferred shares or common shares, in each case, until the 12th month (in the case of the SLEECS issued by Sun Life Capital Trust) or 6th month (in the case of SLEECS issued by Sun Life Capital Trust II) following the failure to pay the required distribution in full, unless the required distribution is paid to the holders of SLEECS. Public Preferred Shares means preferred shares issued by Sun Life Assurance which: (a) have been issued to the public (excluding any preferred shares held beneficially by affiliates of Sun Life Assurance); (b) are listed on a recognized stock exchange; and (c) have an aggregate liquidation entitlement of at least $200. As at December 31, 2011, Sun Life Assurance did not have outstanding any shares that qualify as Public Preferred Shares.

The terms of SLF Inc.'s outstanding preferred shares provide that for so long as Sun Life Assurance is a subsidiary of SLF Inc., no dividends on such preferred shares are to be declared or paid if the MCCSR ratio of Sun Life Assurance is then less than 120%.

The terms of SLF Inc.'s outstanding preferred shares also restrict our ability to pay dividends on SLF Inc.'s common shares. Under the terms of our preferred shares, we cannot pay dividends on SLF Inc.'s common shares without the approval of the holders of the preferred shares unless all dividends on the preferred shares for the last completed period for which dividends are payable have been declared and paid or set apart for payment.

Currently, the above limitations do not restrict the payment of dividends on SLF Inc.'s preferred or common shares.

The declaration and payment of dividends on SLF Inc.'s shares are at the sole discretion of the board of directors and will be dependent upon our earnings, financial condition and capital requirements. Dividends may be adjusted or eliminated at the discretion of the board on the basis of these or other considerations.

16.A Common Shares

The changes in shares issued and outstanding common shares for the years ended December 31 are as follows:

Common Shares (In Millions of Shares)	2011 Number of Shares	2011 Amount	2010 Number of Shares	2010 Amount
Balance, January 1	574	$7,407	564	$7,126
Stock options exercised (Note 20)	2	48	1	18
Common shares issued to non-controlling interest (Note 17)	2	37	—	—
Shares issued under the dividend reinvestment and share purchase plan[i]	10	243	9	263
Balance, December 31	588	$7,735	574	$7,407

[i] Under SLF Inc.'s Canadian Dividend Reinvestment and Share Purchase Plan, Canadian-resident common and preferred shareholders may choose to have their dividends automatically reinvested in common shares and may also purchase common shares for cash. For dividend reinvestments, SLF Inc. may, at its option, issue common shares from treasury at a discount of up to 5% to the volume weighted average trading price or direct that common shares be purchased for participants through the Toronto Stock Exchange ("TSX") at the market price. Common shares acquired by participants through optional cash purchases may be issued from treasury or purchased through the TSX at SLF Inc.'s option, in either case at no discount. The common shares issued from treasury for dividend reinvestments during 2011 and 2010 were issued at a discount of 2%. An insignificant number of common shares were issued from treasury for optional cash purchases at no discount.

16.B Preferred Shares

The changes in issued and outstanding preferred shares for the years ended December 31 are as follows:

Class A Preferred Shares (In Millions of Shares)	2011 Number of Shares	2011 Amount	2010 Number of Shares	2010 Amount
Balance, January 1	82	$2,015	71	$1,741
Issued, Series 8R	—	—	11	280
Issued, Series 10R	8	200	—	—
Issued, Series 12R	12	300	—	—
Issuance costs, net of taxes	—	(12)	—	(6)
Balance, December 31	102	$2,503	82	$2,015

Further information on the preferred shares outstanding as at December 31, 2011, is as follows:

Class A Preferred Shares (In Millions of Shares)	Issue Date	Annual Dividend Rate	Annual Dividend Per Share	Earliest Redemption Date[1]	Number of Shares	Face Amount	Net Amount[2]
Series 1	February 25, 2005	4.75%	$1.19	March 31, 2010[3]	16	$400	$394
Series 2	July 15, 2005	4.80%	$1.20	September 30, 2010[3]	13	325	318
Series 3	January 13, 2006	4.45%	$1.11	March 31, 2011[3]	10	250	245
Series 4	October 10, 2006	4.45%	$1.11	December 31, 2011[3]	12	300	293
Series 5	February 2, 2007	4.50%	$1.13	March 31, 2012[3]	10	250	245
Series 6R[4]	May 20, 2009	6.00%	$1.50	June 30, 2014[5]	10	250	246
Series 8R[6]	May 25, 2010	4.35%	$1.09	June 30, 2015[7]	11	280	274
Series 10R[8]	August 12, 2011	3.90%	$0.98	September 30, 2016[9]	8	200	195
Series 12R[10]	November 10, 2011	4.25%	$1.06	December 31, 2016[11]	12	300	293
Total preferred shares					102	$2,555	$2,503

[1] Redemption of all preferred shares is subject to regulatory approval.

[2] Net of after-tax issuance costs.

[3] On or after the earliest redemption date, SLF Inc. may redeem these shares in whole or in part, at a premium that declines from 4% of the par amount to Nil over the next following four years.

[4] On June 30, 2014, and every five years thereafter, the annual dividend rate will reset to an annual rate equal to the 5-year Government of Canada bond yield plus 3.79%. Holders of the Series 6R Shares will have the right, at their option, to convert their Series 6R Shares into Class A Non-Cumulative Floating Rate Preferred Shares Series 7QR ("Series 7QR Shares") on June 30, 2014 and every five years thereafter. Holders of Series 7QR Shares will be entitled to receive floating non-cumulative quarterly dividends at an annual rate equal to the then 3-month Government of Canada treasury bill yield plus 3.79%.

[5] On June 30, 2014 and June 30 each fifth year thereafter, SLF Inc. may redeem these shares in whole or in part, at par.

[6] On June 30, 2015, and every five years thereafter, the annual dividend rate will reset to an annual rate equal to the 5-year Government of Canada bond yield plus 1.41%. Holders of the Series 8R Shares will have the right, at their option, to convert their Series 8R Shares into Class A Non-Cumulative Floating Rate Preferred Shares Series 9QR ("Series 9QR Shares") on June 30, 2015 and every five years thereafter. Holders of Series 9QR Shares will be entitled to receive floating non-cumulative quarterly dividends at an annual rate equal to the then 3-month Government of Canada treasury bill yield plus 1.41%.

[7] On June 30, 2015 and June 30 each fifth year thereafter, SLF Inc. may redeem these shares in whole or in part, at par.

[8] On September 30, 2016, and every five years thereafter, the annual dividend rate will reset to an annual rate equal to the 5-year Government of Canada bond yield plus 2.17%. Holders of the Series 10R Shares will have the right, at their option, to convert their Series 10R Shares into Class A Non-Cumulative Floating Rate Preferred Shares Series 11QR ("Series 11QR Shares") on September 30, 2016 every five years thereafter. Holders of Series 11QR Shares will be entitled to receive floating non-cumulative quarterly dividends at an annual rate equal to the then 3-month Government of Canada treasury bill yield plus 2.17%.

[9] On September 30, 2016 and September 30 each fifth year thereafter, SLF Inc. may redeem these shares in whole or in part, at par.

[10] On December 31, 2016, and every five years thereafter, the annual dividend rate will reset to an annual rate equal to the 5-year Government of Canada bond yield plus 2.73%. Holders of the Series 12R Shares will have the right, at their option, to convert their Series 12R Shares into Class A Non-Cumulative Floating Rate Preferred shares Series 13QR ("Series 13QR Shares") on December 31, 2016 and on every five years thereafter. Holders of Series 13QR Shares will be entitled to receive floating non-cumulative quarterly dividends at an annual rate equal to the then 3-month Government of Canada treasury bill yield plus 2.73%.

[11] On December 31, 2016 and December 31 each fifth year thereafter, SLF Inc. may redeem these shares in whole or in part, at par.

17. Non-Controlling Interests in Subsidiaries

Non-controlling interests in our Consolidated Statements of Financial Position, Consolidated Statements of Changes in Equity, and Net income (loss) attributable to non-controlling interests in our Consolidated Statements of Operations, consisted of non-controlling interests in McLean Budden Limited until the fourth quarter of 2011.

In the fourth quarter of 2011, we purchased the minority shares of McLean Budden Limited, our investment management subsidiary for consideration of approximately $144 plus additional consideration which will be based on the attaining of performance targets. The consideration consisted of cash of $48, common shares of SLF Inc. of $37 with the remaining amount payable in promissory notes. The difference between the consideration paid and the non-controlling interest acquired was recorded as an adjustment to the equity attributable to the SLF Inc. shareholders. Subsequent to the purchase of the minority shares, all of the shares of McLean Budden Limited were transferred to our subsidiary MFS.

Hybrid Securities—Issue, Dividends, and Repayment

4.15

Woori Finance Holdings Co., Ltd. (Dec 2011)

CONSOLIDATED STATEMENTS OF CHANGES IN EQUITY (in part)

Korean Won (In Millions)	Capital Stock	Hybrid Securities	Capital Surplus	Other Equity	Retained Earnings	Controlling Interests	Non-Controlling Interests	Total Equity
January 1, 2011	4,030,077	—	180,105	1,002,019	10,489,339	15,701,540	4,563,214	20,264,754
Net income	—	—	—	—	2,136,828	2,136,828	296,452	2,433,280
Dividends	—	—	—	—	(201,503)	(201,503)	(36,687)	(238,190)
Changes in investment in consolidated subsidiaries	—	—	295	—	—	295	(217)	78
Changes in other capital surplus	—	—	(4,632)	—	—	(4,632)	355,418	350,786
Variation of available-for-sale financial assets	—	—	—	(403,737)	—	(403,737)	28,860	(374,877)
Changes in equity of jointly controlled entities and associates	—	—	—	(20,030)	—	(20,030)	(17,572)	(37,602)
Cash flow hedge	—	—	—	13,449	—	13,449	11,142	24,591
Foreign currency translation	—	—	—	3,149	—	3,149	(635)	2,514
Changes in other equity	—	—	—	(8,428)	—	(8,428)	(16,340)	(24,768)
Changes in equity of non-controlling interests	—	—	—	—	—	—	22,292	22,292
Dividends to hybrid securities	—	—	—	—	(1,942)	(1,942)	(156,532)	(158,474)
Issue of hybrid securities	—	309,010	—	—	—	309,010	—	309,010
Repayment of hybrid securities	—	—	—	(1)	—	(1)	(499,999)	(500,000)
December 31, 2011	4,030,077	309,010	175,768	586,421	12,422,722	17,523,998	4,549,396	22,073,394

NOTES TO THE CONSOLIDATED FINANCIAL STATEMENTS (in part)

1. General (in part)

(1) Woori Finance Holdings Co., Ltd.

Woori Finance Holdings Co., Ltd. (hereinafter referred to "Woori Finance Holdings" or "Parent" or the "Company") was incorporated under the laws of the Republic of Korea on March 27, 2001, to manage the following five financial institutions: Woori Bank, Kyongnam Bank, Kwangju Bank, Woori Credit Card Co., Ltd. (formerly known as Peace Bank of Korea which merged into Woori Bank on March 31, 2004) and Woori Investment Bank (which merged into Woori Bank on July 31, 2003), whose shares were contributed to the Company by the Korea Deposit Insurance Corporation (the "KDIC") in accordance with the provisions of the Financial Holding Company Act. As of December 31, 2011, the Company controls the following entities: three commercial banks, which include Woori Bank (formerly known as Hanvit Bank), Kyongnam Bank and Kwangju Bank (collectively referred to as the "Bank Subsidiaries"); Woori FIS Co., Ltd. (formerly known as Woori Finance Information System Co., Ltd., "Woori FIS"); Woori F&I Co., Ltd. ("Woori F&I"); Woori Investment & Securities Co., Ltd. ("Woori Investment & Securities"); Woori Asset Management Co., Ltd. ("Woori Asset Management," formerly known as Woori Credit Suisse Asset Management Co., Ltd.); Woori Private Equity Co., Ltd. ("Woori PE"); Woori Financial Co.,

Ltd. ("Woori Financial," formerly known as Hanmi Capital Co., Ltd.) and Woori FG Savings Bank; all collectively referred to as "Woori Subsidiaries." Several of the Woori Subsidiaries also have other subsidiaries of which the Company is now the ultimate financial holding company. As a result of its functional restructuring, as of December 31, 2011, the Company consolidates Woori Bank, nine other subsidiaries, and 133 2nd-tier subsidiaries including Woori Credit Information Co., Ltd.

Upon incorporation, the Company's stock amounted to 3,637,293 million Won, consisting of 727,458,609 common shares (5,000 Won per share). As a result of several capital increases, exercise of warrants and conversion rights since incorporation, as of December 31, 2011, the Company's stock amounted to 4,030,077 million Won, consisting of 806,015,340 common shares issued and outstanding of which KDIC owns 459,198,609 shares (56.97% ownership).

On June 24, 2002, the Company listed its common shares on the Korea Exchange. On September 29, 2003, the Company registered with the Securities and Exchange Commission in the United States of America and listed its American Depositary Shares on the New York Stock Exchange.

2. Significant Basis of Preparation and Accounting Policies (in part)

(1) Basis of Presentation

The Group has adopted International Financial Reporting Standards ("IFRS") as issued by the International Accounting

Standards Board ("IASB") for the annual periods beginning on January 1, 2011. In accordance with IFRS 1 *First-time adoption of International Financial Reporting Standards*, the transition date to IFRS is January 1, 2010. An explanation of how the transition to IFRS has affected the consolidated statements of financial position as of January 1, 2010 (date of transition) and December 31, 2010, and the consolidated statements of comprehensive income for the year ended December 31, 2010 of the Group are provided in Note 47 "Transition to IFRSs."

The Group operates primarily in Korea and its official accounting records are maintained in Korean Won. The United States dollar ("U.S. dollar" or "US$" or "USD") amounts are provided herein as supplementary information solely for the convenience of readers outside Korea. Korean Won amounts are expressed in U.S. Dollars at the rate of 1,158.5 Korean Won to US$1.00, the noon buying exchange rate in effect on December 30, 2011, as quoted by the Federal Reserve Bank of New York in the United States. Such convenience translation into U.S. Dollars should not be construed as representa-

tions that Korean Won amounts have been, could have been, or could in the future be, converted at this or any other rate of exchange.

The Group's consolidated financial statements have been prepared based on the historical cost method except for specific non-current assets and certain financial assets or liabilities reported at fair value.

(23) Earnings per Share ("EPS")

Basic EPS is calculated by earnings subtracting the dividends paid to holders of preferred stock and hybrid securities from the net income attributable to ordinary shareholders from the statements of comprehensive income and dividing by the weighted average number of common shares outstanding. Diluted EPS is calculated by adjusting the earnings and number of shares for the effects of all dilutive potential common shares.

27. Capital Stock and Capital Surplus

(1) The number of authorized shares is as follows:

	January 1, 2010	December 31, 2010	December 31, 2011
Authorized shares of common stock	2,400,000,000 shares	2,400,000,000 shares	2,400,000,000 shares
Par value	5,000 Won	5,000 Won	5,000 Won
Issued shares of common stock	806,015,340 shares	806,015,340 shares	806,015,340 shares

As of January 1, 2010, December 31, 2010 and December 31, 2011, the Group holds 2,560 shares (18 million Won), 2,561 shares (18 million Won), 1,999 shares (14 million Won) of its treasury stock, respectively, acquired as a buyback of

odd-lot share when exchanging the stock of Woori Investment & Securities.

(2) Capital surplus are as follows (Unit: Korean Won in millions):

	January 1, 2010	December 31, 2010	December 31, 2011
Capital in excess of par value	109,025	109,025	109,025
Other capital surplus	71,448	71,080	66,743
Total	180,473	180,105	175,768

28. Hybrid Securities

The bond-type hybrid securities classified as shareholder's equity are as follows (Unit: Korean Won in millions):

	Issuance Date	Maturity	Annual Interest Rate (%)	Amount
The 1st bond-type hybrid securities	November 22, 2011	November 22, 2041	5.91	310,000
Expense of issuance				(990)
				309,010

Although these instruments have a contractual maturity date, November 22, 2041 and stipulated contractual interest payments, the contractual agreements allow Group to indefinitely extend the maturity date and defer the payment of interest without a modification of the other terms of the instrument

such as interest rate, etc. In addition, the Group has the ability to not pay dividends on ordinary stock and there are no other agreements that would require the Group to pay interest on the hybrid securities.

30. Retained Earnings

(1) Retained earnings are as follows (Unit: Korean Won in millions):

	January 1, 2010	December 31, 2010	December 31, 2011
Legal reserves	783,301	885,903	1,005,401
Voluntary reserves	6,539,000	7,379,000	8,256,000
Retained earnings carried forward	1,958,046	2,224,436	3,161,321
	9,280,347	10,489,339	12,422,722

Pursuant to Article 53 of the Financial Holding Company Act, legal reserves are appropriated at no less than 10% of net income until reaching an amount equal to the Company's capital.

(2) Changes in retained earnings are as follows (Unit: Korean Won in millions):

	For the Years Ended December 31	
	2010	2011
Beginning balance	9,280,347	10,489,339
Net income	1,288,856	2,136,828
Dividends on common stock	(80,601)	(201,503)
Dividends on hybrid securities	—	(1,942)
Others	737	—
Ending balance	10,489,339	12,422,722

31. Planned Regulatory Reserve for Credit Loss

In accordance with the Regulations for Supervision of Financial Holding Companies ("RSFHC"), if the estimated provision for credit loss determined in accordance with IAS 39 *Financial instruments: Recognition and Measurement* is lower than those in accordance with the RSFHC, the Group shall disclose the difference as the regulatory reserve for credit loss.

(1) Balances of the planned regulatory reserve for credit loss are 553,010 million Won and 1,351,766 million Won as of December 31, 2010 and 2011, respectively.

(2) Reserve, net income attributable to shareholders and earning per share after the reserve provided are as follows (Unit: Korean Won in millions, except for earning per share):

	For the Years Ended December 31	
	2010	2011
Planned regulatory reserve for credit loss	(553,010)	(798,756)
Net income after the planned reserve provided	735,846	1,338,072
Earnings per share after the planned reserve provided[*]	913	1,658

[*] Earnings per share after the planned reserve provided is calculated by deducting dividends on hybrid securities from net income after the planned reserve provided.

41. Earnings Per Share ("EPS")

Basic EPS is calculated by dividing net income by weighted average number of common shares outstanding (Unit: Korean Won in millions except for EPS):

	For the Years Ended December 31	
	2010	2011
Net income attributable to common shareholders	1,288,856	2,136,828
Dividends to hybrid securities	—	(1,942)
Net income attributable to common shareholders	1,288,856	2,134,886
Weighted average number of common shares outstanding	806,012,779 shares	806,012,901 shares
Basic EPS	1,599	2,649

Diluted EPS is equal to basic EPS because there is no dilution effect for the years ended December 31, 2010 and 2011, respectively.

Cash Dividends and Dividends to Non-Controlling Interests, Increase in Share Capital From Dividends Paid in Shares, Purchases of Treasury Stock, Reduction in Share Capital From Resissue of Treasury Stock

4.16

Sanofi (formerly Sanofi-Aventis) (Dec 2011)

CONSOLIDATED STATEMENTS OF CHANGES IN EQUITY (in part)

(€ Million)	Share Capital	Additional Paid-In Capital and Retained Earnings	Treasury Shares	Stock Options and Other Share-Based Payment	Other Compre-hensive Income[1]	Attributable to Equity Holders of Sanofi	Attributable to Non-Controlling Interests	Total Equity
Balance at December 31, 2010	2,622	50,169	(371)	1,829	(1,152)	53,097	191	53,288
Other comprehensive income for the period	—	(539)	—	—	192	(347)	(12)	(359)
Net income for the period	—	5,693	—	—	—	5,693	241	5,934
Comprehensive income for the period	—	5,154	—	—	192	5,346	229	5,575
Dividend paid out of 2010 earnings (€2.50 per share)	—	(3,262)	—	—	—	(3,262)	—	(3,262)
Payment of dividends and equivalent to non-controlling interests	—	—	—	—	—	—	(252)	(252)
Increase in share capital—dividends paid in shares[2]	76	1,814	—	—	—	1,890	—	1,890
Share repurchase program[2]	—	—	(1,074)	—	—	(1,074)	—	(1,074)
Reduction in share capital[2]	(21)	(488)	509	—	—	—	—	—
Share-based payment plans:	—	—	—	—	—			
• Exercise of stock options	4	66	—	—	—	70	—	70
• Issuance of restricted shares	1	(1)	—	—	—	—	—	—
• Proceeds from sale of treasury shares on exercise of stock options	—	—	3	—	—	3	—	3
• Value of services obtained from employees	—	—	—	143	—	143	—	143
• Tax effects on the exercise of stock options	—	—	—	8	—	8	—	8
Change in non-controlling interests without loss of control	—	(2)	—	—	—	(2)	2	—
Balance at December 31, 2011	2,682	53,450	(933)	1,980	(960)	56,219	170	56,389

[1] See Note D.15.7.
[2] See Notes D.15.3., D.15.4. and D.15.5.

NOTES TO THE CONSOLIDATED FINANCIAL STATEMENTS (in part)

Introduction

Sanofi and its subsidiaries ("Sanofi" or "the Group") is a diversified global healthcare leader engaged in the research, development and marketing of therapeutic solutions focused on patient needs. Sanofi has fundamental strengths in the healthcare field, operating via six growth platforms: Emerging Markets, Diabetes Solutions, Human Vaccines, Consumer Health Care (CHC), Animal Health and Innovative Products. Sanofi, the parent company, is a société anonyme (a form of limited liability company) incorporated under the laws of France. The registered office is at 54, rue La Boétie, 75008 Paris, France.

Sanofi is listed in Paris (Euronext: SAN) and New York (NYSE: SNY).

The consolidated financial statements for the year ended December 31, 2011, and the notes thereto, were adopted by the Sanofi Board of Directors on February 7, 2012.

A. Basis of Preparation (in part)

A.1. International Financial Reporting Standards (IFRS)

The consolidated financial statements cover the twelve-month periods ending December 31, 2011, 2010 and 2009.

In accordance with Regulation No. 1606/2002 of the European Parliament and Council of July 19, 2002 on the application of international accounting standards, Sanofi has presented its consolidated financial statements in accordance with IFRS since January 1, 2005. The term "IFRS" refers collectively to international accounting and financial reporting standards (IASs and IFRSs) and to interpretations of the interpretations committees (SIC and IFRIC), mandatorily applicable as of December 31, 2011.

The consolidated financial statements of Sanofi as of December 31, 2011 have been prepared in compliance with IFRS as issued by the International Accounting Standards Board (IASB) and with IFRS endorsed by the European Union as of December 31, 2011.

IFRS endorsed by the European Union as of December 31, 2011 are available under the heading "IAS/IFRS, Standards and Interpretations" via the following web link:

http://ec.europa.eu/internal_market/accounting/ias/index_en.htm

The consolidated financial statements have been prepared in accordance with the IFRS general principles of fair presentation, going concern, accrual basis of accounting, consistency of presentation, materiality, and aggregation.

New standards, amendments and interpretations applicable in 2011 with an impact on the consolidated financial statements are described in Note A.2. For standards, amendments and interpretations issued by the IASB that are not mandatorily applicable in 2011, refer to Note B.28.

B. Summary of Significant Accounting Policies (in part)

B.24.3. Restricted Share Plans

Sanofi may award restricted share plans to certain of its employees. The terms of these plans may make the award contingent on performance criteria for some grantees.

In accordance with IFRS 2, an expense equivalent to the fair value of such plans is recognized on a straight line basis over the vesting period of the plan, with the matching entry credited to equity. Depending on the country, the vesting period of such plans is either two or four years. Plans with a two-year vesting period are subject to a two-year lock-up period.

The fair value of stock option plans is based on the fair value of the equity instruments granted, representing the fair value of the services received during the vesting period. The fair value of an equity instrument granted under a plan is the market price of the share at the grant date, adjusted for expected dividends during the vesting period.

D. Presentation of the Financial Statements (in part)

D.15. Consolidated Shareholders' Equity (in part)

D.15.1. Share Capital

The share capital of €2,681,837,622 consists of 1,340,918,811 shares with a par value of €2.

Treasury shares held by the Group are as follows:

	Number of Shares in Millions	%
December 31, 2011	17.2	1.28%
December 31, 2010	6.1	0.46%
December 31, 2009	9.4	0.71%
January 1, 2009	10.0	0.76%

Treasury shares are deducted from shareholders' equity. Gains and losses on disposals of treasury shares are taken directly to equity and not recognized in net income for the period.

Movements in the share capital of the Sanofi parent company over the last three years are presented below:

Date	Transaction	Number of Shares	Share Capital[1]	Additional Paid-In Capital[1]
January 1, 2009		1,315,525,463	2,631	6,604
During 2009	Capital increase by exercise of stock subscription options	2,953,589	6	134
December 31, 2009		1,318,479,052	2,637	6,738
During 2010	Capital increase by exercise of stock subscription options	430,033	1	17
Board of Directors meeting of April 28, 2010	Capital reduction by cancellation of treasury shares	(7,911,300)	(16)	(404)
December 31, 2010		1,310,997,785	2,622	6,351
During 2011	Capital increase by exercise of stock subscription options	1,593,369	4	66
During 2011	Capital increase by issue of restricted shares	587,316	1	(1)
June 16, 2011	Capital increase by payment of dividends in shares	38,139,730	76	1,814
Board of Directors meeting of July 27, 2011	Capital reduction by cancellation of treasury shares	(2,328,936)	(5)	(116)
Board of Directors meeting of November 2, 2011	Capital reduction by cancellation of treasury shares	(8,070,453)	(16)	(372)
December 31, 2011		1,340,918,811	2,682	7,742

[1] € million amounts.

For equity related disclosures as required under IFRS 7, refer to Note B.27.

Following the exercise of Sanofi stock options, 1,593,369 shares were issued in the 2011 fiscal year.

In addition, 585,782 bonus shares under the 2009 France restricted share plan were vested and issued in 2011.

D.15.2. Restricted Share Plans

Restricted share plans are accounted for in accordance with the policies described in Note B.24.3.

- The Board of Directors meeting held on March 9, 2011, approved a restricted share plan with performance conditions for 3,330,650 shares, including 1,934,610 shares vested at the end of a four-year service period, and 1,396,040 shares vested at the end of a two-year service period and then non-transferable for a two-year period. The fair value of a share awarded is the market price of the share as of the grant date (€50.28), adjusted for the dividends expected during the vesting period.

The fair value of this restricted share plan is €125 million.

- The Board of Directors meeting held on October 27, 2010 decided to award a worldwide restricted share plan, under which 20 shares were granted to each employee of the Group. The fair value per share granted is the market price of the share as of the date of grant (€49.53), adjusted for expected dividends during the vesting period. A total of 2,101,340 shares were granted under this plan.

The fair value of this restricted share plan is €67 million.

- The Board of Directors meeting held on March 1, 2010 decided to award a discretionary restricted share plan. A total of 1,231,249 shares were granted, 699,524 of which will vest after a four-year service period and 531,725 of which will vest after a two-year service period but will be subject to a further two-year lock-up period. The fair value per share granted is the market price of the share as of the date of grant (€54.82), adjusted for expected dividends during the vesting period.

The fair value of this restricted share plan is €50 million.

- The Board of Directors meeting held on March 2, 2009 decided to award a restricted share plan. A total of 1,194,064 shares were granted, 604,004 of which will vest after a four-year service period and 590,060 of which will vest after a two-year service period but will be subject to a further two-year lock-up period (including 65,000 shares which are also contingent upon performance conditions). The fair value per share granted is the market price per share as of the date of grant (€41.10), adjusted for expected dividends during the vesting period.

The fair value of this restricted share plan is €37 million.

At December 31, 2011, the total expense for the restricted share plans amounted to €84 million compared with €36 million at December 31, 2010 and €11 million at December 31, 2009.

The number of restricted shares outstanding at December 31, 2011 was 7,062,324, including 3,266,840 under the plan approved in March 2011, 2,063,440 under the plan approved in October 2010, 1,176,038 under the plan approved in March 2010 and 556,006 under the 2009 plan. There were 4,467,968 restricted shares outstanding at December 31, 2010 and 1,181,049 at December 31, 2009.

D.15.3. Capital Increase

On May 6, 2011, the General Meeting of Sanofi shareholders approved the payment of a €2.50 dividend per share for the 2010 fiscal year, with an option for payment in cash or in newly-issued shares of the Company. As a result of the exercise of this option by shareholders representing 57.8% of the shares, 38,139,730 new shares were issued for payment of the dividend in shares. The shares issued represent 2.9% of the capital, which is an increase of €76 million in capital and €1,814 million in additional paid-in capital (net of transactions costs to issue dividends in shares).

There were no share issues reserved for employee share ownership plans in 2009, 2010 or 2011.

D.15.4. Repurchase of Sanofi Shares

The Sanofi Shareholders' Annual General Meeting of May 6, 2011 authorized a share repurchase program for a period of 18 months. Under this program, the Group repurchased 21,655,140 shares in 2011 for a total amount of €1,074 million.

The Sanofi Shareholders' Annual General Meeting of May 17, 2010 authorized a share repurchase program for a period of 18 months. The Group has not repurchased any of its own shares under this program.

Under the share repurchase program authorized by the Shareholders' Annual General Meeting of April 17, 2009, the Group repurchased 5,871,026 shares in 2010 for a total of €321 million.

There were no stock buybacks in 2009.

D.15.5. Reduction in Share Capital

The Board of Directors on November 2, 2011 approved the cancellation of 8,070,453 treasury shares (€388 million), representing 0.60% of the share capital as of that date.

The Sanofi Board of Directors meeting held on July 27, 2011 decided to cancel 2,328,936 treasury shares (€121 million), representing 0.17% of the share capital as of that date.

The Sanofi Board of Directors on April 28, 2010 decided to cancel 7,911,300 treasury shares (€420 million), representing 0.60% of the share capital as of that date.

These cancellations had no effect on consolidated shareholders' equity.

D.16. Non-Controlling Interests

Non-controlling interests in consolidated companies break down as follows:

(€ Million)	December 31, 2011	December 31, 2010	December 31, 2009
Non-controlling interests of ordinary shareholders:			
• BMS[1]	34	41	104
• Zentiva	21	28	32
• Aventis Pharma Ltd India	58	75	73
• Maphar	7	7	7
• Sanofi-aventis Korea	7	7	5
• Shantha Biotechnics	10	9	12
• Other	33	24	25
Total	170	191	258

[1] Under the terms of the agreements with BMS (see Note C.1.), the BMS share of the net assets of entities majority-owned by Sanofi is recognized in Non-controlling interests (refer to the statement of changes in equity).

Private Placement of Convertible Debentures, Conversion of Preferred Shares, Share Issue for Business Acquisition, Exercise of Share Options, Share Purchase Loans Issued to Key Employees

4.17

Counsel Corporation (Dec 2011)

CONSOLIDATED STATEMENT OF CHANGES IN EQUITY (in part)

(In thousands of Canadian dollars)

	Attributable to Shareholders of the Company								
	Share Capital (Note 19) $	Share Based Compensation $	Foreign Currency Translation $	Contributed Surplus $	Accumulated Other Comprehensive Income (Loss) $	Retained Earnings (Deficit) $	Total $	Non-Controlling Interest $	Total Shareholders' Equity $
Balance—January 1, 2010	170,523	5,179	—	48,690	75	(190,584)	33,883	73,146	107,029
Common shares purchased for cancellation	(716)	—	—	734	—	—	18	—	18
Net investment by non-controlling interest	—	—	—	(333)	—	—	(333)	1,950	1,617
Share based compensation	—	163	—	—	—	—	163	—	163
Foreign currency translation adjustment	—	—	(330)	—	—	—	(330)	—	(330)
Net income (loss)	—	—	—	—	—	(4,655)	(4,655)	2,995	(1,660)
Balance—December 31, 2010	169,807	5,342	(330)	49,091	75	(195,239)	28,746	78,091	106,837
Conversion of Series B preferred shares	11,490	—	—	—	—	—	11,490	—	11,490
Issuance of common shares	6,196	—	—	—	—	—	6,196	—	6,196
Exercise of stock options	543	—	—	—	—	—	543	—	543
Net investment by non-controlling interest	—	—	(206)	16	—	—	(190)	(28,860)	(29,050)
Share based compensation	—	1,436	—	—	—	—	1,436	—	1,436
Foreign currency translation adjustment	—	—	1,565	—	—	—	1,565	(206)	1,359
Net income (loss)	—	—	—	—	—	25,511	25,511	7,773	33,284
Balance—December 31, 2011	188,036	6,778	1,029	49,107	75	(169,728)	75,297	56,798	132,095

NOTES TO THE CONSOLIDATED FINANCIAL STATEMENTS (in part)

(In thousands of Canadian dollars, except per share data)

1. General Information

Counsel Corporation ("Counsel" or "the Company"), founded in 1979, is a financial services company that operates through its individually branded businesses, primarily in mortgage lending, distressed and surplus capital asset transactions, real estate finance and private equity investments. The address of its registered office is 1 Toronto Street, Suite 700, P.O. Box 3, Toronto, Ontario, M5C 2V6.

Counsel currently operates in four business sectors: mortgage lending, asset liquidation, private equity (which includes our case goods business), and real estate.

Counsel carries on its mortgage lending business ("Mortgage Lending") through its subsidiary, Street Capital Financial Corporation ("Street Capital"). Street Capital is a Canadian prime residential mortgage lender. Counsel acquired Street Capital on May 31, 2011.

Counsel's asset liquidation business ("Asset Liquidation") is carried on through a U.S. subsidiary, Counsel RB Capital LLC ("Counsel RB"). Counsel RB specializes in the acquisition and disposition of distressed and surplus assets throughout the United States and Canada, including industrial machinery and equipment, real estate, inventories, accounts receivable and distressed debt.

Counsel carries on its private equity business ("Private Equity") through its wholly-owned subsidiary, Knight's Bridge Capital Partners Inc. ("Knight's Bridge"). Knight's Bridge is responsible for sourcing and managing Counsel's portfolio investment opportunities. Knight's Bridge is an opportunistic and diversified financial service provider with a focus on building portfolio companies into market leaders.

Counsel's case goods business ("Case Goods") is carried on through a Canadian limited partnership, Fleetwood Fine Furniture LP ("Fleetwood"), which was acquired effective April 30, 2006. Fleetwood provides high quality customized case goods for large, upscale hotel chains, primarily in North America, with over 90% of its revenues generated in the United States. Fleetwood serves a focused niche, being the "upscale" and "upper upscale" strata of the hospitality industry.

Counsel's real estate business ("Real Estate") consists of the ownership and development of its own properties as well as the provision of real estate property and asset management services to third parties.

2. Basis of Preparation

The Company prepares its financial statements in accordance with Canadian generally accepted accounting principles as set out in the Handbook of the Canadian Institute of Chartered Accountants ("CICA Handbook"). In 2010, the CICA Handbook was revised to incorporate International Financial Reporting Standards ("IFRS"), and requires publicly accountable enterprises to apply such standards effective for years beginning on or after January 1, 2011. Accordingly the Company has commenced reporting on this basis in its 2011 consolidated financial statements. In these financial statements, the term "Canadian GAAP" refers to Canadian GAAP before the adoption of IFRS.

These consolidated financial statements have been prepared in accordance with IFRS applicable to the preparation of financial statements. Subject to certain transition elections disclosed in Note 32, the Company has consistently applied the same accounting policies in its opening IFRS consolidated statement of financial position at January 1, 2010 and throughout all the periods presented, as if these policies had always been in effect. Note 32 discloses the impact of the transition to IFRS on the Company's reported statement of financial position, financial performance and cash flows, including the nature and effect of significant changes in accounting policies from those used in the Company's consolidated financial statements for the year ended December 31, 2010 prepared in accordance with Canadian GAAP. Comparative figures for 2010 in these financial statements have been restated to give effect to these changes.

The policies applied in these consolidated financial statements are based on IFRS issued and outstanding as of March 22, 2012, the date the Board of Directors approved the financial statements.

The consolidated financial statements should be read in conjunction with the Company's Canadian GAAP annual financial statements for the year ended December 31, 2010. Note 32 discloses IFRS information for the year ended December 31, 2010 that is material to an understanding of these consolidated financial statements.

17. Convertible Debentures

	December 31, 2011 $	December 31, 2010 $	January 1, 2010 $
Liability component of convertible debentures	12,000	—	—
Less: Deferred financing costs	107	—	—
	11,893	—	—

Counsel partially financed the acquisition of Street Capital (Note 5) by a non-brokered private placement of convertible unsecured subordinated debentures (the "Debentures") for gross proceeds of $12,000 on May 31, 2011. The Debentures are convertible at $1.25 per common share. The Debentures bear interest at 8% per annum, payable quarterly, in cash on the last day of March, June, September and December of each year, commencing September 30, 2011, and mature on May 31, 2014. The Company has the right to require conversion of the Debentures when the market price per common share is equal to or greater than $1.75 for 20 consecutive trading days.

19. Share Capital

	Number of Shares			Share Capital		
Issued and Outstanding ('000s)	**December 31, 2011**	**December 31, 2010**	**January 1, 2010**	**December 31, 2011 $**	**December 31, 2010 $**	**January 1, 2010 $**
Common shares, without par value	85,148	61,520	61,820	$191,226	$172,997	$173,865
Share purchase loans	—	—	—	(3,190)	(3,190)	(3,342)
Total share capital	85,148	61,520	61,820	$188,036	$169,807	$170,523

The authorized capital stock consists of an unlimited number of common and preferred shares. See below for details on preferred shares.

During 2010, the Company purchased 300,000 common shares for cancellation.

On January 25, 2011, all the Series B preferred shares were converted into common shares at $0.75 per share. This resulted in the issuance of 15,384,617 common shares.

On May 31, 2011, the Company issued 6,883,331 common shares as part of the purchase price for Street Capital and related acquisition expenses. See Note 5 for details of the acquisition.

In June 2011, 1,350,000 stock options to purchase common shares were exercised, and in October 2011, an additional 10,000 stock options were exercised.

At September 30, 2010 the Company had share purchase loans receivable of $3,190 (December 31, 2010—$3,190 and January 1, 2010—$3,342). The share purchase loans were granted to certain key employees and former employees. The loans are collateralized by the shares purchased and personal guarantees. At September 30, 2011, the share purchase loans outstanding were for the purchase of 1,590,511 (December 31, 2010—1,590,511 and January 1, 2010—1,890,511) common shares of the Company. These loans have various maturity dates through to January 19, 2016. All the loans are non-interest bearing.

20. Convertible Preferred Shares

	December 31, 2011	December 31, 2010	January 1, 2010
Liability component of convertible preferred shares Series B	—	11,538	11,538

The number of Series B preferred shares outstanding at December 31, 2010 and January 1, 2010 was 6,009,616. On January 25, 2011, all the Series B preferred shares were converted into common shares at $0.75 per share. This resulted in the issuance of 15,384,617 common shares.

On December 19, 2003, the Company completed a private placement of a new series of convertible preferred shares for proceeds of US$15,000, comprised of 10 million Series A preferred shares at a price of US$1.50 per share. On July 24, 2009 the Series A preferred shares were redeemed in full from proceeds from a private placement of common shares and a new series, Series B, of preferred shares, for aggregate proceeds of approximately

$23,700. Under the private placement, Counsel issued 16,164,471 common shares at $0.75 per share and 6,009,616 Series B preferred shares for $1.92 per share. The Series B preferred shares were convertible into common shares at a price of $0.75 per common share, subject to typical anti-dilution adjustments. The Series B preferred shares were entitled to a cumulative cash dividend of 6% per annum, payable semi-annually. The Series B preferred shares were redeemable at their original issue price plus accrued and unpaid dividends.

In 2010, the Company declared and paid cash dividends of $648 on its Series B shares. In January 2011, the Company declared and paid cash dividends of $396 on its Series B preferred shares.

Adjustment for Hyperinflation

4.18

Turkcell Iletisim Hizmetleri AS (Dec 2011)

CONSOLIDATED STATEMENT OF CHANGES IN EQUITY (in part)

(Amounts expressed in thousands of US Dollars unless otherwise indicated except share amounts)

	Attributable to equity holders of the Company											
	Share Capital	Capital Contri-bution	Share Premium	Legal Reserves	Fair Value Reserve	Cash Flow Hedge Reserves	Reserve for Non-Control-ling Interest Put Option	Translation Reserve	Retained Earnings	Total	Non-Controlling Interest	Total Equity
Balance at 1 January 2011	1,636,204	22,772	434	534,943	—	—	(263,984)	(931,080)	5,258,327	6,257,616	(24,019)	6,233,597
Total comprehensive income												
Profit for the year	—	—	—	—	—	—	—	751,709	751,709	(26,596)	725,113	
Other comprehensive income/(expense)												
Foreign currency translation differences, net of tax	—	—	—	—	—	—	(10,717)	(1,281,157)	—	(1,291,874)	(6,473)	(1,298,347)
Change in cash flow hedge reserve	—	—	—	—	—	(459)	—	—	—	(459)	—	(459)
Net change in fair value of available-for-sale securities, net of tax	—	—	—	—	—	—	—	—	—	—	—	—
Total other comprehensive income/(expense)	—	—	—	—	—	(459)	(10,717)	(1,281,157)	—	(1,292,333)	(6,473)	(1,298,806)
Total comprehensive income/(expense)	—	—	—	—	—	(459)	(10,717)	(1,281,157)	751,709	(540,624)	(33,069)	(573,693)
Transfers from legal reserves	—	—	—	(1,004)	—	—	—	—	1,004	—	—	—
Dividend paid (Note 22)	—	—	—	—	—	—	—	—	—	—	(3,989)	(3,989)
Effects of inflation accounting (Note 2b)	—	—	—	—	—	—	—	—	42,662	42,662	—	42,662
Change in non-controlling interest	—	—	—	—	—	—	—	—	—	—	544	544
Change in reserve for non-controlling interest put option (Note 30)	—	—	—	—	—	—	32,484	—	—	32,484	—	32,484
Balance at 31 December 2011	1,636,204	22,772	434	533,939	—	(459)	(242,217)	(2,212,237)	6,053,702	5,792,138	(60,533)	5,731,605

NOTES TO THE CONSOLIDATED FINANCIAL STATEMENTS (in part)

1. Reporting Entity

Turkcell Iletisim Hizmetleri Anonim Sirketi (the "Company") was incorporated in Turkey on 5 October 1993 and commenced its operations in 1994. The address of the Company's registered office is Turkcell Plaza, Mesrutiyet Caddesi No: 71, 34430 Tepebasi/Istanbul. It is engaged in establishing and operating a Global System for Mobile Communications ("GSM") network in Turkey and regional states.

In April 1998, the Company signed a license agreement (the "2G License") with the Ministry of Transport, Maritime Affairs and Communications of Turkey (the "Turkish Ministry"), under which it was granted a 25 year GSM license in exchange for a license fee of $500,000. The License permits the Company to operate as a stand-alone GSM operator and releases it from some of the operating constraints in the Revenue Sharing Agreement, which was in effect prior to the 2G License. Under the 2G License, the Company collects all of the revenue generated from the operations of its GSM network and pays the Undersecretariat of Treasury (the "Turkish Treasury") a treasury share equal to 15% of its gross revenue from Turkish GSM operations. The Company continues to build and operate its GSM network and is authorized to, among other things, set its own tariffs within certain limits, charge peak and off-peak rates, offer a variety of service and pricing packages, issue invoices directly to subscribers, collect payments and deal directly with subscribers. Following the 3G tender held by the Information Technologies and Communications Authority ("ICTA") regarding the authorization for providing IMT-2000/UMTS services and infrastructure, the Company has been granted the A-Type license (the "3G License") providing the widest frequency band, at a consideration of EUR 358,000 (excluding Value Added Tax ("VAT")). Payment of the 3G license was made in cash, following the necessary approvals, on 30 April 2009.

On 25 June 2005, the Turkish Government declared that GSM operators are required to pay 10% of their existing monthly treasury share to the Turkish Ministry as a universal service fund contribution in accordance with Law No: 5369.

As a result, starting from 30 June 2005, the Company pays 90% of the treasury share to the Turkish Treasury and 10% to the Turkish Ministry as universal service fund.

In July 2000, the Company completed an initial public offering with the listing of its ordinary shares on the Istanbul Stock Exchange and American Depositary Shares, or ADSs, on the New York Stock Exchange.

As at 31 December 2011, two significant founding shareholders, Sonera Holding BV and Cukurova Group, directly and indirectly, own approximately 37.1% and 13.8%, respectively of the Company's share capital and are ultimate counterparties to a number of transactions that are discussed in the related parties footnote. Alfa Group holds 13.2% of the Company's shares indirectly through Cukurova Holdings Limited and Turkcell Holding AS.

The consolidated financial statements of the Company as at and for the year ended 31 December 2011 comprise the Company and its subsidiaries (together referred to as the "Group") and the Group's interest in one associate and one joint venture. Subsidiaries of the Company, their locations and their business are given in Note 35. The Company's and each of its subsidiaries', associate's and joint venture's financial statements are prepared as at and for the year ended 31 December 2011.

2. Basis of Preparation (in part)

(a) Statement of Compliance

The consolidated financial statements have been prepared in accordance with International Financial Reporting Standards ("IFRSs") as issued by the International Accounting Standards Board ("IASB").

The Company selected the presentation form of "function of expense" for the statement of comprehensive income in accordance with IAS 1 "Presentation of Financial Statements".

The Company reports cash flows from operating activities by using the indirect method in accordance with IAS 7 " Statement of Cash Flows, "whereby profit or loss is adjusted for the effects of transactions of a non-cash nature, any deferrals or accruals of past or future operating cash receipts or payments, and items of income or expense associated with investing or financing cash flows.

Authority for restatement and approval of consolidated financial statements belongs to the Board of Directors. Consolidated financial statements are approved by the Board of Directors by the recommendation of Audit Committee of the Company.

The Group's audited consolidated financial statements prepared as at and for the year ended 31 December 2010 were approved by the Audit Committee and the Board of Directors (Board Resolution dated 23 February 2011 and numbered 797), however not approved by the General Assembly on 21 April 2011 and the Extraordinary General Assemblies of Shareholders held on 11 August 2011 and 12 October 2011.

The consolidated financial statements as of and for the year ended 31 December 2011 were authorized for issue on 22 February 2012 by the Board of Directors and updated by the management for any subsequent events up until 20 April 2012.

(b) Basis of Measurement

The accompanying consolidated financial statements are based on the statutory records, with adjustments and reclassifications for the purpose of fair presentation in accordance

with IFRSs as issued by the IASB. They are prepared on the historical cost basis adjusted for the effects of inflation during the hyperinflationary periods in accordance with International Accounting Standard No. 29. ("Financial Reporting in Hyperinflationary Economies") ("IAS 29"), where applicable, except that the following assets and liabilities are stated at their fair value: put option liability, derivative financial instruments and financial instruments classified as available-for-sale. The methods used to measure fair value are further discussed in Note 4. Hyperinflationary period lasted by 31 December 2005 in Turkey and commenced on 1 January 2011 in Belarus. In the financial statements of subsidiaries operating in Belarus, restatement adjustments have been made to compensate the effect of changes in the general purchasing power of the Belarusian Ruble in accordance with IAS 29. IAS 29 requires that financial statements prepared in the currency of a hyperinflationary economy be stated in terms of the measuring unit current at the balance sheet date. One characteristic that necessitates the application of IAS 29 is a cumulative three-year inflation rate approaching or exceeding 100%. Such cumulative rate in Belarus was 152% for the three years ended 31 December 2011 based upon the consumer price index ("CPI") announced by the National Statistical Committee of the Republic of Belarus. Such index and the conversion factors used to adjust the financial statements of the subsidiaries operating in Belarus for the effect of inflation as at 31 December 2011 are given below:

Dates	Index	Conversion Factor
31 December 2008	1.3524	2.5221
31 December 2009	1.4856	2.2959
31 December 2010	1.6345	2.0867
31 December 2011	3.4109	1.0000

The annual change in the BYR exchange rate against USD and Euro can be compared with the rates of general price inflation in Belarus according to the CPI as set out below:

Years	2009	2010	2011
Currency change USD (%)	30%	5%	178%
Currency change Euro (%)	33%	(3)%	172%
CPI inflation (%)	10%	10%	109%

As at 31 December 2011 the exchange rate announced by the National Bank of the Republic of Belarus was BYR 8,350 = USD 1, BYR 10,800 = Euro 1 (31 December 2010: BYR 3,000 = USD 1, BYR 3,973 = Euro 1).

The main guidelines for the IAS 29 restatement are as follows:

- All statement of financial position items, except for the ones already presented at the current purchasing power level, are restated by applying a general price index.
- Monetary assets and liabilities of the subsidiaries operating in Belarus are not restated because they are already expressed in terms of the current measuring unit at the balance sheet date. Monetary items presents money held and items to be received or paid in money.
- Non-monetary assets and liabilities of the subsidiaries operating in Belarus are restated by applying, to the initial acquisition cost and any accumulated depreciation, the change in the general price index from the date of acquisition or initial recording to the balance sheet date.

Hence, property, plant and equipment, investments and similar assets are restated from the date of their purchase, not to exceed their market value. Depreciation is similarly restated. The components of shareholders' equity are restated by applying the applicable general price index from the dates the components were contributed or arose otherwise.

- All items in the statement of income of the subsidiaries operating in Belarus, except non-monetary items in the statement of financial position that have effect over statement of income, are restated by applying the relevant conversion factors from the dates when the income and expense items were initially recorded in the financial statements.

- The gain or loss on the net monetary position is the result of the effect of general inflation and is the difference resulting from the restatement of non-monetary assets, shareholders' equity and statement of income items. The gain or loss on the net monetary position is included in net income.

The comparative amounts relating to the subsidiaries operating in Belarus in the 2010 consolidated financial statements are not restated. Only the current period amounts reported in the consolidated financial statements are affected by the subsidiaries operating in Belarus. Since the carrying value of Belarusian Telecom as of 1 January 2011 is limited by the value in use determined in accordance with the impairment analysis as of the same date, the net effect amounting to $42,662 as a result of the inflation accounting effect on the carrying value of Best as of 1 January 2011 less reassessed corresponding additional impairment charge amounting to $87,341 is presented as "Effects of Hyperinflation" within the opening balance of retained earnings for the financial year 2011.

(d) Use of Estimates and Judgments

The preparation of the consolidated financial statements in conformity with IFRS requires management to make judgments, estimates and assumptions that affect the application of accounting policies and the reported amounts of assets, liabilities, income and expenses. Actual results may differ from these estimates.

Estimates and underlying assumptions are reviewed on an ongoing basis. Revisions to accounting estimates are recognized in the period in which the estimates are revised and in any future periods affected.

Information about significant areas of estimation, uncertainty and critical judgments in applying accounting policies that have the most significant effect on the amounts recognized in the consolidated financial statements are described in Notes 4 and 33 and detailed analysis with respect to accounting estimates and critical judgments of allowance for doubtful receivables, useful lives or expected patterns of consumption of the future economic benefits embodied in depreciable assets, commission fees, revenue recognition, income taxes and impairment testing for cash-generating unit containing goodwill are provided below:

Key Sources of Estimation Uncertainty

The economic environment in Belarus has deteriorated significantly since the second quarter of financial year 2011. Interest rates are linked to the prime refinance rate of the National Bank of Belarus, which has been gradually increased during 2011 and prices for goods and services denominated

in BYR have been revisited several times in 2011 based on the change of market exchange rates. As of the balance sheet date cumulative inflation in the last three years exceeds 100% and therefore Belarus is considered a hyperinflationary economy. IAS 29 *"Reporting in Hyperinflationary Economies"* is applied by subsidiaries operating in Belarus in financial statements for the year ending 31 December 2011 as detailed Note 2(b).

While the National Bank of the Republic of Belarus has taken certain measures aimed at stabilizing the situation and preventing negative trends in the domestic foreign exchange market, including speculative pressure on the BYR, there exist the potential for economic uncertainties to continue in the foreseeable future.

Current and potential future political and economic changes in Belarus could have an adverse effect on the subsidiaries operating in this country. The economic stability of Belarus depends on the economic measures that will be taken by the government and the outcomes of the legal, administrative and political processes in the country. These processes are beyond the control of the subsidiaries established in the country.

Consequently, the subsidiaries operating within Belarus may be subject to the risks, i.e. foreign currency and interest rate risks related to borrowings and the subscriber's purchasing power and liquidity and increase in corporate and personal insolvencies, that may not necessarily be observable in other markets. The accompanying consolidated financial statements contain the Group management's estimations on the economic and financial positions of its subsidiaries operating in Belarus. The future economic situation of Belarus might differ from the Group's expectations. As of 31 December 2011, the Group's management believes that their approach is appropriate in taking all the necessary measures to support the sustainability of these subsidiaries' businesses in the current circumstances.

3. Significant Accounting Policies (in part)

The accounting policies set out below have been applied consistently to all periods presented in these consolidated financial statements, and have been applied consistently by the Group entities.

(b) Foreign Currency

(i) Foreign Currency Transactions

Transactions in foreign currencies are translated to the respective functional currencies of Group entities at exchange rates at the dates of the transactions. Monetary assets and liabilities denominated in foreign currencies at the reporting date are retranslated to the functional currency at the exchange rate at that date. Foreign currency differences arising on translation of foreign currency transactions are recognized in the statement of income. The foreign currency gain or loss on monetary items is the difference between amortized cost in the functional currency at the beginning of the period, adjusted for effective interest and payments during the period, and the amortized cost in foreign currency translated at the exchange rate at the end of the period.

Non-monetary assets and liabilities denominated in foreign currencies that are measured at fair value are retranslated to the functional currency at the exchange rate at the date that the fair value was determined. Foreign currency differences arising on retranslation are recognized in the statement of

IFRS-BPPD 4.18

income, except for differences arising on the retranslation of available-for-sale equity instruments, which are recognized directly in equity.

(ii) Foreign Operations

The assets and liabilities of foreign operations, including goodwill and fair value adjustments arising on acquisition, are translated to USD from the functional currency of the foreign operation at foreign exchange rates ruling at the reporting date. The income and expenses of foreign operations are translated to USD at monthly average exchange rates excluding foreign operations in hyperinflationary economies which are translated to USD at exchange rates at the reporting date.

The income and expenses of foreign operations in hyperinflationary economies are translated to USD at the exchange rate at the reporting date. Prior to translating the financial statements of foreign operations in hyperinflationary economies, their financial statements for the current period are restated to account for changes in the general purchasing power of the local currency. The restatement is based on relevant price indices at the reporting date.

Foreign currency differences arising on retranslation are recognized directly in the foreign currency translation reserve, as a separate component of equity. Since 1 January 2005, the Group's date of transition to IFRSs, such differences have been recognized in the foreign currency translation reserve. When a foreign operation is disposed of, partially or fully, the relevant amount in the foreign currency translation reserve is transferred to the statement of income.

Foreign exchange gains and losses arising from a monetary item receivable from or payable to a foreign operation, the settlement of which is neither planned nor likely in the foreseeable future, are considered to form part of a net investment in a foreign operation and are recognized directly in equity in the foreign currency translation reserve.

(iii) Translation From Functional to Presentation Currency

Items included in the financial statements of each entity are measured using the currency of the primary economic environment in which the entities operate, normally under their local currencies.

The consolidated financial statements are presented in USD, which is the presentation currency of the Group. The Group uses USD as the presentation currency for the convenience of investor and analyst community.

Assets and liabilities for each statement of financial position presented (including comparatives) are translated to USD at exchange rates at the statement of financial position date. Income and expenses for each statement of income (including comparatives) are translated to USD at monthly average exchange rates excluding operations in hyperinflationary economies which are translated to USD at exchange rates at the reporting date.

22. Capital and Reserves

Share Capital

As at 31 December 2011, common stock represented 2,200,000,000 (31 December 2010: 2,200,000,000) authorized, issued and fully paid shares with a par value of TL 1 each. In accordance with the Law No. 5083 with respect to TL, on 9 May 2005, par value of each share is registered to be one TL.

In connection with the redenomination of the TL and as per the related amendments of Turkish Commercial Code, in order to increase the nominal value of the shares to TL 1, 1,000 units of shares, each having a nominal value of TL 0.001 shall be merged and each unit of share having a nominal value of TL 1 shall be issued to represent such shares. The Company is still in the process of merging 1,000 existing ordinary shares, each having a nominal value of TL 0.001 to one ordinary share having a nominal value of TL 1 each. After the share merger which appears as a provisional article in the Articles of Association to convert the value of each share with a nominal value of TL 0.001 to TL 1, all shares will have a value of TL 1. Although the merger process has not been finalized, the practical application is to state each share having a nominal value of TL 1 which is consented by Capital Markets Board of Turkey ("CMB"). Accordingly, number of shares data is adjusted for the effect of this merger.

The holders of shares are entitled to receive dividends as declared and are entitled to one vote per share at meetings of the Company.

As at 31 December 2011, total number of pledged shares held by various institutions is 1,132,709 (31 December 2010: 137,200).

Capital Contribution

Capital contribution comprises the contributed assets and certain liabilities that the government settled on behalf of the Group that do not meet the definition of a government grant which the government is acting in its capacity as a shareholder.

Translation Reserve

The translation reserve comprises all foreign currency differences arising from the translation of the financial statements of foreign and domestic operations from their functional currencies to presentation currency of USD.

Fair Value Reserve

The fair value reserve comprises the cumulative net change in the fair value of available-for-sale financial assets until the investments are derecognized or the asset is impaired.

Legal Reserve

Under the Turkish Commercial Code, Turkish companies are required to set aside first and second level legal reserves out of their profits. First level legal reserves are set aside 5% of the distributable income per statutory accounts each year. The ceiling on the first legal reserves is 20% of the paid-up capital. The reserve requirement ends when the 20% of paid-up capital level has been reached. Second legal reserves correspond to 10% of profits actually distributed after the deduction of the first legal reserves and the minimum obligatory dividend pay-out (5% of the paid-up capital). There is no ceiling for second legal reserves and they are accumulated every year.

Cash Flow Hedging Reserve

The cash flow hedging reserve represents the cumulative effective portion of gains or losses arising on changes in fair value of hedging instruments entered into for cash flow hedges. The cumulative gain or loss arising on changes in fair value of the hedging instruments that are recognized and accumulated under the heading of cash flow hedging reserve will be reclassified to profit or loss only when the hedged transaction affects the profit or loss, or included as a basis adjustment to the non-financial hedged item, consistent with the relevant accounting policy.

Reserve for Non-Controlling Interest Put Option Liability

The reserve for non-controlling interest put option liability includes the difference between the put option liability granted to the non-controlling shareholders in existing subsidiaries recognized and the amount of non-controlling interest derecognized. Subsequent changes in the fair value of the put option liability are also recognized in this reserve.

Dividends

The Company has adopted a dividend policy, which is set out in its corporate governance guidance. As adopted, the Company's general dividend policy is to pay dividends to shareholders with due regard to trends in the Company's operating performance, financial condition and other factors.

The Board of Directors intends to distribute cash dividends in an amount of not less than 50% of the Company's lower of distributable profit based on the financial statements prepared in accordance with the accounting principles accepted by the CMB or statutory records, for each fiscal year starting with profits for fiscal year 2004. However, the payment of dividends will still be subject to cash flow requirements of the Company, compliance with Turkish law and the approval of and amendment by the Board of Directors and the General Assembly of Shareholders.

On 23 March 2011, the Company's Board of Directors has proposed a dividend distribution for the year ended 31 December 2010 amounting to TL 1,328,697 (equivalent to $703,424 as at 31 December 2011), which represented 75% of distributable income. This represents a net cash dividend of full TL 0.6039532 (equivalent to full $0.32 as at 31 December 2011) per share. This dividend proposal was discussed but not approved at the Ordinary General Assembly of Shareholders held on 21 April 2011 and the Extraordinary General Assemblies of Shareholders held on 11 August 2011 and 12 October 2011.

	2011		2010		2009	
	TL	USD	TL	USD*	TL	USD*
Cash dividends	1,328,697	703,424	859,259	573,451	1,098,193	713,297

* USD equivalents of dividends are computed by using the Central Bank of the Republic of Turkey's TL/USD exchange rate on 29 April 2010 and 8 May 2009 which are the dates that the General Assembly of Shareholders approved the dividend distribution, respectively.

In the Ordinary General Assemblies of Shareholders Meeting of Inteltek Internet Teknoloji Yatirim ve Danismanlik AS ("Inteltek") held on 4 April 2012 and 6 April 2011, it has been decided to distribute dividends amounting to TL 34,061 (equivalent to $18,032 as at 31 December 2011) and TL 16,744 (equivalent to $8,864 as at 31 December 2011), respectively. The 2010 dividend amounting to TL 16,744 was paid on 2 May 2011.

SECTION 5: STATEMENT OF CASH FLOWS AND RELATED DISCLOSURES[1]

IAS 7, *STATEMENT OF CASH FLOWS*

Author's Note

In 2011, the International Accounting Standards Board amended International Accounting Standard (IAS) 7, *Statement of Cash Flows*, by issuing the following standards:

- International Financial Reporting Standard (IFRS) 10, *Consolidated Financial Statements* (issued May 2011 and effective for annual periods beginning on or after 1 January 2013)
- IFRS 11, *Joint Arrangements* (issued May 2011 and effective for annual periods beginning on or after 1 January 2013)

The amendments to IAS 7 only update the titles of the standards related to the scope exclusion for subsidiaries, associates, and joint ventures to IFRS 10; IAS 27, *Separate Financial Statements*; and IAS 28, *Investments in Associates and Joint Ventures*.

Because these standards are effective for annual periods beginning on or after 1 January 2012, these amendments are not reflected in the commentary in this section. However, these amendments would not affect the availability of illustrative excerpts from survey companies' financial statements.

IFRSs Overview and Comparison to U.S. GAAP

5.01 IAS 1, *Presentation of Financial Statements*, requires a statement of cash flows as an integral part of a complete set of financial statements for each period for which financial statements are presented. IAS 7 establishes the requirements for the preparation and presentation of a statement of cash flows.

Presentation

IFRSs

5.02 The statement of cash flows reports the changes to the balance sheet account, cash, and cash equivalents (as those terms are defined in IAS 7). In IAS 7, *cash* is defined as cash on hand and demand deposits. *Cash equivalents* are defined as short-term, highly liquid investments, readily convertible to known amounts of cash, and subject to insignificant risk of

changes in value. An investment normally qualifies as short-term only when it has a maturity date of three months or less from the date of acquisition.

5.03 Entities that use bank overdrafts repayable on demand as part of their normal cash management activities may include those amounts as a component of cash and cash equivalents. IAS 7 does not prohibit an equity instrument from being included in cash equivalents if it is, in substance, a cash equivalent (that is, it meets the definition of a cash equivalent). An example of an equity instrument that could meet the definition of a cash equivalent is a preferred share that has a specified redemption date and is acquired within three months of its maturity.

5.04 Preparation of a statement of cash flows requires an entity to classify the inflows and outflows of cash and cash equivalents into three categories: operating activities, investing activities, and financing activities. An entity should exclude movements within cash and cash equivalents from this classification exercise because these movements are part of an entity's cash management activities rather than its operating, investing, and financing activities. This treatment is consistent with the principle set forth in IAS 7 that cash management includes the investment of excess cash in cash equivalents.

5.05 Operating activities are primarily derived from an entity's principal revenue producing activities (for example, collections from customer and payments to suppliers of goods or services, payments to employees, and payments of income taxes). IAS 7 provides entities two alternatives for presenting cash flows from operating activities: the direct method and the indirect method. However, the standard encourages, but does not require, entities to use the direct method. The *direct method* results in a presentation of gross cash collections and payments, except to the extent that the cash inflows and outflows are either with the same customer and reflect the activities of the customer rather than those of the entity, or for items with quick turnover, in large amounts, and with short maturities. Under the *indirect method*, an entity derives the net cash flow from operating activities by adjusting profit or loss (either before or after income taxes) for the effects of the following:

- Noncash income and expense items (for example, depreciation and amortization, deferred taxes, provisions, and share based payment expense)
- Changes in the entity's working capital balance sheet accounts (for example, changes in accounts receivable, inventories, accounts payable, and accrued liabilities)
- Items for which the cash effects are reported as investing or financing cash flows (for example, purchases and sales of property, plant, and equipment [PPE] and proceeds from and repayments of loans)

Entities should report cash flows arising from income taxes separately as an operating activity unless they can be specifically identified with financing and investing activities. Entities should also report cash payments to manufacture or acquire assets held for rental to others and subsequently held for sale (as described in paragraph 68A of IAS 16, *Property,*

[1] Unless otherwise indicated, references to International Accounting Standards Board (IASB) standards and interpretations throughout this 2012 edition of *IFRS Financial Statements—Best Practices in Presentation and Disclosure* refer to the version of those standards and interpretations included in the *IFRS 2012* bound volume, the official printed consolidated text of IASB standards and interpretations, including revisions, amendments, and supporting documents, issued as of 1 January 2012.

Plant and Equipment) in cash flows from operating activities. An entity should also classify cash receipts from rentals and subsequent sales of such assets as cash flows from operating activities.

5.06 Investing activities represent the extent to which the entity has made expenditures to support future income and cash flows (for example, acquisition and disposal of noncurrent assets, such as PPE, and investments in business combinations, joint ventures, and associates).

Author's Note

Improvements to IFRSs, issued in April 2009, clarified that only expenditures that result in a recognized asset in the statement of financial position are eligible for classification as investing activities. This amendment to IAS 7 is effective for annual reporting periods beginning on or after 1 January 2010, with early application permitted.

5.07 Financing activities represent sources of funding for both operations and investing activities and result in changes in the size and composition of the equity capital and borrowings of the entity (for example, issues and repurchases of share capital, and proceeds and repayments of principal on borrowings).

5.08 Entities should report cash flows from investing and financing activities by major class of gross proceeds and gross cash payments unless an exception permitting net presentation applies. One exception to separate presentation of the cash inflows and outflows is the same exception previously described for operating activities presented under the direct method. Another exception applies to financial institutions for cash flows arising from acceptance or repayment of deposits with a fixed maturity date, cash flows arising from the placement or withdrawal of deposits from other financial institutions, or from cash advances and loans to customers and the respective repayments.

5.09 An entity should translate cash flows denominated in a foreign currency and cash flows of a foreign operation into its functional currency using the relevant exchange rate at the dates of the cash flows. An entity should report cash flows denominated in a foreign currency consistent with IAS 21, *The Effects of Changes in Foreign Exchange Rates*. Although its objective is to translate these transactions using the relevant exchange rate between the entity's functional currency and foreign currency, IAS 21 permits the use of a weighted-average exchange rate that approximates the actual rate. IAS 21 does not permit the use of an end-of-period exchange rate in translating the cash flows of a foreign subsidiary. Gains and losses arising on translation are not cash flows but IAS 7 requires these translation effects to be presented separately in the statement of cash flows.

5.10 Entities should disclose separately interest paid, interest received, dividends paid, and dividends received and classify each consistently from period to period as an operating, investing, or financing activity. IAS 7 requires entities to disclose the total amount of interest paid during the period whether expensed in the statement of comprehensive income or capitalized in accordance with IAS 23, *Borrowing Costs*.

5.11 When accounting for an investment in another entity using the equity or cost method, an entity should only report those cash flows between itself and the investee (for example, dividends and advances). When using the proportionate consolidation method of accounting for a jointly controlled entity, the entity should include its proportionate share of the jointly controlled entity's cash flows in the relevant line item of its own cash flow statement.

5.12 Entities should report separately aggregate cash flows from gaining and losing control of subsidiaries and other businesses, classified as an *investing activity*. IFRS 5, *Noncurrent Assets Held for Sale and Discontinued Operations*, requires separate disclosure of cash flows attributable to the operating, investing, and financing activities of discontinued operations either in the statement of cash flows or in the notes.

U.S. GAAP

5.13 The Financial Accounting Standards Board (FASB) *Accounting Standards Codification* (ASC) glossary definitions of *cash* and *cash equivalents* are similar to those used in IAS 7, except that FASB ASC definitions do not explicitly give entities the ability to include bank overdrafts in cash and cash equivalents. Paragraphs 5 and 7 of FASB ASC 230-10-45 explain that gross cash flows are generally more relevant than net cash flows unless the cash flows are part of the entity's cash management activities rather than its operating, and financing activities. Paragraphs 8–9 of FASB ASC 230-10-45 discuss the relevance of net cash flows on demand deposits of a bank or customer accounts payable of a broker-dealer, as well as investments (other than cash equivalents), loans receivable, and debt (provided that the original maturity of the asset or liability is three months or less). Despite no explicit prohibition in FASB ASC, current practice dictates that bank overdrafts are not considered cash or cash equivalents and are classified as a financing activity.

5.14 In addition, IFRSs are more lenient than FASB ASC and permit an entity to include equity instruments in cash equivalents. According to the FASB ASC glossary, generally, only investments with original maturities of three months or less qualify under the definition of *cash equivalent*, which would disqualify equity instruments, except for some mandatorily redeemable equity instruments.

5.15 The basic structure of the cash flow statement is the same under both IFRSs and U.S. generally accepted accounting principles (U.S. GAAP). FASB ASC 230, *Statement of Cash Flows*, requires an entity to classify cash flows as operating, financing, or investing activities and contains similar examples of events included in these classifications. However, paragraphs 16–17 of FASB ASC 230-10-45 require entities to classify interest paid, interest and dividends received (except dividends with long term donor restrictions), and income taxes paid as operating activities, even when associated with an investing or financing transaction. According to FASB ASC 230-10-45-15, entities should classify dividends paid as a financing activity.

Disclosure

IFRSs

5.16 IAS 7 requires entities to disclose the components of cash and cash equivalents and its policy for determining these components. An entity should reconcile the amount shown in the statement of cash flows with the equivalent balance sheet amount. Entities also should disclose any restricted amounts of cash and cash equivalents. When its policy for cash and cash equivalents changes, the entity should account for the change retrospectively as a change in accounting policy in accordance with IAS 8, *Accounting Policies, Changes in Accounting Estimates and Errors.*

5.17 An entity should not report noncash financing and investing activities (for example, the acquisition of an asset by assuming a mortgage or by means of a finance lease) in the statement of cash flows. However, an entity should disclose these activities elsewhere in the financial statements in order to provide information relevant to understanding these significant financing and investing activities.

5.18 When an entity gains or loses control of a subsidiary (or other business), in addition to reporting cash flows as previously described, it also should disclose the total consideration paid or received (including the portion consisting of cash and cash equivalents), the amount of the subsidiary's cash and cash equivalents, and the amounts of the subsidiary's other assets and liabilities (that is, assets and liabilities other than cash or cash equivalents) by major class of asset and liability.

5.19 IAS 7 encourages entities to report additional information about the types of cash flows when relevant to users' understanding of the financial statements, including the following:

- Undrawn borrowing facilities
- Aggregate cash flows of proportionately consolidated joint ventures
- Aggregate amount of cash flows representing increases in operating capacity
- Operating, investing, and financing cash flows by segment

U.S. GAAP

5.20 Like IAS 7, FASB ASC 230-10-50-1 requires an entity to disclose its policy with respect to cash and cash equivalents and to account for any changes as a change in accounting principle with retrospective application and restatement of the comparative periods presented.

5.21 Like IFRSs, entities reporting under FASB ASC 230-10-45 can present operating activities using either the direct or indirect method. However, FASB ASC 230-10-45–30 also requires entities using the direct method to provide a reconciliation of net income to net cash flow from operating activities in a separate schedule. Essentially, this requirement results in an entity disclosing both the direct and indirect method of presenting its operating activities. IAS 7 does not require this additional disclosure. FASB ASC 230-10-45-24 states that separate disclosure of cash flows of extraordinary items or discontinued operations is not required. However, Securities and Exchange Commission registrants that elect to separately disclose cash flows of discontinued operations should classify the related cash receipts and payments as operating, investing, and financing activities.

5.22 FASB ASC 230-10-45-3 prohibits reporting cash flow per share in the financial statements. Cash flow per share is not discussed in IFRSs.

TABLE 5-1: METHOD OF REPORTING CASH FLOWS FROM OPERATING ACTIVITIES

	2011	2010	2009
Survey entities electing the indirect method....	151	147	141
Survey entities electing the direct method.......	23	23	19
Total...	**175**	**170**	**160**

TABLE 5-2: CLASSIFICATIONS OF REPORTED INCOME TAX, INTEREST, AND DIVIDEND CASH FLOWS

	2011	2010	2009
Survey Entities Reporting Income Tax Paid or Received			
Operating..	173	164	159
Investing...	0	0	0
Financing...	0	0	0
Presented in both operating and investing.......	0	0	1
No taxes paid or received presented..............	2	6	0
Total...	**175**	**170**	**160**
Survey Entities Reporting Interest Received			
Operating..	92	91	86
Investing[2]...	38	53	52
Financing...	2	2	2
Presented in both operating and investing.......	2	1	0
No interest received presented......................	41	23	20
Total...	**175**	**170**	**160**
Survey Entities Reporting Interest Paid			
Operating..	106	112	110
Investing...	1	0	1
Financing[3]..	46	48	46
Presented in both operating and financing.......	3	2	1
Presented in both operating and investing.......	2	0	0
Presented in both investing and financing.......	0	1	0
No interest paid presented............................	17	7	2
Total...	**175**	**170**	**160**
Survey Entities Reporting Dividends Received			
Operating..	51	55	53
Investing...	37	38	36
Financing...	1	0	0
Presented in both operating and investing.......	1	1	0
Presented in both operating and financing.......	1	0	0
No dividends received presented....................	84	76	71
Total...	**175**	**170**	**160**

(continued)

TABLE 5-2: CLASSIFICATIONS OF REPORTED INCOME TAX, INTEREST, AND DIVIDEND CASH FLOWS—CONTINUED

	2011	2010	2009
Survey Entities Reporting Dividends Paid			
Operating	2	2	3
Investing	0	0	0
Financing	143	142	128
Presented in both operating and financing	0	1	0
Presented between operating and investing	2	2	2
No dividends paid presented	28	23	27
Total	**175**	**170**	**160**
Survey Entities Reporting Dividends Paid to Minority Interest			
Operating	1	3	4
Investing	0	1	1
Financing	49	47	45
No dividends paid to minority interest	125	119	110
Total	**175**	**170**	**160**

Presentation and Disclosure Excerpts

Presentation of Operating Activities Using the Direct Method—Reconciliation of Net Income to Cash From Operating Activities Provided in a Note Disclosure, Additional Disclosure of Cash Flows for Investing Events

5.23

DRDGOLD Limited (Jun 2011)

CONSOLIDATED STATEMENT OF CASH FLOWS

For the year ended June 30, 2011

	Note	2011 R'000	2010 R'000	2009 R'000
Cash Flows From Operating Activities				
Cash received from sales of precious metals		2,565,319	1,990,522	1,910,738
Cash paid to suppliers and employees		(2,249,516)	(1,942,786)	(1,745,805)
Cash generated by operations	27	315,803	47,736	164,933
Finance income		13,384	23,436	88,964
Dividends received		6,013	—	4,829
Finance expenses		(4,975)	(4,862)	(3,605)
Income tax paid		(6,212)	(12,698)	(46,889)
Net cash inflow from operating activities		324,013	53,612	208,232
Cash Flows From Investing Activities				
Proceeds on sale of investments		—	—	47,467
Additions to property, plant and equipment		(317,250)	(194,018)	(345,132)
Proceeds on disposal of property, plant and equipment		4,662	13,873	10,816
Environmental trust funds and rehabilitation payments		(22,577)	(5,674)	(6,049)
Cash flow on acquisition of subsidiaries, net of cash	28	—	(40,396)	(277,821)
Cash flow on acquisition/disposal of joint ventures, net of cash	29	—	(166)	(20,000)
Cash flow on acquisition of associate	30	—	—	(2,700)
Net cash outflow from investing activities		(335,165)	(226,381)	(593,419)
Cash Flows From Financing Activities				
Proceeds from the issue of shares		—	30,881	6,707
Share issue expenses		(714)	(2,043)	(433)
Advances of loans and borrowings		109,636	—	—
Repayments of loans and borrowings		(8,332)	(2,101)	(54,438)
Dividends paid		(19,244)	(18,954)	(37,658)
Net cash inflow/(outflow) from financing activities		81,346	7,783	(85,822)
Net increase/(decrease) in cash and cash equivalents		70,194	(164,986)	(471,009)
Cash and cash equivalents at beginning of the year		188,152	352,731	845,587
Foreign exchange movements		766	407	(21,847)
Cash and cash equivalents at the end of the year	31	259,112	188,152	352,731

NOTES TO THE CONSOLIDATED FINANCIAL STATEMENTS (in part)

1. Accounting Policies (in part)

DRDGOLD Limited ('the company') is a company domiciled in South Africa. The consolidated financial statements of the company for the year ended June 30, 2011 comprise the company and its subsidiaries, (together referred to as the group) and the group's interests in associates and jointly controlled entities.

Statement of Compliance

The consolidated financial statements have been prepared in accordance with International Financial Reporting Standards (IFRS) and its interpretations adopted by the International Accounting Standards Board (IASB).

The financial statements were approved by the Board of Directors on September 19, 2011.

Financial Instruments (in part)

Financial instruments recognized in the statement of financial position include investments, available-for-sale financial instruments, trade and other receivables, cash and cash equivalents, long- and short-term interest-bearing borrowings, trade and other payables and bank overdrafts. Financial instruments are initially recognized at fair value and include any directly attributable transaction costs, except those financial instruments measured at fair value through profit or loss. Subsequent to initial recognition, financial instruments are measured as described below.

Financial assets and liabilities are off-set and the net amount presented in the statement of financial position when, and only when, the group has the legal right to off-set the amounts, and intends either to settle on a net basis, or to realize the assets and settle the liabilities simultaneously.

Financial assets are derecognized when the contractual rights to the cash flows from the financial asset expire or to the extent that the company transfers substantially all the risks and rewards of ownership of the financial asset. Financial liabilities are derecognized when the obligation specified in the contract is discharged or cancelled or has expired. Any gain or loss on derecognition is taken to profit or loss.

Cash and Cash Equivalents

Cash and cash equivalents comprise cash on hand, demand deposits, and highly liquid investments with an original maturity of three months or less. Subsequent to initial recognition, cash and cash equivalents are measured at amortized cost, which is equivalent to their fair value. Bank overdrafts that are repayable on demand and form an integral part of the group's cash management are included as a component of cash and cash equivalents for the purpose of the statement of cash flows.

2. Operating Segments (in part)

2011	Blyvoor R'000	Crown[1] R'000	Ergo[2] R'000	Corporate Head Office and All[3] Other Expenses R'000	Total R'000
Reconciliation of assets					
Reportable segment assets	26,046	330,154	1,125,162	58,641	1,540,003
Other assets	148,096	150,262	116,437	333,863	748,658
Total assets	174,142	480,416	1,241,599	392,504	2,288,661
Reconciliation of liabilities					
Reportable segment liabilities	174,115	322,647	206,673	243,299	946,734
Taxation and deferred taxation	27	7,715	114,806	213	122,761
Total liabilities	174,142	330,362	321,479	243,512	1,069,495
Other material information					
Depreciation	(32,638)	(11,247)	(86,917)	(117)	(130,919)
Impairment of assets	(546,566)	—	—	(1,090)	(547,656)
Reconciliation of revenues					
Total revenues for reportable segments	1,185,860	910,867	468,592	—	2,565,319
Statement of cash flows					
Cash flows from operating activities	89,400	203,508	126,093	(94,988)	324,013
Cash flows from investing activities	(94,323)	(152,399)	(78,497)	(9,946)	(335,165)
Cash flows from financing activities	—	—	—	81,346	81,346
Reconciliation of (loss)/profit					
Segment working profit/(loss) before capital expenditure	70,493	248,147	149,139	(77,746)	390,033
—Depreciation	(32,638)	(11,247)	(86,917)	(117)	(130,919)
—Movement in provision for environmental rehabilitation	(5,649)	(27,198)	(9,154)	(10,566)	(52,567)
—Impairments	(546,566)	—	—	(1,090)	(547,656)
—Net gain/(loss) on financial liabilities measured at amortized cost	30,856	—	—	(6,048)	24,808
—Growth in environmental rehabilitation trust funds	1,769	3,096	—	3,526	8,391
—Unwinding of provision for environmental rehabilitation	(1,049)	(3,631)	(3,672)	(1,053)	(9,405)
—Unwinding of discount on financial liabilities measured at amortized cost	(3,550)	—	—	(4,117)	(7,667)
—Borrowing costs capitalized	—	1,011	—	5,409	6,420
—Ongoing rehabilitation expenditure	(1,453)	(25,197)	(7,114)	(9,214)	(42,978)
—Actuarial gain on post-retirement and other employee benefits	—	5,651	—	—	5,651
—Net other operating (costs)/income	(8,559)	(3,552)	2,279	(23,764)	(33,596)
—Deferred tax	(2,532)	(18,502)	53,332	(58,191)	(25,893)
(Loss)/profit for the year	(498,878)	168,578	97,893	(182,971)	(415,378)

[1] Crown includes ERPM's Cason surface retreatment operations.

[2] Includes 100% of ErgoGold and the Ergo JV.

[3] Corporate head office expenses are taken into consideration in the strategic decision-making process of the CODM and are therefore included in the disclosure here, even though they do not earn revenue.

27. Cash Generated by Operations

	2011 R'000	2010 R'000	2009 R'000
(Loss)/profit before taxation	(383,226)	211,626	82,240
Adjusted for:			
Depreciation	130,919	190,769	99,217
Movement in provision for environmental rehabilitation	52,567	(88,034)	19,545
Movement in gold in process	15,612	(29,941)	(7,018)
Impairments	547,656	6,224	75,138
Profit on disposal of property, plant and equipment	(3,255)	(13,722)	(10,266)
Share-based payments	3,519	4,115	7,873
Rehabilitation trust fund adjustment	339	—	—
Post-retirement and other employee benefits	(3,038)	5,015	2,673
(Reversal of impairment)/impairment on trade receivables	(5,617)	4,568	113
Actuarial (gain)/loss on post-retirement and employee benefits	(5,651)	(35,290)	18,226
Finance income	(52,792)	(200,273)	(205,991)
Finance expenses	22,047	24,132	41,743
Operating cash flows before working capital changes	319,080	79,189	123,493
Working capital changes	(3,277)	(31,453)	41,440
Change in trade and other receivables	(56,087)	19,650	156,042
Change in inventories	(10,417)	(10,070)	(16,648)
Change in trade and other payables	63,227	(41,033)	(97,954)
Cash generated by operations	315,803	47,736	164,933

28. Cash Flow on Acquisition of Subsidiaries, Net of Cash

	2011 R'000	2010 R'000	2009 R'000
Total net cash flow on acquisition of subsidiaries			
DRDGOLD Limited (Cell No. 170)	—	—	(100)
ErgoGold	—	—	(277,721)
Ergo Mining (Pty) Limited	—	(40,396)	—
Blyvooruitzicht Gold Mining Company Limited	—	—	—
	—	(40,396)	(277,821)

Acquisition of DRDGOLD Limited (Cell No. 170)

In July 1, 2008, DRDGOLD acquired 100% of a separate class of share in Guardrisk Insurance Company Limited known as DRDGOLD Limited (Cell No 170).

	2011 R'000	2010 R'000	2009 R'000
Cash flow on acquisition of subsidiary	—	—	(100)

Acquisition of ErgoGold

On March 31, 2009, East Rand Proprietary Mines Limited and DRDGOLD acquired 15% and 35% respectively, of ErgoGold from Mogale Gold (Proprietary) Limited.

The fair value of the net assets acquired net of non-controlling interest were as follows:

	2011 R'000	2010 R'000	2009 R'000
Property, plant and equipment	—	—	409,118
Inventories	—	—	8,236
Trade and other receivables	—	—	438
Amounts owing by group companies	—	—	13,975
Cash and cash equivalents	—	—	768
Deferred tax liability	—	—	(85,586)
Trade and other payables	—	—	(15,389)
Carrying value at time of acquisition	—	—	331,560
Less: Cash and cash equivalents acquired	—	—	(833)
Negative goodwill on acquisition	—	—	(53,006)
Cash flow on acquisition of subsidiary net of cash acquired	—	—	(277,721)

Acquisition of Ergo Mining (Pty) Limited

On April 30, 2010 DRDGOLD acquired the remaining 50% interest in Ergo Mining (Pty) Limited (Ergo JV) from Ergo Uranium (Pty) Limited for a total consideration of R82.1 million, R62.1 million settled in cash and the balance in shares in Witfontein Mining (Pty) Limited. A further R0.3 million was incurred on transaction cost. DRDGOLD has consolidated 100% of the Ergo JV from May 1, 2010. Prior to the acquisition, the Ergo JV was accounted for as a joint venture (refer note 13).

	2011 R'000	2010 R'000	2009 R'000
Total cash consideration paid	—	(62,438)	—
Add: Cash and cash equivalents of acquired entity	—	22,042	—
Cash flow on acquisition of subsidiary, net of cash acquired	—	(40,396)	—

Acquisition of Blyvooruitzicht Gold Mining Company Limited (Blyvoor)

Effective September 30, 2010, DRDGOLD acquired a 74% interest in Blyvoor from Ergo Mining Operations for a total consideration of R75.7 million settled against Ergo Mining Operation's inter-company loan with DRDGOLD. The acquisition has been accounted for as an acquisition of an entity under common control (refer note 12).

	2011 R'000	2010 R'000	2009 R'000
Total cash consideration paid	—	—	—

29. Cash Flow on Acquisition/Disposal of Joint Ventures, Net of Cash

Acquisition of Witfontein Mining (Pty) Limited

On February 28, 2009, DRDGOLD through its subsidiary Argonaut Financial Services (Pty) Limited acquired a 50% interest in Witfontein Mining (Pty) Limited and entered into a joint venture agreement with Mintails SA (Pty) Limited which owns the remaining 50%.

	2011 R'000	2010 R'000	2009 R'000
Cash flow on acquisition of joint venture	—	—	(20,000)

Disposal of Witfontein Mining (Pty) Limited

On April 30, 2010, Argonaut Financial Services (Pty) Limited disposed of its 50% interest in the Witfontein Mining (Pty) Limited joint venture for R20.0 million. No cash consideration was received as this disposal formed part of the purchase consideration paid (value of R20.0 million) for the acquisition of the remaining 50% interest in the Ergo JV.

The carrying value of the net asset disposed of were as follows:

	2011 R'000	2010 R'000	2009 R'000
Property, plant and equipment	—	28,809	—
Trade and other receivables	—	47	—
Cash and cash equivalents	—	166	—
Trade and other payables	—	(10,522)	—
Carrying value at time of disposal	—	18,500	—
Total cash consideration received	—	—	—
Less: Cash and cash equivalents of disposed entity	—	(166)	—
Cash flow on disposal of joint venture	—	(166)	—

Acquisition of Chizim Gold (Pvt) Limited

During the year ended June 30, 2011, the group entered into a 50:50 joint enture in a start-up company called Chizim Gold (Pvt) Limited for a nominal cash consideration amounting to $1 (refer note 13).

	2011 R'000	2010 R'000	2009 R'000
Cash flow on acquisition of joint venture	—	—	—

30. Cash Flow on Acquisition of Associate

Acquisition of West Wits SA (Pty) Limited.

In January 2009, DRDGOLD acquired a 28.33% interest in West Wits SA (Pty) Limited.

	2011 R'000	2010 R'000	2009 R'000
Cash flow on investment in associate	—	—	(2,700)

31. Cash and Cash Equivalents

Cash and cash equivalents comprise cash on hand, demand deposits and highly liquid investments with an original maturity of three months or less. Included in cash and cash equivalents is restricted cash in a form of a guarantee relating to the rehabilitation of the Brakpan tailings dam, given to AngloGold Ashanti Limited amounting to R43.0 million (2010: R43.0 million and 2009: R34.4 million). Further guarantees are held by Guardrisk amounting to R8.3 million (2010: R8.3 million and 2009: R9.7 million), and by Standard Bank of South Africa Limited, amounting to R24.3 million (2010: R17.9 million and 2009: R18.1 million).

	2011 R'000	2010 R'000	2009 R'000
Cash and cash equivalents	259,112	188,152	353,555
Bank overdrafts	—	—	(824)
	259,112	188,152	352,731

32. Cash Flows Relating to Exploration Assets

	2011 R'000	2010 R'000	2009 R'000
Investing cash flow	17,210	57,993	27,401

Presentation of Operating Activities Using the Direct Method—Tax Refund, Cash From Settlement of Currency Forward Contracts and Cash for Cross-Currency Swap Contracts Presented as Operating Activities

5.24

PT Indosat Tbk (Dec 2011)

Author's Note

An excerpt from PT Indosat's financial statements regarding its derivative contracts is provided in Section 8, *Financial Instruments and Related Disclosures*.

CONSOLIDATED STATEMENTS OF CASH FLOWS

(Expressed in millions of rupiah)

	Notes	2009 Rp	2010 Rp	2011 Rp
Cash Flows From Operating Activities				
Cash received from:				
Customers		18,415,890	19,678,609	20,620,790
Refund of taxes	6	84,650	41,753	141,271
Interest income		146,826	145,067	81,336
Settlement from currency forward contracts	32c, 32h, 32i-j, 32k, 32aa-ap	—	—	55,371
Settlement from derivative contracts	32c, 32h-k	—	—	20,626
Cash paid to/for:				
Authorities, other operators, suppliers and others		(10,061,275)	(9,051,275)	(9,102,182)
Employees		(1,359,817)	(1,310,556)	(2,003,642)
Financing cost		(1,730,149)	(2,175,997)	(1,739,810)
Income taxes		(878,137)	(215,874)	(563,320)
Interest rate swap contracts	32m-z	(47,715)	(117,231)	(119,521)
Swap cost from cross currency swap contracts	32a-l	(125,748)	(121,449)	(70,838)
Settlement from derivative contract	32b, 32g	—	(24,431)	—
Long-term prepaid licenses	2f19	(338,408)	—	—
Net cash provided by operating activities		4,106,117	6,848,616	7,320,081
Cash Flows From Investing Activities				
Cash dividend received from other long-term investment	12a	26,774	19,281	13,790
Proceeds from sale of property and equipment	8	2,253	7,741	6,708
Acquisitions of property and equipment	8	(10,684,690)	(6,495,146)	(6,047,958)
Acquisition of intangible assets	9	(15,044)	(40,052)	(10,452)
Proceeds of Palapa D-Satellite insurance claim	8	—	537,657	—
Purchase of investment in an associated company		—	(194)	—
Net cash used in investing activities		(10,670,707)	(5,970,713)	(6,037,912)
Cash Flows From Financing Activities				
Proceeds from long-term loans	18	3,892,786	1,092,059	2,322,900
Proceeds from short-term loan	14	—	—	1,500,000
Repayment of long-term loans	18	(632,814)	(4,098,277)	(3,505,063)
Repayment of bonds payable	19	(14,453)	(3,720,815)	(1,100,000)
Cash dividend paid by the Company	31	(939,255)	(749,122)	(323,591)
Cash dividend paid by subsidiaries to non-controlling interest		(9,291)	(21,436)	(29,692)
Proceeds from bonds payable	19	1,500,000	5,851,301	—
Settlement from derivative contract	32a	—	59,925	—
Decrease (increase) in restricted cash and cash equivalents		(18,206)	2,846	—
Swap cost from cross currency swap contract	32a	(54,116)	(46,136)	—
Net cash provided by (used in) financing activities				
		3,724,651	(1,629,655)	(1,135,446)

	Notes	2009 Rp	2010 Rp	2011 Rp
Net foreign exchange differences from cash and cash equivalents		(54,908)	(9,732)	2,213
Net increase (decrease) in cash and cash equivalents		(2,894,847)	(761,484)	148,936
Cash and cash equivalents of liquidated subsidiary*		(7,020)	—	—
Cash and cash equivalents of acquired subsidiary	1b	—	755	—
Cash and cash equivalents at beginning of year		5,737,866	2,835,999	2,075,270
Cash and cash equivalents at end of year	4	2,835,999	2,075,270	2,224,206
Details of cash and cash equivalents:				
Time deposits with original maturities of three months or less and deposits on call		2,611,529	1,791,783	1,919,227
Cash on hand and in banks		224,470	283,487	304,979
Cash and cash equivalents as stated in the consolidated statements of financial position		2,835,999	2,075,270	2,224,206

* PT Satelindo Multi Media ("SMM") was liquidated on June 23, 2009.

NOTES TO THE CONSOLIDATED FINANCIAL STATEMENTS (in part)

(Expressed in millions of rupiah and thousands of U.S. dollar, except share and tariff data)

1. General (in part)

a. Company's Establishment

PT Indosat Tbk ("the Company") was established in the Republic of Indonesia on November 10, 1967 within the framework of the Indonesian Foreign Investment Law No. 1 of 1967 based on the notarial deed No. 55 of Mohamad Said Tadjoedin, S.H. The deed of establishment was published in Supplement No. 24 of State Gazette No. 26 dated March 29, 1968 of the Republic of Indonesia. In 1980, the Company was sold by American Cable and Radio Corporation, an International Telephone & Telegraph subsidiary, to the Government of the Republic of Indonesia ("the Government") and became a State-owned Company (*Persero*).

On February 7, 2003, the Company received the approval from the Capital Investment Coordinating Board (BKPM) in its letter No. 14/V/PMA/2003 for the change of its legal status from a State-owned Company (*Persero*) to a Foreign Capital Investment Company. Subsequently, on March 21, 2003, the Company received the approval from the Ministry of Justice and Human Rights of the Republic of Indonesia on the amendment of its Articles of Association to reflect the change of its legal status.

The Company's Articles of Association has been amended from time to time. The latest amendment was covered by notarial deed No. 123 dated January 28, 2010 of Aulia Taufani, S.H., (as a substitute notary of Sutjipto, S.H.) as approved in the Stockholders' Extraordinary General Meeting held on January 28, 2010, in order to comply with the Indonesian Capital Market and Financial Institutions Supervisory Agency (BAPEPAM-LK) Rule No. IX.J.1 dated May 14, 2008 on the Principles of Articles of Association of Limited Liability Companies that Conduct Public Offering of Equity Securities and Public Companies and Rule No. IX.E.1 on Affiliate Transactions and Certain Conflict of Interests Transactions. The latest amendment of the Company's Articles of Association has been approved by and reported to the Ministry of Law and Human Rights of the Republic of Indonesia based on its letters No. AHU-09555.AH.01.02 Year 2010 dated February 22, 2010 and No. AHU-AH.01.10-04964 dated February 25, 2010. The amendments relate to, among others, the changes in the Company's purposes, objectives and business activities, appointment of acting President Director if the incumbent President Director is unavailable and definition of conflict of interests.

The address of the Company's registered office is at Jl. Medan Merdeka Barat 21 Jakarta and it has 4 regional offices located in Jakarta, Surabaya, Batam and Balikpapan.

According to article 3 of its Articles of Association, the Company's purposes and objectives are to provide telecommunications networks, telecommunications services as well as information technology and/or convergence technology services by carrying out the following main business activities:

a. To provide telecommunications networks, telecommunications services as well as information technology and/or convergence technology services, including but not limited to providing basic telephony services, multimedia services, internet telephony services for public use, interconnection internet services, internet access services, mobile telecommunications networks and fixed telecommunications networks; and

b. To engage in payment transactions and money transfer services through telecommunications networks as well as information technology and/or convergence technology.

The Company can provide supporting business activities in order to achieve the purposes and objectives, and to support its main businesses, as follows:

a. To plan, to procure, to modify, to build, to provide, to develop, to operate, to lease, to rent, and to maintain infrastructures/facilities including resources to support the Company's business in providing telecommunications networks, telecommunications services as well as information technology and/or convergence technology services;

b. To conduct business and operating activities (including development, marketing and sales of telecommunications networks, telecommunications services as well as information technology and/or convergence technology services by the Company), including research, customer services, education and courses (both domestic and overseas); and

c. To conduct other activities necessary to support and/or related to the provision of telecommunications networks, telecommunications services as well as information technology and/or convergence technology services including but not limited to electronic transactions and provision of hardware, software, content as well as telecommunications-managed services.

The consolidated financial statements of the Company and its subsidiaries (collectively referred to hereafter as "the Group") as of January 1, 2010 and December 31, 2010 and 2011 and for each of the three years in the period ended December 31, 2011 were approved and authorized for issue by the Board of Directors on April 25, 2012, as reviewed and recommended for approval by the Audit Committee.

2. Summary of Significant Accounting Policies (in part)

The significant accounting policies applied consistently in the preparation of the consolidated financial statements are as follows:

c. Statement of Compliance

The consolidated financial statements of the Group have been prepared in accordance with International Financial Reporting Standards ("IFRS") as issued by the International Accounting Standards Board ("IASB").

f. Significant Accounting Policies and Practices (in part)

f8. Financial Assets (in part)

- Loans and receivables

Loans and receivables are non-derivative financial assets with fixed or determinable payments that are not quoted in an active market. After initial measurement, such financial assets are subsequently measured at amortized cost using the effective interest rate method (EIR), less impairment. Amortized cost is calculated by taking into account any discount or premium on acquisition and fees or costs that are an integral part of the EIR. The EIR amortization is included in the consolidated statements of comprehensive income. The losses arising from impairment are recognized in the consolidated statements of comprehensive income.

The Group's cash and cash equivalents, trade and other accounts receivables, due from related parties, other current financial assets and other non-current financial assets are included in this category.

Time deposits with original maturities of three months or less at the time of placement and deposits on call are considered as "Cash Equivalents."

Cash in banks and time deposits which are pledged as collateral for bank guarantees are not classified as part of "Cash and Cash Equivalents." These are presented as part of either "Other Current Financial Assets" or "Other Non-current Financial Assets."

f19. Leases

Group as a Lessee

A finance lease that transfers to the Group substantially all the risks and benefits incidental to ownership of the leased item, is capitalized at the commencement of the lease at the fair value of the leased property or, if lower, at the present value of the minimum lease payments. Lease payments are apportioned between finance charges and reduction of the lease liability so as to achieve a constant rate of interest on the remaining balance of the liability. Finance charges are recognized as part of finance costs in the consolidated statements of comprehensive income.

A leased asset is depreciated over the useful life of the asset. However, if there is no reasonable certainty that the Group will obtain ownership by the end of the lease term, the asset is depreciated over the shorter of the estimated useful life of the asset and the lease term.

Current Portion of Obligation under Finance Lease is presented as part of Other Current Financial Liabilities.

Operating lease payments are recognized as an operating expense in the consolidated statements of comprehensive income on a straight-line basis over the lease term.

Group as a Lessor

A lease in which the Group does not transfer substantially all the risks and benefits of the ownership of an asset is classified as an operating lease. Initial direct costs incurred in negotiating an operating lease are added to the carrying amount of the leased asset and recognized over the lease term on the same basis as rental income. Contingent rents are recognized as revenue in the period which they are earned.

A lease in which the Group transfers substantially all the risks and benefits of the ownership of an asset is classified as a finance lease. Leased asset is recognized as asset held under a finance lease in the consolidated statements of financial position and presented as a receivable at an amount equal to the net investment in the lease. Selling profit or loss is recognized in the period, in accordance with the policy followed by the Group for outright sales. Costs incurred by the Group in connection with negotiating and arranging a lease are recognized as an expense when the selling profit is recognized.

The current portion of Finance Lease Receivables is presented as part of Other Current Financial Assets—Net.

4. Cash and Cash Equivalents

This account consists of the following:

	January 1, 2010	December 31 2010	December 31 2011
Cash on hand (including US$10 on January 1, 2010, US$12 on December 31, 2010 and US$13 on December 31, 2011)	1,581	1,792	1,580
Cash in banks			
Related parties (Note 29) (including US$4,365 on January 1, 2010, US$4,726 on December 31, 2010 and US$3,805 on December 31, 2011)	91,783	116,107	93,880
Third parties (including US$9,759 on January 1, 2010, US$12,885 on December 31, 2010 and US$13,506 on December 31, 2011)	131,106	165,588	209,519
	222,889	281,695	303,399

(continued)

		December 31	
	January 1, 2010	2010	2011
Time deposits and deposits on call			
Related parties (Note 29) (including US$265 on January 1, 2010, US$81,705 on December 31, 2010 and US$11,115 on December 31, 2011)	1,976,259	1,499,544	884,080
Third parties (including US$22,725 on January 1, 2010, US$12,454 on December 31, 2010 and US$24,917 on December 31, 2011)	635,270	292,239	1,035,147
	2,611,529	1,791,783	1,919,227
Total	2,835,999	2,075,270	2,224,206

Time deposits and deposits on call denominated in rupiah earned interest at annual rates ranging from 2.50% to 14.50% in 2009, from 2.50% to 10.00% in 2010 and from 2.50% to 9.75% in 2011, while those denominated in U.S. dollar earned interest at annual rates ranging from 0.001% to 6.00% in 2009, from 0.05% to 4.75% in 2010 and from 0.01% to 2.75% in 2011.

The interest rates on deposits on call and time deposits in related parties are comparable to those offered by third parties.

6. Taxes Receivable

This account consists of claims for tax refund as of January 1, 2010 and December 31, 2010 and 2011 amounting to Rp396,581, Rp479,786 and Rp514,934, respectively, mainly consisting of the Company's corporate income tax for fiscal years 2004, 2005, 2006, 2009, 2010 and 2011 and Satelindo's corporate income tax for fiscal year 2002.

On April 13, 2010, the Company received the tax refund from the Tax Office amounting to Rp41,753 for the remaining tax overpayment of 2004 corporate income tax based on the Tax Court's Decision Letter dated December 4, 2009 on the 2004 corporate income tax.

On July 15, 2010, the Company received Decision Letter No. KEP-357/WPJ.19/BD.05/2010 from the Directorate General of Taxation ("DGT") declining the Company's objection to the correction on Satelindo's corporate income tax for fiscal year 2002 amounting to Rp105,809 (including penalties and interest). On October 14, 2010, the Company submitted an appeal letter to the Tax Court concerning the Company's objection to the correction on Satelindo's corporate income tax for fiscal year 2002. As of April 25, 2012, the Company has not received any decision from the Tax Court on such appeal.

On October 12, 2010, the Company received the Decision Letter from the Tax Court which accepted the Company's objection to the correction of the 2005 corporate income tax amounting to Rp38,155, which was offset against the underpayment of the Company's 2008 and 2009 income tax article 26 based on Tax Collection Letters ("STPs") received by the Company on September 17, 2010 (Note 16). On February 24, 2011, the Company received a copy of a Memorandum for Reconsideration Request (Memori Permohonan Peninjauan Kembali) from the Tax Court to the Supreme Court on the Tax Court's Decision Letter dated October 29, 2010 for the 2005

corporate income tax. On March 25, 2011, the Company submitted a Counter Memorandum for Reconsideration Request to the Supreme Court. As of April 25, 2012, the Company has not received any decision from the Supreme Court on such request.

On April 21, 2011, the Company received the assessment letter on tax overpayment ("SKPLB") from the DGT for the Company's 2009 corporate income tax amounting to Rp29,272, which amount is lower than the amount recognized by the Company in its financial statements. The Company accepted a part of the corrections amounting to Rp835, which was charged to current operations. On May 31, 2011, the Company received the tax refund of its claim for 2009 corporate income tax amounting to Rp23,695 after being offset with the accepted amount of tax correction of VAT for the period January—December 2009 (Note 16). On July 20, 2011, the Company submitted an objection letter to the Tax Office regarding the remaining correction on the Company's 2009 corporate income tax. As of April 25, 2012, the Company has not received any decision from the Tax Office on such letter.

On April 25, 2011, IMM received SKPLB from the Tax Office for IMM's 2009 corporate income tax amounting to Rp34,950, which amount is lower than the amount recognized by IMM in its financial statements. IMM charged the unapproved 2009 claim for tax refund amounting to Rp597 to current operations. On the same date, IMM also received the assessment letters on tax underpayment ("SKPKBs") for IMM's 2009 income tax articles 21 and 23 and VAT totalling Rp4,512 (including penalties and interest). On May 26 2011, IMM received the refund of its claim for 2009 corporate income tax amounting to Rp30,438, after being offset with above underpayment of IMM's 2009 income tax articles 21 and 23 and VAT.

On April 26, 2011, the Company received the Tax Court's Decision Letter which accepted the Company's appeal on the remaining correction of the 2006 corporate income tax. On June 21, 2011, the Company received the tax refund amounting to Rp82,626. On August 22, 2011, the Company received a copy of a Memorandum for Reconsideration Request (Memori Permohonan Peninjauan Kembali) from the Tax Court to the Supreme Court on the Tax Court's Decision Letter dated April 26, 2011 for the 2006 corporate income tax. On September 21, 2011, the Company submitted a Counter-Memorandum for Reconsideration Request to the Supreme Court. As of April 25, 2012, the Company has not received any decision from the Supreme Court on such request.

Presentation of Operating Activities Using the Indirect Method—Interest Received Explicitly Presented in Operating and Investing Activities, Interest Paid Explicitly Presented in Operating and Financing Activities, and Taxes Paid Explicitly Presented in Operating Activities, Change in Accounting Policy for Dividends Received

Author's Note

As noted previously, IAS 7 permits reporting entities to classify cash flows from interest, dividends, and taxes as follows, as long as the classification is consistent from period to period:

- Interest and dividends received as operating or investing activities
- Interest paid and dividends paid as operating or financing activities

- Taxes received and paid as operating unless the cash flows are readily identifiable with an investing or financing activity

When an entity uses the indirect method to present operating activities and classifies some or all of its interest, dividend and tax cash flows as operating, it should also disclose the related amounts received and paid. These disclosures were traditionally provided outside the financial statement itself. Many companies are now explicitly presenting these specific cash flows in the operating section; that is, the adjustment to net income is for the entirety of the income or expense item and replaced with the cash flows. No adjustment is made for the change in the related receivable or payable. In consequence, the method for presentation of operating activities is a hybrid of the direct and indirect methods. The first two excerpts that follow illustrate this type of presentation.

5.25

Banco Bradesco, S.A. (Dec 2011)

CONSOLIDATED STATEMENT OF CASH FLOWS
(in part)

| | Years Ended December 31 | | |
R$ Thousand	2011	2010	2009
Operating Activities			
Income before income taxes	14,683,469	15,324,117	12,565,173
Adjustments to reconcile income before income tax to net cash flow from operating activities:			
Impairment of loans and advances	8,296,151	5,756,125	10,809,611
Changes in the insurance technical provisions and pension plans	18,212,405	14,294,976	12,768,473
Net gains from disposals on assets available for sale	(238,606)	(645,216)	(549,038)
Depreciation	990,092	956,092	824,899
Amortization of intangible assets	1,130,243	1,010,341	691,630
Impairment of intangible assets	5,126	26,493	36,511
Equity in the earnings of associates	(682,122)	(577,053)	(728,867)
Losses on disposal of non-current assets held for sale	237,727	292,595	315,248
Net losses from disposal of property and equipment	8,596	12,148	14,355
Gains on sale of investments in associated companies	—	—	(2,409,619)
Changes in assets and liabilities:			
Increase in compulsory deposits in the Central Bank	(6,013,739)	(47,273,389)	(4,722,952)
Increase in loans and advances to banks	(25,693,398)	(29,473,272)	(22,935,353)
Increase in loans and advances to customers	(88,088,656)	(81,584,730)	(44,996,235)
(Increase)/decrease in financial assets held for trading	(75,106,993)	(36,900,513)	2,166,148
(Increase)/decrease in other assets	(6,508,618)	(1,578,591)	18,752,963
Net increase in deposits from banks	50,571,306	62,708,679	26,705,387
Net increase in deposits from customers	38,975,249	32,148,572	14,716,268
Increase/(decrease) in financial liabilities held for trading	14,243	200,545	(1,523,248)
Decrease in insurance technical provisions and pension plans	(2,593,130)	(3,398,827)	(2,739,259)
Increase in other provisions	4,598,584	2,475,383	893,781
Increase/(decrease) in other liabilities	8,852,270	9,209,750	(8,749,105)
Interest received	64,161,337	52,844,025	48,030,114
Interest paid	(33,332,306)	(20,474,472)	(15,892,066)
Income and social contribution taxes paid	(5,383,283)	(3,196,072)	(3,791,506)
Other changes in taxes	(4,156,577)	(500,862)	(1,551,228)
Net cash provided by/(used in) operating activities (Revised—See Note 2 (z))	(37,060,630)	(28,343,156)	38,702,085

(continued)

R$ Thousand	Years Ended December 31		
	2011	2010	2009
Investing Activities			
Acquisitions of subsidiaries, net of cash and cash equivalents paid	(214,676)	(226,765)	35,779
Acquisitions of financial assets available for sale	(19,055,607)	(41,287,204)	(15,854,009)
Proceeds from sale of financial assets available for sale	32,753,402	9,405,730	754,251
Acquisitions of investments held to maturity	—	—	(14,554)
Redemption of investments held to maturity	105,722	89,844	62,828
Disposal of non-current assets held for sale	228,958	327,377	324,246
Acquisition of investments in associated companies	(111,826)	(786,688)	(339,902)
Disposal of investments in associated companies	—	—	2,519,272
Dividends received from investments in associated companies (Revised—See Note 2 (z))	489,200	496,698	560,965
Acquisition of property and equipment	(1,698,704)	(1,356,856)	(1,299,292)
Disposal of property and equipment	102,079	123,876	252,150
Acquisition of intangible assets	(3,232,620)	(1,695,177)	(1,058,075)
Dividends received	126,696	109,200	208,217
Interest received	7,190,077	5,494,551	2,736,771
Net cash provided by/(used in) investing activities (Revised—See Note 2 (z))	16,682,701	(29,305,414)	(11,111,353)
Financing Activities			
Funds from securities issued	28,212,490	12,815,608	3,565,694
Payment of funds from securities issued	(5,679,892)	(3,725,745)	(3,705,243)
Issuance of subordinated debts	9,505,799	1,282,600	2,628,271
Payment of subordinated debts	(6,542,624)	(828,351)	—
Premium on share subscription	11,441	—	—
Capital increase in cash	1,500,000	—	—
Acquisition of treasury shares	(173,060)	(14,789)	(184,021)
Increase/(decrease) of non-controlling interest	42,483	(448,060)	19,131
Interest paid	(2,342,856)	(1,611,252)	(2,933,162)
Interest on equity and dividends paid	(3,568,337)	(2,914,982)	(2,829,871)
Net cash provided by/(used in) financing activities	20,965,444	4,555,029	(3,439,201)
Increase/(decrease) in cash and cash equivalents	587,515	(53,093,541)	24,151,531
Cash and cash equivalents			
At the beginning of the year	36,265,611	89,359,152	65,207,621
At the end of the year	36,853,126	36,265,611	89,359,152
Increase/(decrease) in cash and cash equivalents	587,515	(53,093,541)	24,151,531
Non-cash transactions			
Credit operations transferred to non-current assets	758,757	988,702	1,054,613
Dividends and interest on equity declared but not yet paid	2,519,378	2,029,222	1,548,141
Unrealized gains/losses on securities available for sale	468,447	(390,638)	(2,091,932)
Exchange of shares on acquisition of Odontoprev	—	—	327,302

NOTES TO THE CONSOLIDATED FINANCIAL STATEMENTS (in part)

1) General Information

Banco Bradesco S.A. ("Bradesco," the "Bank," the "Company" or the "Organization") is a publicly-traded company established according to the laws of the Federative Republic of Brazil with headquarters in the city of Osasco, state of São Paulo, Brazil.

Bradesco is a bank that provides multiple services within two segments: banking and insurance. The Bank complies with Brazilian banking regulations and operates throughout all of Brazil. The banking segment includes a number of areas in the banking activities, serving individual and corporate customers in the following operations: investment banking, national and international banking operations, asset management operations and consortium administration. The insurance segment covers auto, health, life, accident and property insurance and pension plans as well as capitalization bonds.

The retail banking products include demand deposits, savings deposits, time deposits, mutual funds, foreign exchange services and a range of credit operations, including overdrafts, credit cards and loans with repayments in installments.

The services provided to corporate entities include fund management and treasury services, foreign exchange operations, corporate finance and investment banking services, hedge and finance operations including working capital financing, leasing and loans with repayments in installments. These services are provided, mainly, in domestic markets, but also include international services on a smaller scale.

The Organization was originally listed on the São Paulo Stock Exchange ("BM&FBovespa") and then subsequently on the New York Stock Exchange ("NYSE").

The consolidated financial statements were approved by the Board of Directors on April 30, 2012.

2) Significant Accounting Practices (in part)

These consolidated financial statements of the Organization were prepared in accordance with the International Financial Reporting Standards (IFRS) issued by the International Accounting Standards Board (IASB). The consolidated financial statements include the consolidated statement of financial position, consolidated statement of income, consolidated statement of comprehensive income, consolidated statement of changes in equity and consolidated statement of cash flows as well as the notes to the consolidated financial statements.

The consolidated financial statements have been prepared on the historical cost basis except for the following material items in the statement of financial position: financial assets available for sale measured at fair value, assets and liabilities held for trading measured at fair value, and financial instruments at fair value through profit or loss that are measured at fair value and the liability for defined benefit obligations is recognized as the present value of the defined benefit obligation less the net total of the plan assets, plus unrecognized actuarial gains, less unrecognized past service cost and unrecognized actuarial losses.

The Organization has classified its expenses according to their nature.

The consolidated statement of cash flows shows the changes in cash and cash equivalents during the year arising from operating, investing and financing activities. Cash and cash equivalents include highly liquid investments. Note 19 details the accounts of the consolidated statement of financial position comprising cash and cash equivalents. The consolidated statement of cash flows is prepared using the indirect method. Accordingly, the income before taxes and the participation of non-controlling interests were adjusted by non-cash items such as gains or losses, on provisions, depreciation, amortization and losses due to impairment of loans and advances. The interests received and paid are classified as operating cash flows.

c) Cash and Cash Equivalents

Cash and cash equivalents include: cash, bank deposits, unrestricted balances held with the Central Bank and other highly liquid short–term investments, with original maturities of three months or less and are subject to insignificant risk of changes in fair value, used by the Organization to manage its short-term commitments. See Note 19 (b)—"Cash and cash equivalents."

Cash and cash equivalents are held at amortized cost in the statement of financial position.

t) Interest

Interest income and expenses are recognized on an accrual basis in the consolidated statement of income using the effective interest rate method. The effective interest rate is the rate that discounts estimated future cash payments and receipts throughout the expected life of the financial asset or liability (or, when appropriate, a shorter period) to the carrying amount of the financial asset or liability. When calculating the effective rate of, the Organization estimates future cash flows considering all contractual terms of the financial instrument, but not future credit losses.

The calculation of the effective interest rate includes all commissions, transaction costs, discounts or bonuses which are an integral part of such rate. Transaction costs are incremental costs directly attributable to the acquisition, issuance or disposal of a financial asset or liability.

z) Change in Classification in the Statement of Cash Flows

In these financial statements the Organization has voluntarily elected to change its accounting policy with respect to the classification in the cash flow statements of dividends received from investments in associated companies. This accounting policy change did not affect the amounts that were previously recorded as assets, liabilities, equity, net income or other comprehensive income.

In the previously issued financial statements for the years ended December 31, 2010 and 2009 dividends received from investments in associated companies were presented as a cash inflow from operating activities. In these financial statements dividends received from investments in associated companies are presented as a cash inflow from investing activities and prior periods have been revised to be presented on a consistent basis. Management believes that this presentation provides more relevant information by including as cash flows from investing activities all cash inflows and outflows related to its associated companies including the purchase and sale of interests as well as dividends received.

As a result of the change in accounting policy there was a decrease in the 2010 and 2009 previously reported cash flow statements in the line "Net cash provided by (used in) operating activities" and a corresponding increase in the line "Net cash provided by (used in) investing activities" in the amounts of R$ 496,698 thousand and R$ 560,965 thousand, respectively.

19) Cash and Balances With Banks

a) Balances

R$ Thousand	December 31 2011	2010
Cash in local currency	16,123,156	13,941,186
Cash in foreign currency	6,443,564	1,821,837
Restricted deposits in the Brazilian Central Bank [1]	71,210,757	65,197,018
Others	100	86
Total	93,777,577	80,960,127

[1] Compulsory deposits in the Brazilian Central Bank refer to a minimum balance that financial institutions must maintain at the Brazilian Central Bank based on a percentage of deposits received from third parties.

b) Cash and Cash Equivalents

R$ Thousand	December 31 2011	2010
Cash in local currency	16,123,156	13,941,186
Cash in foreign currency	6,443,564	1,821,837
Short-term interbank investments[1]	14,286,306	20,502,502
Others	100	86
Total	36,853,126	36,265,611

[1] Refers to operations with maturity date on the effective date of investment equal to or less than 90 days and insignificant risk of change in the fair value.

Presentation of Operating Activities Using the Indirect Method—Interest Received and Paid, Dividends Received, and Tax Received and Paid Explicitly Presented in Operating Activities, Reconciliation of Profit (Loss) to Net Cash Flows From Operating Activities Provided in a Note Disclosure

5.26

KT Corporation (Dec 2011)

CONSOLIDATED STATEMENTS OF CASH FLOWS
(in part)

Years ended December 31, 2010 and 2011

(In Millions of Korean Won)	Notes	2010	2011	(In Thousands of U.S. Dollars) 2011
Cash Flows From Operating Activities				(Note 2)
Cash generated from operations	33	(Won) 3,272,059	(Won) 2,905,037	$2,518,891
Interest paid		(554,054)	(512,643)	(444,501)
Interest received		252,161	156,932	136,072
Dividends received		50,194	15,330	13,293
Income tax paid		(79,470)	(414,631)	(359,517)
Income tax refund received		32,218	284	246
Net cash generated from operating activities		2,973,108	2,150,309	1,864,484
Cash Flows From Investing Activities				
Collection of loans		13,523	66,713	57,845
Origination of loans		(53,621)	(71,450)	(61,953)
Disposal of available-for-sale financial assets		74,363	65,760	57,019
Acquisition of available-for-sale financial assets		(86,289)	(188,752)	(163,663)
Disposal of investments in jointly controlled entities and associates		48,703	102,563	88,930
Acquisition of investments in jointly controlled entities and associates		(276,404)	(65,055)	(56,407)
Disposal of current and non-current financial instruments		476,443	240,779	208,774
Acquisition of current and non-current financial instruments		(252,035)	(257,619)	(223,376)
Disposal of property and equipment		181,425	594,250	515,261
Acquisition of property and equipment		(2,713,358)	(3,208,337)	(2,781,875)
Disposal of intangible assets		6,008	14,763	12,801
Acquisition of intangible assets		(331,779)	(476,888)	(413,499)
Acquisition of subsidiaries, net of cash acquired		(2,749)	208,752	181,004
Cash inflow (outflow) from changes in scope of consolidation		(33,298)	326,524	283,121
Net cash used in investing activities		(2,949,068)	(2,647,997)	(2,296,018)
Cash Flows From Financing Activities				
Proceeds from borrowings and bonds		5,698,981	7,224,666	6,264,342
Repayments of borrowings and bonds		(5,575,825)	(6,025,054)	(5,224,186)
Settlement of derivative assets and liabilities, net		8,959	130,119	112,823
Cash inflow from consolidated capital transaction		1,205	83,855	72,709
Cash outflow from consolidated capital transaction		(300)	(2,213)	(1,919)
Dividends paid to shareholders		(486,393)	(586,150)	(508,237)
Dividends paid to non-controlling interest		(6,792)	(9,050)	(7,847)
Decrease in finance leases liabilities		(38,183)	(47,701)	(41,360)
Net cash provided by (used in) financing activities		(398,348)	768,472	666,325
Effect of exchange rate change on cash and cash equivalents		(6,923)	12,744	11,050
Net increase (decrease) in cash and cash equivalents		(381,231)	283,528	245,841
Cash and cash equivalents				
Beginning of the period	6	1,542,872	1,161,641	1,007,232
End of the period	6	(Won) 1,161,641	(Won) 1,445,169	$1,253,073

NOTES TO THE CONSOLIDATED FINANCIAL STATEMENTS (in part)

1. General Information (in part)

The consolidated financial statements include the accounts of KT Corporation, which is the controlling company as defined under IAS 27, *Consolidated and Separate Financial Statements*, and its 51 controlled subsidiaries as described in Note 1.2 (collectively referred to as the "Company").

The Controlling Company

KT Corporation (the "Controlling Company") commenced operations on January 1, 1982, when it spun off from the Korea Communications Commission (formerly the Korean Ministry of Information and Communications) to provide telephone services and to engage in the development of advanced communications services under the Act of Telecommunications of Korea. The headquarters are located in Seongnam-si, Gyeonggi-do, Republic of Korea, and the address of its registered head office is 206, Jungja-dong, Bundang-gu, Seongnam-si, Gyeonggi-do.

On October 1, 1997, upon the announcement of the Government-Investment Enterprises Management Basic Act and the Privatization Law, the Controlling Company became a government-funded institution under the Commercial Code of Korea.

On December 23, 1998, the Controlling Company's shares were listed on the Korea Exchange.

On May 29, 1999, the Controlling Company issued 24,282,195 additional shares and issued American Depository Shares (ADS), representing new shares and government-owned shares, at the New York Stock Exchange and the London Stock Exchange. On July 2, 2001, the additional ADS representing 55,502,161 government-owned shares were issued at the New York Stock Exchange and London Stock Exchange.

In 2002, the Controlling Company acquired 60,294,575 government-owned shares in accordance with the Korean government's privatization plan. As of December 31, 2011, the Korean government does not own any share in the Controlling Company.

On June 1, 2009, the Controlling Company, which is an existing company, was merged with KT Freetel Co., Ltd., which was a subsidiary, to enhance the efficiency of business management.

2. Significant Accounting Policies (in part)

The following is a summary of significant accounting policies followed by the Company in the preparation of its financial statements. These policies have been consistently applied to all the periods presented, unless otherwise stated.

2.5 Cash and Cash Equivalents

Cash and cash equivalents include cash on hand, deposits held at call with banks, and other short-term highly liquid investments with original maturities of less than three months.

6. Cash and Cash Equivalents

Cash and cash equivalents as of January 1, 2010 and December 31, 2010 and 2011 are as follows:

(In Millions of Korean Won)	1.1.2010	12.31.2010	12.31.2011
Cash on hand	(Won) 3,212	(Won) 8,646	(Won) 11,330
Cash in banks	351,243	418,984	652,374
Money market trust	108,000	320,000	464,000
Other financial instruments	1,080,417	414,011	317,465
Total	(Won) 1,542,872	(Won) 1,161,641	(Won) 1,445,169

Cash and cash equivalents in the statement of financial position equal cash and cash equivalents in the statements of cash flows.

Restricted cash and cash equivalents as of January 1, 2010 and December 31, 2010 and 2011 are as follows:

(In Millions of Korean Won)	Type	1.1.2010	12.31.2010	12.31.2011	Description
Cash and cash equivalents	Restricted deposit	(Won) 10,341	(Won) 9,494	(Won) 8,707	Deposit restricted for governmental project

33. Cash Generated From Operations

Cash flows from operating activities for the years ended December 31, 2010 and 2011 are as follows:

(In Millions of Korean Won)	2010	2011
1. Profit for the period	(Won) 1,314,884	(Won) 1,452,019
2. Adjustments to reconcile net income		
Income tax expenses	396,369	316,735
Interest income[1]	(257,483)	(325,028)
Interest expense[1]	585,462	588,366
Depreciation	2,972,503	2,671,858
Amortization of intangible assets	266,299	319,875
Provision for severance benefits	160,095	250,576
Bad debt expenses	204,009	168,096
Income or losses from jointly controlled entities and associates[2]	(33,182)	473
Gain or loss on disposal of jointly controlled entities and associates	(16,727)	(190,631)
Impairment on jointly controlled entities and associates	—	5,107
Impairment on property and equipment	10,464	18,594
Gain or loss on disposal of property and equipment	62,425	(226,571)
Contribution of provisions	58,253	59,116
Reversal of provisions	(12,909)	(4,963)
Foreign currency translation gain (loss)	(33,339)	79,189
Gain or loss on valuation of derivatives	(5,405)	(28,101)
Others	(83,628)	(282,083)
3. Changes in operating assets and liabilities		
Increase in trade receivables	(1,033,307)	(1,412,493)
Decrease in other receivables	208	879,746
Increase in loans receivable	(285,207)	(152,497)
Increase in finance lease receivables	(156,863)	(183,669)
Increase in other assets	(167,179)	(79,175)
Decrease in inventories	55,954	32,113
Increase in trade payables	142,014	98,761
Decrease in other payables	(393,388)	(1,077,806)
Increase in other liabilities	(3,034)	62,579
Decrease in provisions	264,900	29,365
Increase in deferred revenue	219,629	196,507
Increase in contribution on plan assets	(3,848)	(125,984)
Payment of severance benefits	(955,910)	(235,037)
4. Net cash provided by operating activities (1 + 2 + 3)	(Won) 3,272,059	(Won) 2,905,037

[1] Interest income of (Won) 173,740 million (2010: (Won) 160,043 million) recognized as operating revenues and interest expense (Won) 106,951 million (2010: (Won) 95,537 million) recognized as operating expense are included.

[2] Operating revenue of (Won) 2,701 million (2010: (Won) 622 million) and operating expenses of (Won) 136 million (2010: (Won) 126 million) from jointly controlled entities and associates are included.

Significant transactions not affecting cash flows for the years ended December 31, 2010 and 2011, are as follows:

(In Millions of Korean Won)	2010	2011
Reclassification of the current portion of bonds payable	(Won) 1,920,773	(Won) 1,080,549
Reclassification of construction-in-progress to property and equipment	2,383,898	3,165,808

Presentation of Operating Activities Using the Indirect Method—Adjustments for Depreciation, Amortization of Program Rights and Video Rentals, Asset Impairment, Settlement of Pension Obligations, Pension and Stock-Based Compensation Expense, Amortization of Fair Value Adjustment of Long-Term Debt on Transition to IFRSs

5.27

Rogers Communications Inc. (Dec 2011)

CONSOLIDATED STATEMENTS OF CASH FLOWS
(in part)

(In millions of Canadian dollars)

Years Ended December 31	2011	2010
Cash Provided by (Used in):		
Operating Activities:		
Net income for the year	$1,563	$1,502
Adjustments to reconcile net income to net cash flows from operating activities:		
Depreciation and amortization	1,743	1,639
Impairment of assets	—	11
Program rights amortization	57	74
Video rental amortization	26	54
Finance costs	738	768
Income tax expense	535	612
Pension contributions, net of expense	(41)	(35)
Settlement of pension obligations	11	—
Stock-based compensation expense	64	50
Amortization of fair value decrement (increment) on long-term debt	1	(2)
Share of the income of associates and joint ventures accounted for using the equity method, net of tax	(7)	(2)
Other	8	12
	4,698	4,683
Change in non-cash operating working capital items	(169)	(386)
	4,529	4,297
Income taxes paid	(99)	(152)
Interest paid	(639)	(651)
	3,791	3,494

Cash and cash equivalents (bank advances) are defined as cash and short-term deposits, which have an original maturity of less than 90 days, less bank advances.

See accompanying notes to consolidated financial statements.

NOTES TO THE CONSOLIDATED FINANCIAL STATEMENTS (in part)

(Tabular amounts in millions of Canadian dollars, except per share amounts)

1. Nature of the Business:

Rogers Communications Inc. ("RCI") is a diversified Canadian communications and media company, incorporated in Canada, with substantially all of its operations and sales in Canada. Through its Wireless segment ("Wireless"), RCI is engaged in wireless voice and data communications services. RCI's Cable segment ("Cable") consists of Cable Operations, Rogers Business Solutions ("RBS") and Rogers Video ("Video"). Through Cable Operations, RCI provides television, high-speed Internet and telephony products primarily to residential customers; RBS provides local and long-distance telephone, enhanced voice and data networking services, and IP access to medium and large Canadian businesses and governments; and Video offers digital video disc ("DVD") and video game sales and rentals. RCI is engaged in radio and television broadcasting, televised shopping, consumer, trade and professional publications, sports entertainment, and digital media properties through its Media segment ("Media"). RCI and its subsidiary companies are collectively referred to herein as the "Company."

The Company's registered office is located at 333 Bloor Street East, 10th Floor, Toronto, Ontario, M4W 1G9.

RCI Class A Voting and Class B Non-Voting shares are traded in Canada on the Toronto Stock Exchange ("TSX") and its Class B Non-Voting shares are also traded on the New York Stock Exchange ("NYSE").

2. Significant Accounting Policies: (in part)

(a) Statement of Compliance:

These consolidated financial statements have been prepared in accordance with International Financial Reporting Standards ("IFRS") as issued by the International Accounting Standards Board ("IASB"). These are the Company's first annual consolidated financial statements prepared in accordance with IFRS, and the Company has elected January 1, 2010 as the date of transition to IFRS (the "Transition Date"). IFRS 1, First-time Adoption of IFRS ("IFRS 1"), has been applied. An explanation of how the transition to IFRS has affected the consolidated financial statements is included in note 3.

The consolidated financial statements of the Company for the years ended December 31, 2011 and 2010 and as at January 1, 2010 were approved by the Board of Directors on February 21, 2012.

(b) Basis of Presentation:

The consolidated financial statements include the accounts of the Company. Intercompany transactions and balances are eliminated on consolidation.

The consolidated financial statements have been prepared mainly under the historical cost convention. Other measurement bases used are described in the applicable notes. The Company's financial year corresponds to the calendar year. The consolidated financial statements are prepared in millions of Canadian dollars.

Presentation of the consolidated statements of financial position differentiates between current and non-current assets and liabilities. The consolidated statements of income are presented using the nature classification for expenses.

Concurrent with the impact of the transition to IFRS described in note 3, the Company underwent a change in strategy which impacted the Company's management reporting resulting in changes to the Company's reportable segments. Commencing January 1, 2011, the results of the former Rogers Retail segment are segregated as follows: the results of operations of the Video business are presented as a separate operating segment and the former Rogers Retail segment results of operations related to wireless and cable products and services are included in the results of operations of Wireless and Cable Operations, respectively. In addition, certain intercompany transactions between the Company's RBS segment and other operating segments, which were previously recorded as revenue in RBS and operating expenses in the other operating segments, are recorded as cost recoveries in RBS beginning January 1, 2011. The effect of these changes in management reporting on the comparatives for 2010 was a decrease in RBS revenue of $108 million and a decrease in RBS operating costs of $108 million, and a decrease in Video revenue of $212 million and a decrease in Video operating costs of $206 million. These transactions were offset by elimination entries resulting in no effect to the consolidated revenue or operating costs.

3. Transition to IFRS: (in part)

As stated in note 2(a), these are the Company's first annual consolidated financial statements prepared in accordance with IFRS.

The accounting policies set out in note 2 have been applied in preparing the consolidated financial statements as at and for the year ended December 31, 2011, the comparative information presented in these consolidated financial statements as at and for the year ended December 31, 2010, and for the opening IFRS statement of financial position at January 1, 2010 (the Company's Transition Date to IFRS). In preparing its opening and comparative IFRS statements of financial positions, the Company has adjusted amounts reported previously in financial statements prepared in accordance with previous Canadian GAAP.

In addition to the changes required to adjust for the accounting policy differences described in the following notes, interest paid and income taxes paid have been moved into the body of the consolidated statements of cash flows as part of operating activities, whereas they were previously disclosed as supplementary information. There are no other material differences related to presentation of the consolidated statements of cash flows.

(g) Financial Instruments—Transaction Costs:

The Company has applied IAS 39, Financial Instruments: Recognition and Measurement ("IAS 39"), at January 1, 2010, which requires directly attributable costs to be added to certain acquired financial assets and liabilities and amortized to the consolidated statements of income over the life of the asset or liability. Under previous Canadian GAAP, these costs were expensed as incurred. Unamortized transaction costs of $58 million related to the Company's long-term debt were adjusted upon transition. Additionally, unamortized discounts recognized on long-term debt have been reclassified from other long-term assets to conform with IFRS presentation requirements.

The impact of the change is summarized as follows:

Year Ended December 31	2010
Consolidated statement of comprehensive income:	
Finance costs—amortization	$ 13
Finance costs—debt issuances	(10)
Adjustment before income taxes	$ 3

	January 1, 2010	December 31, 2010
Consolidated statements of financial position:		
Other long-term assets—reclassify unamortized discounts	$ (9)	$ (9)
Long-term debt—reclassify unamortized discounts	9	9
Long-term debt—unamortized transaction costs	58	55
Adjustment to retained earnings before income taxes	58	55
Related income tax effect	(16)	(15)
Adjustment to retained earnings	$42	$40

Operating Activities: Exploration and Evaluation, Depletion and Depreciation, Gain on Divestiture of Oil and Gas Properties, Asset Retirement Expenditures

5.28

Baytex Energy Corp. (Sep 2011)

CONSOLIDATED STATEMENTS OF CASH FLOWS (in part)

Years Ended December 31	2011	2010
(Thousands of Canadian Dollars)		
Cash Provided by (Used in):		
Operating Activities		
Net income for the year	$217,432	$231,615
Adjustments for:		
Share-based or unit-based compensation (note 17)	33,845	94,199
Unrealized foreign exchange loss (gain) (note 22)	8,490	(8,999)
Exploration and evaluation	10,130	18,913
Depletion and depreciation	248,468	202,796
Unrealized loss on financial derivatives (note 23)	16,166	43,312
Gain on divestitures of oil and gas properties	(37,946)	(16,227)
Deferred income tax expense (recovery) (note 19)	52,141	(124,240)
Financing costs (note 21)	44,611	34,570
Change in non-cash working capital (note 22)	(10,889)	(11,704)
Asset retirement expenditures (note 15)	(10,588)	(2,829)
	571,860	461,406

NOTES TO THE CONSOLIDATED FINANCIAL STATEMENTS (in part)

(All tabular amounts in thousands of Canadian dollars, except per common share and per trust unit amounts)

1. Reporting Entity

Baytex Energy Corp. (the "Company" or "Baytex") is an oil and gas corporation engaged in the acquisition, development and production of oil and natural gas in the Western Canadian Sedimentary Basin and the United States. The Company's common shares are traded on the Toronto Stock Exchange and the New York Stock Exchange under the symbol BTE. The Company's head and principal office is located at 2800, 520—3 rd Avenue S.W., Calgary, Alberta, T2P 0R3, and its registered office is located at 2400, 525—8 th Avenue S.W., Calgary, Alberta, T2P 1G1.

Baytex Energy Trust (the "Trust") completed the conversion of its legal structure from an income trust to a corporation at year-end 2010 pursuant to a Plan of Arrangement under the Business Corporations Act (Alberta) (the "Arrangement"). Pursuant to the Arrangement, (i) on December 31, 2010, the trust units of the Trust were exchanged for common shares of Baytex on a one-for-one basis and (ii) on January 1, 2011, the Trust was dissolved and terminated, with Baytex being the successor to the Trust. The reorganization into a corporation

has been accounted for on a continuity of interest basis, and accordingly, the consolidated financial statements reflect the financial position, results of operations and cash flows as if the Company had always carried on the business formerly carried on by the Trust.

2. Basis of Presentation

The consolidated financial statements have been prepared in accordance with International Financial Reporting Standards ("IFRS") as issued by the International Accounting Standards Board. Canadian generally accepted accounting principles have been revised to incorporate IFRS and publicly accountable enterprises are required to apply such standards for years beginning on or after January 1, 2011. Accordingly, these consolidated financial statements were prepared in accordance with IFRS 1, First-time Adoption of IFRS. The significant accounting policies set out below were consistently applied to all the periods presented.

In these financial statements, the term "previous GAAP" refers to Canadian generally accepted accounting principles prior to the adoption of IFRS. Previous GAAP differs in some areas from IFRS. In preparing these consolidated financial statements, management has amended certain accounting, valuation and consolidation methods applied in the previous GAAP financial statements to comply with IFRS. The date of transition to IFRS was January 1, 2010 and the comparative figures for 2010 were restated to reflect these adjustments. Reconciliations and descriptions of the effect of the transition from previous GAAP to IFRS on equity, net income and comprehensive income are included in note 29.

The consolidated financial statements were approved and authorized by the Board of Directors on March 13, 2012.

The consolidated financial statements have been prepared on the historical cost basis, except for derivative financial instruments which have been measured at fair value. The consolidated financial statements are presented in Canadian dollars, which is the Company's functional currency. All financial information is rounded to the nearest thousand, except per share or per trust unit amounts and when otherwise indicated.

3. Significant Accounting Policies (in part)

Exploration and Evaluation Assets, Oil and Gas Properties and Other Plant and Equipment

a) Pre-License Costs

Pre-license costs are costs incurred before the legal rights to explore a specific area have been obtained. These costs are expensed in the period in which they are incurred.

b) Exploration and Evaluation ("E&E") Costs

Once the legal right to explore has been acquired, costs directly associated with an exploration well are capitalized as an intangible asset until the drilling of the well program/project is complete and the results have been evaluated. Such E&E costs may include costs of license acquisition, technical services and studies, seismic acquisition, exploration drilling and testing. E&E costs are not depleted and are carried forward until technical feasibility and commercial viability of extracting a mineral resource is considered to be determined. The technical feasibility and commercial viability of extracting a mineral resource is considered to be determined when proved and/or probable reserves are determined to exist. All such carried costs are subject to technical, commercial and management review quarterly to confirm the continued intent to develop or otherwise extract value from the discovery. When this is no longer the case, the impairment costs are charged to exploration and evaluation expense. Upon determination of proven and/or probable reserves, E&E assets attributable to those reserves are first tested for impairment and then reclassified to oil and gas properties.

c) Development Costs

Costs incurred subsequent to the determination of technical feasibility and commercial viability are recognized as oil and gas properties only when they increase the future economic benefits embodied in the specific asset to which they relate. Such capitalized petroleum and natural gas interests generally represent costs incurred in developing proved and/or probable reserves and bringing in or enhancing production from such reserves and are accumulated on a geotechnical area basis.

Major maintenance and repairs consist of the cost of replacement assets or parts of assets, inspection costs and overhaul costs. Where an asset or part of an asset that was separately depreciated and has been completely written off is replaced and it is probable that there are future economic benefits associated with the item, the expenditure is capitalized. The costs of the day-to-day servicing of property, plant and equipment are recognized in net income as incurred.

The carrying amount of any replaced or sold component of an oil and gas property is derecognized and included in net income in the period in which the item is derecognized.

d) Borrowing Costs and Other Capitalized Costs

Borrowing costs that are directly attributable to the acquisition, construction or production of a qualifying asset form part of the cost of that asset. A qualifying asset is an asset that requires a period of one year or greater to get ready for its intended use or sale. Baytex has had no qualifying assets that would allow for borrowing costs to be capitalized to the asset. All such borrowing costs are expensed as incurred.

No general and administrative expenses have been capitalized since Baytex's inception.

e) Depletion and Depreciation

The net carrying value of oil and gas properties is depleted using the units of production method using estimated proved and probable petroleum and natural gas reserves, by reference to the ratio of production in the year to the related proven and probable reserves at forecast prices, taking into account estimated future development costs necessary to bring those reserves into production. For purposes of this calculation, petroleum and natural gas reserves are converted to a common unit of measurement on the basis of their relative energy content where six thousand cubic feet of natural gas equates to one barrel of oil. Future development costs are estimated as the costs of development required to produce the reserves. These estimates are prepared by independent reserve engineers at least annually.

The depreciation methods and estimated useful lives for other assets for other plant and equipment are as follows:

Classification	Method	Rate or Period
Motor Vehicles	Diminishing balance	15%
Office Equipment	Diminishing balance	20%
Computer Hardware	Diminishing balance	30%
Furniture and Fixtures	Diminishing balance	10%
Leasehold Improvements	Straight-line over life of the lease	Various
Other Assets	Diminishing balance	Various

The expected lives of other plant and equipment are reviewed on an annual basis and, if necessary, changes in expected useful lives are accounted for prospectively.

Asset Retirement Obligations

The Company recognizes a liability at the discounted value for the future asset retirement costs associated with its oil and gas properties using the risk free interest rate. The present value of the liability is capitalized as part of the cost of the related asset and depleted to expense over its useful life. The discount in the liability unwinds until the date of expected settlement of the retirement obligations and is recognized as a finance cost in the statements of income and comprehensive income. The liability will be revised for the effect of any changes to timing related to cash flow or undiscounted abandonment costs. Actual expenditures incurred for the purpose of site reclamation are charged to the asset retirement obligations to the extent that the liability exists on the statements of financial position.

7. Exploration and Evaluation Assets (in part)

Cost	
As at December 31, 2010	$113,082
Capital expenditures	9,104
Corporate acquisition	14,944
Property acquisition	18,013
Exploration and evaluation expense	(10,130)
Transfer to oil and gas properties	(14,398)
Divestitures	(2,058)
Foreign currency translation	1,217
As at December 31, 2011	$129,774

8. Oil and Gas Properties

Cost

As at December 31, 2010	$1,819,351
Capital expenditures	364,578
Corporate acquisition	131,635
Property acquisitions	61,137
Transferred from exploration and evaluation assets	14,398
Change in asset retirement obligations	84,879
Divestitures	(10,233)
Foreign currency translation	5,674
As at December 31, 2011	$2,471,419
Accumulated depletion	
As at December 31, 2010	$ 194,722
Depletion for the period	244,893
Divestitures	(667)
Foreign currency translation	311
As at December 31, 2011	$ 439,259
Carrying value	
As at December 31, 2011	$2,032,160

22. Supplemental Information (in part)

Change in Non-Cash Working Capital Items

	Years Ended December 31	
	2011	**2010**
Trade and other receivables	$(55,159)	$(14,638)
Crude oil inventory	905	(418)
Trade and other payables	40,992	(2,678)
Foreign exchange	(180)	74
	$(13,442)	$(17,660)
Changes in non-cash working capital related to:		
Operating activities	$(10,889)	$(11,704)
Investing activities	(2,553)	(5,956)
	$(13,442)	$(17,660)

Foreign Exchange

	Years Ended December 31	
	2011	**2010**
Unrealized foreign exchange loss (gain)	$8,490	$(8,999)
Realized foreign exchange gain	(656)	(149)
Foreign exchange loss (gain)	$7,834	$(9,148)

29. First-Time Adoption of International Financial Reporting Standards (in part)

O) Statements of Cash Flows

With the exception of a $28.5 million interest paid reclass from operating activities to financing activities for the year ended December 31, 2010, the transition from previous GAAP to IFRS had no material effect on the reported cash flows generated by the Company.

Investing Activities: Increases in Investments in Subsidiaries and Other Investees; Acquisition, Construction and Development of Investment Property; Investments in Fixed Assets; Proceeds From the Sale of Investment Property and Fixed Assets; Grants and Collections of Long-Term Loans

5.29

Gazit-Globe Ltd (Dec 2011)

CONSOLIDATED CASH FLOW STATEMENT (in part)

	Convenience Translation Into U.S. Dollars (Note 2d(1)) Year Ended December 31, 2011	Year Ended December 31,		
		2011	**2010**	**2009**
	In Millions	**NIS in Millions (Except for Per Share Data)**		
Cash flows from investing activities:				
Acquisition of initially consolidated subsidiaries (a)	24	92	—	8
Initial consolidation of investment previously accounted for using proportionate consolidation (b)	(2)	(8)	—	—
Initial proportionate consolidation of company previously accounted for using the equity method (c)	—	—	—	1,262
Increase in holding interest in proportionate consolidated company (d)	(23)	(87)	—	—
Proceeds from realization of consolidated subsidiary (e)	3	11	—	—
Investment in investees	(14)	(54)	(9)	(166)
Acquisition, construction and development of investment property	(1,913)	(7,308)	(3,550)	(2,706)
Investments in fixed assets	(9)	(36)	(24)	(72)
Proceeds from sale of investment property and investment property under development	834	3,186	988	95
Proceeds from sale of fixed assets	3	13	55	*)—
Grant of long-term loans	(61)	(234)	(121)	(16)
Collection of long-term loans	5	20	26	8
Short-term investments, net	21	80	(39)	19
Investment in financial assets	(269)	(1,029)	(422)	(177)
Proceeds from sale of financial assets	132	506	478	1,068
Net cash used in investing activities	(1,269)	(4,848)	(2,618)	(677)

	Convenience Translation Into U.S. Dollars (Note 2d(1)) Year Ended December 31, 2011	Year Ended December 31,		
		2011	2010	2009
	In Millions	NIS in Millions (Except for Per Share Data)		
(a) Acquisition of initially consolidated subsidiaries (Notes 9c6 and 9c7):				
Working capital (excluding cash and cash equivalents):				
Current assets	(4)	(14)	—	(18)
Assets held for sale	(122)	(465)	—	—
Current liabilities	82	311	—	261
	(44)	(168)	—	243
Investment property and other non-current assets	(468)	(1,791)	—	(1,690)
Carrying amount of previous investment	—	—	—	241
Long-term liabilities	279	1,066	—	976
Non-controlling interests in initially consolidated subsidiaries	194	742	—	130
Issue of shares to non-controlling interests in EQY	69	265	—	51
Contingent obligation to issue shares of EQY	—	—	—	37
Gain from bargain purchase (goodwill)	(6)	(22)	—	20
Increase in cash and cash equivalents	24	92	—	8
(b) Initial consolidation of investment previously accounted for using proportionate consolidation (Note 9m):				
Working capital (excluding cash and cash equivalents):				
Current assets	(196)	(747)	—	—
Current liabilities	151	576	—	—
	(45)	(171)	—	—
Non-current assets	(49)	(188)	—	—
Non-current liabilities	49	186	—	—
Non-controlling interests	41	158	—	—
Realization of exchange differences reserve	3	12	—	—
Loss on revaluation of previous investment	(8)	(31)	—	—
Gain from bargain purchase	7	26	—	—
Decrease in cash and cash equivalents	(2)	(8)	—	—
(c) Initial proportionate consolidation of company previously accounted for using the equity method (Note 9g)				
Working capital (excluding cash and cash equivalents):				
Current assets	—	—	—	(255)
Current liabilities	—	—	—	194
	—	—	—	(61)
Investment property	—	—	—	(2,409)
Investment property under development	—	—	—	(1,090)
Other non-current assets	—	—	—	(60)
Non-current liabilities	—	—	—	1,068
Non-controlling interests	—	—	—	20
Investment in shares, convertible debentures and warrants	—	—	—	3,574
Gain from bargain purchase	—	—	—	220
Increase in cash and cash equivalents	—	—	—	1,262
(d) Increase in holding rate in proportionate consolidated company (Note 9g)				
Working capital (excluding cash and cash equivalents):				
Current assets	(4)	(15)	—	—
Current liabilities	3	11	—	—
	(1)	(4)	—	—

(continued)

	Convenience Translation Into U.S. Dollars (Note 2d(1)) Year Ended December 31, 2011	Year Ended December 31,		
		2011	2010	2009
	In Millions	NIS in Millions (Except for Per Share Data)		
Non-current assets	(54)	(206)	—	—
Non-current liabilities	12	46	—	—
Non-controlling interests	*)—	1	—	—
Gain from bargain purchase	20	76	—	—
Decrease in cash and cash equivalents	(23)	(87)	—	—
(e) Proceeds from realizing an investment in a subsidiary (Note 9m)				
Working capital (excluding cash and cash equivalents):	(1)	(3)	—	—
Investment in a company treated according to equity method of accounting	(2)	(9)	—	—
Warrants exercisable into shares in jointly controlled entity	*)—	*)—	—	—
Receipts on account of shares in a subsidiary	(2)	(7)	—	—
Gain from loss of control in a former subsidiary	8	30	—	—
Increase in cash and cash and cash equivalents	3	11	—	—
(f) Significant non-cash transactions: (in part)				
Acquisition of subsidiary's shares and other investments for an issuance of shares by subsidiaries	69	265	37	126

*) Represents an amount of less than NIS 1 million and less than U.S. $1 million.

NOTES TO THE CONSOLIDATED FINANCIAL STATEMENTS (in part)

Note 1:—General (in part)

a. The Company and its business activities

The Company, through its investees (collectively, the "Group"), is the owner, operator and developer of income producing properties in North America, Europe, Israel and Brazil and focuses mainly on the supermarket-anchored shopping center sector. In addition, the Group operates in the medical office buildings sector in North America, the senior housing facilities sector in the U.S., as well as in the development and construction of real estate projects in Israel and Eastern Europe. Furthermore, the Group continues to seek and realize business opportunities by acquiring properties and/or companies that operates within its core business or in similar fields, both in regions where it currently operates and also in new regions.

The Company's securities are listed for trading on the Tel Aviv and New York Stock Exchanges.

b. Initial public offering in the United States

On December 19, 2011 the Company completed the process of registering its shares for trade on the New York Stock Exchange ("NYSE") under the symbol GZT pursuant to a prospectus that was published in the U.S. on December 14, 2011, with initial public offering in the U.S. of 10,350,000 ordinary shares in gross consideration of NIS 350 million. For additional details, refer to Note 27d.

c. As of December 31, 2011 (the "reporting date"), the Group has a working capital deficiency of New Israeli Shekels ("NIS") 958 million. The Group has unutilized approved lines of credit in total amount of NIS 5.4 billion that can be used over the coming year. In addition, as of the reporting date, the Group has unencumbered investment property presented in the consolidated financial statements at its fair value of NIS 33.6 billion. As for the raising of capital and long-term debt by the Group companies after the reporting date, see Note 40. The Company's management believes that the noted sources, as well as the positive cash flow generated from operating activities, will allow each of the Group's companies to repay its current liabilities when due.

Note 2:—Significant Accounting Policies (in part)

a. Basis of presentation of the financial statements

The consolidated financial statements of the Group have been prepared on a cost basis, except for investment property, investment property under development, senior housing facilities and certain financial instruments including derivative instruments that are measured at fair value.

The Company has elected to present profit or loss items using the "function of expense" method.

The basis of preparation of the financial statements

These consolidated financial statements have been prepared in accordance with International Financial Reporting Standards ("IFRS") as issued by the International Accounting Standards Board ("IASB"). These Standards include:

1. International Financial Reporting Standards ("IFRS").
2. International Accounting Standards ("IAS").
3. Interpretations issued by the IFRS Interpretations Committee ("IFRIC") and by the Standing Interpretations Committee ("SIC").

Note 3:—Cash and Cash Equivalents

a. Composition:

NIS in Millions	December 31 2011	December 31 2010
Cash in banks and on hand	901	751
Cash equivalents—short-term deposits	1,060	570
	1,961	1,321

b. Part of the cash in banks bears floating interest based on daily bank deposits rates (as of the reporting date—0.1%—1.78%).

c. The deposits earn annual interest at the rate of 0.15%—5.5%, based on the respective term of the deposits.

d. As for the linkage basis of cash and cash equivalents, refer to Note 37.

Note 9:—Investments in Investees (in part)

c. Investment in Equity One Inc. ("EQY") (a subsidiary)

1. As of December 31, 2011, the Group has a 42.1% interest in EQY's voting rights and the Group's economic interest in EQY's share capital (calculated net of non-controlling interests in Gazit America Inc) is 43.4% (38.2% on a fully diluted basis) of the share capital of EQY. EQY's shares are listed for trading on the New York Stock Exchange. The market price of EQY shares as of December 31, 2011 was U.S. $ 16.98 and close to the date of the approval of the financial statements—U.S. $ 20.12. As of December 31, 2011, EQY has approximately 112.6 million shares outstanding.

The Company consolidates EQY in its financial statements, although its ownership interest in EQY is less than 50%, due to effective control over EQY, refer to Note 2c.

2. Share options of EQY outstanding as of December 31, 2011:

Series	Average Exercise Price Per Share	Expiration Date	Number of Share Options in Thousands
Options to employees and officers[*]	$20.62	2012–2022	3,565

[*] Includes all the share options granted to employees and officers, including 890 thousand options that are unvested. It also includes share options which were granted as part of the employment contract between the Company's Chairman of the Board and EQY, refer to Note 38c(2).

3. EQY has issued restricted shares to directors, officers and employees with various restriction periods. As of December 31, 2010, the share capital of EQY includes 1,178 thousand shares that are unvested. These shares bear voting rights and are entitled to receive dividends. In addition, EQY issued 800 thousand restricted shares to executives that do not bear voting rights and rights to receive dividends.

4. On March 28, 2011, the Company completed an agreement through a wholly-owned subsidiary, for the purchase of 2 million ordinary shares of EQY from Alony-Hetz Properties and Investments Ltd ("Alony-Hetz"), in consideration for U.S. $ 36.5 million (NIS 125 million).

On May 18, 2011, EQY announced a capital-raising through a public offering of 5 million shares in the U.S. at the price of U.S. $ 19.42 per share and in total consideration of U.S. $ 97.1 million (NIS 332 million). Simultaneously, wholly-owned subsidiaries of the Company purchased from EQY an additional 1.0 million EQY shares in a private placement at the offering price and in total consideration of U.S. $ 19.4 million (NIS 66 million).

In a separate transaction, wholly-owned subsidiaries of the Company also purchased from an entity controlled by Alony-Hetz an additional 1.0 million EQY shares, for a total consideration of U.S. $ 19.3 million (NIS 66 million).

As a result of the offering and the purchase, the Group's voting rights in EQY decreased to 40.1% and its economic interest decreased to 41.2% and the Group recognized subsequent to the reporting date a capital decrease amounting to NIS 2 million charged to capital reserve from transactions with non-controlling interests.

5. During the second half of 2011 the Company through wholly-owned subsidiaries, purchased approximately 2.2 million EQY shares during the trade on the NYSE for a total consideration of U.S. $ 36.0 million (NIS 138 million). As a result of the purchases, the Group's voting rights increased to 42.1% and its economic interest increased to 43.4% and the Group recognized a capital decrease amounting to U.S. $ 7.6 million (NIS 28 million) charged to capital reserve from transactions with non-controlling interests.

6. In May 2010 EQY entered into an agreement for the acquisition of C&C US No. 1 Inc. ("CapCo") through a joint venture (the "Joint Venture") with Liberty International Holdings Limited ("LIH"), a subsidiary of Capital Shopping Centers Group Plc ("CSC"). On January 4, 2011 (the "closing date"), CapCo held 13 income-producing properties in California with a total area of 240 thousand square meters, comprised of shopping centers, offices, residential buildings and medical office buildings. On the closing date, LIH contributed all of CapCo's outstanding share capital to the Joint Venture in return for the allocation of 11.4 million units in the Joint Venture ("Units"), granting LIH, a 22% interest in the Joint Venture, which can be converted by LIH into 11.4 million shares of EQY's common stock (subject to certain adjustments) or into cash, at EQY's sole discretion. Furthermore, a 78% interest in the Joint Venture, which consists of approximately 70% of the Class A Joint Venture shares and all of the Class B Joint Venture shares were allocated to EQY in exchange for the issuance of a U.S. $ 600 million promissory note. Class B shares were allocated to EQY as a preferred return instrument. In addition, 4.1 million shares of EQY's common stock were allocated to LIH in exchange for an assignment of a U.S. $ 67 million CapCo's promissory note.

Moreover, EQY allocated to LIH one class A share which was converted in June 2011 according to its terms, into 10,000 shares of EQY's common stock and which under certain limitations confer upon LIH voting rights in EQY, according to its holdings in the Joint Venture's Units. A mortgage-secured debt amounting to approximately U.S. $ 243 million (net of U.S. $ 84.3 million which was repaid in cash by EQY), bearing annual weighted average interest of 5.7%, was assigned to the Joint Venture within the framework of the transaction. Upon the closing of the transaction, the Group's interest in EQY's voting rights reached 38.8% (including all of EQY shares held by GAA) and 39.3% economic rights in EQY's share capital. On the closing date, LIH held a 3.85% interest in EQY's share capital and 13.16% in EQY's voting rights.

As for the Group's shareholders' agreement with LIH and CSC, and with EQY, refer to Note 26a(1). As for EQY's offering of the 4.1 million shares that were allocated to LIH, see Note 40g.

Following the closing of the transaction, the Company continued to consolidate EQY's accounts, due to effective control over EQY.

EQY executed a provisional allocation of the cost of the acquisition to the identifiable net assets of CapCo. Presented below is the fair value of the identifiable assets and liabilities of CapCo at the acquisition date, after being retroactively adjusted following the measurement period adjustment of the fair value of the identifiable assets and liabilities, as permitted pursuant to the provisions of IFRS 3:

NIS in Millions	Provisional Allocation	Measurement Period Adjustment	Fair Value
Cash and cash equivalents	92	—	92
Assets held for sale	465	—	465
Other current assets	14	—	14
Investment property and other non-current assets	1,770	21	1,791
	2,341	21	2,362
Current liabilities	(302)	(9)	(311)
Deferred taxes[2]	(139)	(2)	(141)
Other non-current liabilities	(925)	—	(925)
	(1,366)	(11)	(1,377)
Net assets	975	10	985
Goodwill (gain from bargain purchase)[3]	(63)	85	22
Total acquisition cost[1]	912	95	1,007

[1] The total acquisition cost amounting to U.S. $ 279.8 million (NIS 1,007 million) is comprised of the issuance of 4.1 million shares of EQY's common stock valued at U.S. $ 73.7 million (NIS 265 million) (according to EQY's share price on the issuance date of U.S. $ 18.15) and the fair value of the 11.4 million Units presented as non-controlling interest in CapCo, which was estimated by reference to the amount LIH would be entitled to receive upon redeeming its Joint Venture Units for shares of EQY ("Units' fair value").

The Units' fair value was first estimated at U.S. $ 15.83 per share, or U.S. $ 179.8 million (NIS 647 million) in aggregate, representing a 12.8% discount on EQY's share price, mainly due to the restriction on transferability imposed on the Units and the probability that the Units would not be redeemed for EQY shares for at least five years due to tax obligations, which EQY erroneously believed needed to be taken into account in the valuation.

After performing a reexamination of this matter and conducting consultations with its professional advisors, EQY came to the conclusion that the Units' fair value needed to be calculated without any component of "discount" on EQY's share price. Hence, the interim financial statements for the six month period ended 30 June, 2011 and for the three months ended on March 31, 2011 were restated to reflect the estimation of the Units' fair value at EQY's closing share price on the date of closing the transaction, namely U.S. $ 18.15 per Unit, or U.S. $ 206.1 million (NIS 742 million) in aggregate.

[2] The deferred tax liability solely represents the tax effect of the temporary difference between the fair value and the tax base of CapCo's net identifiable assets, which was recorded only the Company's share, due to the fact that EQY and CapCo are REITs for tax purposes, and as such they do not provide for deferred taxes in their financial statements.

[3] Prior to correcting the aforementioned error, the gain from bargain purchase recognized in 2011, in the amount of NIS 63 million, was fully allocated to the non-controlling interests, since the portion allocable to the Company had been eliminated by the provision for deferred taxes as discussed in (2) above. Following the correction of the error and the measurement period adjustment, goodwill in an amount of NIS 22 million has been recorded in the statement of financial position, which has been allocated in full to the equity holders of the Company, after creating the provision for deferred taxes discussed in (2) above and after setting off bargain purchase gain which had been allocated to the non-controlling interests in amount of NIS 66 million.

As a result of the decrease in the holding interest in EQY, the Group recognized a NIS 16 million increase in equity, which was charged to the capital reserve from transactions with non-controlling interests.

CapCo's revenues and net income during 2011 regarding the properties acquired on the closing date, totaled U.S. $ 57 million (NIS 203 million) and U.S. $ 36 million (NIS 128 million), respectively.

7. Investment in DIM

On January 9, 2009 (the "closing date"), EQY entered into an agreement with Homburg Invest Inc. ("Homburg") to acquire approximately 2,004 thousand Ordinary shares of DIM Vastgoed N.V. ("DIM"). DIM was incorporated in the Netherlands, and was listed for trading on the Euronext Stock Exchange in Amsterdam, the Netherlands until August 2010. At closing Homburg transferred to EQY approximately 1,238 thousand Ordinary shares of DIM in consideration for the issuance by

EQY of approximately 866 thousand shares (representing an exchange ratio of 0.7). On such date, EQY obtained voting rights with respect to another 766 thousand Ordinary shares of DIM (the "additional shares") which Homburg has an option to acquire on October 1, 2010 and which conferred it voting rights. Subject to fulfillment of certain conditions by January 1, 2011, EQY has undertaken to acquire from Homburg the additional shares in consideration for the issuance by EQY of approximately 537 thousand Ordinary shares. Subsequent to this transaction, EQY had a voting interest of approximately 74.6% in DIM. Commencing from the closing date, EQY consolidates the accounts of DIM in its financial statements since its holdings in DIM confer control to EQY.

In February 2010, EQY exercised its right to purchase an additional 766 thousand shares of DIM in exchange for the issuance of 537 thousand EQY Ordinary shares. EQY also issued a purchase offer for the remaining DIM shares owned by the public, at a cash price of U.S. $ 7.3 per share. During 2010, the purchase offer was completed for approximately 1,904 thousand DIM shares in return for approximately U.S. $ 13.7 million (including additional shares purchased on the stock exchange during 2010 and 2011), and EQY's share in DIM increased to 97.8% as of December 31, 2011. EQY is seeking to carry out a forced purchase of the remaining publicly-held DIM shares. In July 2010, a request to approve the forced purchase was submitted to the authorities in the Netherlands and on August 2, 2010 DIM's shares were delisted from trading on the Amsterdam Stock Exchange.

g. Investment in Atrium European Real Estate Limited ("ATR") (A Jointly Controlled Entity)

As of December 31, 2011, the Company owns, through wholly-owned subsidiaries, approximately 31.6% (31.4% on a fully diluted basis) of the share capital of ATR. ATR's shares are listed for trading on the Vienna Stock Exchange and on the Euronext Stock Exchange in Amsterdam. The market price of ATR shares as of December 31, 2011 was €3.48 and close to the date of the approval of the financial statements—€3.71. As of December 31, 2011, ATR has approximately 372.9 million shares outstanding.

The Company proportionally consolidates ATR in its financial statements due to joint control over ATR, pursuant to a shareholders' agreement with CPI European Fund ("CPI"), a member of Apollo Global Real Estate Management L.P, as detailed in Note 26a(4).

The share options of ATR outstanding as of December 31, 2011:

Series	Average Exercise Price Per Share	Expiration Date	Number of Share Options (In Thousands)
Options to employees and officers[*]	€2.99	2012-2015	5,372

[*] As of December 31, 2011, 2,052 thousand share options are fully vested.

In addition, ATR operates a restricted share plan to directors, as a substitute to a cash director remuneration, at the directors' discretion. As of the reporting date, 24 thousand restricted shares were granted under the plan.

Additional Information About the Investment in ATR

On March 20, 2008, the Company and CPI entered into a series of agreements for a joint investment in ATR (collectively, the "original investment agreement") (Company's share 54%; CPI share 46%). The transaction was completed on August 1, 2008. ATR, which is incorporated in the Island of Jersey in the Channel Islands ("Jersey"), is a property real estate investment company focused on the acquisition and development of supermarket-anchored shopping centers. ATR is engaged in the rental, management and development of shopping centers in 11 countries in Central and Eastern Europe, primarily in Poland, the Czech Republic, Russia, Slovakia and Hungary.

Description of the Original Investment Agreement in ATR

Pursuant to the original investment agreement, the Company and CPI (collectively: the "Investors") invested in ATR securities as follows:

1. At the date of closing, €500 million (the Company's share—€270 million) was invested in non-listed debentures of ATR which are convertible into ATR shares at the conversion price of €9 per share, subject to the usual adjustments. The debentures bear interest at the rate of 10.75%, which was paid on a quarterly basis. The debentures provided the Investors the right to vote at the general shareholders' meeting even prior to their conversion into shares.

2. It was provided that ATR would issue rights to its shareholders within six months from closing in the scope of €300 million, at a price of €7 per share and if the shareholders do not take up their rights in full, the investors would acquire the shares issuable pursuant to the rights not taken up (the "Underwriting Commitment").

3. The Investors were granted an option to acquire, within six months from the closing date of the aforementioned rights issue, ATR shares at a per share price of €7 in the total amount of €200 million, less amounts invested, if and when invested, by the Investors as part of the Underwriting Commitment.

4. Upon closing, the Investors were issued, without additional consideration, warrants to purchase 30 million shares of ATR at an exercise price of €7 and exercisable over a period of four years from the issue date (the Company's share—warrants to purchase 16.2 million shares).

According to the original investment agreement, the Investors (pursuant to the articles of association of ATR) received a right to appoint four directors of ATR (out of ten Board members), including the Chairman of the Board of Directors. This right was subject to their joint investment in ATR (including the aforementioned debentures) not falling below €300 million. The other directors of the Board were to be independent directors who are nominated by a committee whose composition was such that the Investors had the right to appoint the majority of its members and whose election was approved by the general shareholders' meeting. Upon closing, Mr. Chaim Katzman, the Company's Chairman of the Board, became Chairman of the Board of Directors of ATR.

In addition, according to the original investment agreement, provided that the scope of the investment of the joint entity does not decrease below €200 million, the Investors were provided with extensive consent rights with respect to ATR, including rights regarding the appointment of a CEO of ATR (which is approved by ATR's Board), the extent of ATR's liabilities, changes in its articles of association, the issuance of securities under certain circumstances, liabilities in excess of €200 million, approval of other transactions and other rights.

As of the closing date of the original investment agreement, the Investors held 23.8% of the voting rights in ATR (the Company's share—14.3%) and 3.9% of ATR's capital (the Company's share—3.9%).

Description of the Additional Investment Agreement in ATR

On January 13, 2009, the Investors and ATR signed an agreement which was completed on January 30, 2009, that set the terms of the additional investment in ATR, the principal terms of which are as follows:

1. The planned issuance by ATR of rights amounting to €300 million was cancelled and the Underwriting Commitment and the Investors' option to acquire, under certain conditions, additional shares in the amount of €200 million, were cancelled. ATR issued to the Investors 10.3 million shares at a price of €7 per

share (the Company's share was approximately 5.6 million shares). This number of shares increased the Investors' holdings in ATR to approximately 29.9%, which effectively constituted a partial fulfillment of the Underwriting Commitment. The balance of the Underwriting Commitment was cancelled. The issuance took place on January 30, 2009 in consideration of approximately €38.9 million par value of convertible debentures of ATR which were issued to the Company in August 2008.

2. Warrants to purchase approximately 25 million shares of ATR (out of 30 million issued to the investors in August 2008) were returned to ATR for no consideration and were cancelled.

3. The Investors undertook not to acquire until August 1, 2010, without ATR's consent, shares or convertible securities of ATR in a manner that would trigger a change of control in ATR, subject to the terms set in the agreement.

Further, according to the agreement, ATR was to acquire from the Company approximately €103 million of its debentures (non-convertible) for an amount of approximately €77.3 million which was the cost incurred by the Company to acquire them, plus accrued interest on the debentures to the date of purchase by ATR. The acquisition was completed on January 30, 2009.

As of the closing date of the additional investment agreement, the Investors held 29.1% of the voting rights in ATR (Company's share—19.1%) and 13.9% of ATR's capital (Company's share—11.5%).

An Agreement to Exchange Debentures for ATR Shares

On September 2, 2009, the Investors and ATR entered into an additional agreement, completed and executed on December 1, 2009 (the "exchange agreement") pursuant to which the investors delivered to ATR the remaining €427.9 million par value of convertible debentures (the Company's share was €231.1 million par value) and the remaining warrants to purchase 4,933 thousand shares of ATR (the Company's share was 2,664 thousand) that had been issued to them by ATR in August 2008 in exchange for the issuance of approximately 144.9 million shares of ATR (the Company's share is approximately 79.6 million shares) and for approximately €9.3 million in cash (to CPI only). The parties also agreed as follows:

1. ATR declared a special dividend of €0.50 per share. In addition, it was agreed that ATR will act to maintain an annual dividend distribution policy of no less than €0.12 per share to be paid on a quarterly basis, subject to any legal and business considerations. The quarterly and special dividends were paid in December 2009.

2. The agreement determining the Investors' consent rights with respect to ATR and ATR's articles of association were amended such that the number of items pursuant to which ATR requires the Investors' consent was reduced. Additionally, some matters were added to ATR's articles of association that require a special 2/3 majority vote in ATR's general meeting of shareholders.

3. The Investors' rights regarding the appointment of directors of ATR were amended (including in ATR's articles of association) such that the investors are entitled to appoint (out of a board of directors not exceeding ten members) four directors as long as they hold (in aggregate) 80 million shares; three directors as long as they hold 60 million shares; two directors as long as they hold 40 million shares; and one director as long as they hold 20 million shares.

4. It was agreed that the Investors' rights to appoint the majority of the members of the Board's nominations committee, which recommends the appointment of the remaining members of the Board, and the appointment of the Chairman of the Board will be maintained as long as the Investors hold, in aggregate, at least 55 million shares.

5. The Investors undertook not to take any steps that will lead to a breach of the terms of the debentures (series 2006) regarding change of control as long as the balance of the debentures is €100 million par value or until 20 months from the closing date have elapsed, whichever is earlier. ATR was to announce a purchase offer for the said debentures at a price equivalent to 95% of their par value, at a total cost of up to €120 million.

In 2009, the Company recognized a gain from bargain purchase, amounting to €116 million (NIS 631 million), due to acquisition of ATR shares on the stock exchange, and due to the issuances of shares in January and December 2009, as described above. This amount includes €23.2 million (NIS 123 million) from realization of the remainder of the Underwriting Commitment as of December 31, 2008. The Company also recognized in 2009 a gain from the exchange of convertible debentures of ATR in January and December 2009, amounting to €190 million (NIS 1,055 million), which was included in finance income.

The Company accounted for the Underwriting Commitment, the remaining warrants and the conversion component of the debentures until their exercise date, as derivatives measured at fair value through profit or loss. In 2009, the Company recognized a gain of approximately €15.2 million (approximately NIS 84 million) relating to the remeasurement of the warrants and the conversion component of the debentures.

Commencing from the closing date of the original investment agreement (August 1, 2008), the Company accounted for its investment in ATR in the financial statements using the equity method, since the original investment agreement conferred on the Company significant influence over ATR.

Based on the Investors' rights pursuant to the agreements with ATR and ATR's articles of association, as amended under the exchange agreement described above, and based on the increase in the Investors' interest in ATR following the exchange agreement above the threshold of 1/3 in ATR's voting rights in a manner that ATR's articles of association cannot be amended without the Investors' approval, commencing at the closing date of the exchange agreement, the Investors jointly control ATR, even though their joint holdings in the voting rights of ATR on that date were less than 50%. Since a joint control agreement is in place between the Company and CPI, as described in Note 26a(4), the Company proportionately consolidates ATR in its financial statements beginning at the end of 2009.

The fair values of the net identifiable assets of ATR at the closing date of the exchange transaction (December 1, 2009), according the Company's share, were as follows:

	Fair Value NIS in Millions
Net assets acquired	3,794
Investment previously presented at equity	1,386
Net assets acquired	2,408
Gain from bargain purchase	(220)
Total acquisition cost(*)	2,188

(*) The cost of the exchange transaction represents the fair value of the debentures and warrants of ATR.

During 2011 the Company through wholly-owned subsidiaries, purchased approximately 6.0 million ATR shares (1.6% of ATR's share capital) during the trade on the Vienna stock exchange for total consideration of EUR 20.8 million (NIS 103 million). As a result of the purchases the Company recognized a gain from bargain purchase amounting to EUR 15.7 million (NIS 77 million), measured as the difference between the fair value of ATR's net identifiable assets acquired and the consideration paid and presented in other income.

As of December 31, 2011, the Company owns through wholly-owned subsidiaries 117.9 million shares of ATR, which constitute 31.6% of the share capital and voting rights of ATR. To the best of the Company's knowledge, CPI owns, as of December 31, 2011, about 72.5 million shares of ATR, representing about 19.4% of the share capital and voting rights of ATR.

As for lawsuits filed with regards to the investment in ATR, and the engagement in a compromise agreement refer to Note 26d.

As for the purchase of additional 6.7 million ATR shares after the reporting date, see Note 40h.

m. Investment in Acad Building and Investments Ltd. ("Acad")

In September 2007, a wholly-owned subsidiary of the Company acquired 50% of the share capital and voting rights of Acad, thus obtaining joint control over Acad, for a consideration of approximately NIS 184 million. Since the acquisition date, Acad has been accounted for as a jointly controlled entity, using proportionate consolidation.

Acad's primary activity is the direct and indirect holding of the share capital and voting rights of U. Dori Ltd. ("Dori Group"), a public company listed on the Tel-Aviv Stock Exchange which is primarily engaged in the development and construction (both as an initiator and as a contractor for third parties) of residential and commercial buildings and as a contractor performing construction contracts in the field of infrastructure. Dori Group operates in Israel and in Eastern Europe. Dori Group is also operating (along with others) to build a power station in Israel for the production of electricity. Besides the holdings in Dori Group, Acad had a construction contracts activity in Nigeria (50%) that was sold after the reporting date with estimated gain of NIS 10 million, and owns 26% interest in an income producing property in Israel (26%).

On March 10, 2011 the other shareholders of Acad at that time (the "Partners") submitted an offer to the Company, to buy or sell 50% of Acad's share capital, according to the Buy and Sell ("BMBY") mechanism set out in Acad's shareholders agreement. On April 3, 2011 the Company notified the Partners that it would purchase their 50% interest in Acad at the price indicated in their offer (NIS 82 million (the "transaction price") reflecting a total value of NIS 164 million for Acad). On April 17, 2011 the transaction closed and commencing on that date Acad is fully consolidated in the Company's financial statements.

The acquisition was accounted for as a business combination achieved in stages under IFRS 3, with the previously owned interest in Acad revalued to its fair value at the acquisition date according to the transaction price. As a result of such revaluation, the Company recognized a NIS 31 million loss (including the currency translation reserve realization amounted to NIS 12 million) charged to profit or loss.

The Company engaged an external valuer to execute a provisional allocation of the purchase price to Acad's net identifiable assets at the acquisition date. The fair value of the identifiable assets and liabilities of Acad at the acquisition date are as follows:

	Fair Value NIS in Million
Cash and cash equivalents	150
Inventory of buildings and apartments for sale	819
Other current assets	674
Non-current assets	311
	1,954
Current liabilities	1,152
Non-current liabilities	343
Non-controlling interests	269
	1,764
Net assets acquired	190
Gain from bargain purchase	(26)
Total acquisition cost	164

On June 6, 2011, the Company completed an agreement for the sale of 100% of Acad's share capital to Gazit Development, in which it holds a 75% interest in consideration for NIS 200 million, including NIS 20 million for the assignment of loans that were granted to Acad by the Company.

Acad's revenues and net income for 2011, which were consolidated in these financial statements, totaled NIS 1,257 million and NIS 54 million, respectively.

The Company's total revenues and net income for 2011, assuming a full consolidation of Acad as from the beginning of 2011, totaled NIS 6,673 million and NIS 1,897 million, respectively.

In January 27, 2011, Dori Energy (a wholly-owned subsidiary of Dori Group), which owns 18.75% of the share capital of Dorad Energy Ltd., completed a share issuance of 40% of its share capital and granted a call option with a fair value of NIS 0.4 million, to purchase additional 10% of its share capital, to Alumey Clean Energy Ltd., in consideration for NIS 50 million. As a result of the share issuance, and due to the loss of control over Dori Energy, Dori Group has recognized a NIS 60 million gain, which is presented in the other income section (the Company's share—NIS 22 million). After the transaction, Dori Energy is proportionately consolidated in the financial statements of Dori Group.

As of December 31, 2011, Acad holds 73.8% of the share capital of Dori Group and consolidates Dori Group in its financial statements. The Company's share of Acad's ownership of Dori Group is 55.4% (50.8% on a fully diluted basis). The market price of Dori Group shares as of December 31, 2011 was NIS 1.32 and close to the date of approval of these financial statements—NIS 1.325. The number of Dori Group's shares outstanding as of December 31, 2011 is 115.3 million. At the reporting date, 1,905 thousand share options which were granted to officers in Dori Group are outstanding. The share options are exercisable into Dori Group shares at an exercise price of NIS 3.87, and expire during 2012.

As for rights offering completed by Dori Group after the reporting date, with participation of Gazit Development, see Note 40b.

Investing Activities: Interest and Dividends Received, Purchases and Sales of Investments, Deposits and Realization of Margin Money and Restricted Deposits, Loans to and Repayment of Loans From Equity Accounted Investees, Purchases and Sales of Tangible and Intangible Long-Lived Assets

5.30

Tata Motors Limited (Mar 2011)

CONSOLIDATED STATEMENTS OF CASH FLOWS
(in part)

(In Millions)	Year Ended March 31			
	2012	2012	2011	2010
Cash Flows From Investing Activities:				
Deposits with banks	US$ (257.5)	Rs. (13,102.6)	Rs. (12,451.5)	Rs. (4,150.3)
Realization of deposits with banks	173.6	8,830.1	8,903.3	21.5
Repayment of loans/Loans (given) to equity accounted investees and others	(0.6)	(29.6)	48.0	(93.8)
Purchases of available-for-sale investments (net)	(1,149.2)	(58,464.6)	(332.0)	(9,895.5)
Purchases of other investments	(7.0)	(355.7)	(1,139.0)	—
Proceeds from sale of available-for-sale investments	0.4	20.2	64.3	10,056.5
Proceeds from sale of investments classified as loans and receivables	0.1	7.5	69.0	55.9
Proceeds from sale of controlling equity interest in subsidiary, net of cash	—	—	—	11,144.8
Proceeds from sale of other investments	—	—	2.0	—
Deposits of margin money and other restricted deposits	(243.8)	(12,404.5)	(9,053.8)	(14,417.9)
Realization of margin money and other restricted deposits	99.5	5,062.3	18,285.2	11,421.6
Investments in equity accounted investees	(10.1)	(514.1)	(2,056.8)	(1,324.3)
Dividends received from equity accounted investees	9.2	465.9	399.9	94.7
Interest received	92.8	4,723.5	3,451.7	2,585.0
Dividend received	4.6	236.1	654.3	351.4
Payments for property, plant and equipment	(1,288.3)	(65,543.8)	(33,852.8)	(37,714.0)
Proceeds from sale of property, plant and equipment	18.2	926.3	384.4	311.0
Payments for intangible assets	(1,438.8)	(73,200.7)	(48,245.2)	(44,013.3)
Proceeds from sale of intangible assets	—	—	—	11.9
Part payment of purchase consideration for acquisition of subsidiaries	—	—	—	(426.0)
Payments for acquisitions, net of cash acquired	—	—	(119.4)	—
Net cash used in investing activities	(3,996.9)	(203,343.7)	(74,988.4)	(75,980.8)

NOTES TO THE CONSOLIDATED FINANCIAL STATEMENTS *(in part)*

1. Background and Operations

Tata Motors Limited and its subsidiaries, collectively referred to as ("the Company" or "Tata Motors"), designs, manufactures and sells a wide range of automotive vehicles. The Company provides financing for the vehicles sold by dealers of the Company in certain markets. The Company also manufactures engines for industrial and marine applications, aggregates such as axles and transmissions for commercial vehicles and factory automation equipment, and provides information technology services (also refer note 30 regarding sale of controlling equity interest in Telco Construction Equipment Company Limited (Telcon)—a subsidiary engaged in manufacture and sale of construction equipment).

Tata Motors Limited is a public limited company incorporated and domiciled in India and has its registered office at Mumbai, Maharashtra, India.

The consolidated financial statements were approved by the Board of Directors and authorised for issue on July 30, 2012.

In financial year 2008-09, the Company acquired Jaguar Land Rover businesses (referred to as "JLR") which included three manufacturing facilities and two advanced engineering centers in the UK, and a worldwide sales network.

As on March 31, 2012, Tata Sons Limited (or Tata Sons), together with its subsidiaries, owns 29.02% of the ordinary shares and 3.85% of 'A' ordinary shares of Tata Motors Limited, and has the ability to significantly influence the Company's operations (refer note 25 for voting rights relating to ordinary shares and 'A' ordinary shares).

2. Significant Accounting Policies (in part)

a. Statement of Compliance

These consolidated financial statements have been prepared in accordance with International Financial Reporting Standards (referred to as "IFRS") as issued by the International Accounting Standards Board (referred to as "IASB").

3. Cash and Cash Equivalents

Cash and cash equivalents consist of the following:

	As of March 31		
(In Millions)	**2012**	**2012**	**2011**
Cash balances	US$ 4.2	Rs. 215.5	Rs. 246.1
Balances with banks (including deposits with original maturity of up to three months)	2,864.6	145,736.9	90,424.8
Total	US$ 2,868.8	Rs. 145,952.4	Rs. 90,670.9

Cash and cash equivalents includes Rs. 36,974.1 million and Rs. 15,765.6 million as of March 31, 2012 and 2011 respectively, held by a subsidiary that operates in a country where exchange control restrictions prevent the balances being available for general use by Tata Motors Limited and other subsidiaries.

7. Other Financial Assets—Current

Other financial assets—current consist of the following:

	As of March 31		
(In Millions)	**2012**	**2012**	**2011**
Derivative financial instruments	US$ 77.6	Rs. 3,950.4	Rs. 3,648.4
Advances and other receivables recoverable in cash	74.0	3,764.7	3,969.5
Inter corporate deposits	9.9	504.2	474.6
Margin money with banks	8.0	405.0	2,297.2
Restricted bank deposits	249.2	12,676.7	823.4
Total	US$ 418.7	Rs. 21,301.0	Rs. 11,213.1

Margin money with banks is restricted cash deposits, and consists of collateral provided for transfer of finance receivables. Restricted bank deposits include Rs.10,709.1 million and Rs. Nil as of March 31, 2012 and 2011 respectively, held as security in relation to bank borrowings. The deposits are pledged till the maturity of the respective borrowings.

10. Other Financial Assets—Non-Current

Other financial assets—non-current consist of the following:

	As of March 31		
(In Millions)	**2012**	**2012**	**2011**
Margin money with banks	US$ 42.9	Rs. 2,184.4	Rs. 5,293.7
Restricted deposits	129.3	6,577.2	4,677.2
Loans to employees	9.4	476.1	518.3
Loan to the equity accounted investee	52.1	2,650.0	2,650.0
Derivative financial instruments	37.3	1,897.0	—
Others	64.9	3,305.2	1,879.0
Total	US$ 335.9	Rs. 17,089.9	Rs. 15,018.2

Margin money with banks is restricted cash deposits, and consists of collateral provided for transfer of finance receiv-

ables. Restricted deposits are held as security in relation to vehicles ultimately sold on lease. The amount is pledged until the leases reach their respective maturity.

Loan to the equity accounted investee represents loan given to a joint venture of the Company. This loan is subordinated to other borrowings of the joint venture. Subject to certain conditions, the loan is convertible into equity of the joint venture at the option of the joint venture.

Financing Activities: Issue of Common Stock and Debt, Securitization of Trade Receivables, Increase in Noncurrent Liabilities, Derivative Instruments

5.31

Cemex, S.A.B. de C.V. (Dec 2011)

CONSOLIDATED STATEMENTS OF CASH FLOWS (in part)

(Millions of Mexican pesos)

		Years Ended December 31	
	Notes	**2011**	**2010**
Financing Activities			
Issuance of common stock	19A	11	5
Derivative instruments		(5,464)	69
Issuance (repayment) of debt, net	15A	5,702	(9,615)
Securitization of trade receivables		2,890	121
Non-current liabilities, net		1,430	140
Net cash flows provided by (used in) financing activities		4,569	(9,280)
Increase (decrease) in cash and investments		9,563	(4,478)
Cash conversion effect, net		(1,789)	(1,272)
Cash and investments at beginning of year		8,354	14,104
Cash and Investments at end of year	7	Ps 16,128	8,354

NOTES TO THE CONSOLIDATED FINANCIAL STATEMENTS (in part)

(Millions of Mexican pesos)

1. Description of Business

CEMEX, S.A.B. de C.V., a public stock corporation with variable capital (S.A.B. de C.V.) organized under the laws of the United Mexican States, or Mexico, is a holding company (parent) of entities whose main activities are oriented to the construction industry, through the production, marketing, distribution and sale of cement, ready-mix concrete, aggregates and other construction materials.

CEMEX, S.A.B. de C.V. was founded in 1906 and was registered with the Mercantile Section of the Public Register of Property and Commerce in Monterrey, N.L., Mexico in 1920 for a period of 99 years. In 2002, this period was extended to the year 2100. The shares of CEMEX, S.A.B. de C.V. are listed on the Mexican Stock Exchange ("MSE") as Ordinary Participation Certificates ("CPOs"). Each CPO represents two series "A" shares and one series "B" share of common stock of CEMEX, S.A.B. de C.V. In addition, CEMEX, S.A.B. de C.V.'s shares are listed on the New York Stock Exchange ("NYSE") as American Depositary Shares ("ADSs") under the symbol "CX." Each ADS represents ten CPOs.

The terms "CEMEX, S.A.B. de C.V." or the "Parent Company" used in these accompanying notes to the financial statements refer to CEMEX, S.A.B. de C.V. without its consolidated subsidiaries. The terms the "Company" or "CEMEX" refer to CEMEX, S.A.B. de C.V. together with its consolidated subsidiaries. The issuance of these consolidated financial statements was authorized by the Company's management and its Board of Directors on April 27, 2012, for their inclusion in CEMEX's 2011 annual report in accordance with the *Circular Única de Emisoras* to the Mexican National Banking and Securities Commission ("CNBV" for its abbreviation in Spanish) and the MSE, as well as for their inclusion in CEMEX's 2011 annual report on Form 20-F to the U.S. Securities and Exchange Commission ("SEC").

2. Significant Accounting Policies (in part)

A) Basis of Presentation and Disclosure

In November 2008, the CNBV issued regulations requiring registrants whose shares are listed on the MSE, to begin preparing their consolidated financial statements using International Financial Reporting Standards ("IFRS"), as issued by the International Accounting Standards Board ("IASB"), no later than January 1, 2012 and to stop the use of Mexican Financial Reporting Standards ("MFRS"). In connection with this requirement, the consolidated financial statements as of December 31, 2011 and 2010 and January 1, 2010 and for the years ended December 31, 2011 and 2010, represent CEMEX's first consolidated financial statements prepared in accordance with IFRS, as these standards were effective on December 31, 2011.

Prior to the issuance of these consolidated financial statements, CEMEX issued its consolidated financial statements under MFRS on January 26, 2012, covering the same periods, which were the last consolidated financial statements of CEMEX prepared in accordance with MFRS, and were used by CEMEX to comply with its financial information obligations from December 31, 2011 until the issuance of these IFRS financial statements.

CEMEX determined its opening balance sheet under IFRS as of January 1, 2010, following the guidance set forth by IFRS 1, *First time adoption* ("IFRS 1"). The options elected by CEMEX in the migration to IFRS and the effects on its opening balance sheet as of January 1, 2010, according to IFRS 1, as well as the effects on CEMEX's balance sheets as of December 31, 2011 and 2010, and its statements of operations, statements of comprehensive loss and statements of cash flows for the years ended December 31, 2011 and 2010, as compared to CEMEX's previously reported amounts under MFRS, are described in note 27.

Statements of Cash Flows

The statements of cash flows present cash inflows and outflows, excluding unrealized foreign exchange effects, as well as the following transactions that did not represent sources or uses of cash:

- In 2011, the decrease in debt and in perpetual debentures within non-controlling interest for approximately Ps239 and Ps1,391, respectively, in connection with the gains resulting from the difference between the notional amount and the fair value of CEMEX's debt and perpetual instruments held by subsidiaries (note 15A);
- In 2011, the increases in property, plant and equipment for approximately Ps1,519 and in debt for approximately Ps1,558, associated with the negotiation of capital leases during the year (note 15B);
- In 2011, the increase in debt for Ps1,352 related mainly to the acquisition of Ready Mix USA LLC (note 14A);
- In 2011, the exchange of a portion of CEMEX's perpetual debentures for new notes for US$125, and in 2010, the exchange of a portion of CEMEX's perpetual debentures for new notes for US$1,067 and €115 (note 15A), which represented a net increase in debt of Ps1,486 in 2011 and Ps15,361 in 2010, a reduction in equity's non controlling interest of Ps1,937 in 2011 and Ps20,838 in 2010 and an increase in equity's controlling interest of Ps446 in 2011 and Ps5,401 in 2010; and
- In 2011 and 2010, the increases in stockholders' equity associated with: (i) the capitalization of retained earnings for Ps4,216 and Ps5,481, respectively (note 19A); and (ii) CPOs issued as part of the executive stock-based compensation for Ps495 and Ps312, respectively (note 19A).

E) Cash and Investments (Note 7)

The balance in this caption is comprised of available amounts of cash and cash equivalents, mainly represented by highly-liquid short-term investments, which are easily convertible into cash, and which are not subject to significant risks of changes in their values, including overnight investments, which yield fixed returns and have maturities of less than three months from the investment date. These fixed-income investments are recorded at cost plus accrued interest. Other investments which are easily convertible into cash are recorded at their market value. Gains or losses resulting from changes in market values and accrued interest are included in the statements of operations as part of other financial income (expense), net.

The amount of cash and investments in the balance sheet includes restricted cash and investments, comprised of deposits in margin accounts that guarantee several of CEMEX's obligations, to the extent that the restriction will be lifted in less than three months from the balance sheet date. When the restriction period is greater than three months, such restricted cash and investments are not considered cash equivalents and are included within short-term or long-term "Other accounts receivable," as appropriate. When contracts contain provisions for net settlement, these restricted amounts of cash and investments are offset against the liabilities that CEMEX has with its counterparties.

F) Trade Accounts Receivable and Other Current Accounts Receivable (Notes 8, 9)

According to IAS 39, *Financial instruments: recognition and measurement* ("IAS 39"), items under this caption are classified as "loans and receivables," which are recorded at their amortized cost, which is represented by the net present value of the consideration receivable or payable as of the transaction date. Due to their short-term nature, CEMEX initially recognizes these receivables at the original invoiced amount less an estimate of doubtful accounts. Allowances for doubtful accounts as well as impairment of other current accounts receivable are recognized against administrative and selling expenses.

Trade receivables sold under securitization programs, in which CEMEX maintains a residual interest in the trade accounts receivable sold in case of recovery failure, as well as continued involvement in such assets, do not qualify for derecognition and are maintained on the balance sheet.

7. Cash and Investments

Consolidated cash and investments consisted of:

	December 31, 2011	December 31, 2010	January 1, 2010
Cash and bank accounts	Ps 6,123	3,659	11,295
Fixed-income securities and other cash equivalents[1]	10,005	4,695	2,809
	Ps 16,128	8,354	14,104

[1] As of December 31, 2011 and 2010, this caption includes approximately Ps4,103 and Ps195, respectively, for the Mexican promissory notes ("*Certificados Bursátiles*" or "CBs") reserve (note 15A), as well as restricted deposits related to insurance contracts for approximately Ps425 and Ps185, respectively.

Based on net settlement agreements, as of December 31, 2011 and 2010 and January 1, 2010, the balance of cash and investments excludes deposits in margin accounts that guarantee several obligations of CEMEX for approximately Ps4,010, Ps2,918 and Ps3,962, respectively, which are offset against the corresponding CEMEX's obligations with the counterparties.

8. Trade Accounts Receivable

Consolidated trade accounts receivable consisted of:

	December 31, 2011	December 31, 2010	January 1, 2010
Trade accounts receivable	Ps 28,376	24,407	25,578
Allowances for doubtful accounts	(2,171)	(2,246)	(2,571)
	Ps 26,205	22,161	23,007

As of December 31, 2011 and 2010 and January 1, 2010, trade accounts receivable include receivables of Ps12,733 (US$912), Ps9,968 (US$807) and Ps9,624 (US$735), respectively, that were sold under securitization programs for the sale of trade accounts receivable established in Mexico, the United States, Spain, France and the United Kingdom; the latter forms part of the program in France and was initiated in 2011. Under these programs, CEMEX effectively surrenders control associated with the trade accounts receivable sold and there is no guarantee or obligation to reacquire the assets. However, CEMEX retains certain residual interest in the programs and/or maintains continuing involvement with the accounts receivable; therefore, the amounts received are recognized within "Other financial obligations." Trade accounts receivable qualifying for sale exclude amounts over certain days past due or concentrations over certain limits to any one customer, according to the terms of the programs. The portion of the accounts receivable sold maintained as reserves amounted to Ps3,181 as of December 31, 2011, Ps3,306 as of December 31, 2010 and Ps3,083 as of January 1, 2010. Therefore, the funded amount to CEMEX was Ps9,552 (US$684) as of December 31, 2011, including approximately Ps656 (US$47) of accounts receivable in France sold through factoring programs with recourse, Ps6,662 (US$539) as of December 31, 2010 and Ps6,541 (US$500) as of January 1, 2010. The discount granted to the acquirers of the trade accounts receivable is recorded as financial expense and amounted to approximately Ps390 (US$31) in 2011 and Ps368 (US$29) in 2010. CEMEX's securitization programs are negotiated for specific periods and should be renewed at their maturity. The securitization programs outstanding as of December 31, 2011 in Mexico, the United States, Spain, France and the United Kingdom, were initiated or renewed during 2011 and mature in October 2015, May 2013, May 2016, March 2013 and March 2013, respectively.

15. Financial Instruments (in part)

15A) Short-Term and Long-Term Debt (in part)

Consolidated debt by interest rates, currencies and type of instrument was summarized as follows:

	December 31, 2011			December 31, 2010			January 1, 2010		
	Short-Term	Long-Term	Total	Short-Term	Long-Term	Total	Short-Term	Long-Term	Total
Floating rate debt	Ps 2,997	106,943	109,940	Ps 4,785	120,303	125,088	Ps 7,254	150,091	157,345
Fixed rate debt	1,676	96,855	98,531	833	68,473	69,306	20	53,081	53,101
	Ps 4,673	203,798	208,471	Ps 5,618	188,776	194,394	Ps 7,274	203,172	210,446
Effective rate[1]									
Floating rate	5.0%	5.3%		5.2%	5.0%		5.1%	5.0%	
Fixed rate	10.5%	8.4%		7.7%	8.3%		5.7%	7.8%	

15B) Other Financial Obligations (in part)

IV. Liabilities Secured with Accounts Receivable

As mentioned in note 8, as of December 31, 2011 and 2010, CEMEX maintains securitization programs for the sale of trade accounts receivable established in Mexico, the United States, Spain, France and the United Kingdom, by means of which, CEMEX effectively surrenders control associated with the trade accounts receivable sold and there is no guarantee or obligation to reacquire the assets. However, CEMEX retains certain residual interest in the programs and/or maintains continuing involvement with the accounts receivable. Based on IAS 39, CEMEX recognizes cash flows received, that is the funded amounts of the trade receivables sold within "Other financial obligations."

19. Stockholders' Equity

As of December 31, 2011 and 2010 and January 1, 2010, the balances of consolidated stockholders' equity exclude investments in shares of CEMEX, S.A.B. de C.V. held by subsidiaries of approximately Ps129 (17,334,881 CPOs), Ps220 (16,668,156 CPOs) and Ps187 (16,107,081 CPOs). These amounts are canceled within "Other equity reserves." The increase in the number of CPOs held by subsidiaries during 2011 and 2010 relates to CPOs received by subsidiaries as a result of the recapitalization of retained earnings as described below.

19A) Common Stock and Additional Paid-In Capital

As of December 31, 2011 and 2010 and as of January 1, 2010, the breakdown of common stock and additional paid-in capital was as follows:

	December 31, 2011	December 31, 2010	January 1, 2010
Common stock	Ps 4,135	4,132	4,127
Additional paid-in capital	109,309	104,590	98,797
	Ps113,444	108,722	102,924

The common stock of CEMEX, S.A.B. de C.V. was represented as follows:

Shares[1]	December 31, 2011 Series A[2]	December 31, 2011 Series B[3]	December 31, 2010 Series A[2]	December 31, 2010 Series B[3]	January 1, 2010 Series A[2]	January 1, 2010 Series B[3]
Subscribed and paid shares	20,939,727,526	10,469,863,763	20,043,602,184	10,021,801,092	19,224,300,330	9,612,150,165
Unissued shares authorized for stock compensation programs	250,782,926	125,391,463	345,164,180	172,582,090	395,227,442	197,613,721
Shares that guarantee the issuance of convertible securities[4]	5,932,438,520	2,966,219,260	1,896,584,924	948,292,462	344,960,064	172,480,032
Shares authorized for the issuance of stock or convertible securities[5]	7,561,480	3,780,740	3,415,076	1,707,538	1,055,039,936	527,519,968
	27,130,510,452	13,565,255,226	22,288,766,364	11,144,383,182	21,019,527,772	10,509,763,886

[1] As of December 31, 2011 and 2010 and January 1, 2010, 13,068,000,000 shares correspond to the fixed portion, and 27,627,765,678 shares as of December 31, 2011, 20,365,149,546 shares as of December 31, 2010 and 18,461,291,658 shares as of January 1, 2010, correspond to the variable portion.

[2] Series "A" or Mexican shares must represent at least 64% of CEMEX's capital stock.

[3] Series "B" or free subscription shares must represent at most 36% of CEMEX's capital stock.

[4] Shares that guarantee the conversion of both the voluntary and mandatorily convertible securities (note 15B).

[5] Shares authorized for the issuance of stock through a public offer or through the issuance of convertible securities.

On February 24, 2011, stockholders at the extraordinary shareholders' meeting approved an increase in the variable portion of our capital stock of up to 6 billion shares (2 billion CPOs). Pursuant to the resolution approved by CEMEX, S.A.B. de C.V.'s stockholders, the subscription and payment of the new shares may occur through a public offer of CPOs and/or the issuance of convertible securities. These shares are kept in CEMEX's treasury as a guarantee for the potential issuance of shares through CEMEX's convertible securities (note 15B).

On February 24, 2011, stockholders at the annual ordinary shareholders' meeting approved resolutions to: (i) increase the variable common stock through the capitalization of retained earnings, issuing up to 1,202.6 million shares (400.9 million CPOs) based on a price of Ps10.52 per CPO. Stockholders received 3 new shares for each 75 shares held (1 new CPO for each 25 CPOs held), through the capitalization of retained earnings. As a result, shares equivalent to approximately 401 million CPOs were issued, representing an increase in common stock of approximately Ps3, considering a nominal value of Ps0.00833 per CPO, and additional paid-in capital of approximately Ps4,213; and (ii) increase the variable common stock by up to 60 million shares (20 million CPOs) issuable as a result of antidilution adjustments upon conversion of CEMEX's convertible securities (note 15B). These shares are kept in CEMEX's treasury. There was no cash distribution and no entitlement to fractional shares.

Financing Activities: Dividends Paid on Ordinary Share Capital and Preference Shares, Interest Paid, Increase in Short-Term Borrowings, Issue and Repayment of Financial Liabilities, Repayment of Principal on Capital Lease Obligations

5.32

Unilever N.V. and Unilever plc (Dec 2011)

CONSOLIDATED CASH FLOW STATEMENT (in part)

	€ Million 2011	€ Million 2010	€ Million 2009
Dividends paid on ordinary share capital	(2,485)	(2,323)	(2,106)
Interest and preference dividends paid	(496)	(494)	(517)
Net change in short-term borrowings	1,261	(46)	(227)
Additional financial liabilities	3,419	86	3,140
Repayment of financial liabilities	(907)	(1,391)	(4,456)
Capital element of finance lease rental payments	(16)	(22)	(24)
Other movements on treasury stock	30	(124)	103
Other financing activities	(395)	(295)	(214)
Net cash flow (used in)/from financing activities	411	(4,609)	(4,301)
Net increase/(decrease) in cash and cash equivalents	1,396	(283)	210
Cash and cash equivalents at the beginning of the year	1,966	2,397	2,360
Effect of foreign exchange rate changes	(384)	(148)	(173)
Cash and cash equivalents at the end of the year 15	2,978	1,966	2,397

NOTES TO THE CONSOLIDATED FINANCIAL STATEMENTS (in part)

1. Accounting Information and Policies (in part)

The accounting policies adopted are the same as those which were applied for the previous financial year, except as set out below under the heading 'Recent accounting developments'.

Unilever

The two parent companies, NV and PLC, together with their group companies, operate as a single economic entity (the Unilever Group, also referred to as Unilever or the Group). NV and PLC have the same Directors and are linked by a series of agreements, including an Equalisation Agreement, which are designed so that the positions of the shareholders of both companies are as closely as possible the same as if they held shares in a single company.

The Equalisation Agreement provides that both companies adopt the same accounting principles. It also requires that dividends and other rights and benefits attaching to each ordinary share of NV, be equal in value to those rights and benefits attaching to each ordinary share of PLC, as if each such unit of capital formed part of the ordinary capital of one and the same company.

Basis of Consolidation

Due to the operational and contractual arrangements referred to above, NV and PLC form a single reporting entity for the purposes of presenting consolidated financial statements. Accordingly, the financial statements of Unilever are presented by both NV and PLC as their respective consolidated financial statements. Group companies included in the consolidation are those companies controlled by NV or PLC. Control exists when the Group has the power to govern the financial and operating policies of an entity so as to obtain benefits from its activities.

The net assets and results of acquired businesses are included in the consolidated financial statements from their respective dates of acquisition, being the date on which the Group obtains control. The results of disposed businesses are included in the consolidated financial statements up to their date of disposal, being the date control ceases.

Intra-group transactions and balances are eliminated.

Companies Legislation and Accounting Standards

The consolidated financial statements have been prepared in accordance with International Financial Reporting Standards (IFRS) as adopted by the European Union (EU), IFRIC Interpretations and in accordance with Part 9 of Book 2 of the Civil Code in the Netherlands and the United Kingdom Companies Act 2006 applicable to companies reporting under IFRS. They are also in compliance with IFRS as issued by the International Accounting Standards Board.

5. Net Finance Costs

Net finance costs is the net of finance costs and finance income, including net finance costs in relation to pensions and similar obligations.

Finance income includes income on cash and cash equivalents and income on other financial assets. Finance costs include interest costs in relation to financial liabilities.

Borrowing costs which are not capitalised are recognised based on the effective interest method.

Net Finance Costs	€ Million 2011	€ Million 2010	€ Million 2009
Finance costs	(540)	(491)	(504)
Bank loans and overdrafts	(59)	(38)	(47)
Bonds and other loans	(472)	(441)	(429)
Dividends paid on preference shares	(5)	(6)	(7)
Net gain/(loss) on derivatives for which hedge accounting is not applied[a]	(4)	(6)	(21)
On foreign exchange derivatives	(379)	(601)	(168)
Exchange difference on underlying items	375	595	147
Finance income	92	77	75
Pensions and similar obligations[b]	71	20	(164)
	(377)	(394)	(593)

[a] For further details of derivatives for which hedge accounting is not applied please refer to note 16D on page 98.

[b] Net finance costs in respect of pensions and similar obligations are analysed in note 4B on page 76.

15. Financial Assets and Liabilities (in part)

15A. Financial Assets (in part)

Cash and Cash Equivalents

Cash and cash equivalents in the balance sheet include deposits, investments in money market funds and highly liquid investments. To be classified as cash and cash equivalents, an asset must:

- be readily convertible into cash; and
- have an insignificant risk of changes in value; and
- have a maturity period of three months or less at acquisition.

Cash and cash equivalents in the cash flow statement also includes bank overdrafts.

Financial Assets[a]	€ Million Current 2011	€ Million Non-Current 2011	€ Million Total 2011	€ Million Current 2010	€ Million Non-Current 2010	€ Million Total 2010
Cash and cash equivalents						
Cash at bank and in hand	1,139	—	1,139	732	—	732
Short-term deposits with maturity of less than 3 months	2,243	—	2,243	888	—	888
Other cash equivalents[b]	102	—	102	696	—	696
	3,484	—	3,484	2,316	—	2,316

[a] For the purposes of notes 15 and 16, financial assets and liabilities exclude trade and other current receivables and liabilities which are covered in notes 13 and 14 respectively.

[b] Other cash equivalents include investments in money market funds of €20 million (2010: €603 million) for which the risk of changes in value are insignificant.

[c] Current loans and receivables include short-term deposits with banks with maturities of longer than three months.

[d] Current available-for-sale financial assets include government securities and A-minus or higher rated money and capital market instruments. Also included are investments in money market funds of €116 million (2010: €nil) for which the risk of changes in value is insignificant. Non-current available-for-sale financial assets predominantly consist of investments in a number of companies and financial institutions in Europe and the US, including €110 million (2010: €128 million) of assets in a trust to fund benefit obligations in the US (see also note 4B on page 77).

Cash and Cash Equivalents Reconciliation to the Cash Flow Statement	€ Million 2011	€ Million 2010
Cash and cash equivalents per balance sheet	3,484	2,316
Less: bank overdrafts	(506)	(350)
Cash and cash equivalents per cash flow statement	2,978	1,966

Other Income From Non-Current Investments	€ Million 2011	€ Million 2010	€ Million 2009
Income from other non-current investments	76	76	47
Profit on disposal of investments[e]	—	—	327
	76	76	374

[e] For 2009, profit on disposal of investments relates to the disposal of the majority of the Group's equity interest in JohnsonDiversey.

SECTION 6: NON-CURRENT ASSETS HELD FOR SALE AND DISCONTINUED OPERATIONS[1]

IFRS 5, *NON-CURRENT ASSETS HELD FOR SALE AND DISCONTINUED OPERATIONS*

Author's Note

The International Accounting Standards Board amended International Financial Reporting (IFRS) 5, *Non-current Assets Held for Sale and Discontinued Operations*, by issuing the following standards:

- IFRS 9, *Financial Instruments* (issued November 2009 and October 2010 and effective for annual periods beginning on or after 1 January 2015)
  When an entity adopts IFRS 9, this amendment excludes financial assets within the scope of IFRS 9 from the measurement provisions of IFRS 5.
- IFRS 11, *Joint Arrangements* (issued May 2011 and effective for annual periods beginning on or after 1 January 2013)
  This amendment requires an entity to include an adjustment to the carrying amount of a subsidiary, joint venture, or associate in profit or loss from continuing operations when that subsidiary, joint venture, or associate ceases to be classified as held for sale. The entity should adjust the financial statements for all periods since classification as held for sale.
- IFRS 13, *Fair Value Measurements* (issued May 2011 and effective for annual periods beginning on or after 1 January 2013)
  IFRS 13 amended the definition of fair value in appendix A of IFRS 5.

Because these standards are effective after 1 January 2012, they are not discussed in the commentary in this section. In addition, the timing of the effective dates of these standards affects the availability of illustrative excerpts from survey companies' financial statements. Accordingly, the excerpts appearing later in this section may not reflect all or some of these revisions.

IFRSs Overview and Comparison to U.S. GAAP

6.01 IFRS 5 specifically addresses the accounting, classification, presentation, and disclosure of noncurrent assets and disposal groups held for sale and discontinued operations.

IFRS 5 was developed as part of a Financial Accounting Standards Board (FASB) convergence project and with consideration of the requirements of FASB *Accounting Standards Codification* (ASC) 360, *Property, Plant, and Equipment*.

6.02 IFRS 5 applies to all noncurrent assets (assets that are not expected to be realized within 12 months after the reporting period or the entity's normal operating cycle) and disposal groups (groups of assets with associated liabilities expected to be disposed of in a single transaction), with the following exceptions:

- Deferred tax assets, assets arising from employee benefits
- Financial assets within the scope of International Accounting Standard (IAS) 39, *Financial Instruments: Recognition and Measurement*
- Noncurrent assets accounted for using the fair value model in IAS 40, *Investment Property*, or measured at fair value through profit and loss in IAS 41, *Agriculture*
- Contractual rights under insurance contracts in IFRS 4, *Insurance Contracts*

6.03 IFRS 5 requires an entity to test assets within the scope of IFRSs for impairment in accordance with all applicable IFRSs immediately prior to classification as held for sale or discontinued operations. For example, an entity would test items of property, plant, and equipment (PPE) in accordance with IAS 36, *Impairment of Assets*, which establishes the requirements of the impairment test and measurement of impairment losses and also permits reversals of impairment losses, recognized at the time of reclassification, that occur prior to disposal of an asset or disposal group.

Recognition and Measurement

IFRSs

6.04 An entity should classify noncurrent assets or disposal groups as *held for sale* if the carrying amount(s) will be recovered through a sale transaction rather than continued use. To be eligible for classification as *held for sale*, IFRS 5 requires that an asset or disposal group be available for immediate sale in its present condition subject only to the usual and customary terms for sales of such assets or disposal groups. Completion of the sale should be highly probable.

6.05 The entity can conclude that sale is highly probable if the appropriate level of management is committed to a plan to sell the asset or disposal group and has initiated an active program to locate a buyer. The entity should actively market an asset or disposal group at a reasonable price in relation to its current fair value. The entity should expect completion of the sale within one year of the classification, although the standard recognizes and allows for extension of this period when there is sufficient evidence that the entity remains committed to the sale. Actions required to complete the plan should indicate that it is unlikely the plan will be withdrawn or changed significantly. An entity should not reclassify as held for sale any assets to be abandoned.

---

[1] Unless otherwise indicated, references to International Accounting Standards Board (IASB) standards and interpretations throughout this 2012 edition of *IFRS Financial Statements—Best Practices in Presentation and Disclosure* refer to the version of those standards and interpretations included in the *IFRS 2012* bound volume, the official printed consolidated text of IASB standards and interpretations, including revisions, amendments, and supporting documents, issued as of 1 January 2012.

6.06 At initial recognition as held for sale, an entity should measure assets and disposal groups within the scope of IFRS 5 at the lower of the carrying amount prior to reclassification and fair value less cost to sell as defined in IAS 36. If the asset or disposal group was acquired in a business combination, an entity should measure the asset at fair value less cost to sell when classified as held for sale. An entity should not record depreciation and amortization while the asset is classified as held for sale even if the asset or disposal group continues to be used in operations.

6.07 Disposal groups may include assets that are outside the scope of IFRS 5 (for example, investment property held at fair value in accordance with IAS 40 or financial instruments within the scope of IAS 39). IFRS 5 requires an entity to measure such assets in accordance with the relevant standards before measuring the disposal group as a whole at fair value less cost to sell.

6.08 An entity should recognize impairment losses for any write-downs of assets or disposal groups before or after classification as held for sale. An entity should first allocate any impairment losses on disposal groups (cash generating units) to any related goodwill, then to other assets on a pro rata basis. An entity should recognize reversals of impairment losses for increases in fair value less cost to sell that may occur after classification as held for sale. However, reversals of impairment losses are limited to the cumulative amount of impairment losses recognized either under IFRS 5 or previously under IAS 36. An entity should not reverse impairment losses allocated to goodwill.

6.09 Normally, an entity should recognize gains or impairment losses in the income statement (profit and loss) except when they relate to an asset held under a revaluation model (for example, in accordance with IAS 16, *Property, Plant and Equipment*). Gains or losses recognized on revalued assets are considered revaluations and an entity should recognize such gains or losses in the appropriate other comprehensive income account.

6.10 A discontinued operation is a *component of an entity*, defined as "operations and cash flows that can be clearly distinguished both operationally and for financial reporting purposes." Consequently, IFRS 5 concludes from this definition that a discontinued operation is a single cash generating unit or group of cash generating units. To be presented as a discontinued operation, IFRS 5 also requires the component to be a major line of business, geographical area of operations, or a subsidiary acquired solely with a view to resell (that either is classified as held for sale or has already been disposed of).

6.11 When an asset or disposal group no longer meets the IFRS 5 criteria to be classified as held for sale or discontinued operations, an entity should remove the assets or disposal groups from this classification and measure them at the lower of the carrying amount before reclassification, less the depreciation and amortization that the entity would otherwise have recorded, and recoverable amount on the date the decision to sell was rescinded. An entity should recognize any adjustments to carrying amounts in profit and loss from continuing operations in the current year.

U.S. GAAP

6.12 For assets classified as held for sale or discontinued operations, both IFRSs and FASB ASC 360 and 205-20 are similar with respect to measurement, timing of classification, and presentation within the financial statements. Although IFRS 5 narrowed the differences substantially between IFRSs and FASB ASC with respect to assets held for sale, some significant differences remain. Specifically, the FASB ASC glossary defines a *component of an entity* as one that comprises operations and cash flows that can be clearly distinguished, operationally and for financial reporting purposes, from the rest of the entity. A component of an entity may be a reportable segment or an operating segment, a reporting unit, a subsidiary, or an asset group. Although this definition is similar to the definition in IFRSs, entities may apply the definitions differently. For example, IFRS 5 does not prohibit classification as discontinued operations when the entity retains a noncontrolling interest (for example, by an equity method investment) (see paragraph 6.19). However, for Securities and Exchange Commission (SEC) registrants, SEC *Codification of Staff Accounting Bulletins* topic 5(Z)(4), "Disposal of Operation With Significant Interest Retained," states that when the entity retains significant influence (equity method investment), it should not account for the disposal as a discontinued operation, only as a disposal of a group of assets classified within continuing operations.

6.13 Similarly, because FASB ASC does not permit measurement at fair value for assets that meet the definition of an investment property under IFRSs and biological assets, all items of PPE can be classified as held for sale or discontinued operations and would be subject to the same impairment and measurement requirements. FASB ASC 350-20-50-1 permits an entity to include goodwill in a disposal group classified as held for sale.

6.14 As noted previously, the definition of a *component of an entity* in the FASB ASC glossary is essentially the same as the definition in IFRS 5. However, FASB ASC 205-20-45-1 contains the following additional criteria, not included in IFRS 5, that an entity should meet before reporting a component as a discontinued operation:

- The entity has or will eliminate the operations and cash flows of the component from its continuing operations as a result of the disposal transaction.
- The entity will not have any significant continuing involvement in the operations of the component after the disposal transaction.

As a result of these criteria, fewer components of a business held for sale may qualify as discontinued operations under FASB ASC 205-20.

6.15 The IFRS 5 convergence project does not address impairment recognition and measurement and significant differences remain. For example, under FASB ASC 350-20-35-31, an entity recognizes impairment losses on assets within disposal groups without first allocating these losses to any allocated goodwill. An entity should test separately any goodwill allocated to the disposal group for impairment only after recording impairment losses on individual assets.

Presentation

IFRSs

6.16 An entity should present assets classified as held for sale separately from other assets as a single line item in the statement of financial position. Similarly, the entity should present any liabilities included in disposal groups separately from other liabilities as a single line item. An entity should not offset or show assets and liabilities as a single net asset or liability. IFRS 5 also requires an entity to show separately any cumulative income and expense recognized directly in other comprehensive income in respect of assets and disposal groups classified as held for sale.

6.17 Although further disaggregation is permitted, IFRS 5 requires presentation of a separate line item on the face of the statement of comprehensive income consisting of the sum of
- posttax profit or loss of the discontinued operations,
- posttax gain or loss on measurement to fair value less cost to sell, or
- posttax gain or loss on disposal of the relevant assets or disposal groups.

6.18 Comparative information should reflect the new classification for assets or disposal groups classified as discontinued operations, but not for those classified as held for sale.

6.19 IFRS 5 also requires an entity that is committed to a sale plan involving loss of control of a subsidiary to classify all the assets and liabilities of that subsidiary as held for sale when the relevant criteria are met, regardless of whether the entity will retain a noncontrolling interest in the former subsidiary after the sale. In these circumstances, the entity should provide the same disclosures required for a discontinued operation. This amendment is included in *Improvements to IFRSs*, issued in May 2008 and effective for annual reporting periods beginning on or after 1 July 2009, and will apply to most survey companies.

U.S. GAAP

6.20 For those assets classified as held for sale or discontinued operations under IFRSs or FASB ASC 360-10-45, respectively, presentation requirements are essentially the same, except that under FASB ASC 230-10-45-24, an entity that chooses to report separately operating cash flows of discontinued operations should do so consistently for all periods affected, which may include periods long after sale or liquidation of the operations. In addition, unlike IFRS 5, FASB ASC 205-20-45-3 requires presentation of both pretax and posttax income from discontinued operations on the face of the income statement.

Disclosure

IFRSs

6.21 An entity may present the following disclosures either on the face of the financial statements or in the notes:
- Major classes of assets and liabilities classified as held for sale, unless the disposal group is a newly acquired subsidiary classified as held for sale

- Disaggregation of the posttax profit or loss on discontinued operations into the revenue, expenses, pretax profit and loss, gains or losses on measurement to fair value less cost to sell or on disposal, and related income tax effects of these two items respectively
- Net cash flows attributable to operating, financing, and investing activities of discontinued operations
- Amount of income from continuing operations and from discontinued operations attributable to the equity holders of the parent and the noncontrolling interest

When this information is provided in the notes, an entity should disclose the caption of the relevant line item in the financial statements.

6.22 When noncurrent assets or disposal groups are classified as held for sale or discontinued operations, IFRS 5 requires extensive narrative disclosures, including a description of the assets or disposal groups, facts and circumstances leading to the sale, the sale itself, and the expected manner and timing of disposal.

6.23 If applicable, an entity should disclose the reportable segment in which the asset or disposal group was previously reported and should also present the asset or disposal group in accordance with IFRS 8, *Operating Segments*. A disposal group classified as a discontinued operation often qualifies as a separate reportable segment under IFRS 8. IFRS 8 also requires the entity to disclose a reconciliation of the total profit and loss of reportable segments to the entity's profit and loss before tax and discontinued operations.

U.S. GAAP

6.24 Although disclosure requirements are essentially converged with IFRSs, several differences remain, including the following:
- According to FASB ASC 230-10-45-24, separate presentation or disclosure of cash flows from discontinued operations is not required.
- According to FASB ASC 205-20-50-2, an entity should disclose the major classes of assets and liabilities classified as held for sale. Unlike IFRS 5, entities are not exempt from this requirement for newly acquired subsidiaries classified as held for sale.

TABLE 6-1: NONCURRENT ASSETS HELD FOR SALE	2011	2010	2009
Survey entities reporting assets classified as held for sale..	27	35	31
Survey entities reporting assets and associated liabilities as held for sale........	21	35	35
Total..	48	70	66
Survey entities not reporting assets classified as held for sale........................	127	100	94
Total..	175	170	160

TABLE 6-2: DISCONTINUED OPERATIONS

	2011	2010	2009
Survey entities reporting discontinued operations...	32	45	41
Survey entities not reporting discontinued operations...	143	125	119
Total..	**175**	**170**	**160**

Presentation and Disclosure Excerpts

Noncurrent Assets Held for Sale

6.25

Viña Concha y Toro S.A. (Dec 2011)

CONSOLIDATED STATEMENT OF FINANCIAL POSITION (in part)

Assets	Note	As of December 31, 2011 Th$	As of December 31, 2010 Th$
Current assets			
Cash and cash equivalents	(6)	20,855,397	16,757,549
Other current financial assets	(7)	8,336,813	10,721,894
Other non-financial current assets		6,654,074	9,729,058
Trade and other accounts receivable, current net	(8)	130,693,605	108,358,712
Accounts receivable from related parties, current	(9)	417,813	609,117
Inventories	(10)	173,973,666	107,877,080
Current biologic assets	(15)	12,407,775	10,944,784
Current tax assets	(21)	16,794,392	9,740,456
Total current assets other than assets or groups of assets for disposition classified as maintained for sale or as maintained to distribute to owners		370,133,535	274,738,650
Assets held for sale	(16)	2,350,168	82,500
Total current assets		372,483,703	274,821,150

NOTES TO THE CONSOLIDATED FINANCIAL STATEMENTS (in part)

Note 1. General Considerations (in part)

The Company's name is Viña Concha y Toro S.A. ID No. 90.227.000—0, and is registered as an Open Corporation. The Company is located in Avda. Nueva Tajamar 481, North Tower, Floor N° 15, Las Condes, Santiago, Chile, phone (56-2) 476-5000, fax (56-2) 203-6740, postal box No. 213, Central Post Office, Santiago, e-mail webmaster@conchaytoro.cl, Website www.conchaytoro.com, it uses the ticker Conchatoro in the Chilean stock market and VCO for the NYSE.

Viña Concha y Toro S.A. was formed as a public limited company by means of a Public Deed dated December 31, 1921, before the Notary Public of Santiago Mr. Pedro N. Cruz. The summary was inscribed under file 1,051 numbers 875 and 987 both of the Business Registry of Santiago from the Santiago Real Estate Custodian corresponding to year 1922 and was published in the Official Gazette under N°13,420, dated November 6, 1922. The Existence Authorization Decree has N°1.556, dated October 18, 1922.

The Company is currently registered under file 15,664 N°12,447 in the Business Registry from the Santiago Real Estate Custodian, corresponding to year 1999; and in the Securities Register of the Superintendence of Securities and Insurance under N°0043.

Viña Concha y Toro is the biggest wine producing and exporting company in Chile. The Company is vertically integrated and operates its own vineyards, wineries and bottling plants. The Company also operates in Argentina, through Trivento Bodegas y Viñedos S.A. and in the United States of America through Fetzer Vineyards.

The Company has developed a wide wine portfolio using the brand Concha y Toro. Likewise, the Company has fostered innovating projects through its subsidiaries Viña Cono Sur, Viña Quinta de Maipo (formerly—Viña Palo Alto), Viña Maycas del Limarí and Trivento Bodegas y Viñedos. Additionally, together with the prestigious French winery Barón Philippe de Rothschild through a joint venture, Viña Almaviva S.A., produces the Almaviva icon, a first class wine.

The Company has presence in the main vineyard valleys of Chile: Valle del Limarí, Casablanca, San Antonio, Maipo, Cachapoal, Colchagua, Curicó and Maule.

In the distribution business, the Company operates through the subsidiaries, Comercial Peumo Ltda. (which has the most extensive on network for the distribution of wines in the domestic market), Concha y Toro UK Limited (United Kingdom) in 2008, in order to strengthen its distribution, the Company established its own distribution offices in Brazil, Sweden, Norway and Finland; which began operation during 2009. In other export markets, the Company maintains strategic relationships with significant specialized dealers.

Note 2. Basis of Preparation and Presentation of the Financial Statements (in part)

2.1 Basis of Preparation (in part)

2.1.1 Financial Statements

The consolidated financial statements of Viña Concha y Toro and subsidiaries as of December 31, 2011 have been prepared in conformity with International Financial Reporting Standards (IFRSs), as issued by the International Accounting Standards Board (IASB). The consolidated financial statements have been authorized for issue by the Board of Directors on April 26, 2012.

2.7 Assets Held for Sale

Non-current assets, Property, Plant and equipment whose carrying amount will be recovered through a sales operation and not through its ongoing use, are classified as held for sale. This condition is considered as complied solely when the sale is highly probable and the asset is available for immediate sale in its current state and transferred to the current group.

These are included in non-current assets when the investment is not intended to be disposed of in the twelve months following year-end.

These assets are valued at the lower of carrying amount and the estimated sales value deducting the costs required for realization, and are no longer depreciated from the time in which they are classified as non-current assets held-for-sale.

Note 16. Non-Financial Assets Held for Sale

These assets were classified as held for sale, as per the Company's regulations this requires the previous approval of the managers responsible of the areas involved with these assets. This decision was mainly based on the need to replace these assets with others with higher productivity.

The sale of these assets is expected to be completed during the first quarter of 2012. As reported in Note 2.7, these assets have been recorded at the lowest value between the book value and the estimated sale value.

As of December 31, 2011 assets maintained for sale are as follows:

Non-Financial Assets Maintained for Sale	As of December 31, 2011 Th$	As of December 31, 2010 Th$
Plant and equipment	50,712	82,447
Land	2,299,403	—
Fixed facilities and accessories	53	53
Total	2,350,168	82,500

Withdrawal of Business From Held for Sale and Reclassification as Property, Plant and Equipment

6.26

DRDGOLD Limited (Jun 2011)

CONSOLIDATED STATEMENT OF FINANCIAL POSITION (in part)

At June 30, 2011

	Note	2011 R'000	2010 R'000
Assets			
Non-current assets		1,778,646	2,178,190
Property, plant and equipment	10	1,540,003	1,857,646
Non-current investments and other assets	11	159,312	174,223
Non-current inventories	15	10,099	5,579
Deferred tax asset	21	69,232	140,742
Current assets		510,015	402,102
Inventories	15	122,922	132,636
Trade and other receivables	16	126,410	64,521
Current tax asset		1,571	1,793
Cash and cash equivalents		259,112	188,152
Assets classified as held for sale	17	—	15,000
Total assets		2,288,661	2,580,292

NOTES TO THE CONSOLIDATED FINANCIAL STATEMENTS (in part)

1. Accounting Policies (in part)

DRDGOLD Limited ('the company') is a company domiciled in South Africa. The consolidated financial statements of the company for the year ended June 30, 2011 comprise the company and its subsidiaries, (together referred to as the group) and the group's interests in associates and jointly controlled entities.

Statement of Compliance

The consolidated financial statements have been prepared in accordance with International Financial Reporting Standards (IFRS) and its interpretations adopted by the International Accounting Standards Board (IASB).

The financial statements were approved by the Board of Directors on September 19, 2011.

Significant Accounting Policies (in part)

The accounting policies set out below have been applied consistently by all entities in the group to all periods presented, except as explained below under 'New standards, interpretations and amendments to standards and interpretations adopted'.

Non-Current Assets Held for Sale and Discontinued Operations

A held-for-sale asset is classified as such if it is a non-current asset, or disposal group comprising assets and liabilities, that is expected to be recovered primarily through sale rather than through continuing use. Immediately before classification as held-for-sale, the assets (or components of a disposal group) are remeasured in accordance with the group's accounting policies. Thereafter, in general, the non-current assets or disposal groups are measured at the lower of carrying amount and fair value less costs to sell. Impairment losses on initial classification as held-for-sale are included in profit or loss. The same applies to gains and losses on subsequent measurement. Gains are not recognized in excess of any cumulative impairment loss.

A discontinued operation in the group is a component of the group's business that represents a separate major line of business, a geographical area of operations which has been disposed of or is held-for-sale, or a subsidiary acquired exclusively for resale. When an operation is classified as a discontinued operation, the comparative statement of comprehensive income is restated as if the operation had been discontinued from the start of the comparative period.

10. Property, Plant and Equipment (in part)

	2011 R'000	2010 R'000
Total		
Cost	3,548,479	3,191,996
Opening balance	3,191,996	2,901,436
Acquired through purchase of subsidiaries	—	131,205
Additions	340,064	200,405
Borrowing costs capitalized	6,420	32
Disposals	(4,766)	(41,082)
Transfer from non-current assets held-for-sale (refer note 17)	15,000	—
Foreign exchange movement	(235)	—
Accumulated depreciation and impairment	(2,008,476)	(1,334,350)
Opening balance	(1,334,350)	(1,168,217)
Current depreciation	(130,919)	(190,769)
(Impairment)/reversal of impairment (refer note 4)	(546,566)	12,514
Disposals	3,359	12,122
Carrying value	1,540,003	1,857,646
Mining property		
Cost	332,197	314,309
Opening balance	314,309	284,800
Acquired through purchase of subsidiaries	—	21,656
Additions	4,204	7,853
Disposals	(1,316)	—
Transfer from non-current assets held-for-sale (refer note 17)	15,000	—
Accumulated depreciation and impairment	(219,720)	(159,179)
Opening balance	(159,179)	(151,527)
Current depreciation	(5,407)	(7,652)
Impairment	(55,134)	—
Carrying value	112,477	155,130
Mine development		
Cost	2,095,084	1,970,999
Opening balance	1,970,999	1,806,500
Acquired through purchase of subsidiaries	—	54,384
Additions (b)	127,107	122,174
Disposals	(3,022)	(12,059)
Accumulated depreciation and impairment	(1,237,325)	(717,586)
Opening balance	(717,586)	(614,272)
Current depreciation	(104,923)	(115,373)
Impairment	(417,838)	—
Disposals	3,022	12,059
Carrying value	857,759	1,253,413

17. Assets Classified as Held for Sale

Mining property of R15.0 million, being the DRDGOLD mine village, was presented as held for sale following the decision of the group's management to sell this disposal group as part of the closure of the old Durban Deep mine. A sale was initially expected by June 30, 2011, however this did not take place due to ongoing litigation between Dino Properties (Pty) Limited and the group (refer note 23). The group does not believe that a sale of the property is highly probable within the next year and it has therefore been reclassified to property, plant and equipment.

For the year ended June 30, 2010, the disposal group was carried at the lower of carrying amount or fair value less costs to sell and was included within 'Corporate head office and all other expenses' for operating segmental reporting purposes (refer note 2).

	2011 R'000	2010 R'000
Assets classified as held for sale		
Property, plant and equipment	—	15,000
	—	15,000

Discontinued Operations, Assets and Associated Liabilities Classified as Held for Sale

6.27

Veolia Environnement (Dec 2011)

CONSOLIDATED STATEMENT OF FINANCIAL POSITION (in part)

(€ Million)	Notes	As of December 31 2011	As of December 31 2010[1]	As of December 31 2009[1]	As of January 1 2009[1]
Assets					
Inventories and work-in-progress	14	1,020.8	1,130.6	978.0	1,013.1
Operating receivables	14	11,427.6	12,488.7	12,241.3	13,093.2
Current operating financial assets	11	357.0	373.3	376.6	452.3
Other current financial assets	12	114.6	132.3	217.7	321.4
Current derivative instruments—Assets	30	48.1	34.6	45.6	142.8
Cash and cash equivalents	15	5,723.9	5,406.8	5,614.4	3,849.6
Assets classified as held for sale	25	3,256.5	805.6	722.6	203.0
Current assets		21,948.5	20,371.9	20,196.2	19,075.4
Total assets		50,405.6	51,427.3	49,754.7	49,086.2
Equity and Liabilities					
Operating payables	14	12,598.6	13,773.9	13,076.9	13,591.8
Current provisions	15	604.8	689.9	749.2	773.1
Current borrowings	18	3,942.3	2,827.1	2,983.1	3,219.7
Current derivative instruments—Liabilities	30	81.5	51.7	84.8	125.9
Bank overdrafts and other cash position items	15	440.2	387.0	454.9	465.7
Liabilities directly associated with assets classified as held for sale	25	2,012.8	386.8	309.4	98.2
Current liabilities		19,680.2	18,116.4	17,658.3	18,274.4
Total equity and liabilities		50,405.6	51,427.3	49,754.7	49,086.2

[1] Amounts as of December 31, 2010, December 31, 2009 and January 1, 2009 re-presented pursuant to IAS 8, *Accounting Policies, Changes in Accounting Estimates and Errors*—See Note 1 to the Consolidated Financial Statements.

CONSOLIDATED INCOME STATEMENT (in part)

(€ Million)	Notes	Year Ended December 31 2011[2]	Year Ended December 31 2010[2][3]	Year Ended December 31 2009[1][2][3]
Net income (loss) from continuing operations		(314.2)	819.7	791.2
Net income (loss) from discontinued operations	25	(2.4)	29.3	25.6
Net income (loss) for the year		(316.6)	849.0	816.8

[1] In 2009, as part of ongoing efficiency measures, the Group reclassified certain expenses from cost of sales to selling costs and general and administrative expense. These reclassifications had no impact on operating income (see Note 20, Operating income).

[2] In accordance with IFRS 5, Non-current assets held for sale and discontinued operations, the Income Statements of:
- the whole Transportation business, in the process of being sold (see Note 4)
- Water activities in the Netherlands, divested in December 2010 and Environmental Services activities in Norway, divested in March 2011;
- German operations in the Energy Services division, partially divested in May 2011,
- household assistance services (Proxiserve) held jointly by the Water and Energy Services divisions, divested in December 2011,
- urban lighting activities (Citelum) in the Energy Services division,

are presented in a separate line, Net income from discontinued operations, for the years ended December 31, 2011, 2010 and 2009.

Furthermore, as the divestiture process for Water activities in Gabon and Pinellas incineration activities in the United States was interrupted in the first and second semesters of 2011 respectively, these activities are no longer presented in Net income from discontinued operations.

[3] Amounts as of December 31, 2010 and December 31, 2009 re-presented pursuant to IAS 8, Accounting Policies, Changes in Accounting Estimates and Errors—See Note 1 to the Consolidated Financial Statements.

CONSOLIDATED CASH FLOW STATEMENT

(€ Million)	Notes	Year Ended December 31		
		2011	2010[2]	2009[1][2]
Net income (loss) for the year		(316.6)	849.0	816.8
Operating depreciation, amortization, provisions and impairment losses	20	2,842.5	1,884.2	1,869.1
Financial amortization and impairment losses		5.6	18.6	7.2
Gains/losses on disposal	20	(592.4)	(277.2)	(306.1)
Share of net income of associates	9	(13.4)	(18.4)	0.9
Dividends received	22	(4.9)	(6.9)	(8.7)
Finance costs and finance income	21	796.1	811.2	792.0
Income tax expense	23	558.3	362.4	319.1
Other items		77.7	95.8	69.1
Operating cash flow before changes in working capital		3,352.9	3,718.7	3,559.4
Changes in working capital	14	(40.7)	105.8	450.4
Income taxes paid		(368.2)	(367.9)	(408.5)
Net cash from operating activities		2,944.0	3,456.6	3,601.3
Including Net cash from operating activities of discontinued operations		187.8	365.3	416.3
Industrial investments	42	(2,258.3)	(2,083.7)	(2,104.8)
Proceeds on disposal of intangible assets and property, plant and equipment		168.9	205.2	258.7
Purchases of investments		(372.1)	(426.3)	(177.9)
Proceeds on disposal of financial assets		1,286.9	498.6	522.3
Operating financial assets				
—New operating financial assets	11	(363.5)	(489.1)	(483.1)
—Principal payments on operating financial assets	11	441.0	424.1	455.2
Dividends received	9 & 22	12.4	12.9	14.8
New non-current loans granted		(160.3)	(59.8)	(43.8)
Principal payments on non-current loans		110.5	31.8	65.8
Net decrease/increase in current loans		(3.1)	69.1	140.9
Net cash used in investing activities		(1,137.6)	(1,817.2)	(1,351.9)
Including Net cash used in investing activities of discontinued operations		878.1	(170.2)	17.7
Net increase/decrease in current borrowings	18	(534.5)	(938.2)	(1,323.9)
New non-current borrowings and other debts	18	745.1	537.6	3,301.2
Principal payments on non-current borrowings and other debts	18	(315.0)	(148.8)	(1,514.8)
Proceeds on issue of shares		2.5	128.8	157.1
Share capital reduction				
Transactions with non-controlling interests: partial purchases and sales		24.4	91.8	50.9
Purchases of/proceeds from treasury shares		2.2	7.9	4.9
Dividends paid		(547.0)	(735.6)	(434.0)
Interest paid		(753.6)	(821.9)	(729.8)
Net cash used in financing activities		(1,375.9)	(1,878.4)	(488.4)
Including Net cash used (provided) in financing activities of discontinued operations		(19.5)	(4.2)	(138.6)
Net cash at the beginning of the year		5,019.8	5,159.5	3,383.9
Effect of foreign exchange rate changes and other		(166.6)	99.3	14.6
Net cash at the end of the year		5,283.7	5,019.8	5,159.5
Cash and cash equivalents	15	5,723.9	5,406.8	5,614.4
Bank overdrafts and other cash position items	15	440.2	387.0	454.9
Net cash at the end of the year		5,283.7	5,019.8	5,159.5

[1] Figures for the year ended December 31, 2009 have been adjusted for the application of the amendments to IAS 7 as follows:
  — replacement costs are now included in Net cash from operating activities: the impact of this reclassification between "Operating depreciation, amortization, provisions and impairment losses" in cash flows from operating activities and "Industrial investments" in investing activities is −€360.9 million in the year ended December 31, 2009;
  — transactions with non-controlling interests without a change in control are now recorded in cash flows from financing activities: the impact of this reclassification between "Proceeds on disposals of financial assets" in investing flows and "Transactions with non–controlling interests: partial purchases and sales" in financing flows is €50.9 million in the year ended December 31, 2009.

[2] 2010 and 2009 amounts re-presented pursuant to IAS 8, Accounting Policies, Changes in Accounting Estimates and Errors—See Note 1 to the Consolidated Financial Statements.

Net cash flows attributable to discontinued operations as defined in IFRS 5 primarily concern the Veolia Transdev combination (see Note 4).

  Discontinued operations are presented in Note 25.

IFRS-BPPD 6.27

NOTES TO THE CONSOLIDATED FINANCIAL STATEMENTS (in part)

1 Accounting Principles and Methods (in part)

1.1 Accounting Standards Framework (in part)

1.1.1 Basis Underlying the Preparation of the Financial Information

Pursuant to Regulation no.1606/2002 of July 19, 2002, as amended by European Regulation no. 297/2008 of March 11, 2008, the consolidated financial statements for the year ended December 31, 2011 are presented in accordance with IFRS (International Financial Reporting Standards) as adopted by the European Union and IFRS as published by the International Accounting Standards Board (IASB). These standards may be consulted at the following European Union website: http://ec.europa.eu/internal_market/accounting/ ias/ index_en.htm.

These financial statements are accompanied, for comparative purposes, by financial statements for fiscal years 2010 and 2009 drawn up in accordance with the same standards framework.

In the absence of IFRS standards or interpretations and in accordance with IAS 8, *Accounting Policies, Changes in Accounting Estimates and Errors*, Veolia Environnement refers to other IFRS dealing with similar or related issues and the conceptual framework. Where appropriate, the Group may use other standard references and in particular U.S. standards.

2 Use of Management Estimates in the Application of Group Accounting Standards (in part)

Veolia Environnement may be required to make estimates and assumptions that affect the reported amounts of assets, liabilities, revenue and expenses, and the disclosures of contingent assets and liabilities. Future results may be different from these estimates.

Underlying estimates and assumptions are determined based on past experience and other factors considered as reasonable given the circumstances. They act as a basis for making judgments necessary to the determination of the carrying amount of assets and liabilities, which cannot be obtained directly from other sources. Future values could differ from these estimates.

Underlying estimates and assumptions are reviewed on an ongoing basis. The impact of changes in accounting estimates is recognized in the period the change is made if it affects this period only and in the period the change is made and prior periods if they are also affected by the change.

Notes 5 on goodwill and 25 on discontinued operations present the impact of − €440 million impairment on the Veolia Transdev goodwill,in the course of being sold. This value adjustment is the result of a downturn in the performance of the subsidiary and a decrease in implicit market transaction valuation multiples in this sector. The value adjustment is based on non-binding offers received on January 27, 2012 and also incorporates the potential impact on the transaction price of current legal proceedings concerning one of the assets of this group, SNCM (see Note 38, Contingent liabilities).

3 Significant Events (in part)

3.2 Changes in the Group Structure

Veolia Transdev Combination

This transaction is presented in detail in Note 4.

Acquisitions

On July 26, Dalkia Polska won the privatization bid for the Warsaw urban heating network. The European Commission issued a favorable opinion on the takeover by Dalkia Polska, a subsidiary of Dalkia International of an 85% stake in SPEC. The deal was closed on October 11, 2011 for an enterprise value of €227 million (Group share). The company is consolidated from this date and the fair value measurement of identifiable assets and liabilities acquired was determined on a provisional basis as of December 31, 2011.

This acquisition is presented in detail in Note 32.

Divestitures

- On February 14, 2011, the Group signed an agreement for the disposal of its sorting-recycling activities in Norway. The divestiture was completed on March 25, 2011.
- In May and August 2011, the activities of the Energy Services division in Germany were sold for an enterprise value of €29 million (Group share).
- On May 5, 2011, the Group sold its transportation activities in Norway for an enterprise value of €36 million (Group share).
- On May 23, 2011, the Group sold 5% of Dalkia Ceska Republica to J&T Group for an enterprise value of €32 million.
- On June 29, 2011, the EBRD and IFC acquired a 5% interest each in the Baltic-Russian activities of the Energy Services division in the amount of €38 million.
- On July 1, 2011, the Group sold its United Kingdom activities previously owned by Veolia Transport.
- On August 10, 2011, the Group sold its solid waste activities in Belgium in the Environmental Services division.
- On December 16, 2011, the Group sold its household assistance services business ("Veolia Habitat Services" or Proxiserve) for an enterprise value of €118 million.
- On December 20, 2011, the Group sold its cogeneration activities in Estonia for an enterprise value of €69 million (Group share).
- On December 22, 2011, the Group sold its residual 15% stake in Dalkia Usti nad Labem to CEZ Group for an enterprise value of €26 million (Group share). Accordingly, in fiscal years 2010 and 2011, cumulative divestitures of Dalkia Usti nad Labem activities, comprising a cogeneration (heat and electricity) plant and the primary district heating system for the city of Usti nad Labem, represented a total enterprise value of €171 million (Group share).

The divestiture of Norwegian recycling activities in the Environmental Services division, German activities in the Energy Services division, United Kingdom and Norwegian activities in the Transportation division and Proxiserve household assistance services is presented in discontinued operations.

Investor Day

During its Investor Day held in Paris on December 6, 2011, the Group presented its strategic plan and mid-term outlook based primarily on refocusing the activity and business portfolio, with in particularly €5 billion in assets divestitures over the next two years, the restructuring of activities on the three core businesses (Water, Environmental Services and Energy Services) and the sale of regulated Water activities in the United Kingdom and solid waste activities in the United States.

4 Veolia Transdev Combination

On May 4, 2010, the Caisse des dépôts et consignations and Veolia Environnement concluded their agreement on the Transdev-Veolia Transport combination by the creation of a 50/50 joint venture combining Transdev and Veolia.

As part of this transaction, the companies Veolia Transport and Transdev were transferred respectively by their shareholders to the newly created joint venture, Veolia Transdev. Prior to completing the transaction, the Caisse des dépôts et consignations subscribed to a €200 million share capital increase by Transdev.

Following completion of the combination, Veolia Environnement became the industrial operator of the new entity and Caisse des dépôts et consignations a long-term strategic partner.

On March 3, 2011, the transaction was effectively completed:

- following authorization of the combination by the relevant anti-monopoly authorities and approval by the French Ministry of the Economy of the privatization of Transdev.
- following the final amendments to the shareholders' agreement in order to simplify measures regarding the governance of the new entity.

Following the changes in the shareholders' agreement, the new entity has a single Chief Executive, Mr. Jérôme Gallot, with full operational responsibilities. Veolia Environnement and the Caisse des dépôts et consignations exercise joint control over the new entity.

From this date and pursuant to IAS/IFRS, Veolia Environnement lost exclusive control of Veolia Transport in exchange for a 50% investment in the Veolia Transdev joint venture, which is proportionately consolidated.

On December 6, 2011, during the Investor Day, the Group presented its strategic plan encompassing the refocusing of its activities and business portfolio and leading to the decision to withdraw progressively from the Transportation sector.

The communication of these decisions and progress with the withdrawal process as of December 31, 2011, led the Company to classify the Transportation business as a group of assets held for sale and consider the Transportation business as a discontinued operation as defined by IFRS 5, *Non-Current Assets Held for Sale and Discontinued Operations*.

The accounting impacts of these transactions in the Group financial statements are quantified below:

Impact on the Main Income Statement Headings

The main accounting impacts of the combination break down as follows:

- the net income and expenses of Veolia Transport were recorded in a separate income statement line, *Net income from discontinued operations*. Amounts presented in *Net income from continued operations* in fiscal years 2010 and 2009 were also restated retrospectively on the same line. Income and expenses reclassified in fiscal year 2011 consist of 100% of Veolia Transport income and expenses for the period January 1 to March 3, 2011 and 50% of Veolia Transdev income and expenses for the period March 3 to December 31 (including income and expenses incurred in transactions with other Group entities).
- the recognition of a gain on disposal of €429.8 million following the loss of control of Veolia Transport on March 3, 2011, comprising:
  — the Veolia Transport disposal gain of €391.5 million;
  — items recorded directly in other comprehensive income of €38.3 million (mainly a foreign exchange translation gain of €34.2 million).

The recognition of an impairment as of December 31 of €440 million on Veolia Transdev goodwill. This value adjustment is the result of a downturn in the performance of the subsidiary and a decrease in implicit market transaction valuation multiples in this sector. The value adjustment is based on non-binding offers received on January 27, 2012 and also incorporates the potential impact on the transaction price of current legal proceedings concerning one of the assets of this group, SNCM (see Note 38, Contingent liabilities).

(€ Millions)	Year Ended December 31, 2011	Year Ended December 31, 2010	Year Ended December 31, 2009
Revenue	4,259.0	5,764.7	5,860.7
Operating income	(449.0)	119.7	152.9
Financial items	(40.4)	(47.0)	(65.9)
Income tax expense	(9.8)	(20.7)	(43.8)
Share of net income of associates	0.5	0.3	(10.0)
Net income (loss) reclassified in discontinued operations	(498.7)	52.3	33.2
Capital gains and losses on disposals	443.0	—	—
Tax impacts on disposal	—	—	—
Disposal gain after tax reclassified in Net income (loss) from discontinued operations	443.0	—	—
Total reclassified in Net income (loss) from discontinued operations	(55.7)	52.3	33.2

Transaction-related costs expensed in the accounts of Veolia Transdev totaled €13.7 million and are recognized in *Net income from discontinued operations*.

Impact on the Main Consolidated Statement of Financial Position Headings

The main accounting impacts break down as follows:

- the derecognition of all Veolia Transport assets and liabilities, fully consolidated in the accounts, following loss of control by the Group on March 3, 2011 and as a consequence the Group recognized a disposal gain amounted €429.8 million.
- the fair value remeasurement of the assets and liabilities held in the Veolia Transdev joint venture, following

the acquisition of 50% joint control by the Group. The fair value allocation primarily concerned contracts and contract portfolios, brands, real-estate sites and travelling systems.

- the recognition of an impairment loss of €440 million on Veolia Transdev goodwill.
- the reclassification of the entire assets and liabilities of the Veolia Transdev joint venture consolidated using the proportionate method in assets and liabilities held for sale following the withdrawal decided by the Group.

(€ Million)	100% De-recognition of Veolia Transport (a)	50% Recognition of Veolia Transdev (b)	Impact Presented in Change in Consolidation Scope (a) + (b)	Flows During the Period	Transfers to Assets/Liabilities Classified as Held for Sale
Assets					
Goodwill	(543.6)	730.0	186.4	(446.1)	(283.9)
Concession intangible assets	(14.2)	7.1	(7.1)	6.1	(13.2)
Other intangible assets	(125.0)	159.5	34.5	2.4	(161.9)
Property, plant and equipment	(1,607.1)	1,163.6	(443.5)	(149.4)	(1,014.2)
Investments in associates	(2.5)	3.2	0.7	0.8	(4.0)
Non-consolidated investments	(13.0)	20.2	7.2	(2.8)	(17.4)
Non-current operating financial assets	(87.8)	35.3	(52.5)	64.1	(99.4)
Derivative instruments—Assets	(2.6)	5.3	2.7	(2.4)	(2.9)
Other non-current financial assets	(81.0)	53.6	(27.4)	(5.3)	(48.3)
Deferred tax assets	(192.8)	181.0	(11.8)	3.4	(184.4)
Total non-current assets	(2,669.6)	2,358.8	(310.8)	(529.2)	(1,829.6)
Inventories and work-in-progress	(96.8)	58.4	(38.4)	0.5	(58.9)
Operating receivables	(1,145.2)	769.7	(375.5)	(74.0)	(695.7)
Current operating financial assets	(15.9)	7.9	(8.0)	13.3	(21.2)
Other current financial assets	(29.9)	19.2	(10.7)	12.0	(31.2)
Current derivative instruments	(1.7)	1.7	—	0.7	(2.4)
Cash and cash equivalents	(252.9)	282.3	29.4	(130.5)	(151.8)
Assets classified as held for sale	(18.6)	19.2	0.6	(12.1)	2,790.8
Total current assets	(1,561.0)	1,158.4	(402.6)	(190.1)	1,829.6
Total assets	(4,230.6)	3,517.2	(713.4)	(719.3)	—
Equity and Liabilities					
Equity attributable to owners of the Company	(304.8)	691.1	386.3		
Equity attributable to non-controlling interests	(118.9)	86.4	(32.5)		
Equity	(423.7)	777.5	353.8	—	—
Non-current provisions	(258.9)	136.4	(122.5)	10.0	(146.4)
Non-current borrowings	(166.7)	230.9	64.2	(24.0)	(206.9)
Derivative instruments—Liabilities	(2.1)	1.7	(0.4)	4.3	(6.0)
Deferred tax liabilities	(256.6)	262.0	5.4	(3.7)	(258.3)
Total non-current liabilities	(684.3)	631.0	(53.3)	(13.4)	(617.6)
Current borrowings	(85.3)	235.3	150.0	(101.0)	(134.3)
Operating payables	(1,354.7)	973.8	(380.9)	(9.1)	(964.7)
Current provisions	(94.3)	61.5	(32.8)	(18.4)	(43.1)
Current derivative instruments—Liabilities	7.3	(7.7)	(0.4)	7.1	(0.6)
Bank overdrafts and other cash position items	(28.7)	60.0	31.3	(44.9)	(15.1)
Group financing	(1,537.6)	771.3	(766.3)	—	—
Liabilities directly associated with assets classified as held for sale	(29.3)	14.5	(14.8)	(14.1)	1,775.4
Total current liabilities	(3,122.6)	2,108.7	(1,013.9)	(180.4)	617.6
Total equity and liabilities	(4,230.6)	3,517.2	(713.4)	(193.8)	—

Impact on Cash Flows

(€ Million)	Year Ended December 31, 2011	Year Ended December 31, 2010	Year Ended December 31, 2009
Net cash from operating activities	163.0	298.9	335.6
Net cash used (from) in investing activities	621.7	(219.8)	(126.0)
Net cash used (from) in financing activities	(129.4)	20.1	(88.2)
Net increase (decrease) in cash and cash equivalents reclassified in net cash flows of discontinued operations	655.3	99.2	121.4

Impact on Group Debt and Cash and Cash Equivalents

(€ Million)	Veolia Transport at 100%	Veolia Transdev at 50%	Net Impact as of March 3	Impact of Transfers to Assets/Liabilities Classified as Held for Sale as of December 31, 2011
Non-current borrowings	(166.7)	230.9	64.2	(206.9)
Current borrowings	(85.3)	235.3	150.0	(134.3)
Group financing	(1,537.6)	771.3	(766.3)	
Bank overdrafts and other cash position items	(28.7)	60.0	31.3	(15.1)
Gross borrowings	(1,818.3)	1,297.5	(520.8)	(356.3)
Cash and cash equivalents	252.9	(282.3)	(29.4)	151.8
Net debt	(1,565.4)	1,015.2	(550.2)	(204.5)

The Veolia Transdev combination reduced Group net financial debt by €550 million in the first quarter of 2011, primarily due to the refinancing of the new entity by both Veolia Environnement and the Caisse des dépôts et consignations. The loans granted by Veolia Environnement and the Caisse des dépôts et consignations are granted jointly to Veolia Transdev. The cash and cash equivalents of Veolia Transdev and its subsidiaries is pooled and managed by Veolia Environnement.

As of December 31, 2011, external financing and net cash and cash equivalents were reclassified in assets and liabilities held for sale in the amount of €205 million.

Other Comprehensive Income of Discontinued Operations

(€ Million)		Year Ended December 31, 2011	Year Ended December 31, 2010	Year Ended December 31, 2009
Actuarial gains and losses on pension obligations	Net of tax	(9.3)	(6.5)	(6.7)
Fair value reserve	Net of tax	1.4	2.7	36.1
Foreign exchange gains and losses	Net of tax	(41.2)	31.6	32.1
Other comprehensive income		(49.1)	27.8	61.5
—attributable to owners of the Company		(40.0)	25.3	60.9
—attributable to non-controlling interests		(9.1)	2.5	0.6

Other comprehensive income released to net profit consists of the foreign exchange translation reserve and the fair value reserve, net of tax, attributable to owners of the Company.

5 Goodwill (in part)

Movements in the net carrying amount of goodwill by division are as follows:

(€ Million)	As of December 31, 2010	Changes in Consolidation Scope	Foreign Exchange Translation	Impairment Losses	Transfers to Assets Classified as Held for Sale	Other	As of December 31, 2011
Water	2,408.0	(19.2)	24.3	(58.6)	13.0	0.8	2,368.3
Environmental Services	2,691.2	(3.2)	45.9	(78.1)	(3.3)	0.7	2,653.2
Energy Services	1,161.6	(12.1)	(26.7)	(366.1)	(12.9)	—	743.8
Transportation	549.0	173.9	0.8	(440.0)[1]	(283.9)	0.2	0.0
Incl. VeoliaTransdev		717.5	6.2	(440.0)[1]	(283.9)	0.2	
Incl. VeoliaTransport	549.0	(543.6)	(5.4)	—	—	—	—
Other	30.4	—	0.2	—	—	—	30.6
Goodwill	6,840.2	139.4	44.5	(942.8)	(287.1)	1.7	5,795.9

[1] Reclassified as discontinued operations.

Changes in consolidation scope primarily concern the disposal of Veolia Transportation (− €543.6 million), the acquisition of joint control of the Veolia Transdev joint venture (€730.0 million) (see Note 4) and the sale of Transportation activities in Norway (− €20.9 million).

Acquisitions during the year are presented in Note 32, Main acquisitions, and primarily concern the acquisition of SPEC by the Energy Services division.

Transfers to Assets classified as held for sale mainly concern the assets of the Veolia Transdev group reclassified as discontinued operation (€283.9 million, see Note 4).

Impairment losses recognized in the year total €942.8 million of which €440.0 million on Veolia Transdev reclassified as discontinued operations (see Note 25) and €502.8 million recorded in operating income and detailed in Note 20.

9 Investments in Associates (in part)

The principal investments in associates with a value of greater than €10 million as of December 31, 2011 are as follows:

	As of December 31								
	% Control			Share in Equity			Share of Net Income		
	2011	2010	2009	2011	2010	2009	2011	2010	2009
Fovarosi Csatomazasi Muvek	25.00%	25.00%	25.00%	80.7	89.6	91.1	1.7	1.0	0.1
Regaz (Gaz de Bordeaux)	24.00%	24.00%	24.00 %	27.1	27.0	23.8	1.6	4.1	4.0
Cie Méridionale de Navigation[1]				—	—		—	—	(10.2)
Mayflower	10.00%	10.00%		27.1	26.7		0.5	0.4	
Kraftwerk Mehrum[2]	16.70%			19.9			(1.6)		
Doshion VWS	30.00%	30.00%	30.00%	16.8	19.2	16.8	0.1	0.4	0.4
TIRU	24.00%	24.00%	24.00%	16.3	15.0	13.0	1.5	1.5	1.1
Berlinwasser China Holding (BWI)[4]	—	49.00%	49.00%	—	13.3	12.0	0.5	0.7	0.2
Stadtereinigung Holtmeyer GmbH[3]			40.00%		—	11.9		—	(0.4)
SDC PTE	30.32%	30.32%	30.32%	12.1	8.8	—	3.0	—	—
CIACG	41.97%	41.97%	41.97%	11.5	10.1	8.7	1.7	1.8	(2.5)
Acqua Campania	47.90%	23.71%	—	10.8	5.5	—	0.9	—	—
Other amounts < €10 million in 2011				102.9	96.5	91.2	3.5	8.6	6.4
Investments in associates				325.2	311.7	268.5	13.4[5]	18.5[5]	(0.9)[5]

[1] Companies sold in 2009.
[2] Change in consolidation method (from proportionate consolidation to equity accounting).
[3] Companies sold in 2010.
[4] Companies sold in 2011.
[5] Pursuant to IFRS 5, a portion of this net income is reclassified in Net income from discontinued operations in the amount of €1.1 million in 2011, €0.5 million in 2010 and − €9.7 million in 2009 (see Note 25).

Movements in investments in associates during 2011 are as follows:

(€ Million)	% Control as of December 31, 2011	2010	Net Income	Dividend Distribution	Foreign Exchange Translation	Changes in Consolidation Scope	Other	2011
Fovarosi Csatomazasi Muvek	25.00%	89.6	1.7	—	(10.6)	—	—	80.7
Regaz (Gaz de Bordeaux)	24.00%	27.0	1.6	(1.5)	—	—	—	27.1
Mayflower	10.00%	26.7	0.5	(0.9)	0.8	—	—	27.1
Kraftwerk Mehrum	16.70%	—	(1.6)	(0.1)	—	21.6	—	19.9
Doshion VWS	30.00%	19.2	0.1	—	(2.5)	—	—	16.8
Berlinwasser China Holding (BWI)	—	13.3	0.5	—	(0.5)	0.9	(14.2)	—
TIRU	24.00%	15.0	1.5	—	(0.1)	—	(0.1)	16.3
SDC PTE	30.32%	8.8	3.0	—	0.3	—	—	12.1
CIACG	41.97%	10.1	1.7	(0.3)	—	—	—	11.5
Acqua Campania	47.90%	5.5	0.9	(1.1)	—	5.5	—	10.8
Other amounts < €10 million in 2011		96.5	3.5	(3.6)	(0.4)	10.4	(3.5)	102.9
Investments in associates		311.7	13.4	(7.5)	(13.0)	38.4	(17.8)	325.2

No material amounts were transferred to Assets classified as held for sale in 2009, 2010 or 2011.

10 Non-Consolidated Investments (in part)

In accordance with IAS 39, non-consolidated investments are recognized at fair value. Unrealized gains and losses are taken directly through other comprehensive income, except for unrealized losses considered long-term or material which are expensed in the Consolidated Income Statement in "Other financial income and expenses" (see Note 22).

Movements in non-consolidated investments during 2011 are as follows:

(€ Million)	As of December 31, 2010	Additions	Disposals	Changes in Consolidation Scope	Fair Value Adjustments	Impairment Losses	Foreign Exchange Translation	Transfers to Assets Classified as Held for Sale	Other	As of December 31, 2011
Non-consolidated investments	130.7	25.6	(17.9)	(2.3)	(1.6)	(4.3)	0.7	(18.2)	(6.4)	106.3

The Group did not hold any investment lines in excess of €20 million as of December 31, 2011.

Transfers to Assets classified as held for sale mainly concern the non-consolidated investments of the Veolia Transdev group as part of the reclassification of this joint venture in discontinued operations (− €17.4 million, see Note 4).

17 Non-Current and Current Provisions (in part)

Movements in non-current provisions during 2011 are as follows:

(€ Million)	As of December 31, 2010	Addition/ Charge	Repayment/ Utilization	Reversal	Actuarial Gains (Losses)	Unwinding of the Discount	Changes in Consolidation Scope	Foreign Exchange Translation	Non-Current/ Current Reclassification	Other	As of December 31, 2011
Tax litigation	109.6	14.9	—	(6.5)	—	0.1	1.4	(0.2)	(32.6)	(0.3)	86.4
Employee litigation	9.8	3.1	—	(1.0)	—	—	(1.8)	(0.0)	(0.5)	(5.5)	4.1
Other litigation	114.6	16.4	—	(12.4)	—	0.6	(0.6)	0.4	(55.0)	(16.5)	47.5
Contractual commitments	180.9	179.7	(177.4)	(1.8)	—	1.4	3.1	0.2	—	92.9	279.0
Provisions for work-in-progress and losses to completion on long-term contracts	205.8	16.2	—	(11.2)	—	4.6	(57.1)	1.1	(25.1)	3.7	138.0
Closure and postclosure costs	615.5	3.5	—	(3.7)	—	65.8	(24.5)	4.7	(62.0)	3.7	603.0
Restructuring provisions	1.2	0.5	—	(0.0)	—	(0.0)	0.8	(0.0)	(1.3)	(0.6)	0.6
Self-insurance provisions	116.8	34.9	—	(12.4)	—	1.8	(9.4)	0.6	(17.6)	(16.0)	98.7
Other provisions	78.9	35.0	—	(3.7)	—	1.5	(10.1)	(0.3)	(11.9)	(21.6)	67.8
Non-current provisions excl pensions and other employee benefits	1,433.1	304.2	(177.4)	(52.7)	—	75.8	(98.2)	6.5	(206.0)	39.8	1,325.1
Provisions for pensions and other employee benefits	880.8	103.0	(120.9)	(28.2)	33.8	22.1	(54.7)	3.3	—	(87.2)	752.0
Non-current provisions	2,313.9	407.2	(298.3)	(80.9)	33.8	97.9	(152.9)	9.8	(206.0)	(47.4)	2,077.1

Changes in consolidation scope mainly concern the Veolia Transdev joint venture (− €122.5 million, see Note 4) and the divestiture of solid waste activities in Belgium in the Environmental Services division (− €30.5 million).

Other movements mainly concern the transfer to "Liabilities classified as held for sale" of provisions of the Veolia Transdev group as part of the reclassification of this joint venture as discontinued operations (− €146.4 million, including €91.7 million in respect of provisions for pensions and other employee benefits) and the impact of the interruption of the divestiture process for Water division activities in Gabon (+ €95.2 million, including €10.3 million in respect of provisions for pensions and other employee benefits).

18 Non-Current and Current Borrowings (in part)

18.4 Finance Leases (in part)

The Group uses finance leases to finance the purchase of certain operating property, plant and equipment and real estate assets recognized as assets in the Consolidated Statement of Financial Position.

Assets financed by finance lease break down by category as follows:

(€ Million)	Property, Plant and Equipment	Concession Intangible Assets	Operating Financial Assets	Total
As of December 31, 2011	258.4	114.9	220.1	593.4
As of December 31, 2010	343.5	131.1	237.0	711.6
As of December 31, 2009	381.2	146.2	267.6	795.0

The decrease in property, plant and equipment is mainly due to the transfer to assets classified as held for sale of the assets of the Veolia Transdev group as part of the reclassification of this joint venture in discontinued operations (see Note 4).

19 Revenue (in part)

As for other Income Statement headings, Revenue does not include amounts relating to discontinued operations, in accordance with IFRS 5, *Non-Current Assets Held for Sale and Discontinued Operations* (see Note 25). Such amounts concern:

- the whole Transportation business, in the process of divestiture (see Note 4);
- Water activities in the Netherlands, divested in December 2010 and Environmental Services activities in Norway, divested in March 2011;

- German operations in the Energy Services division, divested in May and August 2011;
- household assistance services (Proxiserve) held jointly by the Water and Energy Services divisions, divested in December 2011;
- urban lighting activities (Citelum) in the Energy Services division.

These amounts are presented in a separate line, "Net income from discontinued operations", in fiscal year 2011 and fiscal years 2010 and 2009 presented for comparison purposes (see Note 25).

Furthermore, as the divestiture process for Water activities in Gabon and Pinellas incineration activities in the United States in the Environmental Services division was interrupted in the first and second semesters of 2011 respectively, these activities are reclassified in continuing operations.

20 Operating Income

Operating income is calculated as follows:

(€ Million)	Year Ended December 31, 2011	Year Ended December 31, 2010	Year Ended December 31, 2009
Revenue	29,647.3	28,764.2	27,847.7
Cost of sales[1]	(24,919.0)	(23,255.0)	(22,677.9)
O/w:			
• impairment losses on goodwill, net of negative goodwill recognized in the Consolidated Income Statement	(502.8)	0.2	(0.9)
• impairment losses (excl. working capital) and provisions	(136.3)	(38.7)	(94.9)
• replacement costs	(399.5)	(364.0)	(360.9)
Selling costs[1]	(595.1)	(574.8)	(539.9)
General and administrative expenses[1]	(3,176.0)	(3,139.5)	(3,021.1)
• Research and development costs	(111.7)	(87.4)	(89.3)
Other operating revenue and expenses	60.0	187.2	180.1
O/w:			
• Capital gains (losses) on disposal of financial assets	59.9	179.5	170.6
• Other	0.1	7.7	9.5
Operating income	1,017.2	1,982.1	1,788.9

[1] In 2009, as part of ongoing efficiency measures, the Group reclassified certain expenses from cost of sales to selling costs and general and administrative expenses. These reclassifications had no impact on operating income. The impact of these reclassifications on Cost of sales, Selling costs and General and administrative expenses is €181.1 million, − €6.9 million and − €174.2 million, respectively, in 2009.

Breakdown of Capital Gains and Losses on Disposal

(€ Million)	Year Ended December 31, 2011	Year Ended December 31, 2010	Year Ended December 31, 2009
Capital gains and losses on disposals of property, plant and equipment	25.4	27.3	20.4
Capital gains and losses on disposals of financial assets	59.9	179.5	170.6
Capital gains and losses on disposals recognized in operating income	85.3	206.8	191.0
Capital gains and losses on disposals recognized in financial income (loss)	(2.3)	(2.7)	(1.1)
Capital gains and losses on disposals of PP&E and financial assets	8.5	15.7	23.8
Capital gains and losses on disposals of discontinued operations	500.9	57.4	92.4
Capital gains and losses on disposals recognized in net income (loss) from discontinued operations	509.4	73.1	116.2
Total capital gains and losses on disposals in the cash flows statement	592.4	277.2	306.1

The capital gains or losses on disposals of discontinued operations are described in Note 25.

*Breakdown of Impairment Losses on Goodwill and
Non-Current Assets*

The main impairment losses recognized as of December 31,
2011 break down as follows:

Operating Segment	Country	Indication of Loss in Value	Discount Rate	Assets Impaired	Amount (€ Million)
Energy Services	Italy	—Economic crisis —Non realization of the budget —New management reorganization, rationalization and restructuring plan	7.8%	Goodwill, intangible assets and PP&E	(242.8)
Environmental Services	Italy	—Uncertainty regarding the political environment, and in particular regional politics —Cessation of Group refinancing —Termination of Calabria contract —Decision to place the company in voluntary liquidation	7.8%	Goodwill, intangible assets and operating financial assets	(169.6)
Water	Italy	—Regulatory uncertainty —Request of the termination of the Calabria contract	8.5%[1]	Goodwill, intangible assets and concession intangible assets	(75.5)
Water	Portugal	—Economic and financial crisis		Intangible assets	(11.2)
Energy Services	Spain	—Regulatory change in the solar energy sector —Economic and financial crisis	8.4%	Goodwill and intangible assets	(20.4)
Sub-total	Southern Europe				(519.5)
Water	Morocco	Preliminary conclusions of the Audit Commission	9.1%	Goodwill, and intangible assets	(59.0)
Energy Services	United States	—Decrease in development potential	6.6%	Goodwill	(153.1)
Environmental Services	United States	—Economic context in the Gulf of Mexico	6.6%	PP&E	(26.3)
Environmental Services/ Energy Services	France	—Failure of client negotiations	6.6%	Concession intangible assets	(25.3)
Impairment losses					(783.2)

[1] The discount rate is the rate for the Southern Europe cash-generating unit comprising these two countries.

*Breakdown of Operating Depreciation, Amortization,
Provisions and Impairment Losses*

Operating depreciation, amortization, provisions and impairment losses included in operating income in 2011 break down
as follows:

(€ Million)	Charge	Reversal	Year Ended December 31, 2011	Year Ended December 31, 2010	Year Ended December 31, 2009
Operating depreciation, amortization and provisions, net	(2,723.4)	1,022.5	(1,700.9)	(1,553.8)	(1,629.8)
Depreciation and amortization	(1,552.4)	2.9	(1,549.5)	(1,475.2)	(1,516.3)
Property, plant and equipment	(1,054.9)	2.9	(1,052.0)	(1,021.5)	(1,085.7)
Intangible assets	(497.5)	—	(497.5)	(453.7)	(430.6)
Impairment losses	(559.6)	239.8	(319.8)	(80.5)	(152.1)
Property, plant and equipment	(112.7)	9.4	(103.3)	(19.5)	(5.6)
Intangible assets and operating financial assets	(221.0)	7.7	(213.3)	(25.5)	(74.9)
Inventories	(28.4)	41.7	13.3	(6.1)	1.1
Trade receivables	(184.7)	165.8	(18.9)	(34.4)	(58.8)
Other operating and non-operating receivables	(12.8)	15.2	2.4	5.0	(13.9)
Non-current and current operating provisions	(611.4)	779.8	168.4	1.9	38.6
Non-current operating provisions	(348.0)	337.0	(11.0)	(107.0)	(14.6)
Current operating provisions	(263.4)	442.8	179.4	108.9	53.2
Impairment losses and impact of disposals on goodwill and negative goodwill recognized in the consolidated income statement			(502.8)	0.2	(0.9)
Operating depreciation, amortization, provisions and impairment losses			(2,203.7)	(1,553.6)	(1,630.7)

IFRS-BPPD 6.27

Operating depreciation, amortization, charges to provisions and impairment losses in the Consolidated Cash Flow Statement include operating depreciation, amortization, provisions and impairment losses transferred to Net income from discontinued operations in the amount of €648.1 million in 2011, €367.6 million in 2010 and €284.7 million in 2009. Impairment losses on inventories and receivables are recorded in changes in working capital in the Consolidated Cash Flow Statement.

21 Net Finance Costs (in part)

The income and expense balances making up net finance costs are as follows:

(€ Million)	Year Ended December 31, 2011	Year Ended December 31, 2010	Year Ended December 31, 2009
Finance income	113.1	92.7	92.1
Finance costs	(861.5)	(851.6)	(817.5)
Net finance costs	(748.4)	(758.9)	(725.4)

Finance costs and finance income represent the cost of borrowings net of cash and cash equivalents. In addition, net finance costs include net gains and losses on derivatives allocated to borrowings, irrespective of whether they qualify for hedge accounting.

Net finance costs total €748.4 million in 2011, compared to €758.9 million in 2010. This increase is due to the rise in the financing rate (defined as net finance costs excluding fair value adjustments to instruments not qualifying for hedge accounting, divided by average monthly net financial debt during the period, including the net finance costs of discontinued operations) from 5.09% in 2010 to 5.39% in 2011, which was mainly the result of:

- the increase in average low-yield cash investments;
- the increase in short-term rates on the floating portion of the debt;
- the cost of buying back the 2013 USD bond line.

25 Assets Classified as Held for Sale, Discontinued Operations and Divestitures

Discontinued Operations

In the Consolidated Income Statements presented for comparative purposes, the net income (loss) of operations sold or in the course of being sold was reclassified to "Net income (loss) from discontinued operations". This concerns the following operations:

- the whole Transportation business, in the process of divestiture (see Note 4, Veolia Transdev combination);
- Water activities in the Netherlands, divested in December 2010 and Environmental Services activities in Norway, divested in March 2011;
- German operations in the Energy Services division, divested in May and August 2011;
- household assistance services (Proxiserve) held jointly by the Water and Energy Services divisions, divested in December 2011 for an enterprise value of €118 million;
- urban lighting activities (Citelum) in the Energy Services division, in the course of being sold.

Furthermore, as the divestiture process for Water activities in Gabon and Pinellas incineration activities in the United States in the Environmental Services division was interrupted during the first and second semesters of 2011 respectively, these activities are reclassified in continuing operations.

Movements in net income (loss) from discontinued operations are as follows:

(€ Million)	Year Ended December 31, 2011	Year Ended December 31, 2010	Year Ended December 31, 2009
Income (loss) from discontinued operations	(503.3)	63.8	3.6
Capital gains and losses on disposals	500.9	(32.2)	92.4
Income tax expense	—	(2.3)	(70.4)
Net income (loss) from discontinued operations	(2.4)	29.3	25.6

Net income (loss) from discontinued operations in 2011 breaks down by division as follows:

(€ Million)	Water	Energy Services	Environmental Services	Transportation	Total
Income (loss) from discontinued operations	0.9	(5.2)	(0.3)	(498.7)[1]	(503.3)
Capital gains and losses on disposals	1.8	(6.1)	62.2	443.0	500.9
Income tax expense	—	—	—	—	—
Net income (loss) from discontinued operations	2.7	(11.3)	61.9	(55.7)	(2.4)

[1] Include impairment losses of €440 million on goodwill of the Transportation business (see Notes 4 and 5).

The main Consolidated Income Statement items for discontinued operations for the year ended December 31, 2011 break down by division as follows:

(€ Million)	Water	Energy Services	Environmental Services	Transportation	Total
Revenue	131.9	448.7	—	4,259.0	4,839.6
Operating income	4.8	6.5	—	(449.0)[(1)]	(437.7)
Financial items	(0.9)	(5.7)	(0.3)	(40.4)	(47.3)
Income tax expense	(3.2)	(6.3)	—	(9.8)	(19.3)
Share of net income of associates	0.2	0.3	—	0.5	1.0
Net income (loss) from discontinued operations	0.9	(5.2)	(0.3)	(498.7)	(503.3)

[(1)] Include impairment losses of €440 million on goodwill of the Transportation business (see Notes 4 and 5).

Furthermore, the decision to interrupt the divestiture process for Water activities in Gabon and Pinellas incineration activities in the United States in the Environmental Services division led to the inclusion of the results of these activities in "Net income from continuing operations" in 2011. The main items included in net income (loss) from discontinued operations in 2010 and 2009 were as follows:

(€ Million)	Year Ended December 31, 2010	Year Ended December 31, 2009
Revenue	260.4	218.6
Operating income	29.4	9.4
Financial items	(4.0)	(4.5)
Income tax expense	(10.1)	(2.6)
Share of net income of associates	—	—
Net income of water activities in Gabon	15.3	2.3

(€ Million)	Year Ended December 31, 2010	Year Ended December 31, 2009
Revenue	25.0	35.4
Operating income	(2.0)	(8.8)
Financial items	(0.1)	(0.1)
Income tax expense	—	—
Share of net income of associates	—	—
Net loss of pinellas incineration activities	(2.1)	(8.9)

Net income (loss) from discontinued operations in 2010 breaks down by division as follows:

(€ Million)	Water	Energy Services	Environmental Services	Transportation	Total
Income (loss) from discontinued operations	0.6	10.0	11.5	41.7	63.8
Capital gains and losses on disposals	(3.2)	(56.2)	56.5	(29.3)	(32.2)
Income tax expense	5.0	—	(7.3)	—	(2.3)
Net income (loss) from discontinued operations	2.4	(46.2)	60.7	12.4	29.3

The main Consolidated Income Statement items for discontinued operations for the year ended December 31, 2010 break down by division as follows:

(€ Million)	Water	Energy Services	Environmental Services	Transportation	Total
Revenue	157.1	462.5	408.5	5,822.4	6,850.5
Operating income	12.7	18.3	23.5	106.5	161.0
Financial items	(10.6)	(2.7)	(3.7)	(44.5)	(61.5)
Income tax expense	(1.6)	(5.7)	(8.3)	(20.6)	(36.2)
Share of net income of associates	0.1	0.1	—	0.3	0.5
Net income (loss) from discontinued operations	0.6	10.0	11.5	41.7	63.8

IFRS-BPPD 6.27

Net income (expense) from discontinued operations in 2009 breaks down by division as follows:

(€ Million)	Water	Energy Services	Environmental Services	Transportation	Total
Income (loss) from discontinued operations	3.0	11.5	8.5	(19.4)	3.6
Capital gains and losses on disposals			134.6	(42.2)	92.4
Income tax expense	—	—	(70.4)	—	(70.4)
Net income (loss) from discontinued operations	3.0	11.5	72.7	(61.6)	25.6

The main Consolidated Income Statement items for discontinued operations for the year ended December 31, 2009 break down by division as follows:

(€ Million)	Water	Energy Services	Environmental Services	Transportation	Total
Revenue	154.1	414.5	432.8	6,108.4	7,109.8
Operating income	14.4	21.6	13.2	108.6	157.8
Financial items	(9.8)	(4.6)	(4.0)	(75.1)	(93.5)
Income tax expense	(1.8)	(5.7)	(0.8)	(42.7)	(51.0)
Share of net income of associates	0.2	0.2	0.1	(10.2)	(9.7)
Net income (loss) from discontinued operations	3.0	11.5	8.5	(19.4)	3.6

Assets/Liabilities Classified as Held for Sale (in part)

Assets classified as held for sale and Liabilities directly associated with assets classified as held for sale are presented separately in the Group Consolidated Statement of Financial Position as follows:

(€ Million)	As of December 31, 2011	As of December 31, 2010	As of December 31, 2009
Assets classified as held for sale	3,256.5	805.6	722.6
Liabilities directly associated with assets classified as held for sale	2,012.8	386.8	309.4

Assets classified as held for sale and Liabilities directly associated with assets classified as held for sale as of December 31, 2011 primarily concern the assets and liabilities of the Veolia Transdev group (see Note 4), those of Citelum in the Energy Services division and those of Marine Services in the Environmental Services division, pursuant to the restructuring of the Group's activities announced on December 6, 2011.

Assets classified as held for sale and Liabilities directly associated with assets classified as held for sale as of December 31, 2010 primarily concerned Water division activi-ties in Gabon and Environmental Services division activities in Norway, sold in 2011.

Assets classified as held for sale and Liabilities directly associated with assets classified as held for sale as of December 31, 2009, primarily concerned certain French subsidiaries held jointly with Suez Environnement, Renewable Energy activities, Transportation activities in the United Kingdom and Dalkia Usti businesses (Czech Republic).

In 2011, the main asset and liability categories recorded in assets classified as held for sale, break down by division as follows:

(€ Million)	Energy Services	Environmental Services	Transportation	Total
Assets				
Non-current assets	90.5	89.2	1,836.6	2,016.3
Current assets	226.0	20.8	809.5	1,056.3
Cash and cash equivalents	32.1		151.8	183.9
Assets classified as held for sale	348.6	110.0	2,797.9	3,256.5
Liabilities				
Non-current liabilities	14.8	—	633.5	648.3
Current liabilities	169.5	52.7	1,142.3	1,364.5
Liabilities directly associated with assets classified as held for sale	184.3	52.7	1,775.8	2,012.8

SECTION 7: OPERATING SEGMENTS[1]

IFRS 8, *OPERATING SEGMENTS*

IFRSs Overview and Comparison to U.S. GAAP

Author's Note

In May 2011, the International Accounting Standards Board issued a revised International Accounting Standard (IAS) 19, *Employee Benefits*, which is effective for annual periods beginning on or after 1 January 2013. Early application is permitted. IAS 19 amended the disclosure requirements of IFRS 8 by replacing the phrase "post-employment benefit assets" with "net defined benefit assets" to describe assets excluded from the amounts of specific assets to be disclosed when regularly provided to the chief operating decision maker (CODM).

Because this standard is effective for annual periods beginning on or after 1 January 2012, these amendments are not reflected in the commentary in this section. However, these amendments would not affect the content or availability of illustrative excerpts from survey companies' financial statements.

7.01 International Financial Reporting Standard (IFRS) 8, *Operating Segments*, establishes requirements for disclosures about an entity's operating segments, its products and services, the geographic areas in which it operates, and its major customers. Although IFRS 8 is the result of a short-term convergence project to reduce the differences between IAS 14, *Segment Reporting*, and Financial Accounting Standards Board (FASB) *Accounting Standards Codification* (ASC) 280, *Segment Reporting*, several minor differences between IFRS 8 and FASB ASC remain.

7.02 IFRS 8 applies to the financial statements, whether consolidated or separate, of a parent entity whose debt or equity is traded in a public market or who files, or is in the process of filing, with a regulatory organization for the purpose of issuing any class of instruments in a public market. A public market includes domestic or foreign exchanges and both local and regional over-the-counter markets. Entities not required to apply IFRS 8 can voluntarily provide information labeled as segment information, only if that information fully complies with IFRS 8.

7.03 An *operating segment* is a component of the entity with the following characteristics:
- It engages in business activities that may earn revenues and incur expenses. These revenues and expenses need not be generated externally but may be solely generated

through transactions with other components of the same entity.
- The entity's CODM regularly reviews its operating results when making resource allocation and performance assessment decisions (the CODM is a function within the entity, not necessarily an individual).
- Discrete financial information is available about the component's activities.

Note that the term *component of an entity* is not a defined term in IFRS 8. It is defined in IFRS 5, *Non-current Assets Held for Sale and Discontinued Operations*, and in the glossary of the *IFRS 2012* bound volume, the latter in which its definition reflects the meaning as used in IFRS 5.

Recognition and Measurement

Author's Note

IFRS 8 is a disclosure standard. Its requirements do not affect recognition and measurement of items in the financial statements themselves. However, the standard does contain criteria for identifying the components of the entity to be shown in the required disclosures and for measuring the financial information provided. These criteria are described in this section.

IFRSs

7.04 IFRS 8 requires disclosure of information about reportable segments. *Reportable segments* are operating segments or aggregations of operating segments that meet certain specified criteria. The standard takes the management approach to identifying reportable segments and for measuring the required financial information to be disclosed.

7.05 Entities should identify operating segments based on information in internal reports reviewed by the CODM when making resource allocation and performance assessment decisions. An operating segment is not required to have revenues from external customers. Therefore, an entity can consider different stages of a vertically integrated operation to be separate operating segments if they meet the definition. Start-up operations that have not yet earned revenues, but are incurring expenses, also can be an operating segment.

7.06 However, not every part of an entity is necessarily an operating segment or part of an operating segment. For example, corporate headquarters or certain functional departments, such as human resources or accounting, may not earn revenues or may earn revenues that are only incidental to the activities of the entity and would not meet the definition of an operating segment. IFRS 8 specifically excludes an entity's postemployment benefit plan from identification as a separate operating segment.

7.07 In matrix and similar forms of organization, managers are held responsible for two or more overlapping sets of components of an entity. For example, some managers are responsible for specific products or services, and other managers are responsible for specific geographic areas in which

---

[1] Unless otherwise indicated, references to International Accounting Standards Board (IASB) standards and interpretations throughout this 2012 edition of *IFRS Financial Statements—Best Practices in Presentation and Disclosure* refer to the version of those standards and interpretations included in the *IFRS 2012* bound volume, the official printed consolidated text of IASB standards and interpretations, including revisions, amendments, and supporting documents, issued as of 1 January 2012.

the products and services are offered. Therefore, the CODM reviews financial reports for both types of components and discrete information is available for both. In this situation, IFRS 8 permits the entity to determine the identifying characteristics of the operating segments in accordance with the objective of the standard rather than providing more prescriptive guidance.

7.08 A reportable segment is either an individual operating segment or an aggregation of operating segments that meets or exceeds the following quantitative thresholds:
- *Revenue threshold.* The reported revenue, whether generated from sales to external customers or intersegment transactions, meets or exceeds 10 percent of the combined revenue (internal and external) of all operating segments.
- *Profit and loss threshold.* The absolute amount of profit and loss meets or exceeds 10 percent of the greater of the absolute amount of combined reported profit of all segments that did not report a loss and the combined reported loss of all segments that did not report a profit.
- *Asset threshold.* The assets meet or exceed 10 percent of the combined assets of all operating segments.

7.09 Entities can aggregate operating segments in order to meet the criteria for a reportable segment if the segments have similar economic characteristics with respect to the nature of segment products or services; the nature of the production process; the type or class of customer; distribution methods; and, when applicable, the nature of the regulatory environment.

7.10 Two circumstances exist in which entities should identify additional reportable segments, even if the operating segments do not meet the preceding thresholds:
- Total external revenue from reportable segments should meet or exceed 75 percent of the entity's reported revenue. An entity should identify additional operating segments as reportable until this criterion is met.
- If management believes that users of the financial statements would find information about an operating segment useful, the entity can choose to identify that operating segment as reportable.

7.11 Despite these criteria for identifying reportable segments, IFRS 8 also recognizes that there may be a practical limit (more than 10) to the number of reportable segments, after which the information disclosed is likely to be too detailed to be useful.

7.12 With respect to measurement of the financial information disclosed, the entity should use the same measurement bases that are reported internally to the CODM. Therefore, the measurements in the required disclosures are not necessarily based on the accounting policies used in the preparation of the consolidated financial statements.

U.S. GAAP

7.13 FASB ASC 280 normally requires more entities to provide segment disclosures than IFRS 8. Under FASB ASC 280-10-15, segment disclosures are required for all public entities, with certain exceptions noted in FASB 280-10-15-3 (such as not-for-profit entities, regardless of whether the entity meets the definition of a *public entity*, as defined within the FASB ASC glossary). The FASB ASC glossary defines

public entities as business entities or not-for-profit entities that (*a*) have debt or equity securities or are a conduit bond obligor for conduit debt securities that are traded in a public market, (*b*) are required to file financial statements with a regulatory organization, or (*c*) provide financial statements for the purpose of issuing securities in a public market. The FASB ASC definition is similar to IFRSs, except that IFRSs do not apply to not-for-profit entities or specifically address conduit bond obligors for conduit debt securities. Conduit debt securities are issued by state or local governments on behalf of the obligor, not itself a governmental entity. The issuer itself has no obligation beyond resources provided by a lease or loan agreement with the obligor.

7.14 Like IFRSs, FASB ASC 280 uses the management approach to identify operating segments and measure the financial information disclosed based on information reported internally to the CODM to make resource allocation and performance assessment decisions. However, according to FASB ASC 280-10-50-9, entities that have a matrix organization should identify operating segments based on products and services when more than one type of component is reviewed by the CODM.

Disclosure

IFRSs

7.15 The core principle underlying IFRS 8 disclosure requirements is that an entity should disclose information to enable users of the financial statements to evaluate the nature and financial effects of its business activities and its economic environment. IFRS 8 requires the following types of disclosures:
- General descriptive information about reportable segments
- Information about segment profit or loss, segment assets, and segment liabilities
- Information about the measurement bases used
- Entity-wide disclosures about revenues from products and services, geographical areas, and major customers
- Reconciliations to reported financial statement amounts
- Restatements of prior period information

7.16 Required general descriptive information includes a description about the factors used to identify the entity's reportable segments. These factors include the basis of organization (for example, how segments are organized around products and services, geographical areas, regulatory environments, or a combination of these factors). The entity also should disclose whether operating segments are aggregated to arrive at reportable segments. Additionally, IFRS 8 requires an entity to describe the types of revenues generated by each reportable segment. Often this particular disclosure is included with other accounting policy disclosures.

7.17 IFRS 8 requires disclosure of a measure of segment profit or loss and, if regularly reported to the CODM, a measure of total segment assets and total segment liabilities. In addition, an entity should disclose the following additional measures when these amounts are included in the measure of profit or loss reported to the CODM or otherwise regularly reported to the CODM:
- Revenue, distinguished between external customers and intersegment transactions

- Interest revenue and expense (reported separately)
- Depreciation and amortization, and other similar non-cash items
- Material items of income and expense in accordance with IAS 1, *Presentation of Financial Statements*
- Entity's interest in the profit or loss of associates and joint ventures accounted for using the equity method
- Income tax expense or income

7.18 The entity should disclose the following amounts when they are included in the measure of segment assets or are otherwise regularly provided to the CODM:

- Amount of investments in associates and joint ventures accounted for by the equity method
- Additions to noncurrent assets, except financial instruments, deferred tax assets, postemployment benefit assets, rights under insurance contracts, and long-term customer relationships of financial institutions

7.19 IFRS 8 takes the management approach to measurement as well as segment identification. Because the entity need not use its accounting policies as the measurement basis for the quantitative disclosures, IFRS 8 requires a description of the measurement basis used and discussion of various policies that affect those measurements (for example, transfer pricing policies and differences between segment amounts and amounts reported in the financial statement). This discussion includes the accounting policies and any policies that the entity used to allocate centrally incurred costs that are necessary for an understanding of the reported segment information, as well as any asymmetrical allocations.

7.20 An entity should measure the entity-wide disclosures about revenues based on the accounting policies used in the consolidated financial statements, rather than the bases used for internal measurements. Revenue disclosures include revenue from external customers by product or service (or group of products and services) by geographic area, and by major customer. Entities also should disclose noncurrent assets except financial instruments, deferred tax assets, postemployment benefit assets, and rights under insurance contracts by geographic area.

7.21 An entity should disclose information about the extent to which it relies on its major customers. When revenues from a single major customer equal or exceed 10 percent of the entity's revenues, IFRS 8 requires the entity to disclose that fact, although not the customer's identity, and the total amount of such revenues, and the relevant segment or segments. The standard cautions that an entity use judgment to assess whether it should consider a government, including governmental agencies (whether local, national, or international) and entities known to be under that government's control, to be a single customer for the purposes of this disclosure. One consideration would be the extent of economic integration among the government and these entities.

7.22 IFRS 8 requires a reconciliation of the total amounts of segment revenues, reported segment profit or loss, segment assets, segment liabilities, and other material segment items to the corresponding reported financial statements amounts. These reconciliations are required for each statement of financial position presented.

7.23 IFRS 8 requires an entity to discuss changes in the composition of reportable segments and changes in measurement bases used. An entity should restate comparative information when there is a change in the composition of segments or measurement basis, unless the information is not available or is excessively costly to develop. If the comparative information is not restated, the entity should present the current period's information on both the old and new basis, unless the information is not available or is excessively costly to develop.

U.S. GAAP

7.24 FASB ASC 280 and IFRS 8 requirements are largely converged. FASB ASC 280-10-50-22 requires disclosure of a measure of segment profit or loss and segment assets, but does not explicitly require disclosure of segment liabilities.

7.25 IFRS 8 requires disclosure of additional material items whereas FASB ASC 280-10-50-22(f) requires disclosure of unusual items of income and expense. This difference in choice of words is likely to lead to a difference in the items disclosed. FASB ASC 280-10-55-22(i) also requires disclosure of extraordinary items, which are prohibited in IFRSs.

7.26 IFRS 8 and FASB ASC 280 both require disclosure of additions to noncurrent assets with certain exclusions. In addition to the assets excluded from this requirement by IFRS 8, FASB ASC 280-10-50-25(b) also excludes mortgage and other servicing rights and certain other noncurrent assets (for example, financial instruments and deferred policy acquisition costs).

Presentation and Disclosure Excerpts

Operating Segments Based Primarily on Business Activities

7.27

Sociedad Quimica y Minera de Chile S.A. (Dec 2010)

NOTES TO THE CONSOLIDATED FINANCIAL STATEMENTS (in part)

Note 1—Corporate Information for Sociedad Química y Minera de Chile S.A. and Subsidiaries

Historical Background

Sociedad Química y Minera de Chile S.A. and subsidiaries (collectively the "Company") is a public corporation organized in accordance with the laws of the Republic of Chile, ID N° 93.007.000-9. The Company was constituted by public deed issued on June 17, 1968 by the Notary Public of Santiago Mr. Sergio Rodríguez Garcés. Its existence was approved by Decree No. 1,164 of the Ministry of Finance on June 22, 1968, and it was registered on June 29, 1968 in the Business Registry of Santiago, on page 4,537 N° 1,992. The parent company is located at El Trovador 4285, 6th Floor, Las Condes, Santiago, Chile. Its phone No. is (56-2) 425-2000.

The Company is registered with the Securities Registry of the Chilean Superintendence of Securities and Insurance (SVS) under No. 0184 dated March 18, 1983 and is subject to inspection by the SVS.

The Company's operating segments are divided into six main categories, as follows:

Specialty plant nutrients: In this business line, the Company provides advice in practices for fertilization according to each type of crop, soil and climate. In this business category, potassium derivative products and especially potassium nitrate have played a leading role, given the contribution they make to developing crops, ensuring an improvement in post-crop life in addition to improving quality, flavor and fruit color. Potassium nitrate, which is sold in multiple formats and as a part of other specialty mixtures, is complemented by sodium nitrate, potassium sodium nitrate, and other mixtures.

Iodine: The Company is an important producer of iodine worldwide. Iodine is a product that is widely used in the pharmaceutical industry, in technology and in nutrition. Additionally, Iodine is also used in x-ray contrast media and polarizing film for LCD displays.

Lithium: The Company's Lithium is mainly used in rechargeable batteries for cell phones, cameras and laptops. Through the preparation of lithium-based products, the Company provides significant raw materials to face great challenges such as the efficient use of energy and raw material. Lithium is not only used for rechargeable batteries and in new technologies for electric vehicles, but is also used in industrial applications to lower melting temperatures and to help save costs and energy.

Industrial Chemicals: Industrial chemicals are products used as supplies for a number of production processes. The Company participates in this line of business, producing sodium nitrate, potassium nitrate, boric acid and potassium chloride. Industrial nitrates are also used as a means for the storage of thermal energy at solar energy plants, which are widely used in countries such as Spain and the United States in their search for decreasing CO_2 emissions.

Potassium: Potassium is a primary essential macro-nutrient, and even though it does not form part of a plant's structure, it has a significant role in the development of its basic functions, validating the quality of a crop, increasing post-crop life, improving the crop flavor, its vitamin content and its physical appearance. Within this business line, the Company also produces potassium chlorate and potassium sulfate, both extracted from the salt layer located under the Atacama Salar (the Atacama Saltpeter Deposit).

Other products and services: This segment includes those revenues derived from commodities, rendering of services, interests, royalties and dividends.

Note 2—Basis of Presentation for Consolidated Financial Statements and Summary of Significant Accounting Policies (in part)

2.4 Basis of Consolidation (in part)

2.6 Financial Information by Operating Segment

IFRS 8 requires that companies adopt a "management approach" to disclose information on the operations generated by its operating segments. In general, this is the information that management uses internally for the evaluation of segment performance and making the decision on how to allocate resources for this purpose.

An operating segment is a group of assets and operations responsible for providing products or services subject to risks and performance different from those of other business segments. A geographical segment is responsible for providing products or services in a given economic environment subject to risks and performance different from those of other segments that operate in other economic environments.

The following operating segments have been identified by the Company:
- Specialty plant nutrients
- Industrial chemicals
- Iodine and derivatives
- Lithium and derivatives
- Potassium
- Other products and services

The Company has not been able to allocate all assets and liabilities to each operating segment because the same productive plants and process are often related to more than one operating segment. Such assets and liabilities are classified as non-allocated in Note 26.

Note 26—Operating Segments

26.1 Operating Segments (in part)

The balance of each item presented in each operating segment is equal to that reported to the maximum authority who makes decisions regarding the operation, in order to decide on the allocation of resources to the defined segments and to assess its performance. The reported information in each segment is obtained from the consolidated financial statements of the company and, therefore, no consolidation is required between the abovementioned data and that reported in the corresponding operating segments, according to what is set forth in paragraph 28 of IFRS N° 8, "Operating Segments."

Operating segments relate to the following groups of products that generate revenue and for which the Company incurs expenses and the result of which is regularly reviewed by the Company's maximum authority in the decision-making process:

1. Specialty plant nutrients
2. Iodine and its derivatives
3. Lithium and its derivatives
4. Industrial chemicals
5. Potassium
6. Other products and services

Information relative to assets, liabilities and profit and expenses that cannot be assigned to the segments indicated above, due to the nature of production processes, is included under the "Corporate Unit" category of disclosures.

The indicator used by management to performance measurement and resource allocation to each segment, is related to the margin of each segment.

Sales between segments are made in the same conditions as those made to third parties, and are consistently measured as presented in the income statement.

26.2 Statement of Income Classified by Operating Segments
Based on Groups of Products as of December 31, 2011:

Items in the Statement of Income	Specialty Plant Nutrients ThUS$	Iodine and Its Derivatives ThUS$	Lithium and Its Derivatives ThUS$	Industrial Chemicals ThUS$	Potassium ThUS$	Other Products and Services ThUS$	Corporate Unit ThUS$	Total Segments and Corporate Unit ThUS$
Sales	721,696	454,468	183,403	139,508	555,742	90,469	—	2,145,286
Cost of sales	(494,220)	(192,107)	(98,173)	(83,503)	(337,478)	(85,013)	—	(1,290,494)
Gross profit	227,476	262,361	85,230	56,005	218,264	5,456	—	854,792
Other income by function	—	—	—	—	—	—	47,681	47,681
Administrative expenses	—	—	—	—	—	—	(91,760)	(91,760)
Other expenses by function	—	—	—	—	—	—	(63,047)	(63,047)
Other gains	—	—	—	—	—	—	5,787	5,787
Interest income	—	—	—	—	—	—	23,210	23,210
Interest expenses	—	—	—	—	—	—	(39,335)	(39,335)
Interest in gains from associates and joint ventures accounted for using the equity method	—	—	—	—	—	—	21,808	21,808
Foreign currency transactions	—	—	—	—	—	—	(25,307)	(25,307)
Profit (loss) before taxes	227,476	262,361	85,230	56,005	218,264	5,456	(120,963)	733,829
Income tax expense	—	—	—	—	—	—	(179,710)	(179,710)
Net income (loss) from continuing operations	227,476	262,361	85,230	56,005	218,264	5,456	(300,673)	554,119
Net income (loss) from discontinued operations	—	—	—	—	—	—	—	—
Net income (loss)	227,476	262,361	85,230	56,005	218,264	5,456	(300,673)	554,119
Net income attributable to:								
Owners of the parent	—	—	—	—	—	—	—	545,758
Non-controlling interests	—	—	—	—	—	—	—	8,361
Net income for the year	—	—	—	—	—	—	—	554,119

26.3 Revenues From Ordinary Activities From Transactions
With Other Operating Segments of the Company at
December 31, 2011 are Detailed as Follows:

Specialty Plant Nutrients ThUS$	Iodine and Its Derivatives ThUS$	Lithium and Its Derivatives ThUS$	Industrial Chemicals ThUS$	Potassium ThUS$	Other Products and Services ThUS$	Corporate Unit ThUS$	Total Segments and Corporate Unit ThUS$
268,628	620,516	136,894	265,298	568,393	365,225	—	2,224,954

26.3 Revenues From Ordinary Activities From Transactions
With Other Operating Segments of the Company at
December 31, 2010 are Detailed as Follows:

Specialty Plant Nutrients ThUS$	Iodine and Its Derivatives ThUS$	Lithium and Its Derivatives ThUS$	Industrial Chemicals ThUS$	Potassium ThUS$	Other Products and Services ThUS$	Corporate Unit ThUS$	Total Segments and Corporate Unit ThUS$
233,064	416,758	91,675	227,567	468,169	225,402	—	1,662,635

26.3 Revenues From Ordinary Activities From Transactions With Other Operating Segments of the Company at December 31, 2009 are Detailed as Follows:

Specialty Plant Nutrients ThUS$	Iodine and Its Derivatives ThUS$	Lithium and Its Derivatives ThUS$	Industrial Chemicals ThUS$	Potassium ThUS$	Other Products and Services ThUS$	Corporate Unit ThUS$	Total Segments and Corporate Unit ThUS$
125,924	336,743	62,677	144,184	365,940	275,429	—	1,310,897

26.4 Disbursements of Non-Monetary Assets of the Segment as of December 31, 2011:

Identification of Disbursements of Non-Monetary Assets	Chile ThUS$	Latin America and the Caribbean ThUS$	Europe ThUS$	North America ThUS$	Asia and Others ThUS$	Balances According to the Statement of Financial Position ThUS$
Investments in joint ventures	—	—	—	—	4,909	4,909
Coromandel SQM India	—	—	—	—	409	409
SQM Migao Sichuan	4,500	4,500				
Amounts in addition of non-current assets	500,118	—	—	—	—	501,118
—Property, plant and equipment	500,895	—	—	—	—	500,895
—Intangible assets	223	—	—	—	—	223
Total segments	501,118	—	—	—	4,909	506,027

26.5 Information on Products and Services of External Customers

Revenues from operating activities with external customers by group of product and service as of December 31, 2011 are detailed as follows:

Items in the Statement of Income	Specialty Plant Nutrients ThUS$	Iodine and Its Derivatives ThUS$	Lithium and Its Derivatives ThUS$	Industrial Chemicals ThUS$	Potassium ThUS$	Other Products and Services ThUS$	Total Segments and Corporate Unit ThUS$
Revenue	721,696	454,468	183,403	139,508	555,742	90,469	2,145,286

Revenues from operating activities from external customers by group of product and service as of December 31, 2010 are detailed as follows:

Items in the Statement of Income	Specialty Plant Nutrients ThUS$	Iodine and Its Derivatives ThUS$	Lithium and Its Derivatives ThUS$	Industrial Chemicals ThUS$	Potassium ThUS$	Other Products and Services ThUS$	Total Segments and Corporate Unit ThUS$
Revenue	603,678	316,253	150,810	149,706	528,151	81,815	1,830,413

Revenues from operating activities from external customers by group of product and service as of December 31, 2009 are detailed as follows:

Items in the Statement of Income	Specialty Plant Nutrients ThUS$	Iodine and Its Derivatives ThUS$	Lithium and Its Derivatives ThUS$	Industrial Chemicals ThUS$	Potassium ThUS$	Other Products and Services ThUS$	Total Segments and Corporate Unit ThUS$
Revenue	526,953	190,915	117,844	115,385	399,109	88,453	1,438,659

26.6 Information on Geographical Areas

As indicated in paragraph 33 of IFRS 8, the entity discloses geographical information on its revenue from operating activities with external customers and from non-current assets that are not financial instruments, deferred income tax assets, assets related to post-employment benefits or rights derived from insurance contracts.

26.7 Revenues From Operating Activities From External Customers Classified by Geographical Areas as of December 31, 2011:

Identification of Revenue From External Customers	Chile ThUS$	Latin America and the Caribbean ThUS$	Europe ThUS$	North America ThUS$	Asia and Others ThUS$	Balances According to the Statement of Income ThUS$
Revenue	247,510	284,605	837,126	445,048	330,997	2,145,286

26.8 Non-Current Assets Classified by Geographical Area as of December 31, 2011:

Non-Current Asset Items	Chile ThUS$	Latin America and the Caribbean ThUS$	Europe ThUS$	North America ThUS$	Asia and Others ThUS$	Balances According to the Statement of Financial Position ThUS$
Investments in associates accounted for using the equity method	1,444	—	16,919	14,867	27,464	60,694
Intangible assets other than goodwill	3,877	—	—	439	—	4,316
Goodwill	27,146	86	11,373	—	—	38,605
Property, plant and equipment, net	1,752,991	1,433	389	29	200	1,755,042
Investment property	—	—	—	—	—	—
Other non-current assets	24,413	238	—	—	—	24,651
Total assets	1,809,871	1,757	28,681	15,335	27,664	1,883,308

26.9 Information on Main Customers

With respect to the degree of dependency of the Company on its customers, in accordance with paragraph N° 34 of IFRS N° 8, the Company has no external customers who individually represent 10% or more of its income from operating activities. Credit risk concentrations with respect to trade and other accounts receivable are limited due to the significant number of entities in the Company's portfolio and its worldwide distribution. The Company's policy requires guarantees (such as letters of credit, guarantee clauses and others) and/or to maintain insurance policies for certain accounts as deemed necessary by the Company's Management.

26.10 Property, Plant and Equipment Classified by Geographical Area as of December 31, 2011:

12.31.2011 Property, Plant and Equipment	Chile ThUS$	Latin America and the Caribbean ThUS$	Europe ThUS$	North America ThUS$	Asia and Others ThUS$	Total ThUS$
Production and Port Facilities:						
Coya Sur	279,416	—	—	—	—	279,416
María Elena	150,046	—	—	—	—	150,046
Nueva Victoria	242,758	—	—	—	—	242,758
Pampa Blanca	17,998	—	—	—	—	17,998
Pedro de Valdivia	104,662	—	—	—	—	104,662
Salar de Atacama	648,303	—	—	—	—	648,303
Salar del Carmen	210,955	—	—	—	—	210,955
Tocopilla (port premises)	74,629	—	—	—	—	74,629
Sub total Production and Port facilities	1,728,767	—	—	—	—	1,728,767
Corporate Facilities:						
Santiago	16,752	—	—	—	—	16,752
Antofagasta	5,907	—	—	—	—	5,907
Subtotal corporate facilities	22,659	—	—	—	—	22,659
Subtotal business offices	1,565	1,433	389	29	200	3,616
Total segments	1,752,991	1,433	389	29	200	1,755,042

Operating Segments Based Primarily on Geographic Areas; Allocation of Property, Plant and Equipment to Operating Segments

7.28

Canadian Natural Resources Limited (Dec 2011)

NOTES TO THE CONSOLIDATED FINANCIAL STATEMENTS (in part)

(Tabular amounts in millions of Canadian dollars, unless otherwise stated)

1. Accounting Policies (in part)

Canadian Natural Resources Limited (the "Company") is a senior independent crude oil and natural gas exploration, development and production company. The Company's exploration and production operations are focused in North America, largely in Western Canada; the United Kingdom ("UK") portion of the North Sea; and Côte d'Ivoire, Gabon, and South Africa in Offshore Africa.

The Horizon Oil Sands Mining and Upgrading segment ("Horizon") produces synthetic crude oil through bitumen mining and upgrading operations.

Within Western Canada, the Company maintains certain midstream activities that include pipeline operations and an electricity co-generation system.

The Company was incorporated in Alberta, Canada. The address of its registered office is 2500, 855-2 Street S.W., Calgary, Alberta.

In 2010, the Canadian Institute of Chartered Accountants ("CICA") Handbook was revised to incorporate International Financial Reporting Standards ("IFRS") and require publicly accountable enterprises to apply IFRS effective for years beginning on or after January 1, 2011. The 2011 fiscal year is the first year in which the Company has prepared its consolidated financial statements in accordance with IFRS as issued by the International Accounting Standards Board.

The accounting policies adopted by the Company under IFRS are set out below and are based on IFRS issued and outstanding as at December 31, 2011. Subject to certain transition elections disclosed in note 22, the Company has consistently applied the same accounting policies in its opening IFRS balance sheet at January 1, 2010 and throughout all periods presented, as if these policies had always been in effect.

Comparative information for 2010 has been restated from Canadian Generally Accepted Accounting Principles ("Canadian GAAP") to comply with IFRS. In these consolidated financial statements, Canadian GAAP refers to Canadian GAAP before the adoption of IFRS. Note 22 discloses the impact of the transition to IFRS on the Company's reported financial position, net earnings and cash flows, including the nature and effect of significant changes in accounting policies from those used in the Company's Canadian GAAP consolidated financial statements for the year ended December 31, 2010.

(E) Property, Plant and Equipment (in part)

Exploration and Production

Property, plant and equipment is measured at cost less accumulated depletion and depreciation and impairment provisions. When significant components of an item of property, plant and equipment, including crude oil and natural gas interests, have different useful lives, they are accounted for separately.

The cost of an asset comprises its acquisition, construction and development costs, costs directly attributable to bringing the asset into operation, the estimate of any asset retirement costs, and applicable borrowing costs. Property acquisition costs are comprised of the aggregate amount paid and the fair value of any other consideration given to acquire the asset. The capitalized value of a finance lease is also included in property, plant and equipment.

The cost of property, plant and equipment at January 1, 2010, the date of transition to IFRS, was determined as described in note 22.

Crude oil and natural gas properties are depleted using the unit-of-production method over proved reserves. The unit-of-production rate takes into account expenditures incurred to date, together with future development expenditures required to develop proved reserves.

Midstream and Head Office

The Company capitalizes all costs that expand the capacity or extend the useful life of the assets. Midstream assets are depreciated on a straight-line basis over their estimated useful lives ranging from 5 to 30 years. Head office assets are amortized on a declining balance basis.

Useful Lives

The expected useful lives of property, plant and equipment are reviewed on an annual basis, with changes in useful lives accounted for prospectively.

Derecognition

An item of property, plant and equipment is derecognized upon disposal or when no future economic benefits are expected to arise from the continued use of the asset. Any gain or loss arising on derecognition of the asset (calculated as the difference between the net disposal proceeds and the carrying amount of the item) is recognized in net earnings.

Major Maintenance Expenditures

Inspection costs associated with major maintenance turnarounds are capitalized and amortized over the period to the next major maintenance turnaround. All other maintenance costs are expensed as incurred.

Oil Sands Mining and Upgrading

Capitalized costs for the Oil Sands Mining and Upgrading segment are reported separately from the Company's North America Exploration and Production segment. Capitalized costs include property acquisition, construction and development costs, the estimate of any asset retirement costs, and applicable borrowing costs.

Mine-related costs and costs of the upgrader and related infrastructure located on the Horizon site are amortized on the unit-of-production method based on Horizon proved reserves or productive capacity, respectively. Other equipment is depreciated on a straight-line basis over its estimated useful life ranging from 2 to 15 years.

6. Property, Plant and Equipment

| | Exploration and Production | | | | | | |
	North America	North Sea	Offshore Africa	Oil Sands Mining and Upgrading	Midstream	Head Office	Total
Cost							
At December 31, 2011	$46,120	$4,147	$3,044	$15,211	$298	$234	$69,054
Accumulated depletion and depreciation							
At January 1, 2010	$16,427	$2,054	$1,008	$ 207	$ 81	$152	$19,929
Expense	2,473	295	298	396	8	13	3,483
Impairment[2]	—	—	637	—	—	—	637
Disposals/derecognitions	—	(5)	—	—	—	(11)	(16)
Foreign exchange adjustments and other	(5)	(139)	(39)	4	—	(5)	(184)
At December 31, 2010	18,895	2,205	1,904	607	89	149	23,849
Expense	2,826	248	242	266	7	15	3,604
Impairment[1]	—	—	—	396	—	—	396
Disposals/ derecognitions[1]	—	—	(29)	(503)	—	—	(532)
Foreign exchange adjustments and other	—	59	35	10	—	2	106
At December 31, 2011	$21,721	$2,512	$2,152	$ 776	$ 96	$166	$27,423
Net Book Value							
—at December 31, 2011	$24,399	$1,635	$ 892	$14,435	$202	$ 68	$41,631
—at December 31, 2010	$21,966	$1,608	$1,024	$13,562	$202	$ 67	$38,429
—at January 1, 2010	$19,732	$1,812	$1,658	$13,551	$203	$ 62	$37,018

[1] During 2011, the Company derecognized certain property, plant and equipment related to the coker fire at Horizon in the amount of $411 million based on estimated replacement cost, net of accumulated depletion and depreciation of $15 million. There was a resulting impairment charge of $396 million. For additional information, refer to note 10.

[2] During 2010, the Company recognized a $637 million impairment relating to the Gabon CGU, in Offshore Africa, which was included in depletion, depreciation and amortization expense. The impairment was based on the difference between the December 31, 2010 net book value of the assets and their recoverable amounts. The recoverable amounts were determined using fair value less costs to sell based on discounted future cash flows of proved and probable reserves using forecast prices and costs.

Development Projects Not Subject to Depletion

At December 31, 2011	$1,443
At December 31, 2010	$ 934
At January 1, 2010	$1,270

The Company acquired a number of producing crude oil and natural gas assets in the North American Exploration and Production segment for total cash consideration of $1,012 million during the year ended December 31, 2011 (2010—$1,482 million), net of associated asset retirement obligations of $ 79 million (2010—$22 million). Interests in jointly controlled assets were acquired with full tax basis. No working capital or debt obligations were assumed.

During the year ended December 31, 2011, the Company capitalized directly attributable administrative costs of $44 million (2010—$43 million) in the North Sea and Offshore Africa, related to development activities and $60 million (2010—$33 million) in North America, primarily related to Oil Sands Mining and Upgrading.

The Company capitalizes construction period interest for qualifying assets based on costs incurred and the Company's cost of borrowing. Interest capitalization to a qualifying asset ceases once construction is substantially complete. For the year ended December 31, 2011, pre-tax interest of $59 million was capitalized to property, plant and equipment (2010—$28 million) using a capitalization rate of 4.7% (2010—4.9%).

9. Other Long-Term Liabilities (in part)

Segmented Asset Retirement Obligations

	December 31, 2011	December 31, 2010	January 1, 2010
Exploration and Production			
North America	$1,862	$1,390	$ 905
North Sea	723	670	630
Offshore Africa	192	137	129
Oil Sands Mining and Upgrading	798	426	549
Midstream	2	1	1
	$3,577	$2,624	$2,214

10. Horizon Asset Impairment Provision and Insurance Recovery

Due to property damage resulting from a fire in the Horizon primary upgrading coking plant on January 6, 2011, the Company recognized an asset impairment provision in the Oil Sands Mining and Upgrading segment of $396 million, net of accumulated depletion and amortization. Insurance proceeds of $393 million were also recognized, offsetting the property damage. Production resumed in August 2011. As at December 31, 2011, the Company finalized its property damage insurance claim with certain of its insurers. The Company believes that the remaining portion of the property damage insurance claim will be settled without further adjustment.

The Company also maintains business interruption insurance to reduce operating losses related to its ongoing Horizon operations. The Company finalized its business interruption insurance claim for $333 million.

11. Income Taxes (in part)

The provision for income tax is as follows:

	2011	2010
Current corporate income tax—North America	$ 315	$ 431
Current corporate income tax—North Sea	245	203
Current corporate income tax—Offshore Africa	140	64
Current PRT[1] expense—North Sea	135	68
Other taxes	25	23
Current income tax expense	860	789
Deferred corporate income tax expense	412	408
Deferred PRT recovery—North Sea	(5)	(9)
Deferred income tax expense	407	399
Income tax expense	$1,267	$1,188

[1] Petroleum Revenue Tax.

Taxable income from the Exploration and Production business in Canada is primarily generated through partnerships, with the related income taxes payable in periods subsequent to the current reporting period. North America current and deferred income taxes have been provided on the basis of this corporate structure. In addition, current income taxes in each operating segment will vary depending upon available income tax deductions related to the nature, timing and amount of capital expenditures incurred in any particular year.

20. Segmented Information

The Company's exploration and production activities are conducted in three geographic segments: North America, North Sea and Offshore Africa. These activities include the exploration, development, production and marketing of crude oil, natural gas liquids and natural gas.

The Company's Oil Sands Mining and Upgrading activities are reported in a separate segment from exploration and production activities as the bitumen will be recovered through mining operations.

Midstream activities include the Company's pipeline operations and an electricity co-generation system. Production activities that are not included in the above segments are reported in the segmented information as other. Intersegment eliminations include internal transportation, electricity charges and natural gas sales.

Sales between segments are made at prices that approximate market prices, taking into account the volumes involved. Segment revenues and segment results include transactions between business segments. These transactions and any unrealized profits and losses are eliminated on consolidation, unless unrealized losses provide evidence of an impairment of the asset transferred. Sales to external customers are based on the location of the seller.

Operating segments are reported in a manner consistent with the internal reporting provided to senior management.

	Exploration and Production					
	North America		North Sea		Offshore Africa	
	2011	2010	2011	2010	2011	2010
Segmented product sales	$11,806	$ 9,713	$1,224	$1,058	$ 946	$ 884
Less: royalties	(1,538)	(1,267)	(3)	(2)	(114)	(62)
Segmented revenue	10,268	8,446	1,221	1,056	832	822
Segmented expenses						
Production	1,933	1,675	412	387	186	167
Transportation and blending	2,301	1,761	13	8	1	1
Depletion, depreciation and amortization	2,840	2,484	249	297	242	935
Asset retirement obligation accretion	70	52	33	36	7	7
Realized risk management activities	101	(110)	—	—	—	—
Horizon asset impairment provision	—	—	—	—	—	—
Insurance recovery—property damage (note 10)	—	—	—	—	—	—
Insurance recovery—business interruption (note 10)	—	—	—	—	—	—
Total segmented expenses	7,245	5,862	707	728	436	1,110
Segmented earnings (loss) before the following	$ 3,023	$ 2,584	$ 514	$ 328	$ 396	$ (288)
Non–segmented expenses						
Administration						
Share-based compensation						
Interest and other financing costs						
Unrealized risk management activities						
Foreign exchange loss (gain)						
Total non–segmented expenses						
Earnings before taxes						
Current income tax expense						
Deferred income tax expense						
Net earnings						

	Oil Sands Mining and Upgrading		Midstream		Inter-Segment Elimination and Other		Total	
	2011	2010	2011	2010	2011	2010	2011	2010
Segmented product sales	$1,521	$2,649	$88	$79	$(78)	$(61)	$15,507	$14,322
Less: royalties	(60)	(90)	—	—	—	—	(1,715)	(1,421)
Segmented revenue	1,461	2,559	88	79	(78)	(61)	13,792	12,901
Segmented expenses								
Production	1,127	1,208	26	22	(13)	(10)	3,671	3,449
Transportation and blending	62	61	—	—	(50)	(48)	2,327	1,783
Depletion, depreciation and amortization	266	396	7	8	—	—	3,604	4,120
Asset retirement obligation accretion	20	28	—	—	—	—	130	123
Realized risk management activities	—	—	—	—	—	—	101	(110)
Horizon asset impairment provision	396	—	—	—	—	—	396	—
Insurance recovery—property damage (note 10)	(393)	—	—	—	—	—	(393)	—
Insurance recovery—business interruption (note 10)	(333)	—	—	—	—	—	(333)	—
Total segmented expenses	1,145	1,693	33	30	(63)	(58)	9,503	9,365
Segmented earnings (loss) before the following	$ 316	$ 866	$55	$49	$(15)	$ (3)	4,289	3,536
Non–segmented expenses								
Administration							235	211
Share-based compensation							(102)	203
Interest and other financing costs							373	448
Unrealized risk management activities							(128)	(24)
Foreign exchange loss (gain)							1	(163)
Total non–segmented expenses							379	675
Earnings before taxes							3,910	2,861
Current income tax expense							860	789
Deferred income tax expense							407	399
Net earnings							$ 2,643	$ 1,673

	2011			2010		
Capital Expenditures[1]	Net Expenditures	Non Cash and Fair Value Changes[2]	Capitalized Costs	Net Expenditures	Non Cash and Fair Value Changes[2]	Capitalized Costs
Exploration and Evaluation Assets						
Exploration and Production						
North America	$ 309	$(233)	$ 76	$ 563	$ (299)	$ 264
North Sea	1	(6)	(5)	6	—	6
Offshore Africa	2	—	2	3	(154)	(151)
	$ 312	$(239)	$ 73	$ 572	$ (453)	$ 119
Property, Plant and Equipment						
Exploration and Production						
North America	$4,427	$ 832	$5,259	$3,806	$ 896	$4,702
North Sea	226	15	241	143	42	185
Offshore Africa	31	16	47	246	162	408
	4,684	863	5,547	4,195	1,100	5,295
Oil Sands Mining and Upgrading[3][4]	1,182	(140)	1,042	543	(132)	411
Midstream	5	2	7	7	—	7
Head office	18	—	18	18	(11)	7
	$5,889	$ 725	$6,614	$4,763	$ 957	$5,720

[1] This table provides a reconciliation of capitalized costs and does not include the impact of accumulated depletion and depreciation.

[2] Asset retirement obligations, deferred income tax adjustments related to differences between carrying amounts and tax values, transfers of exploration and evaluation assets, and other fair value adjustments.

[3] Net expenditures for Oil Sands Mining and Upgrading also include capitalized interest, share-based compensation, and the impact of intersegment eliminations.

[4] During 2011, the Company derecognized certain property, plant and equipment related to the coker fire at Horizon in the amount of $411 million. This amount has been included in non cash and fair value changes.

Segmented Assets	2011	2010
Exploration and Production		
North America	$28,554	$25,486
North Sea	1,809	1,759
Offshore Africa	1,070	1,263
Other	23	15
Oil Sands Mining and Upgrading	15,433	14,026
Midstream	321	338
Head office	68	67
	$47,278	$42,954

Change in Reported Segments From Change in Organizational Structure, Allocation of Goodwill to Operating Segments

7.29

Sun Life Financial, Inc. (Dec 2011)

NOTES TO THE CONSOLIDATED FINANCIAL STATEMENTS (in part)

(Amounts in millions of Canadian dollars except for per share amounts and where otherwise stated)

1. Accounting Policies (in part)

1. A Significant Accounting Policies (in part)

Description of Business

Sun Life Financial Inc. ("SLF Inc.") is a publicly traded company domiciled in Canada and is the holding company of Sun Life Assurance Company of Canada ("Sun Life Assurance"). Both companies are incorporated under the Insurance Companies Act of Canada, and are regulated by the Office of the Superintendent of Financial Institutions, Canada ("OSFI"). SLF Inc. and its subsidiaries are collectively referred to as "us", "our", "ours", "we" or "the Company." We are an internationally diversified financial services organization providing savings, retirement and pension products, and life and health insurance to individuals and groups through our operations in Canada, the United States, the United Kingdom and Asia. We also operate mutual fund and investment management businesses, primarily in Canada, the United States and Asia.

Statement of Compliance

We prepare our Consolidated Financial Statements using International Financial Reporting Standards as issued by the International Accounting Standards Board ("IASB") and the former International Accounting Standards Committee, which includes International Financial Reporting Standards, International Accounting Standards ("IAS"), and interpretations developed by the International Financial Reporting Interpretations Committee ("IFRIC") and the former Standing Interpretations Committee ("SIC"). These various standards are collectively referred to as "IFRS." Our Consolidated Financial Statements are prepared in accordance with IFRS 1 *First Time Adoption of International Financial Reporting Statements*. The accounting policies have been applied consistently within our Consolidated Financial Statements and our opening Consolidated Statement of Financial Position at the transition date of January 1, 2010 ("the Transition Date") prepared for the purposes of transition to IFRS, which are our first annual financial statements in accordance with IFRS. Note 2 contains the required disclosures with regards to our first time adoption of IFRS and the differences from our previous basis of accounting, Canadian generally accepted accounting principles ("GAAP").

Basis of Presentation

Our Consolidated Statements of Financial Position have been presented in the order of liquidity and each statement of financial position line item includes both current and non-current balances, as applicable.

We have defined our reportable segments and the amounts disclosed for those segments based on our management structure and the manner in which our internal financial reporting is conducted. Transactions between segments are executed and priced on an arm's-length basis in a manner similar to transactions with third parties.

The significant accounting policies used in the preparation of our Consolidated Financial Statements are summarized below and are applied consistently by us.

4. Segmented Information (in part)

We have five reportable segments: Sun Life Financial Canada ("SLF Canada"), Sun Life Financial United States ("SLF U.S."), MFS, Sun Life Financial Asia ("SLF Asia") and Corporate. These reportable segments operate in the financial services industry and reflect our management structure and internal financial reporting. Corporate includes the results of our U.K. business unit, our Corporate Support operations, which includes life retrocession and run-off reinsurance as well as investment income, expenses, capital and other items not allocated to our other business groups. In the fourth quarter of 2011, we transferred McLean Budden Limited to our subsidiary MFS. As a result, the results of McLean Budden Limited are reported as part of the MFS segment instead of the SLF Canada segment and the related goodwill and intangible assets previously reported in SLF Canada are now reported as part of Corporate. Prior period information has been restated to reflect this change in organization.

Revenues from our reportable segments are derived principally from life and health insurance, investment management and annuities, mutual funds, and life retrocession. Revenues not attributed to the strategic business units are derived primarily from Corporate investments and earnings on capital.

Transactions between segments are executed and priced on an arm's-length basis in a manner similar to transactions with third parties. These transactions consist primarily of internal financing agreements. They are measured at fair values prevailing when the arrangements are negotiated. Intersegment revenue consists of interest income and fee income and is presented in the consolidation adjustments column in the tables that follow.

Results by segment for the years ended December 31 are as follows:

	SLF Canada	SLF U.S.	MFS	SLF Asia	Corporate	Consolidation Adjustments	Total
2011							
Gross premiums:							
Annuities	$ 1,840	$1,234	$ —	$ —	$ 202	$ —	$ 3,276
Life insurance	3,249	2,111	—	674	116	—	6,150
Health insurance	3,376	1,504	—	9	10	—	4,899
Total gross premiums	8,465	4,849	—	683	328	—	14,325
Less: ceded premiums	4,551	384	—	49	27	—	5,011
Net Investment income (loss)	4,958	3,327	—	684	1,057	(112)	9,914
Fee income	746	757	1,640	119	171	(80)	3,353
Total revenue	$ 9,618	$8,549	$1,640	$1,437	$1,529	$(192)	$22,581
Total benefits and expenses	$ 9,172	$9,827	$1,305	$1,266	$1,834	$(192)	$23,212
Income tax expense (benefit)	$ (10)	$ (388)	$ 140	$ 33	$ (222)	$ —	$ (447)
Total net income (loss)	$ 456	$ (890)	$ 195	$ 138	$ (83)	$ —	$ (184)

Assets and liabilities by segment are as follows:

	SLF Canada	SLF U.S.	MFS	SLF Asia	Corporate	Consolidation Adjustments	Total
As at December 31, 2011							
Total general fund assets	$64,192	$44,490	$1,180	$8,122	$12,165	$(305)	$129,844
Investments for account of segregated fund holders	$47,245	$29,804	$ —	$1,198	$ 9,936	$ —	$ 88,183
Total general fund liabilities	$57,615	$38,196	$ 973	$6,336	$11,299	$(305)	$114,114
As at December 31, 2010							

The results of our reportable segments differ from geographic segments primarily due to segmenting the results of our Corporate segment.

The following table shows revenue, net income (loss), assets and liabilities by country for Corporate:

For the Years Ended December 31	2011	2010
Revenue:		
United States	$ 225	$ 518
United Kingdom	1,336	1,354
Canada	(55)	204
Other countries	23	18
Total revenue	$1,529	$2,094
Total net income (loss):		
United States	$ (72)	$ 65
United Kingdom	156	237
Canada	(173)	(142)
Other countries	6	14
Total net income (loss)	$ (83)	$ 174

IFRS-BPPD 7.29

As at	December 31, 2011	December 31, 2010	January 1, 2010
Total general fund assets:			
United States	$ 2,866	$ 3,107	$ 4,987
United Kingdom	8,635	8,047	8,690
Canada	553	1,480	2,638
Other countries	111	115	116
Total general fund assets	$12,165	$12,749	$16,431
Investment for account of segregated fund holders:			
United Kingdom	$ 9,936	$10,764	$11,240
Total investment for account of segregated fund holders	$ 9,936	$10,764	$11,240
Total general fund liabilities:			
United States	$ 2,216	$ (16)	$ 548
United Kingdom	7,620	7,062	7,820
Canada	1,374	3,114	4,136
Other countries	89	93	108
Total general fund liabilities	$11,299	$10,253	$12,612

Management considers its external customers to be the individual policyholders and as such we are not reliant on any individual customer.

10. Goodwill and Intangible Assets (in part)

10.A Goodwill (in part)

This note analyzes the changes to the carrying amount of goodwill during the year and details the result of our impairment testing on goodwill.

Changes in the carrying amount of goodwill acquired through business combinations by reportable segment are as follows:

	SLF Canada	SLF U.S.	SLF Asia	Corporate	Total
Balance, January 1, 2010[1]	$2,765	$450	$463	$ 912	$4,590
Disposition (Note 3)	—	—	—	(309)	(309)
Foreign exchange rate movements	—	(24)	(25)	(32)	(81)
Balance, December 31, 2010[1]	$2,765	$426	$438	$ 571	$4,200
Impairment[2]	(194)	(94)	—	—	(288)
Foreign exchange rate movements	—	10	10	10	30
Balance, December 31, 2011	$2,571	$342	$448	$ 581	$3,942

[1] January 1, 2010 and December 31, 2010 balances for SLF Canada and Corporate have been restated by $74 as a result of the transfer of McLean Budden from SLF Canada to MFS Holdings within Corporate. See Note 17 for details.

[2] The goodwill relating to the variable annuities CGU within SLF U.S. was impaired as a result of the restructuring that took place during the fourth quarter of 2011. See Note 21 for details on the impact of the restructuring. The goodwill relating to the Individual Wealth CGU within SLF Canada was impaired by $194.

Addition of Operating Segment after Business Acquisition

7.30

Philippine Long Distance Telephone Company (Dec 2011)

NOTES TO THE CONSOLIDATED FINANCIAL STATEMENTS (in part)

1. Corporate Information

The Philippine Long Distance Telephone Company, or PLDT, or Parent Company, was incorporated under the old Corporation Law of the Philippines (Act 1459, as amended) on November 28, 1928, following the merger of four telephone companies under common U.S. ownership. Under its amended Articles of Incorporation, PLDT's corporate term is currently limited through 2028. In 1967, effective control of PLDT was sold by the General Telephone and Electronics Corporation, then a major shareholder since PLDT's incorporation, to a group of Filipino businessmen. In 1981, in furtherance of the then existing policy of the Philippine government to integrate the Philippine telecommunications industry, PLDT purchased substantially all of the assets and liabilities of the Republic Telephone Company, which at that time was the second largest telephone company in the Philippines. In 1998, certain subsidiaries of First Pacific Company Limited, or First Pacific, and its Philippine affiliates (collectively the First Pacific Group and its Philippine affiliates), acquired a significant interest in PLDT. On March 24, 2000, NTT Communications Corporation, or NTT Communications, through its wholly-owned subsidiary NTT Communications Capital (UK) Ltd., or NTTC-UK, became PLDT's strategic partner with approximately 15% economic and voting interest in the issued and outstanding common stock of PLDT at that time. Simultaneous with NTT Communications' investment in PLDT, the latter acquired 100% of Smart Communications, Inc., or Smart. On March 14, 2006, NTT DOCOMO, Inc., or NTT DOCOMO, acquired from NTT Communications approximately 7% of PLDT's then outstanding common shares held by NTT Communications with NTT Communications retaining ownership of approximately 7% of PLDT's common shares. Since March 14, 2006, NTT DOCOMO has made additional purchases of shares of PLDT and together with NTT Communications beneficially owned approximately 21% of PLDT's outstanding common stock as at December 31, 2010. NTT Communications and NTT DOCOMO are subsidiaries of NTT Holding Company. On February 28, 2007, Metro Pacific Asset Holdings, Inc., a Philippine affiliate of First Pacific, completed the acquisition of an approximately 46% interest in Philippine Telecommunications Investment Corporation, or PTIC, a shareholder of PLDT. This investment in PTIC represents an attributable interest of approximately 6% of the then outstanding common shares of PLDT and thereby raised First Pacific Group's and its Philippine affiliates' beneficial ownership to approximately 28% of PLDT's outstanding common stock as at that date. Since then, First Pacific Group's beneficial ownership interest in PLDT decreased by approximately 2%, mainly due to the holders of Exchangeable Notes, which were issued in 2005 by a subsidiary of First Pacific and exchangeable into PLDT shares owned by First Pacific Group, who fully exchanged their notes. First Pacific Group and its Philippine affiliates had beneficial ownership of approximately 26% in PLDT's outstanding common stock as at December 31, 2010.

On October 26, 2011, PLDT completed the acquisition of a controlling interest in Digital Telecommunications Phils., Inc., or Digitel, from JG Summit Holdings, Inc., or JGS, and certain other seller-parties. As payment for the assets acquired from JGS, PLDT issued approximately 27.7 million common shares. In November 2011, JGS sold 5.81 million and 4.56 million PLDT shares to a Philippine affiliate of First Pacific and NTT DOCOMO, respectively, pursuant to separate option agreements that JGS had entered into with a Philippine affiliate of First Pacific and NTT DOCOMO, respectively. As at February 29, 2012, the JG Summit Group, First Pacific Group and its Philippine affiliates, and NTT Group (NTT DOCOMO, together with NTTC-UK) owned approximately 8%, 26% and 20% of PLDT's outstanding common shares, respectively. See *Note 13—Business Combinations—PLDT's Acquisition of Digitel.*

The common shares of PLDT are listed and traded on the Philippine Stock Exchange, Inc., or PSE. On October 19, 1994, an American Depositary Receipt, or ADR, facility was established, pursuant to which Citibank N.A., as the depositary, issued ADRs evidencing American Depositary Shares, or ADSs, with each ADS representing one PLDT common share with a par value of Php5 per share. Effective February 10, 2003, PLDT appointed JP Morgan Chase Bank as successor depositary for PLDT's ADR facility. The ADSs are listed on the New York Stock Exchange, or NYSE, in the United States and are traded on the NYSE under the symbol "PHI." There are approximately 55 million ADSs outstanding as at December 31, 2011.

PLDT and our Philippine-based fixed line and wireless subsidiaries operate under the jurisdiction of the Philippine National Telecommunications Commission, or NTC, which jurisdiction extends, among other things, to approving major services offered and certain rates charged to customers.

We are the leading telecommunications service provider in the Philippines. Through our three principal business segments, wireless, fixed line and business process outsourcing, or BPO, we offer the largest and most diversified range of telecommunications services across the Philippines' most extensive fiber optic backbone and wireless, fixed line and satellite networks. Our principal activities are discussed in *Note 4—Operating Segment Information.*

Our registered office address is Ramon Cojuangco Building, Makati Avenue, Makati City, Philippines.

Our consolidated financial statements as at December 31, 2011 and 2010 and for each of the three years in the period ended December 31, 2011 were approved and authorized for issuance by the Board of Directors on March 22, 2012, as reviewed and recommended for approval by the Audit Committee.

2. Summary of Significant Accounting Policies

Reorganization of SPi Global

On July 25, 2011, ePLDT sold its 100% equity interest in SPi Global to PLDT to serve as the new holding company for BPO business segment of the PLDT Group. Subsequently, on December 6, 2011, ePLDT also sold its 100% equity interest in SPi, SPi CRM and Infocom to SPi Global. The transaction was made at carrying values and has no impact in our consolidated financial statements. See discussion in *Note 4—Operating Segment Information.*

Change in the Presentation of our Outbound Revenues

In 2011, we changed the presentation of our outbound revenues to gross amounts before charges billed to us, where applicable, by other carriers. In doing so, interconnection costs are then presented as a separate line item in the expense section of our consolidated income statements. Prior to 2011, we presented outbound revenues net of the share of other carriers. We made this change to present outbound revenues on a gross basis to more correctly present and align our consolidated income statement presentation with the predominant global practice in the telecommunications industry.

We accounted for the change retroactively and accordingly restated our comparative consolidated income statements. The change is for presentation only, and has no impact on our consolidated net income, earnings per share, cash flows and statements of financial position. The table below shows the affected line items in our financial information for the years ended December 31, 2010 and 2009.

(In million pesos)	2010			2009		
	As Restated	As Previously Presented	Change	As Restated	As Previously Presented	Change
Revenues	158,387	144,459	13,928	162,023	147,993	14,030
Expenses	102,831	88,903	13,928	104,141	90,111	14,030
Adjusted EBITDA margin[(1)]	54%	59%	(5%)	54%	59%	(5%)

[(1)] See discussion in Note 4—Operating Segment Information.

3. Management's Use of Accounting Judgments, Estimates and Assumptions (in part)

The preparation of our consolidated financial statements in conformity with IFRS requires us to make judgments, estimates and assumptions that affect the reported amounts of our revenues, expenses, assets and liabilities and disclosure of contingent liabilities at the end of each reporting period. The uncertainties inherent in these assumptions and estimates could result in outcomes that could require a material adjustment to the carrying amount of the assets or liabilities affected in the future years.

Judgments

In the process of applying the PLDT Group's accounting policies, management has made the following judgments, apart from those including estimations and assumptions, which have the most significant effect on the amounts recognized in our consolidated financial statements.

Determination of Functional Currency

The functional currencies of the entities under the PLDT Group are the currency of the primary economic environment in which each entity operates. It is the currency that mainly influences the revenue from and cost of rendering products and services.

The presentation currency of the PLDT Group is the Philippine peso. Based on the economic substance of the underlying circumstances relevant to the PLDT Group, the functional currency of all entities under PLDT Group is the Philippine peso, except for, SMHC, SMI, TSI, FECL Group, PLDT Global and certain of its subsidiaries, PGNL, DCPL, SPi Global and certain of its subsidiaries, and certain subsidiaries of Chikka, which use the U.S. dollar. SHPL, SGP, 3rd Brand, and certain subsidiaries of AGS use the Singapore dollar as functional currency.

As a result of the internal reorganization within PLDT wherein BPO is now classified as an independent operating segment under SPi Global, management undertook a review of the functional currency exposures of SPi Global and certain of its subsidiaries. Based on management's assessment, SPi Global and SPi CRM's new currency exposures are now largely U.S. dollars. Based on the aforementioned consideration, which is set forth in *IAS 21,* SPi Global and SPi CRM commenced adopting U.S. dollars as its functional currency starting on December 6, 2011. See discussions in *Note 2—Summary of Significant Accounting Policies* and *Note 4—Operating Segment Information.*

Estimates and Assumptions (in part)

The key estimates and assumptions concerning the future and other key sources of estimation uncertainty at the end of the reporting period that have a significant risk of causing a material adjustment to the carrying amounts of assets and liabilities recognized in the consolidated financial statements within the next financial year are discussed below. We based our estimates and assumptions on parameters available when the consolidated financial statements were prepared. Existing circumstances and assumptions about future developments, however, may change due to market changes or circumstances arising beyond the control of PLDT. Such changes are reflected in the assumptions when they occur.

Asset Impairment (in part)

IFRS requires that an impairment review be performed when certain impairment indicators are present. In the case of goodwill, at a minimum, such asset is subject to an annual impairment test and more frequently whenever there is an indication that such asset may be impaired. This requires an estimation of the value in use of the CGUs to which the goodwill is allocated. Estimating the value in use requires us to make an estimate of the expected future cash flows from the CGU and to choose a suitable discount rate in order to calculate the present value of those cash flows.

Determining the recoverable amount of property, plant and equipment, investments in associates and joint ventures, intangible assets and other noncurrent assets, requires us to make estimates and assumptions in the determination of future cash flows expected to be generated from the continued use and ultimate disposition of such assets. Future events could cause us to conclude that property, plant and equipment, investments in associates and joint ventures, intangible assets and other noncurrent assets associated with an acquired business are impaired. Any resulting impairment loss could have a material adverse impact on our financial condition and financial performance.

The preparation of estimated future cash flows involves significant estimations and assumptions. While we believe that our assumptions are appropriate and reasonable, significant changes in our assumptions may materially affect our assessment of recoverable values and may lead to future additional impairment charges under IFRS.

Total asset impairment on noncurrent assets amounted to Php8,517 million, Php1,496 million and Php2,337 million for the years ended December 31, 2011, 2010 and 2009, respectively. See *Note 4—Operating Segment Information, Note 5—Income and Expenses* and *Note 9—Property, Plant and Equipment.*

Estimating Useful Lives of Property, Plant and Equipment

We estimate the useful lives of our property, plant and equipment based on the periods over which our assets are expected to be available for use. Our estimate of the useful lives of our property, plant and equipment is based on our collective assessment of industry practice, internal technical evaluation and experience with similar assets. The estimated useful lives of our property, plant and equipment are reviewed every year-end and are updated if expectations differ from previous estimates due to physical wear and tear, technical or commercial obsolescence and legal or other limitations on the use of our assets. It is possible, however, that future results of operations could be materially affected by changes in our estimates brought about by changes in the factors mentioned above. The amounts and timing of recorded expenses for any period would be affected by changes in these factors and circumstances. A reduction in the estimated useful lives of our property, plant and equipment would increase our recorded depreciation and amortization and decrease our property, plant and equipment.

The total depreciation and amortization of property, plant and equipment amounted to Php27,957 million, Php26,277 million and Php25,607 million for the years ended December 31, 2011, 2010 and 2009, respectively. Total carrying values of property, plant and equipment, net of accumulated depreciation and amortization, amounted to Php197,731 million and Php163,184 million as at December 31, 2011 and 2010, respectively. See *Note 4—Operating Segment Information* and *Note 9—Property, Plant and Equipment*.

Recognition of Deferred Income Tax Assets and Liabilities

We review the carrying amounts of deferred income tax assets at the end of each reporting period and reduce these to the extent that these are no longer probable that sufficient taxable income will be available to allow all or part of the deferred income tax assets to be utilized. Our assessment on the recognition of deferred income tax assets on deductible temporary differences is based on the level and timing of forecasted taxable income of the subsequent reporting periods. This forecast is based on our past results and future expectations on revenues and expenses as well as future tax planning strategies. However, there is no assurance that we will generate sufficient taxable income to allow all or part of our deferred income tax assets to be utilized. We also review the level of projected gross margin for the use of Optional Standard Deduction, or OSD method, and assess the future tax consequences for the recognition of deferred income tax assets and deferred income tax liabilities. Based on Smart's and Wolfpac's projected gross margin, they expect to continue using the OSD method in the foreseeable future.

Based on the above assessment, our consolidated unrecognized deferred income tax assets amounted to Php16,098 million and Php1,477 million as at December 31, 2011 and 2010, respectively. In addition, our unrecognized net deferred income tax assets for items which would not result in future tax benefits when using the OSD method amounted to Php4,240 million and Php2,803 million as at December 31, 2011 and 2010, respectively. Total consolidated benefit from deferred income tax amounted to Php1,261 for the year ended December 31, 2011 and total consolidated provision for deferred income tax amounted to Php1,198 million and Php656 million for the years ended December 31, 2010 and 2009, respectively. Total consolidated net deferred income tax assets amounted to Php5,975 million and Php6,110 million as at December 31, 2011 and 2010, respectively, while total consolidated net deferred income tax liabilities amounted to Php2,902 million and Php1,099 million as at December 31, 2011 and 2010, respectively. See *Note 4—Operating Segment Information* and *Note 7—Income Taxes*.

Estimating Allowance for Doubtful Accounts

If we assessed that there is an objective evidence that an impairment loss has been incurred in our trade and other receivables, we estimate the allowance for doubtful accounts related to our trade and other receivables that are specifically identified as doubtful of collection. The amount of allowance is evaluated by management on the basis of factors that affect the collectibility of the accounts. In these cases, we use judgment based on the best available facts and circumstances, including, but not limited to, the length of our relationship with the customer and the customer's credit status based on third party credit reports and known market factors, to record specific reserves for customers against amounts due in order to reduce our receivables to amounts that we expect to collect. These specific reserves are re-evaluated and adjusted as additional information received affect the amounts estimated.

In addition to specific allowance against individually significant receivables, we also assess a collective impairment allowance against credit exposures of our customer which were grouped based on common credit characteristic, which, although not specifically identified as requiring a specific allowance, have a greater risk of default than when the receivables were originally granted to customers. This collective allowance is based on historical loss experience using various factors, such as historical performance of the customers within the collective group, deterioration in the markets in which the customers operate, and identified structural weaknesses or deterioration in the cash flows of customers.

Total provision for doubtful accounts for trade and other receivables recognized in our consolidated income statements amounted to Php1,549 million, Php834 million and Php2,335 million for the years ended December 31, 2011, 2010 and 2009, respectively. Trade and other receivables, net of allowance for doubtful accounts, amounted to Php16,245 million and Php16,428 million as at December 31, 2011 and 2010, respectively. See *Note 4—Operating Segment Information, Note 5—Income and Expenses, Note 16—Trade and Other Receivables* and *Note 27—Financial Assets and Liabilities*.

Estimating Net Realizable Value of Inventories and Supplies

We write-down the cost of inventories whenever the net realizable value of inventories becomes lower than cost due to damage, physical deterioration, obsolescence, change in price levels or other causes. The lower of cost and net realizable value of inventories is reviewed on a periodic basis. Inventory items identified to be obsolete or unusable are written-off and charged as expense in our consolidated income statement.

Total write-down of inventories and supplies amounted to Php143 million, Php108 million and Php389 million for the years ended December 31, 2011, 2010 and 2009, respectively. The carrying values of inventories and supplies amounted to Php3,827 million and Php2,219 million as at December 31, 2011 and 2010, respectively. See *Note 4—Operating Segment Information, Note 5—Income and Expenses* and *Note 17—Inventories and Supplies*.

4. Operating Segment Information (in part)

Operating segments are components of the PLDT Group that engage in business activities from which they may earn revenues and incur expenses (including revenues and expenses relating to transactions with other components of PLDT Group), which operating results are regularly reviewed by the chief operating decision maker to make decisions about how resources are to be allocated to each of the segments and to assess their performances, and for which discrete financial information is available.

For management purposes, we are organized into business units based on our products and services and based on the reorganization as discussed below. We have four reportable operating segments, as follows:

- Wireless—wireless telecommunications services provided by Smart, CURE, and DMPI, which is the operator of the *Sun Cellular* business and is a wholly-owned subsidiary of Digitel (PLDT acquired a controlling interest in Digitel on October 26, 2011 and through a series of transactions holds approximately 99.5% of the outstanding common stock of Digitel as at March 22, 2012); our cellular service providers; SBI and PDSI, our wireless broadband service providers; Wolfpac and Chikka Group, our wireless content operators; and ACeS Philippines, our satellite operator;

- Fixed Line—fixed line telecommunications services primarily provided by PLDT. We also provide fixed line services through PLDT's subsidiaries, namely, ClarkTel, SubicTel, Philcom Group, Maratel, SBI, PDSI, BCC, PLDT Global and Digitel, all of which together account for approximately 17% of our consolidated fixed line subscribers; information and communications infrastructure and services for internet applications, internet protocol-based solutions and multimedia content delivery provided by ePLDT and AGS Group; netGames; and bills printing and other VAS-related services provided by ePDS (ePLDT increased its equity interest in ePDS from 50% to 67% on August 24, 2011). ePLDT disposed of its 75% interest in Digital Paradise, a provider of internet access services on April 1, 2011 and disposed of its 57.51% interest in Level Up!, a publisher of online games on July 11, 2011;

- BPO—knowledge processing solutions provided by the SPi Group; and customer relationship management provided by SPi CRM and Infocom (ePLDT transferred the internet business of Infocom to PLDT on July 1, 2011); and

- Others—PCEV, an investment holding company.

See *Note 2—Summary of Accounting Policies* and *Note 13— Business Combinations* for further discussion.

The primary effects of the acquisition of the Digitel Group on our operating segments is the addition of DMPI to our wireless business and the addition of Digitel to our fixed line business. We have agreed with the NTC that we will continue to operate *Sun Cellular* as a separate brand.

On July 7, 2010, our Board of Directors approved the reorganization of the ePLDT Group into two business groups: (i) the information and communications technology, or ICT business group, which provides data center services, internet and online gaming services and business solutions and applications, and which was subsequently incorporated into our fixed line business; and (ii) the BPO business group, which covers customer relationship management or call center operations

under SPi CRM; and content solutions, medical billing and coding and medical transcription services under SPi.

With our objective to grow the BPO business segment, and for ePLDT to focus on its core business of IT infrastructure and services, our Board of Directors approved on July 5, 2011 to spin off SPi and SPi CRM from ePLDT and transfer the ownership of SPi Global to PLDT, and to place both SPi and SPi CRM under SPi Global. The reorganization was completed on December 6, 2011.

PCEV transferred its cellular business to Smart in August 2009 and acquired 223 million common shares, or about 20% equity interest, in Manila Electric Company, or Meralco, in March 2010. PCEV subsequently transferred to Beacon Electric Asset Holdings, Inc., or Beacon, in which PCEV acquired 50% equity interest effective March 31, 2010, 154.2 million and 68.8 million Meralco common shares to Beacon on May 12, 2010 and October 25, 2011, respectively. As a result, PCEV became an investment/holding company and reclassified PCEV from Wireless to Others business segment.

As at December 31, 2011, our chief operating decision maker views our business activities in four business units: Wireless, Fixed Line, BPO and Others, compared to three business units in 2010: Wireless, Fixed Line and ICT. The remaining ICT businesses, which did not form part of our BPO, were reclassified into our fixed line segment. We have retroactively implemented the above changes in our segment reporting and restated our comparative operating segment information accordingly.

The chief operating decision maker and management monitor the operating results of each business unit separately for purposes of making decisions about resource allocation and performance assessment. Segment performance is evaluated based on net income (loss) for the year; earnings before interest, taxes and depreciation and amortization, or adjusted EBITDA; adjusted EBITDA margin; and core income. Net income (loss) for the year is measured consistent with net income (loss) in the consolidated financial statements.

Adjusted EBITDA is measured as net income excluding depreciation and amortization, amortization of intangible assets, asset impairment on noncurrent assets, financing costs, interest income, equity share in net earnings (losses) of associates and joint ventures, foreign exchange gains (losses)— net, gains (losses) on derivative financial instruments—net, provision for (benefit from) income tax and other income (expenses).

Adjusted EBITDA margin is measured as adjusted EBITDA divided by service revenues for the year.

Core income for the year is measured as net income attributable to equity holders of PLDT (net income less net income attributable to noncontrolling interests), excluding foreign exchange gains (losses)—net, gains (losses) on derivative financial instruments—net (excluding hedge costs), asset impairment on noncurrent assets, other nonrecurring gains (losses), net of tax effect of aforementioned adjustments, as applicable, and similar adjustments to equity share in net earnings (losses) of associates and joint ventures.

Transfer prices between operating segments are on an arm's length basis similar to transactions with third parties. Segment revenues, segment expenses and segment results include transfers between business segments. These transfers are eliminated in full upon consolidation.

Core earnings per common share, or core EPS, is measured as core income divided by the weighted average number of common shares for the year. See *Note 8—Earnings Per*

Common Share for the weighted average number of common shares for the year.

Adjusted EBITDA, adjusted EBITDA margin, core income and core EPS are non-IFRS measures.

The amount of segment assets and liabilities are based on measurement principles that are similar to those used in measuring the assets and liabilities in the consolidated statement of financial position, which is in accordance with IFRS.

The segment revenues, net income for the year, assets, liabilities, and other segment information of our reportable operating segments as at and for the years ended December 31, 2011, 2010 and 2009 are as follows:

(In Million Pesos)	Wireless	Fixed Line	BPO	Others	Inter-Segment Transactions	Consolidated
December 31, 2011						
Revenues						
External customers:	97,984	50,495	8,124	—	—	156,603
Service revenues (Note 3)	96,515	49,319	8,124	—	—	153,958
Non-service revenues (Notes 3 and 5)	1,469	1,176	—	—	—	2,645
Inter-segment transactions:	5,554	9,511	464	—	(15,529)	—
Service revenues (Note 3)	5,554	9,466	464	—	(15,484)	—
Non-service revenues (Notes 3 and 5)	—	45	—	—	(45)	—
Total revenues	103,538	60,006	8,588	—	(15,529)	156,603

(In Million Pesos)	Wireless	Fixed Line	BPO	Others	Inter-Segment Transactions	Consolidated
Depreciation and amortization (Notes 3 and 9)	14,295	13,244	418	—	—	27,957
Asset impairment (Notes 3, 5, 9, 10, 16, 17 and 27)	9,197	1,003	9	—	—	10,209
Equity share in net earnings (losses) of associates and joint ventures (Note 10)	(115)	307	—	1,843	—	2,035
Interest income (Note 5)	677	590	15	90	—	1,372
Financing costs—net (Notes 5, 9, 20 and 27)	2,744	3,710	37	—	—	6,491
Provision for income tax (Notes 3 and 7)	8,429	2,491	118	2	—	11,040
Net income/Segment profit	22,366	6,302	984	1,985	—	31,637
Adjusted EBITDA	55,393	22,675	1,558	(11)	344	79,959
Adjusted EBITDA margin	54%	39%	18%	(100%)	—	52%
Core income	29,903	5,765	906	2,461	—	39,035
Assets and Liabilities						
Operating assets	136,821	281,770	13,211	9,982	(69,978)	371,806
Investments in associates and joint ventures (Notes 3, 5, 10 and 27)	—	1,272	—	16,593	—	17,865
Deferred income tax assets—net (Notes 3, 7 and 27)	1,071	4,672	232	—	—	5,975
Consolidated total assets	137,892	287,714	13,443	26,575	(69,978)	395,646
Operating liabilities	133,344	190,569	3,277	754	(87,419)	240,525
Deferred income tax liabilities—net (Notes 3, 7 and 27)	1,158	1,363	107	—	274	2,902
Consolidated total liabilities	134,502	191,932	3,384	754	(87,145)	243,427
Other Segment Information						
Capital expenditures, including capitalized interest (Notes 5, 9, 20 and 21)	17,152	13,654	400	1	—	31,207

(In Million Pesos)	Wireless	Fixed Line	BPO	Others	Inter-Segment Transactions	Consolidated
Adjusted EBITDA margin[1]	56%	42%	11%	—	—	54%
Core income	31,715	8,344	(230)	1,311	(2)	41,138
Assets and Liabilities						
Operating assets	95,826	222,652	12,507	12,074	(92,865)	250,194
Investments in associates and joint ventures (Notes 3, 5, 10 and 27)	—	813	—	21,420	—	22,233
Deferred income tax assets—net (Notes 3, 7 and 27)	187	7,515	19	—	—	7,721
Consolidated total assets	96,013	230,980	12,526	33,494	(92,865)	280,148
Operating liabilities	95,132	112,955	15,410	1,062	(44,857)	179,702
Deferred income tax liabilities—net (Notes 3, 7 and 27)	640	26	323	—	332	1,321
Consolidated total liabilities	95,772	112,981	15,733	1,062	(44,525)	181,023
Other Segment Information						
Capital expenditures, including capitalized interest (Notes 5, 9, 20 and 21)	16,257	11,419	369	24	—	28,069

[1] The 2010 and 2009 results have been restated to reflect the change in the presentation of our outbound revenues and the implementation of the reorganization of our business segments. See Note 2—Summary of Significant Accounting Policies.

The following table shows the reconciliation of our consolidated adjusted EBITDA to our consolidated net income for the years ended December 31, 2011, 2010 and 2009:

(In Million Pesos)	2011	2010	2009
Consolidated adjusted EBITDA	79,959	83,717	86,194
Equity share in net earnings of associates and joint ventures (Note 10)	2,035	1,408	2
Interest income (Notes 5 and 15)	1,372	1,200	1,539
Gains (losses) on derivative financial instruments—net (Note 27)	197	(1,741)	(1,006)
Amortization of intangible assets (Notes 3 and 14)	(264)	(388)	(368)
Foreign exchange gains (losses)—net (Notes 9 and 27)	(744)	1,807	909
Financing costs—net (Notes 5, 9, 20 and 27)	(6,491)	(6,698)	(6,556)
Asset impairment on noncurrent assets (Notes 3, 5 and 9)	(8,517)	(1,496)	(2,337)
Depreciation and amortization (Notes 3 and 9)	(27,957)	(26,277)	(25,607)
Other income (Note 18)	3,087	2,153	2,069
Consolidated income before income tax	42,677	53,685	54,839
Provision for income tax (Notes 3 and 7)	11,040	13,426	14,744
Consolidated net income	31,637	40,259	40,095

The following table shows the reconciliation of our consolidated core income to our consolidated net income for the years ended December 31, 2011, 2010 and 2009:

(In Million Pesos)	2011	2010	2009
Consolidated core income	39,035	42,028	41,138
Gains (losses) on derivative financial instruments—net, excluding hedge cost (Note 27)	560	(1,307)	(407)
Core income adjustment on equity share in net earnings of associates and joint ventures	(476)	(699)	(136)
Foreign exchange (losses) gains—net (Notes 9 and 27)	(750)	1,819	908
Asset impairment on noncurrent assets—net of share of noncontrolling interest (Notes 3, 5 and 9)	(8,517)	(1,492)	(1,948)
Others	233	—	(381)
Net tax effect of aforementioned adjustments	1,612	(132)	607
Net income attributable to equity holders of PLDT (Notes 6 and 8)	31,697	40,217	39,781
Net income (loss) attributable to noncontrolling interests	(60)	42	314
Consolidated net income	31,637	40,259	40,095

The following table shows the reconciliation of our consolidated basic and diluted core EPS to our consolidated basic and diluted EPS attributable to common equity holder of PLDT for the years ended December 31, 2011, 2010 and 2009:

	Basic			Diluted		
	2011	2010	2009	2011	2010	2009
Consolidated core EPS	201.58	222.55	217.65	201.41	222.55	217.62
Adjustments:						
Losses (gains) on derivative financial instruments—net, excluding hedge cost (Note 27)	2.05	(4.90)	(1.53)	2.05	(4.90)	(1.52)
Core income adjustment on equity share in net earnings of associates and joint ventures (Note 10)	(2.48)	(3.74)	(0.73)	(2.48)	(3.74)	(0.73)
Foreign exchange losses (gains)—net (Notes 9 and 27)	(2.71)	6.81	3.40	(2.71)	6.81	3.40
Asset impairment on noncurrent assets—net of share of noncontrolling interest (Notes 3, 5 and 9)	(36.49)	(7.87)	(6.37)	(36.46)	(7.87)	(6.37)
Others	1.29	—	(2.04)	1.29	—	(2.04)
	(38.34)	(9.70)	(7.27)	(38.31)	(9.70)	(7.26)
EPS attributable to common equity holder of PLDT (Note 8)	163.24	212.85	210.38	163.10	212.85	210.36

The following table presents our revenues from external customers by category of products and services for the years ended December 31, 2011, 2010 and 2009:

(In Million Pesos)	2011	2010	2009
		(As Restated—Note 2)	
Wireless Services			
Service revenues:			
Cellular	88,091	90,629	93,352
Broadband, satellite and others	8,424	8,504	8,144
	96,515	99,133	101,496
Non-service revenues:			
Sale of cellular handsets, cellular subscriber identification module, or SIM,-packs and broadband data modems	1,469	1,357	1,695
Total wireless revenues	97,984	100,490	103,191
Fixed Line Services			
Services revenues:			
Local exchange	15,003	15,226	15,530
International long distance	11,011	11,071	11,538
National long distance	5,032	6,317	7,722
Data and other network	17,351	15,120	13,564
Miscellaneous	922	1,730	1,856
	49,319	49,464	50,210
Non-service revenues:			
Sale of computers	658	342	233
Point-product-sales	518	518	498
Total fixed line revenues	50,495	50,324	50,941
BPO Services			
Service revenues:			
Knowledge processing solutions	5,721	5,289	5,215
Customer relationship management	2,403	2,284	2,676
Total BPO revenues	8,124	7,573	7,891
Total products and services from external customers	156,603	158,387	162,023

Disclosure of the geographical distribution of our revenues from external customers and the geographical location of our total assets are not provided since the majority of our consolidated revenues are derived from our operations within the Philippines.

In each of the years ended December 31, 2011, 2010 and 2009, no revenue transactions with a single external customer had accounted for 10% or more of our consolidated revenues from external customers.

14. Goodwill and Intangible Assets (In part)

Impairment Testing of Goodwill

Goodwill from Acquisition of SBI, CURE, Airborne Access, PDSI and Chikka

The organizational structure of Smart and its subsidiaries is designed to monitor financial operations based on fixed line and wireless segmentation. Management provides guidelines and decisions on resource allocation, such as continuing or disposing of asset and operations by evaluating the performance of each segment through review and analysis of available financial information on the fixed and wireless segments. As at December 31, 2011, Smart's goodwill comprised of goodwill resulting from Smart's acquisition of SBI in 2004, CURE in 2008, SBI's acquisition of a 99.4% equity interest in Airborne Access from ePLDT in 2008 and Smart's acquisition of PDSI and Chikka in 2009. The test for recoverability of Smart's goodwill was applied to the wireless asset group, which represents the lowest level for which identifiable cash flows are largely independent of the cash inflows from other groups of assets and liabilities.

Although revenue streams may be segregated among Smart, CURE, SBI and PDSI through subscribers availing themselves of their respective cellular (for Smart and CURE) and wireless broadband (for SBI and PDSI) services, the cost items and cash flows are difficult to carve out due largely to the significant portion of shared and common-used network/platform. In the case of CURE, it provides cellular services to its subscribers using Smart's 2G network. SBI, on the other hand, provides broadband wireless access to its subscribers using Smart's cellular base stations and fiber optic and IP backbone, as well as the Worldwide Interoperability for Microwave Access technology of PDSI. With the common use of wireless assets of Smart in providing 3G cellular and wireless broadband access, the lowest level of assets of CURE, SBI and PDSI for which cash flows are clearly identifiable from other groups of assets is Smart's wireless business segment. On the other hand, Chikka's mobile applications and content are developed mainly for the cellular subscribers of Smart and CURE.

The recoverable amount of this segment had been determined using the value in use approach calculated using cash flow projections based on the financial budgets approved by the Board of Directors, covering a five-year period from 2012 to 2016. The pre-tax discount rate applied to cash flow projections is 8.8% and cash flows beyond the five-year period are determined using a 2.5% growth rate that is the same as the long-term average growth rate for the telecommunications industry.

With regard to the assessment of value-in-use of the entire operations, management believes that no reasonably possible change in the discount of 1% would cause the carrying value of the unit to materially exceed its recoverable amount. The recoverable amount exceeded the carrying amount of the CGU, which as a result, no impairment was recognized by Smart for the years ended December 31, 2011 and 2010.

SECTION 8: FINANCIAL INSTRUMENTS AND RELATED DISCLOSURES[1]

IFRS 7, *FINANCIAL INSTRUMENTS: DISCLOSURES*

IAS 32, *FINANCIAL INSTRUMENTS: PRESENTATION*

IAS 39, *FINANCIAL INSTRUMENTS: RECOGNITION AND MEASUREMENT*

IFRSs Overview and Comparison to U.S. GAAP

Author's Note

Accounting for financial instruments is a major convergence project of the International Accounting Standards Board (IASB) and the Financial Accounting Standards Board (FASB). The objective of this project is to improve the usefulness for users of financial statements by simplifying the classification and measurement requirements for financial instruments. However, the boards have chosen not to issue joint exposure drafts and are proceeding with their respective projects on different schedules.

The following discussion provides a brief overview of the state of this project as of 1 May 2012. Readers can find more information about decisions to date and the expected publication of IASB due process documents under the "Standards development" section of its website at www.ifrs.org. The latest information about International Financial Reporting Standard (IFRS) 9, *Financial Instruments* (replacement of IAS 39), can be found under the "Work Plan for IFRSs" section of IASB's website at www.ifrs.org. Additional information about FASB's project can be found under the "Projects" section of FASB's website at www.fasb.org.

IASB Project

For IASB, accomplishing the project's objective involves replacing International Accounting Standard (IAS) 39, *Financial Instruments: Recognition and Measurement*, which is organized in the following phases:

1. *Classification and measurement.* In November 2009, IASB issued IFRS 9. As IASB completes phase 1 and the other phases of the project, it plans

to delete sections of IAS 39 and replace them with new sections in IFRS 9.

In brief, IFRS 9 originally addressed the classification and measurement of financial assets only. IFRS 9 requires an entity to classify all financial assets on the basis of the entity's business model for managing financial assets and the contractual cash flow characteristics of the particular financial asset under consideration. The standard reduces the number of classifications for financial assets and requires an entity to measure a financial asset initially at fair value, including, in the case of a financial asset not at fair value through profit or loss (FVTPL), particular transaction costs. Subsequently, an entity should measure the financial asset at either cost or fair value.

In October 2010, IASB added requirements for financial liabilities to IFRS 9. Although IASB carried forward most requirements for financial liabilities from IAS 39 unchanged, IASB made some changes to the fair value option for financial liabilities to address the issue of an entity's own credit risk.

In November 2011, IASB tentatively decided to consider expediting limited modifications to IFRS 9 for three reasons:

- Constituents who have early adopted or are in the process of adopting IFRS 9 raised application issues with regard to classifying certain financial instruments and stating that simply clarifying the existing application guidance will resolve these issues.
- Because the insurance contracts model is sufficiently developed, IASB believes it is ready to consider the interaction between this model and the IFRS 9 model for financial assets.
- FASB is near to finalizing its classification and measurement model. In the interest of achieving increased comparability between the boards' respective standards, IASB and FASB will jointly discuss some issues with the goal of reducing key differences in their respective models. In January 2012, the boards announced they would work together in this regard.

In December 2011, IASB issued *Mandatory Effective Date of IFRS 9 and Transition Disclosures*, which defers the effective date of IFRS 9 to annual periods beginning on or after 1 January 2015. This amendment to IFRS 9 also provides relief to entities with respective to comparative information and adds several disclosures to help users better understand the effect of applying the classification and measurement model in IFRS 9.

Throughout 2012, IASB and FASB have been working together to achieve a more converged solution to classification and measurement of financial assets. During early meetings, the boards agreed on the following criteria for classification:

---

[1] Unless otherwise indicated, references to International Accounting Standards Board (IASB) standards and interpretations throughout this 2012 edition of *IFRS Financial Statements—Best Practices in Presentation and Disclosure* refer to the version of those standards and interpretations included in *IFRS 2012* bound volume, the official printed consolidated text of IASB standards and interpretations, including revisions, amendments, and supporting documents, issued as of 1 January 2012.

- *Individual debt instrument.* The entity would classify an individual instrument based on that instrument's characteristics; that is, to be eligible for measurement at either amortized cost or fair value with changes in fair value reported in other comprehensive income, the contractual cash flows of the debt instrument can consist only of principal and interest payments.
- *Portfolio.* The entity would classify the portfolio of debt instruments based on business strategy.

In May 2012, FASB and IASB agreed on a three-category model for debt instruments (for example, loans and debt securities) when IASB agreed to add a third category for instruments measured at fair value with changes in fair value reported in other comprehensive income. The three categories for investments in debt instruments are the following:

- *Amortized cost.* The entity's primary objective for the investment is to collect contractual cash flows.
- *Fair value with changes in fair value reported in other comprehensive income.* The entity's primary objective for the investment is both to collect contractual cash flows and realize changes in fair value from sale of the asset. Therefore, the entity would report (recycle) the changes in fair value to profit or loss when the asset is sold.
- *Fair value with changes in fair value reported in profit or loss.* The entity uses this category for investments that either do not pass the individual instrument characteristics criteria described previously or do not meet one of the other characteristics of the category.

The boards also agreed to prohibit bifurcation of hybrid financial assets. However, an entity would still be required to bifurcate hybrid financial liabilities. The boards do not plan to address differences in their respective approaches to classification and measurement of equity instruments that are not accounted for using the equity method.

2. *Amortized cost and impairment of assets.* In November 2009, IASB published an exposure draft, *Financial Instruments: Amortised Cost and Impairment*, with a comment deadline of 30 June 2010. This document provided the following measurement principles for amortized cost, including impairment:

- Amortized cost is the present value of expected future cash flows over the remaining life of the financial instrument, discounted using the effective interest rate.
- Estimates of the amounts and timing of expected future cash flows are probability weighted.
- The effective interest method is the method by which an entity allocates interest revenue and expense and reflects the nature of the financial instrument's interest formula.

In January 2011, IASB issued a supplementary document, *Financial Instruments: Impairment*, with a comment deadline of 1 April 2011. Because IASB and FASB are committed to enhancing comparability in accounting for financial instruments and achieving a common solution to the accounting for impairment, this supplement was published jointly by IASB and FASB. However, although sympathetic to each other's primary objectives, they each continue to stress their own. IASB continues to stress the importance of the relationship between pricing and expected credit losses, and FASB continues to stress the importance of adequacy of the allowance for credit losses to cover expected credit losses. This document partly satisfies these two objectives by incorporating a minimum allowance for credit losses into IASB's discounted cash flow model described previously.

3. *Hedge accounting.* In December 2010, IASB issued an exposure draft, *Hedge Accounting*, with a comment deadline of 9 March 2011. This document proposed that the objective of hedge accounting is to represent the effect of an entity's risk management activities in its financial statements with the goal of conveying the context in which the entity uses hedging instruments so that users understand their purpose and effect. In part, IASB proposed the following changes to the existing requirements for hedge accounting, including portfolio hedge accounting, by permitting an entity to designate

- nonderivative financial assets and nonderivative financial liabilities measured at fair value through profit or loss as hedging instruments.
- an aggregated exposure that is a combination of an exposure and a derivative as the hedged item.
- all changes in cash flows or fair value of an item as the hedged item.
- separately identifiable and reliably measurement risk components as the hedged item.
- a layer component of the nominal amount of an item as the hedged item.

IASB also proposed that a hedging relationship should meet the objective of hedge effectiveness assessment and be expected to achieve other than accidental offsetting of the risk. When the hedging relationship is no longer effective but the entity's risk management objective remains the same, an entity should rebalance the hedging relationship to meet the hedging effectiveness objective. Finally, the entity should discontinue hedge accounting prospectively when all or part of the hedging relationship no longer meets the proposed criteria for hedging effectiveness.

4. *Forthcoming documents.* IASB expects to issue the following documents in the latter half of 2012:

- Exposure draft on classification and measurements issues
- Second exposure draft on impairment
- IFRS on general hedge accounting
- Discussion paper or exposure draft on macro-hedging

FASB Project

In contrast to IASB, because the issues are interrelated, FASB decided that a comprehensive, rather than phased, approach to the financial instruments project would be more coherent and easier for constituents to understand and respond. Therefore, in May

2010, FASB issued an exposure draft proposing a new comprehensive FASB Accounting Standards Update (ASU), *Accounting for Financial Instruments and Revisions to the Accounting for Derivative Instruments and Hedging Activities*. This exposure draft addressed the issues in all phases of the IASB project: classification and measurement of financial assets and financial liabilities, impairment methodology, and hedge accounting. The comment period ended 30 September 2010. In this document, FASB proposed to apply a fair value measurement model for many financial assets and financial liabilities. This model differed from the mixed measurement model in IFRS 9.

As discussed previously under the IASB's project on classification and measurement, in May 2012, the boards agreed on a converged approach to classification and measurement of debt instruments. See the discussion in that part of this author's note for more details of that agreement.

FASB also made the following decisions on impairment of financial assets:

- When the entity accounts for a nonmarketable equity security under the practicability exception, it would apply a single-step approach to assess qualitative factors (that is, impairment indicators) to determine whether it is more likely than not that the fair value of the nonmarketable equity security is less than its carrying amount (that is, an impairment exists). When an impairment exists, the entity would recognize an impairment loss in earnings equal to the entire difference between the investment's carrying value and its fair value.
- Impairment for debt instruments would follow a "three-bucket" approach based on deterioration in the instrument's credit quality. All originated and purchased financial assets would initially start in Bucket 1 and would move into Bucket 2 and Bucket 3 as the instrument's credit quality deteriorates. An entity would measure the credit loss allowance for instruments in Bucket 1 at an amount based on either 12 or 24 months' worth of expected losses. However, an entity would measure the credit loss allowance for instruments in Buckets 2 and 3 at an amount based on an estimate of remaining lifetime expected losses.

FASB has not begun to redeliberate hedge accounting. In February 2011, FASB issued an invitation to comment to solicit input on the IASB exposure draft on hedge accounting published in December 2010 (discussed previously).

In addition to classification and measurement, impairment, and hedging, FASB also made the following decisions related to financial statement presentation of financial instruments:

- An entity would separately present financial assets and financial liabilities on the statement of financial position by classification and measurement category.
- Public entities would present parenthetically on the face of the statement of financial position the fair value for financial instruments measured at amortized cost, except for demand deposit liabilities, receivables, and payables due in less than a year. An entity would disclose the present value of demand deposit liabilities in the notes to the financial statements.
- All entities would present parenthetically on the face of the statement of financial position the amortized cost of an entity's own debt measured at fair value.
- In the income statement, an entity would present in net income an aggregate amount for realized and unrealized gains or losses for financial assets measured at fair value with all changes in fair value included in net income.
- For both financial assets measured at fair value with changes in value recognized in other comprehensive income and financial assets measured at amortized cost, an entity would present in net income the following items separately:
  —Current-period interest income
  —Current-period credit losses
  —Realized gains and losses
- For financial liabilities measured at fair value with all changes in fair value recognized in net income, an entity would present in net income an aggregate amount for realized and unrealized gains or losses.
- For financial liabilities measured at amortized cost, an entity would present in net income the following items separately:
  —Current-period interest expense
  —Realized gains and losses.

FASB would not require an entity to present the changes in the fair value of financial liabilities attributable to changes in the entity's own credit risk separately from other changes in fair value. As discussed previously in the discussion of the IASB project, in January 2011, the boards proposed a common solution for impairment accounting. Both boards are currently deliberating the results on the comments received on this document.

Other Changes to IFRSs

IASB also had a separate project on derecognition of financial instruments that addressed both the existing derecognition criteria in IAS 39 and the related disclosures in IFRS 7, *Financial Instruments: Disclosures*. In July 2010, IASB finalized the disclosure requirements proposed in the March 2009 exposure draft, *Derecogntion*, and, in October 2010, issued *Disclosures—Transfers of Financial Assets (Amendments to IFRS 7)*. These amendments are effective for annual periods beginning on or after 1 July 2011. Although the commentary that follows discusses these amendments, the timing of the effective date of these amendments affects the availability of illustrative excerpts from survey companies' financial statements. Accordingly, the excerpts appearing later in this section may not reflect all or some of these revisions.

In May 2011, IASB also issued the following standards which amended the standards related to accounting for financial instruments:

1. *Offsetting Financial Assets and Financial Liabilities* (Amendments to IAS 32) (issued December 2011 with an effective date of 1 January 2014)

2. *Disclosures—Offsetting Financial Assets and Financial Liabilities* (Amendments to IFRS 7) (issued December 2011 with an effective date of 1 January 2013)

These two standards are discussed in an author's note later in the commentary under the headings titled "Presentation" and "Disclosure," respectively.

3. IFRS 10, *Consolidated Financial Statements* (issued May 2011 with an effective date of 1 January 2013)

4. IFRS 11, *Joint Arrangements* (issued May 2011 with an effective date of 1 January 2013)

These two standards replace references to IAS 27, *Consolidated and Separate Financial Statements*, and IAS 31, *Interests in Joint Ventures*, with references to IFRS 10 and IFRS 11 respectively and add a reference to IAS 27, *Separate Financial Statements,* as appropriate.

5. IFRS 13, *Fair Value Measurement* (issued May 2011 with an effective date of 1 January 2013)

This standard amends the accounting for financial instruments by requiring an entity to apply the requirements of IFRS 13 to financial assets and financial liabilities, whether by designation or otherwise, measured at fair value or whose fair value is disclosed.

6. *Presentation of Items of Other Comprehensive Income* (Amendments to IAS 1) (issued June 2011 with an effective date of 1 July 2012)

These amendments replace the phrase "statements of comprehensive income or the separate income statement" in IFRS 7 and IAS 32, *Financial Instruments: Presentation*, with "statements of profit or loss and other comprehensive income."

Because these standards are effective for annual periods beginning on or after 1 January 2012, these amendments are not reflected in the commentary in this section. The timing of the effective dates affects the availability of illustrative excerpts from survey companies' financial statements. Accordingly, the excerpts appearing later in this section may not reflect these revisions.

8.01 IFRSs define a *financial instrument* as a contract that gives rise to a financial asset of one entity and a financial liability of another. IFRSs establish the accounting and disclosure requirements and application guidance for both the financial asset and financial liability created by such contracts in the following three standards:

- IAS 32 establishes the principles for distinguishing a liability from an equity instrument and for presenting financial assets and liabilities net on the balance (offsetting).
- IAS 39 establishes the principles for recognizing and measuring financial assets and financial liabilities as well as for some contracts to buy or sell nonfinancial items. IAS 39 also establishes the principles under which an entity would have an effective hedging relationship and be able to apply hedge accounting.
- IFRS 7 establishes the disclosures that an entity should provide about the significance of financial instruments to their balance sheet and statement of comprehensive income and the risks from these instruments to which it is exposed.

8.02 In addition, IASB has issued several interpretations that are applicable to the financial instruments covered by the previous standards, including the following:

- International Financial Reporting Interpretations Committees (IFRIC) 2, *Members' Shares in Co-operative Entities and Similar Instruments*

  IFRIC 2 describes how an entity should evaluate redemption terms when deciding whether to classify a financial instrument as debt or equity. An entity should classify member shares as equity if the entity has an unconditional right to refuse redemption of the members' shares or if the redemption is unconditionally prohibited by local law, regulation, or the entity's governing charter.

- IFRIC 9, *Reassessment of Embedded Derivatives*

  When an entity first becomes party to a contract that includes an embedded derivative, IFRIC 9 requires an entity to assess whether to separate an embedded derivative from the host contract and account for that derivative separately. IFRIC 9 also prohibits the entity to reassess this separation unless either the terms of the contract change resulting in a significant modification of the cash flows otherwise required by the contract or the entity reclassifies the financial asset out of fair value through profit or loss which requires reassessment.

- IFRIC 10, *Interim Financial Reporting and Impairment*

  IFRIC 10 prohibits an entity from reversing impairment losses recognized in a previous interim period with respect to goodwill, investments in equity instruments, or investments in a financial asset carried at cost.

- IFRIC 16, *Hedges of a Net Investment in a Foreign Operation*

  In part, IFRIC 16 allows an entity to apply hedge accounting only to foreign exchange differences arising between the functional currencies of the foreign operation and the parent entity and only once in the consolidated financial statements. The parent entity can designate an amount equal to or less than the carrying amount of the net assets of the foreign operation as the hedged item. An entity is constrained by whether a lower-level parent in the group has used hedge accounting to this hedged item and whether this hedge accounting is maintained in the consolidated financial statements.

- IFRIC 19, *Extinguishing Financial Liabilities with Equity Instruments*

  IFRIC 19 requires an entity to consider equity instruments issued to extinguish a financial liability to be consideration paid and to measure these instruments initially at their fair value, unless fair value cannot be measured reliably. In the latter case, the entity should measure the fair value of the equity instruments to reflect the fair value of the financial liability extinguished, including any demand features. If the entity does not extinguish the financial liability in its entirety, it should first assess whether some of the consideration paid relates to a modification of terms of the remaining liability. If so, the consideration paid is allocated between the amount of the liability extinguished and the amount remaining. The entity should recognize in profit or loss the difference between the carrying amount of the financial liability extinguished and the amount of consideration paid to extinguish the liability. The interpretation also addresses the circumstances when modification of terms is so substantial that the entity should extinguish the original liability and recognize a new liability.

Author's Note

The commentary that follows in this section collectively refers to the aforementioned standards and interpretations as *IFRSs for financial instruments*. Recognition and measurement of financial instruments is extremely complex. Therefore, commentary under this heading primarily focuses on the disclosures that entities provide in their financial statements and provides only a brief description of the issues that an entity must address when accounting for these items. Although differences between IFRSs and FASB *Accounting Standards Codification*™ (ASC) exist at a high level, many additional transaction-specific differences also exist. See the author's note at the beginning of this section for information about the IASB and FASB convergence project on accounting for financial instruments.

8.03 IAS 32 applies to all financial instruments, except the following:

- Interests in subsidiaries, associates, or joint ventures accounted for in accordance with IAS 27; IAS 28, *Investments in Associates*; and IAS 31, respectively, unless the entity is permitted to account for these investments in accordance with IAS 39
- Rights and obligations under employee benefit plans, accounted for in accordance with IAS 19, *Employee Benefits*
- Insurance contracts within the scope of IFRS 4, *Insurance Contracts* (except when IAS 32 specifically provides otherwise)
- Financial instruments, contracts, and obligations accounted for in accordance with IFRS 2, *Share-based Payment* (except certain requirements of IAS 32 may continue to apply)

However, IAS 32 does apply to certain contracts to buy or sell a nonfinancial item when the entity can settle the contract net in cash or another financial instrument or by exchanging financial instruments, as if the contracts themselves were financial instruments.

8.04 IFRSs for financial instruments contain definitions that are critical for determining the application of the requirements of IFRSs for financial instruments to a particular instrument, transaction, or circumstance. These definitions are dispersed among the different standards and interpretations previously noted. IAS 32 defines the following terms: *financial instrument, financial asset, financial liability, equity instrument, fair value,* and *puttable instrument*. IAS 39 defines the following terms: *financial instrument, financial asset, financial liability, equity instrument, fair value,* and *puttable instrument*. IAS 39 defines the following terms: *amortized cost for a financial asset or financial liability; effective interest method; derecognition; derivative; financial guarantee contract; regular way purchase or sale; transaction costs;* and, in the context of hedge accounting, *firm commitment, forecast transaction, hedged item,* and *hedging effectiveness*.

Recognition and Measurement

IFRSs

8.05 IAS 39 establishes the recognition and measurement requirements for financial instruments. In addition to the scope exclusions in IAS 32, IAS 39 includes the following additional scope exclusions:

- Rights and obligations accounted for in accordance with IAS 17, *Leases*, except for certain lease receivables, finance lease payables, and embedded derivatives
- Forward contracts to buy or sell an acquiree that will result in a business combination
- Certain loan commitments
- Reimbursement rights for previously recognized provisions

However, the scope of IAS 39 includes other loan commitments: those designated at FVTPL, those that can be settled net in cash and by delivery or exchange of financial instruments (settled net), and commitments to provide a loan at a below-market rate. Entities should apply IAS 39 to contracts to buy or sell a nonfinancial item that can be settled net, except when the entity enters into and continues to hold such contracts for receipt or delivery as part of its normal expected sale, purchase, or usage requirements.

8.06 In addition to the defined terms previously mentioned, IAS 39 also defines the following four categories that entities should use to classify financial instruments:

- Financial asset or financial liability at FVTPL, such as the following:
  - Held for trading
  - Designated on initial recognition (designated at FVTPL)
- Held to maturity (HTM)
- Loans and receivables
- Available for sale financial assets (AFS)

An entity should classify its financial instruments in one of these four categories to determine the appropriate recognition, initial and subsequent measurements on the balance sheet, and derecognition, as well as the nature of the effects on the statement of comprehensive income.

8.07 IAS 39 requires recognition of a financial asset or financial liability in the balance sheet only when the entity becomes a party to the instrument's contractual provisions. However, IAS 39 includes more extensive guidance on derecognition. Entities should evaluate whether to derecognize a financial asset by first determining whether they should apply the derecognition criteria to the financial asset, to part of the financial asset, to a group of financial assets, or to part of a group based on criteria in IAS 39. After making this assessment, the entity should derecognize a financial asset when, and only when, (*a*) the contractual rights to the asset's cash flows expire or (*b*) the entity transfers the financial asset and the transfer meets the criteria in IAS 39. IAS 39 requires the entity to conduct an evaluation of the extent to which the entity retains the risks and rewards of ownership of the financial asset as part of this assessment.

8.08 When a transfer of a financial asset qualifies for derecognition and the entity retains servicing rights for a fee, the entity should recognize either a servicing asset (when the entity expects the fee to adequately compensate it for its services) or a servicing liability (when the entity does not expect the fee to adequately compensate it for its services).

8.09 When an entity derecognizes a financial asset, it should recognize a gain or loss equal to the difference between the asset's carrying amount and the sum of consideration received and the cumulative gain or loss, if any, previously recognized in comprehensive income. When the derecognized financial asset is a component of a larger financial asset, the entity should allocate the larger asset's carrying value between the derecognized component and the carrying value of the retained asset.

8.10 Not all transfers of financial assets will qualify for derecognition. When an entity retains substantially all of the risks and rewards of ownership or, by the extent of its continuing involvement, is exposed to changes in the value of the transferred asset, it should not derecognize the asset. In the former case, the entity should continue to recognize the entire asset and also recognize a liability for the consideration received. In the latter case, the entity should recognize an asset to the extent of its continuing involvement and an associated liability. IAS 39 provides guidance for measuring the carrying amount of this retained asset and the liability. IAS 39 also provides guidance on accounting for any noncash collateral provided to the transferee.

Author's Note

The criteria for determining whether a transfer of a financial asset qualifies for derecognition is complex and too lengthy to cover comprehensively in this commentary.

8.11 Entities have an option under IAS 39 to recognize regular way purchases of financial assets or derecognize sales using either trade date or settlement date accounting, consistently applied.

8.12 An entity should derecognize all or part of a financial liability when the entity has discharged or cancelled its obligation under the contract or when the obligation expires. The entity should consider an exchange of financial instruments as an extinguishment of the original and should consider recognition of a new liability only if the terms of the instruments are substantially different. Similarly, when the terms of the original obligation are substantially modified, the entity should account for the modification as an extinguishment of the existing liability and recognition of a new liability. The entity should recognize a gain or loss in profit or loss for the difference between the carrying value of the existing liability and the sum of the carrying value of the new liability and any consideration or noncash assets paid or transferred.

8.13 IAS 39 requires entities to recognize a financial asset or financial liability initially at the sum of its fair value and transaction costs, except when the instrument is classified as FVTPL. When instruments are held at FVTPL, an entity should recognize any transaction costs directly attributable to acquisition or issue of the instrument in profit or loss when incurred.

8.14 Subsequent measurement depends on the classification of the financial instrument on initial recognition. After initial recognition, unless designated as a hedged item, an entity should measure its financial assets, including derivatives, at fair value, excluding transaction costs, with the following exceptions:

- Loans, receivables, and HTM investments at amortized cost using the effective interest method

- Other financial instruments at cost, including the following:
  — Investments in equity instruments without a quoted market price in an active market and whose fair value cannot be measured reliably
  — Derivatives linked to and with required settlement by such unquoted instruments

8.15 Similarly, unless designated as a hedged item, entities should subsequently measure financial liabilities, including derivatives, at amortized cost using the effective interest method, with the following exceptions:

- Derivatives linked to, and with required settlement by, delivery of an unquoted equity instrument whose fair value cannot be reliably measured should be measured at cost.
- Financial liabilities at FVTPL should be measured at fair value.
- Financial guarantee contracts and commitments to provide a loan at below fair market value should be measured at the higher of
  — the amount determined in accordance with IAS 37, *Provisions, Contingent Liabilities and Contingent Assets*, or
  — the amount initially recognized, less any cumulative amortization recognized in accordance with IAS 18, *Revenue*.

8.16 IAS 39 contains substantive application guidance on recognition and measurement including fair value measurement. Appendix A, "Application Guidance," is considered an integral part of the standard and is mandatory. In contrast, the implementation guidance that accompanies the standard is not considered part of the standard and is not mandatory.

8.17 Entities may need to reclassify a financial asset or financial liability because the entity's intention with respect to the instrument may change or its fair value can no longer be measured reliably. IAS 39 prohibits entities from reclassifying financial assets or financial liabilities in the following circumstances:

- Out of the FVTPL category:
  — Derivatives when held or issued
  — Instruments designated at FVTPL at initial recognition, generally
- Into the FVTPL category:
  — Any financial instruments after initial recognition

However, in certain circumstances, IAS 39 permits an entity to reclassify nonderivative financial assets (other than those designated at FVTPL at initial recognition) out of the FVTPL category. The standard also permits an entity to transfer a financial asset from the available-for-sale category to the loans and receivables category when the following two criteria are met: (*a*) the financial asset would have met the definition of loans and receivables if the entity had not classified it as AFS and (*b*) the entity has the intention and ability to hold that financial asset for the foreseeable future. However, in rare circumstances when specific conditions are met, entities may reclassify a financial asset no longer held for trading (selling or repurchasing in the near term) out of the FVTPL category.

8.18 When an entity no longer has the intent or ability to hold an investment to maturity, it should reclassify an HTM investment as AFS and remeasure the investment at fair value. The entity should recognize the difference between the carrying amount and fair value in other comprehensive income until the entity derecognizes the asset. However, when an entity reclassifies more than an insignificant amount of HTM investments, it should reclassify all of its remaining HTM investments and not classify any new investments as HTM until two years have elapsed.

8.19 Entities should recognize gains or losses from changes in fair value on instruments that are not part of a hedging relationship depending on their classification. Entities should recognize such gains or losses in profit or loss when the instrument is classified as FVTPL, and in other comprehensive income when the instrument is classified as AFS. For instruments held at amortized cost, an entity should recognize a gain or loss in profit or loss when the financial asset or financial liability is derecognized or impaired, and also through the amortization process, unless the instrument is part of a hedging relationship.

Author's Note

See section 3, "Statement of Comprehensive Income and Related Disclosures," for excerpts illustrating items recognized in profit or loss and recognized in other comprehensive income.

8.20 At the end of each reporting period, an entity should review its financial assets or groups of such assets and determine whether objective evidence of impairment exists. When such evidence exists for financial assets held at amortized cost, the entity should measure the amount of the loss as the difference between the carrying value of the asset and the present value of future cash flows discounted at the original effective interest rate. The entity should recognize this loss in profit or loss. The entity may reduce the carrying amount of the asset directly or use a valuation allowance. Entities should recognize a reversal of this impairment loss if they can attribute the decrease in the loss to an event that occurred after the original loss was recognized. Entities should not increase the carrying amount of the asset above the amount that would have resulted if the impairment had not been recognized. When the entity determines that an AFS financial asset is impaired, it should reclassify the cumulative loss previously recognized in equity to profit or loss as a reclassification adjustment. An entity should not reverse an impairment loss recognized on equity instruments classified as AFS. However, the entity should reverse an impairment loss on an AFS debt instrument subject to the same constraints as a reversal on an instrument held at amortized cost.

8.21 In accordance with IAS 32, entities should recognize in profit or loss interest and dividend income and interest expense on financial instruments within the scope of IFRSs for financial instruments.

Author's Note

See section 3 for excerpts illustrating items recognized in profit or loss and other comprehensive income.

8.22 IAS 39 provides special accounting treatment for hedged items and hedging instruments in a designated hedging relationship. Hedge accounting permits the offsetting of gains or losses from changes in fair value of the hedged item and hedging instrument. Certain conditions and constraints exist for an instrument to qualify as either a hedging instrument or hedged item and for designation of the hedging relationship. The hedging relationship should also meet an effectiveness test in order for the entity to apply hedge accounting. IAS 39 recognizes two types of hedging relationships: fair value hedge and cash flow hedge. When the hedged item is a forecast transaction, only a cash flow hedge can be designated. An entity that hedges its net investment in a foreign operation should account for the hedging relationship similar to a cash flow hedge.

U.S. GAAP

8.23 Unlike IFRSs, in which requirements for most financial instruments are contained in three standards, guidance in FASB ASC covering recognition, measurement, presentation, and disclosure requirements is widely dispersed. Although the primary topic is FASB ASC 825, *Financial Instruments*, FASB ASC has specific guidance for various types of receivables, investments in debt and equity instruments, payables, debt, financial instruments held under the fair value option, and derivatives and hedging within other topics (for example FASB ASC 310, *Receivables*, or FASB ASC 320, *Investments—Debt and Equity Securities*). In addition, FASB ASC includes many transaction- and circumstance-specific requirements and a significant amount of industry specific guidance. For example, with respect to transfers of assets, FASB ASC 860-20 provides guidance on accounting for transfers of financial assets, including accounting for transfers of receivables in securitization transactions, transfers of receivables with recourse, and factoring arrangements.

Author's Note

In April 2011, FASB issued ASU No. 2011-03, *Transfers and Servicing (Topic 860): Reconsideration of Effective Control for Repurchase Agreements*. FASB issued ASU No. 2011-03 to improve the accounting for repurchase agreements and other agreements that both entitle and obligate a transferor to repurchase or redeem financial assets before their maturity. The main provision of ASU No. 2011-03 removes the following criterion from the required reassessment of control: the transferor should have the ability to repurchase or redeem the financial assets on substantially all of the agreed terms, even in the event of default by the transferee. Consequently, ASU No. 2011-03 also removes the implementation guidance related to this criterion which required the transferor to possess adequate collateral to fund substantially all of the cost of purchasing replacement assets. IAS 39 does not include this criterion. Therefore, by eliminating this criterion, FASB also improved convergence. ASU No. 2011-03 is effective for annual periods beginning on or after December 15, 2011. Early adoption is prohibited.

8.24 Definitions in the FASB ASC glossary also differ from those in IFRSs in subtle ways that may cause differences in classification and accounting treatments. For example, the FASB ASC glossary defines a *derivative instrument* as a financial instrument or other contract with all of the following characteristics:

- The instrument has an underlying, and a notional amount or payment provision, or both. (As defined in the FASB ASC glossary, an *underlying* is a specified interest rate, security price, commodity price, foreign exchange rate, index of prices or rates, or other variable [including the occurrence or nonoccurrence of a specified event such as a scheduled payment under a contract]. An underlying may be a price or rate of an asset or liability but is not the asset or liability itself. An underlying is a variable that, along with either a notional amount or a payment provision, determines the settlement of a derivative instrument.)

- The instrument requires no initial net investment or one smaller than required on other contracts expected to have a similar response to market factors.
- The entity can settle the instrument net in one of following three specific ways:
  — Terms implicitly or explicitly require or permit net settlement.
  — Entity can readily settle by a means outside the contract.
  — Delivery of the asset puts the recipient in a position not substantially different from net settlement.

Derivative instruments also include embedded derivatives that have been separated from a host contract in accordance with FASB ASC 815-15-25-1.

8.25 The characteristics of a derivative under IFRSs compare and contrast with characteristics previously mentioned in the following ways:

- The instrument's value changes in response to changes in a variable (underlying). However, IFRSs do not require a notional amount or payment provision.
- The instrument requires no initial net investment or one smaller than required on other contracts expected to have a similar response to market factors and is the same as U.S. generally accepted accounting principles (U.S. GAAP).
- The instrument is settled at a future date. IFRSs have no requirement for net settlement in any form.

8.26 Like IFRSs, derivatives, securities classified as trading or AFS, and instruments that the entity has elected to measure at FVTPL are measured initially at fair value. Unlike IFRSs, investments in equity method investees may be measured at fair value using the fair value option in FASB ASC 825-10-15-1. Other financial instruments are measured initially at cost. Key differences between IFRSs and FASB ASC guidance also exist for subsequent measurement.

8.27 In addition to the dispersion of guidance on financial instruments throughout FASB ASC, differences in scope between items meeting the definition of a financial instrument under IFRSs and FASB ASC make comparisons between the two sets of standards difficult. For example, unless the receivables have been securitized, the FASB ASC glossary does not consider either of the following to meet the definition of a debt security (financial instrument):

- Trade accounts receivable from credit sales by industrial or commercial entities
- Loans receivable from consumer, commercial, and real estate lending activities of financial institutions

Presentation

Author's Note

On 28 January 2011, IASB published for public comment an exposure draft, *Offsetting Financial Assets and Financial Liabilities*, and FASB published for public comment a proposed ASU, *Balance Sheet Offsetting*. The comment period ended on 28 April 2011, with a target for release of a final standard in the third quarter of 2011. According to the joint exposure drafts, the differences in the existing offsetting requirements in IFRSs and U.S. GAAP account for the single largest quantitative difference in the amounts presented in statements of financial position. Therefore, IASB and FASB seek to align the respective guidance in IFRSs and FASB ASC on the criteria that would determine when offsetting in the balance sheet is appropriate.

In December 2011, both boards issued amendments to their respective guidance on offsetting of assets and liabilities. IASB issued *Offsetting Financial Assets and Financial Liabilities* (Amendments to IAS 32) and *Disclosures—Offsetting Financial Assets and Financial Liabilities* (Amendments to IFRS 7), and FASB issued ASU No. 2011-11, *Balance Sheet (Topic 210): Disclosures about Offsetting Assets and Liabilities*. Although both boards decided to retain their respective models for offsetting, they agreed that disclosure of both gross and net information would help users. Therefore, they agreed on common disclosure requirements. IASB also added application guidance to IAS 32 to address some identified inconsistencies in applying the offsetting criteria. The amendments to IAS 32 and IFRS 7 are effective for annual periods beginning on or after 1 January 2014. The amendments to the FASB ASC are effective for annual periods beginning on or after 1 January 2013.

An author's note under the section titled "Disclosure" later in this section addresses the amendments to disclosure requirements in IFRS 7 and FASB ASC.

IFRSs

8.28 IAS 32 requires an entity, on initial recognition, to classify a financial instrument or its components as a financial asset, a financial liability, or an equity instrument in accordance with the substance of the contractual arrangement and the definitions applicable to those respective items. When distinguishing between a financial liability and an equity instrument, entities should only classify the item as equity when the following two conditions are met:

- The entity has no contractual obligation to deliver cash or to exchange financial assets or liabilities under potentially unfavorable conditions.
- If the entity may settle the instrument with its own shares, the instrument is either a nonderivative with no contractual obligation to deliver a variable number of shares or a derivative that will be settled by a fixed number of shares.

If the instrument does not meet these conditions, the entity should classify the instrument as a financial liability.

8.29 A *puttable instrument* is a financial instrument that either gives the holder the right to return (put back) the instrument to the issuer for cash or another financial asset or is automatically put back to the issuer on the occurrence of an uncertain future event or the death or retirement of the instrument holder. This is an exception to the definition of a *financial liability*. Entities should classify this instrument as equity when it has certain features established in IAS 32, including the following:

- In the event of liquidation, the holder is entitled to a pro rata share of the entity's net assets.
- The instrument is subordinate to all other financial instruments (that is, it has, and conversion is unnecessary for it to have, no priority over other claims).

8.30 Entities should reclassify an instrument as equity or financial liability as of the date that the necessary conditions for these classifications are met or are no longer met, respectively. IAS 32 also provides guidance on liability or equity classification when contingent settlement provisions and settlement options exist. Certain instruments, known as *compound financial instruments*, contain both a liability and an equity component. Based on the measurement criteria identified in IAS 32, entities should classify each component separately as financial assets, financial liabilities, or equity and account for each component accordingly.

8.31 Entities should account for treasury shares as a reduction of equity. Entities should not recognize gains or losses on treasury share transactions in profit or loss. IAS 1, *Presentation of Financial Statements*, requires entities to disclose treasury shares separately either on the face of the balance sheet or in the notes.

8.32 Entities should offset a financial asset and financial liability only when they have a legally enforceable right to offset and intend to settle net or simultaneously. When a transferred financial asset does not qualify for derecognition under IAS 39, an entity should not offset the transferred asset against any related liabilities. IAS 32 provides examples of situations, including synthetic instruments, that would generally not qualify for a net presentation on the balance sheet.

U.S. GAAP

8.33 Like IFRSs, FASB ASC 480, *Distinguishing Liabilities from Equity*, contains guidance, which all entities should apply, for determining when an entity should classify a financial instrument with characteristics of both liabilities and equity as a financial liability or an equity instrument. However, certain instruments are outside the scope of FASB ASC 480 (for example, registration prepayment arrangements or nonderivative embedded features). In these circumstances, an entity should also consider the requirements of FASB ASC 405, *Liabilities*, or FASB ASC 825 to determine proper classification. In contrast to IFRSs, FASB ASC includes more guidance for instruments with specific features. Only by analyzing the respective guidance in both forms of GAAP and the particular features of the instrument under consideration, can an entity know whether the classification and, hence, recognition and measurement would be the same under IFRSs and FASB ASC.

8.34 Like IFRSs, FASB ASC 505-30 notes that treasury shares are classified as a reduction of equity and an entity should not recognize in income any gains and losses on resale of such shares. However, FASB ASC 505-30-25-2 further explains that the laws of some states govern the circumstances under which an entity may acquire its own stock, and these laws may prescribe an accounting treatment. When these laws conflict with the requirements of certain paragraphs in FASB ASC 505-30-25 and 505-30-30, the entity should comply with the state law.

8.35 FASB ASC 210-20-45-1 includes conditions similar to those in IFRSs that permit entities to offset assets and liabilities (right of setoff). A right of setoff exists at the balance sheet date when all of the following conditions are met:

- The respective counterparties each owe the other determinable amounts.
- The reporting entity has a right to offset the amount owed with the amount owed by the other party.
- The reporting party intends to offset (settle net).
- The right of setoff is enforceable by law.

Disclosure

Author's Note

As discussed previously in the author's note following paragraph 8.27, in December 2011, IASB and FASB issued amendments to enhance their respective disclosures about recognized financial instruments subject to enforceable master netting arrangements and similar agreements, regardless of whether they are presented net in the financial statements. These enhanced disclosures resulted from a joint project related to requirements for offsetting financial assets and financial liabilities. The additional disclosures will enable financial statement users to better understand the effect of such arrangements on its financial position. The amendments to IFRS 7 are effective for annual reporting periods beginning on or after 1 January 2013. The amendments to FASB ASC 210-20-45 and FASB ASC 815-10-45 are effective for annual reporting periods beginning on or after 1 January 2013. An entity should apply these amendments retrospectively.

These converged disclosures require an entity to disclose the following with respect to financial instruments, including derivatives, subject to enforceable master netting arrangements and similar agreements:

1. Information to enable users of financial statements to evaluate the effect or potential effect, including rights of setoff associated with recognized financial assets and recognized financial liabilities, of netting arrangements on its financial position
2. The following quantitative information:
   a. Gross amounts of those recognized financial assets and recognized financial liabilities
   b. Amounts offset to determine the net amount presented in the statement of financial position
   c. Net amounts presented in the statement of financial position
   d. Amounts subject to enforceable master netting arrangements or similar agreements not otherwise included in (*b*) (for example, that do not meet the offsetting criteria in the relevant standards), including amounts related to financial collateral
   e. Net amount after deducting amounts in (*d*) from amounts in (*c*)

Accordingly, an entity should

- present this required quantitative information in a tabular format, separately for assets and liabilities, unless another format is more appropriate. The total is limited to the net amount presented in the statement of financial position.

- include a description of the rights of setoff associated with the recognized financial assets and financial liabilities subject to master netting arrangements and similar agreements, including the nature of those rights.
- cross-reference note disclosures when it includes this information in more than one note.

IFRSs

8.36 IFRS 7 applies to all financial instruments not excluded from the scope of IAS 32, except instruments required to be classified as equity instruments in accordance with paragraph 16(A)–(D) of IAS 32. The standard also applies to share-based payment contracts that are within the scope of IAS 39, rather than IFRS 2.

8.37 IFRS 7 requires certain disclosures by class of financial instrument. A class of instrument is different from the IAS 39 categories previously discussed (for example, HTM or FVTPL). A *class of instrument* is a grouping of instruments that is appropriate to the information disclosed (for example, corporate bonds). Instruments in the same class may be included in different categories depending on the entity's intentions. For example, an entity may designate a particular bond at FVTPL and classify all other bond investments as AFS while considering all bonds to be a class of financial assets. IFRS 7 requires entities to provide sufficient detail so users can reconcile the information in the note disclosures to the amounts on the balance sheet.

8.38 Entities should separately disclose the amounts of financial assets and the amounts of financial liabilities in each IAS 39 category. When financial assets or financial liabilities are designated at FVTPL, entities should disclose additional information. When a loan or receivable or financial liability is classified at FVTPL, an entity should disclose information about various risks, including changes in fair value due to changes in credit risk, changes in market conditions that give rise to market risk (such as, changes in interest rates), and the methods used to determine these effects.

8.39 Entities should also disclose additional information about any reclassifications during the period, including the amounts reclassified, carrying amounts and fair values, and amounts that would have been recognized in profit or loss if they had not reclassified the instrument.

8.40 When an entity has transferred financial assets that did not qualify for derecognition, it should disclose the nature of these assets, the nature of the risks and rewards to which it remains exposed, the carrying amount of the recognized assets, and the amount of the original assets when the remaining balance sheet measurement relates only to its continuing involvement.

8.41 With respect to the balance sheet, entities should also disclose information about collateral, allowances for credit losses, defaults, and breaches.

8.42 With respect to the statement of comprehensive income, entities should separately disclose net gains or losses recognized for each IAS 39 category of financial assets and liabilities, total interest income, total interest expense on instruments not held at FVTPL, fee income and expense separately for instruments not held at FVTPL, trust and fiduciary activities, interest income on impaired financial assets, and the amount of any impairment losses for each class of financial asset.

8.43 Entities should disclose their accounting policies in accordance with IAS 1, including the measurement bases applied.

8.44 With respect to hedge accounting, entities should disclose descriptions of the hedge and the hedging instruments used with fair values and the nature of the risks hedged, separately, for fair value hedges, cash flow hedges, and hedges of net investments. IAS 39 requires additional disclosures for each type of hedge. In addition, for each class of financial asset and financial liability, an entity should disclose the fair value of the class in such a way that it can be compared with the carrying amounts of these classes.

8.45 An entity should disclose the fair value of each class of financial asset and liability and the methods, valuation techniques (if any), and assumptions used in determining fair value, except when the financial instrument
- has a carrying amount that approximates fair value,
- is held at cost under IAS 39 because its fair value cannot be measured reliably, or
- contains a discretionary feature and the fair value of that feature cannot be measured reliably.

In providing these disclosures, the entity should also classify fair value measurements using the following fair value hierarchy:
- *Level 1*: Fair values obtained from quoted prices (unadjusted) in active markets for identical assets or liabilities.
- *Level 2*: Fair values obtained using inputs other than quoted prices included within level 1 that are observable for the asset or liability, either directly or indirectly.
- *Level 3*: Fair values are obtained using inputs for the asset or liability that are not based on observable market data.

For fair value measurements disclosed in the balance sheet, the entity should disclose the relevant level in this hierarchy, disclose and explain any significant transfers between levels 1 and 2, and reconcile the beginning and ending balances in the balance sheet account for level 3 measurements. For level 3 measurements, the entity should disclose the sensitivity of the measurement to changes in inputs and how this change was calculated.

8.46 Entities should also disclose both qualitative and quantitative information about the nature and extent of their risk exposure arising from financial instruments. These risks include, but IAS 39 does not limit these risks to, credit risk, liquidity risk, and market risk. Entities should provide both qualitative and quantitative disclosures about these risks. *Qualitative disclosures* include the entity's objective, policies, and processes used to manage that particular risk and any changes from the prior period. Entities should base *quantitative disclosures* on the information provided internally to management (for example, the board of directors). Entities should disclose when the required information is not provided because the effect is not material and should discuss concentrations of risk not apparent from the other disclosures provided. IAS 39 also requires sensitivity analysis for market risks.

8.47 Entities should also disclose any additional information required by IAS 1.

U.S. GAAP

8.48 FASB ASC 825-10-50-14 does not require entities to disclose fair value information for trade receivables and payables when their carrying amounts approximate fair value.

8.49 FASB ASC 825-10-50 requires all entities to disclose the following general information about financial instruments:

- Fair value
- Concentrations of credit risk
- Market risk

In addition, FASB ASC 825-10-50 requires additional disclosures about fair values, regardless of whether the entity recognized the instruments in the statement of financial position, except for the following exceptions noted in FASB ASC 825-10-50-8:

- Employer and plan obligations for postretirement benefits
- Substantively extinguished debt
- Insurance contracts and other financial guarantee and investment contracts
- Lease contracts
- Warranty obligations
- Unconditional purchase obligations
- Equity method investments, noncontrolling interests, and equity investments in consolidated subsidiaries
- Equity instruments issued by the entity and classified as stockholders' equity

All of these instruments are excluded from the scope of the required fair value disclosures for financial instruments within FASB ASC.

8.50 Similar to IFRSs, FASB ASC 825-10-50-10 states that entities should disclose, either on the face of the relevant financial statement or in the notes, the following information about fair values of financial instruments for which it is practicable to estimate that value:

- Methods and significant assumptions used to estimate fair value
- Description of changes in these methods or assumptions, if any, during the period

When information is presented in the notes FASB ASC 825-10-50-11 requires entities to include both the carrying amounts and fair values, clearly indicate whether these amounts represent assets or liabilities, and explain how the carrying amounts relate to the amounts reported in the balance sheet. Unlike IFRSs, if information is dispersed in several notes, FASB ASC 825-10-50-12 requires an entity to provide a summary table with the fair values and related carrying amounts with cross references to the related notes where users can find the additional information.

8.51 In disclosing the fair value of a financial instrument, under FASB ASC 825-10-50-15, an entity should not net that fair value with the fair value of other financial instruments, even if those financial instruments are of the same class or otherwise considered to be related, except to the extent that the offsetting of carrying amounts in the statement of financial position is permitted under the general principle for offsetting (as previously described in paragraph 8.35)

or under the exceptions for master netting arrangements in FASB ASC 815-10-45-5 and for amounts related to certain repurchase and reverse repurchase agreements in paragraphs 11–17 of FASB ASC 210-20-45. This contrasts with IFRSs in which a master netting arrangement is not an exception to the general prohibition against offsetting and the assets and liabilities within the agreement should meet the necessary terms and conditions to be shown net.

8.52 When it is not practicable for an entity to estimate the fair value, FASB ASC 825-10-50-16 requires an entity to explain why it is not practicable and to disclose information pertinent to estimating the fair value of the financial instrument or class (such as the carrying amount, effective interest rate, and maturity). When it is practicable to estimate fair value for only a subset of a class of financial instruments, FASB ASC 825-10-50-19 requires the entity to estimate and disclose fair value for that subset.

8.53 Like IFRSs, FASB ASC 825-10-50 requires an entity to disclose information about risk exposures, specifically credit risk, and to provide certain quantitative and qualitative information. FASB ASC 825-10-50-23 encourages, but does not require, an entity to disclose quantitative information about the market risk of financial instruments. Like IFRSs, FASB ASC 815, *Derivatives and Hedging*, requires disclosures about the use of derivatives and hedging activities, with specific disclosure for each type of hedge. These disclosures are supplemented for Securities and Exchange Commission (SEC) registrants by those required by Item 305 of SEC Regulation S-K. However, unlike IFRSs, Item 305 only requires SEC registrants to provide these disclosures outside the financial statements (for example, in the management discussion and analysis).

TABLE 8-1: TYPE OF FINANCIAL INSTRUMENTS

Categories of Financial Instruments	2011	2010	2009
Cash	175	170	160
Loans and receivables	175	170	160
Available-for-sale financial assets	105	114	111
Held-to-maturity financial assets (measured at amortized cost)	37	36	29
Financial assets measured at fair value through profit or loss			
Derivatives	101	105	101
Nonderivatives (including those classified as held-for-trading)	79	71	70
Derivatives designated as hedges	76	90	82
Trade payables	163	158	147
Financial liabilities measured at amortized cost	167	159	150
Financial liabilities measured at fair value through profit or loss			
Derivatives	107	35	114
Nonderivatives (including those classified as held-for-trading)	51	117	37
Derivatives designated as hedges	84	90	94

Presentation and Disclosure Excerpts

Early Adoption of IFRS 9—First-Time Adoption of IFRS

8.54

Fairfax Financial Holdings Limited (Dec 2011)

Author's Note

Fairfax Financial Holdings Limited implemented IFRSs effective December 31, 2011, with a date of transition of January 1, 2010. The excerpt that follows reflects both the early application of IFRS 9 and the initial application of IFRSs.

CONSOLIDATED BALANCE SHEETS (in part)

As at December 31, 2011, December 31, 2010 and January 1, 2010

(US$ Millions)	Notes	December 31, 2011	December 31, 2010	January 1, 2010
Assets				
Holding company cash and investments (including assets pledged for short sale and derivative obligations—$249.0; December 31, 2010—$137.4; January 1, 2010—$78.9)	5, 28	1,026.7	1,540.7	1,251.6
Portfolio investments				
Subsidiary cash and short term investments	5, 28	6,199.2	3,513.9	3,244.8
Bonds (cost $9,515.4; December 31, 2010—$11,456.9; January 1, 2010—$10,516.2)	5	10,835.2	11,748.2	10,918.3
Preferred stocks (cost $555.6; December 31, 2010—$567.6; January 1, 2010—$273.0)	5	563.3	583.9	292.8
Common stocks (cost $3,867.3; December 31, 2010—$3,198.0; January 1, 2010—$4,081.1)	5	3,663.1	4,133.3	4,893.2
Investments in associates (fair value $1,271.8; December 31, 2010—$976.9; January 1, 2010—$604.3)	5, 6	924.3	707.9	423.7
Derivatives and other invested assets (cost $511.4; December 31, 2010—$403.9; January 1, 2010—$122.5)	5, 7	394.6	579.4	142.7
Assets pledged for short sale and derivative obligations (cost $810.1; December 31, 2010—$698.3; January 1, 2010—$138.3)	5, 7	886.3	709.6	151.5
		23,466.0	21,976.2	20,067.0
Liabilities				
Subsidiary indebtedness	15	1.0	2.2	12.1
Accounts payable and accrued liabilities	14	1,656.2	1,263.1	1,290.8
Income taxes payable	18	21.4	31.7	77.6
Short sale and derivative obligations (including at the holding company—$63.9; December 31, 2010—$66.5; January 1, 2010—$8.9)	5, 7	170.2	216.9	57.2
Long term debt	15	3,017.5	2,726.9	2,301.2

CONSOLIDATED STATEMENTS OF EARNINGS
(in part)

For the years ended December 31, 2011 and 2010

(US$ Millions Except Per Share Amounts)	Notes	2011	2010
Revenue			
Interest and dividends	5	705.3	711.5
Share of profit of associates	5	1.8	46.0
Net gains (losses) on investments	5	691.2	(3.0)
Expenses			
Interest expense		214.0	195.5

CONSOLIDATED STATEMENTS OF COMPREHENSIVE INCOME (in part)

For the years ended December 31, 2011 and 2010

(US$ Millions)	Notes	2011	2010
Net earnings		47.8	338.0
Other comprehensive income (loss), net of income taxes			
Change in unrealized foreign currency translation gains (losses) on foreign operations[1]		(40.8)	121.0
Change in gains and losses on hedge of net investment in foreign subsidiary[2]	7	33.2	(28.2)

[1] Net of income tax expense of $9.0 (2010—$11.5).
[2] Net of income tax recovery of nil (2010—nil).

NOTES TO THE CONSOLIDATED FINANCIAL STATEMENTS (in part)

(In US$ and $ millions except per share amounts and as otherwise indicated)

1. Business Operations

Fairfax Financial Holdings Limited ("the company" or "Fairfax") is a financial services holding company which, through its subsidiaries, is principally engaged in property and casualty insurance and reinsurance and the associated investment management. The holding company is federally incorporated and domiciled in Ontario, Canada.

These consolidated financial statements were approved for issue by the company's Board of Directors on March 9, 2012.

2. Basis of Presentation

The consolidated financial statements of the company for the year ended December 31, 2011 represent the first annual financial statements of the company prepared in accordance with International Financial Reporting Standards ("IFRS") as issued by the International Accounting Standards Board ("IASB"). The accounting policies used to prepare the consolidated financial statements comply with IFRS effective as at December 31, 2011 (except IFRS 9 which was early adopted as described in note 30). Where IFRS does not contain clear guidance governing the accounting treatment of certain transactions including those that are specific to insurance products, IFRS requires judgment in developing and applying an accounting policy, which may include reference to another comprehensive body of accounting principles. In these cases, the company considers the hierarchy of guid-

ance in International Accounting Standard 8 *Accounting Policies, Changes in Accounting Estimates and Errors* and may refer to accounting principles generally accepted in the United States ("US GAAP"). The consolidated financial statements have been prepared on a historical cost basis, except for derivative financial instruments and as at fair value through profit and loss ("FVTPL") financial assets and liabilities that have been measured at fair value.

The preparation of consolidated financial statements in accordance with IFRS requires management to make estimates and assumptions that affect the reported amounts of assets and liabilities at the date of the consolidated financial statements, the reported amounts of revenue and expenses during the reporting periods covered by the consolidated financial statements and the related disclosures. Critical accounting estimates and judgments are described in note 4.

As a financial services holding company, the consolidated balance sheet is presented on a non-classified basis. Assets expected to be realized and liabilities expected to be settled within the company's normal operating cycle of one year would typically be considered as current, including the following balances: cash, short term investments, insurance contract receivables, deferred premium acquisition costs, subsidiary indebtedness, income taxes payable, and short sale and derivative obligations.

The following balances are generally considered as non-current: deferred income taxes and goodwill and intangible assets.

The following balances are generally comprised of current and non-current amounts: bonds, preferred and common stocks, derivatives and other invested assets, recoverable from reinsurers, other assets, accounts payable and accrued liabilities, funds withheld payable to reinsurers, insurance contract liabilities and long term debt.

The company adopted IFRS in accordance with International Financial Reporting Standard 1 *First-time Adoption of International Financial Reporting Standards.* Reconciliations and explanations of the impact of the transition from Canadian Generally Accepted Accounting Principles ("Canadian GAAP") to IFRS as at January 1, 2010 on the financial position and financial results of the company for the year ended December 31, 2010 are provided in note 30. In these consolidated financial statements the term 'Canadian GAAP' refers to Canadian GAAP before the adoption of IFRS.

3. Summary of Significant Accounting Policies

The principal accounting policies applied to the presentation of these consolidated financial statements are set out below. These policies have been consistently applied to all periods presented unless otherwise stated.

Investments

Investments include cash and cash equivalents, short term investments, non-derivative financial assets, derivatives, real estate held for investment and investments in associates. Management determines the appropriate classifications of investments in fixed income and equity securities at their acquisition date.

Classification of non-derivative financial assets— Investments in equity instruments and those debt instruments that do not meet the criteria for amortized cost (see below) are classified as at fair value through profit or loss ("FVTPL"). Financial assets classified as at FVTPL are carried at fair value on the consolidated balance sheet with realized and unrealized gains and losses recorded in net gains (losses) on investments in the consolidated statement of earnings and as an operating activity in the consolidated statement of cash flows. Dividends and interest earned, net of interest incurred are included in the consolidated statement of earnings in interest and dividends and as an operating activity in the consolidated statement of cash flows except for interest income from mortgage backed securities. Interest income from mortgage backed securities is included in net gains (losses) on investments in the consolidated statement of earnings and as an operating activity in the consolidated statement of cash flows.

A debt instrument is measured at amortized cost if (i) the objective of the company's business model is to hold the instrument in order to collect contractual cash flows and (ii) the contractual terms of the instrument give rise on specified dates to cash flows that are solely payments of principal and interest on the principal amount outstanding. Alternatively, debt instruments that meet the criteria for amortized cost may be designated as at FVTPL on initial recognition if doing so eliminates or significantly reduces an accounting mismatch. The company's business model currently does not permit any of its investments in debt instruments to be measured at amortized cost.

Investments in equity instruments that are not held for trading may be irrevocably designated at fair value through other comprehensive income ("FVTOCI") on initial recognition. The company has not designated any of its equity instruments at FVTOCI.

*Recognition and measurement of non-derivative financial assets—*The company recognizes purchases and sales of financial assets on the trade date, which is the date on which the company commits to purchase or sell the asset. Trans-actions pending settlement are reflected in the consolidated balance sheet in other assets or in accounts payable and accrued liabilities.

Transaction costs related to financial assets classified or designated as at FVTPL are expensed as incurred.

A financial asset is derecognized when the rights to receive cash flows from the investment have expired or have been transferred and when the company has transferred substantially the risks and rewards of ownership of the asset.

*Determination of fair value—*Fair values for substantially all of the company's financial instruments are measured using market or income approaches. Considerable judgment may be required in interpreting market data used to develop the estimates of fair value. Accordingly, actual values realized in future market transactions may differ from the estimates presented in these consolidated financial statements. The use of different market assumptions and/or estimation methodologies may have a material effect on the estimated fair values. The fair values of financial instruments are based on bid prices for financial assets and ask prices for financial liabilities. The company categorizes its fair value measurements according to a three level hierarchy described below:

Level 1—Inputs represent unadjusted quoted prices for identical instruments exchanged in active markets. The fair values of the majority of the company's common stocks, equity call options and certain warrants are based on published quotes in active markets.

Level 2—Inputs include directly or indirectly observable inputs (other than Level 1 inputs) such as quoted prices for similar financial instruments exchanged in active markets, quoted prices for identical or similar financial instruments exchanged in inactive markets and other market observable inputs. The fair value of the majority of the company's investments in bonds, derivative contracts (total return swaps and credit default swaps) and certain warrants are based on third party broker-dealer quotes.

The fair values of investments in certain limited partnerships classified as common stocks on the consolidated balance sheet are based on the net asset values received from the general partner, adjusted for liquidity as required and are classified as Level 2 when they may be liquidated or redeemed within three months or less of providing notice to the general partner. Otherwise, investments in limited partnerships are classified as Level 3 within the fair value hierarchy.

Level 3—Inputs include unobservable inputs used in the measurement of financial instruments. Management is required to use its own assumptions regarding unobservable inputs as there is little, if any, market activity in these instruments or related observable inputs that can be corroborated at the measurement date. Investments in consumer price indices ("CPI") linked derivatives are classified as Level 3 within the company's fair value hierarchy.

Transfers between fair value hierarchy categories are considered effective from the beginning of the reporting period in which the transfer is identified.

The reasonableness of pricing received from third party broker-dealers and independent pricing service providers is assessed by comparing the fair values received to recent transaction prices for similar assets where available, to industry accepted discounted cash flow models (that incorporate estimates of the amount and timing of future cash flows and market observable inputs such as credit spreads and discount rates) and to option pricing models (that incorporate market observable inputs including the quoted price, volatility and dividend yield of the underlying security and the risk free rate).

Short term investments—Short term investments are investments with maturity dates between three months and twelve months when purchased. Short term investments are classified as at FVTPL and their carrying values approximate fair value.

Accounts Receivable and Accounts Payable

Accounts receivable and accounts payable are recognized initially at fair value. Due to their short-term nature, carrying value is considered to approximate fair value.

Securities Sold Short and Derivative Financial Instruments

Securities sold short—Securities sold short represent obligations to deliver securities which were not owned at the time of the sale. These obligations are carried at fair value with changes in fair value recorded in net gains (losses) on investments where fair value is determined based on Level 1 inputs (described above).

Derivative financial instruments—Derivative financial instruments may include interest rate, credit default, currency and total return swaps, CPI-linked, futures, forwards, warrants and option contracts all of which derive their value mainly from changes in underlying interest rates, foreign exchange rates, credit ratings, commodity values or equity instruments. A derivative contract may be traded on an exchange or over-the-counter ("OTC"). Exchange-traded derivatives are standardized and include futures and certain warrants and option contracts. OTC derivative contracts are individually negotiated between contracting parties and may include the company's forwards, CPI-linked derivatives and swaps.

The company uses derivatives principally to mitigate financial risks arising from its investment holdings and reinsurance recoverables. Derivatives that are not specifically designated or that do not meet the requirements for hedge accounting are carried at fair value on the consolidated balance sheet with changes in fair value recorded in net gains (losses) on investments in the consolidated statement of earnings and as an operating activity in the consolidated statement of cash flows. Derivatives are monitored by the company for effectiveness in achieving their risk management objectives. The determination of fair value for the company's derivative financial instruments where quoted market prices in active markets are unavailable is described in the "Investments" section above. The company has not designated any financial assets or liabilities (including derivatives) as accounting hedges except for the hedge of its net investment in Northbridge as described in note 7.

The fair value of derivatives in a gain position is presented on the consolidated balance sheet in derivatives and other invested assets in portfolio investments and in cash and investments of the holding company. The fair value of derivatives in a loss position and obligations to purchase securities sold short, if any, are presented on the consolidated balance sheet in short sale and derivative obligations. The initial premium paid for a derivative contract, if any, would be recorded as a derivative asset and subsequently adjusted for changes in the market value of the contract at each balance sheet date. Changes in the market value of a contract are recorded as net

gains (losses) on investments in the consolidated statement of earnings at each balance sheet date, with a corresponding adjustment to the carrying value of the derivative asset or liability.

The fair value of the majority of the company's equity call options and certain warrants are based on published quotes in an active market considered to be Level 1 inputs. The fair value of the majority of the company's derivative contracts and certain warrants are based on third party broker-dealer quotes considered to be Level 2 inputs. Included in Level 3 are investments in CPI-linked derivatives that are valued using broker-dealer quotes which management has determined utilize market observable inputs except for the inflation volatility input which is not market observable.

Cash collateral received from or paid to counterparties as security for derivative contract assets or liabilities respectively is included in liabilities or assets on the consolidated balance sheet. Securities received from counterparties as collateral are not recorded as assets. Securities delivered to counterparties as collateral continue to be reflected as assets on the consolidated balance sheet as assets pledged for short sale and derivative obligations.

Equity contracts—The company's long equity total return swaps allow the company to receive the total return on a notional amount of an equity index or individual equity security (including dividends and capital gains or losses) in exchange for the payment of a floating rate of interest on the notional amount. Conversely, short equity total return swaps allow the company to pay the total return on a notional amount of an equity index or individual equity security in exchange for the receipt of a floating rate of interest on the notional amount. The company classifies dividends and interest paid or received related to its long and short equity total return swaps on a net basis as derivatives and other in interest and dividends in the consolidated statement of earnings. The company's equity and equity index total return swaps contain contractual reset provisions requiring counterparties to cash-settle on a monthly or quarterly basis any market value movements arising subsequent to the prior settlement. Any cash amounts paid to settle unfavourable market value changes and, conversely, any cash amounts received in settlement of favourable market value changes, are recorded as net gains (losses) on investments in the consolidated statement of earnings. To the extent that a contractual reset date of a contract does not correspond to the balance sheet date, the company records net gains (losses) on investments in the consolidated statement of earnings to adjust the carrying value of the derivative asset or liability associated with each total return swap contract to reflect its fair value at the balance sheet date. Final cash settlements of total return swaps are recognized as net gains (losses) on investments net of any previously recorded unrealized market value changes since the last quarterly reset date. Total return swaps require no initial net investment and at inception, their fair value is zero.

Credit contracts—The initial premium paid for a credit contract is recorded as a derivative asset and is subsequently adjusted for changes in the unrealized fair value of the contract at each balance sheet date. Changes in the unrealized fair value of a contract are recorded as net gains (losses) on investments in the consolidated statement of earnings at each balance sheet date, with a corresponding adjustment to the carrying value of the derivative asset. As the average remaining life of a contract declines, the fair value of the contract (excluding the impact of credit spreads) will generally decline.

CPI-linked contracts—The initial premium paid for a CPI-linked contract is recorded as a derivative asset and is subsequently adjusted for changes in the unrealized fair value of the contract at each balance sheet date. Changes in the unrealized fair value of a contract are recorded as net gains (losses) on investments in the consolidated statement of earnings at each balance sheet date, with a corresponding adjustment to the carrying value of the derivative asset. As the average remaining life of a contract declines, the fair value of the contract (excluding the impact of changes in the underlying CPI) will generally decline. The reasonableness of the fair values of CPI-linked derivative contracts are assessed by comparing the fair values received from broker-dealers to values determined using option pricing models that incorporate market observable and unobservable inputs such as the current value of the relevant CPI index underlying the derivative, the inflation swap rate, nominal swap rate and inflation volatility and by comparing to recent market transactions where available. The fair values of CPI-linked derivative contracts are sensitive to assumptions such as market expectations of future rates of inflation and related inflation volatilities.

5. Cash and Investments

Cash and short term investments, portfolio investments and short sale and derivative obligations are classified as at FVTPL, except for investments in associates and other invested assets which are classified as other, and are shown in the table below:

	December 31, 2011	December 31, 2010	January 1, 2010
Holding Company:			
Cash and cash equivalents (note 28)	43.5	337.3	115.4
Short term investments	244.0	111.3	256.0
Cash and cash equivalents pledged for short sale and derivative obligations	—	—	24.5
Short term investments pledged for short sale and derivative obligations	249.0	137.4	54.4
Bonds	188.1	513.5	403.2
Preferred stocks	45.0	43.4	64.8
Common stocks	166.4	343.2	235.8
Derivatives (note 7)	90.7	54.6	97.5
	1,026.7	1,540.7	1,251.6
Short sale and derivative obligations	(63.9)	(66.5)	(8.9)
	962.8	1,474.2	1,242.7
Portfolio Investments:			
Cash and cash equivalents (note 28)	1,995.0	3,022.1	2,093.3
Short term investments	4,204.2	491.8	1,151.5
Bonds	10,835.2	11,748.2	10,918.3
Preferred stocks	563.3	583.9	292.8
Common stocks	3,663.1	4,133.3	4,893.2
Investments in associates (note 6)	924.3	707.9	423.7
Derivatives (note 7)	364.4	547.8	127.7
Other invested assets	30.2	31.6	15.0
	22,579.7	21,266.6	19,915.5
Assets pledged for short sale and derivative obligations:			
Cash and cash equivalents (note 28)	6.2	14.6	—
Short term investments	132.5	—	4.6
Bonds	747.6	695.0	146.9
	886.3	709.6	151.5
	23,466.0	21,976.2	20,067.0
Short sale and derivative obligations	(106.3)	(150.4)	(48.3)
	23,359.7	21,825.8	20,018.7

Common stocks include investments in certain limited partnerships with a carrying value of $321.2 at December 31, 2011 ($265.3 at December 31, 2010, $134.0 at January 1, 2010).

Restricted cash and cash equivalents at December 31, 2011 of $134.7 ($98.9 at December 31, 2010, $76.3 at January 1, 2010) was comprised primarily of amounts required to be maintained on deposit with various regulatory authorities to support the subsidiaries' insurance and reinsurance operations. Restricted cash and cash equivalents are included in the consolidated balance sheets in holding company cash and investments, or in subsidiary cash and short term investments and assets pledged for short sale and derivative obligations in portfolio investments.

The company's subsidiaries have pledged cash and investments, inclusive of trust funds and regulatory deposits, as security for their own obligations to pay claims or make premium payments (these pledges are either direct or to support letters of credit). In order to write insurance business in certain jurisdictions (primarily U.S. states) the company's subsidiaries must deposit funds with local insurance regulatory authorities to provide security for future claims payments as ultimate protection for the policyholder. Additionally, some of the company's subsidiaries provide reinsurance to primary insurers, for which funds must be posted as security for losses that have been incurred but not yet paid. These pledges are in the normal course of business and are generally released when the payment obligation is fulfilled.

The table that follows summarizes pledged assets (excluding assets pledged in favour of Lloyd's) by the nature of the pledge requirement:

	December 31, 2011	December 31, 2010	January 1, 2010
Regulatory deposits	2,171.3	1,779.5	1,424.9
Security for reinsurance and other	722.4	889.4	794.3
	2,893.7	2,668.9	2,219.2

Fixed Income Maturity Profile

Bonds are summarized by the earliest contractual maturity date in the table below. Actual maturities may differ from maturities shown below due to the existence of call and put features. At December 31, 2011, securities containing call and put features represented approximately $6,032.3 and $1,069.9 respectively ($5,444.0 and $1,286.0 at December 31, 2010 respectively) of the total fair value of bonds in the table below.

	December 31, 2011		December 31, 2010	
	Amortized Cost	Fair Value	Amortized Cost	Fair Value
Due in 1 year or less	442.5	413.7	555.4	525.1
Due after 1 year through 5 years	2,288.5	2,505.0	1,618.0	1,809.3
Due after 5 years through 10 years	3,884.5	4,446.4	4,870.1	5,223.6
Due after 10 years	3,751.0	4,405.8	5,596.6	5,398.7
	10,366.5	11,770.9	12,640.1	12,956.7
Effective interest rate		6.2%		5.7%

The calculation of the effective interest rate of 6.2% (December 31, 2010—5.7%) is on a pre-tax basis and does not give effect to the favourable tax treatment which the company expects to receive with respect to its tax advantaged bond investments of approximately $4.9 billion ($4.4 billion at December 31, 2010) included in U.S. states and municipalities.

Fair Value Disclosures

The company's use of quoted market prices (Level 1), valuation models using observable market information as inputs (Level 2) and valuation models without observable market information as inputs (Level 3) in the valuation of securities and derivative contracts were by type of issuers as follows:

	December 31, 2011				December 31, 2010			
	Total Fair Value Asset (Liability)	Quoted Prices (Level 1)	Significant Other Observable Inputs (Level 2)	Significant Unobservable Inputs (Level 3)	Total Fair Value Asset (Liability)	Quoted Prices (Level 1)	Significant Other Observable Inputs (Level 2)	Significant Unobservable Inputs (Level 3)
Cash and cash equivalents	2,044.7	2,044.7	—	—	3,374.0	3,374.0	—	—
Short term investments:								
Canadian provincials	408.9	408.9	—	—	88.6	88.6	—	—
U.S. treasury	4,071.0	4,071.0	—	—	364.2	364.2	—	—
Other government	288.0	267.4	20.6	—	252.2	248.6	3.6	—
Corporate and other	61.8	—	61.8	—	35.5	6.3	29.2	—
	4,829.7	4,747.3	82.4	—	740.5	707.7	32.8	—
Bonds:								
Canadian government	21.1	—	21.1	—	393.5	—	393.5	—
Canadian provincials	1,038.7	—	1,038.7	—	1,251.3	—	1,251.3	—
U.S. treasury	2,082.3	—	2,082.3	—	2,824.7	—	2,824.7	—
U.S. states and municipalities	6,201.5	—	6,201.5	—	5,425.6	—	5,425.6	—
Other government	934.7	—	934.7	—	954.6	—	954.6	—
Corporate and other	1,492.6	—	1,432.6	60.0	2,107.0	—	2,045.1	61.9
	11,770.9	—	11,710.9	60.0	12,956.7	—	12,894.8	61.9

(continued)

	December 31, 2011				December 31, 2010			
	Total Fair Value Asset (Liability)	Quoted Prices (Level 1)	Significant Other Observable Inputs (Level 2)	Significant Unobservable Inputs (Level 3)	Total Fair Value Asset (Liability)	Quoted Prices (Level 1)	Significant Other Observable Inputs (Level 2)	Significant Unobservable Inputs (Level 3)
Preferred stocks:								
Canadian	105.5	—	103.5	2.0	134.6	—	134.6	—
U.S.	457.3	—	451.0	6.3	451.0	—	450.7	0.3
Other	45.5	—	45.5	—	41.7	—	41.7	—
	608.3	—	600.0	8.3	627.3	—	627.0	0.3
Common stocks:								
Canadian	711.8	673.3	13.7	24.8	814.8	784.3	14.6	15.9
U.S.	1,785.0	1,507.6	33.8	243.6	2,539.4	2,345.0	47.4	147.0
Other	1,332.7	886.1	290.6	156.0	1,122.3	665.9	324.7	131.7
	3,829.5	3,067.0	338.1	424.4	4,476.5	3,795.2	386.7	294.6
Derivatives and other invested assets[1]	462.3	—	254.1	208.2	609.4	—	280.8	328.6
Short sale and derivative obligations	(170.2)	—	(170.2)	—	(216.9)	—	(216.9)	—
Holding company cash and investments and portfolio investments measured at fair value	23,375.2	9,859.0	12,815.3	700.9	22,567.5	7,876.9	14,005.2	685.4
	100.0%	42.2%	54.8%	3.0%	100.0%	34.9%	62.1%	3.0%

[1] Excluded from these totals are real estate investments of $23.0 ($24.6 at December 31, 2010) which are carried at cost less any accumulated amortization and impairment.

Included in Level 3 are investments in CPI-linked derivatives, certain private placement debt securities and common and preferred shares. CPI-linked derivatives are classified within derivatives and other invested assets on the consolidated balance sheets and are valued using broker-dealer quotes which management has determined utilize market observable inputs except for the inflation volatility input which is not market observable. Private placement debt securities are classified within holding company cash and investments and bonds on the consolidated balance sheets and are valued using industry accepted discounted cash flow and option pricing models that incorporate certain inputs that are not market observable; specifically share price volatility (for convertible se-

curities) and credit spreads of the issuer. Common shares are classified within holding company cash and investments and common stocks on the consolidated balance sheets and include common shares of private companies as well as investments in certain private equity funds and limited partnerships. These investments are valued by third party fund companies using observable inputs where available and unobservable inputs, in conjunction with industry accepted valuation models, where required. In some instances the private equity funds and limited partnerships may require at least three months' notice to liquidate.

A summary of changes in the fair values of Level 3 financial assets measured at fair value on a recurring basis for the years ended December 31 follows:

	2011					2010				
	Bonds	Common Stocks	Preferred Stocks	Derivatives and Other Invested Assets	Total	Bonds	Common Stocks	Preferred Stocks	Derivatives and Other Invested Assets	Total
Balance—January 1	61.9	294.6	0.3	328.6	685.4	47.2	146.2	—	—	193.4
Total net realized and unrealized gains (losses) included in net gains (losses) on investments	(1.2)	38.5	—	(243.0)	(205.7)	32.3	13.0	4.6	(64.6)	(14.7)
Purchases	15.0	146.8	8.0	122.6	292.4	63.9	72.5	100.0	37.1	273.5
Acquisition of Zenith National	—	—	—	—	—	1.0	78.2	0.3	—	79.5
Sales	(15.7)	(55.5)	—	—	(71.2)	(82.5)	(30.3)	—	—	(112.8)
Transfer in (out) of category	—	—	—	—	—	—	15.0	(104.6)	356.1	266.5
Balance—December 31	60.0	424.4	8.3	208.2	700.9	61.9	294.6	0.3	328.6	685.4

Purchases of $292.4 of investments classified as Level 3 within the fair value hierarchy during 2011 were primarily comprised of certain limited partnerships and CPI-linked derivative contracts. Total net realized and unrealized losses of $205.7 during 2011 were primarily comprised of $233.9 of unrealized losses (excluding the effect of foreign exchange) recognized on CPI-linked derivative contracts.

7. Short Sale and Derivative Transactions

The following table summarizes the notional amount and fair value of the company's derivative instruments:

| | December 31, 2011 | | | | December 31, 2010 | | | | January 1, 2010 | | | |
| | | Notional | Fair Value | | | Notional | Fair Value | | | Notional | Fair Value | |
	Cost	Amount	Assets	Liabilities	Cost	Amount	Assets	Liabilities	Cost	Amount	Assets	Liabilities
Equity derivatives:												
Equity index total return swaps—short positions	—	5,517.6	25.8	59.6	—	5,463.3	10.3	133.7	—	1,582.7	9.2	—
Equity total return swaps—short positions	—	1,617.6	68.8	47.7	—	624.5	18.0	28.3	—	232.2	—	1.2
Equity total return swaps—long positions	—	1,363.5	2.4	49.2	—	1,244.3	0.7	8.3	—	214.6	8.7	7.7
Equity call options	—	—	—	—	—	—	—	—	46.2	79.3	46.0	—
Warrants	11.7	44.6	15.9	—	21.6	158.8	171.1	—	10.1	127.5	71.6	—
Credit derivatives:												
Credit default swaps	66.8	3,059.6	49.8	—	70.8	3,499.3	67.2	—	114.8	5,926.2	71.6	—
Warrants	24.3	340.2	50.0	—	16.6	340.2	6.5	—	15.8	340.2	2.8	—
CPI-linked derivative contracts	421.1	46,518.0	208.2	—	302.3	34,182.3	328.6	—	8.8	1,490.7	8.2	—
Foreign exchange forward contracts	—	—	32.9	8.2	—	—	—	25.5	—	—	1.6	48.0
Other derivative contracts	—	—	1.3	5.5	—	—	—	21.1	—	—	5.5	0.3
Total			455.1	170.2			602.4	216.9			225.2	57.2

The company is exposed to significant market risk through its investing activities. Market risk is the risk that the fair value or future cash flows of a financial instrument will fluctuate because of changes in market prices. Market risk is comprised of currency risk, interest rate risk and other price risk. The company's derivative contracts, with limited exceptions, are used for the purpose of managing these risks. Derivative contracts entered into by the company are considered economic hedges and are not designated as hedges for financial reporting purposes.

Equity Contracts

The company holds significant investments in equities and equity-related securities. The market value and the liquidity of these investments are volatile and may vary dramatically either up or down in short periods, and their ultimate value will therefore only be known over the long term or on disposition. Short positions in equity and equity index total return swaps are held primarily to provide protection against significant declines in the value of the company's equities and equity-related securities. As a result of volatility in the equity markets and international credit concerns, the company protected its equity and equity-related holdings against a potential decline in equity markets by way of short positions effected through equity and equity index total return swaps including short positions in certain equities, the Russell 2000 index and the S&P 500 index as set out in the table below.

During 2011, the company increased the net original notional amount of its short equity and equity index total return swaps by $1,332.7. At December 31, 2011, equity hedges represented 104.6% of the company's equity and equity-related holdings (80.2% at December 31, 2010). The excess of the equity hedges over the company's equity and equity-related holdings at December 31, 2011 arose principally as a result of the company's decision in the third quarter of 2011 to fully hedge its equity and equity-related holdings by adding to the notional amount of its short positions in certain equities effected through equity total return swaps and also reflected some non-correlated performance of the company's equity and equity-related holdings in 2011 relative to the performance of the economic equity hedges used to protect those holdings. The company's exposure to basis risk is discussed further in note 24. The company's objective is that the equity hedges be reasonably effective in protecting that proportion of the company's equity and equity-related holdings to which the hedges relate should a significant correction in the market occur; however, due to the lack of a perfect correlation between the hedged items and the hedging items, combined with other market uncertainties, it is not possible to predict the future impact of the company's economic hedging programs related to equity risk. During 2011, the company received net cash of $293.2 (2010—paid net cash of $797.0) in connection with the reset provisions of its short equity and equity index total return swaps. During 2011, the company paid net cash of $22.6 (2010—received net cash of $91.9) to counterparties in connection with the reset provisions of the company's long equity total return swaps.

	December 31, 2011			December 31, 2010		
Underlying Equity Index	Units	Original Notional Amount[1]	Weighted Average Index Value	Units	Original Notional Amount[1]	Weighted Average Index Value
Russell 2000	52,881,400	3,501.9	662.22	51,355,500	3,377.1	657.60
S&P 500	12,120,558	1,299.3	1,071.96	12,120,558	1,299.3	1,071.96

[1] The aggregate notional amounts on the dates that the short positions were first initiated.

As at December 31, 2011, the company had entered into long equity total return swaps on individual equity securities for investment purposes with an original notional amount of $1,280.0 ($1,114.3 at December 31, 2010).

At December 31, 2011, the fair value of the collateral deposited for the benefit of derivative counterparties included in assets pledged for short sale and derivative obligations was $1,135.3 ($847.0 at December 31, 2010), comprised of collateral of $962.6 ($733.2 at December 31, 2010) required to be deposited to enter into such derivative contracts (principally related to total return swaps) and net collateral of $172.7 ($113.8 at December 31, 2010) securing amounts owed to counterparties to the company's derivative contracts arising in respect of changes in the fair values of those derivative contracts since the most recent reset date.

Equity warrants were acquired in conjunction with the company's investment in debt securities of various Canadian companies. At December 31, 2011, the warrants have expiration dates ranging from 2 years to 5 years (2 years to 4 years at December 31, 2010).

Credit Contracts

Since 2003, the company's investments have included credit default swaps referenced to various issuers in the financial services industry as an economic hedge of certain financial and systemic risks. Effective January 1, 2011, the company no longer considers credit default swaps to be an economic hedge of its financial assets. At December 31, 2011, the company's remaining credit default swaps have a weighted average life of 1.3 years (2.4 years at December 31, 2010) and a notional amount and fair value of $3,059.6 ($3,499.3 at December 31, 2010) and $49.8 ($67.2 at December 31, 2010) respectively.

The company holds, for investment purposes, various bond warrants that give the company an option to purchase certain long dated corporate bonds. At December 31, 2011, the warrants have expiration dates averaging 35.1 years (35.8 years at December 31, 2010).

CPI-Linked Derivative Contracts

The company has purchased derivative contracts referenced to consumer price indices ("CPI") in the geographic regions in which it operates, which serve as an economic hedge against the potential adverse financial impact on the company of decreasing price levels. At December 31, 2011, these contracts have a remaining weighted average life of 8.6 years (9.4 years at December 31, 2010) and a notional amount and fair value as shown in the table below. In the event of a sale, expiration or early settlement of any of these contracts, the company would receive the fair value of that contract on the date of the transaction. The company's maximum potential loss on any contract is limited to the original cost of that contract. The following table summarizes the notional amounts and weighted average strike prices of CPI indices underlying the company's CPI-linked derivative contracts:

	December 31, 2011			December 31, 2010		
	Notional Amount		Weighted Average	Notional Amount		Weighted Average
Underlying CPI Index	Original Currency	U.S. Dollars	Strike Price	Original Currency	U.S. Dollars	Strike Price
United States	18,175.0	18,175.0	216.95	16,250.0	16,250.0	216.58
United Kingdom	550.0	854.8	216.01	550.0	861.1	216.01
European Union	20,425.0	26,514.6	109.74	12,725.0	17,071.2	108.83
France	750.0	973.6	120.09	—	—	—
		46,518.0			34,182.3	

During 2011, the company purchased $13,596.7 (2010—$32,670.2) notional amount of CPI-linked derivative contracts at a cost of $122.6 (2010—$291.4) and recorded net mark-to-market losses of $233.9 (2010—mark-to-market gains of $28.1) on positions remaining open at the end of the year.

The CPI-linked derivative contracts are extremely volatile, with the result that their market value and their liquidity may vary dramatically either up or down in short periods, and their ultimate value will therefore only be known upon their disposition or settlement. The company's purchase of these derivative contracts is consistent with its capital management framework designed to protect its capital in the long term. Due to the uncertainty of the market conditions which may exist many years into the future, it is not possible to predict the future impact of this aspect of the company's risk management program.

Foreign Exchange Forward Contracts

A significant portion of the company's business is conducted in currencies other than the U.S. dollar. The company is also exposed to currency rate fluctuations through its equity accounted investments and its net investment in subsidiaries that have a functional currency other than the U.S. dollar. Long and short foreign exchange forward contracts primarily denominated in the Euro, the British pound sterling and the Canadian dollar are used to manage certain foreign currency exposures arising from foreign currency denominated transactions. The contracts have an average term to maturity of less than one year and may be renewed at market rates.

Counterparty Risk

The company endeavours to limit counterparty risk through the terms of agreements negotiated with the counterparties to its derivative contracts. The fair value of the collateral deposited for the benefit of the company at December 31, 2011 consisted of cash of $50.5 ($26.1 at December 31, 2010)

and government securities of $156.8 ($94.4 at December 31, 2010) that may be sold or repledged by the company. The company has recognized the cash collateral within subsidiary cash and short term investments and recognized a corresponding liability within accounts payable and accrued liabilities. The company had not exercised its right to sell or repledge collateral at December 31, 2011. The company's exposure to counterparty risk and the manner in which the company manages counterparty risk are discussed further in note 24.

Hedge of Net Investment in Northbridge

The company has designated the carrying value of Cdn$1,075.0 principal amount of its Canadian dollar denominated unsecured senior notes with a fair value of $1,114.6 (principal amount of Cdn$675.0 with a fair value of $736.2 at December 31, 2010) as a hedge of its net investment in Northbridge for financial reporting purposes. In 2011, the company recognized pre-tax gains of $33.2 (2010—pre-tax losses of $28.2) related to foreign currency movements on the unsecured senior notes in change in gains and losses on hedge of net investment in foreign subsidiary in the consolidated statements of comprehensive income.

14. Accounts Payable and Accrued Liabilities

Accounts payable and accrued liabilities are comprised as follows:

	December 31, 2011	December 31, 2010	January 1, 2010
Payable to reinsurers	409.8	359.1	290.7
Pension and post retirement liabilities	154.1	139.4	138.9
Salaries and employee benefit liabilities	209.8	185.2	187.5
Ceded deferred premium acquisition costs	79.0	47.4	63.7
Accrued legal and professional fees	39.4	39.4	46.0
Accounts payable for securities purchased but not yet settled	23.5	45.4	39.0
Amounts withheld and accrued taxes	64.7	57.9	52.0
Accrued interest expense	35.8	36.4	34.0
Amounts payable to agents and brokers	41.2	38.0	44.6
Accrued commissions	55.2	42.8	40.0
Accrued premium taxes	66.1	56.8	39.5
Other reporting segment payables	63.7	40.4	37.8
Other	413.9	174.9	277.1
	1,656.2	1,263.1	1,290.8
Current	1,008.8	646.0	755.1
Non-current	647.4	617.1	535.7
	1,656.2	1,263.1	1,290.8

15. Subsidiary Indebtedness, Long Term Debt and Credit Facilities

	December 31, 2011			December 31, 2010		
	Principal	Carrying Value[a]	Fair Value[b]	Principal	Carrying Value[a]	Fair Value[b]
Subsidiary indebtedness consists of the following balances:						
Ridley secured revolving term facility:						
Cdn $30.0 or U.S. dollar equivalent at floating rate	—	—	—	1.0	0.9	0.9
U.S. $20.0 at floating rate	1.0	1.0	1.0	1.3	1.3	1.3
	1.0	1.0	1.0	2.3	2.2	2.2
Long term debt consists of the following balances:						
Fairfax unsecured notes:						
7.75% due April 15, 2012[1]	86.3	86.1	87.4	157.3	156.1	165.2
8.25% due October 1, 2015[3]	82.4	82.2	89.4	82.4	82.2	89.0
7.75% due June 15, 2017[1][4]	48.4	46.4	52.5	275.6	261.7	289.4
7.375% due April 15, 2018[3]	144.2	143.9	154.3	144.2	143.8	151.4
7.50% due August 19, 2019 (Cdn $400.0)[5]	392.8	389.2	427.7	402.6	398.5	441.1
7.25% due June 22, 2020 (Cdn $275.0)[2]	270.1	268.0	289.7	276.8	274.4	295.1
5.80% due May 15, 2021[1]	500.0	494.3	467.5	—	—	—
6.40% due May 25, 2021 (Cdn $400.0)[1]	392.8	389.0	397.2	—	—	—
8.30% due April 15, 2026[3]	91.8	91.4	90.9	91.8	91.4	91.8
7.75% due July 15, 2037[3]	91.3	90.1	83.6	91.3	90.0	91.1
TIG Note[2]	201.4	152.7	152.7	201.4	143.8	143.8
Trust preferred securities of subsidiaries[12]	9.1	9.1	8.1	9.1	9.1	7.0
Purchase consideration payable[11]	152.2	152.2	152.2	158.6	158.6	158.6
Long term debt—holding company borrowings	2,462.8	2,394.6	2,453.2	1,891.1	1,809.6	1,923.5
OdysseyRe unsecured senior notes:						
7.65% due November 1, 2013[1][2][6]	182.9	181.7	200.2	218.8	216.4	239.9
6.875% due May 1, 2015[2][7]	125.0	123.7	131.3	125.0	123.3	134.4
Series A, floating rate due March 15, 2021[8]	50.0	49.8	42.2	50.0	49.8	47.3
Series B, floating rate due March 15, 2016[8]	50.0	49.8	47.5	50.0	49.7	48.7
Series C, floating rate due December 15, 2021[9]	40.0	39.8	34.3	40.0	39.8	38.7
Crum & Forster unsecured senior notes:						
7.75% due May 1, 2017[1][2][10]	6.2	5.6	6.5	330.0	306.4	346.5
First Mercury trust preferred securities:						
Trust III, floating rate due December 14, 2036[1]	25.8	25.8	25.8	—	—	—
Trust IV, 8.25% through December 15, 2012, floating rate thereafter, due September 26, 2037[1]	15.6	15.6	15.6	—	—	—
Zenith National redeemable debentures:						
8.55% due August 1, 2028[2]	38.4	38.0	38.0	38.4	38.0	38.0
Advent subordinated notes:						
Floating rate due June 3, 2035	34.0	33.0	28.1	34.0	33.0	32.2
€12.0 million, floating rate due June 3, 2035	15.6	15.1	12.9	16.0	15.5	15.1
Advent unsecured senior notes:						
Floating rate due January 15, 2026	26.0	25.1	26.0	26.0	25.1	26.1
Floating rate due December 15, 2026	20.0	19.4	19.3	20.0	19.4	20.1
Ridley economic development loan at 1% due August 10, 2019	0.6	0.5	0.5	0.7	0.6	0.6
MFXchange, equipment loans at 7.3% due April 1, 2011	—	—	—	0.3	0.3	0.3
Long term debt—subsidiary company borrowings	630.1	622.9	628.2	949.2	917.3	987.9
	3,092.9	3,017.5	3,081.4	2,840.3	2,726.9	2,911.4

[a] Principal net of unamortized issue costs and discounts.
[b] Based principally on market prices, where available, or discounted cash flow models.

Current and non-current portions of long term debt principal
are comprised as follows:

	December 31, 2011	December 31, 2010
Current	90.6	7.1
Non-current	3,002.3	2,833.2
	3,092.9	2,840.3

(1) During 2011, the company or one of its subsidiaries completed the following transactions with respect to its debt:

(a) First Mercury

The company acquired First Mercury on February 9, 2011, pursuant to the transaction described in note 23. At the acquisition date, the company's consolidated balance sheet included the $67.0 carrying value of trust preferred securities issued by First Mercury Capital Trust I, II, III and IV (statutory business trust subsidiaries of First Mercury) in long term debt. These securities are redeemable at First Mercury's option at 100% of the principal amount together with accrued and unpaid interest on any interest payment date on or after the redemption dates as set out in the table below. First Mercury fully and unconditionally guarantees the distributions and redemptions of these trust preferred securities.

Issuer	Issue Date	Interest	Redemption Date
First Mercury Capital Trust I	April 29, 2004	Payable quarterly at three month LIBOR plus 3.75%	On or after April 29, 2009
First Mercury Capital Trust II	May 24, 2004	Payable quarterly at three month LIBOR plus 4.00%	On or after May 24, 2009
First Mercury Capital Trust III	December 14, 2006	Payable quarterly at three month LIBOR plus 3.00%	On or after December 14, 2011
First Mercury Capital Trust IV	September 26, 2007	Payable quarterly at 8.25% fixed through December 15, 2012; three month LIBOR plus 3.30% thereafter	On or after December 15, 2012

On May 15, 2011, First Mercury redeemed for cash all $8.2 principal amount of its outstanding Trust I trust preferred securities due April 2034 for cash consideration of $8.7.

On May 24, 2011, First Mercury redeemed for cash all $12.4 principal amount of its outstanding Trust II trust preferred securities due May 2034 for cash consideration of $13.1.

On May 27, 2011, First Mercury repurchased for cash $5.0 principal amount of its outstanding Trust IV trust preferred securities due September 2037 for cash consideration of $4.9.

(b) Debt and Tender Offerings

On May 9, 2011, the company completed a private placement debt offering of $500.0 principal amount of 5.80% unsecured senior notes due May 15, 2021 at an issue price of $99.646 for net proceeds after discount, commissions and expenses of $493.9. Commissions and expenses of $4.3 were included as part of the carrying value of the debt. The notes are redeemable at the company's option, in whole or in part, at any time at a price equal to the greater of (a) 100% of the principal amount to be redeemed or (b) the sum of the present values of the remaining scheduled payments of principal and interest thereon (exclusive of interest accrued to the date of redemption) discounted to the redemption date on a semi-annual basis at the treasury rate plus 50 basis points, together, in each case, with accrued interest thereon to the date of redemption.

On May 25, 2011, the company completed a public debt offering of Cdn$400.0 principal amount of 6.40% unsecured senior notes due May 25, 2021 at an issue price of $99.592 for net proceeds after discount, commissions and expenses of $405.6 (Cdn$396.0). Commissions and expenses of $2.4 (Cdn$2.4) were included as part of the carrying value of the debt. The notes are redeemable at the company's option, in whole or in part, at any time at the greater of a specified redemption price based upon the then current yield of a Government of Canada bond with a term to maturity equal to the remaining term to May 25, 2021 and par, together, in each case, with accrued and unpaid interest to the date fixed for redemption. The company has designated these senior notes as a hedge of a portion of its net investment in Northbridge.

Pursuant to the tender offer as amended on May 20, 2011 (the "Amended Tender Offer"), the net proceeds of the debt offerings described above were used to purchase for cash the following debt during May and June of 2011:

	Principal Amount	Cash Consideration
Fairfax unsecured senior notes due 2012 ("Fairfax 2012 notes")	71.0	75.6
Fairfax unsecured senior notes due 2017 ("Fairfax 2017 notes")	227.2	252.9
Crum & Foster unsecured senior notes due 2017	323.8	357.8
OdysseyRe unsecured senior notes due 2013 ("OdysseyRe 2013 notes")	35.9	40.8
Total	657.9	727.1

Unsecured senior notes repurchased in connection with the Amended Tender Offer were accounted for as an extinguishment of debt. Accordingly, other expenses during 2011 included a charge of $104.2 recognized on the repurchase of long term debt (including the release of $35.0 of unamortized issue costs and discounts and other transaction costs incurred in connection with the Amended Tender Offer). The principal amount of $657.9 in the table above is net of $7.0, $23.3 and $6.2 aggregate principal amounts of Fairfax 2017, Fairfax 2012, and OdysseyRe 2013 notes respectively, which were owned in Zenith National's investment portfolio prior to being acquired by Fairfax and tendered to the Amended Tender Offer by Zenith National. Similarly, the $727.1 of cash consideration in the table above is net of $39.7 of total consideration paid to Zenith National in connection with the Amended Tender Offer. The notes tendered by Zenith National were eliminated within Fairfax's consolidated financial reporting since the acquisition date of Zenith National.

(continued)

(footnote continued)

(2) During 2010, the company or one of its subsidiaries completed the following transactions with respect to its debt:

(a) During 2010, holders of OdysseyRe's 7.65% senior notes due 2013 and 6.875% senior notes due 2015 and Crum & Forster's 7.75% senior notes due 2017 provided their consent to amend the indentures governing those senior notes to allow OdysseyRe and Crum & Forster to make available to senior note holders certain specified financial information and financial statements in lieu of the reports OdysseyRe and Crum & Forster previously filed with the Securities and Exchange Commission ("SEC"). In exchange for their consent to amend the indentures, OdysseyRe and Crum & Forster paid cash participation payments of $2.7 and $3.3 respectively to the senior note holders which were recorded as a reduction of the carrying value of the senior notes and will be amortized as an adjustment to the effective interest rate on the senior notes through interest expense in the consolidated statements of earnings. Transaction costs of $1.2, comprised of legal and agency fees incurred in connection with the consent solicitations, were recognized as an expense in the consolidated statements of earnings.

(b) On August 17, 2010, in connection with the acquisition of GFIC as described in note 23, TIG issued a non-interest bearing contingent promissory note with an acquisition date fair value of $140.6. The TIG Note is non-interest bearing (except interest of 2% per annum will be payable during periods, if any, when there is an increase in the United States consumer price index of six percentage points or more) and is due following the sixth anniversary of the closing of the GFIC Transaction. The principal amount of the TIG Note will be reduced based on the cumulative adverse development, if any, of GFIC's loss reserves at the sixth anniversary of the closing of the GFIC Transaction. The principal amount will be reduced by 75% of any adverse development up to $100, and by 90% of any adverse development in excess of $100 until the principal amount is nil. The fair value of the TIG Note was determined as the present value of the expected payment at maturity using a discount rate of 6.17% per annum due to the long term nature of this financial instrument. Fairfax has guaranteed TIG's obligations under the TIG Note. Amortization of the discount on the TIG Note is recognized as interest expense in the consolidated statement of earnings.

(c) On June 22, 2010, the company completed a public debt offering of Cdn$275.0 principal amount of 7.25% unsecured senior notes due June 22, 2020, issued at par for net proceeds after commissions and expenses of $267.1 (Cdn$272.5). Commissions and expenses of $2.5 (Cdn$2.5) were included as part of the carrying value of the debt. The notes are redeemable at the company's option, in whole or in part, at any time at the greater of a specified redemption price based on the then current yield of a Government of Canada bond with a term to maturity equal to the remaining term to June 22, 2020 and par. The company has designated these senior notes as a hedge of a portion of its net investment in Northbridge.

(d) Effective May 20, 2010, the company consolidated the assets and liabilities of Zenith National, pursuant to the transaction described in note 23. As a result, the carrying value of $38.0 of redeemable securities issued by a statutory business trust subsidiary of Zenith National, was included in long term debt. These securities mature on August 1, 2028, pay semi-annual cumulative cash distributions at an annual rate of 8.55% of the $1,000 liquidation amount per security and are redeemable at Zenith National's option at any time prior to their stated maturity date at a redemption price of 100% plus the excess of the then present value of the remaining scheduled payments of principal and interest over 100% of the principal amount together with the accrued and unpaid interest. Zenith National fully and unconditionally guarantees the distributions and redemptions of these redeemable securities. On May 26, 2010, holders of the redeemable securities provided their consent to amend the indenture governing these securities to allow Zenith National to make available to the security holders certain specified financial information and financial statements in lieu of the reports Zenith National previously filed with the SEC.

The acquisition of Zenith National resulted in the consolidation of aggregate principal amount of $38.7 and $6.3 of debt securities issued by Fairfax and OdysseyRe respectively, which were recorded in Zenith National's investment portfolio as at FVTPL on the acquisition date. Accordingly, the $47.5 fair value of these debt securities was eliminated against long term debt. As a result, the carrying value of long term debt—holding company borrowings and long term debt—subsidiary company borrowings decreased by $38.0 and $6.3 respectively and the company recorded a pre-tax loss of $3.2 in net gains (losses) on investments in the consolidated statement of earnings.

On September 17, 2010, Zenith National purchased $7.0 principal amount of its redeemable debentures due 2028 for cash consideration of $7.0. On June 9, 2010, Zenith National purchased $13.0 principal amount of its redeemable debentures due 2028 for cash consideration of $13.0.

(3) During 2002, the company closed out the swaps for this debt and deferred the resulting gain which is amortized to earnings over the remaining term to maturity. The unamortized balance at December 31, 2011 is $26.6 ($28.5 at December 31, 2010).

(4) Redeemable at Fairfax's option at any time on or after June 15, 2012, June 15, 2013, June 15, 2014 and June 15, 2015 at $103.9, $102.6, $101.3 and $100.0 per bond, respectively.

(5) Redeemable at Fairfax's option, at any time at the greater of a specified redemption price based upon the then current yield of a Government of Canada bond with a term to maturity equal to the remaining term to August 19, 2019 and par.

(6) Redeemable at OdysseyRe's option at any time at a price equal to the greater of (a) 100% of the principal amount to be redeemed or (b) the sum of the present values of the remaining scheduled payments of principal and interest thereon (exclusive of interest accrued to the date of redemption) discounted to the redemption date on a semi-annual basis at the treasury rate plus 50 basis points, plus, in each case, accrued interest thereon to the date of redemption.

(7) Redeemable at OdysseyRe's option at any time at a price equal to the greater of (a) 100% of the principal amount to be redeemed or (b) the sum of the present values of the remaining scheduled payments of principal and interest thereon (exclusive of interest accrued to the date of redemption) discounted to the redemption date on a semi-annual basis at the treasury rate plus 40 basis points, plus, in each case, accrued interest thereon to the date of redemption.

(8) The Series A and Series B notes are callable by OdysseyRe on any interest payment date on or after March 15, 2011 and March 15, 2009 respectively, at their par value plus accrued and unpaid interest. The interest rate on each series of debenture is equal to three month LIBOR, which is calculated on a quarterly basis, plus 2.20%.

(9) The Series C notes are due in 2021 and are callable by OdysseyRe on any interest payment date on or after December 15, 2011 at their par value plus accrued and unpaid interest. The interest rate is equal to three month LIBOR plus 2.50% and is reset after every payment date.

(10) Redeemable at Crum & Forster's option at any time beginning May 1, 2012 at specified redemption prices.

(11) On December 16, 2002, the company acquired Xerox's 72.5% economic interest in TRG, the holding company of International Insurance Company ("IIC"), in exchange for payments over the next 15 years of $424.4 ($203.9 at December 16, 2002 using a discount rate of 9.0% per annum), payable approximately $5.0 a quarter from 2003 to 2017 and approximately $128.2 on December 16, 2017.

(12) TIG Holdings had issued 8.597% junior subordinated debentures to TIG Capital Trust (a statutory business trust subsidiary of TIG Holdings) which, in turn, has issued 8.597% mandatory redeemable capital securities, maturing in 2027.

IFRS-BPPD 8.54

Consolidated interest expense on long term debt amounted to $213.9 (2010—$195.3). Interest expense on Ridley's indebtedness amounted to $0.1 (2010—$0.2).

Principal repayments on long term debt-holding company borrowings and long term debt-subsidiary company borrowings are due as follows:

2012	90.6
2013	187.4
2014	5.0
2015	212.8
2016	257.4
Thereafter	2,339.7

Credit Facilities

On January 31, 2012, Ridley entered into a three-year revolving credit agreement replacing its recently expired credit facility. Ridley may borrow the lesser of $50.0 or a calculated amount based on the level of eligible trade accounts receivable and inventory. The credit agreement is secured by first-ranking general security agreements covering substantially all of Ridley's assets.

On November 10, 2010, Fairfax entered into a three year $300.0 unsecured revolving credit facility (the "credit facility") with a syndicate of lenders to enhance its financial flexibility. On December 16, 2011, Fairfax extended the term of the credit facility until December 31, 2015. As of December 31, 2011, no amounts had been drawn on the credit facility. In accordance with the terms of the credit facility agreement, Northbridge terminated its five-year unsecured revolving credit facility with a Canadian chartered bank on November 10, 2010.

As at December 31, 2009 and until February 23, 2010, OdysseyRe maintained a five-year $200.0 credit facility with a syndicate of lenders maturing in 2012. As at February 24, 2010, the size of this credit facility was reduced to $100.0 with an option to increase the size of the facility by an amount up to $50.0, to a maximum facility size of $150.0. Following such a request, each lender has the right, but not the obligation, to commit to all or a portion of the proposed increase. As at December 31, 2011, there was $34.3 utilized under this credit facility, all of which was in support of letters of credit.

30. Transition From Canadian GAAP to International Financial Reporting Standards (in part)

Adjustments Upon Adoption of IFRS

IFRS permits exemptions from full retrospective application of certain standards. In preparing these consolidated financial statements in accordance with IFRS, the company has applied the mandatory exceptions and certain of the optional exemptions to full retrospective application of IFRS as at the transition date of January 1, 2010.

Other Measurement Adjustments Between Canadian GAAP and IFRS

(4) Adoption of IFRS 9 Financial Instruments: Classification and Measurement

As permitted by the transition rules for first-time adopters of IFRS, the company has early adopted IFRS 9 *Financial Instruments: Classification and Measurement* ("IFRS 9") effective January 1, 2010. This standard replaces the guidance in IAS 39 *Financial Instruments: Recognition and Measurement* for the classification and measurement of financial assets and liabilities. IFRS 9 eliminates the available for sale and held to maturity categories, and the requirement to bifurcate embedded derivatives with respect to hybrid contracts. Under IFRS 9 hybrid contracts are measured as a whole as at FVTPL. Equity instruments are measured as at FVTPL by default. Fixed income investments are measured at amortized cost if both of the following criteria are met: (i) the financial asset is held within a business model whose objective is to hold financial assets in order to collect contractual cash flows; and (ii) the contractual terms of the financial asset give rise on specified dates to cash flows that are solely payments of principal and interest on the principal outstanding, otherwise fixed income investments are measured as at FVTPL. Under this standard, the company's business model requires that its investment portfolio be primarily measured as at FVTPL.

The effect of adopting IFRS 9 as at January 1, 2010 is to recognize all unrealized gains and losses on financial instruments in accumulated other comprehensive income to retained earnings. The impact on individual financial statement lines is as follows:

Financial Statement Line	As at January 1, 2010 Increase (Decrease)	As at December 31, 2010 Increase (Decrease)
Retained earnings	747.1	611.1
Accumulated other comprehensive income	(747.1)	(611.1)

	For the Year Ended December 31, 2010 Increase (Decrease)
Share of profit (loss) of associates	1.8
Net gains (losses) on investments	(204.9)
Provision for (recovery of) income taxes	(67.1)
Other comprehensive income, net of income taxes	136.0

Financial Assets—Accounts Receivable and Payable and Accounts Receivable and Payable From Related Parties

8.55

GRUMA, S.A.B. de C.V. (Dec 2011)

CONSOLIDATED BALANCE SHEETS (in part)

(In thousands of Mexican pesos)
(Notes 1, 2 and 4)

	Note	As of January 1, 2010	As of December 31, 2010	As of December 31, 2011
Assets				
Current:				
Cash and cash equivalents	7	Ps. 1,880,663	Ps. 21,317	Ps. 1,179,651
Accounts receivable, net	8	5,670,752	5,017,797	7,127,208
Non-current:				
Long-term notes and accounts receivable	10	543,295	598,961	626,874
Liabilities				
Current:				
Short-term debt	15	Ps. 2,203,392	Ps. 2,192,871	Ps. 1,633,207
Trade accounts payable		3,564,372	3,601,829	5,544,105
Other current liabilities	17	2,368,388	2,894,694	2,732,215

NOTES TO THE CONSOLIDATED FINANCIAL STATEMENTS (in part)

(In thousands of Mexican pesos, except where otherwise indicated)

1. Entity and Operations

Gruma, S.A.B. de C.V. (GRUMA) is a Mexican company with subsidiaries located in Mexico, the United States of America, Central America, Venezuela, Europe, Asia and Oceania, together referred to as the "Company." The Company's main activities are the production and sale of corn flour, wheat flour, tortillas and related products.

Gruma, S.A.B. de C.V. is a publicly held corporation (*Sociedad Anónima Bursátil de Capital Variable*) organized under the laws of Mexico. The address of its registered office is Rio de la Plata 407 in San Pedro Garza García, Nuevo León, Mexico.

The consolidated financial statements were authorized by the Chief Corporate Office and the Chief Administrative Office of the Company on April 30, 2012.

2. Basis of Preparation (in part)

The consolidated financial statements of Gruma, S.A.B. de C.V. and Subsidiaries as of December 31, 2011 have been prepared for the first time in accordance with the International Financial Reporting Standards (IFRS) as issued by the International Accounting Standards Board (IASB). The IFRS also include the International Accounting Standards (IAS) in force, as well as all the related interpretations issued by the International Financial Reporting Interpretations Committee (IFRIC), including those previously issued by the Standing Interpretations Committee (SIC).

In accordance with the amendments to the Rules for Public Companies and Other Participants in the Mexican Stock Exchange, issued by the Mexican Banking Securities Exchange Commission on January 27, 2009, the Company is required to prepare its financial statements under IFRS starting in 2012.

The Company decided to adopt IFRS earlier, starting January 1, 2011, therefore, these are the Company's first consolidated financial statements prepared in accordance with IFRS as issued by the IASB.

For comparative purposes, the consolidated financial statements as of and for the year ended December 31, 2010 have been prepared in accordance with IFRS, as required by the IFRS 1—First-Time Adoption of International Financial Reporting Standards.

The Company modified its accounting policies from Mexican Financial Reporting Standards (Mexican FRS) in order to comply with IFRS starting January 1, 2011. The transition from Mexican FRS to IFRS was recognized in accordance with IFRS 1, setting January 1, 2010 as the transition date. The reconciliation of the effects of the transition from Mexican FRS to IFRS in equity as of January 1, 2010 and December 31, 2010, in net income and cash flows for the year ended December 31, 2010 are disclosed in Note 28 to these financial statements.

4. Summary of Significant Accounting Policies (in part)

D) Accounts Receivable

Trade receivables are initially recognized at fair value and subsequently valued at amortized cost using the effective interest rate method, less provision for impairment. The Company has determined that the amortized cost does not represent significant differences with respect to the invoiced amount from short-term trade receivables, since the transactions do not have relevant associated costs.

Allowances for doubtful accounts or impairment represent the Company's estimates of losses that could arise from the failure or inability of customers to make payments when due. These estimates are based on the ageing of customers' balances, specific credit circumstances and the Company's historical bad receivables experience.

K) Financial Instruments (in part)

Regular purchases and sales of financial instruments are recognized in the balance sheet on the trade date, which is the date when the Company commits to purchase or sell the instrument.

a. Financial Assets

Classification

In its initial recognition and based on its nature and characteristics, the Company classifies its financial assets in the following categories: (i) financial assets at fair value through profit or loss, (ii) loans and receivables, (iii) financial assets held until maturity, and (iv) available-for-sale financial assets. The classification depends on the purpose for which the financial assets were acquired.

ii. Loans and Receivables

Loans and receivables are non-derivative financial assets with fixed or determinable payments that are not quoted in an active market. They are included in current assets, except for assets with maturities greater than 12 months. Initially, these assets are carried at fair value plus any transaction costs directly attributable to them; subsequently, these assets are recognized at amortized cost using the effective interest rate method.

b. Debt and Financial Liabilities

Debt and financial liabilities that are non-derivatives are initially recognized at fair value, net of transaction costs directly attributable to them: subsequently, these liabilities are recognized at amortized cost. The difference between the net proceeds and the amount payable is recognized in the income statement during the debt term, using the effective interest rate method.

c. Impairment of Financial Assets

The Company assesses at each reporting date whether there is any objective evidence that a financial asset or a group of financial assets is impaired. A financial asset or a group of financial assets is deemed to be impaired if, and only if, there is objective evidence of impairment as a result of one or more events that have occurred after the initial recognition of the asset (an incurred "loss event") and that loss event has an impact on the estimated future cash flows of the financial asset or the group of financial assets that can be reliably estimated. See Note 4-D for the accounting policy for the impairment of accounts receivable.

5. Risk and Capital Management

Credit Risk

The Company's regular operations expose it to potential defaults when customers, suppliers and counterparties are unable to comply with their financial or other commitments. The Company seeks to mitigate this risk by entering into transactions with a diverse pool of counterparties. However, the Company continues to remain subject to unexpected third party financial failures that could disrupt its operations.

The Company is also exposed to risks in connection with its cash management activities and temporary investments, and any disruption that affects its financial intermediaries could also adversely affect its operations.

The Company's exposure to risk due to trade receivables is limited given the large number of its customers located in different parts of Mexico, the United States, Central America, Venezuela, Europe, Asia and Oceania. However, the Company still maintains reserves for potential credit losses. Risk control assesses the credit quality of the customer, taking into account its financial position, past experience and other factors.

Since a portion of the clients do not have an independent rating of credit quality, the Company's management determines the maximum credit risk for each one, taking into account its financial position, past experience, and other factors. Credit limits are established according to policies set by the Company, which also includes controls that assure its compliance.

During 2010 and 2011, credit limits were complied with and, consequently, management does not expect any important losses from trade accounts receivable.

At December 31, 2011 the Company has certain accounts receivable that are neither past due or impaired. The credit quality of such receivables does not present indications of impairment, since the sales are performed to a large variety of clients that include supermarkets, government institutions, commercial businesses and tortilla sellers. At December 31, 2011, none of these accounts receivable presented non-performance by these counterparties.

The Company has centralized its treasury operations in Mexico, and in the United States for its operations in that country. Liquid assets are invested primarily in government bonds and short term debt instruments with a minimum grade of "A1/P1" in the case of operations in the United States and "A" for operations in Mexico. The Company faces credit risk from potential defaults of their counterparts with respect to financial instruments they use. Substantially all of these financial instruments are not guaranteed. Additionally, it minimizes the risk of default by the counterparts contracting derivative financial instruments only with major national and international financial institutions using contracts and standard forms issued by the International Swaps and Derivatives Association, Inc. ("ISDA") and operations standard confirmation formats. For operations in Central America and Venezuela, the Company only invests cash reserves with leading local banks and local branches of international banks. Additionally, they maintain small investments abroad.

8. Accounts Receivable

Accounts receivable comprised the following:

	At January 1, 2010	At December 31, 2010	At December 31, 2011
Trade accounts and notes receivable	Ps. 4,707,528	Ps. 4,350,763	Ps. 6,434,327
Related parties	500,669	238,289	—
Employees	26,752	17,567	31,628
Recoverable value-added tax	216,737	260,308	368,239
ASERCA receivables (Note 5)	30,518	61,097	321,958
Other debtors	440,484	380,152	287,168
Allowance for doubtful accounts	(251,936)	(290,379)	(316,112)
	Ps. 5,670,752	Ps. 5,017,797	Ps. 7,127,208

The age analysis of accounts receivable is as follows:

			Past Due Balances		
	Total	Not Past Due Date Balances	1 to 120 Days	121 to 240 Days	More Than 240 Days
Accounts receivable	Ps. 5,922,688	Ps. 3,351,286	Ps. 1,599,902	Ps. 339,089	Ps. 632,411
Allowance for doubtful accounts	(251,936)	—	(27,062)	(49,637)	(175,237)
Total at January 1, 2010	Ps. 5,670,752	Ps. 3,351,286	Ps. 1,572,840	Ps. 289,452	Ps. 457,174

			Past Due Balances		
	Total	Not Past Due Date Balances	1 to 120 Days	121 to 240 Days	More Than 240 Days
Accounts receivable	Ps. 5,308,176	Ps. 3,166,147	Ps. 1,571,514	Ps. 116,407	Ps. 454,108
Allowance for doubtful accounts	(290,379)	—	(30,583)	(36,765)	(223,031)
Total at December 31, 2010	Ps. 5,017,797	Ps. 3,166,147	Ps. 1,540,931	Ps. 79,642	Ps. 231,077

			Past Due Balances		
	Total	Not Past Due Date Balances	1 to 120 Days	121 to 240 Days	More Than 240 Days
Accounts receivable	Ps. 7,443,320	Ps. 4,635,346	Ps. 2,174,062	Ps. 255,623	Ps. 378,289
Allowance for doubtful accounts	(316,112)	—	(31,130)	(48,289)	(236,693)
Total at December 31, 2011	Ps. 7,127,208	Ps. 4,635,346	Ps. 2,142,932	Ps. 207,334	Ps. 141,596

For the years ended December 31, 2010 and 2011, the movements on the allowance for doubtful accounts are as follows:

	2010	2011
Beginning balance	Ps. (251,936)	Ps. (290,379)
Allowance for doubtful accounts	(73,976)	(130,885)
Receivables written off during the year	26,232	117,254
Exchange differences	9,301	(12,102)
Ending balance	Ps. (290,379)	Ps. (316,112)

10. Long-Term Notes and Accounts Receivable

Long-term notes and accounts receivable are as follows:

	At January 1, 2010	At December 31, 2010	At December 31, 2011
Long-term recoverable asset tax	Ps. 119,996	Ps. 119,996	Ps. 209,940
Long-term notes receivable from sale of tortilla machines	8,768	175,653	189,044
Prepaid rent deposits	—	124,127	111,396
Guarantee deposits	119,217	118,842	38,827
Long-term recoverable value-added tax	—	—	35,019
Others	295,314	60,343	42,648
	Ps. 543,295	Ps. 598,961	Ps. 626,874

At December 31, 2011 long-term notes receivable are de-nominated in pesos, maturing from 2013 to 2016 and bearing an average interest rate of 16.5%.

20. Financial Instruments (in part)

A) Financial Instruments by Category (in part)

	At December 31, 2011			
	Loans, Receivables and Liabilities at Amortized Cost	Financial Assets at Fair Value Through Profit or Loss	Hedge Derivatives	Total Categories
Financial assets:				
Cash and cash equivalents	Ps. 1,179,651	Ps. —	Ps. —	Ps. 1,179,651
Trading investments	—	140,255	—	140,255
Derivative financial instruments	—	88,537	14,876	103,413
Accounts receivable	7,127,208	—	—	7,127,208
Non-current notes and accounts receivable	515,478	—	—	515,478
Financial liabilities:				
Current debt	Ps. 1,633,207	Ps. —	Ps. —	Ps. 1,633,207
Trade accounts payable and other accounts payable	5,544,105	—	—	5,544,105
Derivative financial instruments	—	46,013	—	46,013
Long-term debt	11,472,110	—	—	11,472,110
Other liabilities (excludes non-financial liabilities)	45,734	—	—	45,734

26. Related Parties (in part)

Related party transactions were carried out at market value.

D) Balances with Related Parties

At January 1, 2010 and at December 31, 2010 and 2011, the balances with related parties were as follows:

	Nature of the Transaction	At January 1, 2010	At December 31, 2010	At December 31, 2011
Receivables from related parties:				
Entities that have significant influence over the entity	Commercial and services	Ps. 500,669	Ps. 238,289	Ps. —
Payables from related parties:				
Entities that have significant influence over the entity	Commercial and services	Ps. 207,559	Ps. 75,999	Ps. 131,772

The balances payable to related parties at December 31, 2011 expired during 2012 and do not bear interest.

Additionally, during 2011 the Company obtained financing for Ps.600 million from a subsidiary of GFNorte, bearing an interest rate of 7.335%.

Financial Assets—Current and Noncurrent Held to Maturity and Available for Sale, Including Amounts Due From a Joint Venture

8.56

CNOOC Limited (Dec 2011)

CONSOLIDATED STATEMENTS OF FINANCIAL POSITION (in part)

(All amounts expressed in millions of Renminbi/US$)

	Notes	2010 RMB Million Note 2.2	2011 RMB Million	2011 US$ Million
Non-Current Assets				
Property, plant and equipment	15	186,678	220,567	35,045
Intangible assets	16	1,148	1,033	164
Investments in associates	17	1,781	2,822	448
Investments in a joint venture	18	20,823	20,175	3,205
Available-for-sale financial assets	19, 33	8,616	7,365	1,170
Other non-current assets		—	379	60
Total non-current assets		219,046	252,341	40,092
Current Assets				
Inventories and supplies	20	3,975	4,380	696
Trade receivables	21	10,311	10,604	1,685
Due from related companies		9,548	10,312	1,638
Held-to-maturity financial assets		3,040	23,467	3,729
Available-for-sale financial assets	19, 33	18,940	27,576	4,381
Other current assets		14,307	7,430	1,181
Time deposits with maturity over three months	22	11,976	24,476	3,889
Cash and cash equivalents	22	27,287	23,678	3,762
Total current assets		99,384	131,923	20,961

CONSOLIDATED STATEMENTS OF COMPREHENSIVE INCOME (in part)

	Notes	2009 RMB Million	2010 RMB Million Note 2.2	2011 RMB Million	2011 US$ Million
Profit from operating activities		40,325	71,145	90,607	14,397
Interest income	8	638	618	1,196	190
Exchange gains, net	8	54	995	637	101
Investment income	8	200	427	1,828	290
Profit before tax	8	40,821	72,603	92,565	14,708
Other comprehensive (loss)/income					
Net (loss)/gain on available-for-sale financial assets, net of tax	19	(74)	5,590	(800)	(127)

NOTES TO THE CONSOLIDATED FINANCIAL STATEMENTS (in part)

3. Summary of Significant Accounting Policies (in part)

Investments and Other Financial Assets

Initial Recognition and Measurement

Financial assets within the scope of IAS 39/HKAS 39 are classified as financial assets at fair value through profit or loss, loans and receivables, held-to-maturity investments, and available-for-sale financial assets, as appropriate. The Group determines the classification of its financial assets at initial recognition. When financial assets are recognized initially, they are measured at fair value plus transaction costs, except in the case of financial assets recorded at fair value through profit or loss.

Purchases or sales of financial assets that require delivery of assets within a time frame established by regulation or convention in the marketplace (regular way purchases or sales) are recognised on the trade date, that is, the date that the Group commits to purchase or sell the asset.

The Group's financial assets include cash and bank balances, trade and other receivables, quoted and unquoted financial instruments, and derivative financial instruments.

Subsequent Measurement (in part)

The subsequent measurement of financial assets depends on their classifications as follows:

(c) Held-to-Maturity Investments

Non-derivative financial assets with fixed or determinable payments and fixed maturity are classified as held to maturity when the Group has the positive intention and ability to hold them to maturity. Held-to-maturity investments are subsequently measured at amortized cost using the effective interest rate method less any allowance for impairment. Amortized cost is calculated by taking into account any discount or premium on acquisition and fees or costs that are an integral part of the effective interest rate. Gains and losses are recognized in profit or loss when the investments are derecognized or impaired, as well as through the amortization process.

(d) Available-for-Sale Financial Assets

Available-for-sale financial assets are non-derivative financial assets in listed and unlisted equity investments and debt securities. Equity investments classified as available for sale are those which are neither classified as held for trading nor designated at fair value through profit or loss. Debt securities in this category are those which are intended to be held for an indefinite period of time and which may be sold in response to needs for liquidity or in response to changes in market conditions.

After initial recognition, available-for-sale financial assets are measured at fair value, with unrealized gains or losses recognized as other comprehensive income in the available-for-sale investment revaluation reserve until the investment is derecognized, at which time the cumulative gain or loss is recognized in profit or loss, or until the investment is determined to be impaired, when the cumulative gain or loss is reclassified from the available-for-sale investment revaluation reserve to profit or loss. Interest and dividends earned whilst holding the available-for-sale financial investments are reported as interest income and dividend income, respectively and are recognized in profit or loss in accordance with the policies set out for "Revenue recognition" below.

When the fair value of unlisted equity investments cannot be reliably measured because (a) the variability in the range of reasonable fair value estimates is significant for that investment or (b) the probabilities of the various estimates within the range cannot be reasonably assessed and used in estimating fair value, such investments are stated at cost less any impairment losses.

Fair Value

The fair value of financial instruments that are traded in active markets at each reporting date is determined by reference to quoted market prices or dealer price quotations, without any deduction for transaction costs.

For financial instruments not traded in an active market, the fair value is determined using appropriate valuation techniques. Such techniques may include using recent arm's length market transactions; reference to the current fair value

of another instrument that is substantially the same; a discounted cash flow analysis or other valuation models.

An analysis of fair values of financial instruments and further details as to how they are measured are provided in note 33.

Impairment of Financial Assets

The Group assesses at each reporting date whether there is any objective evidence that a financial asset or a group of financial assets is impaired.

(a) Assets Carried at Amortized Cost

If there is objective evidence that an impairment loss on loans and receivables or held-to-maturity investments carried at amortized cost has been incurred, the amount of the loss is measured as the difference between the asset's carrying amount and the present value of estimated future cash flows (excluding future credit losses that have not been incurred) discounted at the financial asset's original effective interest rate (the effective interest rate computed at initial recognition). The carrying amount of the asset is reduced either directly or through the use of an allowance account. The amount of the impairment loss is recognized in profit or loss.

If, in a subsequent year, the amount of the estimated impairment loss increases or decreases and the decrease can be related objectively to an event occurring after the impairment was recognized, the previously recognized impairment loss is increased or reduced by adjusting the allowance account. Any subsequent reversal of an impairment loss is recognized in profit or loss, to the extent that the carrying value of the asset does not exceed amortized cost at the reversal date.

In relation to trade and other receivables, a provision for impairment is made when there is objective evidence (such as the probability of insolvency or significant financial difficulties of the debtor and significant changes in the technological, market, economic or legal environment that have an adverse effect on the debtor) that the Group will not be able to collect all of the amounts due under the original terms of an invoice.

(b) Assets Carried at Cost

If there is objective evidence that an impairment loss has been incurred on an unquoted equity instrument that is not carried at fair value because its fair value cannot be reliably measured, the amount of the loss is measured as the difference between the asset's carrying amount and the present value of estimated future cash flows discounted at the current market rate of return for a similar financial asset. Impairment losses on these assets are not reversed.

(c) Available-for-Sale Financial Assets

If an available-for-sale asset is impaired, an amount comprising the difference between its cost (net of any principal payment and amortization) and its current fair value, less any impairment loss previously recognized in the profit or loss, is removed from other comprehensive income and recognized in profit or loss.

Equity investments are impaired if there is a significant or prolonged decline in fair value of the investment below its cost or where other objective evidence of impairment exists. Impairment of debt instruments is assessed based on the same criteria as assets carried at amortised cost. Impairment losses on equity instruments are not reversed through profit or loss; increases in their fair value after impairments are recognised directly in equity. Impairment losses on debt instruments are reversed through the profit or loss, if the increase in fair value of the instruments can be objectively related to an event occurring after the impairment loss was recognized in profit or loss.

Derecognition of Financial Assets

A financial asset (or, where applicable a part of a financial asset or part of a group of similar financial assets) is derecognized where:

i) the rights to receive cash flows from the asset have expired;

ii) the Group retains the rights to receive cash flows from the asset, but has assumed an obligation to pay the received cash flows in full without material delay to a third party under a "pass-through" arrangement; or

iii) the Group has transferred its rights to receive cash flows from the asset and either (a) has transferred substantially all the risks and rewards of the asset, or (b) has neither transferred nor retained substantially all the risks and rewards of the asset, but has transferred control of the asset.

Where the Group has transferred its rights to receive cash flows from an asset and has neither transferred nor retained substantially all the risks and rewards of the asset nor transferred control of the asset, the asset is recognized to the extent of the Group's continuing involvement in the asset. Continuing involvement that takes the form of a guarantee over the transferred asset is measured at the lower of the original carrying amount of the asset and the maximum amount of consideration that the Group could be required to repay.

8. Profit Before Tax

The Group's profit before tax is arrived at after charging/ (crediting):

	2009	2010	2011
Crediting:			
Interest income from bank deposits	(638)	(618)	(1,196)
Exchange gains, net	(54)	(995)	(637)
Investment income:			
—Net gain from available-for-sale financial assets	(200)	(425)	(1,695)
—Net gain from held-to-maturity financial assets	—	(2)	(133)
	(200)	(427)	(1,828)

19. Available-for-Sale Financial Assets

	2010	2011
Current:		
Non-publicly traded investments, at fair value:		
Private equity funds	16	15
Corporate wealth management products (1)	13,000	18,500
Liquidity funds (2)	5,924	9,061
	18,940	27,576
Non-current:		
Publicly traded investments, at fair value:		
Equity investment in MEG (3)	8,616	7,365
	8,616	7,365

The fair values of publicly traded investments are based on quoted market prices. The fair values of non-publicly traded investments are based on fund managers' quotations. The directors believe that the estimated fair values quoted by fund managers are reasonable, and that they are the most appropriate values at the reporting date.

(1) The corporate wealth management products matured from February 17, 2012 to June 21, 2012.

(2) The liquidity funds have no fixed maturity date and no coupon rate.

(3) The equity investment represents investment in the equity securities of MEG Energy Corporation ("MEG"). As at December 31, 2011, the investment in MEG was stated at the quoted market price. MEG is principally engaged in the exploitation and production of oil sands.

During the year, the gross loss of the Group's available-for-sale investments recognised directly in other comprehensive loss amounted to RMB800 million (2010: other comprehensive income RMB5,590 million, and 2009 other comprehensive loss: RMB22 million).

In addition, there were no realized gains of the Group, transferred from other comprehensive income to the profit and loss for the year (2010: nil, and 2009: 52 million) upon the disposal of the related available-for-sale financial assets.

None of the financial assets above is either past due or impaired.

29. Related Party Transactions (in part)

(v) Balances with a Joint Venture

	2010	2011
Amounts due from a joint venture		
—Included in held-to-maturity financial assets	—	44
—Included in other current assets	11,688	—
	11,688	44

33. Financial Instruments (in part)

Fair Value of Financial Instruments

The carrying values of the Group's cash and cash equivalents, time deposits, trade receivables, other current assets, trade and accrued payables and other payables approximated to their fair values at the reporting date due to the short maturity of these instruments.

The fair value of the Group's long term bank loans with floating interest rates approximated to the carrying amount of RMB4,063 million as at December 31, 2011 (2010: RMB8,950 million).

The estimated fair value of the Group's long term guaranteed notes based on current market interest rates was approximately RMB20,097 million as at December 31, 2011 (2010: RMB6,989 million), which was determined by reference to the market price as at December 31, 2011.

Fair Value Hierarchy

The Group uses the following hierarchy that reflects the significance of the inputs used in making the measurement:

Level 1: quoted prices (unadjusted) in active markets for identical assets or liabilities;

Level 2: inputs other than quoted prices included within Level 1 that are observable for the asset or liability, either directly or indirectly; and

Level 3: inputs for the asset or liability that are not based on observable market data (unobservable inputs).

As at December 31, 2011 and 2010, the Group held the following financial instruments measured at fair value for each hierarchy respectively:

Assets Measured at Fair Value	December 31 2011	Level 1	Level 2	Level 3
Available-for-sale financial assets-current				
Private equity funds*	15	—	15	—
Corporate wealth management products*	18,500	—	18,500	—
Liquidity funds**	9,061	9,061	—	—
	27,576	9,061	18,515	—
Available-for-sale financial assets-non current				
Equity investment in MEG**	7,365	7,365	—	—
	7,365	7,365	—	—

* The fair values of private equity funds and corporate wealth management products are based on the fund managers' quotations.
** The fair values of liquidity funds and equity investment in MEG are based on quoted market prices.

Financial Liabilities—Trade and Other Payables, Held for Trading, Held at Fair Value Through Profit and Loss, Hedging Derivatives

8.57

Empresa Nacional de Electricidad S.A. (Endesa-Chile) (Dec 2011)

Author's Note

Endesa-Chile provides a detailed list of all borrowings in Note 16, Other Financial Liabilities, which has not been included in this excerpt.

CONSOLIDATED STATEMENTS OF FINANCIAL POSITION (in part)

Liabilities and Equity	Note	12-31-2011 ThCh$	12-31-2010 ThCh$
Current Liabilities			
Other current financial liabilities	16	305,557,690	252,708,694
Trade and other current payables	19	357,781,381	377,477,705
Accounts payable to related companies	8	135,386,489	223,038,793
Non-Current Liabilities			
Other non-current financial liabilities	16	1,728,093,903	1,538,650,097
Other non-current payables	19	—	3,738,357

CONSOLIDATED STATEMENTS OF COMPREHENSIVE INCOME (in part)

	Note	2011 ThCh$	2010 ThCh$	2009 ThCh$
Financial income	28	28,039,261	10,083,190	25,315,918
Financial costs	28	(137,535,382)	(142,256,150)	(188,368,384)
Profit (loss) from indexed assets and liabilities	28	(5,332,672)	(3,162,695)	9,275,308

NOTES TO THE CONSOLIDATED FINANCIAL STATEMENTS (in part)

(In thousands of Chilean pesos)

1. The Group's Activities and Financial Statements (in part)

Empresa Nacional de Electricidad S.A. (hereinafter the Parent Company or the Company) and its subsidiaries comprise the Endesa Group Chile (hereinafter Endesa or the Group).

Endesa Chile is a publicly traded corporation with registered address and head office located at Avenida Santa Rosa, No.76, in Santiago, Chile. The Company is registered in the securities register of the Superintendency of Securities and Insurance of Chile (Superintendencia de Valores y Seguros or SVS) under number 114. In addition, the Company is registered with the Securities and Exchange Commission of the United States of America (hereinafter U.S. SEC), and with Spain's Comisión Nacional del Mercado de Valores. The Company's shares have been listed on the New York Stock Exchange since 1994 and on the Latibex since 2001.

Endesa Chile is a subsidiary of Enersis S.A., a Spanish company controlled by Enel S.p.A. (hereinafter Enel).

2. Basis of Presentation of Consolidated Financial Statements (in part)

2.1 Accounting Principles (in part)

The December 31, 2011 consolidated financial statements of Endesa Chile and its subsidiaries have been prepared in accordance with International Financial Reporting Standards (IFRS), issued by the International Accounting Standards Board (hereinafter "IASB"), and approved by its Board of Directors at its meeting held on January 31, 2012.

The consolidated financial statements have been prepared from accounting records maintained by the Company and its subsidiaries. Each entity prepares its financial statements according to the accounting principles and standards in force in each country, so the necessary adjustments and reclassifications have been made in the consolidation process in order to present the consolidated financial statements in accordance with IFRS and the criteria of the IFRS Interpretation Committee (hereinafter IFRIC).

3. Accounting Principles Applied (in part

The main accounting policies used in preparing the accompanying consolidated financial statements were the following

f) Financial Instruments (in part)

Financial instruments are contracts that give rise to both a financial asset in one company and a financial liability or equity instrument in another company.

f.3) Financial Liabilities Other Than Derivatives

Financial liabilities are generally recorded based on cash received, net of any costs incurred in the transaction. In subsequent periods, these obligations are valued at their amortized cost, using the effective interest rate method (see Note 3.f.1).

In the particular case that a liability is the underlying item of a fair value hedge derivative, as an exception, such liability will be valued at its fair value for the portion of the hedged risk.

In order to calculate the fair value of debt, both in the cases when it is recorded in the statement of financial position and for fair value disclosure purposes as seen in Note 16, debt has been divided into fixed interest rate debt (hereinafter "fixed-rate debt") and variable interest rate debt (hereinafter "floating-rate debt"). Fixed-rate debt is that on which fixed-interest coupons established at the beginning of the transaction are paid explicitly or implicitly over its term. Floating-rate debt is that issued at a variable interest rate, i.e., each coupon is established at the beginning of each period based on the reference interest rate. All debt has been valued by discounting expected future cash flows with a market-interest rate curve based on the payment's currency.

f.4) Derivative Financial Instruments and Hedge Accounting

Derivatives held by Endesa Chile and its subsidiaries are primarily transactions entered into to hedge interest and/or exchange rate risk, intended to eliminate or significantly reduce these risks in the underlying transactions being hedged.

Derivatives are recorded at fair value as of the date of the statement of financial position as follows: if their fair value is positive, they are recorded within "Other financial assets" and if their fair value is negative, they are recorded within "Other financial liabilities." For derivatives on commodities, the positive value is recorded in "Trade and other current receivables," and negative values are recorded in "Trade and other current liabilities."

Changes in fair value are recorded directly in income except when the derivative has been designated for accounting purposes as a hedge instrument and all of the conditions established under IFRS for applying hedge accounting are met, including that the hedge be highly effective. In this case, changes are recorded as follows:

- Fair value hedges: The underlying portion for which the risk is being hedged is valued at its fair value, as is the hedge instrument, and any changes in the value of both are recorded in the comprehensive income statement by netting the effects in the same comprehensive income statement account.
- Cash flow hedges: Changes in the fair value of the effective portion of derivatives are recorded in an equity reserve known as "Reserve of cash flow hedges." The cumulative loss or gain in this account is transferred to the comprehensive income statement to the extent that

the underlying item impacts the comprehensive income statement because of the hedged risk, netting the effect in the same comprehensive income statement account. Gains or losses from the ineffective portion of the hedge are recorded directly in the comprehensive income statement.

A hedge is considered highly effective when changes in the fair value or the cash flows of the underlying item directly attributable to the hedged risk, are offset by changes in the fair value or the cash flows of the hedging instrument, with effectiveness ranging from 80% to 125%.

The Company does not apply hedge accounting to its investments abroad.

As a general rule, long-term commodity purchase or sale agreements are recorded in the consolidated statement of financial position at their fair value as of period end, recording any differences in value directly in income, except when all of the following conditions are met:

- The sole purpose of the agreement is for the Group's own use.
- The future projections of Endesa Chile and its subsidiaries justify the existence of these agreements for its own use.
- Past experience with agreements shows that they have been utilized for the Group's own use, except in certain isolated cases when they had to be used for exceptional reasons or reasons associated with logistical issues beyond the control and projection of Endesa Chile and its subsidiaries.
- The agreement does not stipulate settlement by differences and the parties do not make it a practice to settle similar contracts by differences in the past.

The long-term commodity purchase or sale agreements maintained by Endesa Chile and its subsidiaries, which are mainly for electricity, fuel, and other supplies, meet the conditions described above. Thus, the purpose of fuel purchase agreements is to use them to generate electricity, the electricity purchase contracts are used to make sales to end-customers, and the electricity sale contracts are used to sell the company's own product.

The Company also evaluates the existence of derivatives embedded in contracts or financial instruments to determine if their characteristics and risk are closely related to the principal contract, provided that the set is not being accounted for at fair value. If they are not closely related, they are recorded separately and changes in value are accounted for directly in the comprehensive income statement.

f.5) Fair Value Measurement and Classification of Financial Instruments

The fair value of the various derivative financial instruments is calculated as follows:

- For derivatives traded on a formal market, by its quoted price as of year-end.
- Endesa Chile and its subsidiaries value derivatives not traded on formal markets by using discounted expected cash flows and generally accepted options valuation models, based on current and future market conditions as of year-end.

Using the procedures described, the Group classifies financial instruments at the following levels:

Level 1: Quoted price (unadjusted) in active markets for identical assets or liabilities;

Level 2: Inputs other than quoted prices included within Level 1 that are observable for the asset or liability, either directly (i.e. as prices) or indirectly (i.e. derived from prices); and

Level 3: Inputs for assets or liabilities that are not based on observable market data (unobservable inputs).

16. Other Financial Liabilities (in part)

The balance of other financial liabilities as of December 31, 2011 and 2010 is as follows:

Other Financial Liabilities	Balance at December 31, 2011		Balance at December 31, 2010	
	Current ThCh$	Non-Current ThCh$	Current ThCh$	Non-Current ThCh$
Interest-bearing loans	302,006,286	1,712,294,737	249,185,637	1,523,141,821
Hedging derivatives[*]	184,042	6,555,571	908,928	4,487,602
Other financial liabilities	3,367,362	9,243,595	2,614,129	11,020,674
Total	305,557,690	1,728,093,903	252,708,694	1,538,650,097

[*] See Note 18.2a.

Interest-Bearing Liabilities

1. The detail of current and non-current interest-bearing borrowings as of December 31, 2011 and 2010 is as follows:

Classes of Loans that Accrue Interest	Balance at December 31, 2011		Balance at December 31, 2010	
	Current ThCh$	Non-Current ThCh$	Current ThCh$	Non-Current ThCh$
Bank loans	145,464,457	194,087,333	74,236,476	238,314,148
Unsecured obligations	83,118,154	1,403,000,187	110,611,465	1,145,282,214
Secured obligations	10,660,476	9,635,108	9,522,288	17,703,710
Finance leases	9,178,783	54,985,624	8,571,797	57,785,278
Other loans	53,584,416	50,586,485	46,243,611	64,056,471
Total	302,006,286	1,712,294,737	249,185,637	1,523,141,821

2. Liabilities by currency and contractual maturity as of December 31, 2011 and 2010 are as follows:
- Summary of Bank Loans by currency and contractual maturity

The fair value of current and non-current bank borrowings totaled ThCh$ 332,248,376 at December 31, 2011 and ThCh$ 388,248,122 at December 31, 2010.

| | | | | | Current | | | Non-Current | | | |
| | | | | | Maturity | | | Maturity | | | |
Country	Currency	Amortization	Nominal Rate	Secured/ Unsecured	One to Three Months ThCh$	Three to Twelve Months ThCh$	Total Current at 12-31-2011 ThCh$	One to Three Years ThCh$	Three to Five Years ThCh$	More Than Five Years ThCh$	Total Non-Current at 12-31-2011 ThCh$
Chile	US$	Semi-annual	2.83%	Unsecured	84,500	1,607,710	1,692,210	106,555,130	849,449	—	107,404,579
Peru	US$	Quarterly	3.44%	Unsecured	2,354,628	8,838,878	11,193,506	4,296,544	19,212,039	26,158,087	49,666,670
Peru	Soles	Quarterly	3.85%	Unsecured	3,068	1,541,618	1,544,686	—	—	—	—
Argentina	US$	Semi-annual	5.10%	Unsecured	494,597	6,393,975	6,888,572	17,983,101	1,598,484	—	19,581,585
Argentina	Ar$	Semi-annual	17.66%	Unsecured	28,051,669	9,299,019	37,350,688	15,020,415	2,414,084	—	17,434,499
Colombia	CPs	Semi-annual	6.48%	Unsecured	—	86,794,795	86,794,795	—	—	—	—
				Total	30,988,462	114,475,995	145,464,457	143,855,190	24,074,056	26,158,087	194,087,333

3. The detail of Unsecured Liabilities by currency and maturity as of December 31, 2011 and 2010 is as follows:
- Summary of Unsecured Liabilities by currency and maturity

| | | | | | Current | | | Non-Current | | | | |
| | | | | | Maturity | | | Maturity | | | | |
Country	Currency	Amortization	Nominal Rate	Secured/ Unsecured	One to Three Months ThCh$	Three to Twelve Months ThCh$	Total Current at 12-31-2011 ThCh$	One to Three Years ThCh$	Three to Five Years ThCh$	More Than Five Years ThCh$	More Than Ten Years ThCh$	Total Non-Current at 12-31-2011 ThCh$
Chile	US$	Semi-annual	8.36%	Unsecured	16,296,727	—	16,296,727	206,726,825	102,843,263	—	157,356,125	466,926,213
Chile	Ch$	Quarterly	5.17%	Unsecured	31,548,592	6,789,214	38,337,806	9,274,316	9,274,316	83,987,692	275,252,070	377,788,394
Peru	US$	Semi-annual	6.98%	Unsecured	853,625	60,597	914,222	13,692,084	14,632,944	5,195,251	5,049,784	38,570,063
Peru	Soles	Quarterly	6.60%	Unsecured	437,080	57,158	494,238	23,760,221	—	4,817,555	4,817,555	33,395,331
Colombia	CPs	Semi-annual	9.11%	Unsecured	—	27,075,161	27,075,161	—	37,890,242	212,561,450	235,868,494	486,320,186
				Total	49,136,024	33,982,130	83,118,154	244,811,146	163,699,905	315,999,641	678,489,495	1,403,000,187

4. The detail of Secured Liabilities by currency and maturity as of December 31, 2011 and 2010 is as follows:
- Summary of Secured Liabilities by currency and maturity

| | | | | | Current | | | Non-Current | | | |
| | | | | | Maturity | | | Maturity | | | |
Country	Currency	Amortization	Nominal Rate	Secured/ Unsecured	One to Three Months ThCh$	Three to Twelve Months ThCh$	Total Current at 12-31-2011 ThCh$	One to Three Years ThCh$	Three to Five Years ThCh$	More Than Five Years ThCh$	Total Non-Current at 12-31-2011 ThCh$
Peru	US$	Semi-annual	6.15%	Secured	—	10,463,994	10,463,994	—	—	—	—
Peru	Soles	Semi-annual	6.35%	Secured	135,886	60,596	196,482	9,635,108	—	—	9,635,108
				Total	135,886	10,524,590	10,660,476	9,635,108	—	—	9,635,108

- Detail of Financial Lease Obligations

| | | | | | | | | 12-2011 | | | | | | | |
| | | | | | | | | Current | | | Non-Current | | | | |
Taxpayer ID No. (RUT)	Company	Country	ID No. Financial Institution	Financial Institution	Country	Currency	Nominal Interest Rate	Less Than 90 Days	More Than 90 Days	Total Current	One to Three Years	Three to Five Years	More Than Five Years	More Than Ten Years	Total Non-Current
91,081,000-6	Endesa Chile	Chile	87,509,100-K	Leasing Abengoa Chile	Chile	US$	6.50%	1,041,741	—	1,041,741	2,291,023	2,598,536	8,126,396	5,639,145	18,655,100
Foreign	Edegel	Peru	Foreign	Banco Scotiabank	Peru	US$	2.02%	1,918,477	6,218,565	8,137,042	10,519,276	14,415,305	11,395,943	—	36,330,524
96,830,980-3	Inversiones Gas Atacama Holding	Chile	96,976,410-5	Gasred S.A.	Chile	US$	8.27%	—	—	—	—	—	—	—	—
				Total ThCh$						9,178,783					54,985,624

- Detail of Other Obligations

Taxpayer ID No. (RUT)	Company	Country	Financial Institution ID No.	Financial Institution	Country	Currency	Nominal Interest Rate	Current			Non-Current			
								Less Than 90 Days	More Than 90 Days	Total Current	One to Three Years	Three to Five Years	More Than Five Years	Total Non-Current
Foreign	Endesa Costanera	Argentina	Foreign	Mitsubishi (secured debt)	Argentina	US$	7.42%	7,749,998	14,969,290	22,719,288	12,851,153	37,735,332	—	50,586,485
Foreign	Endesa Costanera	Argentina	Foreign	Mitsubishi (unsecured debt)	Argentina	US$	7.42%	—	13,925,511	13,925,511	—	—	—	—
Foreign	Endesa Costanera S	Argentina	Foreign	Others	Argentina	Ar$	11.50%	679,866	1,133,110	1,812,976	—	—	—	—
91,081,000-6	Endesa Chile	Chile	N/A	Others	Chile	Ch$	4.74%	27	—	27	—	—	—	—
96,830,980-3	Inversiones Gas Atacama Holding	Chile	96,963,440-6	SC GROUP	Chile	US$	7.50%	10,104,537	—	10,104,537	—	—	—	—
96,830,980-3	Inversiones Gas Atacama Holding	Chile	96,963,440-6	SC GROUP	Chile	US$	N/A	1,092,804	—	1,092,804	—	—	—	—
96,589,170-6	Pangue	Chile	N/A	Others	Chile	Ch$	N/A	2	—	2	—	—	—	—
96,827,970-K	Endesa Eco	Chile	96,601,250-1	Inversiones Centinela S.A.	Chile	US$		3,929,271	—	3,929,271	—	—	—	—
				Total ThCh$						53,584,416				50,586,485

5. Hedged Debt

Of Endesa Chile's US dollar denominated debt, as of December 31, 2011, ThCh$ 739,686,386 is related to future cash flow hedges for the Group's US dollar-linked operating income (see Note 3.k). As of December 31, 2010, this amount totaled ThCh$ 679,999,810.

The following table details movements in "Reserve of cash flow hedges" during 2011, 2010, and 2009 due to exchange differences of this debt:

	December 31, 2011 ThCh$	December 31, 2010 ThCh$	December 31, 2009 ThCh$
Balance in hedging reserves (hedging income) at the beginning of the year, net	101,149,888	85,798,007	(96,503,511)
Foreign currency exchange differences recorded in equity, net	(47,549,956)	26,100,215	187,292,646
Recognition of foreign currency exchange differences in profit (loss), net	(12,505,769)	(10,748,334)	(4,991,128)
Foreign currency translation differences	1,055,579	—	—
Balance in hedging reserves (hedging income) at the end of the year, net	42,149,742	101,149,888	85,798,007

6. Other Information

As of December 31, 2011 and 2010, Endesa Chile has long-term lines of credit available for use amounting to ThCh$ 199,892,000 and ThCh$ 144,776,000, respectively.

Various of the Company's and its subsidiaries' credit facilities contain certain financial ratio covenants, customary In these types of contracts. These agreements also include affirmative and negative covenants that require ongoing monitoring. Additionally, there are certain restrictions in the events of default sections that also require compliance.

Some of Endesa Chile's credit facilities include cross default provisions. Endesa Chile's loan, syndicated under the State of New York law, subscribed in 2008 and expiring in 2014, and which contains a disbursed balance of US$ 200 million to date, does not make reference to Endesa Chile's subsidiaries, so cross default can only originate if Endesa Chile defaults on other of its own debt. For debt repayments to become accelerated due to cross default, the amount in default must exceed US$ 50 million, or its equivalent in other currencies. Additionally, other conditions must be met before debt repayments can be accelerated, including expiration of the grace period (if any) and a formal notice documenting intention to accelerate debt repayment from the lenders that represent more than 50% of the balance owed under the credit facility. Additionally, in December 2009, Endesa Chile subscribed loans under Chilean law that stipulate that a cross default will arise only by the debtor's default. In these loans, the amount in default must also exceed the US$ 50 million threshold aforementioned or its equivalent in foreign currency. Note that since their subscription, these credit facilities have never been disbursed.

Regarding Endesa Chile's bonds registered with the U.S. SEC, commonly known as "Yankee Bonds," the cross default for nonpayment can arise from other debt affecting the same company, or from any of its Chilean subsidiaries, regardless of the amount, as long as the principal that originated the cross default exceeds US$ 30 million, or its equivalent in other currency. The acceleration of the debt repayment caused by the cross default provision does not happen automatically; instead, bondholders of at least 25% of a certain series of the Yankee Bonds must demand this. Additionally, the bankruptcy or insolvency of a foreign subsidiary does not have a contractual impact on Endesa Chile's Yankee Bonds.

Endesa Chile's Chilean bonds stipulate that a cross default can only arise if the "Issuer" of the debt instrument is in default when the amount in default exceeds US$ 50 million or its equivalent in another currency. Furthermore, the acceleration of the debt repayment must be requested by at least 50% of the bondholders of a particular series.

As of December 31, 2011 and 2010, Endesa Chile and its respective subsidiaries were in full compliance with all above-described financial and other covenants and restrictions.

18. Financial Instruments (in part)

18.1 Financial Instruments, Classified by Type and Category

a) The detail of financial assets, classified by type and category, as of December 31, 2011 and 2010, is as follows:

December 31, 2011

	Financial Assets Held for Trading ThCh$	Financial Assets at Fair Value With Change in Net Income ThCh$	Held-to-Maturity Investments ThCh$	Loans and Receivables ThCh$	Available-for-Sale Financial Assets ThCh$	Hedge Derivatives ThCh$
Equity instruments	—	—	—	—	—	—
Derivative instruments	47,504	—	—	—	—	723,067
Other financial assets	—	—	—	379,534,910	—	—
Total Current	47,504	—	—	379,534,910	—	723,067
Equity instruments	—	—	—	—	2,865,405	—
Derivative instruments	—	—	—	—	—	9,385,907
Other financial assets	—	—	—	152,956,126	—	—
Total Non-current	—	—	—	152,956,126	2,865,405	9,385,907
Total	47,504	—	—	532,491,036	2,865,405	10,108,974

b) The detail of financial liabilities, classified by type and category, as of December 31, 2011 and 2010, is as follows:

December 31, 2011

	Financial Liabilities Held for Trading ThCh$	Financial Liabilities at Fair Value With Change in Net Income ThCh$	Loans and Payables ThCh$	Hedge Derivatives ThCh$
Interest-bearing loans	—	3,929,271	298,077,015	—
Derivative instruments	807,105	—	—	184,042
Other financial liabilities	—	—	495,728,127	—
Total current	807,105	3,929,271	793,805,142	184,042
Interest-bearing loans	—	—	1,712,294,737	—
Derivative instruments	—	—	—	6,555,571
Other financial liabilities	—	—	9,243,595	—
Total non-current	—	—	1,721,538,332	6,555,571
Total	807,105	3,929,271	2,515,343,474	6,739,613

18.2 Derivative Instruments

The risk management policy of the Group uses primarily interest rate and foreign exchange rate derivatives to hedge its exposure to interest rate and foreign currency risks.
The Company classifies its hedges as follows:
- Cash flow hedges: Those that hedge the cash flows of the underlying hedged item.
- Fair value hedges: Those that hedge the fair value of the underlying hedged item.

- Non-hedge derivatives: Financial derivatives that do not meet the requirements established by IFRS to be designated as hedge instruments are recorded at fair value with changes in net income (assets held for trading).

a) Assets and Liabilities for Hedge Derivative Instruments

As of December 31, 2011 and 2010, financial derivative transactions that qualify as hedge instruments resulted in recognition of the following assets and liabilities in the statement of financial position:

| | December 31, 2011 | | | | December 31, 2010 | | | |
| | Assets | | Liabilities | | Assets | | Liabilities | |
	Current ThCh$	Non-Current ThCh$	Current ThCh$	Non-Current ThCh$	Current ThCh$	Non-Current ThCh$	Current ThCh$	Non-Current ThCh$
Interest rate hedge:	—	—	91,829	6,454,964	54,650	—	334,843	4,487,602
Cash flow hedge	—	—	91,829	6,454,964	54,650	—	334,843	4,487,602
Exchange rate hedge:	723,067	9,385,907	92,213	100,607	—	25,387,885	574,085	—
Fair value hedge	723,067	9,385,907	92,213	100,607	—	25,387,885	574,085	—
Total	723,067	9,385,907	184,042	6,555,571	54,650	25,387,885	908,928	4,487,602

- General information on hedge derivative instruments

Hedging derivative instruments and their corresponding hedged instruments are shown in the following table:

Detail of Hedge Instruments	Description of Hedge Instruments	Description of Hedged Instruments	Fair Value of Hedged Instruments 12-31-2011 ThCh$	Fair Value of Hedged Instruments 12-31-2010 ThCh$	Type of Risks Hedged
SWAP	Interest rate	Bank borrowings	(6,546,793)	(4,822,445)	Cash flow
SWAP	Exchange rate	Bank borrowings	—	(519,435)	Cash flow
SWAP	Exchange rate	Unsecured obligations (bonds)	9,916,154	25,387,885	Cash flow

At the close of the years ending December 31, 2011 and 2010, the Group has not recognized significant gains or losses for ineffective cash flow hedges.

b) Financial Derivative Instrument Assets and Liabilities at Fair Value with Changes in Net Income

As of December 31, 2011 and 2010, financial derivative transactions recorded at fair value with changes in net income, resulted in the recognition of the following assets and liabilities in the statement of financial position:

| | December 31, 2011 | | | | December 31, 2010 | | | |
	Current Assets ThCh$	Current Liabilities ThCh$	Non-Current Assets ThCh$	Non-Current Liabilities ThCh$	Current Assets ThCh$	Current Liabilities ThCh$	Non-Current Assets ThCh$	Non-Current Liabilities ThCh$
Non-hedging derivative instruments	47,504	807,105	—	—	17,551	—	91,262	—

c) Other Information on Derivatives:

The following tables present the fair value of hedging and non-hedging derivatives entered into by the Group as well as the remaining contractual maturities as of December 31, 2011 and 2010:

| | December 31, 2011 | | | | | | | |
| | | Notional Value | | | | | | |
Financial Derivatives	Fair Value ThCh$	Less Than 1 Year ThCh$	1–2 Years ThCh$	2–3 Years ThCh$	3–4 Years ThCh$	4–5 Years ThCh$	Subsequent Years ThCh$	Total ThCh$
Interest rate hedge:	(6,546,793)	9,479,132	5,731,377	107,702,257	5,292,723	5,292,723	8,368,224	141,866,438
Cash flow hedge	(6,546,793)	9,479,132	5,731,377	107,702,257	5,292,723	5,292,723	8,368,224	141,866,438
Exchange rate hedge:	9,916,154	—	—	209,977,060	—	—	—	209,977,060
Cash flow hedge	9,916,154	—	—	209,977,060	—	—	—	209,977,060
Derivatives not designated for hedge accounting	(759,601)	17,569,294	—	—	—	—	—	17,569,294
Total	2,609,760	27,048,426	5,731,377	317,679,317	5,292,723	5,292,723	8,368,224	369,412,792

18.3 Fair Value Hierarchies

a) Financial instruments recognized at fair value in the consolidated statement of financial position are classified based on the hierarchies described in Note 3.f.5.

The following table presents financial assets and liabilities measured at fair value as of December 31, 2011 and 2010:

Financial Instruments Measured at Fair Value		Fair Value Measured at End of Reporting Period Using		
	12-31-2011 ThCh$	Level 1 ThCh$	Level 2 ThCh$	Level 3 ThCh$
Financial Assets				
Cash flow hedge derivatives	10,108,974	—	10,108,974	—
Derivatives not designated for hedge accounting	47,504	—	47,504	—
Borrowings and receivables (commodities hedge)	3,338	—	3,338	—
Available-for-sale financial assets, non-current	61,676	61,676	—	—
Total	10,221,492	61,676	10,159,816	—
Financial Liabilities				
Cash flow hedge derivatives	6,739,613	—	6,739,613	—
Derivatives not designated for hedge accounting	807,105	—	807,105	—
Other non-current financial liabilities	3,929,271	—	—	3,929,271
Total	11,475,989	—	7,546,718	3,929,271

b) The following is the reconciliation between opening and closing balances for financial instruments whose fair value is classified at Level 3:

Non-Current Interest-Bearing Loans	ThCh$
Balance at January 1, 2010	11,953,000
Total losses recognized in financial profit or loss	442,250
Balance at December 31, 2010	12,395,250
(Profit) recognized in financial profit or loss	(8,465,979)
Balance at December 31, 2011	3,929,271

The fair value of Level 3 has been calculated by applying a traditional discounted cash flow method. These projected cash flows include assumptions from within the company that are primarily based on estimates for prices and levels of energy production and firm capacity, as well as the costs of operating and maintaining some of our plants.

None of the possible reasonable scenarios foreseeable in the assumptions mentioned in the above paragraph would result in a significant change in the fair value of the financial instruments included at this level.

19. Trade and Other Payables

Trade and other payables as of December 2011 and 2010 is as follows:

Trade and Other Payables	Current		Non-Current	
	12-31-2011 ThCh$	12-31-2010 ThCh$	12-31-2011 ThCh$	12-31-2010 ThCh$
Trade payables	109,707,264	156,322,891	—	—
Other payables	248,074,117	221,154,814	—	3,738,357
Total	357,781,381	377,477,705	—	3,738,357

The breakdown of Trade Accounts and other Payables as of December 31, 2011 and 2010 is as follows:

Trade and Other Payables	Current		Non-Current One to Five Years	
	12-31-2011 ThCh$	12-31-2010 ThCh$	12-31-2011 ThCh$	12-31-2010 ThCh$
Energy suppliers	71,605,183	118,514,681	—	—
Fuel and gas suppliers	38,102,081	37,808,210	—	—
Payables for goods and services	170,243,991	64,586,392	—	—
Dividends payable to third parties	39,053,184	142,992,486	—	—
Prepayments to clients (mining companies)	7,698,967	8,877,873	—	—
Mitsubishi contract	—	3,397,620	—	3,288,535
Other accounts payable	31,077,975	1,300,443	—	449,822
Total	357,781,381	377,477,705	—	3,738,357

See Note 17.4 for the description of the liquidity risk management policy.

28. Financial Results

Financial income and costs as of December 31, 2011, 2010, and 2009 are as follows:

	Balance at		
Financial Income	**12-31-2011** **ThCh$**	**12-31-2010** **ThCh$**	**12-31-2009** **ThCh$**
Cash and cash equivalents	23,153,501	4,716,032	19,525,214
Other financial income	4,885,760	5,367,158	5,790,704
Total	28,039,261	10,083,190	25,315,918

	Balance at		
	12-31-2011 **ThCh$**	**12-31-2010** **ThCh$**	**12-31-2009** **ThCh$**
Financial costs	(137,535,382)	(142,256,150)	(188,368,384)
Bank loans	(24,427,040)	(27,969,118)	(44,385,051)
Secured and unsecured obligations	(109,225,126)	(96,485,135)	(110,024,240)
Financial leasing	(2,698,665)	(2,735,638)	(3,666,191)
Valuation of financial derivatives	(6,450,352)	(9,733,581)	(4,255,054)
Post-employment benefit obligations	(2,544,632)	(2,693,816)	(3,014,451)
Capitalized borrowing costs	29,922,494	11,744,123	4,745,501
Others	(22,112,061)	(14,382,985)	(27,768,898)
Gain (loss) from indexed assets and liabilities	(5,332,672)	(3,162,695)	9,275,308
Foreign currency exchange differences, net	(6,466,655)	15,618,964	(17,017,325)
Positive	17,737,642	33,103,786	28,293,419
Negative	(24,204,297)	(17,484,822)	(45,310,744)
Total financial costs	(149,334,709)	(129,799,881)	(196,110,401)
Total financial results	(121,295,448)	(119,716,691)	(170,794,483)

Financial Liabilities—Convertible Redeemable Preference Shares, Member Shares

8.58

Silver Fern Farms Limited (Sep 2011)

BALANCE SHEET (in part)

		Parent		Consolidated	
NZD in Thousands ($000)	**Notes**	**As at 30 Sept 11**	**As at 30 Sept 10**	**As at 30 Sept 11**	**As at 30 Sept 10**
Liabilities—Non-current liabilities					
Provisions	21	9,683	8,633	9,683	8,633
Interest bearing loans and borrowings	19	550	41,832	550	41,832
Bonds payable	20	—	—	—	—
Deferred income tax	9	20,724	11,265	21,225	11,895
Total Non-current liabilities excluding members' shares		30,957	61,730	31,458	62,360
Total liabilities excluding members' shares		300,695	256,154	279,730	232,470
Net assets excluding members' shares		406,838	378,004	394,767	367,771
Convertible redeemable preference shares	19,22	1,584	1,595	1,584	1,595
Supplier investment shares	22	7,155	7,203	7,155	7,203
Members' ordinary shares	22	19,601	20,360	19,601	20,360
Total members' shares		28,340	29,158	28,340	29,158
Net assets		378,498	348,846	366,427	338,613

STATEMENT OF COMPREHENSIVE INCOME
(in part)

		Parent		Consolidated	
NZD in Thousands ($000)	Notes	12 Months to 30 Sept 11	13 Months to 30 Sept 10	12 Months to 30 Sept 11	13 Months to 30 Sept 10
Continuing Operations					
Finance costs	7	20,072	22,322	20,215	22,845

NOTES TO THE CONSOLIDATED FINANCIAL STATEMENTS *(in part)*

1 Corporate Information

The financial statements of Silver Fern Farms Limited for the 12 months ended 30 September 2011 were authorised for issue in accordance with a resolution of the directors on 18 November 2011.

Silver Fern Farms Limited (the Parent) is registered under the Companies Act 1993 and the Co-operative Companies Act 1996. Silver Fern Farms Limited is an issuer for the purposes of the Financial Reporting Act 1993.

On 29 April 2010, Silver Fern Farms Limited announced a change of balance date to 30 September. The later 30 September balance date better reflects Silver Fern Farm Limited's financial performance from the sales of meat and associated products supplied in the season. Financial statements for the Parent and Group have been prepared for the 12 months ended 30 September 2011. The comparative period is for the 13 months ended 30 September 2010 and therefore the comparative amounts shown in the statement of comprehensive income, statement of changes in equity, balance sheet, the cash flow statement and related notes may not be directly comparable.

The nature of the operations and principal activities of the Group are described in note 4.

2 Summary of Significant Accounting Policies *(in part)*

A Basis of Preparation

The financial statements have been prepared in accordance with generally accepted accounting practice in New Zealand (NZ GAAP) and the requirements of the Companies Act 1993 and the Financial Reporting Act 1993.

The financial statements have also been prepared on a historical cost basis, except for operational land and buildings which are measured at fair value. Derivative financial instruments and available for sale financial assets have been measured at fair value.

The financial statements are presented in New Zealand dollars and all values are rounded to the nearest thousand dollars ($'000).

B Statement of Compliance

The financial statements have been prepared in accordance with NZ GAAP. They comply with New Zealand equivalents to International Financial Reporting Standards (NZ IFRS) and other applicable Financial Reporting Standards, as appropriate for profit-oriented entities. These financial statements comply with International Financial Reporting Standards (IFRS).

V Convertible Redeemable Preference Shares

The convertible preference shares exhibit characteristics of a liability, and are therefore recognised as a liability in the balance sheet.

The convertible redeemable preference shares are measured initially at cost, being the fair value of the consideration received net of issue costs associated with the borrowing. After initial recognition, these shares are subsequently measured at amortised cost using the effective interest method which allocates the cost through the expected life of the loan or borrowing. Amortised cost is calculated taking into account any issue costs.

W Members' Shares

i. Members Ordinary Shares

The Co-operative's share capital includes the amount of shares issued to the members of the Co-operative. From time to time, existing members leave the Co-operative and new members join the Co-operative. Members who leave the Co-operative are entitled, after a length of time, to have their share capital amounts repaid to them. New members are required to subscribe to shares in the Co-operative.

Silver Fern Farms Limited has two classes of Members' shares: Members' ordinary shares which are issued to suppliers who supply stock under the Silver Fern Farms rebate system and Supplier investment shares, which are issued to all suppliers of stock to Silver Fern Farms (subject to certain restrictions). All Members' shares have a nominal value of one dollar per share. Supplier investment shares are paid to ninety cents by the supplier with the balance of ten cents being paid by way of a dividend from retained earnings.

Members' ordinary shares carry full voting rights subject to the shareholder being a Current Supplier (as defined in Silver Fern Farms constitution) at the time of voting. Supplier investment shares carry voting rights in relation to director elections only. Members' shares participate equally on winding up.

The current maximum shareholdings for Members' ordinary shares and Supplier investment shares are 17,500 and 15,000 respectively.

Members' shares are eligible to receive a dividend subject to profitability, although any such dividend is likely to be restricted to fully paid Supplier investment shares. Members' ordinary shares shareholders are eligible to receive a rebate based on the profit earned from stock supplied.

Due to the obligations of the Co-operative set out above, the Co-operative share capital meets the definition of a financial liability as per NZ IAS 32: Financial Instruments Disclosure and Presentation, and hence, the issued and paid up capital is classified as a financial liability.

ii. New Ordinary Shares

New ordinary shares are classified as equity. Incremental costs attributable to the issue of new shares are shown in equity as a deduction, net of tax, from the proceeds.

7 Expenses (in part)

NZD in Thousands ($000)	Parent		Consolidated	
	12 Months to 30 Sept 11	13 Months to 30 Sept 10	12 Months to 30 Sept 11	13 Months to 30 Sept 10
Finance costs				
Bank facility fees	5,264	4,897	5,264	4,897
Bank interest cost	13,326	8,151	13,367	8,193
Other interest cost	249	229	351	710
Bond interest cost and similar expenses	1,233	9,045	1,233	9,045
Total finance costs	20,072	22,322	20,215	22,845

10 Members' Distributions Paid and Proposed

NZD in Thousands ($000)	Parent and Consolidated 12 Months to 30 Sept 11	Parent and Consolidated 13 Months to 30 Sept 10
Recognised amounts		
Declared and paid during the year:		
Dividends on convertible redeemable preference shares	96	98
Members' ordinary shares issued	—	—
Total members' distributions paid and proposed	96	98

22 Convertible Redeemable Preference Shares, Members' Shares and New Ordinary Shares

In October 2009 the change in the capital structure was finalised resulting in the issue of new ordinary shares. These shares began trading on the Unlisted exchange on 27 October 2009. As the new ordinary shares are not redeemable, they have been classified as equity. The details of the members shares and new ordinary shares movements as a result of the capital raising are as follows:

NZD in Thousands ($000)	Convertible Redeemable Preference Shares	Supplier Investment Shares	Members' Ordinary Shares	New Ordinary Shares	Total
Balance as at 1 September 2009	1,622	24,754	47,769	—	74,145
Shares issued during the year	—	(17,235)	(25,669)	117,560	74,656
Shares surrendered	(27)	(316)	(1,740)	—	(2,083)
Balance as at 30 September 2010	1,595	7,203	20,360	117,560	146,718
Taxable bonus issue of ordinary shares (non-cash)				16,287	16,287
Total of transactions associated with capital raising	—	—	—	16,287	16,287
Shares issued during the year	—	—	—	—	—
Shares surrendered	(11)	(48)	(759)	—	(818)
Balance as at 30 September 2011	1,584	7,155	19,601	133,847	162,187
Called/Uncalled					
19.601 m Members' ordinary shares of $1 each	—	—	19,601	—	19,601
79.741 m New ordinary shares—fully paid	—	—	—	109,209	109,209
17.990 m New ordinary shares—partly paid	—	—	—	24,638	24,638
Issued and fully paid	—	—	19,601	133,847	153,448

a Convertible Redeemable Preference Shares

Convertible redeemable preference shares were issued on 1 December 2002. A dividend of 6% (or as otherwise determined by the board) plus any available imputation credits, is paid on the anniversary of their issue. Convertible redeemable preference shares were repaid subsequent to year end, see note 33.

Convertible redeemable preference shares are currently finite and subject to a fixed term with rights of renewal.

b Members Shares

Silver Fern Farms Limited has two classes of Members' shares: Members' ordinary shares which are issued to suppliers who supply stock under Silver Fern Farms Limited's rebate system and Supplier investment shares, which are issued to all suppliers of stock to Silver Fern Farms (subject to certain restrictions). All Members' shares have a nominal value of one dollar per share. Supplier investment shares are paid to ninety cents by the supplier with the balance of ten cents being paid by way of a dividend from retained earnings. Members' shares are currently classified as a financial liability as Silver Fern Farms does not have the unconditional right to refuse redemption.

Members' ordinary shares carry full voting rights subject to the shareholder being a Current Supplier (as defined in the constitution of Silver Fern Farms Limited) at the time of voting. Supplier investment shares carry voting rights in relation to director elections only. Ordinary Shares participate equally on winding up.

The maximum shareholding for Members' ordinary shares and Supplier investment shares is 17,500 (2010: 17,500) and 15,000 (2010: 15,000) respectively.

Silver Fern Farms Limited's Members' shares are eligible to receive a dividend subject to profitability, although any such dividend is likely to be restricted to fully paid Supplier investment shares. Members' ordinary shares shareholders

are eligible to receive a rebate based on the profit earned from stock supplied.

c New Ordinary Shares Issued

As part of the change in the capital structure in October 2009, shareholders could elect to exchange Members' ordinary shares and Supplier investment shares for New ordinary shares on a one for one basis; no cash was payable on exchange. In addition to the exchange of shares, shareholders could elect to participate in a two for one rights issue. Under the terms of the rights issue, shareholders were entitled to subscribe in cash for two New ordinary shares for every one New ordinary share issued to them under the exchange offer.

The rights issue price per New ordinary share of $1.00 was payable either in full on application or under a deferred payment option, over a period of approximately three years by way of deduction from proceeds of the sale of livestock. Under the deferred payment option, the New ordinary shares must be fully paid by February 2013. The deferred payments due are held at their fair value based on their discounted expected future cashflows. The discount rate applied is 7.3%. The outstanding balance of deferred payments due is as follows:

NZD in Thousands ($000)	Parent and Consolidated As at 30 Sept 11	Parent and Consolidated As at 30 Sept 10
Deferred payments due within 12 months	7,788	6,486
Deferred payments due after 12 months	513	6,192
Total deferred payments	8,301	12,678

25 Financial Instruments (in part)

Detail of the significant accounting policies and methods adopted, including the criteria for recognition and the basis in which income and expenses are recognised, in respect of each class of financial asset and financial liability instrument, are disclosed in the Statement of Accounting Policies.

a Categories of Financial Instruments

NZD in Thousands ($000)		Parent As at 30 Sept 11	Parent As at 30 Sept 10	Consolidated As at 30 Sept 11	Consolidated As at 30 Sept 10
Financial liabilities					
Bank overdraft	Loans and receivables	7,283	860	9,807	2,847
Derivatives	Fair value through profit and loss	5,956	705	5,956	705
Trade and other payables	Recorded at amortised cost	118,786	95,145	102,556	77,263
Members' shares	Recorded at amortised cost	28,340	29,158	28,340	29,158
Bonds payable	Recorded at amortised cost	—	75,052	—	75,052
Interest bearing loans and borrowings	Recorded at amortised cost	111,057	397	111,057	397
Interest bearing loans and borrowings (non-current)	Recorded at amortised cost	550	41,832	550	41,832
Total financial liabilities		271,972	243,149	258,266	227,254
Net exposure		(94,086)	(117,272)	(90,991)	(92,004)

b Maturity Profile in Contractual Cashflow Order

Consolidated NZD in Thousands ($000)	6 Months or Less	Between 6–12 Months	Between 1–5 Years	>5 Years	Total
As at 30 September 2011					
Financial liabilities					
Bank overdraft	9,807	—	—	—	9,807
Derivatives	5,956	—	—	—	5,956
Trade and other payables	102,556	—	—	—	102,556
Secured loans	—	111,057	550	—	111,607
Convertible redeemable preference shares	1,587	—	—	—	1,584
Supplier investment shares	—	—	—	7,155	7,155
Members' ordinary shares	—	—	—	19,601	19,601
Total financial liabilities	119,903	111,057	550	26,756	258,266
Net maturity	29,320	(106,520)	10,968	(24,759)	(90,991)

Consolidated NZD in Thousands ($000)	6 Months or Less	Between 6–12 Months	Between 1–5 Years	>5 Years	Total
As at 30 September 2010					
Financial liabilities					
Bank overdraft	2,847	—	—	—	2,847
Derivatives	705	—	—	—	705
Trade and other payables	77,263	—	—	—	77,263
Secured loans	—	—	42,229	—	42,229
Bonds payable	76,922	—	—	—	76,922
Convertible redeemable preference shares	—	—	1,595	—	1,595
Supplier investment shares	—	—	—	7,203	7,203
Members' ordinary shares	—	—	—	20,360	20,360
Total financial liabilities	157,737	—	43,824	27,563	229,124
Net maturity	(47,316)	10,831	(30,733)	(25,383)	(92,601)

As at 30 September 2011 the Parent and Group each report financial liabilities in excess of financial assets. Over time, inventory that is not recorded as a financial asset will convert to trade receivables. Bank funding facilities will be rolled over at their expiry date. Longer term members' ordinary shares, classified as financial liabilities by virtue of their terms of issue will remain on issue, convert to ordinary shares or be redeemed and replaced based on a shareholders livestock supply.

The financial instruments in the table above are prioritised in order of payment.

Members who leave the Co-operative are entitled, after a length of time, to have their share capital amounts repaid to them. This requires the recognition of the outstanding shares as a financial liability. Due to the uncertain timing of the surrender of shares, and the small levels of redemption each year, Members Ordinary Shares have been classified as having a maturity date of over five years.

c Fair Values of Financial Instruments

Set out below is a comparison of carrying amounts and fair values of all of the Group's financial instruments that are carried in the financial statements at other than fair values.

The fair value for members' ordinary shares has been calculated by applying a discount factor of 10% (2010: 10%), with an estimated repayment date of 10 years (2010: 10 years).

The carrying values of all other financial assets and financial liabilities recorded in the financial statements approximates their fair values.

Parent and Consolidated NZD in Thousands ($000)	Carrying Amount		Fair Value	
	As at 30 Sept 11	As at 30 Sept 10	As at 30 Sept 11	As at 30 Sept 10
Financial liabilities				
Members' ordinary shares	19,601	20,360	7,557	7,850
SFF030 Bonds	—	75,052	—	74,474

Silver Fern Farm bonds were issued and are redeemable at $1 per unit, however at balance date the fair value was represented by the market price as traded through the New Zealand Debt Securities market.

d Fair Values of Financial Assets and Financial Liabilities

The fair values of the Group's financial instruments are disclosed in hierarchy levels depending on the nature of the inputs used in determining the fair values as follows:

- Level 1: Quoted prices (unadjusted) in active markets for identical assets or liabilities.
- Level 2: Inputs other than quoted prices included within level 1, that are observable for the asset or liability, either directly or indirectly.
- Level 3: Inputs for the asset or liability that are not based on observable market data.

The Group measures the fair value of foreign currency forward exchange contract based on dealer quotes of market forward rates and reflects the amount that the Group would receive or pay at their maturity dates for contracts involving the same currencies and maturity dates.

The Group does not have any significant financial assets or liabilities measured at fair value using Level 3 inputs as of 30 September 2011 or 30 September 2010.

Parent and Consolidated NZD in Thousands ($000)	Level 1	Level 2	Level 3	Total
As at 30 September 2011				
Financial liabilities				
Forward currency contracts	—	(5,956)	—	(5,956)
Net fair values of financial assets and financial liabilities	—	(2,905)	—	(2,905)

Compound Financial Instruments—Convertible Notes, Debt Component Classified as Loans, Option Component Classified at Fair Value Through Profit and Loss

8.59

Sequans Communications S.A. (Dec 2011)

CONSOLIDATED STATEMENTS OF FINANCIAL POSITION (in part)

(In Thousands)	Note	At December 31 2009	2010	2011
Equity and Liabilities				
Equity:				
Issued capital euro 0.02 nominal value, 34,667,339 shares issued and outstanding at December 31, 2011 (27,720,013 and 23,696,451 at December 31, 2010 and 2009, respectively)	12	$ 606	$ 710	$ 912
Share premium	12	47,671	68,972	129,283
Other capital reserves	13	4,063	5,194	9,368
Accumulated deficit		(51,570)	(54,262)	(54,691)
Other components of equity		123	85	(628)
Total equity		893	20,699	84,244
Non-current liabilities:				
Interest-bearing loans and borrowings	14	6,935	—	—
Government grant advances and interest-free loans	15	1,101	1,278	385
Provisions	16	777	184	259
Deferred tax liabilities	5	—	—	55
Other non-current financial liabilities	14	4,925	—	—
Total non-current liabilities		13,738	1,462	699
Current liabilities:				
Trade payables	17	3,384	15,508	8,580
Interest-bearing loans and borrowings	14	3,754	3,564	—
Government grant advances and interest-free loans	15	1,744	1,889	717
Other current financial liabilities	17	3,380	5,270	5,846
Deferred revenue	17	1,651	893	869
Provisions	16	269	432	75
Total current liabilities		14,182	27,556	16,087
Total equity and liabilities		$28,813	$49,717	$101,030

CONSOLIDATED STATEMENTS OF OPERATIONS
(in part)

(In Thousands, Except Share and Per Share Amounts)	Note	2009	At December 31 2010 Adjusted (1)	2011
Financial income (expense):				
Interest expense	4.1	(912)	(1,190)	(470)
Interest income	4.1	131	311	81
Foreign exchange gain (loss)	4.1	(315)	925	(744)
Change in the fair value of Category E convertible notes option component	4.1	(569)	(2,109)	—

NOTES TO THE CONSOLIDATED FINANCIAL STATEMENTS (in part)

1. Corporate Information

Sequans Communications S.A. ("Sequans") is organized as a limited liability company ("*société anonyme*") incorporated and domiciled in the Republic of France, with its principal place of business at 19 Le Parvis, 92073 Paris-La Défense, France. Sequans, together with its subsidiaries (the "Company"), is a leading fabless designer, developer and supplier of 4G semiconductor solutions for wireless broadband applications. The Company's semiconductor solutions incorporate baseband processor and radio frequency transceiver integrated circuits along with our proprietary signal processing techniques, algorithms and software stacks.

2. Summary of Significant Accounting and Reporting Policies (in part)

2.1. Basis of Preparation (in part)

The Consolidated Financial Statements are prepared on a historical cost basis, except for fair value through profit and loss financial assets, derivative financial instruments and available for sale financial assets that are measured at fair value. The Consolidated Financial Statements are presented in U.S. dollars and all values are rounded to the nearest thousand ($000) except where otherwise indicated.

On April 15, 2011 the Company's ordinary shares (as evidenced by American Depositary Shares) began trading on the New York Stock Exchange following its initial public offering of 6,666,666 new ordinary shares.

Statement of Compliance

The Consolidated Financial Statements of the Company have been prepared in accordance with International Financial Reporting Standards ("IFRS") as issued by the International Accounting Standard Board ("IASB") and whose application is mandatory for the year ending December 31, 2011. Comparative figures are presented for December 31, 2009 and 2010.

The accounting policies are consistent with those of the same period of the previous financial year, except for the changes disclosed in Note 2.2 to the Consolidated Financial Statements.

The Consolidated Financial Statements of the Company for the years ended December 31, 2009, 2010 and 2011 have been authorized for issue in accordance with a resolution of the board of directors on March 28, 2012.

Financial Income and Expense

Financial income and expense include:
- interest expense related to financial debt (financial debt consists of notes, the debt component of compound or hybrid instruments, other borrowings and finance-lease liabilities);
- other expenses paid to financial institutions for financing operations;
- foreign exchange gains and losses associated with operating and financing transactions; and
- changes in fair value connected with financial assets and liabilities at fair value through profit and loss.

In accordance with revised IAS 23 *Borrowing Costs*, the Company capitalizes borrowing costs for all eligible assets where construction was commenced on or after January 1, 2009. To date, the Company has not incurred such costs.

From January 1, 2011, the Company reflects the classification of foreign exchange gains and losses related to hedges of euro-based operating expenses in operation expenses instead of financial result.

Financial Liabilities

Convertible Notes and Borrowings

Interest-bearing bank loans are initially recognized at fair value, plus any transaction costs directly attributable to the issue of the liability. These financial liabilities are subsequently measured at amortized cost, using the effective interest rate method. Certain financial instruments, such as notes including an option to convert into shares, include both a financial debt component and an option component.

For convertible notes whose option component is recorded as an equity component (mainly when this component permits or requires the exchange of a fixed number of equity instruments for a fixed amount in cash), a "split accounting" is performed in accordance with IAS 32 *Financial Instruments: Presentation* for compound instruments (paragraphs 28 to 32):
- On the date of issue, the debt component equals the present value of future contractual cash flows for a similar instrument with the same conditions (maturity, cash flows) excluding any option or any obligation for conversion or redemption in shares. Consequently, the value of the option conversion is the residual amount after deducting the debt component from the compound financial instrument nominal amount. In accordance with paragraph 31 of IAS 32 *Financial Instruments: Presentation*, the sum of the carrying amounts assigned to the liability and option components on initial recognition is

always equal to the fair value that would be ascribed to the instrument as a whole.

- Subsequently, the debt component is re-measured at amortized cost, using the effective interest rate calculated at the date of issue and the option component is accounted for as an equity instrument.

In other circumstances, the option component cannot be classified in equity and a derivative is recorded as a financial liability under IAS 39 *Financial Instruments: Recognition and Measurement*. This is specifically applicable to the convertible notes issued in a foreign currency which is different from the Company's functional currency (as described in Notes 14.1 and 14.2 to the Consolidated Financial Statements). In such circumstances, a "split accounting" is performed in accordance with IAS 39 *Financial Instruments: Recognition and Measurement* for "hybrid instruments" (paragraphs 10 to 13).

2.4. Significant Accounting Judgments, Estimates and Assumptions (in part)

In the process of applying the Company's accounting policies, management must make judgments and estimates involving assumptions. These judgments and estimates can have a significant effect on the amounts recognized in the financial statements and the Company reviews them on an ongoing basis taking into consideration past experience and other relevant factors. The evolution of the judgments and assumptions underlying estimates could cause a material adjustment to the carrying amounts of assets and liabilities as recognized in the financial statements. The most significant management judgments and assumptions in the preparation of these financial statements are:

Fair Value of Financial Instruments

Fair value corresponds to the quoted price for listed financial assets and liabilities. Where no active market exists, the Company establishes fair value by using a valuation technique determined to be the most appropriate in the circumstances, for example:

- available-for-sale assets: comparable transactions, multiples for comparable transactions, discounted present value of future cash flows;
- loans and receivables, financial assets at fair value through profit and loss: net book value is deemed to be approximately equivalent to fair value because of their relatively short holding period;
- trade payables: book value is deemed to be approximately equivalent to fair value because of their relatively short holding period;
- convertible notes: some of the Company's convertible notes had optional redemption periods/dates occurring before their contractual maturity, as described in Notes 12 and 14 to the Company's Consolidated Financial Statements. Holders of our Category E convertible notes had the right to request conversion at any time from their issue. As from the expiration of an 18 month period from issue of the Category E convertible notes, the Company had the right to request the conversion of all the convertible notes then held; and
- derivatives: either option pricing models or discounted present value of future cash flows. Specifically and as described in Note 14.1 to the Consolidated Financial Statements, the option component of the Category E convertible notes was recorded as a derivative at fair value in accordance with the provisions of AG 28 of

IAS 39 *Financial Instruments: Recognition and Measurement*. The fair value was determined using a valuation model that requires judgment, including estimating the change in value of the Company at different dates and market yields applicable to the Company's straight debt (without the conversion option). The assumptions used in calculating the value of the conversion represent the Company's best estimates based on management's judgment and subjective future expectations.

4. Other Revenues and Expenses (in part)

4.1. Financial Income and Expenses (in part)

Financial Expenses:

(In Thousands)	Year Ended December 31		
	2009	2010 Adjusted[1]	2011
Interest on loans and finance leases	$ 472	$ 637	$ 134
Other bank fees and financial charges	440	553	336
Change in fair value of Category E Convertible notes option component	569	2,109	—
Foreign exchange loss	1,826	2,682	1,836
Total financial expenses	$3,307	$5,981	$2,306

[1] As adjusted to reflect the classification of foreign exchange gains and losses related to hedges of euro-based operating expenses from financial result to operating expenses. The effect on the year ended December 31, 2010 was to increase foreign exchange loss by $213,000.

The net foreign exchange loss of $744,000 for the year ended December 31, 2011 (2010: net foreign exchange gain $925,000; 2009: net foreign exchange loss $315,000) arises primarily from euro-based monetary assets. This includes a loss of $206,000 corresponding to the inefficiency of foreign exchange hedge (losses of $19,000 in 2010 and $42,000 in 2009).

For the year ended December 31, 2010, the loss of $2,109,000 was related to the change in fair value of the option of the component of the Category E convertible notes, calculated prior to their conversion. (See Note 14.1 to the Consolidated Financial Statements).

6. Earnings (Loss) Per Share

Basic earnings (loss) per share amounts are calculated by dividing net income (loss) for the year attributable to all shareholders of the Company by the weighted average number of all shares outstanding during the year. Since prior to April 12, 2011 there are no ordinary shares outstanding and all categories of preference shares had the same voting and dividend rights, were convertible to ordinary shares at any time, and were the most subordinate class of equity instruments outstanding, all preference shares were treated as ordinary shares in the calculation in all years presented.

Diluted earnings per share amounts are calculated by dividing the net earnings attributable to equity holders of the Company by the weighted average number of shares outstanding during the year plus the weighted average number of shares that would be issued on the exercise of all the dilutive stock options and warrants and the conversion of all convertible notes. Dilution is defined as a reduction of earnings per share or an increase of loss per share. As the exercise of all outstanding stock options and warrants and conversion of convertible notes would decrease loss per share, they are considered to be anti-dilutive and excluded from the calculation of loss per share.

The following reflects the income and share data used in the basic and diluted earnings (loss) per share computations:

	Year Ended December 31		
(In Thousands, Except Share and Per Share Data)	2009	2010	2011
Profit (Loss)	$ (16,872)	$ (2,692)	$ (429)
Weighted average number of shares outstanding for basic EPS	23,257,434	24,980,139	32,610,380
Net effect of dilutive stock options	—	—	—
Net effect of dilutive warrants	—	—	—
Net effect of dilutive convertible notes	—	—	—
Weighted average number of shares outstanding for diluted EPS	23,257,434	24,980,139	32,610,380
Basic earnings (loss) per share	$ (0.73)	$ (0.11)	$ (0.01)
Diluted earnings (loss) per share	$ (0.73)	$ (0.11)	$ (0.01)

12. Issued Capital and Reserves (in part)

Capital Transactions

On October 14, 2009, the Company's shareholders approved a capital increase of €4,847 through the issue of 242,342 Category E preference shares (each with one anti-dilution warrant attached), at an issue price of €4,048 per share for a total amount of €981,000. On the same date, the shareholders approved the issue of Category E convertible notes convertible into 992,836 Category E preference shares, with one anti-dilution warrant attached.

The Category E convertible notes were convertible immediately upon demand of the noteholder or, after the expiration of an 18-month period from the authorizing shareholder meeting, upon demand of the Company. Each Category E convertible note was convertible to one Category E preference share (each with one anti-dilution warrant attached). The purchase price was €4.048 per Category E convertible note. The fair value of each of the debt and conversion option portions of the Category E convertible notes has been determined as described in Note 14.1 to the Consolidated Financial Statements.

On July 16, 2010, the Company's shareholders approved a capital increase of €34,585 through the issue of 1,729,249 Category E preference shares, each with one anti-dilution warrant attached, at an issue price of €4.048 per share for a total subscription amount of €7,000,000.

On September 15, 2010, the Category E convertible notes convertible into 1,069,664 Category E preference shares with attached anti-dilution warrant which had been issued in 2008 were converted at the request of the Company (see Note 14.1 to the Consolidated Financial Statements). This resulted in an increase in capital of €21,393.

On December 30, 2010, the Company converted Category E convertible notes issued in 2009 into 992,836 Category E preference shares with attached anti-dilution warrant (see Note 14.1 to the Consolidated Financial Statements), resulting in an increase in capital of €19,857.

In preparation for the initial public offering, on April 12, 2011 all preference shares were converted into ordinary shares, with all preference share categories being cancelled, and a 1-for-2 reverse split of the Company's share capital was made effective.

On April 20, 2011, the Company increased its capital in connection with the initial public offering by issuing 6,666,666 ordinary shares at $10 per share for a total offering amount of $66,666,660. $193,533 was recorded in share capital in the Consolidated Statement of Financial Position and $66,473,127 in share premium. IPO costs directly attributable to the equity transaction amounting to approximately $7.5 million were deducted from the share premium.

In the years ended December 31, 2009, 2010 and 2011, Category A preference shares and ordinary shares were issued upon exercise of options and warrants as described in Note 13 to the Consolidated Financial Statements.

14. Interest-Bearing Loans and Borrowings

		At December 31		
(In Thousands)	Note	2009	2010	2011
Current				
Bank convertible notes	14.2	$3,601	$3,340	$—
Accrued interests	14.1, 14.2	153	188	—
Factoring	14.3	—	36	—
Total current portion		$3,754	$3,564	$—
Non-current				
Category E convertible notes	14.1	$6,935	$ —	$—
Bank convertible notes	14.2	—	—	—
Total non-current portion		$6,935	$ —	$—

14.1. Interest-Bearing Debt—Category E Convertible Notes

On October 14, 2009, the shareholders approved the issue of notes convertible into 992,836 Category E preference share with an anti-dilution warrant attached, at a subscription price of €4.048 per Category E convertible note, for a total of €4,019,000 ($6,037,000). The Category E convertible notes bore interest at 2.0% per year, paid annually on the anniversary of the subscription date, or, in the event of early settlement or conversion, on a pro rata basis on the settlement or conversion date. The conversion features are described in Note 12 to the Consolidated Financial Statements. If not converted, the Category E convertible notes were to be reimbursed on the 10th anniversary of the subscription date.

The fair value of the Category E convertible notes—debt component was initially determined by discounting the cash flows, including allocated financing transaction costs of $132,000 for the 2009 issue, assuming a market rate of interest for a non-convertible debt with otherwise similar terms. The market rates used were 8.05%, resulting in a fair value of €2,302,992 ($3,459,094) for the 2009 issue.

The option component was recorded as a derivative at fair value in accordance with the provisions of AG 28 of IAS 39 *Financial Instruments: Recognition and Measurement.* In each instance, the Company's issuances of convertible notes were made at fair value. Accordingly, at each issuance date, the fair value of the convertible note as a whole was equal to the sum of the fair value of the conversion option and the fair value of the host contract (without the conversion option).

The fair value of the Category E convertible notes—option component was recalculated at the end of each reporting period, resulting in a fair value of €3,225,751 ($4,283,797) at December 30, 2010 (before conversion in capital), and €3,418,979 ($4,925,381) at December 31, 2009. The change of this fair value was recorded in the Consolidated Statement of Operations.

Accrued interest related to the Category E convertible notes totalled $132,000 at December 31, 2010 (2009: $396,000).

On July 30, 2010, the Company converted the 884,387 and 185,277 Category E convertible notes issued respectively on January 31, 2008 and July 10, 2008 into 1,069,664 Category E preference shares with attached anti-dilution warrant. As of that conversion date, the aggregate carrying amounts of the debt and option components (respectively $3,358,110 and $2,305,026) were transferred to equity, without any impact on net income, in applying the provisions of IAS 32.AG.32. These amounts were recorded in share capital for $27,871 and in share premium for $5,635,265.

On December 30, 2010, the Company converted the 992,836 Category E convertible notes issued on October 14, 2009 into 992,836 Category E preference shares with attached anti-dilution warrant. As of that conversion date, the carrying amounts of the debt and option components (respectively $3,241,391 and $4,244,988) were transferred to equity without any impact on net income, in applying the provisions of AG 32 of IAS 32. These amounts were recorded in share capital for $26,344 and in share premium for $7,460,036.

As at December 31, 2010, the Company no longer had any Category E convertible notes.

14.2. Interest-Bearing Debt—Bank Convertible Notes

In January 2008, the shareholders of the Company approved the issue of 100,000 notes to a French bank ("bank convertible notes"). The Company had the right but not the obligation to issue the bank convertible notes at a subscription price of €100 per note for a total amount of up to €10.0 million ($14.7 million), with the requirement that the first tranche not be less than €2,500,000 ($3,479,000) and that such first tranche be issued by December 31, 2008. In October 2008, the Company issued the first tranche of €2,500,000 ($3,479,000) in bank convertible notes.

The bank convertible notes could be converted, at the election of the financial institution, into ordinary shares only in the event of an initial public offering of the Company's shares, and at the IPO offering price. If there was no conversion, all outstanding bank convertible notes were (prior to amendment in 2010) to be repaid on June 30, 2010.

In June 2010, the Company and the bank agreed to amend the terms of the instrument whereby the repayment date, if the note was not converted, was extended to June 30, 2011, the interest rate was increased and the non-conversion penalty was modified. Such modification of the initial terms of the existing financial liability was not considered substantial under the provisions of AG 62 of IAS 39 and did not trigger the recognition of a new financial liability.

Following the Company's initial public offering in April 2011, the notes became convertible at $10.00 per ordinary share. The conversion option, according to the terms of the instrument, had a term of six months after the IPO date. In October 2011, the conversion option expired unexercised and the Company repaid the €2,500,000 balance due.

The bank convertible notes bore interest at Euribor 3-month rate plus 225 basis points through June 30, 2010. After amendment in 2010, the interest rate increased to Euribor 3-month rate plus 525 basis points. Interest on the outstanding bank convertible notes was payable on the last day of each calendar year quarter. In the event of non-conversion, the Company was to pay a non-conversion penalty at the time the principal was reimbursed up to a maximum of 6% of the amount of bank convertible notes issued. After amendment in 2010, the non-conversion penalty was modified to become an early repayment penalty (not payable at maturity date in the absence of a conversion) and reduced to 5%.

The outstanding amount of bank convertible notes would have become payable immediately in the event that financial covenants were not met:

- The Company was to maintain a net cash balance at the end of each quarter equal to at least 30% of any issued bank convertible notes and other financial debt. Net cash balance was defined as cash and cash equivalents less financial debt (excluding the bank and other convertible notes issued). This financial covenant was met at the end of each quarter during 2010 and 2009 and at the end of the first three quarters of 2011.
- Operating result, excluding the impact of depreciation, amortization and LTE development costs, was required to be positive.

Until September 30, 2010, given that the conversion option was primarily under the control of the Company (as the option was exercisable only if the Company decided to launch an IPO), such option did not qualify as a financial liability under paragraph 25 of IAS 32. At December 31, 2010, the recognition of the option component was required under IFRS since the IPO process had been officially launched by the Company during the last quarter of 2010. Such component was treated as a derivative financial liability, which was measured at nil fair value at December 31, 2010, since the conversion option was deeply out-of-the money (the current value of the Company's shares was much lower than the value of the debt component) and the time value of the option was considered to be close to nil (because of the short maturity and low volatility of the Company's value).

The effective rate of interest applied in 2011 was 4.56% (2010: 4.49%. 2009: 3.84%). Accrued interest of $52,000 was recorded in "Interest on convertible loan" as of December 31, 2010 (2009: $28,000). No interest was accrued as of December 31, 2011 due to the repayment of the bank convertible notes in 2011.

As of December 31, 2011, the Company had no other drawn or undrawn committed borrowing or overdraft facilities in place.

18. Information about Financial Instruments

18.1. Financial Assets and Liabilities

(In Thousands)	Carrying Amount December 31			Fair Value December 31		
	2009	2010	2011	2009	2010	2011
Financial assets:						
Trade and other receivables	$ 7,045	$14,368	$ 8,387	$ 7,045	$14,368	$ 8,387
Loans and other receivables						
Deposits	398	1,485	531	398	1,485	531
Available for sale instruments						
Long-term investments	463	432	677	463	432	677
Cash and cash equivalents	7,792	9,739	57,220	7,792	9,739	57,220
Total financial assets	$15,698	$26,024	$66,815	$15,698	$26,024	$66,815
Total current	$14,837	$24,107	$65,607	$14,837	$24,107	$65,607
Total non-current	$ 861	$ 1,917	$ 1,208	$ 861	$ 1,917	$ 1,208
Financial liabilities:						
Interest-bearing loans and borrowings:						
Bank convertible notes	3,629	3,392	—	3,629	3,392	—
Category E convertible notes—debt component	7,060	132	—	7,060	132	—
Factoring	—	36	—	—	36	—
Interest-free loans	1,552	1,158	—	1,463	1,149	—
Trade and other payables	3,384	15,508	8,580	3,384	15,508	8,580
Financial instruments at fair value through other comprehensive income:						
Cash flow hedges	21	129	1,007	21	129	1,007
Financial instruments at fair value through profit and loss:						
Category E convertible notes—option component	4,925	—	—	4,925	—	—
Total financial liabilities	$20,571	$20,355	$ 9,587	$20,482	$20,346	$ 9,587
Total current	$ 8,110	$19,731	$ 9,587	$ 8,055	$19,727	$ 9,587
Total non-current	$12,461	$ 624	$ —	$12,426	$ 619	$ —

The carrying values of current financial instruments (cash and cash equivalents, trade receivables and trade and other payables, and factoring) approximate their fair values, due to their short-term nature.

Available for sale long-term investments are primarily related to a bank guarantee issued by the Company in favor of the owners of leased office space to secure annual lease payments by the Company for its office space in Paris and a bank credit line used in connection with the purchase of hedging instruments. This guarantee, which is expected to be renewed annually until the end of the lease in May 2014, is secured by pledges of investments in money market funds.

In addition, the Company has pledged money market funds to secure a bank credit line used in connection with the purchase of hedging instruments.

New interest-free loans received from Oséo in 2010 were recorded as financial instruments in compliance with IAS 20 *Accounting for Government Grants and Disclosure of Government Assistance.*

The bank convertible notes bear interest at a variable rate which was reset each quarter; therefore their carrying value was considered to approximate fair value.

The Category E convertible notes were hybrid financial instruments. The fair value of the option component had been revalued at each reporting period.

Fair Value Hierarchy (in part)

The Group uses the following hierarchy for determining and disclosing the fair value of financial instruments by valuation technique:

- Level 1: quoted (unadjusted) prices in active markets for identical assets or liabilities

- Level 2: other techniques for which all inputs which have a significant effect on the recorded fair value are observable, either directly or indirectly
- Level 3: techniques which use inputs that have a significant effect on the recorded fair value that are not based on observable market data

As at December 31, 2011, the Company held the following financial instruments carried at fair value on the statement of financial position:

Liabilities Measured at Fair Value

(In Thousands)	At December 31, 2009	Level 1	Level 2	Level 3
Financial instruments at fair value through other comprehensive income:				
Cash Flow hedges	$ 21	$—	$21	$ —
Financial instruments at fair value through profit and loss:				
Category E convertible notes—option component	4,925	$—	$—	4,925

Reconciliation of Fair Value Measurements of Level 3 Financial Instruments

A reconciliation of the beginning and closing balances disclosing movements separately is disclosed hereafter:

(In Thousands)	Category E Option Component
January 1, 2009	$1,920
Issuances of Convertible Notes	2,445
Total gains and losses recognized in profit and loss	560
December 31, 2009	4,925
Total gains and losses recognized in profit and loss	1,663
Conversion of Convertible Notes	(6,588)
December 31, 2010	—
Total gains and losses recognized in profit and loss	—
December 31, 2011	—

18.2. Financial Instruments at Fair Value (in part)

The Company uses financial instruments, including derivatives such as foreign currency forward and options contracts,

to reduce the foreign exchange risk on cash flows from firm and highly probable commitments denominated in euros.

The use of different estimations, methodologies and assumptions could have a material effect on the estimated fair value amounts. The methodologies are as follows:

- Cash, cash equivalents, accounts receivable, accounts payable, other receivable and accrued liabilities: due to the short-term nature of these balances, carrying amounts approximate fair value.
- Long-term investments are composed of debt-based mutual funds with traded market prices. Their fair values amounted to $463,000, $432,000 and $677,000 at December 31, 2009, 2010 and 2011, respectively.
- Foreign exchange forward and option contracts: the fair values of foreign exchange forward and option contracts were calculated using the market price that the Company would pay or receive to settle the related agreements, by reference to published exchange rates.
- Convertible notes: the fair value of the derivative instrument is estimated using the listed market value of comparable companies. See Note 14.2 to the Consolidated Financial Statements.

Securitization and Assignment of Receivables

8.60

Veolia Environnement (Dec 2011)

CONSOLIDATED STATEMENT OF FINANCIAL POSITION (in part)

Assets

(€ Million)	Notes	As of December 31			As of January 1,
		2011	2010[1]	2009[1]	2009[1]
Non-current operating financial assets	11	5,088.3	5,255.3	5,275.2	5,298.9
Non-current derivative instruments—Assets	30	742.8	621.1	431.9	508.4
Other non-current financial assets	12	736.5	773.1	753.9	817.3
Non-current assets		28,457.1	31,055.4	29,558.5	30,010.8
Operating receivables	14	11,427.6	12,488.7	12,241.3	13,093.2
Current operating financial assets	11	357.0	373.3	376.6	452.3
Other current financial assets	12	114.6	132.3	217.7	321.4
Current derivative instruments—Assets	30	48.1	34.6	45.6	142.8
Cash and cash equivalents	15	5,723.9	5,406.8	5,614.4	3,849.6
Current assets		21,948.5	20,371.9	20,196.2	19,075.4
Total assets		50,405.6	51,427.3	49,754.7	49,086.2

[1] Amounts as of December 31, 2010, December 31, 2009 and January 1, 2009 re-presented pursuant to IAS 8, *Accounting Policies, Changes in Accounting Estimates and Errors*—See Note 1 to the Consolidated Financial Statements.

CONSOLIDATED INCOME STATEMENT (in part)

(€ Million)	Notes	Year Ended December 31		
		2011[2]	2010[2] [3]	2009[1] [2] [3]
Finance costs	21	(861.5)	(851.6)	(817.5)
Income from cash and cash equivalents	21	113.1	92.7	92.1
Other financial income and expenses	22	(56.3)	(102.5)	(83.2)

[1] In 2009, as part of ongoing efficiency measures, the Group reclassified certain expenses from cost of sales to selling costs and general and administrative expense. These reclassifications had no impact on operating income (see Note 20, Operating income).

[3] Amounts as of December 31, 2010 and December 31, 2009 re-presented pursuant to IAS 8, *Accounting Policies, Changes in Accounting Estimates and Errors*—See Note 1 to the Consolidated Financial Statements.

NOTES TO THE CONSOLIDATED FINANCIAL STATEMENTS (in part)

1 Accounting Principles and Methods

1.1 Accounting Standards Framework (in part)

1.1.1 Basis Underlying the Preparation of the Financial Information

Pursuant to Regulation no.1606/2002 of July 19, 2002, as amended by European Regulation no. 297/2008 of March 11, 2008, the consolidated financial statements for the year ended December 31, 2011 are presented in accordance with IFRS (International Financial Reporting Standards) as adopted by the European Union and IFRS as published by the International Accounting Standards Board (IASB). These standards may be consulted at the following European Union website: http://ec.europa.eu/internal_market/accounting/ias/index_en.htm.

These financial statements are accompanied, for comparative purposes, by financial statements for fiscal years 2010 and 2009 drawn up in accordance with the same standards framework.

In the absence of IFRS standards or interpretations and in accordance with IAS 8, *Accounting Policies, Changes in Accounting Estimates and Errors*, Veolia Environnement refers to other IFRS dealing with similar or related issues and the conceptual framework. Where appropriate, the Group may use other standard references and in particular U.S. standards.

1.14. Financial Instruments (in part)

1.14.1 Financial Assets and Liabilities

Financial assets include assets classified as available-for-sale and held-to-maturity, assets at fair value through the Consolidated Income Statement, asset derivative instruments, loans and receivables and cash and cash equivalents.

Financial liabilities include borrowings, other financing and bank overdrafts, liability derivative instruments and operating payables.

The recognition and measurement of financial assets and liabilities is governed by IAS 39.

IFRS-BPPD 8.60

Loans and Receivables

This category includes loans to non-consolidated investments, operating financial assets, other loans and receivables and trade receivables. After initial recognition at fair value, these instruments are recognized and measured at amortized cost using the effective interest method.

An impairment loss is recognized if, where there exists an indication of impairment, the carrying amount of these assets exceeds the present value of future cash flows discounted at the initial EIR. The impairment loss is recognized in the Consolidated Income Statement.

The impairment of trade receivables is calculated using two methods:

- a statistical method: this method is based on past losses and involves the application of a provision rate by category of aged receivables. The analysis is performed for a group of similar receivables, presenting similar credit characteristics as a result of belonging to a client category and country;
- an individual method: the probability and amount of the loss is assessed on an individual case basis in particular for non-State public debtors (past due period, other receivables or payables with the counterparty, rating issued by an external rating agency, geographical location).

Net gains and losses on loans and receivables consist of interest income and impairment losses.

Derecognition of Financial Assets

The Group derecognizes a financial asset when the contractual rights to the cash flows from the asset expire or when it transfers the contractual rights to the cash flows from the financial asset in a transaction under which nearly all the rights and obligations inherent to ownership of the financial asset are transferred. Any interest created or retained by the Group in a financial asset is recognized separately as an asset or liability.

1.18 Financial Items in the Consolidated Income Statement

Finance costs consist of interest payable on borrowings calculated using the amortized cost method and losses on interest rate derivatives, both qualifying and not qualifying as hedges.

Interest costs included in payments under lease finance contracts are recorded using the effective interest method.

Finance income consists of gains on interest rate derivatives, both qualifying and not qualifying as hedges and income from cash investments and equivalents.

Interest income is recognized in the Consolidated Income Statement when earned, using the effective interest method.

Other financial income and expenses primarily include income on financial receivables calculated using the effective interest method, dividends, foreign exchange gains and losses, impairment losses on financial assets and the unwinding of discounts on provisions.

11 Non-Current and Current Operating Financial Assets (in part)

Operating financial assets comprise financial assets resulting from the application of IFRIC 12 on accounting for concession arrangements and from the application of IFRIC 4 (see Notes 1.20 and 1.21).

Movements in the net carrying amount of non-current and current operating financial assets during 2011 are as follows:

(€ Million)	As of December 31, 2010	New Financial Assets	Repayments/ Disposals	Impairment Losses[1]	Changes in Consolidation Scope	Foreign Exchange Translation	Non-Current/ Current Reclassification	Transfers to Assets Classified as Held for Sale	Other	As of December 31, 2011
Gross	5,317.3	381.0	(36.9)	—	(64.7)	33.3	(406.6)	(135.2)	48.3	5,136.5
Impairment losses	(62.0)	—	—	(4.3)	—	(0.1)	5.0	—	13.2	(48.2)
Non-current operating financial assets	5,255.3	381.0	(36.9)	(4.3)	(64.7)	33.2	(401.6)	(135.2)	61.5	5,088.3
Gross	373.3	0.2	(404.1)	—	(9.3)	2.0	406.6	(24.9)	13.2	357.0
Impairment losses	—	—	—	5.0	—	—	(5.0)	—	—	—
Current operating financial assets	373.3	0.2	(404.1)	5.0	(9.3)	2.0	401.6	(24.9)	13.2	357.0
Non-current and current operating financial assets	5,628.6	381.2	(441.0)	0.7	(74.0)	35.2	—	(160.1)	74.7	5,445.3

[1] Impairment losses are recorded in operating income.

The principal new operating financial assets in 2011 mainly concern:

- the Water division and in particular projects in Berlin (€129 million);
- the Energy Services division and in particular cogeneration plants (€66.9 million);
- the Environmental Services division and in particular new Private Finance Initiative (PFI) contracts for the processing and disposal of residual waste in the United Kingdom (€47.4 million).

The principal repayments and disposals of operating financial assets in 2011 concern:

- the Water division and in particular projects in Berlin (– €141.3 million);
- the Energy Services division and in particular cogeneration plants (– €110.0 million);
- the Environmental Services division and in particular the non-recourse assignment of Valomed receivables to the Royal Bank of Scotland (– €28.5 million).

Foreign exchange translation gains and losses on current and non-current operating financial assets mainly concern the Water division (€20.8 million) and the Environmental Services division (€17.4 million), primarily due to the appreciation of the Chinese renminbi yuan and the pound sterling against the euro.

Non-current/current reclassifications mainly concern:
- the Water division and in particular projects in Berlin (€140.8 million);
- the Energy Services division and in particular cogeneration plants (€85.4 million).

Changes in consolidation scope mainly concern the impacts of the Veolia Transdev combination (− €60.5 million, including − €52.5 million classified as non-current, see Note 4).

Transfers to Assets classified as held for sale mainly concern the assets of the Veolia Transdev group reclassified as discontinued operation (− €120.6 million, see Note 4) and the placing of Citelum in the Energy Services division for sale (− €46.7 million).

The breakdown of operating financial assets by division is as follows:

	As of December 31								
	Non-Current			Current			Total		
(€ Million)	2011	2010	2009	2011	2010	2009	2011	2010	2009
Water	3,873.9	3,889.2	3,870.3	215.6	197.7	188.8	4,089.5	4,086.9	4,059.1
Environmental Services	697.4	698.0	711.8	51.2	47.2	42.8	748.6	745.2	754.6
Energy Services	416.0	488.3	528.4	86.8	110.0	126.0	502.8	598.3	654.4
Transportation	—	89.7	86.7	—	17.2	18.7	—	106.9	105.4
Other	101.0	90.1	78.0	3.4	1.2	0.3	104.4	91.3	78.3
Operating financial assets	5,088.3	5,255.3	5,275.2	357.0	373.3	376.6	5,445.3	5,628.6	5,651.8

IFRIC 12 Operating Financial Assets Maturity Schedule:

(€ Million)	1 Year	2 to 3 Years	4 to 5 Years	More Than 5 Years	Total
Water	184.8	370.4	394.6	2,699.7	3,649.5
Environmental Services	49.1	97.6	99.2	475.6	721.5
Energy Services	2.6	4.3	3.4	9.8	20.1
Other	0.4	1.1	1.6	2.2	5.3
Total	236.9	473.4	498.8	3,187.3	4,396.4

IFRIC 4 Operating Financial Assets Maturity Schedule:

(€ Million)	1 Year	2 to 3 Years	4 to 5 Years	More Than 5 Years	Total
Water	30.9	73.5	79.3	256.3	440.0
Environmental Services	2.0	5.0	6.1	14.1	27.2
Energy Services	84.2	105.8	80.9	211.7	482.6
Other	3.0	6.4	7.5	82.2	99.1
Total	120.1	190.7	173.8	564.3	1,048.9

14 Working Capital (in part)

Movements in net working capital during 2011 are as follows:

(€ Million)	As of December 31, 2010	Changes in Business	Impairment Losses	Changes in Consolidation Scope	Foreign Exchange Translation	Transfers to Assets/ Liabilities Classified as Held for Sale	Other	As of December 31, 2011
Inventories and work-in-progress, net	1,130.6	28.1	13.9	(76.1)	2.1	(59.6)	(18.2)	1,020.8
Operating receivables, net	12,488.7	330.8	(23.5)	(481.6)	28.0	(829.8)	(85.0)	11,427.6
Operating payables	13,773.9	305.1	—	(436.9)	53.0	(1,007.4)	(89.1)	12,598.6
Net working capital	(154.6)	53.8	(9.6)	(120.8)	(22.9)	118.0	(14.1)	(150.2)

Amounts transferred to "Assets classified as held for sale" and "Liabilities directly associated with assets classified as held for sale" mainly concern the Veolia Transdev group reclassified as discontinued operation (€210.1 million in net working capital, see Note 4) and urban lighting activities (Citelum) in the Energy Services division (− €71.8 million in net working capital). These amounts also include the impact of the interruption of the divestiture process for Water division activities in Gabon (− €21.0 million in net working capital).

Changes in consolidation scope mainly concern the Veolia Transdev combination (− €33.0 million in net working capital, see Note 4), the acquisition of SPEC in the Energy Services division (− €26.1 million in net working capital, see Note 32) and the divestiture of the household assistance services business (Proxiserve) held jointly by the Water and Energy Services divisions (− €18.3 million in net working capital).

Net working capital includes "operating" working capital (inventories, trade receivables, trade payables and other operating receivables and payables, tax receivables and payables other than current tax), "tax" working capital (current tax receivables and payables) and "investment" working capital (receivables and payables in respect of industrial investments). Movements in each of these working capital categories in 2011 are as follows:

(€ Million)	As of December 31, 2010	Changes in Business	Impairment Losses	Changes in Consolidation Scope	Foreign Exchange Translation	Transfers to Assets/Liabilities Classified as Held for Sale	Other	As of December 31, 2011
Inventories and work-in-progress, net	1,130.6	28.1	13.9	(76.1)	2.1	(59.6)	(18.2)	1,020.8
Operating receivables (including tax receivables other than current tax)	12,287.9	262.2	(23.2)	(446.0)	27.2	(824.8)	(48.4)	11,234.9
Operating payables (including tax payables other than current tax)	(13,135.2)	(240.3)	0.0	439.3	(41.4)	975.4	5.8	(11,996.4)
Operating working capital [1]	283.3	50.0	(9.3)	(82.8)	(12.1)	91.0	(60.8)	259.3
Tax receivables (current tax)	176.6	72.2	—	(15.4)	0.5	(3.9)	(55.5)	174.5
Tax payables (current tax)	(221.0)	(31.4)	—	17.9	(0.6)	19.3	59.8	(156.0)
Tax working capital	(44.4)	40.8	—	2.5	(0.1)	15.4	4.3	18.5
Receivables on non-current asset disposals	24.2	(3.6)	(0.3)	(20.2)	0.3	(1.1)	18.9	18.2
Industrial investment payables	(417.7)	(33.4)	—	(20.3)	(11.0)	12.7	23.5	(446.2)
Investment working capital	(393.5)	(37.0)	(0.3)	(40.5)	(10.7)	11.6	42.4	(428.0)
Net working capital	(154.6)	53.8	(9.6)	(120.8)	(22.9)	118.0	(14.1)	(150.2)

[1] The change in working capital presented in the Consolidated Cash Flow Statement is equal to the sum of operating working capital changes in business activity and impairment losses presented above.

Movements in operating receivables during 2011 are as follows:

Operating Receivables (€ Million)	As of December 31, 2010	Changes in Business	Impairment Losses[1]	Reversal of Impairment Losses[1]	Changes in Consolidation Scope	Foreign Exchange Translation	Transfers to Assets Classified as Held for Sale	Other	As of December 31, 2011
Trade receivables	9,852.8	165.3	—	—	(346.2)	14.4	(561.5)	(27.2)	9,097.6
Impairment losses on trade receivables	(600.4)	—	(194.8)	173.0	12.0	(1.3)	10.5	(3.7)	(604.7)
Trade receivables, net[2]	9,252.4	165.3	(194.8)	173.0	(334.2)	13.1	(551.0)	(30.9)	8,492.9
Other current operating receivables	1,187.5	(112.4)	—	—	(73.8)	4.2	(149.2)	14.4	870.7
Impairment losses on other current operating receivables	(77.9)	—	(17.8)	16.1	3.9	(0.4)	8.2	2.0	(65.9)
Other operating receivables, net[2]	1,109.6	(112.4)	(17.8)	16.1	(69.9)	3.8	(141.0)	16.4	804.8
Other receivables[3]	800.1	109.6	—	—	(19.6)	14.1	(48.2)	(11.9)	844.1
Tax receivables	1,326.6	168.3	—	—	(57.9)	(3.0)	(89.6)	(58.6)	1,285.8
Operating receivables, net	12,488.7	330.8	(212.6)	189.1	(481.6)	28.0	(829.8)	(85.0)	11,427.6

[1] Impairment losses are recorded in operating income and included in the line "Changes in working capital" in the Consolidated Cash Flow Statement.

[2] Financial assets as defined by IAS 39, valued in accordance with the rules applicable to loans and receivables.

[3] Receivables recognized on a percentage completion basis in respect of construction activities and prepayments.

Short-term commercial receivables and payables without a declared interest rate are recognized at nominal value, unless discounting at the market rate has a material impact.

Changes in consolidation scope mainly concern the Veolia Transdev combination (– €375.5 million, see Note 4) and the divestiture of the household assistance services business (Proxiserve) held jointly by the Water and Energy Services divisions (– €108.0 millions).

Transfers to Assets classified as held for sale mainly concern the Veolia Transdev group reclassified as discontinued operation (– €695.7 million, see Note 4) and urban lighting activities (Citelum) in the Energy Services division (– €205.5 million). These amounts also include the impact of the interruption of the divestiture process for Water division activities in Gabon (+ €71.8 million).

Securitization of Receivables in France

Securitized debts total €482.9 million as of December 31, 2011 compared to €487.1 million as of December 31,

2010 and €499.7 million as of December 31, 2009 (Water division).

The risks associated with these securitized receivables (principally credit risk and late payment risk) are retained by the Group, justifying their retention as assets in the Consolidated Statement of Financial Position. The financing secured is recognized in "Current borrowings" (see Note 18, Current borrowings).

Assignment of Receivables

Receivables definitively assigned to third parties in the Energy Services division total €257 million as of December 31, 2011, including €139 million in France and €110 million in Italy. Assigned receivables total €192 million as of December 31, 2010, including €62 million in France and €123 million in Italy. They total €134 million as of December 31, 2009 and solely concern Italy.

Movements in operating payables during 2011 are as follows:

Operating Payables (€ Million)	As of December 31, 2010	Changes in Business	Changes in Consolidation Scope	Foreign Exchange Translation	Transfers to Liabilities Classified as Held for Sale	Other	As of December 31, 2011
Trade payables	5,535.3	80.9	(140.3)	15.1	(344.9)	(6.0)	5,140.1
Other operating payables [1]	5,332.0	0.5	(213.7)	35.3	(450.7)	17.2	4,720.6
Other liabilities [2]	1,340.2	180.7	(28.3)	2.8	(105.7)	(35.9)	1,353.8
Tax and employee-related liabilities	1,566.4	43.0	(54.6)	(0.2)	(106.1)	(64.4)	1,384.1
Operating payables	13,773.9	305.1	(436.9)	53.0	(1,007.4)	(89.1)	12,598.6

[1] Financial liabilities as defined by IAS 39, measured at amortized cost.
[2] Primarily deferred income.

Trade payables are recognized as liabilities at amortized cost in accordance with IAS 39 for accounting purposes. Short-term commercial payables without a declared interest rate are recognized at nominal value, unless discounting at the market rate has a material impact.

Changes in consolidation scope mainly concern the Veolia Transdev combination (– €380.9 million, see Note 4) and the divestiture of the household assistance services business

(Proxiserve) held jointly by the Water and Energy Services divisions (– €100.6 million).

Transfers to Assets classified as held for sale mainly concern the Veolia Transdev group reclassified as discontinued operation (– €964.7 million, see Note 4) and urban lighting activities (Citelum) in the Energy Services division (– €148.6 million). These amounts also include the impact of the interruption of the divestiture process for Water division activities in Gabon (+ €106.8 million).

18 Non-Current and Current Borrowings (in part)

(€ Million)	Non-Current			Current			Total		
	2011	2010	2009	2011	2010	2009	2011	2010	2009
Bond issues	13,076.2	13,625.7	13,264.5	690.8	17.1	36.9	13,767.0	13,642.8	13,301.4
• maturing in < 1 year	—	—	—	690.8	17.1	36.9	690.8	17.1	36.9
• maturing in 2–3 years	2,400.9	2,004.5	1,045.2	—	—	—	2,400.9	2,004.5	1,045.2
• maturing in 4–5 years	2,127.1	2,382.0	2,951.7	—	—	—	2,127.1	2,382.0	2,951.7
• maturing in > 5 years	8,548.2	9,239.2	9,267.6	—	—	—	8,548.2	9,239.2	9,267.6
Other borrowings	3,630.5	4,270.4	4,382.8	3,251.5	2,810.0	2,946.2	6,882.0	7,080.4	7,329.0
• maturing in < 1 year	—	—	—	3,251.5	2,810.0	2,946.2	3,251.5	2,810.0	2,946.2
• maturing in 2–3 years	1,050.2	1,429.8	1,511.1	—	—	—	1,050.2	1,429.8	1,511.1
• maturing in 4–5 years	493.4	572.2	779.7	—	—	—	493.4	572.2	779.7
• maturing in > 5 years	2,086.9	2,268.4	2,092.0	—	—	—	2,086.9	2,268.4	2,092.0
Total non-current and current borrowings	16,706.7	17,896.1	17,647.3	3,942.3	2,827.1	2,983.1	20,649.0	20,723.2	20,630.4

18.2 Movements in Other Borrowings (in part)

(€ Million)	As of December 31, 2010	Increases/ Subscrip- tions	Repay- ments	Changes in Consoli- dation Scope	Fair Value Adjust- ments[1]	Foreign Exchange Trans- lation	Non- Current/ Current Reclassi- fication	Transfers to Liabilities Classified as Held for Sale	Other	As of December 31, 2011
Other non-current borrowings	4,270.4	666.2	(120.4)	51.4	1.6	18.4	(1,079.6)	(206.1)	28.6	3,630.5
Other current borrowings	2,810.0	385.2	(881.7)	50.4	7.0	21.1	1,079.6	(165.4)	(54.7)	3,251.5
Other borrowings	7,080.4	1,051.4	(1,002.1)	101.8	8.6	39.5	—	(371.5)	(26.1)	6,882.0

[1] Fair value adjustments are recorded in financial income and expenses.

The decrease in other non-current borrowings in 2011 breaks down as follows:

Increases and repayments mainly concern draw-downs on project debt and on the Polish zloty syndicated loan facility.

Changes in consolidation scope mainly concern the Veolia Transdev combination (+ €64.2 million, see Note 4).

Non-current/current reclassifications primarily reflect the impact of the refinancing of the syndicated loan facilities maturing April 2012 and April 2011 in the amount of €345 million (see Note 3).

Transfers to liabilities classified as held for sale mainly concern the transfer to Liabilities directly associated with assets classified as held for sale of the other borrowings of the Veolia Transdev group classified as discontinued operation (− €206.9 million, see Note 4).

Breakdown of Other Non-Current Borrowings by Main Component:

(€ Million)	As of December 31, 2009	As of December 31, 2010	As of December 31, 2011	Maturing In 2 to 3 Years	Maturing In 4 to 5 Years	Maturing In > 5 Years
BWB and SPE debts[a]	1,344.7	1,334.9	1,325.8	228.9	117.6	979.3
Finance lease obligations[b]	650.4	571.1	434.5	135.6	78.6	220.3
Multi-currency syndicated loan facility[c]	305.4	345.5	307.3	307.3	—	—
Delfluent[d]	108.4	—	—	—	—	—
Shenzhen[e]	99.1	107.8	112.6	11.6	16.7	84.3
Non-controlling interest put options (Note 1.14.5)[f]	95.2	18.1	34.8	28.3	6.5	—
VSA Tecnitalia[g]	94.5	76.8	—	—	—	—
Redal[h]	92.7	90.4	82.3	19.3	22.9	40.1
Cogevolt[i]	91.0	34.7	—	—	—	—
Syndicated loan facility in CZK[j]	75.4	59.9	—	—	—	—
Glen Water Holding Ltd.[k]	75.8	77.5	78.4	4.9	6.0	67.5
VID[l]	67.1	78.9	73.8	7.5	10.0	56.3
Other amounts < €70 million	1,283.1	1,474.9	1,181.0	306.8	235.1	639.1
Other non-current borrowings	4,382.8	4,270.4	3,630.5	1,050.2	493.4	2,086.9

[i] Cogevolt: This securitization of future receivables was organized to finance cogeneration installations in the Energy Services division. The debt reflects payments due in respect of the amortization of future receivables over the period to May 2012 and was therefore transferred to current borrowings as of December 31, 2011. The average fixed rate of interest payable on this debt is 5.24%.

Derivatives and Hedging, Collateralized Accounts Receivable

8.61

Embraer S.A. (Dec 2011)

CONSOLIDATED BALANCE SHEET *(in part)*

	Note	12.31.2011	12.31.2010
Assets			
Current			
Cash and cash equivalents	6	1,350.2	1,393.1
Financial assets	7	753.6	733.5
Trade accounts receivable, net	8	505.8	348.6
Derivative financial instruments	39	8.2	6.8
Customer and commercial financing	9	12.0	20.4
Collateralized accounts receivable	10	14.9	11.6
Non-Current			
Trade accounts receivable	8	0.2	0.7
Financial assets	7	54.7	52.1
Customer and commercial financing	9	90.2	50.1
Collateralized accounts receivable	10	472.7	526.6
Derivative financial instruments	39	22.7	15.5
Liabilities			
Current			
Trade accounts payable	20	829.9	750.2
Loans and financing	19	251.8	72.6
Non-recourse and recourse debt	10	312.8	111.8
Other payables	21	81.2	84.4
Derivative financial instruments	39	1.0	0.8
Non-Current			
Loans and financing	19	1,406.3	1,362.2
Non-recourse and recourse debt	10	149.8	358.5
Other payables	21	14.0	27.6
Derivative financial instruments	39	0.2	1.4

CONSOLIDATED STATEMENTS OF INCOME
(in part)

	Note	12.31.2011	12.31.2010	12.31.2009
Operating profit before financial income (expense)		318.2	391.7	379.4
Financial income (expense), net	34	(90.7)	17.5	10.2
Foreign exchange gain (loss), net	35	20.0	(1.1)	(68.8)

NOTES TO THE CONSOLIDATED FINANCIAL STATEMENTS (in part)

In millions of US dollars, unless otherwise stated

1. Operations

Embraer S.A. (the "Company" or "Embraer") is a publicly-held company incorporated under the laws of the Federative Republic of Brazil with headquarters in São José dos Campos, State of São Paulo, Brazil. The corporate purpose of the Company is:

- The development, production and sale of jet and turboprop aircraft for civil and defense aviation, aircraft for agricultural use, structural components, mechanical and hydraulic systems, aviation services and technical activities related to the production and maintenance of aerospace material;

- The design, construction and sale of equipment, materials, systems, software, accessories and components to the defense, security and energy industries and the promotion or performance of technical activities related to production and maintenance, keeping the highest technological and quality standards;
- The performance of other technological, industrial, commercial and service activities related to the defense, security and energy industries; and
- Contribution to the formation of technical professionals necessary to the aerospace industry.

The Company's shares are listed on the enhanced corporate governance segment of the Stock Exchange in Brazil ("BM&FBOVESPA"), known as the New Market ("Novo Mercado"). The Company also has American Depositary Shares (evidenced by American Depositary Receipts-ADRs) which are registered with the Securities and Exchange Commission

("SEC") and are listed on the New York Stock Exchange ("NYSE"). The Company has no controlling group and its capital comprises only common shares.

The Company has consolidated wholly-owned and jointly controlled entities and/or commercial representation offices which are located in Brazil, the United States of America ("United States"), France, Spain, Portugal, China and Singapore. Their activities comprise sales, marketing, and after sales and maintenance services.

The presented Financial Statements were approved by the Board of Directors of the Company on March 15, 2012.

2. Presentation of the Financial Statements and Accounting Practices (in part)

2.1 Presentation of the Financial Statements

Basis of Preparation

The consolidated financial statements have been prepared in conformity with International Financial Reporting Standards ("IFRS") issued by the International Accounting Standards Board ("IASB") which comprise (i) IFRS, (ii) the International Accounting Standard ("IAS"), and (iii) the International Financial Reporting Interpretations Committee ("IFRIC") or its predecessor the Standing Interpretations Committee ("SIC"). For the purposes of these consolidated financial statements presented in accordance with IFRS there are no differences in relation to the current accounting practices adopted in Brazil ("Brazilian GAAP") for the periods presented.

These consolidated financial statements were prepared under the historical cost convention and adjusted to reflect assets and liabilities measured at fair value through profit or loss or marked to market when available for sale.

The preparation of financial statements in conformity with IFRS requires the use of certain critical accounting estimates. It also requires management of the Company ("Management") to exercise its judgment in the process of applying the Company's accounting policies. The areas which involve a higher degree of judgment or complexity, or assumptions and estimates significant to the consolidated financial statements are disclosed in Note 3. The actual results may differ from these estimates and assumptions.

2.2 Summary of Significant Accounting Policies (in part)

(g) Financial Instruments (in part)

Financial Assets

Financial instrument assets are Financial assets acquired by the Company, principally for the purpose of selling in the short-term. Usually, this classification includes securities with original maturities over 90 days from the date of application.

The Company classifies its Financial assets among the following categories: (i) measured at fair value through profit or loss, including assets held for trading (ii) available for sale, (iii) held to maturity (iv) loans and receivables and (v) hedge accounting. The classification depends on the purpose for which the financial assets were acquired. Management decides on the classification of its financial assets at initial recognition.

Regular purchases and sales of financial assets are recognized on the trade date—the date on which the Company commits to purchase or sell the asset.

Financial assets are initially recognized at fair value plus transaction costs for all financial assets not carried at fair value through profit or loss. Financial assets carried at fair value through profit or loss are initially recognized at fair value, and transaction costs are expensed in the statement of income.

Financial assets are derecognized when the rights to receive cash flows from the investments have expired or have been transferred. Derecognition occurs if the Company has transferred substantially all risks and rewards of the asset ownership.

(iv) Loans and Receivables

This category includes loans granted and receivables that are non-derivative financial assets with fixed or determinable payments, not quoted in an active market. They are classified as current assets, except for maturities greater than 12 months after the end of the reporting period. These are classified as non-current assets.

The Company's loans and receivables comprise loans to associates, trade accounts receivable, customer financing and other accounts receivable.

The Company assesses at the end of each reporting period whether there is objective evidence that a financial asset or group of financial assets is impaired. When applicable, a loss allowance is recorded.

A financial asset or a group of financial assets is impaired and impairment losses are incurred only if there is objective evidence of impairment as a result of one or more events that occurred after the initial recognition of the asset (a 'loss event') and that loss event (or events) has an impact on the estimated future cash flows of the financial asset or group of financial assets that can be reliably estimated.

(j) Derivatives and Hedge Operations

Derivatives are initially recognized at fair value on the date on which a derivatives contract is signed and are, subsequently, re-measured at fair value. The differences in fair value are recorded in the statement of income as Foreign Exchange Gains (Losses), Net, except when the derivative is designated as a hedge instrument.

The Company holds instruments for fair value and cash flow accounting hedges:

(i) Fair Value Hedges

Changes in the fair value of derivatives that are designated and qualify as fair value hedges are recorded in the statement of income, together with any changes in the fair value of the hedged asset or liability that are attributable to the hedged risk. The Company only applies fair value hedge accounting to hedge fixed interest risk on borrowings. Changes in the fair value of the hedged fixed rate borrowings attributable to interest rate risk are recognized in the statement of income within Financial income (expense).

If the hedge no longer meets the criteria for hedge accounting, the adjustment to the carrying amount of a hedged item for which the effective interest method is used is amortized to profit or loss over the period to maturity.

(ii) Cash Flow Hedges

The effective portion of changes in the fair value of derivatives that are designated and qualified as cash flow hedges is recognized in Other comprehensive income. The gain or loss related to the ineffective portion is recognized immediately in the statement of income as Financial income (expense).

Amounts accumulated in equity are reclassified to the statement of income in the periods when the hedged item affects profit or loss. However, when the forecasted transaction that is hedged results in the recognition of a non-financial asset, the gains and losses previously deferred in equity are transferred from equity and included in the initial measurement of the cost of the asset.

When a hedging instrument expires or is sold, or when a hedge no longer meets the criteria for hedge accounting, any cumulative gain or loss existing in equity at that time remains in equity and is reclassified to profit or loss when the forecast transaction is ultimately in the statement of income. When a forecasted transaction is no longer expected to occur, the cumulative gain or loss that was reported in equity is immediately transferred to the statement of income within Financial income (expense).

(k) Trade Accounts Receivable

Trade accounts receivable are recognized initially at present value and include revenues recorded using the percentage-of-completion method, net of the respective customer advances. They are subsequently recorded at amortized cost using the effective interest rate method, less provision for doubtful accounts.

A provision for doubtful accounts of trade receivable is recorded when there is objective evidence that the Company will not be able to recover all the amounts owed by its customers. Significant financial difficulties of the debtor, probability of the debtor filing for bankruptcy or reorganization proceedings and failure to pay or default (overdue 180 days or more) are considered indicators that the trade receivables are impaired. The amount of the provision is the difference between the book value and the recoverable value. The book value of the asset is reduced by the amount of the provision, and the amount of the loss is recorded in the statement of income as Selling expenses. When a trade receivable is deemed totally unrecoverable, it is written off against a provision for trade receivables. Subsequent recovery of amounts previously written off is registered in the statements of income, as Selling expenses.

The present value calculation, where applicable, is made on the date of the transaction based on an interest rate that reflects the timing and market conditions at the time. The Company does not record the adjustment to present value because they do not have a material effect on the financial statements.

(m) Collateralized Accounts Receivable and Recourse and Non-Recourse Debt

Certain Company sales are made under structured financing arrangements whereby an SPE purchases the aircraft, pays the Company the purchase price on delivery or at the end of the structured sales financing period, and transfers the purchased aircraft to the final customer. A financial institution finances the purchase of the aircraft by a SPE and bears part of the credit risk; the Company offers financial guarantees and/or residual value guarantees in favor of the institution.

The Company classifies the risks of this transaction as non-recourse when the financing institution bears the risk and as recourse when the Company bears the risk (Note 10).

(mm) Financial Income and Expenses

Financial income and expenses primarily comprise earnings on short-term investments, financial charges on loans, interest on contested taxes and contingencies (Note 26), as well as foreign exchange gains/losses (Note 35) on assets and liabilities expressed in currencies other than the functional currency (dollar), on an accrual basis.

Financial income and expenses exclude borrowing costs attributable to acquisitions, buildings or the production of qualifying assets that require a substantial period of time to be ready for use or sale which are capitalized as part of the cost of the asset.

5. Financial Instruments (in part)

a) Financial Instruments by Category (in part):

	Note	Loans and Receivables	Assets Measured at Fair Value Through Profit or Loss	Available for Sale	Investments Held to Maturity	Hedge Accounting	Total
			12.31.2011				
Cash and cash equivalents	6	—	1,350.2	—	—	—	1,350.2
Financial assets	7	—	748.1	8.3	51.9	—	808.3
Collateralized accounts receivable	10	487.6	—	—	—	—	487.6
Trade accounts receivable	8	506.0	—	—	—	—	506.0
Customer and commercial financing	9	102.2	—	—	—	—	102.2
Derivative financial instruments	39	—	28.8	—	—	—	28.8
Derivative Instrument—Designated as fair value hedge		—	—	—	—	2.1	2.1
		1,095.8	2,127.1	8.3	51.9	2.1	3,285.2

b) Credit Rating of Financial Instruments:

	12.31.2011	12.31.2010
Cash and cash equivalents	1,350.2	1,393.1
Financial assets	808.3	785.6
Total	2,158.5	2,178.7
Based on external appraisal:		
AAA	1,870.2	1,825.4
AA	126.0	233.1
A	156.6	120.2
BBB	5.7	—
Total	2,158.5	2,178.7

	12.31.2011	12.31.2010
Collateralized accounts receivable	487.6	538.2
Trade accounts receivable, net	506.0	349.3
Customer and commercial financing	102.2	70.5
Total	1,095.8	958.0
Based on internal appraisal:		
Group 1	1.2	2.0
Group 2	103.6	176.4
Group 3	991.0	779.6
Total	1,095.8	958.0

Group 1: New customers (less than one year).
Group 2: Customers (more than one year) impaired.
Group 3: Customers (more than one year) not impaired.

10. Collateralized Accounts Receivable and Recourse and Non-Recourse Debt

(a) Collateralized Accounts Receivable

	12.31.2011	12.31.2010
Minimum lease payments receivable	366.9	455.3
Estimated residual value of leased assets	458.4	458.4
Unearned income	(337.7)	(375.5)
Investment in sales-type lease	487.6	538.2
Less—current portion	14.9	11.6
Long-term portion	472.7	526.6

At December 31, 2011, the maturities of the amounts classified as non-current assets are as follows:

Year	
2013	14.0
2014	11.6
2015	10.6
2016	14.4
2017	30.2
Thereafter 2017	391.9
	472.7

(b) Recourse and Non-Recourse Debt

	12.31.2011	12.31.2010
Recourse Debt	437.2	443.2
Non Recourse Debt	25.4	27.1
	462.6	470.3
Less—current portion	312.8	111.8
Long-term portion	149.8	358.5

At December 31, 2011, the maturities of the amounts classified as non-current liabilities are as follows:

Year	
2013	10.4
2014	10.8
2015	10.6
2016	14.4
2017	30.2
Thereafter 2017	73.4
	149.8

34. Financial Income (Expense), Net

	12.31.2011	12.31.2010	12.31.2009
Financial Income:			
Interest on cash and cash equivalents and financial assets	133.8	115.5	98.5
Interest on receivables	25.9	23.6	47.0
Residual value guarantee			1.1
Gains on financial transactions	0.3	0.7	0.8
Other	0.6	0.5	5.2
Total financial income	160.6	140.3	152.6
Financial Expenses:			
Interest on loans and financing	(100.7)	(90.3)	(117.1)
Interest on taxes, social charges and contributions	(13.8)	(11.4)	(9.5)
Financial restructuring costs	(10.4)	(8.4)	—
IOF tax on financial transactions	(3.1)	(1.6)	(2.9)
Residual value guarantee[i]	(110.0)	(2.7)	—
Other	(13.3)	(8.4)	(12.9)
Total financial expenses	(251.3)	(122.8)	(142.4)
Financial income, net	(90.7)	17.5	10.2

[i] In 2011, the residual value guarantee provisions were complemented to meet the increased exposure to loss caused by some certain customers filing for Chapter 11 (Note 38).

39. Financial Instruments (in part)

a) Fair Value of Financial Instruments

The fair value of the Company's financial assets and liabilities were determined using available market information and appropriate valuation methodologies. However, considerable judgment was required in interpreting market data to generate estimates of fair values. Accordingly, the estimates presented below are not necessarily indicative of the amounts that might be realized in a current market exchange. The use of different assumptions and/or methodologies could have a material effect on the estimated realizable values.

The following methods were used to estimate the fair value of each category of financial instrument for which it is possible to estimate the fair value.

The book values of cash, cash equivalents, and commercial papers debt securities, accounts receivable and current liabilities are approximately their fair values. The fair value of securities held to maturity is estimated by the discounted cash flow methodology. The fair value of noncurrent loans is based on the discounted value of the contractual cash flows. The discount rate used, when applicable, is based on the future market yield curve for the cash flows of each liability.

The fair values of financial instruments at December 31 are as follows:

	12.31.2011		12.31.2010	
	Carrying Amounts	Fair Value	Carrying Amounts	Fair Value
Financial assets				
Cash and cash equivalents	1,350.2	1,350.2	1,393.1	1,393.1
Financial assets	808.3	808.3	785.6	785.6
Collateralized accounts receivable	487.6	487.6	538.2	538.2
Trade accounts receivable, net	506.0	506.0	349.3	349.3
Customer and commercial financing	102.2	102.3	70.5	70.5
Derivative financial instruments	28.7	28.8	22.3	22.3
Hedge accounting—fair value	2.2	2.2	—	—
Financial liabilities				
Loans and financing	1,658.1	1,733.1	1,434.8	1,485.2
Trade accounts payable and other liabilities	1,387.7	1,387.8	1,332.5	1,332.5
Financial guarantee and residual value	494.9	494.9	219.5	219.5
Derivative financial instruments	1.2	1.2	2.2	2.2

b) Classification (in part)

The Company considers "fair value" to be the price that would be received to sell an asset or paid to transfer a liability in an orderly transaction between market participants at the measurement date (exit price). The Company utilizes market data or assumptions that market participants would use in pricing the asset or liability, including assumptions about risk and the risks inherent in the inputs to the valuation technique. The Company primarily applies the market approach for recurring fair value measurements and endeavors to utilize the best available information. Accordingly, the Company utilizes valuation techniques that maximize the use of observable inputs and minimize the use of unobservable inputs. The Company is able to classify fair value balances based on the observable inputs. A fair value hierarchy is used to prioritize the inputs used to measure fair value. The three levels of the fair value hierarchy are as follows:

(i) Level 1—quoted prices are available in active markets for identical assets or liabilities as of the reporting date. Active markets are those in which transactions for the asset or liability occur in sufficient frequency and volume to provide pricing information on an ongoing basis. Level 1 primarily consists of financial instruments such as exchange-traded derivatives and listed equities.

(ii) Level 2—pricing inputs are other than quoted prices in active markets included in level 1, which are either directly or indirectly observable as of the reported date. However, they can be directly or indirectly observable at the balance sheet date. Level 2 includes those

financial instruments that are valued using models or other valuation methodologies. These models are primarily industry-standard models that consider various assumptions, including quoted forward prices for commodities, time value, volatility factors and current market and contractual prices for the underlying instruments, as well as other relevant economic measures. Substantially all of these assumptions are observable in the marketplace throughout the full term of the instrument, can be derived from observable data or are supported by observable levels at which transactions are executed in the marketplace. Instruments in this category include non-exchange traded derivatives such as over-the-counter forwards and options.

(iii) Level 3—pricing inputs include significant inputs that are generally less observable from objective sources. These inputs may be used with internally developed methodologies that result in Management's best estimate of fair value. At each balance sheet date, the Company performs an analysis of all instruments and includes in Level 3 all of those instruments whose fair value is based on significant unobservable inputs.

The following table sets forth by level within the fair value hierarchy the Company's financial assets and liabilities that were accounted for at fair value on a recurring basis as of December 31, 2011. The Company's assessment of the significance of a particular input to the fair value measurement requires judgment and may affect the valuation of fair value assets and liabilities and their placement within the fair value hierarchy levels.

	Fair Value Measurements at December 31, 2011			
	Quoted Prices in Active Markets for Identical Assets (Level 1)	Significant Other Observable Inputs (Level 2)	Significant Unobservable Inputs (Level 3)	Total
Assets				
Held for trading	666.2	0.4	89.8	756.4
Derivative financial instruments	—	28.8	—	28.8
Fair value hedge	—	2.1	—	2.1
Liabilities				
Derivative financial instruments	—	1.2	—	1.2

Fair Value Measurements Using Significant Unobservable Inputs (Level 3) for the Year Ended December 31, 2011	
Beginning balance	103.4
Purchases (sales)	(13.5)
Profits (losses)	
unreallized	(0.1)
Ending balance	89.8

Financial Risk Management Policy

The Company has and follows a risk management policy to direct transactions, which involves the diversification of transactions and counterparties. This policy provides for regular monitoring and management of the nature and general situation of the financial risks in order to assess the results and the financial impact on cash flows. The credit limits and risk rating of the counterparties are also reviewed periodically.

The Company's risk management policy was established by the Executive Directors and submitted to the Statutory Board of Directors, and provides for a Financial Management Committee. Under this policy, the market risks are mitigated when there is no counterparty in the Company's operations and when it is considered necessary to support the corporate strategy. The Company's internal control procedures provide for a consolidated monitoring and supervision of the financial results and of the impact on cash flows.

The Financial Management Committee assists the Financial Department in examining and reviewing information in relation to the economic scenario and its potential impact on the Company's operations, including significant risk management policies, procedures and practices.

The financial risk management policy includes the use of derivative financial instruments to mitigate the effects of interest rate fluctuations and to reduce the exposure to exchange rate risk. The use of these instruments for speculative purposes is forbidden.

(a) Capital Risk Management

The Company uses capital management to ensure the continuity of its investment program and offer a return to its shareholders and benefits to its stakeholders and also to maintain an optimized capital structure in order to reduce costs.

The Company may review its dividends payment policy, pay back capital to the shareholders, issue new shares or sell assets in order to maintain or adjust its capital structure (to reduce the financial indebtedness, for instance).

Liquidity and the leverage level are constantly monitored in order to mitigate refinance risk and to maximize the return to the shareholders. The ratio between the liquidity and the return to the shareholders may be changed pursuant to the assessment of Management.

Accordingly, the Company has been able to maintain cash surpluses over the balance of financial indebtedness and to assure liquidity by establishing and maintaining a standby credit line (Note 19).

The capital management may be changed due to economy scenario alterations or to strategic repositioning of the Company.

At December 31, 2011, cash and cash equivalents exceeded the Company's financial indebtedness by US$ 445.7 (US$ 691.8 in 2010) resulting, on a net basis, in a leverage-free capital structure.

Of the total financial indebtedness at December 31, 2011, 15.2% was short-term (5.1% in 2010) and the average weighted term was equivalent to 4.8 years (6.3 years in 2010). Own capital accounted for 35.2% and 37.3% of the total liabilities at the end of 2011 and 2010, respectively.

(b) Credit Risk

The Company may incur losses on amounts receivable from sales of spare parts and services. To reduce this risk, customer credit analyses are made continuously. In relation to accounts receivable from aircraft sales, the Company may have credit risks until the financing structure has been completed. To minimize this credit risk, the Company operates with financial institutions to facilitate structuring of the financing.

To cover risk of loss from doubtful accounts, the Company has recorded an allowance in an amount considered sufficient by management to cover expected losses on realization of the receivables.

The financial management policy establishes that assets in the investment portfolios in Brazil and overseas should have a minimum risk classification as investment grade, and also establishes a maximum exposure level of 15% of the shareholders' equity of the issuing financial institution and, in the case of a non-financial institution, a maximum of 5% of the total amount of the issue.

Counterparty risks in derivative transactions are managed by contracting transactions through highly-rated financial institutions and registration with the Clearing House for the Custody and Financial Settlement of Securities ("CETIP").

(c) Liquidity Risk (in part)

This is the risk of the Company not having sufficient liquid funds to honor its financial commitments as a result of a mismatch of terms or volumes of estimated receipts and payments.

To manage the liquidity of cash in Dollar and Real, Management has established projections and assumptions based on contracts for future disbursements and receipts, which are monitored daily by the Company, aiming to detect possible mismatches well in advance allowing the Company to adopt mitigation measures in advance, always trying to reduce the risk and financial cost.

The following table provides additional information related to undiscounted contractual obligations and commercial commitments and their respective maturities.

	Total	Less Than One Year	One to Three Years	Three to Five Years	More Than Five Years
At December 31, 2011					
Loans	2,113.9	313.7	464.9	213.3	1,122.0
Suppliers	829.9	829.9	—	—	—
Recourse and Non Recourse Debt	462.6	312.8	31.8	44.6	73.4
Financial Guarantees	494.9	317.3	85.2	69.7	22.7
Other Liabilities	161.4	5.9	37.5	70.9	47.1
Capital Lease	3.2	1.4	1.6	0.2	—
Total	4,065.9	1,781.0	621.0	398.7	1,265.2

The above table shows the outstanding principal and anticipated interest due at maturity date. For the fixed rate liabilities, the interest expenses were calculated based on the rate established in each debt contract. For the floating rate liabilities, the interest expenses were calculated based on a market forecast for each period (e.g. LIBOR 6m—12m) at December 31, 2011

(d) Market Risk

(i) Interest Rate Risk

This risk arises from the possibility that the Company might incur losses on account of interest rate fluctuations that increase the financial expense of liabilities and related to floating interest rates that reduce the assets income subject to floating interest rates and/or when the fluctuation in the determination of fair value price of assets or liabilities that are marked to market by fixed rates.

Financial investments—Company policy for managing the risk of fluctuations in interest rates on financial investments is to measure market risk by the Value-At-Risk—VAR methodology, analyzing a variety of risk factors that might affect the return on the investments. The financial income determined in the period already reflects the effects of marking the assets in the Brazilian and foreign investment portfolios to market.

Loans and financing—the Company uses derivative contracts to hedge against the risk of fluctuations in interest rates on certain transactions, and also continuously monitors market interest rates to evaluate the potential need to contract new derivative transactions to protect against the risk of volatility in these rates.

At December 31, 2011, the Company's consolidated financial investments and loans and financing are indexed as follows:

	Pre-Fixed		Post-Fixed		Total	
	Amount	%	Amount	%	Amount	%
Financial assets	923.1	42.77%	1,235.4	57.23%	2,158.5	100.00%
• In reais	—	0.00%	919.1	42.58%	919.1	42.58%
• In U.S. dollars	821.4	38.06%	316.3	14.65%	1,137.7	52.71%
• In other currencies	101.7	4.71%	—	0.00%	101.7	4.71%
Loans	1,475.5	88.99%	182.6	11.01%	1,658.1	100.00%
• In reais	526.2	31.73%	94.8	5.72%	621.0	37.45%
• In U.S. dollars	919.7	55.48%	87.8	5.29%	1,007.5	60.77%
• In other currencies	29.6	1.78%	—	0.00%	29.6	1.78%

	Pre-Fixed		Post-Fixed		Total	
After Derivatives	Amount	%	Amount	%	Amount	%
Financial investments	923.1	42.77%	1,235.4	57.23%	2,158.5	100.00%
• In reais	—	0.00%	919.1	42.58%	919.1	42.58%
• In U.S. dollars	821.4	38.06%	316.3	14.65%	1,137.7	52.71%
• In other currencies	101.7	4.71%	—	0.00%	101.7	4.71%
Loans	1,370.7	82.66%	287.4	17.34%	1,658.1	100.00%
• In reais	415.3	25.05%	205.7	12.40%	621.0	37.45%
• In U.S. dollars	925.8	55.83%	81.7	4.94%	1,007.5	60.77%
• In other currencies	29.6	1.78%	—	0.00%	29.6	1.78%

On December 31, 2011, the financial assets and loans post-fixed were indexed as follows:

	Without Derivative Effect		With Derivative Effect	
	Amount	%	Amount	%
Financial assets	1,235.4	100.00%	1,235.4	100.00%
• CDI	919.1	74.40%	919.1	74.40%
• LIBOR	316.3	25.60%	316.3	25.60%
Loans	182.6	100.00%	287.5	100.00%
• TJLP	93.7	51.35%	93.8	32.62%
• LIBOR	87.8	48.06%	81.9	28.50%
• CDI	1.1	0.59%	111.8	38.88%

(ii) Foreign Exchange Rate Risk

The Company adopts the dollar as functional currency (Note 2.2.(c)).

Consequently, the Company's operations which are most exposed to foreign exchange gains/losses are those denominated in Real (labor costs, local expenses, financial investments and loans and financing) as well as investments in subsidiaries in currencies other than the US dollar.

Company policy for protection against foreign exchange risks on assets and liabilities is mainly based on seeking to maintain a balance between assets and liabilities indexed in each currency and daily management of foreign currency purchases and sales to ensure that, on realization of the transactions contracted, this natural hedge will occur. This policy minimizes the effect of exchange rate changes on assets and liabilities already contracted, but does not protect against the risk of fluctuations in future results due to the appreciation or depreciation of the Real that can, when measured in dollars, show an increase or reduction of the share of costs when Real denominated.

The Company, in certain market conditions, may protect itself against future expenses and revenues, denominated in foreign currency, mismatches seeking to minimize future exchange rate gains/losses effects in the results.

Efforts to minimize the foreign exchange risk for rights and liabilities denominated in currencies other than the functional currency may involve transactions with derivatives, such as swaps, exchange options and Non-Deliverable Forwards ("NDF") to balance the portion of the Company's expenses and obligations denominated in Real.

At December 31, the Company's assets and liabilities, denominated by currency, were as follows:

	Without the Effect of Derivative Transactions		With the Effect of Derivative Transactions	
	12.31.2011	12.31.2010	12.31.2011	12.31.2010
Loans				
Brazilian reais	621.0	400.5	621.0	400.5
U.S. dollars	1,007.5	1,024.2	1,007.5	1,024.2
Euro	29.6	10.1	29.6	10.1
	1,658.1	1,434.8	1,658.1	1,434.8
Trade accounts payable				
Brazilian reais	56.7	38.2	56.7	38.2
U.S. dollars	706.8	668.0	706.8	668.0
Euro	65.7	41.4	65.7	41.4
Other currencies	0.7	2.6	0.7	2.6
	829.9	750.2	829.9	750.2
Total (1)	2,488.0	2,185.0	2,488.0	2,185.0
Cash and cash equivalents and financial assets				
Brazilian reais	919.1	1,051.9	919.1	1,051.9
U.S. dollars	1,137.7	1,039.1	1,137.7	1,039.1
Euro	20.2	20.6	20.2	20.6
Other currencies	81.5	67.1	81.5	67.1
	2,158.5	2,178.7	2,158.5	2,178.7
Trade accounts receivable:				
Brazilian reais	55.0	44.7	55.0	44.7
U.S. dollars	402.8	252.7	402.8	252.7
Euro	48.1	51.5	48.1	51.5
Other currencies	0.1	0.4	0.1	0.4
	506.0	349.3	506.0	349.3
Total (2)	2,664.5	2,528.0	2,664.5	2,528.0
Net exposure (1–2):				
Brazilian reais	(296.4)	(657.9)	(296.4)	(657.9)
U.S. dollars	173.8	400.4	173.8	400.4
Euro	27.0	(20.6)	27.0	(20.6)
Other currencies	(80.9)	(64.9)	(80.9)	(64.9)

The Company has other financial assets and liabilities that are also subject to exchange variation, not included in the previous note; however, they are used to minimize exposure in the currencies reported.

(iii) Derivatives

The Company uses derivatives to protect its operations against the risk of fluctuations in foreign exchange and interest rates; they are not used for speculative purposes.

Gains and losses on derivative transactions are recorded monthly in income, taking into account the realizable value of these instruments. The provision for unearned gains and losses is recorded in the balance sheet under Derivative financial instruments, and the contra item under Foreign exchange gain (loss), net, except for the operations designed as hedge accounting.

Hedge Accounting—Fair Value

At the time of designation of the hedge, the Company formally documents the relationship between hedging instruments and items that are hedged, including the risk management objectives and strategy in the conduct of the transaction, together with the methods to be used for evaluating the effectiveness of the relationship. The Company makes a continual assessment of the contract to conclude whether the instrument is "highly effective" in offsetting changes in fair value of the respective items of the subject contract during the period for which the hedge is designated, and actual results of each hedge are within the range 80% to 125%.

On December 31, 2011 the Company designated for hedge accounting the derivative financial instruments (swap) designed to convert financing operations subject to fixed interest rate of 9.00% p.a. into a floating rate equivalent to a CDI (Interbank Deposit Certificate) rate of 75.08% p.a. The amount of funding and the reference value of the derivative correspond to R$ 200.0 millions.

Hedge Accounting of Cash Flow

At the time of initial designation of the hedge, the Company formally documents the relationship between hedging instruments and hedged items, including risk management objectives and strategy in the conduct of the transaction, together with the methods to be used for evaluating the effectiveness of the relationship. The Company continually evaluates the hedging relationship to conclude whether this relationship will be "highly effective" in offsetting changes in fair value of its hedging instruments and hedge during the period for which the hedge is designated as high performers and actual results of each hedging relationship within the range 80 to 125%.

The objective of hedge accounting of cash flow is to protect more probable flow of salaries, besides medical plan expenses that are Real denominated against the exchange rate risk. The related cash flow is expected to be realized monthly, initiating on January 2012 and finishing on January 2013. The projected cash flow will impact the statement of income in the moment the expenses are recognized.

On December, 31 2011, the Company designated as hedge accounting cash flow derivative financial instruments in the zero-cost collar form. Those instruments consist of the purchase of puts with strike price of R$ 1.75 and the sale of calls with average strike price of R$ 2.3490; have been contracted with the same counterparty and with zero net premium. The reference value of contracted instruments totaled R$ 756.0 millions (equivalent to US$ 432.0 converted to the exchange rate of R$ 1.75). The fair value of hedge accounting instruments on December 31, 2011 is presented in the "exchange swap contracts" section.

The fair value of hedge accounting instruments is determined through the Garman–Kohlhagen model, which is commonly used by market participants to measure similar instruments.

Cross-Currency Interest Rate Swaps

These cross-currency interest rate swaps are contracted with the main objective of exchanging the debt at floating rates for fixed interest rates, and exchanging US dollars for Real or vice-versa, as applicable. At December 31, 2011, the Company had no contracts subject to margin calls.

On December 31, 2011, the Company had hired a swap designated as fair value hedge, by which the debt with the reference value at Real in the amount of R$ 200.0 million equivalent to US$ 106.6 of a fixed rate of 9.00% p.a. for a floating rate of 75.08% p.a. CDI (Interbank Deposit Certificate).

On December 31, 2011, the Company contracted swaps which effectively converted US$ 159.6 of obligations with and without recourse from a fixed interest rate of 5.98% p.a. to a floating interest rate of LIBOR + 1.21% p.a., and through a subsidiary hired a swap transaction in the amount of U$ 5.9 converting financing transactions subject to floating interest rate of LIBOR 1 month + 2.44% p.a. to fixed rates of 5.23% p.a.

The swap operations were as follows:

Underlying Transactions	Type	Original Currency	Present Currency	Notional Amount (In Thousands)	Average Rate Agreed—%	Gain (loss) Book Value 12.31.2011	Gain (loss) Fair Value 12.31.2011	Gain (loss) Book Value 12.31.2010	Gain (loss) Fair Value 12.31.2010
Recourse and Non-Recourse Debt									
Company asset	"Swap"	US$	US$	159.6	5.98% a.a.	28.6	28.6	20.9	20.9
Company liability	"Swap"			159.6	Libor + 1.21% a.a.				
Counterparty									
Natixis						28.6	28.6	20.9	20.9
Export financing— Designated for Fair Value Hedging									
Company asset	"Swap"	R$	R$	106.6	9.00% a.a.	2.2	2.2	—	—
Company liability	"Swap"			106.6	75.08% CDI a.a.				
Counterparty									
Bradesco						1.1	1.1		
Goldman Sachs						1.1	1.1	—	—
Acquisition Property, Plant and Equipment									
Company asset	"Swap"	US$	US$	5.9	Libor 1M + 2.44% a.a.	(0.7)	(0.7)	(0.4)	(0.4)
Company liability	"Swap"			5.9	5.23% a.a.				
Counterparty									
Compass Bank						(0.7)	(0.7)	(0.4)	(0.4)
					Total	30.1	30.1	20.5	20.5

Swaps—these are valued at present value, at the market rate on the base date, of the future flows determined by applying the contractual rates up to maturity and discounting to present value on the date of the financial statements at the current market rates.

Exchange Swap Contracts

At December 31, 2011 the Company had contracted option operations that have been designated as a cash flow hedge in the amount of R$ 756.0 million equivalent to US$ 432.0

by purchasing a put option with the average exercise price of R$ 1.75 and selling a call option with average price of R$ 2.4390. At December 31, 2011 the closing rate between the put option and call option values generated no gain or loss.

Other Derivatives

At December 31, 2011, the Company had swaps, equivalent to US$ 25.0 through which it has an asset linked to Exchange Coupon and a liability at a pre-fixed interest rate, as shown below:

Underlying Transactions	Type	Original Currency	Present Currency	Notional Amount (In Thousands)	Average Rate Agreed—%	Gain (Loss) Book Value 12.31.2011	Gain (Loss) Book Value 12.31.2011	Gain (Loss) Book Value 12.31.2010	Gain (Loss) Book Value 12.31.2010
Other									
Company asset	"Swap"	US$	US$	25.0	Coupon Fixed US dollar	(0.2)	(0.2)	(0.4)	(0.4)
Company liability	"Swap"			25.0					
Counterparty									
JP Morgan						(0.2)	(0.2)	(0.4)	(0.4)
					Total	(0.2)	(0.2)	(0.4)	(0.4)

These swap contracts are subject to Brazilian sovereign risk, and in case of an event that limits the convertibility of the Brazilian Real and or change the in taxes, could result in the redemption of the operation in Brazil in the form of bonds issued by the Brazilian Government ("LTN's"—National Treasury Bills) with a swap transaction into dollar for such securities.

Sensitivity Analysis

In order to present a positive and negative variation of 25% and 50% in the risk variable considered, a sensitivity analysis of the financial instruments is presented below, including derivatives, describing the effects on the monetary and foreign exchange variations on the financial income and expense determined on the balances recorded at December 31, 2011, in the event of the occurrence of such variations in the risk component.

However, statistical simplifications were made in isolating the variability of the risk factor in question. Consequently, the following estimates do not necessarily represent the amounts that might be determined in future financial statements. The use of different hypotheses and/or methodologies could have a material effect on the estimates presented below.

Methodology:

Based on the balances shown in the tables in item (c) above, and assuming that these remain constant, the Company calculated the interest and exchange variation differential for each of the projected scenarios.

In the evaluating of the amounts exposed to the interest rate risk, only the financial statements risks were considered, that is, the operations subject to prefixed interest rates were not included.

The probable scenario is based on the Company's estimates for each of the variables indicated, and positive and negative variations of 25% and 50% were applied to the rates in force at the balance sheet dates.

In the sensitivity analysis of derivative contracts, positive and negative variations of 25% and 50% were applied to the market yield curve (BM&FBOVESPA) at the balance sheet dates.

a. Interest Risk Factor

			Changes in Book Balances[*]				
	Risk Factor	Exposure at 12.31.2011	− 50%	− 25%	Probable Scenario—%	25%	50%
Financial investments	CDI	919.1	(50.0)	(24.9)	(10.3)	24.9	50.0
Loans	CDI	1.1	0.1	—	—	—	(0.1)
Net impact	CDI	918.0	(49.9)	(24.9)	(10.3)	24.9	49.9
Financial investments	Libor	316.3	(0.4)	(0.2)	0.4	0.2	0.4
Loans	Libor	87.8	0.1	—	(0.1)	—	(0.1)
Net impact	Libor	228.5	(0.3)	(0.2)	0.3	0.2	0.3
Financial investments	TJLP	—	—	—	—	—	—
Loans	TJLP	93.7	2.8	1.4	—	(1.4)	(2.8)
Net impact	TJLP	(93.7)	2.8	1.4	—	(1.4)	(2.8)
Rates considered—%	CDI	10.87%	5.44%	8.15%	9.75%	13.59%	16.31%
Rates considered—%	Libor	0.22%	0.11%	0.17%	0.35%	0.28%	0.33%
Rates considered—%	TJLP	6.00%	3.00%	4.50%	6.00%	7.50%	9.00%

[*] The positive and negative variations of 25% and 50% were applied on the rates in effect at 12.31.2011.

b. Foreign Exchange Risk Factor

			Changes in Book Balances[*]				
	Risk Factor	Exposure at 12.31.2011	− 50%	− 25%	Probable Scenario—%	25%	50%
Assets		1,351.1	675.5	337.8	90.6	(337.8)	(675.5)
Financial assets	BRL	919.1	459.5	229.8	61.6	(229.8)	(459.5)
Other assets	BRL	432.0	216.0	108.0	29.0	(108.0)	(216.0)
Liabilities		1,513.7	(756.9)	(378.4)	(101.5)	378.4	756.9
Loans and financing	BRL	621.0	(310.5)	(155.2)	(41.6)	155.2	310.5
Other liabilities	BRL	892.7	(446.4)	(223.2)	(59.9)	223.2	446.4
Net impact		(162.6)	(81.4)	(40.6)	(10.9)	40.6	81.4
Exchange rate considered		1.8758	0.9379	1.4069	1.7500	2.3448	2.8137

[*] The positive and negative variations of 25% and 50% were applied on the rates in effect at 12.31.2011.

c. Derivative Contracts

		Risk Factor	Exposure at 12.31.2011	Changes in Book Balances[*]				
				− 50%	− 25%	Probable Scenario—%	25%	50%
Interest swap	Libor	LIBOR	27.8	6.7	3.3	(2.0)	(3.0)	(6.1)
Interest swap—fair value hedge	CDI	CDI	2.2	6.9	3.2	0.2	(3.0)	(5.8)
Cash flow hedge	US$	US$	—	—	—	—	(6.7)	(23.9)
Others derivatives	Cupom Cambial	Exchange coupon	(0.2)	0.1	—	(0.1)	(0.3)	(0.4)
Total			29.8	13.7	6.5	(1.9)	(13.0)	(36.2)
Rate considered	CDI	LIBOR	10.87%	5.44%	8.15%	9.75%	13.59%	16.31%
Rate considered	Libor	CDI	0.29%	0.15%	0.22%	0.35%	0.36%	0.44%
Rate considered	US$	US$	1.8758	0.9379	1.4069	1.7500	2.3448	2.8137
Rate considered	Cupom Cambial	Exchange coupon	2.65%	1.33%	1.99%	2.97%	3.31%	3.98%

[*] The positive and negative variations of 25% and 50% were applied on the rates in effect at 12.31.2011.

d. Residual Value Guarantees

The residual value guarantees are reported in a manner similar to financial derivative instruments (Note 2.2 (ee)).

Methodology:

Based on residual value guarantee contracts in force, the Company ascertains any changes in values based on third party appraisals. The probable scenario is based on the Company's expectation of recording the provisions on a statistical basis, and the positive and negative variations of 25% and 50% have been applied to the third party appraisals at the balance sheet date.

Certain statistical simplifications were made in to isolating the variability of the risk factors in question. Consequently, the actual results may differ from these estimates. The following estimates do not necessarily represent the amounts that might be determined in future financial statements. The use of different hypotheses and/or methodologies could have a material effect on the estimates presented below.

(a) Description of Derivative Instruments Held by the Funds

Type	N° of Contracts	Due Date	Unit Market Price	Reference Value at 12.31.2011
Purchase—Forward DI	331	July-12	50.8	(16.8)
Sales—Forward DI	5	October-12	49.6	0.2
Sales—Forward DI	178	January-13	48.4	8.6
Purchase—Forward DI	193	April-13	47.3	(9.1)
Purchase—Forward DI	117	July-13	46.1	(5.4)
Sales—Forward DI	44	January-14	43.7	1.9
Purchase—Forward DI	8	January-15	39.2	(0.3)
Purchase—Forward Dolar	169	January-12	1.0	(8.5)
Purchase—Forward Dolar	13	February-12	1.0	(0.7)
Purchase—Forward Euro	2	January-12	1.3	(0.1)
Sales—Forward Reais to Australian	2	January-12	1.0	0.1
Sales—Forward Reais to Australian	2	February-12	1.0	0.1
Sales—Forward Reais to Canadian	3	January-12	1.0	0.2
Sales—Forward Reais to Canadian	2	February-12	1.0	0.1
Sales—Liber	3	January-12	1.5	0.2
Purchase—Forward Reais to New Z	5	January-12	0.8	(0.3)
Purchase—Forward Reais to New Z	4	February-12	0.8	(0.2)
Total				(30.0)

(b) Sensitivity Analysis

Risk Factor	Reference Value 12.31.2011	Additional Variations in the Return of the Fund		Probable Scenario		
		− 50%	− 25%	Probable Scenario	25%	50%
CDI	(20.9)	(0.8)	(0.4)	(0.1)	0.4	0.7
USD	(9.1)	4.6	2.3	(0.5)	(2.3)	(4.6)
Euro	(0.1)	0.2	0.2	0.3	0.3	0.3
Canadian Dolar	0.3	(0.1)	(0.1)	—	0.1	0.1
Pound Sterling	0.2	(0.1)	—	—	—	0.1
Australian Dolar	0.2	(0.1)	(0.1)	—	0.1	0.1
New Zealand Dolar	(0.5)	0.3	0.1	—	(0.1)	(0.3)
Total	(29.9)	4.0	2.0	(0.3)	(1.5)	(3.6)
Rates used						
CDI	10.87%	5.44%	8.15%	9.75%	13.59%	16.31%
Dolar	1.8758	0.9379	1.4069	1.7500	2.3448	2.8137
Euro	2.4342	1.2171	1.8257	2.4800	3.0428	3.6513
Canadian Dolar	1.8401	0.9201	1.3801	1.8360	2.3001	2.7602
Pound Sterling	2.9148	1.4574	2.1861	2.9100	3.6435	4.3722
Australian Dolar	1.9116	0.9558	1.4337	1.9200	2.3895	2.8674
New Zealand Dolar	1.4537	0.7269	1.0903	1.4600	1.8171	2.1806

SECTION 9: BUSINESS COMBINATIONS[1]

IAS 3, *BUSINESS COMBINATIONS*

IFRSs Overview and Comparison to U.S. GAAP

Author's Note

The International Accounting Standards Board (IASB) amended International Financial Reporting Standard (IFRS) 3, *Business Combinations*, through the issuance of the following standards:

- IFRS 9, *Financial Instruments* (issued November 2009 and October 2010 and effective for annual periods beginning on or after 1 January 2015) These amendments to IFRS 9
  —replace references to International Accounting Standard (IAS) 39, *Financial Instruments: Recognition and Measurement*, with references to IFRS 9;
  —eliminate the classification "available for sale;" and
  —replace the "fair value through profit or loss" with "fair value."
  With the elimination of the classification "available for sale," changes in fair value of financial assets or liabilities classified and measured at fair value are by definition recognized in profit or loss.
- IFRS 10, *Consolidated Financial Statements* (issued May 2011 and effective for annual periods beginning on or after 1 January 2013) This standard amends IFRS 3 by replacing references to IAS 27, *Consolidated and Separate Financial Statements*, with references to IFRS 10.
- IFRS 13, *Fair Value Measurement* (issued May 2011 and effective for annual periods beginning on or after 1 January 2013) This standard amends the definition of fair value in IFRS 3 and amends several paragraphs to add clarity using language that is consistent with that in IFRS 13.

Early application is permitted. Because the effective dates of these standards are after 1 January 2012, these amendments are not reflected in the commentary in this section. The timing of the effective dates of these standards also affects the availability of illustrative excerpts from survey companies' financial statements. Accordingly, the excerpts appearing later in the section may not reflect some or all of these revisions.

9.01 IFRS 3, issued January 2008, is the result of the second phase of the joint project between IASB and the Financial

Accounting Standards Board (FASB). The first phase of this project resulted in the issuance of the original IFRS 3 in 2004 and reflected IASB's conclusion that most business combinations should be accounted for using the acquisition method. The second phase had the objective of reaching the same conclusions as FASB with respect to the application of the acquisition method. Although IASB and FASB reached similar conclusions on most matters, several significant differences between the two standards remain.

9.02 IFRS 3 established two important changes in terminology, including the following:
- "Acquisition method" replaced "purchase method"
- "Noncontrolling interest" replaced "minority interest"

9.03 IFRS 3 establishes principles for recognition and measurement of identifiable assets acquired, liabilities assumed, and any noncontrolling interest in the acquired entity, as well as any goodwill acquired in the business combination or any gain from a bargain purchase. IFRS 3 also establishes disclosure requirements aimed at enabling users of the financial statements to adequately evaluate the nature and financial effects of the business combination.

9.04 IFRS 3 uses the term *acquisition method* to describe the method of accounting for business combinations, rather than the term previously used, *purchase method*. In making this change, IASB expressed its preference for describing the accounting method in terms of an economic event rather than in terms of consolidation accounting.

Recognition and Measurement

IFRSs

9.05 IFRS 3 applies to a transaction or other event that meets the definition of a *business combination*, defined in IFRSs as a transaction or other event in which an acquirer obtains control of one or more businesses. IFRS 3 requires the use of the acquisition method and identification of one of the combining entities as the acquirer. The *acquirer* is the entity that obtains control of the other entities (acquirees). IFRS 3 does not apply to any of the following transactions:
- Formation of a joint venture
- Acquisition of an asset or a group of assets that does not constitute a business
- Combination of entities or businesses under common control, as it is described in paragraphs B1–B4 of appendix B, "Application Guidance," of IFRS 3

9.06 IFRS 3 requires the entity identified as the acquirer to recognize, separately from goodwill, the identifiable assets acquired, liabilities assumed, and any noncontrolling interest in the acquiree. The entity should measure each identifiable asset acquired and liability assumed at their acquisition date fair value rather than at an allocated amount of the cost of the transaction.

9.07 IFRS 3 permits the acquirer to measure at the acquisition date, components of any noncontrolling interest in the

---

[1] Unless otherwise indicated, references to International Accounting Standards Board (IASB) standards and interpretations throughout this 2012 edition of *IFRS Financial Statements—Best Practices in Presentation and Disclosure* refer to the version of those standards and interpretations included in the *IFRS 2012* bound volume, the official printed consolidated text of IASB standards and interpretations, including revisions, amendments, and supporting documents, issued as of 1 January 2012.

acquiree that are present ownership interests and that entitle their holders to a proportionate share of the acquiree's net assets in the event of liquidation at either

- fair value, or
- the present ownership instruments' proportionate share of the acquiree's net identifiable assets.

The acquirer should measure all other components of non-controlling interests at their acquisition date fair values, unless IFRSs require another measurement basis.

9.08 Limited exceptions exist to these general recognition and measurement principles for certain assets and liabilities. These exceptions include the following:

- *Classification.* Classify leases and insurance contracts based on the contracts' terms at their inception rather than their acquisition date, as necessary to apply other IFRSs subsequently.
- *Contingent liabilities.* Recognize contingent liabilities assumed that constitute a present obligation and can be measured reliably, even if it is not probable that an outflow of resources embodying economic benefits will be required to settle the obligation.
- *Income taxes.* Recognize and measure deferred tax assets and liabilities and potential tax effects of temporary differences and carryforwards of an acquiree existing at the date of acquisition or arising from the business combination in accordance with IAS 12, *Income Taxes.*
- *Employee benefits.* Recognize and measure any liability or asset related to employee benefits in accordance with IAS 19, *Employee Benefits.*
- *Indemnification assets.* Recognize and measure indemnification assets on the same basis as the indemnified item, subject to a valuation allowance for uncollectible amounts.
- *Share-based payments.* Measure at the acquisition date a liability or equity instrument related to share-based payment transactions of the acquiree or the replacement of an acquiree's share-based payment awards transactions with share-based payment awards transactions of the acquirer, in accordance with the method in IFRS 2, *Share-based Payment.*
- *Reacquired rights.* Measure reacquired rights based on the remaining contractual term of the related contract.

9.09 An entity should recognize the difference between the sum of the fair values of the consideration transferred, the noncontrolling interest, any previously held equity interest in the acquiree, and the net identifiable assets acquired, measured in accordance with this standard, either as goodwill or, in certain circumstances, as a gain on a bargain purchase.

9.10 IFRS 3 eliminated the concept of negative goodwill. Prior to these revisions, an entity initially recognized the identifiable assets acquired and liabilities assumed (net assets acquired) at cost by allocating the consideration paid using relative fair values. When the consideration paid was more than the total fair value of the net assets acquired, the entity recognized the difference as goodwill. When the consideration paid was less than the total fair value, the entity allocated the difference and proportionately reducing carrying values. IFRS 3 now requires an entity to recognize the net assets acquired initially at fair value. Therefore, when the consideration paid is less than the fair value of the net assets, an entity recognizes this difference in profit or loss on the acquisition date and refers to this difference as a *gain on a bargain purchase.*

9.11 Paragraphs B19–B27 in appendix B of IFRS 3 include application guidance on accounting for reverse acquisitions in which the entity that issues securities (the legal acquirer) is identified as the acquiree for accounting purposes. IFRS 3 requires the accounting acquiree to meet the definition of a *business* in order for the business combination to be accounted for as a reverse acquisition. IFRS 3 requires the accounting acquirer to measure the acquisition date fair value of the consideration that it transferred for its interest in the accounting acquiree based on the number of equity interests that the legal subsidiary would have had to issue to give the owners of the legal parent the same percentage equity interest in the combined entity that results from the reverse acquisition. The accounting acquirer uses the fair value of the number of equity interests calculated in this way as the fair value of consideration transferred in exchange for the acquiree.

U.S. GAAP

Author's Note

Although IFRS 3 is the result of a convergence project between IASB and FASB, differences between IFRS 3 and FASB *Accounting Standards Codification* (ASC) 805, *Business Combinations*, remain. The text of IFRS 3 includes a detailed comparison of the differences between the two standards. This section only describes several key recognition and measurement differences.

9.12 Unlike IFRS 3, FASB ASC 805-20-30-1 requires an entity to measure the noncontrolling interest in the acquired entity at the acquisition date fair value on initial recognition. No alternative measurement is permitted.

9.13 Additionally, measurement differences exist between IFRSs and FASB ASC 805-20-30 even when the boards reached the same conclusions because there are differences in the measurement requirements of other standards (for example, deferred tax assets and employee benefit obligations). Disclosure requirements also can differ either because the entities within the scope of IFRS 3 are different from those entities subject to the comparable guidance under FASB ASC 805 or disclosure requirements are different for the various types of entities. For example, unlike FASB ASC 805-10-15-4, IFRS 3 does not provide a scope exception for not-for-profit entities that elect to prepare financial statements in accordance with IFRSs.

9.14 Like IFRS 3, an entity should not adjust assets and liabilities that arose from business combinations whose acquisition dates preceded the application of FASB ASC 805.

9.15 FASB ASC 805-40 provides more guidance than IFRSs on reverse acquisitions. Like IFRSs, FASB ASC 805-40-25-1 requires that the accounting acquiree must meet the definition of a *business*. FASB ASC 805-40-30-2 prescribes the identical measurement of the acquisition date fair value of the consideration transferred, as described in paragraph 9.11.

Presentation

IFRSs

9.16 IFRS 3 does not contain separate presentation requirements for normal business acquisitions beyond those found in IAS 1, *Presentation of Financial Statements*. However, because the consolidated financial statements following a reverse acquisition are issued under the name of the legal parent (accounting acquiree), appendix B of IFRS 3 requires the entity to describe in the notes to the consolidated financial statements a continuation of the financial statements of the legal subsidiary (accounting acquirer), with a retroactive adjustment of the accounting acquirer's legal capital to reflect the legal capital of the accounting acquiree. IFRS 3 also requires the legal parent to present comparative information, which is also retroactively adjusted to reflect the legal capital of the legal parent (accounting acquiree).

U.S. GAAP

9.17 Like IFRSs, FASB ASC 805-10 does not include specific presentation requirements for normal business acquisition. Presentation requirements in FASB ASC 805-40-45 are identical to those in appendix B of IFRS 3, with respect to reverse acquisitions.

Disclosure

Author's Note

Although an entity should apply IFRS 3 prospectively, some disclosures regarding changes in accounting policies required by IAS 8, *Accounting Policies, Changes in Accounting Estimates and Errors*, are relevant.

IFRSs

9.18 Prior to the 2008 revision, IFRS 3 had the following three disclosure objectives:
- Disclose information that permits evaluation of the nature and financial effect of business combinations that occurred during the reporting period or after the reporting date but before the financial statements were issued.
- Disclose information that permits evaluation of gains, losses, error corrections, and other adjustments related to business combinations that were recognized in the current period.
- Disclose information that permits evaluation of changes in the carrying amount of goodwill during the period.

9.19 The 2008 revisions to IFRS 3 resulted in the latter two objectives being combined into one objective to disclose information that permits evaluation of adjustments related to business combinations recognized during the current reporting period.

9.20 Disclosure requirements that remain unchanged in the 2008 revisions to IFRS 3 include information about the nature of the combination including the following:
- Name and description of the acquiree
- Acquisition date
- Percentage of voting equity interests acquired
- Primary reasons for the business combination and a description of how the acquirer obtained control of the acquiree

9.21 Additional disclosures, including those resulting from the 2008 revisions to IFRS 3, include the following:
- Acquisition date fair value of the total consideration transferred

- Acquisition date fair value of each major class of consideration (for example, cash, other assets, liabilities assumed, and equity instruments transferred)
- Amounts recognized for each major class of assets acquired and liabilities assumed
- Information about contingent liabilities recognized and, if not recognized for lack of measurement reliability, the reasons that the contingency could not be measured reliably
- Goodwill expected to be tax deductible
- Descriptions for assets and liabilities recognized separately from the business combination
- Amounts of any gains on bargain purchases, the line item in which gain is reported, and the reasons that the combination resulted in a gain
- Noncontrolling interest, such as the following:
  — Amounts of noncontrolling interest, if any
  — Measurement basis used
  — If the measurement basis is fair value, information about valuation models used and key model inputs
- Information about combinations achieved in stages, including the amount of equity interest held before the acquisition date
- Additional information also is disclosed for each individually material combination, such as the following:
  — Information about incomplete accounting
  — Changes in rights to contingent consideration
  — Reconciliation of the carrying amount of goodwill
  — Qualitative description of the factors that make up the goodwill recognized (for example, expected synergies from combined operations and intangible assets that did not qualify for separate recognition)
- Amounts of revenues and profit or loss of the acquiree subsequent to the acquisition date that are included in the acquirer's consolidated statement of comprehensive income, unless disclosure is impracticable (If impracticable, disclose this fact and provide an explanation.)
- Information in the aggregate for individually immaterial business combinations that are material in aggregate, such as the following:
  — Information about incomplete accounting
  — Changes in rights to contingent consideration
  — Reconciliation of the carrying amount of goodwill
- Amounts and explanations of gains or losses recognized during the period related to assets assumed and liabilities incurred that are relevant to an understanding of the combined entity's financial performance
- Amounts of revenue and profit and loss of the combined entity for all business combinations in total for the current reporting period as if the acquisition date was as of the beginning of the reporting period
- Acquired receivables, including fair values; gross contractual amounts; and estimated uncollectible amounts
- Contingent consideration arrangements and indemnification assets

9.22 The revised IFRS 3 retains the disclosure requirements of IFRS 3 as originally issued with modifications to reflect the shift from the original cost-based approach to the acquisition date fair value approach of IFRS 3 revised. New disclosure requirements required by the 2008 revisions were added either in response to requests from commentators during review of the exposure draft or to converge with FASB ASC 805 disclosures.

U.S. GAAP

9.23 Most of the required disclosures are similar to those required by IFRS 3. Both IFRSs and FASB ASC 805-10-50 require supplemental pro forma disclosures for the current period. However, FASB ASC 805-10-50-2 requires these disclosures for public entities only, whereas IFRSs require them for all entities. Such disclosures include the following:

- Name and description of the acquiree
- Acquisition date
- Percentage of voting equity interests acquired
- Primary reason for business combination and description of how acquirer gained control of the acquiree
- For a business combination achieved in stages:
  — Acquisition date fair value of the equity interest in the acquiree held by the acquirer immediately before the acquisition
  — Amount of any gain or loss recognized as a result of remeasuring to fair value the equity interest that the acquirer held immediately before the business combination
  — Line item in the income statement in which that gain or loss is recognized
  — Valuation technique(s) used to measure the acquisition date fair value of the equity interest the acquirer held immediately before the business combination
  — Other information helpful to users in assessing the inputs used to develop the fair value measurement of the equity interest in the acquiree held by the acquirer immediately before the business combination
- For acquirers that are public entities:
  — Amounts of revenue and earnings of the acquiree since the acquisition date included in the consolidated income statement for the period
  — Pro forma information that differs depending upon whether the entity presents comparative financial statements. If an entity presents comparative financial statements, it should provide pro forma disclosures for the comparative prior period for revenue and earnings of the combined entity. IFRS 3 has no such requirement. Nature and amount of any material, nonrecurring pro forma adjustments directly attributable to the business combination, that are included in the reported pro forma revenue and earnings.

9.24 Paragraphs 5–6 of FASB ASC 805-10-50 require an acquirer to disclose information about the financial effects of adjustments recognized in the current period that relate to business combinations completed in the current or prior periods. Unlike IFRSs, these paragraphs do not specifically require the disclosure of gains or losses recognized in the current period that relate to the identifiable assets acquired or liabilities assumed in the business combination. However, these paragraphs, in conjunction of FASB ASC 805-10-25-17, require an entity to disclose changes to prior measurements. Both IFRSs and FASB ASC 805-10-50 include a general requirement for acquirers to disclose information that would be relevant to users' understanding of the business combination.

9.25 FASB ASC 805-20-50 disclosures about contingencies differ from those required by IFRS 3 because the recognition criteria differ.

Presentation and Disclosure Excerpts

Multiple Business Acquisitions for Cash in 2011 and 2010, Gains on Bargain Purchases and Revaluation of Previously Held Equity Interest in 2010, Change in Accounting Policy for Common Control Transactions

9.26

Absa Group Limited (Dec 2011)

CONSOLIDATED STATEMENT OF COMPREHENSIVE INCOME (in part)

	Note	Group 2011 Rm	2010 Rm
Net interest income		24 429	23 340
Interest and similar income	30	51 221	54 241
Interest expense and similar charges	31	(26 792)	(30 901)
Impairment losses on loans and advances	10.1	(5 081)	(6 005)
Net interest income after impairment losses on loans and advances		19 348	17 335
Non-interest income		21 403	19 474
Net fee and commission income		15 293	14 391
Fee and commission income	32	17 422	16 454
Fee and commission expense	32	(2 129)	(2 063)
Net insurance premium income	33	5 209	4 602
Net insurance claims and benefits paid	34	(2 517)	(2 405)
Changes in investment contract and insurance contract liabilities	35	(914)	(1 059)
Gains and losses from banking and trading activities	36	2 594	2 349
Gains and losses from investment activities	37	966	884
Other operating income	38	772	712
Operating profit before operating expenditure		40 751	36 809
Operating expenditure		(26 581)	(24 949)
Operating expenses	39	(25 458)	(24 070)
Other impairments	40	(52)	(108)
Indirect taxation	41	(1 071)	(771)
Share of post-tax results of associates and joint ventures	13.1	40	(9)
Operating profit before income tax		14 210	11 851

CONSOLIDATED STATEMENT OF CHANGES IN EQUITY (in part)

	Number of Ordinary Shares '000	Ordinary Share Capital Rm	Ordinary Share Premium Rm	Retained Earnings Rm	Total Other Reserves Rm	General Credit Risk Reserve Rm	Available-For-Sale Reserve Rm	Cash Flow Hedging Reserve Rm	Foreign Currency Translation Reserve Rm	Insurance Contingency Reserve Rm	Share-Based Payment Reserve Rm	Associates' and Joint Ventures' Reserve Rm	Total Equity Attributable to Ordinary Equity Holders of the Group Rm	Non-Controlling Interest—Ordinary Shares Rm	Non-Controlling Interest—Preference Shares Rm	Total Rm
Group 2011																
Balance at the beginning of the year	716 590	1 433	4 590	47 958	2 309	63	(196)	2 258	(640)	305	285	234	56 290	1 215	4 644	62 149
Total comprehensive income for the year	—	—	—	9 623	168	—	(17)	(237)	422	—	—	—	9 791	326	284	10 401
Profit for the year	—	—	—	9 674	—	—	—	—	—	—	—	—	9 674	226	284	10 184
Other comprehensive income	—	—	—	(51)	168	—	(17)	(237)	422	—	—	—	117	100	—	217
Dividends paid during the year	—	—	—	(3 744)	—	—	—	—	—	—	—	—	(3 744)	(173)	(284)	(4 201)
Share buy-back in respect of equity-settled share-based payment schemes	—	—	(281)	—	—	—	—	—	—	—	—	—	(281)	—	—	(281)
Elimination of the movement in treasury shares held by Absa Group Limited Share Incentive Trust	681	2	26	—	—	—	—	—	—	—	—	—	28	—	—	28
Options exercised by employees		2	26	—	—	—	—	—	—	—	—	—	28	—	—	28
Shares issued to the trust		—	—	—	—	—	—	—	—	—	—	—	—	—	—	—
Elimination of the movement in treasury shares held by Group subsidiaries	(257)	(1)	167	—	—	—	—	—	—	—	—	—	166	—	—	166
Movement in share-based payment reserve	—	0	174	—	(116)	—	—	—	—	—	(116)	—	58	—	—	58
Transfer from share-based payment reserve		0	174	—	(174)	—	—	—	—	—	(174)	—	—	—	—	—
Value of employee services		—	—	—	58	—	—	—	—	—	58	—	58	—	—	58
Movement in general credit risk reserve	—	—	—	48	(48)	(48)	—	—	—	—	—	—	—	—	—	—
Movement in insurance contingency reserve	—	—	—	(19)	19	—	—	—	—	19	—	—	—	—	—	—
Share of post-tax results of associates and joint ventures	—	—	—	(40)	40	—	—	—	—	—	—	40	—	—	—	—
Disposal of associates and joint ventures—release of reserves	—	—	—	(13)	13	—	—	—	—	—	—	13	—	—	—	—
Increase in the interest of non-controlling equity holders	—	—	—	—	—	—	—	—	—	—	—	—	—	21	—	21
Non-controlling interest arising from business combinations	—	—	—	—	—	—	—	—	—	—	—	—	—	64	—	64
Balance at the end of the year	717 014	1 434	4 676	53 813	2 385	15	(213)	2 021	(218)	324	169	287	62 308	1 453	4 644	68 405
Notes	27	27	27			28	28	28	28	28	28	28			29	

IFRS-BPPD 9.26

CONSOLIDATED STATEMENT OF CASH FLOWS
(in part)

		Group	
	Note	2011 Rm	2010[1] Rm
Cash flow from investing activities			
Purchase of investment properties	15	(255)	(288)
Purchase of property and equipment	16	(1 729)	(2 351)
Proceeds from sale of property and equipment		119	255
Purchase of intangible assets	14	(482)	(718)
Disposal of investment properties		4	—
Proceeds from sale of intangible assets		4	—
Acquisition of businesses, net of cash	56.1, 56.2	(290)	470
Disposal of businesses, net of cash	56.4	—	(6)
Acquisition of associates and joint ventures	13.5, 56.1	(3)	(95)
Disposal of associates and joint ventures	8, 13.6	356	95
Net (increase)/decrease in loans to associates and joint ventures	13.1	(7)	4
Net decrease in investment securities		1 642	3 397
Dividends received from investment activities		130	117
Net cash (utilised)/generated from investing activities		(511)	880

NOTES TO THE CONSOLIDATED FINANCIAL STATEMENTS *(in part)*

1. Summary of Significant Accounting Policies *(in part)*

The significant accounting policies applied in the preparation of these consolidated financial statements are set out below. These policies comply with IFRS, Interpretations issued by the International Financial Reporting Interpretation Committee (IFRIC) and the requirements of the Companies Act. Certain new disclosures have been added in the consolidated financial statements in order to comply with the new provisions as required by the recently effective Companies Act, which is mandatory for the first time for this financial year under review.

Standards and Amendments to Standards Mandatory for the First Time for This Financial Year Under Review

IFRS 3 *Business Combinations* (IFRS 3) (amendments): clarify that contingent consideration arising in a business combination previously accounted for in accordance with IFRS 3 (2004) that remains outstanding at the adoption date of IFRS 3 (2008), continues to be accounted for in accordance with IFRS 3 (2004); limit the accounting policy choice to measure non-controlling interests upon initial recognition at fair value or at the non-controlling interest's proportionate share of the acquiree's identifiable net assets to instruments that give rise to a present ownership interest and that currently entitle the holder to a share of net assets in the event of liquidation; and expand the current guidance on the attribution of the market-based measure of an acquirer's share-based payment awards issued in exchange for acquiree awards between consideration transferred and post-combination compensation cost, when an acquirer is obliged to replace the acquiree's existing awards to encompass voluntarily replaced unexpired acquiree awards.

These amendments were specifically considered for business acquisitions within the scope of IFRS 3 for the current year or prior year (where applicable) and had no material impact on the consolidated financial statements of the Group.

1.3 Consolidation (in part)

1.3.5 Business Combinations Achieved in Stages (Step Acquisitions)

When the Group purchases additional interests in an entity in which it does not have control prior to acquisition, the previously held equity interest in the acquiree is remeasured at its acquisition-date fair value and the resulting gain or loss, if any, is recognised in profit or loss. If in any prior periods, any changes in the value of the equity interest in the acquiree have previously been recognised in other comprehensive income, then that change is recognised on the same basis as if the Group had disposed directly of the previously held interest.

1.3.6 Common Control

Common control transactions are business combinations in which the combining entities are ultimately controlled by the Group. The Group applies the predecessor accounting method when accounting for common control transactions.

The assets and liabilities of the combining entities are not adjusted to fair value but reflected at their carrying amounts at the date of the transaction. Any difference between the consideration paid/transferred and the net asset value 'acquired' is reflected within retained earnings. No new goodwill will be recognised as a result of the common control transaction.

The comparative statement of financial position and statement of comprehensive income will be restated as if the entities had always been combined, regardless of the date of the transaction.

1.27 Change in Accounting Policy (in part)

The application of the Group's accounting policies are consistent with those adopted in the prior year, except for the following:

During the year, the Group adopted the predecessor accounting method as the method for the treatment of common control transactions. The Group previously accounted for common control transactions, where the transaction had substance, using the acquisition method under IFRS 3.

This change has been adopted in order to be consistent with the Group's parent, Barclays Bank PLC.

The change in accounting policy did not impact the consolidated results, nor did it have any impact on basic or diluted earnings per share as previously reported. Furthermore, the change did not impact any line item on the statement of financial position for any financial periods prior to the comparative information presented.

14. Goodwill and Intangible Assets

	Group					
	2011			**2010**		
	Cost Rm	Accumulated Amortisation and/or Impairments Rm	Carrying Value Rm	Cost Rm	Accumulated Amortisation and/or Impairments Rm	Carrying Value Rm
Computer software development costs	2 322	(906)	1 416	1 738	(616)	1 122
Customer lists	270	(125)	145	191	(96)	95
Goodwil	719	(150)	569	693	(122)	571
Other	10	(5)	5	10	(4)	6
	3 321	(1 186)	2 135	2 632	(838)	1 794

	Group						
	2011						
	Opening Balance Rm	Additions Rm	Additions Through Business Combinations Rm	Disposals Rm	Foreign Exchange Movements Rm	Amortisation Rm	Impairment Charge Rm	Closing Balance Rm
Reconciliation of goodwill and intangible assets							
Computer software development costs	1 122	482	—	(6)	80	(262)	—	1 416
Customer lists	95	—	76	—	—	(26)	—	145
Goodwill	571	—	26	—	—	—	(28)	569
Other	6	—	—	—	—	(1)	—	5
	1 794	482	102	(6)	80	(289)	(28)	2 135

	2010						
	Opening Balance Rm	Additions Rm	Additions Through Business Combinations Rm	Disposals Rm	Foreign Exchange Movements Rm	Amortisation Rm	Impairment Charge Rm	Closing Balance Rm
Reconciliation of goodwill and intangible assets							
Computer software development costs	543	718	—	—	(3)	(132)	(4)	1 122
Customer lists	124	—	1	—	—	(30)	—	95
Goodwil	571	—	—	—	—	—	—	571
Other	7	—	2	—	—	3	—	6
	1 245	718	3	—	(3)	(165)	(4)	1 794

Refer to note 1.14 for useful lives, amortisation methods and amortisation rates. The majority of computer software development costs were internally generated with the remainder externally acquired.

Included in computer software development costs is R168 million (2010: R325 million) relating to assets still under construction. No borrowing costs were capitalised during the year under review.

	Group	
	2011 Rm	2010 Rm
Composition of goodwill		
Absa Vehicle and Management Solutions Proprietary Limited	112	112
Abseq Properties Proprietary Limited	—	25
Abvest Holdings Proprietary Limited	30	30
Glenrand MIB employee benefits and healthcare	22	22
Global Alliance Seguros S.A.	23	—
Ngwenya River Estate Proprietary Limited	18	18
Woolworths Financial Services Proprietary Limited	364	364
	569	571

Significant Assumptions Made in Reviewing Impairments

Management has to consider at least annually whether the current carrying value of goodwill is impaired. This calculation is based on discounting expected risk adjusted pre-tax cash flows at a risk adjusted pre-tax interest rate appropriate to the operating unit, the determination of which requires the exercise of judgement. The estimation of pre-tax cash flows is sensitive to the periods for which detailed forecasts are available, normally capped at five years, and to assumptions regarding the growth rate, although this is usually capped at inflation growth where higher growth is forecasted by the CGU. While forecasts are compared with actual performance and external sources of data, expected cash flows naturally reflect management's best estimate of future performance. The discount rate used in the impairment calculations is 14% (2010: 14%). Growth rates used in the impairment calculations range from 4% to 7% (2010: 4% to 7%).

44. Headline Earnings

Headline earnings are determined as follows:

	Group			
	2011		2010	
	Gross Rm	Net[1] Rm	Gross Rm	Net[1] Rm
Profit attributable to ordinary equity holders of the Group		9 674		8 118
Total headline earnings adjustment:		45		(77)
IFRS 3—Goodwill impairment (gain on bargain purchase) (refer to notes 40 and 56)	28	28	(72)	(72)
IAS 16[2]—Profit on disposal of property and equipment (refer to note 38)	(33)	(30)	(41)	(37)
IAS 28 and 31—Headline earnings component of share of post-tax results of associates and joint ventures	(0)	(0)	(1)	(1)
IAS 28 and 31—Profit on disposal of investments in associates and joint ventures (refer to note 36)	—	—	(42)	(42)
IAS 28 and 31—Impairment (reversal)/charge of investments in associates and joint ventures (refer to note 40)	(2)	(1)	29	21
IAS 36[3]—Impairment of equipment (refer to note 40)	—	—	13	9
IAS 38[4]—Loss on disposal and impairment of intangible assets (refer to note 38 and 40)	2	1	4	3
IAS 39—Release of available-for-sale reserves (refer to note 36)	20	14	92	66
IAS 39—Impairment of available-for-sale assets (refer to note 40)	—	—	25	18
IAS 40[5]—Change in fair value of investment properties (refer to notes 38 and 39)	39	33	(50)	(42)
Headline earnings/diluted headline earnings		9 719		8 041
Headline earnings per share (cents)		1 355,9		1 122,6
Diluted headline earnings per share (cents)		1 350,0		1 115,7

56. Acquisitions and Disposals of Businesses

56.1 Acquisitions of Businesses During the Year Under Review

A summary of the total net cash outflow and cash and cash equivalents related to business combinations is included below:

	Group	
	2011 Rm	2010 Rm
Summary of net cash (outflow)/inflow due to acquisitions	(331)	61
Summary of total cash and cash equivalents acquired	38	409

56.1.1 During April 2011, the Group acquired 76% of the units in Absa Property Equity Fund (APEF) and, as a result, has taken on a majority share of the risks and rewards of the fund. APEF operates as a SPE specifically for the investment in community upliftment projects and is consolidated in terms of SIC-12. The APEF was disposed of in 2010 and reacquired in 2011.

Details of the net assets acquired are as follows:

	Group
	2011 Fair Value Recognised on Acquisition Rm
Cash, cash balances and balances with central banks	0
Other assets	1
Investment securities	277
Other liabilities	0
Non-controlling interest	(67)
Net assets acquired	211
Satisfied by:	
Cash outflow on acquisition	211
Fair value of net assets acquired	(211)
Goodwill	—
Net cash outflow due to acquisition	211
Total cash and cash equivalents acquired	0

Since its acquisition, the APEF contributed revenue of R10 million and a net profit before tax of R13 million to the Group for the period 1 April 2011 to 31 December 2011. If the acquisition occurred on 1 January 2011, the Group's revenue would have been R17 million higher and the net profit before tax for the year would have been R18 million higher.

56.1.2 During September 2011, the Group acquired a 100% shareholding in Global Alliance Seguros S.A. (GA), a leading provider of non-life insurance in Mozambique. The acquisition of GA will enable the Group to offer a full suite of insurance products and services in the Mozambican market. As at the acquisition date, the accounting for the business combination was provisionally determined since all the fair values of identifiable assets and liabilities are in the process of being finalised as part of the due diligence process. Acquisition-related costs amounted to R3 million in the statement of comprehensive income.

Details of the net assets acquired are as follows:

	Group
	2011 Fair Value Recognised on Acquisition Rm
Cash, cash balances and balances with central banks	38
Intangible assets	72
Investment properties	28
Property and equipment	24
Other assets	91
Other liabilities	(139)
Deferred tax liabilities	(20)
Net assets acquired	94
Satisfied by:	
Cash outflow on acquisition	117
Fair value of net assets acquired	(94)
Goodwill	23
Net cash outflow due to acquisition	117
Total cash and cash equivalents acquired	38

Since its acquisition, GA has contributed revenue of R31 million and a net profit before tax of R16 million to the Group for the period 1 September 2011 to 31 December 2011. If the acquisition occurred on 1 January 2011, the Group's revenue would have been R86 million higher and the net profit before tax for the year would have been R39 million higher.

56.1.3 During October 2011, the Group acquired the operations of Takafol South Africa Proprietary Limited (Takafol), (an underwriting management agent) for which Absa Insurance Company underwrote the Islamic insurance policies administered by Takafol, for R3 million.

Details of the net assets acquired are as follows:

	Group
	2011 Fair Value Recognised on Acquisition Rm
Intangible assets—customer relationships	4
Deferred tax liabilities	(1)
Net assets acquired	3
Satisfied by:	
Cash outflow on acquisition	3
Fair value of net assets acquired	(3)
Goodwill	—
Net cash outflow due to acquisition	3
Total cash and cash equivalents acquired	—

56.1.4 The Group, together with two other parties, have a shareholding in Barrie Island Investments Proprietary Limited (Barrie Island). During January 2011, the Group entered into an agreement to purchase an additional 30% of the shares in Barrie Island from another shareholder who wished to exit the arrangement. Following this purchase, the Group owns 70% of the shares of Barrie Island. At the acquisition date, the investment was recognised at Rnil. A fair value adjustment of R3 million was processed as a loss in the statement of comprehensive income when the additional shares in Barrie Island were acquired. Barrie Island holds property in Alberton. The property is zoned for commercial and residential use. The goodwill in Barrie Island has been impaired as Barrie Island has been consistently making losses and is not expected to be profitable in the near future.

Details of the net assets acquired are as follows:

	Group
	2011
	Fair Value Recognised on Acquisition
	Rm
Cash, cash balances and balances with central banks	0
Investment properties	40
Other liabilities	(50)
Deferred tax asset	1
Fair value of existing interest	3
Non-controlling interest	3
Net liabilities incurred	(3)
Satisfied by:	
Cash outflow on acquisition	0
Fair value of net liabilities incurred	3
Goodwill	3
Net cash outflow due to acquisition	0
Total cash and cash equivalents acquired	0

Since the additional purchase of shares in Barrie Island, there was no revenue and profit before tax impact to the Group for the period to 31 December 2011.

56.2.1 On 30 June 2010, the Virgin Money South Africa Proprietary Limited (VMSA) joint venture arrangement was terminated. This was a result of a contractually agreed arrangement where its future existence depended on the financial performance of the joint venture. Due to the underperformance of the joint venture, the arrangement was terminated and the Group acquired the underlying business. The termination resulted in the Group selling its 50% interest in VMSA for R1, while acquiring VMSA's credit and home loan business for R1. VMSA's credit card and home loan business contributed a net profit before tax of R40 million and revenue of R57 million to the Group for the period from 30 June 2010 to 31 December 2010. If the acquisition occurred on 1 January 2010, the Group's revenue would have been R116 million higher and the net profit before tax for the year would have been R21 million higher.

Details of the net assets acquired and the gain on bargain purchase are as follows:

	Group
	2010
	Fair Value Recognised on Acquisition
	Rm
Intangible assets	3
Other liabilities	(1)
Deferred tax liabilities	(1)
Net assets acquired	1
Satisfied by:	
Cash flow on acquisition	0
Fair value of net assets acquired	(1)
Gain on bargain purchase	(1)
Net cash outflow due to acquisition	0
Total cash and cash equivalents acquired	0

This bargain purchase gain arose primarily due to the underperformance of the underlying VMSA credit card and home loan portfolio. No contingent liabilities were recognised as a result of the acquisition, and no contingent consideration is payable. No identifiable assets were identified of which the fair values could not be reliably measured. No material receivables were acquired as part of the transaction.

56.2.2 The Group previously had a 50% share in the preference shares of Sanlam Home Loans Proprietary Limited (SHL), the holding company of three securitisation vehicles. The investment in SHL has previously been equity accounted as the Group and Sanlam had joint control over SHL. On 1 August 2010, the Group acquired the remaining 50% preference shares in SHL, which resulted in the Group controlling and consolidating SHL. SHL contributed a net profit before tax of R39 million and revenue of R12 million to the Group for the period from 1 August 2010 to 31 December 2010. If the acquisition had occurred on 1 January 2010, the Group's revenue would have been R84 million higher and the net profit before tax for the year would have been R70 million higher.

Details of the net assets acquired and the gain on bargain purchase are as follows:

	Group
	2010
	Fair Value Recognised on Acquisition
	Rm
Cash, cash balances and balances with central banks	409
Other assets	11
Loans and advances to customers	4 621
Other liabilities	(9)
Debt securities in issue	(3 687)
Shareholders' loans	(1 325)
Previously held interest	(10)
Net assets acquired	10
Satisfied by:	
Cash inflow on acquisition	(61)
Fair value of net assets acquired	(10)
Gain on bargain purchase	(71)
Net cash inflow on acquisition	61
Total cash and cash equivalents acquired	409

56.2.2 No goodwill resulted from the transaction and the excess of R71 million, together with the gain of R10 million recognised as a result of remeasuring the previously held interest to fair value, was realised in the statement of comprehensive income in other operating income. No contingent liabilities were recognised as a result of the acquisition, and no contingent consideration was payable. No identifiable assets were identified of which the fair values could not be reliably measured.

Subsequent to the acquisition, the debt securities in issue were redeemed in full.

Mortgage loans with a fair value of R4 621 million were acquired as a result of the acquisition. The gross contractual capital amounts receivable were R4 685 million on the acquisition date and an impairment provision of R64 million was carried against these loans on the acquisition date.

The joint venture agreement was terminated due to the underperformance of the mortgage loan portfolio and consequently the Group obtained full control of SHL. The underperformance of the mortgage loan portfolio gave rise to the gain on bargain purchase as the joint venture partner was willing to sell its 50% stake at below the fair value of the underlying assets and liabilities.

56.3 Disposal of Businesses During the Year Under Review

There were no disposals during the current year under review.

56.4 Disposal of Businesses During the Prior Year

56.4.1 APEF operated as a SPE for the investment of community upliftment projects. This fund was previously consolidated under SIC-12 as the Group held between 75% and 93% of units (depending on the total number of units in issue at a specific point in time) and was thereby exposed to the majority of risks and rewards of the fund.

Between January 2010 and August 2010, the Group disposed of some of its units, thereby decreasing its effective shareholding to below 50% of the units in issue. At this point, the fund was deconsolidated due to the Group no longer being exposed to the majority of the risks and rewards of the fund.

No gain or loss was recognised on deconsolidation of the fund due to the underlying assets being measured at fair value.

The remainder of the investment retained after deconsolidation was disposed of during September 2010 and October 2010.

Details of the net assets disposed of are as follows:

	Group 2010 Rm
Cash, cash balances and balances with central banks	22
Investment securities	136
Net assets disposed of	158
Satisfied by:	
Non-controlling interest	(78)
Fair value of interest retained	(64)
Net cash inflow on disposal	16
Total cash and cash equivalents disposed of	(22)
Net cash outflow on disposal	(6)

Non-Controlling Interest Measured at the Proportionate Share of the Net Identifiable Assets of the Acquiree, Call Option Agreement

9.27

Author's Note

VimpelCom Ltd implemented IFRSs effective December 31, 2010, with a date of transition of January 1, 2009. Prior to adopting IFRSs, VimpelCom prepared its financial statements in accordance with U.S. GAAP. In its 2011 financial statements, VimpelCom explains the effect of adopting IFRS 3 retrospectively to June 26, 2008. The excerpt that follows includes the relevant parts of note 4, First time adoption of IFRS.

VimpelCom Ltd (Dec 2011)

CONSOLIDATED STATEMENT OF CHANGES IN EQUITY (in part)

(In Millions of US Dollars)	Foot-note	Number of Shares Outstanding	Issued Capital	Capital Surplus	Treasury Shares	Other Capital Reserves	Retained Earnings	Foreign Currency Trans-lation	Total	Non-Con-trolling Interest	Total Equity
As at December 31, 2009		1,014,291,577	1	1,432	(224)	(30)	3,370	(384)	4,165	37	4,202
Profit for the period							1,806		1,806	67	1,873
Other comprehensive income	17							(81)	(81)	(10)	(91)
Total comprehensive income							1,806	(81)	1,725	57	1,782
Dividends	21						(594)		(594)	(73)	(667)
Issuance of shares for KyivStar acquisition		301,653,080		5,595					5,595		5,595
Effect of exchange offer	1	(24,764,218)		(501)					(501)		(501)
Issuance of shares	1	50,000		1					1		1
Repurchase of noncontrolling interest in OJSC	1			30					30		30
Acquisition of non-controlling interest	7					(4)			(4)	(6)	(10)
Changes in a parent's ownership interest in a subsidiary that do not result in a loss of control	17					(11)			(11)	(24)	(35)
Exercise of options	22	820,261			8	—			8		8
Share-based payment transactions	22					7			7		7
As at December 31, 2010		1,292,050,700	1	6,557	(216)	(38)	4,582	(467)	10,421	(9)	10,412

(In Millions of US Dollars)	Foot-note	Number of Shares	Issued Capital	Capital Surplus	Treasury Shares	Other Capital Reserves	Retained Earnings	Foreign Currency Transla-tion	Total	Non-Con-trolling Interest	Total Equity
						Attributable to Owners of the Parent					
As at December 31, 2010		1,292,050,700	1	6,557	(216)	(38)	4,582	(467)	10,421	(9)	10,412
Profit for the period							543		543	(274)	269
Total other comprehensive income						(276)		(603)	(879)	(125)	(1,004)
Total comprehensive income						(276)	543	(603)	(336)	(399)	(735)
Dividends							(1,216)		(1,216)		(1,216)
Issuance of shares	1	325,639,827	1	4,988					4,989		4,989
Acquisition of treasury shares		(50,000)			(1)				(1)		(1)
Non-controlling interest arising on a business combination	7					(13)		—	(13)	2,124	2,111
Restructuring of shareholding in consolidated subsidiaries	7					268		(5)	263	(37)	226
Changes in a parent's ownership interest in a subsidiary that do not result in a loss of control	17					(54)			(54)	(49)	(103)
Effect of deconsolidation OTH spin-off assets	7								—	(765)	(765)
Exercise of options	22	480,000		4		(3)			1		1
Share-based payment transactions	22					(17)			(17)		(17)
As at December 31, 2011		1,618,120,527	2	11,545	(213)	(133)	3,909	(1,075)	14,037	865	14,902

CONSOLIDATED STATEMENT OF CASH FLOWS
(in part)

(In Millions of US Dollars)	Note	2011	2010	2009
		Year Ended December 31		
Investing Activities				
Proceeds from sale of property, plant and equipment and intangible assets		34	14	—
Purchase of property, plant and equipment and intangible assets		(6,260)	(1,814)	(1,022)
Payments of loans granted		(118)	(33)	—
Receipts/(payments) from deposits and loans granted		212	478	(489)
Receipts from/(investments in) associates		25	—	(13)
Acquisition of subsidiaries, net of cash acquired	7	(838)	(27)	—
Net cash flows used in investing activities		(6,945)	(1,382)	(1,524)
Financing Activities				
Net proceeds from exercise of share options		5	7	18
Acquisition of non-controlling interest		—	(13)	(18)
Proceeds from borrowings net of fees paid		10,389	1,170	1,217
Repayment of borrowings		(6,581)	(2,898)	(2,433)
Purchase of treasury shares		(1)	(480)	—
Dividends paid to equity holders of the parent		(1,216)	(578)	(316)
Dividends paid to non-controlling interests		(13)	(72)	(31)
Net cash flows used in financing activities		2,583	(2,864)	(1,563)

NOTES TO THE CONSOLIDATED FINANCIAL STATEMENTS *(in part)*

1 General Information

VimpelCom Ltd. ("VimpelCom," the "Company," and together with its consolidated subsidiaries the "Group" or "we") was incorporated in Bermuda on 5 June 2009, as an exempted company under the name New Spring Company Ltd., which was subsequently changed to VimpelCom Ltd. on 1 October 2009. VimpelCom Ltd. was formed to recapitalize Open Joint Stock Company "Vimpel-Communications" ("OJSC Vimpel-Com") and acquire CJSC "Kyivstar G.S.M." ("Kyivstar") (Note 7). Altimo Holdings & Investments Limited ("Altimo") and

Telenor ASA ("Telenor") together with certain of their respective affiliates were the two major shareholders in each of the companies. The registered office of VimpelCom Ltd. is Victoria Place, 31 Victoria Street, Hamilton HM 10, Bermuda. VimpelCom Ltd.'s headquarters and principal place of business are located at Claude Debussylaan 88, 1082 MD Amsterdam.

In these notes U.S. dollar amounts are presented in millions, except for share and per share (or ADS) amounts and as otherwise indicated.

On 21 April 2010, VimpelCom Ltd. successfully completed an exchange offer ("Exchange Offer") for OJSC VimpelCom shares (including shares represented by American Depositary Shares ("ADSs")), and acquired approximately 98% of OJSC VimpelCom's outstanding shares (including shares represented by ADSs). Therefore, effective 21 April 2010, OJSC VimpelCom is a subsidiary of VimpelCom Ltd. As the continuation of the existing Group, VimpelCom Ltd. is the accounting successor to OJSC VimpelCom, and therefore accounting data and disclosures related to the period prior to 21 April 2010 represent accounting data and disclosures of OJSC VimpelCom. Information about the number of shares prior to 21 April 2010 has been adjusted to reflect the effect of the recapitalization due to the Exchange Offer.

On 25 May 2010, VimpelCom Ltd. served a squeeze-out demand notice to OJSC VimpelCom demanding that the remaining shareholders of OJSC VimpelCom sell their shares to VimpelCom Ltd. The squeeze-out process was completed on 6 August 2010. As a result, VimpelCom Ltd. became the sole shareholder of OJSC VimpelCom. The increase in capital surplus of USD 31 represents the difference between the amount recorded as liability to noncontrolling interest in OJSC VimpelCom on 21 April 2010 in the amount of USD 501 and the amount recorded on 25 May 2010 when a squeeze-out demand notice was served (effectively this transaction represented a purchase of own shares legally affected through purchase of non-controlling interest in OJSC VimpelCom).

VimpelCom Ltd. ADS began trading on the New York Stock Exchange ("NYSE") on 22 April 2010 while OJSC VimpelCom ADS were delisted from the NYSE on 14 May 2010.

On 4 October 2010, the Company and Weather Investments S.p.A. ("Weather") signed an agreement to combine their two groups (the "Transaction"). The Transaction terms provided that at the closing of the Transaction, the Company will own, through Weather, 51.7% of Orascom Telecom Holding S.A.E. ("Orascom Telecom," or "OTH") and 100% of Wind Telecomunicazioni S.p.A. ("Wind Italy").

At its meeting on 16 January 2011, the Supervisory Board approved new terms of the Transaction, under which shareholders of Wind Telecom S.p.a. ("Wind Telecom," formerly Weather) would contribute to VimpelCom their shares in Wind Telecom in exchange for consideration consisting of 325,639,827 newly-issued VimpelCom common shares, 305,000,000 newly-issued VimpelCom convertible preferred shares and USD1,495 in cash. The newly-issued convertible preferred shares have the same rights as the existing convertible preferred shares. In addition, pursuant to the terms of the Transaction, at or shortly after the closing of the Transaction, certain assets were spun off from the Wind Telecom group and transferred back to Weather Investments II S.a. r.l., the 72.65% shareholder of Wind Telecom ("Weather II") prior to completion of the Transaction. These assets included certain assets from OTH, which VimpelCom committed to transfer back to Weather II, or in the event the assets could not be transferred, VimpelCom would have had to pay up to USD 770. These assets were transferred to Weather II in February 2012.

On 17 March 2011, the shareholders of the Company approved the issuance of common and convertible preferred shares to Wind Telecom's shareholders and the related increase in the Company's share capital.

On 15 April 2011, VimpelCom successfully completed the Transaction and obtained control over Wind Telecom. As a result of the Transaction, VimpelCom owns, through Wind Telecom, 51.9% of Orascom Telecom and 100% of Wind Italy (Note 7).

VimpelCom earns revenues by providing voice, data and other telecommunication services through a range of wireless, fixed and broadband internet services, as well as selling equipment and accessories. As of 31 December 2011, the Company operated telecommunications services in Russia, Italy, Algeria, Kazakhstan, Ukraine, Pakistan, Bangladesh, Armenia, Tajikistan, Uzbekistan, Georgia, Kyrgyzstan, Laos, Central African Republic, Burundi, Canada, Zimbabwe, Vietnam and Cambodia.

The consolidated financial statements of the Company for the year ended 31 December 2011 were authorized for issue in accordance with a resolution of the directors on 24 April 2012.

2 Basis of the Consolidated Financial Statements (in part)

2.1 Basis of Preparation (in part)

These consolidated financial statements of the Company have been prepared in accordance with International Financial Reporting Standards ("IFRS") as issued by the International Accounting Standards Board ("IASB"), effective at the time of preparing the consolidated financial statements and applied by VimpelCom.

For all periods up to and including the year ended 31 December 2010, VimpelCom Ltd. and OJSC VimpelCom, the accounting predecessor of the Company, prepared its consolidated financial statements in accordance with generally accepted accounting principles in the United States ("U.S. GAAP"). VimpelCom is a formal foreign company in the Netherlands which falls under the Formal Foreign Companies Act ("FFCA") and is therefore subject to certain parts of the Dutch Civil Code. VimpelCom was considered a first-time adopter of IFRS for the 2010 financial statements filed for the Dutch statutory purposes. Therefore in the first VimpelCom group consolidated IFRS financial statements as of 31 December 2010, VimpelCom stated that the consolidated financial statements have been prepared in accordance with IFRS as adopted by the European Commission and also comply with the IFRS as issued by the IASB. These financial statements include certain supplemental disclosures in the form of reconciliations from US GAAP to IFRS as issued by the IASB to disclose the changes in the basis of presentation from US GAAP basis-financial statements. Refer to Note 4 for information on the Company's adoption of IFRS.

The consolidated financial statements have been prepared on a historical cost basis, unless disclosed otherwise.

2.2 Basis of Consolidation

The consolidated financial statements comprise the financial statements of the Company and its subsidiaries as at 31 December 2011.

Subsidiaries (Note 26) are fully consolidated from the date of acquisition, being the date on which the Company obtains control, and continue to be consolidated until the date when such control ceases. The financial statements of the subsidiaries are prepared for the same reporting period as the parent company, using consistent accounting policies.

All intercompany accounts and transactions within the Company have been eliminated in full.

Non-controlling interests are reported in the consolidated statement of financial position as a separate component of equity. Non-controlling interests represent the equity in subsidiaries not attributable, directly or indirectly, to the Company. We refer to Note 17 for the effect of options over non-controlling interests.

As stated in Note 1 'General information' the Company successfully completed an exchange offer for OJSC VimpelCom shares and acquired approximately 98% of OJSC Vimpel-Com's outstanding shares. Therefore, effective 21 April 2010, OJSC VimpelCom is a subsidiary of VimpelCom Ltd.

In the consolidated financial statements the acquisition of OJSC VimpelCom is accounted for as the continuation of the existing Group. VimpelCom is therefore the accounting successor to OJSC VimpelCom. Accounting data and disclosures related to the period prior to 21 April 2010, represent accounting data and disclosures of OJSC VimpelCom.

3 Significant Accounting Policies (in part)

Business Combinations

Business combinations are accounted for using the acquisition method. The cost of the acquisition, being the total consideration transferred, is measured at the aggregate of the fair values, at the date of exchange, of assets given, liabilities incurred or assumed, and equity instruments issued by the Group in exchange for control of the acquiree and the amount of any non-controlling interest in the acquiree. The aggregate consideration transferred is allocated to the underlying assets acquired, including any intangible assets identified, and liabilities assumed based on their respective estimated fair values. Determining the fair value of assets acquired and liabilities assumed requires the use of significant estimates and assumptions, including assumptions with respect to future cash inflows and outflows, discount rates, licenses and other assets' lives and market multiples, among other items. The results of operations of acquired companies are included in the consolidated financial statements from the date of acquisition.

For each business combination VimpelCom elects whether it measures the non-controlling interest in the acquiree either at fair value or at the proportionate share in the recognized amounts of the acquiree's identifiable net assets. Acquisition costs are expensed in the income statement as incurred.

If the business combination is achieved in stages, the acquisition date fair value of the acquirer's previously held equity interest in the acquiree is remeasured to fair value at the acquisition date and the difference is recognized through profit or loss.

Any contingent consideration to be transferred by the Group is recognized at fair value at the acquisition date. Subsequent changes to the fair value of the contingent consideration that is deemed to be an asset or liability is recognized in accordance with IAS 39 *Financial Instruments: Recognition and Measurement* either in profit or loss or as a change to other comprehensive income depending on the classification of financial instrument. If the contingent consideration is classified as equity, it is not remeasured. Subsequent settlement is accounted for within equity. In instances where the contingent consideration does not fall within the scope of IAS 39, it is measured in accordance with the appropriate IFRS standards.

Goodwill is initially measured at cost, being the excess of the sum of the consideration transferred, the amount of any non-controlling interests in the acquiree and the fair value of the Group's previously held equity interest in the acquiree, if any, over the fair value of the net amounts of identifiable assets acquired and liabilities assumed at the acquisition date. After initial recognition, goodwill is carried at cost less any accumulated impairment losses.

In the event the acquisition is achieved in stages, goodwill is recognized at the time when the company obtains control over the entity.

If the consideration is lower than the fair value of the net assets of the subsidiary acquired, the difference is recognized in profit or loss.

Goodwill is not amortised but is tested for impairment on at least an annual basis or when impairment indicators are observed.

The Group may enter into business combinations which include options (call, put, or a combination of both) over the shares of the non-controlling interest.

Where there are call options, the Group considers the implications on control. Where call options lead to the establishment of control, then the proportions of the acquiree's subsequent profits or losses and changes in equity allocated to the parent and non-controlling interests will be based on the present ownership interest, only to the extent that the Group does not have current access to the economic benefits of the shares of non-controlling interest. To the extent the call option provides a present ownership (through current access to the underlying economic benefits) a gross liability is recognized, whereby any changes in the liability are recognized in profit and loss. If the call option does not provide present ownership it is recorded as a derivative asset at fair value through profit and loss.

Where there are put options granted to the non-controlling interest, then a financial liability is recognized. These liabilities are initially measured at the present value of the redemption amount and are subsequently measured in accordance with *International Accounting Standard* No. 39, *Financial Instruments; Recognition and Measurement* ("IAS 39"). Where the Group does not have a present ownership interest in the outstanding shares, then at each period end the difference between the financial liability and the non-controlling interest (which reflects its share of the profit and losses, and changes in equity, of the acquiree) is accounted for as an equity transaction. Where the put option does provide a present ownership interest, the changes in the liability are recognized in profit or loss.

Common-Control Transactions

For business combinations exercised under common-control VimpelCom measures the net assets of the transaction at the carrying amounts in the accounts of the transferor.

4 First Time Adoption of IFRS (in part)

The consolidated financial statements of the Company have been prepared in accordance with IFRS as issued by the IASB, effective at the time of preparing the consolidated financial statements and applied by VimpelCom. The first consolidated financial statements of the Company prepared in accordance with IFRS were for the year ended December 31, 2010, filed in accordance with the Dutch Civil Law. Disclosed below is a reconciliation from US GAAP to IFRS as at 31 December 2010 and 2009 as well as the elections taken by the Company in its adoption of IFRS.

In preparing these consolidated financial statements, the Company's opening statement of financial position was prepared as at 1 January 2009, the date of transition to IFRS.

IFRS has been applied retrospectively, except for certain optional and mandatory exemptions from full retrospective application, as provided for by *IFRS 1 (Revised 2009) First-Time Adoption of International Financial Reporting Standards*, as detailed below.

Business Combinations

The Company has elected to apply *IFRS 3 (Revised) Business Combinations* ("IFRS 3") retrospectively starting from 26 June 2008. As a result, *IFRS 3* is applied to all subsequent business combinations. Accordingly, IAS 27, *Consolidated and Separate Financial Statements* ("IAS 27") is applied from 26 June 2008 onwards. Business combinations that occurred prior to 26 June 2008 have not been converted to IFRS.

Upon adoption of IFRS, transaction costs that were capitalized are recorded to equity. Under IFRS the Company has a policy choice to recognize the net assets of the non-controlling interest at fair value or at the proportionate share in the recognized amounts of the acquiree's identifiable net assets, whereas under US GAAP these were measured at historical cost.

Concurrently with the election to apply IFRS 3, the Company also applies IAS 27 as of the same date. Therefore an increase in the Company's ownership interest that does not result in a loss of control is accounted for as an equity transaction as of that date, whereas under US GAAP increases in the Company's ownership interest were accounted for applying acquisition accounting.

Had the Company not elected to apply IFRS 3 and IAS 27 to prior business combinations occurred before the date of transition to IFRS, there would be no adjustments related to such transactions as compared to US GAAP.

Notes to the Reconciliation of Equity as at 31 December 2009 and 31 December 2010 and Profit for the Years Ended 31 December 2009 and 31 December 2010.

Note 1—Limnotex Acquisition and Limnotex Options

The Company elected to restate business combinations starting from the acquisition of LLC Komtel in June 2008 and to apply IAS 27 as of that date. In accordance with IFRS a change in ownership interest without loss of control leads to the carrying amounts of the controlling and non-controlling interest being adjusted to reflect the changes in their relative interest in the subsidiary. The difference between the fair value of the consideration paid and the amount by which the non-controlling interest is adjusted is recognized in equity, while US GAAP effective in 2008 required purchase accounting.

On July 1, 2008 VimpelCom acquired 25% of Limnotex in addition to existing controlling stake of 50% plus one share. In addition VimpelCom entered into a put and call option agreement over the remaining 25% shares. The agreement was recognized as a redeemable noncontrolling interest under US GAAP. Under IFRS the put option granted to the non-controlling interest gives rise to a financial liability. As the Company concluded that they do not have present access to the benefits of all the shares held by the non-controlling shareholders, changes in the carrying amount of the financial liability (Note 16) are recognized in equity.

For the year ended 31 December 2009 the amortization expense decreased by USD 18 and deferred tax decreased by USD 15. Net profit of USD 1 was attributable to non-controlling interest and USD 2 to the owners of the parent.

For the year end 31 December 2010 the amortization expense decreased by USD 18 with a corresponding deferred tax decrease of USD 4. Net profit of USD 4 was attributable to non-controlling interest and USD 11 to the owners of the parent.

Note 2—Menacrest Consolidation

In comparison to US GAAP effective in 2009 the definition of control differs under IAS 27. As a result Menacrest Limited ("Menacrest") and its subsidiaries Aridus and Sky Mobile are included as subsidiaries in the consolidated financial statements in accordance with IFRS that were not included in the consolidated financial statements in accordance with US GAAP. In addition the Company received two call options to acquire up to 100% of interest in Menacrest which were Investments Limited ("Crowell"), the owner of Menacrest, a loan of USD 350 on 13 February 2008 (the "Original Crowell Loan Agreement") and subsequently re-negotiated its terms by decreasing the interest rate and increasing the maturity of the loan (the "Revised Crowell Loan Agreement") which resulted in required de-recognition of the original loan and recognition of the new one.

The original terms were bearing interest rate of 10% and the loan was secured by 25% of the shares of Limnotex Developments Limited ("Limnotex"). The revised terms were bearing fixed annual amount and the security was amended to 100% of Menacrest, which owned 100% of the share capital of Sky Mobile, a mobile operator in Kyrgyzstan, holding GSM and 3G licenses to operate over the entire territory of Kyrgyzstan.

Crowell granted the Company two call options (the "Call Option Agreement") over the issued share capital of Menacrest.

On 29 May 2009, VimpelCom agreed to amend the Revised Crowell Loan Agreement in that the term of the loan facility was extended until 11 February 2014 and interest rate has been changed to be a fixed amount per annum starting from the effective date of the amendment. Also, the security interest granted by Crowell to VimpelCom over 25% of the shares of Limnotex was replaced by a security interest over 100% of the shares of Menacrest.

As a result of the Call Option Agreement, control is deemed to have been established over Menacrest, and Sky Mobile as its subsidiary, on the basis that the call options were exercisable at the date of acquisition in February 2008. Since that date precedes June 2008, after which the business combinations have been converted under IFRS 3R, in accordance with IFRS1. C4j, the financial statements of VimpelCom as of 1 January 2009 have been adjusted to include the original Sky Mobile carrying values as of 28 March 2008 (the date at which Menacrest acquired Sky Mobile) plus the subsequent movements to 1 January 2009. At transition date, the Company had present access to the benefits of 50.1% of the non controlling interest. Since the call option over Menacrest was in the money and likely to be exercised a liability has been recognized of USD 330. VimpelCom has elected to measure the non-controlling interest in the acquiree at the proportionate share of net assets of Menacrest. The difference between the carrying values of the assets and liabilities of Sky Mobile, the non-controlling interest of Menacrest and the liability recognized has been recognized as goodwill.

The values of the consolidated assets and liabilities of Menacrest and Sky Mobile as of 1 January 2009 in accordance with IFRS 1 were as follows:

	As of 1 January 2009
Assets	
Cash and cash equivalents	20
Other current non-financial assets	12
Property and equipment (6 years weighted average remaining useful life)	96
Intangible assets	37
Other non-current non-financial assets	5
	170
Liabilities	
Current non-financial liabilities	56
Non-current non-financial liabilities	57
	113
Total identifiable net assets acquired	57
Non-controlling interest	28
Goodwill arising on acquisition	301
Purchase consideration transferred	330

The recognized goodwill is expected to be realized from the potential of the Kyrgyzstan telecommunication market development.

Before June 2009, 49.9% of equity over Menacrest was classified as non-controlling interest, after that date, when the Company had lost the present access to the benefits of interest ownership of Menacrest—100% of equity over Menacrest was classified as non-controlling interest.

On October 20, 2010, the Company exercised the first call option to acquire 50.1% of the issued share capital of Menacrest. The remaining 49.9% of Menacrest is owned by Crowell. On the same date the pledge over 100% of Menacrest shares was released by the Company.

The consideration for the 50.1% share capital of Menacrest in the amount of USD 150 has been set off against part of the debt of Crowell to the Company under the Crowell Loan Agreement (Note 17). As Menacrest was already consolidated at the time the first call option was exercised, the transaction was accounted for as a repayment of liability instead of as an equity transaction under US GAAP.

7 Business Combinations and Other Significant Transactions (in part)

Acquisitions in 2011

Wind Telecom Acquisition

On 15 April 2011, VimpelCom successfully completed the acquisition of 100% shares of Wind Telecom (the "Transaction"). As a result of the Transaction, VimpelCom owns, through Wind Telecom, 51.9% of Orascom Telecom and 100% of Wind Italy.

On 3 May 2011, the Company and Weather II completed the spin-off of certain assets from Wind Italy. As part of the Transaction VimpelCom agreed to execute a legal demerger at the OTH level and created a new entity ("OTMT") to hold the spin-off assets. OTMT was demerger from OTH in the end of 2011 to fulfill its obligation to transfer the OTMT assets. The main demerged assets are: Mobinil and ECMS, telephone service providers in Egypt, Orascom Telecom Ventures (including Orascom Telecom Lebanon), Koryolink, mobile service provider in North Korea, Menacable and Trans World Associates, fixed-line operators around the Mediterranean Sea. In the event that the OTMT spin-off had not taken place, the Company would have been obliged to pay up to USD 770 in contingent consideration which was equal to the fair value on the date of acquisition and respective assets are classified as held for sale. On 16 February 2012 VimpelCom fulfilled its obligation to transfer the remaining spin-off assets to Weather II by transferring its interests in OTMT to Weather II.

Under the Share Sale and Exchange Agreement with Weather II, which governed the Transaction, Weather II and VimpelCom indemnify each other for a number of items, including Weather's indemnification of VimpelCom against certain fines and penalties from the Italian Tax Authorities (Note 28). The indemnification asset recognized in this respect was USD 51.

The acquisition of Wind Telecom by VimpelCom Ltd. is accounted for as a business combination under the "acquisition method," as defined by IFRS 3. The acquisition method requires the consideration transferred to be based on the fair value on the acquisition date. The consideration transferred was USD 7,253, which was calculated based on the market value of VimpelCom shares on 15 April, 2011 (USD 14.55 per share), fair value of convertible preferred shares based on a recent transaction among market participants, the fair value of the spin-off assets and cash.

	Number of Shares	Quoted Bid Price on 15 April 2011	Fair Value on 15 April 2011	Total
Equity Consideration:				
Shares transferred:				
VimpelCom common shares	325,639,827	14.55		4,738
VimpelCom convertible preferred shares	305,000,000		0.82	250
Equity consideration transferred	630,639,827			4,988
Cash Consideration:				
Cash payment at closing				1,495
Cash consideration transferred				1,495
Other Consideration:				
Contingent consideration for Orascom Telecom spin-off assets				770
Other consideration transferred				770
Total consideration transferred				7,253

The fair values of acquired identifiable assets and liabilities as well as non-controlling interest of Wind as of 15 April 2011, were as follows:

	15 April 2011
Cash and cash equivalents	1,197
Trade accounts receivable (gross amount of 2,758, net of allowance of 693)	2,065
Other current assets	1,701
Total current assets acquired	4,963
Property and equipment (with the average remaining useful life of 8.9 years)	7,248
Telecommunications licenses (with the average remaining useful life of 16.2 years)	3,129
Goodwill	10,878
Customer relationships (with the average remaining useful life of 7.7 years)	3,750
Brandnames and trademarks (with the average remaining useful life of 18.4 years)	2,059
Other intangible assets	1,133
Deferred income taxes	1,123
Other assets	1,432
Total non-current assets acquired	30,752
Assets held for sale	1,810
Total assets acquired	37,525
Accounts payable	3,059
Short-term debt	1,408
Other accrued liabilities	2,125
Total current liabilities assumed	6,592
Deferred income taxes	2,162
Long-term debt	18,581
Other non-current liabilities	794
Total non-current liabilities assumed	21,537
Liabilities associated to assets held for sale	264
Non-controlling interest	1,878
Total consideration transferred	7,253

The acquisition-related costs incurred in the transaction at the amount of USD 80 were treated as expenses under IFRS 3 with no impact on goodwill.

Non-controlling interest was valued based on the market values of Orascom Telecom shares as of 15 April 2011.

Goodwill is calculated as the excess of the purchase consideration and the fair value of the non controlling interest in Wind Telecom, over the identifiable net assets acquired. The goodwill recorded as part of the acquisition of Wind Telecom primarily reflects the value of adding Wind Telecom to create a more fully integrated supply chain and go-to-market business model, as well as any intangible assets that do not qualify for separate recognition. Goodwill is not amortizable nor deductible for tax purposes. The allocation of the goodwill to CGU's is presented in the following table:

CGU's	As at 15 April 2011
Italy	5,789
Algeria	2,174
Russia	1,851
Pakistan	560
Kazakhstan	234
Uzbekistan	110
Ukraine	45
Kyrgyzstan	41
Armenia	33
Georgia	31
Tadjikistan	9
Bangladesh	1
Total goodwill	10,878

The allocation of goodwill was performed based on the synergies to be benefited by the respective CGU's. The synergies mainly represent future development of the local markets where Wind Telecom has operations as well as a decrease in future capital expenditures due to favourable prices to be negotiated with vendors in all of our markets. The determination how much synergies are applicable to existing VimpelCom CGU's was performed based on projected cash flows pre and after the Transaction.

Millicom Lao

On 9 March 2011 VimpelCom acquired 100% ownership interest in VimpelCom Holding Laos B.V. (Netherlands), formerly Millicom Holding Laos B.V. which holds a 78% interest in VimpelCom Lao Co., Ltd., formerly Millicom Lao Co., Ltd., a cellular telecom operator with operations in the Lao People's Democratic Republic ("Millicom Lao"). The remaining 22% of Millicom Lao is owned by the Government of the Lao PDR, as represented by the Ministry of Finance.

The reason for the acquisition was gaining access to the new market of Lao PDR.

The acquisition of Millicom Lao is accounted for as a business combination under the "acquisition method," as defined by IFRS 3. The consideration transferred was measured at fair value on the acquisition date. The total cash consideration transferred was approximately USD 70.

The fair values of consolidated identifiable assets and liabilities of Millicom Lao as of 9 March 2011, were as follows:

	As of 9 March 2011
Cash and cash equivalents	3
Other current non-financial assets	9
Property and equipment	48
Licenses (remaining useful life of 11 years)	9
Goodwill	65
Other non-current non-financial assets	5
Total assets acquired	139
Current liabilities	(36)
Non-current liabilities	(13)
Total liabilities assumed	(49)
Non-controlling interest	(20)
Total consideration transferred	70

The non-controlling interest was valued based on the fair value of 22% stake using discounted cash flows analysis ("DCF") adjusted for a control premium.

The excess of the purchase consideration over the fair value of the identifiable net assets of Millicom Lao amounted to USD 75 and was recorded as goodwill. The goodwill was assigned to the Lao CGU and is expected to be realized from the potential development of telecommunication market in Lao as well as synergies with VimpelCom's operations in South-East Asia. This goodwill is not deductible for tax purposes.

GTEL-Mobile

On 29 March 2011, VimpelCom agreed with GTEL, its local partner in Vietnam, on a financing plan for their investment, GTEL-Mobile, that could result in the Company providing investments in total of up to USD 500 through 2013. The Company completed the first stage of the financing plan by paying USD 196 for the newly issued shares and thereby increasing its stake in GTEL-Mobile from 40% to 49% on 26 April 2011. All proceeds from this financing will be used for GTEL-Mobile's development.

The Company agreed to invest another USD 304 under this plan, which would increase its economic interest in GTEL-Mobile from 49% to 65%. The additional financing and equity increase are subject to meeting certain performance targets by GTEL-Mobile and obtaining further regulatory approvals. Based on 2011 performance those targets have not been met and as a result the Company was released from its obligation to finance GTEL-Mobile.

The primary reason for the increase in ownership was expanding VimpelCom's operations in Vietnam.

In conjunction with the financing agreements described above, VimpelCom and GTEL agreed on certain changes to the joint venture agreement and charter of GTEL-Mobile. Under the revised agreement, VimpelCom is assigned with the operational management of GTEL-Mobile, by way of substantial control over adoption of annual budgets and appointment of the General Director of GTEL-Mobile who is granted with wide authority with respect of day-to-day operations.

Based on these agreed changes, VimpelCom has started consolidating GTEL-Mobile from 26 April 2011 onwards.

The increase in ownership in GTEL-Mobile and subsequent consolidation is accounted for as a business combination achieved in stages, as defined by IFRS 3. The acquisition achieved in stages requires remeasurement of previously held equity interest in the acquiree at its acquisition-date fair value and recognizing the resulting gain or loss, if any, in earnings. As of the acquisition date the fair value of previously held interest was USD 157 representing the fair value of 40% stake based on DCF adjusted for a control premium. The resulting loss of USD 40 was recognized as other non-operating losses item of accompanied income statement. In prior reporting periods, the Company recognized a portion of changes in the value of its equity interest in GTEL-Mobile associated with foreign currency translation in other comprehensive income. As of the acquisition date, the respective accumulated foreign currency translation adjustment of USD

43 was reclassified from other comprehensive income and included in the current period earnings as other expenses item of accompanied income statement.

The fair values of consolidated identifiable assets and liabilities of GTEL-Mobile as of 26 April 2011, were as follows:

	As of 26 April 2011
Cash and cash equivalents	206
Other current non-financial assets	7
Property and equipment	147
Licenses (14.6 years weighted average remaining useful life)	143
Goodwill	127
Other non-current non-financial assets	2
Total assets acquired	632
Current liabilities	(39)
Non-current liabilities	(4)
Total liabilities assumed	(43)
Non-controlling interest	(236)
Previously held 40% interest	(157)
Total cash contribution	196

The non-controlling interest was valued based on the 51% stake of total value of the equity based on DCF adjusted for a control premium.

The excess of the purchase consideration over the fair value of the identifiable net assets of GTEL-Mobile amounted to USD 126 and was recorded as goodwill. The goodwill was assigned to the Vietnam CGU and was expected to be realized from the potential development of telecommunication market in Vietnam as well as synergies with VimpelCom's operations in South-East Asia. This goodwill is not deductible for tax purposes. This goodwill was impaired as of October 1, 2011, due to negative market trends in Vietnamese market in late 2011 which resulted in a negative business enterprise value of Vietnam CGU. (Note 15)

NTC

On 7 June 2011, VimpelCom acquired 90% of the share capital of OJSC "New Telephone Company" ("NTC") for the total consideration of RUR10,835 million (the equivalent to USD 390 as of 7 June 2011). On 21 October 2011, VimpelCom completed the acquisition of an additional 10% of the outstanding NTC shares. The total acquisition price is USD 438. The total consideration was paid in cash.

The primary reason for the acquisition was to enhance VimpelCom's presence in Primorskiy region telecommunication market and to increase VimpelCom's local mobile subscribers base.

The acquisition of NTC is accounted for as a business combination under the "acquisition method," as defined by IFRS 3. The consideration transferred was measured at fair value on the acquisition date.

The fair values of consolidated identifiable assets and liabilities of NTC as of 7 June 2011, were as follows:

	As of 7 June 2011
Cash and cash equivalents	2
Other current non-financial assets	25
Property and equipment	123
Trademarks (3 years weighted average remaining useful life)	6
Customer Relationships (7.7 years weighted average remaining useful life)	22
Licenses (10.3 years weighted average remaining useful life)	56
Number capacity (10.3 years weighted average remaining useful life)	1
Other non-current non-financial assets	5
Goodwill	231
Total assets acquired	471
Current liabilities	(13)
Non-current liabilities	(20)
Total liabilities assumed	(33)
Total consideration transferred	438

The excess of the purchase consideration over the fair value of the identifiable net assets of NTC amounted to USD 231 and was recorded as goodwill. The goodwill was assigned to Russia CGU and is expected to be realized from the potential of "business to business" telecommunication market development in the future, as well as synergies with VimpelCom's operations. This goodwill is not deductible for tax purposes. The acquisition-related costs incurred in the transactions were treated as expenses under IFRS 3.

Restructuring of Shareholding in Kazakhstan and Kyrgyzstan

On 24 August 2011, a restructuring transaction ("Restructuring transaction") with Crowell was completed. As a result of the Restructuring transaction, VimpelCom Finance B.V. became the legal and beneficial owner of 71.5% shares in the issued share capital of the combined Limnotex (resulting in 71.5% indirect shareholding of VimpelCom Finance B.V. in KaR-Tel and Sky Mobile), while the non-controlling 28.5% of Limnotex shares are now held by Crowell. Before the transaction, VimpelCom Group (via OJSC Vimpel-Communications and VimpelCom Finance B.V.) held indirectly 75.0% in KaR-Tel and 50.1% in Sky Mobile.

At the same time, the Company's call option to acquire 49.9% of the issued share capital of Menacrest was terminated, while Crowell's put and VimpelCom's call options for the 25% of Limnotex shares (Note 17) were amended. After the amendments, Crowell holds two put options for Limnotex shares: the first put option for 13.5% is exercisable during 2013 at a fixed price of USD 297 and the second put option for 15% is exercisable during 2017 at a fixed price of USD 330. In turn the Company holds two call options for Limnotex shares (for 13.5% and 15%) and both are exercisable during the period between April 2012 and May 2018. As a part of the transaction, VimpelCom terminated the loan agreement with Crowell and was released from its commitment to exercise the call option for the 25% of Limnotex shares.

The existing dividend mandate from Crowell to Menacrest (allowing VimpelCom to receive 49.9% Menacrest dividends payable to Crowell) was cancelled. In accordance with new dividend mandates VimpelCom Finance B.V. will receive 100% Menacrest dividends payable to Limnotex and 3.5% Limnotex dividends payable to Crowell.

The Restructuring transaction was accounted for as an equity transaction reflecting exchange of 21.4% in Menacrest for 3.5% in Limnotex. Simultaneously the termination of the loan was offset by the release of liability to exercise the call option for the 25% of Limnotex shares. In addition the fair value of the call options for the total 28.5% of Limnotex shares at the amount of USD 68 were recognized as financial assets and the redemption value of the put options for the total of 28.5% of Limnotex shares at the amount of USD 391 was recorded as financial liabilities.

Other Transactions 2011

Eltel

On January 21, 2011, VimpelCom acquired 100% of the share capital of Closed Joint Stock Company Eltel ("Eltel"), one of the leading alternative fixed-line providers in Saint Petersburg, for the total cash consideration of RUR1,000 million (the equivalent to USD 33 as of January 21, 2011). The fair values of consolidated identifiable assets and liabilities of Eltel as of January 21, 2011, were USD 16 of assets, USD 3 of liabilities resulting in excess of consideration over the fair value of net assets acquired of USD 20. This amount was recorded as goodwill, was assigned to the Russia CGU and is subject to annual impairment tests. The recognized goodwill is expected to be realized primarily from the synergies of combining of VimpelCom's and Eltel's regional operations.

Tacom

On 21 November 2011, VimpelCom acquired from its local partner additional 8% participatory interest in LLC "Tacom," a cellular telecom operator with operations in Tajikistan, for the total cash consideration of USD 9.2, thus increasing its total indirect shareholding in Tacom to 98%.

14 Intangible Assets

The total gross carrying value and accumulated amortization of VimpelCom's intangible assets consisted of the following at 31 December:

	Telecommuni- cations Licenses, Frequencies and Permissions	Goodwill	Software	Brands and Trademarks	Customer Relationships	Telephone Line Capacity	Other Intangible Assets	Total
Cost								
At 31 December 2010	1,600	6,722	1,148	193	1,430	159	261	11,513
Additions	331	—	137	—	1	10	1,891	2,370
Acquisition of a subsidiary (Note 7)	3,330	11,331	9	2,308	2,937	1	1,390	21,306
Disposals	(80)	—	(33)	—	—	(1)	(28)	(142)
Transfer	2	—	3	—	(14)	(10)	12	(7)
Other	10	—	15	(4)	(25)	(14)	47	29
Translation adjustment	(277)	(1,151)	(43)	(174)	(242)	(2)	(261)	(2,150)
At 31 December 2011	4,916	16,902	1,236	2,323	4,087	143	3,312	32,919
Amortization and Impairment								
At 31 December 2010	(933)	—	(726)	(19)	(346)	(56)	(216)	(2,296)
Amortization charge for the year	(387)	—	(183)	(118)	(1,083)	(43)	(246)	(2,060)
Disposals	71	—	30	5	—	—	25	131
Impairment (Note 15)	(128)	(126)	(4)	—	—	—	—	(258)
Other	(1)	—	(9)	2	11	8	(7)	4
Translation adjustment	7	—	35	7	83	3	26	161
At 31 December 2011	(1,371)	(126)	(857)	(123)	(1,335)	(88)	(418)	(4,318)
Net book value								
At 31 December 2011	3,545	16,776	379	2,200	2,752	55	2,894	28,601

24 Other Non-Operating (Gains)/Losses (in part)

Other non-operating (gains)/losses consisted of the following for the years ended 31 December

	2011	2010	2009
Change of fair value of derivatives over non-controlling interest	(2)	(38)	52
Remeasurement of previously held investment in GTEL-Mobile	40	—	—

Provisional Assessment of Acquisition Date Fair Values of the Net Assets Acquired

9.28

OAO Gazprom (Dec 2011)

CONSOLIDATED STATEMENT OF CASH FLOWS (in part)

In millions of Russian Roubles)

Notes		Year Ended 31 December 2011	2010
	Operating Activities		
30	Net cash provided by operating activities	1,637,450	1,460,116
	Investing activities		
12	Capital expenditures	(1,553,118)	(1,042,642)
	Net change in loans issued	(6,469)	(9,113)
	Interest received	14,950	13,233
12	Interest paid and capitalised	(58,507)	(62,392)
	Acquisition of subsidiaries, net of cash acquired	(111,001)	(73,696)

(continued)

Notes		Year Ended 31 December	
		2011	**2010**
36	Decrease of cash and cash equivalents from deconsolidation of banking subsidiaries	—	(32,504)
13	Investment in associated undertakings and jointly controlled entities	(18,405)	(32,817)
38	Proceeds from sales of interest in subsidiaries	12,307	34,540
37	Proceeds from disposal of interest in OAO NOVATEK	—	57,462
13	Proceeds from associated undertakings and jointly controlled entities	118,495	93,894
	Net change of long-term available-for-sale financial assets	(1,369)	317
	Change in other long-term financial assets	(2,128)	3,411
	Net cash used for investing activities	(1,605,245)	(1,050,307)

NOTES TO THE CONSOLIDATED FINANCIAL STATEMENTS (in part)

(In millions of Russian Roubles)

1 Nature of Operations

OAO Gazprom and its subsidiaries (the "Group") operate one of the largest gas pipeline systems in the world and are responsible for major part of gas production and high pressure gas transportation in the Russian Federation. The Group is also a major supplier of gas to European countries. The Group is engaged in oil production, refining activities, electric and heat energy generation. The Government of the Russian Federation is the ultimate controlling party of OAO Gazprom and has a controlling interest (including both direct and indirect ownership) of over 50% in OAO Gazprom.

The Group is involved in the following principal activities:
* Exploration and production of gas;
* Transportation of gas;
* Sales of gas within Russian Federation and abroad;
* Gas storage;
* Production of crude oil and gas condensate;
* Processing of oil, gas condensate and other hydrocarbons, and sales of refined products; and
* Electric and heat energy generation and sales.

Other activities primarily include production of other goods, works and services.

The weighted average number of employees during 2011 and 2010 was 401 thousand and 393 thousand, respectively.

2 Economic Environment in the Russian Federation

The Russian Federation displays certain characteristics of an emerging market. Tax, currency and customs legislation is subject to varying interpretations and contributes to the challenges faced by companies operating in the Russian Federation (Note 41).

The international sovereign debt crisis, stock market volatility and other risks could have a negative effect on the Russian financial and corporate sectors. Management determined impairment provisions by considering the economic situation and outlook at the end of the reporting period.

The future economic development of the Russian Federation is dependent upon external factors and internal measures undertaken by the government to sustain growth, and to change the tax, legal and regulatory environment. Management believes it is taking all necessary measures to support the sustainability and development of the Group's business in the current business and economic environment.

3 Basis of Presentation

These consolidated financial statements are prepared in accordance with, and comply with, International Financial Reporting Standards, including International Accounting Standards and Interpretations issued by the International Accounting Standards Board ("IFRS") and effective in reporting period.

The consolidated financial statements of the Group are prepared under the historical cost convention except for certain financial instruments as described in Note 5. The principal accounting policies applied in the preparation of these consolidated financial statements are set out below. These policies have been consistently applied to all the periods presented, unless otherwise stated.

4 Scope of Consolidation (in part)

As described in Note 5, these financial statements include consolidated subsidiaries, associated undertakings and jointly controlled entities of the Group. Significant changes in the Group's structure in 2011 and 2010 are described below.

In November 2011 the Group entered into a share purchase agreement with the State Property Committee of the Republic of Belarus to acquire an additional 50% interest in OAO Beltransgaz for cash consideration of USD 2,500 million. In December 2011 the transaction was finalised. As a result the Group increased its ownership interest up to 100% and obtained control over OAO Beltransgaz (see Note 33).

In November 2010 the Group sold its entire 51% controlling interest in OOO Severenergiya to the OOO Yamal razvitie—jointly controlled entity which is owned on a fifty-fifty basis by the Group (OAO Gazprom Neft) and OAO Novatek (see Note 38).

In August 2010 the reorganization in the form of the merger of ZAO Gazenergoprombank to OAO AB Rossiya was finalized. As a result of the reorganization the Group received a non-controlling interest in OAO AB Rossiya (see Note 36).

In February 2011 the Board of Directors of Sibir Energy Ltd. adopted a resolution to reduce the share capital by 86.25 million shares (22.39%). OAO Central Fuel Company, an affiliate to the Moscow Government, made a decision to withdraw membership in Sibir Energy Ltd. for a compensation of USD 740 million. As a result of the transaction starting from 15 February 2011 the Group has 100% interest in Sibir Energy Ltd. (see Note 35).

5. Summary of Significant Accounting Policies

The principal accounting policies followed by the Group are set out below.

5.1 Group Accounting

Subsidiary Undertakings

The Group's subsidiaries are entities over which the Group has the power to govern the financial and operating policies so as to obtain benefits from the activities of those entities. Subsidiary undertakings in which the Group, directly or indirectly, has an interest of more than 50% of the voting rights and is able to exercise control over the operations have been consolidated. Also subsidiary undertakings include entities in which the Group controls 50% and less of the voting share capital but where the Group controls the entity through other means. This may include a history of casting the majority of the votes at the meetings of the board of directors or equivalent governing body.

Certain entities in which the Group has an interest of more than 50% are recorded as investments in associated undertakings as the Group is unable to exercise control due to certain factors, for example restrictions stated in foundation documents.

The consolidated financial statements of the Group reflect the results of operations of any subsidiaries acquired from the date control is established. Subsidiaries are no longer consolidated from the date from which control ceases. All intercompany transactions, balances and unrealized surpluses and deficits on transactions between group companies have been eliminated. Separate disclosure is made for non-controlling interests.

The acquisition method of accounting is used to account for the acquisition of subsidiaries, including those entities and businesses that are under common control. The cost of an acquisition is measured at the fair value of the assets given up, equity instruments issued and liabilities incurred or assumed at the date of exchange. Acquisition-related costs are expensed as incurred. The date of exchange is the acquisition date where a business combination is achieved in a single transaction, and is the date of each share purchase where a business combination is achieved in stages by successive share purchases.

An acquirer should recognise at the acquisition date a liability for any contingent purchase consideration. Changes in the value of that liability which relate to measurement period adjustments are adjusted against goodwill. Changes which arise due to events occurring after the acquisition date will be recognised in accordance with other applicable IFRSs, as appropriate, rather than by adjusting goodwill.

Goodwill and Non-Controlling Interest

The excess of the consideration transferred, the amount of any non-controlling interest in the acquiree and the acquisition-date fair value of any previous equity interest in the acquiree over the fair value of the group's share of the identifiable net assets acquired is recorded as goodwill. If this is less than the fair value of the net assets of the subsidiary acquired in the case of a bargain purchase, the difference is recognized directly in the statement of comprehensive income. Goodwill is tested annually for impairment as well as when there are indications of impairment. For the purpose of impairment testing goodwill is allocated to the cash generating units that are expected to benefit from synergies from the combination.

Non-controlling interest represents that portion of the profit or loss and net assets of a subsidiary attributable to equity interests that are not owned, directly or indirectly through subsidiaries, by the parent. The group treats transactions with non-controlling interests as transactions with equity owners of the group. In accordance with IFRS 3 "Business Combinations," the acquirer recognises the acquiree's identifiable assets, liabilities and contingent liabilities that satisfy the recognition criteria at their fair values at the acquisition date, and any non-controlling interest in the acquiree is stated at the non-controlling interest proportion of the net fair value of those items.

6 Critical Judgments and Estimates in Applying Accounting Policies (in part)

6.7 Fair Value Estimation for Acquisitions

In accounting for business combinations, the purchase price paid to acquire a business is allocated to its assets and liabilities based on the estimated fair values of the assets acquired and liabilities assumed as of the date of acquisition. The excess of the purchase price over the fair value of the net tangible and identifiable intangible assets acquired is recorded as goodwill. A significant amount of judgment is involved in estimating the individual fair values of property, plant and equipment and identifiable intangible assets. We use all available information to make these fair value determinations and, for certain acquisitions, engage third-party consultants for assistance.

The estimates used in determining fair values are based on assumptions believed to be reasonable but which are inherently uncertain. Accordingly, actual results may differ from the projected results used to determine fair value.

32 Non-Controlling Interest

Notes		Year Ended 31 December	
		2011	**2010**
	Non-controlling interest at the beginning of the year	286,610	322,806
	Non-controlling interest share of net profit of subsidiary undertakings	35,424	29,436
35	Acquisition of the additional interest in Sibir Energy Ltd.	(23,022)	(17,026)
	Disposal of the interest in OAO Teploset Sankt-Peterburga	6,468	—
38	Disposal of the controlling interest in OOO SeverEnergiya	—	(41,677)
	Purchase of the non-controlling interest in OAO Daltransgaz	—	(3,619)
	Changes in the non-controlling interest as a result of other disposals and acquisitions	(105)	(3,074)
	Dividends	(9,453)	(1,110)
	Translation differences	1,498	874
	Non-controlling interest at the end of the year	297,420	286,610

33 Acquisition of the Controlling Interest in OAO Beltransgaz

During the period from June 2007 to February 2010 as a result of series of transactions, the Group acquired a 50% interest in OAO Beltransgaz. Four equal installments in the amount of USD 625 million were paid by the Group for each 12.5% share acquired. Since February 2008, when the Group's interest in OAO Beltransgaz increased to 25%, the Group started to exercise significant influence and applied the equity method of accounting for its investment in OAO Beltransgaz.

In November 2011 the Group entered into a share purchase agreement with the State Property Committee of the Republic of Belarus to acquire the remaining 50% interest in OAO Beltransgaz for cash consideration of USD 2,500 million. In December 2011 the transaction was finalised. As a result the Group increased its ownership interest up to 100% and obtained control over OAO Beltransgaz.

In accordance with IFRS 3 "Business Combinations," the Group recognized the acquired assets and liabilities based upon their fair values. In these consolidated financial statements, management made a preliminary assessment on a provisional basis. Management is required to finalise the accounting within 12 months from the date of acquisition. Any revisions to the provisional values will be reflected as of the acquisition date.

Purchase consideration includes 50% share in OAO Beltransgaz acquired in December 2011 in amount of RR 78.3 billion (USD 2,500 million) and fair value of previously acquired 50% share in OAO Beltransgaz accounted for using the equity method in amount of RR 34.3 billion.

As a result of the Group obtaining control over OAO Beltransgaz, the Group's previously held 50% interest was remeasured to fair value, resulting in a loss of RR 9.63 billion. This has been recognised in the line item 'Share of net income of associated undertakings and jointly controlled entities' in the consolidated statement of comprehensive income.

Details of the assets acquired and liabilities assumed are as follows:

	Book Value	Provisional Fair Value
Cash and cash equivalents	8,187	8,187
Accounts receivable and prepayments	34,046	34,046
VAT recoverable	1,907	1,907
Inventories	4,490	4,490
Other current assets	365	365
Current assets	48,995	48,995
Property, plant and equipment	30,905	79,091
Construction in progress	763	763
Other non-current assets	251	251
Non-current assets	31,919	80,105
Total assets	80,914	129,100
Accounts payable and accrued charges	41,891	41,891
Short-term borrowings, promissory notes and current portion of long-term borrowings	9,627	9,627
Current liabilities	51,518	51,518
Long-term borrowings	301	301

(continued)

	Book Value	Provisional Fair Value
Deferred tax liabilities	—	8,674
Other non-current liabilities	5	5
Non-current liabilities	306	8,980
Total liabilities	51,824	60,498
Net assets at acquisition date	29,090	68,602
Provisional fair value of Net assets at acquisition date		68,602
Purchase consideration		112,605
Provisional goodwill		44,003

If the acquisition had occurred on 1 January 2011, the Group' sales for year ended 31 December 2011 would have been RR 4,695,157. The Group's profit for the year ended 31 December 2011 would have been RR 1,336,248 respectively.

Goodwill is attributable to enabling effective integration of the Russian and Belarusian gas transmission systems, reducing transit risks, providing additional security of gas sales in the respective markets over the long term. The acquisition of OAO Beltransgaz also allowed the Group to play an active role in the gas infrastructure development in the Republic of Belarus—which is very important for its synchronization with the Company's facilities development in Russia.

34 Merger of OAO WGC-2 and OAO WGC-6

In June 2011 the Annual general shareholders meeting of OAO WGC-2 took a decision to reorganize OAO WGC-2 in the form of a merger with OAO WGC-6. As a result of this reorganization, completed in November 2011, all assets and liabilities of OAO WGC-6 were transferred to OAO WGC-2. The share capital of OAO WGC-2 was increased in form of an additional ordinary shares issue. Placement of shares was performed by conversion of all shares of OAO WGC-6 into ordinary shares of OAO WGC-2. As the result of this reorganization, the share of Gazprom Group in OAO WGC-2 amounts to 58%.

35 Purchase of Non-Controlling Interest in Sibir Energy Ltd.

On 14 February 2011 the Board of Directors of Sibir Energy Ltd. adopted a resolution to reduce the share capital by 86.25 million shares (22.39%). OAO Central Fuel Company, an affiliate to the Moscow Government, made a decision to withdraw membership in Sibir Energy Ltd. for a compensation of USD 740 million. As a result of the transaction starting from 15 February 2011 the Group has 100% interest in Sibir Energy Ltd.

Following the reduction in share capital of Sibir Energy Ltd. the Group has increased its effective interest in OAO Gazpromneft-MNPZ from 66.04% to 74.36%.

As a result of this transaction the difference between the non-controlling interest acquired and consideration paid has been recognized in equity in amount of RR 5,405 and is included within retained earnings and other reserves.

SECTION 10: REPORTING IN HYPERINFLATIONARY ECONOMIES[1]

IAS 29, *FINANCIAL REPORTING IN HYPERINFLATIONARY ECONOMIES*

Author's Note

In December 2010, the International Accounting Standards Board (IASB) issued *Severe Hyperinflation and Removal of Fixed Dates for First-time Adopters: Amendments to IFRS 1*, which is effective for annual reporting periods beginning on or after 1 July 2011. Early application is permitted. The timing of the effective date of these amendments affects the availability of illustrative excerpts from survey companies' financial statements. Accordingly, the excerpts appearing later in the section may not reflect some or all of these revisions.

These amendments define a currency of a hyperinflationary economy to be subject to severe hyperinflation if it has both of the following characteristics:

a. No reliable general price index available to all entities with transactions and balances in the currency

b. No exchangeability between the currency and a relatively stable foreign currency

First-time adopters of International Financial Reporting Standards (IFRSs) with a functional currency that is subject to severe hyperinflation and that elect to measure assets and liabilities at fair value and use that fair value as deemed cost on the date of transition should disclose the circumstances that support their functional currency meeting the characteristics of a currency subject to severe hyperinflation.

In addition, with respect to derecognition of financial assets and liabilities, these amendments replaced the fixed date of 1 January 2004 with the entity's date of transition.

IFRSs Overview and Comparison to U.S. GAAP

10.01 A fundamental element of historical cost measurements is the assumption that the money value or purchasing power associated with these measurements in the entity's functional currency is maintained over fairly long periods of time. In contrast, fair value measurements do not require an assumption of long-term stability of the entity's functional currency. As defined in both the Financial Accounting Standards Board (FASB) *Accounting Standards Codification* (ASC) glossary and IFRSs, an entity's *functional currency* is the currency of the primary economic environment in which the entity operates.

10.02 International Accounting Standard (IAS) 29, *Financial Reporting in Hyperinflationary Economies*, recognizes that the assumption described in the previous paragraph is violated for measurements denominated in the currency of hyperinflationary environments. In addition, the standard recognizes that in a hyperinflationary economy, reporting the results of an entity's financial position and results of operations without restatement is both meaningless and misleading to the users of financial statements.

10.03 In a hyperinflationary economy, money loses its purchasing power at such a fast rate that comparisons of measurements from different periods, even within the same accounting period, will significantly skew the results. Therefore, when an entity's functional currency is that of a hyperinflationary economy, it is necessary to restate an entity's financial position, results of operations, and other financial statement information to provide users of the financial statements with useful information.

10.04 Because judgment is required in determining whether or not an economy is hyperinflationary, IAS 29 provides the following indicators of the characteristics of such an economy:

- The general population tends to keep its wealth in non-monetary assets or a stable currency. In addition, available funds in the local currency are immediately invested in order to maintain purchasing power.
- The general population does not refer to prices in the local currency, and prices may actually be quoted in a more stable currency.
- Prices for credit purchase and credit sale transactions take into account estimated changes in purchasing power even when the time between delivery and payment is short.
- Prices, including interest rates, wages, and so on, may be linked to a price index.
- The cumulative inflation rate over a three-year period approaches or exceeds 100 percent.

Recognition and Measurement

IFRSs

10.05 Although there are several potential approaches to address the challenges that entities face in providing useful financial reporting information in hyperinflationary economies, IAS 29 requires the restatement approach. Entities whose functional currency is the local currency of a hyperinflationary economy should restate the local currency measurements at the end of the reporting period by applying a general price index. International Financial Reporting Interpretations Committee (IFRIC) 7, *Applying the*

---

[1] Unless otherwise indicated, references to International Accounting Standards Board (IASB) standards and interpretations throughout this 2012 edition of *IFRS Financial Statements—Best Practices in Presentation and Disclosure* refer to the version of those standards and interpretations included in the *IFRS 2012* bound volume, the official printed consolidated text of IASB standards and interpretations, including revisions, amendments, and supporting documents, issued as of 1 January 2012.

Restatement Approach under IAS 29 Financial Reporting in Hyperinflationary Economies, clarifies the application of IAS 29 to nonmonetary items measured at historical cost and those carried in the opening statement of financial position at amounts current at dates other than those of acquisition or incurrence. IFRIC 7 also addresses an entity's accounting for opening deferred tax items in its restated financial statements. Application of IAS 29 is mandatory for all entities whose functional currency is hyperinflationary.

10.06 IAS 21, *The Effects of Changes in Foreign Exchange Rates*, is also relevant for most entities applying IAS 29. Consistent with FASB ASC glossary, IAS 21 defines *functional currency* to be the currency of the primary economic environment in which the entity operates. It also establishes the requirements for translation of foreign operations and foreign subsidiaries for inclusion in consolidated financial statements and for translation of either consolidated or separate financial statements from a functional currency to a different presentation currency. IAS 21 prohibits entities with hyperinflationary functional currencies from using a stable or hard currency as their measurement unit of account.

10.07 An entity undertaking a restatement in accordance with IAS 29 would normally take the following actions:
 a. Identify a general price index.
 b. Restate nonmonetary assets and liabilities on the statement of financial position.
 c. Restate items on the statement of comprehensive income.
 d. Calculate any gain or loss on the change in the net monetary position.
 e. Restate the statement of cash flows.
 f. Restate any comparative financial statements by applying the general price index.
 g. Restate comparative information included in note disclosures.

10.08 When an entity's functional currency first becomes hyperinflationary, IFRSs require the application of IAS 29 to the financial statements. IAS 29 is applied retrospectively as if the functional currency has always been hyperinflationary. Therefore, in accordance with IAS 1, *Presentation of Financial Statements*, the entity should present a restated opening balance sheet for the earliest period presented and a restated comparative balance sheet(s), as necessary.

10.09 For consolidation purposes, a reporting entity (parent) restates the financial statements of a foreign subsidiary in accordance with IAS 29 before translation of these statements into the parent's functional currency. The financial statements of a foreign operation also are restated in accordance with IAS 29. A *foreign operation*, as defined in IFRSs, is an entity that is a subsidiary, associate, joint venture, or branch of a reporting entity, the activities of which are based or conducted in a country or currency other than that of the reporting entity. Similarly, a *foreign currency* is a currency other than the functional currency of the entity.

10.10 In accordance with IAS 21, all assets, liabilities, equity items, income, and expenses are translated at the closing rate at the reporting date of the most recent statement of financial position, including comparatives, except when the financial statements are translated into a *stable currency* (the currency of a nonhyperinflationary economy). When the *presentation currency* (the currency in which the financial statements are presented) is a stable currency, the comparative financial statement amounts are those that were presented previously as current year amounts in the relevant prior year financial statements rather than being adjusted for either subsequent changes in the price level or subsequent changes in exchange rates.

U.S. GAAP

10.11 FASB ASC 830, *Foreign Currency Matters*, applies to reporting entities with a reporting currency other than the U.S. dollars in financial statements that are prepared in conformity with U.S. GAAP. However, FASB ASC 830 does not address the scenario under which a reporting entity preparing U.S. GAAP consolidated financial statements would itself have a reporting and functional currency from a highly inflationary economy. FASB ASC 830-10-45-11 only addresses the circumstances in which a reporting entity (parent) translates the financial reporting information of a foreign operation or subsidiary whose functional currency is that of a highly inflationary economy into the presentation currency of the parent in order to prepare consolidated financial statements. Generally, when applying both FASB ASC 830 and IFRSs, an entity would determine the same economies to be highly inflationary or hyperinflationary, even though the criteria for making the determination are more prescriptive under FASB ASC 830-10-45-12.

10.12 Paragraphs 11–14 of FASB ASC 830-10-45 provide guidance to entities with a functional currency in highly inflationary economies. FASB ASC 830-10-45 requires an entity with a functional currency in a highly inflationary economy to remeasure its financial statements as if the functional currency was the reporting currency. When the local currency financial statements of a foreign operation or foreign subsidiary are consolidated in the financial statements of a U.S. GAAP parent, then the local currency financial statements are remeasured as if the functional currency were the parent's reporting currency, in accordance with FASB ASC 830-10-45-11. Such remeasurement is prohibited under IFRSs.

10.13 Unlike IFRSs, when an entity's functional currency becomes hyperinflationary, FASB ASC 830-10-45-10 establishes that restatements are to be made prospectively; therefore, an entity does not restate either its comparative financial statements or other comparative information.

Disclosure

IFRSs

10.14 IAS 29 requires disclosure that the financial statements and prior period comparative information are restated for the changes in the general purchasing power of the functional currency and, as a result, are stated in terms of the measuring unit at the end of the reporting period. IAS 29 also requires an entity to disclose whether the financial statements are based on a historical cost approach or a current cost approach. The identity and level of the price index at the end of the reporting period and the movement in the index during the current and prior reporting periods also are disclosed.

U.S. GAAP

10.15 FASB ASC 830 does not address the scenario in which the consolidated financial statements would be presented in the currency of a hyperinflationary economy. Therefore, this topic does not require disclosures comparable with those required by IAS 29 are necessary.

10.16 However, foreign entities that prepare U.S. GAAP financial statements in the currency of the country in which the reported operations are conducted and that operate in countries with hyperinflationary economies are included in the scope of FASB ASC 255, *Changing Prices*. Entities are encouraged, but not required, to disclose the following information on the effects of changing prices for each of the five most recent years:

- Net sales and other operating revenues
- Income from continuing operations on a current cost basis
- Purchasing power gain or loss on net monetary items
- Increase or decrease in the current cost or lower recoverable amount of inventory and property, plant, and equipment, net of inflation
- Aggregate foreign currency translation adjustment on a current cost basis, if applicable

- Net assets at year-end on a current cost basis
- Income per common share from continuing operations on a current cost basis
- Cash dividends declared per common share
- Market price per common share at year-end

Presentation and Disclosure Excerpts

Foreign Subsidiary Adjusted for Inflation Prior to Translation into Presentation Currency

10.17

Telekom Austria Aktiengesellschaft (Dec 2011)

CONSOLIDATED STATEMENT OF OPERATIONS (in part)

Notes		2011	2010
(4)	Operating revenues	4,454,626	4,650,843
(5)	Other operating income	100,379	89,161
	Operating expenses		
	Materials	− 442,044	− 403,617
	Employee expenses, including benefits and taxes	− 805,042	− 806,836
(6)	Other operating expenses	− 1,780,575	− 1,883,659
	EBITDA comparable	1,527,343	1,645,892
(22)	Restructuring	− 233,703	− 124,061
(17)(18)(19)	Impairment and reversal of impairment	− 248,906	− 18,342
	EBITDA incl. effects from restructuring and impairment tests	1,044,735	1,503,489
(18)(19)	Depreciation and amortization	− 1,052,376	− 1,065,585
	Operating Income	− 7,641	437,903
	Financial result		
(7)	Interest income	16,942	13,078
(7)	Interest expense	− 216,773	− 207,093
(7)	Foreign exchange differences	− 43,533	− 1,665
(7)	Other financial result	− 4,544	205
(15)	Equity in earnings of affiliates	1,089	− 790
	Earnings Before Taxes	− 254,460	241,638

CONSOLIDATED STATEMENT OF COMPREHENSIVE INCOME (in part)

Notes		2011	2010
	Net result	− 252,806	195,173
(8)(16)	Unrealized result on securities available-for-sale	− 647	363
	Income tax benefit (expense)	163	− 91
(7)	Realized result on securities available-for-sale	18	39
	Income tax benefit (expense)	− 5	− 10
(33)	Unrealized result on hedging activities	− 27,365	8,292
	Income tax benefit (expense)	6,841	− 773
(29)	Foreign currency translation adjustment	− 5,096	− 8,293
	Other comprehensive (loss) income	− 26,090	− 471
	Total comprehensive (loss) income	− 278,896	194,702

CONSOLIDATED STATEMENT OF FINANCIAL POSITION *(in part)*

Notes		December 31, 2011	December 31, 2010
	Stockholders' equity		
(29)	Common stock	− 966,183	− 966,183
(29)	Treasury shares	8,196	8,196
(29)	Additional paid-in capital	− 582,896	− 582,896
(29)	Retained earnings	219,772	− 346,341
(29)	Available-for-sale reserve	805	335
(29)	Hedging reserve	27,887	7,363
(29)	Translation adjustments	410,243	405,146
	Equity attributable to equity holders of the parent	− 882,177	− 1,474,379

CONSOLIDATED STATEMENT OF CASH FLOWS *(in part)*

	2011	2010
Cash flow from operating activities	1,213,275	1,397,535
Cash flow from investing activities	− 854,751	− 616,930
Cash flow from financing activities	− 3,673	− 1,388,441
Effect of exchange rate changes	1,274	− 2,023
Monetary loss on cash and cash equivalents	− 16,367	0
Change in cash and cash equivalents	339,756	− 609,858
Cash and cash equivalents at beginning of the year	120,196	730,054
Cash and cash equivalents at end of the year	459,952	120,196

CONSOLIDATED STATEMENT OF CHANGES IN STOCKHOLDERS' EQUITY *(in part)*

	Retained Earnings	Translation Reserve	Total	Non-Controlling Interests	Total Stockholders' Equity
Balance at December 31, 2010	346,341				
Net result	− 251,972	0	− 251,972	− 834	− 252,806
Other comprehensive income (loss)					
Net unrealized result on securities	0	0	− 483	0	− 483
Net realized result on securities	0	0	14	0	14
Net unrealized result on hedging activities	0	0	− 20,524	0	− 20,524
Foreign currency translation adjustment	0	− 5,096	− 5,096	0	− 5,096
Other comprehensive income (loss)	0	− 5,096	− 26,090	0	− 26,090
Total comprehensive income	− 251,972	− 5,096	− 278,062	− 834	− 278,896
Distribution of dividends	− 331,923	0	− 331,923	0	− 331,923
Hyperinflation adjustment	17,783	0	17,783	0	17,783
Acquisition of minority interests	0	0	0	− 777	− 777
Balance at December 31, 2011	− 219,772	− 410,243	882,177	934	883,111

NOTES TO THE CONSOLIDATED FINANCIAL STATEMENTS *(in part)*

Consolidated Segment Reporting *(in part)*

2011	Austria	Bulgaria	Croatia	Belarus	Additional Markets	Corporate & Other	Eliminations	Consolidated
External revenues	2,919,434	500,021	403,046	260,774	371,351	0	0	4,454,626
Intersegmental revenues	22,630	27,670	17,685	99	25,004	0	− 93,089	0
Total revenues	2,942,064	527,692	420,731	260,873	396,355	0	− 93,089	4,454,626
Other operating income	95,825	19,069	2,770	5,252	6,219	20,790	− 49,545	100,379
Segment expenses	− 2,065,304	− 284,865	− 288,982	− 159,546	− 312,171	− 59,172	142,379	− 3,027,662

(continued)

2011	Austria	Bulgaria	Croatia	Belarus	Additional Markets	Corporate & Other	Eliminations	Consolidated
EBITDA comparable	972,584	261,896	134,519	106,580	90,403	− 38,383	− 255	1,527,343
Restructuring	− 233,703	0	0	0	0	0	0	− 233,703
Impairment and reversal of impairment	0	− 19,300	0	− 278,985	49,379	0	0	− 248,906
EBITDA incl. effects from restructuring and impairment tests	738,881	242,596	134,519	− 172,405	139,782	− 38,383	− 255	1,044,735
Depreciation and amortization	− 609,175	− 200,343	− 66,576	− 82,782	− 96,351	0	2,851	− 1,052,376
Operating income	129,706	42,253	67,943	− 255,188	43,431	− 38,383	2,596	− 7,641
Interest income	10,661	2,465	1,242	4,129	2,004	30,678	− 34,237	16,942
Interest expense	− 57,056	− 7,515	− 4,063	− 3,024	− 987	− 178,832	34,703	− 216,773
Equity in earnings of affiliates	1,089	0	0	0	0	0	0	1,089
Other financial income	− 5,195	− 46	− 1,909	− 7,886	93	481,709	− 514,842	− 48,077
Earnings before income taxes	79,205	37,157	63,212	− 261,968	44,541	295,173	− 511,779	− 254,460
Income taxes								1,654
Net result								− 252,806
Segment assets	4,308,424	1,513,857	516,776	560,105	834,065	7,693,395	− 7,977,817	7,448,804
Segment liabilities	− 2,737,458	− 270,628	− 264,837	− 88,855	− 165,517	− 5,147,829	2,109,430	− 6,565,693
Capex other intangible assets	101,701	19,723	5,030	3,347	16,365	0	0	146,166
Capex property, plant and equipment	383,371	50,788	45,506	41,603	71,545	0	0	592,813
Total capital expenditures	485,073	70,511	50,536	44,950	87,910	0	0	738,979
Cost to acquire property, plant and equipment and intangible assets	489,439	71,111	51,171	48,268	88,805	0	0	748,794
Other non-cash items	260,049	48,300	7,283	276,402	− 44,335	33,144	0	580,843

(1) The Company and Significant Accounting Policies (in part)

Description of Business, Organization and Relationship With the Federal Republic of Austria

Telekom Austria AG is incorporated as a joint stock corporation ("Aktiengesellschaft") under the laws of the Republic of Austria and is located in Austria, Lassallestrasse 9, 1020 Vienna. Telekom Austria AG and its subsidiaries ("Telekom Austria Group") are engaged as full service telecommunications providers of long distance, local and wireless services, corporate data communications services as well as internet services and television broadcasting. Telekom Austria Group also supplies telephones and technical equipment for telephone communications. These activities are conducted primarily in Austria, Croatia, Slovenia, Bulgaria, Serbia, Macedonia and Belarus.

The Federal Republic of Austria, through Österreichische Industrieholding AG ("ÖIAG"), is a significant shareholder of Telekom Austria Group. ÖIAG's stake in Telekom Austria Group is disclosed in Note (29).

In addition to the related party transactions described in Note (10), the Federal Republic of Austria authorizes and supervises the Rundfunk und Telekom Regulierungs–GmbH ("RTR"), which regulates certain activities of Telekom Austria Group. In addition, the government holds the taxing authority for the Austrian operations of Telekom Austria Group and imposes taxes such as corporate income tax and value-added taxes on Telekom Austria Group.

The use of automated calculation systems may give rise to rounding differences.

Basis of Presentation

Telekom Austria Group prepared the accompanying consolidated financial statements as of December 31, 2011 in compliance with the provisions of the International Financial Reporting Standards ("IFRS/IAS"), issued by the International Accounting Standards Board ("IASB"), the interpretations of the International Financial Reporting Interpretation Committee ("IFRIC") and the interpretation of the Standards Interpretation Committee ("SIC"), effective as of December 31, 2011 and as endorsed by the European Union.

Foreign Currency Translation

The consolidated financial statements of Telekom Austria Group are expressed in thousand Euros ("EUR").

Financial statements of subsidiaries where the functional currency is a currency other than the Euro are translated using the functional currency principle. For these entities, assets and liabilities are translated using the year-end exchange rates, while revenues and expenses are translated using the average exchange rates prevailing during the year except for subsidiaries located in a hyperinflationary economy for which the year-end exchange rates are applied. All items of shareholders' equity are translated at historical exchange rates. Until the disposal of the respective operation, the foreign currency translation adjustment classified in equity, is recognized in other comprehensive income (OCI).

Transaction gains and losses that arise from exchange rate fluctuations on transactions denominated in a currency other than the functional currency are included in the financial result.

The following table provides the exchange rates for the currencies in which Telekom Austria Group conducts most of its transactions:

	Exchange Rates at December 31		Average Exchange Rates for the Period Ended December 31	
	2011	2010	2011	2010
Bulgarian Lev (BGN)	1.9558	1.9558	1.9558	1.9558
Croatian Kuna (HRK)	7.5370	7.3830	7.4387	7.2889
Hungarian Forint (HUF)	314.5800	277.9500	279.3587	275.4534
Serbian Dinar (CSD)	104.6409	105.4982	101.9674	103.0016
Swiss Franc (CHF)	1.2156	1.2504	1.2330	1.3799
Rumanian Leu (RON)	4.3233	4.2620	4.2381	4.2121
Turkish Lira (TRY)	2.4432	2.0694	2.3374	1.9965
Macedonian Denar (MKD)	61.5050	61.5085	61.5292	61.5181
Belarusian Ruble (BYR)*	10,800.0000	3,972.6000	10,800.0000	3,951.7641
US Dollar (USD)	1.2939	1.3362	1.3921	1.3257

* Year-end rates are used for the translation of revenues and expenses if IAS 29 "Financial Reporting in Hyperinflationary Economies" is applied.

Financial Reporting in Hyperinflationary Economies

Financial statements of subsidiaries located in hyperinflationary economies are restated before translation to the reporting currency of the group and before consolidation in order to reflect the same value of money for all items. Items recognized in the statement of financial position which are not measured at the applicable year-end measuring unit are restated based on the general price index. All non-monetary items measured at cost or amortized cost are restated for the changes in the general price index from the date of transaction to the reporting date. Monetary items are not restated. All items of shareholders' equity are restated for the changes in the general price index since their addition until the end of the reporting period. All items of comprehensive income are restated for the change in a general price index from the date of initial recognition to the reporting date. Gains and losses resulting from the net-position of monetary items are reported in the consolidated statement of operations in financial result in exchange differences. In accordance with IAS 21.42 (b) prior year financial statements were not restated.

The financial statements of the subsidiary in Belarus are generally based on historic cost. In 2011, this basis had to be restated due to changes in the value of money of its functional currency. The financial statements of the subsidiary in Belarus are therefore reported at the applicable measuring unit at the reporting date. The consumer price indexes published by the Belarusian "National Statistical Committee" were applied. The following table provides the inflation rates used in the calculation:

Years	Inflation %
2008	13.4
2009	9.8
2010	10.1
2011	108.7

2011-Monthly	Inflation %
January	1.4
February	2.7
March	1.9
April	4.5
May	13.1
June	8.6
July	3.5
August	8.9
September	13.6
October	8.2
November	8.1
December	2.3

Assets and liabilities as well as revenues and expenses of these foreign subsidiaries are translated using the year-end exchange rates for the purpose of consolidation.

(3) Operating Segments

Reporting on operating segments (see table "Consolidated Operating Segments") has been prepared in accordance with IFRS 8. The accounting policies of the segments are the same as those described in Note (1).

Telekom Austria Group has aligned its management structure and the resulting segment reporting due to the demand for convergent products. As a result, operating segments are based on geographical markets. Telekom Austria Group reports separately on its five operating segments: Austria, Bulgaria, Croatia, Belarus and Additional Markets.

The segment Austria comprises convergent products for voice telephony, internet access, data and IT solutions, value added services, wholesale services, television broadcasting (A1 TV), mobile business and payment solutions in Austria.

The segment Bulgaria comprises voice telephony (mobile and fixed line telephone service), access to emergency services, directory services, internet access, data and IT solutions, value added services, wholesale services, the sale of end-user terminal equipment, IP television and other IP based services and payment solutions in Bulgaria.

The segment Croatia provides mobile and fixed line telephony, value added services and mobile and fixed line internet access and cable television in Croatia.

The segment Belarus comprises mobile communication services in Belarus. In 2011, hyperinflation accounting in accordance with IAS 29 was initially applied for the segment Belarus, which results in the restatement of non monetary assets, liabilities and all items of the statement of comprehensive income for the change in a general price index and the translation of these items applying the year-end exchange rate. In accordance with IAS 21.42 comparative amounts for 2010 were not restated.

The segment Additional Markets comprises the mobile communication companies in Slovenia, Liechtenstein, the Republic of Serbia and the Republic of Macedonia.

The segment Corporate & Other performs strategic and cross-divisional management functions and takes responsibility for the connection to the capital markets.

Segment revenues, segment expenses and segment results include transfers between operating segments. Such transfers are accounted for at transfer prices corresponding to competitive market prices charged to unaffiliated customers for similar products. Those transfers are eliminated in consolidation.

The segments are reported on a consolidated basis. Segment assets and segment liabilities do not include deferred tax assets or liabilities, income tax receivables or income tax payables. The elimination column contains the reconciliation of segment assets and liabilities to consolidated total assets and liabilities. Capital expenditures, as well as depreciation and amortization, relate to property, plant and equipment and other intangible assets.

Other non-cash items mainly consist of restructuring expenses, pension and severance expense, accrued interest, accretion expense related to the asset retirement obligations, bad debt expenses and impairment charges. Additionally in 2011, unrealized foreign exchange losses, the reversal of impairment and the net monetary gain in the segment Belarus resulting from the application of hyperinflation accounting are included in other non-cash items.

None of the segments records revenues from transactions with a single external customer amounting to at least 10% or more of an entity's revenues.

For information on restructuring in the segment Austria see Note (22). In 2011, impairment charges recorded in the segment Bulgaria related to the brand name "Mobiltel" (see Note (18)), in the segment Belarus to the goodwill of velcom (see Note (17)) and to the reversal of the impairment on the license in Serbia recognized in 2009 in the segment Other Markets (see Note (18)). In 2010, impairment charges recorded in the Segment Austria relate to the impairment of the goodwill, software and equipment of Mass Response Service (see Note (17), (18) and (19)).

The item other financial result includes other financial result as well as foreign exchange differences. In 2011, other financial result in the segment Corporate & Other relate to dividend income from subsidiaries which are consolidated in eliminations, thus having no impact on the consolidated financial statements. In 2010, other financial result reported in the segments Austria as well and in the segment Holding & Other, mainly results from the reorganization within Telekom Austria Group and additionally in the segment Holding & Other to dividend income from subsidiaries, which were consolidated in eliminations, thus having no impact on the consolidated financial statements.

The following table sets out revenues from external customers for each product line:

	2011	2010
Monthly fee and traffic	3,193,557	3,306,321
Data and ICT Solutions	202,551	215,840
Wholesale (incl. Roaming)	248,011	250,521
Interconnection	519,672	597,335
Equipment	243,894	213,044
Other revenues	46,941	67,781
Total revenues	4,454,626	4,650,843

(29) Stockholders' Equity (in part)

Reserve for Available-for-Sale Marketable Securities, Hedging Reserve and Translation Adjustment

The development of the reserve for available-for-sale marketable securities and the hedging reserve as well as the translation adjustment are presented in the consolidated statement of comprehensive income and consolidated statement of changes in stockholder's equity. The foreign currency translation adjustment mainly relates to the consolidation of velcom in Belarus and Vip mobile in Serbia. The currency appreciation of the Serbian Dinar in 2011 resulted in a positive adjustment of EUR 1,351, the translation adjustment as of December 31, 2011 amounts to EUR 102,826. Due to the application of IAS 29 "Financial Reporting in Hyperinflationary Economies" to the subsidiaries in Belarus in 2011, the relating translation adjustment of EUR 302,063 as of December 31, 2011 remains unchanged compared to December 31, 2010.

(33) Financial Instruments (in part)

Financial Risk Management (in part)

Overview

Telekom Austria Group is exposed to market risks, including liquidity risk, interest rate and foreign currency exchange rate risk and credit risk associated with underlying financial assets, liabilities and anticipated transactions. Telekom Austria Group selectively enters into derivative financial instruments to manage the related risk exposures in areas such as foreign exchange rates and interest rate fluctuations. These policies are laid down in the Treasury Guidelines. Telekom Austria Group does not hold or issue derivative financial instruments for trading or speculative purposes.

Exchange Rate Risk

As of December 31, 2011 and 2010, a remaining purchase price liability from the acquisition of SBT in 2007 (see Note (2)) amounts to 74,887 TUSD and 95,253 TUSD. This liability was not hedged but Telekom Austria Group invested US Dollars resulting from the initial forward exchange contract which expired in 2010.

As of December 31, 2011 and 2010, of all accounts receivable—trade and accounts payable—trade, only the following are denominated in a currency other than the functional currency of the reporting entities or their sub-sidiaries (for foreign exchange rates, see Note (1)):

At December 31	2011 EUR	2011 USD	Other	2010 EUR	2010 USD	Other
Accounts receivable—trade	14,110	7,943	14,767	13,476	4,986	13,441
Accounts payable—trade	43,360	21,045	13,733	90,967	14,199	7,106

A change of 5% in the exchange rate of EUR to HRK would have increased (decreased) foreign exchange rate differ-ences by EUR 2,313 and EUR 3,131 in 2011 and 2010, re-spectively. A change of 10% in the exchange rate of EUR to RSD would have increased (decreased) foreign exchange rate differences by EUR 551 and EUR 314 in 2011 and 2010, respectively. A sensitive analysis for a change of the BYR was not performed due to the application of accounting in hyperin-flationary economies. No sensitivity analysis was performed for other accounts receivable or for accounts payable—trade, denominated in foreign currencies, as there is no significant risk due to diversification.

Foreign Exchange Agreements

Forward exchange contracts entered into by Telekom Austria Group serve as economic hedges of Telekom Austria Group's transactions in foreign currencies. As of December 31, 2011 and 2010, hedge accounting was not applied to foreign ex-change agreements.

As of December 31, 2011 and 2010, Telekom Austria Group entered into forward exchange contracts which served as hedges of Telekom Austria Group's operating exposure to fluctuations in foreign currencies, but for which hedge ac-counting was not applied. Changes in the fair value of these derivative instruments are recognized immediately in the con-solidated statement of operations as foreign exchange gains or losses.

The following tables indicate the types of foreign exchange agreements in use at December 31, 2011 and 2010 (amounts to be received are stated negative):

At December 31	2011	2010
Forward exchange contract—EUR long		
Notional amount in BYR	0	4,095,510
Notional amount in EUR	0	−1,000
Forward exchange rate (weighted)	0	4,095.51
Exchange rate as of the reporting date	0	3,972.60
Longest term of the contracts	0	August, 2011

At December 31	2011	2010
Forward exchange contract—USD long		
Notional amount in EUR	8,682	0
Notional amount in USD	11,495	0
Forward exchange rate (weighted)	1.3240	0
Exchange rate as of the reporting date	1.2939	0
Longest term of the contracts	February, 2012	0

Elimination of the Price-Level Adjustment on Transition to IFRSs Except for Property, Plant and Equipment Under the Deemed Cost Exemption in IFRS 1

10.18

GRUMA, S.A.B. de C.V. (Dec 2011)

CONSOLIDATED STATEMENTS OF CASH FLOWS (in part)

	2010	2011
Income before taxes	Ps. 1,479,047	Ps. 7,622,394
Restatement effect from companies in hyperinflationary environment	64,899	27,771
Foreign exchange loss (gain) from working capital	434,326	(59,187)
Net cost of the year for employee benefit obligations	56,148	35,347
Items related with investing activities:		
Depreciation and amortization	1,502,534	1,596,643
Impairment of long-lived assets	—	93,808
Written-down fixed assets	—	52,271
Interest income	(7,531)	(86,846)
Foreign exchange (gain) loss from cash	(9,635)	36,797
Share of profit of associates	(592,235)	(3,329)
Gain from the sale of shares of associate	—	(4,707,804)
Loss in sale of fixed assets and damaged assets	64,659	20,812
Items related with financing activities:		
Derivative financial instruments	82,525	(207,816)
Foreign exchange gain from bank borrowings	(561,821)	(23,953)
Interest expense	1,391,631	965,128
	3,904,547	5,362,036

(continued)

	2010	2011
Accounts receivable, net	(275,595)	(1,422,010)
Inventories	(747,758)	(3,063,148)
Prepaid expenses	(126,655)	101,106
Trade accounts payable	759,773	1,623,802
Accrued liabilities and other accounts payable	561,910	(341,743)
Income taxes paid	(786,796)	(561,279)
Employee benefits obligations and others, net	1,712	52,550
	(613,409)	(3,610,722)
Net cash flows from operating activities	3,291,138	1,751,314
Net (decrease) increase in cash and cash equivalents	(1,745,501)	1,101,384
Exchange differences and effects from inflation on cash and cash equivalents	(113,845)	56,950
Cash and cash equivalents at the beginning of the year	1,880,663	21,317
Cash and cash equivalents at the end of the year	Ps. 21,317	Ps. 1,179,651

NOTES TO THE CONSOLIDATED FINANCIAL STATEMENTS (in part)

1. Entity and Operations

Gruma, S.A.B. de C.V. (GRUMA) is a Mexican company with subsidiaries located in Mexico, the United States of America, Central America, Venezuela, Europe, Asia and Oceania, together referred to as the "Company". The Company's main activities are the production and sale of corn flour, wheat flour, tortillas and related products.

Gruma, S.A.B. de C.V. is a publicly held corporation (*Sociedad Anónima Bursátil de Capital Variable*) organized under the laws of Mexico. The address of its registered office is Rio de la Plata 407 in San Pedro Garza García, Nuevo León, Mexico.

The consolidated financial statements were authorized by the Chief Corporate Office and the Chief Administrative Office of the Company on April 30, 2012.

2. Basis of Preparation

The consolidated financial statements of Gruma, S.A.B. de C.V. and Subsidiaries as of December 31, 2011 have been prepared for the first time in accordance with the International Financial Reporting Standards (IFRS) as issued by the International Accounting Standards Board (IASB). The IFRS also include the International Accounting Standards (IAS) in force, as well as all the related interpretations issued by the International Financial Reporting Interpretations Committee (IFRIC), including those previously issued by the Standing Interpretations Committee (SIC).

In accordance with the amendments to the Rules for Public Companies and Other Participants in the Mexican Stock Exchange, issued by the Mexican Banking Securities Exchange Commission on January 27, 2009, the Company is required to prepare its financial statements under IFRS starting in 2012.

The Company decided to adopt IFRS earlier, starting January 1, 2011, therefore, these are the Company's first consolidated financial statements prepared in accordance with IFRS as issued by the IASB.

For comparative purposes, the consolidated financial statements as of and for the year ended December 31, 2010 have been prepared in accordance with IFRS, as required by the IFRS 1—First-Time Adoption of International Financial Reporting Standards.

The Company modified its accounting policies from Mexican Financial Reporting Standards (Mexican FRS) in order to comply with IFRS starting January 1, 2011. The transition from Mexican FRS to IFRS was recognized in accordance with IFRS 1, setting January 1, 2010 as the transition date. The reconciliation of the effects of the transition from Mexican FRS to IFRS in equity as of January 1, 2010 and December 31, 2010, in net income and cash flows for the year ended December 31, 2010 are disclosed in Note 28 to these financial statements.

A) Basis of Measurement

The consolidated financial statements have been prepared on the basis of historical cost, except for the fair value of certain financial instruments as described in the policies below.

The preparation of financial statements requires that management make judgments, estimates and assumptions that affect the application of accounting policies and the reported amounts of assets, liabilities, income and expenses. Actual results could differ from those estimates.

B) Functional and Presentation Currency

The consolidated financial statements are presented in Mexican pesos, which is the functional currency of Gruma, S.A.B. de C.V.

4. Summary of Significant Accounting Policies (in part)

B) Foreign Currency

a. Transactions in Foreign Currency

Foreign currency transactions are translated into the functional currency of the Company using the exchange rates prevailing at the dates of the transactions. Monetary assets and liabilities denominated in foreign currencies are translated at year-end exchange rates. The differences that arise from the translation of foreign currency transactions are recognized in the income statement.

b. Foreign Currency Translation

The financial statements of the Company's entities are measured using the currency of the main economic environment where the entity operates (functional currency). The consolidated financial statements are presented in Mexican pesos, currency that corresponds to the presentation currency of the Company.

The financial position and results of all of the group entities that have a functional currency which differs from the presentation currency are translated as follows:

- Assets and liabilities are translated at the closing rate of the period.
- Income and expenses are translated at average exchange rates.
- All resulting exchange differences are recognized in other comprehensive income as a separate component of equity denominated "Foreign currency translation adjustments."

The Company applies hedge accounting to foreign exchange differences originated between the functional currency of a foreign subsidiary and the functional currency of the Company. Exchange differences resulting from the translation of a financial liability designated as hedge for a net investment in a foreign subsidiary, are recognized in other comprehensive income as a separate component denominated "Foreign currency translation adjustments" while the hedge is effective. See Note 4-L for the accounting of the net investment hedge.

Previous to the peso translation, the financial statements of foreign subsidiaries with functional currency from a hyper-inflationary environment are adjusted by inflation in order to reflect the changes in purchasing power of the local currency. Subsequently, assets, liabilities, equity, income, costs, and expenses are translated to the presentation currency at the closing rate at the date of the most recent balance sheet. To determine the existence of hyperinflation, the Company evaluates the qualitative characteristics of the economic environment, as well as the quantitative characteristics established by IFRS of an accumulated inflation rate equal or higher than 100% in the past three years.

The exchange rates used for preparing the financial statements are as follows:

	As of January 1, 2010	As of December 31, 2010	As of December 31, 2011
Pesos per U.S. dollar	13.07	12.35	13.95
Pesos per Euro	18.7358	16.4959	18.0764
Pesos per Swiss franc	12.63	13.22	14.87
Pesos per Venezuelan bolivar	6.0791	2.8721	3.2442
Pesos per Australian dollar	11.7565	12.6341	14.2178
Pesos per Chinese yuan	1.9145	1.8692	2.2161
Pesos per Pound sterling	21.1041	19.3352	21.6797
Pesos per Malaysian ringgit	3.8143	4.0313	4.4035
Pesos per Costa Rica colon	0.0231	0.0239	0.0270
Pesos per Ukrainian hryvnia	—	1.5550	1.7553
Pesos per Russian ruble	—	—	0.4341
Pesos per Turkish lira	—	—	7.3935

5. Risk and Capital Management (in part)

A) Risk Management (in part)

The Company is exposed to a variety of financial risks: market risk (including currency risk, interest rate risk, and commodity price risk), credit risk and liquidity risk. The group's overall risk management focuses on the unpredictability of financial markets and seeks to minimize potential adverse effects on financial performance. The Company uses derivative financial instruments to hedge some of these risks.

Currency Risk

The Company operates internationally and thus, is exposed to currency risks, particularly with the U.S. dollar. Currency risks arise from commercial operations, recognized assets and liabilities and net investments in foreign subsidiaries.

The following tables detail the exposure of the Company to currency risks at January 1, 2010 and at December 31, 2010 and 2011. The tables show the carrying amount of the Company's financial instruments denominated in foreign currency.

At January 1, 2010:

			Amounts in Thousands of Mexican Pesos			
	U.S. Dollar	Pound Sterling	Venezuelan Bolivar	Euros	Costa Rica Colons and Others	Total
Monetary assets:						
Current	Ps. 2,061,769	Ps. 38,249	Ps. 1,722,114	Ps. 234,904	Ps. 555,074	Ps. 4,612,110
Non-current	27,536	—	13,822	1,973	15,712	59,043
Monetary liabilities:						
Current	(3,908,767)	(146,826)	(2,261,136)	(145,376)	(364,208)	(6,826,313)
Non-current	(16,898,484)	(745)	(47,316)	(58,442)	(46,246)	(17,051,233)
Net position	Ps. (18,717,946)	Ps. (109,322)	Ps. (572,516)	Ps. 33,059	Ps. 160,332	Ps. (19,206,393)

At December 31, 2010:

	Amounts in Thousands of Mexican Pesos					
	U.S. Dollar	Pound Sterling	Venezuelan Bolivar	Euros	Costa Rica Colons and Others	Total
Monetary assets:						
Current	Ps. 1,777,322	Ps. 82,151	Ps. 1,057,283	Ps. 129,748	Ps. 454,600	Ps. 3,501,104
Non-current	24,021	1,270	8,089	2,793	3,642	39,815
Monetary liabilities:						
Current	(4,069,370)	(158,958)	(1,392,016)	(222,625)	(332,376)	(6,175,345)
Non-current	(13,550,278)	(20,049)	(26,713)	(34,963)	(53,075)	(13,685,078)
Net position	Ps. (15,818,305)	Ps. (95,586)	Ps. (353,357)	Ps. (125,047)	Ps. 72,791	Ps. (16,319,504)

At December 31, 2011:

	Amounts in Thousands of Mexican Pesos					
	U.S. Dollar	Pound Sterling	Venezuelan Bolivar	Euros	Costa Rica Colons and Others	Total
Monetary assets:						
Current	Ps. 2,867,933	Ps. 313,652	Ps. 1,085,573	Ps. 172,257	Ps. 935,694	Ps. 5,375,109
Non-current	20,809	1,428	522	33,608	42,170	98,537
Monetary liabilities:						
Current	(4,627,116)	(173,062)	(1,970,433)	(273,115)	(515,808)	(7,559,534)
Non-current	(11,615,016)	(1,074)	(22,356)	(33,253)	(69,899)	(11,741,598)
Net position	Ps. (13,353,390)	Ps. 140,944	Ps. (906,694)	Ps. (100,503)	Ps. 392,157	Ps. (13,827,486)

For the years ended December 31, 2010 and 2011, the effects of exchange rate differences on the Company's monetary assets and liabilities were recognized as follows:

	2010	2011
Exchange differences arising from foreign currency liabilities accounted for as a hedge of the Company's net investment in foreign subsidiaries, recorded directly to equity as an effect of foreign currency translation adjustments	Ps. 296,636	Ps. (813,101)
Exchange differences arising from foreign currency transactions recognized in the income statement	143,852	40,885
	Ps. 440,488	Ps. (772,216)

Net sales are denominated in Mexican pesos, U.S. dollars, and other currencies. During 2011, 34% of sales were generated in Mexican pesos and 38% in U.S. dollars. Additionally, at December 31, 2011, 67% of total assets were denominated in different currencies other than Mexican pesos, mainly in U.S. dollars. An important portion of operations are financed through debt denominated in U.S. dollars. For the years ended December 31, 2010 and 2011, net sales in foreign currency amounted to Ps. 30,732,369 and Ps.37,819,919, respectively.

An important currency risk for the debt denominated in U.S. dollars is present in subsidiaries that are not located in the United States, which represented 83% of total debt denominated in U.S. dollars.

During 2010 and 2011, the Company carried out forward transactions with the intention of hedging the currency risk of the Mexican peso with respect to the U.S. dollar, related with the price of corn purchases for domestic and imported har-

vest. These foreign exchange derivative instruments that did not qualify for hedging accounting were recognized at their fair value. At December 31, 2010 and 2011, the open positions of these instruments represented an unfavorable effect of approximately Ps.4,863 and a favorable effect of approximately Ps.88,537, respectively, which was recognized in the income statement.

At December 31, 2011 the Company had foreign exchange derivative instruments for a nominal amount of U.S.$106 million with different maturities, ranging from January to March 2012. The purpose of these instruments is to hedge the risks related to foreign exchange differences in the price of corn, which is denominated in U.S. dollars.

The effect of foreign exchange differences recognized in the income statements for the years ended December 31, 2010 and 2011, related with the assets and liabilities denominated in foreign currency, totaled a gain of Ps.143,852 and Ps.40,885, respectively. Considering the exposure at December 31, 2010 and 2011, and assuming an increase or decrease of 10% in the exchange rates while keeping constant the rest of the variables such as interest rates, the effect after taxes in the Company's consolidated results will be Ps.605,597 and Ps.128,673, respectively.

Investment Risk in Venezuela

The Company's operations in Venezuela represented approximately 16% of consolidated net sales and 14% of total consolidated assets as of December 31, 2011. The recent political and civil instability that has prevailed in Venezuela represents a risk to the business that cannot be controlled and that cannot be accurately measured or estimated.

Also, in recent years the Venezuelan authorities have imposed foreign exchange controls and price controls on certain products such as corn flour and wheat flour. These price controls may limit the Company's ability to increase prices in order to compensate for the higher cost of raw materials. The foreign exchange controls may limit the Company's capacity to convert bolivars to other currencies and also transfer funds outside Venezuela.

Various fixed exchange rates have been established by the Venezuelan Government since 2003. Effective January 1, 2010, the Venezuelan Government established an exchange rate of 4.30 bolivars per U.S. dollar.

The Company does not have insurance for the risk of expropriation of its investments. See Note 25 for additional information about the expropriation proceedings of MONACA assets and the measures taken by the People's Defense Institute for the Access of Goods and Services of Venezuela (Instituto para la Defensa de las Personas en el Acceso a los Bienes y Servicios de Venezuela, or INDEPABIS) in Demaseca.

Given the Company's operations in Venezuela, the financial position and results of the Company may be negatively affected by a number of factors, including:

a. Decrease in consolidated income due to a possible devaluation of the Venezuelan bolivar against the U.S. dollar;
b. Subsidiaries in Venezuela manufacture products subject to price controls;
c. The enactment of the Just Costs and Prices Law (Ley de Costos y Precios Justos) on July 18, 2011, that controls the prices of products affecting the Company's sales;
d. It may be difficult for subsidiaries in Venezuela to pay dividends, as well as to import some of their requirements of raw materials as a result of the foreign exchange control;
e. The costs of some raw materials used by the Venezuelan subsidiaries may increase due to import tariffs, and
f. Inability to obtain a just and reasonable compensation for MONACA's assets subject to expropriation and if obtained, whether such compensation could be collected.

28. First Time Adoption of International Financial Reporting Standards (in part)

Until 2010, the Company prepared its consolidated financial statements in accordance with Mexican Financial Reporting Standards. Starting in 2011, the Company prepared its consolidated financial statements in accordance with International Financial Reporting Standards (IFRS) as issued by the International Accounting Standards Board (IASB).

In accordance with IFRS 1, "First-time adoption of International Financial Reporting Standards", the Company considered January 1, 2010 as the transition date and January 1, 2011 as the adoption date. The amounts included in the consolidated financial statements for the year 2010 have been reconciled in order to be presented with the same standards and criteria applied in 2011.

In order to determine the balances for adoption of IFRS, the Company considered January 1, 2010 as the date of transition. In preparing these consolidated financial statements in accordance with IFRS 1, the Company applied certain optional exceptions from full retrospective application of IFRS.

IFRS Optional Exceptions

The Company applied the following optional exceptions allowed by IFRS:

a. The accounting of business combinations occurred prior to January 1, 2010 was not modified (exception for IFRS 3).
b. The depreciated cost for property, plant and equipment at January 1, 2010 was considered the deemed cost on transition to IFRS, including asset revaluations held in the different countries in which the Company operates (exception for IAS 16).
c. Foreign currency translation adjustments recognized prior to January 1, 2010 were classified in retained earnings (exception to IAS 21).
d. The Company recognized accumulated actuarial gains and losses within retained earnings at the date of transition (exception for IAS 19).

E) Description of the Effects from the Transition to IFRS

a. Recognition of Effects of Inflation

In accordance with IAS 29, "Financial reporting in hyper-inflationary economies", the effects of inflation in the financial information must be recognized for hyper-inflationary economies, when the accumulated inflation rate for the last three years exceeds 100%. Since the Company and its main subsidiaries are located in non-hyper-inflation economies, the effects of inflation recognized under Mexican FRS until 2007 were cancelled for the non-hyper-inflationary periods, except for "Property, plant and equipment" (due to the deemed cost exception of IFRS 1) and for "Goodwill" (due to the business combinations exception).

Retrospective Application of IAS 29, Discussion of Devaluation of the Venezuelan Bolivar in 2010

10.19

East Asiatic Company Ltd. A/S (Dec 2011)

CONSOLIDATED STATEMENT OF COMPREHENSIVE INCOME (in part)

DKK Million	2011	2010
Net profit for the year	242	761
Other comprehensive income:		
Foreign exchange adjustments, etc.:		
Foreign currency translation adjustments, foreign entities	6	274
Foreign currency translation adjustments, transferred to profit from discontinued operations		− 36
Foreing currency translation adjustments, transferred to gain on disposal of associates		9
Devaluation of the Bolivar (VEF) in Plumrose, January 2010		− 855
Inflation adjustment for the year (and at 1 January)	338	299

CONSOLIDATED STATEMENT OF CHANGES IN EQUITY (in part)

DKK Million	Share Capital	Hedging Reserve	Translation Reserves	Treasury Shares	Retained Earnings	Proposed Dividend for The Year	EAC's Share of Equity	Non-Controlling Interests	Total Equity
Equity at 1 January 2011	960	0	103	− 76	1,306	69	2,362	95	2,457
Comprehensive income for the year									
Profit for the year					100	62	162	80	242
Other comprehensive income									
Foreign currency translation adjustments, foreign entities			0				0	6	6
Inflation adjustment for the year			316				316	22	338
Tax on other comprehensive income			0				0		0
Total other comprehensive income	0	0	316		0	0	316	28	344
Total comprehensive income for the year	0	0	316		100	62	478	108	586

CONSOLIDATED CASH FLOW STATEMENT (in part)

DKK Million	Note	31.12.2011	31.12.2010
Changes in cash and cash equivalents		− 437	574
Cash and cash equivalents at beginning of year		1,054	604
Translation adjustments of cash and cash equivalents including devaluation impact		12	− 124
Cash and cash equivalents at end of period		629	1,054
Bank balances		629	1,054
Cash and cash equivalents at end of period		629	1,054

The Group's cash balance included DKK 471m (2010: DKK 252m) relating to cash in subsidiaries in countries with currency control or other legal restrictions. Accordingly this cash is not available for immediate use by the Parent Company or other subsidiaries.

NOTES TO THE CONSOLIDATED FINANCIAL STATEMENTS (in part)

1. Accounting Policies for the Consolidated Financial Statements (in part)

General Information

The East Asiatic Company Ltd. A/S (the Company) and its subsidiaries (together the EAC Group or the Group) have the following two lines of business:

- Santa Fe Group provides moving, value-added reloca-tion and records management services to corporate and individual clients.
- Plumrose is an integrated manufacturer and distributor of processed meat products in Venezuela.

The Company is a limited liability company incorporated and domiciled in Denmark. The address of its registered office is 20 Indiakaj, DK-2100 Copenhagen Ø, Denmark.

The annual report comprises both consolidated financial statements and separate Parent Company financial statements.

The Company has its listing on NASDAQ OMX Copenhagen A/S.

On 23 February 2012, the Supervisory Board approved this annual report for publication and approval by the shareholders at the annual general meeting to be held on 27 March 2012.

The financial statements are presented in DKK million unless otherwise stated.

Refer to page 37 for further details about the EAC Group and page 83 for details about the Parent Company.

Basis of Preparation of the Consolidated Financial Statements (in part)

The consolidated financial statements of EAC for 2011 are prepared in accordance with International Financial Reporting Standards (IFRS) as adopted by the EU and Danish disclosure requirements for listed companies.

In addition, the annual report has been prepared in compliance with IFRS as issued by the IASB.

Accounting estimates and judgements considered material for the preparation of the consolidated financial statements are described in note 2.

Hyperinflation

Venezuela is classified as a hyperinflationary economy. As a consequence, the accounting figures for Plumrose's activities in Venezuela have been adjusted for inflation prior to translation to the Group's presentation currency. The effect of the inflation adjustment is further described in note 38.

Foreign Currency Translation and Hyperinflation

Items included in the financial statements of each of the EAC Group's entities are measured using the currency of the primary economic environment in which the entity operates ('functional currency'). As the EAC Group is a Danish listed group, the consolidated financial statements are presented in DKK ('presentation currency').

Transactions and Balances

Foreign currency transactions are translated into the functional currency using the exchange rates prevailing at the dates of the transactions. Foreign currency translation adjustments resulting from the settlement of such transactions and from the translation at year-end exchange rates of monetary assets and liabilities denominated in foreign currencies are recognised in the income statement.

EAC Group Companies

The items of the income statements and balance sheets of foreign subsidiaries and associates with a functional currency other than DKK are translated into the presentation currency as follows:

- (i) assets and liabilities are translated at the closing rate at the date of the balance sheet;
- (ii) income and expenses are translated at the rate of the transaction date or at an approximate average rate; and
- (iii) all resulting foreign currency translation adjustments are recognised as a separate component of equity.

In foreign subsidiaries and associates that operate in hyperinflationary economies, income and expenses are, however, translated at the exchange rate at the balance sheet date. Prior to translating the financial statements of foreign operations in hyperinflationary economies, the income statement and non-monetary balance sheet items are restated taking into account changes in the general purchasing power of the functional currency based on the inflation up to the balance sheet date ('inflation adjustment'). The effect of the inflation adjustment is recognised as a separate item in the EAC Group's equity in the translation reserve. In the income statement, gain/loss on the monetary net position in the foreign entities is recognised as financial income or expense. The assessment as to when an economy is hyperinflationary is based on qualitative as well as quantitative factors, including whether the accumulated inflation over a three-year period is in the region of 100%.

Foreign currency translation adjustments of a loan or payable to subsidiaries which are neither planned nor likely to be settled in the foreseeable future and which are therefore considered to form part of the net investment in the subsidiary are recognised directly in equity.

When a foreign operation is sold, the EAC Group's share of accumulated foreign exchange adjustments are recognised in the income statement as part of the gain or loss on the sale.

Goodwill arising on the acquisition of a foreign entity is treated as assets of the foreign entity and translated at the rate of the balance sheet date.

Dual Exchange Rates

Where a system of dual exchange rates exists, individual transactions and monetary items denominated in foreign currencies are translated into the functional currency at the expected settlement rate of the transaction.

Foreign subsidiaries and associates with a functional currency other than DKK are translated into the presentation currency using the translation rate which is expected to apply for capital repatriation in the form of royalties and dividends to the EAC Group.

Shareholders' Equity (in part)

Translation reserve comprises foreign exchange differences arising on translation to DKK of financial statements of foreign entities and the effect of inflation adjustments regarding foreign subsidiaries and associated companies operating in hyperinflationary economies.

2. Significant Accounting Estimates and Judgements (in part)

In connection with the preparation of the consolidated financial statements, Management has made accounting estimates and judgements that affect the assets and liabilities reported at the balance sheet date as well as the income and expenses reported for the financial period. Management continuously reassesses these estimates and judgements based on a number of other factors in the given circumstances.

The following judgements in relation to the application of the group accounting policies apart from the above estimates are considered significant for the financial reporting:

- In connection with the preparation of the consolidated financial statements, Management decides which foreign exchange rate to apply for translation of the financial statements of foreign entities into DKK. Foreign entities operating under dual exchange rate regimes use the translation rate in which return in the form of royalties and dividends is repatriated. Uncertainty in this respect may in subsequent reporting periods lead to significant changes in the carrying amount of the activities in these foreign entities measured in DKK. In connection with the financial reporting for 2011, Management estimated that the financial statements of foreign entities in Venezuela (Plumrose) are to be translated at the official exchange rate of VEF/USD 4.30 as this is the exchange rate expected to be applied for royalties as well as dividends. As the EAC Group did not receive royalty or dividend payments from Plumrose during 2011, this is subject to uncertainty. The alternative parallel exchange rate at 14 May 2010 (prior to the suspension of the parallel exchange market) was in the region of VEF/USD 7.50. The amount of outstanding royalties and dividends is disclosed in note 28.

- The decision as to whether foreign entities operate in hyperinflationary economies is based on qualitative as well as quantitative factors, including whether the accumulated inflation over a three-year period is in the region of 100%. In connection with the financial reporting for 2011, Management assessed that Venezuela where Plumrose operates—continues to be a hyperinflationary economy. As a consequence, adjustments for inflation are made to the foreign entity's income statement and non-monetary balance sheet items taking into consideration changes in the purchasing power based on the inflation up to the balance sheet date. Since the VEF exchange rate has been fixed against the USD during 2011, the hyperinflation adjustments have not been offset by a corresponding devaluation of the VEF exchange rate. Accordingly, the hyperinflation adjustments have correspondingly increased the consolidated accounting figures reported in DKK including revenue, non-current assets and equity. See note 38 for further details.

4. Operating Segments (in part)

Segments (Products and Services) DKK Million	Plumrose (Processed Meat Products)		Santa Fe Group (Moving & Relocation Services)		Reportable Segments		Parent and Unallocated Activities		EAC Group, Pro Forma, Continuing Operations Historical Accounting Policy		Inflation Adjustment Plumrose		Reported EAC Group, Continuing Operations (IAS 29)	
	2011	2010	2011	2010	2011	2010	2011	2010	2011	2010	2011	2010	2011	2010
Income statement														
External revenue	3,743	2,956	1,797	640	5,540	3,596			5,540	3,596	734	262	6,274	3,858
Operating profit before interests, taxes, depreciation and amortisation (EBITDA) and other taxes	543	425	155	69	698	494	−54	−57	644	437	−71	−108	573	329
Other taxes	47	17			47	17			47	17	10	2	57	19
Operating profit before interests, taxes, depreciation and amortisation (EBITDA)	496	408			651	477			597	420	−81	−110	516	310
Depreciation and amortisation	69	51	28	12	97	63	1	1	98	64	88	60	186	124
Reportable segment operating profit (EBIT)	427	357	127	57	554	414	−55	−58	499	356	−169	−170	330	186
Financial income	30	10	4	1	34	11	14	10	48	21	203	55	251	76
Financial expenses	189	89	11	9	200	98	5	24	205	122	39	1	−244	121
Share of profit from associates			0	1	0	1	2	12	2	13	0	0	2	13
Gain on disposal of associates			0	3	0	3		194		197	0	0	0	197
Profit before tax	268	278	120	53	388	331	−44	134	344	465	−5	−114	339	351
Income tax expense	−75	33	38	14	−37	47	23	31	−14	78	111	59	97	137
Reportable segment profit from continuing operations	343	245	82	39	425	284	−67	103	358	387	−116	−173	242	214
Balance sheet														
Goodwill	0	0	654	361	654	361	0	0	654	361	0	0	654	361
Other intangible assets	2	0	471	217	473	217	10	0	483	217	3	2	486	219
Property, plant and equipment and livestock	992	663	158	87	1,150	750	12	13	1,162	763	710	440	1,872	1,203
Deferred tax asset	264	108	21	13	285	121	0	1	285	122	−223	−107	62	15
Other financial fixed assets	0	0	9	1	9	1	12	11	21	12	0	0	21	12
Investment in associates	0	0	1	0	1	0	24	25	25	25	0	0	25	25
Inventories	966	489	19	10	985	499	0	0	985	499	51	15	1,036	514
Trade receivables	559	387	433	208	992	595	0	0	992	595	0	0	992	595
Cash	471	252	144	118	615	370	14	684	629	1,054	0	0	629	1,054
Other current assets	164	93	141	71	305	164	12	21	317	185	1	0	318	185
Total assets	3,418	1,992	2,051	1,086	5,469	3,078	84	755	5,553	3,833	542	350	6,095	4,183

(continued)

Segments (Products and Services) DKK Million	Plumrose (Processed Meat Products)		Santa Fe Group (Moving & Relocation Services)		Reportable Segments		Parent and Unallocated Activities		EAC Group, Pro Forma, Continuing Operations Historical Accounting Policy		Inflation Adjustment Plumrose		Reported EAC Group, Continuing Operations (IAS 29)	
	2011	2010	2011	2010	2011	2010	2011	2010	2011	2010	2011	2010	2011	2010
Non-current liabilities excl. interest bearing debt	52	20	124	26	176	46	38	31	214	82	−4	12	210	89
Current liabilities excl. interest bearing debt	514	345	638	310	1,152	655	18	41	1,170	691	7	1	1,177	697
Interest bearing debt	1,650	784	154	154	1,804	938	58	2	1,862	940	0	0	1,862	940
Liabilities	2,216	1,149	916	490	3,132	1,639	114	74	3,246	1,713	3	13	3,249	1,726
Non-controlling interests	88	41	20	17	108	58	1	1	109	59	57	36	166	95
Equity													2,680	2,362
Total equity and liabilities													6,095	4,183
Invested capital	2,125	1,267	1,209	630	3,334	1,897	17	−38	3,351	1,859			4,114	2,347
Working capital employed	1,306	712	65	45	1,371	757	−1	−1	1,370	756			1,423	772
Cash flows														
Cash flows from operations	−251	83	115	34									−213	59
Cash flows from investing activities	−358	−223	−516	−426									−890	477
Cash flows from financing activities	822	219	424	415									666	32
Cash flows from discontinued operations														6
Changes in cash & cash equivalents	213	79	23	23									−437	574
Financial ratios in %														
Operating margins:														
EBITDA excl. other taxes	14.5	14.4	8.6	10.8					11.6	12.2			9.1	8.5
EBITDA	13.3	13.8							10.8	11.7			8.2	8.0
EBIT	11.4	12.1	7.1	8.9					9.0	9.9			5.3	4.8
Return on average invested capital (ROIC) including goodwill	29.2	26.2	16.9	18.3					22.9	22.0			16.0	13.2
Return on average invested capital (ROIC) excluding goodwill	29.2	26.2	37.6	43.4					28.5	24.8			19.0	14.5

The segment reporting is based on the internal management reporting in which pro forma figures are prepared under the historical accounting policies without any hyperinflation adjustments. Such adjustments are presented separately.

EAC's operating segments comprise strategic business units which sell different products and services. The segments are managed independently of each other and have different customers. No inter segment sales occur. Each segment comprises of a set of units and none of these are of a magnitude which requires them to be viewed as a separate reportable segment.

Consolidated revenue includes sale of goods in the amount of DKK 4,478m (DKK 3,218m). Remaining revenue is related to sale of services.

Reconciliation items in "Parent and unallocated items" are primarily related to corporate costs and corporate assets including cash and cash equivalents held by the Parent Company.

15. Property, Plant and Equipment (in part)

DKK Million	Land and Buildings Etc.	Plants Etc.	Other Assets, Installations, Vehicles Etc.	IT Equipments	Construction in Progress	Total
2011						
Cost:						
01.01.	917	661	246	66	223	2,113
Translation adjustment	23	19	9	1	5	57
Inflation adjustment	256	230	32	16	63	597
Additions	2	0	24	3	326	355
Additions due to business combinations	29	50	49	0	0	128
Disposals	9	1	11	2	6	29
Reclassification	133	91	15	42	−285	−4
31.12.	1,351	1,050	364	126	326	3,217
Depreciation						
01.01.	350	397	139	39	0	925
Translation adjustment	9	10	4	1		24
Inflation adjustment	95	137	30	9		271
Depreciation for the year	45	64	37	16		162
Disposals	8	1	8	2		19
Reclassification	4	−1	−5	1		−1
31.12.	495	606	197	64	0	1,362
Carrying amount 31.12.	856	444	167	62	326	1,855
Financial leases						8

DKK Million	Land and Buildings Etc.	Plants Etc.	Other Assets, Installations, Vehicles Etc.	IT Equipments	Construction in Progress	Total
2010						
Cost:						
01.01.	1,186	788	337	78	340	2,729
Translation adjustment including devaluation loss	− 477	− 360	− 87	− 25	− 155	− 1,104
Inflation adjustment	157	143	6	9	50	365
Additions	1		10	1	236	248
Additions due to business combinations	2		43	1		46
Disposals	2	1	19	1	1	24
Disposals, discontinued operations	72	4	56	12	3	147
Reclassification	122	95	12	15	− 244	0
31.12.	917	661	246	66	223	2,113
Depreciation						
01.01.	469	492	211	57	0	1,229
Translation adjustment including devaluation loss	− 185	− 226	− 54	− 17		− 482
Inflation adjustment	62	89	3	6		160
Depreciation for the year	37	42	29	8		116
Disposals	2		16	5		23
Disposals, discontinued operations	31		34	10		75
31.12.	350	397	139	39	0	925
Carrying amount 31.12.	567	264	107	27	223	1,188
Financial leases						0

The EAC Group was at 31 December 2011 contractually committed to investments related to production machinery, etc., primarily in Plumrose in the total amount of DKK 192m (DKK 103m).

16. Livestock

DKK Million	2011	2010
Reconciliation of Carrying Amounts of Reproducing Livestock		
Carrying amount 1.1	15	21
Translation adjustment including devaluation loss	1	− 10
Inflation adjustment	4	3
Increase due to purchases	22	16
Gain/loss arising from changes in fair value less estimated point-of-sale costs attributable to physical changes	− 15	− 11
Decrease due to sales	11	4
Reclassification	1	
Carrying amount 31.12	17	15

The reproducing livestock is presented at cost net of accumulated amortisation since there is no available market price and no other reliable alternatives to determine the fair value. The assets comprise pig herds and stock of cattle with an amortisation period of 2.5 and 5 years, respectively.

As of 31 December 2011, Plumrose owns 12,000 reproducing livestock (31 December 2010: 12,000).

28. Credit Risk, Currency Risk and Interest Rate Risk (in part)

Group Policy for Managing Risk and Capital

Given the international scope of EAC's business activities, the Group is exposed to financial market risk, i.e. the risk of losses as a result of adverse movements in currency exchange rates, interest rates and/or commodity prices. It also encompasses financial counterparty credit risk, liquidity and funding risk.

EAC operates in relatively volatile markets in South America and Asia Pacific where sudden currency and interest movements can be expected. Consequently EAC maintains a conservative debt-equity ratio providing management with sufficient flexibility to act in support of its businesses, if and when so required. EAC will continuously strive to achieve an efficient debt-equity ratio in the operating businesses, while aming at maintaining a cautious cash position and equity ratio in the Parent Company.

EAC's financial risk management activities are decentralised, although co-ordinated by the EAC Group within a policy framework approved by the Supervisory Board. It is the EAC Group's policy not to engage in any active speculation in financial risks. Therefore, the Group's financial management is focused on managing or eliminating financial risks relating to operations and funding, in particular on reducing the volatility of the EAC Group's cash flows in local currencies. The Group does currently not apply any material financial derivatives for hedging.

There are no changes to the Group's risk exposure and risk management compared to 2010.

Currency Risk

The EAC Group is exposed to translation risks from currency translation into the Group reporting currency (DKK). EAC's business activities are conducted in different currencies: Venezuelan Bolivar, Asia Pacific currencies, and European curencies. In order to minimise the currency risk, EAC seeks to match the currency denomination of income and expenses and of assets and liabilities on a country-by-country basis. Consequently, EAC's functional currency varies from country to country and is typically different from the reporting currency in DKK of the listed entity, EAC Ltd. A/S. The objective of EAC's currency management strategies is to min-imise currency risks relating to the functional currencies, i.e. to protect profit margins in local currency.

Due to the significance of Plumrose's activities in Venezuela the currency exposure to the Bolivar (VEF) is rel-atively high. The devaluation of the VEF in 2010 is detailed in note 39.

From a Group point of view, net assets in Plumrose are translated at the official rate of VEF/USD 4.30. Outstanding dividends from Plumrose are summarised below.

Outstanding Dividends From Plumrose:

Period	Exchange Rate	USD '000
2007	VEF/USD 4,30	22,866
2008	VEF/USD 4,30	14,163
2009	VEF/USD 4,30	152
2010	VEF/USD 4,30	19,597
Total		56,778

Due to uncertainty, the Parent Company only recognises div-idends from Venezuela upon receipt.

EAC Parent royalty receivable at exchange rate VEF/USD 4,30 from Plumrose are summarised below:

Period	USD '000
Q4 2009	4,286
2010	17,996
2011	23,803
Total	46,085

During 2011, CADIVI did not approve payment of any out-standing royalties or dividends.

The EAC Group has foreign exchange risk on balance sheet items, partly in terms of translation of debt denomi-nated in a currency other than the functional currency for the relevant Group entity, and partly in terms of translation of net investments in entities with a functional currency other than DKK. The former risk affects the operating profit.

Developments in exchange rates between DKK and the functional currencies of subsidiaries had an impact on the EAC Group's revenue and EBITDA for 2011 reported in DKK. In a number of countries (particularly in Asia Pacific) where the EAC Group has significant activities, the currency corre-lates partly with the USD. In 2011, the average DKK/USD rate (532.29) was 5.6 per cent below 2010 (DKK/USD 563.62). As a consequence of the depreciation of a number of key cur-rencies compared to DKK, revenue and EBITDA for 2011 decreased in Santa Fe Group by DKK 36m and DKK 3m respectively.

In foreign subsidiaries that operate in hyperinflationary economies, income and expenses are translated at the ex-change rate at the balance sheet date which had a positive impact in Plumrose due to the appreciation of the exchange rate from DKK/USD 561.33 end of 2010 to DKK/USD 574.56 end of 2011. The associated impact on revenue and EBITDA was an increase of DKK 103m and DKK 11m respectively.

29. Other Non-Cash Items

DKK million	2011	2010
Gains/losses on disposal of intangible and tangible assets		−4
Changes in provisions	39	−6
Share based payments	4	10
Net monetary gain	195	60
of which relates to borrowings	−227	−126
Foreign currency & other adjustments	16	53
Total	27	−13

38. Accounting Impact of Venezuela's Status as a Hyperinflationary Economy

DKK Million

As described in the accounting policies for the consolidated financial statements, the assessment as to when an economy is hyperinflationary is based on qualitative as well as quanti-tative factors.

Due to recent years' rising inflation in Venezuela, the coun-try was considered a hyperinflationary economy for account-ing purposes effective from 30 November 2009. This was based on the fact that the cumulative inflation for the three years ending 30 November 2009 exceeds 100 per cent and that the other qualitative characteristics of a hyperinflationary economy all was met.

Based on this assessment, the EAC Group has retrospec-tively from 1 January 2009 onwards applied IAS 29 "Financial Reporting in Hyperinflationary Economies" for the activities of Plumrose as if the economy has always been hyperinflation-ary.

IAS 29 requires the financial reporting of Plumrose to be restated to reflect the current purchasing power at the end of the reporting period, and as a result all non-monetary as-sets, such as property, plant and equipment and inventories, should be restated to the current purchasing power as of 31 December using a general price index from the date when they were first recognised in the accounts (or 1 January 2004 when IFRS was first applied as basis of preparation of the consolidated financial statements). Monetary assets and liabilities are by their nature stated at their current pur-chasing power and accordingly a gain/loss on the monetary net position from 1 January to 31 December is recognised as financial income or expense for the year representing the gain/loss obtained from maintaining a monetary liability or asset position respectively during an inflationary period. For the income statement, all items are restated for changes in the general price index from the date of the transaction to the reporting date of 31 December except for items related to non-monetary assets such as depreciation and amortization and consumption of inventories, etc. Deferred tax is adjusted accordingly.

IAS 29 and IAS 21 require the end-of-period reporting ex-change rate to be applied when translating both the income statement and the balance sheet from the hyperinflationary currency, VEF, into the presentation currency of the EAC Group, DKK.

At 31 December 2011, the applicable rate for translation purposes was the official exchange rate of VEF/USD 4.30 (VEF/USD 4,30) as the Group expects to receive future roy-alties as well as dividends at this exchange rate. The alterna-tive parallel exchange rate in May 2010 (prior to suspension of the parallel exchange market) was in the region of VEF/USD 7.50. The implied VEF/USD exchange rate trough issuance of bonds by the Venezuelan republic and PDVSA during 2011 was approximately VEF/USD 6.12 (based on bond purchases/sales by Plumrose in February 2011).

Since the EAC Group's presentation currency, DKK, is non-inflationary, comparatives are not adjusted for the effects of inflation in the current period. The net impact from inflation adjustment of EAC Foods' net asset is taken directly to the equity (as part of other comprehensive income for the year).

The inflation adjustment for 2011 is based on available data for changes in the Consumer Price Index (CPI) for the Metropolitan Area of Caracas until December 2007 and the National Consumer Price Index (NCPI) as from January 2008 published by the Central Bank of Venezuela (BCV). Based on these indices, the inflation for 2011 is 27.6 per cent (27.2 per cent) and the hyperinflation closing index at 31 December 2011 was 266 (208).

The hyperinflation adjustment during 2011 is not offset by a corresponding devaluation of the VEF exchange rate as this, since the devaluation on 8 January 2010, has been fixed against the USD at the official rate of VEF/USD 4.30. Accordingly, the hyperinflation adjustment under IAS 29 has correspondingly increased the consolidated accounting figures reported in DKK including revenue, non-current assets and equity.

The impact from applying IAS 29 on the consolidated financial statements for 2011 is summarised in a separate column in note 4, to which reference is made.

The most material inflation accounting adjustments between the historical accounting policies of Plumrose (now applied for internal management reporting) as well as recognition and measurement after IAS 29 can be explained as follows:

- Revenue increases as it is restated for changes in the general price index from the date of the transaction until 31 December.
- Gross profit decreases due to higher costs of goods sold and fixed costs following restatement for changes in the general price index from the date of the transaction until 31 December.
- Operating profit decreases due to higher depreciation charges following the restatement of property, plant and equipment for changes in the general price index from the date of the transaction until 31 December.
- Profit before income tax is impacted, in addition to as set out above, by the recognition of a gain on the net monetary position which is due to the purchasing power impact resulting from Plumrose having monetary liabilities in excess of monetary assets as of 31 December.

- Net profit is further impacted by changes to deferred tax following the change in the accounting values of the non-monetary assets (hyperinflated).
- Total equity increases primarily due to the restatement of the fixed assets to a higher inflation adjusted level.
- Total assets and equity increase primarily due to restatement of non-current assets to a higher inflation-adjusted level.

For 2011, the gain on the net monetary position amounts to DKK 195 m (DKK 60 m) which has been recognised as financial income.

39. Devaluation of the Bolivar in 2010

Devaluation in January 2010

On 8 January 2010, the Venezuelan government announced a devaluation of the official exchange rate of the Bolivar (VEF) to the USD, which had been pegged at VEF/USD 2.15 since March 2005, to a new split rate of VEF/USD 2.60 for the importation of food, pharmaceuticals and other essential goods and VEF/USD 4.30 for all other items. The existence of a third floating rate—known as the parallel rate—was officially acknowledged and managed through central bank intervention to avoid excessive speculation with this initiative. The government aimed to stabilise the parallel rate at a rate close to VEF/USD 4.30.

As all future royalties and dividends will be received at VEF/USD 4.30, this exchange rate has consequently been applied as of 1 January 2010 for translation of the financial statements of Plumrose into the reporting currency of the EAC Group, DKK.

Suspension of the Parallel Exchange Market and Introduction of the SITME Allocation System

On 14 May 2010, the Venezuelan government announced that it would take over management of the VEF/USD parallel market. As a consequence, purchase of USD could henceforth only be made from CADIVI and via the Central Bank of Venezuela through the SITME allocation system at a rate of VEF/USD 5.30 and subject to a number of restrictions.

Simplification of the Venezuelan Exchange Rate System in December

On 30 December 2010, the Venezuelan government announced the elimination of the preferential VEF/USD 2.60 exchange rate used for importation of certain product categories including Plumrose' imports. The elimination will primarily impact future import transactions into Venezuela, and now will take place at VEF/USD 4.30.

SECTION 11: SERVICE CONCESSION ARRANGEMENTS[1]

IFRIC COMMITTEE 12, *SERVICE CONCESSION ARRANGEMENTS*

SIC 29, *DISCLOSURE—SERVICE CONCESSION ARRANGEMENTS*

Author's Note

International Financial Reporting Standard (IFRS) 9, *Financial Instruments*, issued November 2009 and October 2010, and effective for annual periods beginning on or after 1 January 2015, amends the classification and measurement requirements for financial assets recognized in accordance with International Financial Reporting Interpretations Committee (IFRIC) 12, *Service Concession Arrangements*. In accordance with IFRS 9, an entity measures the amount due from, or at the direction of, the grantor at either amortized cost or fair value through profit or loss. If the financial asset is carried at amortized cost, IFRS 9 requires the entity to use the effective interest method and to recognize interest income in profit or loss. Early adoption of IFRS 9 is permitted. See a more extensive discussion of the financial instruments convergence project in section 8, "Financial Instruments and Related Disclosures."

Because these standards are effective for annual periods beginning on or after 1 January 2012, these amendments are not reflected in the commentary in this section. The timing of the effective date of IFRS 9 also affects the availability of illustrative excerpts from survey companies' financial statements. Accordingly, the excerpts appearing later in the section may not reflect these revisions.

IFRSs Overview and Comparison to U.S. GAAP

11.01 *Service concession arrangements* are a mechanism by which a public sector entity (such as a governmental agency) or an entity acting as an agent for a public sector entity procures public services by entering into an arrangement with a private sector entity. Rather than the public entity developing, funding, building, operating, and maintaining infrastructure assets alone, the public sector entity contracts some or all of these activities to one or more private sector entities. Examples of service concession arrangements include developing, funding, building, operating, and maintaining

roads, bridges, tunnels, hospitals, railroads, and prisons, among other arrangements.

11.02 As part of these arrangements, private sector entities provide one or more, but not necessarily all, of the services necessary to make the infrastructure asset operational. In some cases, the private sector entity constructs the infrastructure asset (a road, for example). In other cases, the infrastructure asset may already exist, such as an airport, and the public sector entity contracts with a private sector entity to manage and operate the asset.

11.03 When providing high quality, transparent, and comparable information, the accounting challenge is to reflect the substance of the arrangement between the public sector entity (grantor) and private sector entity (operator). IFRIC 12, establishes the requirements and provides guidance for reporting public-to-private service concession arrangements on the financial statements of service concession operators. Standing Interpretations Committee (SIC) 29, *Disclosure— Service Concession Arrangements*, establishes the disclosure requirements.

11.04 IFRIC 12 is effective for annual periods beginning on or after 1 January 2008. If an entity early adopts IFRIC 12, it should disclose that fact in the relevant financial statements.

Recognition and Measurement

IFRSs

11.05 IFRIC 12 establishes requirements and provides guidance for private sector operators on accounting for public-to-private service concession arrangements. It does not provide accounting guidance to the public sector grantor of the service concession. This interpretation applies to those arrangements in which the grantor controls (*a*) the services that the operator will provide with the infrastructure asset, to whom those services will be provided, and the price for those services and (*b*) any significant residual interest in the infrastructure asset at the end of the term of the arrangement. The grantor's control of the residual interest in the infrastructure asset may exist through ownership, beneficial entitlement, or other means. As long as both conditions are met, IFRIC 12 applies to infrastructure assets used in service concession arrangements for the entirety of these assets' economic lives.

11.06 IFRIC 12 addresses recognition and measurement of the following:
- Operator's rights over the infrastructure asset
- Arrangement consideration
- Construction or upgrade services
- Operating services
- Borrowing costs
- Subsequent treatment of recognized financial assets and intangible assets
- Items provided to the operator by the grantor

11.07 When a service concession arrangement meets the two conditions previously described, IFRIC 12 concludes

---

[1] Unless otherwise indicated, references to International Accounting Standards Board (IASB) standards and interpretations throughout this 2012 edition of *IFRS Financial Statements—Best Practices in Presentation and Disclosure* refer to the version of those standards and interpretations included in the *IFRS 2012* bound volume, the official printed consolidated text of IASB standards and interpretations, including revisions, amendments, and supporting documents, issued as of 1 January 2012.

that the arrangement only gives the operator a right of access to, not a right to use, the infrastructure asset. The right of access allows the operator to provide services on behalf of the grantor in accordance with the contractual terms of the arrangement. This conclusion is significant because the interpretation does not permit the infrastructure assets to be recognized as property, plant, and equipment (PPE) under International Accounting Standard (IAS) 16, *Property, Plant and Equipment*, or as a leased asset under IAS 17, *Leases*. The infrastructure asset itself does not meet the definition of PPE in IAS 16, which requires the asset to be held for use, or the definition of a leased asset in IAS 17, which requires a lease to convey the right to use an asset.

11.08 Therefore, IFRIC 12 requires the operator to recognize either a financial asset or an intangible asset. The operator should recognize a financial asset to the extent that it has an unconditional right to receive cash or another financial asset. The operator should recognize an intangible asset to the extent that consideration is dependent upon the use of the asset to provide services. In some cases, the operator might recognize both a financial and an intangible asset. An entity classifies a financial asset as a loan or receivable, an available-for-sale financial asset, or designated at fair value through profit and loss in accordance with IAS 39, *Financial Instruments: Recognition and Measurement*.

11.09 In accordance with IAS 11, *Construction Contracts*, when the outcome of a construction contract can be measured reliably, an entity should recognize revenues and contract costs for construction and upgrade services using the percentage of completion method. An entity should recognize revenue for providing services in accordance with IAS 18, *Revenue*. Revenue is measured at the fair value of the consideration received or receivable. If the operator provides more than one service, then the entity should allocate the consideration to the different services based on the relative fair values of the delivered services when separately identifiable.

Author's Note

In June 2010, the International Accounting Standards Board (IASB) and the Financial Accounting Standards Board (FASB) issued an exposure draft, *Revenue from Contracts with Customers*, proposing to create a single revenue recognition standard that would replace the requirements of both IAS 18 and FASB *Accounting Standards Codification* (ASC) 605, *Revenue Recognition*. Entities would apply the new standard across various industries and capital markets. The boards believe that "publication of this joint proposal represents a significant step forward toward global convergence in one of the most important and pervasive areas in financial reporting." In June 2011, the boards decided to re-expose their revised proposals for a common revenue recognition standard to give constituents an opportunity to comment on the revisions to the draft issued in 2010. IASB issued a revised exposure draft in November 2011 and plans to consider the comments received through the third quarter of 2012. As of May 2012, IASB work plan does not include a target date for issuing a final standard. See the discussion of the proposals in section 3, "Statement of Comprehensive Income and Related Disclosures."

11.10 To the extent that the infrastructure asset is a qualifying asset under IAS 23, *Borrowing Costs*, an operator should capitalize interest in accordance with that standard. Otherwise, the operator should expense borrowing costs.

11.11 When the grantor provides assets that the operator can, at his or her sole discretion, retain or dispose of, the operator should recognize the assets separately and measure them at fair value on initial recognition, with a corresponding liability representing the obligations it has assumed in exchange.

11.12 An entity should recognize and measure maintenance obligations in accordance with IAS 37, *Provisions, Contingent Liabilities and Contingent Assets*.

U.S. GAAP

11.13 Service concession arrangements are not defined in the FASB ASC glossary, and FASB ASC does not include specific guidance on the applicable accounting treatment. As a result, there is likely to be diversity in practice. For example, although service concession arrangements, as defined in IFRIC 12, are excluded from the scope of IAS 17, some of these types of arrangements may be accounted for as leases under FASB ASC 840, *Leases*.

11.14 As reflected in current practice, operators generally do not recognize infrastructure assets as PPE under FASB ASC. However, if an operator determined that lease accounting was appropriate under FASB ASC 840 and concluded that the lease constituted a finance (capital) lease under FASB ASC 840-30, the entity effectively accounts for the leased infrastructure asset as PPE and depreciates the asset accordingly. Operators generally do not recognize intangible assets in connection with service concessions.

11.15 A potentially significant difference between IFRSs and FASB ASC affecting revenue and expense recognition is the requirement under FASB ASC 605-25 to evaluate the arrangement to determine whether it is a multiple element arrangement. In a *multiple element arrangement*, the entity allocates the consideration received or receivable to individual elements and determines the timing of revenue and expense recognition separately for each element. FASB ASC 605-25-25-2 requires the consideration received or receivable for delivery of multiple services to be allocated, in most cases, to the identified elements by reference to relative selling prices, referred to as the "relative selling price method." When using this method, en entity determines selling prices based on vendor-specific objective evidence of selling price or, in its absence, on third-party evidence. If neither evidence of selling price exists for an element in the arrangement, the entity should use its best estimate of selling price for that element.

11.16 FASB ASC 605-25 requirements for multiple element arrangements differ from IFRSs in two ways. First, under FASB ASC 605-25-30-2, consideration is allocated only by reference to the relative selling prices of the individual services to be delivered. Second, although IAS 18 requires an entity to separately identify components of a single transaction in order to reflect the substance of the transaction, IFRSs provide little guidance for this process. Therefore, it is likely that entities would recognize revenue differently under FASB ASC 605-25 and IFRSs.

11.17 Absent specific guidance in FASB ASC, an operator would generally not recognize as separate assets items provided by the grantor as part of the consideration for services to be provided and which the operator has the discretion to retain or dispose of. Instead, the operator would allocate these items in the same manner as other consideration. Similarly, an entity would not recognize liabilities unless cash is received in advance.

11.18 Although not separately defined, a receivable meets the definition of a *financial asset* in the FASB ASC glossary (that is, a contract that conveys to one entity a right to receive cash or another financial instrument from a second entity). Therefore, consistent with IFRSs and in the absence of more specific guidance, it is generally agreed an operator should recognize a receivable to the extent that it has an unconditional right to receive cash irrespective of the infrastructure's use.

Disclosure

IFRSs

11.19 SIC 29 applies not only to all public-to-private service concession arrangements within the scope of IFRIC 12 but also to private-to-private service concession arrangements, as long as the services provided give the public access to major economic or social infrastructure assets. However, outsourcing of internal services of a public sector entity (for example, building maintenance and technology) is excluded.

11.20 Arrangements with the following rights and obligations of the service concession operator are subject to the disclosures required by SIC 29:
- Rights to provide services that give the public access to major economic or social facilities
- Rights to use specified tangible assets, intangible assets, and financial assets (in some cases)
- Obligations to provide services according to the terms and conditions of the agreement over the concession period

- Obligations to return any rights received at the end of the concession period (when applicable)

11.21 Additional disclosures may be required by other standards and interpretations depending on the nature of the asset or liability recognized (for example, IAS 38, *Intangible Assets*, or IFRS 7, *Financial Instruments: Disclosures*).

U.S. GAAP

11.22 Because there is no separate standard or interpretation for service concession arrangements, disclosures would depend on the specific FASB ASC topic or other U.S. GAAP guidance applied. For example, FASB ASC 605-25-50-2 requires vendors to disclose information about multiple element arrangements. See paragraph 3.53 in section 3.

Presentation and Disclosure Excerpts

Service Concession—Financial Assets and Intangible Assets

11.23

Empresas ICA S.A. de C.V. (Dec 2011)

Author's Note

Empresas ICA S.A. de C.V. implemented IFRSs effective December 31, 2011, with a date of transition of January 1, 2010. The excerpt that follows reflects the initial application of IAS 38, *Intangible Assets;* IAS 39, *Financial Instruments—Recognition and Measurement;* in addition to IFRIC 12 and SIC 29. Empresas ICA did not early adopt IFRS 9.

CONSOLIDATED STATEMENTS OF FINANCIAL POSITION (in part)

(Thousands of Mexican pesos)

	Millions of U.S. Dollars (Convenience Translation Note 4) December 31, 2011	2011	2010	January 1, 2010 (Transition Date)
Current assets:				
Cash and cash equivalents (Note 7)	$ 347	Ps. 4,844,965	Ps. 2,975,384	Ps. 2,677,581
Restricted cash (Note 7)	428	5,973,082	1,401,090	1,419,572
Customers, net (Note 8)	1,897	26,462,594	8,681,432	8,352,364
Other receivables, net (Note 12)	252	3,513,951	2,696,667	2,196,759
Inventories, net (Note 10)	77	1,077,308	815,643	679,357
Real estate inventories (Note 11)	270	3,767,898	4,119,415	2,473,885
Advances to subcontractors and other	159	2,218,125	1,269,026	1,739,036
Current assets	3,430	47,857,923	21,958,657	19,538,554

(continued)

	Millions of U.S. Dollars (Convenience Translation Note 4) December 31, 2011	2011	2010	January 1, 2010 (Transition Date)
Non-current assets:				
Restricted cash (Note 7)	$ 6	Ps. 81,667	Ps. 142,488	Ps. 413,514
Customers, net (Note 8)	590	8,236,276	14,672,708	9,928,265
Real estate inventories (Note 11)	324	4,517,614	3,218,830	2,821,949
Financial assets from concessions (Note 13)	608	8,488,478	4,655,476	3,415,788
Intangible assets from concessions, net (Note 13)	1,059	14,768,140	17,373,385	15,401,554
Investment in associated companies (Note 13)	393	5,485,563	3,238,755	3,335,435
Property, plant and equipment, net (Note 14)	327	4,565,736	4,258,110	4,287,123
Derivative financial instruments (Note 20)	23	318,427	7,618	64,750
Prepaid expenses	61	848,292	1,104,246	1,176,411
Other assets, net (Note 15)	25	348,901	280,062	199,902
Deferred income taxes (Note 23)	242	3,371,056	1,625,304	1,612,541
Non-current assets	3,658	51,030,150	50,576,982	42,657,232
Total assets	$7,088	Ps. 98,888,073	Ps. 72,535,639	Ps. 62,195,786

CONSOLIDATED STATEMENTS OF COMPREHENSIVE INCOME (in part)

	Millions of U.S. Dollars (Convenience Translation Note 4) December 31, 2011	2011	2010
Continuing operations:			
Revenues:			
Construction	$2,431	Ps. 33,920,383	Ps. 27,849,781
Concessions	224	3,129,808	2,102,123
Sales of goods and other	410	5,718,594	4,524,158
Total revenues	3,065	42,768,785	34,476,062
Costs:			
Construction	2,204	30,741,641	24,940,301
Concessions	160	2,236,438	1,533,548
Sales of goods and other	229	3,201,299	3,019,269
Total costs (Note 29)	2,593	36,179,378	29,493,118
Gross profit	472	6,589,407	4,982,944

CONSOLIDATED STATEMENTS OF CASH FLOWS (in part)

	Millions of U.S. Dollars (Convenience Translation Note 4) December 31, 2011	2011	2010
Net cash used in operating activities	(728)	(10,155,163)	(4,530,866)
Investing activities:			
Investment in machinery and equipment	(29)	(405,306)	(492,040)
Dividends received	15	211,139	5,319
Other long term assets	(7)	(91,683)	(55,609)
Investment in concessions	(114)	(1,586,682)	(1,993,063)
Sale of property, plant and equipment	6	86,080	390,128
(Grants) collections of loans	(7)	(100,810)	86,075
Business acquisitions	(5)	(74,000)	(261,122)
Activities of discontinued operations	204	2,851,393	(82,785)
Net cash provided by (used) in investing activities	63	890,131	(2,403,097)

NOTES TO THE CONSOLIDATED FINANCIAL STATEMENTS (in part)

(Thousands of Mexican pesos except as otherwise indicated)

1. Activities

Empresas ICA, S.A.B. de C.V. and subsidiaries ("ICA" or, together with its subsidiaries, "the Company") is a holding company incorporated in Mexico with over 64 years experience, the subsidiaries of which are engaged in a wide range of construction and related activities including the construction of infrastructure facilities as well as industrial, urban and housing construction, for both the Mexican public and private sectors. ICA's subsidiaries are also involved in the construction, maintenance and operation of highways, bridges and tunnels granted by the Mexican government and foreign governments under concessions. Through its subsidiaries and affiliates, the Company also manages and operates airports and municipal services under concession arrangements. In addition, some of ICA's subsidiaries are engaged in real estate and housing development. ICA's shares are traded on the Mexican Stock Exchange and the New York Stock Exchange. Its registered address is 36 Boulevard Manuel Avila Camacho, Piso 15, Lomas de Chapultepec, 11000 Mexico, D. F.

2. Adoption of International Financial Reporting Standards (in part)

a. In January 2009, the National Banking and Securities Commission ("CNBV" for its acronym in Spanish) issued amendments to the Single Circular for Issuers to include the obligation to file financial statements based on the International Financial Reporting Standards ("IFRS") issued by the International Accounting Standards Board ("IASB") as of the year ending December 31, 2012, with the option of early adoption. The Company's management decided to early adopt IFRS for the year ended December 31, 2011.

b. Based on above, the consolidated financial statements for the year ended December 31, 2010 were the last annual consolidated financial statements of the Company to be prepared in conformity with Mexican Financial Reporting Standards ("MFRS") for public use. The first consolidated financial statements prepared in accordance with IFRS are for the year ended December 31, 2011, with January 1, 2010 as the date of transition to IFRS. Guidance regarding the initial adoption of IFRS is included in IFRS 1, *First-time Adoption of International Financial Reporting Standards* ("IFRS 1").

4. Basis of Presentation and Consolidation (in part)

a. Statement of Compliance

The consolidated financial statements have been prepared in accordance with IFRS as issued by the IASB. Included in subsection (g) is the Company's policy regarding consolidation and included in Note 5 are the Company's accouting policies and valuation principles applied in preparing the consolidated financial statements.

The accompanying consolidated financial statements include all financial reporting standards and valuation requirements that affect the Company's consolidated financial information, as well as the alternatives allowed by IFRS.

b. Basis of Preparation

The consolidated financial statements have been prepared on the historical cost basis except for the revaluation of certain non-current assets and financial instruments at fair value. Historical cost is generally based on the fair value of the consideration given in exchange for assets. The consolidated financial statements are prepared in pesos, the legal currency of the United Mexican States and are presented in thousands, except where otherwise noted.

5. Significant Accounting Policies (in part)

The consolidated financial statements are prepared in accordance with IFRS. Preparation of financial statements under IFRS requires management of the Company to make certain estimates and use assumptions to value certain of the items in the consolidated financial statements as well as their related disclosures required therein. The areas with a high degree of judgment and complexity or areas where assumptions and estimates are significant in the consolidated financial statements are described in Note 6. The estimates are based on information available at the time the estimates are made, as well as the best knowledge and judgment of management based on experience and current events. However, actual results could differ from those estimates. The Company has implemented control procedures to ensure that its accounting policies are appropriate and are properly applied. Although actual results may differ from those estimates, the Company's management believes that the estimates and assumptions used were adequate under the circumstances.

i. Investment in Concessions

Under all of the Company's concession arrangements, (i) the grantor controls or regulates what services the Company must provide with the infrastructure, to whom it must provide them, and at what price; and (ii) the grantor controls, through ownership, any significant residual interest in the infrastructure at the end of the term of the arrangement. Accordingly, the Company classifies the assets derived from the construction, administration and operation of the service concession arrangements either as intangible assets, financial assets (accounts receivable) or a combination of both.

A financial asset results when an operator constructs or makes improvements to the infrastructure, in which the operator has an unconditional right to receive a specific amount of cash or other financial assets during the contract term. An intangible asset results when the operator constructs or makes improvements and is allowed to operate the infrastructure for a fixed period after construction is complete, in which the future cash flows of the operator have not been specified, because they may vary depending on the use of the asset, and are therefore considered contingent. Both a financial asset and an intangible asset may result when the return/gain for the operator is provided partially by a financial asset and partially by an intangible asset. The cost of financing incurred during the construction period is capitalized.

Financial assets are recorded at nominal value and subsequently valued at amortized cost by calculating interest through the effective interest method at the date of the financial statements, based on the yields determined for each of the concession contracts. Investments in concessions resulting in the recognition of an intangible asset are recorded at acquisition value or construction cost and are amortized over the concession period based on utilization rates (vehicle traffic during the concession period for toll roads; volume of water treated for water treatment plants).

The Company recognizes and measures contractual obligations for major maintenance of the infrastructure in accordance with IAS 37, *Provisions, Contingent Liabilities and Contingent Assets*. The Company considers that periodic maintenance plans for infrastructure, whose cost is recorded in expense in the period in which the obligation arises, are sufficient to maintain the concession in good operating condition, in accordance with the obligations specified by the grantor and to ensure the delivery of the related infrastructure in good operating use at the end of the term of the concession, ensuring that no additional significant maintenance costs will arise as a result of the reversion to the grantor.

j. Government Grants

Agencies of the Mexican government have given grants to ICA to finance projects, mainly investments in water supply. The conditions set out in relevant resolutions which award the grants are accredited to the competent agencies.

ICA identifies government grants with assets for which the concession implies the purchase of the asset or the construction or acquisition of other assets, restricting the type or location of such assets or the periods during which they are to be acquired or held.

Grants for the acquisition of assets are presented net against the related asset, and are applied to results over the same period and using the same amortization criteria as that of the related asset. When no basis exists to amortize a grant over a specific period, the grant is recognized in results when it becomes receivable.

Government grants are not recognized until there is reasonable assurance that the Company will comply with the conditions attached to them and that the grants will be received. Receipt of a grant does not provide conclusive evidence that the conditions attached to it have been or will be fulfilled.

q. Derivative Financial Instruments (in part)

The Company underwrites a variety of financial instruments to manage its exposure to interest rate risk and foreign exchange related to the financing of its concession projects and construction. Note 20 includes a more detailed explanation of derivative financial instruments.

Derivatives are initially recognized at fair value at the date the derivative contract is entered into and are subsequently remeasured at fair value at the end of each reporting period. Fair value is determined based on recognized market prices. When the derivative is not listed on a market, fair value is based on valuation techniques accepted in the financial sector.

The resulting gain or loss from remeasurement to fair value is recognized in profit or loss unless the derivative is designated and effective as a hedging instrument, in which event the timing of the recognition in profit or loss depends on the nature of the hedge relationship. The Company designates certain derivatives as either fair value hedges of recognized assets or liabilities or firm commitments (fair value hedges), hedges of highly probable forecasted transactions or hedges of foreign currency risk of firm commitments (cash flow hedges). The decision to apply hedge accounting depends on economic or market conditions and economic expectations in the national or international markets.

A derivative with a positive fair value is recognized as a financial asset; a derivative with a negative fair value is recognized as a financial liability. A derivative is presented as a non-current asset or a non-current liability if the remaining maturity of the instrument is greater than 12 months and it is not expected to be realized or settled within 12 months. Other derivatives are presented as current assets or current liabilities.

w. Revenue Recognition (in part)

Revenues are recognized when it is likely that the Company will receive the economic benefits associated with the transaction. Revenue is measured at the fair value of the consideration received or receivable and represents the amounts receivable for goods and services provided in the normal course of activities. Revenues are reduced for estimated customer returns, rebates and other similar allowances.

By type of activity, revenue is recognized based on the following criteria.

Infrastructure Concessions

In accordance with IFRIC 12, both for the financial assets and intangible assets, the revenues and costs related to construction or improvements during the construction phase are recognized in revenues and construction costs.

Revenues stemming from the financing of concessions are recorded in the income statement as they accrue and are recorded within finance income from continuing operations.

Revenues from the operation of concession projects are recognized as concession revenues, as they accrue, which is generally at the time vehicles make use of the highway and pay the respective toll in cash or electronically at toll collection booths. Revenues are derived directly from users of the concession, or at times, from the grantor of the concession. Aeronautical services revenues consist of the right of use of airports. These revenues are recognized when services are provided. Prices for the services rendered are regulated by the grantor. In concessions involving toll revenues, tariff revisions do not apply until their effective date of application.

6. Critical Accounting Judgments and Key Sources of Estimation Uncertainty (in part)

In the application of the Company's accounting policies, which are described in Note 5, management is required to make judgments, estimates and assumptions about the carrying amounts of assets and liabilities that are not readily apparent from other sources. The estimates and associated assumptions are based on historical experience and other factors that are considered to be relevant. Actual results may differ from these estimates.

The estimates and underlying assumptions are reviewed on an ongoing basis. Revisions to accounting estimates are recognized in the period in which the estimate is revised if the revision affects only that period or in the period of the revision and future periods if the revision affects both current and future periods.

The following transactions are those in which management has exercised its professional judgment to apply accounting policies with a material effect on the amount recorded in the consolidated financial statements:

- The long-lived assets owned by the Company relate to buildings, machinery and equipment and concessions granted by the Mexican government and foreign governments for the construction, operation and maintenance of roads, bridges and tunnels, airport management and municipal services. The Company reviews the estimated useful life and depreciation or amortization methods used for tangible and intangible assets derived from the concession (described in Note 13) at the end of each reporting period. The effects of any modifications to estimates are recognized prospectively. Similarly, at the end of each reporting period, the Company reviews the carrying values of its tangible and intangible assets to detect indications of impairment losses (see Note 5m). Determining both the recoverable value of assets and their useful life and depreciation or amortization methods are estimates with a significant impact on the consolidated financial statements of the Company.

- Management prepares estimates to determine and recognize the provision necessary for the maintenance and repair of highways and other infrastructure under concession, which affects the results of the periods in which the infrastructure under concession becomes available for use and through the date on which the maintenance and/or repair work is performed.

7. Cash and Cash Equivalents (in part)

b. Restricted cash and cash equivalents are as follows:

	December 31, 2011	December 31, 2010	January 1, 2010
Cash	Ps. 5,973,082	Ps. 1,237,181	Ps. 1,405,424
Government securities	4,774	160,191	127,766
Other	76,893	146,206	299,896
Total[1]	6,054,749	1,543,578	1,833,086
Long-term	81,667	142,488	413,514
Short-term	Ps. 5,973,082	Ps. 1,401,090	Ps. 1,419,572

[1] At December 31, 2011 and 2010 and January 1, 2010 the total cash, cash equivalents and restricted are Ps. 10,899 million, Ps. 4,519 million and Ps. 4,511 million, respectively.

Restricted cash is composed principally by trusts that have been created to administer the amounts received from tolls and other related services generated by the concessions, which guarantee and are primarily utilized to pay the debt contracted and the maintenance of the concessions.

At December 31, 2011, Ps. 4,838 million of restricted cash corresponds to the funds recdeived from the placement of bond securities in an Issuer Trust mentioned in Note 21, that are administered by the issuing trust and will be used to build infrastructure in the preoperating stage.

To date, there have been no signs of deterioration in real estate inventories.

12. Other Receivables

	December 31, 2011	December 31, 2010	January 1, 2010
Sundry debtors	Ps. 525,220	Ps. 310,704	Ps. 624,235
Notes receivable	185,689	73,310	74,420
Guarantee deposits	219,183	117,980	97,453
Financial assets from concessions	13,982	274,940	93,701
Recoverable taxes	1,055,950	1,134,416	552,116
Amounts receivable from related parties	1,498,253	792,195	769,532
Others	41,704	32,066	19,241
Allowance for doubtful accounts	(26,030)	(38,944)	(33,939)
	Ps. 3,513,951	Ps. 2,696,667	Ps. 2,196,759

13. Investment in Concessions

a. The classification and integration of investment in concessions is as follows:

Financial Asset:

		Ownership Percentage		Balance as of		
Description of Project	Date of Concession Agreement	2011	2010	December 31, 2011	December 31, 2010	January 1, 2010
Water treatment plant in Cd. Acuña[1] [4]	September 1998	100%	100%	Ps. 226,439	Ps. 267,485	Ps. 262,050
Irapuato—La Piedad Highway[1] [7]	August 2005	—	100%	—	697,825	710,759
Querétaro—Irapuato Highway[1] [7]	June 2006	—	100%	—	571,581	476,601
Acueducto II Querétaro—Water supply[1] [2] [3]	May 2007	42%	42%	612,441	611,086	528,551
Nuevo Necaxa—Tihuatlán Highway[1] [2]	June 2007	50%	50%	1,970,911	1,261,360	550,469
Río Verde—Cd. Valles Highway[1]	July 2007	100%	100%	2,352,062	1,516,701	980,304
San Luis Potosí, El Realito, Water supply[1] [2]	July 2009	51%	51%	93,971	3,785	755
PTAR Wastewater Agua Prieta[2]	September 2009	50%	50%	487,154	—	—
Mitla Tehuantepec Highway[1]	June 2010	100%	—	3,906	593	—
Social infrastructure Sarre,	December 2010	100%	100%	1,288,366	—	—
Social infrastructure Pápagos,	December 2010	100%	100%	1,467,210	—	—
				8,502,460	4,930,416	3,509,489
Total short-term financial assets				13,982	274,940	93,701
Total long-term financial assets				8,488,478	4,655,476	3,415,788
Intangible Asset:						
Kantunil—Cancun Highway	October 1990	100%	100%	2,309,172	2,426,706	2,586,266
Acapulco Tunnel	May 1994	100%	100%	848,253	870,810	894,361
Corredor Sur in Panamá[6]	August 1996	—	100%	—	2,007,152	2,178,894
Water treatment plant in Cd. Acuña[1] [4]	September 1998	100%	100%	35,750	39,722	42,705
North Central Airport Group	November 1998	59%	59%	7,051,236	6,901,100	6,758,592
Irapuato—La Piedad Highway[1] [7]	August 2005	—	100%	—	94,609	99,273
Querétaro—Irapuato Highway [1] [7]	June 2006	—	100%	—	2,052,493	1,394,908
Acueducto II Querétaro—Water supply[1] [2] [3]	May 2007	42%	42%	620,430	607,175	378,985
Nuevo Necaxa—Tihuatlán Highway[1] [2]	June 2007	50%	50%	840,878	536,785	232,118
Rio Verde—Cd. Valles Highway[1]	July 2007	100%	100%	1,210,998	773,381	461,612
Parking lots—Perú[2]	September 2008	50%	50%	121,294	92,013	12,200
Libramiento La Piedad, Highway	January 2009	100%	100%	1,672,312	968,077	361,210
San Luis Potosí, El Realito, Water supply[1] [2]	July 2009	51%	51%	57,032	2,028	430
Agua Prieta, Water treatment plant[2]	September 2009	50%	50%	—	1,213	—
Mitla Tehuantepec Highway[1]	June 2010	100%	—	785	121	—
Total intangible assets				Ps. 14,768,140	Ps. 17,373,385	Ps. 15,401,554

Investment in Associated Companies:

		Ownership Percentage		Balance as of		
Investment	Acquired Since	2011	2010	December 31, 2011	December 31, 2010	January 1, 2010
Autopistas Concesionadas del Altiplano, S.A. de C.V. [5]	September 1991	—	19.38%	—	146,127	31,822
Red de Carreteras de Occidente, S.A.P.I.B. de C.V.	October 2007	18.70%	13.63%	4,537,867	2,547,194	2,799,142
Distribuidor Vial San Jerónimo Muyuguarda	December 2010	30%	30%	392,768	—	—
Proactiva Medio Ambiente México, S.A. de C.V.	Various	49.00%	49.00%	533,767	521,138	485,104
Other	Various	—	—	21,161	24,296	19,367
Total investment in associated companies				5,485,563	3,238,755	3,335,435
Total				Ps. 28,742,181	Ps. 25,267,616	Ps. 22,152,777

[1] Combination of both financial and intangible assets.
[2] Proportionately consolidated.
[3] Includes 5% indirect participation.
[4] During 2009, partially renegotiated which such portion represents an intangible asset.
[5] In December 2010, this associated company sold its concession asset obtaining a profit of Ps. 609 million, of which Ps. 120 million belongs to the Company.
[6] This concesion was sold to the Government of Panama in September 2011, see Note 3.
[7] Concessions were sold to RCO in September 2011, see Note 4.h.

b. For the years ended December 31, 2011 and 2010, the Company recognized construction costs and related revenues in exchange for a financial asset, an intangible asset or a combination of both, in relation to construction on its concessions for Ps. 1,768 million and Ps. 1,459 million, respectively.

c. The changes in investment in concessions in the consolidated statement of financial position at December 31, 2011 and 2010 and January 1, 2010 were as follows:

	Cost	Amortization	Net
Balance at January 1, 2010	Ps. 16,675,086	Ps. (1,273,532)	Ps. 15,401,554
Acquisition or increases	2,580,374	—	2,580,374
Decreases	(40,387)	—	(40,387)
Amortization	—	(313,279)	(313,279)
Transferred	(128,452)	—	(128,452)
Translation effects	(126,425)	—	(126,425)
Balance at December 31, 2010	18,960,196	(1,586,811)	17,373,385
Acquisition or increases	1,948,908	—	1,948,908
Sales	(5,758,715)	1,738,193	(4,020,522)
Decreases	(17,329)	—	(17,329)
Amortization	—	(528,027)	(528,027)
Translation effects	11,725	—	11,725
Balance at December 31, 2011	Ps. 15,144,785	Ps. (376,645)	Ps. 14,768,140

d. An analysis of the concessions classified as intangible assets is as follows:

	December 31, 2011	December 31, 2010	January 1, 2010
Projects completed and in operation:			
Construction cost	Ps. 3,180,900	Ps. 8,103,411	Ps. 7,756,104
Rights to use airport facilities	5,479,205	5,519,257	5,559,306
Improvements in concessioned assets	2,987,488	2,663,609	2,249,636
Financing costs capitalized	(28,124)	(3,292)	17,944
Government grants	—	(135,910)	(111,615)
Accumulated amortization	(1,569,166)	(2,903,705)	(2,801,573)
	10,050,303	13,243,370	12,669,802
Construction in-progress:			
Construction cost	5,148,782	4,130,015	2,731,752
Government grants	(430,945)	—	—
	Ps. 14,768,140	Ps. 17,373,385	Ps. 15,401,554

e. Government grants that have been amortized to results in the years 2011 and 2010, classified within cost of concessions in the consolidated statements of comprehensive income amounted to Ps. 845 million and Ps. 69 million, respectively.

f. Related interest income corresponding to concessions classified as financial assets was $1,062 million and $634 million for the years ended December 31, 2011 and 2010, respectively, which is classified within revenues in the accompanying statement of comprehensive income.

g. Below is a description of the primary concessions held by the subsidiaries of the Company:

Grupo Aeroportuario Centro Norte (GACN)

GACN is engaged in administration, operation and, when applicable, construction of airports under the concession granted by the Mexican Federal Government through the Communications and Transportation Ministry ("SCT") for a 50-year period beginning on November 1, 1998. As these airports are state-owned, after the termination of the concession period, any improvements and additional installations permanently attached to the concessioned assets and created during the concession period will revert to the state. The concessioned airports are: Acapulco International Airport, Ciudad Juárez International Airport, Culiacán International Airport, Chihuahua International Airport, Durango International Airport, Mazatlán International Airport, Monterrey International Airport, Reynosa International Aiport, San Luis Potosí International Airport, Tampico International Airport, Torreón International Airport, Zacatecas International Airport and Zihuatanejo International Airport.

At December 31, 2010, accumulated financing cost amounted to Ps. 213 million. The annual average capitalization rate was 17% in the year 2010.

In September 2011, the company sold its shares of COVIQSA to RCO, associated company, and thereby transferred the PPS to RCO; at December 31, 2011, the concession is recognized through recognition of RCO through the equity method (see paragraph g below).

Nuevo Necaxa-Tihuatlán Highway ("AUNETI")

In June 2007, the SCT granted a 30-year concession for: (i) construction, operation, maintenance and conservation of the Nuevo Necaxa—Ávila Camacho highway of 36.6 kilometers; (ii) operation, maintenance and conservation of the Ávila Camacho—Tihuatlán highway of 48.1 kilometers; and (iii) long-term service contract for the Nuevo Necaxa—Ávila Camacho highway capacity service.

At December 31, 2011 and 2010 and January 1, 2010, accumulated financing cost amounted to Ps. 485 million, Ps. 247 million and Ps. 106 million, respectively. The annual average capitalization rate was 11.67%, 18.7% and 23.29%.

Río Verde—Ciudad Valles Highway ("RVCV")

In July 2007, the SCT granted the Company a 20-year concession of the highway between Río Verde and Ciudad Valles covering a length of 113.2 kilometers for: (i) operation, maintenance upgrade, conservation and extension of the Río Verde—Rayón highway of 36.6 kilometers; (ii) construction, operation, maintenance and conservation of the Rayón—La Pitaya II highway of 68.6 kilometers; and (iii) operation, maintenance upgrade, conservation and extension of the La Pitaya—Ciudad Valles III highway of 8.0 kilometers.

At December 31, 2011 and 2010, and January 1, 2010, accumulated financing cost amounted to Ps. 622 million, Ps. 345 million, and Ps. 145 million, respectively. The annual average capitalization rate was 12.49%, 15.71% and 13.31%, respectively.

Acueducto II Water System in Queretaro ("SAQSA")

Suministro de Agua de Querétaro, S.A. de C.V. was created on May, 2007, for the purpose of rendering water pipeline and purification services for the Acueducto II System. In May 2007, SAQSA signed the concession contract to provide the pipeline and purification service for the Acueducto II system, together with the respective operation and maintenance, to carry water from the El Infiernillo source on the Rio Moctezuma. The project includes the construction of a collection reservoir, two pumping plants, a tunnel 4,840 meters long through the mountain and an 84 kilometer section downwards, a purification plant and a storage tank. This system will supply 50 million of cubic meters of drinking water a year, equal to 75% of the current supply of water for the metropolitan zone of Querétaro. The Acueducto began operations in February 2011.

At December 31, 2011 and 2010 and January 1, 2010, accumulated financing cost amounted to Ps. 254 million, Ps. 161 million and Ps. 80 million, respectively. The annual average capitalization rate was 15.36%, 14.03% and 14.23%, respectively.

Kantunil-Cancún Highway

In March 2008, ICA acquired 100% of the stock of Consorcio del Mayab, S.A. de C.V., which holds the concession Kantunil-Cancun.

The concession was granted in 1990 to construct, operate, and maintain the 241.5 kilometer highway that connects those cities in the states of Yucatán and Quintana Roo, respectively. The term of the concession is for 30 years and expires in December 2020.

During the third quarter of 2011, the Company signed an amendment to the concession which adds to the terms of the concession the construction, operation, conservation and maintenance of an additional 54 kilometers related to the Kantunil-Cancun highway to Playa del Carmen. This additiona highway project will connect Lazaro Cardenas with the Playa del Carmen municipality, which would be a branch of the toll road from Cancun to Merida. It is estimated that the additional 54 kilometers, which begain construction in January 2012, will have two phases: 7 km into the municipality of Solidaridad (Playa del Carmen) and another 47 kilometers into Lazaro Cardenas, which will have two lanes, one for each direction of 3.5 meters each with a width of 2.5 meters; with a right of way of 40 meters and a maximum speed of 110 kilometers per hour. The first section, called Cedral-Tintal, will be starting at the Trunk Cedral junction, which connects with Highway Kantunil in the town of Lazaro Cardenas, bound for Playa del Carmen; while the beginning of the branch-Playa del Carmen Tintal will be built in the second grade-separated junction-called Tintal junction-, that the project will also connect with the toll road Mérida-Cancún. The term of the concession is extended 30 years, terminating in 2050.

In early 2012, the Company requested the extension of the concession to connect the tourist destinations of Playa del Carmen with Chiquilá and Holbox, Lazaro Cardenas, which will connect with the capital of Yucatan in an effort to decrease travel time.

Toll revenues provided by this concession guarantee the redeemable participation certificates that will be amortized over a 17-year period (see Note 21).

Libramiento La Piedad Highway ("LIPSA")

In March 2009, the SCT granted to the Company's subsidiary, Libramiento ICA La Piedad, S.A. de C.V., the concession to construct, operate, conserve and maintain the Libramiento de La Piedad (La Piedad Bypass), which is 21.388 km long. The concession is for 30 years and includes the modernization of the federal highways 110 and 90, for a length of 38.8 km and 7.32 km, respectively, located in the States of Guanajuato and Michoacán. The Libramiento de La Piedad will form part of the major junction joining the highway corridors of Mexico City-Nogales and Querétaro-Ciudad Juárez and will free the city of La Piedad from the long-haul traffic moving between the Bajío region and Western Mexico. The construction period under the original plan was 22 months to conclude during 2011. However, due to problems related to the delivery of rights of way, the concession was renegotiated and construction is anticipated to conclude in July 2012.

At December 31, 2011 and 2010, accumulated financing cost amounted to Ps. 74 million and Ps. 25 million, respectively. The annual average capitalization rate was 13.24% and 10.61%, respectively.

Mitla-Tehuantepec Highway

In June 2010, the SCT executed agreements for the construction and operation of the Mitla-Tehuantepec highway in Oaxaca for the next 20 years, under the PPS program, with the subsidiaries Caminos y Carreteras Del Mayab, S.A.P.I. de C.V. and Controladorra de Operaciones de Infraestructura, S.A. de C.V. (CONOISA). Construction work is valued at Ps. 9,318 million. The project includes the concession for the construction, operation, maintenance and expansion, as well as the exclusive right to execute the PPS contract with the Federal Government for the 169 kilometers of the Mitla-Entronque Tehuantepec II, Mitla-Santa María Albarradas, and La Chiguiri-Entronque Tehuantepec II highways.

The construction work will be performed over an approximate 40-month period.

No financing costs have been capitalized through December 31, 2011.

El Realito Aqueduct

In July 2009, the Comisión Estatal del Agua (the State Water Commission) of San Luis Potosí awarded the rendering of services contract for the construction and operation of the El Realito aqueduct for 25 years to the association led by CONOISA, a subsidiary company, and Fomento de Construcciones y Contratas ("FCC"). The total contract amount is Ps. 2,382 million.

At December 31, 2011, accumulated financing cost amounted to Ps. 7 million. The annual average capitalization rate was 5.29% for the year 2011.

Agua Prieta Waste Water Treatment Plant

In September 2009, the State Water Commission (Comisión Estatal del Agua) of Jalisco signed a contract with Consorcio Renova Atlatec, (ICA, Renova and Mitsui) for the construction and operation of the Agua Prieta waste water treatment plant for 20 years. The total value of the contract is Ps. 2,318 million, through a private and public resource investment scheme from the Fondo Nacional para el Desarrollo de Infraestructura ("FONADIN").

At December 31, 2011, accumulated financing cost amounted to Ps. 3 million. The annual average capitalization rate was 6% for the year 2011.

SARRE y Pápagos—Social Infraestructure

On December 27, 2010, the Company executed Servicing Contracts ("CPS") with the Ministry of Public Security ("Secretary") of the United Mexican States ("Federal Government"). The purpose of CPS is for Sarre Infraestructura y Servicios, S.A. de C.V. ("Sarre") and Pápagos Servicios para la Infraestructura, S.A. de C.V. ("Pápagos"), subsidiaries of ICA, to construct and operate social infrastructure and provide to the Federal Government the services associated with infra-structure, under the understanding that at no time the Company will be responsible for those functions and public services that are the sole responsibility of the Federal Government. In accordance with the CPS, the services to be provided by the Company only consist of the construction and maintenance of the infrastructure, and ongoing services related to cleaning, pest control, landscaping, stores, food, laundry and laboratory services. The construction of social infrastructure will be in accordance with the provisions of the contract, amounting to Ps. 21,190 million and Ps. 21,401, million for Sarre and Papagos, respectively. Construction is expected not to exeed 24 months, with an estimated completion date in August 2012.

Once the social infrastructure is built and accepted by the client, payments under the CPS will begin. The maximum term for the CPS is 20 years beginning when services commence.

At December 31, 2011, accumulated financing cost amounted to Ps. 214 million. The annual average capitalization rate was 11% for the year 2011.

h. Investments in concessions through associated companies are as follows:

Red de Carreteras de Occidente (RCO)

RCO, an associated company, was formed on August 13, 2007, with an initial participation of 20% by ICA of RCO's capital stock. In October 2007, the SCT granted to RCO a 30-year concession for the construction, operation, maintenance and conservation of the Maravatío—Zapotlanejo and Guadalajara—Aguascalientes—León highways covering a length of 558 kilometers, in the states of Michoacán, Jalisco, Guanajuato and Aguascalientes. Additionally, the concession includes up to Ps. 1,500 million of additional investments for extension of the four highways to be carried out in the future.

As a result of the sale mentioned in Note 4, the Company transferred to RCO the Irapuato-La Piedad highway (non-toll), with a length of 74.3 km, and the Querétaro-Irapuato highway (non-toll), a length of 108 km. located in the states of Guanajuato and Queretaro.

At the end of the concession, the assets subject thereto will revert to the Mexican government.

Condensed financial information of RCO is as follows:

Statement of Financial Position	December 31, 2011	December 31, 2010	January 1, 2010
Current assets	Ps. 3,329,459	Ps. 1,594,383	Ps. 2,200,935
Investment in concession	47,077,420	44,508,994	44,352,585
Other non-current assets	3,848,089	3,169,597	2,249,287
Current liabilities	1,438,584	508,317	651,425
Long-term debt	29,296,986	27,320,336	26,449,890
Other non-current liabilities	3,100,935	2,255,398	1,149,966
Stockholders' equity	20,418,463	19,188,923	20,551,526

Statement of Operations	Year Ended December 31, 2011	Year Ended December 31, 2010
Revenues	Ps. 3,771,418	Ps. 4,135,987
Operating income	2,068,518	1,516,208
Net loss	(551,874)	(665,941)

Long-term debt of RCO includes a loan received in September 2007 from financial institutions for Ps. 31,000 million, which is guaranteed by the toll revenues provided by this concession. The loan has a seven-year term with the possibility to be extended by ten years, with monthly interest payments at the Mexican Interbank Equilibrium Offered rate ("TIIE") plus 1.20% to 1.65% in the first year and gradually increasing in subsequent years up to a range of 1.80% to 2.25% in the sixth and seventh years. The loan includes additional credit lines for liquidity and capital expenditures for Ps. 3,100 million and Ps. 3,000 million, respectively.

The long-term credit entered into by RCO includes certain restrictive covenants which bar the acquisition of new bank loans, granting security, assuming obligations for payment of taxes, the sale of fixed assets and other noncurrent assets, making capital reimbursements, and require the maintenance of certain financial ratios. These financial ratios include a certain requirement of total liabilities to stockholders' equity; current assets to current liabilities; current assets, less the accounts receivable from affiliates, to current liabilities; and

operating income plus depreciation to net expenses. As of December 31, 2011 and 2010, RCO has complied with these requirements.

In October 2009, the trust that was created specifically for investing in the Series B share capital of RCO, placed Ps. 6,550 million in Long-Term Infrastructure Development Equity Certificates (CKDes) with Mexican institutional investors. In November 2009, the stockholders of RCO owning the Series A shares made equity contributions of Ps. 4,000 million; consequently, the equity percentage held by ICA as of December 31, 2010 was reduced to 13.63%. As a result of the sale of the shares of COVIQSA and CONIPSA mentioned in Note 4, ICA's participation increased to 18.70%, under which it continues to maintain significant influence.

Proactiva Medio Ambiente México (PMA)

Proactiva Medio Ambiente México ("PMA México") is a consortium comprised of Constructoras ICA, S.A. de C.V. ("CICASA") and Proactiva Medio Ambiente, S.A. de C.V. ("Proactiva"), whose principal activities are the operation of water supply distribution, treatment and management systems, as well as the disposal of solid waste to landfill sites, through concessions granted by governmental organizations.

Condensed financial information of PMA is as follows:

Statement of Financial Position	December 31, 2011	December 31, 2010	January 1, 2010
Current assets	Ps. 921,042	Ps. 967,197	Ps. 803,915
Investment in concession	893,817	872,537	863,926
Other non-current assets	225,022	263,948	233,591
Current liabilities	364,612	497,556	502,934
Long-term debt	327,027	226,493	144,835
Other non-current liabilities	127,205	180,349	181,184
Stockholders' equity	1,221,037	1,199,284	1,072,479

Statement of Operations	Year Ended December 31, 2011	Year Ended December 31, 2010
Revenues	Ps. 1,586,606	Ps. 1,417,758
Operating income	230,136	177,380
Net income	147,850	126,805

San Jerónimo-Muyuguarda-Dealer Road

On December 17, 2010, the Mexico City Government signed the concession contract for the design, construction, use, development, operation and management of the property identified in the public domain as the Via Peripheral High in the upper Peripheral Manuel Avila Camacho (Anillo Periférico) in the tranche between San Jeronimo avenue and Distribuidor Vial Muyuguarda, with Concesionaria Distribuidor Vial San Jerónimo Muyuguarda, S.A. de C.V, a consortium formed by Promotora del Desarrollo de América Latina, S.A. de C.V. and Controladora de Operaciones de Infraestructura, S.A. de C.V. The concession contract has a term of 30 years.

Atotonilco—Waste Water Treatment Plant

This is a consortium comprised of Promotora del Desarrollo de América Latina, S.A. de C.V., as project leader with 40.8%, Acciona Agua, S.A. with 24.26%, Atlatec, S.A. de C.V. (a subsidiary of Mitsui & Co., Ltd.) with 24.26%, CONOISA

with 10.2%, and other minority partners; in January 2010 it executed a contract with the National Water Commission (Comisión Nacional del Agua) ("CONAGUA"), for the construction and operation of the Atotonilco waste water treatment plant ("PTAR") in Tula, Hidalgo. The total contract value is Ps. 9,300 million and the term is for 25 years.

18. Provisions

The Company recognizes provisions for those present obligations that result from a past event, which upon the expiration of the obligation, it is probable the Company will incur a probable outflow of economic resources in order to settle the obligation. Provisions are recognized as accrued at an amount that represents the best estimate of the present value of future disbursements required to settle the obligation, at date of the accompanying consolidated financial statements.

At December 31, 2011 the composition and changes of principal provisions is as follows:

a. Short-Term:

Provision for:	December 31, 2010	Additions	Provisions Used and Transfers	Reversals	December 31, 2011
Costs expected to be incurred at the end of the project	Ps. 539,097	Ps. 339,376	Ps. (23,515)	Ps. (295,971)	Ps. 558,987
Repairs and maintenance of machinery	476,030	2,158,389	(1,898,615)	(125,290)	610,514
Estimated contract loss	3,147	—	(2,899)	—	248
Claims	13,132	13,279	(11,195)	—	15,216
Contingencies and warranty reserves for construction contracts	312,366	503,735	(1,294)	(8,901)	805,906
	Ps. 1,343,772	Ps. 3,014,779	Ps. (1,937,518)	Ps. (430,162)	Ps. 1,990,871

	January 1, 2010	Additions	Provisions Used and Transfers	Reversals	December 31, 2010
	Ps. 894,987	Ps. 2,219,791	Ps. (1,756,959)	Ps. (14,047)	Ps. 1,343,772

b. Long Term:

The long-term provisions are as follows:

	December 31, 2010	Additions	Provisions Used and Transfers	December 31, 2011
Contingencies and warranty reserves for construction contracts	Ps. 35,419	Ps. 11,903	Ps. (8,090)	Ps. 39,232
Major maintenance	814,599	226,666	(422,737)	618,528
	Ps. 850,018	Ps. 238,569	Ps. (430,827)	Ps. 657,760

	January 1, 2010	Additions	Provisions Used and Transfers	December 31, 2010
Contingencies and warranty reserves for construction contracts	Ps. 23,541	Ps. 25,330	Ps. (13,452)	Ps. 35,419
Major maintenance	982,619	124,714	(292,734)	814,599
	Ps.1,006,160	Ps.150,044	Ps. (306,186)	Ps.850,018

The provision related to costs expected to be incurred at the end of the project refers to costs that are originated under construction projects that the Company anticipates it will incur through the time the projects are finished and ultimately paid for by the customer. Such amounts are determined systematically based on a percentage of the value of the work completed, over the performance of the contract, based on the experience gained from construction activity.

Due to the nature of the industry in which the Company operates, projects are performed with individual specifications and guarantees, which require the Company to create guarantee and contingency provisions that are continually reviewed and adjusted during the performance of the projects until they are finished, or even after termination. The increases, applications and cancellations shown in the previous table represent the changes derived from the aforementioned reviews and adjustments, as well as the adjustments for expiration of guarantees and contingencies.

The Company recognizes a provision for the costs expected to be incurred for major maintenance, mainly at airports, which affect the results of periods from the commencement of operation of the concession, until the year in which the maintenance and/or repair work is performed. This provision is recognized in accordance with IAS 37, *Provisions and Contingent Liabilities and Assets* and IFRIC 12. A portion is recorded as short-term and the remainder as long-term depending on the period in which the Company expects to perform the major maintenance.

The provision for lawsuits and claims covers the risks of the subsidiaries involved in a given administrative-law proceedings due to the inherent responsibilities of the activities that they perform. While the overall number of lawsuits may be significant, they involve immaterial amounts when considered individually.

The provision for repairs and maintenance of machinery under lease agreements is accrued based on the estimated hours used. The provision is used to cover the expenses related to conditioning, missing equipment and repairs for its return to the lessor in accordance with the terms of the lease agreement.

21. Long-Term Debt (in part)

a. Debt to credit institutions and debentures and other securities at December 31, 2011, December 2010 and January 1, 2010, which amounted to Ps. 44,796 million, Ps. 27,644 milliona and Ps. 19,453 million, respectively, net of Ps. 588 million, Ps. 341 million and Ps. 347 million, from

financing commissions or expenses, respectively, is detailed
as follows:

	December 31, 2011	December 31, 2010	January 1, 2010
Payable in U.S. Dollars:			
Concessions:			
Secured bond, with a fixed annual interest rate of 6.95% and maturity in 2025, to refinance the debt contracted for Corredor Sur, which is guaranteed by toll revenues. This loan was pre-paid in August 2011 (see Note 26).	Ps. —	Ps. 1,764,641	Ps. 1,898,443
Credit granted to Aeroinvest maturing in January 2015. The contracted rate is LIBOR plus 6% margin (6.5698% at December 31, 2011).	629,649	—	—
Payable in Mexican Pesos:			
Concessions and airports:			
TUCA performed a new issuance of securitization certificates, which is guaranteed by collection rights and toll revenues of the Acapulco Tunnel, by issuing a share certificate program trust with a term of up to 25 years. Principal and interest are paid semiannually and bear interest at a rate of the 91-day TIIE plus 265 basis points (7.48%, 7.61% and 7.73% at December 31, 2011 and 2010 and January 1, 2010, respectively) and the 91-day TIIE plus 295 basis points, respectively (7.78%, 7.91% and 8.03% at December 31, 2011 and 2010 and January 1, 2010, respectively). The loan is also guaranteed by a letter of credit of Ps. 75 million.	1,243,250	1,249,143	1,250,000
Consorcio del Mayab, holder of the Kantunil—Cancún highway concession, issued 78,858,900 redeemable participation certificates (CPOAs), each equivalent to one UDI, separated into three types. The CPOAs will be amortized over a 17-year period and are payable on February and August 7 of each year. They mature in 2019 and 2020 and bear interest at 9.50%, 9.50% and 9.25% at December 31, 2011 and 2010 and January 1, 2010, respectively. This loan is guaranteed with toll revenues.	2,445,524	2,478,422	2,429,986
Loan granted for modernization and extension of the Irapuato—La Piedad highway, granted as a concession by the SCT to CONIPSA, maturing in November 2019, bearing interest at the 28-day TIIE plus 2.5% (7.62% as of December 31, 2010). The loan is guaranteed with toll revenues. This loan was transferred in September 2011 as a result of the sale of shares mentioned in Note 3.	—	520,378	539,400

23. (Benefit) Expense for Income Taxes (in part)

d. At December 31, 2011, 2010 and January 1, 2010, the main
items comprising the balance of the deferred ISR liability are:

Liabilities	December 31, 2011	December 31, 2010	January 1, 2010
Customers	Ps. (3,083,149)	Ps. (2,007,436)	Ps. (2,487,012)
Property, plant and equipment	(26,180)	(40,306)	(168,895)
Real estate inventories	(482,579)	(812,425)	(719,119)
Intangible assets from concessions	(1,888,716)	(1,752,358)	(1,904,038)
Total liabilities	(5,480,624)	(4,612,525)	(5,279,064)

e. The main items comprising the liability balance of deferred
IETU at December 31, 2011 and 2010 and January 1, 2010
are as follows:

Liabilities	December 31, 2011	December 31, 2010	January 1, 2010
Customers	Ps. (1,095,965)	Ps. (1,900,713)	Ps. (2,327,403)
Inventories, net	(297,848)	(178,303)	(451,030)
Real estate inventories	(45,363)	(31,408)	(280,402)
Investments in concessions	(1,337,506)	(449,747)	(109,975)
Property, plant and equipment, and others	(750,093)	(548,718)	(1,081,873)
Total liabilities	(3,526,775)	(3,108,889)	(4,250,683)

24. Contingencies (in part)

c. *Airports*—A lawsuit was filed against Aeropuerto de Ciudad Juárez, S. A. de C. V., a subsidiary of the Company, on November 15, 1995, claiming a portion of plots of land (240 hectares) where the Ciudad Juárez International Airport is located, because such plots were claimed to have been incorrectly transferred to the Mexican government. The plaintiff sought a payment of US$120 million (approximately Ps. 1,486 million) as an alternative to recovery of the land. In May 2005, an appeals court ruled that Aeropuerto de Ciudad Juárez, S. A. de C. V., had to return this land. The airport filed an amparo (constitutional claim), which was granted requiring the appellate court to re-analyze the case and the related evidence. On November 8, 2007, the Appeals Court issued a ruling declaring the previous sentence null, after which the plaintiffs filed an amparo, which was granted to them permitting them to continue the trial with the Mexican federal government as a party. The SCT filed an appearance in the case, responded to the complaint and requested removal to federal court due to lack of jurisdiction by the current court. On May 11, 2010, the court ruled in favor of the SCT´s motion and remanded the case to federal court. On June 2, 2010, the plaintiffs filed another amparo (constitutional claim) with the First District Court of the State of Chihuahua, which on November 10, 2010 confirmed the ruling removing the case from state court. On November 29, 2010, the plaintiffs filed a motion for review of the November 10, 2010 ruling, which will be heard by a Circuit Court, and is still pending.

As of the date of these consolidated financial statements, the Company reports this matter as a contingency due to the fact that the substance of the claim has not been definitively ruled upon even though the SCT has now appeared in the case. The Company believes that in the event of an unfavorable ruling, the economic repercussions of the lawsuit will be borne by the Federal government, as established in the concession title. Accordingly, the Company has not recorded any provisions for this matter.

There are several administrative-law enforcement actions against the airports of Ciudad Juárez, Culiacán, Zihuatanejo, and Reynosa. In November 2009, the Municipality of Ciudad Juárez once again requested payment from the Ciudad Juárez airport, stating the existence of a debt of Ps. 8 million. A new proceeding for annulment was filed by the Company and is still unresolved. In June 2010, the Municipality of Culiacán requested payment of property taxes by the Company (Aeropuerto de Culiacán, S. A. de C. V.) for Ps. 4 million. An action for annulment was filed against this request with the Administrative-Law Court of the State of Sinaloa, and is still unresolved. In October 2010, the Municipality of Zihuatanejo requested payment of Ps. 2 million from the Zihuatanejo airport. An action for annulment was filed with the Tax Court of the State of Guerrero by the airport, which is still unresolved. In February 2011, the Municipality of Reynosa once again requested payment of property taxes of Ps. 118 million from the Reynosa Airport (Aeropuerto de Reynosa, S.A. de C.V.). An action for annulment will again be filed by the airport. The Company does not believe that an unfavorable outcome is probable and thus, has not recognized any provisions related to these contingencies.

e. *Performance guarantees*—In the ordinary course of business, the Company is required to secure construction obligations, mainly related to the completion of construction contracts or the quality of its work, by granting letters of credit or bonds. At December 31, 2011, the Company had granted bonds to its customers for Ps. 20,401 million and U.S. $277 million, respectively.

Additionally, the Company has issued letters of credit to guarantee its performance obligations under certain concession arrangements and construction contracts, in the amount of Ps. 2,835 million, U.S. $143 million dollars and $10 million euros.

25. Risk Management (in part)

a. Significant Accounting Policies

The significant accounting policies and adopted methods of recognition, valuation and basis of recognition of related income and expenses for each class of financial asset, financial liability and equity instrument is disclosed in Note 4.

b. Categories of Financial Instruments and Risk Management Policies (in part)

The main categories of financial instruments are:

Financial Assets	Classification of Risk	December 31, 2011	December 31, 2010	January 1, 2010
Cash		Ps. 1,913,510	Ps. 813,309	Ps. 889,395
Restricted cash		6,054,749	1,543,578	1,833,086
Cash equivalents	Interest rate	2,931,455	2,162,075	1,788,186
Customers[1]	Credit and Operating	14,721,637	2,306,258	4,143,773
Other receivables	Credit and Operating	3,513,951	2,696,667	2,196,759
Customers—non current[1]	Credit and Operating	6,443,952	12,329,801	7,549,646
Financial assets from concessions	Credit and Interest rate	8,488,478	4,655,476	3,415,788

[1] Cost and estimated earnings in excess of billings on uncompleted contracts is not considered a financial instrument, therefore it is not included.

c. Market Risk

The Company is exposed to price risks, mainly for the following activities:

Concessions

The return to the Company on any investment in a concession for a highway, bridge, tunnel or wastewater treatment plant is based on the duration of the concession and the amount of capital invested, as well as the amount of the revenues obtained from use, debt servicing costs and other factors. For example, traffic volumes and, consequently, the revenues from highway tolls, are affected by several factors, including toll rates, the quality and proximity of alternate free highways, the price of fuel, taxes, environmental regulations, the purchasing power of the consumer and general economic conditions. The traffic volume of a highway is also strongly influenced by its integration into other highway networks.

Generally, the concession contracts and the Service Provision Projects (PPS) stipulate that the grantor must deliver the right-of-way to the land involved in the project in accordance with the construction program. If the grantor does not timely release such rights-of-way, the Company might be required to incur additional investments and suffer delays at the start of the operations and could therefore find it necessary to seek amendments to the concession contract or PPS. The Company cannot ensure that it will reach agreement on the amendments to any of such contracts. Particularly in relation to new projects, in which it absorbs construction costs, cost overruns may generate a capital base higher than that expected, which results in a lower capital return. Based on these factors, there is no assurance that its return on any investment in a highway, bridge, tunnel or residual water treatment plant concession matches the estimates established in the respective concession contract or PPS.

The concession titles are some of the principal assets of the Company, and it could not continue with the operations of any specific concession without the concessionaire rights granted by the governments involved. The granting governments may revoke any concession as established in the titles themselves and in the law applicable to the concession, which reasons might include that the development and/or maintenance programs were not duly fulfilled, that the operations were temporarily or permanently suspended, that the Company was unable to pay damages resulting from the operations, that it exceeded the maximum rates or that it did not comply with any significant other condition of a concession.

Additionally, the Mexican government may also terminate a concession, at any time, through a reversal of rights if, in accordance with applicable Mexican laws, it were considered to be in the public interest. The Mexican government may also assume the operation of a concession in the event of war, public unrest or a threat to national security. Furthermore, in the event of force majeure, the Mexican government may demand that the Company make specific changes in its operations. In the event of a reversal of assets in the public domain that were subject to the concessions held by the Mexican government, under Mexican laws, generally the

Company may demand compensation for the value of the concessions or the extra costs incurred. By the same token, if the government took over the operations of the Company, provided that it was not for reasons of war, compensation is demanded from the government and from any third parties involved, for any resulting damages. Other governments generally have a similar condition in their construction contracts and in the applicable law. The Company cannot ensure that it would receive any compensation in a timely fashion or for an amount equivalent to the value of its investment in the concession, plus the respective lost profits or damages.

28. Discontinued Operations

a. As discussed in Note 3, on August 24, 2011, ICA negotiated the sale of the "Corredor Sur" toll highway, a concession segment subsidiary, to Empresa Nacional de Autopistas, S.A. de C.V. ("ENA"). Amounts are presented within discontinued operations in the consolidated statement of comprehensive financing. Consideration received exceeded the carrying value of the related net assets. Details of the assets and liabilities sold and the related gain generated by the sale are discussed below.

b. Condensed financial information of Corredor Sur is as follows:

	Eight Months Ended August 31, 2011	Year Ended December 31, 2010
Revenues	Ps. 476,145	Ps. 646,750
Services cost	(114,749)	(198,629)
Gross profit	361,396	448,121
Operation expenses	(25,976)	(40,176)
Operating income	335,420	407,945
Financing cost	(661,038)	(125,184)
(Loss) income before income taxes	(325,618)	282,761
Income taxes	20,752	(36,770)
(Loss) income from discontinued operations	Ps. (304,866)	Ps. 245,991

c. Assets and liabilities on which control was lost:

	December 31, 2010	January 1, 2010
Assets:		
Cash and cash equivalents	Ps. 322,474	Ps. 703,028
Accounts receivable	31,375	30,552
Investment in concession	1,938,790	2,094,629
Other assets	364,870	614,920
	2,657,509	3,443,129
Liabilities:		
Note payables	1,752,798	1,898,444
Other liabilities	313,755	356,674
	2,066,553	2,255,118
Net assets sold	Ps. 590,956	Ps. 1,188,011

d. Income from sale of subsidiary:

	September 2011
Consideration received	Ps. 3,277,147
Less:	
Net assets sold	64,211
Others[1]	372,584
Loss for the period from discontinued operation	304,866
Income tax attributable to the operation	1,051,627
Gain on sale of subsidiary	Ps. 1,483,859

[1] Includes gain from foreign operations for Ps. 73 million generated through the date of disposal and provision for legal indemnizations for Ps. 333 million.

Gain sale of subsidiary is presented in income from discontinued operations in the consolidated statement of comprehensive income.

e. Cash flows from discontinued operations

	December 31, 2011
Consideration received in cash	Ps. 3,277,147
Less: balance of cash and equivalents from discontinued operations	322,474
Net cash from discontinued operation	Ps. 2,954,673

f. Basic earnings and diluted earnings per share from discontinued operations for the year ended December 31, 2011 and 2010, amounts to Ps. 2.349 and Ps. 0.379, respectively.

35. Business Segment Data (in part)

For management purposes, the Company is organized into six reportable segments, which are: Civil Construction, Industrial Construction, Housing Development, Airports, Concessions and Corporate and Other. These segments are the basis on which the Company reports its segment information. The segment reporting is presented considering internal reports on the business units of the Company, which are reviewed regularly by management for decision-making in the operating area in order to allocate resources to segments and assessing their yield.

Airports

Through GACN, ICA operates 13 airports in the Central North region of Mexico pursuant to concessions granted by the Mexican government, including the Monterrey airport, which accounted for approximately 6% of our revenues in 2011 and 7% in 2010. The airports serve a major metropolitan area (Monterrey), three tourist destinations (Acapulco, Mazatlan and Zihuatanejo), two border cities (Ciudad Juarez and Reynosa) and seven regional centers (Chihuahua, Culiacan, Durango, San Luis Potosi, Tampico, Torreon and Zacatecas).

All of the airports are designated as international airports under Mexican law, meaning that they are all equipped to receive international flights and maintain customs, refueling and immigration services managed by the Mexican government.

Concessions

The concessions segment focuses on the construction, development, maintenance and operation of long-term concessions of toll roads, tunnels and water projects and accounted for 8% of total revenues in 2011. The construction work we perform on the concessions is included in the Civil Construction segment. During 2011, ICA participated in six operating concessioned highways and one operating concessioned tunnel (the Acapulco tunnel) that are consolidated in the financial statements, and in the management and operation of a water treatment plant in Ciudad Acuña and other water supply systems, including the Aqueduct II water supply system that we began proportionally consolidating in 2008.

Mexican state and municipal governments and the governments of certain foreign countries award concessions for the construction, maintenance and operation of infrastructure facilities. The Mexican government actively pursues a policy of granting concessions to private parties for the construction, maintenance and operation of highways, bridges and tunnels to promote the development of Mexico's infrastructure without burdening the public sector's resources and to stimulate private-sector investment in the Mexican economy. A long-term concession is a license of specified duration (typically between 20 and 40 years), granted by a federal, state or municipal government to finance, build, establish, operate and maintain a public means of communication or transportation.

The return on any investment in a concession is based on the duration of the concession, in addition to the amount of toll revenues collected or government payments based on operation volume, operation and maintenance costs, debt service costs and other factors. Recovery of the investment in highway concessions is typically accomplished through the collection of toll tariffs or, if under the Public Private Partnership (PPP) contract structure, a fixed payment for highway availability (together with a smaller shadow tariff based on traffic volume), or a combination of the two methods. The return on investment in the water treatment concessions is generally based on the volume of water supplied or treated.

To finance the obligations of the projects, ICA typically provides a portion of the equity and the rest is arranged through third party financing in the form of loans and debt securities. Recourse on the indebtedness is typically limited to the subsidiary engaged in the project. The investment of equity is returned over time once the project is completed. Generally, ICA contributes equity to a project by accepting deferred payment of a portion of its construction contract price. Depending on the requirements of each specific infrastructure concession project, ICA typically seeks to form a consortium with entities that have expertise in different areas and that can assist us in obtaining financing from various sources.

A summary of certain segment information is as follows (amounts may not add or tie to other accompanying information due to rounding) (in part):

	Airports	Concessions	Consolidated
December 31, 2011:			
External revenues	Ps. 2,776,283	Ps. 3,129,808	Ps. 42,768,785
Intersegment revenues	2,295,690	9,292,325	34,530,876
Operating income	916,807	917,221	3,696,425
Financing income	(20,957)	(220,853)	(286,111)
Financing cost	224,789	647,427	3,747,614
Income tax expense (benefit)	153,881	389,870	(33,205)
Statutory employee profit sharing expense	3,491	—	64,487
Share in operations of associated companies	—	29,864	38,303
Segment assets	10,229,352	35,363,545	98,888,073
Investments in associated companies	—	(455)	193,893
Segment liabilities[1]	1,927,962	6,321,815	27,502,099
Capital expenditures[2]	387,673	1,603,155	6,469,765
Depreciation and amortization	160,306	283,740	1,267,200
Net cash provided by (used in) operating activities	595,722	(3,945,795)	(10,505,572)
Net cash provided by (used in) investing activities	(814,323)	(4,690,793)	890,131
Net cash provided by (used in) financing activities	251,821	14,140,193	15,913,429

[1] Segment liabilities include only the operating liabilities attributable to each segment.
[2] Capital expenditures include purchases of property, plant and equipment, investments in concessions and other assets.

The Company's segments operate in four principal geographical areas in the world: Mexico, its home country, Spain, United States and Latin America. The Company's operations by geographic area were as follows (amounts may not add or tie to another balance due to rounding):

		Foreign					
	Mexico	Spain	United States	Latin America	Sub-Total	Intersegment Eliminations	Total
2011:							
Revenues:							
Construction	Ps. 32,105,604	Ps. 1,044,046	Ps. —	Ps. 770,732	Ps. 33,920,382	Ps. —	Ps. 33,920,382
Concessions	3,091,710	—	—	38,098	3,129,808	—	3,129,808
Sales of goods and other	4,826,835	—	—	891,759	5,718,594	—	5,718,594
Total revenues	40,024,149	1,044,046	—	1,700,590	42,768,785	—	42,768,785
Capital expenditures	5,437,835	—	20,081	1,011,849	6,469,765	—	6,469,765
Fixed assets	3,841,411	242,175	—	476,147	4,559,733	6,000	4,565,733
Total assets	94,706,047	988,758	2,655,452	3,323,189	101,673,446	(2,785,373)	98,888,073

SECTION 12: FIRST-TIME ADOPTION OF INTERNATIONAL FINANCIAL REPORTING STANDARDS[1]

IFRS 1, *FIRST-TIME ADOPTION OF INTERNATIONAL FINANCIAL REPORTING STANDARDS*

Author's Note

U.S. generally accepted accounting principles (U.S. GAAP) have no comparable standard for an entity adopting U.S. GAAP or transitioning to U.S. GAAP from another set of accounting principles.

IFRSs Overview and Comparison to U.S. GAAP

12.01 The International Accounting Standards Board (IASB) issued International Financial Reporting Standard (IFRS) 1, *First-time Adoption of International Financial Reporting Standards*, to ensure that an entity's first IFRSs financial statements, as well as any interim statements issued in the same reporting period, provide a suitable starting point for accounting in accordance with IFRSs. The objective of IFRS 1 is for an entity's first IFRSs financial statements to provide high quality information that is transparent to users and comparable over all periods presented, subject to the constraint that cost should not exceed benefits.

Author's Note

IFRS 1 is not a static standard. As new jurisdictions permit or require companies to adopt IFRSs, the entities affected bring additional issues to IASB. In November 2008, IASB issued a revised IFRS 1 with an effective date of 1 July 2009. Subsequently, IASB amended IFRS 1 both directly, by specific amendments, and indirectly, by issuing new and revised standards. Early application of all of these revisions is permitted. This note includes a list of the standards and amendments that revised the standard itself, excluding those that only revised the basis for conclusions.

The requirements of the following documents are effective for annual periods beginning on or after 1 January 2011 and, therefore, affect the financial statements of most of the entities included in the survey sample. These requirements are discussed within the commentary of this section.

- International Financial Reporting Interpretations Committee (IFRIC) 18, *Transfers of Assets from Customers* (issued January 2009 with an effective date of 1 July 2009)
- *Additional Exemptions for First-time Adopters: Proposed amendments to IFRS 1* (issued July 2009 with an effective date of 1 January 2010)
- IFRIC 19, *Extinguishing Financial Liabilities with Equity Instruments* (issued November 2009 with an effective date of 1 July 2010)
- *Limited Exemption from Comparative IFRS 7 Disclosures for First-time Adopters: Amendment to IFRS 1* (issued January 2010 with an effective date of 1 January 2010)
- *Improvements to IFRSs* (issued May 2010 with an effective date of 1 January 2011)

The commentary in this section also addresses the following amendments, which are effective for annual periods beginning before 1 January 2012. However, the timing of the effective dates of these revisions affects the availability of illustrative excerpts from survey companies' financial statements. Accordingly, the excerpts appearing later in this section may not reflect all or some of these revisions.

- *Severe Hyperinflation and Removal of Fixed Dates for First-time Adopters: Amendments to IFRS 1* (issued December 2010 with an effective date of 1 July 2011)
- *Disclosures—Transfers of Financial Assets: Amendments to IFRS 7* (issued October 2010 with an effective date of 1 July 2011)

In contrast, the following amendments are effective for annual periods beginning on or after 1 January 2012 and are not discussed in the commentary in this section. Instead, this author's note includes a brief description of the revision. As noted previously, the timing of the effective dates of these revisions affects the availability of illustrative excerpts from survey companies' financial statements. Accordingly, the excerpts appearing later in this section may not reflect all or some of these revisions.

- IFRS 9, *Financial Instruments* (issued November 2009 and October 2010 with an effective date of 1 January 2015)

  This amendment incorporates the requirements of paragraph 8 of IFRIC 9, *Reassessment of Embedded Derivatives in IFRS 9*. IFRS 9 now requires a first-time adopter to assess whether an embedded derivative is required to be separated from the host contract and accounted for as a derivative on the basis of conditions that exist at the later of the date on which the entity first became a party to the contract or the date a reassessment is required. IFRS 9 permits reassessment only when a change in the contract's terms significantly modify the cash flows required by the contract or when the entity reclassifies the contract out of the fair value through profit or loss.

- IFRS 10, *Consolidated Financial Statements* (issued May 2011 with an effective date of 1 January 2013)

---

[1] Unless otherwise indicated, references to International Accounting Standards Board (IASB) standards and interpretations throughout this 2012 edition of *IFRS Financial Statements—Best Practices in Presentation and Disclosure* refer to the version of those standards and interpretations included in *IFRS 2012* bound volume, the official printed consolidated text of IASB standards and interpretations, including revisions, amendments, and supporting documents, issued as of 1 January 2012.

This amendment requires a first-time adopter to apply the following requirements of IFRS 10 prospectively from the date of transition to IFRSs:

— Allocating total comprehensive income to the owners of the parent entity and the noncontrolling interest even if this allocation results in a deficit balance in the noncontrolling interest

— Accounting for changes in the parent's ownership interest in a subsidiary that do not result in loss of control

— Accounting for a loss of control over a subsidiary together with the relevant requirements of IFRS 5, *Non-current Assets Held for Sale and Discontinued Operations*

However, if a first-time adopter elects to apply IFRS 3, *Business Combinations*, retrospectively to past business combinations, it should also apply IFRS 10 as of the same date.

- IFRS 11, *Joint Arrangements* (issued May 2011 with an effective date of 1 January 2013)

This amendment provides a first-time adopter to elect to apply the transition provisions of IFRS 11 except that, when changing from proportionate consolidation to the equity method, a first-time adopter should test assets for impairment in accordance with International Accounting Standard (IAS) 36, *Impairment of Assets*, as at the beginning of the earliest period presented, even when no indicator of impairment exists. When this test results in an impairment loss, the entity should adjust retained earnings at the beginning of the earliest period presented.

- IFRS 13, *Fair Value Measurement* (issued May 2011 with an effective date of 1 January 2013)

This amendment requires a first-time adopter to apply the definition of fair value as amended by IFRS 13 and permits a first-time adopter to measure an investment at deemed cost at the date of transition determined as fair value in accordance with IFRS 13.

- *Presentation of Items of Other Comprehensive Income* (Amendments to IAS 1) (issued June 2011 with an effective date of 1 July 2012)

This amendment revised the titles of the income statement component of the "statement of comprehensive income" to the "statement of profit or loss" and the "statement of comprehensive income" to the "statement of profit or loss and other comprehensive income."

- IAS 19, *Employee Benefits* (issued June 2011 with an effective date of 1 January 2013)

This amendment eliminates the employee benefits exemption in IFRS 1 and permits a first-time adopter to apply the transition provision which relieves an entity from presenting comparative information for the required disclosures about the sensitivity of the defined benefit obligation. See the author's note following the discussion of the employee benefits exemption at paragraph 12.07.

- *Government Loans (Amendments to IFRS 1)* (issued October 2011 with an effective date of 1 January 2013)

This amendment requires a first-time adopter to use the previous generally accepted accounting principles (GAAP) carrying amount of government loans as at the date of transition to IFRSs as the IFRSs carrying amount of such loans at that date. A first-time adopter should also apply IAS 32, *Financial Instruments: Presentation*, to determine the classification of this loan as either a financial liability or an equity instrument.

The amendments previously mentioned are effective for periods beginning on or after the effective dates noted. Earlier application is permitted. The timing of the effective dates of these revisions affects the availability of illustrative excerpts from survey companies' financial statements. Accordingly, the excerpts appearing later in the section may not reflect some or all of these revisions. The following commentary only addresses the requirements of IFRSs effective on or before 1 January 2010.

12.02 An entity should apply IFRS 1 in its first IFRSs financial statements. It should also apply IFRS 1 in any interim financial statements presented in accordance with IAS 34, *Interim Financial Reporting*, for part of the period covered by its first IFRSs financial statements. IFRS 1 considers an entity to present its first IFRSs financial statements when these financial statements contain an explicit, unreserved statement of compliance with IFRSs. Unless an entity makes this explicit, unreserved statement of compliance, it has not yet presented its first IFRSs financial statements. IFRS 1 identifies several cases that do not relieve or disqualify an entity from applying IFRS 1 in the first set of financial statements in which full compliance is claimed. One such case is a subsidiary that prepares an IFRSs-compliant consolidation package for a parent that issues IFRSs-compliant consolidated financial statements. However, the subsidiary only issues financial statements in its national GAAP. Because the subsidiary itself has not issued a complete set of financial statements as defined in IAS 1, *Presentation of Financial Statements*, with an explicit unreserved statement of compliance, it would still be eligible to apply IFRS 1 if it chooses, or is required, to adopt IFRSs in the future.

12.03 A first-time adopter of IFRSs is required to comply with IFRS 1. However, an entity has one, and only one, opportunity to apply IFRS 1 to its financial statements to take advantage of the various exemptions available to first-time adopters. Even if an entity fails to provide IFRSs-compliant financial statements in some period after its first IFRSs financial statements, it should not apply IFRS 1 subsequently.

12.04 An entity already reporting under IFRSs should only apply the requirements of IAS 8, *Accounting Policies, Changes in Accounting Estimates and Errors*, to a change in accounting policy. IFRS 1 should not be applied.

Recognition and Measurement

IFRSs

12.05 At the date of transition to IFRSs, IFRS 1 requires an entity to prepare and present its opening balance sheet in accordance with IFRSs. Additionally, the entity should apply the same accounting policies in its opening IFRSs balance sheet and throughout all periods presented in its first IFRSs financial statements. These accounting policies should comply with each IFRSs that is effective at the end of its first

IFRSs reporting period, except as otherwise permitted by IFRS 1. The standards effective at the end of the entity's first IFRSs reporting period may be different from those that were in effect at the entity's transition date, which is the date of its opening IFRSs balance sheet.

12.06 Unless IFRS 1 provides a specific exemption or requires an exception, IAS 8 requires retrospective application for all changes in accounting policy. Retrospective application involves preparation of the financial statements as if the entity always applied the new accounting policy. Retrospective application may be costly or impracticable for an entity to accomplish or may permit an entity to use hindsight to achieve an advantageous result. For the benefit of first-time adopters of IFRSs, IFRS 1 provides both relief (exemptions) and prohibitions (exceptions) from retrospective application, as explained in more detail subsequently.

12.07 Exemptions from retrospective application are voluntary. An entity should explicitly identify, elect, and then discuss the elected exemptions in disclosures required by IFRS 1. Exemptions exist for the following:

- *Business combinations.* An entity may elect to apply IFRS 3 prospectively to all subsequent business combinations either from the date of transition or a specifically selected earlier date. When elected, this exemption permits an entity to avoid restating any business combination that occurred before the selected date, regardless of the method(s) of accounting used at the original dates of prior combinations (for example, combinations accounted for as a pooling of interests would not be restated). In addition, an entity may elect to apply IAS 21, *The Effects of Changes in Foreign Exchange Rates,* prospectively to fair value adjustments and goodwill arising from business combinations before the date of transition. However, if the entity chooses to apply IFRS 3 retrospectively for any business combination that occurred prior to the date of transition, it should also apply IFRS 3 to all subsequent business combinations.
- *Share-based payments.* This exemption relieves a first-time adopter from applying IFRS 2, *Share-based Payments,* to equity instruments granted on or before 7 November 2002. However, if an entity decides to apply IFRS 2 to instruments granted before this date, it should disclose the instruments' fair value. An additional exemption relieves a first-time adopter from applying IFRS 2 to equity instruments granted after 7 November 2002 and vested before the later of its date of transition to IFRSs or 1 January 2005.
- *Insurance contracts.* An entity may elect the transition provisions of IFRS 4, *Insurance Contracts.*
- *Deemed cost for property, plant, and equipment (PPE); investment property; and intangible assets.* An entity may elect to measure at fair value individual assets of PPE, investment property, and intangible assets that meet the criteria for revaluation and use the cost model for subsequent measurement in accordance with the relevant standard. Alternative measures of fair value under this exemption are a revaluation under the entity's previous GAAP done at or before the date of transition if that revaluation is broadly comparable to fair value, and cost or depreciated cost, in accordance with IFRSs, adjusted to reflect, for example, changes in a general or specific price index. An entity may also use as deemed cost an event-driven fair value determined previously (for example, at the time of a privatization or initial public offering.)
- *Deemed cost for oil and gas assets.* When an entity transitions from a previous GAAP in which exploration and development costs for oil and gas properties in the development or production phases are accounted for in cost centers that include all properties in a large geographical area, the entity may elect to measure the exploration and evaluation assets at the amount determined under the entity's previous GAAP and the assets in the development or production phases at the amount determined for the cost center under the entity's previous GAAP. The entity should allocate the amount to the cost center's underlying assets on a pro rata basis using reserve volumes or reserve values as of the date of transition.
- *Deemed cost for operations subject to rate regulation.* An entity may hold and use items of PPE or intangible assets, either currently or previously, in operations subject to rate regulation. The carrying amount of these assets may include amounts measured under the previous GAAP that would not qualify for capitalization under IFRSs. This exemption permits an entity to use the previous GAAP carrying amount as deemed cost at the date of transition on an item-by-item basis. However, the entity should test each of these items for impairment, in accordance with IAS 36, as of the date of transition. IFRS 1 describes operations subject to rate regulation as those that provide goods or services to customers at prices (that is, rates) established by an authorized body empowered to establish rates binding on customers and designed both to recover the specific costs the entity incurs in providing the regulated goods or services and to earn a specified return, which could be a minimum or range rather than a fixed or guaranteed return.
- *Leases.* An entity may elect the transitional provisions in IFRIC 4, *Determining whether an Arrangement contains a Lease,* which permits an entity to apply IFRIC 4 to arrangements existing at the date of transition based on the facts and circumstances existing at that date. Under this exemption, an entity is not required to reassess any arrangements for which it had made the same assessment required by IFRIC 4 at some time prior to its date of transition.
- *Actuarial gains or losses on defined benefit plans.* If an entity uses the corridor approach to recognize actuarial gains and losses under IAS 19, some gains and losses remain unrecognized. This exemption permits an entity to recognize all unrecognized cumulative actuarial gains and losses existing at the date of transition, even if it will use the corridor approach after transition.

Author's Note

In June 2011, IASB issued a revised IAS 19 eliminating the option of deferring recognition of changes in an entity's net defined benefit liability through use of the corridor method and amending some disclosure requirements for defined benefit plans and multi-employer plans. In accordance with IAS 8, an entity should apply this amendment retrospectively to all assets and liabilities within the scope of IAS 19. With elimination of the corridor method, IASB also eliminated any need for the IFRS 1 exemption for actuarial gains or losses on defined benefit plans. On adoption of IAS 19 revised, either when the standard is effective or early adopted, an entity recognizes all unrecognized actuarial gains or losses in equity.

- *Cumulative translation differences.* This exemption permits an entity to set the cumulative translation adjustment account to zero at the date of transition. Therefore, gains or losses on subsequent disposal of a foreign operation will exclude all foreign currency translation adjustments that occurred before transition.

- *Investments in subsidiaries, associates, and jointly controlled entities.* This exemption applies to the separate (unconsolidated) financial statements of a parent entity. Separate financial statements may be required by regulatory authorities or issued voluntarily. Sometimes company-only (parent-only) financial statements are included within consolidated financial statements. In these separate financial statements, an entity may measure its investments in subsidiaries, associates, and jointly controlled entities at cost or in accordance with IAS 39, *Financial Instruments: Recognition and Measurement.* This exemption permits cost to be determined either in accordance with IAS 27, *Consolidated and Separate Financial Statements,* or at deemed cost (that is, either the fair value in accordance with IAS 39 at the entity's date of transition to IFRSs in its separate financial statements or the previous GAAP carrying amount at that date).

- *Assets and liabilities of subsidiaries, associates, and jointly controlled entities.* When a subsidiary, associate, or jointly controlled entity adopts IFRSs later than its parent, this exemption permits the subsidiary, associate, or jointly controlled entity to apply either IFRS 1 in its first IFRSs financial statements or to use the carrying amounts that would be included in the parent's consolidated IFRSs financial statements. However, when the parent becomes a first-time adopter later than a subsidiary, associate, or jointly controlled entity, the parent should use the carrying amounts reported in that investment's IFRSs financial statements.

- *Compound financial instruments.* When the liability component of a compound financial instrument is no longer outstanding, an entity is not required to retrospectively separate the liability and equity components to determine the carrying amount of the equity component at the date of transition.

- *Designation of previously recognized financial instruments.* In most cases, IAS 39 limits an entity's ability to reclassify financial assets and liabilities after initial recognition. This exemption permits an entity to designate, as of the date of transition, a financial instrument as available for sale or as at fair value through profit or loss, provided that the relevant criteria for designation are met.

- *Fair value measurement of financial assets or financial liabilities at initial recognition.* This exemption permits an entity to apply the last sentence of paragraphs AG76

and AG76A[2] in IAS 39, prospectively, to transactions entered into after the date of transition to IFRSs.

- *Decommissioning liabilities included in the cost of PPE.* An entity that elects this exemption should measure the decommissioning liability in accordance with IAS 37, *Provisions, Contingent Liabilities and Contingent Assets.* To the extent that the liability is within the scope of IFRIC 1, *Changes in Existing Decommissioning, Restoration and Similar Liabilities,* the entity should estimate the amount that would have been included in the carrying value of the asset when the liability first arose (using a historical risk-adjusted interest rate) and calculate a carrying amount of accumulated depreciation based on its current estimates of the asset's useful life and residual value and its chosen depreciation method. When an entity applies the exemption described previously with respect to oil and gas assets accounted for in cost centers that include properties in a large geographical area, it may elect to apply IFRIC 1 or to measure its decommissioning, restoration, and similar liabilities at the date of transition, in accordance with IAS 37 and recognize directly in retained earnings the difference between that amount and the carrying amount of those liabilities at the date of transition determined under its previous GAAP.

- *Financial assets or intangible assets accounted for in accordance with IFRIC 12,* Service Concession Arrangements. An entity may elect to apply the transitional requirements in IFRIC 12. When retrospective application is impracticable, these transition requirements permit an entity to recognize financial assets and intangible assets as of the date of transition and to use the previous carrying amounts of these assets in the opening balance sheet. The entity should test these assets for impairment at the date of transition or, if impracticable, at the start of the current reporting period.

- *Borrowing costs.* An entity may elect to apply the transitional provisions in IAS 23, *Borrowing Costs,* which permit the entity to capitalize interest on qualifying assets as of a designated date but not later than the date of transition.

- *Transfers of assets from customers.* A first-time adopter may elect to apply the transitional provisions of IFRIC 18, which requires an entity to apply the interpretation prospectively on or after 1 July 2009 or the date of transition to IFRSs, whichever is later. A first-time adopter

---

[2] The text of the relevant paragraphs in International Accounting Standard (IAS) 39, *Financial Instruments: Recognition and Measurement,* reads as follows:

AG76 (in part): The best evidence of the fair value of a financial instrument at initial recognition is the transaction price (that is, the fair value of the consideration given or received) unless the fair value of that instrument is evidenced by comparison with other observable market transactions in the same instrument (without modification or repackaging) or based on a valuation technique whose variables include only data from observable markets.

AG76A: The subsequent measurement of the financial asset or financial liability and the subsequent recognition of gains or losses should be consistent with the requirements of this Standard or IFRS 9 as appropriate. The application of paragraph AG76 may result in no gain or loss being recognized on the initial recognition of a financial asset or liability. In such a case, IAS 39 requires that a gain or loss should be recognized after initial recognition only to the extent that it arises from a change in a factor (including time) that market participants would consider in setting a price.

may apply IFRIC 18 to all transfers of assets from customers received on or after a designated date before the date of transition.

- *Extinguishing financial liabilities with equity instruments.* A first-time adopter may apply the transitional provisions of IFRIC 19, which requires an entity to apply the requirements of this interpretation from 1 July 2010 with early application permitted. An entity should apply a change in accounting policy in accordance with IAS 8 as of the beginning of the earliest comparative period presented.

- *Severe hyperinflation.* This amendment defines two characteristics that together identify when a currency in a hyperinflationary economy is subject to severe hyperinflation. First, all entities with transactions and balances in the currency do not have a reliable general price index available, and, second, there is no exchangeability between the currency and a relatively stable foreign currency. The amendment also defines the *functional currency normalization date* as the date on which the currency no longer has either or both of these characteristics. When an entity's date of transition to IFRSs is on or after the functional currency normalization date, the entity may elect to measure all assets and liabilities held before that date at fair value on the date of transition to IFRSs. The entity may also use that fair value as deemed cost of these assets and liabilities in its opening IFRSs statement of financial position.

12.08 IFRS 1 also provides for a short term exemption from the required disclosures about financial instruments in IFRS 7, *Financial Instruments: Disclosures*, by affording first-time adopters the option of applying the same transitional provisions as entities already applying IFRSs.

Author's Note

In 2007, the Institute of Chartered Accountants in England and Wales published a study, *EU Implementation of IFRS and the Fair Value Directive: A Report for the European Commission*, that it conducted for the European Commission regarding application of IFRS 1 exemptions and other applications of IFRSs in European-listed companies' first IFRSs financial statements. The study of 151 companies reports that when an exemption was applicable, all companies surveyed used the following exemptions:

- Business combinations
- Deemed cost (for PPE or investment property, although practice varied over the amounts used as deemed cost)
- Actuarial gains and losses on defined benefit plants (when the entity elected to use the corridor after transition)
- Cumulative translation differences
- Compound financial instruments
- Share-based payments

No first-time adopters used the deemed cost exemption for intangible assets.

- *Transfers of assets from customers.* This exemption permits a first-time adopter to apply the transitional provisions in paragraph 22 of IFRIC 18. An entity should interpret the reference in that paragraph to the effective date to be the later of

1 July 2009 or the date of transition to IFRSs. In addition, a first-time adopter may designate any date before the date of transition to IFRSs and apply IFRIC 18 to all transfers of assets from customers received on or after that date.

- *Extinguishing financial liabilities with equity instruments.* This exemption permits a first-time adopter to use the transition provisions in IFRIC 19.

12.09 IFRS 1 includes two categories of exceptions to retrospective application: estimates and retrospective application of other IFRSs. Essentially, these exceptions prohibit the use of hindsight to achieve a potentially preferable accounting treatment. With respect to estimates, this exception requires an entity's estimates at the date of transition to be consistent with those applied under its previous GAAP at the same date (after adjustments for changes in accounting policy), unless there is objective evidence that the previous GAAP estimates were in error. With respect to retrospective application in accordance with other IFRSs, IFRS 1 prohibits an entity from using retrospective application in the following circumstances:

- Designating hedging relationships
- Recognizing previously derecognized financial assets or financial liabilities, unless they would qualify for recognition as a result of a later transaction or event
- Applying IFRS 27 at a date earlier than it elects to apply IFRS 3 to business combinations (Refer to the previous discussion of the exemption related to IFRS 3.)

Presentation

IFRSs

12.10 To comply with IAS 1, IFRS 1 states that a first time adopter's financial statements should include at least three statements of financial position (which includes this statement as of the date of transition), two statements of comprehensive income, two separate income statements (if presented), two statements of cash flows, and two statements of changes in equity and related notes, including comparative information.

12.11 IFRS 1 does not require an entity to restate information prior to the date of transition when such information is included in historical summaries of selected data. An entity should clearly label any information prepared under previous GAAP and describe the main adjustments needed to comply with IFRSs.

Disclosure

IFRSs

12.12 An entity should explain how the transition from its previous GAAP to IFRSs affected its reported financial position, financial performance, and cash flows. In addition to narrative discussions, this explanation should include reconciliations of equity in accordance with previous GAAP to equity in accordance with IFRSs, at both the date of transition and the date of the most recent financial statements prepared under the previous GAAP. This explanation also includes a reconciliation of comprehensive income in accordance with previous GAAP to comprehensive income in accordance with IFRSs for the year of the most recent financial statements prepared under the previous GAAP. These reconciliations should include sufficient detail to enable users of the financial statements to understand the material adjustments to the balance sheet and the statement of comprehensive income.

12.13 If the entity recognized any impairment losses or reversals in its opening balance sheet, it should provide disclosures in accordance with IAS 36 or other applicable IFRSs.

12.14 An entity should clearly distinguish error corrections from changes in accounting principle.

12.15 An entity should explain the IFRS 1 exemptions that it elected. Additional disclosures are required when an entity elects the exemptions for derecognition of financial assets or financial liabilities and deemed cost.

12.16 Interim reports in the period covered by an entity's first IFRS financial statements prepared under IAS 34 should include reconciliations similar to those required in the first IFRS financial statements for the current interim period and comparable interim period of the immediately preceding financial year.

Presentation and Disclosure Excerpts

Author's Note

The following excerpts illustrating the required disclosures under IFRS 1 are all taken from survey companies whose 2011 financial statements were their first IFRS financial statements, regardless of the date of transition. At a minimum, the date of transition is two years prior to a company's first IFRS financial statements.

Securities regulators in different jurisdictions impose different requirements on companies to discuss a forthcoming transition to IFRS. Disclosures required prior to those in a company's first IFRS financial statements are not illustrated.

Transition From Canadian GAAP to IFRSs—IFRS 1 Exemptions Elected

12.17

Rogers Communications Inc. (Dec 2011)

CONSOLIDATED STATEMENTS OF FINANCIAL POSITION

(in millions of Canadian dollars)

	December 31, 2011	December 31, 2010	January 1, 2010
Assets			
Current assets:			
Cash and cash equivalents	$ —	$ —	$ 378
Accounts receivable	1,574	1,443	1,289
Other current assets (note 11)	322	315	277
Current portion of derivative instruments (note 18)	16	1	4
	1,912	1,759	1,948
Property, plant and equipment (note 12)	9,114	8,437	8,136
Goodwill (note 13)	3,280	3,108	3,011
Intangible assets (note 13)	2,721	2,591	2,640
Investments (note 14)	1,107	933	715
Derivative instruments (note 18)	64	6	78
Other long-term assets (note 15)	134	147	113
Deferred tax assets (note 9)	30	52	84
	$18,362	$17,033	$16,725
Liabilities and Shareholders' Equity			
Current liabilities:			
Bank advances	$ 57	$ 45	$ —
Accounts payable and accrued liabilities	2,085	2,133	2,066
Income tax payable	—	238	147
Current portion of provisions (note 16)	35	21	14
Current portion of long-term debt (note 17)	—	—	1
Current portion of derivative instruments (note 18)	37	67	80
Unearned revenue	335	329	335
	2,549	2,833	2,643

(continued)

	December 31, 2011	December 31, 2010	January 1, 2010
Provisions (note 16)	38	62	58
Long-term debt (note 17)	10,034	8,654	8,396
Derivative instruments (note 18)	503	840	1,004
Other long-term liabilities (note 19)	276	229	177
Deferred tax liabilities (note 9)	1,390	655	291
	14,790	13,273	12,569
Shareholders' equity (note 21)	3,572	3,760	4,156
	$18,362	$17,033	$16,725

Guarantees (note 18(e)(ii))
Commitments (note 25)
Contingent liabilities (note 26)
Subsequent events (note 27)

NOTES TO THE CONSOLIDATED FINANCIAL STATEMENTS (in part)

(Tabular amounts in millions of Canadian dollars, except per share amounts)

1. Nature of the Business:

Rogers Communications Inc. ("RCI") is a diversified Canadian communications and media company, incorporated in Canada, with substantially all of its operations and sales in Canada. Through its Wireless segment ("Wireless"), RCI is engaged in wireless voice and data communications services. RCI's Cable segment ("Cable") consists of Cable Operations, Rogers Business Solutions ("RBS") and Rogers Video ("Video"). Through Cable Operations, RCI provides television, high-speed Internet and telephony products primarily to residential customers; RBS provides local and long-distance telephone, enhanced voice and data networking services, and IP access to medium and large Canadian businesses and governments; and Video offers digital video disc ("DVD") and video game sales and rentals. RCI is engaged in radio and television broadcasting, televised shopping, consumer, trade and professional publications, sports entertainment, and digital media properties through its Media segment ("Media"). RCI and its subsidiary companies are collectively referred to herein as the "Company."

The Company's registered office is located at 333 Bloor Street East, 10th Floor, Toronto, Ontario, M4W 1G9.

RCI Class A Voting and Class B Non-Voting shares are traded in Canada on the Toronto Stock Exchange ("TSX") and its Class B Non-Voting shares are also traded on the New York Stock Exchange ("NYSE").

2. Significant Accounting Policies: (in part)

(a) Statement of Compliance:

These consolidated financial statements have been prepared in accordance with International Financial Reporting Standards ("IFRS") as issued by the International Accounting Standards Board ("IASB"). These are the Company's first annual consolidated financial statements prepared in accordance with IFRS, and the Company has elected January 1, 2010 as the date of transition to IFRS (the "Transition Date"). IFRS 1, First-time Adoption of IFRS ("IFRS 1"), has been applied. An explanation of how the transition to IFRS has affected the consolidated financial statements is included in note 3.

The consolidated financial statements of the Company for the years ended December 31, 2011 and 2010 and as at January 1, 2010 were approved by the Board of Directors on February 21, 2012.

(b) Basis of Presentation:

The consolidated financial statements include the accounts of the Company. Intercompany transactions and balances are eliminated on consolidation.

The consolidated financial statements have been prepared mainly under the historical cost convention. Other measurement bases used are described in the applicable notes. The Company's financial year corresponds to the calendar year. The consolidated financial statements are prepared in millions of Canadian dollars.

Presentation of the consolidated statements of financial position differentiates between current and non-current assets and liabilities. The consolidated statements of income are presented using the nature classification for expenses.

Concurrent with the impact of the transition to IFRS described in note 3, the Company underwent a change in strategy which impacted the Company's management reporting resulting in changes to the Company's reportable segments. Commencing January 1, 2011, the results of the former Rogers Retail segment are segregated as follows: the results of operations of the Video business are presented as a separate operating segment and the former Rogers Retail segment results of operations related to wireless and cable products and services are included in the results of operations of Wireless and Cable Operations, respectively. In addition, certain intercompany transactions between the Company's RBS segment and other operating segments, which were previously recorded as revenue in RBS and operating expenses in the other operating segments, are recorded as cost recoveries in RBS beginning January 1, 2011. The effect of these changes in management reporting on the comparatives for 2010 was a decrease in RBS revenue of $108 million and a decrease in RBS operating costs of $108 million, and a decrease in Video revenue of $212 million and a decrease in Video operating costs of $206 million. These transactions were offset by elimination entries resulting in no effect to the consolidated revenue or operating costs.

3. Transition to IFRS:

As stated in note 2(a), these are the Company's first annual consolidated financial statements prepared in accordance with IFRS.

The accounting policies set out in note 2 have been applied in preparing the consolidated financial statements as at and for the year ended December 31, 2011, the comparative information presented in these consolidated financial statements

as at and for the year ended December 31, 2010, and for the opening IFRS statement of financial position at January 1, 2010 (the Company's Transition Date to IFRS). In preparing its opening and comparative IFRS statements of financial positions, the Company has adjusted amounts reported previously in financial statements prepared in accordance with previous Canadian GAAP.

Reconciliation of Financial Position and Shareholders' Equity at January 1, 2010:

	Canadian GAAP	Reclassification for IFRS Presentation	Note	Adjustments to Shareholders' Equity	Note	IFRS Balance
Assets						
Current assets:						
Cash and cash equivalents	$ 383	$ (5)	(f)	$ —		$ 378
Accounts receivable	1,310	(21)	(f)	—		1,289
Other current assets	338	(61)	(f), (l)	—		277
Current portion of derivative instruments	4	—		—		4
Current portion of deferred tax assets	220	(220)	(m)	—		—
	2,255	(307)		—		1,948
Property, plant and equipment	8,197	(50)	(f)	(11)	(e)	8,136
Goodwill	3,018	(7)	(f)	—		3,011
Intangible assets	2,643	(3)	(f), (l)	—		2,640
Investments	547	167	(f)	1	(i)	715
Derivative instruments	78	—		—		78
Other long-term assets	280	(46)	(f), (g), (l)	(121)	(b)	113
Deferred tax assets	—	84	(f), (m)	—		84
	$17,018	$(162)		$(131)		$16,725
Liabilities and Shareholders' Equity						
Current liabilities:						
Accounts payable and accrued liabilities	$ 2,175	$(118)	(d), (f), (h)	$ 9	(c)	$ 2,066
Income tax payable	147	—		—		147
Current portion of provisions	—	4	(h)	10	(h)	14
Current portion of long-term debt	1	—		—		1
Current portion of derivative instruments	80	—		—		80
Unearned revenue	284	55	(d)	(4)	(d)	335
	2,687	(59)		15		2,643
Provisions	—	39	(h)	19	(h)	58
Long-term debt	8,463	(9)	(g)	(58)	(g)	8,396
Derivative instruments	1,004	—		—		1,004
Other long-term liabilities	133	—		44	(b), (c), (f)	177
Deferred tax liabilities	458	(133)	(m)	(34)	(m)	291
	12,745	(162)		(14)		12,569
Shareholders' equity	4,273	—		(117)	(n)	4,156
	$17,018	$(162)		$(131)		$16,725

Reconciliation of Financial Position and Shareholders'
Equity at December 31, 2010:

	Canadian GAAP	Reclassification for IFRS Presentation	Note	Adjustments to Shareholders' Equity	Note	IFRS Balance
Assets						
Current assets:						
Accounts receivable	$ 1,480	$ (37)	(f)	$ —		$ 1,443
Other current assets	365	(50)	(f), (l)	—		315
Current portion of derivative instruments	1	—		—		1
Current portion of deferred tax assets	159	(159)	(m)	—		—
	2,005	(246)		—		1,759
Property, plant and equipment	8,493	(46)	(f)	(10)	(e)	8,437
Goodwill	3,115	(7)	(f)	—		3,108
Intangible assets	2,669	(73)	(f), (l)	(5)	(l)	2,591
Investments	721	213	(f)	(1)	(i)	933
Derivative instruments	6	—		—		6
Other long-term assets	321	(37)	(g), (l)	(137)	(b)	147
Deferred tax assets	—	52	(m)	—		52
	$17,330	$(144)		$(153)		$17,033
Liabilities and Shareholders' Equity						
Current liabilities:						
Bank advances	$ 40	$ 5	(f)	$ —		$ 45
Accounts payable and accrued liabilities	2,256	(137)	(d), (f), (h)	14	(c)	2,133
Income tax payable	238	—		—		238
Current portion of provisions	—	12	(h)	9	(h)	21
Current portion of derivative instruments	67	—		—		67
Unearned revenue	274	56	(d)	(1)	(d)	329
	2,875	(64)		22		2,833
Provisions	—	36	(h)	26	(h)	62
Long-term debt	8,718	(9)	(g)	(55)	(g)	8,654
Derivative instruments	840	—		—		840
Other long-term liabilities	124	—		105	(b), (c), (f)	229
Deferred tax liabilities	814	(107)	(m)	(52)	(m)	655
	13,371	(144)		46		13,273
Shareholders' equity	3,959	—		(199)	(n)	3,760
	$17,330	$(144)		$(153)		$17,033

Reconciliation of Comprehensive Income for the Year
Ended December 31, 2010:

	Canadian GAAP	Reclassification for IFRS Presentation	Note	Adjustment	Note	IFRS
Operating revenue	$12,186	$(41)	(f)	$ (3)	(d)	$12,142
Operating expenses:						
Operating costs	7,594	(19)	(f)	(4)	(b), (c), (h)	7,571
Integration, restructuring and acquisition costs	40	—		—		40
Depreciation and amortization	1,645	(12)	(f)	6	(e), (f)	1,639
Impairment of assets	6	—		5	(l)	11
Operating income	2,901	(10)		(10)		2,881

(continued)

	Canadian GAAP	Reclassification for IFRS Presentation	Note	Adjustment	Note	IFRS
Finance costs	(762)	—		(6)	(e), (g), (j)	(768)
Other income (expense), net	(1)	—		—		(1)
Share of the income (loss) of associates and joint ventures accounted for using the equity method, net of tax	—	10	(f)	(8)	(h)	2
Income before income taxes	2,138	—		(24)		2,114
Income tax expense	610	—		2	(m)	612
Net income for the year	1,528	—		(26)		1,502
Other comprehensive income (loss):						
Defined benefit pension plans:						
Actuarial gain (loss)	—	—		(80)	(b)	(80)
Related income tax recovery	—	—		21	(m)	21
	—	—		(59)		(59)
Change in fair value of available-for-sale investments:						
Increase (decrease) in fair value	104	—		(2)	(i)	102
Related income tax expense	(13)	—		—		(13)
	91	—		(2)		89
Cash flow hedging derivative instruments:						
Change in fair value of derivative instruments	(227)	—		6	(j)	(221)
Reclassification to net income for foreign exchange gain on long-term debt	264	—		—		264
Reclassification to net income of accrued interest	97	—		—		97
Related income tax expense	(24)	—		(1)	(m)	(25)
	110	—		5		115
Other comprehensive income for the year	201	—		(56)		145
Comprehensive income for the year	$1,729	$—		$(82)		$1,647

In addition to the changes required to adjust for the accounting policy differences described in the following notes, interest paid and income taxes paid have been moved into the body of the consolidated statements of cash flows as part of operating activities, whereas they were previously disclosed as supplementary information. There are no other material differences related to presentation of the consolidated statements of cash flows.

(a) Principal Exemptions Elected on Transition to IFRS:

IFRS 1 sets out the requirements that the Company must follow when it adopts IFRS for the first time as the basis for preparing its consolidated financial statements. The Company established its IFRS accounting policies for the year ended December 31, 2011, and has applied retrospectively these policies to the opening consolidated statement of financial position at the date of transition of January 1, 2010, except for specific exemptions available to the Company outlined as follows:

(i) Business Combinations:

The Company has elected to apply IFRS 3, Business Combinations ("IFRS 3"), retrospectively to all business combinations that took place on or after the date of transition, January 1, 2010. Under previous Canadian GAAP, the Company had elected to early adopt The Canadian Institute of Chartered Accountants' Handbook Section 1582, Business Combinations, effective January 1, 2010, the requirements of which

are converged with IFRS. As a condition under IFRS 1 of applying this exemption, goodwill relating to business combinations that occurred prior to January 1, 2010 was tested for impairment even though no impairment indicators were identified. No impairment existed at the date of transition.

(ii) Leases:

The Company has elected to apply the transitional provisions in International Financial Reporting Interpretations Committee ("IFRIC") 4, Determining Whether an Arrangement Contains a Lease ("IFRIC 4"), thereby determining whether the Company has any arrangements that exist at the date of transition to IFRS that contain a lease on the basis of facts and circumstances existing at January 1, 2010. No such arrangements were identified.

(iii) Changes in Existing Decommissioning, Restoration and Similar Liabilities Included in the Cost of PP&E:

The Company has elected to apply the exemption to full retrospective application of IFRIC 1, Changes in Existing Decommissioning, Restoration and Similar Liabilities ("IFRIC 1"). This election allows the Company to measure the impact of any changes to its decommissioning and restoration liabilities using estimates applicable at the date of transition to IFRS, and no adjustment was required to the opening consolidated statement of financial position as a result of applying this election and IFRIC 1.

(iv) Borrowing Costs:

The Company has elected to apply the transitional provisions of IAS 23, Borrowing Costs ("IAS 23"), prospectively from the date of transition.

(v) Transfers of Assets from Customers:

The Company has elected to apply the transitional provisions of IFRIC 18, Transfers of Assets from Customers ("IFRIC 18"), prospectively from the date of transition.

(b) Employee Benefits:

(i) Upon adoption of IFRS, actuarial gains and losses, as described in the significant accounting policies note are recognized immediately in OCI, as permitted by IAS 19, Employee Benefits ("IAS 19"). Under previous Canadian GAAP, the Company used the corridor method to amortize actuarial gains or losses over the average remaining service life of the employees. At the date of transition, all previously unrecognized cumulative actuarial gains and losses, including the unamortized transitional obligation, were recognized in retained earnings, resulting in a reduction of retained earnings of $149 million. Actuarial losses of $76 million were recognized in OCI for the year ended December 31, 2010.

(ii) In compliance with IAS 19, past service costs are recognized immediately if vested, or on a straight-line basis over the average remaining vesting period if unvested. Under Canadian GAAP, past service costs were recognized over the expected average remaining service period of active employees expected to receive benefits under the plan. At the date of transition, all previously unrecognized past service costs amounting to $9 million were fully vested and as such were recognized in retained earnings.

(iii) Furthermore, IAS 19 requires that the defined benefit obligation and plan assets be measured at the consolidated statement of financial position date. Accordingly, the defined benefit obligation and plan assets have been measured at January 1, 2010 and December 31, 2010, resulting in an $8 million reduction to retained earnings at the Transition Date.

(iv) In addition, IAS 19 and IFRIC 14, The Limit on a Defined Benefit Asset, Minimum Funding Requirement and their Interaction, limit the amount that can be recognized as an asset on the consolidated statement of financial position to the present value of available contribution reductions or refunds plus unrecognized actuarial losses and unrecognized past service costs. This restriction has resulted in a limit on the asset that can be recorded for one of the Company's defined benefit plans, which resulted in a further reduction of $8 million that has been recognized in retained earnings at the Transition Date. For the year ended December 31, 2010, $4 million was recognized in OCI.

The impact arising from the changes is summarized as follows:

Year Ended December 31	2010
Consolidated statement of comprehensive income:	
Operating costs	$ (5)
Other comprehensive income	80
Adjustment before income taxes	$ 75

	January 1, 2010	December 31, 2010
Consolidated statements of financial position:		
Other long-term assets	$(121)	$(137)
Other long-term liabilities	(53)	(112)
Adjustment to retained earnings before income taxes	(174)	(249)
Related income tax effect	44	64
Adjustment to retained earnings	$(130)	$(185)

(c) Stock-Based Compensation:

As described in note 22, the Company has granted stock-based compensation to employees. The Company applied IFRS 2 to its unsettled stock-based compensation arrangements at January 1, 2010, which requires that stock-based compensation be measured based on the fair values of the awards. Under previous Canadian GAAP, the Company accounted for these arrangements at intrinsic value.

The impact arising from the change is summarized as follows:

Year Ended December 31	2010
Consolidated statement of comprehensive income:	
Operating costs	$3
Adjustment before income taxes	$3

	January 1, 2010	December 31, 2010
Consolidated statements of financial position:		
Accounts payable and accrued liabilities	$ (9)	$(14)
Other long-term liabilities	(6)	(4)
Adjustment to retained earnings before income taxes	(15)	(18)
Related income tax effect	4	—
Adjustment to retained earnings	$(11)	$(18)

(d) Customer Loyalty Programs:

The Company applied IFRIC 13, Customer Loyalty Programmes ("IFRIC 13"), retrospectively. IFRIC 13 requires that the fair value of the awards given to a customer be identified as a separate component of the initial sales transaction and the revenue be deferred until the awards are redeemed. Under previous Canadian GAAP, the Company took a liability-based approach in accounting for customer loyalty programs.

Consistent with the requirements of IFRS, the liability balance has been reclassified from accounts payable and accrued liabilities to unearned revenue upon transition.

The impact arising from the change is summarized as follows:

Year Ended December 31	2010
Consolidated statement of comprehensive income:	
Operating revenue	$(3)
Adjustment before income taxes	$(3)

	January 1, 2010	December 31, 2010
Consolidated statements of financial position:		
Accounts payable and accrued liabilities	$ 55	$ 56
Unearned revenue	(51)	(55)
Adjustment to retained earnings before income taxes	4	1
Related income tax effect	(1)	—
Adjustment to retained earnings	$ 3	$ 1

(e) Property, Plant and Equipment:

The Company has applied IAS 16, Property, Plant and Equipment, which requires that the Company identify the significant components of its PP&E and depreciate these parts separately over their respective useful lives which results in a more detailed approach than was used under previous Canadian GAAP. The Company has also applied IAS 23 which requires the capitalization of interest and other borrowing costs as part of the cost of certain qualifying assets which take a substantial period of time to get ready for its intended use. Under previous Canadian GAAP, the Company elected not to capitalize borrowing costs.

The impact arising from these changes is summarized as follows:

Year Ended December 31	2010
Consolidated statement of comprehensive income:	
Depreciation and amortization	$ 2
Finance costs–capitalized interest	(3)
Adjustment before income taxes	$(1)

	January 1, 2010	December 31, 2010
Consolidated statements of financial position:		
Property, plant and equipment	$(11)	$(10)
Related income tax effect	3	3
Adjustment to retained earnings	$ (8)	$ (7)

As noted previously, the Company has elected to apply IAS 23 prospectively from the date of transition, January 1, 2010;

consequently, there was no impact to the consolidated statements of financial position at that date.

(f) Joint Ventures:

(i) The Company applied IAS 31, Interests in Joint Ventures ("IAS 31"), at January 1, 2010. The Company has elected to use the equity method to recognize interests in joint ventures as described in note 2(c). Previous Canadian GAAP required that the Company proportionately consolidate its interests in joint ventures. This change had no impact on the Company's net assets and consequently is presented as a reclassification difference.

(ii) IFRS requires that the Company immediately recognize any gains that arise on non-monetary contributions to a joint venture to the extent of the other venturers' interest in the joint venture when certain conditions are met. Under previous Canadian GAAP, these gains were deferred and amortized into income over the life of the assets contributed. The impact of this difference was to recognize $15 million of unamortized gains in opening retained earnings. Depreciation and amortization increased by $4 million for the year ended December 31, 2010 as a result of eliminating the amortization of the gain under previous Canadian GAAP.

The impacts of applying IAS 31 are summarized as follows:

Year Ended December 31	2010
Consolidated statement of comprehensive income:	
Operating revenue	$ 41
Operating costs	(19)
Depreciation and amortization–change from proportionate consolidation	(12)
Depreciation and amortization–remove amortization of deferred gain	4
Share of the loss of associates and joint ventures accounted for using the equity method	(10)
Adjustment before income taxes	$ 4

	January 1, 2010	December 31, 2010
Consolidated statements of financial position:		
Cash and cash equivalents	$ (5)	$ —
Accounts receivable	(21)	(37)
Other current assets	—	(1)
Property, plant and equipment	(50)	(46)
Goodwill	(7)	(7)
Intangible assets	(103)	(150)
Investments	167	213
Other long-term assets	2	—
Deferred tax assets	(3)	—
Bank advances	—	(5)
Accounts payable and accrued liabilities	20	33
Other long-term liabilities— remove deferred gain	15	11
Adjustment to retained earnings before income taxes	15	11
Related income tax effect	(10)	(9)
Adjustment to retained earnings	$ 5	$ 2

(g) Financial Instruments—Transaction Costs:

The Company has applied IAS 39, Financial Instruments: Recognition and Measurement ("IAS 39"), at January 1, 2010, which requires directly attributable costs to be added to certain acquired financial assets and liabilities and amortized to the consolidated statements of income over the life of the asset or liability. Under previous Canadian GAAP, these costs were expensed as incurred. Unamortized transaction costs of $58 million related to the Company's long-term debt were adjusted upon transition. Additionally, unamortized discounts recognized on long-term debt have been reclassified from other long-term assets to conform with IFRS presentation requirements.

The impact of the change is summarized as follows:

Year Ended December 31	2010
Consolidated statement of comprehensive income:	
Finance costs—amortization	$ 13
Finance costs—debt issuances	(10)
Adjustment before income taxes	$ 3

	January 1, 2010	December 31, 2010
Consolidated statements of financial position:		
Other long-term assets— reclassify unamortized discounts	$ (9)	$ (9)
Long-term debt—reclassify unamortized discounts	9	9
Long-term debt—unamortized transaction costs	58	55
Adjustment to retained earnings before income taxes	58	55
Related income tax effect	(16)	(15)
Adjustment to retained earnings	$ 42	$ 40

(h) Provisions:

IAS 37, Provisions, Contingent Liabilities and Contingent Assets ("IAS 37"), requires separate disclosure of provisions on the face of the consolidated statements of financial position and also requires recognition of a provision for onerous contracts; that is any contract where the costs to fulfill the contract exceed the benefits to be received under the contract, neither of which were required under previous Canadian GAAP. Therefore, upon transition, all provisions were reclassified from accounts payable and accrued liabilities and the Company recognized an onerous contract provision of $29 million.

The impact of the changes is summarized as follows:

Year Ended December 31	2010
Consolidated statement of comprehensive income:	
Operating costs	$(2)
Share of the income of associates and joint ventures accounted for using the equity method	8
Adjustment before income taxes	$ 6

	January 1, 2010	December 31, 2010
Consolidated statements of financial position:		
Accounts payable and accrued liabilities	$ 43	$ 48
Current portion of provisions— reclassification	(4)	(12)
Current portion of provisions— onerous contract	(10)	(9)
Provisions—reclassification	(39)	(36)
Provisions—onerous contract	(19)	(26)
Adjustment to retained earnings before income taxes	(29)	(35)
Related income tax effect	10	8
Adjustment to retained earnings	$(19)	$(27)

(i) Financial Instruments—Investments:

IAS 39 requires that the Company measure at fair value its investments in equity instruments that do not have a quoted market price in an active market classified as available-for-sale. Under previous Canadian GAAP, these investments were classified as available-for-sale and measured at cost, as cost closely approximated fair value.

The impact of this change is summarized as follows:

Year Ended December 31	2010
Consolidated statement of comprehensive income:	
Increase in fair value of available-for-sale investments	$2
Adjustment before income taxes	$2

	January 1, 2010	December 31, 2010
Consolidated statements of financial position:		
Investments	$1	$(1)
Available-for-sale equity reserve	(1)	1
Adjustment to retained earnings	$—	$—

There is no impact on retained earnings at January 1, 2010 or December 31, 2010 as a result of this change.

(j) Financial Instruments—Hedge Accounting:

IAS 39 requires that the Company include credit risk when measuring the ineffective portion of its cross-currency interest rate exchange agreements. Under previous Canadian GAAP, the Company elected not to include credit risk in the determination of the ineffective portion of its cross-currency interest rate exchange agreements.

The impact of this change is summarized as follows:

Year Ended December 31	2010
Consolidated statement of comprehensive income:	
Finance costs—change in fair value of derivative instruments	$ 6
Change in fair value of derivative instruments	(6)
Adjustment before income taxes	$—

	January 1, 2010	December 31, 2010
Consolidated statements of financial position:		
Equity reserves—hedging	$ 7	$ 1
Adjustment to retained earnings before income taxes	7	1
Related income tax effect	(1)	—
Adjustment to retained earnings	$ 6	$ 1

(k) Share of the Income or Loss of Associates:

IAS 1, Presentation of Financial Statements ("IAS 1"), requires that the share of the income or loss of associates accounted for using the equity method are presented as a separate line item on the face of the consolidated statements of income. Under previous Canadian GAAP, the share of the income or loss of associates was included with other income.

For the year ended December 31, 2010, the impacts of applying IAS 1 was less than $1 million.

(l) Intangible Assets and Impairment of Assets:

IAS 36, Impairment of Assets ("IAS 36"), uses a one-step approach for both testing for and measurement of impairment, with asset carrying values compared directly with the higher of fair value less costs to sell and value in use (which uses discounted future cash flows) and assets are tested for impairment at the level of cash generating units, which is the lowest level of assets that generate largely independent cash flows. Canadian GAAP, however, uses a two-step approach to impairment testing: first comparing asset carrying values with undiscounted future cash flows to determine whether impairment exists; and then measuring any impairment by comparing asset carrying values with fair values, and assets are grouped at the lowest level for which identifiable cash flows are largely independent of the cash flows of other assets and liabilities for impairment testing purposes.

The impact of this change is summarized as follows:

Year Ended December 31	2010
Consolidated statement of comprehensive income:	
Impairment of assets	$5
Adjustment before income taxes	$5

	January 1, 2010	December 31, 2010
Consolidated statements of financial position:		
Intangible assets	$—	$(5)
Adjustment to retained earnings before income taxes	—	(5)
Related income tax effect	—	1
Adjustment to retained earnings	$—	$(4)

IAS 38, Intangible Assets ("IAS 38"), requires acquired program rights to be classified as intangible assets. Under previous Canadian GAAP, these amounts were classified as other current assets and other long-term assets. Therefore, upon transition, the Company reclassified an amount of $100 million at January 1, 2010 and $77 million at December 31, 2010 to intangible assets.

The impact of the changes is summarized as follows:

	January 1, 2010	December 31, 2010
Consolidated statements of financial position:		
Other current assets	$(61)	$(49)
Intangible assets	100	77
Other long-term assets	(39)	(28)
Adjustment to retained earnings	$—	$—

(m) Income Taxes:

The above changes decreased (increased) the net deferred tax liability as follows:

	Note	January 1, 2010	December 31, 2010
Employee benefits	(b)	$44	$64
Stock-based compensation	(c)	4	—
Customer loyalty programs	(d)	(1)	—
Property, plant and equipment	(e)	3	3
Joint ventures	(f)	(10)	(9)
Financial instruments— transaction costs	(g)	(16)	(15)
Provisions	(h)	10	8
Impairment of assets	(l)	—	1
Decrease in net deferred tax liability		$34	$52

The effect on the consolidated statement of comprehensive income for the year ended December 31, 2010 was to decrease the previously reported tax charge for the period by $18 million.

Under IFRS, all deferred tax balances are classified as non-current, regardless of the classification of the underlying assets or liabilities, or the expected reversal date of the temporary difference. The effect of this change, including the impact of netting deferred tax assets and liabilities, is to reclassify the current deferred tax asset of $220 million at January 1, 2010 and $159 million at December 31, 2010 to non-current and reclassify $87 million at January 1, 2010 and $52 million at December 31, 2010 from deferred tax liability to deferred tax asset.

IFRS requires that subsequent changes to the tax effect of items recorded in OCI in previous years be also recorded in OCI, where previously this was recorded in the consolidated statements of income. The impact of this difference on transition is to reduce equity reserves by $16 million and increase opening retained earnings by $16 million.

In addition, the Company reclassified an amount of $61 million at January 1, 2010 and $138 million at December 31, 2010 from income tax payable to deferred tax liability as compared to amounts previously reported under Canadian GAAP relating to its investment in its wholly-owned operating partnership.

(n) The Above Changes Decreased (Increased) Shareholders' Equity (Each Net of Related Tax) as Follows:

	Note	January 1, 2010	December 31, 2010
Employee benefits	(b)	$130	$185
Stock-based compensation	(c)	11	18
Customer loyalty programs	(d)	(3)	(1)
Property, plant and equipment	(e)	8	7
Joint ventures	(f)	(5)	(2)
Financial instruments–transaction costs	(g)	(42)	(40)
Provisions	(h)	19	27
Financial instruments–hedge accounting	(j)	(6)	(1)
Impairment of assets	(l)	—	4
Income tax impact transferred from equity reserves		(16)	(16)
Adjustment to retained earnings		96	181
Equity reserves–available-for-sale investments	(i)	(1)	1
Equity reserves–hedging	(j)	6	1
Income tax impact transferred to retained earnings		16	16
Adjustment to shareholders' equity		$117	$199

Transition From South Korean GAAP to IFRSs—IFRS 1 Exemptions Elected

12.18

SK Telecom Co., Ltd. (Dec 2011)

CONSOLIDATED STATEMENTS OF FINANCIAL POSITION

	Notes	Korean Won January 1, 2010	Korean Won December 31, 2010	Korean Won December 31, 2011	Translation Into U.S. Dollars (Note 2) December 31, 2011
		(In Millions)			(In Thousands)
Assets					
Current assets:					
Cash and cash equivalents	4, 29	(Won) 905,561	(Won) 659,405	(Won) 1,650,794	$1,424,941
Short-term financial instruments	4, 29	471,970	567,152	979,564	845,545
Short-term investment securities	4, 7	376,722	400,531	94,829	81,855
Accounts receivable—trade, net	4, 5, 28	1,832,967	1,949,397	1,823,170	1,573,733
Short-term loans, net	4, 5, 28	75,941	94,924	100,429	86,689
Accounts receivable—other, net	4, 5, 28	2,421,874	2,531,847	908,836	784,494
Prepaid expenses		172,225	182,091	118,200	102,028
Derivative assets	4, 30	—	—	148,038	127,784
Inventories, net	6, 29	119,317	149,223	219,590	189,547
Advanced payments and other	4, 5, 7	65,391	119,422	74,029	63,902
Total Current Assets		6,441,968	6,653,992	6,117,479	5,280,518

(continued)

	Notes	Korean Won January 1, 2010	Korean Won December 31, 2010	Korean Won December 31, 2011	Translation Into U.S. Dollars (Note 2) December 31, 2011
		(In Millions)	(In Millions)	(In Millions)	(In Thousands)
Non-current assets:					
Long-term financial instruments	4, 29	6,565	117	7,628	6,584
Long-term investment securities	4, 7	2,443,978	1,680,582	1,537,945	1,327,531
Investments in associates	8	549,913	1,204,692	1,384,605	1,195,170
Property and equipment, net	9, 28, 29	8,027,678	8,153,413	9,030,998	7,795,423
Investment property	10	212,742	197,307	271,086	233,997
Goodwill	11	1,736,733	1,736,649	1,749,933	1,510,516
Intangible assets	12	2,004,218	1,884,956	2,995,803	2,585,933
Long-term loans, net	4, 5, 28	81,109	84,323	95,565	82,490
Long-term accounts receivable—other	4, 5	761,735	527,106	5,393	4,655
Long-term prepaid expenses	29	449,906	411,509	567,762	490,084
Guarantee deposits	4, 5, 28	232,975	250,333	245,218	211,669
Long-term derivative assets	4, 30	314,658	203,382	105,915	91,424
Deferred income tax assets	24	28,646	106,860	227,578	196,442
Other	4, 5	43,900	37,168	23,128	19,965
Total non-current assets		16,894,756	16,478,397	18,248,557	15,751,883
Total assets		(Won) 23,336,724	(Won) 23,132,389	(Won) 24,366,036	$21,032,401
Liabilities and Stockholders' Equity					
Current liabilities:					
Short-term borrowings	4, 13, 29	(Won) 554,469	(Won) 523,710	(Won) 700,713	$604,845
Accounts payable—trade	4, 28	164,314	195,777	195,391	168,659
Accounts payable—other	4, 28	1,307,236	1,434,329	1,507,877	1,301,577
Withholdings	4	288,455	408,261	496,860	428,882
Accrued expenses	4	419,816	677,480	744,673	642,791
Income tax payable	24	395,503	259,871	293,725	253,539
Unearned revenue		341,538	311,365	290,791	251,006
Derivative liabilities	4, 30	36,318	15,393	4,645	4,009
Provisions	15	516,382	652,889	657,198	567,284
Current portion of long-term debt, net	4, 13, 14, 16	1,262,383	1,601,231	1,662,841	1,435,340
Advanced receipts and other		96,364	121,864	118,876	102,612
Total current liabilities		5,382,778	6,202,170	6,673,590	5,760,544
Non-current liabilities:					
Bonds payable, net	4, 13	4,453,300	3,658,546	3,229,009	2,787,233
Long-term borrowings	4, 13, 29	844,640	235,968	323,852	279,544
Long-term payables—other	4, 14	170,953	54,783	847,496	731,546
Long-term unearned revenue		274,876	241,892	212,172	183,144
Finance lease liabilities	4, 16	77,709	60,075	41,940	36,202
Retirement benefit obligation	17	53,659	67,870	85,941	74,183
Long-term derivative liabilities	4, 30	34,495	14,761	—	—
Long-term provisions	15	121,097	112,227	142,361	122,884
Long-term advanced receipts and other	4, 28	75,172	76,098	76,966	66,435
Total non-current liabilities		6,105,901	4,522,220	4,959,737	4,281,171
Total liabilities		11,488,679	10,724,390	11,633,327	10,041,715
Equity:					
Share capital	1, 18	44,639	44,639	44,639	38,532
Share premium	18, 19	167,876	(78,953)	(285,347)	(246,307)
Retained earnings	20	9,563,940	10,721,249	11,642,525	10,049,655
Reserves	21	919,835	643,056	260,064	224,483
Non-controlling interests		1,151,755	1,078,008	1,070,828	924,323
Total equity		11,848,045	12,407,999	12,732,709	10,990,686
Total liabilities and equity		(Won) 23,336,724	(Won) 23,132,389	(Won) 24,366,036	$21,032,401

NOTES TO THE CONSOLIDATED FINANCIAL STATEMENTS (in part)

1. General

SK Telecom Co., Ltd. ("SK Telecom") was incorporated in March 1984 under the laws of Korea to engage in providing cellular telephone communication services in the Republic of Korea. SK Telecom Co., Ltd. and its subsidiaries (the "Company") mainly provide wireless telecommunications in the Republic of Korea. The Company's common shares and depositary receipts (DRs) are listed on the Stock Market of Korea Exchange, the New York Stock Exchange and the London Stock Exchange. As of December 31, 2011, the Company's total issued shares are held by the following:

	Number of Shares	Percentage of Total Shares Issued (%)
SK Holdings, Co., Ltd.	20,363,452	25.22
Tradewinds Global Investors, LLC	4,050,518	5.02
POSCO Corp.	2,341,569	2.90
Institutional investors and other minority stockholders	42,939,460	53.17
Treasury stock	11,050,712	13.69
	80,745,711	100.00

2. Summary of Significant Accounting Policies (in part)

The Company maintains its official accounting records in Republic of Korean won ("Won") and prepares consolidated financial statements in conformity with International Financial Reporting Standards ("IFRS") as issued by International Accounting Standard Board ("IASB"). The Company has adopted IFRS as issued by IASB for the annual period beginning on January 1, 2011. In accordance with IFRS 1 First-time adoption of IFRS, the Company's transition date to IFRS is January 1, 2010. Refer to Note 3, for transition adjustments to IFRS.

The accompanying consolidated financial statements are stated in Korean won, the currency of the country in which the Company is incorporated and operates. The translation of Korean won amounts into U.S. dollar amounts is included solely for the convenience of readers of financial statements and has been made at the rate of (Won)1,158.50 to US$1.00, the Noon Buying Rate in the City of New York for cable transfers in Korean won as certified for customs purposes by the Federal Reserve Bank of New York on the last business day of the year ended December 30, 2011.

The consolidated financial statements have been prepared on a historical cost basis except for certain non-current assets and financial instruments that are measured at revalued amounts or at fair values. Major accounting policies used for the preparation of the consolidated financial statements are stated below and these accounting policies have been applied consistently to the financial statements for the current period and comparative periods. Historical cost is generally based on the fair value of the consideration paid in exchange for assets. The consolidated financial statements were approved by the board of directors on February 9, 2012.

3. Transition to International Financial Reporting Standards ("IFRS")

The Company's financial statements are prepared in accordance with the requirements of IFRS on or after January 1, 2010, the date of transition, for IFRSs effective as of December 31, 2011. The consolidated statements of financial position as of December 31, 2010 and the consolidated statements of comprehensive income for the year ended December 31, 2010, which are comparatively presented, were previously prepared in accordance with previous GAAP("Korean GAAP") but were restated in accordance with IFRS 1, *First-time adoption of International Financial Reporting Standard*.

For the opening IFRS statement of financial position, the Company has applied the following exemptions from the requirements of IFRS and exceptions to the retrospective application of some aspects of IFRS as permitted by IFRS 1, *First-time adoption of International Financial Reporting Standard*.

a. Exemptions From IFRS

Business Combinations

The Company has elected not to apply IFRS 3, *Business Combinations*, retrospectively to past business combinations that occurred before January 1, 2010, the date of transition to IFRS. The Company has recorded the value of goodwill at transition date of IFRS at its carrying value under Korean GAAP after any impairment on goodwill. No intangible assets were identified that might have been embedded in the goodwill.

Fair Value or Revaluation as Deemed Cost

The Company has elected to measure its certain property, plant and equipments at their fair value at the date of transition to IFRS and use that fair value as their deemed cost at that date.

Effect of revaluation in certain property, plant and equipment as of January 1, 2010 are as follows (in millions of Korean won)

Korean GAAP	Revaluation Increase	IFRS
(Won) 8,165,879	(Won) 69,538	(Won) 8,235,417

Leases

The Company has elected to apply the transitional provisions in International Financial Reporting Interpretations Committee ("IFRIC") 4, Determining Whether an Arrangement Contains a Lease ("IFRIC 4"); thereby determining whether the Company has any arrangements that exist at the date of transition to IFRS that contain a lease on the basis of facts and circumstances existing at January 1, 2010. No such arrangements were identified.

Borrowing Costs

The Company has elected to apply the transitional provisions of IAS 23, Borrowing Costs ("IAS 23"), prospectively from the date of transition.

Cumulative Translation Differences

The Company has reset the cumulative currency translation adjustments for all foreign operations to zero as of the date of transition to IFRS.

b. Significant Differences Between IFRS and Korean GAAP in Accounting Policies

Korean GAAP	IFRS
(1) Scope of Consolidation	
The definition of control is similar to those in IFRS. However, some of the scope of consolidation is restricted by the Act on External Audit of Stock Companies as below. • An entity that another entity owns more than 30% of shares as the largest shareholder is included in consolidation. • A subsidiary with less than 10 billion Won in its total assets as of the previous fiscal year end is excluded from consolidation. • An unincorporated entity such as a partnership is excluded from consolidation.	Control is the power to govern the financial and operating policies of an entity so as to obtain benefits from its activities. All entities controlled by the Company are consolidated regardless of quantitative significance. As a result, at transition date to IFRS, the Company's change in scope of consolidation as compared with those of Korean GAAP. Added : Broadband D&M Co., Ltd 　　　　Broadband CS Co., Ltd Excluded : F&U Credit Information Co., Ltd 　　　　IHQ, Inc 　　　　BMC Movie Expert Fund 　　　　BMC Digital Culture and Contents Fund
(2) Employ benefits and retirement benefit obligation	
Allowances for retirement benefits accrued equal to the amounts to be paid at the end of reporting period, assuming that all entitled employees with a service year more than a year would retire at once. Retirement benefit expenses incur at the point when the payment obligation is fixed. The Company recognized allowances for long-term employee benefit at the point when the payment obligation is fixed.	The Company has defined benefit plans and the amounts of defined benefit obligation are measured based on actuarial assumptions. The Company recognizes the expected cost of long-term employee benefit when the employees render service that increases their entitlement to future long-term employee benefit.
(3) Property and Equipment	
Under Korean GAAP, the Company uses the cost model in the measurement after initial recognition. The depreciation method is required to be applied consistently at each period and cannot be changed unless there are justified reasons. For a newly acquired asset, the same depreciation methods applied to the existing, similar assets are applied consistently.	The Company revalued its property and equipment as at January 1, 2010 and used their fair values as deemed cost in the opening IFRS statement of financial position. For the measurement after initial recognition, IAS 16, Property, Plant and Equipment allows for an entity to choose either the cost model or the revaluation model by the class of property and equipment and the Company has chosen the cost model. The residual value, the useful life and the depreciation method of property and equipment are required to be reviewed at least at each financial year-end and, if expectations differ from previous estimates, the changes should be accounted for as a change in an accounting estimate in accordance with IAS 8, Accounting Policies, Changes in Accounting Estimates and Errors. The Company changed its depreciation method of equipment from a declining balance method to a straight-line method in connection with the adoption of IFRS.
(4) Goodwill	
Under Korean GAAP, the Company amortized Goodwill acquired as a result of business combination on a straight line method basis over 5–20 years.	Under IFRS, goodwill is not amortized. Impairment test was performed at the reporting date.
(5) Transfer of financial assets	
Under Korean GAAP, when the Company transferred a financial asset to a financial institution and it was determined that the control over such asset had been transferred; the Company derecognized the financial asset.	Under IFRS, if the Company substantially retains all the risks and rewards of ownership of the asset, the asset is not derecognized but instead the related cash proceeds are recognized as financial liabilities.
(6) Deferral of non-refundable activation fees	
Under Korean GAAP, the Company recognized non-refundable activation revenue when the activation service was performed.	Under IFRS, the Company defers such revenue and recognizes it over the expected term of the customer relationship.

(continued)

Korean GAAP	IFRS
(7) Income tax Under Korean GAAP, deferred tax assets and liabilities were classified as either current or non-current based on the classification of their underlying assets and liabilities assuming that all differences from one entity are recovered or settled together. If there are no corresponding assets or liabilities, deferred tax assets and liabilities were classified based on the periods the temporary differences were expected to reverse. Under Korean GAAP, differences between the carrying value and the tax base of the investments in subsidiaries, associates and interest in joint ventures were considered as temporary differences and recognized as deferred tax assets and liabilities.	Under IFRS, deferred tax assets and liabilities are all classified as non-current on the statement of financial position. Under IFRS, the temporary differences associated with investments in subsidiaries, and associates and interest in joint ventures is recognized as deferred assets and liabilities reflecting the manner in which Company expects, at the end of the reporting period, to recover or settle the carrying amount of its assets and liabilities.
(8) Other reclassifications 1) Membership Under Korean GAAP, facility-use memberships were classified as other non-current assets	Under IFRS, facility-use memberships are recognized as intangible assets with an indefinite useful life.
2) Investment property Under Korean GAAP, properties acquired for earning rental income and/or for capital appreciation were classified as property and equipment.	Under IFRS, the properties owned to earn rentals or for capital appreciation or both is classified and accounted for as investment property in accordance with IAS 40, Investment Property.
(9) Effects on equity method investments	The aggregate effects of IFRS transition related to the Company's equity method investments in associates.

In connection with the opening IFRS statements of financial position, the effects on the Company's financial position, management performance and cash flows due to the adoption of IFRS are as follows:

c. Reconciliations to IFRS From Korean GAAP

(1) Reconciliations of Equity at January 1, 2010 (Date of Transition to IFRS) (In Million of Korean Won)

	Note	Total Assets	Total Liabilities	Net Equity
Based on Korean GAAP		(Won) 23,206,256	(Won) 10,861,631	(Won) 12,344,625
Adjustments:				
Changes in scope of consolidation	b-(1)	(62,440)	3,735	(66,175)
Property and equipment	b-(3)	69,538	—	69,538
Employee benefits and retirement benefit obligation	b-(2)	15	25,048	(25,033)
Transfer of financial assets	b-(5)	416,242	400,753	15,489
Non-refundable activation fees	b-(6)	—	593,981	(593,981)
Other adjustments	b-(8)	(107,730)	(73,521)	(34,209)
Deferred tax and tax effect of adjustments	b-(7)	(185,157)	(322,948)	137,791
Total adjustment		130,468	627,048	(496,580)
Based on IFRS		(Won) 23,336,724	(Won) 11,488,679	(Won) 11,848,045

(2) Reconciliations of Equity at December 31, 2010 and
Total Comprehensive Income for the Year Ended December
31, 2010 (In Million of Korean Won):

	Note	Total Assets	Total Liabilities	Net Equity	Total Comprehensive Income
Based on Korean GAAP		(Won) 22,651,704	(Won) 10,173,055	(Won) 12,478,649	(Won) 1,021,501
Adjustments:					
Changes in scope of consolidation	b-(1)	(103,743)	(13,053)	(90,690)	1,247
Property and equipment	b-(3)	477,044	—	477,044	407,811
Goodwill	b-(4)	151,900	—	151,900	142,176
Employee benefits and retirement benefit obligation	b-(2)	17	38,799	(38,782)	(5,514)
Transfer of financial assets	b-(5)	—	—	—	(15,489)
Effects on equity method investments	b-(9)	18,430	—	18,430	7,717
Nonrefundable activation fees	b-(6)	—	533,783	(533,783)	60,199
Other adjustments	b-(8)	44,507	94,943	(50,436)	598
Deferred tax and tax effect of adjustments	b-(7)	(107,470)	(103,137)	(4,333)	(140,695)
Total adjustment		480,685	551,335	(70,650)	458,050
Based on IFRS		(Won) 23,132,389	(Won) 10,724,390	(Won) 12,407,999	(Won) 1,479,551

(3) Details of Cash Flow Adjustments

Under IFRS, dividends received, interest received, interest paid, and income tax paid which were not presented separately in the consolidated statement of cash flows under Korean GAAP, are now separately presented and the related income (expense) and assets (liabilities) have been adjusted for accordingly. Also, under IFRS, foreign currency translation amounts are presented gross as part of the related transactions and deducted against the effects of foreign exchange rate changes on the balance of cash held in foreign currencies. No other significant differences between the consolidated statements of cash flows prepared under Korean GAAP compared to IFRS have been noted.

(4) For Details on Reclassification From Operating to Non-Operating Income Due to the Transition to IFRS From Korean GAAP, Refer to FN 22 Other Operating Income and Expense.

IFRS-BPPD 12.18

COMPANY INDEX

Company Name	Accounting Technique Illustration
Daimler AG	
Danubius Hotel and Spa Nyrt.	
Deutsche Bank Aktiengesellschaft	
Deutsche Telekom AG	
DHT Holdings, Inc	
Diploma Group Limited	1.72
Dr. Reddy's Laboratories Limited	1.133
DRDGOLD Limited	5.23, 6.26
East Asiatic Company Ltd. A/S	3.107, 10.19
Elbit Imaging Ltd.	1.194
Embraer S.A.	1.77, 1.137, 3.58, 3.238, 8.61
Empresa Nacional de Electricidad S.A. (Endesa-Chile)	2.115, 3.286, 8.57
Empresas ICA, S.A.B. de C.V.	2.30, 3.55
Eni S.p.A	
Etablissements Delhaize Frères et Cie "Le Lion" (Groupe Delhaize) S.A.	1.132, 2.257
Fairfax Financial Holdings Limited	8.54
Fibria Cellulose S.A.	1.75, 2.28, 2.210, 2.303, 3.315
France Telecom	
Gazit-Globe Ltd.	2.74, 3.89, 5.28
GrainCorp Limited	
Gruma, S.A.B. de C.V.	2.111, 3.108, 8.55, 10.18
Grupo Radio Centro, S.A.B. de C.V.	3.56
Grupo TMM, S.A.B.	1.110, 1.171, 2.73
Guangshen Railway Company Limited	
Harmony Gold Mining Company Limited	
Harry Winston Diamond Corporation	1.70, 2.363
Hemisphere GPS Inc.	
HGL Limited	
Huaneng Power International, Inc.	2.165
ING Groep N.V.	2.395
InterContinental Hotels Group plc	
JSC Halyk Bank	
Kazakhstan Kagazy PLC	1.74, 3.139
KB Financial Group Inc.	1.111, 3.136
Koninklijke Philips Electronics NV	
Korea Electric Power Corporation	2.301
KT Corporation	1.138, 2.50, 3.382, 5.26
Lan Airlines S.A.	
Leisureworld Senior Care Corporaton	
LG Display Co., Ltd.	2.17, 3.301
Linamar Corporation	2.49
Lloyds Banking Group plc	2.113, 3.216
Luxottica Group S.p.A	2.350
Maple Leaf Foods Inc.	2.21
Martinrea International Inc.	
Medical Facilities Corporation	2.351
MFC Industrial Ltd.	2.51, 3.110
Millicom International Cellular S.A.	1.81, 3.342
Mondi Limited and Mondi plc[3]	2.256
N Brown Group plc	
Nestlé SA	
Newcrest Mining Limited	
Nokia Corporation	
Nortel Inversora S.A.	
Novartis AG	
Novo Nordisk A/S	
OAO Gazprom	9.28
Pargesa Holding AG	
Perusahaan Perseroan (Persero) PT Telekomunikasi Indonesia Tbk	1.134, 3.109
PetroChina Company Limited	

Note that paragraph references ending with "n" refer to an author's note following the numbered paragraph.

International Accounting Standards Board (IASB) Statements

Laws and Legislation

Other IFRS Guidance

SEC GUIDANCE

Securities and Exchange Commission (SEC) Regulations and Interpretations

Codification of Staff Accounting Bulletins

SUBJECT INDEX

Note that paragraph references ending with "n" refer to an author's note following the numbered paragraph.

C

F

O

S

Powerful Online Research Tools

The AICPA Online Professional Library offers the most current access to comprehensive accounting and auditing literature, as well business and practice management information, combined with the power and speed of the Web. Through your online subscription, you'll get:

- Cross-references within and between titles — smart links give you quick access to related information and relevant materials
- First available updates — no other research tool offers access to new AICPA standards and conforming changes more quickly, guaranteeing that you are always current with all of the authoritative guidance!
- Robust search engine — helps you narrow down your research to find your results quickly
- And much more…

Choose from two comprehensive libraries or select only the titles you need!

With the *Essential A&A Research Collection*, you gain access to the following:
- AICPA Professional Standards
- AICPA Technical Practice Aids
- PCAOB Standards & Related Rules
- All current AICPA Audit and Accounting Guides
- All current Audit Risk Alerts
One-year individual online subscription
Item # ORS-XX

OR

***Premium A&A Research Collection* and get everything from the *Essential A&A Research Collection* plus:**
- AICPA Audit & Accounting Manual
- All current Checklists & Illustrative Financial Statements
- eXacct: Financial Reporting Tools & Techniques
- IFRS Accounting Trends & Techniques
One-year individual online subscription
Item # WAL-BY

You can also add the FASB *Accounting Standards Codification*™ and the GASB Library to either collection.

Take advantage of a 30-day free trial!
See for yourself how these powerful online libraries can improve your productivity and simplify your accounting research.

Visit **cpa2biz.com/library** for details or to subscribe.

Additional Publications

Audit Risk Alerts/Financial Reporting Alerts
Find out about current economic, regulatory and professional developments before you perform your audit engagement. AICPA industry-specific Audit Risk Alerts will make your audit planning process more efficient by giving you concise, relevant information that shows you how current developments may impact your clients and your audits. For financial statement preparers, AICPA also offers a series of Financial Reporting Alerts. For a complete list of Audit Risk Alerts available from the AICPA, please visit **cpa2biz.com/ara**.

Checklists and Illustrative Financial Statements
Updated to reflect recent accounting and auditing standards, these industry-specific practice aids are invaluable tools to both financial statement preparers and auditors. For a complete list of Checklists available from the AICPA, please visit **cpa2biz.com/checklists**.